West's Legal Environment of Business

Text
Cases
Ethical, Regulatory, and International Issues

Third Edition

Frank B. Cross
Associate Director, Center for Legal and Regulatory Studies
University of Texas at Austin

Roger LeRoy Miller
Institute for University Studies
Arlington, Texas

WEST

WEST EDUCATIONAL PUBLISHING
An International Thomson Publishing Company

Publisher/Team Director: Jack Calhoun
Acquisitions Editor: Rob Dewey
Development Editor: Jan Lamar
Production Editor: Bill Stryker
Marketing Manager: Scott Person
Cover Design: Doug Abbott
Internal Design: Bill Stryker

I(T)P® *An International Thomson Publishing Company*

Library of Congress Cataloging-in-Publication Data
Cross, Frank B.
West's legal environment of business: text, cases, ethical, regulatory, and international issues / Frank B. Cross, Roger LeRoy Miller,—3rd ed.
p. cm.
Includes index.
ISBN 0–538–87965–3 (hc)
1. Industrial laws and legislation—United States. 2. Trade regulation—United States. 3. Commercial law—United States.
I. Miller, Roger LeRoy. II. Title.
KF1600.C76 1998
346.7307—dc21

97–22498
CIP

23456789 WCBS 543210987

Printed in the United States of America

I(T)P®

International Thomson Publishing
West Educational Publishing is an ITP Company.
The ITP trademark is used under license.

Contents in Brief

UNIT ONE

The Foundations 1

UNIT TWO

The Public and International Environment 95

UNIT THREE

The Private Environment 173

UNIT FOUR

The Employment Environment 389

UNIT FIVE

The Regulatory Environment 477

Appendices

Contents

UNIT ONE

The Foundations 1

UNIT TWO

The Public and International Environment 95

UNIT FOUR

The Employment Environment 389

UNIT FIVE

The Regulatory Environment 477

Concept Summaries List

Exhibits List

Emerging Trends

PREFACE TO THE INSTRUCTOR

The legal environment of business has universal applicability. A student entering virtually any field of business must have at least a passing understanding of the legal environment of business in order to function in the real world. Additionally, students preparing for a career in accounting, government and political science, economics, and even medicine can fruitfully use much of the information they learn in a business law and legal environment course.

KEY AREAS OF EMPHASIS

To make sure that instructors and students alike can rely on the coverage, accuracy, and applicability of *West's Legal Environment of Business*, Third Edition, we emphasize the following throughout the text:

- **Cyberlaw**—Your students will find that the Third Edition of *West's Legal Environment of Business* offers the most up-to-date coverage of technological developments as they affect business law. Throughout this text, whenever relevant, we have incorporated discussions of the new legal challenges created by cyberspace transactions via the Internet and the growing body of *cyberlaw* governing such transactions.
- **Access to Technology**—Most of the chapters in the text conclude with a special section, called *Accessing the Internet: The Legal Environment of Business.* These sections describe—and provide Internet addresses for—resources available on the Internet relating to topics covered in the chapters. Finally, instructors and students alike can access the *West's Legal Environment of Business* Home Page at **http://www.westbuslaw.com** (see below).
- **Comprehensiveness**—Virtually every important topic in the legal environment is covered in this book. We have made the text extremely comprehensive to allow instructors complete flexibility in choosing those areas of the legal environment that they wish to emphasize.
- **Authoritativeness**—We have fully researched every aspect of the legal environment included in this text. Instructors can rely on its accuracy and can find references to case and statutory law, as needed, for any authority. Complete parallel citations are given throughout the text. An extensive set of appendices includes excerpts from uniform codes and statutes. Accuracy is the watchword of *West's Legal Environment of Business.*
- **Ethics**—Because of the importance of ethics, there is an early chapter on the subject, with continuing references to ethics throughout. Many of the cases presented in the text conclude with a section entitled *Ethical Considerations,* in which the authors indicate some of the ethical implications of the issue being addressed by the court. Additionally, a special question, called *A Question of Ethics,* concludes the *Questions and Case Problems* sections in all of the chapters. Finally, *Focus on Ethics* sections, which conclude all of the units in the text, deal solely with ethical aspects of selected topics covered within the unit.
- **International and Comparative Law**—As the world gets smaller, a knowledge of the international and comparative aspects of the law must become part of any student's background. To this end, *West's Legal Environment of Busines* includes a full chapter on comparative law (Chapter 7) and presents a full chapter on international law (Chapter 8). Additionally, *International Considerations,* which conclude many of the cases presented in the text, offer further glimpses at comparative law. Finally, as will be discussed next, several of the cases are preceded by a special section entitled *Historical and International Setting.*
- **AACSB Curriculum Requirements**—This text explicitly addresses the AACSB's broad array of curriculum requirements by focusing on the global, political, ethical, social, environmental, technological, and cultural-diversity context of

many of the cases presented. Specifically, selected cases are preceded by a *Historical and [Social, Economic, Political, Technological, Environmental,* or *International] Setting,* which places the case in a particular political, ethical, social, or other setting. Additionally, *Company Profiles* precede many of the cases in this edition. Finally, the materials in all units explore virtually every facet of the AACSB's curriculum requirements. The AACSB's emphasis on the global and ethical context of the law is addressed throughout the rest of the text in features already mentioned: the *International* and *Ethical Considerations* that follow many of the cases and the *Focus on Ethics* section found at the end of each unit.

WEST'S LEGAL ENVIRONMENT OF BUSINESS ON THE WEB

When you visit us at **http://www.westbuslaw.com** you will find, at a minimum, the following:

- Current legal events updated regularly and keyed to chapters in this text.
- Summaries of new cases from various West legal publications, as well as many other legal publications, all linked to this text.
- Professors' Exchange: You will be able to e-mail your questions about *West's Legal Environment of Business* to Frank Cross.
- Online with Frank Cross: At scheduled times, you will be able to chat with Frank Cross about issues relating to *West's Legal Environment of Business.*
- A variety of classroom material will be made available.
- There will be more as we continue to improve our Home Page to make it better for you and your students.

AN EFFECTIVE CASE FORMAT

To ensure that *West's Legal Environment of Business,* Third Edition, meets the needs of instructors and students alike, we have devoted significant efforts to finding cases that not only effectively illustrate the principles of the legal environment discussed in the text but also are of high interest to students. Our selection includes classic, landmark cases as well as some of the most modern examples of the legal environment. For those instructors who like to see the entire court opinions for cases presented in the text, we also offer a supplement called *Case Printouts to Accompany West's Business Law,* Seventh Edition. This supplement contains the output from WESTLAW (without headnotes) for virtually every case that is included in each chapter. If the instructor wishes, the full court opinions may be copied and handed out to students.

BASIC CASE FORMAT

Each case in *West's Business Law* is presented in the following basic format:

- *Case Title and Full Case Citation*—The case title and full case citation (including all parallel citations) are presented at the beginning of each case.
- *Background and Facts*—This section contains a summary, in the authors' own words, of the events leading up to the lawsuit.
- *In the Language of the Court*—Following the summary of the background of the case, an excerpt from the actual court opinion is presented—in a contrasting type size to differentiate it from the surrounding textual material. Whenever the court opinion contains a term or phrase that may be difficult for the student to understand, we provide a brief explanation of the term in brackets. When important phrases and sentences are italicized, bracketed notes clearly indicate that the emphasis was added by the authors, not by the court.
- *Decision and Remedy*—In this section, the authors summarize, in their own words, the outcome of the case.

ADDITIONAL SECTIONS IN THE CASES

Many cases include one of the following sections, which have already been described.

- *Company Profiles*—Numerous companies are profiled before appropriate cases. Each profile, which describes the history of the company involved in a particular case, is designed to give your students the real-world context of the case before the court.
- *Historical and [Social or Other] Settings*—When appropriate, the global, political, ethical, social, environmental, technological, or cultural context of a case is presented in one of these *Settings.*
- *Ethical Considerations*—These sections, as mentioned previously, discuss ethical aspects of the law or laws under consideration.

- *International Considerations*—As explained above, these sections let your students know how the particular issue at bar is treated in other countries.

OTHER SPECIAL FEATURES OF THIS TEXT

We have included in *West's Legal Environment of Business*, Third Edition, a number of additional pedagogical devices and special features, including those discussed here.

EMERGING TRENDS

Many chapters in this edition include a special feature entitled *Emerging Trends*. These two-page spreads emphasize policy issues that are currently arising with respect to certain aspects of the legal environment. The following *Emerging Trends* are among those included in this edition:

- Jurisdictional Issues in Cyberspace (Chapter 3).
- Electronic Sales Contracts (Chapter 11).
- The Use of "Intelligent Agents" (Chapter 19).

CONCEPT SUMMARIES

Whenever key areas of the legal environment need additional emphasis, we provide a *Concept Summary*. These summaries have always been a popular pedagogical tool in this text. There are many such summaries, including the following:

- The Common Law Tradition (Chapter 1).
- Pretrial Procedures (Chapter 3).
- Intentional Torts (Chapter 12).

EXHIBITS

When appropriate, we have illustrated important aspects of the legal environment in graphic or summary form in exhibits. In all, forty-six exhibits are featured in *West's Legal Environment of Business*, Third Edition, including the following:

- Civil and Criminal Law Compared (Exhibit 1–3).
- Stages in a Typical Lawsuit (Exhibit 3–4).
- The Legal Systems of Nations (Exhibit 7–2).
- Multilateral International Organizations in Which the United States Participates (Exhibit 8–1).
- Federal Environment Statutes (Exhibit 24–1).
- Comparison of Coverage, Application, and Liabilities under Rule 10b-5 and Section 16(b) (Exhibit 28–7).

VOCABULARY STRESSED

In addition to including bracketed explanations of difficult terms and phrases within the court opinions presented in the text, we also boldface and fully define every important legal term when it is first introduced. Additionally, at the end of each chapter, all terms that were boldfaced within the chapter are listed in alphabetical order under the heading *Terms and Concepts to Review*. The page on which the term is defined is given after each term. For selected terms, particularly those of Latin origin, a special pronunciation guide has been included in footnotes within the chapters as well as in the Glossary at the end of the text. For the Third Edition, we have also increased, by almost 30 percent, the number of terms included in the Glossary.

QUESTIONS AND CASE PROBLEMS

Nearly every chapter of this text ends with ten or more questions and case problems. The first three to six of these are hypothetical questions. The remainder are actual case problems, many of which are from 1995, 1996, and 1997. Complete answers are given in a separate manual for all questions and case problems in the text, including the ethical questions and case briefing assignments.

ALTERNATE PROBLEM SETS WITH ANSWERS

To expand the number of case problems available to instructors, for each chapter of *West's Legal Environment of Business*, Third Edition, we have created a set of five or more alternate case problems. These alternate case problems, along with their answers, are included at the end of the *Answers to Questions and Case Problems and Alternate Problem Sets with Answers*. They are presented on perforated pages for easy removal and copying.

CASE BRIEFING ASSIGNMENTS

Some professors prefer to have their students brief a few cases. To make these assignments more manageable for both students and professors, we provide in Appendix A a short explanation of how to brief a case, followed by a briefed version of the sample court case presented in the appendix to Chapter 1 as Exhibit 1A–3. We then present selected cases for briefing. Case briefing assignments, including questions that should be answered for each of the cases chosen for briefing, are found at the end of the problem sets in eleven of the chapters in the text (one for each unit). Sample answers to the questions listed in the case briefing assignments are found in the *Answers to Questions and Case Problems* manual.

UNIT-ENDING HYPOTHETICALS

New to this edition are unit-ending cumulative hypothetical questions. These questions first posit a scenario—such as a small business just getting underway—and then pose a series of questions for the student to answer. The questions provide an excellent means of reviewing legal concepts covered throughout the unit. Suggested answers for these hypotheticals are included in the *Answers to Questions and Case Problems.*

APPENDICES

Because the majority of students keep their business law texts as a reference source, we have included a full set of appendices. Due to the growing importance of the limited liability company as a business organizational form, we have added a special new appendix to this edition. This appendix (Appendix Q) presents excerpts from the Uniform Limited Liability Company Act. In all, the following appendices are included in *West's Legal Environment of Business Law,* Third Edition:

- **A** Briefing Cases—Instructions and Selected Cases.
- **B** The Constitution of the United States.
- **C** The Administrative Procedure Act of 1946 (Excerpts).
- **D** The Uniform Commercial Code (Excerpts).
- **E** The National Labor Relations Act of 1914 (Excerpts).
- **F** The Sherman Act of 1890 (Excerpts).
- **G** The Clayton Act of 1914 (Excerpts).
- **H** The Federal Trade Commission Act of 1914 (Excerpts).
- **I** The Robinson-Patman Act of 1936 (Excerpts).
- **J** Securities Act of 1933 (Excerpts).
- **K** Securities Exchange Act of 1934 (Excerpts).
- **L** Title VII of the Civil Rights Act of 1964 (Excerpts).
- **M** Civil Rights Act of 1991 (Excerpts).
- **N** Americans with Disabilities Act of 1990 (Excerpts).
- **O** The Uniform Partnership Act.
- **P** The Revised Uniform Partnership Act (Excerpts).
- **Q** The Uniform Limited Liability Company Act (Excerpts).
- **R** The General Agreement on Tariffs and Trade of 1994 (Excerpts).
- **S** The North American Free Trade Agreement of 1993 (Excerpts).
- **T** The Small Business Regulatory Enforcement Fairness Act of 1996 (Excerpts).
- **U** Spanish Equivalents for Important Legal Terms in English.

THE COMPLETE SUPPLEMENTS PACKAGE

This edition of *West's Legal Environment of Business* is accompanied by a vastly expanded number of teaching and learning supplements. For further information on the *West's Legal Environment of Business* teaching/learning package, contact your local West/ITP sales representative. An additional source of information is our *West's Legal Environment of Business* Home Page at

http://www.westbuslaw.com

PRINTED SUPPLEMENTS

- *Instructor's Course Planning Guide and Media Handbook.*
- *Instructor's Manual* (also available in computerized form).
- *Study Guide and Test Preparation with Quicken Business Law Partner CD-ROM* (prepared by Aaron Abrams, William Eric Hollowell, and text author Roger LeRoy Miller)—Includes a value-added CD-ROM, *Quicken Business Law Partner.* Exercises based on the CD-ROM are included in this *Study Guide.*
- A comprehensive *Test Bank* (co-written by text author Roger LeRoy Miller)—Contains approximately 1,000 multiple-choice questions with answers and over 950 true-false questions with answers; also available on software.
- *Answers to Questions and Case Problems and Alternate Problem Sets with Answers.*
- *Case Printouts.*
- *Internet Activities for West's Legal Environment of Business.*
- *Lecture Outline System.*
- *Law and the Entrepreneur.*

- *Landmark Cases in Business Law and the Legal Environment.*
- *Advanced Topics and Contemporary Issues: Expanded Coverage*, Third Edition, by Frank B. Cross.
- *Personal Law Handbook.*
- *Handbook of Selected Statutes.*
- *Handbook on Critical Thinking and Writing in Business Law and Legal Environment.*
- *Instructor's Manual* for the *Drama of the Law* video series.
- Transparency Acetates.
- Regional Reporters.

SOFTWARE AND VIDEO SUPPLEMENTS

- *Quicken Business Law Partner* (business forms on CD-ROM).
- Computerized *Instructor's Manual.*
- *WESTEST* (computerized versions of the Test Banks).
- *Lecture Outline System.*
- PowerPoint slides.
- "The Legal Tutor on Contracts" software.
- "The Legal Tutor on Sales" software.
- Interactive software—Contracts.
- Interactive software—Sales.
- "You Be the Judge" software.
- Case-Problem Cases on Diskette.
- WESTLAW.
- CD-ROM Resources for Business Law and Legal Environment.
- West's Business Law and Legal Environment Audiocassette Library.
- Videocassettes, including those discussed next.

CNN LEGAL ISSUES UPDATE VIDEO

You can update your coverage of legal issues, as well as spark lively classroom discussion and deeper understanding of business law, by using the *CNN Legal Issues* update video. This video is produced by Turner Learning, Inc., using the resources of CNN, the world's first twenty-four-hour, all-news network.

With the introduction of the *CNN Legal Issues* update video, West Educational Publishing is proud to be the educational partner of CNN for textbook/video integration for legal issues. By making use of the *CNN Legal Issues* update video, you can bring the power of CNN, the network known for providing live, in-depth coverage and analysis of breaking news events, to your classroom.

ADDITIONAL VIDEOS

South-Western's *Business Law* video series, a set of situational videos, covers a range of topics for the full legal environment course, including the Uniform Commercial Code and employment law.

FOR USERS OF THE SECOND EDITION

First of all, we want to thank you for helping make *West's Legal Environment of Business* the best-selling legal environment text in America today. Second, we want to make you aware of the numerous additions and changes that we have made in this edition. The major additions and changes are summarized below.

SIGNIFICANTLY REVISED CHAPTERS

- Chapter 1 (Business and Its Legal Environment)—This chapter has been revised and reorganized to streamline the presentation and to make the chapter more relevant to legal environment students. The section discussing jurisprudential thought has been condensed and rewritten. A new subsection explains the steps involved in the legal reasoning process and shows students how they can use this process when working through case problems or other assignments. We have also expanded the discussion of civil law versus criminal law—and added an exhibit—to clarify the differences between civil and criminal law actions.
- Chapter 2 (Business Ethics)—This chapter has been extensively revised to place more emphasis on the process of ethical decision making in the real-world context. New sections focus on how businesspersons can determine whether their actions are not only profitable and legal but also ethical; the distinction between maximum profits and optimum profits; and the role played by public opinion in establishing the boundaries of ethical business behavior. Also included in the chapter is a fold-out exhibit showing PriceCostco's Code of Ethics, which we have annotated to show how it relates to legal environment topics covered in this text.
- Chapter 3 (The Court System)—This chapter has been reorganized and rewritten as necessary to ensure that the topics covered flow more logically from one to another. The chapter now opens with a section explaining the judiciary's role in American government. A first-level section on

"Basic Judicial Requirements" includes subsections focusing on the concepts of jurisdiction, venue, and standing to sue. The chapter also includes an *Emerging Trends* dealing with jurisdictional issues posed by online transactions.

- Chapter 5 (Constitutional Laws)—The sections on freedom of speech and freedom of religion were revised to create more clarity and to make them more relevant to students. For example, the freedom of speech section was revised so that protected speech was discussed first; then commercial speech (advertising) and corporate political speech; and, finally, unprotected speech. In the freedom of religion section, we included some examples of church-state issues, such as prayer in the schools, evolution versus creation, and government aid to parochial schools. A major section entitled "Constitutional Law in Cyberspace" looks at some of the free speech issues that have arisen in the online context. The section discusses the latest case law on the topic, including the United States Supreme Court's June 1997 decision on the unconstitutionality of key provisions of the 1996 Communications Decency Act.
- Chapter 6 (Administrative Law)—This chapter has been reorganized and, to a significant extent, rewritten to make it more manageable for business law students in terms of readability and clarity. A new exhibit entitled "Organization of the Federal Trade Commission" has been added, and the exhibit showing a page from the *Federal Register* (Exhibit 6–4) now shows a page from the Environmental Protection Agency's recently proposed rule on particulate standards.
- Chapter 11 (Sales and Leases)—This chapter now covers both sales and lease contracts and includes references to Article 2A of the Uniform Commercial Code (UCC), as well as references to Article 2.
- Chapter 12 (Torts and Strict Liability) and Chapter 13 (Torts and Crimes Related to Business)—Both of these chapters now include sections discussing online defamation, including (in Chapter 13) the liability of online service providers.
- Chapter 15 (Intellectual Property and Cyberlaw)—Now included in this chapter is an entirely new section entitled "Cyberlaw: Protecting Intellectual Property in Cyberspace." Topics discussed in this section include domain names and trademark law, patents for cyberproducts, and copyrights in cyberspace. This section is followed by an *Emerging Trends* discussing online copyright infringement. Also included in the chapter are discussions of the Lanham Act, the Trademark Dilution Act of 1995, and an updated and expanded section on international protection for intellectual property.
- Chapter 16 (Creditor-Debtor Relations and Bankruptcy)—This chapter has been rewritten as necessary to conform with the Bankruptcy Code as amended by the 1994 Bankruptcy Reform Act. A new exhibit entitled "Collection and Distribution of Property in Most Voluntary Bankruptcies" has been added.
- Chapter 17 (Business Organizations)—This chapter has been reorganized and rewritten as necessary to include limited liability companies (LLCs), limited liability partnerships (LLPs), and limited liability limited partnerships (LLLPs), as well as major business forms. Major sections on LLCs and LLPs present up-to-date discussions of the increased use of these business forms and their significance for businesspersons. Additionally, an *Emerging Trends* looks at the implications of recent Internal Revenue Service tax rules that will make the use of LLCs even simpler in the future.
- Chapter 20 (Employment Relationships)—This chapter now opens with a discussion of the employment-at-will doctrine. A discussion of AIDS testing in the employment context has been added to the section discussing privacy issues.
- Chapter 21 (Employment Discrimination)—An examination of the major provisions of the Equal Pay Act of 1963 has been added, as has a brief discussion of English-language-only policies in the workplace. The section on the Americans with Disabilities Act of 1990 has been expanded, and the *Emerging Trends* on this topic has been totally rewritten to reflect current concerns. Also discussed are the latest developments in the area of affirmative action.
- Chapter 28 (Securities Regulation and Investor Protection)—This chapter has been extensively revised and updated to include the latest developments in this area—including the United States Supreme Court's June 1997 ruling on the misappropriation theory of liability. The key functions and expanding powers of the Securities and Exchange Commission (SEC) are now given fuller treatment, and the discussion of exempt transactions under the 1993 Securities Act has been streamlined to make these exemptions more understandable for students. The chapter also now

offers expanded coverage of the sanctions and penalties that can be imposed for violations of securities laws and a discussion of the key provisions of the 1995 Private Securities Litigation Reform Act. The section on state securities now includes references to Article 8 of the UCC and examines the effect of the National Securities Markets Improvement Act of 1996 on state authority to regulate investment securities traded on national markets. Concluding the chapter is a new major section, entitled "Technology and Securities Law," that discusses online developments with respect to securities transactions and applicable SEC rules.

WHAT ELSE IS NEW?

In addition to the changes already noted, we have included in the Third Edition text a number of new pedagogical features and have expanded the supplements package. The new features and elements are listed below.

NEW FEATURES We have added the following entirely new features to the Third Edition:

- *Accessing the Internet: The Legal Environment of Business.*
- Unit-ending cumulative hypothetical questions.

NEW *EMERGING TRENDS* All of these features have been either newly created for the Third Edition or completely rewritten.

NEW EXHIBITS Of the forty-six exhibits in this edition, the following sixteen exhibits are new to the Third Edition:

- *Exhibit 1–1*—Equitable Maxims.
- *Exhibit 1–3*—Civil and Criminal Law Compared.
- *Exhibit 1A–3*—A Sample Court Case.
- *Fold-Out Exhibit*—PriceCostco's Code of Ethics, Annotated.
- *Exhibit 3–2*—The Federal and State Court Systems.
- *Exhibit 3–4*—Stages in a Typical Lawsuit.
- *Exhibit 6–1*—Organization of the Federal Trade Commission.
- *Exhibit 6–4*—A Page from the *Federal Register.*
- *Exhibit 6–6*—The Process of Formal Administrative Adjudication.
- *Exhibit 7–4*—Hourly Labor Costs in Manufacturing in Selected Countries.
- *Exhibit 12–1*—Tort Lawsuit and Criminal Prosecution for the Same Act.
- *Exhibit 16–1*—Collection and Distribution of Property in Most Voluntary Bankruptcies.
- *Exhibit 22–1*—Unfair Labor Practice Complaint Form.
- *Exhibit 22–2*—Basic Unfair Labor Practices.
- *Exhibit 25–1*—Tenancy in Common and Joint Tenancy.
- *Exhibit 26–1*—FTC Notification Form.

NEW CASES Of the over 150 cases presented in the chapters of this text, over half are new to the Third Edition. In all, approximately 65 percent of the cases presented in *West's Legal Environment of Business*, Third Edition, are from 1995, 1996, and 1997. Many classic cases have been retained from the Second Edition, and some others have been added.

NEW CASE PROBLEMS Of the over 200 case problems included in this text, over a third are new to the Third Edition. Of the new case problems, over two dozen are from 1995, 1996, and 1997. In addition, alternate sets of five or more case problems (and answers) for each chapter are now available—see the list of new supplements below.

NEW APPENDICES We have added to this edition two new appendices: Appendix Q, entitled "The Uniform Limited Liability Company Act (Excerpts)," and Appendix T, entitled "The Small Business Regulatory Enforcement Fairness Act of 1996 (Excerpts)."

A NEW LIST OF ABBREVIATIONS For the Third Edition, we have added a list of selected abbreviations to the inside front cover of the book.

EXPANDED GLOSSARY The Glossary of the Third Edition lists and defines about 30 percent more terms than were included in the Second Edition.

NEW SUPPLEMENTS AND SPECIAL RESOURCES

- CNN *Legal Issues* update video.
- South-Western's *Business Law* video series.
- "The Legal Tutor on Contracts" software.
- "The Legal Tutor on Sales" software.
- *Alternate Problem Sets with Answers*—Included, on perforated sheets, at the end of the *Answers to*

Questions and Case Problems and Alternate Problem Sets with Answers.
- *Internet Activities for West's Legal Environment of Business.*
- *Lecture Outline System.*
- PowerPoint slides.
- *Law and the Entrepreneur.*
- *Landmark Cases in Business Law and the Legal Environment.*
- *Advanced Topics and Contemporary Issues:* Expanded Coverage, Third Edition, by Frank Cross.
- *Quicken Business Law Partner* (business forms on CD-ROM).
- *West's Legal Environment of Business* Internet Home Page.

ACKNOWLEDGMENTS FOR SECOND EDITION

The extensive revision of *West's Legal Environment of Business* could never have been done without the extremely helpful criticisms, comments, and suggestions that we received from the following professors:

Wm. Dennis Ames
Indiana University of Pennsylvania

Wayne L. Anderson
SW Missouri State University

Betty Kendall
North Adams State College

Anne C. Levy
Michigan State University

Richard A. Mills
Cypress College

Michael J. O'Hara
University of Nebraska at Omaha

Larry D. Strate
University of Nevada at Las Vegas

Daphyne Saunders Thomas
James Madison University

ACKNOWLEDGMENTS FOR THE THIRD EDITION

In preparing the Third Edition of *West's Legal Environment of Business*, we worked closely with the following reviewers, each of whom offered us valuable suggestions for how to improve the text.

Wm. Dennis Ames
Indiana University of Pennslyvania

Angela Cerino
Villanova University

David Cooper
Fullerton College

Gamewell Gant
Idaho State University

Arlene M. Hibschweiler
SUNY Fredonia

Marty Salley McGee
South Carolina State University

Kathleen A. Phillips
University of Houston

Brian Terry
Johnson and Wales University

Michael G. Walsh
Villanova University

As in all past editions, we owe a debt of extreme gratitude to the numerous individuals who worked directly with us or at West Publishing Company. We especially wish to thank Lavina Leed Miller for her management of the entire project, as well as for the application of her superb editorial skills. William Eric Hollowell, who also coauthored the *Instructor's Manual, Study Guide*, and *Test Bank*, helped with much of the research. We were again fortunate enough to have the copyediting services of Beverly Peavler. Literally dozens of individuals helped proofread the galleys and pages of this edition over many, many months. They include Lavina Leed Miller, William Eric Hollowell, Suzie Franklin DeFazio, and Roxanna Lee.

We continue to be the fortunate recipients of an incredibly skilled and dedicated editorial, production, and printing and manufacturing team at West Publishing Company. In particular, we wish to thank Clyde Perlee, Jr., for his helpful advice and guidance during the planning stages of *West's Legal Environment of Business*, Third Edition. We also wish to thank Rob Dewey and Scott Person for their overall supervision of the project. Our long-time developmental editor, Jan Lamar, also helped us plan this project and made sure we addressed all reviewers' criticisms and suggestions. She additionally made sure that the preparation of supplements went smoothly and on time. Also, we would like to thank the following content specialists: Kathleen M. Knutson (contributor), College of St. Catherine; and John T. Wendt (author of *Drama of the Law Interactivity*), University of St. Thomas. Their contributions are greatly appreciated.

Our production manager at West, Bill Stryker, made sure that we came out with an error-free, visually appealing edition. We will always be in his debt.

Through the years, we have enjoyed a continuing correspondence with many of you who have found points on which you wish to comment. We continue to welcome all comments and promise to respond promptly. By incorporating your ideas, we can continue to write a business law text that is best for you and best for your students.

R.L.M.
F.B.C.

Dedication

To my parents and sisters.

Frank B. Cross

R.L.M. dedicates this edition to Mike Elia. Thanks for your support and friendship for so many years.

R.L.M.

UNIT ONE

THE FOUNDATIONS

CONTENTS

CHAPTER 1

BUSINESS AND ITS LEGAL ENVIRONMENT

CIVILIZED SOCIETIES REQUIRE ORDER and some degree of certainty. The law generates both. If any society is to survive, its citizens must be able to determine what is legally right and legally wrong. When citizens believe that a legal wrong has occurred, they must have some idea of how to seek redress. The law provides such a vehicle.

In this introductory chapter, we first look at the nature of law and then examine the foundation and basic characteristics of the American legal system. We next describe the basic sources of American law and the distinction between civil law and criminal law. In the appendix to this chapter, we provide sections offering practical guidance on several topics, including how to find the sources of law discussed in this chapter (and referred to throughout the text), how to read and understand court opinions, and legal reasoning.

The legal environment of business includes the American court system, administrative agencies, and alternatives to litigation, as well as the laws and legal systems of other nations and the international community. The legal environment is a significant part of the world of business, influencing contracts, leases, creditor-debtor relations, employment relationships, real property transactions, business organizations, and the conduct of competitors. The remainder of this book addresses these and other topics with special emphasis on business ethics and on the effect of the legal environment in the area of electronic communications.

SECTION 1

WHAT IS LAW?

There have been and will continue to be different definitions of law. Although the numerous definitions vary in their particulars, they all are based on the general observation that, at a minimum, **law** consists of *enforceable rules governing relationships among individuals and between individuals and their society*.

This broad statement may serve as a basic definition of law, but for those who embark on a study of law, it is only a starting point. It leaves unanswered some important questions concerning the nature of law. In this section, we examine some of those questions and how they have been answered in the past by legal philosophers and jurists. You may think that legal philosophy is far removed from the practical study of business law and the legal environment. In fact, it is not. As you will learn in the chapters of this text, how judges apply the law to specific disputes, including disputes relating to the business world, depends in part on their personal philosophical views.

NATURAL LAW AND POSITIVE LAW

An age-old question in regard to the nature of law has to do with the finality of **positive law** (the written law of a particular society at a particular point in time). For example, what if a positive law of a particular nation is deemed to be a "bad" law by a substantial number of that nation's citizens? Must a citizen obey the law if it goes against his or her conscience to do so? Is there a higher or universal law to which they can appeal?

THE NATURAL LAW TRADITION One who adheres to the natural law tradition would answer this question in the affirmative. **Natural law** denotes a system of moral and ethical principles that are inherent in human nature and that can be discovered by humans through the use of their natural intelligence. The natural law tradition is one of the oldest and most significant schools of jurisprudence. It dates to the Greek philosopher Aristotle (384–322 B.C.E.), who distinguished between natural law (which applies universally to all humankind) and positive law. The notion that people have "natural rights" (expressed in the Declaration of Independence as "unalienable rights" to "life, liberty, and the pursuit of happiness") stems from the natural law tradition. In essence, the natural law tradition presupposes that the legitimacy of positive, or conventional, law derives from a higher law—natural law. Whenever positive law conflicts with natural law, positive law loses its legitimacy.

Those who claim that a specific foreign government is depriving certain citizens of their human rights, notwithstanding the fact that the government's actions are legal in that country, implicitly are appealing to a higher law that has universal applicability. The question of the universality of basic human rights also comes into play in the context of international business operations. Should rights that extend to workers in this country, such as the right to be free of discrimination in the workplace, be applied to a U.S. firm doing business in another country that does not provide for such rights? Implicitly, this question is rooted in a concept of universal rights that has its origins in the natural law tradition.

LEGAL POSITIVISM At the other end of the spectrum are the legal positivists. **Legal positivists** believe that there can be no higher law than a nation's positive law. Whether a particular law is bad or good is irrelevant. The merits or demerits of a given law can be discussed, and laws can be changed—in an orderly manner through a legitimate lawmaking process—but as long as a law exists, it must be obeyed.

From the positivist perspective, then, the significance of positive law is greater than in the natural law tradition. The positivist approach is rooted in the assumption that there is no such thing as "natural rights." Rather, human rights exist solely because of laws. If the laws are not enforced, anarchy will result. A judge with positivist leanings probably would be more inclined to defer to an existing law than would a judge who adheres to the natural law tradition.

LEGAL REALISM

Another significant question about the nature of law can be phrased as follows: To what extent should changing social customs and practices affect the law? Prior to the 1920s, jurists and legal theorists commonly assumed that the law should change only slowly, if at all, and that sociological and economic data had little relevance in the making of judicial decisions. The idea was that the law should be applied impartially, logically, and uniformly to all similar situations, regardless of the social and economic context in which a particular dispute arose.

In the 1920s and 1930s, a number of jurists and scholars, known as **legal realists,** rebelled against this conception of the law. The legal realists pointed out that law is a human enterprise and not a set of abstract rules that can be applied uniformly to all cases involving similar facts. Given that judges are human beings with unique personalities, value systems, and intellects, it would be impossible for any two judges to engage in an identical reasoning process when evaluating the same case. Additionally, each case involves a unique set of circumstances—no two cases, no matter how similar, are ever exactly the same. Therefore, judges must take into account the specific circumstances of each case when making their decisions. When making decisions, judges also should consider extra-legal sources, such as economic and sociological data, to the extent that such sources can illuminate the circumstances and issues involved in specific cases. In other words, the law should take social and economic realities into account.

United States Supreme Court Justice Oliver Wendell Holmes, Jr. (1841–1935), and Karl Llewellyn (1893–1962) were both influential proponents of legal realism. Llewellyn is best known for his dominant role in drafting the Uniform Commercial Code (UCC), a set of rules for commercial transactions that will be discussed later in this chapter. The UCC reflects the influence of legal realism in its emphasis on practicality, flexibility, reasonability, and customary trade practices.

JUDICIAL INTERPRETATION OF THE LAW

Oliver Wendell Holmes, Jr., once stated that "the prophecies of what the courts will do in fact, and nothing more pretentious, are what I mean by the law." The final question we explore has to do with the implications of this statement.

Clearly, judges are not free to decide cases solely on the basis of their personal philosophical views or their opinions on the issues before the court. A judge's function is not to make the laws—that is the function of the legislative branch of government—but to interpret and apply them. From a practical point of view, however, the courts play a significant role in defining what the law is. This is because the law is not an exact science, and legal rules tend to be expressed in general terms. Judges thus have some flexibility in interpreting and applying the law. It is because of this flexibility that different courts can—and often do—arrive at different conclusions in cases that involve nearly identical issues, facts, and applicable laws. This flexibility also means that each judge's unique personality, legal philosophy, set of values, and intellectual attributes necessarily frame the judicial decision-making process to some extent.

Part of the study of law is discovering how different approaches to law affect judicial decision making. As you read the cases presented and discussed in this book, keep in mind that how a particular judge or panel of judges approaches an issue in a particular case necessarily has an impact on the outcome of the case. Because of our common law tradition (discussed next), the courts—and thus the personal views and philosophies of judges—play a paramount role in the American legal system. This is particularly true of the United States Supreme Court, which has the final say on how a particular law or legal principle should be interpreted and applied.

SECTION 2

THE COMMON LAW TRADITION

Because of our colonial heritage, much of American law is based on the English legal system, which originated in medieval England and continued to evolve in the following centuries. A knowledge of this system is necessary to an understanding of the American legal system today.

EARLY ENGLISH COURTS

The origins of the English legal system—and the U.S. legal system—date to 1066, when the Normans conquered England. William the Conqueror and his successors began the process of unifying the country under their rule. One of the means they used to this end was the establishment of the king's courts, or *curiae regis.* Before the Norman Conquest, disputes had been settled according to the local legal customs and traditions in various regions of the country. The king's courts sought to establish a uniform set of customs for the country as a whole. What evolved in these courts was the beginning of the **common law**—a body of general rules that prescribed social conduct and applied throughout the entire English realm.

COURTS OF LAW AND REMEDIES AT LAW In the early English king's courts, the kinds of **remedies** (the legal means to recover a right or redress a wrong) that could be granted were severely restricted. If one person wronged another in some way, the king's courts could award as compensation one or more of the following: (1) land, (2) items of value, or (3) money. The courts that awarded this compensation became known as **courts of law,** and the three remedies were called **remedies at law.** (Today, the remedy at law normally takes the form of **damages**—money given to a party whose legal interests have been injured.) Even though the system introduced uniformity in the settling of disputes, when a complaining party wanted a remedy other than economic compensation, the courts of law could do nothing, so "no remedy, no right."

COURTS OF EQUITY AND REMEDIES IN EQUITY Equity is a branch of law, founded on what might be described as notions of justice and fair dealing, that seeks to supply a remedy when there is no adequate remedy available at law. When individuals could not obtain an adequate remedy in a court of law because of strict technicalities, they petitioned the king for relief. Most of these petitions were decided by an adviser to the king, called a **chancellor,** who was said to be the "keeper of the king's conscience." When the chancellor thought that the claims were fair, new and unique remedies were granted. Eventually, formal chancery courts, or **courts of equity,** were established.

The remedies granted by equity courts became known as **remedies in equity,** or equitable remedies. These remedies include *specific performance* (ordering a party to perform an agreement as promised), an *injunction* (ordering a party to cease engaging in a specific activity or to undo some wrong or injury), and *rescission* (the cancellation of a contractual obligation). We discuss these and other equitable remedies in more detail at appropriate points in the chapters that follow. As a general rule, today's courts, like the early English courts, will not grant equitable remedies unless the remedy at law—money damages—is inadequate.

In fashioning appropriate remedies, judges often were (and continue to be) guided by so-called **equitable maxims**—propositions or general statements of equitable rules. Exhibit 1–1 lists some important equitable maxims. The last maxim listed in that exhibit—"Equity aids the vigilant, not those who rest on their rights"—merits special attention. It has become known as the equitable doctrine of **laches,** and it can be used as a defense. A **defense** is an argument raised by the **defendant** (the party being sued) indicating why the **plaintiff** (the suing party) should not obtain the remedy sought. The doctrine of laches arose to encourage people to bring lawsuits while the evidence was fresh. What constitutes a reasonable time, of course, varies according to the circumstances of the case. Time periods for different types of cases are now usually fixed by **statutes of limitations.** After the time allowed under a statute of limitations has expired, no action can be brought, no matter how strong the case was originally.

LEGAL AND EQUITABLE REMEDIES TODAY

The establishment of courts of equity in medieval England resulted in two distinct court systems: courts of law and courts of equity. The systems had different sets of judges and granted different types of remedies. Parties who sought legal remedies, or remedies at law, would bring their claims before courts of law. Parties seeking equitable relief, or remedies in equity, would bring their claims before courts of equity. During the nineteenth century, however, in the United States, most states adopted rules of procedure that resulted in combined courts of law and equity—although some states, such as Arkansas, still retain the distinction. A party now may request both legal and equitable remedies in the same action, and the trial court judge may grant either form or both forms of relief.

The distinction between legal and equitable remedies remains relevant to students of business

EXHIBIT 1–1 ■ EQUITABLE MAXIMS

- *Whoever seeks equity must do equity.* (Anyone who wishes to be treated fairly must treat others fairly.)
- *When there is equal equity, the law must prevail.* (The law will determine the outcome of a controversy in which the merits of both sides are equal.)
- *One seeking the aid of an equity court must come to the court with clean hands.* (Plaintiffs must have acted fairly and honestly.)
- *Equity will not suffer a right to exist without a remedy.* (Equitable relief will be awarded when there is a right to relief and there is no adequate remedy at law.)
- *Equity regards substance rather than form.* (Equity is more concerned with fairness and justice than with legal technicalities.)
- *Equity aids the vigilant, not those who rest on their rights.* (Equity will not help those who neglect their rights for an unreasonable period of time.)

Statute of limitations

law, however, because these remedies differ. To seek the proper remedy for a wrong, one must know what remedies are available. Additionally, certain vestiges of the procedures used when there were separate courts of law and equity still exist. For example, a party has the right to demand a jury trial in an action at law, but not in an action in equity. In the old courts of equity, the chancellor heard both sides of an issue and decided what should be done. Juries were considered inappropriate. In actions at law, however, juries participated in determining the outcome of cases, including the amount of damages to be awarded. Exhibit 1–2 summarizes the procedural differences (applicable in most states) between an action at law and an action in equity.

THE DOCTRINE OF *STARE DECISIS*

A unique feature of the common law is that it is *judge-made* law. The body of principles and doctrines that form the common law emerged over time as judges decided actual legal controversies.

CASE PRECEDENTS AND CASE REPORTERS When possible, judges attempted to be consistent and to base their decisions on the principles suggested by earlier cases. They sought to decide similar cases in a similar way and considered new cases with care, because they knew that their decisions would make new law. Each interpretation became part of the law on the subject and served as a legal **precedent**—that is, a decision that furnished an example or authority for deciding subsequent cases involving similar legal principles or facts.

By the early fourteenth century, portions of the more important decisions of each year were being gathered together and recorded in *Year Books*, which became useful references for lawyers and judges. In the sixteenth century, the *Year Books* were discontinued, and other types of publications of cases became available. Today, cases are published, or "reported," in volumes called **reporters,** or *reports*. We describe today's case reporting system in detail later in this chapter.

STARE DECISIS* AND THE COMMON LAW TRADITION** The practice of deciding new cases with reference to former decisions, or precedents, became a cornerstone of the English and American judicial systems. The practice forms a doctrine called ***stare decisis[1] (a Latin phrase meaning "to stand on decided cases"). Under this doctrine, judges are obligated to follow the precedents established within their jurisdictions.

For example, if the Supreme Court of California (that state's highest court) has ruled in a certain way on an issue, that decision will control the outcome of future cases on that issue brought before the California courts. Similarly, a decision on a given issue by the United States Supreme Court (the nation's highest court) is binding on all inferior courts. Case precedents, as well as statutes and other laws that must be followed, are referred to as **binding authorities.** (Nonbinding legal authorities on which judges may rely for guidance, such as precedents established in other jurisdictions, are referred to as *persuasive authorities.*)

The doctrine of *stare decisis* helps the courts to be more efficient, because if other courts have carefully reasoned through a similar case, their legal reasoning and opinions can serve as guides. *Stare decisis* also makes the law more stable and predictable. If the law on a given subject is well settled, someone bringing a case to court can usually rely on the court to make a decision based on what the law has been.

DEPARTURES FROM PRECEDENT Although courts are obligated to follow precedents, sometimes

1. Prononunced *ster*-ay dih-*si*-ses.

EXHIBIT 1–2 ■ PROCEDURAL DIFFERENCES BETWEEN AN ACTION AT LAW AND AN ACTION IN EQUITY

PROCEDURE	ACTION AT LAW	ACTION IN EQUITY
Initiation of lawsuit	By filing a complaint	By filing a petition
Decision	By jury or judge	By judge (no jury)
Result	Judgment	Decree
Remedy	Monetary damages	Injunction, specific performance, or rescission

a court will depart from the rule of precedent if it decides that the precedent should no longer be followed. If a court decides that a ruling precedent is simply incorrect or that technological or social changes have rendered the precedent inapplicable, the court might rule contrary to the precedent. Cases that overturn precedent often receive a great deal of publicity.[2]

WHEN THERE IS NO PRECEDENT Occasionally, cases come before the courts for which no precedents exist. Such cases, called "cases of first impression," often result when new practices or technological developments in society create new types of legal disputes. In the last several years, for example, the courts have had to deal with disputes involving transactions conducted via the Internet. When existing laws governing free speech, pornography, fraud, jurisdiction, and other areas were drafted, cyberspace did not exist. Although new laws are being created to govern such disputes, in the meantime the courts have to decide, on a case-by-case basis, what rules should be applied.

Generally, in deciding cases of first impression, courts may consider a number of factors, including legal principles and policies underlying previous court decisions or existing statutes, fairness, social values and customs, **public policy** (governmental policy based on widely held societal values), and data and concepts drawn from the social sciences. Which of these sources is chosen or receives the greatest emphasis depends on the nature of the case being considered and the particular judge or judges hearing the case. As mentioned previously, judges are not free to decide cases on the basis of their own personal views. In cases of first impression, as in all cases, judges must have legal reasons for deciding as they do on particular issues. When a court issues a written opinion on a case (we discuss court opinions later in this chapter), the opinion normally contains a carefully reasoned argument justifying the decision.

2. For example, when the United States Supreme Court held in the 1950s that racial segregation in the public schools was unconstitutional, it expressly overturned a Supreme Court precedent upholding the constitutionality of "separate-but-equal" segregation. The Supreme Court's departure from precedent received a tremendous amount of publicity as people began to realize the ramifications of this change in the law. See *Brown v. Board of Education of Topeka*, 347 U.S. 483, 74 S.Ct. 686, 98 L.Ed. 873 (1954). (Legal citations are explained later in the appendix at the end of this chapter.)

STARE DECISIS AND LEGAL REASONING

Legal reasoning is the reasoning process used by judges in deciding what law applies to a given dispute and then applying that law to the specific facts or circumstances of the case. Through the use of legal reasoning, judges harmonize their decisions with decisions that have been made before—which the doctrine of *stare decisis* requires.

Students of business law also engage in legal reasoning. For example, you may be asked to provide answers for some of the case problems that appear at the end of every chapter in this text. Each problem describes the facts of a particular dispute and the legal question at issue. If you are assigned a case problem, you will be asked to determine how a court would answer that question and why. In other words, you will need to give legal reasons for whatever conclusion you reach. We look here at the basic steps involved in legal reasoning and then describe some forms of reasoning commonly used by the courts in making their decisions.

BASIC STEPS IN LEGAL REASONING At times, the legal arguments set forth in court opinions are relatively simple and brief. At other times, the arguments are complex and lengthy. Regardless of the brevity or length of a legal argument, however, the basic steps of the legal reasoning process remain the same in all cases. These steps, which you also can follow when analyzing cases and case problems, can best be described as a series of questions.

1. *What are the key facts and issues?* For example, suppose that a plaintiff comes before the court claiming *assault* (a wrongful and intentional action, or *tort*, in which one person makes another fearful of immediate physical harm). The plaintiff claims that the defendant threatened her while she was sleeping. Although the plaintiff was unaware that she was being threatened, her roommate heard the defendant make the threat. The legal issue, or question, raised by these facts is whether the defendant's actions in fact constitute the tort of assault, given that the plaintiff was not aware of those actions at the time they occurred.
2. *What are the relevant rules of law?* Because the plaintiff **alleges** (claims) that the defendant committed a tort, the applicable law is the common law of torts—specifically, tort law governing assault (see Chapter 12 for more detail on torts). Case precedents

involving similar facts and issues thus would be relevant.

3. *How do the relevant rules of law apply to the particular facts and circumstances of this case?* This step is often the most difficult one, because each case presents a unique set of facts, circumstances, and parties. Although there may be similar cases, no two cases are ever identical in all respects. Normally, judges (and lawyers and law students) try to find **cases on point**—previously decided cases that are as similar as possible to the one under consideration. (Because of the difficulty—and importance—of this step in the legal reasoning process, we discuss it in more detail in the next subsection.)

4. *What conclusion should be drawn?* This step normally presents few problems. Usually, the conclusion is evident if the previous three steps have been followed carefully.

FORMS OF LEGAL REASONING Judges use many types of reasoning when following the third step of the legal reasoning process—applying the law to the facts of a particular case. Three common forms of reasoning are deductive reasoning, linear reasoning, and reasoning by analogy.

Deductive Reasoning. Deductive reasoning is sometimes called *syllogistic* reasoning because it employs a **syllogism**—a logical relationship involving a major premise, a minor premise, and a conclusion. For example, consider the example given earlier, in which the plaintiff alleged that the defendant committed assault by threatening her while she was sleeping. The judge might point out that "under the common law of torts, an individual must be *aware* of a threat of danger for the threat to constitute civil assault" (major premise); "the plaintiff in this case was unaware of the threat at the time it occurred" (minor premise); and "therefore, the circumstances do not amount to a civil assault" (conclusion).

Linear Reasoning. A second important form of commonly employed legal reasoning might be thought of as "linear" reasoning, because it proceeds from one point to another, with the final point being the conclusion. An analogy will help make this form of reasoning clear. Imagine a knotted rope, with each knot tying together separate pieces of rope to form a tight length. As a whole, the rope represents a linear progression of thought logically connecting various points, with the last point, or knot, representing the conclusion. For example, suppose that a tenant in an apartment building sues the landlord for damages for an injury resulting from an allegedly dimly lit stairway. The court may engage in a reasoning process involving the following "pieces of rope":

1. The landlord, who was on the premises the evening the injury occurred, testifies that none of the other nine tenants who used the stairway that night complained about the lights.
2. The fact that none of the tenants complained is the same as if they had said the lighting was sufficient.
3. That there were no complaints does not prove that the lighting was sufficient but proves that the landlord had no reason to believe that it was not.
4. The landlord's belief was reasonable, because no one complained.
5. Therefore, the landlord acted reasonably and was not negligent in respect to the lighting in the stairway.

On the basis of this reasoning, the court concludes that the tenant is not entitled to compensation on the basis of the stairway's lighting.

Reasoning by Analogy. Another important form of reasoning that judges use in deciding cases is reasoning by *analogy*. To reason by **analogy** is to compare the facts in the case at hand to the facts in other cases and, to the extent that the patterns are similar, to apply the same rule to the case at hand. To the extent that the facts are unique, or "distinguishable," different rules may apply. For example, in case A, it is held that a driver who crosses a highway's center line is negligent. In case B, a driver crosses the line to avoid hitting a child. In determining whether case A's rule applies in case B, a judge would consider what the reasons were for the decision in A and whether B is sufficiently similar for those reasons to apply. If the judge holds that B's driver is not liable, that judge must indicate why case A's rule does not apply to the facts presented in case B.

THERE IS NO ONE "RIGHT" ANSWER

Many persons believe that there is one "right" answer to every legal question. In most situations involving a legal controversy, however, there is no single correct result. Good arguments can often be made to support either side of a legal controversy. Quite often, a case does not present the situation of a "good" person suing a "bad" person. In many cases, both parties

CONCEPT SUMMARY 1.1 The Common Law Tradition

ELEMENT	DESCRIPTION
Origins of the Common Law	The American legal system is based on the common law tradition, which originated in medieval England. Following the conquest of England in 1066 by William the Conquerer, king's courts were established throughout England, and the common law was developed in these courts.
Legal and Equitable Remedies	The distinction between remedies at law (money or items of value, such as land) and remedies in equity (including specific performance, injunction, and rescission of a contractual obligation) originated in the early English courts of law and courts of equity, respectively.
Case Precedents and the Doctrine of *Stare Decisis*	In the king's courts, judges attempted to make their decisions consistent with previous decisions, called precedents. This practice gave rise to the doctrine of *stare decisis.* This doctrine, which became a cornerstone of the common law tradition, obligates judges to abide by precedents established in their jurisdictions.
Stare Decisis and Legal Reasoning	Legal reasoning refers to the reasoning process used by judges in applying the law to the facts and issues of specific cases. Legal reasoning involves becoming familiar with the key facts of a case, identifying the relevant legal rules, linking those rules to the facts, and forming a conclusion. In linking the legal rules to the facts of a case, judges may use deductive reasoning, linear reasoning, or reasoning by analogy.

have acted in good faith in some measure or have acted in bad faith to some degree.

Additionally, as already mentioned, each judge has his or her own personal beliefs and philosophy, which shape, at least to some extent, the process of legal reasoning. What this means is that the outcome of a particular lawsuit before a court can never be predicted with absolute certainty. In fact, in some cases, even though the weight of the law would seem to favor one party's position, judges, through creative legal reasoning, have found ways to rule in favor of the other party in the interests of preventing injustice.

SECTION 3

SOURCES OF AMERICAN LAW

There are numerous sources of American law. *Primary sources of law,* or sources that *establish* the law, include the following:

1. The U.S. Constitution and the constitutions of the various states.
2. Statutes, or laws, passed by state legislatures.
3. Regulations created by administrative agencies, such as the Food and Drug Administration.
4. Case law and common law doctrines.

We describe each of these important sources of law in the following pages.

Secondary sources of law are books and articles that summarize and clarify the primary sources of law. Examples are legal encyclopedias, treatises, and articles in law reviews. Courts often refer to secondary sources of law for guidance in interpreting and applying the primary sources of law discussed here.

CONSTITUTIONAL LAW

The federal government and the states have separate written constitutions that set forth the general organization, powers, and limits of their respective governments. **Constitutional law** is the law as expressed in these constitutions.

The U.S. Constitution is the supreme law of the land. As such, it is the basis of all law in the United States. A law in violation of the Constitution, no matter what its source, will be declared unconstitutional and will not be enforced. Because of its importance in the American legal system, we present the complete text of the U.S. Constitution in Appendix B.

The Tenth Amendment to the U.S. Constitution reserves all powers not granted to the federal government to the states. Each state in the union has its own constitution. Unless it conflicts with the U.S. Constitution or a federal law, a state constitution is supreme within the state's borders.

STATUTORY LAW

Statutes enacted by legislative bodies at any level of government make up another source of law, which is generally referred to as **statutory law.** When a legislature passes a statute, that statute ultimately is included in the federal code of laws or the relevant state code of laws (these codes are discussed later in this chapter). Statutory law also includes local **ordinances**—statutes (laws, rules, or orders) passed by municipal or county governing units to govern matters not covered by federal or state law. Ordinances commonly have to do with city or county land use (zoning ordinances), building and safety codes, and other matters affecting the local unit.

A federal statute, of course, applies to all states. A state statute, in contrast, applies only within the state's borders. State laws thus may vary from state to state. No federal statute may violate the U.S. Constitution, and no state statute or local ordinance may violate the U.S. Constitution or the relevant state constitution.

UNIFORM LAWS

The differences among state laws were particularly notable in the 1800s, when conflicting state statutes frequently made the rapidly developing trade and commerce among the states very difficult. To counter these problems, in 1892 a group of legal scholars and lawyers formed the National Conference of Commissioners (NCC) on Uniform State Laws to draft **uniform laws,** or model laws, for the states to consider adopting. The NCC still exists today and continues to issue uniform laws.

Each state has the option of adopting or rejecting a uniform law. *Only if a state legislature adopts a uniform law does that law become part of the statutory law of that state.* Note that a state legislature may adopt all or part of a uniform law as it is written, or the legislature may rewrite the law however the legislature wishes. Hence, even when a uniform law is said to have been adopted in many states, those states' laws may not be entirely "uniform."

The earliest uniform law, the Uniform Negotiable Instruments Law, had been completed by 1896 and adopted in every state by the early 1920s (although not all states used exactly the same wording). Over the following decades, other acts were drawn up in a similar manner. In all, over two hundred uniform acts have been issued by the NCC since its inception. The most ambitious uniform act of all, however, was the Uniform Commercial Code.

THE UNIFORM COMMERCIAL CODE (UCC)

The Uniform Commercial Code (UCC), which was created through the joint efforts of the NCC and the American Law Institute,[3] was first issued in 1952. The UCC has been adopted in all fifty states,[4] the District of Columbia, and the Virgin Islands. The UCC facilitates commerce among the states by providing a uniform, yet flexible, set of rules governing commercial transactions. The UCC assures businesspersons that their contracts, if validly entered into, normally will be enforced. Because of its importance in the area of commercial law, we cite the UCC frequently in this text. We also present excerpts from the latest version of the UCC in Appendix C.

ADMINISTRATIVE LAW

An important source of American law consists of **administrative law**—the rules, orders, and decisions of administrative agencies. An **administrative agency** is a federal, state, or local government agency established to perform a specific function. Administrative law and procedures, which will be examined in detail in Chapter 6, constitute a dominant element in the regulatory environment of business. Rules issued by various administrative agencies now affect virtually every aspect of a business's operation, including the firm's capital structure and financing, its hiring and firing procedures, its relations with employees and unions, and the way it manufactures and markets its products.

At the national level, numerous **executive agencies** exist within the cabinet departments of the executive branch. The Food and Drug Administration, for example, is an agency within the Department of Health and Human Services. Executive agencies are subject to the authority of the president, who has the power to appoint and remove officers of federal agencies. There are also major **independent regulatory**

3. This institute was formed in the 1920s and consists of practicing attorneys, legal scholars, and judges.

4. Louisiana has adopted only Articles 1, 3, 4, 5, 7, 8, and 9. All states have, of course, modified the UCC.

agencies at the federal level, such as the Federal Trade Commission, the Securities and Exchange Commission, and the Federal Communications Commission. The president's power is less pronounced in regard to independent agencies, whose officers serve for fixed terms and cannot be removed without just cause.

There are administrative agencies at the state and local levels as well. Commonly, a state agency (such as a state pollution-control agency) is created as a parallel to a federal agency (such as the Environmental Protection Agency). Just as federal statutes take precedence over conflicting state statutes, so federal agency regulations take precedence over conflicting state regulations.

CASE LAW AND COMMON LAW DOCTRINES

As is evident from the earlier discussion of the common law tradition, another basic source of American law consists of the rules of law announced in court decisions. These rules of law include interpretations of constitutional provisions, of statutes enacted by legislatures, and of regulations created by administrative agencies. Today, this body of law is referred to variously as the common law, judge-made law, or **case law.**

THE RELATIONSHIP BETWEEN THE COMMON LAW AND STATUTORY LAW Common law doctrines and principles govern all areas not covered by statutory or administrative law. In a dispute concerning a particular employment practice, for example, if a statute regulates that practice, the statute will apply rather than the common law doctrine that applied prior to the enactment of the statute.

Even though the body of statutory law has expanded greatly since the beginning of this nation, thus narrowing the applicability of common law doctrines, there is a significant overlap between statutory law and the common law. For example, many statutes essentially codify existing common law rules, and thus the courts, in interpreting the statutes, often rely on the common law as a guide to what the legislators intended.

Additionally, how the courts interpret a particular statute determines how that statute will be applied. If you wanted to learn about the coverage and applicability of a particular statute, for example, you would, of course, need to locate the statute and study it. You would also need to see how the courts in your jurisdiction have interpreted the statute—in other words, what precedents have been established in regard to that statute. Often, the applicability of a newly enacted statute does not become clear until a body of case law develops to clarify how, when, and to whom the statute applies.

RESTATEMENTS OF THE LAW The American Law Institute has drafted and published compilations of the common law called *Restatements of the Law*, which generally summarize the common law rules followed by most states. There are *Restatements of the Law* in the areas of contracts, torts, agency, trusts, property, restitution, security, judgments, and conflict of laws. The *Restatements*, like other secondary sources of law, do not in themselves have the force of law but are an important source of legal analysis and opinion on which judges often rely in making their decisions.

Many of the *Restatements* are now in their second or third editions. We refer to the *Restatements* frequently in subsequent chapters of this text, indicating in parentheses the edition to which we are referring. For example, we refer to the second edition of the *Restatement of the Law of Contracts* simply as the *Restatement (Second) of Contracts*.

SECTION 4

CIVIL LAW VERSUS CRIMINAL LAW

The body of law is huge. To study it, one must break it down by some means of classification, and a number of classification systems have been devised. Here we look at one of the most significant classifications: the division of law into civil law and criminal law.

CIVIL LAW

Civil law is concerned with the duties that exist between persons or between citizens and their governments, excluding the duty not to commit crimes. Typically, in a civil case, a private party sues another private party (although the government can also sue a party for a civil law violation) to make that other party comply with a duty or pay for the damage caused by failure to comply with a duty. For example, if a seller **breaches** (fails to perform) a contract with a buyer, the buyer may bring a lawsuit against the seller either to compel performance or to obtain money damages for the seller's failure to perform.

CONCEPT SUMMARY 1.2 Sources of American Law

SOURCE	DESCRIPTION
Constitutional Law	The law as expressed in the U.S. Constitution and the various state constitutions. The U.S. Constitution is the supreme law of the land. State constitutions are supreme within state borders to the extent that they do not violate a clause of the U.S. Constitution or a federal law.
Statutory Law	Laws (statutes and ordinances) created by federal, state, and local legislatures and governing bodies. None of these laws may violate the U.S. Constitution or the relevant state constitution. Uniform laws, when adopted by a state, become statutory law in that state.
Administrative Law	The rules, orders, and decisions of federal or state government administrative agencies.
Case Law and Common Law Doctrines	Judge-made law, including interpretations of constitutional provisions, of statutes enacted by legislatures, and of regulations created by administrative agencies. The common law—the doctrines and principles embodied in case law—governs all areas not covered by statutory or administrative law.

Each state court system, as well as the federal court system, has a set of rules governing civil procedures. You will read about these procedures in detail in Chapter 3. Generally, in a civil case, the plaintiff presents evidence (including the testimony of witnesses, documents, and so on) supporting his or her allegation to the court, and the defendant then offers evidence to show why the plaintiff should not obtain the remedy sought. Based on the evidence presented, the court makes its decision. Usually, the plaintiff must prove his or her case by a *preponderance of the evidence.* Under this standard, the plaintiff must convince the court that, based on the evidence presented by both parties, it is more likely than not that the plaintiff's allegation is true.

Much of the law that we discuss in this text is civil law. Contract law, for example, which we discuss in Chapters 9 and 10, is civil law. The whole body of tort law, which is covered in Chapters 12 through 15, is civil law.

CRIMINAL LAW

In contrast to civil law, **criminal law** is concerned with wrongs committed *against the public as a whole.* Criminal acts are defined and prohibited by local, state, or federal government statutes. Criminal defendants thus are prosecuted by public officials, such as a district attorney (D.A.), on behalf of the state, not by their victims or other private parties. Whereas in a civil case the object is to obtain remedies (such as money damages) to compensate the injured party, in a criminal case the object is to punish the wrongdoer in an attempt to deter others from similar actions. Penalties for violations of criminal statutes consist of fines and/or imprisonment—and, in some cases, death.

Because the state has extensive resources at its disposal when prosecuting criminal cases, there are numerous procedural safeguards to protect the rights of defendants. One of these safeguards is the higher standard of proof that applies in criminal cases. As you can see in Exhibit 1–3, which summarizes some of the key differences between civil law and criminal law, in a criminal case the state must prove its case *beyond a reasonable doubt,* not just by a preponderance of the evidence. Every juror in a criminal case must be convinced, beyond a reasonable doubt, of the defendant's guilt. This safeguard and others will be discussed in more detail in Chapter 13, in the section discussing criminal procedures.

Although business law primarily has to do with civil law, as mentioned, criminal law is also an important component of the legal environment of business. This is because many of the statutes regulating the business world provide for both civil and criminal sanctions. Additionally, even though the corporate structure shields corporate directors and officers from personal liability for corporate crimes, increasingly the courts are finding ways to hold key corporate personnel personally liable for such crimes.

EXHIBIT 1–3 ■ CIVIL AND CRIMINAL LAW COMPARED

ISSUE	CIVIL LAW	CRIMINAL LAW
Area of concern	Rights and duties between individuals	Offenses against society as a whole
Wrongful act	Harm to a person or to a person's property	Violation of a statute that prohibits some type of activity
Party who brings suit	Person who suffered harm	The state
Standard of proof	Preponderance of the evidence	Beyond a reasonable doubt
Remedy	Damages to compensate for the harm or an equitable remedy	Punishment (fine or imprisonment)

TERMS AND CONCEPTS TO REVIEW

administrative agency 10
administrative law 10
allege 7
analogy 8
binding authority 6
breach 11
case law 11
case on point 8
chancellor 5
civil law 11
common law 4
constitutional law 9
court of equity 5
court of law 5
criminal law 12
damages 5
defendant 5
defense 5
equitable maxims 5
executive agency 10
independent regulatory agency 10
laches 5
law 3
legal positivists 3
legal realists 4
legal reasoning 7
natural law 3
ordinance 10
plaintiff 5
positive law 3
precedent 6
public policy 7
remedy 4
remedy at law 5
remedy in equity 5
reporter 6
stare decisis 6
statute of limitations 5
statutory law 10
syllogism 8
uniform law 10

QUESTIONS AND CASE PROBLEMS

1–1. PHILOSOPHY OF LAW. In the middle of the nineteenth century, the United States declared war on Mexico and levied taxes to support the war effort. Henry David Thoreau (author of *Walden*), who felt that the war was unjust, refused to pay taxes to support it and was subsequently imprisoned for violating the law. Thoreau maintained that obeying the law in these circumstances would be unethical. Which of the schools of legal philosophy discussed in this chapter would be the most sympathetic toward Thoreau's views on law? Explain.

1–2. STATUTORY VERSUS COMMON LAW. How does statutory law come into existence? How does it differ from the common law? If statutory law conflicts with the common law, which law will govern?

1–3. READING CITATIONS. Assume that you want to read the entire court opinion in the case of *Mazda Motor of America, Inc. v. Rogowski*, 105 Md.App. 318, 659 A.2d 391 (1995). The case deals with a consumer's complaint that a car manufacturer failed to adequately warn consumers of the fact that seat belts might not prevent injuries in head-on collisions. Explain specifically where you would find the court's opinion. (Read the appendix to this chapter.)

1–4. Sources of American Law. This chapter discussed a number of sources of American law. Which source of law takes priority in the following situations, and why?

(a) A federal statute conflicts with the U.S. Constitution.

(b) A federal statute conflicts with a state constitutional provision.

(c) A state statute conflicts with the common law of that state.

(d) A state constitutional amendment conflicts with the U.S. Constitution.

1–5. *Stare Decisis*. In the text of this chapter, we stated that the doctrine of *stare decisis* "became a cornerstone of the English and American judicial systems." What does *stare decisis* mean, and why has this doctrine been so fundamental to the development of our legal tradition?

1–6. Court Opinions. What is the difference between a concurring opinion and a majority opinion? Between a concurring opinion and a dissenting opinion? Why do judges and justices write concurring and dissenting opinions, given the fact that these opinions will not affect the outcome of the case at hand, which has already been decided by majority vote? (Read the appendix to this chapter.)

1–7. Common Law versus Statutory Law. Courts can overturn precedents and thus change the common law. Should judges have the same authority to overrule statutory law? Explain.

1–8. *Stare Decisis*. "The judge's role is not to make the law but to uphold and apply the law." Do you agree or disagree with this statement? Discuss fully the reasons for your answer.

1–9. Remedies. Arthur Rabe is suing Xavier Sanchez for breaching a contract in which Sanchez promised to sell Rabe a Van Gogh painting for $150,000. What remedy will Rabe seek if he wants Sanchez to perform the contract as promised? What remedy will Rabe seek if he wants to cancel the contract because Sanchez fraudulently misrepresented the painting as an original Van Gogh when in fact it is a copy? Will the remedy Rabe seeks in either case be a remedy at law or a remedy in equity?

1–10. Terminology. In the Rabe-Sanchez lawsuit above, which party is the plaintiff? If Rabe loses in the trial court and appeals that court's decision, which party will be the appellant (or petitioner), and which party will be the appellee (or respondent)? Assume that one of the three appellate judges reviewing the case disagrees with the other two judges. What is the written opinion representing the decision of this court called—a unanimous opinion, a concurring opinion, a majority opinion, or a dissenting opinion?

Accessing the Internet
The Legal Environment of Business

Many chapters of *West's Legal Environment of Business*, Third Edition, end with a list of Internet resources and addresses. Once you are on the Internet, you can use the addresses, or uniform resource locators (URLs), listed in the *Accessing the Internet* sections in this text to access the ever-growing number of resources available on the "Net."

Internet sites tend to come and go, and there is no guarantee that a site included in one of *Accessing the Internet* features in this text will be there by the time this book is in print. We have tried, though, to include sites that have so far proved to be fairly stable. If you do have difficulty reaching a site (that is, if your *Destination* is "Not Found!"), do not immediately assume that the site does not exist. First recheck the URL shown in your browser. Remember, you have to type the URLs exactly as written: upper case and lower case are important. If it appears that the URL has been keyed correctly, then try the following technique: delete all of the information to the right of the forward slash that is farthest to the right and press enter.

For example, suppose that you are trying to reach the WashLaw site listed toward the bottom of page 15. If you have difficulty reaching the site, first check the URL as you keyed it in. Then try deleting the final "washlaw.html" from the URL and press enter. If you still have problems, delete "washlaw," which is now the farthest to the right. Eventually, you will get back to the home page and can again start your search.

You can go to the Internet sites listed here to find many of the sources of American law discussed in this chapter, as well as other useful information on legal topics.

- FindLaw (a directory of law-related Web sites):

http://www.findlaw.com/

- The Legal Information Institute, Cornell University School of Law (a good place to begin researching cases and statutes, including decisions of the United States Supreme Court, the U.S. Code, and selected state statutory codes):

  http://www.law.cornell.edu

- The Internet Law Library (sponsored by the U.S. House of Representatives, this site offers links to federal and state legislative and regulatory materials, including the U.S. Code and the Code of Federal Regulations):

  http:/www.house.gov/

- Law Guru (a "meta-search" site that allows you to access more than 160 legal search engines and indexes from a single location):

  http://www.lawguru.com

- Law Journal EXTRA! (one of the largest and most comprehensive commercial legal sites on the Internet):

  http://www.ljx.com/

- The 'Lectric Law Library (a comprehensive collection of law-related materials, including legal forms, law outlines, a high-quality law dictionary, and a lawyer-joke library):

  http://www.lectlaw.com

- The Legal List (law-related resources on the Internet):

  http://www.lcp.com/The-Legal-List/TLL-home.html

- The Legal Web: Law Journals (an index of electronic law journals):

  http://www.law.vill.edu/vcilp/legalweb.lawjournals.html

- The Library of Congress (offers extensive links to state and federal government resources):

  http://www.loc.gov/

- Nolo Press Online (offers updated information on legal sites on the Internet):

  http://www.nolo.com

- Villanova Center for Information Law and Policy (provides access to numerous legal resources, including opinions from the federal appellate courts):

  http://www.law.vill.edu

- The Virtual Law Library Index, created and maintained by the Indiana University School of Law (provides an index of legal sources categorized by subject):

  http://www.law.indiana.edu/

- WashLaw (offers links to numerous law-related resources on the Internet):

  http://lawlib.wuacc.edu/washlaw/washlaw.html

- Yahoo (a general Internet directory/search tool):

  http://www.yahoo.com/Government/Law/

APPENDIX TO CHAPTER 1

FINDING AND ANALYZING THE LAW

This text includes numerous citations to primary sources of law—federal and state statutes, regulations issued by administrative agencies, and court cases. (A *citation* is a reference to a publication in which a legal authority—such as a statute or a court decision—or other source can be found.) In this section, we explain how you can use these citations to find these sources.

SECTION 1

FINDING STATUTORY LAW

When Congress passes laws, they are collected in a publication titled *United States Statutes at Large.* When state legislatures pass laws, they are collected in similar state publications. Most frequently, however, laws are referred to in their codified form—that is, the form in which they appear in the federal and state codes.

In these codes, laws are compiled by subject. The *United States Code* (U.S.C.) arranges all existing federal laws of a public and permanent nature by subject. Each of the fifty subjects into which the U.S.C. arranges the laws is given a title and a title number. For example, laws relating to commerce and trade are collected in Title 15, "Commerce and Trade." Titles are subdivided by sections. A citation to the U.S.C. includes title and section numbers. Thus, a reference to "15 U.S.C. Section 1" means that the statute can be found in Section 1 of Title 15. ("Section" may also be designated by the symbol §, and "Sections," by §§.) Sometimes a citation includes the abbreviation *et seq.*—as in "15 U.S.C. Sections 1 *et seq.*" The term is an abbreviated form of *et sequitur,* which in Latin means "and the following"; when used in a citation, it refers to sections that concern the same subject as the numbered section and follow it in sequence.

State codes follow the U.S.C. pattern of arranging law by subject. They may be called codes, revisions, compilations, consolidations, general statutes, or statutes, depending on the preference of the states. In some codes, subjects are designated by number. In others, they are designated by name. For example, "13 Pennsylvania Consolidated Statutes Section 1101" means that the statute can be found in Title 13, Section 1101, of the Pennsylvania code. "California Commercial Code Section 1101" means the statute can be found under the subject heading "Commercial Code" of the California code in Section 1101. Abbreviations may be used. For example, "13 Pennsylvania Consolidated Statutes Section 1101" may be abbreviated "13 Pa. C.S. §1101," and "California Commercial Code Section 1101" may be abbreviated "Cal. Com. Code §1101."

Commercial publications of these laws and regulations are available and are widely used. For example, West Publishing Company publishes the *United States Code Annotated* (U.S.C.A.). The U.S.C.A. contains the complete text of laws included in the U.S.C., as well as notes on court decisions that interpret and apply specific sections of the statutes, plus the text of presidential proclamations and executive orders. The U.S.C.A. also includes research aids, such as cross-references to related statutes, historical notes, and library references. A citation to the U.S.C.A. is similar to a citation to the U.S.C.: "15 U.S.C.A. Section 1."

SECTION 2

FINDING ADMINISTRATIVE LAW

Rules and regulations adopted by federal administrative agencies are initially published in the *Federal Register,* a daily publication of the U.S. government. Later, they are incorporated into the *Code of Federal Regulations* (C.F.R.). Like the U.S.C., the C.F.R. is divided into fifty titles. Rules within each title are assigned section numbers. A full citation to the C.F.R. includes title and section numbers. For example, a reference to "17 C.F.R. Section 230.504" means that the rule can be found in Section 230.504 of Title 17.

SECTION 3

FINDING CASE LAW

To understand how to read citations to court cases, we need first to look briefly at the court system. As will be discussed in Chapter 3, there are two types of courts in the United States, federal courts and state courts. Both the federal and state court systems consist of several levels, or tiers, of courts.

Trial courts, in which evidence is presented and testimony given, are on the bottom tier (which also includes lower courts handling specialized issues). Decisions from a trial court can be appealed to a higher court, which commonly would be an intermediate *court of appeals,* or an *appellate court.* Appellate courts are known as *reviewing courts,* because they do not hear evidence or testimony, as trial courts do; rather, an appellate court reviews all of the records relating to a case to determine whether the trial court's decision was correct. Decisions from these intermediate courts of appeals may be appealed to an even higher court, such as a state supreme court or the United States Supreme Court.

STATE COURT DECISIONS Most state trial court decisions are not published. Except in New York and a few other states that publish selected opinions of their trial courts, decisions from the state trial courts are merely filed in the office of the clerk of the court, where they are available for public inspection. Written decisions of the appellate, or reviewing, courts are published and distributed. The reported appellate decisions are published in volumes called *Reports,* which are numbered consecutively.

Reporters Containing State Court Decisions. Decisions of the appellate courts of a particular state are found in the state reports of that state. A few states—including those with intermediate appellate courts, such as California, Illinois, and New York—have more than one reporter for opinions given by their courts.

Additionally, state court opinions appear in regional units of the *National Reporter System,* published by West Publishing Company. Most lawyers and libraries have the West reporters because they report cases more quickly, and are distributed more widely, than the state-published reports. In fact, many states have eliminated their own reporters in favor of West's National Reporter System. The National Reporter System divides the states into the following geographical areas: *Atlantic* (A. or A.2d), *South Eastern* (S.E. or S.E.2d), *South Western* (S.W. or S.W.2d), *North Western* (N.W. or N.W.2d), *North Eastern* (N.E. or N.E.2d), *Southern* (So. or So.2d), and *Pacific* (P. or P.2d). (The *2d* in the preceding abbreviations refers to *Second Series.*) The states included in each of these regional divisions are indicated in Exhibit 1A–1, which illustrates West's National Reporter System.

Case Citations. After an appellate decision has been published, it is normally referred to (cited) by the name of the case (called the *style* of the case); the volume, name, and page of the state's official reporter (if different from West's National Reporter System); the volume, unit, and page number of the National Reporter; and the volume, name, and page number of any other selected reporter. (Citing a reporter by volume number, name, and page number, in that order, is common to all citations.) When more than one reporter is cited for the same case, each reference is called a *parallel citation.*

For example, consider the following case citation: *J-Mart Jewelry Outlets, Inc. v. Standard Design,* 218 Ga.App. 459, 462 S.E.2d 406 (1995). We see that the opinion in this case may be found in Volume 218 of the official *Georgia Appeals Reports,* on page 459. The parallel citation is to Volume 462 of the *South Eastern Reporter, Second Series,* page 406. In reprinting appellate opinions in this text, in addition to the reporter, we give the name of the court hearing the case and the year of the court's decision.

Sample citations to state court decisions are listed and explained in Exhibit 1A–2.

FEDERAL COURT DECISIONS Federal district (trial) court decisions are published unofficially in West's *Federal Supplement* (F.Supp.), and opinions from the circuit courts of appeals are reported unofficially in West's *Federal Reporter* (F., F.2d, or F.3d). Cases concerning federal bankruptcy law are published unofficially in West's *Bankruptcy Reporter* (Bankr.).

The official edition of all decisions of the United States Supreme Court for which there are written opinions is the *United States Reports* (U.S.), which is published by the federal government. The series includes reports of Supreme Court cases dating from the August term of 1791, although many of the Supreme Court's decisions were not reported in the early volumes.

Unofficial editions of Supreme Court cases include West's *Supreme Court Reporter* (S.Ct.), which includes cases dating from the Court's term in October 1882; and the *Lawyers' Edition of the Supreme Court Reports* (L.Ed.), published by the Lawyers Cooperative Publishing Company. The latter contains many of the decisions not reported in the early volumes of the *United States Reports.*

Sample citations for federal court decisions are listed and explained in Exhibit 1A–2.

EXHIBIT 1A–1 ■ NATIONAL REPORTER SYSTEM—REGIONAL/FEDERAL

Regional Reporters	Coverage Beginning	Coverage
Atlantic Reporter (A. or A.2d)	1885	Connecticut, Delaware, Maine, Maryland, New Hampshire, New Jersey, Pennsylvania, Rhode Island, Vermont, and District of Columbia.
North Eastern Reporter (N.E. or N.E.2d)	1885	Illinois, Indiana, Massachusetts, New York, and Ohio.
North Western Reporter (N.W. or N.W.2d)	1879	Iowa, Michigan, Minnesota, Nebraska, North Dakota, South Dakota, and Wisconsin.
Pacific Reporter (P. or P.2d)	1883	Alaska, Arizona, California, Colorado, Hawaii, Idaho, Kansas, Montana, Nevada, New Mexico, Oklahoma, Oregon, Utah, Washington, and Wyoming.
South Eastern Reporter (S.E. or S.E.2d)	1887	Georgia, North Carolina, South Carolina, Virginia, and West Virginia.
South Western Reporter (S.W. or S.W.2d)	1886	Arkansas, Kentucky, Missouri, Tennessee, and Texas.
Southern Reporter (So. or So.2d)	1887	Alabama, Florida, Louisiana, and Mississippi.
Federal Reporters		
Federal Reporter (F., F.2d, or F.3d)	1880	U.S. Circuit Court from 1880 to 1912; U.S. Commerce Court from 1911 to 1913; U.S. District Courts from 1880 to 1932; U.S. Court of Claims (now called U.S. Court of Federal Claims) from 1929 to 1932 and since 1960; U.S. Court of Appeals since 1891; U.S. Court of Customs and Patent Appeals since 1929; and U.S. Emergency Court of Appeals since 1943.
Federal Supplement (F.Supp.)	1932	U.S. Court of Claims from 1932 to 1960; U.S. District Courts since 1932; and U.S. Customs Court since 1956.
Federal Rules Decisions (F.R.D.)	1939	U.S. District Courts involving the Federal Rules of Civil Procedure since 1939 and Federal Rules of Criminal Procedure since 1946.
Supreme Court Reporter (S.Ct.)	1882	U.S. Supreme Court since the October term of 1882.
Bankruptcy Reporter (Bankr.)	1980	Bankruptcy decisions of U.S. Bankruptcy Courts, U.S. District Courts, U.S. Courts of Appeals, and U.S. Supreme Court.
Military Justice Reporter (M.J.)	1978	U.S. Court of Military Appeals and Courts of Military Review for the Army, Navy, Air Force, and Coast Guard.

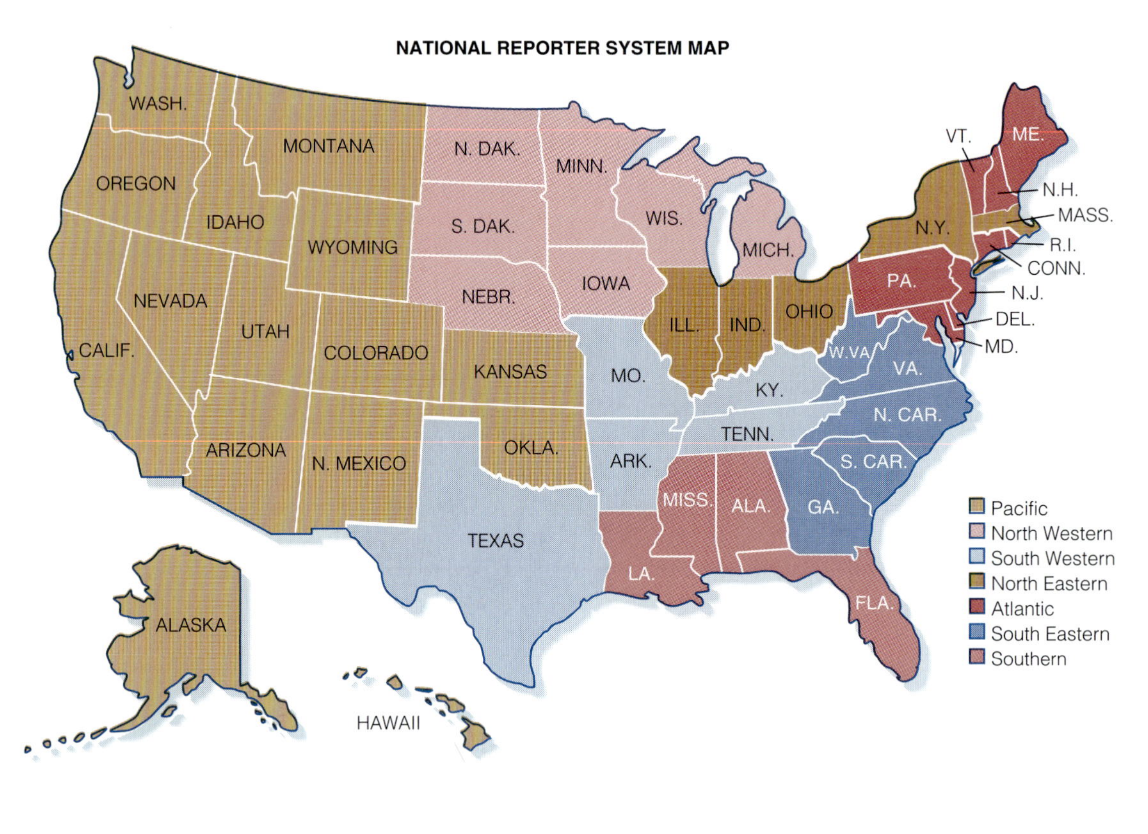

EXHIBIT 1A–2 ■ HOW TO READ CITATIONS

State Courts

251 Neb. 411, 558 N.W.2d 40 (1997)[a]

N.W. is the abbreviation for West's publication of state court decisions rendered in the northwestern region of the National Reporter System. *2d* indicates that this case was included in the second series of those reports. The number 558 refers to the volume number of the reporter; the number 40 refers to the first page in that volume on which this case can be found.

Neb. is an abbreviation for *Nebraska Reports,* Nebraska's official reports of the decisions of its highest court, the Nebraska Supreme Court.

14 Cal.4th 968, 60 Cal.Rptr.2d 93 (1997)

Cal.Rptr. is the abbreviation for West's unofficial reports—titled *California Reporter*—of the decisions of California courts.

85 N.Y.2d 549, 650 N.E.2d 829, 626 N.Y.S.2d 982 (1995)

N.Y.S. is the abbreviation for West's unofficial reports—titled *New York Supplement*—of the decisions of New York courts.

N.Y. is the abbreviation for *New York Reports,* New York's official reports of the decisions of its court of appeals. The New York Court of Appeals is the state's highest court, analogous to other states' supreme courts. In New York, a supreme court is a trial court.

108 Md.App. 527, 672 A.2d 667 (1996)

Md.App. is the abbreviation for *Maryland Appellate Reports,* Maryland's official reports of the decisions of its court of appeals.

Federal Courts

___ U.S. ___, 117 S.Ct. 843, 136 L.Ed.2d 808 (1997)

L.Ed. is an abbreviation for *Lawyers' Edition of the Supreme Court Reports,* an unofficial edition of decisions of the United States Supreme Court.

S.Ct. is the abbreviation for West's unofficial reports—titled *Supreme Court Reporter*—of United States Supreme Court decisions.

U.S. is the abbreviation for *United States Reports,* the official edition of the decisions of the United States Supreme Court. Volume and page numbers are not included in this citation because they have not yet been assigned.

a. The case names have been deleted from these citations to emphasize the publications. It should be kept in mind, however that the name of a case is as important as the specific numbers of the volumes in which it is found. If a citation is incorrect, the correct citation may be found in a publication's index of case names. The date of a case is also important. First, the date provides a check on errors in citations. Second, a recent case is likely to have more value as an authority than earlier cases.

EXHIBIT 1A–2 ■ HOW TO READ CITATIONS (CONTINUED)

Federal Courts (Continued)

105 F.3d 248 (8th Cir. 1997)

8th Cir. is an abbreviation denoting that this case was decided in the United States Court of Appeals for the Eighth Circuit.

915 F.Supp. 663 (E.D.N.Y. 1996)

E.D.N.Y. is an abbreviation indicating that the United States District Court for the Eastern District of New York decided this case.

Statutory and Other Citations

15 U.S.C. Section 1262(e)

U.S.C. denotes *United States Code,* the codification of *United States Statutes at Large.* The number 15 refers to the statute's U.S.C. title number and 1262 to its section number within that title. The letter *e* refers to a subsection within the section.

UCC 2–206(1)(a)

UCC is an abbreviation for *Uniform Commercial Code.* The first number 2 is a reference to an article of the UCC, and 206 refers to a section within that article. The number 1 refers to a subsection within the section and the letter *a* to a subdivision within the subsection.

Restatement (Second) of Torts, Section 568

Restatement (Second) of Torts refers to the second edition of the American Law Institute's *Restatement of the Law of Torts.* The number 568 refers to a specific section.

16 C.F.R. Section 453.2

C.F.R. is an abbreviation for *Code of Federal Regulations,* a compilation of federal administrative regulations. The number 16 is a reference to the regulation's title number and 453.2 to a specific section within that title.

OLD CASE LAW On a few occasions, this text cites opinions from old, classic cases dating to the nineteenth century or earlier; some of these are from the English courts. The citations to these cases appear not to conform to the descriptions given above, because the reporters in which they were published have since been replaced. Whenever we cite an unfamiliar reporter in this text, we include with the citation a brief description of that reporter's full name and the time period it covers.

CASE DIGESTS AND LEGAL ENCYCLOPEDIAS The body of American case law consists of nearly five million decisions, to which more than forty thousand decisions are added each year. Because judicial decisions are published in chronological order, finding relevant precedents would be a Herculean task if it were not for case digests, legal encyclopedias, and many other publications that classify decisions according to subject.

SECTION 4

HOW TO READ AND UNDERSTAND CASE LAW

The decisions made by the courts establish the boundaries of the law as it applies to business firms and business relationships. It thus is essential that businesspersons know how to read and understand case law. The cases that we present in this text have been condensed from the full text of the courts' opinions—that is, in each case we have summarized the background and facts, as well as the court's decision and remedy, in our own words and have included only selected portions of the court's opinion ("in the language of the court"). For those who wish to review court cases to perform research projects or to gain additional legal information, however, the following sections will provide useful insights into how to read and understand case law.

CASE TITLES

The title of a case, such as *Adams v. Jones,* indicates the names of the parties to the lawsuit. The *v.* in the case title stands for *versus,* which means "against." In the trial court, Adams was the plaintiff—the person who filed the suit. Jones was the defendant. If the case is appealed, however, the appellate court will sometimes place the name of the party appealing the decision first, so that the case may be called *Jones v. Adams* if Jones is appealing. Because some appellate courts retain the trial court order of names, it is often impossible to distinguish the plaintiff from the defendant in the title of a reported appellate court decision. You must carefully read the facts of each case to identify the parties. Otherwise, the discussion by the appellate court will be difficult to understand.

TERMINOLOGY

The following terms, phrases, and abbreviations are frequently encountered in court opinions and legal publications. Because it is important to understand what is meant by these terms, phrases, and abbreviations, we define and discuss them here.

PARTIES TO LAWSUITS As mentioned previously, the party initiating a lawsuit is referred to as the *plaintiff,* and the party against whom a lawsuit is brought is the *defendant.* Lawsuits frequently involve more than one plaintiff and/or defendant. (Sometimes, a party that initiates a lawsuit is referred to as the *petitioner,* and the party against whom the suit is brought is referred to as the *respondent.*) When a case is appealed from the original court or jurisdiction to another court or jurisdiction, the party appealing the case is called the *appellant.* The *appellee* is the party against whom the appeal is taken.

JUDGES AND JUSTICES The terms *judge* and *justice* are usually synonymous and represent two designations given to judges in various courts. All members of the United States Supreme Court, for example, are referred to as *justices,* and *justice* is the formal title usually given to judges of appellate courts, although this is not always the case. In New York, a *justice* is a judge of the trial court (which is called the Supreme Court), and a member of the Court of Appeals (the state's highest court) is called a *judge.* The term *justice* is commonly abbreviated to J., and *justices,* to JJ. A Supreme Court case might refer to Justice Kennedy as Kennedy, J., or to Chief Justice Rehnquist as Rehnquist, C.J.

DECISIONS AND OPINIONS Most decisions reached by reviewing, or appellate, courts are explained in written *opinions.* The opinion contains the court's reasons for its decision, the rules of law that apply, and the judgment.

When all judges or justices unanimously agree on an opinion, the opinion is written for the entire court and can be deemed a *unanimous opinion.* When there is not a unanimous opinion, a *majority opinion* is written; it outlines the views of the majority of the judges or justices deciding the case. If a judge agrees, or concurs, with the majority's decision, but for different reasons, that judge may write a *concurring opinion.* A *dissenting opinion* is written by one or more judges who disagree with the majority's decision. The dissenting opinion is important because it may form the basis of the arguments used years later in overruling the precedential majority opinion.

Occasionally, a court issues a *per curiam* opinion. *Per curiam* is a Latin phrase meaning "of the court." In *per curiam* opinions, there is no indication of which judge or justice authored the opinion. This term may also be used for an announcement of a court's disposition of a case that is not accompanied by a written opinion. Sometimes, the cases presented in this text are *en banc* decisions. When an appellate court reviews a case *en banc,* which is Latin for "in the bench," generally all of the judges sitting on the bench of that court review the case.

A SAMPLE COURT CASE

To illustrate the various elements contained in a court opinion, we present in Exhibit 1A–3 an annotated court opinion. The opinion is from an actual case that was heard by the United States Supreme Court in 1997. The lawsuit was initiated by an individual who claimed that his former employer, by giving him a negative job reference, had discriminated against him in violation of a federal statute. The relevant provision in the statute prohibits discrimination against employees but says nothing about *former* employees. Thus, the issue before the Court is one of statutory interpretation: Does the statute also prohibit discrimination against former employees?

You will note that triple asterisks (* * *) and quadruple asterisks (* * * *) frequently appear in the

EXHIBIT 1A–3 ■ A SAMPLE COURT CASE

ROBINSON v. SHELL OIL COMPANY
Supreme Court of the United States, 1997.
____ U.S. ____ ,
117 S.Ct. 843.
136 L.Ed. 2d 808.

This line gives the name of the justice who authored the opinion for the Court.

Justice *THOMAS* delivered the opinion of the Court.

A federal statute that prohibits employment discrimination based on race, color, national origin, religion, or gender.

The first paragraph of the opinion states the issue to be decided by the Court. An issue is a disputed point of fact or law. The issue here is a disputed point of law—how a statute should be interpreted.

The federal administrative agency that handles claims of employment discrimination.

Section 704(a) of **Title VII of the Civil Rights Act of 1964** makes it unlawful "for an employer to discriminate against any of its employees or applicants for employment" who have either availed themselves of Title VII's protections or assisted others in so doing. We are asked to decide in this case whether the term "employee," as used in [Section] 704(a), includes former employees, such that petitioner may bring suit against his former employer for postemployment actions allegedly taken in retaliation for petitioner's having filed a charge with the **Equal Employment Opportunity Commission (EEOC).** * * *

The Court divides the opinion into three sections, headed by roman numerals. In this first section, the Court summarizes the factual and procedural background to the case.

I

The party responding to the appeal.

The party bringing the appeal.

Respondent Shell Oil Co. fired **petitioner** Charles T. Robinson, Sr., in 1991. Shortly thereafter, petitioner filed a charge with the EEOC, alleging that respondent had discharged him because of his race. While that charge was pending, petitioner applied for a job with another company. That company contacted respondent, as petitioner's former employer, for an employment reference. Petitioner claims that respondent gave him a negative reference in retaliation for his having filed the EEOC charge.

A federal trial court in which a lawsuit is initiated.

A *precedent* is a decision in a previous case that is binding on courts within the jurisdiction; in this case, the precedent was set by the U.S. Court of Appeals for the Fourth Circuit, one of thirteen federal appellate courts.

An appellate court will reverse the trial court's judgment if it concludes that the trial court erred in some way.

An appellate court will affirm (give legal force to) the trial court's judgment if the court concludes that the trial court did not err in any way.

Petitioner subsequently sued under [Section] 704(a) * * *. [T]he **District Court** dismissed the action, adhering to previous **Fourth Circuit precedent** holding that [Section] 704(a) does not apply to former employees. Petitioner appealed, and a divided panel of the Fourth Circuit **reversed** the District Court. The Fourth Circuit granted rehearing* * *and thereafter **affirmed** the District Court's determination that former employees may not bring suit under [Section] 704(a) for retaliation occurring after termination of their employment.

EXHIBIT 1A–3 ■ A SAMPLE COURT CASE (CONTINUED)

A Latin term [pronounced sur-shee-uh-*rah*-ree] meaning that the United States Supreme Court ordered the appellate court to send it the record of the case for review.

We granted ***certiorari*** in order to resolve a conflict among the Circuits on this issue.

The Court now moves to a second major section of the opinion, in which it analyzes the issue before the Court.

II

A basic rule of statutory interpretation is that if the meaning of a statute or clause is plain and clear from the wording of the statute or clause itself, the courts give effect to that meaning. If the meaning is not clear, then the courts look at other factors.

A. Our first step in interpreting a statute is to determine whether the language at issue has a **plain and unambiguous meaning** with regard to the partcular dispute in the case. Our inquiry must cease if the statutory language is unambiguous and "the statutory scheme is coherent and consistent."

* * * *

These mechanisms include filing a claim with the EEOC—and filing suit against the employer if the EEOC decides not to do so—in order to obtain job reinstatement, back pay, money damages, or other remedies available under Title VII to victims of employment discrimination.

B. Finding that the term "employees" in [Section] 704(a) is ambiguous, we are left to resolve that ambiguity. The broader context provided by other sections of the statute provides considerable assistance in this regard. * * * [S]everal sections of the statute plainly contemplate that former employees will make use of the **remedial mechanisms of Title VII.** Indeed, [Section] 703(a) expressly includes discriminatory "discharge" as one of the unlawful employment practices against which Title VII is directed. Insofar as [Section] 704(a) expressly protects employees from retaliation for filing a "charge" under Title VII, and a charge under [Section] 703(a) alleging unlawful discharge would necessarily be brought by a former employee, it is far more consistent to include former employees within the scope of "employees" protected by [Section] 704(a).

* * * *

In this final section of the opinion, the Court summarizes its conclusions and gives its order.

III

We hold that the term "employees," as used in [Section] 704(a) of Title VII, is ambiguous as to whether it includes former employees. It being more consistent with the broader context of Title VII and the primary purpose of [Section] 704(a), we hold that former employees are included within [Section] 704(a)'s coverage. Accordingly, the decision of the Fourth Circuit is reversed.

It is so ordered.

opinion. The triple asterisks indicate that we have deleted a few words or sentences from the opinion for the sake of readability or brevity. Quadruple asterisks mean that an entire paragraph (or more) has been omitted. Additionally, when the opinion cites another case or legal source, the citation to the case or other source has been omitted to save space and to improve the flow of the text. These editorial practices are continued in the other court opinions presented in this text. In addition, whenever a court opinion presented in this text includes a term or phrase that may not be readily understandable, we have added a bracketed definition or paraphrase.

Knowing how to read and understand court opinions and the legal reasoning used by the courts is an essential step in undertaking accurate legal research. Yet a further step is "briefing," or summarizing, the case. Legal researchers routinely brief cases by reducing the texts of the opinions to their essential elements. Instructions on how to brief a case are given in Appendix A, which also includes selected cases for briefing and a briefed version of the sample court case presented in Exhibit 1A–3.

Chapter 2

Business Ethics

Few people today would claim that it is unethical to seek profits. In fact, successful businesspersons are often ranked among the most admired individuals in our society. Nonetheless, there always has been—and continues to be—an underlying tension between the pursuit of profits and the welfare of those groups affected by this pursuit. Generally, businesspersons have to walk a fine line to ensure that their profit-making activities do not exceed the ethical boundaries established by society.

In the past, these boundaries were often regarded as being coterminous with the law—that is, if something was legal, it was ethical. In the past few decades, however, the ethical boundaries within which business firms must operate have narrowed significantly. In the rights-conscious world of today, a business firm that decides it has no duties other than those prescribed by law may find it difficult to survive. If a firm's behavior is perceived as unethical—even though it may be legal—that firm may suffer negative publicity, boycotts, lost profits, and even government sanctions.

In preparing for a career in business, you will find that a background in business ethics and a commitment to ethical behavior is just as important as a knowledge of the specific laws that you will read about in this text. In the first part of this chapter, we examine the nature of business ethics and the process of ethical decision making in the business context. We then discuss some specific examples of ethical issues that commonly arise in the business world.

PriceCostco Background

PriceCostco was formed on October 21, 1993, by merging The Price Company and the Costco Wholesale Corporation, two of the top three membership discount retailers in the United States.

PriceCostco operates a chain of cash-and-carry membership warehouses that sell high-quality, nationally branded, and selected private-label merchandise at low prices. Its target markets include both businesses that buy goods for commercial use or resale and individuals who are employees of specific organizations. The company tries to reach high sales volume and fast inventory turnover by offering a limited choice of merchandise in many product groups at competitive prices.

The company takes a strong position on behaving ethically in all transactions and relationships. It expects employees to behave ethically. For example, no one can accept gratuities from vendors. The company also expects to behave ethically, according to domestic ethical standards, in any country in which it operates.

PRICE COSTCO™

CODE OF ETHICS

By Jim Sinegal

OBEY THE LAW

The law is irrefutable! Absent a moral imperative to challenge a law, we must conduct our business in total compliance with the laws of every community where we do business.

- Comply with all statutes.
- Cooperate with authorities.
- Respect all public officials and their positions.

OBEY THE LAW

TAKE CARE OF OUR EMPLOYEES

To claim "people are our most important asset" is true and an understatement. Each employee has been hired for a very important job. Jobs such as stocking the shelves, ringing members' orders, buying products, and paying our bills are jobs we would all choose to perform because of their importance. The employees hired to perform these jobs are performing as management's "alter egos." Every employee, whether they are in a Price Club or Costco warehouse, or whether they work in the regional or corporate offices, is a PriceCostco ambassador trained to give our members professional, courteous treatment.

Today we have warehouse managers who were once stockers and callers, and vice presidents who were

- Avoid all conflict of interest issues with public officials.
- Comply with all disclosure and reporting requirements.
- Comply with safety and security standards for all products sold.
- Exceed ecological standards required in every community where we do business.
- Comply with all applicable wage and hour laws.
- Comply with all applicable anti-trust laws.
- Protect "inside information" that has not been released to the general public.

TAKE CARE OF OUR MEMBERS

The member is our key to success. If we don't keep our members happy, little else that we do will make a difference.

- Provide top-quality products at the best prices in the market.
- Provide a safe shopping environment in our warehouses.
- Provide only products that meet applicable safety and health standards.
- Sell only products from manufacturers who comply with "truth in advertising/packaging" standards.
- Provide our members with a 100% satisfaction guaranteed warranty on every product and service we sell, including their membership fee.
- Assure our members that every product we sell is authentic in make and in representation of performance.
- Make our shopping environment a pleasant experience by making our members feel welcome as our guests.
- Provide products to our members that will be ecologically sensitive.

TAKE CARE OF OUR MEMBERS

Our member is our reason for being. If they fail to show up, we cannot survive. Our members have extended a "trust" to PriceCostco by virtue of paying a fee to shop with us. We can't let them down or they will simply go away. We must always operate in the following manner when dealing with our members:
Rule #1– The member is always right.
Rule #2 – In the event the member is ever wrong, refer to rule #1.

There are plenty of shopping alternatives for our members. We will succeed only if we do not violate the trust they have extended to us. We must be committed at every level of our company, with every ounce of energy and grain of creativity we have, to constantly

rently working in our warehouses, depots, buying offices, and accounting departments, as well as in our home offices.

To that end, we are committed to these principles:

- Provide a safe work environment.
- Pay a fair wage.
- Make every job challenging, but make it fun!
- Consider the loss of any employee as a failure on the part of the company and a loss to the organization.
- Teach our people how to do their jobs and how to improve personally and professionally.
- Promote from within the company to achieve the goal of a minimum of 80% of management positions being filled by current employees.
- Create an "open door" attitude at all levels of the company that is dedicated to "fairness and listening."

RESPECT OUR VENDORS

Our vendors are our partners in business and for us to prosper as a company, they must prosper with us. It is important that our vendors understand that we will be tough negotiators, but fair in our treatment of them.

- Treat all vendors and their representatives as you would expect to be treated if visiting their places of business.
- Pay all bills within the allocated time frame.
- Honor all commitments.
- Protect all vendor property assigned to PriceCostco as though it were our own.
- Always be thoughtful and candid in negotiations.
- Provide a careful review process with at least two levels of authorization before terminating business with an existing vendor of more than two years.
- Do not accept gratuities of any kind from a vendor

RESPECT OUR VENDORS

These guidelines are exactly that - guidelines, some common sense rules for the conduct of our business. Intended to simplify our jobs, not complicate our lives, these guidelines will not answer every question or solve every problem. At the core of our philosophy as a company must be the implicit understanding that not one of us is required to lie or cheat on behalf of PriceCostco. In fact, dishonest conduct will not be tolerated. To do any less would be unfair to the overwhelming majority of our employees who support and respect PriceCostco's commitment to ethical business conduct.

to varying ethical interpretations, take the high road and do what is right.

If you want our help, we are always available for advice and counsel. That's our job and we welcome your questions or comments.

Our continued success depends on you. We thank each of you for your contribution to our past success and for the high standards you have insisted upon in our company.

9680322

If we do these four things throughout our organization, we will realize our ultimate goal, which is to REWARD OUR SHAREHOLDERS.

"Truth in advertising/packaging" legal standards are part of the statutes and regulations that are discussed in Chapter 45, which deals with consumer law.

Accepting "gratuities" from a vendor might be interpreted as accepting a bribe. This can be a crime (see Chapter 10). In an international context, a bribe can be a violation of the Foreign Corrupt Practices Act. This act and other international laws are discussed in Chapter 55.

If the company did not provide products that comply with safety and health standards, it could be held liable in civil suits on legal grounds that are classified as torts (see Chapters 6, 7, and 8).

If the company fails to honor one of its commitments, it may be sued for breach of contract (see Chapters 19 and 23). Remedies for breaches of contracts are discussed in Chapters 20 and 24.

Disclosure of "inside information" that constitutes *trade secrets* could subject an employee to civil liability or criminal prosecution (see Chapters 9 and 10).

Failing to pay bills when they become due could subject the company to the creditors' remedies discussed in Chapters 30 and 31. The company might even be forced into involuntary bankruptcy (see Chapter 32).

Antitrust laws apply to illegal restraints of trade—an agreement between competitors to set prices, for example, or an attempt by one company to control an entire market. Antitrust laws are discussed in Chapter 47.

Promotions and other benefits of employment cannot be granted or withheld on the basis of discrimination. This is against the law. Employment discrimination is the subject of Chapter 36.

Failure to comply with "ecological" standards could be a violation of environmental laws (see Chapter 46).

Safety standards for the work environment are governed by the Occupational Safety and Health Act and other statutes. Laws regulating safety in the workplace are discussed in Chapter 35.

SECTION 1
WHAT IS ETHICS?

Before we examine the nature of business ethics, we need to discuss what is meant by ethics generally. **Ethics** can be defined as the study of what constitutes right or wrong behavior. It is the branch of philosophy that focuses on morality and the way in which moral principles are derived or the way in which a given set of moral principles apply to one's conduct in daily life. Ethics has to do with questions relating to the fairness, justness, rightness, or wrongness of an action. What is fair? What is just? What is the right thing to do in this situation? These are essentially ethical questions.

Often, moral principles serve as the guiding force in an individual's personal ethical system. Although the terms *ethical* and *moral* often are used interchangeably, the terms refer to slightly different concepts. Whereas ethics has to do with the philosophical, rational basis for conduct, morals are often defined as *universal* rules or guidelines (such as those rooted in religious precepts) that determine our actions and character. Morals generally are "revealed" truths—that is, they are revealed to us by our family, influential mentors, or religious sources, such as the Bible (for Christians) or the Koran (for Muslims). Ethics, in contrast, is a reasoned set of principles of conduct. These principles may be based either on moral truths or on premises derived through logic and reasoning.

SECTION 2
THE NATURE OF BUSINESS ETHICS

Business ethics focuses on what constitutes right or wrong behavior in the world of business and on how moral and ethical principles are applied by businesspersons to situations that arise in their daily activities in the workplace. Note that business ethics is not a separate *kind* of ethics. The ethical standards that guide our behavior as, say, mothers, fathers, or students apply equally well to our activities as businesspersons.

Each individual, when faced with a particular ethical dilemma, engages in **ethical reasoning**—that is, a reasoning process in which the individual links his or her moral convictions or ethical standards to the particular situation at hand. Businesspersons do likewise when making decisions with ethical implications.

How do businesspersons decide whether a given decision is the "right" one for their firms? What ethical standards should be applied? Broadly speaking, ethical reasoning relating to business traditionally has been characterized by two fundamental approaches. One approach defines ethical behavior in terms of *duty*, which also implies certain rights. The other approach determines what is ethical in terms of the *consequences*, or outcome, of any given action. We examine each of these approaches here.

DUTY-BASED ETHICS

Duty-based ethical standards often are derived from revealed truths, such as religious precepts. They can also be derived through philosophical reasoning.

RELIGIOUS ETHICAL STANDARDS In the Judeo-Christian tradition, which is the dominant religious tradition in the United States, the Ten Commandments of the Old Testament establish fundamental rules for moral action. Other religions have their own sources of revealed truth. Religious rules generally are absolute with respect to the behavior of their adherents. For example, the commandment "Thou shalt not steal" is an absolute mandate for a person, such as a Jew or a Christian, who believes that the Ten Commandments reflect revealed truth. Even a benevolent motive for stealing (such as Robin Hood's) cannot justify the act, because the act itself is inherently immoral and thus wrong.

Ethical standards based on religious teachings also involve an element of *compassion*. Therefore, for example, even though it might be profitable for a firm to lay off a less productive employee, if that employee would find it difficult to find employment elsewhere and his or her family would suffer as a result, this potential suffering would be given substantial weight by the decision makers. Compassionate treatment of others is also mandated—to a certain extent, at least—by the Golden Rule of the ancients ("Do unto others as you would have them do unto you"), which has been adopted by most religions.

KANTIAN ETHICS Duty-based ethical standards may also be derived solely from philosophical reasoning. The German philosopher Immanuel Kant (1724–1804), for example, identified some general guiding principles for moral behavior based on what he believed to be the fundamental nature of human beings. Kant held that it is rational to assume that human beings are qualitatively different from other physical objects occupying space. Persons are endowed with moral integrity and the capacity to reason and conduct their affairs rationally. Therefore, their thoughts and actions should be respected. When human beings are treated merely as a means to an end, they are being treated as the equivalent of objects and are being denied their basic humanity.

A central postulate in Kantian ethics is that individuals should evaluate their actions in light of the consequences that would follow if *everyone* in society acted in the same way. This **categorical imperative** can be applied to any action. For example, say that you are deciding whether to cheat on an examination. If you have adopted Kant's categorical imperative, you will decide not to cheat, because if everyone cheated, the examination would be meaningless.

THE PRINCIPLE OF RIGHTS Duty-based ethical standards imply that human beings have basic rights, because a duty cannot exist without a corresponding right. For example, the commandment "Thou shalt not kill" implies that individuals have a right to live. Additionally, religious ethics may involve a rights component because of the belief—characteristic of many religions—that an individual is "made in the image of God" or "Allah." This belief confers on the individual great dignity as a person. For one who holds this belief, not to respect that dignity—and the rights and status that flow from it—would be morally wrong. Kantian ethics also implies fundamental rights based on the personal dignity of each individual. Just as individuals have a duty not to treat others as means to an end, so individuals have a right to have their status and moral integrity as human beings treated with respect.

The principle that human beings have certain fundamental rights (to life, freedom, and the pursuit of happiness, for example) is deeply embedded in Western culture. As discussed in Chapter 1, the natural law tradition embraces the concept that certain actions (such as killing another person) are morally wrong because they are contrary to nature (the natural desire to continue living).

Those who adhere to this **principle of rights,** or "rights theory," believe that a key factor in determining whether a business decision is ethical is how that decision affects the rights of others. These others include the firm's owners, its employees, the consumers of its products or services, its suppliers, the community in which it does business, and society as a whole.

OUTCOME-BASED ETHICS: UTILITARIANISM

"Thou shalt act so as to generate the greatest good for the greatest number." This is a paraphrase of the major premise of the utilitarian approach to ethics. **Utilitarianism** is a philosophical theory developed by Jeremy Bentham (1748–1832) and then advanced, with some modifications, by John Stuart Mill (1806–1873)—both British philosophers. In contrast to duty-based ethics, utilitarianism is outcome oriented. It focuses on the consequences of an action, not on the nature of the action itself or on any set of preestablished moral values or religious beliefs.

Under a utilitarian model of ethics, an action is morally correct, or "right," when, among the people it affects, it produces the greatest amount of good for the greatest number. When an action affects the majority adversely, it is morally wrong. Applying the utilitarian theory thus requires (1) a determination of which individuals will be affected by the action in question; (2) a **cost-benefit analysis**—an assessment of the negative and positive effects of alternative actions on these individuals; and (3) a choice among alternative actions that will produce maximum societal utility (the greatest positive net benefits for the greatest number of individuals).

The utilitarian approach to decision making commonly is employed by businesses, as well as by individuals. Weighing the consequences of a decision in terms of its costs and benefits for everyone affected by it is a useful analytical tool in the decision-making process. At the same time, utilitarianism is often criticized because its objective, calculated approach to problems tends to reduce the welfare of human beings to plus and minus signs on a cost-benefit worksheet and to "justify" human costs that many find totally unacceptable.

SECTION 3 ETHICAL DECISION MAKING

Anyone preparing to enter today's business world must realize that there is an ethical component to virtually every key decision a business firm makes. To ensure that their decisions are ethical, most major companies today ask three questions about any action before it is undertaken: Is the action profitable? It is legal? Is it ethical? The first prong of this test for ethical decision making—determining whether a given course of action will be profitable—is foremost. After all, for-profit firms only remain in business if they make a profit. If the action would not be profitable, it probably will not be undertaken. If the action would be profitable, then the decision makers need to evaluate whether it also would be legal and ethical.

IS THE CONTEMPLATED ACTION LEGAL?

It may seem that answering a question concerning the legality of a given action should be simple. Either something is legal or it is not. In fact, one of the major challenges businesspersons face is that the legality of a particular action is not always clear. In part, this is because there are so many laws regulating business that it is possible to violate one of them without realizing it. There are also numerous "gray areas" in the law, making it difficult to predict with certainty how a court may apply a given law to a particular action.

LAWS REGULATING BUSINESS Today's business firms are subject to extensive government regulation. As mentioned in Chapter 1, virtually every action a firm undertakes—from the initial act of going into business to hiring and firing personnel to selling products in the marketplace—is subject to statutory law and to numerous rules and regulations issued by administrative agencies. Furthermore, these rules and regulations are changed or supplemented frequently.

Determining whether a planned action is legal thus requires the decision makers to keep abreast of the law. Normally, large business firms have attorneys on their staffs to assist them in making key decisions. Small firms must also seek legal advice before making important business decisions—because the consequences of just one violation of a regulatory rule may be costly.

In the following case, a company was charged with a "willful" violation of a regulation issued by the federal Occupational Safety and Health Administration (OSHA). The company argued that it should not be held liable for a willful violation (and the consequent fine) because it was not aware of the specific regulation.

CASE 2.1 Valdak Corp. v. Occupational Safety and Health Review Commission

United States Court of Appeals, Eighth Circuit, 1996. 73 F.3d 1466.

BACKGROUND AND FACTS *Valdak Corporation operated a car wash that used an industrial dryer to spin-dry towels. The dryer was equipped with a device that was supposed to keep it locked while it spun, but the device often did not work. An employee reached into the dryer while it was spinning, and his arm was cut off above the elbow. The Occupational Safety and Health Administration (OSHA) cited Valdak for, among other things, a willful violation of a machine-guarding regulation and assessed a $28,000 penalty. Valdak appealed to the Occupational Safety and Health Review Commission, which upheld the penalty. Valdak then appealed to the U.S. Court of Appeals for the Eighth Circuit, arguing in part that it did not know about the specific regulation and thus could not be cited for a "willful" violation of it.*

IN THE LANGUAGE OF THE COURT

JOHN R. GIBSON, Circuit Judge.

* * * *

Valdak's claimed ignorance of the OSHA standard does not negate a finding of willfulness. Willfulness can be proved by "plain indifference" to the [Occupational Safety and Health Act's] requirements. Plain indifference to the machine guarding requirement is amply demonstrated by the facts that the dryer was equipped with an interlocking device, the interlocking device did not work, and Valdak continued to use the dryer with the broken interlock device.

DECISION AND REMEDY *The U.S. Court of Appeals for the Eighth Circuit upheld the agency's finding that Valdak had willfully violated the OSHA regulation.*

ETHICAL CONSIDERATIONS *This case affirms the adage, "Ignorance of the law is no excuse." One might conclude, though, that even if Valdak's actions had been legal, they would not have been ethical. The fact that the locking device periodically malfunctioned clearly posed a safety risk for Valdak's employees. For both legal and ethical reasons, many employers today not only make sure that their equipment is functioning properly but also create safety programs or manuals to help ensure the safety of their workers.*

"GRAY AREAS" IN THE LAW In many situations, business firms can predict with a fair amount of certainty whether a given action would be legal. For example, firing an employee solely because of that person's race or gender would clearly violate federal laws prohibiting employment discrimination. In some situations, though, the legality of a particular action may be less clear. For example, under federal laws employers must "reasonably accommodate" the religious needs of their employees and the needs of employees or job applicants with disabilities—unless to do so creates an "undue hardship" for the employer. No law, however, spells out exactly what "reasonable accommodation" means or the point at which an employer experiences "undue hardship." Generally, the courts decide these issues on a case-by-case basis.

There are numerous other examples of this legal uncertainty. For example, suppose that a firm decides to launch a new advertising campaign. How far can the firm go in making claims for its product or services? Federal and state laws prohibit firms from engaging in "deceptive advertising." At the federal level, the test for deceptive advertising normally used by the Federal Trade Commission is whether an advertising claim would deceive a "reasonable consumer." At what point, though, would a reasonable consumer be deceived by a particular ad?

In short, whether a given action will be deemed legal or illegal often depends on how an administrative agency or a court in a particular jurisdiction decides to interpret and apply a governing statute or regulation. It is in these areas that business decision makers need to proceed with caution and evaluate the action and its consequences from an ethical perspective. Generally, if a company can demonstrate that it acted in good faith and responsibly in the circumstances, it has a better chance of defending its action successfully in court or before an administrative law judge.

IS THE CONTEMPLATED ACTION ETHICAL?

Even if a company is certain of the legality of a particular action, that does not mean that the action is necessarily ethical. It is true that because the law reflects and codifies a society's ethical values, obeying the law normally is ethical in itself. The law thus makes many of our ethical decisions for us. Nonetheless, in the interest of preserving personal freedom, as well as for practical reasons, the law does not—and cannot—codify all ethical requirements. No law says, for example, that it is *illegal* to lie to one's family, but it may be *unethical* to do so. Likewise, in the business world, numerous actions might be unethical but not necessarily illegal.

Consider the following hypothetical example. A U.S. government agency has declared that a child's toy is dangerous. The toy has caused the deaths of some children. Consequently, the government has banned sales of the toy, leaving the manufacturer with a large unsold inventory. Although the sale of the product is banned in the United States, it may be perfectly legal to export this toy to certain other nations—but would it be ethical to do so?

In today's business world, legal compliance usually is regarded as the **moral minimum.** In other words, the minimal acceptable standard for ethical business behavior is compliance with the law. When the law is silent on an issue, however, as in the above example and in many ethical dilemmas facing business firms, ethical standards must guide the decision-making process. Commonly, some ethical guidance is provided by a company's ethical policies or code of ethics.

CODES OF ETHICS Most corporations today have codes of ethics or established ethical policies to guide their executives and managers (and all company personnel) in making decisions. For example, look at the foldout exhibit in this chapter showing PriceCostco's Code of Ethics. This code clearly indicates PriceCostco's commitment to legal compliance, as well as to the welfare of its members (those who belong to its clubs and purchase its products), its employees, and its vendors (suppliers). The code also details some specific ways in which the interests and welfare of these groups will be protected. If you look closely at the exhibit, you will also see that PriceCostco acknowledges that by protecting these groups' interests, it will realize its "ultimate goal"—which is to reward its shareholders (those who own the company).

PriceCostco's code can guide management and supervisory personnel as they make decisions involving the ethical rights and obligations of each group. What the code does not do, however, and what most codes cannot accomplish satisfactorily, is indicate which group's interests should take priority when the interests of one group conflict with those of another. For example, suppose that a company's employees are pressuring management for a wage increase. If the company agrees to increase employees' wages, this will cut into the firm's profits and thus adversely affect the shareholder-owners' interests. The decision to be made here involves not a choice between an ethical and an unethical action but rather a choice between two conflicting goals.

One of the reasons that ethical decision making is more complex in the business context than in our personal lives is precisely because business firms are perceived to owe duties to a number of groups. These groups include the firm's owners (in a corporation, the shareholders), its employees, its suppliers, those who use its products or services (consumers), the community in which it operates, and, according to many, society at large. These duties often come into conflict, as in the example given above.

ESTABLISHING ETHICAL PRIORITIES An ethical issue involving conflicting duties can only be resolved by establishing which duties should take priority over others. To illustrate: Suppose that the Wellsen Company, a glue-manufacturing firm, learns that thousands of children in several Latin American countries have been inhaling its glue. As a result, many of the children may suffer severe health consequences in the future, including kidney disease and brain damage. Consumer activists have launched a media campaign against Wellsen, accusing it of being unethical by marketing its glue in those countries. What is the right thing to do in this situation? Should Wellsen cease selling its glue in the countries in question even though selling it is legal and profitable?

Assume that Wellsen decides to pull out of those markets. Whose interests would be adversely affected? First of all, the interests of the company's shareholder-owners would be—because the decision probably would result in lower profits. The interests of employees, particularly those with jobs at stake, would also be adversely affected by the decision. Additionally, those firms that supply Wellsen with the materials it needs in the glue-manufacturing process would see decreased profits, at least temporarily, because Wellsen would need fewer materials. Finally, what about the interests of the majority of the consumers in the Latin American countries, who do not misuse the glue? These consumers would also be adversely affected, because they could no longer purchase the glue for home or business purposes.

Clearly, if equal ethical weight were attached to the interests of each group, the right decision would be to continue marketing the product in Latin American countries. Indeed, from a utilitarian perspective, this action might be deemed the most ethical, because the action would benefit the majority of those affected by the decision. From a duty-based (or rights-based) perspective, however, it would be difficult to justify a decision to continue selling a product that was harming some human beings, regardless of the fact that the harm was caused by product misuse.

MAXIMUM VERSUS OPTIMUM PROFITS Today's corporate decision makers are, in a sense, poised on a fulcrum between profitability and ethical responsibility. If they emphasize profits at the expense of perceived ethical responsibilities to other groups, they may become the target of negative media exposure, consumer boycotts, and even lawsuits. If they go too far in the other direction (keep an unprofitable plant open so that the employees do not lose their jobs, invest too heavily in charitable works or social causes, and so on), their profits will suffer and they may have to go out of business.

Striking the right balance on this fulcrum is difficult, and usually some profits must be sacrificed in the process. Instead of maximum profits, many firms today aim for **optimum profits**—the maximum profits a firm can realize while staying within legal *and* ethical limits. In the Wellsen Company's situation, if the decision makers base their reasoning on duty/rights-based ethical standards, they may conclude that they have an ethical duty to pull out of the Latin American markets. In other words, they may decide to settle for optimum profits rather than maximum profits.

Even from a utilitarian perspective, it might be wise to discontinue sales in the Latin American countries in question. Although utilitarian reasoning may lead to the conclusion that there is nothing unethical about continuing sales in those areas—because it would benefit the majority of persons affected by such a decision—Wellsen's reputation could suffer irreparable damage if it did so. In the long run, a decision to continue the sales thus could be an unprofitable one.

PUBLIC OPINION AND BUSINESS ETHICS

Note that in a utilitarian cost-benefit analysis of the ethical issue facing the Wellsen Company, the "cost" of potentially decreased profits in the long run was acknowledged primarily because of the media campaign against Wellsen. In other words, if consumer activists had not created widespread public awareness of Wellsen's actions, the outcome of the utilitarian analysis of the issue would probably be a decision to continue marketing the glue in the Latin American countries.

In the last two decades, the actions of business firms have been much more closely scrutinized by the media and various interest groups (groups supporting human rights, animal rights, the environment, consumers, employees, and so on) than they ever were in the past. What this means is that if a corporation undertakes or continues an action deemed to be unethical by one or more of these groups, the firm's "unethical" behavior will probably become widely known. In the interests of preserving their good reputations, business firms thus pay attention to public opinion. If they do not, they may lose customers, be boycotted by investors concerned about ethical issues, and, ultimately, lose profits.

The ethical reasoning process thus has a practical element. As a manager, you might personally be convinced that there is nothing unethical about a certain business action. If a highly vocal interest group believes otherwise, though, you might want to review your ethical reasoning with a view toward preserving the firm's goodwill and reputation in the community. If you decide to pursue the action regardless of public opinion, you may violate your ethical (and legal) duty to act in the firm's best interests.

ETHICAL DECISION MAKING AND THE CORPORATE ENVIRONMENT

Individuals in their personal lives normally are free to decide ethical issues as they wish and to follow through on those decisions. In the business world, and particularly in the corporate environment, rarely is such a decision made by one person. If you are an officer or a manager of a large company, for example, you will find that the decision as to what is right or wrong for the company is not totally yours to make. Your input may weigh in the decision, but ultimately a corporate decision is a collective undertaking.

In a sense, the corporate environment poses obstacles to ethical decision making because decisions are made collectively. Just as no one person makes a collective decision, so no one person (normally) is held accountable for the decision. The corporate enterprise tends to shield corporate personnel from both personal exposure to the consequences of their decisions (such as direct experience with someone who suffers harm from a corporate product) and personal accountability for those decisions.

Additionally, collective decision making, because it places emphasis on consensus and unity of opinion, tends to hinder individual ethical assertiveness. For example, suppose that a director has ethical misgivings about a planned corporate venture that promises to be highly profitable. If the other directors have no such misgivings, the director who does may be swayed by the enthusiasm of the others for the project and downplay his or her own criticisms.

SECTION 4
ETHICAL ISSUES IN BUSINESS

We now turn to some specific examples of ethical issues that arise in the business world. As you will discover in reading this text, ethics relates to all aspects of business activity. Broadly speaking, though, ethical issues can be categorized as internal issues or external issues. Ethical issues internal to the firm frequently concern the relationship between the firm and its employees. Ethical issues external to the firm predominantly relate to the products or services marketed by the firm and to how marketing decisions affect the welfare of the ultimate consumers of those products and services. We examine both types of issues in the following sections.

Note that external issues also involve a firm's relationship with its suppliers, its creditors, the surrounding community, and other external groups. In the *Focus on Ethics* following Chapter 4, you will read further about both internal and external ethical issues in the context of corporate social responsibility.

EMPLOYMENT RELATIONSHIPS

One of the primary concerns of every employer is the ability to control the workplace environment. After all, it is the employer who is responsible for making the business firm a success, and success requires qualified, competent, loyal employees and efficient operations. Employees, though, also have concerns. They want to earn a fair wage; they want to work in an environment free of health-endangering hazards; they want to be treated fairly and equally by their employers; they want to be free of harassment by co-workers; and increasingly in recent years, they want employers to respect their personal integrity and privacy rights.

By law, employers are required to provide a safe workplace, to pay a minimum wage, and to not discriminate against potential and existing employees. Ethical issues in the employment context often concern compliance with such laws. As mentioned earlier, the minimum ethical standard for all business firms is compliance with the law. Even the most ethical firm, however, may have difficulty in deciding what kind of behavior is mandated by a certain law. Furthermore, employers sometimes, by attempting to fulfill one legal and ethical duty, end up violating another. Other ethical issues in the employment context involve the extent to which a firm's ethical obligations to employees go beyond its legal obligations. We look here at some employment decisions facing employers in which various ethical or legal duties come into conflict. (See Chapters 20 and 21 for other ethical issues that arise in the employment context.)

SEXUAL HARASSMENT VERSUS WRONGFUL DISCHARGE Lawsuits for sexual harassment in the workplace (discussed in Chapter 21) climbed dramatically in number in the past decade and are costly for employers. Under guidelines issued by the Equal Employment Opportunity Commission (EEOC), the regulatory agency that enforces federal laws prohibiting discrimination and sexual harassment, an employer must take "immediate and appropriate corrective action" in response to an employee's complaint of sexual harassment or abuse. An employer that does not do so may be forced to pay costly damages in a subsequent lawsuit.

Consider, though, what might happen if an employer does take "immediate and appropriate corrective action." An employee complains to her supervisor that a co-worker is sexually harassing her—physically touching her in objectionable ways, making lewd comments about her and to her, and so on. The company immediately investigates the claim, and on finding that it is substantiated, promptly fires the harassing employee. In taking this action, the company assumes that it is acting ethically and in compliance with the law. The fired employee, however, then sues the firm for *wrongful discharge* (firing an employee without good cause or for discriminatory reasons—see Chapter 20). Will the fired employee win the lawsuit? Perhaps. Under some state laws and employment agreements, employers are prohibited from firing employees without "just cause," and particular incidents of sexual harassment may or may not constitute just cause for firing the harasser.[1]

In an attempt to shield themselves from liability, most large companies today (and many smaller ones) have created and implemented harassment policies. These policies typically establish procedures that employees can follow if they feel they are being harassed by co-workers or supervisors. The policies also instruct management and supervisory personnel on the proper corrective actions to take in response to employees' complaints. Corrective actions usually involve a series of steps. Initially, the harassing employee is informed of the problem and asked to cease the offensive behavior. If the behavior continues, then the employee may be placed on probation. Finally, if the problem recurs, the employee will be fired. A company that can demonstrate that it established and followed such procedures may be able to avoid liability for either sexual harassment or wrongful discharge.[2]

1. See, for example, *Chrysler Motors Corp. v. International Union, Allied Industrial Workers of America*, 959 F.2d 685 (7th Cir. 1992).

2. See, for example, *Baskerville v. Culligan International Co.*, 50 F.3d 428 (7th Cir. 1995).

CORPORATE RESTRUCTURING AND EMPLOYEE WELFARE Often, ethical issues in employment involve a conflict between making profits and ensuring the welfare of employees. For example, suppose that Jemico, Inc., decides to reduce its costs by downsizing and restructuring its operations. Among other things, this would allow the company to cut back on its overhead by consolidating various supervisory and managerial positions. The question for Jemico is, which employees should be retained and which should be let go? Should the firm retain highly paid employees who have worked for—and received annual raises from—the firm for years? Alternatively, in the interests of cutting costs, should it retain (or hire) younger, less experienced persons at lower salaries?

Jemico would not necessarily be acting illegally if it pursued the second option. Unless a fired employee can prove that the employer has breached an employment contract or violated the Age Discrimination in Employment Act (ADEA) of 1967, he or she will not have a cause of action against the employer. The ADEA prohibits discrimination against workers forty years old and older on the basis of their age, but Jemico can always say that lack of performance or ability, not age, was the deciding factor. The question here is whether such an action would be ethical.

In deciding this issue, remember that Jemico must keep its eye on its profit margin. If it does not, the firm may fail, and the shareholders will lose their investments. Furthermore, why should the firm retain highly paid employees if it can obtain essentially the same work output for a lower price from less highly paid employees? Does Jemico owe an ethical duty to employees who have served the firm loyally over a long period of time? Most people would say yes. Should this duty take precedence over Jemico's duty to the firm's owners to maintain or increase the profitability of the firm? What if the firm faced imminent bankruptcy if it could not lower its operational costs? What if longtime employees were willing to take a slight reduction in pay to help the firm through its financial difficulties? What if they were not?

In the following case, an employer was confronted with a dwindling market and decreasing sales. The employer decided to reduce its costs of doing business by eliminating some of its obligations to its employees.

CASE 2.2 Varity Corp. v. Howe

Supreme Court of the United States, 1996.
__U.S.__,
116 S.Ct. 1065,
134 L.Ed.2d 130.

BACKGROUND AND FACTS *Varity Corporation manufactures and sells farm implements. In 1986, Varity set up a subsidiary, Massey Combines Corporation (MCC), to market its self-propelled combines and four-wheel-drive tractors. The sales of both products were at an all-time low. Varity convinced current and former employees who were, or had been, involved with the products to accept a transfer to MCC of their jobs and retirement benefit plans. Varity did not tell those employees that it expected MCC to fail. Within two years, MCC did fail. Among other consequences, some retirees stopped receiving benefits. The retirees and other ex-employees sued Varity in a federal district court under the Employee Retirement Income Security Act of 1974 (ERISA), a federal act regulating employer-provided pension plans (see Chapter 20). They claimed that Varity owed them a fiduciary duty,*[a] *which it had breached. The court ruled in their favor, the U.S. Court of Appeals for the Eighth Circuit affirmed, and Varity appealed to the United States Supreme Court.*

IN THE LANGUAGE OF THE COURT

Justice *BREYER* delivered the opinion of the Court.

* * * *

* * * ERISA requires a "fiduciary" to "discharge his duties with respect to a [retirement benefit] plan solely in the interest of the participants and beneficiaries."

a. A *fiduciary* is a party who, because of something that he or she has undertaken to do, has a duty to act primarily for another's benefit. Fiduciary duties are imposed by law in many circumstances.

To participate knowingly and significantly in deceiving a plan's beneficiaries in order to save the employer money at the beneficiaries' expense, is not to act "solely in the interest of the participants and beneficiaries." As other courts have held, "[l]ying is inconsistent with the duty of loyalty owed by all fiduciaries * * * ."

DECISION AND REMEDY *The United States Supreme Court affirmed the decision of the lower court. Varity had violated its fiduciary duty to its employees with respect to their retirement benefits.*

ETHICAL CONSIDERATIONS *This case clearly illustrates the flaws in Varity's ethical decision-making process. Although the decision to transfer its employees to MCC appeared to meet the profitability criterion for ethical decision making, it did not, as it turns out, meet the legality requirement. Either Varity knew that it was taking a risk by assuming its decision would be legal, or it (or its attorney) had not researched the issue carefully. Because the legality of the action was not clear cut, Varity should have taken another action that was at least ethically defensible—and lying to employees, as the Supreme Court indicated in this case, is not ethically defensible.*

CONSUMER WELFARE

To a certain extent, product liability laws and warranty laws (discussed in Chapters 14 and 11, respectively), as well as other laws protecting consumers, help to ensure that corporations will market only products that are safe to use or consume. There is a large "gray area," however, in which marketing a certain product is legal but may be considered unethical, particularly if the product is being misused.

PRODUCT MISUSE When a substantial number of consumers are injured by using a product in a way not intended by the manufacturer, an ethical question arises: Should the manufacturer suspend sales of the product even if it has no legal duty to do so? For example, suppose that a corporation that markets baby formula in developing countries has learned that mothers in those countries often mix the formula with impure water, to make the formula go further. As a result, babies there are suffering from malnutrition, diarrhea, and even death. Although the corporation is not violating any law, many would contend that it should suspend sales of the formula in those countries.

Product misuse can occur anywhere, including the United States. The central question raised by product misuse remains the same, however: Who should bear the responsibility for the harms caused by product misuse, the consumer or the manufacturer? At one time, both legally and ethically, it was felt that consumers should assume full responsibility for the consequences of their actions, including product misuse. The prevailing dictum was *caveat emptor* ("let the buyer beware"). In an era of technologically sophisticated products, large corporate enterprises, and a perceived lack of equality in bargaining power between buyers and sellers, society has deemed that this dictum is no longer appropriate. Today, the prevailing dictum is *caveat venditor* ("let the seller beware"). Consumers who are injured by defective products have recourse against sellers under product liability laws (see Chapter 14).

DUTY TO WARN Among other things, product liability laws require manufacturers and sellers to warn consumers of the kinds of injuries that might result from the misuse of their products. An exception to this rule is made, however, when a risk associated with a product is "open and obvious." Sharp knives, for example, can obviously injure their users.

Sometimes, a business has no way of predicting how a court might rule in deciding whether, on the one hand, a particular risk is open and obvious or, on the other hand, consumers should be warned of the risk. Consequently, product liability laws, with respect to the duty to warn, create yet another gray area. A firm's decision makers may conclude that the firm has no legal or ethical duty to warn consumers of what appears to those decision makers to be an open and obvious risk.

Even courts often disagree on such issues. In the following case, for example, the trial court and the appellate court arrived at different conclusions on whether an automobile manufacturer should have warned consumers that seat belts would not necessarily protect them from injuries in head-on collisions.

CASE 2.3 Mazda Motor of America, Inc. v. Rogowski

Court of Special Appeals of Maryland, 1995. 105 Md.App. 318, 659 A.2d 391.

BACKGROUND AND FACTS *Francis Rogowski fell asleep at the wheel of his Mazda pickup truck and collided head-on with a large tree. To recover for the cost of his injuries, Rogowski sued Mazda Motor of America, Inc., and others in a Maryland state court. Rogowski claimed, among other things, that Mazda should have warned him that the seat belts would not protect him from all injuries if he were in an accident. The trial court agreed that Mazda was liable for failure to warn and awarded damages of $601,644 to Rogowski. Mazda appealed.*

IN THE LANGUAGE OF THE COURT

JOHN F. McAULIFFE, Judge.

* * * *

* * * [T]he danger not warned about was clear and obvious. It borders on the absurd to suggest that persons of ordinary intelligence would not appreciate the fact that seat belts, no matter how well designed and made, cannot be expected to protect the occupants of a vehicle from all injury, or even from serious injury, no matter how substantial the impact of a collision. * * * [T]here simply is no necessity to explain that which is obvious—that seat belts do not and cannot protect the occupants of the vehicle from injury no matter how severe the accident. Moreover, the giving of unnecessary warnings should be avoided because the presence of superfluous warnings seriously detracts from the efficacy of warnings that are needed.

* * * Bombarded with nearly useless warnings about risks that rarely materialize in harm, many consumers could be expected to give up on warnings altogether. And the few persons who might continue to take warnings seriously in an environment crowded with warnings of remote risks would probably overreact, investing too heavily in their versions of "safety." Given these limits on the capacity of consumers to react effectively to excessive risk information, the optimal, rather than the highest, levels of risk information, measured both qualitatively and quantitatively, are what is called for.

DECISION AND REMEDY *The Court of Special Appeals of Maryland held that the danger not warned about was clear and obvious, and it reversed and remanded the case to the lower court.*

ETHICAL CONSIDERATIONS *Compliance with the law normally is held to be the moral minimum in business ethics. Because of the many uncertainties and gray areas in the law, such as when a court might consider a risk to be open and obvious, much of business ethical decision making today necessarily must focus on the legality of contemplated actions. Obtaining sound legal advice when making important decisions, then, is important for both practical and ethical reasons.*

SECTION 5
THE EVER-CHANGING ETHICAL LANDSCAPE

Society's determination of what constitutes ethical business behavior changes over time. Consider the ethical landscape of business as it existed seventy-five years ago. At that time, a corporation was perceived to have one major duty: to serve the interests of its shareholders (basically, make profitable decisions) and to act within legal limits when doing so. In other words, in the corporate decision-making process, only two questions normally were asked: Is it profitable? Is it legal? The third question (Is it ethical?) was largely answered by the first two.

Indeed, most of the ethical and social issues discussed in this chapter and elsewhere in this text either did not exist or were of little public concern at that time. In some cases, these issues emerged only as recently as a decade ago. Technological innovations, the communications revolution, pressing environmental problems, and social movements resulting in greater rights for minorities, women, and consumers have all dramatically changed the society in which we live and, consequently, the business and ethical landscape of America. Today, society expects business leaders to acknowledge and fulfill ethical duties to all persons and groups that are affected by the decisions and activities of their firms.

TERMS AND CONCEPTS TO REVIEW

business ethics 25
categorical imperative 26
cost-benefit analysis 26
ethical reasoning 25
ethics 25
moral minimum 28
optimum profits 30
principle of rights 26
utilitarianism 26

QUESTIONS AND CASE PROBLEMS

2–1. BUSINESS ETHICS. Some business ethicists maintain that whereas personal ethics has to do with "right" or "wrong" behavior, business ethics is concerned with "appropriate" behavior. In other words, ethical behavior in business has less to do with moral principles than with what society deems to be appropriate behavior in the business context. Do you agree with this distinction? Do personal and business ethics ever overlap? Should personal ethics play any role in business ethical decision making?

2–2. BUSINESS ETHICS. If a firm engages in "ethical" behavior solely for the purpose of gaining profits from the goodwill it generates, the "ethical" behavior is essentially a means toward a self-serving end (profits and the accumulation of wealth). In this situation, is the firm acting unethically in any way? Which should carry greater weight on the ethical scales in this situation: motive or conduct?

2–3. ETHICAL REASONING. Susan Whitehead serves on the city planning commission. The city is planning to build a new subway system, and Susan's brother-in-law, Jerry, who owns the Custom Transportation Co., has submitted the lowest bid for the system. Susan knows that Jerry could complete the job for the estimated amount, but she also knows that once Jerry completes this job, he will probably sell his company and quit working. Susan is concerned that Custom Transportation's subsequent management might not be as easy to work with if revisions need to be made on the subway system after its completion. She is torn as to whether she should tell the city about the potential changes in Custom Transportation's management. If the city knew about the instability of Custom Transportation, it might prefer to give the contract to one of Jerry's competitors, whose bid was only slightly higher than Jerry's. Does Susan have an ethical obligation to disclose the information about Jerry to the city planning commission? How would you apply duty-based ethical standards to this question? What might be the outcome of a utilitarian analysis? Discuss fully.

2–4. ETHICAL DECISION MAKING. Assume that you are a high-level manager for a shoe manufacturer. You know that your firm could increase its profit margin by producing shoes in Indonesia, where you could hire women for $40 a month to assemble them. You also know, however, that a competing shoe manufacturer recently was accused by human-rights advocates of engaging in exploitative labor practices because the manufacturer sold shoes made by Indonesian women working for similarly low wages. You personally do not believe that paying $40 a month to Indonesian women is unethical, because you know that in that impoverished country, $40 a month is a better-than-average wage rate. Assuming that the decision is yours to make, should you have the shoes manufactured in Indonesia and make higher profits for your company? Or should you avoid the risk of negative publicity and the consequences of that publicity for the firm's reputation and subsequent profits? Are there other alternatives? Discuss fully.

2–5. Ethical Decision Making. Shokun Steel Co. owns many steel plants. One of its plants is much older than the others. Equipment at the old plant is outdated and inefficient, and the costs of production at that plant are now twice what they are at any of Shokun's other plants. The price of steel cannot be increased because of competition, both domestic and international. The plant is located in Twin Firs, Pennsylvania, which has a population of about forty-five thousand, and currently employs over a thousand workers. Shokun is contemplating whether to close the plant. What factors should the firm consider in making its decision? Will the firm violate any ethical duties if it closes the plant? Analyze these questions from the two basic perspectives on ethical reasoning discussed in this chapter.

2–6. Consumer Welfare. Two eight-year-old boys, Douglas Bratz and Bradley Baughn, were injured while riding a mini–trail bike manufactured by Honda Motor Co. Bratz, who was driving the bike while Baughn rode as a passenger behind him, ran three stop signs and then collided with a truck. Bratz's helmet flew off on impact because it was unfastened. Baughn was not wearing a helmet. Both the owner's manual for the mini–trail bike and a label on the bike itself prominently stated that the bike was intended for off-the-road use, that the bike should not be used on public streets or highways, and that users should "Always Wear a Helmet." Bratz's father had repeatedly told the boy not to ride the bike in the street. The parents of the boys sued Honda for damages. Honda claimed it had sufficiently warned consumers of potential dangers that could result if the bike was not used as directed. Should Honda be held responsible for the boys' injuries? Why or why not? [*Baughn v. Honda Motor Co.*, 107 Wash.2d 127, 727 P.2d 655 (1986)]

2–7. Consumer Welfare. The Seven-Up Co., as part of a marketing scheme, placed two glass bottles of "Like" cola at the front entrance of the Gruenemeier residence. Russell Gruenemeier, a nine-year-old boy, began playing while holding one of the bottles. He tripped and fell, and the bottle broke, severely cutting his right eye and causing him to eventually lose the eye. Russell's mother brought an action against the Seven-Up Co. for damages, claiming that the cause of Russell's injury was Seven-Up's negligence. She claimed that the company had been negligent in placing potentially dangerous instrumentalities—glass bottles—within the reach of small children and that the firm should have used unbreakable bottles for its marketing scheme. Are glass bottles so potentially dangerous that the Seven-Up Co. should be held liable for the boy's harm? If you were the judge, how would you decide the issue? [*Gruenemeier v. Seven-Up Co.*, 229 Neb. 267, 426 N.W.2d 510 (1988)]

2–8. Employment Relationships. In 1982, after learning that when pregnant women are exposed to high lead levels their fetuses may be harmed, Johnson Controls, Inc., adopted a "fetal protection policy." The policy prohibited women of childbearing age from working in the company's Battery Division. Employees and their union, United Automobile Workers, brought a suit in a federal court against Johnson, claiming that the policy violated federal law prohibiting employment discrimination on the basis of gender and pregnancy. The relevant statutory provision states that unless pregnant employees differ from others "in their ability or inability to work," they must be "treated the same" as other employees "for all employment related purposes." Does this mean that Johnson's fetal-protection policy is illegal? If you were the judge, how would you decide the issue, and why? [*United Automobile Workers v. Johnson Controls, Inc.*, 499 U.S. 187, 111 S.Ct. 1196, 113 L.Ed.2d 158 (1991)]

2–9. Employment Relationships. Matt Theurer, an eighteen-year-old high school senior, worked part-time at a McDonald's restaurant in Oregon. Theurer volunteered to work an extra shift one day, in addition to his regular shifts (one preceding and one following the extra shift). After working about twelve hours during a twenty-four-hour period, Theurer told the manager that he was tired and asked to be excused from his next regularly scheduled shift so that he could rest. The manager agreed. While driving home from work, Theurer fell asleep at the wheel and crashed into a van driven by Frederic Faverty. Theurer died, and Faverty was severely injured. Faverty sued McDonald's, alleging, among other things, that McDonald's had been negligent in permitting Theurer to drive a car when it should have known that he was too tired to drive safely. Do employers have a duty to prevent fatigued employees from driving home from work? Should such a duty be imposed on them? How should the court decide this issue? How would you decide the issue if you were the judge? [*Faverty v. McDonald's Restaurants of Oregon, Inc.*, 133 Or.App. 514, 892 P.2d 703 (1994)]

2–10. A Question of Ethics

Three-year-old Randy Welch climbed up to a shelf and picked up a disposable butane cigarette lighter. Randy then used the lighter to ignite a flame, which set fire to his pajama top. Welch and his parents brought a product liability suit against the lighter's manufacturer, Scripto-Tokai Corp., for damages. One of the questions raised in this case was whether the risks attending the lighter were sufficiently "open and obvious" that the manufacturer did not need to warn of those risks. [*Welch v. Scripto-Tokai Corp.*, 651 N.E.2d 810 (Ind.App. 1995)]

1. If you were the judge, how would you decide this issue? Explain your reasoning.
2. Generally, how can a court decide what kinds of risks should be open and obvious for the ordinary consumer? How can a business decision maker decide such questions?

ACCESSING THE INTERNET

THE LEGAL ENVIRONMENT OF BUSINESS

The key to running an ethical business enterprise is effective and ethical management. A good source for information on management ethics is Academy of Management (AM) On-Line. AM can be accessed at

http://www.aom.pace.edu/

Mantis Consultants, Ltd., offers a number of services, including case studies, to help businesses better understand strategic management and the importance of management strategies in cultivating an ethical workplace. To access this company's home page, go to

http://northstar/bus/utk/edu/mgmtsci

The Foundation for Enterprise Development (FED) is an organization dedicated to fostering highly productive corporate cultures. FED provides practical guidelines on how companies can integrate employees into their business decision-making processes. To access FED's home page, go to

http://www.fed.org/fed/

A number of socially responsible corporations have taken up residence on the Internet. The Progressive Business Web Pages constitute a valuable source of information concerning these businesses, including information on environmentally conscious firms. To access these pages, go to

http://envirolink.org.

For a wealth of information on philanthropic organizations in the United States, you can access the Internet Non-Profit Center, a project of the American Institute of Philanthropy, at

http://www.nonprofits.org/

Because of its extensive collection of information on corporations in the United States, Hoover's Online is an invaluable resource. For data on more than 1,500 corporations, access Hoover's Online at

http://www.hoovers.com

If you are interested in how another country views business ethics, you should explore Ethical Business, a site originating in Great Britain. You can find this site at

http://www.arq.co.uk/ethicalbusiness

CHAPTER 3

THE COURT SYSTEM

TODAY IN THE UNITED STATES there are fifty-two court systems—one for each of the fifty states, one for the District of Columbia, and a federal system. Keep in mind that the federal courts are not superior to the state courts; they are simply an independent system of courts, which derives its authority from Article III, Section 2, of the U.S. Constitution. Congress has extended the federal court system beyond the boundaries of the United States to U.S. territories such as Guam, the Virgin Islands, and Puerto Rico. (In Guam and the Virgin Islands, territorial courts serve as both federal courts and state courts, whereas in Puerto Rico, they serve only as federal courts.) Congress has established the U.S. territorial courts by its authority under Article I of the U.S. Constitution. As we shall see, the United States Supreme Court is the final controlling voice over all of these fifty-two systems, at least when questions of federal law are involved.

Every businessperson will likely face either a potential or an actual lawsuit at some time in his or her career. It is thus important for anyone involved in business to have an understanding of the American court systems as well as the various methods of dispute resolution that can be pursued outside the courts. In this chapter, after examining the judiciary's overall role in the American governmental scheme, we discuss some basic requirements that must be met before a party may bring a lawsuit before a particular court. We then look at the court systems of the United States in some detail. We conclude the chapter with an overview of the judicial procedures that frame the litigation process.

SECTION 1

THE JUDICIARY'S ROLE IN AMERICAN GOVERNMENT

As you learned in Chapter 1, the body of American law is vast and complex. It includes the federal and state constitutions, statutes passed by legislative bodies, administrative law, and the case decisions and legal principles that form the common law. These laws would be meaningless, however, without the courts to interpret and apply them. This is the essential role of the judiciary—the courts—in the American governmental system: to interpret and apply the laws to specific situations.

As the branch of government entrusted with interpreting the laws, the judiciary can decide, among other things, whether the laws or actions of the other two branches are constitutional. The process for making such a determination is known as **judicial review.** The power of judicial review enables the judicial branch to act as a check on the other two branches of government, in line with the checks and balances system established by the U.S. Constitution.

The power of judicial review is not mentioned in the Constitution, however. Rather, it was established by the United States Supreme Court's decision in *Marbury v. Madison.*[1] In that case, which was decided in 1803, the Supreme Court stated, "It is emphatically the province and duty of the Judicial Department to say what the law is. . . . If two laws conflict with each other, the courts must decide on the operation of each. . . . So if the law be in opposition to the Constitution . . . [t]he Court must determine which of these conflicting rules governs the case. This is the very essence of judicial duty." Since the *Marbury v. Madison* decision, the power of judicial review has remained unchallenged. Today, this power is exercised by both federal and state courts.

SECTION 2

BASIC JUDICIAL REQUIREMENTS

Before a lawsuit can be brought before a court, certain requirements must be met. These requirements relate to jurisdiction, venue, and standing to sue. We examine each of these important concepts here.

1. 5 U.S. (1 Cranch) 137, 2 L.Ed.60 (1803).

JURISDICTION

In Latin, *juris* means "law," and *diction* means "to speak." Thus, "the power to speak the law" is the literal meaning of the term **jurisdiction.** Before any court can hear a case, it must have jurisdiction over the person against whom the suit is brought—that is, the defendant—or over the property involved in the suit. The court must also have jurisdiction over the subject matter.

JURISDICTION OVER PERSONS Generally, a particular court can exercise ***in personam* jurisdiction** (personal jurisdiction) over residents of a certain geographical area. A state trial court, for example, normally has jurisdictional authority over residents of a particular area of the state, such as a county or district. A state's highest court (often called the state supreme court)[2] has jurisdictional authority over all residents within the state.

In some cases, under the authority of a state **long arm statute,** a court can exercise personal jurisdiction over nonresident defendants as well. Before a court can exercise jurisdiction over a nonresident under a long arm statute, though, it must be demonstrated that the nonresident had sufficient contacts, or *minimum contacts,* with the state to justify the jurisdiction.[3] For example, if an individual has committed a wrong within the state, such as causing an automobile injury or selling defective goods, a court can usually exercise jurisdiction even if the person causing the harm is located in another state. Similarly, a state may exercise personal jurisdiction over a nonresident defendant who is sued for breaching a contract that was formed within the state.

In regard to corporations,[4] the minimum-contacts requirement is usually met if the corporation does business within the state, advertises or sells its products within the state, or places its goods into the "stream of commerce" with the intent that the goods be sold in the state. Suppose that a corporation incorporated under the laws of Maine and headquartered in that state has a branch office or manufacturing

2. As will be discussed shortly, a state's highest court is often referred to as the state supreme court, but there are exceptions. For example, in New York, the supreme court is a trial court.

3. The minimum-contacts standard was established in *International Shoe Co. v. State of Washington,* 326 U.S. 310, 66 S.Ct. 154, 90 L.Ed. 95 (1945).

4. In the eyes of the law, corporations are "legal persons"—entities that can sue and be sued.

plant in Georgia. Does this corporation have sufficient contacts with the state of Georgia to allow a Georgia court to exercise jurisdiction over the corporation? Yes, it does. If the Maine corporation advertises and sells its products in Georgia, or places goods within the stream of commerce with the expectation that the goods will be purchased by Georgia residents, those activities may also suffice to meet the minimum-contacts requirement. In the following case, the issue is whether an Italian corporation had sufficient contacts with the state of Arizona to permit a suit against the corporation to be brought in an Arizona state court.

CASE 3.1 A. Uberti and Co. v. Leonardo

Supreme Court of Arizona, 1995. 892 P.2d 1354.

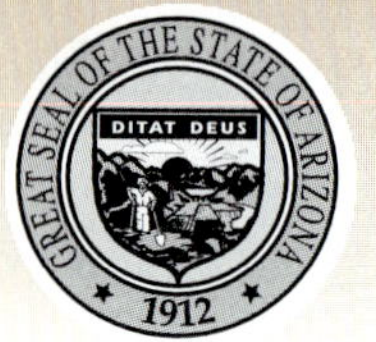

HISTORICAL AND SOCIAL SETTING *Colt Industries manufactured the first Peacemaker, a six-shot, single-action revolver, in 1873. The U.S. government adopted it for service that same year, and the gun became known as "the gun that won the West." In 1892, Colt and other gun manufacturers began making safer, more reliable, and more efficient revolvers. The market for the 1873 model declined until the 1950s, when television Westerns created a new market for replica firearms.*

BACKGROUND AND FACTS *Aldo Uberti and Company, an Italian corporation, manufactures a replica of the Peacemaker known as the Cattleman. Uberti sells its guns to a U.S. distributor for sale throughout the country. Henry Pacho, a resident of Arizona, bought one of the guns, wrapped it in a towel, and put it under the seat of his car. His two-year-old niece, Corrina, was helping to clean the car when the gun fell out of the towel, hit the pavement, and discharged. The bullet struck Corrina in the head and killed her. Corrina's parents filed a suit in an Arizona state court against Uberti, alleging that the company was liable for the "design, manufacture, sale, and distribution of a defective and unreasonably dangerous product." Uberti asked the court to dismiss the suit on the ground (legal basis) that the court did not have personal jurisdiction over Uberti. The court refused, and Uberti appealed. The appellate court reversed. Corrina's parents then appealed to the Supreme Court of Arizona.*

IN THE LANGUAGE OF THE COURT

FELDMAN, Chief Justice.

* * * *

* * * Defendant [Uberti] knew its products, passing through its American distributor[,] * * * would flow into local markets across America.

* * * *

* * * Defendant's catalogs and advertising * * * support the conclusion that the gun, as a replica of an American frontier weapon, was originally and primarily designed and made for the American market. * * *

* * * *

Defendant argues that its activities, at best, focused on the United States in general, not Arizona. Therefore, Arizona exceeds due process by asserting its jurisdiction here. Were this true, then no individual state could assert jurisdiction over Defendant simply because Defendant did not target a particular state or group of states but instead intended to sell its product to all of America. The argument turns common sense on its head. Holding that a defendant intending to sell its products to any and all citizens in the United States could not be held accountable in any jurisdiction where its products caused injury defies any sensible concept of due process. * * *

* * * Thus, we do not believe that Plaintiffs must show Defendant's specific intent to sell in Arizona. An intent to sell across America is enough.

DECISION AND REMEDY *The Supreme Court of Arizona held that Uberti could be sued in an Arizona state court.*

JURISDICTION OVER PROPERTY A court can also exercise jurisdiction over property that is located within its boundaries. This kind of jurisdiction is known as ***in rem* jurisdiction**, or "jurisdiction over the thing." For example, suppose that a dispute arises over the ownership of a boat in dry dock in Fort Lauderdale, Florida. The boat is owned by an Ohio resident, over whom a Florida court cannot normally exercise personal jurisdiction. The other party to the dispute is a resident of Nebraska. In this situation, a lawsuit concerning the boat could be brought in a Florida state court on the basis of the court's *in rem* jurisdiction.

JURISDICTION OVER SUBJECT MATTER Jurisdiction over subject matter is a limitation on the types of cases a court can hear. In both the federal and state court systems, there are courts of *general* (unlimited) *jurisdiction* and courts of *limited jurisdiction.* A court of general jurisdiction can decide virtually any type of case. An example of a court of general jurisdiction is a state or federal trial court. An example of a state court of limited jurisdiction is a probate court. **Probate courts** are state courts that handle only matters relating to the transfer of a person's assets and obligations after that person's death, including matters relating to the custody and guardianship of children. An example of a federal court of limited subject-matter jurisdiction is a bankruptcy court. **Bankruptcy courts** handle only bankruptcy proceedings, which are governed by federal bankruptcy law (discussed in Chapter 16).

A court's jurisdiction over subject matter is usually defined in the statute or constitution creating the court. In both the federal and state court systems, a court's subject-matter jurisdiction can be limited not only by the subject of the lawsuit but also by how much money is in controversy, by whether the case is a felony (a more serious type of crime) or a misdemeanor (a less serious type of crime), or by whether the proceeding is a trial or an appeal.

ORIGINAL AND APPELLATE JURISDICTION The distinction between courts of original jurisdiction and courts of appellate jurisdiction normally lies in whether the case is being heard for the first time. Courts having original jurisdiction are courts of the first instance, or trial courts—that is, courts in which lawsuits begin, trials take place, and evidence is presented. In the federal court system, the *district courts* are trial courts. In the various state court systems, the trial courts are known by various names, as will be discussed shortly.

The key point here is that normally, any court having original jurisdiction is known as a trial court. Courts having appellate jurisdiction act as reviewing courts, or appellate courts. In general, cases can be brought before appellate courts only on appeal from an order or a judgment of a trial court or other lower court.

JURISDICTION OF THE FEDERAL COURTS Because the federal government is a government of limited powers, the jurisdiction of the federal courts is limited. Article III of the U.S. Constitution establishes the boundaries of federal judicial power. Section 2 of Article III states that "[t]he judicial Power shall extend to all Cases, in Law and Equity, arising under this Constitution, the Laws of the United States, and Treaties made, or which shall be made, under their Authority."

Whenever a plaintiff's cause of action is based, at least in part, on the U.S. Constitution, a treaty, or a federal law, then a **federal question** arises, and the case comes under the judicial power of the federal courts. Any lawsuit involving a federal question can originate in a federal court. People who claim that their constitutional rights have been violated can begin their suits in a federal court.

Federal district courts can also exercise original jurisdiction over cases involving **diversity of citizenship.** This term applies whenever a federal court has jurisdiction over a case that does not

EMERGING TRENDS

JURISDICTIONAL ISSUES IN CYBERSPACE

In the good old days, much of the commerce in the United States was quite local in nature. After all, transportation and communication facilities were relatively primitive 150 years ago. By the 1950s, state long arm statutes existed and were applied (as they certainly are today), and the "minimum-contacts" requirement for jurisdiction over an out-of-state defendant had been established. Nonetheless, jurisdictional issues at that time were still far less complicated than they are today.

The issue of minimum contacts started to become sticky when commercial activities did not require physical contact. Specifically, commerce through the mails and over the telephone, particularly as utilized by catalogue companies, raised new jurisdictional issues.

ENTER THE INTERNET

The United States, and indeed the world, is now full of "netizens." They are everywhere, and at the same time, nowhere. How can traditional jurisdictional concepts be applied to the nonphysical landscape of the Internet? Does an entity subject itself to the

jurisdiction of another state's court simply by accessing a Web home page owned by an entity in that other state? In effect, Internet use has turned traditional jurisdictional jurisprudence on its head.

To date, the courts have been mixed in their responses to the jurisdictional issues created by Internet contacts. The trend, though, is toward expanding traditional jurisdictional concepts to cover new forms of communications. Just as modern technology has facilitated cross-border transactions, so it has broadened the permissible scope of jurisdiction. For example, in one case, because a software designer in Texas had repeatedly sent e-mail to CompuServe's headquarters in Columbus, Ohio, he was subjected to personal jurisdiction in Ohio.[a]

An even broader decision was handed down by the federal district court sitting in Los Angeles. That court held that California had jurisdiction over an out-of-state defendant, even though the defendant was not doing business in California—he had simply registered the Internet address (domain name—see Chapter 15) of the Los Angeles plaintiff. The court concluded that California jurisdiction was justified because the effects of the defendant's action were felt in California.[b]

In yet another case, a federal district court held that a New Mexico software company that had allegedly made libelous statements on its Web site and in a CompuServe discussion forum could be sued in Arizona, even though the company had no presence there. The court argued that the defendant "should not be permitted to take advantage of modern technology through an Internet Web page and forum and

a. *CompuServe, Inc. v. Patterson*, 89 F.3d 1257 (6th Cir. 1996).

b. *Panavision International, L.P. v. Toeppen*, 938 F.Supp. 616 (C.D.Cal. 1996).

involve a question of federal law. The most common type of diversity jurisdiction has two requirements:[5] (1) the plaintiff and defendant must be residents of different states, and (2) the dollar amount in controversy must exceed $75,000.[6] For purposes of diversity jurisdiction, a corporation is a citizen of both the state in which it is incorporated and the state in which its principal place of business is located. A

5. Diversity jurisdiction also exists in cases between (1) a foreign country and citizens of a state or of different states and (2) citizens of a state and citizens or subjects of a foreign country. These bases for diversity jurisdiction are less commonly used.

6. This amount was raised from $50,000 to $75,000 in the Federal Courts Improvement Act, which was signed into law on October 19, 1996, by President Bill Clinton and went into effect ninety days later.

EMERGING TRENDS

JURISDICTIONAL ISSUES IN CYBERSPACE (CONTINUED)

simultaneously escape traditional notions of jurisdiction."[c]

The trend in jurisdictional cyberlaw—the emerging body of law governing cyberspace issues—is to focus less on the method of communication or contact and more on the type of activity involved. In other words, the courts tend to look at the type of activity conducted via a particular electronic service and the effects of that activity in the state seeking to exercise jurisdiction over the matter. Indeed, most contracts between online service providers and their users now state explicitly that the users agree to be subject to the jurisdiction of the service provider's state. The courts have upheld such clauses as valid and enforceable, as long as the clauses were reasonable and freely negotiated—so that due process is maintained.

c. *EDIAS Software International, L.L.C. v. BASIS International, Ltd.*, 947 F.Supp. 413 (D.Ariz. 1996).

INTERNATIONAL IMPLICATIONS

The world is becoming more interconnected every day with the increasing use of the Internet. This has serious jurisdictional implications. For example, what if a transaction occurs on the Internet between a U.S. resident and a resident of a foreign country? As another example, consider a person who logs onto the Web through an Internet service provider in Montevideo, Uruguay. What state or country has jurisdictional authority over this person? The server that the user may be accessing could be in Portugal, without the user even being aware of it. Do the Portuguese courts nonetheless have jurisdiction? What about the other countries through which the connection might have been routed?

There are no easy answers to these questions. There certainly will be a trend toward international agreements dealing with basic standards regarding cyberspace. We might also see a United Nations model code that signatory nations would enforce domestically.

IMPLICATIONS FOR THE BUSINESSPERSON

1. Any use of the Internet that involves a business transaction could subject the businessperson to jurisdiction in another state. Thus, there are benefits as well as potential costs to doing business over the Internet.
2. A businessperson could find himself or herself subject to a tort action in another state if he or she chooses to communicate via the Internet.

FOR CRITICAL ANALYSIS

1. In choosing to start up a business via the Internet, what potential cost factors must one take into account?
2. What risks are involved in doing business internationally over the Internet?

case involving diversity of citizenship can be filed in the appropriate federal district court. If the case starts in a state court, it can sometimes be transferred, or "removed," to a federal court. A large percentage of the cases filed in federal courts each year are based on diversity of citizenship.

Note that in a case based on a federal question, a federal court will apply federal law. In a case based on diversity of citizenship, however, a federal court will apply the relevant state law (which is often the law of the state in which the court sits).

EXCLUSIVE VERSUS CONCURRENT JURISDICTION When both federal and state courts have the power to hear a case, as is true in suits involving diversity of citizenship, **concurrent jurisdiction** exists. When cases can be tried only in federal courts or only in state courts, **exclusive jurisdiction** exists.

EXHIBIT 3–1 ■ EXCLUSIVE AND CONCURRENT JURISDICTION

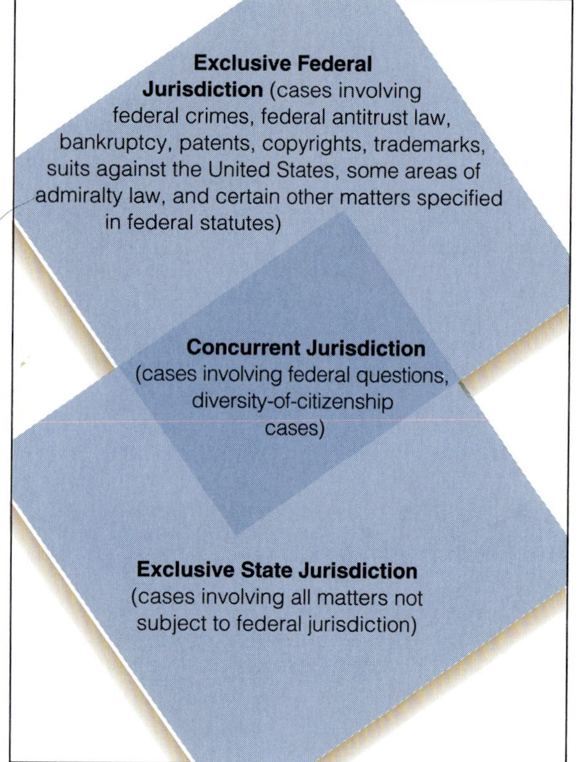

Federal courts have exclusive jurisdiction in cases involving federal crimes, bankruptcy, patents, and copyrights; in suits against the United States; and in some areas of admiralty law (law governing transportation on the seas and ocean waters). States also have exclusive jurisdiction in certain subject matters—for example, divorce and adoption. Exhibit 3–1 illustrates the concepts of concurrent and exclusive jurisdiction.

VENUE

Jurisdiction has to do with whether a court has authority to hear a case involving specific persons, property, or subject matter. **Venue**[7] is concerned with the most appropriate location for a trial. For example, two state courts (or two federal courts) may have the authority to exercise jurisdiction over a case, but it may be more appropriate or convenient to hear the case in one court than in the other.

Basically, the concept of venue reflects the policy that a court trying a suit should be in the geographical neighborhood (usually the county) in which the incident leading to the lawsuit occurred or in which the parties involved in the lawsuit reside. Pretrial publicity or other factors, though, may require a change of venue to another community, especially in criminal cases in which the defendant's right to a fair and impartial jury has been impaired.

For example, a change of venue from Oklahoma City to Denver, Colorado, was ordered for the trials of Timothy McVeigh and Terry Nichols after they had been indicted in connection with the 1995 bombing of the Alfred Murrah Federal Building in Oklahoma City. As a result of the bombing, more than 160 persons were killed, and hundreds of others were wounded. In view of these circumstances, it was felt that to hold the trial in Oklahoma City could prejudice the rights of the defendants to a fair trial.

STANDING TO SUE

In order to bring a lawsuit before a court, a party must have **standing to sue,** or a sufficient "stake" in a matter to justify seeking relief through the court system. In other words, a party must have a legally protected and tangible interest at stake in the litigation in order to have standing. The party bringing the lawsuit must have suffered a harm or been threatened with a harm by the action about which he or she has complained. At times, a person can have standing to sue on behalf of another person. For example, suppose that a child suffers serious injuries as a result of a defectively manufactured toy. Because the child is a minor, a lawsuit can be brought on his or her behalf by another person, such as the child's parent or legal guardian.

Standing to sue also requires that the controversy at issue be a **justiciable**[8] **controversy**—a controversy that is real and substantial, as opposed to hypothetical or academic. For example, in the above example, the child's parent could not sue the toy manufacturer merely on the ground that the toy was defective. The issue would become justiciable only if the child had actually been injured due to the defect in the toy as marketed. In other words, the parent normally could not ask the court to determine, for example, what damages might be obtained if the child had been

7. Pronounced *ven*-yoo.

8. Pronounced jus-*tish*-a-bul.

CONCEPT SUMMARY 3.1 Jurisdiction

TYPE OF JURISDICTION	DESCRIPTION
Personal/Property	Exists when a defendant or a defendant's property is located within the territorial boundaries within which a court has the right and power to decide cases. Jurisdiction may be exercised over out-of-state defendants under state long arm statutes.
Subject Matter	Limits the court's jurisdictional authority to particular types of cases. 1. *Limited jurisdiction*—Exists when a court is limited to a specific subject matter, such as probate or divorce. 2. *General jurisdiction*—Exists when a court can hear any kind of case.
Original	Exists with courts that have the authority to hear a case for the first time (trial courts).
Appellate	Exists with courts of appeal and review; generally, appellate courts do not have original jurisdiction.
Federal	Arises in the following situations: 1. When a federal question is involved (when the plaintiff's cause of action is based at least in part on the U.S. Constitution, a treaty, or a federal law). 2. In diversity-of-citizenship cases between citizens of different states when the amount in controversy exceeds $75,000. (Diversity jurisdiction also exists in cases between a foreign country and citizens of a state or of different states and in cases between citizens of a state and citizens or subjects of a foreign country.)
Concurrent	Exists when both federal and state courts have authority to hear the same case.
Exclusive	Exists when only state courts or only federal courts have authority to hear a

injured, because this would be merely a hypothetical question.

Meeting standing requirements is not always easy. In the following case, for example, an environmental organization sued a company for allegedly discharging pollutants into waterways beyond the amount allowed by the Environmental Protection Agency. At issue in the case was whether the organization had standing to sue under federal environmental laws.

CASE 3.2 Friends of the Earth, Inc. v. Crown Central Petroleum Corp.

United States Court of Appeals, Fifth Circuit, 1996. 95 F.3d 358.

BACKGROUND AND FACTS *Crown Central Petroleum Corporation does business as La Gloria Oil & Gas Company. Under a permit issued by the Environmental Protection Agency (EPA), La Gloria's oil refinery discharges storm-water run-off into Black Fork Creek. Black Fork Creek flows into Prairie Creek, which flows into the Neches River, which flows into Lake Palestine eighteen miles downstream. Friends of the Earth, Inc. (FOE), is a not-for-profit corporation dedicated to the protection of the environment. FOE filed a suit in a federal district court against La Gloria under the Federal Water Pollution Control*

Act.[a] *FOE claimed that La Gloria had violated its EPA permit and that this conduct had directly affected "the health, economic, recreational, aesthetic and environmental interests of FOE's members" who used the lake. La Gloria filed a motion for summary judgment, arguing that FOE lacked standing to bring the suit. The court granted the motion, and FOE appealed.*

IN THE LANGUAGE OF THE COURT

PATRICK E. HIGGINBOTHAM, Circuit Judge:

* * * *

To demonstrate that FOE's members have standing, FOE must show that * * * the injury is "fairly traceable" to the defendant's actions * * * .

* * * *

* * * FOE offered no competent evidence that La Gloria's discharges have made their way to Lake Palestine or would otherwise affect Lake Palestine. * * * FOE and its members relied solely on the truism that water flows downstream and inferred therefrom that any injury suffered downstream is "fairly traceable" to unlawful discharges upstream. At some point this common sense observation becomes little more than surmise. At that point certainly the requirements [for standing] are not met.

DECISION AND REMEDY

The U.S. Court of Appeals for the Fifth Circuit affirmed the lower court's decision. FOE lacked standing to bring a suit against La Gloria.

a. 33 U.S.C. Sections 1251–1387.

SECTION 3

THE STATE AND FEDERAL COURT SYSTEMS

As mentioned earlier in this chapter, each state has its own court system. Additionally, there is a system of federal courts. Although no two state court systems are exactly the same, the right-hand side of Exhibit 3–2 illustrates the basic organizational structure characteristic of the court systems in many states. The exhibit also shows how the federal court system is structured. We turn now to an examination of these court systems, beginning with the state courts.

STATE COURT SYSTEMS

Typically a state court system includes several levels, or tiers, of courts. As indicated in Exhibit 3–2, state courts may include (1) trial courts of limited jurisdiction, (2) trial courts of general jurisdiction, (3) appellate courts, and (4) the state's highest court (often called the state supreme court). Judges in the state court system are usually elected by the voters for specified terms.

Generally, any person who is a party to a lawsuit has the opportunity to plead the case before a trial court and then, if he or she loses, before at least one level of appellate court. Finally, if a federal statute or federal constitutional issue is involved in the decision of a state supreme court, that decision may be further appealed to the United States Supreme Court.

TRIAL COURTS Trial courts are exactly what their name implies—courts in which trials are held and testimony taken. State trial courts have either general or limited jurisdiction. Trial courts that have general jurisdiction as to subject matter may be called county, district, superior, or circuit courts.[9] State trial courts of general jurisdiction have jurisdiction over a wide variety of subjects, including both civil disputes and criminal prosecutions. In some states, trial courts of general jurisdiction may hear appeals from courts of limited jurisdiction.

Courts of limited jurisdiction as to subject matter are often called special inferior trial courts or minor judiciary courts. **Small claims courts** are inferior trial courts that hear only civil cases involving claims of less than a certain amount, such as $2,500 (the

9. The name in Ohio is court of common pleas; the name in New York is supreme court.

EXHIBIT 3–2 ■ FEDERAL COURTS AND STATE COURT SYSTEMS

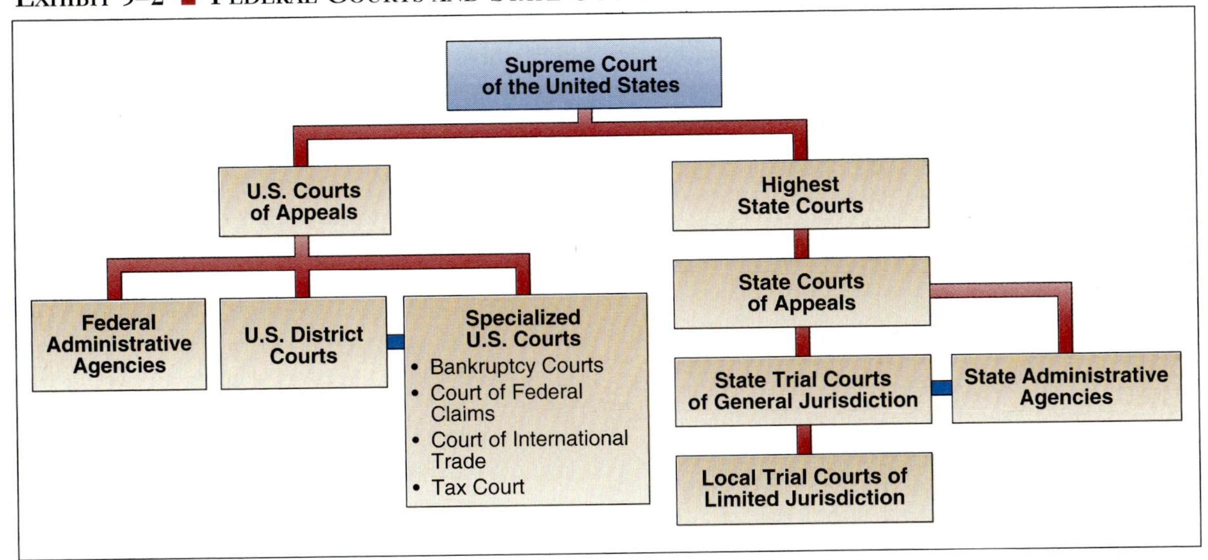

amount varies from state to state). Suits brought in small claims courts are generally conducted informally, and lawyers are not required. In a minority of states, lawyers are not even allowed to represent people in small claims courts for most purposes. Decisions of small claims courts may be appealed to a state trial court of general jurisdiction.

Other courts of limited jurisdiction include domestic relations courts, which handle only divorce actions and child custody cases; local municipal courts, which mainly handle traffic cases; and probate courts, as mentioned earlier.

COURTS OF APPEALS Every state has at least one court of appeals (appellate court, or reviewing court). A court of appeals may be an intermediate appellate court or the state's highest court. About half of the states have intermediate appellate courts. Generally, courts of appeals do not conduct new trials, in which evidence is submitted to the court and witnesses are examined. Rather, an appellate court panel of three or more judges reviews the record of the case on appeal, which includes a transcript of the trial proceedings, and then determines whether the trial court committed an error.

Appellate courts look at questions of law and procedure but usually not at questions of fact. A **question of law** is a question concerning the application or interpretation of the law, on which only a judge, not a jury, can rule. A **question of fact** is a question about what really happened in regard to the dispute being tried. Questions of fact may be decided by a trial judge or jury based on the evidence presented. Normally, an appellate court will defer to the trial court's judgment on questions of fact because the trial court judge and jury were in a better position to evaluate testimony. They directly observed witnesses' gestures, demeanor, and other nonverbal behavior during the trial. At the appellate level, the judges review the written transcript of the trial, which does not include these nonverbal elements.

An appellate court will tamper with a trial court's finding of fact only when the finding is clearly erroneous (that is, when it is contrary to the evidence presented at trial) or when there is no evidence to support the finding. For example, if at trial a jury concluded that a manufacturer's product had harmed the plaintiff but no evidence was submitted to the court to support that conclusion, the appellate court would hold that the trial court's decision was erroneous. The options exercised by appellate courts will be further discussed later in this chapter.

STATE SUPREME (HIGHEST) COURTS The highest state courts usually are called simply supreme courts, but they may be designated by other names. For example, in both New York and Maryland, the highest state court is called the court of appeals. In Maine and Massachusetts, the highest court is labeled the supreme judicial court. In West Virginia, the highest state court is the supreme court of appeals. The decisions of each state's highest court on all questions of state law are final. Only when issues of federal law are involved can a decision made by a state's highest court be overruled by the United States Supreme Court.

THE FEDERAL COURT SYSTEM

The federal court system is basically a three-tiered model consisting of (1) U.S. district courts (trial courts of general jurisdiction) and various courts of limited jurisdiction, (2) U.S. courts of appeals (intermediate courts of appeals), and (3) the United States Supreme Court.

Unlike state court judges, who are usually elected, federal court judges—including the justices of the Supreme Court—are appointed by the president of the United States, subject to the approval of the U.S. Senate. All federal judges receive lifetime appointments (because under Article III they "hold their offices during good Behaviour").

U.S. DISTRICT COURTS At the federal level, the equivalent of a state trial court of general jurisdiction is the district court. There is at least one federal district court in every state. The number of judicial districts can vary over time, primarily owing to population changes and corresponding changes in caseloads. Currently, there are ninety-one federal judicial districts.[10]

U.S. district courts have original jurisdiction in federal matters, and federal cases typically originate in district courts. There are other federal trial courts with original, but special (or limited), jurisdiction, such as the federal bankruptcy courts and others shown in Exhibit 3–2.

U.S. COURTS OF APPEALS In the federal court system, there are thirteen U.S. courts of appeals—also referred to as U.S. circuit courts of appeals. The federal courts of appeals for twelve of the circuits hear appeals from the federal district courts located within their respective judicial circuits. The court of appeals for the thirteenth circuit, called the Federal Circuit, has national appellate jurisdiction over certain types of cases, such as cases involving patent law and cases in which the U.S. government is a defendant.

The decisions of the circuit courts of appeals are binding on all courts within the circuit court's jurisdiction and are final in most cases, but appeal to the United States Supreme Court is possible. Exhibit 3–3 shows the geographical boundaries of U.S. circuit courts of appeals and the boundaries of the U.S. district courts within each circuit.

THE UNITED STATES SUPREME COURT At the highest level in the three-tiered federal court system is the United States Supreme Court. According to the language of Article III of the U.S. Constitution, there is only one national Supreme Court. All other courts in the federal system are considered "inferior." Congress is empowered to create other inferior courts as it deems necessary. The inferior courts that Congress has created include the second tier in our model—the U.S. courts of appeals—as well as the district courts and all other courts of limited, or specialized, jurisdiction.

The United States Supreme Court consists of nine justices. Although the Supreme Court has original, or trial, jurisdiction in rare instances (set forth in Article III, Section 2), most of its work is as an appeals court. The Supreme Court can review any case decided by any of the federal courts of appeals, and it also has appellate authority over some cases decided in the state courts. The Supreme Court is the final arbiter of the Constitution and federal law.

HOW CASES REACH THE SUPREME COURT To bring a case before the Supreme Court, a party requests the Court to issue a writ of *certiorari.* A **writ of *certiorari***[11] is an order issued by the Supreme Court to a lower court requiring the latter to send it the record of the case for review. The Court will not issue a writ unless at least four of the nine justices approve of it. This is called the **rule of four.** Whether the Court will issue a writ of *certiorari* is entirely within its discretion. The Court is not required to issue one, and most petitions for writs are denied. (Thousands of cases are filed with the Supreme Court each year, yet it hears, on average, less than one hundred of these cases.[12]) A denial is not a decision on the merits of a case, nor does it indicate agreement with the lower court's opinion. Furthermore, denial of the writ has no value as a

10. 28 U.S.C. Section 133.

11. Pronounced sur-shee-uh-*rah*-ree.

12. From the mid-1950s through the early 1990s, the Supreme Court reviewed more cases per year than it has in the last few years. In the Court's 1982–1983 term, for example, the Court issued opinions in 151 cases. In contrast, only 75 cases were reviewed during the Court's 1995–1996 term.

EXHIBIT 3–3 ■ U.S. COURTS OF APPEALS AND U.S. DISTRICT COURTS

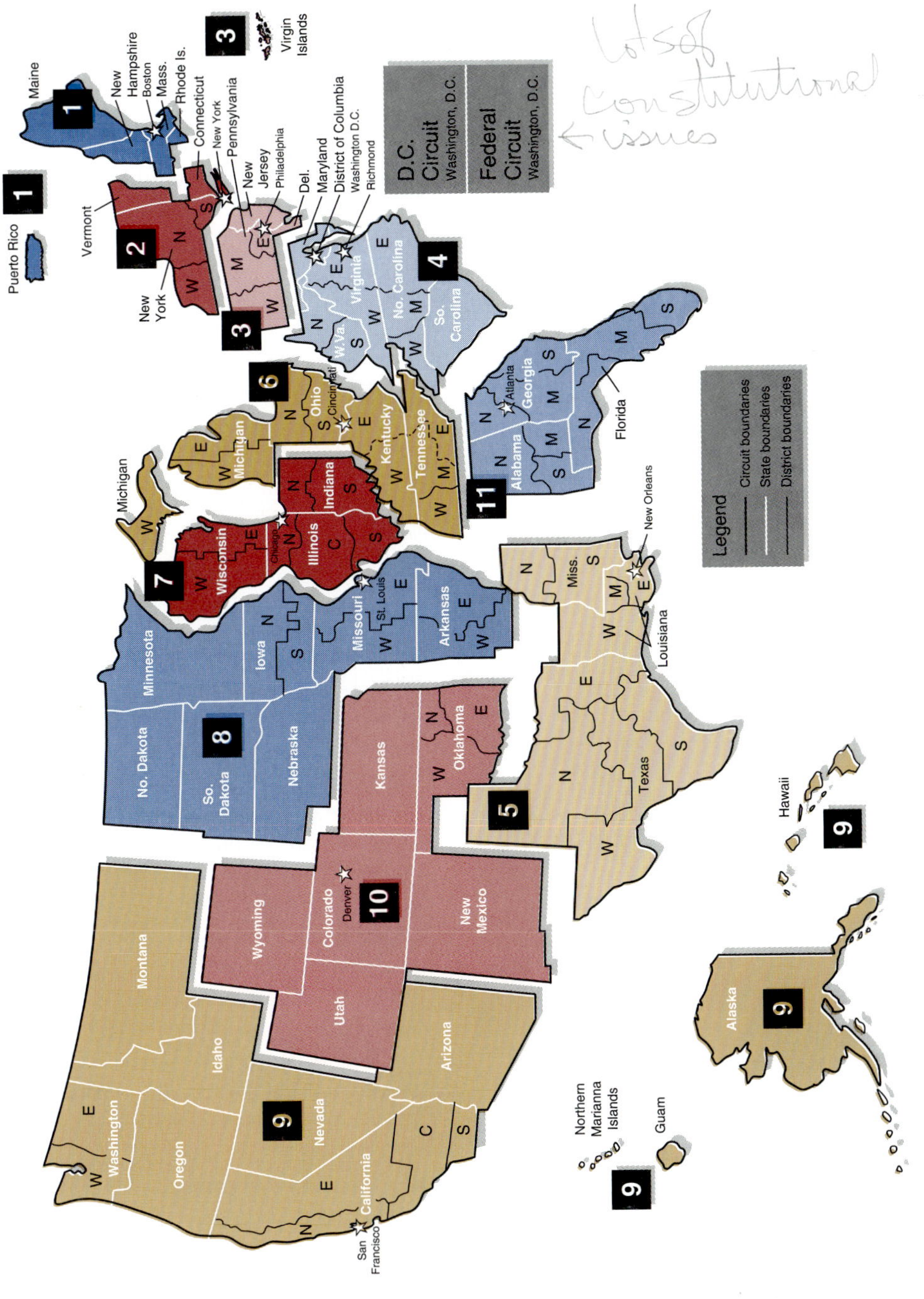

Source: Administrative Office of The United States Courts, January 1983

CONCEPT SUMMARY 3.2 Types of Courts

COURT	DESCRIPTION
Trial Courts	Trial courts are courts of original jurisdiction in which actions are initiated. 1. *State courts*—Courts of general jurisdiction can hear any case that has not been specifically designated for another court; courts of limited jurisdiction include domestic relations courts, probate courts, municipal courts, small claims courts, and others. 2. *Federal courts*—The federal district court is the equivalent of the state trial court. Federal courts of limited jurisdiction include the bankruptcy court and others shown in Exhibit 3–2.
Intermediate Appellate Courts	Courts of appeals are reviewing courts; generally, appellate courts do not have original jurisdiction. Many states have an intermediate appellate court; in the federal court system, the U.S. circuit courts of appeals are the intermediate appellate courts.
Supreme Court	The highest state court is that state's supreme court, although it may be called by some other name. Appeal from a state supreme court to the United States Supreme Court is only possible if a federal question is involved. The United States Supreme Court is the highest court in the federal court system and the final arbiter of the Constitution and federal law.

precedent. A denial of the writ simply means that the decision of the lower court remains the law within that court's jurisdiction.

Typically, the petitions granted by the Court involve cases that raise important constitutional questions or cases that conflict with other state or federal court decisions. Similarly, if federal appellate courts are rendering inconsistent opinions on an important issue, the Supreme Court may review a case involving this issue to define the law on the matter.

SECTION 4

JUDICIAL PROCEDURES: FOLLOWING A CASE THROUGH THE COURTS

American and English courts follow the *adversarial system of justice*. Although clients are allowed to represent themselves in court (called *pro se* representation),[13] most parties to lawsuits hire attorneys to represent them. Each lawyer acts as his or her client's advocate, presenting the client's version of the facts in such a way as to convince the judge (or the judge and jury, in a jury trial) that this version is proper.

In an adversarial system of justice, the judge's role is viewed as nonbiased and mostly passive, but not entirely so. For example, if a defendant chooses to act as his or her own counsel, the judge will often seek to elicit testimony during the trial proceedings to ensure a fair trial. Additionally, judges sometimes ask questions of witnesses, limit the amount of information that can be introduced about an expert witness's qualifications, and even suggest types of evidence to be presented. Judges are responsible for the appropriate application of the law. They do not have to accept the legal reasoning of the attorneys and can base a ruling and a decision on a personal study of the law.

Most of the judicial procedures that you will read about in this chapter are rooted in the adversarial framework of the American legal system. The adversarial system also frames the ethical rules that govern the behavior of attorneys, who are key participants in the litigation process.

In this chapter, after a brief overview of judicial procedures, we illustrate the steps involved in a lawsuit with a hypothetical civil case.

PROCEDURAL RULES

Understanding and meeting procedural requirements are essential in the litigation process. All civil

13. This right was definitively established in *Faretta v. California*, 422 U.S. 806, 95 S.Ct. 2525, 45 L.Ed.2d 562 (1975).

trials held in federal district courts are governed by the **Federal Rules of Civil Procedure (FRCP).**[14] Each state also has rules of civil procedure that apply to all courts within that state. These rules specify what must be done, when, and at which stage of the litigation process. In addition, each court has its own local rules of procedure that supplement the federal or state rules. The parties to a lawsuit must comply with the procedural rules of the court in which the lawsuit is filed.

Although civil trials may vary greatly in terms of complexity, cost, and detail, they all share similar structural characteristics. Even though each case has its own particular set of facts, to which specific laws apply, most civil lawsuits typically follow some version of the course charted in Exhibit 3–4. This exhibit shows that civil litigation typically progresses in very well-defined and discrete stages. Although it may take years for a case to wind its way through court, almost every case follows the same basic steps.

We now turn to our hypothetical case. The case arose from an automobile accident, which occurred when a car driven by Antonio Carvello, a resident of New Jersey, collided with a car driven by Jill Kirby, a resident of New York. The accident took place at an intersection in New York City. Kirby suffered personal injuries, incurring medical and hospital expenses, as well as lost wages for four months. In all, she calculated that the cost to her of the accident was $100,000.[15] Carvello and Kirby have been unable to

14. The United States Supreme Court's authority to promulgate these rules is set forth in 28 U.S.C. Sections 2071–2077.

15. We are ignoring in this example damages for pain and suffering or for permanent disabilities. Often in personal injury cases, plaintiffs seek such damages.

EXHIBIT 3–4 ■ STAGES IN A TYPICAL LAWSUIT

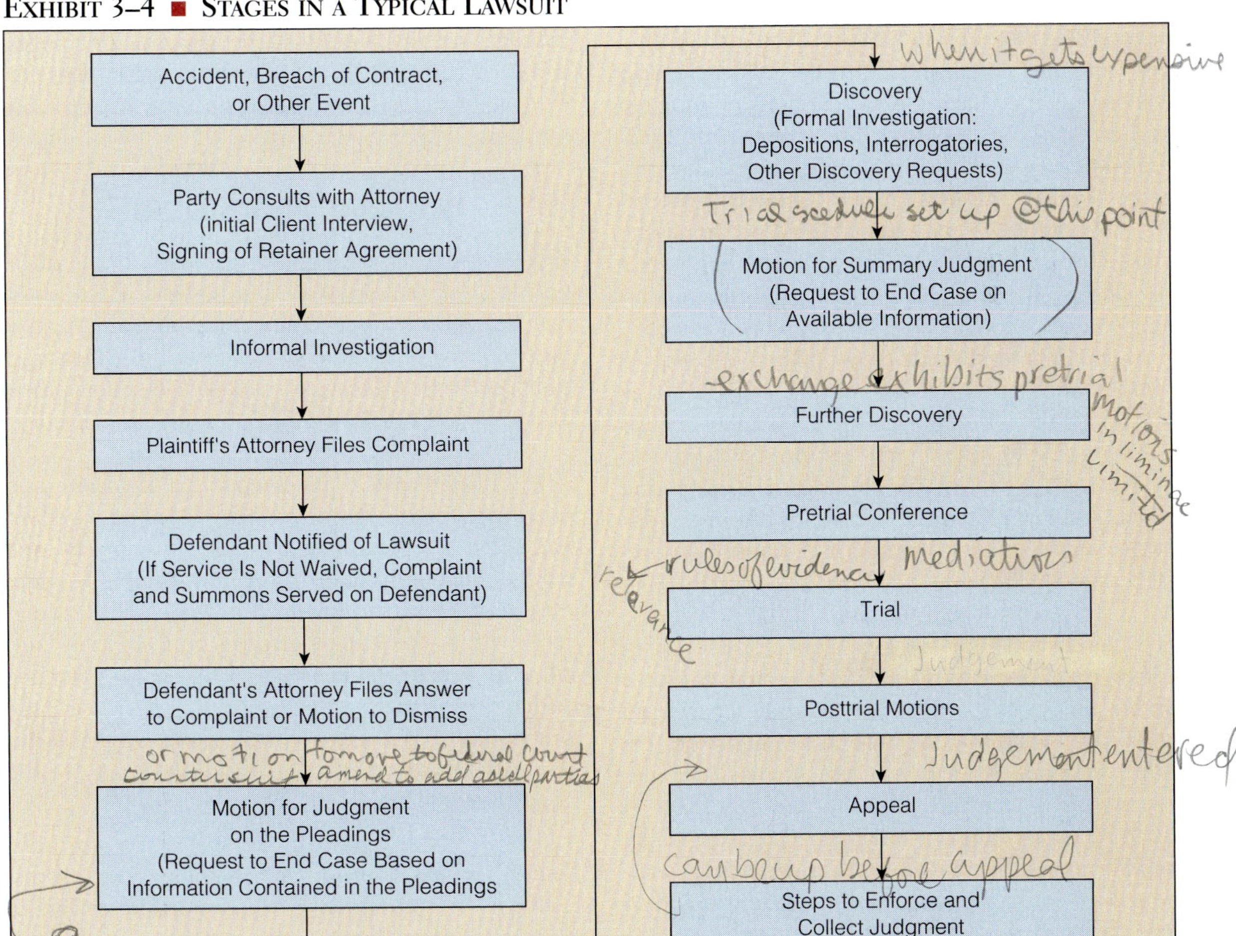

agree on a settlement, and Kirby faces the decision of whether to sue Carvello for the $100,000 compensation that she feels she deserves.

CONSULTING WITH AN ATTORNEY

The first step taken by virtually anyone contemplating a lawsuit is to obtain the advice of a qualified attorney. In the hypothetical Kirby-Carvello case, Kirby may consult with an attorney, who will advise her on what she can expect to gain from a lawsuit, her probability of success if she sues, what procedures will be involved, and how long it may take to resolve the issue through the judicial process. Depending on the court hearing the case, the time costs of the litigation may be enormous. Cases involving personal injuries may take two to three years to resolve, and this is an important factor for Kirby to consider.

LEGAL FEES Another crucial factor that Kirby must consider is, of course, the cost of the attorney's time—the legal fees that she will have to pay to collect damages from the defendant, Carvello. Attorneys base their fees on such factors as the difficulty of a matter, the amount of time involved, the experience and skill of the attorney in the particular area of the law, and the cost of doing business. In the United States, legal fees range from $60 per hour to $450 per hour (the average fee per hour is between $140 and $160). Not included in attorneys' fees are such expenses as court filing charges and other costs directly related to a case.

A particular legal matter may include one type or a combination of several types of fees. *Fixed fees* may be charged for the performance of such services as drafting a simple will. *Hourly fees* may be computed for matters that will involve an indeterminate period of time. Any case brought to trial, for example, may involve an expenditure of time that cannot be precisely estimated in advance. *Contingent fees* (through the initial trial stage) are fixed as a percentage (between 25 and 40 percent) of a client's recovery in certain types of lawsuits, such as personal injury. If the lawsuit is unsuccessful, the attorney receives no fee. If Kirby retains an attorney on a contingency-fee basis, she normally will not have to pay any fees unless she wins the case. She will, however, have to pay the court fees and any other expenses incurred by the attorney on her behalf (such as travel expenses, the cost of expert witnesses and investigators, and so on—often called out-of-pocket costs).

Many state and federal statutes allow for an award of attorneys' fees in certain legal actions, such as probate matters. In these cases, a judge sets the amount of the fee, based on such factors as the results obtained by the attorney and the fee customarily charged for similar services. In some cases, a client may receive an award of attorneys' fees as part of his or her recovery.

SETTLEMENT CONSIDERATIONS A client's decision as to how much money he or she can afford to invest in the resolution of a particular legal problem frequently is the most important factor in determining the extent to which an attorney will pursue a resolution. If a client decides that he or she can afford a lengthy trial and one or more appeals, an attorney may pursue those actions. Often, once a client learns the extent of the costs involved in litigating a claim, he or she is more willing to settle the claim for a lower amount.

Another important factor in deciding whether to pursue litigation is the defendant's ability to pay the damages sought. Even if Kirby is awarded damages, it may be difficult to enforce the court's judgment. (We will discuss the problems involved in enforcing a judgment later in this chapter.)

PRETRIAL PROCEDURES

Broadly speaking, there are three phases of the litigation process: pretrial, trial, and posttrial. Each phase involves specific procedures. The pretrial litigation process involves the filing of *pleadings*, the gathering of evidence (called *discovery*), and possibly other procedures, such as a pretrial conference and jury selection.

THE PLEADINGS The *complaint* and *answer* (and other documents discussed below), taken together, are called the **pleadings.** The pleadings notify each party of the claims of the other and specify the issues (disputed questions) involved in the case. Pleadings remove the element of surprise from a case. They allow lawyers to gather the most persuasive evidence and to prepare better arguments, thus increasing the probability that a just and true result will be forthcoming from the trial. The basic pleadings are the complaint and answer.

The Plaintiff's Complaint. Kirby's action against Carvello will commence when her lawyer files a **complaint** (sometimes called a petition or declaration) with the clerk of the trial court in the appropriate geographical area (the proper venue). In most states, the court would be one having general jurisdiction; in others, it might be a court having special jurisdiction with regard to subject matter. The complaint will contain (1) a statement alleging (asserting) the facts necessary for the court to take jurisdiction, (2) a short statement of the facts necessary to show that the plaintiff is entitled to a remedy, and (3) a statement of the remedy the plaintiff is seeking. A typical complaint is shown in Exhibit 3–5.

The complaint will state that Kirby was driving her car through a green light at the specified intersection, exercising good driving habits and reasonable care, when Carvello negligently drove his vehicle through a red light and into the intersection from a cross street, striking Kirby and causing serious personal injury and property damage. The complaint will go on to state that Kirby is seeking $100,000 in damages.

Service of Process. Before the court can exercise jurisdiction over the defendant (Carvello)—in effect, before the lawsuit can begin—the court must have proof that the defendant was notified of the lawsuit. The process of notifying the defendant of a lawsuit is called **service of process.** Service of process involves serving the defendant with a summons and a copy of the complaint—that is, delivering these items to the defendant. The **summons** notifies defendant Carvello that he is required to prepare an answer to the complaint and to file a copy of his answer with both the court and the plaintiff's attorney within a specified time period (twenty days in the federal courts).

The summons also informs Carvello that if he fails to answer or respond to the plaintiff's complaint within the required time period (unless he can provide a convincing reason to the court why he could not do so), the result will be a default judgment for the plaintiff. A **default judgment** in Kirby's favor would mean that she would be awarded the damages alleged in her complaint. A typical summons is shown in Exhibit 3–6.

How service of process occurs depends on the rules of the court or jurisdiction in which the lawsuit is brought. Under the Federal Rules of Civil Procedure (FRCP), service of process in federal court cases may be effected by anyone who is not a party to the lawsuit and who is at least eighteen years of age. In state courts, the process server is often a sheriff or deputy of the county. Usually, the server effects the service by handing the summons to the defendant personally or by leaving it at the defendant's residence or place of business. In a few states, a summons can be served by mail if the defendant so agrees. When the defendant cannot be reached, special rules sometimes permit serving the summons by leaving it with a designated person, such as the secretary of state.

Serving Corporate Defendants. In cases involving corporate defendants, the summons and complaint may be served on an officer or *registered agent* (representative) of the corporation. The name of a corporation's registered agent can usually be obtained from the secretary of state's office in the state in which the company incorporated its business (and, usually, from the secretary of state's office in any state in which the corporation does business).

Waiver of Formal Service of Process. The FRCP allow formal service of process to be waived by defendants in federal cases, providing that certain procedures are followed. Kirby's attorney, for example, could mail to defendant Carvello a copy of the complaint, along with "Waiver of Service of Summons" forms for Carvello to sign. If Carvello signs and returns the forms within thirty days, formal service of process is waived. To encourage defendants to waive formal service of process, the FRCP provide that defendants who sign and return the waiver are not required to respond to the complaint for sixty days after the date on which the request for waiver of service was sent, instead of the twenty days allowed if formal service of process is undertaken.

The Defendant's Response. The defendant's response to the plaintiff's complaint may take the form of an **answer,** in which the defendant either admits the statements or allegations set out in the complaint or denies them and sets out any defenses that the defendant may have. If Carvello admits to all of Kirby's allegations in his answer, a judgment will be entered for Kirby. If Carvello denies Kirby's allegations, the matter will proceed further.

Carvello can also admit the truth of Kirby's complaint but raise new facts to show that he should not be held liable for Kirby's damages. This is called raising an **affirmative defense.** As will be discussed in subsequent chapters, there are affirmative defenses that can be raised by defendants in both civil and criminal cases. For example, a defendant

EXHIBIT 3–5 ■ A TYPICAL COMPLAINT

IN THE UNITED STATES DISTRICT COURT
FOR THE Southern DISTRICT OF New York

CIVIL NO. 9-1047

Jill Kirby

Plaintiff

vs.

COMPLAINT

Antonio Carvello

Defendant.

The plaintiff brings this cause of action against the defendant, alleging as follows:

1. This action is between the plaintiff, who is a resident of the State of New York, and the defendant, who is a resident of the State of New Jersey. There is diversity of citizenship between the parties.
2. The amount in controversy, exclusive of interest and costs, exceeds the sum of $75,000.
3. On September 10th, 1998, the plaintiff, Jill Kirby, was exercising good driving habits and resonable care in driving her car through the intersection of Boardwalk and Pennsylvania Avenue when the defendant, Antonio Carvello, negligently drove his vehicle through a red light at the intersection and collided with the plaintiff's vehicle.
4. As a result of the collision, the plaintiff suffered severe physical injury, which prevented her from working, and property damage to her car.

WHEREFORE, the plaintiff demands judgment against the defendant for the sum of $100,000 plus interest at the maximum legal rate and the costs of this action.

By Joseph Roe

Joseph Roe
Attorney for Plaintiff
100 Main Street
New York, New York

1/2/99

EXHIBIT 3–6 ■ A TYPICAL SUMMONS

SUMMONS IN A CIVIL ACTION

United States District Court

FOR THE Southern **DISTRICT OF:** New York

CIVIL ACTION FILE NO. 9-1047

Jill Kirby

Plaintiff

v.

Antonio Carvello

Defendant

SUMMONS

To the above named Defendant:

You are hereby summoned and required to serve upon Joseph Roe

100 Main Street

plaintiff's attorney, whose address is New York, New York

an answer to the complaint which is herewith served upon you, within 20 days after service of this summons upon you, exclusive of the day of service. If you fail to do so, judgment by default will be taken against you for the relief demanded in the complaint.

Samuel Raeburn

Clerk of Court

Mary Doakes

Deputy Clerk.

Date: 1/10/99

[Seal of Court]

NOTE:—This summons is issued pursuant to Rule 4 of the Federal Rules of Civil Procedure.

accused of physically harming another might claim that he or she acted in self-defense. A defendant charged with breach of contract might defend on the ground (legal basis) of mistake or the fact that the contract was oral when it was required by law to be in writing. In the Kirby-Carvello case, assume that Carvello has obtained evidence that Kirby was not exercising good driving habits at the time the accident occurred (she was looking at a child in the back of her car instead of watching the road). Carvello could assert Kirby's own negligence as a defense. In some states, a plaintiff's contributory negligence operates as a complete defense. In most states, however, the plaintiff's own negligence constitutes only a partial defense (see Chapter 12).

Carvello could also deny Kirby's allegations and set forth his own claim that the accident occurred as a result of Kirby's negligence, and therefore Kirby owes Carvello money for damages to his car. This is appropriately called a **counterclaim.** If Carvello files a counterclaim, Kirby will have to submit an answer to the counterclaim.

DISMISSALS AND JUDGMENTS BEFORE TRIAL

Many actions for which pleadings have been filed never come to trial. The parties may, for example, negotiate a settlement of the dispute at any stage of the litigation process. There are also numerous procedural avenues for disposing of a case without a trial. Many of them involve one or the other party's attempts to get the case dismissed through the use of various motions.

A **motion** is a procedural request submitted to the court by an attorney on behalf of his or her client. When one party files a motion with the court, that party must also send to, or serve on, the opposing party a *notice of motion.* The notice of motion informs the opposing party that the motion has been filed. **Pretrial motions** include the motion to dismiss, the motion for judgment on the pleadings, and the motion for summary judgment.

Motion to Dismiss. If the defendant challenges the sufficiency of the plaintiff's complaint, the defendant can present to the court a **motion to dismiss** for failure to state a claim for which relief (a remedy) can be granted, or a *demurrer.* (The rules of civil procedure in many states do not use the term *demurrer;* they use only *motion to dismiss.*) The motion to dismiss for failure to state a claim for which relief can be granted is an allegation that even if the facts presented in the complaint are true, their legal consequences are such that there is no reason to go further with the suit and no need for the defendant to present an answer. It is a contention that the defendant is not legally liable even if the facts are as the plaintiff alleges. If, for example, Kirby's complaint had alleged facts that excluded the possibility of negligence on Carvello's part, Carvello could move to dismiss the case.

Defendant Carvello could also file a motion to dismiss if he believed that he had not been properly served, that the complaint had been filed in the wrong court (for example, that the court lacked personal or subject-matter jurisdiction or the venue was improper), or for other specific reasons. A motion to dismiss may be—and often is—filed with the court by a defendant instead of an answer.

The motion to dismiss is often used for purposes of delay (to give the defendant more time to prepare for the lawsuit), because even if the court denies the motion, the defendant generally is given an extension of time to file an answer (or further pleading). If the defendant fails to file the appropriate pleading, a judgment will normally be entered for the plaintiff.

If the court grants a pre-answer motion to dismiss, the defendant is not required to answer the complaint. The plaintiff generally is given time to file an amended complaint. If the plaintiff does not file this amended complaint, a judgment will be entered against the plaintiff solely on the basis of the pleadings, and the plaintiff will not be allowed to bring suit on the matter again.

If Kirby wishes to discontinue the suit because, for example, an out-of-court settlement has been reached, she can likewise move for dismissal. The court can also dismiss a case on its own motion.

Motion for Judgment on the Pleadings. After the pleadings are closed—after the complaint, answer, and any other pleadings have been filed—either of the parties can file a **motion for judgment on the pleadings.** This motion may be filed when it appears from the pleadings that the plaintiff has failed to state a cause of action for which relief may be granted. The motion may also be filed when the pleadings indicate that no facts are in dispute and the only question is how the law applies to a set of undisputed facts. For example, assume for a moment that in the Kirby-Carvello case, defendant Carvello admitted to all of Kirby's allegations in his answer and raised no affirmative defenses. In this situation, Kirby would file a motion for judgment on the pleadings in her favor.

The difference between this motion and a motion for summary judgment, discussed below, is that the party requesting the motion may support a motion for summary judgment with sworn statements and other materials that will be admissible as evidence at trial; on a motion for a judgment on the pleadings, however, a court may consider only what is contained in the pleadings.

Motion for Summary Judgment. The **motion for summary judgment** is similar to a motion for judgment on the pleadings in that the party filing the motion is asking the court to grant a judgment in its favor without a trial. As with a motion for judgment on the pleadings, a court will only grant a motion for summary judgment if it determines that no facts are in dispute and the only question is how the law applies to the facts.

To support a motion for summary judgment, one party can submit, prior to trial, sworn evidence obtained at any point prior to trial (including during the discovery stage of litigation—to be discussed shortly) that refutes the other party's factual claim. The evidence may consist of **affidavits** (sworn statements by parties or witnesses), as well as documents, such as a contract. The evidence must be *admissible* evidence—that is, evidence that the court would allow to be presented during the trial. Hearsay, for example, normally would not be admissible. As mentioned, the use of this additional evidence is one of the features that distinguishes the motion for summary judgment from the motion to dismiss and the motion for judgment on the pleadings.

In the Kirby-Carvello accident, whether or not the light was red is a question of fact. Assume that during discovery, Carvello obtained undisputable evidence that the stoplight was not working when he drove through the intersection. Assume further that Carvello has evidence (a witness's testimony) that he was not exceeding the legal speed limit. Carvello could file a motion for summary judgment on the ground that there was no evidence in the record to support Kirby's claim. The court might grant Carvello's motion, because there would be no genuine factual dispute and Carvello would be entitled to judgment as a matter of law.

A motion for summary judgment can be made before or during a trial, but it will be granted only if, when the evidence is viewed in the light most favorable to the other party, it is clear that there are no factual disputes. The following case illustrates this point.

CASE 3.3 Wohl v. Spectrum Manufacturing, Inc.

United States Court of Appeals, Seventh Circuit, 1996. 94 F.3d 353.

BACKGROUND AND FACTS *Martin Wohl worked for Spectrum Manufacturing, Inc., as the firm's controller. His responsibilities included financial and cost accounting. Billing, which would normally fall under a controller's supervision, was handled by Greg Reuhs, Spectrum's general manager. According to Wohl, Reuhs's unorthodox billing policy (involving "stealing" billing from, and allocating labor to, subsequent months) made it difficult for Wohl to obtain accurate information for his accounting reports. It also prevented management from obtaining an accurate picture of department profit and loss. Wohl discussed the problem with Spectrum's president and others, but he was told to "get along with" Reuhs and to work out the differences. Wohl later stated that it was clear to him "that the company considered Reuhs, who was the younger man, to be a key player in the organization, and that he was to be appeased." When Spectrum fired Wohl, who was then fifty-four years old, and replaced him with a man who was twenty years younger, Wohl sued the company in a federal district court for age discrimination in violation of federal law. Spectrum moved for summary judgment, arguing that it had fired Wohl not because of his age but because of his inability to produce certain accounting reports. The district court granted the motion, and Wohl appealed.*

IN THE LANGUAGE OF THE COURT

ESCHBACH, Circuit Judge.

* * * *

A plaintiff in an age discrimination case may defeat a summary judgment motion brought by the employer if the plaintiff produces evidence that the employer [offered] a phony reason for firing the employee. * * *

* * * *

* * * [The] facts all support Wohl's contention that his failure to produce accurate and reliable reports was not the true reason that he was fired. We recognize that a reasonable fact-finder may infer contrary conclusions, but we reemphasize that all reasonable inferences must be viewed in the light most favorable to the nonmoving party [the party who is not bringing the motion; the opposing party] on summary judgment.

* * * *

Spectrum gave Wohl a substantial raise just before he was fired, Wohl produced financial reports as best he was able, and Spectrum provides no documentary evidence that Wohl did not meet their legitimate expectations. Plaintiff also stated in his affidavit that "[u]ntil I was fired, I had every reason to believe that the company was happy with my performance. I was never given any indication that Spectrum considered my efforts * * * to be deficient." This is essentially a swearing contest. Summary judgment is not the appropriate place to resolve this genuine dispute over a material fact.

DECISION AND REMEDY

The U.S. Court of Appeals for the Seventh Circuit reversed the district court's grant of summary judgment in favor of Spectrum and remanded the case (sent it back to the trial court) for trial.

DISCOVERY Before a trial begins, the parties can use a number of procedural devices to obtain information and gather evidence about the case. Kirby, for example, will want to know how fast Carvello was driving, whether he had been drinking or was under the influence of any medication, whether he was wearing corrective lenses if he was required by law to do so while driving, and so on. The process of obtaining information from the opposing party or from witnesses is known as **discovery.**

The Federal Rules of Civil Procedure and similar rules in the states set forth the guidelines for discovery activity. Discovery includes gaining access to witnesses, documents, records, and other types of evidence. The rules governing discovery are designed to make sure that a witness or a party is not unduly harassed, that privileged material is safeguarded, and that only information relevant to the case at hand—or likely to lead to the discovery of relevant information—are discoverable.

Discovery prevents surprises by giving parties access to evidence that might otherwise be hidden. This allows both parties to learn as much as they can about what to expect at a trial before they reach the courtroom. Discovery also serves to narrow the issues so that trial time is spent on the main questions in the case. Currently, the trend is toward allowing more discovery and thus fewer surprises.[16]

Depositions and Interrogatories. At a minimum, discovery involves the use of depositions, interrogatories, or both. A **deposition** is sworn testimony by a party to the lawsuit or by any witness, recorded by an authorized court official. The person deposed gives testimony and answers questions asked by the attorneys from both sides. The questions and answers are recorded, sworn to, and signed. These answers, of course, will help the attorneys prepare their cases. They can also be used in court to impeach (challenge the credibility of) a party or a witness who changes testimony at the trial. In addition, they can be used as testimony if the witness is not available at trial.

Interrogatories are written questions for which written answers are prepared and then signed under oath. Interrogatories are directed only to parties

16. This is particularly evident in the 1993 revision of the Federal Rules of Civil Procedure. The revised rules provide that each party must disclose to the other, on an ongoing basis, the types of evidence that will be presented at trial, the names of witnesses that may or will be called, and other relevant information.

directly involved in a lawsuit (plaintiffs or defendants), not to witnesses, and the parties can prepare answers with the aid of their attorneys. Whereas depositions are useful for eliciting candid responses from a party and answers not prepared in advance, interrogatories are designed to obtain accurate information about specific topics, such as how many contracts were signed, the specific dates on which certain contracts were signed, and so on.

Request for Admissions. A party can serve a written request to the other party for an admission of the truth of matters relating to the trial. Any matter admitted under such a request is conclusively established as true for the trial. For example, Kirby can ask Carvello to admit that his driver's license was suspended at the time of the accident. A request for admission saves time at trial, because the parties will not have to spend time proving facts on which they already agree.

Request for Documents, Objects, and Entry upon Land. A party can gain access to documents and other items not in his or her possession in order to inspect and examine them. Likewise, a party can gain "entry upon land" to inspect the premises. Carvello, for example, can gain permission to inspect and copy Kirby's repair bills.

Request for Examinations. When the physical or mental condition of one party is in question, the opposing party can ask the court to order a physical or mental examination by an independent examiner. If the court is willing to make the order, the opposing party can obtain the results of the examination. Note that the court will make such an order only when the need for the information outweighs the right to privacy of the person to be examined.

PRETRIAL CONFERENCE After discovery has taken place and before the trial begins, the attorneys may meet with the trial judge in a **pretrial conference.** The purpose of this conference is to clarify the issues that remain in dispute after discovery has taken place and to explore the possibility of settling the dispute without a trial. If a settlement is not possible at this time, the parties and the judge discuss the manner in which the trial will be conducted. In particular, the parties may attempt to establish ground rules to restrict such things as the number of expert witnesses or the admissibility of certain types of evidence.

Once the pretrial conference concludes, both parties will have to turn their attention to the trial itself and, if the trial is to be a jury trial, to the selection of jurors who will hear the case.

THE RIGHT TO A JURY TRIAL The Seventh Amendment to the U.S. Constitution guarantees the right to a jury trial for cases at law in federal courts when the amount in controversy exceeds $20. Most states have similar guarantees in their own constitutions, although many states put a higher minimum-dollar-amount restriction on the guarantee. For example, Iowa requires the dollar amount of damages to be at least $1,000 before there is a right to a jury trial. The right to a trial by jury does not have to be exercised, and many cases are tried without a jury. If there is no jury, the judge determines the truth of the facts alleged in the case. In most states and in federal courts, one of the parties must request a jury, or the right is presumed to be waived.

JURY SELECTION Prior to the commencement of any jury trial, a panel of jurors must be assembled. The clerk of the court will usually notify local residents by mail that they have been selected for jury duty. The process of selecting the names of these prospective jurors varies, but often they are randomly selected by the court clerk from lists of registered voters or those within the state to whom driver's licenses have been issued. These persons then report to the courthouse on the date specified in the notice. There they are gathered into a single pool of jurors, and the process of selecting those jurors who will actually hear the case begins. Although some types of trials require twelve-person juries, most civil matters can be heard by six-person juries.

Voir Dire. The process by which the jury is selected is known as ***voir dire.***[17] In most jurisdictions, *voir dire* consists of oral questions that attorneys for the plaintiff and the defendant ask a group of prospective jurors to determine whether a potential juror is biased or has any connection with a party to the action or with a prospective witness. Usually, jurors are questioned one at a time, although when large numbers of jurors are involved, the attorneys may direct their questions to groups of jurors instead

17. Pronounced *vwahr deehr.* Literally, these French verbs mean "to see, to speak." During the *voir dire* phase of litigation, attorneys do in fact see the jurors speak. In legal language, however, the phrase refers to the process of interrogating jurors to learn about their backgrounds, attitudes, and so on.

CONCEPT SUMMARY 3.3 Pretrial Procedures

PROCEDURE	DESCRIPTION
Pleadings	1. *The plaintiff's complaint*—The plaintiff's statement of the cause of action and the parties involved, filed with the court by the plaintiff's attorney. After the filing, the defendant is notified of the suit through service of process. 2. *The defendant's response*—The defendant's response to the plaintiff's complaint may take the form of an answer, in which the defendant may admit to or deny the plaintiff's allegations. The defendant may raise an affirmative defense and/or assert a counterclaim.
Pretrial Motions	1. *Motion to dismiss*—A motion made by the defendant—often prior to filing an answer to the complaint—requesting the judge to dismiss the case for reasons that are provided in the motion (such as failure to state a claim for which relief can be granted). 2. *Motion for judgment on the pleadings*—May be made by either party; will be granted if no facts are in dispute and only questions of law are at issue. 3. *Motion for summary judgment*—May be made by either party; will be granted if no facts are in dispute and only questions of law are at issue. Unlike the motion for judgment on the pleadings, the motion for summary judgment may be supported by evidence outside the pleadings, such as testimony and other evidence obtained during the discovery phase of litigation.
Discovery	The process of gathering evidence concerning the case; involves (1) *depositions* (sworn testimony by either party or any witness); (2) *interrogatories* (in which parties to the action write answers to questions with the aid of their attorneys); and (3) requests for admissions, documents, examinations, or other information relating to the case.
Pretrial Conference	A pretrial hearing, at the request of either party or the court, to identify the matters in dispute after discovery has taken place and to explore the possibility of settling the dispute without a trial. If no settlement is possible, the parties plan the course of the trial.
Jury Selection	In a jury trial, the selection of members of the jury from a pool of prospective jurors. During a process known as *voir dire,* the attorneys for both sides may challenge prospective jurors either for cause or peremptorily (for no cause).

to minimize the amount of time spent in jury selection. Sometimes, jurors are asked to fill out written questionnaires. Some trial attorneys use psychologists and other professionals to help them pick juries.

Challenges during Voir Dire. During *voir dire,* a party may challenge a certain number of prospective jurors *peremptorily*—that is, ask that these individuals not be sworn in as jurors without providing any reason. The total number of peremptory challenges allowed each side is determined by statute or by the court. Furthermore a party may challenge any juror *for cause*—that is, provide a reason why an individual should not be sworn in as a juror. If the judge grants the challenge, the individual is asked to step down. A prospective juror may not be excluded from participation in the trial process, however, by use of discriminatory challenges, such as those based on racial criteria[18] or gender.[19]

18. *Batson v. Kentucky*, 476 U.S. 79, 106 S.Ct. 1712, 90 L.Ed.2d 69 (1986).

19. *J.E.B. v. Alabama ex rel. T.B.*, 511 U.S. 127, 114 S.Ct. 1419, 128 L.Ed.2d 89 (1994). (*Ex rel.* is Latin for *ex relatione.* The phrase refers to an action brought on behalf of the state, by the attorney general, at the instigation of an individual who has a private interest in the matter.)

After both sides have completed their challenges, those jurors who have been excused will be permitted to leave. The remaining jurors—those who have been found acceptable by both attorneys—will be seated in the jury box.

Alternate Jurors. Because unforeseeable circumstances or illness may necessitate that one or more of the sitting jurors be dismissed, the court, depending on the rules of the particular jurisdiction and the expected length of the trial, might choose to have two or three alternate jurors present throughout the trial. If a juror has to be excused in the middle of the trial, then an alternate may take his or her place without disrupting the proceedings. Once the jury members are seated, the judge will swear in the jury members, and the trial itself can begin.

THE TRIAL

Various rules and procedures govern the trial phase of the litigation process. There are rules governing what kind of evidence will or will not be admitted during the trial, as well as specific procedures that the participants in the lawsuit must follow.

RULES OF EVIDENCE Whether evidence will be admitted at court is determined by the **rules of evidence**—a series of rules that have been created by the courts to ensure that any evidence presented in court is fair and reliable. The Federal Rules of Evidence govern the admissibility of evidence in federal courts.

Relevance. Evidence will not be admitted in court unless it is relevant to the matter in question. **Relevant evidence** is evidence that tends to prove or disprove a fact in question or to establish the degree of probability of a fact or action. For example, evidence that a suspect's gun was in the home of another person when a victim was shot would be relevant—because it would tend to prove that the suspect did not shoot the victim.

Even relevant evidence may not be admitted in court if its reliability is questionable or if its probative (proving) value is substantially outweighed by other important considerations of the court. For example, even though evidence may be relevant and reliable, it may not be necessary—the fact at issue may already have been sufficiently proved or disproved by previous evidence, so that the introduction of further evidence would be a waste of time and cause undue delay in the trial proceedings. Relevant evidence may also be excluded if it would tend to distract the jury from the main issues of the case, mislead the jury, or cause the jury to decide the issue on an emotional basis. A video or a photograph that shows in detail the severity of a victim's injuries, for example, would be relevant evidence, but the court might exclude the evidence on the ground that it would emotionally inflame the jurors.

Hearsay. Generally, hearsay is not admissible as evidence. **Hearsay** is defined as any testimony given in court about a statement made by someone else. Literally, it is what someone heard someone else say. For example, if a witness in the Kirby-Carvello case testified in court concerning what he or she *heard* another observer say about the accident, that testimony would be hearsay—secondhand knowledge. Admitting hearsay into evidence carries many risks because, even though it may be relevant, there is no way to test its reliability. For example, there is the risk that the listener incorrectly perceived the meaning of the statement that he or she heard someone else make. Without the opportunity of cross-examining the originator of the statement, the misperception cannot be challenged. Furthermore, there is the risk of faulty memory and the possibility that the statement was ambiguous or not made sincerely.

OPENING STATEMENTS At the commencement of a trial, both attorneys are allowed to make **opening statements** concerning the facts that they expect to prove during the trial. The opening statement provides an opportunity for each lawyer to give a brief version of the facts and the supporting evidence that will be used during the trial.

EXAMINATION OF WITNESSES Because Kirby is the plaintiff, she has the burden of proving that her claim is correct. Kirby's attorney begins the presentation of Kirby's case by calling the first witness for the plaintiff and examining (questioning) the witness. (For both attorneys, the types of questions and the manner of asking are governed by the rules of evidence.) This questioning is called **direct examination.** After Kirby's attorney is finished, the witness is subject to **cross-examination** by Carvello's attorney. Then Kirby's attorney has another opportunity to question the witness in *redirect examination*, and Carvello's attorney may follow the redirect examination with a *recross*-examination.[20] When both attorneys have

20. The use of recross is extremely limited, however.

finished with the first witness, Kirby's attorney calls the succeeding witnesses in the plaintiff's case, each of whom is subject to examination by the attorneys in the manner just described.

At the conclusion of the plaintiff's case, the defendant's attorney has the opportunity to ask the judge to direct a verdict for the defendant on the ground that the plaintiff has presented no evidence to support the plaintiff's claim. This is called a **motion for a directed verdict** (federal courts use the term *judgment as a matter of law* instead of *directed verdict*). In considering the motion, the judge looks at the evidence in the light most favorable to the plaintiff and grants the motion only if there is insufficient evidence to raise an issue of fact. (Motions for directed verdicts at this stage of trial are seldom granted.)

The defendant's attorney then presents the evidence and witnesses for the defendant's case. Witnesses are called and examined by the defendant's attorney. The plaintiff's attorney has the right to cross-examine them, and there may be a redirect examination and possibly a recross-examination. At the end of the defendant's case, either attorney can move for a directed verdict, and the test again is whether the jury can, through any reasonable interpretation of the evidence, find for the party against whom the motion has been made. After the defendant's attorney has finished present-ing evidence, the plaintiff's attorney can present a **rebuttal,** which includes additional evidence to refute the defendant's case. The defendant's attorney can refute that evidence in a **rejoinder.**

CLOSING ARGUMENTS After both sides have rested their cases, each attorney presents a **closing argument.** In the closing argument, each attorney summarizes the facts and evidence presented during the trial, indicates why the facts and evidence support the client's claim, reveals the shortcomings of the points made by the opposing party during the trial, and generally urges a verdict in favor of the client. Each attorney's comments must be relevant to the issues in dispute.

JURY INSTRUCTIONS After the closing statements, the judge instructs the jury (assuming it is a jury trial) in the law that applies to the case. The instructions to the jury are often called *charges.* A charge is a document that includes statements of the applicable laws, as well as a review of the facts as they were presented during the case. Because the jury's role is to serve as the fact finder, the factual account contained in the charge is not binding on them. Indeed, the jurors may disregard the facts as noted in the charge entirely. They are not free to ignore the statements of law, however. The charge will help to channel the jurors' deliberations.

The importance of accuracy in jury instructions, in order to protect the rights of the accused, cannot be overstated. The reviewing court ordinarily remands, or sends back, the case for a new trial when the trial judge misstated the law in the jury instructions. The following case is illustrative.

CASE 3.4 Ohio v. Lessin

Supreme Court of Ohio, 1993. 67 Ohio St.3d 487, 620 N.E.2d 72.

BACKGROUND AND FACTS *Cheryl Lessin, a member of the Revolutionary Communist Party, participated in a political demonstration over President George Bush's ordering of American troops to the Persian Gulf in 1990. Lessin made prepared political statements to the crowd; assisted in the burning of an American flag to illustrate her own and her party's disapproval of the president's decision; and then pushed, shoved, and punched her way through the crowd until she was arrested by police. In 1989, prior to Lessin's trial, the United States Supreme Court had decided, in* Texas v. Johnson,[a] *that burning an American flag to convey a political message is protected speech under the First Amendment. The trial court in Lessin's case, however, failed to instruct the jury on the law set forth by the Supreme Court in* Johnson *and did not preclude the members of the jury from considering the evidence of political speech, particularly flag burning, in their determination of Lessin's guilt. When Lessin appealed*

a. 491 U.S. 387, 109 S.Ct. 2533, 105 L.Ed.2d 342 (1989).

the court's guilty verdict, the court of appeals affirmed the trial court's decision. Lessin then appealed to the Ohio Supreme Court.

IN THE LANGUAGE OF THE COURT

MOYER, Chief Justice.

* * * *

The risk that a jury will premise its guilty verdict on constitutionally protected conduct is reduced, if not completely eliminated, by an accurate and thorough set of jury instructions which direct the jury to refrain from considering certain evidence as proof of guilt. In this case, the role of the jury instructions was critical in obviating [removing] the possibility that each juror would convict based on his or her personal prejudices against flag burners and Communists. * * *

* * * *

We cannot uphold Lessin's conviction for the crime of inciting violence because it is impossible to say with any degree of certainty that her burning of the United States flag was disregarded by the jury in reaching its verdict. The trial court's instruction given to the jury on free speech did not serve to adequately protect the defendant's rights because it did not inform the jury that (1) flag burning in the absence of a call to violence is protected speech under the First Amendment and (2) the jury is not to consider the fact that Lessin burned the flag in determining whether she is guilty of inciting violence. The necessity of giving a more precise instruction is further underscored because of the * * * exchange which occurred between defense counsel and the trial judge during *voir dire* [in which the trial judge told the defense counsel, "There has been no Supreme Court case, to my knowledge, that permits under any circumstances that it's okay to burn the flag"].

DECISION AND REMEDY

The Ohio Supreme Court reversed the appellate court's decision. The case was sent back for a new trial in which jury instructions reflecting the United States Supreme Court's decision in Johnson *would be given and Lessin's freedom of speech would be protected.*

ETHICAL CONSIDERATIONS

The Supreme Court's position that flag burning is a form of speech protected by the First Amendment has been controversial. Many feel that to allow the flag to be so desecrated is to repudiate the freedom and independence symbolized by the flag. In the Court's judgment, however, to prohibit Americans from freely expressing their political views—symbolically or otherwise—would violate not only the First Amendment to the Constitution but also the basis for democratic government.[b]

b. Flag burning and other forms of symbolic speech are discussed in further detail in Chapter 5.

THE JURY'S VERDICT Following its receipt of instructions, the jury retires to the jury room to deliberate the case. As discussed in Chapter 1, in a civil case, the standard of proof is a *preponderance of the evidence*. That is, the plaintiff (Kirby in our hypothetical case) need not provide indisputable proof that she is entitled to a judgment. She need only show that her factual claim is more likely to be true than the defendant's. (Recall that in a criminal trial, the prosecution has a higher standard of proof to meet—it must prove its case *beyond a reasonable doubt*.)

Note that some civil claims must be proved by a "clear and convincing evidence" standard, under which the evidence must show that the truth of the party's claim is highly probable. This standard applies in suits involving charges of fraud, suits to establish the terms of a lost will, some suits involving oral contracts, and other suits involving circumstances in which there is thought to be a particular danger of deception.

Once the jury has reached a decision, it may issue a **verdict** in favor of one party, which specifies the jury's factual findings and the amount of damages to

CONCEPT SUMMARY 3.4 Trial Procedures

PROCEDURE	DESCRIPTION
Opening Statements	Each party's attorney is allowed to present an opening statement indicating what the attorney will attempt to prove during the course of the trial.
Examination of Witnesses	1. Plaintiff's introduction and direct examination of witnesses, cross-examination by defendant's attorney, possible redirect examination by plaintiff's attorney, and possible recross-examination by defendant's attorney. 2. Defendant's introduction and direct examination of witnesses, cross-examination by plaintiff's attorney, possible redirect examination by defendant's attorney, and possible recross-examination by plaintiff's attorney. 3. Possible rebuttal of defendant's argument by plaintiff's attorney, who presents more evidence. 4. Possible rejoinder by defendant's attorney to meet that evidence.
Closing Arguments	Each party's attorney argues in favor of a verdict for his or her client.
Jury Instructions	The judge instructs the jury as to how the law applies to the issue.
Jury Verdict	The jury renders its verdict, thus bringing the trial to an end.

be paid by the losing party. After the announcement of the verdict, which marks the end of the trial itself, the jurors will be discharged.

POSTTRIAL MOTIONS

After the jury has rendered its verdict, either party may make a posttrial motion. The prevailing party usually files a motion for a judgment in accordance with the verdict. The nonprevailing party frequently files one of the motions discussed next.

MOTION FOR A NEW TRIAL At the end of the trial, a motion can be made to set aside an adverse verdict and any judgment and to hold a new trial. The **motion for a new trial** will be granted only if (a) the judge is convinced, after looking at all the evidence, that the jury was in error but (b) the judge does not feel it is appropriate to grant judgment for the other side. This will usually occur when the jury verdict is the obvious result of a misapplication of the law or a misunderstanding of the evidence.

A new trial can also be granted on the grounds of newly discovered evidence, misconduct by the participants (such as the attorneys, the judge, or the jury) during the trial, or error by the judge. If a motion for a new trial is denied, the judge's denial may be appealed to a higher court. In the following case, the plaintiff filed a motion for a new trial based on allegations of juror misconduct.

CASE 3.5 Powell v. Allstate Insurance Co.

Supreme Court of Florida, 1995. 652 So.2d 354.

BACKGROUND AND FACTS *Derrick and Eugenia Powell, American citizens of Jamaican birth, were in an automobile accident with another motorist, whose insurance liability policy limit was $10,000. Claiming damages in excess of $200,000, the Powells sued their own insurer, Allstate Insurance Company, in a Florida state court to recover the difference. A jury awarded Derrick $29,320 and Eugenia nothing. The next day, one of the jurors—all of whom were white—told the Powells' attorney and the judge that some of the jurors had made racial jokes and statements about the Powells during the trial and the jury deliberations. The Powells filed a motion for a new trial. The court denied the motion, and the appellate court affirmed. The Powells appealed to the Supreme Court of Florida.*

IN THE LANGUAGE OF THE COURT

ANSTEAD, Justice.

* * * *

* * * [W]hen appeals to racial bias are made openly among the jurors, they constitute overt acts of misconduct. * * * This [ruling] may not keep improper bias from being a silent factor with a particular juror, but, hopefully, it will act as a check on such bias and prevent the bias from being expressed so as to overtly influence others.

We also find the conduct alleged herein, if established, to be violative of the guarantees of both the federal and state constitutions which [ensure] all litigants a fair and impartial jury and equal protection of the law.

* * * The obvious difficulty with prejudice in a judicial context is that it prevents the impartial decision making that both the Sixth Amendment and fundamental fair play require. A racially or religiously biased individual harbors certain negative stereotypes which, despite his [or her] protestations to the contrary, may well prevent him or her from making decisions based solely on the facts and law that our jury system requires.

DECISION AND REMEDY

The Supreme Court of Florida held that explicit statements of racial bias made by jurors concerning the parties in a case constitute overt juror misconduct. The court remanded the case for a hearing to determine whether such statements were made about the Powells. If so, the Powells were entitled to a new trial.

MOTION FOR JUDGMENT N.O.V. If Kirby wins, and if Carvello's attorney has previously moved for a directed verdict, Carvello's attorney can now make a **motion for judgment *n.o.v.*** (from the Latin *non obstante veredicto*, "notwithstanding the verdict"; federal courts use the term *judgment as a matter of law* instead of judgment *n.o.v.*). The standards for granting a judgment *n.o.v.* often are the same as those for granting a motion to dismiss or a motion for a directed verdict. Carvello can state that even if the evidence is viewed in the light most favorable to Kirby, a reasonable jury should not have found in Kirby's favor. If the judge finds this contention to be correct or decides that the law requires the opposite result, the motion will be granted. If the motion is denied, Carvello may then appeal the case. (Kirby may also appeal the case, even though she won at trial. She might appeal, for example, if she received a smaller money award than she had sought.)

THE APPEAL

Either party may appeal not only the jury's verdict but also any pretrial or posttrial motion. Many of the appellate court cases that appear in this text involve appeals of motions to dismiss, motions for summary judgment, or other motions that were denied by trial court judges. Note that few trial court decisions are reversed on appeal. In most appealed cases (approximately 90 percent), the trial court's decision is affirmed and thus becomes final.

FILING THE APPEAL If Carvello decides to appeal the verdict in Kirby's favor, then his attorney must file a *notice of appeal* with the clerk of the trial court within a prescribed period of time. Carvello then becomes the *appellant*. The clerk of the trial court sends to the reviewing court (usually an intermediate court of appeals) the *record on appeal*, which contains the following: (1) the pleadings, (2) a transcript of the trial testimony and copies of the exhibits, (3) the judge's rulings on motions made by the parties, (4) the arguments of counsel, (5) the instructions to the jury, (6) the verdict, (7) the posttrial motions, and (8) the judgment order from which the appeal is taken.

Carvello's attorney will file a **brief** with the reviewing court. The brief contains (1) a short statement of the facts; (2) a statement of the issues; (3) the rulings by the trial court that Carvello contends are erroneous and prejudicial (biased in favor of one of the parties); (4) the grounds for reversal of the judgment; (5) a statement of the applicable law; and (6) arguments on Carvello's behalf, citing applicable statutes and relevant cases as precedents. The attorney for the *appellee* (Kirby, in our hypothetical case) usually files an answering brief. Carvello's attorney can file a reply, although it is not required. The reviewing court then considers the case.

CONCEPT SUMMARY 3.5 Posttrial Options

PROCEDURE	DESCRIPTION
Posttrial Motions	1. *Motion for a new trial*—If the judge is convinced that the jury was in error, the motion will be granted. 2. *Motion for judgment* n.o.v. (*"notwithstanding the verdict"*)—The party making the motion must have filed a motion for a directed verdict at the close of all the evidence during the trial; the motion for judgment *n.o.v.* will be granted if the judge is convinced that the jury was in error.
Appeal	Either party can appeal the trial court's judgment to an appropriate court of appeals. 1. *Filing the appeal*—The appealing party must file a notice of appeal with the clerk of the trial court, who forwards to the appellate court the record on appeal. Attorneys' briefs are filed. 2. *Appellate review*—The appellate court does not hear evidence but bases its opinion, which it issues in writing, on the record on appeal and the attorneys' briefs and oral argument. The court may affirm or reverse all (or part) of the trial court's judgment and/or remand the case for further proceedings consistent with its opinion. Most trial court decisions are affirmed on appeal. 3. In some cases, further review may be sought from a higher appellate court, such as a state supreme court. Ultimately, if a federal question is involved, the case may be appealed to the United States Supreme Court.

APPELLATE REVIEW A court of appeals does not hear any evidence. Its decision concerning a case is based on the record on appeal and the briefs. The attorneys can present oral argument, after which the case is taken under advisement. The court then issues a written opinion. In general, the appellate courts do not reverse findings of fact unless the findings are unsupported or contradicted by the evidence.

An appellate court has basically three options after reviewing a case: it can *affirm* the trial court's decision; it can *reverse* the trial court's judgment if it concludes that the trial court erred or that the jury did not receive proper instructions; or it can *remand* (send back) the case to the trial court for further proceedings consistent with its opinion on the matter. The court might also affirm or reverse a decision *in part.* For example, the court might affirm the jury's finding that Carvello was negligent but remand the case for further proceedings on another issue (such as the extent of Kirby's damages). An appellate court can also *modify* a lower court's decision. If the appellate court decided that the jury awarded an excessive amount in damages, for example, the court might reduce the award to a more appropriate, or fairer, amount.

HIGHER APPELLATE COURTS If the reviewing court is an intermediate appellate court, the losing party may be allowed by the court to appeal the decision to the state supreme court. Such a petition corresponds to a petition for a writ of *certiorari* in the United States Supreme Court. If the petition is granted, new briefs must be filed before the state supreme court, and the attorneys may be allowed or requested to present oral argument. Like the intermediate appellate courts, the supreme court may reverse or affirm the appellate court's decision or remand the case. At this point, unless a federal question is at issue, the case has reached its end. If a federal question is involved, the losing party (or the winning party, if that party is dissatisfied with the relief obtained) may appeal the decision to the United States Supreme Court by petitioning the Court for a writ of *certiorari.* (As discussed earlier, the Supreme Court may or may not grant the writ, depending on the type or significance of the issue in dispute.)

ENFORCING THE JUDGMENT

The uncertainties of the litigation process are compounded by the lack of guarantees that any judgment will be enforceable. Even if the jury awarded Kirby the full amount of damages requested ($100,000), for example, she might not, in fact, "win" anything at all. Carvello's auto insurance coverage might have lapsed, in which event the company would not cover any of the damages. Alternatively, Carvello's insurance policy might be limited to $50,000, meaning that Carvello would have to pay personally the remaining $50,000.

If Carvello did not have that amount of money available, then Kirby would need to go back to court and request that the court issue a *writ of execution*—an order, usually issued by the clerk of the court, directing the sheriff to seize and sell Carvello's nonexempt assets (certain assets are exempted by law from creditors' actions). The proceeds of the sale would then be used to pay the damages owed to Kirby. Any excess proceeds of the sale would be returned to Carvello. Alternatively, the nonexempt property itself could be transferred to Kirby in lieu of an outright payment. (Creditors' remedies, including those of judgment creditors, as well as exempt and nonexempt property, will be discussed in more detail in Chapter 16.)

The problem of collecting a judgment is less pronounced, of course, when a party is seeking to satisfy a judgment against a defendant, such as a major corporation, that has substantial assets that can be easily located. Usually, one of the factors considered before a lawsuit is initiated is whether the defendant has sufficient assets to cover the amount of damages sought, should the plaintiff win the case.

TERMS AND CONCEPTS TO REVIEW

QUESTIONS AND CASE PROBLEMS

3–1. ADVERSARIAL JUSTICE. American courts are forums for adversarial justice in which attorneys defend the interests of their respective clients before the court. This means that an attorney may end up claiming before a court that his or her client is innocent, even though the attorney knows that the client acted wrongfully. Is it ethical for attorneys to try to "deceive" the court in these situations? Can the adversarial system of justice really lead to "truth"?

3–2. COURTS OF APPEALS. Appellate courts normally see only written transcripts of trial proceedings when they are reviewing cases. Today, in some states, videotapes are being used as the official trial reports. If the use of videotapes as official reports continues, will this alter the appellate process? Should it? Discuss fully.

3–3. DISCOVERY. In the past, the rules of discovery were very restrictive, and trials often turned on elements of surprise. For example, a plaintiff would not necessarily know until the trial what the defendant's defense was going to be. Within the last twenty-five years, however, new rules of discovery have substantially changed all this. Now each attorney can discover practically all the evidence that the other will be presenting at trial, with the exception of certain information—namely, the opposing attorney's work product. *Work product* is not a clear concept. Basically, it includes all the attorney's thoughts on the case. Can you see any reason why such information should not be made available to the opposing attorney? Discuss fully.

3–4. MOTIONS. When and for what purpose are each of the following motions made? Which of them would be appropriate if a defendant claimed that the only issue between the parties was a question of law and that the law was favorable to the defendant's position?

(a) A motion for judgment on the pleadings.
(b) A motion for a directed verdict.
(c) A motion for summary judgment.
(d) A motion for judgment *n.o.v.*

3–5. PEREMPTORY CHALLENGES. During *voir dire*, the parties or their attorneys select those persons who will serve as jurors during the trial. The parties are prohibited, however, from excluding potential jurors on the basis of race or other discriminatory criteria. An issue concerns whether the prohibition against discrimination extends to potential jurors who have physical or mental disabilities. Federal law prohibits discrimination against an otherwise qualified person with a disability when that person could be accommodated without too much difficulty. Should this law also apply to the jury selection process? For example, should parties be prohibited from excluding blind persons, through either challenges for cause or peremptory challenges, from serving on juries? Discuss.

3–6. JURISDICTION. Marya Callais, a citizen of Florida, was walking near a busy street in Tallahassee, Florida, one day when a large crate flew off a passing truck and hit her, resulting in numerous injuries. She incurred a great deal of pain and suffering, plus significant medical expenses, and she could not work for six months. She wanted to sue the trucking firm for $300,000 in damages. The firm's headquarters were in Georgia, although the company did business in Florida. In what court might Callais bring suit—a Florida state court, a Georgia state court, or a federal court? What factors might influence her decision?

3–7. MOTION TO DISMISS. Martin brought a civil rights action against his employer, the New York Department of Mental Hygiene, when it failed to promote him on several occasions. His complaint stated only that the defendant had discriminated against him on the basis of race by denying him "the authority, salary, and privileges commensurate with this position." The employer made a motion to dismiss the claim for failure to state a cause of action. Discuss whether the employer could be successful. [*Martin v. New York State Department of Mental Hygiene*, 588 F.2d 371 (2d Cir. 1978)]

3–8. JURY TRIALS. On June 16, 1986, the director of the Administrative Office of the U.S. Courts notified all federal district courts that no civil jury trials could be initiated until the end of the fiscal year (September 30) due to lack of funds with which to pay the jurors. Armster and others claimed that the consequent delay (of three and a half months) in scheduling a jury trial violated the Seventh Amendment right to a civil jury trial. The Justice Department maintained that although the Sixth Amendment guarantees a speedy *criminal* jury trial, the Seventh Amendment does not guarantee a speedy *civil* jury trial. The Justice Department further noted that district courts have postponed civil jury trials before, although for other reasons—such as court-calendar congestion, the lack of a sufficient number of judges, and the priority accorded to trying criminal cases before civil actions. Discuss whether the suspension of civil jury trials for a period of three and a half months due to lack of funds to pay jurors violates the constitutional right to a trial by jury. Are people always entitled to a jury trial in civil lawsuits? [*Armster v. U.S. District Court for the Central District of California*, 792 F.2d 1423 (9th Cir. 1986)]

3–9. JURISDICTION. George Rush, a New York resident and columnist for the New York *Daily News*, wrote a critical column about Berry Gordy, the founder and former president of Motown Records. Gordy, a California resident, filed suit in a California state court against Rush and the newspaper (the defendants), alleging defamation (a civil wrong, or tort, that occurs when the publication of false statements harms a person's good reputation). Most of the newspaper's subscribers are in the New York area, and the paper covers mostly New York events. Thirteen copies of its daily edition are

FOLLETT
147

04/20/98 4:00PM
929E#0574

N TEXT $80.00

ITEMS 1Q
CHECK $80.00

...or
...ore
...wledge

...URN
...E
PAGE!

Nature." It distinguished b
desolée," "my blood froze")
for Emerson best represent
...ity,—the Aeolian harp
Hafez,—the foam of the cu
... in whom

The positive degree consis
superlative degree derives fr
poets, which sees or names
... signify." The sup
wo... upon its

I... is no ...vious ce
...tures, apart from the idea
representative, there is rathe
Emerson gave this year. By
call... a kind of Natural H
... England fr
lectures ca... "Mind in th
passag... The lectures
1850, and finally in Emer
(repeated in 1871). After E
published the first three o
(1893). The "Natural Hist
to Emerson's satisfaction,
the frequently recurring
professional, respectabl

In "Natural Histor
mind with some of t
admired the "secu
admiration for hi
"a similar enu
lect?" and he
powers and
of scienc
as the
project of Kant ... his foll
the subject of ...d. Emer
studying ... instrument w

...as of rea... my books
... in my ... tongue
...rsonian ... of an ar-
...nerson is a symbol of any
...fort. He was dismissive of
... to his opinion that "the
...n order."[6]

...llaneous lectures this year
...s from which have been
...ographical Sketches (1883)
...ainst superlatives. Only
...rson, since they do not
...aken, that the positive is
...rson quotes approvingly
... of Wellington's papers,
...d the word glory is not
...he superlative was much
...t was a lecture in praise
...called "The Method of

distributed to California subscribers, however, and the paper does cover events that are of nationwide interest to the entertainment industry. Because of its focus on entertainment, the newspaper also routinely sends reporters to California to gather news from California sources. Can a California state court exercise personal jurisdiction over the New York defendants in this case? What factors will the court consider in deciding this question? If you were the judge, how would you decide the issue, and why? Discuss fully. [*Gordy v. Daily News, L.P.*, 95 F.3d 829 (9th Cir. 1996)]

3–10. Motion for a New Trial. Washoe Medical Center, Inc., admitted Shirley Swisher for the treatment of a fractured pelvis. During her stay, Swisher suffered a fatal fall from her hospital bed. Gerald Parodi, the administrator of her estate, and others filed an action against Washoe in which they sought damages for the alleged lack of care in treating Swisher. During *voir dire*, when the plaintiffs' attorney returned a few minutes late from a break, the trial judge led the prospective jurors in a standing ovation. The judge joked with one of the prospective jurors, whom he had known in college, about the judge's fitness to serve as a judge and personally endorsed another prospective juror's business. After the trial, the jury returned a verdict in favor of Washoe. The plaintiffs moved for a new trial, but the judge denied the motion. The plaintiffs then appealed, arguing that the tone set by the judge during *voir dire* prejudiced their right to a fair trial. Should the appellate court agree? Why or why not? [*Parodi v. Washoe Medical Center, Inc.*, 111 Nev. 365, 892 P.2d 588 (1995)]

3–11. A Question of Ethics

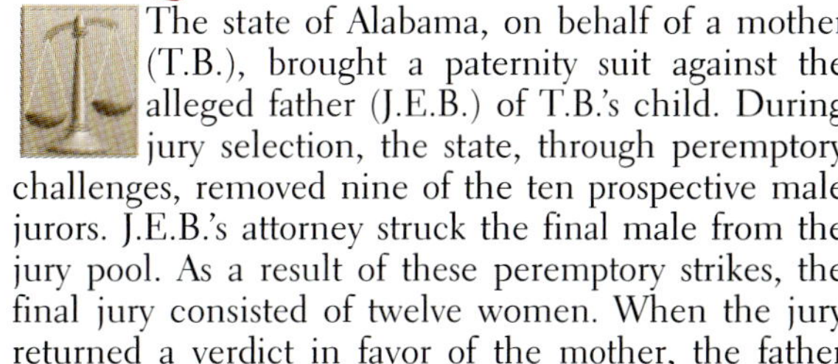

The state of Alabama, on behalf of a mother (T.B.), brought a paternity suit against the alleged father (J.E.B.) of T.B.'s child. During jury selection, the state, through peremptory challenges, removed nine of the ten prospective male jurors. J.E.B.'s attorney struck the final male from the jury pool. As a result of these peremptory strikes, the final jury consisted of twelve women. When the jury returned a verdict in favor of the mother, the father appealed. The father argued that eliminating men from the jury constituted gender discrimination and violated his rights to equal protection and due process (see Chapter 5). The father requested the court to extend the principle enunciated in *Batson v. Kentucky* (cited in footnote 18 of this chapter), which prohibited peremptory strikes based solely on race, to include gender-based strikes. The appellate court refused to do so. [*J.E.B. v. Alabama ex rel. T.B.*, 511 U.S. 127, 114 S.Ct. 1419, 128 L.Ed.2d 89 (1994)]

1. Do you agree with J.E.B. that the state's exercise of its peremptory challenges violated this right to equal protection and due process? Why or why not?
2. If you were the judge, how would you rule?
3. The late Supreme Court Justice Thurgood Marshall urged, when the Court was reviewing the *Batson* case, the peremptory challenges be banned entirely. Do you agree with this proposal? Discuss.

ACCESSING THE INTERNET
THE LEGAL ENVIRONMENT OF BUSINESS

The decisions of the United States Supreme Court and of all of the U.S. Courts of Appeals are now published online shortly after the decisions are rendered (often within hours). You can find these decisions and obtain information about the federal court system by accessing the Federal Court Locator at

http://www.law.vill.edu/

For information on the justices of the United States Supreme Court, go to

http://oyez.nwu.edu/oyez.html

This site offers biographies of the justices, links to opinions they have authored, and, for justices who have served after 1920, video and audio materials. Oral arguments before the Supreme Court are also posted on this site. A planned addition to the site is a video tour of the Court.

To date, the decisions of only one of the federal district courts—the U.S. District Court for the Northern District of Mississippi—are published on the Web. These decisions, which are published by the University of Mississippi School of Law Library in cooperation with the court, can be found at

http://sunset.backbone.olemiss.edu/~llibcoll/ndms

Some of the other federal district courts offer their opinions electronically through the federal judiciary's PACER (Public Access to Court Electronic Records) system. PACER costs 75 cents a minute, but for many it is well worth it. To access PACER, you have to register by calling 1-800-676-6856, Monday through Friday, between 8 A.M. and 5 P.M. You will receive a form that you can mail or fax in. You can sign up with as many federal courts as you wish, out of a total number of over two hundred courts.

Increasingly, decisions of the state courts are also becoming available online. You can search through the texts of state cases that are on the Internet, as well as federal cases and state and federal laws, by accessing WashLaw at

http://lawlib.wuacc.edu/washlaw/searchlaw.html

Numerous rules of procedure and evidence frame the litigation process. If you are interested in learning more about these rules, you can look at the Federal Rules of Civil Procedure (FRCP) and the Federal Rules of Evidence (FRE), both of which are now on the Internet. The FRCP and the FRE can be found at

http://www.cornell.edu/

The federal district courts also have local rules that govern their procedures, although these rules are available online for only a few courts. You can access the local rules for the following federal courts by using the Internet addresses given here:

- The U.S. District Court for the District of Colorado:

  http://www.usa.net/cololaw/features/fedrules.htm

- The U.S. District Courts for the Southern and Eastern Districts of New York (Joint Local Rules):

  http://www.ljextra.com/courthouse/fedrules.html

Procedural rules for several of the state courts are now also online. You can access the rules for selected state courts at the following addresses:

- Alaska Rules of Civil Procedure:

  http://www.alaska.net/~akctlib/homepage.htm

- California Code of Civil Procedure:

  http://www.calbar.org/pub250/relst3.htm

- Indiana Code of Civil Procedure:

  http://www.law.indiana.edu/codes/in/incode.html

- New York Civil Practice Law and Rules:

  http://www.law.cornell.edu/ny/statutes/cplr.htm

- Washington Code of Civil Procedure:

  http://leginfo.leg.wa.gov/pub/rcw/title_04

- Wyoming Rules of Civil Procedure:

  http://courts.state.wy.us/rules.htm

For information on attorneys, you can look at the *Martindale-Hubbell Law Directory*, which is available online at

http://www.martindale.com

This directory lists the names, addresses, telephone numbers, areas of legal practice, and other data for more than 900,000 lawyers and law firms in the United States.

For an example of a typical set of state rules governing attorney conduct, you can access Idaho's Rules of Professional Conduct Governing Lawyers at

http://www.law.cornell.edu:80/lawyers/ruletable.html

CHAPTER 4

ALTERNATIVE DISPUTE RESOLUTION

TRIALS ARE COSTLY AND TIME CONSUMING. It has been said that this is the result of "too many lawyers, too many lawsuits, and too many laws." In fact, since 1960, the number of lawyers has tripled, the number of lawsuits has tripled, and the number of laws has multiplied, while the numbers of judges and courts have not kept pace.

Although it is true that the number of lawsuits filed has grown rapidly, only 5 to 10 percent of lawsuits filed actually go to trial. Most cases are settled or dismissed long before the parties enter a courtroom. Moreover, the number of cases that are litigated does not appear to be growing any faster than the population. When compared with the large number of transactions that occur in our highly complex society, the rate of litigation appears low to some.

Nevertheless, in any individual case, it may be months before a hearing can even be scheduled. Depending on the complexity of the case, the extent of discovery proceedings required, and the delaying tactics of the opposing party, years may be spent in litigation. Even in the best of situations, the civil procedures discussed in Chapter 3 all require much time and money. As the cost and complexity of litigation have grown, businesspersons and other individuals have asked, "Is there a more appropriate way to resolve disputes?"

SECTION 1
THE SEARCH FOR ALTERNATIVES TO LITIGATION

A number of solutions have been proposed, and some have been implemented, to reduce the congestion in our court system and to reduce the litigation costs facing all members of society. The enforcement of arbitration clauses, the use of court-referred arbitration and mediation, and the emergence of an increasing number of private forums for dispute resolution have all helped to reduce the caseload of the courts.

Another possible solution to the problem involves putting caps on damage awards, particularly for pain and suffering. Without the probability of obtaining multimillion-dollar judgments for pain and suffering, some potential litigants will be deterred from undertaking lawsuits to obtain damages. Another avenue of attack is to penalize those who bring frivolous lawsuits. Rule 11 of the Federal Rules of Civil Procedure allows for disciplinary sanctions against lawyers and litigants who bring frivolous lawsuits in federal courts.

Many courts require mediation or arbitration before a case goes to trial. There are proposals to reduce delay and expenses in federal civil cases further, and proposals are being considered by the states as well. Some of the proposals can be viewed as case-management plans. One proposal, for example, would require each federal district court to implement procedures for placing cases on different tracks, with simple cases being handled more quickly than complex ones.

POLITICS AND LAW

Because reforms of any system affect individuals and groups differently, they seldom are accomplished easily and quickly. Reform of the court system is a prime example. At the federal level, members of Congress long have been concerned with bringing court costs and delay under control. These concerns gave rise to the enactment of legislation in the early 1990s that required the federal courts to develop a plan to cut costs and reduce delay within the federal judicial system.

NEW METHODS AND ARRANGEMENTS

The search for alternative means to resolve disputes has produced several distinct methods and arrangements. These range from neighbors' sitting down over a cup of coffee to work out their differences to huge multinational corporations' agreeing to resolve a dispute through a formal hearing before a panel of experts. All of these alternatives to traditional litigation make up what is broadly termed alternative dispute resolution.

Alternative dispute resolution (ADR) describes any procedure or device for resolving disputes other than the traditional judicial process. ADR is normally a less expensive and less time-consuming process than formal litigation. In some cases, it also has the advantage of being more private. Except in cases involving court-annexed arbitration (discussed later in this chapter), no public record of ADR proceedings is created; only the parties directly involved are privy to the information presented during the process. This is a particularly important consideration in many business disputes, because such cases may involve sensitive commercial information.

SECTION 2
NEGOTIATION AND MEDIATION

Alternative dispute resolution methods differ in the degree of formality involved and the extent to which third parties participate in the process. Generally, negotiation is the least formal method and involves no third parties. Mediation may be similarly informal but does involve the participation of a third party.

NEGOTIATION

In the process of negotiation, the parties come together informally, with or without attorneys to represent them. Within this informal setting, the parties air their differences and try to reach a settlement or resolution without the involvement of independent third parties. Because no third parties are involved and because of the informal setting, negotiation is the simplest form of ADR. Even if a lawsuit has been initiated, the parties may continue to negotiate their differences and settle their dispute at any time during the litigation process.

PREPARATION FOR NEGOTIATION Because so many disputes are settled through negotiation, in spite of the informality of this means of dispute resolution, each party must carefully prepare his or her side of the case. The elements of the dispute should be considered, documents and other evidence should be collected, and witnesses should be prepared to testify. Negotiating from a well-prepared position improves the odds of obtaining a favorable result. Even if a dispute is not resolved through negotiation, preparation for negotiation will reduce the effort required to get ready for the next step in the dispute resolution process.

"ASSISTED NEGOTIATION" To facilitate negotiation, various forms of what might be called "assisted negotiation" have been employed. Forms of ADR associated with the negotiation process include minitrials and early neutral case evaluation. Another form of assisted negotiation—the summary jury trial—is discussed later in this chapter.

A **mini-trial** is a private proceeding in which each party's attorney briefly argues the party's case before the other party. Typically, a neutral third party, who acts as an adviser and an expert in the area being disputed, is also present. If the parties fail to reach an agreement, the adviser renders an opinion as to how a court would likely decide the issue. The proceeding assists the parties in determining whether they should negotiate a settlement of the dispute or take it to court.

In **early neutral case evaluation,** the parties select a neutral third party (generally an expert in the subject matter of the dispute) to evaluate their respective positions. The parties explain their positions to the case evaluator however they wish. The evaluator then assesses the strengths and weaknesses of the parties' positions, and this evaluation forms the basis for negotiating a settlement.

MEDIATION

Mediation is similar to negotiation. In the mediation process, as in negotiation, the parties themselves must reach agreement over their dispute. The major difference between negotiation and mediation is that the latter involves a third party, called a mediator. The **mediator** assists the parties in reaching a mutually acceptable agreement. The mediator talks face to face with the parties and allows them to discuss their disagreement, usually in an informal environment. The mediator's role, however, is limited to assisting the parties. The mediator does not decide a controversy; he or she only facilitates the process by helping the parties more quickly find common ground on which they can begin to reach an agreement for themselves.

ADVANTAGES OF MEDIATION Few procedural rules are involved in the mediation process—far fewer than in a courtroom setting. The proceedings can be tailored to fit the needs of the parties—the mediator can be told to maintain a diplomatic role or be asked to express an opinion about the dispute, lawyers can be excluded from the proceedings, and the exchange of a few documents can replace the more expensive and time-consuming process of pretrial discovery. Disputes are often settled far more quickly in mediation than in formal litigation.[1]

There are other benefits. Because the parties reach agreement by mutual consent, the bitterness that often flows from the winner-take-all outcome of a formal trial decision is avoided. Hard feelings are also minimized by the less stressful environment provided by mediation; the absence of the formal rules and adversarial tone of courtroom proceedings lessens the hostility the parties may feel toward one another. Minimizing hard feelings can be very important when the parties have to go on working with one another while the controversy is being resolved or after it has been settled. This is frequently the case when two businesses—say, a supplier and a purchaser—have a long-standing, mutually beneficial relationship that they would like to preserve despite their controversy. Similar considerations are found in the context of management and labor disputes; employee disciplinary matters and grievances are subjects that invite mediation as an alternative to formal litigation.

Another important benefit of mediation is that the mediator is selected by the parties. In litigation, the parties have no control over the selection of a judge. In mediation, the parties may select a mediator on the basis of expertise in a particular field as well as for fairness and impartiality. To the degree that the mediator has these attributes, he or she will effectively aid the parties in reaching an agreement over their dispute.

DISADVANTAGES OF MEDIATION Mediation is not without disadvantages. A mediator is likely to charge a fee. (This can be split between the parties, though, and thus may represent less expense than would both sides' hiring lawyers.)

Informality and the absence of a third party referee can also have disadvantages. (Remember that a mediator can only help the parties reach a decision, not make a decision for them.) Without a deadline hanging over the parties' heads, and without the threat of sanctions if they fail to negotiate in good faith, they may be less willing to make concessions or otherwise strive honestly and diligently to reach a settlement. This can slow the process or even cause it to fail.

1. In Florida alone, as many as fifty thousand disputes that might have ended up in court are instead resolved through mediation each year. Florida's insurance commissioner used mediation to resolve hundreds of insurance claims stemming from 1992's Hurricane Andrew.

SECTION 3
ARBITRATION

A third method of dispute resolution combines the advantages of third party decision making—as provided by judges and juries in formal litigation—with the speed and flexibility inherent in rules of procedure and evidence less rigid than those governing courtroom litigation. This is the process of **arbitration**—the settling of a dispute by an impartial third party (other than a court) who renders a legally binding decision. The third party who renders the decision is called an **arbitrator.**

When a dispute arises, the parties can agree to settle their differences informally through arbitration rather than formally through the court system. Alternatively, the parties may agree ahead of time that, if a dispute should arise, they will submit to arbitration rather than bring a lawsuit. Both parties are obligated to follow the arbitrator's decision regardless of whether or not they agree with it; this is what is meant by saying the decision is legally binding.

The federal government and many state governments favor arbitration over litigation. The federal policy favoring arbitration is embodied in the Federal Arbitration Act (FAA) of 1925.[2] The FAA requires that courts give deference to all voluntary arbitration agreements in cases governed by federal law. Virtually any dispute can be the subject of arbitration. A voluntary agreement to arbitrate a dispute normally will be enforced by the courts if the agreement does not compel an illegal act or contravene public policy.

THE FEDERAL ARBITRATION ACT

The Federal Arbitration Act does not establish a set arbitration procedure. The parties themselves must agree on the manner of resolving their dispute. The FAA provides the means for enforcing the arbitration procedure that the parties have established for themselves.

Section 4 of the FAA allows a party to petition a federal district court for an order compelling arbitration under an agreement to arbitrate a dispute. If the judge is "satisfied that the making of the agreement for arbitration or the failure to comply therewith is not in issue, the court shall make an order directing the parties to proceed with arbitration in accordance with the terms of the agreement."

Under Section 9, the parties to the arbitration may agree to have the arbitrator's decision confirmed in a federal district court. Through confirmation, one party obtains a court order directing another party to comply with the terms of the arbitrator's decision. Section 10 establishes the grounds by which the arbitrator's decision may be set aside (canceled). The grounds for setting aside a decision are limited to misconduct, fraud, corruption, or abuse of power in the arbitration process itself; a court will not review the merits of the dispute or the arbitrator's judgment.

The FAA covers any arbitration clause in a contract that involves interstate commerce. Business activities that have even remote connections or minimal effects on commerce between two or more states are considered to be included. Thus, arbitration agreements involving transactions only slightly connected to the flow of interstate commerce may fall under the FAA. In the following case, the United States Supreme Court considered whether to apply this principle to an arbitration agreement that, at the time of contracting, the parties did not expect to involve interstate commerce.

2. 9 U.S.C. Sections 1–15.

CASE 4.1 Allied-Bruce Terminix Companies, Inc. v. Dobson

Supreme Court of the United States, 1995. 513 U.S. 265, 115 S.Ct. 834, 130 L.Ed.2d 753.

HISTORICAL AND ENVIRONMENTAL SETTING *One of the responsibilities of home ownership is to protect the structure from the elements of nature. Those elements include termites. Termites feed chiefly on wood, such as the wood used to construct houses. The tiny insects can destroy a home that is unprotected or inadequately protected. In the United States, termites cause over $250 million in losses each year. Common methods to prevent the entry of termites into buildings include using chemically treated wood in the construction of the building or chemically treating the soil on which the building is constructed.*

BACKGROUND AND FACTS *Steven Gwin signed a contract with Allied-Bruce Terminix Companies, Inc., to protect his home from termite infestation. The contract specified that any dispute would be resolved by arbitration. After Gwin sold the home to Michael Dobson, the structure became infested with termites. Dobson filed a suit against Gwin and Allied-Bruce in an Alabama state court. Allied-Bruce asked the court to compel arbitration under the Federal Arbitration Act (FAA) section making enforceable a written arbitration provision in "a contract evidencing a transaction involving commerce." The court refused, on the ground that, at the time of contracting, the parties did not expect their contract to involve interstate commerce. Allied-Bruce appealed. The state supreme court affirmed, and the company appealed again—to the United States Supreme Court.*

IN THE LANGUAGE OF THE COURT

Justice *BREYER* delivered the opinion of the Court.

* * * *

The Federal Arbitration Act provides that a " * * * contract evidencing a transaction involving commerce to settle by arbitration a controversy thereafter arising out of such contract or transaction * * * shall be valid, irrevocable, and enforceable * * * ."

* * * Is "involving" the functional equivalent of the word "affecting"? That phrase—"affecting commerce"—normally signals a congressional intent to exercise its Commerce Clause powers to the full. * * *

After examining the statute's language, background, and structure, we conclude that the word "involving" is broad and is indeed the functional equivalent of "affecting." * * *

* * * *

[Interpreting the phrase "evidencing a transaction" to mean that the parties, at the time they entered into the contract, contemplated that it would involve substantial interstate activity] invites litigation about what was, or was not, "contemplated." Why would Congress intend a test that risks the very kind of costs and delay through litigation (about the circumstances of contract formation) that Congress wrote the Act to help the parties avoid?

* * * *

* * * [W]e * * * [read] the [FAA's] language as insisting that the "transaction" in fact "involve" interstate commerce, even if the parties did not contemplate an interstate commerce connection.

DECISION AND REMEDY *The United States Supreme Court held that the FAA extends to the limits of Congress's commerce clause power. The Court reversed the ruling of the state supreme court and remanded the case for further proceedings.*

STATE ARBITRATION STATUTES

Virtually all states follow the federal approach to voluntary arbitration. Thirty-four states and the District of Columbia have adopted the Uniform Arbitration Act, which was drafted by the National Conference of Commissioners on Uniform State Laws in 1955. Those states that have not adopted the uniform act nonetheless follow many of the practices specified in it.

Under the uniform act, the basic approach is to give full effect to voluntary agreements to arbitrate disputes between private parties. The act supplements private arbitration agreements by providing explicit procedures and remedies for enforcing arbitration agreements. The uniform act does not, however, dictate the terms of the agreement. Moreover, under both federal and state statutes, the parties are afforded considerable latitude in deciding the subject matter of the arbitration and the methods for conducting the arbitration process. In the absence of a controlling statute, the rights and duties of the parties are established and limited by their agreement.

THE ARBITRATION PROCESS

The arbitration process begins with a *submission*. **Submission** is the act of referring a dispute to an arbitrator. The next step is the *hearing*, in which evidence and arguments are presented to the arbitrator. The process culminates in an *award*, which is the decision of the arbitrator.

The right to appeal the award to a court of law is limited. If the award was made under a voluntary arbitration agreement, a court normally will not set it aside even if it was the result of an erroneous determination of fact or an incorrect interpretation of law by the arbitrator.

This limitation is based on at least two grounds. First, if an award is not treated as final, then, rather than speeding up the dispute-resolution process, arbitration would merely add one more layer to the process of litigation. Second, the basis of arbitration—the freedom of parties to agree among themselves how to settle a controversy—supports treating an award as final. Having had the opportunity to frame the issues and to set out the manner for resolving the dispute, one party should not complain if the result was not what that party had hoped it would be.

SUBMISSION The parties may agree to submit questions of fact, questions of law, or both to the arbitrator. The parties may even agree to leave the interpretation of the arbitration agreement to the arbitrator. In the case of an existing agreement to arbitrate, the clause itself is the submission to arbitration.

The submission typically states the identities of the parties, the nature of the dispute to be resolved, the monetary amounts involved in the controversy, the place at which the arbitration is to take place, and the intention of the parties to be bound by the arbitrator's award. Exhibit 4–1 contains a sample submission form.

Most states require that an agreement to submit a dispute to arbitration be in writing. Moreover, because the goal of arbitration is speed and efficiency in resolving controversies, most states require that matters be submitted within a definite period of time, generally six months from the date on which the dispute arises.

THE HEARING Because the parties are free to construct the method by which they want their dispute resolved, they must state the issues that will be submitted and the powers that the arbitrator will exercise. The arbitrator may be given power at the outset of the process to establish rules that will govern the proceedings. Typically, these rules are much less restrictive than those governing formal litigation. Regardless of who establishes the rules, the arbitrator will apply them during the course of the hearing.

Restrictions on the kind of evidence and the manner in which it is presented may be less rigid in arbitration, partly because the arbitrator is likely to be an expert in the subject matter involved in the controversy. Restrictions may also be less stringent because there is less fear that the arbitrator will be swayed by improper evidence. In contrast, evidence in a jury trial must sometimes be presented twice: once to the judge, outside the presence of the jury, to determine if the evidence may be heard by the jury, and—depending on the judge's ruling—again, to the jury.

In the typical hearing format, the parties begin as they would at trial by presenting opening arguments to the arbitrator and stating what remedies should or should not be granted. After the opening statements have been made, evidence is presented. Witnesses may be called and examined by both sides. After all the evidence has been presented, the parties give their closing arguments. On completion of these arguments, the arbitrator closes the hearing.

THE AWARD After each side has had an opportunity to present evidence and to argue its case, the arbitrator reaches a decision. The final decision of the arbitrator is called an **award**, even if no money is conferred on a party as a result of the proceedings. Under most statutes, the arbitrator must render an award within thirty days of the close of the hearing.

In most states, the award need not state the arbitrator's findings regarding factual questions in the case. Nor must the award state the conclusions that the arbitrator reached on any questions of law that may have been presented. All that is required for the award to be valid is that it completely resolve the controversy.

Most states do, however, require that the award be in writing, regardless of whether any conclusions of law or findings of fact are included. If the arbitrator does state his or her legal conclusions and factual findings, then a letter or an opinion will be drafted containing the basis for the award. Even when there is no statutory requirement that the arbitrator state the factual and legal basis for the award, the parties

EXHIBIT 4–1 ■ SAMPLE SUBMISSION FORM

American Arbitration Association

SUBMISSION TO DISPUTE RESOLUTION

Date: ________________

The named parties hereby submit the following dispute for resolution under the ______________ ______________________________ Rules* of the American Arbitration Association:

Procedure Selected: ☐ Binding arbitration ☐ Mediation settlement
☐ Other ______________________
(Describe)

FOR INSURANCE CASES ONLY:

________________ Policy Number
________________ to ________________ Effective Dates
________________ Applicable Policy Limits

________________ Date of Incident
________________ Location

Insured: ________________ Claim Number: ________________

Name(s) of Claimant(s)	Check if a Minor	Amount Claimed
________________	☐	________________
________________	☐	________________

Nature of Dispute and/or Injuries Alleged (attach additional sheets if necessary):

Place of Hearing: ______________________________

We agree that, if binding arbitration is selected, we will abide by and perform any award rendered hereunder and that a judgment may be entered on the award.

To Be Completed by the Claimant

____
Name of Party
____
Address
____
City, State, and ZIP Code
(   ) ________________
Telephone Fax
____
Signature†
____
Name of Party's Attorney or Representative
____
Address
____
City, State, and ZIP Code
(   ) ________________
Telephone Fax
____
Signature†

To Be Completed by the Respondent

____
Name of Party
____
Address
____
City, State, and ZIP Code
(   ) ________________
Telephone Fax
____
Signature†
____
Name of Party's Attorney or Representative
____
Address
____
City, State, and ZIP Code
(   ) ________________
Telephone Fax
____
Signature†

Please file three copies with the AAA.

* *If you have a question as to which rules apply, please contact the AAA.*

† *Signatures of all parties are required for arbitration.*

Form G1-7/90

may impose the requirement in their submission or in their pre-dispute agreement to arbitrate.

ENFORCEMENT OF AGREEMENTS TO SUBMIT TO ARBITRATION

The role of the courts in the arbitration process is limited. One important role is played at the prearbitration stage. A court may be called on to order one party to an arbitration agreement to submit to arbitration under the terms of the agreement. The court in this role is essentially interpreting a contract. The court must determine what the parties have committed themselves to before ordering that they submit to arbitration.

When a dispute arises as to whether or not the parties have agreed in an arbitration clause to submit a particular matter to arbitration, one party may file suit to compel arbitration. The court before which the suit is brought will not decide the basic controversy but must decide the issue of arbitrability—that is, whether the issue is one that must be resolved through arbitration. If the court finds that the subject matter in controversy is covered by the agreement to arbitrate, then a party may be compelled to arbitrate the dispute involuntarily.

Although the parties may agree to submit the issue of arbitrability to an arbitrator, the agreement must be explicit; a court will never *infer* an agreement to arbitrate. Unless a court finds an *explicit* agreement to have the arbitrator decide whether a dispute is arbitrable, the court will decide the issue. This is an important initial determination, because no party will be ordered to submit to arbitration unless the court is convinced that the party has consented to do so.

Should claims involving alleged violations of federal statutes protecting employees from employment discrimination be arbitrable? The United States Supreme Court answered this question in the following landmark case.

CASE 4.2 Gilmer v. Interstate/Johnson Lane Corp.

Supreme Court of the United States, 1991. 500 U.S. 20, 111 S.Ct. 1647, 114 L.Ed.2d 26.

BACKGROUND AND FACTS *Interstate/Johnson Lane Corporation required some of its employees, including Robert Gilmer, to register as securities representatives with the New York Stock Exchange (NYSE). The registration application included an agreement to arbitrate when NYSE rules required it. One of the rules requires the arbitration of any controversy arising out of a registrant's termination of employment. Interstate terminated Gilmer's employment at age sixty-two. Gilmer filed a suit in a federal district court, alleging that he had been discharged in violation of the Age Discrimination in Employment Act (ADEA) of 1967.*[a] *(This act attempts to prevent employers from discriminating against older employees—see Chapter 21.) Interstate asked the court to order the arbitration of Gilmer's claim, according to the agreement in Gilmer's registration application with the NYSE. The court denied the employer's request, but on appeal, the appellate court ordered the arbitration. Gilmer appealed to the United States Supreme Court.*

IN THE LANGUAGE OF THE COURT

Justice *WHITE* delivered the opinion of the Court.

* * * *

* * * Although all statutory rights may not be appropriate for arbitration, having made the bargain to arbitrate, the party should be held to it unless Congress itself has evinced an intention to preclude a waiver of judicial remedies for the statutory rights at issue. * * * If such an intention exists, it will be discoverable in the text of the ADEA, its legislative history, or an inherent conflict between arbitration and the ADEA's underlying purposes. Throughout such an inquiry, it should be kept in mind that questions of arbitrability must be addressed with a healthy regard for the federal policy favoring arbitration.

a. 29 U.S.C. Sections 621–634.

* * * *

As Gilmer contends, the ADEA is designed not only to address individual grievances, but also to further important social policies. We do not perceive any inherent inconsistency between those policies, however, and enforcing agreements to arbitrate age discrimination claims. * * *

* * * *

Gilmer also argues that compulsory arbitration is improper because it deprives claimants of the judicial forum provided for by the ADEA. Congress, however, did not explicitly preclude arbitration or other nonjudicial resolution of claims, even in its recent amendments to the ADEA. * * * In addition, * * * arbitration agreements * * * serve to advance the objective of allowing [claimants] a broader right to select the forum for resolving disputes, whether it be judicial or otherwise.

DECISION AND REMEDY *The United States Supreme Court held that the arbitration of an age discrimination claim can be compelled. The Court affirmed the order requiring the parties to arbitrate the claim.*

INTERNATIONAL CONSIDERATIONS **International Arbitration and Public Policy** *International standards for the recognition of arbitration agreements and awards were set by the United Nations Convention on the Recognition and Enforcement of Foreign Arbitral Awards,[b] which has been signed by seventy-three countries, including the United States. Article V(2) of the convention creates an exception to enforcement of arbitration clauses that are "contrary to the public policy" of the relevant country. Thus, the resolution of a case will depend on the strength of a public policy in a given country. International organizations that handle arbitration matters include the United Nations Commission on International Trade Laws, the London Court of International Arbitration, the Euro-Arab Chamber of Commerce, the International Chamber of Commerce in Paris, and the International Trademark Association.*

b. June 10, 1958, 21 U.S.T. 2517 (the New York Convention).

SETTING ASIDE AN ARBITRATION AWARD

After the arbitration has been concluded, the losing party may appeal the arbitrator's award to a court, or the winning party may seek a court order compelling the other party to comply with the award. The scope of review in either situation is much more restricted than in an appellate court's review of a trial court decision. The court does not look at the merits of the underlying dispute, and the court will not add to or subtract from the remedies provided by the award. The court's role is limited to determining whether there exists a valid award. If so, the court will order the parties to comply with the terms. The general view is that because the parties were free to frame the issues and set the powers of the arbitrator at the outset, they cannot complain about the result.

FACT FINDINGS AND LEGAL CONCLUSIONS

The arbitrator's fact findings and legal conclusions are normally final. That the arbitrator may have erred in a ruling during the hearing or made an erroneous fact finding is normally no basis for setting aside an award: the parties agreed that the arbitrator would be the judge of the facts. Similarly, no matter how obviously the arbitrator was mistaken in a conclusion of law, the award is normally nonetheless binding: the parties agreed to accept the arbitrator's interpretation of the law. A court will not look at the merits of the dispute, the sufficiency of the evidence presented, or the arbitrator's reasoning in reaching a particular decision.

This approach is consistent with the underlying view of all voluntary arbitration—that its basis is really contract law. If the parties freely contract with one another, courts will not interfere simply because one side feels that it received a bad bargain. Any party challenging an award must face the presumption that a final award is valid. But is an award final or binding if the parties did not agree that it would be? That was the issue in the following case.

CASE 4.3 Orlando v. Interstate Container Corp.

United States Court of Appeals, Third Circuit, 1996. 100 F.3d 296.

BACKGROUND AND FACTS *Joseph Orlando, an employee of Interstate Container Corporation, underwent heart bypass surgery. For several months, he did not work and collected disability benefits, in part as provided by a collective bargaining agreement.*[a] *When his condition improved, he asked to return to work, but Interstate denied his request. He filed a complaint with the company, which, under the collective bargaining agreement, went to arbitration, culminating in an arbitrator's decision in Interstate's favor. The agreement did not state that the arbitrator's decision would be "final" or "binding," however. In Orlando's subsequent suit against Interstate, a federal district court ruled that the decision was not binding. Interstate appealed.*

IN THE LANGUAGE OF THE COURT

WEIS, Circuit Judge.

* * * *

[Interstate] argues that because the contract makes arbitration mandatory, it must necessarily be final as well. That argument finds support in the policy favoring arbitration as a means of resolving disputes, but fails to meet the requirement of authorization by agreement of the parties. * * *

* * * *

* * * [W]e must give full credit to the language the parties have chosen to include—or not include—in their agreement.

Collective bargaining agreements almost invariably explain that arbitration proceedings will be "final," "binding," or "exclusive," or use other words to that effect. This agreement was drafted by parties well-versed in labor matters and cognizant [aware] of that convention. The omission of any indication that arbitration proceedings should be final and binding leads us to conclude that, if we nevertheless declared them to be so, we would not be enforcing the will of the parties, as expressed in their agreement.

DECISION AND REMEDY *The U.S. Court of Appeals for the Third Circuit affirmed the lower court's decision. An arbitration award may not be final or binding unless the parties agreed that it would be.*

a. A collective bargaining agreement is a contract negotiated by employees and their employer concerning the terms and conditions of employment. See Chapter 22.

PUBLIC POLICY AND ILLEGALITY In keeping with contract law principles, no award will be enforced if compliance with the award would result in the commission of a crime or would conflict with some greater social policy mandated by statute. A court will not overturn an award, however, simply because the arbitrator was called on to resolve a dispute involving a matter of significant public concern.[3] For an award to be set aside, it must call for some action on the part of the parties that would conflict with or in some way undermine public policy. The issue in the following case was whether enforcement of an arbitrator's award would violate public policy.

3. See, for example, *Faherty v. Faherty*, 97 N.J. 99, 477 A.2d 1257 (1984).

CASE 4.4 Meehan v. Nassau Community College

Supreme Court, Appellate Division, Second Department, 1996. 647 N.Y.S.2d 865.

BACKGROUND AND FACTS *Nassau Community College required the faculty in its communications department to possess a master's degree in communications. Michael DeLuca did not have the requisite degree but was nevertheless assigned to teach communications courses. The Middle States Association Commission on Higher Education told the college that its accreditation would be in jeopardy unless its assignment of faculty was based, "first and foremost," on academic credentials. The college reviewed its personnel files, discovered that DeLuca did not have the necessary credentials, and declined to assign him any more courses. DeLuca's subsequent complaint went to arbitration before the New York State Public Employee Relations Board, which ordered DeLuca's reinstatement. The college refused, and DeLuca (through John Meehan, a faculty representative) filed a suit against the college in a New York state court to confirm the award. The court denied DeLuca's request, and he appealed.*

IN THE LANGUAGE OF THE COURT

MEMORANDUM BY THE COURT.

* * * *

* * * [O]nly when [an arbitrator's] award contravenes a strong public policy, almost invariably involving an important constitutional or statutory duty or responsibility, may it be set aside. * * * [H]ere, it is clear that the award the petitioner seeks to confirm contravenes strong public policy, inasmuch as it requires the College to retain DeLuca even though he is undisputably unqualified to teach in the Communications Department because of his lack of certain academic credentials.

DECISION AND REMEDY *The state appellate court affirmed the decision of the trial court setting aside the arbitrator's award. Enforcement of the award would violate public policy. The college did not have to reinstate DeLuca.*

DEFECTS IN THE ARBITRATION PROCESS There are some bases for setting aside an award when there is a defect in the arbitration process. These bases are typified by those set forth in the Federal Arbitration Act. Section 10 of the act provides four grounds on which an arbitration award may be set aside:

1. The award was the result of corruption, fraud, or other "undue means."
2. The arbitrator exhibited bias or corruption.
3. The arbitrator refused to postpone the hearing despite sufficient cause, refused to hear evidence pertinent and material to the dispute, or otherwise acted to substantially prejudice the rights of one of the parties.
4. The arbitrator exceeded his or her powers or failed to use them to make a mutual, final, and definite award.

The first three bases for setting aside the award include actions or decisions that are more than simply mistakes in judgment. Each requires some "bad faith" on the part of the arbitrator. Bad faith actions or decisions are ones that affect the integrity of the arbitration process. The honesty and impartiality, rather than the judgment, of the arbitrator are called into question.

Sometimes it is difficult to make the distinction between honest mistakes in judgment and actions or decisions made in bad faith. A bribe is clearly the kind of "undue means" included in the first basis for setting aside an award. Letting only one side argue its case is likewise a clear violation of the second basis.

Meetings between the arbitrator and one party outside the presence of the other party also taint the arbitration process. Although meetings might not involve the kind of corruption that results from taking a bribe, they do affect the integrity of the process; the third basis for setting aside an award is meant to protect against this.

Not every refusal by an arbitrator to admit certain evidence is grounds for setting aside an award under the third basis. As noted, to provide a basis for overturning an award, the arbitrator's decision must be more than an error in judgment, no matter how obviously incorrect that judgment might appear to another observer. The decision must be so obviously wrong or unfair as to imply bias or corruption. Otherwise, the decision normally cannot be a basis for setting aside an award.

The fourth basis for setting aside an award is that the arbitrator exceeded his or her powers in arbitrating the dispute. This issue involves the question of arbitrability. An arbitrator exceeds his or her powers and authority by attempting to resolve an issue that is not covered by the agreement to submit to arbitration.

WAIVER Although a defect in the arbitration process is sufficient grounds for setting aside an award, a party sometimes forfeits the right to challenge an award by failing to object to the defect in a timely manner. The party must object when he or she learns of the problem. After making the objection, the party can still proceed with the arbitration process and still challenge the award in court after the arbitration proceedings have concluded. If, however, a party makes no objection and proceeds with the arbitration process, then a later court challenge to the award may be denied on the ground that the party *waived* the right to challenge the award on the basis of the defect.

Frequently, this occurs when a party fails to object that an arbitrator is exceeding his or her powers in resolving a dispute because the subject matter is not arbitrable or because the party did not agree to arbitrate the dispute. The question of arbitrability is one for the courts to decide. If a party does not object on this issue at the first demand for arbitration, however, a court may consider the objection waived.

CONFLICTS OF LAW Parties are afforded wide latitude in establishing the manner in which their disputes will be resolved. Nevertheless, an agreement to arbitrate may be governed by the FAA or one of the many state arbitration acts, even though the parties do not refer to a statute in their agreement. Recall that the FAA covers any arbitration clause in a contract that involves interstate commerce. Frequently, however, transactions involving interstate commerce also have substantial connections to particular states, which may in turn have their own arbitration acts. In such situations, unless the FAA and state arbitration law are nearly identical, the acts may conflict. How are these conflicts to be resolved?

As a general principle, the supremacy clause and the commerce clause of the U.S. Constitution are the bases for giving federal law preeminence; when there is a conflict, state law is preempted by federal law. Thus, in cases of arbitration, the strong federal policy favoring arbitration can override a state's laws that might be more favorable to normal litigation.

CHOICE OF LAW Notwithstanding federal preemption of conflicting state laws, the Federal Arbitration Act has been interpreted as allowing the parties to choose a particular state law to govern their arbitration agreement. The parties may choose to have the laws of a specific state govern their agreement by including in the agreement a *choice-of-law clause*. The FAA does not mandate any particular set of rules that parties must follow in arbitration; the parties are free to agree on the manner best suited to their needs. Consistent with this view that arbitration is at heart a contractual matter between private parties, the United States Supreme Court has upheld arbitration agreements containing choice-of-law provisions.

DISADVANTAGES OF ARBITRATION

Arbitration has some disadvantages. The result in any particular dispute can be unpredictable, in part because arbitrators do not need to follow any previous cases in rendering their decisions. Unlike judges, arbitrators do not have to issue written opinions or facilitate a participant's appeal to a court. Arbitrators must decide disputes according to whatever rules have been provided by the parties, regardless of how unfair those rules may be. In some cases, arbitration can be nearly as expensive as litigation. In part, this is because both sides must prepare their cases for presentation before a third party decision maker, just as they would have to do to appear in court. Discovery is usually not available in arbitration, however, which means that during the hearing the parties must take the time to question witnesses whom, in a lawsuit, they would not need to call.[4]

4. One notable dispute concerning computer chip technology was in arbitration for more than seven years and cost the participants more than $100 million. See *Advanced Micro Devices, Inc. v. Intel Corp.*, 9 Cal.4th 362, 885 P.2d 994, 36 Cal.Rptr.2d 581 (1994).

SECTION 4

THE INTEGRATION OF ADR AND FORMAL COURT PROCEDURES

Because of the congestion within the judicial system, many jurisdictions at both the state and federal levels are integrating alternative dispute resolution into the formal legal process. Utilizing methods such as arbitration and mediation within the traditional framework may relieve the logjams afflicting most of the nation's court systems.

COURT-MANDATED ADR

Increasingly, courts are requiring that parties attempt to settle their differences through some form of ADR before proceeding to trial. For example, several federal district courts encourage nonbinding arbitration for cases involving amounts less than $100,000. Less than 10 percent of the cases referred for arbitration ever go to trial. Today, about half of all federal courts have adopted formal rules regarding the use of ADR, and many other courts without such rules use ADR procedures.

Most states have adopted programs that allow them to refer certain types of cases for mediation or arbitration. Typically—as in California and Hawaii—court systems have adopted mandatory mediation or nonbinding arbitration programs for certain types of disputes, usually involving less than a specified threshold dollar amount.[5] Only if the parties fail to reach an agreement, or if one of the parties disagrees with the decision of a third party mediating or arbitrating the dispute, will the case be heard by a court. South Carolina was the first state to institute a voluntary arbitration program at the appellate court level. In the South Carolina system, litigants must waive a court hearing when requesting arbitration. All decisions by the arbitrators are final and binding.

COURT-ANNEXED ARBITRATION

Court-annexed arbitration differs significantly from the voluntary arbitration process discussed above. There are some disputes that courts will not allow to go to arbitration. Most states, for example, do not allow court-annexed arbitration in disputes involving title to real estate or in cases in which a court's equity powers are involved.

A FUNDAMENTAL DIFFERENCE The fundamental difference between voluntary arbitration and court-annexed arbitration is the finality and reviewability of the award. With respect to court-annexed arbitration, either party may reject the award for any reason. In the event that one of the parties does reject the award, the case will proceed to trial, and the court will hear the case *de novo*—that is, the court will reconsider all the evidence and legal questions as though no arbitration had occurred.

Everyone who has a recognizable cause of action or against whom such an action is brought is entitled to have the issue decided in a court of law. Because court-annexed arbitration is not voluntary, there must be some safeguard against using it in a way that denies an individual his or her day in court. This safeguard is provided by permitting either side to reject the award regardless of the reason for so doing.

The party rejecting the award may be penalized, however. Many statutes providing for court-annexed arbitration impose court costs and fees on a party who rejects an arbitration award but does not improve his or her position by going to trial. Thus, for example, if a party rejects an arbitration award, and the award turns out to be more favorable to that party than the subsequent jury verdict, the party may be compelled to pay the costs of the arbitration or some fee for the costs of the trial.

In court-annexed arbitration, discovery of evidence occurs before the hearing. After the hearing has commenced, a party seeking to discover new evidence must usually secure approval from the court that mandated the arbitration. This is intended to prevent the parties from using arbitration as a means of previewing each other's cases and then rejecting the arbitrator's award.

THE ROLE OF THE ARBITRATOR Notwithstanding the differences between voluntary and court-annexed arbitration, the role of the arbitrator is essentially the same in both types of proceedings. The arbitrator determines issues of both fact and law. The arbitrator also makes all decisions concerning applications of the rules of procedure and evidence during the hearing.

5. Hawaii, for example, has a program of mandatory, nonbinding arbitration for disputes involving less than $150,000.

WHICH RULES APPLY Regarding the rules of evidence, there are differences among the states. Most states impose the same rules of evidence on an arbitration hearing as on a trial. Other states, such as New Jersey, allow all evidence relevant to the dispute regardless of whether the evidence would be admissible at trial. Still other jurisdictions, such as Washington, leave it to the arbitrator to decide what evidence is admissible.

WAIVER Once a court directs that a dispute is to be submitted to court-annexed arbitration, the parties must proceed to arbitration. As noted above, either side may reject the award that results from the arbitration for any reason. If a party fails to appear at or participate in the arbitration proceeding as directed by the court, however, that failure constitutes a waiver of the right to reject the award.

COURT-RELATED MEDIATION

Mediation is proving to be more popular than arbitration as a court-related method of ADR. No federal court has adopted an arbitration program since 1991, while mediation programs continue to increase in number in both federal and state courts. Today, more court systems offer or require mediation, rather than arbitration, as an alternative to litigation. In the 1980s, there were only about 200 mediators in the United States. Today, more than 60,000 persons offer mediation services. Mediation is currently being taught in 95 percent of the accredited law schools in the country.

Mediation is often used in disputes relating to employment law, environmental law, product liability, and franchises. One of the most important business advantages of mediation is the lower cost, which can be 25 percent (or less) of the expense of litigation. Another advantage is the speed with which a dispute can go through mediation (possibly one or two days) compared with arbitration (possibly months) or litigation (possibly years).

Part of the popularity of mediation is that its goal, unlike that of litigation and some other forms of ADR, is for opponents to work out a resolution that benefits both sides. The rate of participants' satisfaction with the outcomes in mediated disputes is high. In New Hampshire, for example, where mediation is mandatory for all civil cases in most state trial courts, as many as 70 percent of the participants report satisfaction with the results.

SUMMARY JURY TRIALS

Another means by which the courts have integrated alternative dispute resolution methods into the traditional court process is through the use of summary jury trials. A **summary jury trial** is a mock trial that occurs in a courtroom before a judge and jury. Evidence is presented in an abbreviated form, along with each side's major contentions. The jury then presents a verdict.

The fundamental difference between a traditional trial and a summary jury trial is that in the latter, the jury's verdict is only advisory. The goal of a summary jury trial is to give each side an idea of how it would fare in a full-blown jury trial with a more elaborate and detailed presentation of evidence and arguments. At the end of the summary jury trial, the presiding judge meets with the parties and may encourage them to settle their dispute without going through a standard jury trial.

The U.S. Court of Appeals for the Sixth Circuit recently addressed the question of whether summary jury trials can be mandatory. The court concluded that it would be unfair to litigants to force them to undergo summary jury trials before they were permitted to have their claims heard in a federal court.[6]

ADR AND MASS TORTS

A *tort* is a civil wrong that does not arise from a breach of contract. (Torts are discussed in detail in Chapters 12 and 13. Breach of contract is discussed in Chapter 10.) *Mass tort* is the term applied to civil lawsuits that share such features as scientific or technological complexity and a large number of participants. Such cases often feature a high degree of emotional involvement on the part of the claimants, who may suffer from severe or life-threatening injuries, and on the part of the defendants, whose financial existence may be at stake. Examples of mass torts include litigation involving Agent Orange, the Dalkon Shield, the prescription drug DES, heart valves, and asbestos.

In the 1990s, there has been an explosion in the number of mass torts. For example, more than 300,000 claims have been filed in asbestos-related litigation—in the mid-1990s, new claims were filed at

6. *In re NLO, Inc.*, 5 F.3d 154 (6th Cir. 1993).

the rate of 5,000 every month. Such claims are overwhelming our civil justice system. In attempts to clear the courts, some judges in mass tort cases turn to methods of alternative dispute resolution, including mediation, arbitration, mini-trials, and summary jury trials. ADR may be used to assess the validity or the value of the claims or to sort out or resolve the scientific, technological, or medical issues. ADR may be used to settle large numbers of claims in a speedy, efficient, cost-effective manner. Once a settlement is reached, a neutral third party may coordinate payments to claimants. There may even be provision for an ADR appeals process.

SECTION 5
ADR FORUMS AND SERVICES

Services facilitating dispute resolution outside the courtroom are provided by both government agencies and private organizations. The major source of private arbitration services is the American Arbitration Association (AAA). Most of the largest law firms in the nation are members of this association. Founded in 1926, the AAA now settles more than 72,000 disputes a year and has offices in every state. Cases brought before the AAA are heard by an expert or a panel of experts—of whom usually about half are lawyers—in the area relating to the dispute. To cover its costs, this nonprofit organization charges a fee, paid by the party filing the claim. In addition, each party to the dispute pays a price for each hearing day, as well as a special additional fee in cases involving personal injuries or property loss.

In addition to the AAA, numerous other state and local nonprofit organizations provide arbitration services. For example, the Arbitration Association of Florida provides ADR services in that state. The Better Business Bureau (BBB) offers ADR programs to aid in the resolution of certain types of disagreements. The BBB's latest ADR process involves a mediation program called ComputerCare, through which buyers and sellers of computer equipment and software can settle their disputes. Many industries—including the insurance, automobile, and securities industries—also now have mediation or arbitration programs to facilitate timely and inexpensive settlement of claims. In all, there exist over six hundred ADR entities in the United States.

Those who seek to settle their disputes quickly can turn to private, for-profit organizations to act as mediators or arbitrators. The private system of justice includes hundreds of firms throughout the country offering dispute-resolution services by hired judges. Procedures in these private courts are fashioned to meet the desires of the clients seeking their services. For example, the parties might decide on the date of the hearing, the presiding judge, whether the judge's decision will be legally binding, and the site of the hearing—which could be a conference room, a law-school office, or a leased courtroom complete with flag and Bible. The judges may follow procedures similar to those of the federal courts and use similar rules. Each party to the dispute may pay a filing fee and a designated fee for a half-day hearing session or a special, one-hour settlement conference.

TERMS AND CONCEPTS TO REVIEW

alternative dispute resolution (ADR) 72
arbitration 74
arbitrator 74
award 76
early neutral case evaluation 73
mediation 73
mediator 73
mini-trial 73
submission 76
summary jury trial 84

QUESTIONS AND CASE PROBLEMS

4–1. ARBITRATION. In an arbitration proceeding, the arbitrator need not be a judge or even a lawyer. How, then, can the arbitrator's decision have the force of law and be binding on the parties involved?

4–2. CHOICE OF LAW. Two private U.S. corporations enter into a joint-venture agreement to conduct mining operations in the newly formed Middle Eastern nation of Euphratia. As part of the agreement, the companies include an arbitration clause and a choice-of-law provision. The first states that any controversy arising out of the performance of the agreement will be settled by arbitration. The second states that the agreement is to be governed by the laws of the location of the venture, Euphratia. A dispute arises, and the parties discontinue operations. One of the parties claims sole ownership to the Euphratian mines and orders the other party to remove its equipment from the mines. The other party disputes the claim of sole ownership and seeks an order from a U.S. federal court compelling the parties to submit to arbitration over the ownership issue and alleged breaches of the joint-venture agreement. How should the court rule if the laws of Euphratia state that, whereas arbitration agreements are to be enforced generally, matters of ownership of natural resources can only be resolved in a Euphratian court of law? Does it matter that two U.S. companies engaged in international commerce would be governed by the Federal Arbitration Act?

4–3. CONFIRMATION OF AWARD. Two brothers, both of whom are certified public accountants (CPAs), form a professional association to provide tax-accounting services to the public. They also agree, in writing, that any disputes that arise between them over matters concerning the association will be submitted to an independent arbitrator, whom they designate to be their father, who is also a CPA. A dispute arises, and the matter is submitted to the father for arbitration. During the course of arbitration, which occurs over several weeks, the father asks the older brother, who is visiting one evening, to explain a certain entry in the brothers' association accounts. The younger brother learns of the discussion at the next meeting for arbitration; he says nothing about it, however. The arbitration is concluded in favor of the older brother, who seeks a court order compelling the younger brother to comply with the award. The younger brother seeks to set aside the award, claiming that the arbitration process was tainted by bias because "Dad always liked my older brother best." The younger brother also seeks to have the award set aside on the basis of improper conduct in that matters subject to arbitration were discussed between the father and older brother without the younger brother's being present. Should a court confirm the award or set it aside? Why?

4–4. CALCULATION OF AWARD. After resolving their dispute, the two brothers encountered in Problem 4–3 decide to resume their tax-accounting practice according to the terms of their original agreement. Again a dispute arises, and again it is decided by the father (now retired except for numerous occasions on which he acts as an arbitrator) in favor of the older brother. The older brother files a petition to enforce the award. The younger brother seeks to set aside the award and offers evidence that the father, as arbitrator, made a gross error in calculating the accounts that were material to the dispute being arbitrated. If the court is convinced that the father erred in the calculations, should the award be set aside? Why?

4–5. COMPELLING ARBITRATION. In 1981, AT&T laid off seventy-nine workers in the Chicago area, purportedly because of a slowdown in economic activity. The Communications Workers of America, a union representing some AT&T workers, argued that there was no lack of work and objected to the layoffs as violations of the terms of a collective bargaining agreement between the union and AT&T. The agreement provided that "differences arising with respect to the interpretation of this contract or the performance of any obligation" under the agreement would be resolved through arbitration. The agreement reserved to AT&T the free exercise of managerial functions such as hiring and firing employees. The agreement conditioned such decision making on compliance with the terms of the contract but expressly excluded disputes over those decisions from arbitration. AT&T relied on this exclusion to avoid the union's demand for arbitration over the layoffs. The union sought a court order to compel arbitration. The court held that the issue of whether the dispute over the layoffs was subject to arbitration should be decided by the arbitrator and ordered the parties to submit the question to the arbitrator. An appellate court affirmed the holding, and AT&T appealed to the United States Supreme Court. How should the Court rule? Discuss fully. [*AT&T Technologies v. Communications Workers of America*, 475 U.S. 643, 106 S.Ct. 1415, 89 L.Ed.2d 648 (1990)]

4–6. ARBITRATION. Randall Fris worked as a seaman on an Exxon Shipping Co. oil tanker for eight years without incident. One night, he boarded the ship for duty while intoxicated, in violation of company policy. This policy also allowed Exxon to discharge employees who were intoxicated and thus unfit for work. Exxon discharged Fris. Under a contract with Fris's union, the discharge was submitted to arbitration. The arbitrators ordered Exxon to reinstate Fris on an oil tanker. Exxon filed a suit against the union, challenging the award as contrary to public policy, which opposes having intoxicated persons operate seagoing vessels. Can a court set aside an arbitration award on the ground that the award violates public policy? Should the court set aside the award in this case? Explain. [*Exxon Shipping Co. v. Exxon Seamen's Union*, 11 F.3d 1189 (3d Cir. 1993)]

4–7. ARBITRATION. Phillip Beaudry, who suffered from mental illness, worked in the Department of

Income Maintenance for the state of Connecticut. Beaudry was fired from his job when it was learned that he had misappropriated approximately $1,640 in state funds. Beaudry filed a complaint with his union, Council 4 of the American Federation of State, County, and Municipal Employees (AFSCME), and eventually the dispute was submitted to an arbitrator. The arbitrator concluded that Beaudry had been dismissed without "just cause," because Beaudry's acts were caused by his mental illness and "were not willful or volitional or within his capacity to control." Because Beaudry was disabled, the employer was required, under state law, to transfer him to a position that he was competent to hold. The arbitrator awarded Beaudry reinstatement, back pay, seniority, and other benefits. The state appealed the decision to a court. What public policies must the court weigh in making its decision? How should the court rule? [*State v. Council 4, AFSCME*, 27 Conn.App. 635, 608 A.2d 718 (1992)]

4–8. ARBITRATOR'S AUTHORITY. Hembree purchased a home from Broadway Realty and Trust Co. In the contract of sale, the buyer and seller agreed to arbitrate any claim or controversy "arising out of or relating to this contract." Hembree later claimed that the roof was defective, and the case was arbitrated. The arbitrator decided in favor of Hembree on the basis that the seller had breached an implied warranty. The seller appealed the arbitrator's decision, claiming that the arbitrator had exceeded his authority, because only claims arising out of or relating to the contract were to be arbitrated, and an implied warranty claim did not arise out of or relate to "this contract." Discuss whether the arbitrator was within his authority in addressing the implied warranty claim. [*Hembree v. Broadway Realty and Trust Co.*, 151 Ariz. 418, 728 P.2d 288 (1986)]

4–9. ARBITRATION. Colorado's Mandatory Arbitration Act required that all civil lawsuits involving damages of less than $50,000 be arbitrated rather than tried in court. The act affected eight judicial districts in the state. It provided for a court trial for any party dissatisfied with an arbitrator's decision. It also provided that if the trial did not result in an improvement of more than 10 percent in the position of the party who had demanded the trial, that party had to pay the costs of the arbitration proceeding. The constitutionality of the act was challenged by a plaintiff who maintained in part that the act violated litigants' rights of access to the courts and trial by jury. What will the court decide? Explain your answer. [*Firelock, Inc. v. District Court, 20th Judicial District*, 776 P.2d 1090 (Colo. 1989)]

4–10. ARBITRATION. New York State revised its New Car Lemon Law to allow consumers who complained of purchasing a "lemon" to have their disputes arbitrated before a professional arbitrator appointed by the New York attorney general. Before this revision, the Lemon Law allowed for arbitration of disputes, but the forum in which arbitration took place was sponsored by trade associations within the automobile industry, and consumers often complained of unfair awards. The revised law also provided that consumers could choose between two options: arbitration before a professional arbitrator and suing the manufacturer in court. Manufacturers, however, were compelled to arbitrate claims, if a consumer chose to do so, and could not resort to the courts. Trade associations representing automobile manufacturers and importers brought an action seeking a declaration that the alternative arbitration mechanism of the Lemon Law was unconstitutional because it deprived them of their right to trial by jury. How will the court decide? Discuss. [*Motor Vehicle Manufacturers Association of the United States v. State*, 75 N.Y.2d 175, 550 N.E.2d 919, 551 N.Y.S.2d 470 (1990)]

4–11. A QUESTION OF ETHICS

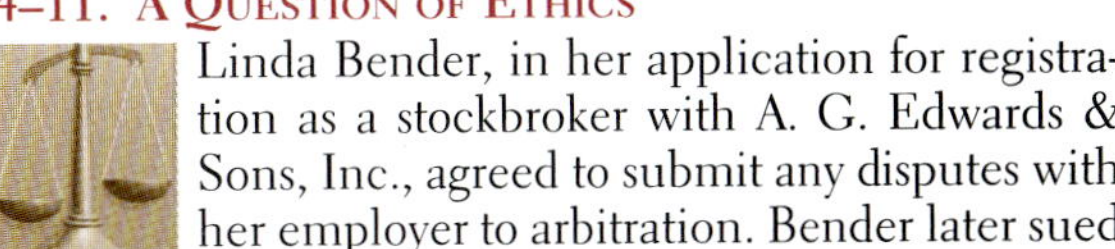

Linda Bender, in her application for registration as a stockbroker with A. G. Edwards & Sons, Inc., agreed to submit any disputes with her employer to arbitration. Bender later sued her supervisor and employer (the defendants) for sexual harassment in violation of Title VII of the Civil Rights Act of 1964, which prohibits, among other things, employment discrimination based on gender. The defendants requested the court to compel arbitration. The district court judge refused to do so, holding that Bender could not be forced to waive her right to adjudicate Title VII claims in a federal court. The appellate court reversed, ruling that Title VII claims are arbitrable. The court held that compelling Bender to submit her claim for arbitration did not deprive her of the right to a judicial forum, because if the arbitration proceedings were somehow legally deficient, she could still take her case to a federal court for review. [*Bender v. A. G. Edwards & Sons, Inc.*, 971 F.2d 698 (11th Cir. 1992)]

1. Does the right to a postarbitration judicial forum equate to the right to initial access to a judicial forum in employment disputes?
2. Should the fact that reviewing courts rarely set aside arbitrators' awards have any bearing on the arbitrability of certain types of claims, such as those brought under Title VII?

4–12. CASE BRIEFING ASSIGNMENT

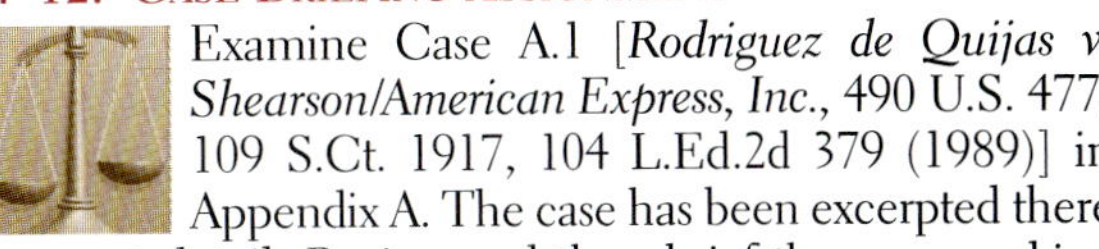

Examine Case A.1 [*Rodriguez de Quijas v. Shearson/American Express, Inc.*, 490 U.S. 477, 109 S.Ct. 1917, 104 L.Ed.2d 379 (1989)] in Appendix A. The case has been excerpted there in great detail. Review and then brief the case, making sure that your brief answers the following questions.

1. What is the legislative policy "embodied in the Arbitration Act"?
2. How did the Court reconcile the protections afforded investors under the Securities Act and the legislative policy advanced by the Arbitration Act? Did the Court believe that by submitting to arbitration, investors forgo "substantive rights" given under the Securities Act?

UNIT ONE—CUMULATIVE HYPOTHETICAL PROBLEM

4–13. *Korman, Inc., a toy manufacturer, has its headquarters in Minneapolis, Minnesota. It markets its toys throughout the United States, as well as in overseas markets. Korman has recently placed on the market a new line of dolls with such irreverent names as "Harass Me," "Spit on Me," "Pull My Hair," "Watch Me Scream," "Cut Me Quick," and "Abuse Me, Please." The dolls are a success commercially and have netted Korman more profits than any of its other toys. Given these "facts," answer the following questions:*

1. Jan's Toy Mart, the California distributor of Korman toys, wants to sue Korman for allegedly breaching a contract. If Jan's Toy Mart brought its suit in a California state court, could that court exercise jurisdiction over Korman? Explain.
2. Suppose that in its contract with Korman, Jan's Toy Mart agreed to submit any dispute that arose between the two companies to binding arbitration. Following the arbitration hearing, the arbitrator concludes that Korman did not breach the contract. Jan's Toy Mart is unsatisfied with the arbitrator's award. Can Jan's Toy Mart appeal the arbitrator's decision to a court?
3. Parents and teachers claim that Korman's dolls encourage children to be violent and that it is unethical of Korman to continue marketing the dolls. Parent-teacher groups are organizing boycotts against Korman and the dolls and have launched a media campaign against the company. Recently, they picketed Korman's headquarters in Minneapolis, bearing such signs as "Korman Hates Kids" and "Watch Korman Scream." If you were a Korman executive, would you recommend that the company cease manufacturing the toys? What factors would Korman's directors need to consider in making this decision?

ACCESSING THE INTERNET
THE LEGAL ENVIRONMENT OF BUSINESS

A preeminent resource on the Internet for information on alternative dispute resolution (ADR) is the American Arbitration Association (AAA), which you can locate at

http://www.adr.org

The AAA's site offers information on ADR in a number of areas, including labor relations, employment, commerce, the construction industry, and international disputes. The site provides the text of AAA rules, samples of several AAA forms, and some useful articles on ADR.

ConflictNet, which describes itself as "a network of people dedicated to promoting the constructive resolution of conflict," provides information on ADR as well as links to other ADR resources on the Internet. To reach this site, go to

http://www.igc.apc.org/conflictnet

You can find publications pertaining to ADR by accessing the Federal Judicial Center at

http://www.fjc.gov

A pilot project involving online dispute resolution is the Virtual Magistrate Project, which is sponsored by several ADR organizations, including the American Arbitration Association, the Villanova Center for Information Law and Policy, and the Cyberspace Law Institute. For information on this project, including its docket and decisions, go to

http://vmag.law.vill.edu:8080

The Global Arbitration Mediation Association (GAMA) was one of the first organizations to offer online arbitration services. GAMA allows for complaints to be filed and served by e-mail, and its "hearings" consist of affidavits and testimony submitted electronically. GAMA's Web page details the arbitration process and contains a library of related forms and sample arbitration clauses. You can access the GAMA's Web page at

http://www.gama.com

FOCUS ON ETHICS

ETHICS AND THE LEGAL ENVIRONMENT OF BUSINESS

Business ethics and business law are closely intertwined concepts, because ultimately the law rests on social beliefs about right and wrong behavior in the business world. Thus, businesspersons, merely by complying with the law, are acting ethically. As pointed out in Chapter 2, though, mere legal compliance (the "moral minimum" in terms of business ethics) is often not enough. This is because the law does not—and cannot—provide the answers for all ethical questions. Rather, the law assumes that those in business will behave ethically in their day-to-day dealings. If they do not, the courts will not come to their assistance.

The main question facing many businesspersons is this: How can they know what constitutes ethical conduct in a particular situation? Furthermore, at what point does unethical conduct cross the line separating unethical from illegal conduct? Often, as mentioned, the laws do not make this line clear—this is left for the courts to decide on a case-by-case basis. In other words, in some cases, businesspersons learn too late that they have violated not just business ethical standards but also the law.

No textbook can provide answers for the many ethical questions that arise in the business context. Nor can it anticipate the types of ethical questions that will arise in the future, as technology continues to

transform the workplace and business relationships. The most we can do is provide examples of the types of ethical issues that businesspersons have faced in the past and that they are facing today. The *Focus on Ethics* sections in this book survey some of the important ethical issues that arise in various areas of business activity. In this *Focus,* we first look at some obstacles to ethical behavior in the business context. We then examine a concept that has become a significant element of the legal environment of business: corporate social responsibility.

OBSTACLES TO ETHICAL BUSINESS BEHAVIOR

People sometimes behave unethically in the business context, just as they do in their private lives. Some businesspersons knowingly engage in unethical behavior because they think that they can "get away with it"—that no one will ever learn of their unethical actions. Examples of this kind of unethical behavior include padding expense accounts, casting doubts on the integrity of a rival co-worker to gain a job promotion, stealing company supplies or equipment, and so on. Obviously, these acts are unethical, and many of them are illegal as well. In other situations, businesspersons who would choose to act ethically may be deterred from doing so because of situational circumstances or external pressures.

Ethics and the Corporate Environment

We looked in Chapter 2 at how the structure of the corporate environment sometimes acts as a deterrent to ethical decision making. This is because (normally) corporate decisions are made collectively. Suppose that a corporation has five directors. One of them, Sarah, is also the corporation's president. Sarah feels that a planned corporate action would be unethical but may be reluctant to voice her opinion because the other directors are clearly committed to going forward with the undertaking. If Sarah declares her misgivings and makes an issue of the matter, the other directors may remove her from her position as president. Alternatively, Sarah may be swayed by the enthusiasm of the others and simply disregard her ethical qualms.

The corporate setting—particularly in a large corporate environment—also tends to distance the individual decision makers from the effects of their decisions on others. For example,

FOCUS ON ETHICS

complaints by product users about a corporation's products rarely affect corporate decision makers personally. Would the corporate actors' views of their ethical responsibilities be significantly different if they were personally involved? At least one person, John Swanson, would answer this question in the affirmative.

Swanson was a high-ranking corporate officer at Dow Corning Corporation, which had manufactured and marketed silicone breast implants since 1963. Swanson's wife was among the implant recipients. For years, the company had been receiving complaints about silicone leakage from the implants and consequent adverse health effects. Dow Corning took a defensive stance, maintaining that there was no convincing evidence that linked silicone to the complex of symptoms experienced by the recipients. Swanson supported Dow's position for years—until 1990, when he finally became convinced that his wife's deteriorating health was the result of the implants. Swanson urged the company to withdraw the implants from the market, but to no avail. The company continued to manufacture the implants until 1992. In the long run, Dow Corning was forced into bankruptcy because of litigation against the firm by implant recipients.

Ethics and Corporate Management

Much unethical business behavior occurs simply because management does not always make it clear what ethical standards and behaviors are expected of the firm's employees. Although most firms now issue ethical policies or codes of conduct, these policies and codes are not always effective in creating an ethical workplace. At times, this is because the firm's ethical policies are not communicated clearly to employees or do not bear on the real ethical issues confronting decision makers. Additionally, particularly in a large corporation, unethical behavior in one corporate department may simply escape the attention of those in control of the corporation or the corporate officials responsible for implementing and monitoring the company's ethics program.

Another deterrent to ethical behavior exists when corporate management, by its own conduct, indicates that ethical considerations take second place. If management makes no attempt to deter unethical behavior—through reprimands or employment terminations, for example—it will be clear to employees that management is not all that serious about ethics. Likewise, if a company doles out promotions or salary increases to those who obviously use unethical tactics to increase the firm's profits, then employees who do not resort to such tactics will be at a disadvantage. An employee in this situation may decide that because "everyone else does it," he or she might as well do it too.

Of course, an even stronger deterrent to ethical behavior occurs when employers engage in blatantly unethical or illegal conduct and expect their employees to do so as well. An employee in this situation faces two options, neither of which is satisfactory: participate in the conduct or "blow the whistle" on (inform authorities of) the employer's actions—and, of course, risk being fired. (See Chapter 20 for a more detailed discussion of this ethical dilemma and its consequences for employees.)

SELF-CRITICAL ANALYSIS

Ironically, even corporate compliance programs can sometimes act as a disincentive to ethical behavior. Such programs are set up so that companies can monitor workplace conduct through internal audits or investigations—a process often referred to as self-critical analysis (SCA).

SCA and the U.S. Sentencing Guidelines

Under the U.S. Sentencing Guidelines, which were created by the U.S. Department of Justice to provide standardized criminal sentences for federal crimes, corporate lawbreakers face sanctions and fines that can be as high as hundreds of millions of dollars. The guidelines allow judges to ease up on penalties, however, if a company can show that it has taken substantial steps to prevent, investigate, and punish wrongdoing by corporate employees. The sentencing guidelines thus provide an incentive for companies to

FOCUS ON ETHICS

establish ethics programs and procedures for implementing and monitoring corporate behavior. The theory is that companies that attempt to regulate their own behavior through SCA should receive more favorable treatment under the law than those that do not.

SCA and "Smoking Guns"

Although laws promoting SCA foster ethical behavior, business owners and managers continue to face significant challenges in attempting to prevent wrongdoing within their companies. An important problem with SCA is that it is virtually impossible to conduct a meaningful internal investigation or undertake an in-depth review process without creating a "paper trail" of some kind. Should the company have to defend itself in a lawsuit, the memos, reports, and other written evidence resulting from an investigation could be subject to discovery (see Chapter 3). If discovered by the plaintiff, these documents could be just the "smoking guns" the plaintiff is seeking—and the company could find it difficult to defend itself.

The SCA Privilege

In an attempt to overcome this disincentive to undertake SCA, an increasing number of states have passed laws that allow certain types of information resulting from internal audits and reviews to be privileged—that is, not admissible as evidence in a legal proceeding against the company. Some courts have also ruled that the results of a company's internal investigation of corporate conduct are protected by the "privilege of self-critical analysis." These courts hold that the SCA privilege furthers the public policy of encouraging self-evaluation on the part of companies.

In one case, for example, a plaintiff alleging gender discrimination on the part of her employer sought access to the employer's records of an investigation it had conducted on the obstacles faced by women within the company. The court, holding that the records were protected by the SCA privilege, stated that "[f]ew, if any, companies would risk commissioning a candid . . . report if these reports could later be used against the company in litigation."[1] Nonetheless, in some states, there are no real guarantees that the results of internal investigations will be kept confidential.

Corporate Social Responsibility

Perhaps no concept is more riddled with ethical perplexities than that of corporate social responsibility—the idea that corporations can and should act ethically and be accountable to society for their actions. We have already examined, in Chapter 2, some of the ethical (and legal) duties that corporations owe to their employees and to the users of their products. Here we look at some problematic aspects of a corporation's responsibilities to other groups, including corporate shareholders, other "stakeholders" in the firm, the community in which the corporation operates, and society at large.

Duty to Shareholders

Corporate directors and officers have a duty to act in the shareholders' interest. Because of the nature of the relationship between corporate directors and officers and the shareholder-owners, the law holds directors and officers to a high standard of care in business decision making (see Chapter 18). Traditionally, it was perceived that this duty to shareholders took precedence over all other corporate duties and that the primary goal of corporations should be profit maximization. Milton Friedman, the Nobel Prize–winning economist and a proponent of the profit-maximization view, saw "one and only one" social responsibility of a corporation: "to use its resources and engage in activities designed to increase its profits, so long as it stays within the rules of the game."[2] The "rules of the game"

1. *Flynn v. Goldman, Sachs & Co.* (S.D.N.Y. 1993)[1993 WL 362380]; this case is not reported in West's *Federal Supplement* reporter, but it can be retrieved on WESTLAW (WL) by use of the WL citation given here. See *Sheppard v. Consolidated Edison Co. of New York*, 893 F.Supp. 6 (E.D.N.Y. 1995), for another example of the application of the SCA privilege. For a discussion of the contrary view—that the SCA privilege should not be applied—see *Warren v. Legg Mason Wood Walker, Inc.*, 896 F.Supp. 540 (E.D.N.C. 1995).

2. *Capitalism and Freedom* (Chicago: University of Chicago Press, 1962), p. 133.

Focus on Ethics

are the "basic rules of society, both those embodied in law and those embodied in ethical custom."[3]

Those who support the profit-maximization view of social responsibility contend that the duty to maximize profits must outweigh any other duty when duties conflict—to the extent, of course, that in maximizing shareholders' profits a firm does not violate the "basic rules of society." The question here is, what are these basic rules?

Duty to Stakeholders

Increasingly, the traditional duty to shareholders is being balanced against a corporation's duty to other groups affected by corporate decisions. In the last decade or so, for example, about half of the states have enacted statutes that allow corporate decision makers to take into consideration not only the welfare of shareholders but also the welfare of *stakeholders*—employees, customers, suppliers, communities, and any group that has a stake in the corporation. Some of the statutes, such as those of Indiana and Pennsylvania, allow corporate management to place the interests of stakeholders above those of shareholders.

The reasoning behind these statutes—and behind what has come to be called "the stakeholder view of corporate social responsibility"—is that in some circumstances, other groups may have a greater stake in company decisions than the shareholders do. Consider an example. A heavily indebted corporation is facing imminent bankruptcy. The shareholder-investors have little to lose in this situation, because their stock is already next to worthless. The corporation's creditors will be first in line for any corporate assets remaining. Because in this situation it is the creditors who have the greatest "stake" in the corporation, under the stakeholder view, corporate directors and officers should give greater weight to the creditors' interests than to those of the shareholders.

Duty to the Community

In some circumstances, the community in which a business enterprise is located has a substantial stake in the firm. Assume, for example, that a company employs two thousand workers at one of its plants. If the company decides that it would be profitable to close the plant or move it to another location, the employees—and the community—would suffer as a result. Today, to be considered socially responsible (and, in some circumstances, to comply with laws governing plant shutdowns), a corporation must take both employees' needs and community needs into consideration when making such a decision.

Another ethical question sometimes arises when a firm moves into a community. Does the company have an obligation to evaluate first how its presence will affect that community? This question has surfaced in regard to the expansion of Wal-Mart Stores, Inc., into smaller communities. Generally, most people in such communities welcome the lower prices and wider array of goods that Wal-Mart offers relative to other, smaller stores in the area. A vocal minority of people in some communities, however, claim that smaller stores often find it impossible to compete with Wal-Mart's prices and thus are forced to go out of business. Many of these smaller stores have existed for years and, according to Wal-Mart's critics, enhance the quality of community life. These critics claim that it is unethical of Wal-Mart to disregard a town's interest in the quality and character of its community life.

In the past several years, beginning in Oklahoma, Wal-Mart has been consolidating some of its smaller stores into large "superstores." In the process of this consolidation, Wal-Mart is closing stores in some of the very towns in which it drove its smaller competitors out of business. This development raises yet another ethical question: Does a store such as Wal-Mart have an obligation to continue operations in a community once it has driven its competitors out of business?

Duty to Society

Perhaps the most disputed area in the controversy surrounding corporate social responsibility is the nature of a corporation's duty to society at large. Generally, the question turns less on whether corporations owe a duty to society than on how that duty can best be fulfilled.

3. Milton Friedman, "Does Business Have Social Responsibility?" *Bank Administration,* April 1971, pp. 13–14.

FOCUS ON ETHICS

Those who contend that corporations should first and foremost attend to the goal of profit maximization would argue that it is by generating profits that a firm can best contribute to society. Society benefits by profit-making activities, because profits can only be realized when a firm markets products or services that are desired by society. These products and services enhance the standard of living, and the profits accumulated by successful business firms generate national wealth. Our laws and court decisions promoting trade and commerce reflect the public policy that the fruits of commerce (wealth) are desirable and good. Because our society values wealth as an ethical goal, corporations, by contributing to that wealth, automatically are acting ethically.

Those arguing for profit maximization as a corporate goal also point out that it would be inappropriate to use the power of the corporate business world to fashion society's goals by promoting social causes. Determinations as to what exactly is in society's best interest involve questions that are essentially political, and therefore the public, through the political process, should have a say in making those determinations. The legislature—not the corporate board room—is thus the appropriate forum for such decisions.

Critics of the profit-maximization view believe that corporations should become actively engaged in seeking and furthering solutions to social problems. Because so much of the wealth and power of this country is controlled by business, business in turn has a responsibility to society to use that wealth and power in socially beneficial ways. Corporations should therefore promote human rights, strive for equal treatment of minorities and women in the workplace, take care to preserve the environment, and generally not profit from activities that society has deemed unethical. The critics also point out that it is ethically irresponsible to leave decisions concerning social welfare up to the government, because many social needs are not being met sufficiently through the political process.

It Pays to Be Ethical

Most corporations today have learned that it pays to be ethically responsible—even if it means less profit in the short run (and it often does). Today's corporations are subject to more intensive scrutiny—by both government agencies and the public—than corporations of the past. If a corporation fails to conduct its operations ethically or to respond quickly to an ethical crisis, its goodwill and reputation (and thus future profits) will likely suffer as a result.

There are other reasons as well for a corporation to behave ethically. As mentioned earlier in this *Focus,* companies that demonstrate a commitment to ethical behavior—by implementing ethical programs, complying with environmental regulations, and promptly investigating product complaints, for example—often receive more lenient treatment from government agencies and the courts.

Additionally, investors may shy away from a corporation's stock if the corporation is perceived to be socially irresponsible. Since the 1970s, certain investment funds have guaranteed to the purchasers of their shares that they will invest only in companies that are ethical. For example, some funds invest money only in corporations that are "environmentally kind."

DISCUSSION QUESTIONS

1. What might be some other deterrents to ethical behavior in the business context, besides those discussed in this *Focus*?
2. Can you think of a situation in which a business firm may be acting ethically but not in a socially responsible manner? Explain.
3. Why are consumers and the public generally more concerned with ethical and socially responsible business behavior today than they were, say, fifty years ago?
4. Discuss some of the ethical implications of differing perceptions of social responsibility among countries for American firms that do business abroad.
5. Suppose that an automobile manufacturing company has to choose between two alternatives: contributing $1 million annually to United Way or reinvesting the $1 million in the company. In terms of ethics and social responsibility, which is the better choice?

UNIT TWO

THE PUBLIC AND INTERNATIONAL ENVIRONMENT

CONTENTS

Chapter 5

Constitutional Law

The U.S. Constitution is the supreme law in this country.[1] As mentioned in Chapter 1, neither Congress nor any state may pass a law that conflicts with the Constitution. Laws that govern business have their origin in the lawmaking authority granted by this document.

Before the Constitution was written, a *confederal* form of government existed. The Articles of Confederation, which went into effect in 1781, established a confederation of independent states and a central government of very limited powers. The central government could handle only those matters of common concern expressly delegated to it by the member states, and the national congress had no authority to make laws directly applicable to individuals unless the member states explicitly supported such laws. In short, the *sovereign power*[2] to govern rested essentially with the states. The Articles of Confederation clearly reflected the central tenet of the American Revolution—that a national government should not have unlimited power.

After the Revolutionary War, however, the states began to pass laws that hampered national commerce and foreign trade by preventing the free movement of goods and services. Consequently, in 1787, the Constitutional Convention convened to **amend** (change, alter) the Articles of Confederation. Instead, the Convention created the Constitution and a completely new type of federal government, which it believed was much better equipped than its predecessor to resolve the problems of the nation.

1. See Appendix B for the full text of the U.S. Constitution.
2. *Sovereign power* refers to that supreme power to which no other authority is superior or equal.

SECTION 1

THE CONSTITUTIONAL POWERS OF GOVERNMENT

The U.S. Constitution established a federal form of government. A **federal form of government** is one in which the states form a union and the sovereign power is divided between a central governing authority and the member states. The Constitution delegates certain powers to the national government, and the states retain all other powers. The relationship between the national government and the state governments is a partnership—neither partner is superior to the other except within the particular area of exclusive authority granted to it under the Constitution.

To prevent the possibility that the national government might use its power arbitrarily, the Constitution provided for three branches of government. The legislative branch makes the laws, the executive branch enforces the laws, and the judicial branch interprets the laws. Each branch performs a separate function, and no branch may exercise the authority of another branch.

Each branch, however, has some power to limit the actions of the other two branches. Congress, for example, can enact legislation relating to spending and commerce, but the president can veto that legislation. The executive branch is responsible for foreign affairs, but treaties with foreign governments require the advice and consent of members of the Senate. Although Congress determines the jurisdiction of the federal courts, the federal courts have the power to hold acts of the other branches of the federal government unconstitutional.[3] Thus, with this system of **checks and balances,** no one branch of government can accumulate too much power.

THE COMMERCE CLAUSE

Article I, Section 8, of the U.S. Constitution expressly permits Congress "[t]o regulate Commerce with foreign Nations, and among the several States, and with the Indian Tribes." This clause, referred to as the **commerce clause,** has had a greater impact on business than any other provision in the Constitution. This power was delegated to the federal government to ensure the uniformity of rules governing the movement of goods through the states.

For some time, the commerce power was interpreted as being limited to *inter*state commerce (commerce among the states) and not applicable to *intra*state commerce (commerce within the states). In 1824, however, in *Gibbons v. Ogden*,[4] the United States Supreme Court held that commerce within states could also be regulated by the national government as long as the commerce concerned more than one state.

THE BREADTH OF THE COMMERCE CLAUSE

As a result of the Supreme Court's interpretation of the commerce clause in *Gibbons v. Ogden,* the national government exercised increasing authority over all areas of economic affairs throughout the land. In a 1942 case,[5] for example, the Court held that wheat production by an individual farmer intended wholly for consumption on his own farm was subject to federal regulation. The Court reasoned that the home consumption of wheat reduced the demand for wheat and thus could have a substantial effect on interstate commerce. In *McLain v. Real Estate Board of New Orleans, Inc.*,[6] a 1980 case, the Supreme Court acknowledged that the commerce clause had "long been interpreted to extend beyond activities actually in interstate commerce to reach other activities, while wholly local in nature, which nevertheless substantially affect interstate commerce."

Today, at least theoretically, the power over commerce authorizes the national government to regulate every commercial enterprise in the United States. The breadth of the commerce clause permits the national government to legislate in areas in which there is no explicit grant of power to Congress. Only once in the last sixty years has the Supreme Court held that there was a limit to the reach of the commerce clause. In *United States v. Lopez*,[7] a case decided in 1995, the Supreme Court held that Congress had exceeded its constitutional authority when it passed the Gun-Free School Zones Act in 1990. The Court stated that the act, which banned the possession of guns within one thousand feet of any school, was unconstitutional because it attempted to regulate an area that had "nothing to do with commerce, or any sort of economic enterprise."

---

3. As discussed in Chapter 3, the power of judicial review was established by the United States Supreme Court in *Marbury v. Madison*, 5 U.S. (1 Cranch) 137, 2 L.Ed. 60 (1803).

4. 22 U.S. (9 Wheat.) 1, 6 L.Ed. 23 (1824).

5. See *Wickard v. Filburn*, 317 U.S. 111, 63 S.Ct. 82, 87 L.Ed. 122 (1942).

6. 444 U.S. 232, 100 S.Ct. 502, 62 L.Ed.2d 441 (1980).

7. 514 U.S. 549, 115 S.Ct. 1624, 131 L.Ed.2d 626 (1995).

The decision in the *Lopez* case was a close one (four of the nine justices dissented), and the implications of the decision are as yet unclear. It is notable that just a few days after the *Lopez* case was decided, the Supreme Court again declared that what appeared (to many) to be fundamentally local activities carried on by a gold miner in Alaska sufficiently affected interstate commerce to be subject to a federal statute.[8]

THE REGULATORY POWERS OF THE STATES A problem that frequently arises under the commerce clause concerns a state's ability to regulate matters within its own borders. The U.S. Constitution does not expressly exclude state regulation of commerce, and there is no doubt that states have a strong interest in regulating activities within their borders. As part of their inherent sovereignty, states possess **police powers.** The term does not relate solely to criminal law enforcement but rather refers to the broad right of state governments to regulate private activities to protect or promote the public order, health, safety, morals, and general welfare. Fire and building codes, antidiscrimination laws, parking regulations, zoning restrictions, licensing requirements, and thousands of other state statutes covering virtually every aspect of life have been enacted pursuant to states' police powers.

When state regulations impinge on interstate commerce, courts must balance the state's interest in the merits and purposes of the regulations against the burden placed by the regulations on interstate commerce. Generally, state laws enacted pursuant to a state's police powers carry a strong presumption of validity. If state laws substantially interfere with interstate commerce, however, they will be held to violate the commerce clause of the Constitution.

In *Raymond Motor Transportation, Inc. v. Rice*,[9] for example, the United States Supreme Court invalidated Wisconsin administrative regulations limiting the length of trucks traveling on the state's highways. The Court weighed the burden on interstate commerce against the benefits of the regulations and concluded that the challenged regulations "place a substantial burden on interstate commerce and they cannot be said to make more than the most speculative contribution to highway safety."

Because courts balance the interests involved, it is extremely difficult to predict the outcome in a particular case. The following case concerns an issue that has elicited much controversy in the last decade: whether states have the power to discriminate against shipments of out-of-state waste to intrastate disposal facilities.

8. *United States v. Robertson*, 514 U.S. 669, 115 S.Ct. 1732, 131 L.Ed.2d 714 (1995).

9. 434 U.S. 429, 98 S.Ct. 787, 54 L.Ed.2d 664 (1978).

CASE 5.1 Oregon Waste Systems, Inc. v. Department of Environmental Quality of the State of Oregon

Supreme Court of the United States, 1994. 511 U.S. 93, 114 S.Ct. 1345, 128 L.Ed.2d 13.

BACKGROUND AND FACTS *Oregon Waste Systems, Inc., operates a waste-disposal facility in Gilliam County, Oregon. The facility receives waste from sources in Oregon and from sources outside the state. In 1989, Oregon imposed a fee ($.85 per ton) on all of the solid waste that such facilities receive from sources in Oregon and imposed a higher fee ($2.25 per ton) on solid waste generated outside the state. Oregon Waste, other operators of waste-disposal facilities in Oregon, and Gilliam County filed a suit against the state in an Oregon court, challenging the higher fee as a violation of, among other things, the commerce clause. The court upheld the higher fee, and the plaintiffs appealed. The Oregon Supreme Court affirmed the ruling. The plaintiffs appealed to the United States Supreme Court.*

IN THE LANGUAGE OF THE COURT

Justice *THOMAS* delivered the opinion of the Court.

* * * *

* * * [T]he first step in analyzing any law subject to judicial scrutiny under the * * * Commerce Clause is to determine whether it "regulates evenhandedly

with only 'incidental' effects on interstate commerce, or discriminates against interstate commerce." * * *

* * * Oregon's $2.25 per ton surcharge is discriminatory on its face. The surcharge subjects waste from other States to a fee almost three times greater than the $0.85 per ton charge imposed on solid in-state waste. * * *

* * * *

Respondents' principal defense of the higher surcharge on out-of-state waste is that it is a "compensatory tax" necessary to make shippers of such waste pay their "fair share" of the costs imposed on Oregon by the disposal of their waste in the State. * * *

* * * *

* * * [W]e have little difficulty concluding that the Oregon surcharge is not such a tax. * * * Respondents' failure to identify a specific charge on intrastate commerce equal to or exceeding the surcharge is fatal to their claim.

Respondents argue that * * * intrastate commerce does pay its share of the costs underlying the surcharge through general taxation. * * *

* * * [T]he very fact that in-state shippers of out-of-state waste, such as Oregon Waste, are charged the out-of-state surcharge even though they pay Oregon income taxes refutes respondents' argument * * * .

DECISION AND REMEDY *The United States Supreme Court reversed the judgment of the Oregon Supreme Court and remanded the case.*

THE SUPREMACY CLAUSE

Article VI of the Constitution provides that the Constitution, laws, and treaties of the United States are "the supreme Law of the Land." This article, commonly referred to as the **supremacy clause,** is important in the ordering of state and federal relationships. When there is a direct conflict between a federal law and a state law, the state law is rendered invalid. Because some powers are *concurrent* (shared by the federal government and the states), however, it is necessary to determine which law governs in a particular circumstance.

Preemption occurs when Congress chooses to act exclusively in a concurrent area. In this circumstance, a valid federal statute or regulation will take precedence over a conflicting state or local law or regulation on the same general subject. Congress, however, rarely makes clear its intent to preempt an entire subject area against state regulation; consequently, the courts must determine whether Congress intended to exercise exclusive dominion over a given area.

No single factor is decisive as to whether a court will find preemption. Generally, congressional intent to preempt will be found if the federal law is so pervasive, comprehensive, or detailed that the states have no room to supplement it. Also, when a federal statute creates an agency (such as the Federal Aviation Administration) to enforce the law, the agency's decisions on matters that may come within its jurisdiction will likely preempt state laws.

THE TAXING AND SPENDING POWERS

Article I, Section 8, provides that Congress has the "Power to lay and collect Taxes, Duties, Imposts, and Excises." Section 8 further provides that "all Duties, Imposts and Excises shall be uniform throughout the United States." The requirement of uniformity refers to uniformity among the states, and thus Congress may not tax some states while exempting others.

Traditionally, if Congress attempted to regulate indirectly, by taxation, an area over which it had no authority, the tax would be invalidated by the courts. Today, however, if a tax measure bears some reasonable relationship to revenue production, it is generally held to be within the national taxing power. Moreover, the expansive interpretation of the commerce clause almost always provides a basis for sustaining a federal tax.

Under Article I, Section 8, Congress has the power "to pay the Debts and provide for the common Defence and general Welfare of the United States." Through the spending power, Congress disposes of the revenues accumulated from the taxing power. Congress can spend revenues not only to carry out its enumerated powers but also to promote any objective it deems worthwhile, so long as it does not violate the Bill of Rights. For example, Congress could not condition welfare payments on the recipients' agreement not to criticize government policies. The spending power necessarily involves policy choices, with which taxpayers may disagree.

SECTION 2

BUSINESS AND THE BILL OF RIGHTS

The importance of a written declaration of the rights of individuals eventually caused the first Congress of the United States to submit twelve amendments to the Constitution to the states for approval. The first ten of these amendments, commonly known as the **Bill of Rights,** were adopted in 1791 and embody a series of protections for the individual against various types of interference by the federal government.[10] Some constitutional protections apply to business entities as well. For example, corporations exist as separate legal entities, or *legal persons,* and enjoy many of the same rights and privileges as *natural persons* do.

10. Another of these proposed amendments was ratified 203 years later (in 1992) and became the Twenty-seventh Amendment to the Constitution. See Appendix B.

Summarized in Exhibit 5–1 are the protections guaranteed by these ten amendments.[11] The due process clause of the Fourteenth Amendment, which we discuss later in this chapter, applies many of the rights guaranteed by these first ten amendments to the states. In other words, neither the federal government nor state governments can deprive individuals of those rights.

The rights secured by the Bill of Rights are not absolute. As you can see in the exhibit, many of the rights guaranteed by the first ten amendments are described in very general terms. For example, the Fourth Amendment prohibits unreasonable searches and seizures, but it does not define what constitutes an *unreasonable* search or seizure. Similarly, the Eighth Amendment prohibits excessive bail or fines, but no definition of *excessive* is contained in that amendment. Ultimately, it is the United States Supreme Court, as the final interpreter of the Constitution, that defines our rights and determines their boundaries.

FREEDOM OF SPEECH

A democratic form of government cannot survive unless people can freely voice their political opinions and criticize government actions or policies. Freedom

11. See the Constitution in Appendix B for the complete text of each amendment.

EXHIBIT 5–1 ■ PROTECTIONS GUARANTEED BY THE BILL OF RIGHTS

First Amendment: guarantees the freedoms of religion, speech, and the press and the rights to assemble peaceably and to petition the government.	**Sixth Amendment:** guarantees the accused in a criminal case the right to a speedy and public trial by an impartial jury and with counsel. The accused has the right to cross-examine witnesses against him or her and to solicit testimony from witnesses in his or her favor.
Second Amendment: guarantees the right to keep and bear arms.	
Third Amendment: prohibits, in peacetime, the lodging of soldiers in any house without the owner's consent.	**Seventh Amendment:** guarantees the right to a trial by jury in a civil case involving at least twenty dollars.[a]
Fourth Amendment: prohibits unreasonable searches and seizures of persons or property.	**Eighth Amendment:** prohibits excessive bail and fines, as well as cruel and unusual punishment.
Fifth Amendment: guarantees the rights to indictment by grand jury, to due process of law, and to fair payment when private property is taken for public use. The Fifth Amendment also prohibits compulsory self-incrimination and double jeopardy (trial for the same crime twice if the first trial ends in acquittal or conviction).	**Ninth Amendment:** establishes that the people have rights in addition to those specified in the Constitution. **Tenth Amendment:** establishes that those powers neither delegated to the federal government nor denied to the states are reserved for the states.

a. Twenty dollars was forty days' pay for the average person when the Bill of Rights was written.

of speech, particularly political speech, is thus a prized right, and traditionally the courts have protected this right to the fullest extent possible.

Symbolic speech—gestures, movements, articles of clothing, and other forms of expressive conduct—is also given substantial protection by the courts. For example, in a 1989 case, *Texas v. Johnson*,[12] the United States Supreme Court ruled that state laws that prohibited the burning of the American flag as part of a peaceful protest also violated the freedom of expression protected by the First Amendment. Congress responded by passing the Flag Protection Act of 1989, which was ruled unconstitutional by the Supreme Court in 1990.[13] Congress and George Bush, who was then president, pledged immediately to work for a constitutional amendment to "protect our flag"—an effort that has yet to be successful. In a subsequent case, the Supreme Court ruled that a city statute banning bias-motivated disorderly conduct (including, in this case, the placing of a burning cross in another's front yard as a gesture of hate) was an unconstitutional restriction of speech.[14]

Governments can and do place restraints on free speech, of course, but such restraints are permissible only when they are necessary to protect other substantial interests and rights. It is up to the courts—and ultimately, the United States Supreme Court—to determine the point at which laws restricting free speech can be justified by the need to protect other rights. In the following case, the court had to decide whether the state's interest in providing information to voters and protecting against fraud justified a state law banning the distribution of anonymous political leaflets.

12. 491 U.S. 397, 109 S.Ct. 2533, 105 L.Ed.2d 342 (1989).
13. *United States v. Eichman*, 496 U.S. 310 , 110 S.Ct. 2804, 110 L.Ed.2d 287 (1990).
14. *R.A.V. v. City of St. Paul, Minnesota*, 505 U.S. 377, 112 S.Ct. 2538, 120 L.Ed.2d 305 (1992).

CASE 5.2 McIntyre v. Ohio Elections Commission

Supreme Court of the United States, 1995.
514 U.S. 334,
115 S.Ct. 1511,
131 L.Ed.2d 426.

HISTORICAL AND POLITICAL SETTING *Anonymous pamphlets, leaflets, brochures, and books have played an important role in the political life of the United States. Perhaps the most famous embodiment of this tradition is* The Federalist Papers, *a series of essays published in New York City newspapers in 1787 and 1788. Writing under the name "Publius," James Madison, Alexander Hamilton, and John Jay argued in* The Federalist Papers *for the ratification of the Constitution.*

BACKGROUND AND FACTS *In April 1988, Margaret McIntyre distributed leaflets to persons attending public meetings at the Blendon Middle School in Westerville, Ohio. The leaflets expressed opposition to a proposed school tax. Some of the leaflets did not identify an author but only purported to express the views of "CONCERNED PARENTS AND TAX PAYERS." A school official filed a complaint with the Ohio Elections Commission under a state statute that prohibits the distribution of campaign literature that does not contain the name and address of the person or official issuing it. The commission imposed a fine of $100. McIntyre appealed to an Ohio state court, arguing that the statute was unconstitutional. The court agreed and dropped the fine. An Ohio appellate court reinstated the fine, and the Ohio Supreme Court affirmed. The state supreme court concluded that the statute was reasonable in light of the state's interests in providing voters with information and in preventing fraud. McIntyre appealed to the United States Supreme Court.*

IN THE LANGUAGE OF THE COURT

Justice *STEVENS* delivered the opinion of the Court.

* * * *

* * * [A]n author's decision to remain anonymous, like other decisions concerning omissions or additions to the content of a publication, is an aspect of the freedom of speech protected by the First Amendment.

* * * *

* * * [T]he speech in which Mrs. McIntyre engaged—handing out leaflets in the advocacy of a politically controversial viewpoint—is the essence of First Amendment expression. * * *

When a law burdens * * * political speech, we * * * uphold the restriction only if it is narrowly tailored to serve an overriding state interest.

* * * *

* * * The simple interest in providing voters with * * * information does not justify a state requirement that a writer make statements or disclosures she would otherwise omit. Moreover, in the case of a handbill written by a private citizen who is not known to the recipient, the name and address of the author adds little, if anything, to the reader's ability to evaluate the document's message. * * *

The state interest in preventing fraud and libel stands on a different footing. * * * Ohio does not, however, rely solely on [this statute] to protect that interest. Its Election Code includes detailed and specific prohibitions against making or disseminating false statements during political campaigns. * * *

As this case demonstrates, the prohibition encompasses documents that are not even arguably false or misleading. * * * We recognize that a State's enforcement interest might justify a more limited identification requirement, but Ohio has shown scant cause for inhibiting the leafletting at issue here.

DECISION AND REMEDY *The United States Supreme Court reversed the decision of the lower court, holding that the First Amendment protects the freedom to publish anonymously.*

COMMERCIAL SPEECH A distinction is often made between "normal" speech and "commercial" speech, which is speech by business firms, usually called advertising.

Although commercial speech is protected by the First Amendment, it is not protected as extensively as noncommercial speech. A state may restrict certain kinds of advertising, for example, in the interest of protecting consumers from being misled by the advertising practices. States also have a legitimate interest in the beautification of roadsides, and this interest allows states to place restraints on billboard advertising. Generally, a restriction on commercial speech will be considered valid as long as it meets the following three criteria: (1) it must seek to implement a substantial government interest, (2) it must directly advance that interest, and (3) it must go no further than necessary to accomplish its objective.

Certain types of restrictions on commercial advertising may implement one substantial government interest but be contrary to another government interest. In such cases, the courts have to decide which interest takes priority. Liquor advertising is a good example of this kind of conflict, as illustrated by the following case.

CASE 5.3 Rubin v. Coors Brewing Co.

Supreme Court of the United States, 1995. 514 U.S. 476, 115 S.Ct. 1585, 131 L.Ed.2d 532.

HISTORICAL AND SOCIAL SETTING *In the United States, no federal law regulates the level of alcohol in beer. The most popular beers contain between 3 and 5 percent alcohol. Ice beers typically contain between 5 and 6 percent alcohol, and malt liquors may contain as much as 7 percent. Beer is a popular drink among young consumers, who sometimes prefer the more potent brands. In the 1980s, it was widely—and erroneously—believed that beer brewed by the Coors Brewing Company was less potent than other beers.*

BACKGROUND AND FACTS *In 1987, Coors applied to the Bureau of Alcohol, Tobacco and Firearms (BATF), an agency of the Department of the Treasury, for* *approval of proposed Coors beer labels that disclosed the alcohol content of the beer. The BATF rejected the labels on the ground that the Federal Alcohol Administration Act (FAAA) of 1935[a] prohibits the disclosure of the alcohol content of beer on labels. Coors filed a suit in a federal district court against the government to block the enforcement of the FAAA, on the ground that it violated the First Amendment. The government argued that enforcement of the FAAA suppresses the threat of "strength wars" among brewers, who, without the regulation, would compete in the marketplace based on the potency of their products. The district court granted Coors relief, and the government appealed. When the appellate court affirmed, the government appealed to the United States Supreme Court.*

IN THE LANGUAGE OF THE COURT

Justice *THOMAS* delivered the opinion of the Court.

* * * *

* * * [T]he Government * * * has a significant interest in protecting the health, safety, and welfare of its citizens by preventing brewers from competing on the basis of alcohol strength, which could lead to greater alcoholism and its attendant social costs. * * *

* * * *

We conclude that [the FAAA] cannot directly and materially advance [this] interest * * * . [T]he laws governing labeling * * * prohibit statements of alcohol content in advertising * * * only in States that affirmatively prohibit such advertisements. As only 18 States at best prohibit disclosure of content in advertisements, brewers remain free to disclose alcohol content in advertisements, but not on labels, in much of the country. * * *

* * * While [the FAAA] bans the disclosure of alcohol content on beer labels, it allows the exact opposite in the case of wines and spirits. * * * Further, the Government permits brewers to signal high alcohol content through use of the term "malt liquor." * * *

* * * *

[Finally] the Government's regulation of speech is not sufficiently tailored to its goal. * * * [Coors] suggests several alternatives, such as directly limiting the alcohol content of beers, prohibiting marketing efforts emphasizing high alcohol strength * * * , or limiting the labeling ban only to malt liquors * * * . We agree that the availability of these options, all of which could advance the Government's asserted interest in a manner less intrusive to [Coors's] First Amendment rights, indicates that [the FAAA] is more extensive than necessary.

DECISION AND REMEDY

The Supreme Court held that the FAAA's labeling ban violated the First Amendment's protection of commercial speech.

a. 27 U.S.C. Sections 201–220.

CORPORATE POLITICAL SPEECH Political speech that otherwise would fall within the protection of the First Amendment does not lose that protection simply because its source is a corporation. For example, in *First National Bank of Boston v. Bellotti*,[15] national banking associations and business corporations sought United States Supreme Court review of a Massachusetts statute that prohibited corporations from making political contributions or expenditures that individuals were permitted to make. The Court ruled that the Massachusetts law was unconstitutional because it violated the right of corporations to freedom of speech. Similarly, the Court has held that a law forbidding a corporation from using bill inserts to express its views on

15. 435 U.S. 765, 98 S.Ct. 1407, 55 L.Ed.2d 707 (1978).

controversial issues violates the First Amendment.[16] Although in 1990 a more conservative Supreme Court reversed this trend somewhat,[17] corporate political speech continues to be given significant protection under the First Amendment.

UNPROTECTED SPEECH The United States Supreme Court has made it clear that certain types of speech will not be protected under the First Amendment. Speech that harms the good reputation of another, or defamatory speech (see Chapter 12), is not protected under the First Amendment. Speech that violates criminal laws (threatening speech, pornography, and so on) is not constitutionally protected. Other unprotected speech includes "fighting words" (speech that is likely to incite others to respond violently). Many people think that the "hate speech" exchanged between members of different groups on college campuses should be included in the category of "fighting words." Courts, however, have been reluctant to uphold university codes banning hate speech, concluding that the codes go too far in restricting the free speech of students.[18]

Another category of unprotected speech is obscene speech. Numerous state and federal statutes make it a crime to disseminate obscene materials. The United States Supreme Court has grappled from time to time with the problem of trying to establish an operationally effective definition of obscene speech. Frequently, this determination is left to state and local authorities, who generally base their definitions of obscenity on community standards. Generally, obscenity is still a constitutionally unsettled area. In the interest of protecting against the abuse of children, however, the Supreme Court has upheld state laws prohibiting the sale and possession of child pornography.[19] In the interest of protecting women against sexual harassment in the workplace, at least one court has banned lewd speech and pornographic pinups in the workplace.[20]

In recent years, obscenity issues have also arisen in relation to television shows, movies, the lyrics and covers of music albums, and the content of monologues by "shock" comedians. As will be discussed later in this chapter, a challenging legal issue today is how to regulate the availability of obscene materials on the Internet.

FREEDOM OF RELIGION

The First Amendment states that the government may neither establish any religion nor prohibit the free exercise of religious practices. The first part of this constitutional provision is referred to as the **establishment clause,** which has to do with the separation of church and state. The second part of the provision is known as the **free exercise clause.**

THE SEPARATION OF CHURCH AND STATE The establishment clause prohibits the government from establishing a state-sponsored religion, as well as from passing laws that promote (aid or endorse) religion or that show a preference for one religion over another. Establishment clause issues often involve such matters as the legality of allowing or requiring school prayers, the teaching of evolutionary versus creationist theory, and state and local government aid to religious organizations and schools.

Federal or state laws that do not promote or place a significant burden on religion are constitutional even if they have some impact on religion. "Sunday closing laws," for example, make the performance of some commercial activities on Sunday illegal. These statutes, also known as "blue laws" (from the color of the paper on which an early Sunday law was written), have been upheld on the ground that it is a legitimate function of government to provide a day of rest. The United States Supreme Court has held that the closing laws, although originally of a religious character, have taken on the secular purpose of promoting the health and welfare of workers.[21] Even though closing laws admittedly make it easier for Christians to attend religious services, the Court has viewed this effect as an incidental, not a primary, purpose of Sunday closing laws.

---

16. *Consolidated Edison Co. v. Public Service Commission,* 447 U.S. 530, 100 S.Ct. 2326, 65 L.Ed.2d 319 (1980).

17. See *Austin v. Michigan Chamber of Commerce,* 494 U.S. 652, 110 S.Ct. 1391, 108 L.Ed.2d 652 (1990), in which the Court upheld a state law prohibiting corporations from using general corporate funds for independent expenditures in state political campaigns.

18. See, for example, *Doe v. University of Michigan,* 721 F.Supp. 852 (1989); and *The UWM Post v. Board of Regents of the University of Wisconsin System,* 774 F.Supp. 1163 (E.D.Wis. 1991).

19. See *Osborne v. Ohio,* 495 U.S. 103, 110 S.Ct. 1691, 109 L.Ed.2d 98 (1990).

20. *Robinson v. Jacksonville Shipyards, Inc.,* 760 F.Supp. 1486 (M.D.Fla. 1991).

21. *McGowan v. Maryland,* 366 U.S. 420, 81 S.Ct. 1101, 6 L.Ed.2d 393 (1961).

The First Amendment does not require a complete separation of church and state. On the contrary, it affirmatively mandates *accommodation* of all religions and forbids hostility toward any.[22] An ongoing challenge for the courts is determining the extent to which governments can accommodate a religion without appearing to promote that religion, which would violate the establishment clause. For example, in *Lynch v. Donnelly*,[23] the United States Supreme Court held that a municipality could include religious symbols, such as a Nativity scene, or crèche, in its annual holiday display as long as the religious symbols constituted just one part of a display in which other, nonreligious symbols (such as reindeer and candy-striped poles) were also featured. The Court has applied this same reasoning in subsequent cases and continues to face such issues.[24]

THE FREE EXERCISE OF RELIGION The free exercise clause guarantees that no person can be compelled to do something that is contrary to his or her religious beliefs. For this reason, if a law or policy is contrary to a person's religious beliefs, exemptions are often made to accommodate those beliefs. When, however, religious practices work against public policy and the public welfare, the government can act. For example, children of Jehovah's Witnesses are not required to say the Pledge of Allegiance at school, but their parents cannot prevent these children from accepting medical treatment (such as blood transfusions) if the children's lives are in danger.

Generally, any laws that infringe in any way on the free exercise of religion in public places must be justified by a *compelling state interest*. This standard was affirmed legislatively with the passage of the Religious Freedom Restoration Act of 1993. In that same year, the Supreme Court held that even animal sacrifices cannot be banned by a municipality if those sacrifices are part of established religious practices.[25] Note that to qualify for First Amendment protection, there must be some demonstrable relationship between the practice at issue and religion. In one case, for example, a criminal defendant convicted of illegal drug use and distribution argued that he was the founder of the "Church of Marijuana" and, as such, was commanded by his religion to use, possess, and distribute drugs "for the benefit of mankind and planet earth." A federal appellate court held that the "Church of Marijuana" did not satisfy the requirements for a "religion."[26] Note that in 1997, the Supreme Court ruled that the Religious Freedom Restoration Act was unconstitutional.

For business firms, an important issue involves the accommodation that businesses must make for the religious beliefs of their employees. For example, if an employee's religion prohibits him or her from working on a certain day of the week or at a certain type of job, the employer must make a reasonable attempt to accommodate these religious requirements. Employers must reasonably accommodate an employee's religious belief even if the belief is not based on the tenets or dogma of a particular church, sect, or denomination. The only requirement is that the belief be religious in nature and sincerely held by the employee.[27] (See Chapter 20 for a further discussion of religious freedom in the employment context.)

SELF-INCRIMINATION

The Fifth Amendment guarantees that no person "shall be compelled in any criminal case to be a witness against himself." Thus, in any federal proceeding, an accused person cannot be compelled to give testimony that might subject him or her to any criminal prosecution. Nor can an accused person be forced to testify against himself or herself in state courts, because the due process clause of the Fourteenth Amendment (discussed later in this chapter) incorporates the Fifth Amendment provision against self-incrimination.

The Fifth Amendment's guarantee against self-incrimination extends only to natural persons. Because a corporation is a legal entity and not a natural person, the privilege against self-incrimination does not apply to it. Similarly, the business records of a partnership do not receive Fifth Amendment

22. *Zorach v. Clauson*, 343 U.S. 306, 72 S.Ct. 679, 96 L.Ed. 954 (1952).

23. 465 U.S. 668, 104 S.Ct. 1355, 79 L.Ed.2d 604 (1984).

24. See, for example, *County of Allegheny v. American Civil Liberties Union*, 492 U.S. 573, 109 S.Ct. 3086, 106 L.Ed.2d 472 (1989); and *Capitol Square Review and Advisory Board v. Pinette*, 515 U.S. 753, 115 S.Ct. 2440, 132 L.Ed.2d 650 (1995).

25. *Church of Lukumi Babalu Aye v. Hialeah*, 508 U.S. 520, 113 S.Ct. 2217, 124 L.Ed.2d 472 (1993).

26. *United States v. Meyers*, 95 F.3d 1475 (10th Cir. 1996).

27. *Frazee v. Illinois Department of Employment Security*, 489 U.S. 829, 109 S.Ct. 1514, 103 L.Ed.2d 914 (1989).

protection.[28] When a partnership is required to produce these records, it must give the information even if it incriminates the persons who constitute the business entity. In contrast, sole proprietors and sole practitioners (those who fully own their businesses) who have not incorporated cannot be compelled to produce their business records. These individuals have full protection against self-incrimination, because they function in only one capacity; there is no separate business entity.

SEARCHES AND SEIZURES

The Fourth Amendment protects the "right of the people to be secure in their persons, houses, papers, and effects." Before searching or seizing private property, law enforcement officers must obtain a **search warrant**—an order from a judge or other public official authorizing the search or seizure.

SEARCH WARRANTS AND PROBABLE CAUSE

To obtain a search warrant, the officers must convince a judge that they have reasonable grounds, or probable cause, to believe a search will reveal a specific illegality. **Probable cause** requires law enforcement officials to have trustworthy evidence that would convince a reasonable person that the proposed search or seizure is more likely justified than not. Furthermore, the Fourth Amendment prohibits *general* warrants. It requires a particular description of that which is to be searched or seized. General searches through a person's belongings are impermissible. The search cannot extend beyond what is described in the warrant.

There are exceptions to the requirement for a search warrant, as when it is likely that the items sought will be removed before a warrant can be obtained. For example, if a police officer has probable cause to believe an automobile contains evidence of a crime and it is likely that the vehicle will be unavailable by the time a warrant is obtained, the officer can search the vehicle without a warrant.

SEARCHES AND SEIZURES IN THE BUSINESS CONTEXT Constitutional protection against unreasonable searches and seizures is important to businesses and professionals. As federal and state regulation of commercial activities increased, frequent and unannounced government inspections were conducted to ensure compliance with the regulations. Such inspections were at times extremely disruptive. In *Marshall v. Barlow's, Inc.*,[29] the United States Supreme Court held that government inspectors do not have the right to enter business premises without a warrant, although the standard of probable cause is not the same as that required in nonbusiness contexts. The existence of a general and neutral enforcement plan will justify issuance of the warrant.

Lawyers and accountants frequently possess the business records of their clients, and inspecting these documents while they are out of the hands of their true owners also requires a warrant. A warrant is not required, however, for the seizure of spoiled or contaminated food. In addition, warrants are also not required for searches of businesses in such highly regulated industries as liquor, guns, and strip mining. General manufacturing is not considered to be one of these highly regulated industries, however.

Of increasing concern to many government employers is how to maintain a safe and efficient workplace without jeopardizing the Fourth Amendment rights of employees "to be secure in their persons." Requiring government employees to undergo random drug tests, for example, may be held to violate the Fourth Amendment. In Chapter 20, we discuss Fourth Amendment issues in the employment context, as well as employee privacy rights in general, in greater detail.

SECTION 3

OTHER CONSTITUTIONAL PROTECTIONS

Other constitutional guarantees of great significance to Americans are mandated by the *privileges and immunities clause* and the *full faith and credit clause* of Article IV of the Constitution, the *due process clauses* of the Fifth and Fourteenth Amendments, and the *equal protection clause* of the Fourteenth Amendment.

28. The privilege has been applied to some small family partnerships. See *United States v. Slutsky*, 352 F.Supp. 1005 (S.D.N.Y. 1972).

29. 436 U.S. 307, 98 S.Ct. 1816, 56 L.Ed.2d 305 (1978).

THE PRIVILEGES AND IMMUNITIES CLAUSE

Article IV, Section 2, of the Constitution provides that the "Citizens of each State shall be entitled to all Privileges and Immunities of Citizens in the several States." This clause is often referred to as the interstate **privileges and immunities clause.**[30] When a citizen of one state engages in basic and essential activities in another state (the "foreign state"), such as transferring property, seeking employment, or accessing the court system, the foreign state must have a *substantial reason* for treating the nonresident differently from its own residents. The foreign state must also establish that its reason for the discrimination is substantially related to the state's ultimate purpose in adopting the legislation or activity.[31]

Charging nonresidents $2,500 for a shrimp-fishing license, for example, while residents are charged only $25 for the same license, may be considered unconstitutional discrimination against nonresidents who are pursuing the essential activity of making a living.[32] Similarly, attempting to limit the practice of law to residents only (on the premise that it would help reduce the state's unemployment rate) may unconstitutionally restrict the nonresident's professional pursuit without substantial justification.[33]

The Fourteenth Amendment provides that "[n]o State shall make or enforce any law which shall abridge the privileges or immunities of citizens of the United States." This clause also protects all individuals, as citizens of the United States, from state action that might infringe on such privileges or immunities as the right to travel from state to state and the right to peaceably assemble.[34]

30. The terms *privilege* and *immunity* are commonly used synonymously with regard to the interpretation of this clause. Generally the terms refer to certain rights, benefits, or advantages enjoyed by individuals.

31. *Supreme Court of New Hampshire v. Piper,* 470 U.S. 274, 105 S.Ct. 1272, 84 L.Ed.2d 205 (1985).

32. *Toomer v. Witsell,* 334 U.S. 385, 68 S.Ct. 1156, 92 L.Ed. 1460 (1948).

33. *Hicklin v. Orbeck,* 437 U.S. 518, 98 S.Ct. 2482, 57 L.Ed.2d 397 (1978).

34. Unlike the due process and equal protection clauses (to be discussed shortly), the privileges and immunities clause of the Fourteenth Amendment does not apply to the individual rights found in the Bill of Rights.

THE FULL FAITH AND CREDIT CLAUSE

Article IV, Section 1, of the Constitution provides that "Full Faith and Credit shall be given in each State to the public Acts, Records, and judicial Proceedings of every other State." This clause, which is referred to as the **full faith and credit clause,** applies only to civil matters. It ensures that rights established under deeds, wills, contracts, and the like in one state will be honored by other states. It also ensures that any judicial decision with respect to such property rights will be honored and enforced in all states.

The full faith and credit clause originally was included in the Articles of Confederation to promote mutual friendship among the people of the various states. In fact, it has contributed to the unity of American citizens, because it protects their legal rights as they move about from state to state. It also protects the rights of those to whom they owe obligations, such as judgment creditors. This is extremely important for the conduct of business in a country with a very mobile citizenry.

DUE PROCESS

Both the Fifth and the Fourteenth Amendments provide that no person shall be deprived "of life, liberty, or property, without due process of law." The **due process clause** of these constitutional amendments has two aspects—procedural and substantive.

PROCEDURAL DUE PROCESS

Procedural due process requires that any government decision to take life, liberty, or property must be made fairly. For example, fair procedures must be used in determining whether a person will be subjected to punishment or have some burden imposed on him or her. Fair procedure has been interpreted as requiring that the person have at least an opportunity to object to a proposed action before a fair, neutral decision maker (which need not be a judge). Thus, for example, if a driver's license is construed as a property interest, some sort of opportunity to object to its suspension or termination by the state must be provided.

SUBSTANTIVE DUE PROCESS

Substantive due process focuses on the content, or substance, of legislation. If a law or other governmental action limits a *fundamental right,* it will be held to violate substantive due process unless it promotes a *compelling* or *overriding state interest.* Fundamental rights include interstate travel, privacy, voting, and all First Amendment rights. Compelling state interests could include, for example, the public's safety. Thus, laws designating speed limits may be upheld even though they affect interstate travel, if they are shown to reduce highway fatalities, because the state has a compelling interest in protecting the lives of its citizens.

In all other situations, a law or action does not violate substantive due process if it rationally relates to any legitimate government purpose. It is almost impossible for a law or action to fail this "rational basis" test. Under this test, virtually any business regulation will be upheld as reasonable—the United States Supreme Court has sustained insurance regulations, price and wage controls, banking controls, and controls of unfair competition and trade practices against substantive due process challenges.

Suppose that a state legislature enacted a law imposing a fifteen-year term of imprisonment without a trial on all businesspersons who appeared in their own television commercials. This law would be unconstitutional on both substantive and procedural grounds. Substantive review would invalidate the legislation because it abridges freedom of speech, a fundamental right. Procedurally, the law is constitutionally invalid because it imposes a penalty without giving the accused a chance to defend his or her actions.

EQUAL PROTECTION

Under the Fourteenth Amendment, a state may not "deny to any person within its jurisdiction the equal protection of the laws." The United States Supreme Court has used the due process clause of the Fifth Amendment to make the **equal protection clause** applicable to the federal government. Equal protection means that the government must treat similarly situated individuals in a similar manner.

Both substantive due process and equal protection require review of the substance of the law or other governmental action rather than review of the procedures used. When a law or action limits the liberty of all persons to do something, it may violate substantive due process; when a law or action limits the liberty of some persons but not others, it may violate the equal protection clause. Thus, for example, if a law prohibits all persons from buying contraceptive devices, it raises a substantive due process question; if it prohibits only unmarried persons from buying the same devices, it raises an equal protection issue.

In an equal protection inquiry, when a law or action distinguishes between or among individuals, the basis for the distinction—that is, the classification—is examined by the courts. The courts may use one of three standards: strict scrutiny, intermediate scrutiny, or the "rational basis" test.

STRICT SCRUTINY If a law or action prohibits or inhibits some persons from exercising a fundamental right, the law or action will be subject to "strict scrutiny" by the courts. Under this standard, the classification must be necessary to promote a *compelling state interest.* Also, if the classification is based on a *suspect trait*—such as race, national origin, or citizenship status—the classification must be necessary to promote a compelling state interest. Compelling state interests include remedying past unconstitutional or illegal discrimination but do not include correcting the general effects of "society's" discrimination. Thus, for example, if a city gives preference to minority applicants in awarding construction contracts, the city normally must identify the past unconstitutional or illegal discrimination against minority construction firms that it is attempting to correct. Generally, few laws or actions survive strict-scrutiny analysis by the courts.

INTERMEDIATE SCRUTINY Another standard, that of "intermediate scrutiny," is applied in cases involving discrimination based on gender or legitimacy. Laws using these classifications must be *substantially related to important government objectives.*

For example, an important government objective is preventing illegitimate teenage pregnancies. Therefore, because males and females are not similarly situated in this regard—only females can become pregnant—a law that punishes men but not women for statutory rape will be upheld, even though it treats men and women unequally. A state law requiring illegitimate children to bring paternity suits within six years of their births, however, will be struck down if legitimate children are allowed to seek support from their parents at any time. An important objective behind statutes of limitations is to prevent persons from bringing stale or fraudulent claims, but distinguishing between support claims on the basis of legitimacy has no relation to this objective.

THE "RATIONAL BASIS" TEST In matters of economic or social welfare, the classification will be considered valid if there is any conceivable *rational basis* on which the classification might relate to any legitimate government interest. It is almost impossible for a law or action to fail the rational basis test. Thus, for example, a city ordinance that in effect prohibits all pushcart vendors except a specific few from operating in a particular area of the city will be upheld if the city provides a rational basis—perhaps regulation and reduction of traffic in the particular area—for the ordinance. In contrast, a law that provides unemployment benefits only to people over six feet tall would violate the guarantee of equal protection. There is no rational basis for determining the distribution of unemployment compensation on the basis of height. Such a distinction could not further any legitimate government objective.

PRIVACY RIGHTS

A personal right to privacy is held to be so fundamental as to be applicable at both the state and the federal level. Although there is no specific guarantee of a right to privacy in the Constitution, such a right has been derived from guarantees found in the First, Third, Fourth, Fifth, and Ninth Amendments. Invasion of another's privacy is also a tort, or civil wrong (see Chapter 12), and over the last several decades legislation has been passed at the federal level to protect the privacy of individuals in several areas of concern.

Privacy rights often relate to emotionally charged issues, such as abortion, assisted suicide for terminally ill people, and gay and lesbian relationships. In the business world, issues of privacy often arise in the employment context, a topic we examine in Chapter 20.

SECTION 4
CONSTITUTIONAL LAW IN CYBERSPACE

The growing use of the Internet for both personal and business communications has created new legal challenges in virtually every area of the law, including many of the areas discussed in this text. In the *Emerging Trends* in Chapter 3, we noted how the existence of cyberspace has posed significant jurisdictional issues for the courts. Here we examine selected legal issues relating to constitutional law.

REGULATING ONLINE OBSCENITY

As discussed earlier in this chapter, obscene speech is not protected by the First Amendment. In 1996, in response to public concern over access to pornographic and obscene materials via the Internet, Congress enacted the Communications Decency Act (CDA). This act, which was part of the Telecommunications Act of 1996, made it a criminal offense to transmit "indecent" speech or images to minors (those under the age of eighteen) or to make such speech or images available online to minors. The act defined indecent speech as any communication that depicts or describes sexual or excretory activities or organs in a way that is "patently offensive," as measured by current community standards. Violators of the act could be fined up to $250,000 or imprisoned for up to two years.

A major legal issue raised by the language of the act was that there is no national standard by which to measure "indecent" or "patently offensive" speech. The CDA's definition of these terms followed the traditional practice of measuring obscenity by current community standards. Generally, the United States Supreme Court has held that in a legal action concerning obscene speech, the relevant standard is that of the community in which the information is accessed or the jury sits. With respect to Internet transmissions, however, obscene materials can be accessed by virtually anyone in any community in the United States (as well as globally). In effect, this means that any Internet transmission that is "patently offensive" by even the most restrictive community standards would be illegal under the CDA.

The American Civil Liberties Union (ACLU) and other organizations immediately challenged the constitutionality of the CDA in a lawsuit against the U.S. attorney general, Janet Reno, and the Justice Department. The plaintiffs alleged that the CDA's definition of indecency was unconstitutionally vague and subjected persons to criminal penalties without specifically identifying the crimes to which these penalties attach. In *American Civil Liberties Union v. Reno*,[35] a federal district court in Pennsylvania agreed

35. 929 F.Supp. 824 (E.D.Pa. 1996).

with the plaintiffs and issued a temporary restraining order prohibiting the government from enforcing the section of the CDA pertaining to indecent materials. Shortly thereafter, another federal district court held that the act was unconstitutional because it was overbroad and impermissibly regulated constitutionally protected communications between adults.[36]

In 1997, the United States Supreme Court held that the CDA's provisions regarding "indecent" and "patently offensive" transmissions violated the First Amendment because of their "unprecedented" breadth: although the government has an interest in protecting children from potentially harmful materials, the CDA suppressed a large amount of speech that adults have a constitutional right to send and receive.[37]

CRYPTOGRAPHY AND CONSTITUTIONAL PROTECTIONS

One of the foremost concerns of the business community today is the security of electronic proprietary and commercial information. To protect electronic data from being accessed by unauthorized persons, many companies use hardware or software with encryption capabilities. When data is *encrypted,* the access codes are scrambled to protect against unauthorized use. The widespread practice of encrypting data has created some interesting legal issues.

ENCRYPTED DATA AND CRIMINAL LAW One issue has to do with the Fourth Amendment protection against unreasonable searches and seizures. Suppose that law enforcement personnel obtain a search warrant to search an individual's office or home for certain information. If this information consists of encrypted data stored in a computer's hard drive or on external storage devices, how can it be accessed? A law enforcement agent might succeed in decrypting the data, but whether it would be lawful would depend on whether the information, once known, fell properly within the search warrant's description of the material to be searched and seized.

If law enforcement personnel could not "break" the code and decrypt the data, another issue would arise: Could the owner or possessor of the data be compelled to provide the encryption code? Under the Fifth Amendment, no person can be compelled to give evidence if that evidence would be self-incriminating. Traditionally, persons have been compelled to produce certain types of physical evidence, such as fingerprints, but whether a person can be compelled to use his or her *mind* to assist law enforcement personnel in obtaining incriminating evidence is not clear.

ENCRYPTION SOURCE CODES AND FREE SPEECH A constitutional issue that has recently come before the courts is whether computer source codes used in encryption software constitute "speech" protected by the First Amendment. The issue arose in the context of a controversy over government restrictions on the export of encryption software.

Under the International Traffic in Arms Regulations (ITAR),[38] administered by the U.S. Department of State, any firm that wishes to export encryption software or products containing encryption components must first obtain a license from the government to do so. In the past, it was difficult, if not impossible, to obtain such a license. In 1996, however, the government began to relax the regulations somewhat. Firms are now allowed to sell certain types of high-level encryption software for commercial purposes only. Software manufacturers complain that any restrictions unfairly place them at a disadvantage in the international marketplace. The government, however, contends that restrictions on the export of encryption software are necessary to prevent the software from falling into the hands of terrorists or others who could use it in ways that could threaten national security.

The constitutional issue currently before the courts is whether encryption software—more specifically, the source codes used to encrypt data—constitute speech. If so, then the government's regulation of this speech may be challenged on constitutional grounds. Whether cryptography qualifies as speech falling under the protection of the First Amendment is at issue in the following case.

36. *Shea v. Reno,* 930 F.Supp. 916 (S.D.N.Y. 1996).

37. *Reno v. American Civil Liberties Union,* ___ U.S. ___, 117 S.Ct. 2329, ___ L.Ed.2d ___ (1997).

38. 22 C.F.R. Sections 120–130.

CASE 5.4 Bernstein v. U.S. Department of State

United States District Court, Northern District of California, 1996. 922 F.Supp. 1426.

BACKGROUND AND FACTS *As a graduate student at the University of California at Berkeley in the field of cryptography, Daniel Bernstein developed an encryption system he called "Snuffle." Bernstein asked the U.S. Department of State whether he needed a license to "export" Snuffle—that is, to teach and discuss its source code at conferences, in journals, and in online discussion groups. A license to disclose certain technical data to "foreign person[s]" is required under the Arms Export Control Act (AECA)*[a] *and the International Traffic in Arms Regulations (ITAR). The State Department said that Bernstein did need a license. Bernstein filed a suit in a federal district court against the State Department, contending in part that the AECA and the ITAR were unconstitutional as applied to Snuffle. He asked the court to, among other things, block their enforcement until his claim could be heard. The State Department filed a motion to dismiss, arguing in part that the Snuffle source code was not "speech" and thus was not protected by the First Amendment to the Constitution.*

IN THE LANGUAGE OF THE COURT

PATEL, District Judge.

* * * *

* * * According to defendants, the source code, as a functioning cryptographic product, is not intended to convey a particular message. It cannot be speech, they say, because its purpose is functional rather than communicative.

* * * *

* * * Contrary to defendants' suggestion, the functionality of a language does not make it any less like speech. * * * [E]ven if Snuffle source code, which is easily compiled into object code for the computer to read and easily used for encryption, is essentially functional, that does not remove it from the realm of speech. Instructions, do-it-yourself manuals, recipes, even technical information about hydrogen bomb construction, are often purely functional; they are also speech.

DECISION AND REMEDY *The court held that a cryptographic code is speech protected by the First Amendment. The court denied the State Department's motion to dismiss and granted Bernstein's request to temporarily block enforcement of the AECA and the ITAR.*

a. 22 U.S.C. Section 2278.

FREE SPEECH AND UNWANTED ELECTRONIC MAIL

Many First Amendment cases involve the question of whether the government can prohibit persons from distributing political, religious, or other leaflets or printed materials in public forums. Normally, any law that restricts or prohibits *speech* (that is, the political, religious, or other *message* communicated in the leaflets or other printed materials) must relate to one of the categories of punishable speech (such as "fighting words," obscenity, defamation, and so on) or be justified by a *compelling state interest.*

Any law concerning speech-related conduct (that is, the distribution of leaflets or other printed materials) may reasonably restrict the time, place, or manner in which the conduct takes place. To be constitutional, however, the law must (1) be *content neutral,* (2) be *narrowly tailored* to serve a significant government interest, and (3) leave open sufficient *alternative channels of communication.* Recall that the Bill of Rights, including the First Amendment, protects persons from *government* actions, not actions undertaken by private parties. The rules just stated, however, apply even to certain privately owned facilities, such as shopping malls, because such areas are deemed to be community business centers and thus serve a public function.

ELECTRONIC LEAFLETS What about the transmission of "electronic leaflets" over the Internet? Should the same principles apply? Is the transmission of such material—often referred to as "junk mail" or "spam"—over the Internet significantly different from the distribution of leaflets in a shopping mall or on a public street? This issue arose in a recent dispute between America Online (AOL), the well-known Internet service provider, and Cyber Promotions (CP). CP transmits electronic ads to thousands of e-mail addresses, including AOL subscribers. In response to complaints from its subscribers, AOL blocked all e-mail from CP. AOL also gathered all of CP's e-mail messages together and returned them to CP in an "e-mail bomb" that brought down the computer system of CP's Internet service provider. CP sued AOL, claiming, among other things, that its electronic messages were protected speech under the First Amendment.

AOL claimed that the First Amendment, which prohibits the government from restraining speech-related conduct, does not apply to AOL, which is a private company. Therefore, AOL can block e-mail transmissions directed to its subscribers without violating the First Amendment. CP contended that because the Internet was initially subsidized by the government, speech over the Internet should be constitutionally protected. In CP's suit against AOL, a federal district court declared that CP did not have a constitutional right, under the First Amendment, to send unsolicited e-mail advertisements to AOL subscribers and that AOL was entitled to block CP's attempts to do so.[39]

OTHER ISSUES Some questions raised in this case relate to other areas of the law. For example, in regard to intellectual property law (discussed in Chapter 15), are the e-mail addresses of AOL's subscribers AOL's property, or are they more like the addresses in a telephone book, which anybody can access and use? Additionally, should the government regulate unwanted e-mail just as it does unwanted faxes (see Chapter 23)? After all, recipients of ads and leaflets distributed through the mails or in shopping malls do not have to pay for those materials. In contrast, subscribers of online service providers, such as AOL, pay an hourly fee for the service, which shifts the cost of e-mail ads to the customer.

39. *Cyber Promotions, Inc. v. America Online, Inc.*, 948 F.Supp. 436 (E.D.Pa. 1966). Note that in a similar case brought against CP by CompuServe in 1997, a federal district court held that CP's sending unsolicited e-mail advertisements to CompuServe's proprietary network, after CompuServe had repeatedly demanded CP to cease transmitting such materials, was actionable as a trespass to personal property (a tort, or wrongful act, discussed in Chapter 12). See *CompuServe, Inc. v. Cyber Promotions, Inc.*, 962 F.Supp. 1015 (S.D. Ohio 1997).

Terms and Concepts to Review

amend 96
Bill of Rights 100
checks and balances 97
commerce clause 97
due process clause 107
equal protection clause 108
establishment clause 104
federal form of government 97
free exercise clause 104
full faith and credit clause 107
police powers 98
preemption 99
privileges and immunities clause 107
probable cause 106
search warrant 106
supremacy clause 99
symbolic speech 101

Questions and Case Problems

5–1. Commerce Clause. A Georgia state law requires the use of contoured rear-fender mudguards on trucks and trailers operating within Georgia state lines. The statute further makes it illegal for trucks and trailers to use straight mudguards. In approximately thirty-five other states, straight mudguards are legal. Moreover, in Florida, straight mudguards are explicitly required by law. There is some evidence that suggests that contoured mudguards might be a little safer than straight mudguards. Discuss whether this Georgia statute violates any constitutional provisions.

5–2. COMMERCIAL SPEECH. A mayoral election is about to be held in a large U.S. city. One of the candidates is Luis Delgado, and his campaign supporters wish to post campaign signs on lampposts and utility posts throughout the city. A city ordinance, however, prohibits the posting of any signs on public property. Delgado's supporters contend that the city ordinance is unconstitutional because it violates their right to free speech. Do you agree? In your answer, discuss what factors a court might consider in determining the constitutionality of the ordinance.

5–3. FREEDOM OF RELIGION. A business has a backlog of orders, and to meet its deadlines, management decides to run the firm seven days a week, eight hours a day. One of the employees, Abe Placer, refuses to work on Saturday on religious grounds. His refusal to work means that the firm may not meet its production deadlines and may therefore suffer a loss of future business. The firm fires Placer and replaces him with an employee who is willing to work seven days a week. Placer claims that his employer, in terminating his employment, has violated his constitutional right to the free exercise of his religion. Do you agree? Why or why not?

5–4. GOVERNMENT POWERS. The framers of the Constitution feared the twin evils of tyranny and anarchy. Discuss how specific provisions of the Constitution and the Bill of Rights reflect these fears and protect against both of these extremes.

5–5. FREEDOM OF RELIGION. Thomas worked in the nonmilitary operations of a large firm that produced both military and nonmilitary goods. When the company discontinued the production of nonmilitary goods, Thomas was transferred to a plant producing war materials. Thomas left his job, claiming that it violated his religious principles to participate in the manufacture of materials to be used in destroying life. In effect, he argued, the transfer to the war-materials plant forced him to quit his job. He was denied unemployment compensation by the state because he had not been effectively "discharged" by the employer but had voluntarily terminated his employment. Did the state's denial of unemployment benefits to Thomas violate the free exercise clause of the First Amendment? Explain. [*Thomas v. Review Board of the Indiana Employment Security Division*, 450 U.S. 707, 101 S.Ct. 1425, 67 L.Ed.2d 624 (1981)]

5–6. EQUAL PROTECTION. In 1988, the Nebraska legislature enacted a statute that required any motorcycle operator or passenger on Nebraska's highways to wear a protective helmet. Eugene Robotham, a licensed motorcycle operator, sued the state of Nebraska to block enforcement of the law. Robotham asserted, among other things, that the statute violated the equal protection clause, because it placed requirements on motorcyclists that were not imposed on other motorists. Will the court agree with Robotham that the law violates the equal protection clause? Why or why not? [*Robotham v. State*, 241 Neb. 379, 488 N.W.2d 533 (1992)]

5–7. COMMERCE CLAUSE. Taylor owned a bait business in Maine and arranged to have live baitfish imported into the state. The importation of the baitfish violated a Maine statute. Taylor was indicted under a federal statute that makes it a federal crime to transport fish in interstate commerce in violation of state law. Taylor moved to dismiss the indictment on the ground that the Maine statute unconstitutionally burdened interstate commerce. Maine intervened to defend the validity of its statute, arguing that the law legitimately protected the state's fisheries from parasites and nonnative species that might be included in shipments of live baitfish. Were Maine's interests in protecting its fisheries from parasites and nonnative species sufficient to justify the burden placed on interstate commerce by the Maine statute? Discuss. [*Maine v. Taylor*, 477 U.S. 131, 106 S.Ct. 2440, 91 L.Ed.2d 110 (1986)]

5–8. COMMERCE CLAUSE. South Dakota Disposal Systems, Inc. (SDDS), applied to the South Dakota Department of Water and Natural Resources (DWNR) for a permit to operate a solid waste–disposal facility (Lonetree). It was estimated that 90 to 95 percent of the waste would come from out of state. The DWNR determined that Lonetree would be environmentally safe and issued a permit. Later, a public referendum was held. The state attorney general issued a pamphlet to accompany the referendum that urged the public to vote against "the out-of-state dump" because "South Dakota is not the nation's dumping grounds." The measure was defeated. SDDS filed a suit against the state, challenging the referendum as a violation of, among other things, the commerce clause. Was the referendum unconstitutional? Why or why not? [*SDDS, Inc. v. State of South Dakota*, 47 F.3d 263 (8th Cir. 1995)]

5–9. FREEDOM OF SPEECH. Three members of the International Caucus of Labor Committees (ICLC) were distributing literature from a card table on a sidewalk in Montgomery, Alabama, when police officers told them to leave or they would be arrested. The city's policy was to completely ban placing tables on sidewalks because such tables would impede the orderly flow of pedestrian traffic. The ICLC filed a suit in a federal district court against the city and its police department. In part, the ICLC asked the court to declare that the city's policy violated the ICLC's right to free speech. Is the use of a portable table on a public sidewalk protected by the First Amendment? Why or why not? [*International Caucus of Labor Committees v. City of Montgomery*, 87 F.3d 1275 (11th Cir. 1996)]

5–10. A QUESTION OF ETHICS

Agnes and John Donahue refused to rent an apartment to an unmarried couple, Verna Terry and Robert Wilder. The Donahues were devout Roman Catholics and firmly believed, in accordance with the church's teachings, that engaging in sexual relations outside of marriage was a mortal sin. Agnes Donahue also believed that it would be sinful for her to aid another person in the commission of a sin. Renting an apartment to an unmarried couple would, in Agnes Donahue's mind, be aiding the couple in the commission of a sin, and therefore she refused to rent the apartment to Terry and Wilder. Terry and Wilder filed a complaint with the California Fair Employment and Housing Commission, alleging that the Donahues' refusal to rent them an apartment violated a state statute prohibiting discrimination on the basis of marital status. Eventually, the case was heard by a California appellate court. The question before the court was whether the state's interest in prohibiting discrimination based on marital status outweighed the Donahues' constitutional right to the free exercise of their religion. [*Donahue v. Fair Employment and Housing Commission*, 7 Cal.App.4th 1498, 2 Cal.Rptr.2d 32 (1991)]

1. In your opinion, should the court make an exception to the state statute's applicability in the Donahues' case? Why or why not?
2. In a previous case that involved a conflict between a state statute and the federal constitutional right to the free exercise of religion, the United States Supreme Court stated that "an individual's religious beliefs [do not] excuse him [or her] from compliance with an otherwise valid law." Should the same principle be applied to the Donahues' actions?

5–11. Case Briefing Assignment

Examine Case A.2 [*Austin v. Berryman*, 878 F.2d 786 (4th Cir. 1989)] in Appendix A. The case has been excerpted there in great detail. Review and then brief the case, making sure that you include answers to the following questions in your brief.

1. Who were the plaintiff and the defendant in this action?
2. Why did Austin claim that she had been forced to leave her job?
3. Why was she refused state unemployment benefits?
4. Did the state's refusal to give her unemployment compensation violate her rights under the free exercise clause of the First Amendment?
5. What logic or reasoning did the court employ in arriving at its conclusion?

Accessing the Internet

The Legal Environment of Business

The World Wide Web version of the Constitution provides hypertext links to amendments and other changes. Go to

http://www.law.cornell.edu/constitution/constitution.overview.html

The home page of Emory University School of Law offers access to a number of early American documents, including scanned originals of the Constitution and the Bill of Rights. This page is located at

http://www.law.emory.edu/FEDERAL/

You can obtain all of the decisions of the United States Supreme Court relating to constitutional issues by using a site developed by Cornell University Law School at

http://www.law.cornell.edu/syllabi?constitutional+unconstitutional

Summaries and the full text of constitutional law decisions by the United States Supreme Court are included at the OYEZ site referred to in the *Accessing the Internet* section at the end of Chapter 1. The address for this site is

http://oyez.nwu.edu/oyez.html

For information on the effect of new computer and communications technologies on the constitutional rights and liberties of Americans, go to the Center for Democracy and Technology at

http://www.cdt.org/

The Cyberspace Law Institute (CLI) also focuses on law and communications technology. According to the CLI, it is devoted to studying and helping to develop "the new forms of law and lawmaking required by the growth of global communications networks and online communities." By using the CLI site, you can find articles and information on such topics as privacy, flaming, obscenity, and other issues relating to constitutional law. Go to

http://www.cli.org

CHAPTER 6

ADMINISTRATIVE LAW

GOVERNMENT AGENCIES ESTABLISHED TO ADMINISTER the law have a tremendous impact on the day-to-day operation of the government and the economy. In the early years of our nation, the United States had a relatively simple, nonindustrial economy that required little regulation. Because often the purpose of administrative agencies is to create and enforce such regulations, there were relatively few such agencies. Today, however, there are rules covering virtually every aspect of a business's operation. Consequently, agencies have multiplied.

At the federal level, the Securities and Exchange Commission regulates the firm's capital structure and financing, as well as its financial reporting. The National Labor Relations Board oversees relations between the firm and any unions with which it may deal. The Equal Employment Opportunity Commission also regulates employment relationships. The Environmental Protection Agency and the Occupational Safety and Health Administration affect the way the firm manufactures its products. The Federal Trade Commission affects the way it markets these products.

Added to this layer of federal regulation is a second layer of state regulation that, when not preempted by federal legislation, may cover many of the same activities or regulate independently those activities not covered by federal regulation. Finally, agency regulations at the county or municipal level also affect certain types of business activities.

Administrative agencies issue rules, orders, and decisions. These regulations make up the body of *administrative law*. You were introduced briefly to some of the main principles of administrative law in Chapter 1. In the following pages, we look at these principles in much greater detail.

SECTION 1

AGENCY CREATION AND POWERS

Because Congress cannot possibly oversee the actual implementation of all the laws it enacts, it must delegate such tasks to others, particularly when the issues relate to highly technical areas, such as air and water pollution. By delegating some of its authority to make and implement laws to administrative agencies, Congress can monitor indirectly a particular area in which it has passed legislation without becoming bogged down in the details relating to enforcement—details that are often best left to specialists.

ENABLING LEGISLATION

To create an administrative agency, Congress passes **enabling legislation,** which specifies the name, purposes, functions, and powers of the agency being created. The enabling legislation for the Federal Trade Commission (FTC), for example, is the Federal Trade Commission Act of 1914.[1] The act prohibits unfair methods of competition and deceptive trade practices. It also describes the procedures that the FTC must follow to charge persons or organizations with violations of the act, and it provides for judicial review of agency orders. The act grants the FTC the power to do the following:

1. 15 U.S.C. Sections 41–58.

1. Create "rules and regulations for the purpose of carrying out the Act."
2. Conduct investigations of business practices.
3. Obtain reports from interstate corporations concerning their business practices.
4. Investigate possible violations of federal antitrust statutes.[2]
5. Publish findings of its investigations.
6. Recommend new legislation.
7. Hold trial-like hearings to resolve certain kinds of trade disputes that involve FTC regulations or federal antitrust laws.

The commission that heads the FTC is composed of five members, each of whom the president appoints, with the advice and consent of the Senate, for a term of seven years. The president designates one of the commissioners to be chairperson. Various offices and bureaus within the FTC undertake different administrative activities for the agency. Exhibit 6–1 illustrates the organization of the FTC.

Federal administrative agencies may exercise only those powers that Congress has delegated to them in enabling legislation. Through similar enabling acts, state legislatures create state administrative agencies.

TYPES OF AGENCIES

As discussed in Chapter 1, there are two basic types of administrative agencies: executive agencies and independent regulatory agencies. Federal *executive*

2. The FTC shares enforcement of the Clayton Act with the Antitrust Division of the U.S. Department of Justice.

EXHIBIT 6–1 ■ ORGANIZATION OF THE FEDERAL TRADE COMMISSION

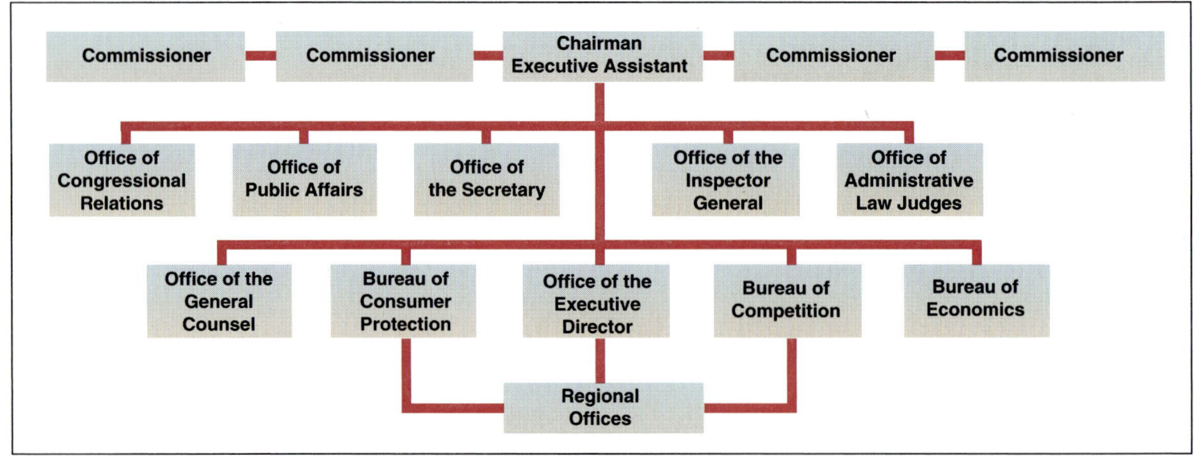

agencies include the cabinet departments of the executive branch, which were formed to assist the president in carrying out executive functions, and the subagencies within the cabinet departments. The Occupational Safety and Health Administration, for example, is a subagency within the Department of Labor. Exhibit 6–2 lists the cabinet departments and their most important subagencies.

EXHIBIT 6–2 ■ EXECUTIVE DEPARTMENTS AND IMPORTANT SUBAGENCIES

DEPARTMENT	DATE FORMED	IMPORTANT SUBAGENCIES
State	1789	Passport Office; Bureau of Diplomatic Security; Foreign Service; Bureau of Human Rights and Humanitarian Affairs; Bureau of Consular Affairs; Bureau of Intelligence and Research.
Treasury	1789	Internal Revenue Service; Bureau of Alcohol, Tobacco, and Firearms; Secret Service; Mint; Customs Service.
Interior	1849	Fish and Wildlife Service; National Park Service; Bureau of Indian Affairs; Bureau of Land Management.
Justice	1870[a]	Federal Bureau of Investigation; Drug Enforcement Administration; Bureau of Prisons; Marshals Service; Immigration and Naturalization Service.
Agriculture	1889	Soil Conservation Service; Agricultural Research Service; Food Safety and Inspection Service; Federal Crop Insurance Corporation; Farmers Home Administration.
Commerce	1913[b]	Bureau of the Census; Bureau of Economic Analysis; Minority Business Development Agency; Patent and Trademark Office; National Oceanic and Atmospheric Administration; Travel and Tourism Administration.
Labor	1913[b]	Occupational Safety and Health Administration; Bureau of Labor Statistics; Employment Standards Administration; Office of Labor-Management Standards; Employment and Training Administration.
Defense	1949[c]	National Guard; Defense Investigative Service; National Security Agency; Joint Chiefs of Staff; Departments of the Air Force, Navy, Army.
Housing and Urban Development	1965	Community Planning and Development; Government National Mortgage Association; Housing—Federal Housing Commissioner; Fair Housing and Equal Opportunity.
Transportation	1967	Federal Aviation Administration; Federal Highway Administration; National Highway Traffic Safety Administration; Coast Guard; Federal Transit Administration.
Energy	1977	Office of Civilian Radioactive Waste Management; Bonneville Power Administration; Office of Nuclear Energy; Energy Information Administration; Office of Conservation and Renewable Energy.
Health and Human Services	1980[d]	Food and Drug Administration; Health Care Financing Administration; Public Health Service.
Education	1980[e]	Office of Special Education and Rehabilitation Services; Office of Elementary and Secondary Education; Office of Postsecondary Education; Office of Vocational and Adult Education.
Veteran's Affairs	1989	Veterans Health Administration; Veterans Benefits Administration; National Cemetery System.

a. Formed from the Office of the Attorney General (created in 1789).
b. Formed from the Department of Commerce and Labor (created in 1903).
c. Formed from the Department of War (created in 1789) and the Department of the Navy (created in 1798).
d. Formed from the Department of Health, Education and Welfare (created in 1953).
e. Formed from the Department of Health, Education and Welfare (created in 1953).

All administrative agencies are part of the executive branch of government, but *independent regulatory agencies* are outside the major executive departments. The Federal Trade Commission and the Securities and Exchange Commission are examples of independent regulatory agencies. These and other selected independent regulatory agencies, as well as their principal functions, are listed in Exhibit 6–3.

The significant difference between the two types of agencies lies in the accountability of the regulators. Agencies that are considered part of the executive branch are subject to the authority of the president, who has the power to appoint and remove federal officers. In theory, this power is less pronounced in regard to independent agencies, whose officers serve for fixed terms and cannot be removed without just cause. In practice, however, the president's power to exert influence over independent agencies is often considerable.

AGENCY POWERS AND THE CONSTITUTION

Administrative agencies occupy an unusual niche in the American legal scheme, because they exercise powers that are normally divided among the three branches of government. Notice that in the FTC's enabling legislation, discussed above, the FTC's grant of power incorporates functions associated with the legislative branch (rulemaking), the executive branch (enforcement of the rules), and the courts (**adjudication,** or the formal resolution of disputes).

The constitutional principle of checks and balances allows each branch of government to act as a check on the actions of the other two branches. Furthermore, the Constitution authorizes only the legislative branch to create laws. Yet administrative agencies, to which the Constitution does not specifically refer, make **legislative rules,** or *substantive rules,* that are as legally binding as laws that Congress passes.

Courts generally hold that Article I of the U.S. Constitution authorizes delegating such powers to administrative agencies. In fact, courts generally hold that Article I is the basis for all administrative law. Section 1 of that article grants all legislative powers to Congress and requires Congress to oversee the implementation of all laws. Article I, Section 8, gives Congress the power to make all laws necessary for executing its specified powers. The courts interpret

EXHIBIT 6–3 ■ SELECTED INDEPENDENT REGULATORY AGENCIES

NAME	DATE FORMED	PRINCIPAL DUTIES
Federal Reserve System Board of Governors (Fed)	1913	Determines policy with respect to interest rates, credit availability, and the money supply.
Federal Trade Commission (FTC)	1914	Prevents businesses from engaging in unfair trade practices; stops the formation of monopolies in the business sector; protects consumer rights.
Securities and Exchange Commission (SEC)	1934	Regulates the nation's stock exchanges, in which shares of stock are bought and sold; enforces the securities laws, which require full disclosure of the financial profiles and companies that wish to sell stock and bonds to the public.
Federal Communications Commission (FCC)	1934	Regulates all communications by telegraph, cable, telephone, radio, satellite, and television.
National Labor Relations Board (NLRB)	1935	Protects employees' rights to join unions and bargain collectively with employers; attempts to prevent unfair labor practices by both employers and unions.
Equal Employment Opportunity Commission (EEOC)	1964	Works to eliminate discrimination in employment based on religion, sex, race, color, disability, national origin, or age; investigates claims of discrimination.
Environmental Protection Agency (EPA)	1970	Undertakes programs aimed at reducing air and water pollution; works with state and local agencies to help fight environmental hazards. (It has been suggested recently that its status be elevated to that of a department.)
Nuclear Regulatory Commission (NRC)	1975	Ensures that electricity-generating nuclear reactors in the United States are built and operated safely; regularly inspects operations of such reactors.

these passages, under what is referred to as the **delegation doctrine,** as granting Congress the power to establish administrative agencies that can create rules for implementing those laws.

The three branches of government exercise certain controls over agency powers and functions, as will be discussed later in this chapter, but in many ways administrative agencies function independently. For this reason, administrative agencies, which constitute the **bureaucracy,** are sometimes referred to as the "fourth branch" of the American government.

SECTION 2
ADMINISTRATIVE PROCESS

The three functions mentioned previously—rulemaking, enforcement, and adjudication—make up what is known as the **administrative process.** Administrative process involves the administration of law by administrative agencies, in contrast to **judicial process,** which involves the administration of law by the courts.

All federal agencies must follow specific procedural requirements in their rulemaking, adjudication, and other functions. Sometimes, Congress specifies certain procedural requirements in an agency's enabling legislation. In the absence of any directives from Congress concerning a particular agency procedure, the Administrative Procedure Act (APA) of 1946[3] applies. The APA is such an integral part of the administrative process that its application will be examined as we go through the basic functions carried out by administrative agencies. In addition, agency procedures are guided indirectly by the courts' interpretation of APA requirements.

RULEMAKING

A major function of an administrative agency is **rulemaking**—the formulation of new regulations. In an agency's enabling legislation, Congress confers the agency's power to make rules. For example, the Occupational Safety and Health Act of 1970 authorized the Occupational Safety and Health Administration (OSHA) to develop and issue rules governing safety in the workplace. In formulating any new rule, OSHA has to follow specific rulemaking procedures required under the APA. The most commonly used rulemaking procedure is called **notice-and-comment rulemaking.** This procedure involves three basic steps: notice of the proposed rulemaking, a comment period, and the final rule.

NOTICE OF THE PROPOSED RULEMAKING

When a federal agency decides to create a new rule, the agency publishes a notice of the proposed rulemaking proceedings in the *Federal Register*, a daily publication of the executive branch that prints government orders, rules, and regulations. The notice states where and when the proceedings will be held, the agency's legal authority for making the rule (usually its enabling legislation), and the terms or subject matter of the proposed rule.

COMMENT PERIOD Following the publication of the notice of the proposed rulemaking proceedings, the agency must allow ample time for persons to comment in writing on the proposed rule. The purpose of this comment period is to give interested parties the opportunity to express their views on the proposed rule in an effort to influence agency policy. The comments may be in writing or, if a hearing is held, may be given orally. The agency need not respond to all comments, but it must respond to any significant comments that bear directly on the proposed rule. The agency responds by either modifying its final rule or explaining, in a statement accompanying the final rule, why it did not make any changes. In some circumstances, particularly when the procedure being used in a specific instance is less formal, an agency may accept comments after the comment period is closed. The agency should summarize these *ex parte* (private, "off-the-record") comments in the record for possible review.

THE FINAL RULE After the agency reviews the comments, it drafts the final rule and publishes it in the *Federal Register*. Exhibit 6–4 shows a sample page from a rule published in the *Federal Register*. The final rule is later compiled with the rules and regulations of other federal administrative agencies in the *Code of Federal Regulations* (C.F.R.). Final rules have binding legal effect unless the courts later overturn them.

3. 5 U.S.C. Sections 551–706.

Exhibit 6–4 ■ A Page from the Federal Register

ENVIRONMENTAL PROTECTION AGENCY
40 CFR Part 50
[AD-FRL-5659-5]
RIN 2060-AE66
National Ambient Air Quality Standards for Particulate Matter: Proposed Decision
Friday, December 13, 1996
AGENCY: Environmental Protection Agency (EPA).
ACTION: Proposed rule.

SUMMARY: In accordance with sections 108 and 109 of the Clean Air Act (Act), EPA has reviewed the air quality criteria and national ambient air quality standards (NAAQS) for particulate matter (PM) and for ozone (O sub3). Based on these reviews, EPA proposes to change the standards for both classes of pollutants. This document describes EPA's proposed changes with respect to the NAAQS for PM. The EPA's proposed actions with respect to O sub3 are being proposed elsewhere in today's Federal Register.

With respect to PM, EPA proposes to revise the current primary PM sub10 standards by adding two new primary PM sub2.5 standards set at 15 MUg/m 3 , annual mean, and 50 MUg/m super3, 24-hour average, to provide increased protection against a wide range of PM-related health effects, including premature mortality and increased hospital admissions and emergency room visits (primarily in the elderly and individuals with cardiopulmonary disease); increased respiratory symptoms and disease (in children and individuals with cardiopulmonary disease such as asthma); decreased lung function (particularly in children and individuals with asthma); and alterations in lung tissue and structure and in respiratory tract defense mechanisms. The proposed annual PM sub2.5 standard would be based on the 3-year average of the annual arithmetic mean PM sub2.5 concentrations, spatially averaged across an area. The proposed 24-hour PM sub2.5 standard would be based on the 3-year average of the 98th percentile of 24-hour PM sub2.5 concentrations at each monitor within an area. The EPA also solicits comment on two alternative approaches for selecting the levels of PM sub2.5 standards. The EPA proposes to revise the current 24-hour primary PM sub10 standard of 150 MUg/m super3 by replacing the 1-expected-exceedance form with a 98th percentile form, averaged over 3 years at each monitor within an area, and solicits comment on an alternative proposal to revoke the 24-hour PM sub10 standard. The EPA also proposes to retain the current annual primary PM sub10 standard of 50 mg/m super3. Further, EPA proposes new data handling conventions for calculating 98th percentile values and spatial averages (Appendix K), proposes to revise the reference method for monitoring PM as PM sub10 (Appendix J), and proposes a new reference method for monitoring PM as PM sub2.5 (Appendix L).

The EPA proposes to revise the current secondary standards by making them identical to the suite of proposed primary standards. In the Administrator's judgment, these standards, in conjunction with the establishment of a regional haze program under section 169A of the Act, would provide appropriate protection against PM-related public welfare effects including soiling, material damage, and visibility impairment.

DATES: Written comments on this proposed rule must be received by February 18, 1997.

ADDRESSES: Submit comments in duplicate if possible on the proposed action to: Office of Air and Radiation Docket and Information Center (6102), Attention: Docket No. A-95-54, U.S. Environmental Protection Agency, 401 M St., SW., Washington, DC 20460.

PUBLIC HEARINGS: The EPA will announce in a separate Federal Register document the date, time, and address of the public hearing on this proposed rule.

FOR FURTHER INFORMATION CONTACT: Ms. Patricia Koman, MD-15, Air Quality Strategies and Standards Division, Office of Air Quality Planning and Standards, U.S. Environmental Protection Agency, Research Triangle Park, North Carolina 27711, telephone: (919) 541-5170.

In the case presented below, the American Dental Association and other health-care providers asked a court to overturn an Occupational Safety and Health Administration (OSHA) rule created in 1991 to contain the spread of blood-borne diseases in the health-care industry. The court discussed some of the considerations that OSHA took into account before formulating its rule. These are illustrative of the factors that any agency must consider in the rulemaking process.

CASE 6.1 American Dental Association v. Martin

United States Court of Appeals, Seventh Circuit, 1993. 984 F.2d 823.

HISTORICAL AND SOCIAL SETTING *Health-care workers are always at risk of being infected with their patients' diseases. For example, viruses, such as those causing acquired immune deficiency syndrome (AIDS) and hepatitis B (a serious liver disease), can be transmitted in the blood of patients. The human immunodeficiency virus (HIV) causes AIDS. Although HIV cannot survive exposure to air, it can be transmitted if, for example, a health-care worker accidentally sticks himself or herself with a needle on which there is fresh blood of an HIV carrier. AIDS appears to be fatal in all cases. The hepatitis B virus (HBV), by contrast, is rarely fatal—about 1 percent of those infected die—but it is more easily transmitted.*

BACKGROUND AND FACTS *In 1991, the Occupational Safety and Health Administration (OSHA) promulgated a rule to protect health-care workers from viruses that can be transmitted in the blood of patients. The rule requires employers in the health-care industry to take certain precautions relating to the handling of contaminated instruments (such as needles), the disposal of contaminated waste, and the use of protective clothing (such as gloves, masks, and gowns). The rule also requires employers to provide vaccinations for hepatitis B for their employees and confidential blood testing of workers following accidental exposures (such as being stuck with a contaminated needle). The American Dental Association (ADA) and two other groups asked a federal court to review the rule. The ADA argued, among other things, that OSHA had failed to establish that dental workers were sufficiently at risk to benefit from the rule. Furthermore, the rule would unnecessarily burden consumers with increased medical costs and, hence, diminished care.*

IN THE LANGUAGE OF THE COURT

POSNER, Circuit Judge.

* * * *

In deciding to impose this extensive array of restrictions on the practice of medicine, nursing, and dentistry, OSHA did not (indeed is not authorized to) compare the benefits with the costs and impose the restrictions on finding that the former exceeded the latter. Instead it asked whether the restrictions would materially reduce a significant workplace risk to human health without imperiling the existence of, or threatening massive dislocation to, the health care industry. * * *

* * * *

OSHA cannot impose onerous requirements on an industry that does not pose substantial hazards to the safety or health of its workers * * * . But neither is the agency required to proceed workplace by workplace, which * * * would require it to promulgate hundreds of thousands of separate rules. It is not our business to pick the happy medium between these extremes. It is OSHA's business. If it provides a rational explanation for its choice, we are bound. * * *

* * * *

* * * [T]he dental association's argument that OSHA's rule is likely to cause a deterioration in dental care as dental patients flee the higher prices resulting from the industry's efforts to shift some of the costs of compliance with the rule to its customers [is untenable]. There are some [costs omitted in OSHA's analysis] * * * but not enough to make a decisive difference * * * .

DECISION AND REMEDY *The U.S. Court of Appeals for the Seventh Circuit denied the ADA's petition to review the rule.*

INVESTIGATION

Administrative agencies conduct investigations of the entities that they regulate. One type of agency investigation occurs during the rulemaking process to obtain information about a certain individual, firm, or industry. The purpose of such an investigation is to ensure that the rule issued is based on a consideration of relevant factors rather than being arbitrary and capricious. After final rules are issued, agencies conduct investigations to monitor compliance with those rules. A typical agency investigation of this kind might begin when a citizen reports a possible violation.

INSPECTIONS Many agencies gather information through on-site inspections. Sometimes, inspecting an office, a factory, or some other business facility is the only way to obtain the evidence needed to prove a regulatory violation. Administrative inspections and tests cover a wide range of activities, including safety inspections of underground coal mines, safety tests of commercial equipment and automobiles, and environmental monitoring of factory emissions. An agency may also ask a firm or individual to submit certain documents or records to the agency for examination.

Normally, business firms comply with agency requests to inspect facilities or business records, because it is in any firm's interest to maintain a good relationship with regulatory bodies. In some instances, however, such as when a firm thinks an agency's request is unreasonable and may be detrimental to the firm's interest, the firm may refuse to comply with the request. In such situations, an agency may resort to the use of a subpoena or a search warrant.

SUBPOENAS There are two basic types of subpoenas. The subpoena *ad testificandum* ("to testify") is an ordinary subpoena. It is a writ, or order, compelling a witness to appear at an agency hearing. The subpoena *duces tecum* ("bring it with you") compels an individual or organization to hand over books, papers, records, or documents to the agency. An administrative agency may use either type of subpoena to obtain testimony or documents.

There are limits on what an agency can demand. To determine whether an agency is abusing its discretion in its pursuit of information as part of an investigation, a court may consider such factors as the following:

1. The purpose of the investigation. An investigation must have a legitimate purpose. An improper purpose is, for example, harassment.
2. The relevance of the information being sought. Information is relevant if it reveals that the law is being violated or if it assures the agency that the law is not being violated.
3. The specificity of the demand for testimony or documents. A subpoena must, for example, adequately describe the material being sought.
4. The burden of the demand on the party from whom the information is sought. In responding to a request for information, a party must bear the costs of, for example, copying the documents that must be handed over, but a business is generally protected from revealing such information as trade secrets.

In the following case, former bank directors challenged the right of an administrative agency to subpoena their personal financial records. The court considered the extent of the agency's investigative powers.

CASE 6.2 Federal Deposit Insurance Corp. v. Wentz

United States Court of Appeals, Third Circuit, 1995. 55 F.3d 905.

HISTORICAL AND ECONOMIC SETTING *Congress created the Federal Deposit Insurance Corporation (FDIC) in 1933 to help prevent commercial bank failures and to protect bank customers' accounts. In 1992, nearly five hundred banks failed. More than half of all bank failures can be attributed to agricultural loans, when the failure of farms leads to default on the loans. Fraud also often plays a role. When a bank fails, the FDIC covers each depositor's loss up to $100,000 and then sells the bank's assets, or takes other steps, to regain some of those funds.*

BACKGROUND AND FACTS *Sidney Wentz and Natalie Koether were directors of Howard Savings Bank of Livingston, New Jersey, when it was declared insolvent in October 1992. The Federal Deposit Insurance Corporation (FDIC) was appointed receiver. In April 1993, the FDIC issued subpoenas* duces tecum *to Wentz, Koether, and others, seeking, among other things, their personal financial records. The directors refused to comply. The FDIC asked a federal district court to enforce the subpoenas, arguing that the records were needed to assess whether any bank losses might be due to breach of the directors' fiduciary duties. The court ordered the directors to produce only those records showing additions to or reductions in their assets. The directors appealed, contending that this order intruded on their privacy.*

IN THE LANGUAGE OF THE COURT

WEIS, Circuit Judge.

* * * *

When personal documents of individuals, as contrasted with business records of corporations, are the subject of an administrative subpoena, privacy concerns must be considered. * * * [R]elevant factors [include] such matters as the type of record requested, the information that it might contain, the potential for harm and subsequent nonconsensual disclosure, the adequacy of safeguards to prevent unauthorized disclosure, the degree of need for access, * * * and the presence of recognizable public interests justifying access.

* * * *

The FDIC has shown a reasonable need for gaining access to the directors' records in order to determine whether they reveal breaches of fiduciary duties through the improper channeling of bank funds for personal benefit. Moreover, the directors have not produced any evidence to show that the information contained in their personal financial records is of such a high degree of sensitivity that the intrusion could be considered severe or that the [directors] are likely to suffer any adverse effects from disclosure to [FDIC] personnel. Finally, we observe that regulatory provisions have been promulgated to guard against subsequent unauthorized disclosure of the subpoenaed information.

DECISION AND REMEDY *The U.S. Court of Appeals for the Third Circuit affirmed the district court's order. The directors were required to produce their records.*

SEARCH WARRANTS The Fourth Amendment protects against unreasonable searches and seizures by requiring that in most instances a physical search for evidence must be conducted under the authority of a search warrant. An agency's search warrant is an order directing law enforcement officials to search a specific place for a specific item and present it to the agency. Although it was once thought that administrative inspections were exempt from the warrant requirement, the United States Supreme Court held in *Marshall v. Barlow's, Inc.*,[4] that the requirement does apply to the administrative process.

Agencies can conduct warrantless searches in several situations. Warrants are not required to conduct searches in highly regulated industries. Firms that sell firearms or liquor, for example, are automatically subject to inspections without warrants. Sometimes, a statute permits warrantless searches of certain types of hazardous operations, such as coal mines. Also, a warrantless inspection in an emergency situation is normally considered reasonable.

ADJUDICATION

After conducting an investigation of a suspected rule violation, an agency may begin to take administrative action against an individual or organization. Most administrative actions are resolved through negotiated settlements at their initial stages, without the need for formal adjudication.

NEGOTIATED SETTLEMENTS Depending on the agency, negotiations may take the form of a simple conversation or a series of informal conferences. Whatever form the negotiations take, their purpose is to rectify the problem to the agency's satisfaction and eliminate the need for additional proceedings.

Settlement is an appealing option to firms for two reasons: to avoid appearing uncooperative and to avoid the expense involved in formal adjudication proceedings and in possible later appeals. Settlement is also an appealing option for agencies. To conserve their own resources and avoid formal actions, administrative agencies devote a great deal of effort to giving advice and negotiating solutions to problems.

FORMAL COMPLAINTS If a settlement cannot be reached, the agency may issue a formal complaint against the suspected violator. If the Environmental Protection Agency (EPA), for example, finds that a factory is polluting groundwater in violation of federal pollution laws, the EPA will issue a complaint against the violator in an effort to bring the plant into compliance with federal regulations. This complaint is a public document, and a press release may accompany it. The factory charged in the complaint will respond by filing an *answer* to the EPA's allegations. If the factory and the EPA cannot agree on a settlement, the case is heard in a trial-like setting before an **administrative law judge (ALJ).** The adjudication process is described below and illustrated graphically in Exhibit 6–5.

THE ROLE OF THE ADMINISTRATIVE LAW JUDGE The ALJ presides over the hearing and has the power to administer oaths, take testimony, rule on questions of evidence, and make determinations of fact. Although formally, the ALJ works for the agency prosecuting the case (in our example, the EPA), the law requires an ALJ to be an unbiased adjudicator (judge).

Certain safeguards prevent bias on the part of the ALJ and promote fairness in the proceedings. For example, the APA requires that the ALJ be separate from an agency's investigative and prosecutorial staff.

EXHIBIT 6–5 ■ THE PROCESS OF FORMAL ADMINISTRATIVE ADJUDICATION

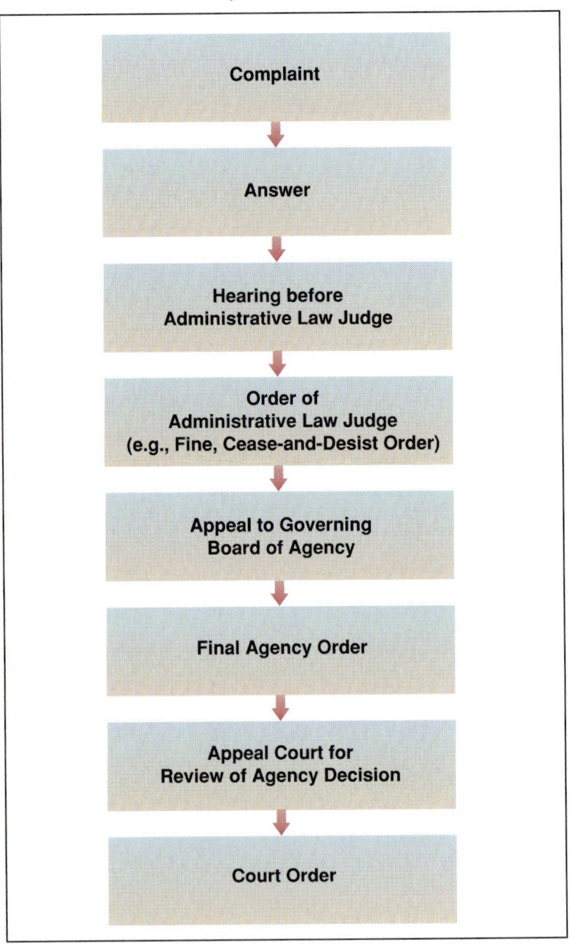

4. 436 U.S. 307, 98 S.Ct. 1816, 56 L.Ed.2d 305 (1978).

The APA also prohibits *ex parte* (private) communications between the ALJ and any party to an agency proceeding, such as the EPA or the factory. Finally, provisions of the APA protect the ALJ from agency disciplinary actions unless the agency can show good cause for such an action.

HEARING PROCEDURES Hearing procedures vary widely from agency to agency. Administrative agencies generally exercise substantial discretion over the type of hearing procedure that will be used. Frequently, disputes are resolved through informal adjudication proceedings. For example, the parties, their counsel, and the ALJ may simply meet at a table in a conference room for the dispute-settlement proceedings.

A formal adjudicatory hearing, in contrast, resembles a trial in many respects. Prior to the hearing, the parties are permitted to undertake extensive discovery (involving depositions, interrogatories, and requests for documents or other information, as described in Chapter 3). During the hearing, the parties may give testimony, present other evidence, and cross-examine adverse witnesses. A significant difference between a trial and an administrative agency hearing, though, is that normally much more information, including hearsay (secondhand information) can be introduced as evidence during an administrative hearing.

AGENCY ORDERS Following a hearing, the ALJ renders an **initial order,** or decision, on the case. Either party can appeal the ALJ's decision to the board or commission that governs the agency. If the factory is dissatisfied with the ALJ's decision, for example, it can appeal the decision to the commission that governs the EPA. If the factory is dissatisfied with the commission's decision, it can appeal the decision to a federal court of appeals. If no party appeals the case, the ALJ's decision becomes the **final order** of the agency. The ALJ's decision also becomes final if a party appeals and the commission and the court decline to review the case. If a party appeals the case and the case is reviewed, the final order comes from the commission's decision or (if that decision is appealed to a federal appellate court) that of the court. In the following case, an ALJ fined a company $2,000 for violating federal regulations governing mine safety. The company eventually asked a federal appellate court to review the order.

CASE 6.3 Buck Creek Coal, Inc. v. Federal Mine Safety and Health Administration

United States Court of Appeals, Seventh Circuit, 1995. 52 F.3d 133.

BACKGROUND AND FACTS *Buck Creek Coal, Inc., operates a coal mine in Sullivan County, Indiana. When James Holland, an inspector for the Mine Safety and Health Administration (MSHA), inspected the mine, he noted an accumulation of loose coal and coal dust in the feeder area, where mined coal is transferred from mine shuttle cars to conveyor belts. Holland issued a citation, charging Buck Creek with violations of federal regulations that require mine operators to keep feeder areas clean. After hearing evidence from both sides, an ALJ found that the evidence supported Holland's conclusions and fined Buck Creek $2,000. Buck Creek asked the Federal Mine Safety and Health Review Commission to review the ALJ's conclusions. When the commission declined, Buck Creek sought review in the courts.*

IN THE LANGUAGE OF THE COURT

ILANA DIAMOND ROVNER, Circuit Judge.

* * * *

* * * [The ALJ] made these findings, based primarily on the testimony of Inspector Holland: "[T]here were substantial accumulations of loose coal, coal fines and float coal dust, in the feeder area * * * . A heated roller turning in that combustible material could easily be an ignition source which could in turn cause a fire. * * * [I]n the event of a fire, smoke and gas inhalation by miners

in the area would cause a reasonably serious injury requiring medical attention." * * * [N]o further evidence was necessary to support the ALJ's conclusion. First, * * * Inspector Holland [is] a federal mine inspector with 32 years of mining experience who specializes in mine ventilation. Nor was anything more than Inspector Holland's opinion necessary to support the common sense conclusion that a fire burning in an underground coal mine would present a serious risk of smoke and gas inhalation to miners who are present. * * * [F]ire is one of the primary safety concerns that has motivated federal regulation of the coal mining industry.

Nor has Buck Creek identified any evidence that tends to undermine the ALJ's conclusion. * * * Buck Creek has relied mainly on * * * testimony [that] pertained to Buck Creek's fire safety systems. * * * The fact that Buck Creek has safety measures in place * * * does not mean that fires do not pose a serious safety risk to miners. Indeed, the precautions are * * * in place * * * precisely because of the significant dangers associated with coal mine fires.

DECISION AND REMEDY *The U.S. Court of Appeals for the Seventh Circuit denied Buck Creek's petition for review. The ALJ's conclusions became the final order for the agency. Buck Creek was ordered to pay the fine.*

SECTION 3 LIMITATIONS ON AGENCY POWERS

Combining the functions normally divided among the three branches of government into an administrative agency concentrates considerable power in a single organization. Because of this concentration of authority, one of the major policy objectives of the government is to control the risks of arbitrariness and overreaching by administrative agencies without hindering the effective use of agency power to deal with particular problem areas, as Congress intends.

The judicial branch of the government exercises control over agency powers through the courts' review of agency actions. The executive and legislative branches of government also exercise control over agency authority.

JUDICIAL CONTROLS

The APA provides for judicial review of most agency decisions, as described above. Agency actions are not automatically subject to judicial review, however. Parties seeking review must demonstrate that they meet certain requirements. The party bringing the action must have *standing to sue* the agency (the party must have a direct stake in the outcome of the judicial proceeding), and there must be an *actual controversy* at issue. These are basic judicial requirements that must be met before a court will hear a case, as discussed in Chapter 3. Furthermore, the party must have *exhausted all possible administrative remedies.* Each agency has its "chain of review," and the party must follow agency appeal procedures before a court will deem that administrative remedies have been exhausted.

Recall from Chapter 3 that appellate courts normally defer to the decisions of trial courts on questions of fact. In reviewing administrative actions, the courts are similarly reluctant to question the factual findings of agencies. In reviewing an administrative agency's decision, a court normally will consider the following types of issues:

1. Whether the agency has exceeded its authority under its enabling legislation.
2. Whether the agency has properly interpreted laws applicable to the agency action under review.
3. Whether the agency has violated any constitutional provisions.
4. Whether the agency has acted in accordance with procedural requirements of the law.
5. Whether the agency's actions were arbitrary, capricious, or an abuse of discretion.
6. Whether any conclusions drawn by the agency are not supported by substantial evidence.

At issue in the following case is whether an agency's action was arbitrary and capricious.

CASE 6.4 Sierra Club v. Thomas

United States Court of Appeals, Sixth Circuit, 1997. 105 F.3d 248.

BACKGROUND AND FACTS *The U.S. Forest Service issued a plan for cutting timber from the Wayne National Forest. Most of the cutting was to be done by a technique known as even-aged management, which requires clearcutting. Clearcutting involves the removal of all trees within areas ranging in size from fifteen to thirty acres. The Sierra Club challenged the plan in an appeal to Jack Ward Thomas, chief of the Forest Service. When Thomas affirmed the plan, the Sierra Club and others filed a suit in a federal district court against Thomas and others, arguing that the plan was arbitrary and capricious because, in making it, the Forest Service had not complied with the National Forest Management Act. The court granted the Forest Service's motion for summary judgment, and the Sierra Club appealed.*

IN THE LANGUAGE OF THE COURT

BOYCE F. MARTIN, JR., Chief Judge.

* * * *

* * * The Forest Service argues that its even-aged management plan is based on evidence that timbering will provide new opportunities for recreation that will, in turn, preserve and enhance the diversity of plant and animal communities in the Wayne National Forest. Most recreation does not require timber harvesting, however. Further, as the Forest Service's own records reflect, the Wayne is surrounded by and intermingled with privately held land which already contains an abundance of diverse plant and animal life. Timbering simply does not promote the kind of recreational activities that are in demand in the Wayne; in fact, recreation like fishing and hiking is harmed by clearcutting. The planners also failed to recognize that cutting is unlikely to stimulate new and valuable forms of recreation because much of the Wayne has already been cut or developed. In that particular environment, clearcutting loses its value.

* * * The National Forest Management Act * * * contemplates that even-aged management techniques will be used only in exceptional circumstances. Yet, the defendants would utilize even-aged management logging as if it were the statutory rule, rather than the exception. By arbitrarily undervaluing the recreational value of wilderness, the Forest Service created a very distorted picture of the Wayne National Forest. Based on false premises such as these, the Forest Service improperly concluded that clearcutting was necessary.

DECISION AND REMEDY *The U.S. Court of Appeals for the Sixth Circuit concluded that the Forest Service plan was arbitrary and capricious. The court reversed the lower court's decision and remanded the case.*

EXECUTIVE CONTROLS

The executive branch of government exercises control over agencies both through the president's power to appoint federal officers and through the president's veto power. The president may veto enabling legislation presented by Congress or congressional attempts to modify an existing agency's authority.

LEGISLATIVE CONTROLS

Congress also exercises authority over agency powers. Through enabling legislation, Congress gives power to an agency. Of course, an agency may not exceed the power that Congress has delegated to it. Through subsequent legislation, Congress can take away that power or even abolish an agency altogether. Legislative authority is required to fund an agency, and enabling legislation usually sets certain time and monetary limits on the funding of particular programs. Congress can always revise these limits.

In addition to its power to create and fund agencies, Congress has the authority to investigate the implementation of its laws and the agencies that it has created. Individual legislators may also affect agency policy through their "casework" activities, which involve attempts to help their constituents deal with agencies.

Congress also has the power to "freeze" the enforcement of most federal regulations before the regulations take effect. Under the Small Business Regulatory Enforcement Fairness Act of 1996,[5] all federal agencies must submit final rules to Congress before the rules become effective. If, within sixty days, Congress passes a joint resolution of disapproval concerning a rule, enforcement of the regulation is frozen while the rule is reviewed by congressional committees.

Another legislative check on agency actions is the Administrative Procedure Act, discussed earlier in this chapter.

SECTION 4 PUBLIC ACCOUNTABILITY

As a result of growing public concern over the powers exercised by administrative agencies, Congress passed several laws to make agencies more accountable through public scrutiny. We discuss here the most significant of these laws.

FREEDOM OF INFORMATION ACT

Enacted in 1966, the Freedom of Information Act (FOIA)[6] requires the federal government to disclose certain "records" to "any person" on request, even if no reason is given for the request. The FOIA exempts certain types of records. For other records, though, a request that complies with the FOIA procedures need only contain a reasonable description of the information sought (see Exhibit 6–6). An agency's failure to comply with a request may be challenged in a federal district court. The media, industry trade associations, public-interest groups, and even companies seeking information about competitors rely on these FOIA provisions to obtain information from government agencies.

Under a 1996 amendment to the FOIA, all federal government agencies now have to make their records available electronically—on the Internet, on computer disks, and in other electronic formats. As of November 1, 1996, any document created by an agency must be available on computer within a year after its creation. Agencies must also provide a clear index to all of their documents.

5. 5 U.S.C. Sections 801–808.
6. 5 U.S.C. Section 552.

GOVERNMENT-IN-THE-SUNSHINE ACT

Congress passed the Government-in-the-Sunshine Act,[7] or open meeting law, in 1976. It requires that "every portion of every meeting of an agency" be open to "public observation." The act also requires the establishment of procedures to ensure that the public is provided with adequate advance notice of scheduled meetings and agendas. Like the FOIA, the sunshine act contains certain exceptions. Closed meetings are permitted when (1) the subject of the meeting concerns accusing any person of a crime, (2) an open meeting would frustrate implementation of agency actions, or (3) the subject of the meeting involves matters relating to future litigation or rulemaking. Courts interpret these exceptions to allow open access whenever possible.

REGULATORY FLEXIBILITY ACT

Concern over the effects of regulation on the efficiency of businesses, particularly smaller ones, led Congress to pass the Regulatory Flexibility Act in 1980.[8] Under this act, whenever a new regulation will have a "significant impact upon a substantial number of small entities," the agency must conduct a regulatory flexibility analysis. The analysis must measure the cost that the rule would impose on small businesses and must consider less burdensome alternatives. The act also contains provisions to alert small businesses—through advertising in trade journals, for example—about forthcoming regulations. The act relieves some record-keeping burdens for small businesses, especially with regard to hazardous waste management.

SMALL BUSINESS REGULATORY ENFORCEMENT FAIRNESS ACT

As mentioned above, the Small Business Regulatory Enforcement Fairness Act (SBREFA) of 1996 allows Congress to review new federal regulations for at least sixty days before they take effect. This period gives opponents of the rules time to present their arguments to Congress.

The SBREFA also authorizes the courts to enforce the Regulatory Flexibility Act. This helps to ensure that federal agencies, such as the Internal Revenue Service, consider ways to reduce the eco-

7. 5 U.S.C. Section 552b.
8. 5 U.S.C. Sections 601–612.

EXHIBIT 6–6 ■ SAMPLE LETTER REQUESTING INFORMATION FROM AN EXECUTIVE DEPARTMENT OR AGENCY

Date

Agency Head or FOIA Officer
Title
Name of Agency
Address of Agency
City, State, Zip

Re: Freedom of Information Act Request.

Dear ______________ :

Under the provisions of the Freedom of Information Act, 5 U.S.C. Section 552, I am requesting access to ____ [identify the records as clearly as possible].

[Optional] I am requesting this information because ________________________ ____ [state the reason for your request if you think it will assist you in obtaining the information].

If there are any fees for searching for, or copying, the records I have requested, please inform me before you fill the request [or:] please supply the records without informing me if the fees do not exceed $ _________.

[or:] As you know, the act permits you to reduce or waive fees when the release of the information is considered as "primarily benefiting the public." I believe that this request fits that category, and I therefore ask that you waive any fees.

If all or any part of this request is denied, please cite the specific exemption(s) that you think justifies your refusal to release the information, and inform me of the appeal procedures available to me under the law.

I would appreciate your handling this request as quickly as possible, and I look forward to hearing from you within 10 days, as the law stipulates.

Sincerely,
[Signature]
Name
Address
City, State, Zip

Source: U.S. Congress, House Committee on Government Operations, *A Citizen's Guide on How to Use the Freedom of Information Act and the Privacy Act Requesting Government Documents*, 95th Congress, 1st session, 1977.

nomic impact of new regulations on small businesses. Federal agencies are required to prepare guides that explain in "plain English" how small businesses can comply with federal regulations.

At the Small Business Administration, the SBREFA set up the National Enforcement Ombudsman to receive comments from small businesses about their dealings with federal agencies. Based on these comments, Regional Small Business Fairness Boards rate the agencies and publicize their findings.

Finally, the SBREFA allows small businesses to recover their expenses and legal fees from the government when an agency makes demands for fines or penalties that a court considers excessive.

SECTION 5 STATE ADMINISTRATIVE AGENCIES

Although most of this chapter deals with federal administrative agencies, state agencies play a significant role in regulating activities within the states. Many of the factors that encouraged the proliferation of federal agencies also fostered the growing presence of state agencies. For example, one reason for the growth of administrative agencies at all levels of government is the inability of Congress and state legislatures to oversee the implementation of their laws.

Another is the greater technical competence of the agencies.

PARALLEL AGENCIES

Commonly, a state creates an agency as a parallel to a federal agency to provide similar services on a more localized basis. Such parallel agencies include the federal Social Security Administration and the state welfare agency, the Internal Revenue Service and the state revenue department, and the Environmental Protection Agency and the state pollution-control agency. Not all federal agencies have parallel state agencies, however. For example, the Federal Bureau of Investigation and the Nuclear Regulatory Commission have no parallel agencies at the state level.

CONFLICTS BETWEEN PARALLEL AGENCIES

If the actions of parallel state and federal agencies conflict, the actions of the federal agency will prevail. For example, if the Federal Aviation Administration specifies the hours during which airplanes may land at and depart from airports, a state or local government cannot issue inconsistent laws or regulations governing the same activities. The priority of federal laws over conflicting state laws is based on the supremacy clause of the U.S. Constitution. Remember from Chapter 5 that this clause, which is found in Article VI of the Constitution, states that the Constitution and "the Laws of the United States which shall be made in Pursuance thereof . . . shall be the supreme Law of the Land."

TERMS AND CONCEPTS TO REVIEW

adjudication 118
administrative law judge (ALJ) 124
administrative process 119
bureaucracy 119
delegation doctrine 119
enabling legislation 116
final order 125
initial order 125
judicial process 119
legislative rule 118
notice-and-comment rulemaking 119
rulemaking 119

QUESTIONS AND CASE PROBLEMS

6–1. RULEMAKING PROCEDURES. Assume that the Securities and Exchange Commission (SEC) has a policy to enforce rules prohibiting insider trading only when the insiders make monetary profits for themselves. Then the SEC modifies this policy by determining that it has the statutory authority to bring an enforcement action against an individual even if he or she does not personally profit from the insider trading. In modifying the policy, the SEC does not conduct a rulemaking but simply announces its new decision. A securities organization objects and says that the policy was unlawfully developed without opportunity for public comment. In a lawsuit challenging the new policy, should the policy be overruled under the Administrative Procedure Act? Discuss.

6–2. RULEMAKING PROCEDURES. Assume that the Food and Drug Administration (FDA), using proper procedures, adopts a rule describing its future investigations. This new rule covers all future cases in which the FDA wants to regulate food additives. Under the new rule, the FDA is not to regulate food additives without giving food companies an opportunity to cross-examine witnesses. Some time later, the FDA wants to regulate methylisocyanate, a food additive. The FDA undertakes an informal rulemaking procedure, without cross-examination, and regulates methylisocyanate. Producers protest, saying that the FDA promised them the opportunity for cross-examination. The FDA responds that the Administrative Procedure Act does not require such cross-examination and that it is free to withdraw the promise made in its new rule. If the producers challenge the FDA in a court, on what basis would the court rule in their favor?

6–3. RULEMAKING AND ADJUDICATION POWERS. For decades, the Federal Trade Commission (FTC) resolved fair trade and advertising disputes through individual adjudications. In the 1960s, the FTC began promulgating rules that defined fair and unfair trade practices. In cases involving violations of these rules, the due process rights of participants were more limited and did not include cross-examination. Although anyone found violating a rule would receive a full adjudication, the legitimacy of the rule itself could not be challenged in the adjudication. Any party charged with violating a rule was almost certain to lose the adjudication. Affected parties complained to a court, arguing that their rights before the FTC were unduly limited by the new rules. What will the court examine to determine whether to uphold the new rules?

6–4. RULEMAKING PROCEDURES. The Department of Commerce issued a flammability standard that required all mattresses, including crib mattresses, to pass a test that involved contact with a burning cigarette. The manufacturers of crib mattresses petitioned the department to exempt their product from the test procedure, but the department refused to do so. The crib manufacturers sued the department and argued that applying such a rule to crib mattresses was arbitrary and capricious because infants do not smoke. On what basis might the court hold that the rule is not arbitrary and capricious? [*Bunny Bear, Inc. v. Peterson*, 473 F.2d 1002 (1st Cir. 1973)]

6–5. RULEMAKING PROCEDURES. The Atomic Energy Commission (AEC) was engaged in rulemaking proceedings for nuclear reactor safety. An environmental group sued the commission, arguing that its proceedings were inadequate. The commission had carefully complied with all requirements of the Administrative Procedure Act. The environmentalists argued, however, that the very hazardous and technical nature of the reactor safety issue required elaborate procedures above and beyond those set forth in the act. A federal court of appeals agreed and overturned the AEC rules. The commission appealed the case to the United States Supreme Court. How should the Court rule? Discuss. [*Vermont Yankee Nuclear Power Corp. v. Natural Resources Defense Council, Inc.*, 435 U.S. 519, 98 S.Ct. 1197, 55 L.Ed.2d 460 (1978)]

6–6. EXECUTIVE CONTROLS. In 1982, the president of the United States appointed Matthew Chabal, Jr., to the position of U.S. marshal. U.S. marshals are assigned to the federal courts. In the fall of 1985, Chabal received an unsatisfactory annual performance rating, and he was fired shortly thereafter by the president. Given that U.S. marshals are assigned to the federal courts, are these appointees members of the executive branch? Did the president have the right to fire Chabal without consulting Congress about the decision? [*Chabal v. Reagan*, 841 F.2d 1216 (3d Cir. 1988)]

6–7. AGENCY INVESTIGATIONS. A state statute required vehicle dismantlers—persons whose business includes dismantling automobiles and selling the parts—to be licensed and to keep records regarding the vehicles and parts in their possession. The statute also authorized warrantless administrative inspections; that is, without first obtaining a warrant, agents of the state department of motor vehicles or police officers could inspect a vehicle dismantler's license and records, as well as vehicles on the premises. Pursuant to this statute, police officers entered an automobile junkyard and asked to see the owner's license and records. The owner replied that he did not have the documents. The officers inspected the premises and discovered stolen vehicles and parts. Charged with possession of stolen property and unregistered operation as a vehicle dismantler, the junkyard owner argued that the warrantless inspection statute was unconstitutional under the Fourth Amendment. The trial court disagreed, reasoning that the junkyard business was a highly regulated industry. On appeal, the highest state court concluded that the statute had no true administrative purpose and impermissibly authorized searches only to discover stolen property. The state appealed to the United States Supreme Court. Should the Court uphold the statute? Discuss. [*New York v. Burger*, 482 U.S. 691, 107 S.Ct. 2636, 96 L.Ed.2d 601 (1987)]

6–8. *EX PARTE* COMMENTS. In 1976, the Environmental Protection Agency (EPA) proposed a rule establishing new pollution-control standards for coal-fired steam generators. The agency gave notice and received comments in the manner prescribed by the Administrative Procedure Act (APA). After the public comments had been received, the EPA received informal suggestions from members of Congress and other federal officials. In 1979, the EPA published its final standards. Several environmental groups protested these standards, arguing that they were too lax. As part of this protest, the groups complained that political influence from Congress and other federal officials, through *ex parte* contracts with EPA officials, had encouraged the EPA to relax the proposed standards. The groups went on to argue that such *ex parte* comments were prohibited by the APA and that such comments should at least have been summarized in the record. What will the court decide? Discuss fully. [*Sierra Club v. Costle*, 657 F.2d 298 (D.C.Cir. 1981)]

6–9. ARBITRARY AND CAPRICIOUS TEST. In 1977, the Department of Transportation (DOT) adopted a passive-restraint standard (known as Standard 208) that required new cars to have either air bags or automatic seat belts. By 1981, it had become clear that all of the major auto manufacturers would install automatic seat belts to comply with this rule. The DOT determined that most purchasers of cars would detach their automatic seat belts, thus making them ineffective. Consequently, the department repealed the regulation. State Farm Mutual Automobile Insurance Co. and other insurance companies sued in the District of Columbia Circuit Court of Appeals for a review of the DOT's repeal of the regulation. That court held that the repeal was arbitrary and capricious because the DOT had reversed its rule without sufficient support. The motor vehicle manufacturers then appealed this decision to the United States Supreme Court. What will result? Discuss fully. [*Motor Vehicle Manufacturers Association v. State Farm Mutual Automobile Insurance Co.*, 463 U.S. 29, 103 S.Ct. 2856, 77 L.Ed.2d 443 (1983)]

6–10. JUDICIAL REVIEW. American Message Centers (AMC) provides answering services to retailers. Calls to a retailer are automatically forwarded to AMC, which pays for the calls. AMC obtains telephone service at a discount from major carriers, including Sprint. Sprint's tariff (a public document setting out rates and rules relating to Sprint's services) states that the "subscriber shall be responsible for the payment of all charges for service." When AMC learned that computer hackers had obtained the access code for AMC's lines and had made nearly $160,000 in long-distance calls, it asked Sprint to absorb the cost. Sprint refused. AMC filed a complaint with the Federal Communications Commission (FCC), claiming in part that Sprint's tariff was vague and ambiguous, in violation of the Communications Act of 1934 and FCC rules. These laws require that a carrier's tariff "clearly and definitely" specify any "exceptions or conditions which in any way affect the rates named in the tariff." The FCC rejected AMC's complaint. AMC appealed the FCC's decision to a federal appellate court, claiming that the FCC's decision to reject AMC's complaint was arbitrary and capricious. What should the court decide? Discuss fully. [*American Message Centers v. Federal Communications Commission*, 50 F.3d 35 (D.C.Cir. 1995)]

6–11. QUESTION OF ETHICS

The Marine Mammal Protection Act was enacted in 1972 to reduce incidental killing and injury of marine mammals during commercial fishing operations. Under the act, commercial fishing vessels are required to allow an employee of the National Oceanic and Atmospheric Administration (NOAA) to accompany the vessels to conduct research and observe operations. In December 1986, after NOAA had adopted a new policy of recruiting female as well as male observers, NOAA notified Caribbean Marine Services Co. that female observers would be assigned to accompany two of the company's fishing vessels on their next voyages. The owners and crew members of the ships (the plaintiffs) moved for an injunction against the implementation of the NOAA directive. The plaintiffs contended that the presence of a female on board a fishing vessel would be very awkward, because the female would have to share the crew's quarters, and crew members enjoyed little or no privacy with respect to bodily functions. Further, they alleged that the presence of a female would be disruptive to fishing operations, because some of the crew members were "crude" men with little formal education who might harass or sexually assault a female observer, and the officers would therefore have to devote time to protecting the female from the crew. Finally, the plaintiffs argued that the presence of a female observer could destroy morale and distract the crew, thus affecting the crew's efficiency and decreasing the vessel's profits. [*Caribbean Marine Services Co. v. Baldrige*, 844 F.2d 668 (9th Cir. 1988)]

1. In general, do you think that the public policy of promoting equal employment opportunity should override the concerns of the vessel owners and crew members? If you were the judge, would you grant the injunction? Why or why not?
2. The plaintiffs pointed out that fishing voyages could last three months or longer. Would the length of a particular voyage affect your answer to the preceding question?
3. The plaintiffs contended that even if the indignity of sharing bunk rooms and toilet facilities with a female observer could be overcome, the observer's very presence in the common areas of the vessel, such as the dining area, would unconstitutionally infringe on the crew members' right to privacy in these areas. Evaluate this claim.

ACCESSING THE INTERNET
THE LEGAL ENVIRONMENT OF BUSINESS

The Internet Law Library, sponsored by the U.S. House of Representatives, offers links to federal and state legislative and regulatory materials, including the Code of Federal Regulations. Go to

http://www.house.gov/

You can find information on federal and state administrative law, links to federal and state administrative procedure acts, and various other resources relating to administrative law at

http://law.fsu.edu/library/adminpro.html

To view the text of the Administrative Procedure Act of 1946, go to

http://www.law.cornell.edu/uscode/5/ch5.html

The Federal Web Locator allows you to search for the names of federal administrative agencies and to find links to agency-related information on the Internet. Go to

http://www.law.vill.edu/Fed-Agency/fedwebloc.html

The State Web Locator provides links to information on state administrative agencies at

http://www.law.vill.edu/State-Agency/statewebloc.html

CHAPTER 7

COMPARATIVE LAW

WHEN DOING BUSINESS ABROAD, a company needs to be aware of how both international law and national law will affect its business activities. **International law** is that body of law that governs relations among or between nations. International customs, treaties, and organizations are all part of the international legal environment of business, which will be discussed in Chapter 8. **National law,** in contrast, is the law of a particular nation, such as the United States, Japan, Germany, or Brazil.

In this chapter, we examine and compare the traditions and legal systems of various nations, as well as specific legal concepts and principles relating to selected areas of substantive law. While it is obviously impossible to discuss here all of the laws of every nation, the following pages will indicate how a variety of nations deal with some of the more important issues facing U.S. businesspersons doing business overseas or conducting business transactions with foreign enterprises.

SECTION 1
DOING BUSINESS ABROAD

The ability to conduct business successfully in a foreign nation requires not only a knowledge of that nation's laws but also some familiarity with its cultural system, economy, and business climate. In this section, we look at some of the ways in which cultural and structural differences can affect transnational business operations.

LANGUAGE AND COMMUNICATION

A crucial part of doing business abroad is understanding the local culture and how it differs from that of the United States. One obvious cultural difference among nations is language. Language differences have occasionally confounded efforts to do business abroad. The following is a list of just a few problems that American businesses have suffered because of language problems:

- Rolls-Royce changed the name of its "Silver Mist" in Germany, because in that country, *mist* translates as "manure."
- In Japan, Esso had difficulty selling gasoline in part because *Esso* sounds like the Japanese word for stalled car.
- Pepsi's "Come Alive with Pepsi" campaign was translated in Taiwan as "Pepsi brings your ancestors back from the grave."
- An airline in Brazil advertised plush "rendezvous lounges" on jets; in Brazil, *rendezvous* implies a special room for making love.
- The Chevy Nova did not go over very well in Spanish-speaking countries because in Spanish *no va* means "it does not go" or "it will not go."

The meaning of nonverbal language (body movements, gestures, facial expressions, and the like) also varies from culture to culture. In the United States, for example, a nod of the head indicates "yes," while in some countries, such as Greece, the same gesture means "no." Similarly, Americans usually indicate "no" by moving the head from side to side, while in India, for example, the same movement means "I'm listening. Please continue."

COLORS AND NUMBERS

Colors also are associated with different meanings in different countries. For example, green is the national color of Egypt, but in Malaysia, green is associated with disease. The same is true for numbers. For example, the number 4 represents bad luck in Japan and Korea.

PERCEPTIONS OF TIME

A frequent source of cultural clashes abroad involves time. For many Americans, punctuality is crucial. In some foreign countries, businesspersons have a more flexible attitude toward time, and Americans seem excessively hurried. Northern Europeans tend to regard time in the same way as U.S. citizens do, but in Latin America, the Middle East, and parts of Asia, meetings may start late and last a long time.

MANAGEMENT STYLES

Researchers have identified certain differences in management style across the continents. The American manager employs a direct, pragmatic, and competitive style. The Latin American manager is more humanistic and indirect, even though Latin American business firms are generally more hierarchical and authoritarian than firms in the United States. The Asian manager is more like the Latin American manager in that Asian management techniques are more indirect and designed to avoid confrontation. The European manager is more like the American, although there are substantial differences in management style between Northern European and Mediterranean nations, with the latter being somewhat less competitive and more family oriented.

ETHICS

Given the varied cultures and religions of the world's nations, one might expect frequent conflicts in ethics between foreign and United States businesspersons. In fact, many of the most important ethical precepts are common to virtually all countries. There are some important ethical differences, however. In Islamic countries, for example, the consumption of alcohol and certain foods is forbidden by the Koran (the sacred book of the Islamic religion, which lies at the heart of Islamic law). It would be thoughtless and imprudent to invite a Saudi Arabian business contact out for a drink. Two notable differences in regard to ethics involve the legitimacy of certain side payments, or gift giving, and the role of women.

GIFT GIVING OR BRIBERY? In many foreign nations, gift giving is a common practice among contracting companies or between companies and government. To Americans, such gift giving may look suspiciously like an unethical (and possibly illegal) bribe. This has been an important source of friction in international business, particularly after the U.S. Congress passed the Foreign Corrupt Practices Act (FCPA) in 1977 (discussed in Chapter 8). The act prohibits American business firms from offering side payments to foreign officials to secure favorable contracts. Payments to minor government officials—to facilitate necessary paperwork relating to a transaction, for example—are not prohibited by the FCPA.

Often, government workers in other countries are paid very little, and the government assumes that these workers will obtain extra income by receiving "grease payments" (to grease the wheels of the bureaucratic machine). Before an American company makes any kind of side payment, it should be sure that it understands local practice. Even when some payment is expected, the form or amount of the payment (if it is too excessive, for example) may violate the ethical rules of the foreign nation itself.

When a businessperson is presented with a gift in his or her official position as a corporate officer, the businessperson may face a dilemma. The company may itself prohibit the receipt of such gifts, for fear of being charged with favoritism by its other employees, yet rejecting the gift may seriously offend the giver. There may be some alternative, though, such as accepting the gift and quietly turning it over to the company or a charity.

WOMEN IN BUSINESS The role played by women in other countries may present some difficult ethical problems for firms doing business internationally. Equal employment opportunity is a fundamental public policy in the United States, and Title VII of the Civil Rights Act of 1964 (discussed in Chapter 20) prohibits discrimination against women in the employment context. Some other countries, however, largely reject any professional role for women, which may cause difficulties for American women conducting business transactions in those countries.

For example, when the World Bank sent a delegation including women to negotiate with the Central Bank of Korea, the Koreans were surprised and offended. They thought that the presence of women meant that the Koreans were not being taken seriously. (This problem might have been cured simply by some advance communication.) In Islamic nations, women are expected to avoid exposing their arms or legs in public. While American women may find it difficult to respect this custom, it may be necessary for them to do so if they wish to succeed in business transactions conducted in those nations.

SECTION 2 COMPARATIVE LEGAL SYSTEMS

When doing business in a foreign nation, a company generally subjects itself to the jurisdiction and laws of that nation. Therefore, a wise businessperson will be familiar with the legal systems of foreign nations in which he or she conducts commercial transactions. The legal systems of foreign nations differ, in widely varying degrees, from that of the United States.

CONSTITUTIONAL FOUNDATIONS

The foundation of a country's legal system is set forth in a governing document that is usually referred to as the nation's constitution. Most nations have several branches of government to exercise legislative, executive, and judicial powers. These systems differ considerably. For example, Taiwan has five independent branches of government. Some nations, including the United States, have federal systems, in which government powers are divided between national and provincial governments. Other nations have **unitary systems,** in which governing authority is concentrated in the hands of a central government and there are no independent local governing units.

In the United States, the Constitution is a single document setting forth powers and rights. The United Kingdom has no single document but considers as its constitution a series of fundamental documents, including the Magna Carta, the Bill of Rights of 1689, and others. One important resulting difference is that British courts have no power to strike down a law as unconstitutional. In the United States, if the United States Supreme Court finds that an act of Congress violates the Constitution, the act will be declared illegal (see the discussion of judicial review in Chapter 3). In the United Kingdom, however, courts cannot invalidate laws passed by Parliament. French courts also lack the power of judicial review of legislative action, although a special constitutional council can invalidate laws. In Germany, laws can be reviewed for constitutionality but only in a special court, and the cases can only be brought by a government body, not individuals. India's constitution is a single document that grants to the courts the power of judicial review over statutory enactments. India also has a supreme court but lacks a fully independent judiciary.

Some nations have specialized commercial law courts to deal with business disputes (in the United States, some jurisdictions are establishing similar courts). France established such courts in 1807, and most nations with commercial codes have done likewise. The United Kingdom also has special commercial courts overseen by judges with expertise in business law.

COMMON LAW AND CIVIL LAW SYSTEMS

Legal systems around the globe generally are divided into *common law* and *civil law* systems.

COMMON LAW SYSTEMS As discussed in Chapter 1, in a common law system, the courts independently develop the rules governing certain areas of law, such as torts and contracts. These common law rules apply to all areas not covered by statutory law. Although the common law doctrine of *stare decisis* obligates judges to follow precedential decisions in their jurisdictions, courts may modify or even overturn precedents when deemed necessary. Additionally, if there is no case law to guide a court, the court may create a new rule of law. Common law systems exist today in countries that were once a part of the British Empire (such as Australia, India, and the United States).

CIVIL LAW SYSTEMS In contrast to Great Britain and the other common law countries, most of the European nations base their legal systems on Roman civil law, or "code law." The term *civil law,* as used here, refers not to civil as opposed to criminal law but to *codified* law—an ordered grouping of legal principles enacted into law by a legislature or other governing body. In a **civil law system,** the only official source of law is a statutory code. Courts are required to interpret the code and apply the rules to individual cases, but courts may not depart from the code and develop their own laws. In theory, the law code will set forth all the principles needed for the legal system.

The best-known example of civil law is the French Napoleonic Code, or *Code Napoléon,* some provisions of which are presented in Exhibit 7–1. This legal system was developed in 1804 by Napoléon Bonaparte, after he became emperor of France. The Napoleonic Code survives to this day, although it has been amended by subsequent French governments. Other significant early law codes are the Spanish Commercial Code of 1885, the Japanese Commercial Code of 1890, and the German Commercial Code of 1900.

Today, civil law systems are followed in most of the continental European countries, as well as in the Latin American, African, and Asian countries that were once colonies of the continental European nations. Japan and South Africa also have civil law systems. Ingredients of the civil law system are found in the Islamic courts of predominantly Muslim countries. In the United States, the state of Louisiana, because of its historical ties to France, has, in part, a civil law system. The legal systems of Puerto Rico, Quebec, and Scotland are similarly characterized as having elements of the civil law system. Exhibit 7–2 lists some of the nations that use common law systems and some that use civil law systems.

LEGAL SYSTEMS COMPARED Common law and civil law systems are not wholly distinct. For example, although the United States has a common law system, crimes are defined by statute as in civil law systems. Civil law systems also may allow considerable room for judges to develop law. Civil law codes cannot be so precise as to address *every* contested issue, so the judiciary must interpret the codes.

Furthermore, there are significant differences among common law countries. The judges of different common law nations have produced differing common law principles. Thus, although the United States and India both derived their legal traditions from England, the common law principles governing contract law differ in some respects between the two countries. Similarly, the laws of nations that have civil law systems vary considerably. For example, the French code tends to set forth general principles of law, while the German code is far more specific and runs to thousands of sections. In some Middle Eastern countries, codes are grounded in the religious law of Islam, called ***sharia.*** The religious basis of these codes makes them far more difficult to alter.

JUDGES AND PROCEDURES

Judges play similar roles in virtually all countries: their primary function is the resolution of litigation. The characteristics and qualifications of judges, which are typically set forth in the nation's constitution, can vary widely, however. The U.S. judge normally does not

EXHIBIT 7–1 ■ EXCERPTS FROM THE CODE NAPOLÉON

Code Napoléon

TITLE III.

OF CONTRACTS OR CONVENTIONAL OBLIGATIONS
IN GENERAL

Decreed the 7th of February 1804. Promulgated the 17th of the same Month.

CHAPTER I.

Preliminary Regulations.

1101.

A contract is an agreement that binds one or more persons, towards another or several others, to give, to do, or not to do something.

* * * *

CHAPTER II.

Of Conditions essential to the Validity of Agreements.

1108.

Four conditions are essential to the validity of an agreement:
The consent of the party who binds himself;
His capacity to contract;
A certain object forming the matter of the contract;
A lawful cause in the bond.

Section I.

Of Consent

1109.

There can be no valid consent if such consent has been given by mistake, or has been extorted through violence or surreptitiously obtained by fraud.

1110.

Mistake is not a cause for annulling the agreement except when it occurs in the very substance of the thing which is the object thereof.

It is not a cause for nullity when it occurs only in the person with whom it is intended to contract, unless the consideration of such person were the principal cause of the agreement.

SOURCE: *The French Civil Code* (Baton Rouge, La.: Claitor's Book Store, 1960 [Reprint]), pp. 302–305.

EXHIBIT 7–2 ■ THE LEGAL SYSTEMS OF NATIONS

CIVIL LAW	COMMON LAW
Argentina	Australia
Austria	Bangladesh
Brazil	Canada
Chile	Ghana
China	India
Egypt	Israel
Finland	Jamaica
France	Kenya
Germany	Malaysia
Greece	New Zealand
Indonesia	Nigeria
Iran	Singapore
Italy	United Kingdom
Japan	United States
Mexico	Zambia
Poland	
South Korea	
Sweden	
Tunisia	
Venezuela	

actively participate in a trial, but many foreign judges involve themselves closely in the proceedings, such as by questioning witnesses. Because U.S. federal judges serve for life and cannot be removed by impeachment except in extreme cases (such as when a judge accepts a bribe), their decisions are less likely to be influenced by politics than may be the case in other countries. In India, for example, judges issuing rulings contrary to the prime minister's views have been transferred or demoted on occasion.

The procedures employed in resolving cases also vary substantially from country to country. A knowledge of a nation's legal procedures is important for a person conducting business transactions in that nation. For example, an American businessperson was on trial in Saudi Arabia for assaulting and slandering a co-worker, an offense for which he might have been jailed or deported. He initially was required to present two witnesses to his version of events, but he had only one. Fortunately, he became aware that he could "demand the oath." In this procedure, he swore before God that he had neither kicked nor slandered the complainant. After taking the oath, he was promptly adjudged not guilty, as lying under oath is one of the most serious sins under Islamic law. Had he failed to demand the oath, he almost certainly would have been found guilty.

LAWYERS AND LITIGATION

The role of lawyers, too, differs from country to country. In the United States, an attorney is required by canons of ethics to serve as a "zealous" advocate for his or her client's interests. In contrast, lawyers in the People's Republic of China are obligated first to further the interests of the government and not necessarily the interests of their clients. Attitudes regarding the function of lawyers also vary. For example, while it is not unusual for American businesspersons to include lawyers and accountants on their negotiating teams, in foreign settings, the presence of these professionals may imply that one is planning some deception.

Tort litigation tends to be more extensive and significant in common law systems than in civil law systems. Indeed, some have blamed America's alleged litigiousness in part on our common law system. Of course, many other factors, such as cultural and business traditions, also affect the legal climate for business. For example, citizens and businesses in some nations, such as Japan, are less disposed to go to court than are their counterparts in the United States.

The total number of lawyers in a country undoubtedly has some effect on litigation, though the vast majority of lawyers do not work directly on lawsuits and do not even appear in court. It is widely believed that the United States has more lawyers (as a percentage of the population) than any other country in the world except Iceland. Comparisons are difficult, however, because there is no uniform global definition of *lawyer.* In Sweden, for example, virtually anyone may serve as a lawyer, without meeting state-mandated educational and other requirements. Exhibit 7–3 shows the number of lawyers in various nations as a percentage of the population.

EXHIBIT 7–3 ■ NUMBER OF LAWYERS PER 100,000 CITIZENS

Iceland	400	Singapore	74
United States	311	Sweden	29
Israel	295	Guyana	17
Venezuela	254	Japan	12
Mexico	153	Kenya	7
England	145	Iran	4
Germany	103	Indonesia	3

SOURCE: Based on information from Euromoney Publications, *The International Financial Law Review 1000* (1993).

SECTION 3

NATIONAL LAWS COMPARED

Certain legal principles are essential to a complex society, and virtually all nations have laws governing torts, contracts, employment, and other areas. Even when the basic principles are fundamentally similar (as in contract law), there are significant variations in the practical application and effect of these laws. This section summarizes some of the similarities and differences among national laws relating to torts, contracts, and employment relationships.

Of course, U.S. businesspersons contemplating any international business transaction should become familiar with the specific legal requirements of the particular country or countries involved. Relevant laws may include those discussed in this section as well as laws governing such areas as corporations, corporate securities, intellectual property, environmental protection, and unfair business practices.

TORT LAW

Tort law, which allows persons to recover damages for harms or injuries caused by the wrongful actions of others, may vary widely among the nations. Common law nations have developed a body of judge-made law regarding what kinds of actions constitute negligence or some other tort that permits recovery. Civil law nations must authorize such recovery in their codes. Exhibit 7–4 shows how the civil law codes of several nations define what constitutes a tort. Even when the statutory language is similar, the application of tort law varies among nations. For example, which party has the burden of proof in a tort lawsuit differs among countries. In the United States, the burden of proof is on the plaintiff. In Russia, the defendant has the burden of proving that he or she was not at fault.

FAILURE TO ACT National tort laws vary considerably with respect to liability for omissions, or failures to act. In some situations, a failure to act will not be regarded as a tort. For example, in the United States, tort law imposes no "duty to rescue," and a person normally is not liable for failing to rescue another person in distress. German law is basically similar. In some countries, though, the failure to rescue another in distress is regarded as negligence.

EXHIBIT 7–4 ■ CIVIL CODE TORT DEFINITIONS

Brazil: He who, by a voluntary act or omission, by negligence or carelessness, violates another's right, or causes him harm, is bound to compensate for the damage.

Egypt: Every culpable act that causes damage to another obliges the person who did it to compensate for it.

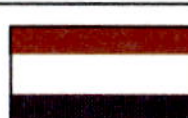
The Netherlands: Every unlawful act by which damage is caused to another obliges the person by whose fault the damage occurred to compensate for it.

Spain: He who by act or omission causes damage to another, either by fault or negligence, is obliged to compensate for the damage caused.

Tunisia: Every act a person does without lawful justification that causes willful and voluntary damage—material or moral—to another obliges the person who did it to compensate for the aforesaid damage, when it is shown that the act is the direct cause.

Uruguay: Every unlawful act a person does which causes damage to another imposes on the person whose malice, fault, or negligence brought it about the obligation to compensate for it. When the unlawful act was done maliciously, i.e., with the intention of causing harm—it amounts to a delict [an intentional tort, discussed in Chapter 6, or a crime], when the intention to cause harm is not present, the unlawful act amounts to a quasi-delict [a tort or a crime caused by negligence]. In either case, the unlawful act can be negative or positive according to whether the breach of duty consists of an act or omission.

SOURCE: Andre Tunc, *International Encyclopedia of Comparative Law*, Vol. XI, Chapter 2, pp. 5–6.

DAMAGES National tort laws also differ in the way in which damages in tort cases are calculated. For example, Swiss law and Turkish law permit a court to reduce damages if an award of full damages would cause undue hardship for a party who was found negligent. In some nations of northern Africa, different amounts of damages are awarded depending on the type of tortious action committed and the degree of intent involved. In the United States, the calculation of actual (compensatory) damages does not depend on whether the tort was negligent or intentional.

STATUTES OF LIMITATIONS Statutes of limitations (deadlines for filing a lawsuit) in other countries also vary and tend to be longer than in the United States. In the United States, state statutes of limitations for tort cases typically run two to three years. In Italy, however, the plaintiff has five years after the tort's commission during which to bring suit. The general French limitations period is ten years.

PRODUCT LIABILITY A growing area of the law in many nations is product liability. As will be discussed in Chapter 14, in the United States, product liability may be imposed on sellers and manufacturers of products based on the tort theories of negligence and strict liability, as well as under warranty theory. Generally, a U.S. manufacturer will be liable for an injury caused by a defective product even though the injury resulted from a defect in a component purchased by the manufacturer from another firm, or supplier. Although other nations also impose product liability on manufacturers and sellers, under some nations' laws, a manufacturer will not be held liable for a defectively designed component purchased from a supplier. The following case illustrates how the German Federal Supreme Court dealt with this issue.

CASE 7.1 Re Product Liability (Case VI ZR 103/89)

Bundesgerichtshof [German Federal Supreme Court], 1991. [1991] ECC 204. [Translated from the German.]

BACKGROUND AND FACTS *The plaintiff purchased an exerciser called the Souplex-Expander from a retail store. The exerciser was manufactured by one company (K-AG), but another company (K-KG) had supplied plastic handle molds for the machine. While the plaintiff was exercising, one of the handles broke, and the expander flew upward, striking the plaintiff in the eye and causing her to lose all sight in that eye. The trial court held that K-KG was liable for damages, including damages for pain and suffering, but found that K-AG was not liable. On appeal, the court reversed and held that K-AG was also liable for these damages. K-AG appealed to the German Federal Supreme Court.*

IN THE LANGUAGE OF THE COURT

DECISION

* * * *

(a) The appeal[s] court made no findings to the effect that the defendant [K-AG] was aware of the dangerous nature of the handle. It evidently proceeded on the basis that the defendant was in a position to find out about the matter, since it explained that the defendant, because of its special knowledge in the field of processing plastics, was not entitled to rely on the molds supplied to it by K-KG being suitable for producing safe and unbreakable handles. This Court cannot agree with that conclusion to such a degree of generality. The [appeals court] is right in objecting that none of the parties to the case has made any submissions to the effect that the defendant had a special knowledge of the weak points in synthetic components under stress. * * *

(b) In the present case the defendant also had no special cause to scrutinize the design of the expander handles inasmuch as the authorized testing office of the Rh-Technical Standards Association had tested the equipment, including the handle produced by the defendant, in accordance with section 3(4) of the Technical Equipment (Safety) Act and granted it the "GS" ("Safety Test") mark, and the B-Technical Standards association had assessed it as "good" after testing it. It is true that a manufacturer who designs his products himself is not exempted from liability for design faults therein solely because a testing institution has examined it and not found defects of the relevant sort. But the position is different for other enterprises that are brought in at various stages of the production process or of the distribution of industrial products; they have lower duties of care in relation to design risks than the actual manufacturer and designer of the product.

DECISION AND REMEDY *The German Federal Supreme Court reversed the appellate court and reinstated the verdict in favor of K-AG.*

ETHICAL CONSIDERATIONS *In the United States, product manufacturers are charged with a high duty of care to all product users. Manufacturers that purchase component parts for their products from other suppliers cannot avoid liability for injuries caused by those defective components. In the United States, if a case involved facts similar to those in the case above, both the manufacturer of the defective component part and the manufacturer of the finished product would be subject to liability. Ultimately, tort liability, including product liability, is based on a society's perception of what is fair and just. As this case indicates, this perception varies from one society to another.*

CONTRACT LAW

Because international business transactions typically involve contracts, businesspersons should familiarize themselves with the contract law of the countries in which they do business. To a degree, the United Nations Convention on Contracts for the International Sale of Goods (CISG) has simplified matters for parties to international sales contracts. As of 1997, thirty-eight countries had ratified or acceded to the CISG, including the United States, Canada, Mexico, some Central and South American countries, and most of the European nations. Four other nations have signed the CISG and have indicated that they intend to ratify it.

Essentially, the CISG is to international sales contracts what the Uniform Commercial Code (UCC) is to domestic sales contracts in the United States. Recall from Chapter 1 that Article 2 of the UCC has been adopted by all of the states except Louisiana as the statutory law governing contracts for the sale of goods. The UCC applies when the parties to a contract for a sale of goods have failed to specify in writing some important term concerning price, delivery, or the like. Similarly, if the parties to international transactions fail to specify in writing the precise terms of a contract, the CISG will be applied.

For many transactions, however, the CISG may not be applicable. For one thing, the CISG applies only to transactions involving firms in countries that have signed the convention, or agreement, and parties (in nonsignatory nations) that have stipulated in their contracts that the CISG will govern any dispute. When transactions involve firms in countries that are not signatory to the CISG, the contract parties need to determine which nation's law will govern any disputes that may arise under the contract. Additionally, even when the CISG would apply, it applies only if the parties have not agreed otherwise in their contract. For example, parties may agree in their contract that German law or U.S. law or some other nation's law will govern any contract dispute that arises. For these reasons, the contract laws of individual nations remain important to businesspersons involved in international contracts.

BASIC CONTRACT REQUIREMENTS IN THE UNITED STATES A *contract* is an agreement that can be enforced in court. As will be discussed in Chapters 9 and 10, in the United States, under the common law of contracts, several requirements must be met for a contract to be valid. The common law of contracts also applies to contracts for the sale of goods, except when the UCC (the statutory law governing sales contracts) has modified common law requirements.

One requirement is *agreement*, which is commonly divided into two events: offer and acceptance. One party, the *offeror*, offers to enter into a contract with another party, the *offeree*. Once the offer is accepted, a valid contract is created—providing the other requirements for a contract are met. Another requirement is *consideration*—each party must give something of legally sufficient value (such as money) to the other party, or the contract will fail. Other requirements include *legality* (the contract must not be contrary to the law or to public policy) and *capacity* (the parties must have the mental capacity to enter into a binding contract). Additionally, the parties' assent to the terms of the contract must be genuine, and certain contracts must be in writing to be enforceable.

Generally, the laws of other nations have similar requirements. There are some important differences, though, particularly with respect to specific aspects of the requirements of agreement, consideration, and legality. Other differences relate to remedies for breach of contract and defenses that can be raised to avoid liability for failing to perform a contract.

AGREEMENT—OFFER AND ACCEPTANCE The requirements of offer and acceptance are common among countries, although what is considered an offer varies by jurisdiction. In the United States, an offer, once made, normally can be revoked (canceled, or taken back) by the offeror at any time prior to the offer's acceptance. Many nations, however, require that an offer must remain open for some minimum period of time. For example, the German Civil Code, which has detailed provisions governing offer and acceptance, requires that a written contractual offer must be held open for a reasonable time, unless the offer specifically states otherwise. Unlike those in the United States, oral contractual offers (those made in person or by telephone) in Germany must be accepted immediately, or they terminate.

Mexico has some special rules for offer and acceptance. If a time for acceptance is not stated in an offer, the offer is deemed to be held open for three days, plus whatever time is necessary for the offer and acceptance to be sent through the mails. If acceptance is desired sooner, the offeror must state the time for acceptance in the offer.

In the United States, a contract's terms must be sufficiently definite that the parties (and a court) can determine whether the contract has been formed or not (see Chapter 9). For contracts for the sale of goods, however, the UCC has substantially relaxed common law requirements in respect to definiteness of contract terms (see Chapter 11). Mexico also has adopted a commercial code, which, like the UCC, liberalizes the traditional requirements of definiteness in mercantile transactions. Under contract law in some countries, such as Saudi Arabia, however, there are strict requirements about the definiteness of a contract's terms. If the terms of an offer are too vague or indefinite, acceptance of that offer normally will not create a valid contract.

CONSIDERATION In contrast to contract law in the United States, contract law in most civil law countries does not require consideration in order for a contract to be legally binding on the parties. German law, for example, does not require the exchange of consideration. An agreement to make a gift may thus be enforceable by the donee (the gift's recipient). In the United States, because consideration is required for a valid contract, promises to make gifts normally are not enforceable (because the donee does not give consideration for the gift).

In other countries, however, such as Saudi Arabia, consideration is required. Similarly, in India, consideration normally is required, although some contracts may be lawful even when the consideration consists of "past consideration" (that is, consideration that consists of an action that occurred in the past). As you will read in Chapter 9, in the United States past consideration is no consideration.

LEGALITY In most nations of the world, as in the United States, contracts to perform illegal acts are void and unenforceable—that is, they are not recognized by the courts as valid contracts. Islamic law, for example, prohibits the consumption of alcohol or pork products. Thus, in Islamic countries, contracts for the sale of those goods are illegal and unenforceable.

In some nations, such as China, certain types of contracts require formal approval by the central government or the relevant provincial government. Failure to obtain such approval will void, or nullify, the contract.

REMEDIES FOR BREACH OF CONTRACT The types of remedies available for breach of contract vary widely throughout the world. In many countries, as in the United States, the normal remedy is damages—money given to the nonbreaching party to compensate that party for the losses incurred owing to the breach (see Chapter 1). The calculation of damages resulting from a breach of contract, however, may differ from one country to another, just as does the calculation of damages under tort law.

National contract laws also differ as to whether and when equitable remedies, such as specific performance (discussed in Chapter 10), will be granted. Germany's typical remedy for a breach of contract is specific performance, which means that the party must go forward and perform the contract. Damages are available only after certain procedures have been employed to seek performance. In contrast, in the United States, the equitable remedy of specific performance will usually not be granted unless the remedy at law (money damages) is inadequate and the subject matter of the contract is unique.

DEFENSES As in the United States, contract law in most nations allows parties to defend against contractual liability by claiming that certain requirements for contract formation have not been met. For example, many nations, including the United States, have laws requiring that certain types of contracts must be in writing. If such contracts are not in writing, they will not be enforced. In Saudi Arabia, the law strongly encourages parties to put all contracts in writing, and any written contract should be formally witnessed by two males or a male and a female. In that country, it may be difficult to enforce an oral contract.

Another common defense is the assertion that a contract was entered into because of fraud or duress, and thus genuineness of assent to the contract's terms was lacking. In some countries, a party may claim that a contract was not formed because the consideration supporting the contract was inadequate—that is, not *enough* value or money was given in exchange for a contractual promise. Indian courts, for example, look to the adequacy of consideration when determining whether the parties' assent to the contract was truly genuine and therefore whether the contract should be enforced. In the United States, in contrast, courts rarely inquire into the adequacy of consideration. Normally, only in cases in which the consideration is so grossly inadequate as to "shock the conscience of the court" will a court refuse to enforce a contract on this basis.

EMPLOYMENT LAW

Employment law is particularly important in many foreign nations. The United States traditionally left the details of the employment relationship to a negotiation between the employer and the employee. Under the common law *employment-at-will* doctrine (discussed in Chapter 20), employers were free to hire and fire employees "at will," meaning that an employee could be fired for any reason or no reason at all. Today, this common law doctrine is less applicable in the United States, because the workplace is regulated extensively by federal and state statutory law. Employment relationships in other nations also are subject to government regulation.

MODIFICATIONS OF THE AT-WILL DOCTRINE

Many other countries, like the United States, have modified their traditional at-will employment rules. In France, for example, the concept of employment at will can be traced back to the original Napoleonic Code. Over the years, the French have modified this doctrine considerably. French courts developed the doctrine of ***abus de droit*** (abuse of rights), which prohibited employers from firing workers for illness, pregnancy, unionization, political beliefs, the exercise of certain rights, or even personal dislike. French courts also began requiring employers to follow customary procedures before terminating workers. French employee-discharge laws were codified in the Dismissal Law of 1973, which also established procedural requirements that employers must follow when discharging workers (to be discussed shortly).

Under the Polish labor code, employment continues to be predominantly "at will." Either party may terminate the employment relationship at any time. Advance notice is generally required, however, and notice requirements vary, depending on the length of the worker's tenure with the employer. An employer may terminate an employee immediately and without notice if the worker has committed a criminal offense, lost a license or other employment qualification, seriously breached his or her duties, or failed to appear regularly at the job site. An employer

EXHIBIT 7–5 ■ HOURLY LABOR COSTS IN MANUFACTURING IN SELECTED COUNTRIES (IN U.S. DOLLARS)

Germany	31.88
Japan	23.66
France	19.34
United States	17.20
Italy	16.48
Canada	16.03
Australia	14.40
Britain	13.77
Spain	12.70
South Korea	7.28
Singapore	7.28
Taiwan	5.82
Hong Kong	4.82
Brazil	4.28
Chile	3.63
Poland	2.09
Hungary	1.70
Argentina	1.67
Malaysia	1.59
Mexico	1.51
Czech Republic	1.30
Philippines	.71
Russia	.60
Thailand	.46
Indonesia	.30
China	.25
India	.25

SOURCE: *The Economist*, November 2, 1996, p. 77.

cannot immediately discharge an employee for the last reason if the employee's absence was due to child-care needs, infectious disease, or entitled sick leave.

WAGES AND BENEFITS One of the reasons U.S. businesspersons decide to establish business operations, such as factories, in other countries is to cut production costs by taking advantage of lower wage rates. As you can see in Exhibit 7–5, hourly labor costs in manufacturing vary significantly from country to country.

Although workers' wages may be lower in some countries than in the United States, typically workers in other countries have many paid holidays plus vacation time. In addition, employers in other countries may be subject to a variety of requirements not found in the United States.

In Mexico, for example, workers have a right to an annual bonus equal to fifteen days' salary and paid at the end of the year. Mexican law requires a minimum amount of paid vacation time (six days in the first year of employment) and also requires that companies give workers a 25 percent bonus above their ordinary pay rates during those vacations. For example, if a worker's ordinary pay is \$200 per week, the vacation pay is \$250 per week. Mexican employers also must periodically give training courses to workers. In some countries, such as Egypt, fringe benefits for employees account for as much as 40 percent of an employer's payroll costs.

INCOME SECURITY AND WORKERS' COMPENSATION Many countries, like the United States, have laws providing for social security and unemployment benefits. The specifics of these programs vary from country to country. Many nations also have some form of workers' compensation laws, much like state workers' compensation laws in the United States (discussed in Chapter 20). These laws compensate employees who are injured on the job. Rules define the nature and scope of workers' compensation and limit it to work-related injuries. In the following case, the issue before the Hong Kong court was whether a worker's death occurred in the course of employment.

CASE 7.2 Fong Fung-Ying and Attorney General

Hong Kong Court of Appeal, 1984. Civil Appeal No. 111 of 1984.

BACKGROUND AND FACTS *A worker agreed to pick up some of his oxy-acetylene welding and cutting equipment at the office of his supervisor at around 8:00 A.M. When his colleagues did not arrive, the worker and his supervisor went to a restaurant and drank wine until 8:50 A.M. The worker left the restaurant and went to a public lavatory in the same block as his office. He was stabbed and killed in the lavatory. His heirs sought to recover for his death under workers' compensation laws. The lower court held that the heirs could not recover under these laws because at the time of his death the worker was not acting in the course of employment. The heirs appealed.*

IN THE LANGUAGE OF THE COURT

SIR ALAN HUGGINS, V.P.

* * * *

Obviously it cannot be right to say that, because a visit to the lavatory might in some circumstances be incidental to the deceased's employment, the deceased was in the course of his employment on every occasion on which he went to that lavatory during working hours. There are two matters to be considered[:] (1) the purpose for which he went there and (2) the circumstances in which he went there. He might have gone there to place a bet with a book-maker, or merely to avoid working, and that would clearly not have been "in the course of" the employment. Of course, one could conceive of numerous possible alternative purposes, and if he went there on another frolic of his own he would have been no more in the course of his employment than he was during his visit to the restaurant. Is it a reasonable and proper assumption on the balance of probabilities that he went there to relieve himself, or was it for the claimant to adduce some evidence to show that that was his intention? * * *

It now being accepted that on the day in question the deceased's visit to the restaurant was not incidental to his employment, it follows that if he had gone from the restaurant to the lavatory with the intention of returning thereafter to the restaurant to continue his unauthorized break, that would equally not have been in the course of his employment.

DECISION AND REMEDY *The Hong Kong Court of Appeal concluded that the survivors bore the burden of proving that the deceased was acting in the course of his employment. Because they were unable to meet this burden, the court dismissed their appeal.*

EQUAL EMPLOYMENT OPPORTUNITY National laws around the globe vary widely with respect to equal employment opportunity. In the United States, employers are prohibited from discriminating against employees or job applicants on the basis of race, color, national origin, gender, religion, age, or disability. U.S. laws prohibiting discrimination on these bases also apply to all U.S. employees working for U.S. employers abroad. Generally, a U.S. employer must abide by U.S. laws prohibiting employment discrimination *unless* to do so would violate the laws of the country in which the employer's workplace is located. This "foreign laws exception" usually allows U.S. employers abroad to avoid being subjected to conflicting laws.

Some other countries also prohibit discriminatory practices. For example, in Indonesia, the Ministry of Manpower, which implements employment laws and regulations, prohibits discrimination in the workplace. Mexican law forbids employers from discriminating against employees on the basis of race, religion, or gender. The Japanese constitution prohibits discrimination based on race, religion, nationality, or gender.

In contrast, some countries, such as Egypt and Turkey, have no laws requiring equal employment opportunity. In Argentina, racial, religious, or other discrimination is not a political issue or a practice prohibited by law. Similarly, in Brazil, equal opportunity is not a factor in employment relationships.

Generally, in those countries that do prohibit employment discrimination, employers retain some flexibility in hiring and firing managerial personnel. In Mexico, for example, employers traditionally have been allowed to hire and fire "confidential" employees—managerial employees—at their discretion. In Italy, workers classified as managers are also less protected by the law.

EMPLOYMENT TERMINATION In many countries, employers find it difficult, and often quite costly, to discharge unwanted or unneeded employees. Employment laws may prohibit the firing of employees for discriminatory reasons, and other laws may also come into play. For example, in France, if an employment contract is for an indefinite term, the employer can fire the worker only for genuine and serious cause or for economic reasons. The law also establishes procedural requirements. Before terminating a worker for cause, the employer must undertake a conciliatory session with labor court mediators. The employer has the burden of proving to the labor court that the cause of the dismissal was serious.

In Egypt, employers commonly use fixed-period employment contracts, which are automatically terminated at the end of the contract period. If an employee continues to work after the end of the contract period and no new contract is created, the employment contract becomes indefinite. It is very difficult to discharge an employee with an indefinite contract. The employee must first commit a serious offense, whereupon the employer must submit a proposal for termination to a committee consisting of representatives of the union, the employer, and the government. Employees may appeal adverse decisions of this committee.

Taiwanese law places clear restrictions on the termination of employment. An employer must provide a reason for discharging an employee. An employer may discharge an employee with advance notice and severance pay for a number of economic reasons or if the worker is incapable of performing the assigned work. The amount of notice and severance pay depends on the worker's tenure with the company. Employers may fire employees without notice or severance pay only for causes such as violence, imprisonment, extensive absenteeism, or lying on a job application should the lie cause the employer to suffer actual harm.

The legal requirements for terminating employment in France, Egypt, and Taiwan are representative of those in many other nations around the world. In practice, employers often circumvent these requirements by offering generous severance benefits to employees to encourage them to resign. Thus, employment termination laws may add substantially to the cost of conducting business abroad.

SECTION 4
THE EUROPEAN UNION

The European Union (EU) arose out of the 1957 Treaty of Rome, which created the Common Market, a free trade zone comprising the nations of Belgium, France, West Germany, Italy, the Netherlands, and Luxembourg. Since 1957, more nations have been added, and the powers of the EU have grown. The EU has added Austria, Denmark, Finland, Greece, Ireland, Portugal, Spain, Sweden, and the United Kingdom to the original Common Market countries. Some Eastern European nations have applied for membership. Some believe that the result will eventually be a "United States of Europe."

The EU has its own governing authorities. One is the Council of Ministers, which coordinates economic policies and includes one representative from each nation. The EU also has a commission that proposes regulations to the council and an elected assembly, which oversees the commission. The community has its own court, the European Court of Justice, which can review each nation's court decisions and is the ultimate authority on EU law.

The EU has gone far toward creating a new body of law to govern all of the member nations, although some of the EU's efforts to create uniform laws have been confounded by nationalism. The council and the commission issue regulations, or directives, that define the EU law in various areas, and these requirements normally are binding on member states. EU directives govern such issues as environmental law, anticompetitive practices, and laws governing corporations. The EU directive on product liability, for example, states that a "producer of an article shall be liable for damage caused by a defect in the article, whether or not he knew or could have known of the defect." Liability extends to anyone who puts a trademark or other identifying feature on the article, and liability may not be excluded, even by contract.

Development of the EU has complicated European business law. A company now must consider international regulations, as well as the rules of the country of operation. This effect is illustrated by the following case.

CASE 7.3 Alsatel - Société Alsacienne et Lorraine de Télécommunications et d'Electronique v. S.A. Novasam

Court of Justice of the European Communities, 1988. Eur. Comm. Rep. 5987. [Translated from the French.]

BACKGROUND AND FACTS *Alsatel - Société Alsacienne et Lorraine de Télécommunications et d'Electronique brought a claim against S.A. Novasam, a temporary employment agency. Novasam had terminated three contracts for the rental of telephone installations. A fifteen-year contract with Alsatel had bound Novasam to deal exclusively with Alsatel for any changes in service, extension of service, additional lines, or other modifications of the installations. The price of such modifications was to be set by Alsatel. Novasam's termination breached this contract under traditional contract law principles, but Novasam claimed that the contract was invalid under Article 86 of the EU treaty, which prohibits a company from abusing its dominant position or market power. The national court in France submitted the issue to the European Court of Justice for clarification.*

IN THE LANGUAGE OF THE COURT

JUDGMENT:

* * * *

Although the obligation imposed on customers to deal exclusively with the installer as regards any modification of the installation may be justified by the fact that the equipment remains the property of the installer, the fact that the price of the supplements to the contract entailed by those modifications is not determined but is unilaterally fixed by the installer and the automatic renewal of the contract for a 15-year term if as a result of those modifications the rental is increased by more than 25% may constitute unfair trading conditions prohibited as abusive practices by Article 86 of the treaty if all the conditions for the application of that provision are met.

The first condition for the application of that provision is that trade between member states must be affected. * * * That condition would be satisfied, in particular, if the contractual clauses referred to above had the effect of restricting imports of telephone equipment from other member states, thereby partitioning the market. There is nothing in the documents before the court which suggests that such is the case. However, it is for the national court to make the necessary findings of fact in that regard.

The second condition laid down by Article 86 is that there must be a dominant position within the common market or in a substantial part of it. The court has defined such a dominant position as a position of economic strength enjoyed by an undertaking which enables it to hinder the maintenance of effective competition on the relevant market by allowing it to behave to an appreciable extent independently of its competitors and customers.

* * * *

There is nothing in the documents before the court that suggests that plaintiff enjoys a dominant position throughout France. The only fact * * * with regard to the plaintiff's economic strength is the large share it holds of the regional market.

A finding of that kind is insufficient to establish that the undertaking in question occupies a dominant position.

DECISION AND REMEDY *The Court of Justice of the European Communities formally ruled that "Article 86 of the [EU] treaty must be interpreted as meaning that contractual practices, even if abusive ones, on the part of an undertaking supplying telephone installations which has a large share of a regional market in a member state do not fall within the prohibition in that article where that undertaking does not occupy a dominant position in the relevant market, in this case the domestic market in telephone installations."*

SECTION 5

EXPANDING BUSINESS OPPORTUNITIES ABROAD

International business transactions have always been attended by more risk than is normally involved in domestic transactions. Since the end of the Cold War following the dissolution of the Soviet Union in 1991, though, the economic climate for business has improved around the globe. In the past, a business involved in overseas investments and operations faced the risk that a socialist government might come into power and nationalize the company, with or without compensation. While the risk of nationalization is still present today, the danger is far less. Additionally, in the past, some countries restricted the ability of U.S. companies to repatriate their profits (take the profits back to the United States), but these restrictions are also disappearing.

Conversely, many countries are now privatizing companies that had been nationalized and run by the government. **Privatization** occurs when a company purchases an entire business that has been operated by the government or moves into competition in a field previously monopolized by the government. For example, Argentina is privatizing its mineral-extractive industries as well as its communications, transportation, and energy industries. Argentina also has eliminated most of the restrictions that it had placed on foreign investment and is eliminating most price controls.

The movement toward privatization is at different stages in other nations. France has gradually undertaken a denationalization program. India is still relatively socialized and requires government approval for much foreign investment. Government approval has become much easier to obtain, however. Egypt offers many investment incentives unavailable elsewhere.

The trend toward privatization has created significant opportunities for businesspersons. It has also created new opportunities for contracting on the basis of price, rather than politics. Other developments that have expanded international business opportunities will be examined in Chapter 8, in the context of the international legal environment of business.

TERMS AND CONCEPTS TO REVIEW

abus de droit 143
civil law system 136
international law 133
national law 133
privatization 147
sharia 136
unitary system 135

QUESTIONS AND CASE PROBLEMS

7–1. ETHICAL CODES OF CONDUCT. A considerable ethical controversy surrounds multinational enterprises (MNEs), which are often beyond the reach of national laws. For ethical or public relations purposes, some MNEs have established internal codes of conduct to govern their behavior toward customers and other populations. Suppose that you were called on to draft such a code for an MNE. What provisions would you include?

7–2. COMPARATIVE EMPLOYMENT LAWS. Assume that you are president of a manufacturing company that intends to expand overseas. Shipping costs and tariffs for your product are uniformly low. Your manufacturing process, however, is highly labor intensive. How would the employment laws of various nations influence your decision on where to situate a new manufacturing plant?

7–3. WOMEN AND BUSINESS. Joe Henderson is the president of an Asian branch of a U.S. bank. His top vice president is a woman, Betty Carter. He would like to take her with him to an important meeting at which he will undertake loan negotiations with a huge company. He has been advised, however, that he will lose respect in the eyes of the overseas company—and perhaps the company's business—if she accompanies him. He talks with her, and she informs him that she does not mind deferring to men at social activities, if local customs demand such deference, but that at the business meetings, she will expect business as usual and will not alter her behavior simply because she is a woman. What should Henderson do? Discuss.

7–4. LEGAL SYSTEMS. As China and formerly communist nations move toward free enterprise, they must develop a new set of business laws. If you could start from scratch, what kind of business law system would you adopt, a civil law system or a common law system? What kind of business regulations would you impose?

7–5. ETHICS AND EXPORTING. AgriChem is a U.S. firm that manufactures pesticides. AgriChem's main product is an effective insecticide called Rodeo. The U.S. Environmental Protection Agency has banned Rodeo because it has the potential to cause cancer. AgriChem has huge inventories of Rodeo that no longer can be sold in the United States. There is a substantial market for Rodeo in many Latin American countries, however, and American law permits the pesticide's export. Moreover, the Latin American countries permit its sale. Should AgriChem export Rodeo for sale in these countries?

7–6. BRIBERY OF FOREIGN OFFICIALS. The Foreign Corrupt Practices Act of 1977 prohibits any U.S. corporation from paying foreign government officials to gain favorable business contracts. UsOil seeks to drill and produce oil and natural gas from a new field found in a foreign nation. The minister of the interior in that nation makes it clear, however, that he will consider granting drilling rights only to companies that make a major contribution to his family-run "charity." Should UsOil make this payment in order to obtain access to the market?

7–7. DOING BUSINESS ABROAD. You are the human resources director for a major American conglomerate. Your company decides that it wants to expand its international presence considerably and asks you to develop a training program for managers. The aim of this training program is to develop managers who can operate more effectively in foreign nations. What components would you include in such a program?

7–8. INTERNATIONAL BUSINESS CONTRACTS. In 1995, France implemented a law making the use of the French language mandatory in certain legal documents. Documents relating to securities offerings, such as prospectuses, for example, must be written in French. So must instruction manuals and warranties for goods and services offered for sale in France. Additionally, all agreements entered into with French state or local authorities, with entities controlled by state or local authorities, and with private entities carrying out a public service (such as providing utilities) must be written in

French. What kinds of problems might this law pose for U.S. businesspersons who wish to form contracts with French persons or business entities?

7–9. EMPLOYMENT DISCRIMINATION. Radio Free Europe and Radio Liberty (RFE/RL), a U.S. corporation doing business in Germany, employs more than three hundred U.S. citizens at its principal place of business in Munich, Germany. The concept of mandatory retirement is deeply embedded in German labor policy, and a contract formed in 1982 between RFE/RL and a German labor union contained a clause that required workers to be retired when they reached the age of sixty-five. When William Mahoney and other American employees (the plaintiffs) reached the age of sixty-five, RFE/RL terminated their employment as required under its contract with the labor union. The plaintiffs sued RFE/RL for discriminating against them on the basis of age, in violation of the Age Discrimination in Employment Act of 1967. Will the plaintiffs succeed in their suit? Discuss fully. [*Mahoney v. RFE/RL, Inc.*, 47 F.3d 447 (D.C. Cir. 1995)]

ACCESSING THE INTERNET
THE LEGAL ENVIRONMENT OF BUSINESS

The International Law Society of the University of Arizona College of Law has an online collection of various resources relating to international law, as well as to the national laws of some other countries. You can access this collection by going to

http://aruba.ccit.arizona.edu/~rdespeld/ils.html

To obtain information on the environmental laws of other countries, you can access the Australian Center for Environmental Law at

http://www.law.usyd.edu.au/~acel

If you are interested in learning about Russia's rules and regulations governing business, access Rules and Regulations in Russia at

http://www.spb.su/rulesreg/

Decisions from the English House of Lords, the final court of appeal in Britain, are now available on the Web. The site also provides general information on the judicial function of the House of Lords, including its jurisdiction and procedures. If you would like to learn more about the British civil and criminal justice system or to find decisions on certain types of cases, go to

http://www.parliament.the-stationery-office.co.uk/pa/ld/ldjudinf.htm

A gopher site that contains civil liberties reports for most countries in the world is

gopher://cyfer.esusda.gov/11/ace/state/hrcr

The Library of Congress's Global Legal Information Network has information on the national laws of more than thirty-five countries, as well as a comprehensive Guide to Law Online. You can access this site at

http://lcweb2.loc.gov/glin/lawhome.html

Chapter 8

International Law

SINCE ANCIENT TIMES, INDEPENDENT PEOPLES and nations have traded their goods and wares with one another. In other words, international business transactions are not unique to the modern world, because people have always found that they can benefit from exchanging goods with others. What is new in our time is the dramatic growth in world trade and the emergence of an increasingly global business community. Just in the last decade, world trade has increased by 80 percent.[1] Today, nearly every major business considers the potential of international markets for its products or services. It is no longer uncommon for a U.S. corporation to have investments or manufacturing plants in a foreign country or for a foreign corporation to have operations in the United States.

Because the exchange of goods, services, and ideas on a global level is now routine, students of business law should be familiar with the laws pertaining to international business transactions. In this chapter, we examine the nature and sources of international law, some of the ways in which U.S. businesspersons commonly do business in or with foreign countries, and how those activities are regulated. The chapter goes on to discuss the application of certain U.S. laws, such as antitrust laws and laws prohibiting discrimination, in a transnational setting. We also look briefly at dispute

1. U.S. Trade Representative Charlene Barshefsky in a statement made to the Ministerial Conference in Singapore, December 9, 1996, as cited in Lucinda A. Low and Kathryn Cameron Atkinson, "Led by the U.S., the World Wages War on Corruption," *The National Law Journal*, March, 3, 1997, p. B9.

settlement in the international context, as well as at a problem of increasing significance for those involved in international business transactions: the bribery of foreign officials.

SECTION 1

THE NATURE AND SOURCES OF INTERNATIONAL LAW

International law, which we mentioned briefly in Chapter 7, was defined there as a body of law—formed as a result of international customs, treaties, and organizations—that governs relations among or between nations. The major difference between *national law* (the laws of specific nations, discussed in detail in Chapter 7) and international law is the fact that national law can be enforced by government authorities. What government, however, can enforce international law? By definition, a *nation* is a sovereign entity—which means that there is no higher authority to which that nation must submit. If a nation violates an international law, the most that other countries or international organizations can do (when persuasive tactics fail) is resort to coercive actions—from severance of diplomatic relations and boycotts to, as a last resort, war—against the violating nation.

In essence, international law is the result of centuries-old attempts to reconcile the traditional need of each nation to be the final authority over its own affairs with the desire of nations to benefit economically from trade and harmonious relations with one another. Sovereign nations can, and do, voluntarily agree to be governed in certain respects by international law for the purpose of facilitating international trade and commerce, as well as civilized discourse. As a result, a body of international law has evolved. In this section, we examine the primary sources and characteristics of that body of law.

INTERNATIONAL CUSTOMS

One important source of international law consists of the international customs that have evolved among nations in their relations with one another. In Article 38(1) of the Statute of the International Court of Justice, an international custom is referred to as "evidence of a general practice accepted as law." The legal principles and doctrines discussed in Section 2 of this chapter are rooted in international customs and traditions that evolved over time in the international arena.

TREATIES AND INTERNATIONAL AGREEMENTS

Treaties and other explicit agreements between or among foreign nations provide another important source of international law. A **treaty** is an agreement or contract between two or more nations that must be authorized and ratified by the supreme power of each nation. Under Article II, Section 2, of the U.S. Constitution, the president has the power "by and with the Advice and Consent of the Senate, to make Treaties, provided two-thirds of the Senators present concur."

A *bilateral* agreement, as the term implies, occurs when two nations form an agreement that will govern their commercial exchanges or other relations with one another. *Multilateral* agreements are those formed by several nations. For example, regional trade associations such as the European Union (EU) and the trading unit established by the North American Free Trade Agreement (NAFTA), both of which are discussed later in this chapter, are the result of multilateral trade agreements. Other regional trade associations that have been created through multilateral agreements include the Association of Southeast Asian Nations (ASEAN) and the Andean Common Market (ANCOM).

INTERNATIONAL ORGANIZATIONS AND CONFERENCES

International organizations and conferences further contribute to international law. In international law, the term **international organization** generally refers to an organization composed mainly of nations and usually established by treaty.

The United States is a member of more than one hundred multilateral and bilateral organizations, including at least twenty through the United Nations (see Exhibit 8–1). These organizations adopt resolutions, declarations, and other types of standards that often require a particular behavior of nations. The General Assembly of the United Nations, for example, has adopted numerous nonbinding resolutions and declarations that embody principles of international law. Disputes with respect to these resolutions and declarations may be brought before the International Court of Justice. That court, however, normally has authority to settle legal disputes only when nations voluntarily submit to its jurisdiction.

The United Nations Commission on International Trade Law has made considerable progress in

EXHIBIT 8–1 ■ MULTILATERAL INTERNATIONAL ORGANIZATIONS IN WHICH THE UNITED STATES PARTICIPATES

NAME	PURPOSE
Customs Cooperation Council	Established in 1950. Supervises the application and interpretation of an international code classifying goods and customs tariffs.
World Trade Organization (WTO)	Established in 1994 during the final round of negotiations of the General Agreement on Tariffs and Trade (GATT). The GATT was created in 1947 and was the first global commercial agreement in history. It became the principal instrument for regulating international trade and limiting tariffs and other barriers to world trade on particular commodities and other items. GATT ceased to exist in 1995, when the WTO came into existence to regulate worldwide trade.
International Bank for Reconstruction and Development	Popularly known as the World Bank; a specialized agency of the United Nations since 1947. Promotes growth, trade, and balance of trade by facilitating and providing technical assistance, particularly in agriculture, energy, transportation, and telecommunications.
International Center for the Settlement of Investment Disputes	Established in 1966. Conciliates and arbitrates disputes between private investors and governments of other countries.
International Civil Aviation Organization	Established in 1947 and became a specialized agency of the United Nations seven months later. Develops international civil aviation by issuing rules and policies for safe and efficient airports and air navigation.
International Court of Justice (World Court)	Established in 1922 and became one of the principal organs of the United Nations in 1945. Jurisdiction comprises all cases that are referred to it. Decides disputes in accord with the rules of international law.
International Maritime Organization	Established in 1948. Promotes cooperation in the areas of government regulation, practices and technical matters of all kinds affecting shipping in international trade, the adoption of standards of maritime safety and efficiency, and the abolition of discrimination and unnecessary restrictions.
International Monetary Fund (IMF)	Created in 1944 at the United Nations Monetary and Financial Conference. Promotes economic stability by aiding the growth of international trade and the stability of currency exchange rates, as well as by providing for a system of international monetary assistance.
International Telecommunications Satellite Organization	Established in 1964. Operates an international public communications satellite system on a commercial, nondiscriminatory basis.
Permanent Court of Arbitration	Established in 1899 to facilitate the settlement of international disputes. The court has jurisdiction over all cases that it is requested to arbitrate.
United Nations (UN)	Established in 1945 to maintain international peace and security. Promotes international cooperation.
World Intellectual Property Organization	Established in 1967 and became a specialized agency of the United Nations in 1974. Promotes protection of intellectual property throughout the world.

establishing more uniformity in international law as it relates to trade and commerce. One of the commission's most significant creations to date is the 1980 Convention on Contracts for the International Sale of Goods (CISG). The CISG is similar to Article 2 of the Uniform Commercial Code (see Chapter 11) in that it is designed to settle disputes between parties to sales contracts. It spells out the duties of international buyers and sellers that will apply if the parties have not agreed otherwise in their contract. The CISG only governs sales contracts between trading partners in nations that have ratified the CISG, however.

SECTION 2

LEGAL PRINCIPLES AND DOCTRINES

Over time, a number of legal principles and doctrines have evolved and have been employed—to a greater or lesser extent—by the courts of various nations to resolve or reduce conflicts that involve a foreign element. The three important legal principles discussed below are based primarily on courtesy and respect and are applied in the interests of maintaining harmonious relations among nations.

THE PRINCIPLE OF COMITY

Under what is known as the principle of **comity,** one nation will defer and give effect to the laws and judicial decrees of another country, as long as those laws and judicial decrees are consistent with the law and public policy of the accommodating nation. For example, assume that a Swedish seller and an American buyer have formed a contract, which the buyer breaches. The seller sues the buyer in a Swedish court, which awards damages. The buyer's assets, however, are in the United States and cannot be reached unless the judgment is enforced by a U.S. court of law. In such a situation, if a U.S. court determined that the procedures and laws applied in the Swedish court were consistent with U.S. national law and policy, the U.S. court would likely defer to, and enforce, the foreign court's judgment.

THE ACT OF STATE DOCTRINE

The **act of state doctrine** is a judicially created doctrine that provides that the judicial branch of one country will not examine the validity of public acts committed by a recognized foreign government within its own territory. This doctrine is premised on the theory that the judicial branch should not "pass upon the validity of foreign acts when to do so would vex the harmony of our international relations with that foreign nation."[2]

The act of state doctrine can have important consequences for individuals and firms doing business with, and investing in, other countries. For example, this doctrine is frequently employed in cases involving **expropriation,** which occurs when a government seizes a privately owned business or privately owned goods for a proper public purpose and awards just compensation. When a government seizes private property for an illegal purpose and without just compensation, the taking is referred to as a **confiscation.** The line between these two forms of taking is sometimes blurred because of differing interpretations of what is illegal and what constitutes just compensation. To illustrate: Tim Flaherty, an American businessperson, owns a mine in Brazil. The government of Brazil seizes the mine for public use and claims that the profits Tim has already realized from the mine constitute just compensation. Tim disagrees, but the act of state doctrine may prevent Tim's recovery in a U.S. court of law.

When applicable, both the act of state doctrine and the doctrine of *sovereign immunity,* which we discuss next, tend to shield foreign nations from the jurisdiction of U.S. courts. What this means is that, generally, firms or individuals who own property overseas have little legal protection against government actions in the countries in which they operate.

THE DOCTRINE OF SOVEREIGN IMMUNITY

When certain conditions are satisfied, the doctrine of **sovereign immunity** exempts foreign nations from the jurisdiction of the U.S. courts. In 1976, Congress codified this rule in the Foreign Sovereign Immunities Act (FSIA).[3] The FSIA also modified previous applications of the doctrine in certain respects by expanding the rights of plaintiff creditors against foreign nations.

The FSIA exclusively governs the circumstances in which an action may be brought in the United States against a foreign nation. Section 1605 of the FSIA sets forth the major exceptions to the jurisdictional immunity of a foreign state. A foreign state is not immune from the jurisdiction of the courts of the United States when the state has "waived its immunity either explicitly or by implication" or when the state has engaged in actions that are taken "in connection with a commercial activity carried on in the United States by the foreign state" or that have "a direct effect in the United States."

Issues frequently arise as to whether particular entities fall within the category of foreign state. Under Section 1603 of the FSIA, a foreign state is defined to include both a political subdivision of a

2. *Libra Bank Ltd. v. Banco Nacional de Costa Rica, S.A.,* 570 F.Supp. 870 (S.D.N.Y. 1983).

3. 28 U.S.C. Sections 1602–1611.

foreign state and an instrumentality of a foreign state (an agency or entity acting for the state). The question of what is a commercial activity has also been the subject of dispute, because the particulars of what constitutes a commercial activity are not defined in the act. Rather, it is left up to the courts to decide whether a particular activity is governmental or commercial in nature.

In the following case, a foreign government claimed immunity from the jurisdiction of U.S. courts on the basis of sovereign immunity. The issue turned on whether the actions of the foreign government were commercial activities.

CASE 8.1 Holden v. Canadian Consulate

United States Court of Appeals, Ninth Circuit, 1996. 92 F.3d 918.

BACKGROUND AND FACTS *Canada closed its consulate in San Francisco and laid off many employees, including Arlene Holden, who had worked for thirteen years as one of the consulate's commercial officers. In place of the consulate, Canada opened a small office staffed with only one commercial officer—Mark Ritchie, a man younger and less experienced than Holden. Holden filed a suit in a U.S. district court against the consulate, alleging, among other things, discrimination. The consulate asked the court to dismiss the suit based on sovereign immunity under the Foreign Sovereign Immunities Act (FSIA). The court concluded that the consulate's employment of Holden was a "commercial activity." The consulate appealed.*

IN THE LANGUAGE OF THE COURT

LEAVY, Circuit Judge:

* * * *

* * * [T]he [FSIA's] legislative history * * * provides a useful framework for analyzing [commercial activity.] The * * * House Report states, " * * * [A] government's * * * employment or engagement of laborers, clerical staff or public relations or marketing agents * * * would be among those [activities] included within the definition [of commercial activity]."

* * * *

The district court examined the nature of Holden's work to determine if she was a civil servant, and found that she was not. * * * Holden did not compete for any examination prior to being hired, was not entitled to tenure, was not provided the same benefits as foreign service officers and did not receive any civil service protections from the Canadian government. * * *

* * * *

Although Holden * * * was a part of the Consulate's staff, her work was not that of a diplomat. As the district court found, Holden's activities were primarily promoting and marketing and she was not involved in any policy making and was not privy to any governmental policy deliberations. She did not engage in any lobbying activity or legislative work for Canada, and she could not speak for the government. * * * Furthermore, as an American, she was not allowed in the Consulate unless in the company of a foreign service officer.

Her employment is more analogous to a marketing agent. * * * The nature of Holden's work, promotion of products, is regularly done by private persons. As such, her employment was a commercial activity, and thus the Consulate is not entitled to sovereign immunity under the FSIA.

DECISION AND REMEDY *The U.S. Court of Appeals for the Ninth Circuit affirmed the lower court's ruling. The appellate court denied the consulate sovereign immunity on the ground that the consulate's employment of Holden was a commercial activity.*

SECTION 3

DOING BUSINESS INTERNATIONALLY

A U.S. domestic firm can engage in international business transactions in a number of ways. Here, we look at some of the ways in which businesspersons extend their business operations into the international arena.

The simplest way of entering into international business operations is to seek out foreign markets for domestically produced products. In other words, U.S. firms can **export** their goods and services to foreign markets. Alternatively, a U.S. firm can establish foreign production facilities so as to be closer to the foreign market or markets in which the firm's products are sold. The advantages may include lower labor costs, fewer government regulations, and lower taxes and trade barriers. A U.S. firm can also obtain business from abroad by licensing technology that it has developed and owns to an existing foreign company. Finally, it is possible to expand abroad by selling franchises to overseas entities. The presence of McDonald's, Burger King, and KFC franchises throughout the world attests to the popularity of franchising.

EXPORTING

Most U.S. companies make the initial foray into international business through exporting. Exporting can take two forms: direct exporting and indirect exporting. In *direct exporting,* a U.S. company signs a sales contract with a foreign purchaser that provides for the conditions of shipment and payment for the goods. If business develops sufficiently in foreign countries, a U.S. company may, through the appointment of a foreign agent or a foreign distributor, develop a specialized marketing organization in the foreign market. This is called *indirect exporting*.

FOREIGN AGENT When a U.S. firm desires a limited involvement in an international market, it will typically establish an agency relationship with a foreign firm. In an agency relationship, one person (the agent) agrees to act on behalf of, or instead of, another (the principal)—see Chapter 19. The foreign agent is thereby empowered to enter into contracts in the agent's country on behalf of the U.S. principal.

FOREIGN DISTRIBUTOR When a substantial market exists in a foreign country, a U.S. firm may wish to appoint a distributor located in that country. The U.S. firm and the distributor enter into a **distribution agreement,** which is a contract between the seller and the distributor setting out the terms and conditions of the distributorship—for example, price, currency of payment, guarantee of supply availability, and method of payment. The terms and conditions primarily involve contract law. Disputes concerning distribution agreements may involve jurisdictional or other issues. In addition, some **exclusive distributorships**—that is, distributorships in which the distributors are given exclusive rights to distribute particular sellers' products in specified areas—have raised antitrust problems (see Chapter 27).

MANUFACTURING ABROAD

An alternative to direct or indirect exporting is the establishment of foreign manufacturing facilities. Typically, U.S. firms want to establish manufacturing plants abroad if they believe that by doing so they will reduce costs—particularly for labor, shipping, and raw materials—and thereby be able to compete more effectively in foreign markets. Apple Computer, IBM, General Motors, and Ford are some of the many U.S. companies that have established manufacturing facilities abroad. Foreign firms have done the same in the United States. Sony, Nissan, and other Japanese manufacturers have established U.S. plants to avoid import duties that the U.S. Congress may impose on Japanese products entering this country.

An American firm can manufacture in other countries in several ways. They include licensing and franchising, as well as investing in a wholly owned subsidiary or a joint venture.

LICENSING U.S. firms can license their technologies to foreign manufacturers. **Technology licensing** may involve a process innovation that lowers the cost of production, or it may involve a product innovation that generates a superior product. Technology licensing may be an attractive alternative to establishing foreign production facilities, particularly if the process or product innovation has been patented, because the patent protects—at least to some extent—against the possibility that the innovation might be pirated. Like any other licensing agreement, a licensing agreement with a foreign-based firm calls for a payment of royalties on some basis—such as so many cents per unit produced or a certain percentage of profits from units sold in a particular geographical territory.

In certain circumstances, even in the absence of a patent, a firm may be able to license the "know-how" associated with a particular manufacturing process—for example, a plant design or a secret formula. The foreign firm that agrees to sign the licensing agreement further agrees to keep the know-how confidential and to pay royalties. For example, the Coca-Cola Bottling Company licenses firms worldwide to use (and keep confidential) its secret formula for the syrup used in that soft drink, in return for a percentage of the income gained from the sale of Coca-Cola by those firms.

The licensing of technology benefits all parties to the transaction: the firm that receives the license can take advantage of an established reputation for quality, and the firm that grants the license receives income from the foreign sales of its products, as well as establishing a worldwide reputation. Also, once a firm's trademark is known worldwide, the demand for other products manufactured or sold by that firm may increase—obviously an important consideration.

FRANCHISING Franchising is a well-known form of licensing. A franchise can be defined as an arrangement in which the owner of a trademark, trade name, or copyright (the franchisor) licenses another (the franchisee) to use the trademark, trade name, or copyright, under certain conditions or limitations, in the selling of goods or services. In return, the franchisee pays a fee, which is usually based on a percentage of gross or net sales. Examples of international franchises include McDonald's, Holiday Inn, Avis, and Hertz. (Franchising will be discussed in more detail in Chapter 17.)

INVESTING IN A WHOLLY OWNED SUBSIDIARY OR A JOINT VENTURE One way to expand into a foreign market is to establish a wholly owned subsidiary firm in a foreign country. The European subsidiary would likely take the form of a *société anonyme* (S.A.), which is similar to a U.S. corporation. In German-speaking nations, it would be called an *Aktiengesellschaft* (A.G.). When a wholly owned subsidiary is established, the parent company, which remains in the United States, retains complete ownership of all the facilities in the foreign country, as well as complete authority and control over all phases of the operation.

The expansion of a U.S. firm into international markets can also take the form of a joint venture. In a joint venture, the U.S. company owns only part of the operation; the rest is owned either by local owners in the foreign country or by another foreign entity. In a joint venture, responsibilities, as well as profits and liabilities, are shared by all of the firms involved in the venture. (See Chapter 17 for a more detailed discussion of joint ventures.)

SECTION 4
THE REGULATION OF SPECIFIC BUSINESS ACTIVITIES

Doing business abroad can affect the economies, foreign policy, domestic politics, and other national interests of the countries involved. For this reason, nations impose laws to restrict or facilitate international business. Controls may also be imposed by international agreements.

INVESTING

Investing in foreign nations involves a risk that the foreign government may expropriate the investment property. As mentioned earlier in this chapter, expropriation occurs when property is taken and the owner is paid just compensation for what is taken. This does not violate generally observed principles of international law. Such principles are normally violated, however, when property is confiscated by a government without compensation (or without adequate compensation).

Few remedies are available for confiscation of property by a foreign government. Claims are often resolved by lump-sum settlements after negotiations between the United States and the taking nation. For example, investors whose claims arose out of confiscations following the Russian Revolution in 1917 were offered a lump-sum settlement by the Union of Soviet Socialist Republics in 1974. Still outstanding are $2 billion in claims against Cuba for confiscations that occurred in 1959 and 1960.

To counter the deterrent effect that the possibility of confiscation may have on potential investors, many countries guarantee compensation to foreign investors if property is taken. A guarantee can be in the form of national constitutional or statutory laws or provisions in international treaties. As further protection for foreign investments, some countries provide insurance for their citizens' investments abroad.

EXPORT CONTROL

The U.S. Constitution provides in Article I, Section 9, that "No Tax or Duty shall be laid on Articles exported from any State." Thus, Congress cannot impose any export taxes. Congress can, however, use a variety of other devices to control exports. Congress may set export quotas on various items, such as grain being sold abroad. Under the Export Administration Act of 1979,[4] restrictions can be imposed on the flow of technologically advanced products and technical data.

Devices to stimulate exports and thereby aid domestic businesses include export incentives and subsidies. The Revenue Act of 1971, for example, gave tax benefits to firms marketing their products overseas through certain foreign sales corporations, exempting income produced by the exports.[5] Under the Export Trading Company Act of 1982,[6] U.S. banks are encouraged to invest in export trading companies. An export trading company consists of exporting firms joined to export a line of goods. The Export-Import Bank provides financial assistance, consisting primarily of credit guaranties given to commercial banks that in turn loan funds to U.S. exporting companies.

IMPORT CONTROL

All nations have restrictions on imports, and the United States is no exception. Restrictions include strict prohibitions, quotas, and tariffs. Under the Trading with the Enemy Act of 1917,[7] for example, no goods may be imported from nations that have been designated enemies of the United States. Other laws prohibit the importation of illegal drugs, books that urge insurrection against the United States, and agricultural products that pose dangers to domestic crops or animals.

Quotas are limits on the amounts of goods that can be imported. At one time, the United States had legal quotas on the numbers of automobiles that could be imported from Japan. Currently, Japan "voluntarily" restricts the numbers of automobiles exported to the United States. **Tariffs** are taxes on imports. A tariff is usually a percentage of the value of the import, but it can be a flat rate per unit (such as per barrel of oil). Tariffs raise the prices of goods, causing some consumers to purchase less expensive, domestically manufactured goods.

The United States has specific laws directed at what it sees as unfair international trade practices. **Dumping,** for example, is the sale of imported goods at "less than fair value." *Fair value* is usually determined by the price of those goods in the exporting country. Dumping is designed to undersell U.S. businesses and obtain a larger share of the U.S. market. To prevent this, an extra tariff—known as an *antidumping duty*—may be assessed on the imports.

The procedure for imposing antidumping duties involves two U.S. government agencies: the International Trade Commission (ITC) and the International Trade Administration (ITA). The ITC is an independent agency that makes recommendations to the president concerning temporary import restrictions. The ITC assesses the effects of dumping on domestic businesses. The ITA is part of the Department of Commerce and decides whether imports were sold at less than fair value. The ITA determination establishes the amount of antidumping duties, which are set to equal the difference between the price charged in the United States and the price charged in the exporting country. A duty may be retroactive to cover past dumping.

THE GATT AND THE WTO

The origins of a worldwide trade liberalization policy date to 1947, when the General Agreement on Tariffs and Trade (GATT) was formed for the purpose of minimizing trade barriers among nations. In subsequent decades, the GATT became the principal instrument for regulating international trade. Between 1964 and 1967, for example, forty-eight countries negotiated tariff reductions of 50 percent on a broad range of products. Between 1973 and 1979, one hundred countries negotiated nearly a dozen agreements relating to other trade barriers. An eighth round of negotiations, called the Uruguay Round, was signed by over one hundred representatives in 1994.

The Uruguay Round resulted in agreements relating to investment policies, dispute resolution, and other topics. One of these agreements, the Trade-Related Aspects of Intellectual Property Rights Agreement (TRIPS), will be discussed in Chapter 15. The Uruguay Round also established the World Trade Organization (WTO), which replaced the GATT beginning in 1995. The agreements reached

4. 50 U.S.C. App. Sections 2401–2420.
5. 26 U.S.C. Sections 991–994.
6. 15 U.S.C. Sections 4001, 4003.
7. 12 U.S.C. Section 95a.

during the final round of the GATT and the establishment of the WTO are expected to result in a cut of roughly 40 percent in tariffs worldwide.

Each member country of the WTO agrees to grant **most-favored-nation status** to other member countries. This means that each WTO member must treat other WTO members at least as well as it treats the country that receives its most favorable treatment with regard to imports or exports. Excerpts from the agreements made during the Uruguay Round of the GATT are presented in Appendix R at the end of this text.

THE EUROPEAN UNION (EU)

Another way of minimizing trade barriers between nations is to form multilateral free trade agreements, or regional trade associations. As discussed in Chapter 7, since the 1950s, European nations have been working toward a real common market by eliminating the financial, technical, and physical barriers that traditionally restrained trade between those nations. A united Europe began in 1951 with the establishment of the European Coal and Steel Community (ECSC), consisting of Belgium, West Germany, France, Italy, Luxembourg, and the Netherlands. In 1957, the European Atomic Energy Community (Euratom) was established, and in the same year, the Treaty of Rome created the European Economic Community (EEC). The Treaty of Rome outlined three goals: (1) to preserve European peace; (2) to establish a European common market—that is, a market in which goods, capital, and labor could move freely from one country to another; and (3) to form a politically unified Europe.

Originally, the ECSC, Euratom, and the EEC functioned separately. Under the Merger Treaty signed in 1965, however, the three entities agreed to have common institutions, and reference was typically made thereafter to the European Community, or EC. By 1968, most tariffs within the EC had been eliminated, and in 1986, the EC countries ratified the Single European Act, which furthered the objective of attaining a unified European market. By 1995, the EC, which is now known as the European Union (EU), had become a single integrated European trading unit made up of fifteen European nations.

THE NORTH AMERICAN FREE TRADE AGREEMENT (NAFTA)

The North American Free Trade Agreement (NAFTA), which was signed in 1993 and became effective on January 1, 1994, created a regional trading unit consisting of Mexico, the United States, and Canada. The primary goal of NAFTA is to eliminate tariffs among the United States, Mexico, and Canada on substantially all goods over a period of fifteen to twenty years. NAFTA gives the three countries a competitive advantage by retaining tariffs on goods imported from countries outside the NAFTA trading unit. Additionally, NAFTA provides for the elimination of barriers that traditionally have prevented the cross-border movement of services, such as financial and transportation services. For example, NAFTA provides that, with some exceptions, U.S. firms do not have to relocate in Mexico or Canada to provide services in those countries. NAFTA also attempts to eliminate citizenship requirements for the licensing of accountants, attorneys, physicians, and other professionals.

Over the last decade, countries competing for international trade have become more evenly matched competitors than in earlier years. In part, this is due to the increased use and success of regional international organizations such as the EU. In the eyes of many, NAFTA presents an opportunity for the United States to increase its global competitiveness and economic growth. Appendix S at the end of this text presents excerpts from NAFTA.

SECTION 5 U.S. LAWS IN A GLOBAL CONTEXT

The internationalization of business raises questions concerning the effect of a country's laws outside the country. To what extent do U.S. domestic laws affect the business activities of other nations? To what extent are U.S. businesses affected by the national laws of other countries when doing business abroad? The following sections discuss these questions in the context of U.S. antitrust and discrimination laws.

U.S. ANTITRUST LAWS

U.S. antitrust laws, which will be discussed in detail in Chapters 26 and 27, have a wide application. They may subject persons in foreign nations to their provisions as well as protect foreign consumers and competitors from violations committed by U.S. business firms. Consequently, *foreign persons*, a term that by definition includes foreign governments, may sue under U.S. antitrust laws in U.S. courts.

Section 1 of the Sherman Act of 1890 provides for the extraterritorial effect of the U.S. antitrust laws. The United States is a major proponent of free competition in the global economy, and thus any conspiracy that has a substantial effect on U.S. commerce is within the reach of the Sherman Act. The violation may even occur outside the United States, and foreign governments as well as persons can be sued for violation of U.S. antitrust laws. Before U.S. courts will exercise jurisdiction and apply antitrust laws, it must be shown that the alleged violation had a *substantial effect* on U.S. commerce. U.S. jurisdiction is automatically invoked, however, when a *per se* violation occurs.

As will be discussed in Chapter 27, certain types of restrictive contracts are deemed inherently anticompetitive and thus in restraint of trade as a matter of law. When such a restrictive contract is entered into, there is said to be a *per se* violation of the antitrust laws. A *per se* violation may consist of price-fixing or tying (tie-in) contracts. If a domestic firm, for example, joins a foreign cartel to control the production, price, or distribution of goods, and this cartel has a *substantial effect* on U.S. commerce, a *per se* violation may exist. Hence, both the domestic firm and the foreign cartel could be sued for violation of the U.S. antitrust laws. Likewise, if foreign firms doing business in the United States enter into a price-fixing or other anticompetitive agreement to control a portion of U.S. markets, a *per se* violation may exist.

In 1982, Congress amended the Sherman Act and the Federal Trade Commission Act of 1914 to limit their application when unfair methods of competition are involved in U.S. export trade or commerce with foreign nations. The acts are not limited, however, when there is a "direct, substantial, and reasonably foreseeable effect" on U.S. domestic commerce that results in a claim for damages.

In the following case, the court considered whether a criminal prosecution under the Sherman Act could be based on price-fixing activities that took place entirely outside the United States but had a substantial effect in this country.

CASE 8.2 United States v. Nippon Paper Industries Co.

United States Court of Appeals, First Circuit, 1997. 109 F.3d 1.

BACKGROUND AND FACTS *A federal grand jury issued a criminal indictment against Nippon Paper Industries Company (NPI) and others, charging the defendants with agreeing to fix the price of thermal fax paper throughout North America. The indictment alleged that the meetings to reach the agreement had occurred entirely in Japan but that the defendants had sold the paper through subsidiaries in the United States at above-normal prices. The indictment stated that these activities had had a substantial adverse effect on commerce in the United States and had unreasonably restrained trade in violation of Section 1 of the Sherman Act. NPI filed a motion to dismiss the indictment. The court granted the motion, declaring that a criminal antitrust prosecution could not be based on wholly extraterritorial conduct. The government appealed.*

IN THE LANGUAGE OF THE COURT

SELYA, Circuit Judge.

* * * *

* * * [C]ivil antitrust actions predicated on wholly foreign conduct which has an intended and substantial effect in the United States come within Section One's jurisdictional reach. * * *

* * * *

* * * [I]n both criminal and civil cases, the claim that Section One applies extraterritorially is based on the same language in the same section of the same statute * * * .

* * * It is a fundamental interpretive principle that identical words or terms used in different parts of the same act are intended to have the same meaning.

* * * It follows, therefore, that if the language upon which the indictment rests were the same as the language upon which civil liability rests but appeared in a different section of the Sherman Act, or in a different part of the same section, we would * * * construe the two iterations [statements] of the language identically. Where, as here, the tie binds more tightly—that is, the text under consideration is not merely a duplicate appearing somewhere else in the statute, but is the original phrase in the original setting— * * * the case for reading the language in a [consistent] manner * * * is irresistible.

DECISION AND REMEDY *The U.S. Court of Appeals for the First Circuit reversed the decision of the lower court. The criminal indictment under the Sherman Act would not be dismissed simply because the actions on which it was based occurred outside the United States.*

U.S. DISCRIMINATION LAWS

There are laws in the United States prohibiting discrimination on the basis of race, color, national origin, religion, sex, age, and disability. These laws, as they affect employment relationships (see Chapter 21), generally apply extraterritorially to U.S. nationals working abroad for U.S. firms or for companies that are controlled by U.S. firms. U.S. discrimination laws protect only U.S. citizens. Citizens of foreign countries are not covered.

In regard to their extraterritorial application, U.S. discrimination laws generally stipulate that U.S. employers must abide by U.S. discrimination laws *unless* to do so would violate the laws of the countries in which their workplaces are located. This "foreign laws exception" allows employers to avoid being subjected to conflicting laws.

What happens if a Japanese firm doing business in the United States allegedly discriminates against U.S. employees in favor of Japanese citizens, which is permitted under a treaty between the United States and Japan? Is discrimination on the basis of citizenship the same thing as discrimination on the basis of national origin? These questions were addressed in the following case.

CASE 8.3 Fortino v. Quasar Co., A Division of Matsushita Electric Corp. of America

United States Court of Appeals, Seventh Circuit, 1991. 950 F.2d 389.

COMPANY PROFILE *In the early years of television, Motorola, Inc., captured a large share of the U.S. television-set market by selling the first sets priced under $200. By the 1970s, however, Motorola had begun losing its television-set market share to Japanese manufacturers. In 1974, the company sold its Quasar television manufacturing facilities in Franklin Park, Illinois, to Matsushita Electric Industrial Company, which is based in Osaka, Japan.*

BACKGROUND AND FACTS *In 1953, the United States and Japan entered into a treaty to provide, among other things, that Japanese companies doing business in the United States and U.S. companies doing business in Japan have the right to choose citizens of their own nations as executives for their firms. Quasar Company, doing business in the United States as a subsidiary of the Japanese company Matsushita Electric Industrial Company, employed U.S. workers and management personnel but was largely controlled by executives of Matsushita. When Matsushita executives restructured Quasar, they cut its work force dramatically. Of eighty-nine managers working for the company, sixty-six were fired, but none of the company's ten Japanese executives was* *laid off. John Fortino and two other American executives who had been fired sued Quasar for, among other things, discriminating against them on the basis of national origin in violation of Title VII. Quasar defended by asserting that discrimination on the basis of citizenship, as allowed under the treaty, did not violate Title VII. The trial court held for the American executives, and Quasar appealed.*

IN THE LANGUAGE OF THE COURT

POSNER, Circuit Judge.

* * * *

* * * [Title VII] protects Americans of non-Japanese origin from discrimination in favor of persons of Japanese origin. Title VII does not, however, forbid discrimination on grounds of citizenship. Of course, especially in the case of a homogeneous country like Japan, citizenship and national origin are highly correlated; almost all citizens of Japan were born there. * * * By virtue of the treaty, "foreign businesses clearly have the right to choose citizens of their own nation as executives because they are such citizens." That right would be empty if the subsidiary could be punished for treating its citizen executives differently from American executives on the ground that, since the former were of Japanese national origin and the latter were not, it was discriminating on the basis of national origin. Title VII would be taking back from the Japanese with one hand what the treaty had given them with the other. This collision is avoided by holding national origin and citizenship separate.

DECISION AND REMEDY

The appellate court reversed the trial court's decision. The plaintiffs had no cause of action under Title VII.

SECTION 6 RESOLVING INTERNATIONAL CONTRACT DISPUTES

Recall from Chapter 4 that the arbitration of civil disputes is becoming an increasingly attractive alternative to costly litigation through the court system. This is true on the international level as well. As already mentioned, arbitration clauses are frequently found in contracts governing the international sale of goods. By means of such clauses, the parties agree in advance to be bound by the decision of a specified third party in the event of a dispute.

The third party may be a neutral entity (such as the International Chamber of Commerce), a panel of individuals representing both parties' interests, or some other group or organization. The United Nations Convention on the Recognition and Enforcement of Foreign Arbitral Awards[8]—which has been implemented in more than fifty countries, including the United States—assists in the enforcement of arbitration clauses, as do provisions in specific treaties between nations. The American Arbitration Association (discussed in Chapter 4) provides arbitration services for international as well as domestic disputes.

When no arbitration clause is contained in a sales contract, a contract dispute may end in litigation. If the contract includes forum-selection and choice-of-law clauses, the lawsuit will be heard by a court in the forum country specified and decided according to that country's law. If no forum or choice of law has been designated, however, legal proceedings will be more complex and attended by much more uncertainty. For example, litigation may take place in two or more countries, with each country applying its own choice-of-law rules to determine which substantive law will be applied to the particular transactions.

Furthermore, even if a plaintiff wins a favorable judgment in a lawsuit litigated in the plaintiff's country, there is no guarantee that the court's judgment will be enforced by judicial bodies in the defendant's country. As discussed earlier in this chapter, under the principle of comity, the judgment may be

8. June 10, 1958, 21 U.S.T. 2517, T.I.A.S. No. 6997 (the "New York Convention").

enforced in the defendant's country, particularly if the defendant's country is the United States and the foreign court's decision is consistent with U.S. national law and policy. Other nations, however, may not be as accommodating as the United States, and the plaintiff may be left empty-handed.

SECTION 7
THE BRIBERY OF FOREIGN OFFICIALS

A major ethical (and legal) problem in international business dealings has to do with the legitimacy of certain side payments to government officials. In the United States, the majority of contracts are formed within the private sector. In many foreign countries, however, decisions on most major construction and manufacturing contracts are made by government officials because of extensive government regulation and control over trade and industry. Side payments to government officials in exchange for favorable business contracts are not unusual in such countries, nor are they considered to be unethical in some areas. In the past, U.S. corporations doing business in developing countries largely followed the maxim, "When in Rome, do as the Romans do."

In the 1970s, however, the U.S. press—and government officials as well—uncovered a number of business scandals involving large side payments by American corporations, such as Lockheed Aircraft, to foreign representatives for the purpose of securing advantageous international trade contracts. In 1977, to prohibit American firms from this unethical conduct, Congress passed the Foreign Corrupt Practices Act (FCPA),[9] which prohibits American businesspersons from bribing foreign officials to secure advantageous contracts. The act has made it difficult for American companies to compete as effectively as they otherwise might in the global marketplace.

MAJOR PROVISIONS OF THE FCPA

The Foreign Corrupt Practices Act (FCPA) of 1977 is divided into two major parts. The first part applies to all U.S. companies and their directors, officers, shareholders, employees, and agents. This part of the FCPA prohibits the bribery of most officials of foreign governments if the purpose of the payment is to get the official to act in his or her official capacity to provide business opportunities.

The FCPA does not prohibit payment of substantial sums to minor officials whose duties are ministerial. These payments are often referred to as "grease," or facilitating, payments. They are meant to ensure that administrative personnel "do what they're supposed to do" and that government services that might otherwise be performed at a slow pace are sped up. Thus, for example, if a firm makes a payment to a minor official to speed up an import-licensing process, the firm has not violated the FCPA. Generally, the act, as amended, permits payments to foreign officials if such payments are lawful within the foreign country. Furthermore, the act does not prohibit payments to private foreign companies or other third parties unless the American firm knows that the payments will be passed on to a foreign government in violation of the FCPA.

The second part of the FCPA is directed toward accountants, because in the past bribes were often concealed in corporate financial records. All companies must keep detailed records that "accurately and fairly" reflect the company's financial activities. In addition, all companies must have an accounting system that provides "reasonable assurance" that all transactions entered into by the company are accounted for and legal. These requirements assist in detecting illegal bribes. The FCPA further prohibits any person from making false statements to accountants or false entries in any record or account.

Business firms that violate the act may be fined up to $2 million. Individual officers or directors who violate the FCPA may be fined up to $100,000 (the fine cannot be paid by the company) and may be imprisoned for up to five years.

MULTINATIONAL INITIATIVES

The FCPA is the only law of its kind in the world. No other country imposes penalties on businesspersons for bribing foreign officials. Increasingly, however, multinational initiatives are being undertaken to stem corruption and bribery in business dealings in the international arena.

Consider, for example, developments that occurred in 1996. The Organization for Economic

9. 15 U.S.C. Sections 78m, 78dd-1, 78dd-2, 78ff. The FCPA was amended by the Foreign Corrupt Practices Act Amendments of 1988. These amendments modified some of the harsher provisions of the act so that U.S. firms could compete more effectively with foreign firms.

Cooperation and Development, to which twenty-six of the world's leading industrialized nations belong, called on its member nations to both criminalize the bribery of foreign officials and eliminate the tax deductibility of bribes. The International Chamber of Commerce also announced that it had updated its "Rules of Conduct to Combat Extortion and Bribery," which were first adopted in 1977. These rules prohibit the payment and receipt of bribes by business firms. In addition, the General Assembly of the United Nations adopted the "Declaration against Corruption and Bribery in International Commercial Transactions." This declaration grew out of efforts begun in 1975 to encourage countries to attack corruption. The 1996 declaration, however, was more forceful than earlier efforts in that it went beyond mere encouragement and committed member nations to action.

Part of the incentive behind these and other multilateral initiatives has to do with the opening up of new markets in Asia and in the Eastern European countries that formerly were part of the Soviet Union. The media attention given to these new markets has led to concerns over real or imagined corruption and bribery. If the momentum of joint international actions to curb such practices continues, eventually U.S. businesspersons may face a more level playing field with respect to international business transactions.

Terms and Concepts to Review

act of state doctrine 153	**exclusive distributorship 155**	**quota 157**
comity 153	**export 155**	**sovereign immunity 153**
confiscation 153	**expropriation 153**	**tariff 157**
distribution agreement 155	**international organization 151**	**technology licensing 155**
dumping 157	**most-favored-nation status 158**	**treaty 151**

Questions and Case Problems

8–1. Bribery of Foreign Officials. Air Flight is a U.S. manufacturer of helicopters. Heise, vice president in charge of sales, wants to sell one hundred helicopters to North Zin, a foreign country. Secretary of Defense Zoro in North Zin has complete authority to purchase helicopters for his country. Zoro usually relies on evaluations made by his subordinates. Air Flight's main competition in the sale of these helicopters is from Top Flight, a European firm. The president of Top Flight has given Zoro his own personal helicopter and deposited $100,000 into Zoro's account. Heise immediately offers Zoro $200,000 in cash and, in addition, gives $10,000 to each of Zoro's subordinates to induce them to process Air Flight's evaluation before they process Top Flight's. ABC accountants, when auditing Air Flight's accounts, discover the payments that have been made to Zoro and his subordinates. Heise and Air Flight claim that without making such payments, Air Flight cannot compete in foreign markets. Discuss whether the payments made by Air Flight are illegal.

8–2. Sovereign Immunity. Section 1610(d)(1) of the Foreign Sovereign Immunities Act (FSIA) provides that property of a foreign state that is used for commercial activity in the United States is not immune from attachment prior to the entry of a judgment if the foreign state has "explicitly waived its immunity from attachment prior to judgment." *Banco Nacional*, an instrumentality of the government of Costa Rica, entered into a written agreement with Libra Bank, Ltd., the plaintiffs. In the agreement, *Banco Nacional* stated that it did not have "any right of immunity from suit with respect to the Borrower's obligations" under this particular agreement. Did *Banco Nacional*, the defendant, "explicitly" waive its immunity from prejudgment attachment, as required by the FSIA? [*Libra Bank, Ltd. v. Banco Nacional de Costa Rica, S.A.*, 676 F.2d 47 (2d Cir. 1982)]

8–3. Dumping. ICC Industries, Inc., was an importer of potassium permanganate from the People's Republic of China. The International Trade Administration (ITA) of the U.S. Department of Commerce conducted an antidumping investigation and concluded that this potassium permanganate was being imported at less than fair value, in violation of U.S. law. Fair value is an estimate of the value of the product in the home market—in this case, the People's Republic of China. As a consequence of its investigation of ICC, the ITA imposed retroactive antidumping duties on ICC's imports of potassium permanganate for the period 1981 to 1983. Imposition of these duties required a finding that ICC knew or should have known that the product was being imported at less than fair value. ICC argued that it was unaware of this fact. ICC emphasized that because the People's Republic of China had a nonmarket economy, the company was unable to ascertain a home market value for potassium permanganate. ICC therefore appealed the ITA's order to the U.S. Court of Appeals for the Federal Circuit. What will result? Discuss fully. [*ICC Industries, Inc. v. United States*, 812 F.2d 694 (Fed.Cir. 1987)]

8–4. SOVEREIGN IMMUNITY. Texas Trading & Milling Corp. and other companies brought an action for breach of contract against the Federal Republic of Nigeria and its central bank. Nigeria, a rapidly developing and oil-rich nation, had overbought huge quantities of cement from Texas Trading and others. Unable to accept delivery of the cement, Nigeria had repudiated the contract, alleging immunity under the Foreign Sovereign Immunities Act of 1976. Because the buyer of the cement was the Nigerian government, did the doctrine of sovereign immunity remove the dispute from the jurisdiction of U.S. courts? [*Texas Trading & Milling Corp. v. Federal Republic of Nigeria*, 647 F.2d 300 (2d Cir. 1981)]

8–5. ANTITRUST CLAIMS. Billy Lamb and Carmon Willis (the plaintiffs) were tobacco growers in Kentucky. Phillip Morris, Inc., and B.A.T. Industries, PLC, routinely purchased tobacco not only from growers in Kentucky but also from producers in several foreign countries. In 1982, subsidiaries of Phillip Morris and B.A.T. (the defendants) entered into an agreement with *La Fundacion Del Nino* (the Children's Foundation) of Caracas, Venezuela. The president of the Children's Foundation was the wife of the president of Venezuela. The agreement provided that the two subsidiaries would donate a total of approximately $12.5 million to the Children's Foundation. In exchange, the subsidiaries were to obtain price controls on Venezuelan tobacco, elimination of controls on retail cigarette prices in Venezuela, tax deductions for the donations, and assurances that existing tax rates applicable to tobacco companies would not be increased. The plaintiffs brought this action, alleging that the Venezuelan arrangement was an inducement designed to restrain trade in violation of U.S. antitrust laws. Such an arrangement, the plaintiffs contended, would result in the artificial depression of tobacco prices to the detriment of domestic tobacco growers, while ensuring lucrative retail prices for tobacco products sold abroad. The trial court held that the plaintiffs' claim was barred by the act of state doctrine. What will result on appeal? Discuss. [*Lamb v. Phillip Morris, Inc.*, 915 F.2d 1024 (6th Cir. 1990)]

8–6. ACT OF STATE DOCTRINE. W. S. Kirkpatrick & Co. learned that the Republic of Nigeria was interested in contracting for the construction and equipment of a medical center in Nigeria. Kirkpatrick, with the aid of a Nigerian citizen, secured the contract as a result of bribing Nigerian officials. Nigerian law prohibits both the payment and receipt of bribes in connection with the awarding of government contracts, and the U.S. Foreign Corrupt Practices Act (FCPA) of 1977 expressly prohibits U.S. firms and their agents from bribing foreign officials to secure favorable contracts. Environmental Tectonics Corporation, International (ETC), an unsuccessful bidder for the contract, learned of the bribery and sued Kirkpatrick in a U.S. federal district court for damages. The district court granted summary judgment for Kirkpatrick, because resolution of the case in favor of ETC would require imputing to foreign officials an unlawful motivation (the obtaining of bribes) and accordingly might embarrass the Nigerian government or interfere with the conduct of U.S. foreign policy. Was the district court correct in assuming that the act of state doctrine barred ETC's action against Kirkpatrick? What should happen on appeal? Discuss fully. [*W. S. Kirkpatrick & Co. v. Environmental Tectonics Corp., International*, 493 U.S. 400, 110 S.Ct. 701, 107 L.Ed.2d 816 (1990)]

8–7. SOVEREIGN IMMUNITY. In 1988, Eckert International, Inc., an American corporation, entered into a three-year contract with the government of Fiji to provide Fiji with public relations consulting services in Washington, D.C., for annual payments of $250,000. In 1991, the contract was renewed without change for three more years. In 1992, Fiji's new prime minister terminated the contract and refused to pay Eckert for the remaining two years. Eckert sued Fiji in a U.S. district court for breach of contract. Fiji moved to dismiss the suit, asserting, among other things, that it was immunized from the jurisdiction of U.S. courts by the Foreign Sovereign Immunities Act (FSIA). Is Fiji immune from the jurisdiction of U.S. courts under the FSIA? Discuss. [*Eckert International, Inc. v. Government of the Sovereign Democratic Republic of Fiji*, 834 F.Supp. 167 (E.D.Va. 1993)]

8–8. SOVEREIGN IMMUNITY. Reed International Trading Corp., a New York corporation, agreed to sell down jackets to Alink, a Russian business. Alink referred Reed to the Bank for Foreign and Economic Affairs of the Russian Federation for payment and gave Reed a letter of credit payable in New York. When Reed tried to collect, the bank refused to pay. Reed (and others) filed a suit in a federal district court against the bank (and others). The bank qualified as a "sovereign" under the Foreign Sovereign Immunities Act and thus claimed in part that it was immune from suit in U.S.

courts. On what basis might the court hold that the bank was not immune? Explain. [*Reed International Trading Corp. v. Donau Bank,* A.G., 866 F.Supp. 750 (S.D.N.Y. 1994)]

8–9. DISCRIMINATION CLAIMS. Radio Free Europe and Radio Liberty (RFE/RL), a U.S. corporation doing business in Germany, employs more than three hundred U.S. citizens at its principal place of business in Munich, Germany. The concept of mandatory retirement is deeply embedded in German labor policy, and a contract formed in 1982 between RFE/RL and a German labor union contained a clause that required workers to be retired when they reached the age of sixty-five. When William Mahoney and other American employees (the plaintiffs) reached the age of sixty-five, RFE/RL terminated their employment as required under its contract with the labor union. The plaintiffs sued RFE/RL for discriminating against them on the basis of age, in violation of the U.S. Age Discrimination in Employment Act of 1967. Will the plaintiffs succeed in their suit? Discuss fully. [*Mahoney v. RFE/RL, Inc.*, 47 F.3d 447 (D.C. Cir. 1995)]

8–10. SOVEREIGN IMMUNITY. George Janini and other former professors and employees of Kuwait University (the plaintiffs) were terminated from their positions following Iraq's invasion of Kuwait in August 1990. Following the invasion, the government of Kuwait issued a decree stating, among other things, that "contracts concluded between the Government and those non-Kuwaiti workers who worked for it . . . shall be considered automatically abrogated because of the impossibility of enforcement due to the Iraqi invasion." The plaintiffs sued Kuwait University in a U.S. court, alleging that their termination breached their employment contracts, which required nine months' notice before termination. The plaintiffs sought back pay and other benefits to which they were entitled under their contracts. The university claimed that, as a government-operated institution, it was immune from the jurisdiction of U.S. courts under the doctrine of sovereign immunity. What exceptions are made to this doctrine? Will an exception apply to the university's activities with respect to the plaintiffs? Discuss fully. [*Janini v. Kuwait University*, 43 F.3d 1534 (D.C. Cir. 1995)]

UNIT TWO—CUMULATIVE HYPOTHETICAL PROBLEM

8–11. *JB Mediquip, Inc., is in the business of manufacturing hospital equipment. JB does business throughout the world and has manufacturing plants in two other countries.*

1. JB agrees to sell fifty hospital beds to a health-care facility operated on a military base in Zamboria, a foreign country. The health-care facility is owned and operated by the Zamborian government. JB ships the beds, but the health-care facility refuses to pay for them. To recover the price of the beds, JB sues the health-care facility in a U.S. district court. Zamboria moves to dismiss JB's action, contending that a U.S. court cannot exercise jurisdiction over the matter. On what ground might Zamboria base its assertion? Is Zamboria correct?
2. Many of the employees in JB's plant in Algoton, a foreign country, are American citizens. JB blatantly discriminates against the female employees in regard to salary and promotions. Several female employees sue JB in a U.S. court, alleging gender-based discrimination in violation of Title VII of the Civil Rights Act of 1964. JB contends that such discrimination is not illegal in Algoton, and therefore its actions are not illegal. Is JB correct? Explain.
3. Suppose that JB does business only within the state of Minnesota. A JB employee claims that the company has violated a federal employment law. JB argues that it is not liable because the law applies only to employees of companies that are engaged in interstate commerce. What might a court decide? Discuss fully.

ACCESSING THE INTERNET

THE LEGAL ENVIRONMENT OF BUSINESS

An index of Internet resources related to international law, including international treaties and conventions, has been published on the Web by the International Law Society of the University of Arizona College of Law at

http://aruba.ccit.arizona.edu/~rdespeld/ils.html

An extensive collection of URLs offering access to various international organizations is offered by the Villanova Center for Information Law and Policy at

http://www.vcilp.org/

Cornell Law School's Legal Information Institute publishes the text of the opinions of the International Court of Justice (World Court) in both English and French. The Cornell site also contains information on the court and links to selected international law sites. You can find this site at

http://www.law.cornell.edu/icj/

You might be interested in the information on foreign policy and international issues compiled by the U.S. Information Agency (USIA). You can find the USIA's site at

http://www.usia.gov/

For information on the World Intellectual Property Organization Arbitration Center, go to

http://www.wto.org

Focus on Ethics

The Public and International Environment

No other areas of law are as dynamic and engender as much controversy as those relating to the public and international environment. This stems from the fact that the law of the public and international environment, more than any other area, involves searching, ethical questions. All areas of law touch on ethical considerations. But many laws have as their basis practical necessity or commercial need. The law of the public environment, however, concerns issues such as the protection of freedom of speech, the promotion of racial equality, and government regulation of behavior for the public welfare versus individual rights. The law of the international environment involves such questions as the influence of foreign and international laws, the impact of divergent cultures, and the effect of different legal, political, and economic systems.

Little guidance is provided by considerations of practicality in resolving these issues. Moreover, these issues do not merely involve questions of ethics; they are in large measure purely ethical questions. In resolving them, one must rely on basic notions of fairness and justice. Yet conceptions of fairness, justice, and equality differ among individuals. Moreover, each individual's conception is a product of his or her circumstances; as circumstances change over time, so, too, basic conceptions change. Not

surprisingly, at any moment in history, there is seldom a broad social consensus over legal issues in the public and international environment.

Free Speech and the Corporation

Free speech is regarded as one of the basic rights of a democratic society. Yet it has never been considered an absolute right. The right of free speech must be balanced against other important rights and the advancement of other important social goals. In that sense the proper extent of freedom of speech, in its many forms, involves ethical considerations.

Because freedom of speech is not absolute, not all forms of expression are protected. Pornography, for example, is not protected by the First Amendment. Nor are utterances protected that would induce an immediate threat of violence or injury. Even within the context of protected speech, the Supreme Court has historically looked to the nature of the speech involved in determining the extent of the protection afforded. Commercial speech, for example, is afforded less protection from government restriction than is noncommercial speech. The lesser degree of protection means in practical terms that it is easier for government to show that the interest it seeks to promote by regulating the speech is more important than protecting the right of speech. But in balancing such conflicting rights and goals, value judgments must be made.

Judging the Source

The nature of the speech involved may be a legitimate concern in assessing the extent of freedom of speech, but is it legitimate to consider the source of the speech? For example, should it make a difference that the speaker, through either a spokesperson or an advertisement, is a corporation? Most corporate "speech" has as its primary purpose the promotion of a product; that is, it is commercial in nature and, as discussed, is afforded a lesser degree of protection. But what if the speech is political in nature? Should it matter in that case that the speaker is a corporation? This issue was addressed by the United States Supreme Court in *First National Bank of Boston v. Bellotti,* a case referred to in Chapter 5. Although the justices deciding the case were applying their concepts of the free speech clause of the First Amendment, the case raises some ethical questions, which are implicit in the Court's decision and in the opinions of the dissenting justices.

Focus on Ethics

First National Bank of Boston v. Bellotti concerned a Massachusetts law that forbade corporations from using their resources to try to influence public opinion on issues submitted to a referendum vote when those issues did not materially relate to the corporation's business. Controversy arose when five corporations announced their intentions to mount a campaign in opposition to a proposed state individual income tax, which was to be submitted to a referendum vote. The state threatened to fine the corporations and punish their executives if the corporations entered the political debate. The corporations sought protection by asking the courts to declare the Massachusetts law unconstitutional. Ultimately, the case was appealed to the United States Supreme Court.

A divided Court decided in favor of the corporations. The majority held that free speech protections extended to corporations and that the Massachusetts law violated those constitutional protections. In deciding the case, the majority recast the issue involved. For the majority, the issue was *not* whether corporations were protected by the free speech clause but, rather, whether the speech involved was protected. Because the speech was political in nature, the majority concluded that the speech could not be restricted in the manner employed by the state. To the majority, it did not matter that the speaker was a corporation. And indeed, as the majority viewed the case, it was not protecting the corporation. Instead, it believed that the political nature of the speech meant that it should be heard.

The Ethical Dimensions

The majority's reasoning has some strong points. After all, political debate is the fundamental ingredient of the democratic political process. One of the few areas of virtually uniform agreement over First Amendment rights is that the authors of the Constitution definitely had the public exchange of political views in mind when they constructed the free speech clause. But there are other considerations, largely of an ethical nature, involved when the speaker is a corporation.

There are ethical considerations in a corporation's using its extensive resources to influence the political process. Certainly, bribing officials is wrong both ethically and legally. But other forms of corporate spending that influence the political process also might be abusive. One concern is that a corporation can "leverage" political power through its economic skills. Corporations acquire resources through skills in marketing, management, and technology. Yet these skills, however beneficial to society's material well-being they may be, do not involve political ideas or necessarily indicate a concern for the public welfare. Should the resources garnered in the economic arena be redeployed in the political arena? Is it fair to allow economic skill to be translated into political power? These were concerns raised in dissent to the majority's opinion in *Bellotti,* but they are as much ethical issues as legal ones.

Notwithstanding these concerns, there are ethical as well as practical considerations that support the majority's view. Recall that the Massachusetts law challenged in *Bellotti* did not ban corporate expenditures on referendum issues that materially related to the corporation's business. The issue was a state individual income tax. The very fact that the corporations would *not* be materially affected by a state *individual* income tax might imply that their political participation was motivated solely by concern for the public welfare rather than their self-interest. Even if they were concerned that the proposed tax might affect the economy of the state and thus the profitability of their businesses, that does not in itself make their views less worthy to be heard. After all, on economic matters, the corporate view of the issues would seem to be extremely relevant. Possibly the corporate view should be heard for that reason alone. And if the corporations choose to subsidize with their own resources the dissemination of important views, maybe they should be praised rather than condemned.

Ethics and the Administrative Process

In Chapter 5 we noted some of the other constitutional protections that apply in the context of business. We looked in Chapter 6 at how some of those protections apply in the administrative process. As noted in Chapter 6, effective

Focus on Ethics

governmental regulation necessitates the gathering of relevant information. Often that information can be obtained only by an on-site inspection of business premises or a first-hand examination of business records. When regulatory need conflicts with constitutional principles, not only are legal issues raised, but ethical ones as well.

Recall that the Fourth Amendment protection from unreasonable searches and seizures applies in the context of business. Within the context of administrative law, this protection has been interpreted as requiring that information sought by a regulatory agency be relevant to the matter under scrutiny. Furthermore, any demand for information must be reasonably specific and not unduly burdensome to the business providing the information.

The Need to Know

The ideals embodied in the Fourth Amendment are deeply ingrained in America's political culture. The image of midnight raids in which innocent families watch helplessly as gruff, heavily armed officers ransack their homes is often invoked when one thinks of a "search and seizure." Protection against such abhorrent practices is fundamental to the American ideal of liberty.

But are the same ideals felt as strongly in other contexts? What about in the business context, especially with regard to agency regulation? Even though the first significant degree of federal economic regulation can be traced as far back as the first half of the nineteenth century, Americans continue to hold extremely ambivalent feelings toward the very idea of government regulation. Americans are prone to look to government to address every new ill society encounters, but then stridently resent, as governmental intrusion, the regulatory schemes designed to cure those ills.

Whatever the sentiments Americans hold regarding government regulation, most accept and many welcome it as an important part of modern society. In accepting such regulation, Americans also accept the fact that regulators must gather information. For example, the Securities and Exchange Commission desires information about proposed stock offerings. The Environmental Protection Agency may request to make an inspection of a chemical plant to ensure compliance with hazardous waste disposal regulations.

Despite acceptance of the need for regulators to gather information, an inherent conflict exists between the regulatory need for information and the individual's right of privacy. Specifically, how much latitude should be afforded to regulators in gathering information and overseeing private activities?

The United States Supreme Court has attempted to resolve the conflict by balancing the regulators' need to know against individual and corporate expectations of freedom from excessive government prying. An important consideration in resolving the conflict is the less intrusive nature of regulatory searches of businesses: most people simply do not have the same degree of concern about protecting places of business as they do about protecting the family dwelling. As a result, the standards for conducting regulatory investigations and searches are different than those imposed when ordinary police investigations and searches are conducted. For example, even though there may be no suspicion of a regulatory violation, an agency may conduct an investigation or search the premises of a business merely to be assured that no violation is occurring. Within industries subject to a history of extensive regulation, searches may be made even without a warrant. Still, though, as noted in Chapter 6 and above, government is restricted in obtaining private information for regulatory purposes only.

The Ethics of Legal Avoidance

In the face of an agency investigation, a business may prevent or delay agency efforts by asserting legal challenges to the nature or manner of the investigation. There remains, however, the question of whether—in an ethical rather than legal sense—business should challenge any such investigation. We would be expected to challenge an unreasonable search of our homes. We would owe it to our families to challenge such abuse. Arguably, it would be one's civic duty to challenge it to protect future abuse of other families in our communities as well.

Focus on Ethics

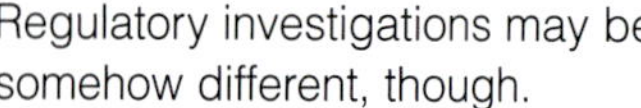

Regulatory investigations may be somehow different, though.

Most regulatory investigations have as their objective ensuring compliance with existing regulatory schemes or gathering information for future ones. Such schemes are designed for the public welfare. Though individuals may disagree about the effectiveness of the scheme or the individual motives of the regulators, society generally accepts the underlying purpose of the regulation—the promotion of public welfare. In such instances, businesses may have an ethical duty not to use legal means to avoid agency action. Indeed, they may have an ethical duty to aid in regulation by compliance, even though they may have a legal right to delay or avoid it.

Ethics and International Law

Differences in the laws and customs of the various nations of the globe present unique ethical issues for firms engaged in international business transactions. Some of these issues were discussed in Chapter 7. Here, we look at a few other problems, focusing particularly on some ethical issues relating to international doctrines and to U.S. laws as they apply to international transactions.

Intellectual Property Rights

The licensing of technology allows U.S. owners of intellectual property (such as patents, trademarks, and copyrights) to benefit from sales of their products in other countries. Much intellectual property, however, is "pirated"—that is, unauthorized copies of the property (such as a software program) are made and sold. In 1994, to protect intellectual property rights on a worldwide basis, more than one hundred nations signed the international agreement on Trade-Related Aspects of Intellectual Property Rights (TRIPS), which is administered by the World Trade Organization. These nations pledged to pass and enforce laws protecting patents, copyrights, and trademarks (see the discussion of TRIPS in Chapter 15).

The attempted enforcement of intellectual property rights on a worldwide basis, however, raises some ethical concerns. For example, in a developing country, the welfare of small business firms and consumers may be enhanced by the ability to purchase pirated (less expensive) copies of high-tech products. Although the owners of the pirated intellectual property lose out, they might have received nothing anyway, if no authorized copies (at higher prices) could have been sold in the poorer country. Therefore, if a developing country's government is somewhat slack in curbing the piracy of intellectual property, it may be because this laxity is in the developing country's interests.

Furthermore, laws governing intellectual property rights are necessarily somewhat arbitrary. For example, if the United States grants copyright protection for a longer period of time than Japan, does this mean that U.S. law is "right" and Japanese law is "wrong"?

Sovereign Immunity

Sometimes, the application of the doctrine of sovereign immunity may lead to seemingly inequitable results. The economy of the United States is primarily controlled by private interests, whereas the economies of many foreign countries, particularly developing nations, are extensively controlled by government. When a U.S. firm does business with a foreign firm in a developing country, therefore, the chances are that the U.S. firm will work closely with foreign government officials. Should a dispute arise between the parties, the question then becomes whether the U.S. firm can bring a lawsuit against the foreign firm. If the foreign defendant raises the defense of sovereign immunity, alleging that it is a government-controlled operation, then it may be immune from liability. The ethical issue in these situations is whether it is fair that U.S. firms be left without any legal recourse when they suffer damages as a result of actions controlled by foreign governments.

Consider, for example, the situation that arose in *Antares Aircraft, L.P. v. Federal Republic of Nigeria.*[1] In that case, Antares Aircraft, a New York limited partnership, had one asset—a DC-8-55 aircraft registered in Nigeria. Antares was required by the Nigerian government to leave the plane at the airport in Lagos, Nigeria, until certain fees (which had been incurred by a previous owner of the plane) were paid. Antares paid the $100,000 in fees,

1. 999 F.2d 33 (2d Cir. 1993).

Focus on Ethics

but the Nigerian government did not release the plane until five months later. In the meantime, the plane had been damaged by exposure to the elements.

Antares filed suit against the Nigerian government for the tort of conversion, alleging that the Nigerian government had wrongfully detained the plane. Antares argued that the Nigerian government's actions fell within the commercial-activity exception to the Foreign Sovereign Immunities Act (FSIA) and therefore the Nigerian government was not immune from the jurisdiction of U.S. courts.

Although the court agreed with Antares that the fees collected by the Nigerian government were connected with a commercial activity, it found that the activity did not have a "direct effect" in the United States—in which case the commercial-activity exception to the FSIA did not apply. The court therefore held that the Nigerian government was immune from liability. The court stated that "the detention of Antares's sole asset affected the financial well-being of the American partnership. However, the fact that an American individual or firm suffers some financial loss from a foreign tort cannot, standing alone, suffice to trigger the [commercial-activity] exception."

Because the FSIA does not define exactly what types of activities on the part of a foreign government fall under the commercial-activity exception, the courts exercise considerable discretion in deciding such issues. Although the majority on the court hearing the *Antares* case concluded that the loss suffered by Antares was not sufficiently significant to constitute a "direct effect in the United States," other courts might have concluded differently.

Certainly, the dissenting judge in *Antares* believed that the detention of the plane did have a direct effect in the United States. The partners lived in the United States and lost money because of a foreign government's interference with their property. The dissent concluded that the partnership's loss should be sufficient to establish an exception to immunity under the FSIA.

The Foreign Corrupt Practices Act

Since its passage by Congress in 1977, the Foreign Corrupt Practices Act (FCPA) has been the target of substantial criticism. Many U.S. firms have complained that the act places them at a competitive disadvantage relative to foreign firms.

For example, assume that your company wants to do business with a foreign firm. A foreign official promises your company the contract, but only if you agree to "contribute," say, $500,000 to the official's bank account in another country. You say no to the deal because you know that the FCPA prohibits you from making such a "bribe." If you agreed to the deal, you could face harsh criminal penalties, including imprisonment. A company from another nation, which has been competing for the contract, faces no such prohibition, however. That company agrees to pay the $500,000 and gets the contract.

As discussed in Chapter 8, for several years, the United States has been encouraging other nations to pass similar antibribery laws, and progress is clearly being made. Even if all nations had laws similar to the FCPA, however, a further issue would remain: How do you prove that a bribe has been tendered (or a side payment requested)?

The crime of bribery occurs not only when a bribe is accepted but also when a bribe is offered. When someone refuses to take a bribe, sometimes the only proof that the bribe was offered or solicited is the word of the person who refused. What would prevent a foreign government from retaliating if a U.S. firm's representative accused a foreign official of requesting a bribe but could not otherwise prove that the bribery occurred?

Discussion Questions

1. You serve as chief executive officer of a large corporation. The state in which your company is headquartered has scheduled a statewide referendum on whether to allow casino gambling to be conducted within the state. Your company is in no way involved in gambling or in the sale of products used in the gaming industry, but you believe that evidence supports the inference that casino gambling, though potentially lucrative for those who operate the casinos, will hurt the state's economy. Some members of the board of directors have expressed similar concerns to you in casual conversation. Should you authorize the use of your company's resources to mount an opposition

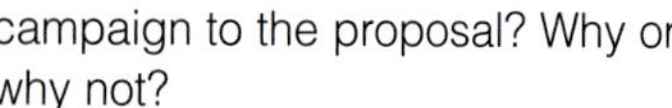

Focus on Ethics

campaign to the proposal? Why or why not?

2. What if, in the situation described in question 1, you knew of no conclusive evidence to support or refute the proposition that casino gambling had any effect on the overall economy of the state? Suppose, though, you had a strong moral conviction that gambling was wrong. How would that change the ethical dimensions of the question of whether you should authorize the use of corporate resources to oppose the gambling initiative?

3. The United States banned the pesticide DDT, primarily because of its adverse effects on wildlife. In Asia, however, DDT has been a critical component of the mosquito control necessary to combat malaria. Should the ban in the United States prevent U.S. firms from manufacturing DDT and shipping it to an Asian country, where it could be used to save lives? Should the U.S. chemical manufacturer be required to produce the DDT in the same country that uses the chemical?

4. What are some of the implications of the doctrine of sovereign immunity for businesspersons doing business internationally? Should the courts make more exceptions to this doctrine?

5. The Foreign Corrupt Practices Act was passed in an attempt to ensure more ethical conduct on the part of U.S. businesspersons doing business abroad. Do you think that the act is fair to U.S. firms in view of the fact that other countries do not—at least as yet—have similar laws? The act permits so-called grease payments to minor government officials to expedite such things as paperwork. Do such payments amount to bribes? Should the act prohibit these kinds of payments as well?

UNIT THREE

THE PRIVATE ENVIRONMENT

CONTENTS

CHAPTER 9

CONTRACTS: PART I

THE NOTED LEGAL SCHOLAR Roscoe Pound once said that "[t]he social order rests upon the stability and predictability of conduct, of which keeping promises is a large item."[1] A **promise** is an assurance that one will or will not do something in the future. A **contract** is "a promise or a set of promises for the breach of which the law gives a remedy, or the performance of which the law in some way recognizes as a duty."[2] Put simply, a contract is an agreement (based on a promise or an exchange of promises) that can be enforced in court.

Like other types of law, contract law reflects our social values, interests, and expectations at a given point in time. It shows, for example, to what extent our society allows people to make promises or commitments that are legally binding. It distinguishes between promises that create only *moral* obligations (such as a promise to take a friend to lunch) and promises that are legally binding (such as a promise to pay for merchandise purchased). Contract law also shows what excuses our society accepts for breaking certain types of promises. In addition, it shows what promises are considered to be contrary to public policy—against the interests of society as a whole—and therefore legally invalid. When a promise is made by a child or a mentally incompetent person, or on the basis of false information, a question will arise as to whether the promise should be enforced. Resolving such questions is the essence of contract law.

1. R. Pound, *Jurisprudence*, Vol. 3 (St. Paul: West Publishing Co., 1959), p. 162.
2. *Restatement (Second) of Contracts.* The *Restatement of the Law of Contracts* is a nonstatutory, authoritative exposition of the common law of contracts compiled by the American Law Institute in 1932. The *Restatement*, which is now in its second edition (a third edition is being drafted), will be referred to throughout the following two chapters on contract law.

The common law governs all contracts except when it has been modified or replaced by statutory law, such as the Uniform Commercial Code (UCC),[3] or administrative agency regulations. Contracts relating to services, real estate, employment, insurance, and so on generally are governed by the common law of contracts. Contracts for the sale of *goods*, however, are governed by the UCC—to the extent that the UCC has modified general contract law. The relationship between general contract law and the law governing sales of goods will be explored in detail in Chapter 11. In the discussion of general contract law that follows, we indicate in footnotes the areas in which the UCC has significantly altered common law contract principles.

SECTION 1 THE BASIC REQUIREMENTS OF A CONTRACT

The many topics that will be discussed in the following chapters on contract law require an understanding of the basic requirements of a contract and the way in which a contract is created. The following list briefly describes the basic requirements of a contract. Each requirement will be explained more fully in subsequent chapters.

1. *Agreement.* An agreement to form a contract includes an *offer* and an *acceptance.* One party must offer to enter into a legal agreement, and another party must accept the terms of the offer.
2. *Consideration.* Any promises made by the parties to the contract must be supported by legally sufficient and bargained-for *consideration* (something of value received or promised, such as money, to convince a person to make a deal).
3. *Contractual capacity.* Both parties entering into the contract must have the contractual *capacity* to do so; the law must recognize them as possessing characteristics that qualify them as competent parties.
4. *Legality.* The contract's purpose must be to accomplish some goal that is *legal* and not against public policy.

These four requirements constitute what are normally known as the elements of a valid contract. If any of these elements is lacking, no contract will have been formed.

Even if all of these elements exist, however, a contract may be unenforceable if the following requirements are not met. These requirements typically are raised as *defenses* to the enforceability of an otherwise valid contract.

1. *Genuineness of assent.* The apparent consent of both parties must be genuine. For example, if a contract was formed as a result of fraud, undue influence, mistake, or duress, the contract may not be enforceable.
2. *Form.* The contract must be in whatever form the law requires; for example, some contracts must be in writing to be enforceable.

SECTION 2 THE OBJECTIVE THEORY OF CONTRACTS

Sometimes, parties claim that they should not be bound in contract because they did not *intend* to form an agreement that would be legally binding. Although the element of intent is of prime importance in determining whether a contract has been formed, it is not the party's *subjective* intent that a court looks to in deciding the issue. In contract law, intent is determined by what is called the *objective theory of contracts,* not by the personal or subjective intent, or belief, of a party. The theory is that intention to enter into a legally binding agreement, or contract, is judged by outward, objective facts as interpreted by a *reasonable* person, rather than by the party's own secret, subjective intentions. Objective facts include (1) what the party said when entering into the contract, (2) how the party acted or appeared (intent may be manifested by conduct as well as by oral or written words), and (3) the circumstances surrounding the transaction.

Consider an example. Jaffe has just purchased a new car for $28,000. A number of his neighbors are admiring his car, and one neighbor, Logan, states that he would like to own a car exactly like Jaffe's. Jaffe, in front of all of his neighbors, says to Logan, "I'll sell you this car for $20,000 in cash." Logan agrees to buy the car, and they put the agreement in writing and sign it. Jaffe immediately tells everyone his agreement to sell the car to Logan was only a joke. Is the agreement legally binding? In other words, do Jaffe and Logan have a contract?

---

3. See Chapter 1 and Chapter 11 for further discussions of the significance and coverage of the Uniform Commercial Code. Excerpts from the UCC are presented in Appendix D at the end of this book.

The answer depends on whether the circumstances (Jaffe's just having purchased a new car, the price of the new car, and the fact that Jaffe agreed in writing to sell the car) and Jaffe's words would, to a reasonable person, manifest Jaffe's intention to form a contract. It is not Jaffe's inner belief or intent to make a joke that determines the answer. If a person in Logan's position could reasonably believe that Jaffe intended to form the contract with him, Jaffe would be legally required to sell the car to Logan.

SECTION 3 TYPES OF CONTRACTS

There are many types of contracts. The categories into which contracts are placed involve legal distinctions as to formation, enforceability, and performance.

BILATERAL VERSUS UNILATERAL CONTRACTS

Every contract involves at least two parties. The *offeror* is the party making the offer. The *offeree* is the party to whom the offer is made. Whether the contract is classified as *unilateral* or *bilateral* depends on what the offeree must do to accept the offer and to bind the offeror to a contract. If to accept the offer the offeree must only *promise* to perform, the contract is a *bilateral contract.* Hence, a bilateral contract is a "promise for a promise." No performance, such as payment of money or delivery of goods, need take place for a bilateral contract to be formed. The contract comes into existence at the moment the promises are exchanged.

In contrast, if the offer is phrased so that the offeree can accept only by completing the contract performance, the contract is a *unilateral contract.* Hence, a unilateral contract is a "promise for an act."[4] A classic example of a unilateral contract is as follows: O'Malley says to Parker, "If you carry this package across the Brooklyn Bridge, I'll give you $10." Only on Parker's complete crossing with the package does she fully accept O'Malley's offer to pay $10. If she chooses not to undertake the walk, there are no legal consequences. Contests, lotteries, and other competitions involving prizes are examples of offers for unilateral contracts. If a person complies with the rules of the contest—such as by submitting the right lottery number at the right place and time—a unilateral contract is formed, binding the organization offering the prize to a contract to perform as promised in the offer.

EXPRESS VERSUS IMPLIED CONTRACTS

An *express contract* is one in which the terms of the agreement are fully and explicitly stated in words, oral or written. A signed lease for an apartment or a house is an express written contract. If a classmate calls you on the phone and agrees to buy your textbooks from last semester for $50, an express oral contract has been made.

A contract that is implied from the conduct of the parties is called an *implied-in-fact contract* or an implied contract. This type of contract differs from an express contract in that the *conduct* of the parties, rather than their words, creates and defines the terms of the contract. (Note that a contract may be a mixture of an express contract and an implied-in-fact contract. In other words, a contract may contain some express terms, while others are implied.) Normally, if the following conditions exist, a court will hold that an implied contract was formed:

1. The plaintiff furnished some service or property.
2. The plaintiff expected to be paid for that service or property, and the defendant knew or should have known that payment was expected.
3. The defendant had a chance to reject the services or property and did not.

For example, suppose that you need an accountant to fill out your tax return this year. You look through the Yellow Pages and find an accountant at an office in your neighborhood, so you drop by to see her. You go into the accountant's office and explain your problem, and she tells you what her fees are. The next day you return, giving her secretary all the necessary information and documents—canceled checks, W-2 forms, and so on. You say nothing expressly to the secretary; rather, you walk out the door. In this situation, you have entered into an implied-in-fact contract to pay the accountant the usual and reasonable fees for her services. The contract is implied by your conduct and by her conduct. She expects to be paid for completing your tax return,

4. Clearly, a contract cannot be "one sided," because, by definition, an agreement implies the existence of two or more parties. Therefore, the phrase *unilateral contract,* if read literally, is a contradiction in terms. As traditionally used in contract law, however, the phrase refers to the kind of contract that results when there is only one promise being made (the promise made by the offeror in return for the offeree's performance).

and by bringing in the records she will need to do the work, you have implied an intent to pay her.

QUASI CONTRACTS—CONTRACTS IMPLIED IN LAW

Quasi contracts, or contracts *implied in law,* are wholly different from actual contracts. Whereas express contracts and implied-in-fact contracts are actual contracts formed by the words or conduct of the parties, quasi contracts are fictional contracts created by courts and imposed on parties in the interests of fairness and justice. Quasi contracts are therefore equitable, rather than contractual, in nature. Usually, quasi contracts are imposed to avoid the *unjust enrichment* of one party at the expense of another. Under the doctrine of quasi contract, a plaintiff may recover in *quantum meruit,*[5] a Latin phrase meaning "as much as he deserves." *Quantum meruit* essentially describes the extent of compensation owed under a contract implied in law.

For example, suppose that a vacationing doctor is driving down the highway and comes upon Potter lying unconscious on the side of the road. The doctor renders medical aid that saves Potter's life. Although the injured, unconscious Potter did not solicit the medical aid and was not aware that the aid had been rendered, Potter received a valuable benefit, and the requirements for a quasi contract were fulfilled. In such a situation, the law will impose a quasi contract, and Potter normally will have to pay the doctor for the reasonable value of the medical services rendered.

EXECUTED VERSUS EXECUTORY CONTRACTS

Contracts are also classified according to the degree to which they have been performed. A contract that has been fully performed on both sides is called an *executed contract.* A contract that has not been fully performed on either side is called an *executory contract.* If one party has fully performed but the other has not, the contract is said to be executed on the one side and executory on the other, but the contract is still classified as executory. For example, assume you agree to buy ten tons of coal from the Northern Coal Company. Further assume that Northern has delivered the coal to your steel mill, where it is now being burned. At this point, the contract is executed on the part of Northern and executory on your part. After you pay Northern for the coal, the contract will be executed on both sides.

VALID, VOID, VOIDABLE, AND UNENFORCEABLE CONTRACTS

A *valid contract* has the elements necessary to entitle at least one of the parties to enforce it in court. Those elements, as mentioned earlier, consist of (1) an agreement, consisting of an offer and an acceptance of that offer, (2) supported by legally sufficient consideration, (3) made by parties who have the legal capacity to enter into the contract, and (4) made for a legal purpose.

A *void contract* is no contract at all. The terms *void* and *contract* are contradictory. A void contract produces no legal obligations on the part of any of the parties. For example, a contract can be void because the purpose of the contract was illegal.

A *voidable contract* is a valid contract but one that can be avoided at the option of one or both of the parties. The party having the option can elect either to avoid any duty to perform or to *ratify* (make valid) the contract. If the contract is avoided, both parties are released from it. If it is ratified, both parties must fully perform their respective legal obligations.

As a general rule, but subject to exceptions, contracts made by minors are voidable at the option of the minor. Contracts entered into under fraudulent conditions are voidable at the option of the defrauded party. In addition, contracts entered into under duress or undue influence are voidable.

An *unenforceable contract* is one that cannot be enforced because of certain legal defenses against it. It is not unenforceable because a party failed to satisfy a legal requirement of the contract; rather, it is a valid contract rendered unenforceable by some statute or law. For example, certain contracts must be in writing, and if they are not, they will not be enforceable except in certain exceptional circumstances.

SECTION 4

AGREEMENT

An essential element for contract formation is **agreement**—the parties must agree on the terms of the contract and manifest to each other their **mutual assent** to the same bargain. Ordinarily, agreement is evidenced by two events: an *offer* and an *acceptance.* One party offers a certain bargain to another party,

5. Pronounced *kwahn*-tuhm *mehr*-oo-whut.

who then accepts that bargain. The agreement does not necessarily have to be in writing. Both parties, however, must manifest their assent to the same bargain. Once an agreement is reached, if the other elements of a contract are present (consideration, capacity, and legality—discussed in subsequent chapters), a valid contract is formed, generally creating enforceable rights and duties between the parties.

Note that not all agreements are contracts. John and Kevin may agree to play golf on a certain day, but a court would not hold that their agreement is an enforceable contract. A *contractual* agreement only arises when the terms of the agreement impose legally enforceable obligations on the parties.

REQUIREMENTS OF THE OFFER

An **offer** is a promise or commitment to do or refrain from doing some specified thing in the future. Under the common law, three elements are necessary for an offer to be effective:

1. The offeror must have a *serious intention* to become bound by the offer.
2. The terms of the offer must be reasonably *certain*, or *definite*, so that the parties and the court can ascertain the terms of the contract.
3. The offer must be communicated by the offeror to the offeree, resulting in the offeree's knowledge of the offer.

Once an effective offer has been made, the offeree has the power to accept the offer. If the offeree accepts, an agreement is formed (and thus a contract, if other essential elements are present).

INTENTION

The first requirement for an effective offer is a serious intent on the part of the offeror. Serious intent is not determined by the *subjective* intentions, beliefs, and assumptions of the offeror. As discussed above, courts generally adhere to the *objective theory of contracts* in determining whether a contract has been formed.

Offers made in obvious anger, jest, or undue excitement do not meet the intent test, because a reasonable person would realize that a serious offer was not being made. Because these offers are not effective, an offeree's acceptance does not create an agreement. For example, suppose you and three classmates ride to school each day in Davina's new automobile, which has a market value of $20,000. One cold morning, the four of you get into the car, but Davina cannot get the car started. She yells in anger, "I'll sell this car to anyone for $500!" You drop $500 in her lap. Given these facts, a reasonable person, taking into consideration Davina's frustration and the obvious difference in value between the market value of the car and the proposed purchase price, would declare that her offer was not made with serious intent and that you did not have an agreement.

The concept of intention can be further clarified through an examination of the types of expressions and statements that are *not* offers.

Expressions of Opinion.

An expression of opinion is not an offer. It does not evidence an intention to enter into a binding agreement. Consider an example. Hawkins took his son to McGee, a doctor, and asked McGee to operate on the son's hand. McGee said that the boy would be in the hospital three or four days and that the hand would *probably* heal a few days later. The son's hand did not heal for a month, but the father did not win a suit for breach of contract. The court held that McGee had not made an offer to heal the son's hand in three or four days. He had merely expressed an opinion as to when the hand would heal.[6]

Statements of Intention.

If Arif says, "I *plan* to sell my stock in Novation, Inc., for $150 per share," a contract is not created if John "accepts" and tenders the $150 per share for the stock. Arif has merely expressed his intention to enter into a future contract for the sale of the stock. If John accepts and tenders the $150 per share, no contract is formed, because a reasonable person would conclude that Arif was only *thinking about* selling his stock, not promising to sell.

Preliminary Negotiations.

A request or invitation to negotiate is not an offer. It only expresses a willingness to discuss the possibility of entering into a contract. Included are statements such as "Will you sell Blythe Estate?" or "I wouldn't sell my car for less than $1,000." A reasonable person in the offeree's position would not conclude that these statements evidenced an intention to enter into a binding obligation. Likewise, when construction work is done for the government and private firms, contractors are invited to submit bids. The *invitation* to submit bids is not an offer, and a contractor does not bind the government or private firm by submitting a bid. (The

6. *Hawkins v. McGee*, 84 N.H. 114, 146 A. 641 (1929).

bids that the contractors submit *are* offers, however, and the government or private firm can bind the contractor by accepting the bid.)

Advertisements, Catalogues, Price Lists, and Circulars. In general, advertisements, mail-order catalogues, price lists, and circular letters are treated not as offers to contract but as invitations to negotiate. Suppose that Loeser advertises a used paving machine. The ad is mailed to hundreds of firms and reads, "Used Loeser Construction Co. paving machine. Builds curbs and finishes cement work all in one process. Price $21,250." If Star Paving calls Loeser and says, "We accept your offer," no contract is formed. Any reasonable person would conclude that Loeser was not promising to sell the paving machine but rather was soliciting offers to buy it. If such an ad were held to constitute a legal offer, and fifty people accepted the offer, there would be no way for Loeser to perform all fifty of the resulting contracts. He would have to breach forty-nine contracts. Obviously, the law seeks to avoid such unfairness.

Price lists are another form of invitation to negotiate or trade. A seller's price list is not an offer to sell at that price; it merely invites the buyer to offer to buy at that price. In fact, the seller usually puts "prices subject to change" on the price list. Only in rare circumstances will a price quotation be construed as an offer.[7]

Although most advertisements and the like are treated as invitations to negotiate, this does not mean that an advertisement can never be an offer. If the advertisement makes a promise so definite in character that it is apparent that the offeror is binding himself or herself to the conditions stated, the advertisement is treated as an offer.

Agreements to Agree. Traditionally, agreements to agree—that is, agreements to agree to a material term of a contract at some future date—were not considered to be binding contracts. More recent cases illustrate the view that agreements to agree serve valid commercial purposes and can be enforced if the parties clearly intended to be bound by such agreements. For example, suppose Zahn Consulting leases office space from Leon Properties, Inc. Their lease agreement includes a clause permitting Zahn to extend the lease at an amount of rent to be agreed on when the lease is extended. Under the traditional rule, because the amount of rent is not specified in the lease clause itself, the clause would be too indefinite in its terms to enforce. Under the modern view, a court could hold that the parties intended the future rent to be a reasonable amount and could enforce the clause.[8]

In other words, under the modern view, the emphasis is on the parties' intent rather than on form. For example, when the Pennzoil Company discussed with the Getty Oil Company the possible purchase of Getty's stock, a "memorandum of agreement" was drafted to reflect the terms of the conversations. After more negotiations over the price, both companies issued press releases announcing an agreement in principle on the terms of the memorandum. The next day, Texaco, Inc., offered to buy all of Getty's stock at a higher price. The day after that, Getty's board of directors voted to accept Texaco's offer, and Texaco and Getty signed a merger agreement. When Pennzoil sued Texaco for tortious interference with its "contractual" relationship with Getty, a jury concluded that Getty and Pennzoil had intended a binding contract before Texaco made its offer, with only the details left to be worked out. Texaco was held liable for interfering with this contract.[9]

DEFINITENESS OF TERMS The second requirement for an effective offer involves the definiteness of its terms. An offer must have reasonably definite terms so that, if it is accepted and a contract formed, a court can determine if a breach has occurred and can provide an appropriate remedy. What specific terms are required depends, of course, on the type of contract. Generally, a contract must include the following terms, either expressed in the contract or capable of being reasonably inferred from it:

1. The identification of the parties.
2. The identification of the object or subject matter of the contract (also quantity, when appropriate),

7. See, for example, *Fairmount Glass Works v. Grunden-Martin Woodenware Co.*, 106 Ky. 659, 51 S.W. 196 (1899).

8. *Restatement (Second) of Contracts*, Section 33. See also UCC 2–204, 2–305.

9. *Texaco, Inc. v. Pennzoil Co.*, 729 S.W.2d 768 (Tex.App—Houston [1st Dist.] 1987, writ ref'd n.r.e.). (Generally, a complete Texas Court of Appeals citation includes the writ-of-error history showing the Texas Supreme Court's disposition of the case. In this case, "writ ref'd n.r.e." is an abbreviation for "writ refused, no reversible error," which means that Texas's highest court refused to grant the appellant's request to review the case, because the court did not consider there to be any reversible error.)

including the work to be performed, with specific identification of such items as goods, services, and land.
3. The consideration to be paid.
4. The time of payment, delivery, or performance.

Courts sometimes are willing to supply a missing term in a contract when the parties have clearly manifested an intent to form a contract. If, in contrast, the parties have attempted to deal with a particular term of the contract but their expression of intent is too vague or uncertain to be given any precise meaning, the court will not supply a "reasonable" term, because to do so might conflict with the intent of the parties. In other words, the court will not rewrite the contract.[10]

Definiteness is also required when a contract is modified. The terms of a contract as modified must be reasonably definite so that a court can determine if there has been a breach. The following case illustrates this point.

10. See Chapter 11 and UCC 2–204. Article 2 of the UCC specifies different rules relating to the definiteness of terms used in a contract for the sale of goods. In essence, Article 2 modifies general contract law by requiring less specificity.

CASE 9.1 Ruud v. Great Plains Supply, Inc.

Supreme Court of Minnesota, 1995. 526 N.W.2d 369.

COMPANY PROFILE *Michael Wigley bought Great Plains Supply, Inc. (GPS), a building materials supplier, in 1989. GPS had suffered losses in nine of the previous ten years. To turn GPS around, Wigley closed unprofitable stores and concentrated business on contractors. In 1994, sales exceeded $100 million—up more than 40 percent over 1993—and sales from GPS's truss manufacturing facilities doubled for the fifth straight year. GPS plants, lumberyards, and distribution centers are located primarily in the Midwest. Successful salespersons are promoted to management, and managers are compensated according to their performance.*

BACKGROUND AND FACTS *The corporate manual of Great Plains Supply, Inc., states that employees can be discharged at any time for any reason. This manual constitutes an employment contract between GPS and its employees. Kevin Ruud was a store manager for GPS. Before accepting an offer to transfer to an unprofitable store, he expressed worries about job security to Michael Wigley, GPS's owner, and Ronald Nelson, a GPS vice president. Wigley and Nelson each responded, "Good employees are taken care of." Ruud accepted the transfer, but when the store closed as he had feared, he was offered only lesser jobs at lower pay. Ruud quit his job and filed a suit in a Minnesota state court against GPS, Wigley, and Nelson for, among other things, breach of contract. Ruud alleged that their statements modified the terms of his contract with GPS to include permanent employment. The court dismissed the claims against Wigley and Nelson and granted GPS's motion for summary judgment. Ruud appealed, and the state intermediate appellate court reversed the trial court's summary judgment on the issue. The case was then appealed to the state supreme court.*

IN THE LANGUAGE OF THE COURT

GARDEBRING, Justice.

* * * *

* * * We conclude that Wigley and Nelson did not intend that GPS offer Kevin Ruud a "permanent" job, but rather were simply making policy statements as to the general goodwill of the company toward Kevin Ruud and its other employees. Furthermore, even if there was an intention to modify the [terms of Ruud's employment] contract, the statements of Wigley and Nelson are so vague as

to leave undeterminable the nature of that modification. Therefore, we conclude that as a matter of law, the statements of Nelson and Wigley are not sufficiently definite to create an offer of permanent employment.

DECISION AND REMEDY *The Supreme Court of Minnesota reinstated the order for summary judgment in favor of GPS.*

COMMUNICATION A third requirement for an effective offer is communication of the offer to the offeree, resulting in the offeree's knowledge of the offer. Ordinarily, one cannot agree to a bargain without knowing that it exists. Suppose that Estrich advertises a reward for the return of his lost dog. Hoban, not knowing of the reward, finds the dog and returns it to Estrich. Hoban cannot recover the reward, because she did not know it had been offered.[11]

TERMINATION OF THE OFFER

The communication of an effective offer to an offeree gives the offeree the power to transform the offer into a binding, legal obligation (a contract) by an acceptance. This power of acceptance, however, does not continue forever. It can be terminated either by the action of the parties or by operation of law.

TERMINATION BY ACTION OF THE PARTIES

An offer can be terminated by the action of the parties in any of three ways: by revocation, by rejection, or by counteroffer.

Revocation of the Offer by the Offeror. The offeror's act of withdrawing an offer is called **revocation.** Unless an offer is irrevocable, the offeror usually can revoke the offer (even if he or she has promised to keep it open), as long as the revocation is communicated to the offeree before the offeree accepts. Revocation may be accomplished by express repudiation of the offer (for example, with a statement such as "I withdraw my previous offer of October 17") or by performance of acts inconsistent with the existence of the offer, which are made known to the offeree.

The general rule followed by most states is that a revocation becomes effective when the offeree or offeree's agent (a person acting on behalf of the offeree) actually receives it. Therefore, a letter of revocation mailed on April 1 and delivered at the offeree's residence or place of business on April 3 becomes effective on April 3.

Irrevocable Offers. Although most offers are revocable, some can be made irrevocable. One type of irrevocable offer involves the option contract. Increasingly, courts also refuse to allow an offeror to revoke an offer when the offeree has changed position because of justifiable reliance on the offer. (In some circumstances, an offer for the sale of goods made by a merchant may also be considered irrevocable—see the discussion of the "merchant's firm offer" in Chapter 11.)

An *option contract* is created when an offeror promises to hold an offer open for a specified period of time in return for a payment (consideration) given by the offeree. An option contract takes away the offeror's power to revoke the offer for the period of time specified in the option. If no time is specified, then a reasonable period of time is implied.

When the offeree justifiably relies on an offer to his or her detriment, the court may hold that this *detrimental reliance* makes the offer irrevocable. The situation is normally called **promissory estoppel.** To *estop* means to bar, impede, or preclude from doing something. Thus, promissory estoppel means that the promisor (the offeror) is barred from revoking the offer, in this case because the offeree has already changed her actions in reliance on the offer. We look again at the doctrine of promissory estoppel later in this chapter, in the context of consideration.

Detrimental reliance on the part of the offeree can also involve partial performance by the offeree in response to an offer looking toward formulation of a unilateral contract. As discussed earlier in this chapter, the offer to form a unilateral contract invites acceptance only by full performance; merely promising to perform does not constitute acceptance.

---

11. A few states allow recovery of the reward, but not on contract principles. Because Estrich wanted his dog to be returned, and Hoban returned it, these few states would allow Hoban to recover on the basis that it would be unfair to deny her the reward just because she did not know it had been offered.

Injustice can result if an offeree expends time and money in partial performance, and then the offeror revokes the offer before performance can be completed. Many courts will not allow the offeror to revoke the offer after the offeree has performed some substantial part of his or her duties.[12] In effect, partial performance renders the offer irrevocable, giving the original offeree reasonable time to complete performance. Of course, once the performance is complete, a unilateral contract exists.

Rejection of the Offer by the Offeree. The offer may be rejected by the offeree, in which case the offer is terminated. Any subsequent attempt by the offeree to accept will be construed as a new offer, giving the original offeror (now the offeree) the power of acceptance. A rejection is ordinarily accomplished by words or conduct evidencing an intent not to accept the offer. As with revocation, rejection of an offer is effective only when it is actually received by the offeror or the offeror's agent.

Merely inquiring about an offer does not constitute rejection. Suppose that a friend offers to buy your CD-ROM library for $300, and you respond, "Is that your best offer?" or "Will you pay me $375 for it?" A reasonable person would conclude that you had not rejected the offer but had merely made an inquiry for further consideration of the offer. You can still accept and bind your friend to the $300 purchase price. When the offeree merely inquires as to the firmness of the offer, there is no reason to presume that he or she intends to reject it.

Counteroffer by the Offeree. A rejection of the original offer and the simultaneous making of a new offer is called a **counteroffer.** Suppose that Duffy offers to sell her home to Wong for $170,000. Wong responds, "Your price is too high. I'll offer to purchase your house for $160,000." Wong's response is a counteroffer, because it terminates Duffy's offer to sell at $170,000 and creates a new offer by Wong to purchase at $160,000.

At common law, the **mirror image rule** requires the offeree's acceptance to match the offeror's offer exactly—to mirror the offer. Any material change in, or addition to, the terms of the original offer automatically terminates that offer and substitutes the counteroffer. The counteroffer, of course, need not be accepted; but if the original offeror does accept the terms of the counteroffer, a valid contract is created.[13]

TERMINATION BY OPERATION OF LAW The power of the offeree to transform the offer into a binding, legal obligation can be terminated by operation of the law through the occurrence of the following events:

1. Lapse of time.
2. Destruction of the specific subject matter of the offer.
3. Death or incompetence of the offeror or the offeree.
4. Supervening illegality of the proposed contract.

An offer terminates automatically by law when the period of time specified in the offer has passed. For example, suppose Alejandro offers to sell his camper to Kelly if she accepts within twenty days. Kelly must accept within the twenty-day period, or the offer will lapse (terminate). The time period specified in an offer normally begins to run when the offer is actually received by the offeree, not when it is sent or drawn up. When the offer is delayed (through the misdelivery of mail, for example), the period begins to run from the date the offeree would have received the offer, but only if the offeree knows or should know that the offer is delayed.[14]

If no time for acceptance is specified in the offer, the offer terminates at the end of a *reasonable* period of time. What constitutes a reasonable period of time depends on the subject matter of the contract, business and market conditions, and other relevant circumstances. An offer to sell farm produce, for example, will terminate sooner than an offer to sell farm equipment because farm produce is perishable and subject to greater fluctuations in market value.

ACCEPTANCE

Acceptance is a voluntary act (either words or conduct) by the offeree that shows assent (agreement) to the terms of an offer. The acceptance must be unequivocal and communicated to the offeror. To

12. *Restatement (Second) of Contracts,* Section 45.

13. The mirror image rule has been greatly modified in regard to sales contracts. Section 2–207 of the UCC provides that a contract is formed if the offeree makes a definite expression of acceptance (such as signing the form in the appropriate location), even though the terms of the acceptance modify or add to the terms of the original offer (see Chapter 11).

14. *Restatement (Second) of Contracts,* Section 49.

exercise the power of acceptance effectively, the offeree must accept unequivocally. This is the *mirror image rule* previously discussed. If the acceptance is subject to new conditions or if the terms of the acceptance materially change the original offer, the acceptance may be deemed a counteroffer that implicitly rejects the original offer. An acceptance may be unequivocal even though the offeree expresses dissatisfaction with the contract. For example, "I accept the offer, but I wish I could have gotten a better price" is an effective acceptance. So, too, is "I accept, but can you shave the price?" In contrast, the statement "I accept the offer but only if I can pay on ninety days' credit" is not an unequivocal acceptance and operates as a counteroffer, rejecting the original offer.

Certain terms when added to an acceptance will not qualify the acceptance sufficiently to constitute rejection of the offer. Suppose that in response to an offer to sell a piano, the offeree replies, "I accept; please send written contract." The offeree is requesting a written contract but is not making it a condition for acceptance. Therefore, the acceptance is effective without the written contract. If the offeree replies, "I accept if you send a written contract," however, the acceptance is expressly conditioned on the request for a writing, and the statement is not an acceptance but a counteroffer. (Notice how important each word is!)

SILENCE AS ACCEPTANCE Ordinarily, silence cannot constitute acceptance, even if the offeror states, "By your silence and inaction you will be deemed to have accepted this offer." This general rule applies because an offeree should not be obligated to act affirmatively to reject an offer when no consideration has passed to the offeree to impose such a duty.

In some instances, however, the offeree does have a duty to speak, in which case his or her silence or inaction will operate as an acceptance. For example, silence may be an acceptance when an offeree takes the benefit of offered services even though he or she had an opportunity to reject them and knew that they were offered with the expectation of compensation.

Silence can also operate as acceptance when the offeree has had prior dealings with the offeror. Suppose that a merchant routinely receives shipments from a certain supplier and always notifies the supplier when defective goods are rejected. In this situation, silence regarding a shipment will constitute acceptance. Additionally, if a person solicits an offer specifying that certain terms and conditions are acceptable, and the offeror makes the offer in response to the solicitation, the offeree has a duty to reject—that is, a duty to tell the offeror that the offer is not acceptable. Failure to reject (silence) operates as an acceptance.

COMMUNICATION OF ACCEPTANCE Whether the offeror must be notified of the acceptance depends on the nature of the contract. In a bilateral contract, communication of acceptance is necessary because acceptance is in the form of a promise (not performance) and the contract is formed when the promise is made (rather than when the act is performed). The offeree must communicate the acceptance to the offeror. Communication of acceptance is not necessary, however, if the offer dispenses with the requirement. Additionally, if the offer can be accepted by silence, no communication is necessary.

Because in a unilateral contract the full performance of some act is called for, acceptance is usually evident, and notification is therefore unnecessary. Exceptions do exist, however. When the offeror requests notice of acceptance or has no adequate means of determining whether the requested act has been performed, or when the law requires notice of acceptance, then notice is necessary.

CONTRACT FORMATION IN THE ELECTRONIC AGE In the last few years, courts have had to deal with such issues as how the rules of contract law can be adapted to an electronic age in which documents are transmitted virtually instantaneously via electronic communications systems, such as fax machines and the Internet. An emerging issue has to do with whether clicking on a "Yes" or "Agreed" box (in response to an online offer) constitutes acceptance by conduct. Generally, the courts tend to extend traditional contract law principles to offers and acceptances made via nontraditional modes of communication.

Faxed Offers and Acceptances. Offers and acceptances commonly are communicated via fax. To date, the courts have held that signatures on faxed documents are legally binding (unless an "original" signature is specifically required), and transmission by fax is now a preferred means of communication for many contracting parties. Often, as part of a contractual arrangement, the parties will provide that a faxed signature is the equivalent of an original signature.

What happens when an acceptance is faxed to the offeror's office but for some reason is not received by the offeror in a timely fashion or is lost? This is similar to a situation in which a letter goes astray because of an incorrect address. In such a situation, the acceptance will not be effective until received by the offeror. Very likely, if a fax transmitted to the offeror failed to reach the offeror for some reason, a court would look closely at the circumstances. For example, if the offeror did not receive the fax because his or her fax machine was out of paper, and the offeree had reason to suspect or know that the offeror did not receive the fax, then the court might hold that the faxed acceptance was not effective.

"Click-on" Acceptances. As noted earlier, under the common law of contracts, an acceptance can be made either expressly or by conduct. The UCC also provides for acceptance by conduct. One of the legal issues concerning contracts formed online is whether clicking "Yes" or "Agreed" on a computer screen constitutes a valid acceptance of a contractual offer. After all, it is possible to click a box on a computer screen accidentally, in which situation it would be unfair to hold that the action bound the offeree in contract.

To date, only a few cases dealing with the validity of "click-on" acceptances have come before the courts. In one case, a federal appellate court held that the offeree had manifested his assent to be bound by the terms and conditions of a Shareware Registration Agreement offered by CompuServe, Inc., by typing "Agree" at various points in the registration agreement.[15] In another case, a different federal appellate court indicated that an online seller, as the master of the offer, could invite online acceptance by conduct in the form of clicking on the appropriate box on the computer screen.[16] Generally, issues concerning the validity of online "click-on" acceptances tend to arise in the context of sales contracts, to which the UCC applies. (For a further discussion of some of the issues that arise in electronic sales contracts, see the *Emerging Trends* in Chapter 11.)

SECTION 5
CONSIDERATION

The fact that a promise has been made does not mean the promise can or will be enforced. No promise is enforceable without consideration. **Consideration** is usually defined as the value (such as money) given in return for a promise (such as the promise to sell a stamp collection on receipt of payment).

Often, consideration is broken down into two parts: (1) something of *legal value* must be given in exchange for the promise, and (2) there must be a *bargained-for* exchange. The "something of legal value" may consist of a return promise that is bargained for. If it consists of performance, that performance may be (1) an act (other than a promise); (2) a forbearance (a refraining from action); or (3) the creation, modification, or destruction of a legal relation.[17]

The following case is one of the classic cases of contract law. The issue before the court is whether refraining from certain behavior at the request of another is sufficient consideration to support a promise to pay a sum of money.

15. *CompuServe, Inc. v. Patterson*, 89 F.3d 1257 (6th Cir. 1996).

16. *ProCD, Inc. v. Zeidenberg*, 86 F.3d 1447 (7th Cir. 1996).

17. *Restatement (Second) of Contracts*, Section 71.

CASE 9.2 Hamer v. Sidway

Court of Appeals of New York, Second Division, 1891. 124 N.Y. 538, 27 N.E. 256.

BACKGROUND AND FACTS *William E. Story, Sr., was the uncle of William E. Story II. In the presence of family members and guests invited to a family gathering, the elder Story promised to pay his nephew $5,000 if he would refrain from drinking, using tobacco, swearing, and playing cards or billiards for money until he reached the age of twenty-one. (Note that in 1869, when this contract was formed, it was legal in New York to drink and play cards for money prior to the age of twenty-one.) The nephew agreed and fully performed his part of the bargain. When he reached the age of twenty-one, he wrote and told his uncle that he had kept his part of the agreement and was therefore entitled to $5,000. The uncle replied that he was pleased with his nephew's performance, writing, "I*

have no doubt but you have, for which you shall have five thousand dollars, as I promised you. I had the money in the bank the day you was twenty-one years old that I intend for you, and you shall have the money certain. . . . P.S. You can consider this money on interest." The nephew received his uncle's letter and thereafter consented that the money should remain with his uncle according to the terms and conditions of the letter. The uncle died about twelve years later without having paid his nephew any part of the $5,000 and interest. The executor of the uncle's estate (Sidway, the defendant in this action) did not want to pay the $5,000 (with interest) to Hamer, a third party to whom the nephew had transferred his rights in the note, claiming that there had been no valid consideration for the promise. The court disagreed with the executor and reviewed the doctrine of detriment and benefit as valid consideration under the law.

IN THE LANGUAGE OF THE COURT

PARKER, J. [Justice]

* * * *

* * * Courts will not ask whether the thing which forms the consideration does in fact benefit the promisee or a third party, or is of any substantial value to any one. It is enough that something is promised, done, forborne, or suffered by the party to whom the promise is made as consideration for the promise made to him. In general a waiver of any legal right at the request of another party is a sufficient consideration for a promise. Any damage, or suspension, or forbearance of a right will be sufficient to sustain a promise. * * * Now, applying this rule to the facts before us, the promisee used tobacco, occasionally drank liquor, and he had a legal right to do so. That right he abandoned for a period of years upon the strength of the promise of the testator that for such forbearance he would give him $5,000. We need not speculate on the effort which may have been required to give up the use of those stimulants. It is sufficient that he restricted his lawful freedom of action within certain prescribed limits upon the faith of his uncle's agreement, and now, having fully performed the conditions imposed, it is of no moment whether such performance actually proved a benefit to the promisor, and the court will not inquire into it; but, were it a proper subject of inquiry, we see nothing in this record that would permit a determination that the uncle was not benefited in a legal sense.

DECISION AND REMEDY

The court ruled that the nephew had provided legally sufficient consideration by giving up smoking, drinking, swearing, and playing cards or billiards for money until he reached the age of twenty-one and was therefore entitled to the money.

ETHICAL CONSIDERATIONS

The Hamer v. Sidway *case is a good illustration of the distinction between benefits to the promisor and detriment to the promisee. Here the court did not inquire as to whether a benefit had flowed to the promisor but required only that there had been a legally sufficient detriment to the promisee. The court did note, however, that arguably the promisor had also benefited by the contract—to the extent that the uncle considered it a benefit that his nephew had given up various vices, protected the family's reputation, and so on.*

ADEQUACY OF CONSIDERATION

Adequacy of consideration refers to the fairness of the bargain. In general, a court will not question the adequacy of consideration if the consideration is legally sufficient. Under the doctrine of freedom of contract, parties are normally free to bargain as they wish. If people could sue merely because they had entered into an unwise contract, the courts would be overloaded with frivolous suits.

EXTREME CASES In extreme cases, a court of law may consider the adequacy of consideration in terms of its amount or worth because inadequate consideration may indicate fraud, duress, undue influence, or a lack of bargained-for exchange. It may also reflect a party's incompetence (for example, an individual might have been too intoxicated or simply too young to make a contract). Suppose Dylan has a house worth $100,000 and he sells it for $50,000. A $50,000 sale could indicate that the buyer unduly pressured Dylan into selling or that Dylan was defrauded into selling the house at far below market value. (Of course, it might also indicate that Dylan was in a hurry to sell and that the amount was legally sufficient.)

In an equity suit, courts will more likely question the adequacy of consideration. (Remember from Chapter 1 that actions at law allow for remedies that consist of some form of compensation. Actions in equity allow for such remedies as specific performance, injunction, and rescission.) In an equity suit, the defendant must show that the transaction was not **unconscionable**[18]—that is, generally speaking, so one sided under the circumstances as to be unfair—and that consideration was exchanged.

PREEXISTING DUTY Under most circumstances, a promise to do what one already has a legal duty to do does not constitute legally sufficient consideration, because no legal detriment is incurred.[19] The preexisting legal duty may be imposed by law or may arise out of a previous contract. A sheriff, for example, cannot collect a reward for providing information leading to the capture of a criminal if the sheriff already has a legal duty to capture the criminal. Likewise, if a party is already bound by contract to perform a certain duty, that duty cannot serve as consideration for a second contract. For example, suppose that Bauman-Bache, Inc., begins construction on a seven-story office building and after three months demands an extra $75,000 on its contract. If the extra $75,000 is not paid, it will stop working. The owner of the land, having no one else to complete construction, agrees to pay the extra $75,000. The agreement is not enforceable, because it is not supported by legally sufficient consideration; Bauman-Bache was under a preexisting contract to complete the building.

18. Pronounced un-*kon*-shun-uh-bul.

19. See *Foakes v. Beer*, 9 App.Cas. 605 (1884).

PAST CONSIDERATION Promises made in return for actions or events that have already taken place are unenforceable. These promises lack consideration in that the element of bargained-for exchange is missing. In short, you can bargain for something to take place now or in the future but not for something that has already taken place. Therefore, *past consideration* is no consideration.

Suppose, for example, that Elsie, a real estate agent, does her friend Judy a favor by selling Judy's house and not charging any commission. Later, Judy says to Elsie, "In return for your generous act, I will pay you $3,000." This promise is made in return for past consideration and is thus unenforceable; in effect, Judy is stating her intention to give Elsie a gift.

DETRIMENTAL RELIANCE, OR PROMISSORY ESTOPPEL

As discussed in the context of irrevocable offers, under the doctrine of *detrimental reliance* (or *promissory estoppel*), a person who has reasonably and substantially relied on the promise of another may be able to obtain some measure of recovery. This doctrine is applied in a wide variety of contexts in which a promise is otherwise unenforceable, including that of a promise not supported by consideration. Under this doctrine, a court may enforce an otherwise unenforceable promise to avoid the injustice that would otherwise result. For the doctrine to be applied, the following elements are required:

1. There must be a clear and definite promise.
2. The promisee must justifiably rely on the promise.
3. The reliance normally must be of a substantial and definite character.
4. Justice will be better served by enforcement of the promise.

If these requirements are met, a promise may be enforced even though it is not supported by consideration. In essence, the promisor will be *estopped* (prevented) from asserting the lack of consideration as a defense. The estoppel arises from the promise, and hence *promissory estoppel* is the term used.

In the following case, a general contractor sought to recover damages under the doctrine of detrimental reliance from a subcontractor that reneged on its bid.

CASE 9.3 Percy J. Matherne Contractor, Inc. v. Grinnell Fire Protection Systems Co.

United States District Court, Middle District of Louisiana, 1995. 915 F.Supp. 818.

BACKGROUND AND FACTS *The St. James Parish School Board invited bids on renovations to Lutcher High School in Lutcher, Louisiana. Before submitting a bid, Percy J. Matherne Contractor, Inc., asked Grinnell Fire Protection Systems Company what it would charge to install a system as part of the renovation. Grinnell responded with a bid of $79,500. Relying on this figure, Matherne bid on, and was awarded, the school contract. Later, Grinnell estimated that its cost could be three times as much as its bid and refused to perform. Matherne hired Superior Sprinkler Corporation to do the work for $192,985. Matherne then filed a suit against Grinnell to recover the difference between Grinnell's bid and the substitute contract price.*

IN THE LANGUAGE OF THE COURT

VANCE, District Judge.

* * * *

* * * [T]he bid submitted by Grinnell constituted a promise. Upon submission of the bid, Grinnell knew that if its bid were the lowest, Matherne would rely to its detriment on the bid by incorporating it into its bid for the prime contract. * * *

* * * *

* * * [A] subcontractor who submits a bid offer to a general contractor, knowing that the general contractor is going to rely on its bid in submitting the general bid, is bound unless it is clearly shown that the subcontractor's bid offer was not final.

DECISION AND REMEDY *The court applied the doctrine of detrimental reliance to hold that Grinnell was bound by its bid. Matherne was entitled to the difference between that bid and the price charged by Superior.*

SECTION 6
CAPACITY

Although the parties TO a contract must assume certain risks, the law indicates that neither party should be allowed to benefit from the other party's lack of *contractual capacity*—the legal ability to enter into a contractual relationship. Courts generally presume the existence of contractual capacity, but there are some situations in which capacity is lacking or may be questionable. In many situations, a party may have the capacity to enter into a valid contract but also have the right to avoid liability under it.

Minors usually are not legally bound by contracts. Subject to certain exceptions, the contracts entered into by a minor are voidable at the option of that minor. The minor has the option of *disaffirming* (renouncing) the contract and setting aside the contract and all legal obligations arising from it. An adult who enters into a contract with a minor, however, cannot avoid his or her contractual duties on the ground that the minor can do so. Unless the minor exercises the option to disaffirm the contract, the adult party is bound by it.

Intoxication is a condition in which a person's normal capacity to act or think is inhibited by alcohol or some other drug. If the person was sufficiently intoxicated to lack mental capacity, then the transaction is voidable at the option of the intoxicated person even if the intoxication was purely voluntary.

If a person has been adjudged mentally incompetent by a court of law and a guardian has been appointed, any contract made by the mentally incompetent person is void—no contract exists. Only the guardian can enter into binding legal duties on the incompetent person's behalf.

SECTION 7

GENUINENESS OF ASSENT

A contract has been entered into by two parties, each with full legal capacity and for a legal purpose. The contract is also supported by consideration. Nonetheless, the contract may be unenforceable if the parties have not genuinely assented to its terms. **Genuineness of assent** may be lacking because of a mistake, misrepresentation, undue influence, or duress—in other words, because there is no true "meeting of the minds."

MISTAKES

We all make mistakes, and it is therefore not surprising that mistakes are made when contracts are formed. It is important to distinguish between mistakes made *in judgment as to value or quality* and mistakes made *as to facts.* Only the latter have legal significance. Suppose that Wong Sun plans to buy ten acres of land in Montana. If he believes the land is worth $100,000, and it is worth only $40,000, his mistake is one of value or quality. If he believes, however, that the land is the ten acres owned by the Boyds, and it is actually the ten acres owned by the Deweys, his mistake is one of fact. Only a mistake as to fact allows a contract to be avoided.

Mistakes occur in two forms—*unilateral* and *mutual (bilateral).* A unilateral mistake is made by only one of the contracting parties; a mutual, or bilateral, mistake is made by both.

UNILATERAL MISTAKES A unilateral mistake occurs when one contracting party makes a mistake as to some *material fact*—that is, a fact important to the subject matter of the contract. The general rule is that a unilateral mistake does not afford the mistaken party any right to relief from the contract. For example, DeVinck intends to sell his motor home for $17,500. When he learns that Benson is interested in buying a used motor home, DeVinck faxes Benson an offer to sell the vehicle to him. When typing the fax, however, DeVinck mistakenly keys in the price of $15,700. Benson immediately sends DeVinck a fax, accepting DeVinck's offer. Even though DeVinck intended to sell his motor home for $17,500, his unilateral mistake falls on him. He is bound in contract to sell the motor home to Benson for $15,700.

There are at least two exceptions to this general rule.[20] First, if the *other* party to the contract knows or should have known that a mistake of fact was made, the contract may not be enforceable. In the above example, if Benson knew that DeVinck intended to sell his motor home for $17,500, then DeVinck's unilateral mistake (stating $15,700 in his offer) may render the resulting contract unenforceable. The second exception arises when a unilateral mistake of fact was due to a mathematical mistake in addition, subtraction, division, or multiplication and was made inadvertently and without gross (extreme) negligence. If a contractor's bid was low because he or she made a mistake in addition when totaling the estimated costs, any contract resulting from the bid may be rescinded. Of course, in both situations, the mistake must still involve some *material* fact.

MUTUAL MISTAKES When both parties are mistaken about the same material fact, the contract can be rescinded by either party.[21] To illustrate: Assume that at Umberto's art gallery, Keeley buys a painting of a landscape. Both Umberto and Keeley believe that the painting is by the artist Van Gogh. Later, Keeley discovers that the painting is a very clever fake. Because neither Umberto nor Keeley was aware of this material fact when they made their deal, Keeley can rescind the contract and recover the purchase price of the painting.

A word or term in a contract may be subject to more than one reasonable interpretation. In that situation, if the parties to the contract attach materially different meanings to the term, their mutual mistake of fact may allow the contract to be rescinded because there has been no "meeting of the minds," or true assent, which is required for a contract to arise. The classic case on mutual mistake involved a ship named *Peerless* that was to sail from Bombay with certain cotton goods on board. More than one ship named *Peerless* sailed from Bombay that winter, however.

20. The *Restatement (Second) of Contracts,* Section 153, liberalizes the general rule to take into account the modern trend of allowing avoidance even though only one party has been mistaken.

21. *Restatement (Second) of Contracts,* Section 152.

CASE 9.4 Raffles v. Wichelhaus

Court of Exchequer, England, 1864. 159 Eng.Rep. 375.

HISTORICAL AND POLITICAL SETTING *Before the Civil War, the states in the southern United States were largely agricultural. By the mid-1800s, the staple of this agricultural area had become cotton. Cotton was important to the economy of the South and to the economy of the European textile industry, which by 1860 was booming. In the 1860s, when the southern states seceded from the United States to form the Confederate States, the United States announced a blockade of southern ports. The states of the Confederacy knew that cotton was important to the European economy, and they were confident that Europe would exert pressure on the United States to lift the blockade. Instead, to obtain cotton, European merchants turned to other sources, including India.*

BACKGROUND AND FACTS *The defendant, Wichelhaus, purchased a shipment of Surat cotton from the plaintiff, Raffles, "to arrive* 'Peerless' *from Bombay." The defendant expected the goods to be shipped on the* Peerless *sailing from Bombay, India, in October. The plaintiff expected to ship the goods on a different* Peerless, *which sailed from Bombay in December. By the time the goods arrived and the plaintiff tried to deliver them, the defendant was no longer willing to accept them.*

IN THE LANGUAGE OF THE COURT

PER CURIAM [by the whole court].

* * * *

[The defendants asserted that the] ship mentioned in the * * * agreement was meant and intended by the defendants to be the ship called the "Peerless," which sailed from Bombay * * * in October; and that the plaintiff was not ready and willing and did not offer to deliver to the defendants any bales of cotton which arrived by the last mentioned ship, but instead thereof was only ready and willing and offered to deliver to the defendants 125 bales of Surat cotton which arrived by another and different ship, which was also called the "Peerless," and which sailed from Bombay * * * in December.

* * * *

There is nothing on the face of the contract to show that any particular ship called the "Peerless" was meant; but the moment it appears that two ships called the "Peerless" were about to sail from Bombay there is latent ambiguity, and parol evidence[a] may be given for the purpose of shewing [showing] that the defendant meant one "Peerless" and the plaintiff another. That being so, there was no consensus ad idem [on the point], and therefore no contract.

DECISION AND REMEDY *The judgment was for the defendant, Wichelhaus. The court held that no mutual assent existed, because the parties had attached materially different meanings to an essential term of the written contract (the ship that was to transport the goods). This being so, oral testimony would have been needed to determine whether the parties had actually meant the same ship. If both had meant the same ship, then the contract would have been enforceable.*

a. With respect to contracts, *parol evidence* is evidence that the document itself does not furnish but that other sources (such as, in this case, oral testimony) provide.

FRAUDULENT MISREPRESENTATION

Although fraud is a tort (see Chapter 12), it also affects the genuineness of the innocent party's consent to the contract. Thus, the transaction is not voluntary in the sense of involving "mutual assent." When an innocent party is fraudulently induced to enter into a contract, the contract normally can be avoided because that party has not *voluntarily* consented to its terms.[22] Normally, the innocent party can either rescind the contract and be restored to his or her original position or enforce the contract and seek damages for any injuries resulting from the fraud.

The word *fraudulent* means many things in the law. Generally, fraudulent misrepresentation refers only to misrepresentation that is consciously false and is intended to mislead another. The perpetrator of the fraudulent misrepresentation knows or believes that the assertion is false or knows that he or she does not have a basis (stated or implied) for the assertion.[23]

What is at issue is whether the defendant believed that the plaintiff was substantially certain to be misled as a result of the misrepresentation. Dantzler, for example, makes a statement to the ABC Credit Rating Company about his financial condition that he knows is untrue. Dantzler realizes that ABC will publish this information for its subscribers. Marchetti, a subscriber, receives the published information. Relying on that information, Marchetti is induced to make a contract to lend money to Dantzler. Dantzler's statement is a fraudulent misrepresentation, and the contract is voidable by Marchetti.

Typically, fraudulent misrepresentation consists of the following elements:

1. A misrepresentation of a material fact must occur.
2. There must be an intent to deceive.
3. The innocent party must justifiably rely on the misrepresentation.

To collect damages, a party must also have been injured. To obtain rescission of a contract, or to defend against the enforcement of a contract on the basis of fraudulent misrepresentation, in most states a party need not have suffered an injury.

22. *Restatement (Second) of Contracts,* Sections 163 and 164.
23. *Restatement (Second) of Contracts,* Section 162.

NONFRAUDULENT MISREPRESENTATION

If a plaintiff seeks to rescind a contract because of *fraudulent* misrepresentation, the plaintiff must prove that the defendant had the intent to deceive. Most courts also allow rescission in cases involving *nonfraudulent* misrepresentation—that is, innocent or negligent misrepresentation—if all of the other elements of misrepresentation exist.

UNDUE INFLUENCE

Undue influence arises from special kinds of relationships in which one party can greatly influence another party, thus overcoming that party's free will. Minors and elderly people, for example, are often under the influence of guardians. If the guardian induces a young or elderly ward to enter into a contract that benefits the guardian, undue influence may have been exerted. Undue influence can arise from a number of confidential or fiduciary relationships:[24] attorney-client, doctor-patient, guardian-ward, parent-child, husband-wife, or trustee-beneficiary. The essential feature of undue influence is that the party being taken advantage of does not, in reality, exercise free will in entering into a contract. A contract entered into under excessive or undue influence lacks genuine assent and is therefore voidable.[25]

DURESS

Assent to the terms of a contract is not genuine if one of the parties is *forced* into the agreement. Forcing a party to do something, including entering into a contract, through fear created by threats is legally defined as *duress.* In addition, blackmail or extortion to induce consent to a contract constitutes duress. Duress is both a defense to the enforcement of a contract and a ground for the rescission of a contract.

Generally, the threatened act must be wrongful or illegal. Threatening to exercise a legal right is not ordinarily illegal and usually does not constitute duress. Suppose that Donovan injures Jaworski in an auto accident. The police are not called. Donovan has no automobile insurance, but she has substantial assets. Jaworski is willing to settle the potential claim out of court for $3,000. Donovan refuses. After much

24. A *fiduciary relationship* is one involving a high degree of trust and confidence—see Chapter 19.
25. *Restatement (Second) of Contracts,* Section 177.

arguing, Jaworski loses her patience and says, "If you don't pay me $3,000 right now, I'm going to sue you for $35,000." Donovan is frightened and gives Jaworski a check for $3,000. Later in the day, she stops payment on the check. Jaworski comes back to sue her for the $3,000. Although Donovan argues that she was the victim of duress, the threat of a *civil* suit is normally not duress.

Economic need is generally not sufficient to constitute duress, even when one party exacts a very high price for an item that the other party needs. If the party exacting the price also creates the need, however, *economic duress* may be found. The Internal Revenue Service, for example, assessed a large tax and penalty against Weller. Weller retained Eyman, the accountant who had filed the tax returns on which the assessment was based, to resist the assessment. Two days before the deadline for filing a reply with the Internal Revenue Service, Eyman declined to represent Weller unless he signed a very high contingency fee agreement for his services. The agreement was unenforceable.[26] Although Eyman had threatened only to withdraw his services, something that he was legally entitled to do, he was responsible for delaying the withdrawal until the last days. Because it would have been impossible at that late date to obtain adequate representation elsewhere, Weller was forced either to sign the contract or lose his right to challenge the IRS assessment.

ADHESION CONTRACTS AND UNCONSCIONABILITY

Questions concerning genuineness of assent may arise when the terms of a contract are dictated by a party with overwhelming bargaining power and the signer must agree to those terms or go without the commodity or service in question. Such contracts are often referred to as *adhesion contracts*. An adhesion contract is written *exclusively* by one party (the dominant party, usually the seller or creditor) and presented to the other party (the adhering party, usually the buyer or borrower) on a take-it-or-leave-it basis—in other words, the adhering party has no opportunity to negotiate the terms of the contract.

Standard-form contracts often contain fine-print provisions that shift a risk naturally borne by one party to the other. Such contracts are used by a variety of businesses and include life insurance policies, residential leases, loan agreements, and employment agency contracts. To avoid enforcement of the contract or of a particular clause, the aggrieved party must show that the parties had substantially unequal bargaining positions and that enforcement would be manifestly unfair or oppressive. If the required showing is made, the contract or particular term is deemed *unconscionable* and not enforced. Technically, unconscionability under Section 2–302 of the Uniform Commercial Code (UCC) applies only to contracts for the sale of goods. Many courts, however, have broadened the concept and applied it in other situations.

Although unconscionability will be discussed in the next chapter, it is important to note here that the great degree of discretion permitted a court to invalidate or strike down a contract or clause as being unconscionable has met with resistance. As a result, some states have not adopted Section 2–302 of the UCC. In those states, the legislature and the courts prefer to rely on traditional notions of fraud, undue influence, and duress. On the one hand, this gives certainty to contractual relationships, because parties know they will be held to the exact terms of their contracts. On the other hand, public policy does require that there be some limit on the power of individuals and businesses to dictate the terms of contracts.

SECTION 8

LEGALITY

For an agreement to be deemed a valid contract, the agreement must not call for the performance of an illegal act—that is, any act that is criminal, tortious, or otherwise opposed to public policy. A contract to do something that is prohibited by federal or state statutory law is illegal and, as such, void from the outset and thus unenforceable.

Although contracts involve private parties, some are not enforceable because of the negative impact they would have on society. These contracts are said to be *contrary to public policy*. Examples include a contract to commit an immoral act (such as a surrogate-parenting contract, which several courts and state statutes equate with "baby selling") and a contract that prohibits marriage. As an example of the latter, suppose that Everett offers a young man $500 if he refrains from marrying Everett's daughter. If the young man accepts, no contract is formed (the contract is void), because such a contract would be

26. *Thompson Crane & Trucking Co. v. Eyman*, 123 Cal.App.2d 904, 267 P.2d 1043 (1954).

contrary to public policy. Thus, if the man marries Everett's daughter, Everett cannot sue him for breach of contract. It is important to note that a contract or a clause in a contract may be illegal even in the absence of a specific statute prohibiting the action promised by the contract.

The following case illustrates the general problem posed by differences among state statutes and policies on gambling, as well as how people from one state (where gambling debts are unenforceable) can avoid responsibility for gambling debts they incur in another state (where gambling debts are enforceable).

CASE 9.5 Metropolitan Creditors Service of Sacramento v. Sadri

California Court of Appeal, First District, 1993. 15 Cal.App.4th 1821, 19 Cal.Rptr.2d 646.

BACKGROUND AND FACTS *Soheil Sadri, a California resident, incurred debts totaling $22,000 over a two-day period in 1991 while gambling at Caesar's Tahoe casino in Nevada. On January 13 and 14, he wrote the casino two personal checks for $2,000 and $10,000. On January 14, he executed two memoranda of indebtedness for $5,000 each. In exchange for the checks and memoranda, Sadri received chips, which he lost playing the game of baccarat. Sadri subsequently stopped payment on the checks and memoranda, which were drawn on his account at a California bank. Caesar's Tahoe transferred its rights in the checks and memoranda to Metropolitan Creditors Service of Sacramento (MCS) for collection, and MCS sued Sadri in California. The court issued a judgment in favor of Sadri, ruling that his gambling debts were unenforceable in California. MCS appealed.*

IN THE LANGUAGE OF THE COURT

KING, Associate Justice.

* * * *

California has always had a strong public policy against judicial enforcement of gambling debts, going back virtually to the inception of statehood. * * *

* * * *

The * * * court [in *Hamilton v. Abadjian*, an earlier California case] stated the anti-enforcement rule within a context * * * specific to the facts of * * * the present case: "The owner of a gambling house who honors a check for the purpose of providing a prospective customer with funds with which to gamble and who then participates in the transaction thus promoted by his act cannot recover on the check."

* * * *

The *Hamilton* rule is on all fours [the facts are similar, and the same questions of law are involved] with the present case. Caesar's Tahoe honored Sadri's checks and memoranda of indebtedness for the purpose of providing him with funds with which to gamble, and then participated in the game. * * * [This rule] precludes judicial enforcement of Sadri's gambling debts in California state courts; * * * the contracts underlying the debts are against public policy * * * and thus the contracts are unlawful and the debts unenforceable.

DECISION AND REMEDY *The appellate court affirmed the lower court's refusal to enforce the debts, on the ground that the enforcement of gambling debts incurred on credit violates California's public policy.*

SECTION 9 STATUTE OF FRAUDS

At early common law, parties to a contract were not allowed to testify. This led to the practice of hiring third party witnesses. As early as the seventeenth century, the English recognized the many problems presented by this practice and enacted a statute to help deal with it. The statute, passed by the English Parliament in 1677, was known as "An Act for the

Prevention of Frauds and Perjuries." The act required that certain types of contracts, to be enforceable, had to be evidenced by a writing and signed by the party against whom enforcement was sought.

MODERN STATUTES OF FRAUDS

Today almost every state has a statute, modeled after the English act, that stipulates what types of contracts must be in writing. In this text, we refer to these statutes collectively—even if a particular state has more than one statute relating to the topic—as the **Statute of Frauds.** The actual name of the Statute of Frauds is misleading because it neither applies to fraud nor invalidates any type of contract. Rather, it denies *enforceability* to certain contracts that do not comply with its requirements.

The primary purpose of the act is *evidentiary*—to provide reliable evidence of the existence and terms of certain classes of contracts deemed historically to be important or complex. Although the statutes vary slightly from state to state, all states require certain types of contracts to be in writing or evidenced by a written memorandum signed by the party against whom enforcement is sought, unless certain exceptions apply. (These exceptions will be discussed later in this chapter.) The following types of contracts are said to fall "under" or "within" the Statute of Frauds and therefore require a writing:

1. Contracts involving interests in land.
2. Contracts that cannot by their terms be performed within one year from the date of formation.
3. Collateral, or secondary, contracts, such as promises to answer for the debt or duty of another and promises by the administrator or executor of an estate to pay a debt of the estate personally—that is, out of his or her own pocket.
4. Promises made in consideration of marriage.
5. Under the UCC, contracts for the sale of goods priced at $500 or more.

PROMISSORY ESTOPPEL AND THE STATUTE OF FRAUDS

In some states, an oral contract that would otherwise be unenforceable under the Statute of Frauds may be enforced under the doctrine of promissory estoppel, or detrimental reliance. Section 139 of the *Restatement (Second) of Contracts* provides that in these circumstances, an oral promise can be enforceable notwithstanding the Statute of Frauds if the reliance was foreseeable to the person making the promise and if injustice can be avoided only by enforcing the promise.

SECTION 10

THIRD PARTY RIGHTS

Once it has been determined that a valid and legally enforceable contract exists, attention can turn to the rights and duties of the parties to the contract. Because a contract is a private agreement between the parties who have entered into it, it is fitting that these parties alone should have rights and liabilities under the contract. This principle is referred to as *privity of contract*, and it establishes the basic rule that only the parties to a contract have rights under that contract. A *third party*—one who is not a direct party to a particular contract—normally does not have rights under that contract.

To illustrate: Suppose that I offer to sell you my watch for $100, and you accept. Later, I refuse to deliver the watch to you, even though you present me with the $100. You decide to overlook my breach, but your close friend, Marie, is unhappy with my action and files suit. Can she receive a judgment? The answer is no, because she was not a party to the contract. You, as a party, have rights under the contract and could file a successful suit, but Marie has no *standing* (right) to sue.

There are exceptions to the rule of privity of contract. One exception allows a party to a contract to transfer the rights or duties arising from the contract to another person through an *assignment* (of rights) or a *delegation* (of duties). The other exception involves a *third party beneficiary contract*—a contract in which the parties to the contract intend that the contract benefit a third party.

ASSIGNMENTS

In a bilateral contract, the two parties have corresponding rights and duties. One party has a *right* to require the other to perform some task, and the other has a *duty* to perform it. The transfer of contractual *rights* to a third party is known as an **assignment.** When rights under a contract are assigned unconditionally, the *rights* of the *assignor* (the party making the assignment) are extinguished. The third party (the *assignee*, or party receiving the assignment) has a right to demand performance from the other original party to the contract. The assignee takes only those rights that the assignor originally had.

As a general rule, all rights can be assigned. Exceptions are made, however, in some circumstances. If a statute expressly prohibits assignment of a particular right, that right cannot be assigned. When a contract is *personal* in nature, the rights under the contract cannot be assigned unless all that remains is a money payment.[27] A right cannot be assigned if assignment will materially increase or alter the risk or duties of the obligor.[28] If a contract stipulates that a right cannot be assigned, then *ordinarily* the right cannot be assigned.

There are several exceptions to the rule that a contract can, by its terms, prohibit any assignment of the contract. These exceptions are as follows:

1. A contract cannot prevent an assignment of the right to receive money. This exception exists to encourage the free flow of money and credit in modern business settings.
2. The assignment of rights in real estate often cannot be prohibited, because such a prohibition is contrary to public policy. Prohibitions of this kind are called restraints against **alienation** (transfer of land ownership).
3. The assignment of *negotiable instruments* (which include checks and promissory notes) cannot be prohibited.
4. In a contract for the sale of goods, the right to receive damages for breach of contract or for payment of an account owed may be assigned even though the sales contract prohibits such assignment.

In the following case, the central issue was whether a covenant not to compete contained in an employment contract could be assigned.

27. *Restatement (Second) of Contracts*, Sections 317 and 318.
28. UCC 2–210(2).

CASE 9.6 Reynolds and Reynolds Co. v. Hardee

United States District Court, Eastern District of Virginia, 1996. 932 F.Supp. 149.

BACKGROUND AND FACTS *Thomas Hardee worked for Jordan Graphics, Inc., as a sales representative under an employment contract that included a covenant not to compete. Reynolds and Reynolds Company contracted to buy most of Jordan's assets. On the day of the sale, Jordan terminated Hardee's employment. Reynolds offered Hardee a new contract that contained a more restrictive covenant not to compete. Hardee rejected the offer and began selling in competition with Reynolds. Reynolds filed a suit in a federal district court against Hardee, seeking, among other things, to enforce the covenant not to compete that was in the contract between Hardee and Jordan. Hardee filed a motion to dismiss the case, asserting that Reynolds was not an assignee of that contract and could not enforce it.*

IN THE LANGUAGE OF THE COURT

REBECCA BEACH SMITH, District Judge.

* * * *

* * * [C]ontracts for personal services are not assignable, unless both parties agree to the assignment. Defendant's [Hardee's] Employment Agreement with Jordan [was] clearly a contract for personal services, based on trust and confidence. Defendant's position involved direct sales to clients; he acted as Jordan's agent in its dealings with customers. A person in such a position must necessarily obtain the trust and confidence of his or her employer. Defendant also placed considerable trust in Jordan by even agreeing to the non-compete clause, namely trusting that Jordan would not fire him and then invoke the covenant not to compete.

* * * *

* * * Without question, an employment contract of the sort involved in this case is not assignable * * * .

DECISION AND REMEDY *The court found that Reynolds was not an assignee of the contract between Hardee and Jordan and thus could not enforce it. The court dismissed this part of Reynolds's claim.*

DELEGATIONS

Just as a party can transfer rights through an assignment, a party can also transfer duties. The transfer of contractual *duties* to a third party is known as a **delegation.** Normally, a delegation of duties does not relieve the party making the delegation (the *delegator*) of the obligation to perform in the event that the party to whom the duty has been delegated (the *delegatee*) fails to perform. No special form is required to create a valid delegation of duties. As long as the delegator expresses an intention to make the delegation, it is effective; the delegator need not even use the word *delegate*.

As a general rule, any duty can be delegated. There are, however, some exceptions to this rule. Delegation is prohibited in the following circumstances:

1. When special trust has been placed in the obligor.
2. When performance depends on the *personal* skill or talents of the *obligor* (the person contractually obligated to perform).
3. When performance by a third party will vary materially from that expected by the obligee (the one to whom performance is owed) under the contract.
4. When the contract expressly prohibits delegation.

If a delegation of duties is enforceable, the *obligee* (the one to whom performance is owed) must accept performance from the *delegatee* (the one to whom the duties have been delegated). The obligee can legally refuse performance from the delegatee only if the duty is one that cannot be delegated. A valid delegation of duties does not relieve the delegator of obligations under the contract.[29] Thus, if the delegatee fails to perform, the delegator is still liable to the obligee.

THIRD PARTY BENEFICIARIES

To have contractual rights, a person normally must be a party to the contract. In other words, privity of contract must exist. As mentioned earlier in this chapter, an exception to the doctrine of privity exists when the original parties to the contract intend at the time of contracting that the contract performance directly benefit a third person. In this situation, the third person becomes a **third party beneficiary** of the contract. As an **intended beneficiary** of the contract, the third party has legal rights and can sue the promisor directly for breach of the contract.

The benefit that an **incidental beneficiary** receives from a contract between two parties is *unintentional*. Because the benefit is unintentional, an incidental beneficiary cannot sue to enforce the contract. For example, Bollow contracts with Coolidge to build a recreational facility on Coolidge's land. Once the facility is constructed, it will greatly enhance the property values in the neighborhood. If Bollow subsequently refuses to build the facility, Tran, Coolidge's neighbor, cannot enforce the contract against Bollow because Tran is an incidental beneficiary.

29. *Crane Ice Cream Co. v. Terminal Freezing & Heating Co.*, 147 Md. 588, 128 A. 280 (1925).

TERMS AND CONCEPTS TO REVIEW

QUESTIONS AND CASE PROBLEMS

9–1. BILATERAL VERSUS UNILATERAL CONTRACTS. Zdanis contacts Joe, who does lawn maintenance work, and makes the following offer: "After my lawn is mowed, I'll pay you $25." Joe responds by saying, "I accept your offer." Is there a contract? Is this an offer to form a bilateral or a unilateral contract? What is the legal significance of the distinction?

9–2. OFFER AND ACCEPTANCE. Ball writes Sullivan and inquires how much Sullivan is asking for a specific forty-acre tract of land Sullivan owns. In a letter received by Ball, Sullivan states, "I will not take less than $60,000 for the forty-acre tract as specified." Ball immediately sends Sullivan a telegram stating, "I accept your offer for $60,000." Discuss whether Ball can hold Sullivan to a contract for sale of the land.

9–3. INTOXICATION. After Kira had had several drinks one night, she sold Charlotte a diamond necklace worth thousands of dollars for one hundred dollars. The next day, Kira offered the one hundred dollars to Charlotte and requested the return of her necklace. Charlotte refused to accept the one hundred dollars or return the necklace, claiming that they had a valid contract of sale. Kira explained that she had been intoxicated at the time the bargain was made and thus the contract was voidable at her option. Was Kira correct? Explain.

9–4. ASSENT. Discuss whether either of the following contracts will be unenforceable on the ground that genuineness of assent is lacking.

(a) Simmons finds a stone in his pasture that he believes to be quartz. Jenson, who also believes that the stone is quartz, contracts to purchase it for $10. Just before delivery, the stone is discovered to be a diamond worth $1,000.

(b) Jacoby's barn is burned to the ground. He accuses Goldman's son of arson and threatens to bring criminal action unless Goldman agrees to pay him $5,000. Goldman agrees to pay.

9–5. OFFER AND ACCEPTANCE. Cora Payne was involved in an automobile accident with Don Chappell, an employee of E & B Carpet Cleaning, Inc. E & B's insurance company offered Payne $18,500 to settle her claim against E & B. Payne did not accept the offer at that time but instead filed suit against E & B and its insurance company (the defendants). Later, Payne offered to settle the case for $50,000, but the defendants refused her offer. Ultimately, Payne told the defendants that she would accept the insurance company's original settlement offer of $18,500, but the insurance company stated that the offer was no longer open for acceptance. When Payne sought to compel the defendants to perform the original settlement offer, the defendants contended that Payne's filing of her lawsuit terminated the insurance company's earlier settlement offer. Will the court agree with the defendants? Discuss. [*Payne v. E & B Carpet Cleaning, Inc.*, 896 S.W.2d 650 (Mo.App. 1995)]

9–6. PROMISSORY ESTOPPEL. An article written by Claudia Dreifus and published in *Glamour Magazine* discussed therapists who sexually exploit their patients. Jill Ruzicka had told Dreifus that she (Ruzicka) was sexually abused as a child by her father and later by her therapist. Dreifus had promised to withhold Ruzicka's identity from the article, and the published article identified Ruzicka by a fictitious name ("Lundquist"). In the article, Dreifus stated that "Lundquist" was an attorney who had served on the Minnesota Task Force against Sexual Abuse. Ruzicka claimed that this detail revealed her true identity because she was, in fact, the only woman on that task force. Ruzicka asserted that she had relied to her detriment on Dreifus's promise and sued Dreifus to recover damages under, among other theories, a theory of promissory estoppel. Under the relevant state law, to support a promissory estoppel theory, the plaintiff must prove (1) that the promise was clear and definite, (2) that the promisor intended to induce reliance on the part of the promisee and such reliance occurred to the promisee's detriment, and (3) that the promise must be enforced to prevent injustice. What should the court decide? Discuss fully. [*Ruzicka v. Conde Nast Publications, Inc.*, 999 F.2d 1319 (8th Cir. 1993)]

9–7. MISTAKE. Kenneth and Linda Whitaker filed an action against Trans Union Corporation and others, alleging violations of the Fair Credit Reporting Act. The lawyer for Trans Union drafted an offer of settlement and presented it to the Whitakers' attorney. The amount of the settlement was supposed to be $500, but the first draft contained a typographical error showing the amount as $500,000. The error went undetected, and the $500,000 figure was typed into the second draft, which was forwarded to Linda Gosnell, Trans Union's attorney, who also did not detect the mistake. Gosnell filed the offer with the clerk of the court and mailed a copy to the Whitakers' lawyer. The Whitakers filed an acceptance of the settlement and forwarded it to Gosnell, who at that time noticed the typing error. The Whitakers refused a substitute offer, and Trans Union filed a motion to set aside the judgment. Can the settlement be set aside on the basis of mistake, notwithstanding the fact that the mistake was unilateral? Explain. [*Whittaker v. Associated Credit Services, Inc.*, 946 F.2d 1222 (6th Cir. 1991)]

9–8. ADHESION CONTRACTS. Patricia Aiken suffered a heart attack and was hospitalized at Phoenix Baptist Hospital and Medical Center, Inc. At the time of her admission, the Aikens told the hospital that they did not have the money to pay for medical care. At the same time, her husband, Thomas, signed an agreement to pay her medical expenses. He did not read what he signed, no one explained the agreement to him, and he later claimed to have been so upset that he could not remember having signed anything. When the bills were not paid, the hospital filed a suit in an Arizona state court against the Aikens. The court ruled in favor of the hospital, and the Aikens appealed. They argued that the agreement was an adhesion contract obtained under circumstances that made it unenforceable. Were the circumstances such that the agreement may have been unenforceable? Discuss fully. [*Phoenix Baptist Hospital & Medical Center, Inc. v. Aiken*, 179 Ariz. 289, 877 P.2d 1345 (1994)]

9–9. ASSIGNMENT. Joseph LeMieux, of Maine, won $373,000 in a lottery operated by the Tri-State Lotto Commission. The lottery is sponsored by the three northern New England states and is administered in Vermont. In accordance with its usual payment plan, Tri-State was to pay the $373,000 to LeMieux in annual installments over a twenty-year period. LeMieux assigned his rights to the lottery installment payments for the years 1996 through 2006 to Singer Freidlander Corp. for the sum of $80,000. LeMieux and Singer Freidlander (the plaintiffs) sought a court judgment authorizing the assignment agreement between them despite Tri-State's regulation barring the assignment of lottery proceeds. The trial court granted Tri-State's motion for summary judgment. On appeal, the plaintiffs argued that Tri-State's regulation was invalid. Is it? Discuss fully. [*LeMieux v. Tri-State Lotto Commission*, 666 A.2d 1170 (Vt. 1995)]

9–10. A QUESTION OF ETHICS

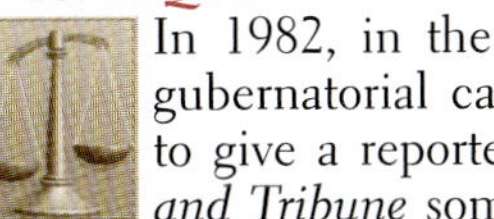

In 1982, in the closing days of Minnesota's gubernatorial campaign, Dan Cohen offered to give a reporter from the *Minneapolis Star and Tribune* some documents—copies of two public court records of a rival party's candidate for lieutenant governor—if the reporter would promise not to reveal the source of the information. The reporter promised to keep the source confidential. The editor of the *Tribune*, however, in spite of the reporter's objections, decided to name Cohen as the source of the information so as not to mislead the public into thinking that the information came from an unbiased source. On the day the newspaper article was published, Cohen was fired by his employer. Cohen sued the newspaper's owner, Cowles Media Co., for breach of contract. Given these facts, discuss the following questions. [*Cohen v. Cowles Media Co.*, 501 U.S. 663, 111 S.Ct. 2513, 115 L.Ed.2d 586 (1991)]

1. Should the editor's ethical duty to provide the reading public with unbiased news coverage have overridden the editor's ethical duty to honor the reporter's promise to Cohen?
2. Did the reporter's promise to keep Cohen's identity confidential create solely an ethical obligation, or did it create an enforceable contract?

ACCESSING THE INTERNET

THE LEGAL ENVIRONMENT OF BUSINESS

Within the legal interest group on the commercial service America Online, there is a subcategory on torts and contracts. If you subscribe to America Online the key word is:

legal

If you wish to partake in discussions of contract law and the teaching of contract law, you can peruse a news group about contracts provided you subscribe to it. To subscribe by e-mail, contact:

listserv@austin.onu.edu

Subject **<anything>**

Message: **Subscribe Contracts <Your Name>**

The 'Lectric Law Library provides information on contract law, including a definition of a contract, the elements required for a contract, and so on. Go to

http://www.lectlaw.com

Then go to the Laypeople's Law Lounge, and scroll down to Contracts.

Findlaw's directory of law-related Web sites offers numerous links to aspects of contract law. Findlaw's URL is

http://findlaw.com/

Look in their index of legal subjects for Contracts, and you will find information ranging from a "Layman's Guide to Drafting and Signing Contracts" to contract law in cyberspace to sample contract forms.

The Law Office's URL is

http://www.thelawoffice.com/

Select the topic of Business Law from the USA Legal Topics list in the left-hand column. Go to Guide to Business Law and then to Contracts.

Law Guru, which allows you to access more than 160 legal search engines and indexes from a single location, can lead you to other sources on contract law. Go to

http:lawguru.com/lawlinks.html

Cornell University's School of Law provides links to online sources of law, including contract law, at

http://www.law.cornell.edu/topics/contracts.html

The Library of Congress offers online links to an extensive menu of topics concerning contract law at

http://www.1oc.gov/

You can find a research project report on the nature and enforceability of electronic contracts at

http://www.uchastings.edu/plri/fall94/whipple.html

The report discusses critical issues with respect to satisfying the writing requirements of the Statute of Frauds.

If you want to do further searching, try the Internet addresses provided in Chapter 1's *Accessing the Internet* feature for general sources of American law. Many of them include links to contract law sources. As mentioned in the *Accessing the Internet* section at the end of Chapter 3, decisions of the courts in several states are now online. Refer to that section for the URLs to use to access relevant sites.

CHAPTER 10

CONTRACTS: PART II

JUST AS RULES ARE NECESSARY TO determine when a legally enforceable contrac are they necessary to determine when one of the parties can justifiably say, " performed, so I am now discharged from my obligations under this contra environment of business requires the identification of some point at which reasonably know that their duties are at an end.

Performance is the most common form of discharge. Duties can be breach of contract, for example, will discharge the duty of the nonb party is in breach of contract whenever he or she fails to perform contract. In this chapter, we will discuss some of the importan discharged. We will also discuss the remedies available on a party.

SECTION 1

PERFORMANCE AND DISCHARGE

The most common way to **discharge,** or terminate, one's contractual duties is by the **performance** of those duties. For example, a buyer and seller have a contract for the sale of a 1994 Buick for $8,000. This contract will be discharged on the performance by the parties of their obligations under the contract—...'s payment of $8,000 to the seller and the ... of possession of the Buick to the

...under a contract may be ... nonoccurrence of ... *...olute*. In the ... ions of

at least $1,000. Jerome accepts Alfonso's offer. Their obligations (promises) are conditioned on the outcome of the appraisal. Should the condition not be satisfied (for example, if the appraiser deems the value of the painting to be only $500), the parties' obligations to each other are discharged and cannot be enforced.

DISCHARGE BY PERFORMANCE

The great majority of contracts are discharged by performance. The contract comes to an end when both parties fulfill their respective duties by performing the acts they have promised. Performance can also be accomplished by **tender.** Therefore, a seller who places goods at the disposal of a buyer has tendered delivery and can demand payment. A buyer who offers to pay for goods has tendered payment and can demand delivery of the goods. Once performance has been tendered, the party making the tender has ...verything possible to carry out the terms of the ... the other party then refuses to perform, ... the tender can sue for breach of

... are two basic ... *...ance* and ... rms

... s ... is ... the ... s sub- ... stantial ... contract. ... apter.) ... ance must ... the contract- ... ision must be ... e performance

... As noted, perform- ... th the terms of a con- ... . Conditions expressly ... fully satisfied for com- ... place. For example, most ... quire the builder to meet ... the specifications are conditions, complete performance is required to avoid material breach. If the conditions are met, the other party to the contract must then fulfill his or her obligation to pay the builder. If the specifications are not conditions and if the builder, without the other party's permission, fails to comply with the standards, performance is not complete. What effect does such a failure have on the other party's obligation to pay? The answer is part of the doctrine of substantial performance.

SUBSTANTIAL PERFORMANCE A party who in good faith performs substantially all of the terms of a contract can enforce the contract against the other party. Note that good faith is required, which means that the failure to fully perform must not be willful. Willfully failing to comply with the terms is a breach of the contract.

There is not an exact point at which performance is considered substantial. As stated above, performance that provides a party with the important and essential benefits of a contract, in spite of any omission or deviation from the terms, is substantial performance. Using this principle to determine whether performance is substantial requires taking into consideration all of the facts. For example, in a construction contract, these facts would include the intended purpose of the structure and the expense required to bring the structure into compliance with the contract.

Because substantial performance is not perfect, the other party is entitled to damages to compensate for the failure to comply with the contract. The measure of the damages is the cost to bring the object of the contract into compliance with the terms, if that cost is reasonable in the circumstances. If the cost is unreasonable, the measure of damages is the difference in value between the performance that was rendered and the performance that would have been rendered if the contract had been performed completely.

The following classic case on substantial performance emphasizes that there is no exact formula for deciding when a contract has been substantially performed. The case also indicates some of the factors that courts consider in deciding the issue.

CASE 10.1 Jacobs & Young, Inc. v. Kent

Court of Appeals of New York, 1921. 230 N.Y. 239, 129 N.E. 889.

BACKGROUND AND FACTS *The plaintiff, Jacobs & Young, Inc., was a builder that had contracted with the defendant, George Kent, to construct a country residence for the defendant. A specification in the building contract required that "[a]ll wrought-iron pipe must be well galvanized, lap welded pipe of the grade known as 'standard pipe' of Reading manufacture." The plaintiff installed substantially similar pipe that was not of Reading manufacture. When the defendant became aware of the difference, he ordered the plaintiff to remove all of the plumbing and replace it with the Reading type. To do so would have required removing finished walls that encased the plumbing—an expensive and difficult task. The plaintiff explained that the plumbing was of the same quality, appearance, value, and cost as Reading pipe. When the defendant refused to pay the plaintiff the $3,483.46 still owed for the work, the plaintiff sued to compel payment. The trial court ruled in favor of the defendant. The plaintiff appealed, and the appellate court reversed the trial court's decision. The defendant then appealed to the Court of Appeals of New York, the state's highest court.*

IN THE LANGUAGE OF THE COURT

CARDOZO, Justice.

* * * *

* * * The courts never say that one who makes a contract fills the measure of his duty by less than full performance. They do say, however, that an omission, both trivial and innocent, will sometimes be atoned for by allowance of the resulting damage, and will not always be the breach of a condition[.] * * *

* * * Where the line is to be drawn between the important and the trivial cannot be settled by a formula. * * * We must weigh the purpose to be served, the desire to be gratified, the excuse for deviation from the letter, [and] the cruelty of

enforced adherence. Then only can we tell whether literal fulfillment is to be implied by law as a condition. * * *

* * * [W]e think the measure of the allowance is not the cost of replacement, which would be great, but the difference in value, which would be either nominal or nothing. * * * The owner is entitled to the money which will permit him to complete, unless the cost of completion is grossly and unfairly out of proportion to the good to be attained.

DECISION AND REMEDY *The Court of Appeals of New York, holding that the plaintiff had substantially performed the contract, affirmed the appellate court's decision. The builder was entitled to the amount owed to it, less the difference in value between the specified and substituted pipe (which the court stated would be "nominal or nothing").*

ETHICAL CONSIDERATIONS *The doctrine of substantial performance, which often applies in construction contracts, is rooted in considerations of fairness. The courts recognize that it is often impossible for a building contractor to perform completely each and every particular requirement of a construction contract. The doctrine is reinforced by practical considerations. If courts routinely held that only strict (complete) performance could discharge contractual obligations, the construction industry would likely come to a standstill.*

MATERIAL BREACH OF CONTRACT A **breach of contract** is the nonperformance of a contractual duty. The breach is *material*[2] when performance is not at least substantial—in other words, when there has been a failure of consideration. In such cases, the nonbreaching party is excused from the performance of contractual duties and has a cause of action to sue for damages caused by the breach. If the breach is *minor* (not material), the nonbreaching party's duty to perform can sometimes be suspended until the breach has been remedied, but the duty to perform is not entirely excused. Once the minor breach has been cured, the nonbreaching party must resume performance of the contractual obligations undertaken. Any breach entitles the nonbreaching party to sue for damages, but only a material breach discharges the nonbreaching party from the contract. The policy underlying these rules allows contracts to go forward when only minor problems occur but allows them to be terminated if major problems occur.

TIME FOR PERFORMANCE If no time for performance is stated in the contract, a *reasonable time* is implied.[3] If a specific time is stated, the parties must usually perform by that time. Unless time is expressly stated to be vital, however, a delay in performance will not destroy the performing party's right to payment. When time is expressly stated to be vital, or when it is construed to be "of the essence," the parties normally must perform within the stated time period. The time element becomes a condition.

DISCHARGE BY AGREEMENT

Any contract can be discharged by agreement of the parties. The agreement can be contained in the original contract, or the parties can form a new contract for the express purpose of discharging the original contract.

DISCHARGE BY RESCISSION *Rescission* is the process by which a contract is canceled or terminated and the parties are returned to the positions they occupied prior to forming it. For **mutual rescission** to take place, the parties must make another agreement, which must also satisfy the legal requirements for a contract. There must be an *offer*, an *acceptance*, and *consideration*.

Ordinarily, in an executory contract in which neither party has yet performed, if the parties agree to

2. *Restatement (Second) of Contracts*, Section 241.
3. See UCC 2–204.

rescind the original contract, their promises not to perform the acts promised in the original contract will be legal consideration for the second contract. The rescission agreement is generally enforceable even if made orally. An exception applies under the UCC to agreements rescinding a contract for the sale of goods regardless of price when the contract requires written rescission.[4]

When one party has fully performed, an agreement to call off the original contract normally will not be enforceable. Because the performing party has received no consideration for the promise to call off the original bargain, additional consideration will be necessary.

In sum, contracts that are *executory on both sides* (contracts on which neither party has performed) can be rescinded solely by agreement.[5] But contracts that are *executed on one side* (contracts on which one party has performed) can be rescinded only if the party who has performed receives consideration for the promise to call off the deal.

DISCHARGE BY SUBSTITUTED AGREEMENT A contractual obligation may also be discharged through novation. A *novation* occurs when both of the parties to a contract agree to substitute a third party for one of the original parties. The requirements of a novation are as follows:

1. A previous valid obligation.
2. An agreement of all the parties to a new contract.
3. The extinguishment of the old obligation (discharge of the prior party).
4. A new contract that is valid.

For example, suppose that Union Corporation contracts to sell its pharmaceutical division to British Pharmaceuticals, Ltd. Before the transfer is completed, Union, British Pharmaceuticals, and a third company, Otis Chemicals, execute a new agreement to transfer all of British Pharmaceutical's rights and duties in the transaction to Otis Chemicals. As long as the new contract is supported by consideration, the novation will discharge the original contract (between Union and British Pharmaceuticals) and replace it with the new contract (between Union and Otis Chemicals).

A novation expressly or impliedly revokes and discharges a prior contract.[6] The parties involved may expressly state in the new contract that the old contract is now discharged. If the parties do not expressly discharge the old contract, it will be *impliedly* discharged because of the change or because of the new contract's different terms, which are inconsistent with the old contract's terms.

A *compromise*, or settlement agreement, that arises out of a genuine dispute over the obligations under an existing contract will be recognized at law. Such an agreement will be substituted as a new contract, and it will either expressly or impliedly revoke and discharge the obligations under any prior contract.

DISCHARGE BY ACCORD AND SATISFACTION
For a contract to be discharged by accord and satisfaction, the parties must agree to accept performance that is different from the performance originally promised. An *accord* is defined as an executory contract to perform some act to satisfy an existing contractual duty.[7] The duty has not yet been discharged. A *satisfaction* is the performance of the accord agreement. An accord and its satisfaction discharge the original contractual obligation.

Once the accord has been made, the original obligation is merely suspended. The obligor (the one owing the obligation) can discharge the obligation by performing the obligation agreed to in the accord or the original obligation. If the obligor refuses to perform the accord, the obligee (the one to whom performance is owed) can bring action on the original obligation or seek a decree compelling specific performance on the accord. These principles are applied in the following case.

4. UCC 2–209(2), (4).

5. Certain sales made to a consumer at home can be rescinded by the consumer within three days for no reason at all. This three-day "cooling-off" period is designed to aid consumers who are susceptible to high-pressure door-to-door sales tactics. See Chapter 23 and 15 U.S.C. Section 1635(a).

6. It is this immediate discharge of the prior contract that distinguishes a novation from an accord and satisfaction, discussed in the next subsection.

7. *Restatement (Second) of Contracts,* Section 281.

CASE 10.2 Ellenbogen & Goldstein, P.C. v. Brandes

Supreme Court, Appellate Division, First Department, 1995. 641 N.Y.S.2d 28.

BACKGROUND AND FACTS *Ellenbogen & Goldstein, P.C., represented Iris Brandes in her divorce action. The law firm sent monthly bills to Brandes, most of which she did not pay. Brandes and the firm agreed to an accord, under which the firm would accept as payment the first $25,000 that she and her husband realized from the sale of their house. The firm sent Brandes a final bill, which went unpaid for four and a half months. Finally, the firm filed a suit in a New York state court against Brandes, seeking $112,281.07. Brandes asserted that the firm had orally agreed to render legal services without charge and orally advised her to ignore its bills. The firm filed a motion for summary judgment, which the court granted. Brandes appealed.*

IN THE LANGUAGE OF THE COURT

MEMORANDUM DECISION.

* * * *

* * * Defendant's [Brandes's] assertions * * * are * * * contradicted by the * * * unsatisfied accord between the parties. * * * While there was clearly an accord that plaintiff would accept defendant's payment of the first $25,000 defendant and her former husband * * * realized from the sale of the marital residence, it is equally clear that there was no satisfaction, and that plaintiff therefore remains free to sue on its original claim.

DECISION AND REMEDY *The Appellate Division of the New York Supreme Court affirmed the judgment of the lower court. The appellate court held that the law firm could sue for its fees because the accord had not been satisfied.*

DISCHARGE BY OPERATION OF LAW

Under certain circumstances, contractual duties may be discharged by operation of law. These circumstances include material alteration of the contract, the running of the statute of limitations, bankruptcy, and the impossibility or impracticability of performance.

ALTERATION OF THE CONTRACT To discourage parties from altering written contracts, the law operates to allow an innocent party to be discharged when the other party has materially altered a written contract without consent. For example, contract terms such as quantity or price might be changed without the knowledge or consent of all parties. If so, the party who was unaware of the alteration can treat the contract as discharged or terminated.[8]

8. The contract is voidable, and the innocent party can also treat the contract as in effect, either on the original terms or on the terms as altered. A buyer who discovers that a seller altered the quantity of goods in a sales contract from 100 to 1,000 by secretly inserting a zero can purchase either 100 or 1,000 of the items.

STATUTES OF LIMITATIONS As mentioned earlier in this text, statutes of limitations limit the period during which a party can sue on a particular cause of action. After the applicable limitations period has passed, a suit can no longer be brought. For example, the limitations period for bringing suits for breach of oral contracts is usually two to three years; for written contracts, four to five years; and for recovery of amounts awarded in judgments, ten to twenty years, depending on state law.

Section 2–725 of the UCC deals with the statute of limitations applicable to contracts for the sale of goods. For purposes of applying this section, the UCC does not distinguish between oral and written contracts. Section 2–725 provides that an action for the breach of any contract for sale must be commenced within four years after the cause of that action has accrued. The cause of action accrues when the breach occurs, regardless of the aggrieved party's lack of knowledge of the breach. By original agreement, the parties can reduce this four-year period to one year. They cannot, however, extend it beyond the four-year limitation period.

Technically, the running of a statute of limitations bars access only to *judicial* remedies; it does not extinguish the debt or the underlying obligation. The statute precludes access to the courts for collection. If, however, the party who owes the debt or obligation agrees to perform (that is, makes a new promise to perform), the cause of action barred by the statute of limitations will be revived. For the old agreement to be revived by a new promise in this manner, many states require that the promise be in writing or that there be evidence of partial performance.

BANKRUPTCY A proceeding in bankruptcy attempts to allocate the assets the debtor owns to the creditors in a fair and equitable fashion. Once the assets have been allocated, the debtor receives a discharge in bankruptcy. A discharge in bankruptcy will ordinarily bar enforcement of most of a debtor's contracts by the creditors. Partial payment of a debt *after* discharge in bankruptcy will not revive the debt. (Bankruptcy is fully discussed in Chapter 16.)

IMPOSSIBILITY OR IMPRACTICABILITY OF PERFORMANCE After a contract has been made, performance may become impossible in an objective sense. This is known as **impossibility of performance** and may discharge a contract.[9]

Objective Impossibility of Performance. *Objective impossibility* ("It can't be done") must be distinguished from *subjective impossibility* ("I'm sorry, I simply can't do it"). Examples of subjective impossibility include cases in which goods cannot be delivered on time because of freight car shortages[10] and cases in which money cannot be paid on time because the bank is closed.[11] In effect, the party in each of these cases is saying, "It is impossible for *me* to perform," not "It is impossible for *anyone* to perform." Accordingly, such excuses do not discharge a contract, and the nonperforming party is normally held in breach of contract. Three basic types of situations generally qualify as grounds for the discharge of contractual obligations based on impossibility of performance:[12]

1. *When one of the parties to a personal contract dies or becomes incapacitated prior to performance.* For example, Fred, a famous dancer, contracts with Ethereal Dancing Guild to play a leading role in its new ballet. Before the ballet can be performed, Fred becomes ill and dies. His personal performance was essential to the completion of the contract. Thus, his death discharges the contract and his estate's liability for his nonperformance.
2. *When the specific subject matter of the contract is destroyed.* For example, A-1 Farm Equipment agrees to sell Gudgel the green tractor on its lot and promises to have it ready for Gudgel to pick up on Saturday. On Friday night, however, a truck veers off the nearby highway and smashes into the tractor, destroying it beyond repair. Because the contract was for this specific tractor, A-1's performance is rendered impossible owing to the accident.
3. *When a change in law renders performance illegal.* An example is a contract to build an apartment building, when the zoning laws are changed to prohibit the construction of residential rental property at this location. This change renders the contract impossible to perform.

Commercial Impracticability. Courts may excuse parties from their performance obligations when the performance becomes much more difficult or expensive than originally contemplated at the time the contract was formed. For someone to invoke successfully the doctrine of **commercial impracticability**, however, the anticipated performance must become *extremely* difficult or costly.[13] For example, in one case, a court held that a contract was discharged because a party would have had to pay ten times more than the original estimate to excavate a certain amount of gravel.[14] Caution should be used in invoking commercial impracticability. The added burden of performing must be *extreme* and, more important, must *not* have been within the cognizance of the parties when the contract was made.

Frustration of Purpose. A theory closely allied with the doctrine of commercial impracticability is the doctrine of **frustration of purpose.** In principle, a contract will be discharged if supervening circumstances make it impossible to attain the purpose both parties

9. *Restatement (Second) of Contracts,* Section 261.
10. *Minneapolis v. Republic Creosoting Co.,* 161 Minn. 178, 201 N.W. 414 (1924).
11. *Ingham Lumber Co. v. Ingersoll & Co.,* 93 Ark. 447, 125 S.W. 139 (1910).
12. *Restatement (Second) of Contracts,* Sections 262–266; UCC 2–615.
13. *Restatement (Second) of Contracts,* Section 264.
14. *Mineral Park Land Co. v. Howard,* 172 Cal. 289, 156 P. 458 (1916).

had in mind when making the contract. The origins of the doctrine lie in the old English "coronation cases." A coronation procession was planned for Edward VII when he became king of England following the death of his mother, Queen Victoria. Hotel rooms along the coronation route were rented at exorbitant prices for that day. When the king became ill and the procession was canceled, a flurry of lawsuits resulted. Hotel and building owners sought to enforce the room-rent bills against would-be parade observers, and would-be parade observers sought to be reimbursed for rental monies paid in advance on the rooms. Would-be parade observers were excused from their duty of payment because the purpose of the room contracts had been "frustrated."

Temporary Impossibility. An occurrence or event that makes performance temporarily impossible operates to *suspend* performance until the impossibility ceases. Then, ordinarily, the parties must perform the contract as originally planned. If, however, the lapse of time and the change in circumstances surrounding the contract make it substantially more burdensome for the parties to perform the promised acts, the contract is discharged.

The leading case on the subject, *Autry v. Republic Productions,*[15] involved an actor who was drafted into the army in 1942. Being drafted rendered the actor's contract temporarily impossible to perform, and it was suspended until the end of the war. When the actor got out of the army, the value of the dollar had so changed that performance of the contract would have been substantially burdensome to him. Therefore, the contract was discharged.

SECTION 2
BREACH OF CONTRACT AND REMEDIES

When one party breaches a contract, the other party—the nonbreaching party—can choose one or more of several remedies. A *remedy* is the relief provided for an innocent party when the other party has breached the contract. It is the means employed to enforce a right or to redress an injury.

The most common remedies available to a nonbreaching party include damages, rescission and restitution, specific performance, and reformation. As discussed in Chapter 1, a distinction is made between *remedies at law* and *remedies in equity.* Today, the remedy at law is normally money damages. Equitable remedies include rescission and restitution, specific performance, and reformation. Usually, a court will not award an equitable remedy unless the remedy at law is inadequate.

DAMAGES

A breach of contract entitles the nonbreaching party to sue for money (damages). Damages are designed to compensate a party for harm suffered as a result of another's wrongful act. In the context of contract law, damages compensate the nonbreaching party for the loss of the bargain. Often, courts say that innocent parties are to be placed in the position they would have occupied had the contract been fully performed.[16] For example, in the famous case of the "hairy hand," a doctor promised to make a boy's scarred hand "a hundred percent perfect." Skin was taken from the boy's chest and grafted onto his thumb and fingers. The hand became infected, and the boy was hospitalized for three months. Use of the hand was greatly restricted, and hair grew out of the grafted skin. In hearing a suit against the doctor, the court explained that the amount of damages was to be determined by the difference between the value to the boy of the "perfect" hand that the doctor had promised and the value of the hand in its condition after the operation.[17]

TYPES OF DAMAGES There are basically four broad categories of damages:

1. Compensatory (to cover direct losses and costs).
2. Consequential (to cover indirect and foreseeable losses).
3. Punitive (to punish and deter wrongdoing).
4. Nominal (to recognize wrongdoing when no monetary loss is shown).

COMPENSATORY DAMAGES Damages compensating the nonbreaching party for the *loss of the*

15. 30 Cal.2d 144, 180 P.2d 888 (1947).

16. *Restatement (Second) of Contracts,* Section 347; UCC 1–106(1).

17. *Hawkins v. McGee,* 84 N.H. 114, 146 A. 641 (1929).

bargain are known as *compensatory damages*. These damages compensate the injured party only for damages actually sustained and proved to have arisen directly from the loss of the bargain caused by the breach of contract. They simply replace what was lost because of the wrong or damage. To illustrate, Wilcox contracts to perform certain services exclusively for Hernandez during the month of March for $2,000. Hernandez cancels the contract and is in breach. Wilcox is able to find another job during the month of March but can only earn $1,000. He can sue Hernandez for breach and recover $1,000 as compensatory damages. Wilcox can also recover from Hernandez the amount that he spent to find the other job.[18] Expenses that are caused directly by a breach of contract—such as those incurred to obtain performance from another source—are known as *incidental damages*.

The measurement of compensatory damages varies by type of contract. In a contract for the sale of goods, the usual measure of compensatory damages is an amount equal to the difference between the contract price and the market price.[19] For example, suppose that Chrysler Corporation contracts to buy ten model UTS 400 network servers from an XEXO Corporation dealer for $8,000 each. The dealer, however, fails to deliver the ten servers to Chrysler. The market price of the servers at the time the buyer learns of the breach is $8,150. Chrysler's measure of damages is therefore $1,500 (10 × $150) plus any incidental damages (expenses) caused by the breach. In a situation in which the buyer breaches and the seller has not yet produced the goods, compensatory damages normally equal lost profits on the sale, not the difference between the contract price and the market price.

Ordinarily, because each parcel of land is unique, the remedy for a seller's breach of a contract for a sale of real estate is *specific performance* (that is, the buyer is awarded the parcel of property for which he or she bargained). When this remedy, which is discussed more fully later in this chapter, is unavailable (for example, when the seller has sold the property to someone else), or when the breach is on the part of the buyer, the measure of damages is ordinarily the same as in contracts for the sale of goods—that is, the difference between the contract price and the market price of the land. The majority of states follow this rule.

A minority of states follow a different rule when the seller breaches the contract and the breach is not deliberate.[20] In such a case, these states allow the prospective purchaser to recover any down payment plus any expenses incurred (such as fees for title searches, attorneys, and escrows). This minority rule effectively places purchasers in the position they occupied prior to the sale.

CONSEQUENTIAL DAMAGES Foreseeable damages that result from a party's breach of contract are called **consequential damages,** or *special damages*. They differ from compensatory damages in that they are caused by special circumstances beyond the contract itself. They flow from the consequences, or results, of a breach.

For example, if a seller fails to deliver goods, and the seller knows that a buyer is planning to resell these goods immediately, consequential damages will be awarded for the loss of profit from the planned resale. The buyer will also recover compensatory damages for the difference between the contract price and the market price of the goods.

To recover consequential damages, the breaching party must know (or have reason to know) that special circumstances will cause the nonbreaching party to suffer an additional loss. This rule was enunciated in the classic case of *Hadley v. Baxendale*, which is presented below. This case established the rule that when damages are awarded, compensation is given only for those injuries that the defendant could *reasonably have foreseen* as a probable result of the usual course of events following a breach.

18. It is one thing to have a court award damages; it is another to collect a judgment. See Chapter 3.

19. That is, the amount is the difference between the contract price and the market price at the time and place at which the goods were to be delivered or tendered. See UCC 2–708 and UCC 2–713.

20. "Deliberate" breaches include the seller's failure to convey the land because the market price has gone up. "Nondeliberate" breaches include the seller's failure to convey the land because an unknown easement (another's right of use over the property) has rendered title unmarketable.

CASE 10.3 Hadley v. Baxendale

Court of Exchequer, 1854.
156 Eng.Rep. 145.

HISTORICAL AND ECONOMIC SETTING *In the mid-1800s in England, it was normal for large flour mills, such as that run by the Hadleys in this case, to have more than one crankshaft in the event the main one broke and had to be repaired. Also, in those days it was common knowledge that flour mills did indeed have spare crankshafts. It is against this background that the parties in the case presented here argued their respective positions on whether the damages resulting from the loss of profits while the crankshaft was out for repair were "too remote" to be recoverable.*

BACKGROUND AND FACTS *The Hadleys (the plaintiffs) ran a flour mill in Gloucester. The crankshaft attached to the steam engine in the mill broke, causing the mill to shut down. The shaft had to be sent to a foundry located in Greenwich so that the new shaft could be made to fit the other parts of the engine. Baxendale, the defendant, was a common carrier that transported the shaft from Gloucester to Greenwich. The freight charges were collected in advance, and Baxendale promised to deliver the shaft the following day. It was not delivered for several days, however. As a consequence, the mill was closed for several days. The Hadleys sued to recover the profits lost during that time. Baxendale contended that the loss of profits was "too remote" to be recoverable. The court held for the plaintiffs, and the jury was allowed to take into consideration the lost profits. The defendant appealed.*

IN THE LANGUAGE OF THE COURT

ALDERSON, B.

* * * *

* * * Where two parties have made a contract which one of them has broken, the damages which the other party ought to receive in respect of such breach of contract should be such as may fairly and reasonably be considered either arising naturally, i.e., according to the usual course of things, from such breach of contract itself, or such as may reasonably be supposed to have been in the contemplation of both parties, at the time they made the contract, as the probable result of the breach of it. Now, if the special circumstances under which the contract was actually made were communicated by the plaintiffs to the defendants, and thus known to both parties, the damages resulting from the breach of such a contract, which they would reasonably contemplate, would be the amount of injury which would ordinarily follow from a breach of contract under these special circumstances so known and communicated. * * * Now, in the present case, if we are to apply the principles above laid down, we find that the only circumstances here communicated by the plaintiffs to the defendants at the time the contract was made, were, that the article to be carried was the broken shaft of a mill, and that the plaintiffs were the millers of that mill. * * * [S]pecial circumstances were here never communicated by the plaintiffs to the defendants. It follows, therefore, that the loss of profits here cannot reasonably be considered such a consequence of the breach of contract as could have been fairly and reasonably contemplated by both the parties when they made this contract.

DECISION AND REMEDY *The Court of Exchequer ordered a new trial. According to the court, the plaintiffs would have to have given express notice of the special circumstances that caused the loss of profits to collect consequential damages.*

MITIGATION OF DAMAGES In most situations, when a breach of contract occurs, the innocent injured party is held to a duty to mitigate, or reduce, the damages that he or she suffers. Under this **mitigation of damages** doctrine, the duty owed depends on the nature of the contract. For example, some states require a landlord to use reasonable means to find a new tenant if a tenant abandons the premises and fails to pay rent. If an acceptable tenant becomes available, the landlord is required to lease the premises to this tenant to mitigate the damages recoverable from the former tenant. The former tenant is still liable for the difference between the amount of the rent under the original lease and the rent received from the new tenant. If the landlord has not used the reasonable means necessary to find a new tenant, presumably a court can reduce the award made by the amount of rent he or she could have received had such reasonable means been used.

In the majority of states, persons whose employment has been wrongfully terminated owe a duty to mitigate damages suffered because of their employers' breach of the employment contract. The damages they receive are their salaries less the incomes they would have received in similar jobs that they could have obtained by reasonable means. The employer must prove both that such a job existed and that the employee could have been hired. As the following case illustrates, however, the employee is under no duty to take a job that is not of the same type and rank.

CASE 10.4 Parker v. Twentieth Century-Fox Film Corp.

Supreme Court of California, 1970. 3 Cal.3d 176, 474 P.2d 689, 89 Cal.Rptr. 737.

BACKGROUND AND FACTS *Twentieth Century-Fox Film Corporation planned to produce a musical,* Bloomer Girl, *and contracted with Shirley MacLaine Parker to play the leading female role. According to the contract, Fox was to pay Parker $53,571.42 per week for fourteen weeks, for a total of $750,000. Fox later decided not to produce* Bloomer Girl *and tried to substitute for the existing contract another contract under which Parker would play the leading role in* Big Country, *a Western movie, for the same amount of money guaranteed by the first contract. Fox gave Parker one week in which to accept the new contract. Parker filed suit against Fox to recover the amount of compensation guaranteed in the first contract because, she maintained, the two roles were not at all equivalent. The* Bloomer Girl *production was a musical, to be filmed in California, and could not be compared with a "Western type" production that was, according to tentative plans, to be produced in Australia. When the trial court held for Parker, Fox appealed.*

IN THE LANGUAGE OF THE COURT

BURKE, Justice.

* * * *

The general rule is that the measure of recovery by a wrongfully discharged employee is the amount of salary agreed upon for the period of service, less the amount which the employer affirmatively proves the employee has earned or with reasonable effort might have earned from other employment. However, before projected earnings from other employment opportunities not sought or accepted by the discharged employee can be applied in mitigation, the employer must show that the other employment was comparable, or substantially similar, to that of which the employee has been deprived * * * .

* * * *

* * * The mere circumstance that "Bloomer Girl" was to be a musical review calling upon plaintiff's talents as a dancer as well as an actress, and was to be produced in the City of Los Angeles, whereas "Big Country" was a straight dramatic role in a "Western Type" story taking place in an opal mine in Australia, demonstrates the difference in kind between the two employments; the female lead as a dramatic actress

in a western style motion picture can by no stretch of imagination be considered the equivalent of or substantially similar to the lead in a song-and-dance production.

DECISION AND REMEDY *The Supreme Court of California affirmed the trial court's ruling. Parker could not be required to accept Fox's offer of the Western-movie role to mitigate the damages she had incurred as a result of the breach of contract.*

INTERNATIONAL CONSIDERATIONS **Mitigation of Damages in France** *Many legal systems, including that of France, have no clear requirement that damages must be mitigated. For example, the French civil law code has no provision stating that an employee must make reasonable efforts to secure comparable employment.*

LIQUIDATED DAMAGES VERSUS PENALTIES

Unliquidated damages are damages that have not been calculated or determined. For example, in a lawsuit, after Jane has proved her right to recover from Sam for his breach of their contract but before she has proved the amount she is entitled to recover, the damages are unliquidated. **Liquidated damages** are damages that are certain in amount. A liquidated damages provision in a contract specifies a certain amount to be paid in the event of a *future* default or breach of contract. For example, a provision requiring a construction contractor to pay $200 for every day he or she is late in completing the construction is a liquidated damages provision. Liquidated damages differ from penalties. **Penalties** specify a certain amount to be paid in the event of a default or breach of contract and are designed to *penalize* the breaching party. Liquidated damages provisions are enforceable; penalty provisions are not.

To determine if a particular provision is for liquidated damages or for a penalty, two questions must be answered. First, when the contract was entered into, was it apparent that damages would be difficult to estimate in the event of a breach? Second, was the amount set as damages a reasonable estimate and not excessive?[21] If both answers are yes, the provision will be enforced. If either answer is no, the provision will not be enforced. Section 2–718(1) of the UCC specifically permits the inclusion of liquidated damages clauses in contracts for the sale of goods as long as both of these tests are met. In construction contracts, it is difficult to estimate the amount of damages that would be caused by a delay in completing construction, so liquidated damages clauses are often used.

The following case involved a contract clause that required a client to pay an attorney substantial damages if the client terminated its relationship with the attorney. The issue before the court was whether the clause was a liquidated damages clause or a penalty clause.

21. *Restatement (Second) of Contracts*, Section 356(1).

CASE 10.5 AFLAC, Inc. v. Williams

Supreme Court of Georgia, 1994. 264 Ga. 351, 444 S.E.2d 314.

HISTORICAL AND SOCIAL SETTING *Historically, lawyers and law firms concentrated their efforts on the practice of law, but they also traditionally held positions as general counselors to their clients. In the 1980s and 1990s, according to some observers, lawyers began to focus too narrowly on legal issues. Consequently, attorneys lost ground, in the traditional role of general counselor, to financial advisers, accounting firms, banks, actuaries, and other consultants who were looking for new areas in which to do business when they found their own traditional markets shrinking.*

BACKGROUND AND FACTS *AFLAC, Inc., hired Peter Williams, an attorney, under a seven-year contract to give the company legal advice as needed. The contract provided that if AFLAC terminated the relationship, it would pay Williams 50 percent of whatever amount was due for the remaining term. After* *four years, AFLAC terminated the contract with Williams and asked a Georgia state court to determine the enforceability of the termination payment provision. The court declared the provision unenforceable, and Williams appealed. The state appellate court reversed this decision, and AFLAC appealed.*

IN THE LANGUAGE OF THE COURT

FLETCHER, Justice.

* * * *

* * * [The contract] requires AFLAC to pay an unreasonably high sum as damages, requires payment without considering Williams' duty to mitigate his damages, and obligates AFLAC to pay even if Williams is discharged for cause. * * * [The] provision is not a reasonable estimate of Williams' damages and instead is a penalty imposed to punish AFLAC * * * .

DECISION AND REMEDY

The Supreme Court of Georgia held that the provision was an unenforceable penalty clause and reversed the decision of the intermediate appellate court. AFLAC thus did not have to pay Williams 50 percent of the amount due for the remainder of the term.

RESCISSION AND RESTITUTION

As discussed earlier in this chapter, *rescission* is essentially an action to undo, or terminate, a contract—to return the contracting parties to the positions they occupied prior to the transaction.[22] When fraud, a mistake, duress, undue influence, misrepresentation, or lack of capacity to contract is present, unilateral rescission is available. Rescission may also be available by statute.[23] The failure of one party to perform entitles the other party to rescind the contract. The rescinding party must give prompt notice to the breaching party. Generally, to rescind a contract, both parties must make **restitution** to each other by returning goods, property, or money previously conveyed.[24] If the goods or property received can be restored *in specie*—that is, if the actual goods or property can be returned—they must be. If the goods or property have been consumed, restitution must be made in an equivalent amount of money.

Essentially, *restitution* refers to the plaintiff's recapture of a benefit conferred on the defendant through which the defendant has been unjustly enriched. For example, Katie pays $10,000 to Bob in return for Bob's promise to design a house for her. The next day Bob calls Katie and tells her that he has taken a position with a large architectural firm in another state and cannot design the house. Katie decides to hire another architect that afternoon. Katie can obtain restitution of the $10,000.

Restitution may be appropriate when a contract is rescinded, but the right to restitution is not limited to rescission cases. Restitution may be sought in actions for breach of contract, tort actions, and other actions at law or in equity. Usually, restitution of money or property transferred by mistake or because of fraud can be awarded. An award in a case may include restitution of money or property obtained through embezzlement, conversion, theft, copyright infringement, or misconduct by a party in a confidential or other special relationship.

SPECIFIC PERFORMANCE

The equitable remedy of **specific performance** calls for the performance of the act promised in the contract. This remedy is quite attractive to the nonbreaching party, because it provides the exact bargain promised in the contract. It also avoids some of the problems inherent in a suit for money damages.

There are three basic reasons for the attractiveness of the remedy of specific performance. First, the nonbreaching party need not worry about collecting the money damages awarded by a court. Second, the nonbreaching party need not look around for

22. The rescission discussed here is *unilateral* rescission, in which only one party wants to undo the contract. In mutual rescission, both parties agree to undo the contract. Mutual rescission discharges the contract; unilateral rescission is generally available as a remedy for breach of contract.

23. The Federal Trade Commission and many states have rules or statutes allowing consumers to unilaterally rescind contracts made at home with door-to-door salespersons. Rescission is allowed within three days for any reason or for no reason at all. See, for example, California Civil Code Section 1689.5.

24. *Restatement (Second) of Contracts*, Section 370.

another contract. Third, the performance is more valuable than the money damages.

Although the equitable remedy of specific performance is often preferable to other remedies, specific performance will not be granted unless the party's legal remedy (money damages) is inadequate.[25] For example, contracts for the sale of goods rarely qualify for specific performance. The legal remedy, money damages, is ordinarily adequate in such situations, because substantially identical goods can be bought or sold in the market. If the goods are unique, however, a court of equity will decree specific performance. For example, paintings, sculptures, or rare books or coins are so unique that money damages will not enable a buyer to obtain substantially identical substitutes in the market.

SALE OF LAND Specific performance is granted to a buyer in a contract for the sale of land. The legal remedy for breach of a land sales contract is inadequate, because every parcel of land is considered to be unique. Money damages will not compensate a buyer adequately, because the same land in the same location obviously cannot be obtained elsewhere. Only when specific performance is unavailable (for example, when the seller has sold the property to someone else) will money damages be awarded instead.

CONTRACTS FOR PERSONAL SERVICES Personal-service contracts require one party to work personally for another party. Courts of equity normally refuse to grant specific performance of personal-service contracts. If a contract is not deemed personal, the remedy at law may be adequate if substantially identical service (for example, lawn mowing) is available from other persons.

In individually tailored personal-service contracts, courts will not order specific performance by the party who was to be employed because public policy strongly discourages involuntary servitude.[26] Moreover, the courts do not want to have to monitor a continuing service contract if supervision would be difficult—as it would be if the contract required the exercise of personal judgment or talent. For example, if you contracted with a brain surgeon to perform brain surgery on you, and the surgeon refused to perform, the court would not compel (and you certainly would not want) the surgeon to perform under those circumstances. A court cannot assure meaningful performance in such a situation.[27]

REFORMATION

Reformation is an equitable remedy used when the parties have *imperfectly* expressed their agreement in writing. Reformation allows the contract to be rewritten to reflect the parties' true intentions. It applies most often when fraud or mutual mistake (for example, a clerical error) is present.

Reformation is almost always sought so that some other remedy may then be pursued. For example, if Gregory contracts to buy a certain parcel of land from Cavendish, but their contract mistakenly refers to a parcel of land different from the one being sold, the contract does not reflect the parties' intentions. Accordingly, a court of equity can reform the contract so that it conforms to the parties' intentions and accurately refers to the parcel of land being sold. Gregory can then, if necessary, show that Cavendish has breached the contract as reformed. She can then request an order for specific performance.

Two other examples deserve mention. The first involves two parties who have made a binding oral contract. They further agree to put the oral contract in writing, but in doing so, they make an error in stating the terms. Universally, the courts will allow into evidence the correct terms of the oral contract, thereby reforming the written contract. The second example deals with written agreements (covenants) not to compete. If the covenant is for a valid and legitimate purpose (such as the sale of a business) but the area or time restraints of the covenant are unreasonable, some courts will reform the restraints by making them reasonable and will enforce the entire contract as reformed. Other courts, however, will throw out the entire restrictive covenant as illegal.

RECOVERY BASED ON QUASI CONTRACT

As stated in Chapter 9, quasi contract is a legal theory under which an obligation is imposed in the absence of an agreement. The courts use this theory to prevent

25. *Restatement (Second) of Contracts*, Section 359.

26. The Thirteenth Amendment to the U.S. Constitution prohibits involuntary servitude, but *negative* injunctions (that is, injunctions prohibiting rather than ordering certain conduct) are possible. Thus, whereas you may not be able to compel a person to perform under a personal-service contract, you may be able to restrain that person from engaging in similar contracts for a period of time.

27. Similarly, courts often refuse to order specific performance of construction contracts because courts are not set up to operate as construction supervisors or engineers.

unjust enrichment. Hence, quasi contract provides a basis for relief when no enforceable contract exists. The legal obligation arises because the law considers that a promise to pay for benefits received is implied by the party accepting the benefits. Generally, when one party has conferred a benefit on another party, justice requires the party receiving the benefit to pay the reasonable value for it. The party conferring the benefit can recover *in quantum meruit*, which means "as much as he deserves" (see Chapter 9).

Quasi-contractual recovery is useful when one party has partially performed under a contract that is unenforceable. It can be used as an alternative to a suit for damages and will allow the party to recover the reasonable value of the partial performance, measured in some cases according to the benefit received and in others according to the detriment suffered.

To recover on a quasi contract, the party seeking recovery must show the following:

1. He or she has conferred a benefit on the other party.
2. He or she conferred the benefit with the reasonable expectation of being paid.
3. He or she did not act as a volunteer in conferring the benefit.
4. The party receiving the benefit would be unjustly enriched by retaining the benefit without making payment.

For example, suppose that Watson contracts to build two oil derricks for Energy Industries. The derricks are to be built over a period of three years, but the parties do not make a written contract. Enforcement of the contract will therefore be barred by the Statute of Frauds.[28] Watson completes one derrick, and then Energy Industries informs him that it will not pay for the derrick. Watson can sue in quasi contract because (1) a benefit has been conferred on Energy Industries, because one oil derrick has been built; (2) Watson built the derrick (conferred the benefit) with the expectation of being paid; (3) Watson did not volunteer to build the derrick but built it under an unenforceable oral contract; and (4) allowing Energy Industries to retain the derrick without paying would enrich the company unjustly. Therefore, Watson should be able to recover the reasonable value of the oil derrick (under the theory of *quantum meruit*). The reasonable value is ordinarily equal to the fair market value.

28. Contracts that by their terms cannot be performed within one year must be in writing to be enforceable. See Chapter 9.

ELECTION OF REMEDIES

In many cases, a nonbreaching party has several remedies available. The party must choose which remedy to pursue. The purpose of the doctrine of *election of remedies* is to prevent double recovery. Suppose McCarthy agrees in writing to sell his land to Tally. Then McCarthy changes his mind and repudiates the contract. Tally can sue for compensatory damages or for specific performance. If she receives damages, she should not be able to get specific performance of the sales contract, because failure to deliver title to the land was the cause of the injury for which she received damages. If Tally could seek compensatory damages in addition to specific performance, she would recover twice for the same breach of contract. The doctrine of election of remedies requires Tally to choose the remedy she wants, and it eliminates any possibility of double recovery. In other words, the election doctrine represents the legal embodiment of the adage "You can't have your cake and eat it, too."

The doctrine has often been applied in a rigid and technical manner, leading to some harsh results. For example, suppose that Wilson is fraudulently induced to buy a parcel of land for $5,000. He spends an additional $4,000 moving onto the land and then discovers the fraud. Instead of suing for damages, Wilson sues to rescind the contract. The court allows Wilson to recover only the purchase price of $5,000. The court denies recovery of the additional $4,000 because the seller, Martin, did not receive the $4,000 and is therefore not required to reimburse Wilson for his moving expenses. So Wilson suffers a net loss of $4,000 on the transaction. If Wilson had elected to sue for damages instead of seeking the remedy of rescission and restitution, he could have recovered the $4,000 as well as the $5,000.[29]

Because of such problems, the doctrine of election of remedies has been eliminated in contracts for the sale of goods. The UCC expressly rejects the doctrine. (See UCC 2–703 and UCC 2–711.) Remedies under the UCC are not exclusive but cumulative in nature and include all the available remedies for breach of contract. Thus, for example, under UCC 2–721, in a suit based on fraud, the defrauded party may obtain rescission of the contract, restitution of the benefits conferred, and any damages due to the fraud. Even though the UCC rejects the doctrine of election of remedies, parties may still not recover

29. See, for example, *Carpenter v. Mason*, 181 Wis. 114, 193 N.W. 973 (1923).

twice for the same harm by seeking, for example, specific performance *and* damages at the same time.

WAIVER OF BREACH

Under certain circumstances, a nonbreaching party may be willing to accept a defective performance of the contract. This knowing relinquishment of a legal right (that is, the right to require satisfactory and full performance) is called a **waiver.** When a waiver of a breach of contract occurs, the party waiving the breach cannot take any later action on it. In effect, the waiver erases the past breach; the contract continues as if the breach had never occurred. Of course, the waiver of breach of contract extends only to the matter waived and not to the whole contract.

Businesspersons often waive breaches of contract to get whatever benefit possible out of the contract. For example, a seller contracts with a buyer to deliver to the buyer ten thousand tons of coal on or before November 1. The contract calls for the buyer's payment to be made by November 10 for coal delivered. Because of a coal miners' strike, coal is scarce. The seller breaches the contract by not tendering delivery until November 5. The buyer may be well advised to waive the seller's breach, accept delivery of the coal, and pay as contracted.

Ordinarily, the waiver by a contracting party will not operate to waive subsequent, additional, or future breaches of contract. This is always true when the subsequent breaches are unrelated to the first breach. For example, an owner who waives the right to sue for late completion of a stage of construction does not waive the right to sue for failure to comply with engineering specifications on the same job. A waiver will be extended to subsequent defective performance if a reasonable person would conclude that similar defective performance in the future will be acceptable. Therefore, a *pattern of conduct* that waives a number of successive breaches will operate as a continued waiver. To change this result, the nonbreaching party should give notice to the breaching party that full performance will be required in the future.

The party who has rendered defective or less-than-full performance remains liable for the damages caused by the breach of contract. In effect, the waiver operates to keep the contract going. The waiver prevents the nonbreaching party from calling the contract to an end or rescinding the contract. The contract continues, but the nonbreaching party can recover damages caused by defective or less-than-full performance.

CONTRACT PROVISIONS LIMITING REMEDIES

A contract may include provisions stating that no damages can be recovered for certain types of breaches or that damages must be limited to a maximum amount. The contract may also provide that the only remedy for breach is replacement, repair, or refund of the purchase price. Provisions stating that no damages can be recovered are called *exculpatory clauses.* Provisions that affect the availability of certain remedies are called *limitation-of-liability clauses.*

Whether these contract provisions and clauses will be enforced depends on the type of breach that is excused by the provision. For example, a provision excluding liability for fraudulent or intentional injury will not be enforced. Likewise, a clause excluding liability for illegal acts or violations of law will not be enforced. A clause excluding liability for negligence may be enforced in certain cases, however. When an exculpatory clause for negligence is contained in a contract made between parties who have roughly equal bargaining positions, the clause usually will be enforced.

TERMS AND CONCEPTS TO REVIEW

breach of contract 202
commercial impracticability 205
condition 200
consequential damages 207
discharge 200
frustration of purpose 205
impossibility of performance 205
liquidated damages 210
mitigation of damages 209
mutual rescission 202
penalty 210
performance 200
reformation 212
restitution 211
specific performance 211
tender 200
waiver 214

QUESTIONS AND CASE PROBLEMS

10–1. IMPOSSIBILITY OF PERFORMANCE. In the following situations, certain events take place after the formation of contracts. Discuss which of these contracts are discharged because the events render the contracts impossible to perform.

(a) Jimenez, a famous singer, contracts to perform in your nightclub. He dies prior to performance.

(b) Raglione contracts to sell you her land. Just before title is to be transferred, she dies.

(c) Oppenheim contracts to sell you one thousand bushels of apples from her orchard in the state of Washington. Because of a severe frost, she is unable to deliver the apples.

(d) Maxwell contracts to lease a service station for ten years. His principal income is from the sale of gasoline. Because of an oil embargo by foreign oil-producing nations, gasoline is rationed, cutting sharply into Maxwell's gasoline sales. He cannot make his lease payments.

10–2. TIME FOR PERFORMANCE. Murphy contracts to purchase from Lone Star Liquors six cases of French champagne for $1,200. The contract states that delivery is to be made at the Murphy residence "on or before June 1, to be used for daughter's wedding reception on June 2." The champagne is carried regularly in Lone Star's stock. On June 1, Lone Star's delivery van is involved in an accident, and the champagne is not delivered that day. On the morning of June 2, Murphy discovers the nondelivery. Unable to reach Lone Star because its line is busy, Murphy purchases the champagne from another dealer. That afternoon, just before the wedding reception, Lone Star tenders delivery of the champagne at Murphy's residence. Murphy refuses tender, and Lone Star sues for breach of contract. Discuss fully the result.

10–3. LIQUIDATED DAMAGES. Cohen contracts to sell his house and lot to Windsor for $100,000. The terms of the contract call for Windsor to pay 10 percent of the purchase price as a deposit toward the purchase price, or a down payment. The terms further stipulate that should the buyer breach the contract, the deposit will be retained by Cohen as liquidated damages. Windsor pays the deposit, but because her expected financing of the $90,000 balance falls through, she breaches the contract. Two weeks later Cohen sells the house and lot to Ballard for $105,000. Windsor demands her $10,000 back, but Cohen refuses, claiming that Windsor's breach and the contract terms entitle him to keep the deposit. Discuss who is correct.

10–4. SPECIFIC PERFORMANCE. In which of the following situations would specific performance be an appropriate remedy? Discuss fully.

(a) Thompson contracts to sell her house and lot to Cousteau. Then, on finding another buyer willing to pay a higher purchase price, she refuses to deed the property to Cousteau.

(b) Amy contracts to sing and dance in Fred's nightclub for one month, beginning May 1. She then refuses to perform.

(c) Hoffman contracts to purchase a rare coin owned by Erikson, as Erikson is breaking up his coin collection. At the last minute, Erikson decides to keep his coin collection intact and refuses to deliver the coin to Hoffman.

(d) There are three shareholders of the ABC Corp.: Panozzo, who owns 48 percent of the stock; Chang, who owns another 48 percent; and Ryan, who owns 4 percent. Ryan contracts to sell her 4 percent to Chang. Later, Ryan refuses to transfer the shares to Chang.

10–5. SUBSTANTIAL PERFORMANCE. Grane, a homeowner, contracted with Butkovich & Sons, Inc., to enlarge Grane's basement and build a new room over the new basement area. Butkovich was also to lay a new garage floor and construct a patio area. The parties agreed to a price of $19,290 for the work. When the construction was completed, Grane refused to pay the contractor the $9,290 balance he still owed, claiming that Butkovich had failed to install water stops and reinforcing wire in one concrete floor, in accordance with Grane's specifications, and that the main floor of the addition was 8⅞ inches lower than the plans had called for. Butkovich sued Grane for recovery of the $9,290. As a mortgage holder on the property, the State Bank of St. Charles was named co-defendant by Butkovich, because its interests would be affected by a judgment against Grane if the latter could not pay. Butkovich claimed that it had substantially performed the contract. Grane claimed that performance was of poor quality and that failure to follow contract specifications constituted a material breach. Discuss who should win. [*Butkovich & Sons, Inc. v. State Bank of St. Charles*, 62 Ill.App.3d 810, 379 N.E.2d 837, 20 Ill.Dec. 4 (1978)]

10–6. DAMAGES. Kerr Steamship Co. delivered to Radio Corp. of America (RCA) a twenty-nine-word coded message to be sent to Kerr's agent in Manila. The message included instructions on loading cargo onto one of Kerr's vessels. Kerr's profits on the carriage of the cargo were to be about $6,600. RCA mislaid the coded message, and it was never sent. Kerr sued RCA for the $6,600 in profits that it lost because RCA never sent the message. Can Kerr recover? Explain. [*Kerr Steamship Co. v. Radio Corp. of America*, 245 N.Y. 284, 157 N.E. 140 (1927)]

10–7. ELECTION OF REMEDIES. Kenneth and Rebecca Palmer wanted to sell their house. Edward and Stephanie Hayes signed a proposed contract of sale, under which they agreed to give the Palmers' real estate agent, Maple Hills Realty, $2,000 as a deposit on the house. The agreement provided that in the event of default, the Palmers could either keep the deposit or sue to enforce their rights. The Palmers accepted the Hayeses' offer and signed the contract. Before the property changed hands, however, the Hayeses changed their minds and asked for the return of their deposit. The Palmers refused and filed a suit against the Hayeses in a Utah state court, seeking damages. The Hayeses filed a motion for summary judgment on the ground that, by not releasing the deposit, the Palmers had elected their remedy. Did the Palmers' failure to release the deposit money before filing their suit for damages constitute an election of remedies? Discuss fully. [*Palmer v. Hayes,* 892 P.2d 1059 (Utah App. 1995)]

10–8. Mitigation of Damages. Charles Kloss had worked for Honeywell, Inc., for over fifteen years when Honeywell decided to transfer the employees at its Ballard facility to its Harbour Pointe facility. Honeywell planned to hire a medical person at the Harbour Pointe facility and promised Kloss that if he completed a nursing program and became a registered nurse (RN), the company would hire him for the medical position. When Kloss graduated from his RN program, however, Honeywell did not assign him to a nursing or medical position. Instead, the company gave Kloss a job in its maintenance department. Shortly thereafter, Kloss left the company and eventually sued Honeywell for damages (lost wages) resulting from Honeywell's breach of the employment contract. One of the issues facing the court was whether Kloss, by voluntarily leaving the maintenance job at Honeywell, had failed to mitigate his damages. How should the court rule on this issue? Discuss. [*Kloss v. Honeywell, Inc.,* 77 Wash.App. 294, 890 P.2d 480 (1995)]

10–9. A Question of Ethics

Robert Ryan, a widower with a ninth-grade education, fell behind in his mortgage payments and in April 1984 faced foreclosure. In May 1984, Norman Weiner, whom Ryan had never met, called on Ryan at his home and told Ryan that he could loan him money to help him keep his house if Ryan signed over the deed to the house as "security" for the loan. When Weiner left, he took Ryan's deed to the property with him for "safekeeping." The next day, Weiner drove Ryan to a lawyer's office, where Ryan signed several papers. Ryan signed the papers without reading them, believing that he was signing loan documents, because he trusted Weiner. In fact, he had signed documents that conveyed ownership of his house to Weiner. Weiner brought the mortgage payments up to date and continued to make the payments on the house. Weiner also paid for electricity and other utilities and services necessary to maintain the house. Ryan continued to live in the house and made monthly payments to Weiner. The payments steadily increased from \$100 to \$310 a month. During that time, the mortgage payments increased also, from \$93 in 1984 to \$120 in 1991. In May 1991, Ryan concluded that he had paid off his mortgage and also his "loan" from Weiner and refused to make further payments. When Weiner initiated legal proceedings to evict Ryan, Ryan sought to rescind his transfer of the deed to Weiner. Based on these facts, answer the following questions. [*Ryan v. Weiner,* 610 A.2d 1377 (Del. 1992)]

1. In view of the fact that Ryan voluntarily signed a document (contract) conveying his property to Weiner, should he be allowed to rescind that contract? What public policies are in conflict here?
2. When the equitable remedy of rescission and restitution is granted, the parties are restored to their status quo prior to the contract's formation. Is it possible to restore the parties to their status quo as of May 1984 in this case? Discuss.

10–10. Case Briefing Assignment

Examine Case A.3 [*Potter v. Oster,* 426 N.W.2d 148 (Ia. 1988)] in Appendix A. The case has been excerpted there in great detail. Review and then brief the case, making sure that you include answers to the following questions in your brief.

1. Why was the plaintiff appealing the trial court's decision?
2. Why did the plaintiff assert that allowing the remedy of rescission and restitution in this case would lead to an inequitable result?
3. According to the court, what three requirements must be met before rescission will be granted?
4. Did the defendant meet these three requirements? If so, why?
5. What reasons did the court give for its conclusion that remedies at law were inadequate in this case?
6. Why are remedies at law presumed inadequate for breach of real estate contracts?

Accessing the Internet
The Legal Environment of Business

The following sites offer information on contract law, including breach of contract and remedies:

http://www.nolo.com/Chunkcm/CM9.html

http://www.law.cornell.edu/topics/contracts.html

Sample Sales Contract for Purchase of Green Coffee

Starbucks Coffee Company was founded in 1971, opening its first store in Seattle's Pike Place Market. Today, Starbucks is North America's leading roaster and retailer of specialty coffee beans and operates more than four hundred stores around the country. In greater Seattle alone, more than a quarter of a mil- people buy their coffee at Starbucks stores every week.

'Our mission as a company," states Howard Schultz, chairman and CEO of Starbucks, "is to lish Starbucks as the premier purveyor of the finest coffees in the world." When Schultz first d the company in the early 1980s as director of retail operations, Starbucks was a local, highly cted roaster and retailer of whole bean and ground coffees. A business trip to Italy opened his to the rich tradition of the espresso bar. Espresso drinks became an irreplaceable element of tz's vision for the company, and when Schultz purchased Starbucks, with the support of local tors, in 1987, Starbucks started brewing. Coffee lovers can now enjoy Starbucks coffee in fine urants in several areas of the United States as well as in a variety of other carefully chosen loca- including high above the ground on Horizon Air flights, at sea with the Washington State Ferry m, and at all major games and events in the Seattle Kingdome. In addition, Starbucks operates l-order business. Starbucks coffee and Pepsi-Cola have recently joined to create unique coffee- l beverages that will be available in the same outlets as Pepsi-Cola soft drinks.

Schultz is committed to maintaining the quality, integrity, and great taste of Starbucks as the pany grows. "I take great pride," continues Schultz, "not in the number of stores we have ed, but in the growth and development of our people." The unusual dedication of Starbucks to tment in its people, believes Schultz, guarantees exceptional quality for the company's cus- rs. The Starbucks mission statement, while recognizing the need for profitability, pledges that ompany will make decisions that foster "respect and dignity" in the workplace. Each employee mes part of an extensive training program that facilitates strong coffee knowledge, product rtise, a commitment to customer service, and well-developed interpersonal skills.

Dedicated to active support of the communities in which it operates, Starbucks helps organiza- that benefit children's welfare, AIDS outreach, and increase environmental awareness. Starbucks is involved in a variety of community cultural events, including jazz and film festivals. The company also has become the largest corporate sponsor of the international aid and relief organization, CARE. Programs, developed through the partnership of Starbucks with CARE, work toward reducing malnutrition in Guatemala, supporting education and literacy programs in Kenya, and lowering the mortality rate of children in Indonesia.

Credit: Jill Doran for Starbucks Coffee

1 This is a contr have their prin be subject to th Goods (CISG) States, the con

2 Quantity is on court may not

3 Weight per un ed, usage of tr

4 Packaging req ments are not for an explana

5 A description Warranties in 11, Section 9. samples.

6 Under the UC set. See Chap determination

7 The terms of p complicated. able in the ord credit). If the to get it. See

8 *Tender* means disposition. W This contract for pickup by place in which For a discussi see Chapter 1

9 The delivery c in breach of th in which to de problems. Th tion (see the " buyer and sell

10 As part of a p when the good out in Chapte

11 In some contr some loss can ple) or to the either of them liability of co

12 Documents ar word-for-word the whole con rated by refere and sets of rul

13 In internation brokers are us commission.

t for a sale of coffee to be *imported* internationally. If the parties pal places of business located in different countries, the contract may United Nations Convention on Contracts for the International Sale of If the parties' principal places of business are located in the United act may be subject to the Uniform Commercial Code (UCC).

of the most important terms to include in a contract. Without it, a e able to enforce the contract. See Chapter 11, Section 3.

(bag) can be exactly stated or approximately stated. If it is not so stat- le in international contracts determines standards of weight.

rements can be conditions for acceptance and payment. Bulk ship- ermitted without the consent of the buyer. See Chapter 10, Section 1, on of the different types of conditions.

f the coffee and the "Markings" constitute express warranties. ontracts for domestic sales of goods are discussed generally in Chapter nternational contracts rely more heavily on descriptions and models or

, parties may enter into a valid contract even though the price is not er 11, Section 3. Under the CISG, a contract must provide for an exact of the price.

yment may take one of two forms: credit or cash. Credit terms can be cash term can be simple, and payment may be by any means accept- nary course of business (for example, a personal check or a letter of eller insists on actual cash, the buyer must be given a reasonable time hapter 11, Section 7.

he seller has placed goods that conform to the contract at the buyer's hat constitutes a valid tender is explained in Chapter 23, Section 2. equires that the coffee meet all import regulations and that it be ready he buyer at a "Bonded Public Warehouse." (A *bonded warehouse* is a goods can be stored without paying taxes until the goods are removed.) n of the responsibilities of the parties when goods are in a warehouse, , Section 6.

ate is significant because, if it is not met, the buyer may hold the seller contract. Under this contract, the seller can be given a "period" with- iver the goods, instead of a specific day, which could otherwise present seller is also given some time to rectify goods that do not pass inspec- Guarantee" clause on page two). For a discussion of the remedies of the r, see Chapter 11, Section 8.

oper tender, the seller (or its agent) must inform the buyer (or its agent) s have arrived at their destination. The responsibilities of agents are set 19.

cts, delivered and shipped weights can be important. During shipping, be attributed to the type of goods (spoilage of fresh produce, for exam- ransportation itself. A seller and buyer can agree on the extent to which will bear such losses. See Chapter 11, Section 6, for a discussion of the mmon carriers for loss during shipment.

often incorporated in a contract by reference, because including them can make a contract difficult to read. If the document is later revised, ract might have to be reworked. Documents that are typically incorpo- nce include detailed payment and delivery terms, special provisions, es, codes, and standards.

l sales transactions, and for domestic deals involving certain products, ed to form the contracts. When so used, the brokers are entitled to a See Chapter 19, Section 3.

OVERLAND COFFEE IMPORT CONTRACT
OF THE
GREEN COFFEE ASSOCIATION
OF
NEW YORK CITY, INC.*
Effective May 9, 1991

SOLD BY: XYZ Co.

TO: Starbucks

QUANTITY: Five Hundred (500) Tons of Bags
weighing about 152.117 lbs. per

PACKAGING: Coffee must be packed in clean sound bags of unif similar woven material, without inner lining or oute and/or machine.
Bulk shipments are allowed if agreed by mutual co

DESCRIPTION: High grown Mexican Altura

PRICE: At Ten/$10.00 dollars U
Upon delivery in Bonded Public Warehouse at

PAYMENT: Cash against warehouse receipts

Bill and tender to DATE when all import requireme and coffee delivered or discharged (as per contract calendar days free time in Bonded Public Warehou

ARRIVAL: During December via truck
(Period)
from Mexico f
(Country of Exportation)
Partial shipments permitted.

ADVICE OF ARRIVAL: Advice of arrival with warehouse name and locatic place of entry, must be transmitted directly, or thro Broker. Advice will be given as soon as known bu at the named warehouse. Such advice may be give same day.

WEIGHTS: (1) DELIVERED WEIGHTS: Coffee covered by t tender. Actual tare to be allowed.
(2) SHIPPING WEIGHTS: Coffee covered by this weight exceeding 1/2 percent at location na
(3) Coffee is to be weighed within fifteen (15) cal account of seller

MARKINGS: Bags to be branded in English with the name of C regulations of the Country of Importation, in effec merchandise. Any expense incurred by failure to Exporter/Seller.

RULINGS: The "Rulings on Coffee Contracts" of the Green C the date this contract is made, is incorporated for a herewith, constitute the entire contract. No variati parties to the contract.
Seller guarantees that the terms printed on the reve are identical with the terms as printed in By-Laws York City, Inc., heretofore adopted.
Exceptions to this guarantee are:

ACCEPTED:
XYZ Co.
Seller
BY
Agent

Starbucks
Buyer
BY
Agent

When this contract is executed by a person acting fully authorized to commit his principal.

* Reprinted with permission of The Green Coffee Association of New York

Contract Seller's No.: 504617
Buyer's No.: P9264
Date: 9/11/98

exican ______ coffee

nade of sisal, henequen, jute, burlap, or
g of any material properly sewn by hand

uyer and Seller.

ncy, per lb. ______ net, (U.S. Funds)
o, TX
(City and State)

overnmental regulations have been satisfied,
eller is obliged to give the Buyer two (2)
ng but not including date of tender.

od of Transportation)
t Laredo, TX
(Country of Importation)

r with the quantity, description, marks and
's Agent/Broker, to the Buyer or his Agent/
than the fifth business day following arrival
with written confirmation to be sent the

ct is to be weighed at location named in

s sold on shipping weights. Any loss in
der is for account of Seller at contract price.
after tender. Weighing expenses, if any, for
______ (Seller or Buyer)
Origin and otherwise to comply with laws and
ne of entry, governing marking of import
th these regulations to be borne by

ociation of New York City, Inc., in effect on
s as a part of this agreement, and together
tion hereto shall be valid unless signed by the

, which by reference are made a part hereof,
of the Green Coffee Association of New

SSION TO BE PAID BY:
ler

Brokerage
Broker(s)
r, such person hereby represents that he is

14 Arbitration is the settling of a dispute by submitting it to a disinterested party (other than a court) that renders a decision. The procedures and costs can be provided for in an arbitration clause or incorporated through other documents. To enforce an award rendered in an arbitration, the winning party can "enter" (submit) the award in a court "of competent jurisdiction." For a general discussion of arbitration and other forms of dispute resolution (other than courts), see Chapter 4.

15 When goods are imported internationally, they must meet certain import requirements before being released to the buyer. Because of this, buyers frequently want a guaranty clause that covers the goods not admitted into the country and that either requires the seller to replace the goods within a stated time or allows the contract for those goods not admitted to be void. See Chapter 11, Section 1.

16 In the "Claims" clause, the parties agree that the buyer has a certain time within which to reject the goods. The right to reject is a right by law and does not need to be stated in a contract. If the buyer does not exercise the right within the time specified in the contract, the goods will be considered accepted. See Chapter 11, Section 7.

17 Many international contracts include definitions of terms so that the parties understand what they mean. Some terms are used in a particular industry in a specific way. Here, the word "chop" refers to a unit of like-grade coffee bean. The buyer has a right to inspect ("sample") the coffee. If the coffee does not conform to the contract, the seller must correct the nonconformity. See Chapter 11, Section 7.

18 The "Delivery," "Insurance," and "Freight" clauses, with the "Arrival" clause on page one, indicate that this is a destination contract. The seller has the obligation to deliver the goods to the destination, not simply deliver them into the hands of a carrier. Under this contract, the destination is a "Bonded Public Warehouse" in a specific location. The seller bears the risk of loss until the goods are delivered at their destination. Typically, the seller will have bought insurance to cover the risk. See Chapter 11, Section 6, for a discussion of the risk of loss.

19 Delivery terms are commonly placed in all sales contracts. Such terms determine who pays freight and other costs, and, in the absence of an agreement specifying otherwise, who bears the risk of loss. International contracts can use delivery terms as provided under the UCC (see Chapter 11, Section 6) or can use INCOTERMS, which are published by the International Chamber of Commerce. INCOTERMS differ slightly from UCC terms in legal effect. For example, the INCOTERM "DDP" ("delivered duty paid") requires the seller to arrange shipment, obtain and pay for import or export permits, and get the goods through customs to a named destination.

20 Exported and imported goods are subject to duties, taxes, and other charges imposed by the governments of the countries involved. International contracts spell out who is responsible for these charges.

21 This clause protects a party if the other party should become financially unable to fulfill the obligations under the contract. Thus, if the seller cannot afford to deliver, or the buyer cannot afford to pay, for the stated reasons, the other party can consider the contract breached. This right is subject to "11 USC 365(e)(1)," which refers to a specific provision of the U.S. Bankruptcy Code dealing with executory contracts. Bankruptcy provisions are covered in Chapter 16.

22 In the "Breach or Default of Contract" clause, the parties agreed that the remedies under this contract are the remedies (except for consequential damages) provided by the UCC, as in effect in the state of New York. The amount and "ascertainment" of damages, as well as other disputes about relief, are to be determined by arbitration. UCC remedies and breach of contract under the UCC is explained in Chapter 11, Sections 7 and 8.

23 Three clauses frequently included in international contracts are omitted here. There is no "Choice of Language" clause designating the official language to be used in interpreting the contract terms. There is no "Choice of Forum" clause designating the place in which disputes will be litigated, except for arbitration (law of New York State). Finally, there is no "*Force Majeure*" clause relieving the sellers or buyers from nonperformance due to events beyond their control.

TERMS AND CONDITIONS

ARBITRATION: All controversies relating to, in connection with, or arising out of this contract, its modification, making or the authority or obligations of the signatories hereto, and whether involving the principals, agents, brokers, or others who actually subscribe hereto, shall be settled by arbitration in accordance with the "Rules of Arbitration" of the Green Coffee Association of New York City, Inc., as they exist at the time of the arbitration (including provisions as to payment of fees and expenses). Arbitration is the sole remedy hereunder, and it shall be held in accordance with the law of New York State, and judgment of any award may be entered in the courts of that State, or in any other court of competent jurisdiction. All notices or judicial service in reference to arbitration or enforcement shall be deemed given if transmitted as required by the aforesaid rules.

GUARANTEE: (a) If all or any of the coffee is refused admission into the country of importation by reason of any violation of governmental laws or acts, which violation existed at the time the coffee arrived at Bonded-Public Warehouse, seller is required, as to the amount not admitted and as soon as possible, to deliver replacement coffee in conformity to all terms and conditions of this contract, excepting only the Arrival terms, but not later than thirty (30) days after the date of the violation notice. Any payment made and expenses incurred for any coffee denied entry shall be refunded within ten (10) calendar days of denial of entry, and payment shall be made for the replacement delivery in accordance with the terms of this contract. Consequently, if Buyer removes the coffee from the Bonded Public Warehouse, Seller's responsibility as to such portion hereunder ceases.

(b) Contracts containing the overstamp "No Pass-No Sale" on the face of the contract shall be interpreted to mean: If any or all of the coffee is not admitted into the country of Importation in its original condition by reason of failure to meet requirements of the government's laws or Acts, the contract shall be deemed null and void as to that portion of the coffee which is not admitted in its original condition. Any payment made and expenses incurred for any coffee denied entry shall be refunded within ten (10) calendar days of denial of entry.

CONTINGENCY: This contract is not contingent upon any other contract.

CLAIMS: Coffee shall be considered accepted as to quality unless within *fifteen* (15) calendar days after delivery at Bonded Public Warehouse or within *fifteen* (15) calendar days after all Government clearances have been received, whichever is later, either:

(a) Claims are settled by the parties hereto, or,

(b) Arbitration proceedings have been filed by one of the parties in accordance with the provisions hereof.

(c) If neither (a) nor (b) has been done in the stated period or if any portion of the coffee has been removed from the Bonded Public Warehouse before representative sealed samples have been drawn by the Green Coffee Association of New York City, Inc., in accordance with its rules, Seller's responsibility for quality claims ceases for that portion so removed.

(d) Any question of quality submitted to arbitration shall be a matter of allowance only, unless otherwise provided in the contract.

DELIVERY: (a) No more than three (3) chops may be tendered for each lot of 250 bags.

(b) Each chop of coffee tendered is to be uniform in grade and appearance. All expense necessary to make coffee uniform shall be for account of seller.

(c) Notice of arrival and/or sampling order constitutes a tender, and must be given not later than the fifth business day following arrival at Bonded Public Warehouse stated on the contract.

INSURANCE: Seller is responsible for any loss or damage, or both, until Delivery and Discharge of coffee at the Bonded Public Warehouse in the Country of Importation.

All Insurance Risks, costs and responsibility are for Seller's Account until Delivery and Discharge of coffee at the Bonded Public Warehouse in the Country of Importation.

Buyer's insurance responsibility begins from the day of importation or from the day of tender, whichever is later.

FREIGHT: Seller to provide and pay for all transportation and related expenses to the Bonded Public Warehouse in the Country of Importation.

EXPORT DUTIES/TAXES: Exporter is to pay all Export taxes, duties or other fees or charges, if any, levied because of exportation.

IMPORT DUTIES/TAXES: Any Duty or Tax whatsoever, imposed by the government or any authority of the Country of Importation, shall be borne by the Importer/Buyer.

INSOLVENCY OR FINANCIAL FAILURE OF BUYER OR SELLER: If, at any time before the contract is fully executed, either party hereto shall meet with creditors because of inability generally to make payment of obligations when due, or shall suspend such payments, fail to meet his general trade obligations in the regular course of business, shall file a petition in bankruptcy or, for an arrangement, shall become insolvent, or commit an act of bankruptcy, then the other party may at his option, expressed in writing, declare the aforesaid to constitute a breach and default of this contract, and may, in addition to other remedies, decline to deliver further or make payment or may sell or purchase for the defaulter's account, and may collect damage for any injury or loss, or shall account for the profit, if any, occasioned by such sale or purchase.

This clause is subject to the provisions of (11 USC 365 (e) 1) if invoked.

BREACH OR DEFAULT OF CONTRACT: In the event either party hereto fails to perform, or breaches or repudiates this agreement, the other party shall subject to the specific provisions of this contract be entitled to the remedies and relief provided for by the Uniform Commercial Code of the State of New York. The computation and ascertainment of damages, or the determination of any other dispute as to relief, shall be made by the arbitrators in accordance with the Arbitration Clause herein.

Consequential damages shall not, however, be allowed.

CHAPTER 11

SALES AND LEASES

WHEN WE TURN TO CONTRACTS for the sale and lease of goods, we move away from common law principles and into the area of statutory law. State statutory law governing sales and lease transactions is based on the Uniform Commercial Code (UCC), which has been adopted as law by all states (Louisiana has not adopted it in its entirety, however). Relevant sections of the UCC are noted in the following discussion of sales and lease contracts. You should refer to Appendix D in the back of the book, which presents excerpts from the most recent version of the UCC, while examining these notations. Many similarities to the contract law discussed in Chapters 9 and 10 will be apparent. Indeed, such similarities should be expected, because the UCC represents the codification of much of the existing common law of contracts.

We open this chapter with a look at the scope of the UCC's Article 2 (on sales) and Article 2A (on leases). Article 2 of the UCC sets out the requirements of sales contracts and how they are formed. It also addresses the sometimes sticky concept of when title passes and who bears the risk of loss for goods in the process of being sold—for example, goods en route from the seller to the buyer—along with the concept of insurable interest. Article 2 regulates performance and obligations required under sales contracts. It also delineates when a breach by either the buyer or the seller occurs and what remedies normally may be sought. A sale of goods usually carries with it at least one type of warranty; sales warranties, express and implied, likewise are governed by the UCC. Article 2A covers similar issues for lease contracts.

SECTION 1

THE SCOPE OF ARTICLE 2—THE SALE OF GOODS

Article 2 of the UCC governs sales contracts, or contracts for the sale of goods. To facilitate commercial transactions, Article 2 modifies some of the common law contract requirements that were discussed in the previous chapters. To the extent that it has not been modified by the UCC, however, the common law of contracts also applies to sales contracts. For example, the common law requirements for a valid contract—agreement (offer and acceptance), consideration, capacity, and legality—are applicable to sales contracts. Thus, you should reexamine these common law principles when studying sales. In general, the rule is that whenever there is a conflict between a common law contract rule and the UCC, the UCC controls. In other words, when a UCC provision addresses a certain issue, the UCC governs; when the UCC is silent, the common law governs.

In regard to Article 2, you should keep in mind two things. First, Article 2 deals with the sale of *goods;* it does not deal with real property (real estate), services, or intangible property such as stocks and bonds. Thus, if the subject matter of a dispute is goods, the UCC governs. If it is real estate or services, the common law applies. Second, in some cases, the rules may vary quite a bit, depending on whether the buyer or the seller is a *merchant.* We look now at how the UCC defines a *sale, goods,* and *merchant status.*

The fold-out exhibit in this chapter, which shows an actual sales contract used by Starbuck's Coffee Company, illustrates many of the terms and clauses that are typically contained in contracts for the sale of goods.

WHAT IS A SALE?

Section 2–102 of the UCC states that Article 2 "applies to transactions in goods." This implies a broad scope—covering gifts, bailments (temporary deliveries of personal property, discussed in Chapter 49), and purchases of goods. In this chapter, however, we treat Article 2 as being applicable only to an actual sale (as would most authorities and courts). The UCC defines a **sale** as "the passing of title from the seller to the buyer for a price," where *title* refers to the formal right of ownership of property [UCC 2–106(1)]. The price may be payable in money or in other goods, services, or realty (real estate).

WHAT ARE GOODS?

To be characterized as a *good,* an item of property must be *tangible,* and it must be *movable.* Tangible property has physical existence—it can be touched or seen. Intangible property—such as corporate stocks and bonds, patents and copyrights, and ordinary contract rights—have only conceptual existence and thus do not come under Article 2. A *movable* item can be carried from place to place. Hence, real estate is excluded from Article 2.

WHO IS A MERCHANT?

Article 2 governs the sale of goods in general. It applies to sales transactions between all buyers and sellers. In a limited number of instances, however, the UCC presumes that in certain phases of sales transactions involving merchants, special business standards ought to be imposed because of the merchants' relatively high degree of commercial expertise.[1] Such standards do not apply to the casual or inexperienced seller or buyer ("consumer").

In general, a person is a merchant when he or she, acting in a mercantile capacity, possesses or uses an expertise specifically related to the goods being sold. This basic distinction is not always clear-cut. For example, courts in some states have determined that farmers may be merchants, while courts in other states have determined that it was not within the contemplation of the drafters of the UCC to include farmers as merchants.

SECTION 2

THE SCOPE OF ARTICLE 2A—LEASES

In the past few decades, leases of personal property (goods) have become increasingly common. Consumers and business firms lease automobiles, industrial equipment, items for use in the home (such as floor polishers), and many other types of goods.

Article 2A of the UCC was created to fill the need for uniform guidelines in this area. Article 2A covers any transaction that creates a lease of goods, as well as subleases of goods [UCC 2A–102, 2A–103(k)]. Article 2A is essentially a repetition of Article 2, except that it applies to leases of goods, rather than

1. The provisions that apply only to merchants deal principally with the Statute of Frauds, firm offers, confirmatory memoranda, warranties, and contract modification. These special rules reflect expedient business practices commonly known to merchants in the commercial setting. They will be discussed later in this chapter.

sales of goods, and thus varies to reflect differences between sales and lease transactions.

Article 2A defines a **lease agreement** as the bargain of the lessor and lessee, as found in their language and as implied by other circumstances [UCC 2A–103(k)]. A **lessor** is one who sells the right to the possession and use of goods under a lease [UCC 2A–103(p)]. A **lessee** is one who acquires the right to the possession and use of goods under a lease [UCC 2A–103(o)]. Article 2A applies to all types of leases of goods, including commercial leases and consumer leases.

SECTION 3
THE FORMATION OF SALES AND LEASE CONTRACTS

In regard to the formation of sales and lease contracts, the UCC modifies the common law in several ways. We look here at how Article 2 and Article 2A of the UCC modify common law contract rules. Remember that parties to sales contracts are free to establish whatever terms they wish. The UCC comes into play when the parties have not, in their contract, provided for a contingency that later gives rise to a dispute. The UCC makes this very clear time and again by its use of such phrases as "unless the parties otherwise agree" and "absent a contrary agreement by the parties."

OFFER

In general contract law, the moment a definite offer is met by an unqualified acceptance, a binding contract is formed. In commercial sales transactions, the verbal exchanges, the correspondence, and the actions of the parties may not reveal exactly when a binding contractual obligation arises. The UCC states that an agreement sufficient to constitute a contract can exist even if the moment of its making is undetermined [UCC 2–204(2), 2A–204(2)].

OPEN TERMS According to contract law, an offer must be definite enough for the parties (and the courts) to ascertain its essential terms when it is accepted. The UCC states that a sales or lease contract will not fail for indefiniteness even if one or more terms are left open as long as (1) the parties intended to make a contract and (2) there is a reasonably certain basis for the court to grant an appropriate remedy [UCC 2–204(3), 2A–204(3)].

Although the UCC has radically lessened the requirement of definiteness of terms, keep in mind that the more terms left open, the less likely a court will find that the parties intended to form a contract.

Open Price Term. If the parties have not agreed on a price, the court will determine a "reasonable price at the time for delivery" [UCC 2–305(1)]. If either the buyer or the seller is to determine the price, the price is to be fixed in good faith [UCC 2–305(2)].

Sometimes the price fails to be fixed through the fault of one of the parties. In that case, the other party can treat the contract as canceled or fix a reasonable price. For example, Johnson and Merrick enter into a contract for the sale of goods and agree that Johnson will fix the price. Johnson refuses to fix the price. Merrick can either treat the contract as canceled or set a reasonable price [UCC 2–305(3)].

Open Payment Term. When parties do not specify payment terms, payment is due at the time and place at which the buyer is to receive the goods [UCC 2–310(a)]. The buyer can tender payment using any commercially normal or acceptable means, such as a check or credit card. If the seller demands payment in cash, however, the buyer must be given a reasonable time to obtain it [UCC 2–511(2)]. This is especially important when the contract states a definite and final time for performance.

Open Delivery Term. When no delivery terms are specified, the buyer normally takes delivery at the seller's place of business [UCC 2–308(a)]. If the seller has no place of business, the seller's residence is used. When goods are located in some other place and both parties know it, delivery is made there. If the time for shipment or delivery is not clearly specified in the sales contract, then the court will infer a "reasonable" time for performance [UCC 2–309(1)].

Open Quantity Term. Normally, if the parties do not specify a quantity, a court will have no basis for determining a remedy. The UCC recognizes two exceptions in requirements and output contracts [UCC 2–306(1)].

In a requirements contract, the buyer agrees to purchase and the seller agrees to sell all or up to a stated amount of what the buyer *needs* or *requires*. In an output contract, the seller agrees to sell and the buyer agrees to buy all or up to a stated amount of what the seller *produces*.

The UCC imposes a *good faith limitation* on requirements and output contracts. The quantity under such contracts is the amount of requirements

EMERGING TRENDS

ELECTRONIC SALES CONTRACTS

In Chapter 9, we discussed contract formation in an electronic age, in which offers and acceptances can be communicated via fax. Additionally, we briefly examined the issue of "click-on" acceptances of online offers. Are such acceptances valid under the Uniform Commercial Code (UCC)? Given that each day more customers use online information services for business use, the issue of "click-on" acceptances is increasingly significant.

"Point-and-click" agreements created electronically involve several legal issues. One has to do with whether the person who assented to the conditions of the agreement actually had the authority to bind his or her principal or employer to the contract. There is, of course, also the issue of whether the agreement meets the signature requirements of the Statute of Frauds—because a point-and-click agreement is not actually signed by the recipient. A similar issue arises with agreements that are included in virtually all shrinkwrapped software. When the purchaser opens the software package, he or she agrees to abide by the terms of the limited license agreement. The equivalent on the Internet is, of course, the point-and-click "Yes, I Agree" box that appears on the computer screen just prior to using downloaded software.

ACCEPTANCE BY CONDUCT

The courts increasingly are holding that limited licenses included with shrinkwrapped software, as well as their equivalents on the Internet, are binding on the buyer. Section 2–204 of the UCC provides that any contract for the sale of goods "may be made in any manner sufficient to show agreement, including *conduct* by both parties which recognizes the existence of a contract." [Emphasis added.] Thus, a buyer's failure to object to terms contained within a shrinkwrapped software package may constitute an acceptance of the terms by conduct.

In a recent case dealing with this issue, *ProCD, Inc. v. Zeidenberg,*[a] a producer of computer software brought an action against users of the software under the Copyright Act (see Chapter 15) and under applicable state contract and tort laws when the users downloaded telephone listings stored in the software and made such listings available on the Internet. Significantly, the Court of Appeals for the Seventh Circuit held that "shrinkwrapped licenses are enforceable unless their terms are objectionable on grounds applicable to contracts in general." The Seventh Circuit applied the same reasoning in a subsequent case, *Hill v. Gateway 2000, Inc.,*[b] in which the plaintiff had ordered a computer via the phone. When the box arrived, it contained a list of terms that would constitute the contract unless the customer returned the computer within thirty days. Because the plaintiff did not return the computer within that time period, the court held that a contract existed on the terms contained in the box.

The court pointed out some of the practical considerations underlying its decision in the *Hill* case: "Practical considerations support allowing vendors to enclose the full legal terms with their products. . . . If the staff at the other end of the phone for direct-sales operations such as Gateway's had to read the four-page statement of terms before taking the buyer's credit-card number, the droning voice would anesthetize rather than enlighten many potential buyers. Others would hang up in a rage over the waste of their time. And oral recitation would not avoid customers' assertions (whether true or feigned) that the clerk did not read term X to them, or that they did not remember or understand it. . . . Customers as a group are better off when

a. 86 F.3d 1447 (7th Cir. 1996).

b. 105 F.3d 1147 (7th Cir. 1997).

EMERGING TRENDS

ELECTRONIC SALES CONTRACTS (CONTINUED)

vendors skip costly and ineffectual steps such as telephonic recitation, and use instead a simple approve-or-return device. Competent adults are bound by such documents, read or unread."

PARTNERING AGREEMENTS

Another online contractual issue involves so-called *partnering agreements.* In a partnering agreement, a seller and a buyer who frequently do business with each other agree in advance on the terms and conditions that will apply to all transactions subsequently conducted via computer modem (or fax). Such partnering agreements often establish special access and identification codes to be used by buyers and sellers when transacting business electronically.

A partnering agreement reduces the likelihood of a "battle of the forms," because the buyer and the seller have agreed to the terms and conditions that will accompany each sale. The terrain for fraud is, of course, a bit more fertile than it is with paper forms. If an unauthorized person uses a purchaser's designated access number and identification code, it may be some time before the problem is discovered. In the meantime, who is liable for the loss—the seller or the buyer? This is an issue that will be decided by the courts in years to come.

DIGITAL SIGNATURES

At issue in partnering agreements, as in other electronic agreements, is the question of digital signatures. Many laws and regulations require a "signature" for regulatory compliance or to validate a transaction and make it enforceable. Unfortunately, the law has never really been settled as to the definition of a "signature." The UCC defines the term *signature* in a very broad fashion, obviously not limiting it to a traditional manual signature. The two functional requirements that most judges would say a signature must fulfill are the following: (1) the signature must establish the identity of the person signing, and (2) the signature must validate or authenticate the document as an intentional legal act of the signer.

Many legal scholars, however, contend that such a definition does not go far enough in defining what should be required for a valid signature in online transactions. What if a digital image of a person's signature can bind that person to a contract, but the digital image can be duplicated exactly without that person's knowledge? Given the low cost and high quality of scanning hardware, it is relatively easy to copy a manual signature on one document and present it online in a fraudulent transaction. Nonetheless, the use of digital signatures in transactions with government bodies has been authorized in some states, including California and Utah, by specific legislation.[c]

c. See California Government Code Section 16.5 (1995) and Utah Code Annotated Section 46-3-101, as well as 31 U.S.C. Section 1501(a)(1).

IMPLICATIONS FOR THE BUSINESSPERSON

1. Any businessperson engaging in the sale of software must make sure that agreements accompanying shrinkwrapped software or provided for online are conspicuously displayed on the package or on the user's screen. Such agreements should be written in simple, straightforward language that can be understood by a nonlawyer, and they should not be unreasonable or overreaching. The agreements should also indicate that the party opening the package or clicking "I Agree" on a computer screen box is duly authorized to bind his or her principal or employer.
2. In an electronic-contracting environment, all communication between the parties should refer to the online terms and conditions as the sole and definitive agreement between the parties with respect to any transaction that was initiated through the online service.

FOR CRITICAL ANALYSIS

1. Who do you think should be responsible for the damages that occur when a computer system fails and orders do not get processed under a partnering agreement?
2. How might an encryption process affect the issue of digital signatures?

or the amount of output that occurs during a *normal* production year. The actual quantity purchased or sold cannot be unreasonably disproportionate to normal or comparable prior requirements or output [UCC 2–306].

MERCHANT'S FIRM OFFER Under regular contract principles, an offer can be revoked at any time before acceptance. The major common law exception is an *option contract,* in which the offeree pays consideration for the offeror's irrevocable promise to keep the offer open for a stated period. The UCC creates a second exception, which applies only to firm offers for the sale or lease of goods made by a merchant (regardless of whether or not the offeree is a merchant). A **firm offer** arises when a merchant-offeror gives assurances in a *signed writing* that the offer will remain open. The merchant's firm offer is irrevocable without the necessity of consideration[2] for the stated period or, if no definite period is stated, a reasonable period (neither to exceed three months) [UCC 2–205, 2A–205].

ACCEPTANCE

The following sections examine the UCC's provisions governing acceptance. Acceptance of an offer to buy, sell, or lease goods generally may be made in any reasonable manner and by any reasonable means. If the offeree's response indicates a *definite* acceptance of the offer, a contract is formed.

If the acceptance includes terms additional to or different from those contained in the offer and one (or both) of the parties is a *nonmerchant,* the contract is formed according to the terms of the original offer submitted by the original offeror and not according to the additional terms of the acceptance [UCC 2–207(2)]. In contracts *between merchants,* the additional terms automatically become part of the contract unless (1) the original offer expressly requires acceptance of its terms, (2) the new or changed terms materially alter the contract, or (3) the offeror objects to the new or changed terms within a reasonable period of time [UCC 2–207(2)].

PROMISE TO SHIP OR PROMPT SHIPMENT The UCC permits acceptance of an offer to buy goods for current or prompt shipment by either a prompt *promise* to ship the goods to the buyer or the prompt *shipment* of conforming goods (that is, goods that accord with the contract's terms) to the buyer [UCC 2–206(1)(b)]. The prompt shipment of *nonconforming goods* constitutes both an *acceptance* (a contract) and a *breach* of that contract. This rule does not apply if the seller seasonably (within a reasonable amount of time) notifies the buyer that the nonconforming shipment is offered only as an *accommodation,* or as a favor. The notice of accommodation must clearly indicate to the buyer that the shipment does not constitute an acceptance and that, therefore, no contract has been formed.

COMMUNICATION OF ACCEPTANCE Under the common law, because a unilateral offer invites acceptance by a performance, the offeree need not notify the offeror of performance unless the offeror would not otherwise know about it. The UCC is more stringent than the common law, stating that when "the beginning of requested performance is a reasonable mode of acceptance[,] an offeror who is not notified of acceptance within a reasonable time may treat the offer as having lapsed before acceptance" [UCC 2–206(2), 2A–206(2)].

SECTION 4
CONSIDERATION

The common law rule that a contract requires consideration also applies to sales and lease contracts. Unlike the common law, however, the UCC does not require a contract modification to be supported by new consideration. The UCC states that an agreement modifying a contract for the sale or lease of goods "needs no consideration to be binding" [UCC 2–209(1), 2A–208(1)].

Of course, contract modification must be made in good faith [UCC 1–203]. For example, Jim agrees to lease certain goods to Louise for a stated price. Subsequently, a sudden shift in the market makes it difficult for Jim to lease the items to Louise at the given price without suffering a loss. Jim tells Louise of the situation, and Louise agrees to pay an additional sum for the goods. Later, Louise reconsiders and refuses to pay more than the original price. Under the UCC, Louise's promise to modify the contract needs no consideration to be binding. Hence, Louise is bound by the modified contract.

In this example, a shift in the market is a *good faith* reason for contract modification. What if there really was no shift in the market, however, and Jim

2. If the offeree pays consideration, then an option contract (not a merchant's firm offer) is formed.

knew that Louise needed the goods immediately but refused to deliver them unless Louise agreed to pay an additional sum of money? This sort of extortion of a modification without a legitimate commercial reason would be ineffective, because it would violate the duty of good faith. Jim would not be permitted to enforce the higher price.

SECTION 5

STATUTE OF FRAUDS

The UCC contains Statute of Frauds provisions covering sales and lease contracts. Under these provisions, sales contracts for goods priced at $500 or more and lease contracts requiring payments of $1,000 or more must be in writing to be enforceable [UCC 2–201(1), 2A–201(1)].

SUFFICIENCY OF THE WRITING

The UCC has greatly relaxed the requirements for the sufficiency of a writing to satisfy the Statute of Frauds. A writing or a memorandum will be sufficient as long as it indicates that the parties intended to form a contract and as long as it is signed by the party (or agent of the party) against whom enforcement is sought. The contract normally will not be enforceable beyond the quantity of goods shown in the writing, however. All other terms can be proved in court by oral testimony. For leases, the writing must reasonably identify and describe the goods leased and the lease term.

SPECIAL RULES FOR CONTRACTS BETWEEN MERCHANTS

Once again, the UCC provides a special rule for merchants. The rule, however, applies only to sales (under Article 2); there is no corresponding rule that applies to leases (under Article 2A).[3] Merchants can satisfy the requirements of a writing for the Statute of Frauds if, after the parties have agreed orally, one of the merchants sends a signed written confirmation to the other merchant. The communication must indicate the terms of the agreement, and the merchant receiving the confirmation must have reason to know of its contents. Unless the merchant who receives the confirmation gives written notice of objection to its contents within ten days after receipt, the writing is sufficient against the receiving merchant, even though he or she has not signed anything [UCC 2–201(2)].

EXCEPTIONS

The UCC defines three exceptions to the writing requirements of the Statute of Frauds. An oral contract for the sale of goods priced at $500 or more or the lease of goods involving payments of $1,000 or more will be enforceable despite the absence of a writing in the following circumstances [UCC 2–201(3), 2A–201(4)].

SPECIALLY MANUFACTURED GOODS An oral contract is enforceable if (1) it is for goods that are specially manufactured for a particular buyer or specially manufactured or obtained for a particular lessee, (2) these goods are not suitable for resale or lease to others in the ordinary course of the seller's or lessor's business, and (3) the seller or lessor has substantially started to manufacture the goods or has made commitments for the manufacture or procurement of the goods. In this situation, once the seller or lessor has taken action, the buyer or lessee cannot repudiate the agreement claiming the Statute of Frauds as a defense.

ADMISSIONS An oral contract for the sale or lease of goods is enforceable if the party against whom enforcement is sought admits in pleadings, testimony, or other court proceedings that a contract for sale was made. In this situation, the contract will be enforceable even though it was oral, but enforceability will be limited to the quantity of goods admitted.

PARTIAL PERFORMANCE An oral contract for the sale or lease of goods is enforceable if payment has been made and accepted or goods have been received and accepted. This is the "partial performance" exception. The oral contract will be enforced at least to the extent that performance *actually* took place.

SECTION 6

TITLE, RISK, AND INSURABLE INTEREST

Before the creation of the Uniform Commercial Code (UCC), *title*—the right of ownership—was the central concept in sales law, controlling all issues of rights and remedies of the parties to a sales contract. There were numerous problems with this concept. For example, frequently it was difficult to determine

3. According to the Comments accompanying UCC 2A–201 (Article 2A's Statute of Frauds), the "between merchants" provision was not included because "the number of such transactions involving leases, as opposed to sales, was thought to be modest."

when title actually passed from seller to buyer, and therefore it was also difficult to predict which party a court would decide had title at the time of a loss. Because of such problems, the UCC divorced the question of title as completely as possible from the question of the rights and obligations of buyers, sellers, and third parties (such as subsequent purchasers, creditors, or the tax collector). In some situations, title is still relevant under the UCC, and the UCC has special rules for locating title. These rules will be discussed in the sections that follow. In most situations, however, the UCC has replaced the concept of title with three other concepts: (1) identification, (2) risk of loss, and (3) insurable interest.

In lease contracts, of course, title to the goods is retained by the lessor-owner of the goods. Hence, the UCC's provisions relating to passage of title do not apply to leased goods. Other concepts discussed in this chapter, though, including identification, risk of loss, and insurable interest, relate to lease contracts as well as to sales contracts.

IDENTIFICATION

Before any interest in specific goods can pass from the seller or lessor to the buyer or lessee, two conditions must prevail: (1) the goods must be in existence, and (2) they must be identified as the specific goods designated in the contract. **Identification** is a designation of goods as the subject matter of a sales or lease contract. Title and risk of loss cannot pass to buyer from seller unless the goods are identified to the contract [UCC 2–105(2)]. (As mentioned, title to leased goods remains with the lessor—or, if the owner is a third party, with that party. The lessee does not acquire title to leased goods.) Identification is significant because it gives the buyer or lessee the right to insure (or obtain an insurable interest in) the goods and the right to recover from third parties who damage the goods.

Once the goods are in existence, the parties can agree in their contract on when identification will take place. If they do not so specify, however, and if the contract calls for the sale or lease of specific and ascertained goods that are already in existence, identification takes place at the time the contract is made. If a sale involves unborn animals to be born within twelve months after contracting, identification takes place when the animals are conceived. If a lease involves any unborn animals, identification occurs when the animals are conceived. If a sale involves crops that are to be harvested within twelve months (or the next harvest season occurring after contracting, whichever is longer), identification takes place when the crops are planted or begin to grow. In a sale or lease of any other future goods, identification occurs when the goods are shipped, marked, or otherwise designated by the seller or lessor as the goods to which the contract refers. Goods that are part of a larger mass are identified when the goods are marked, shipped, or somehow designated by the seller or lessor as the particular goods to pass under the contract.

WHEN TITLE PASSES

Once goods exist and are identified, the provisions of UCC 2–401 apply to the passage of title. In virtually all subsections of UCC 2–401, the words "unless otherwise explicitly agreed" appear, meaning that any explicit understanding between the buyer and the seller determines when title passes. Unless an agreement is explicitly made, title passes to the buyer at the time and the place the seller performs the *physical* delivery of the goods [UCC 2–401(2)]. This rule is applied in the following case.

CASE 11.1 Synergistic Technologies, Inc. v. IDB Mobile Communications, Inc.

United States District Court, District of Columbia, 1994. 871 F.Supp. 24.

HISTORICAL AND TECHNOLOGICAL SETTING *The Soviet Union (now fifteen independent countries, of which the most important is Russia) launched the first artificial satellite, Sputnik I, into orbit around the earth in 1957. Today, several thousand artificial satellites circle our planet. They are used for weather forecasting, for communications, and for military, scientific, and other purposes. For example, the maritime and aviation industries use the International Maritime Satellite (INMARSAT) system for navigation and communication purposes. In the United States, one of the few providers of INMARSAT service is IDB Mobile Communications, Inc.*

BACKGROUND AND FACTS *Synergistic Technologies, Inc. (SynTech), developed three computer software systems for IDB Mobile Communications, Inc., to provide IDB's customers with satellite voice and data communications services. SynTech installed the systems in IDB's computers under a "statement of work" negotiated between the two firms. During the installation, IDB discovered that the systems would not allow it to make back-up copies of the software. If IDB's computers crashed, a return to full operation would thus be delayed. When IDB hired another company to make back-up copies, SynTech filed a suit in a federal district court against IDB, seeking damages and other relief for, among other things, alleged infringement of SynTech's copyrights. IDB responded in part by filing a motion for summary judgment. One of the issues was whether IDB was the "owner" of the software.*

IN THE LANGUAGE OF THE COURT

JOYCE HENS GREEN, District Judge.

* * * *

* * * The Statement of Work is not clear on the issue of transfer of ownership of the software. * * * If this matter turned solely on the Statement of Work, the Court would be unable to resolve the issue of ownership * * * .

However, this question is also governed by [Section] 2–401 of the Uniform Commercial Code, which provides that "[u]nless otherwise explicitly agreed title passes to the buyer at the time and place at which the seller completes his performance with reference to the physical delivery of the goods." The parties not having explicitly agreed otherwise, title to * * * the software passed to IDB at the time of delivery of the goods.

DECISION AND REMEDY *The federal district court granted IDB's motion on this issue. Title to the software passed to IDB when SynTech installed it in IDB's computers.*

SHIPMENT AND DESTINATION CONTRACTS In the absence of agreement, delivery arrangements can determine when title passes from the seller to the buyer. In a shipment contract, the seller is required or authorized to ship goods by carrier, such as a trucking company. Under a shipment contract, the seller is required only to deliver the goods into the hands of a carrier, and title passes to the buyer at the time and place of shipment [UCC 2–401(2)(a)]. Generally, *all contracts are assumed to be shipment contracts if nothing to the contrary is stated in the contract.*

In a destination contract, the seller is required to deliver the goods to a particular destination, usually directly to the buyer, although sometimes the buyer designates that the goods should be delivered to another party. Title passes to the buyer when the goods are *tendered* at that destination [UCC 2–401(2)(b)]. A tender of delivery is the seller's placing or holding of conforming goods at the buyer's disposition (with any necessary notice), enabling the buyer to take delivery [UCC 2–503(1)].

DELIVERY WITHOUT MOVEMENT OF THE GOODS When the contract of sale does not call for the seller's shipment or delivery of the goods (when the buyer is to pick up the goods), the passage of title depends on whether the seller must deliver a document of title, such as a bill of lading or a warehouse receipt, to the buyer. A *bill of lading* is a receipt for goods that is signed by a carrier and that serves as a contract for the transportation of the goods. A *warehouse receipt* is a receipt issued by a warehouser for goods stored in a warehouse. (See Exhibits 11–1 and 11–2.)

When a document of title is required, title passes to the buyer *when and where the document is delivered.* Thus, if the goods are stored in a warehouse, title passes to the buyer when the appropriate documents are delivered to the buyer. The goods never move. In fact, the buyer can choose to leave the goods at the same warehouse for a period of time, and the buyer's title to those goods will be unaffected.

When no documents of title are required, and delivery is made without moving the goods, title

Exhibit 11–1 ■ A Sample Negotiable Bill of Lading

UNIFORM MOTOR CARRIER ORDER BILL OF LADING

1st Sheet

Original—Domestic

Shipper's No. ____________

Agent's No. ____________

CENTRAL FREIGHT LINES INC.

RECEIVED, subject to the classifications and tariffs in effect on the date of the issue of this Bill of Lading,

From ____________ Date ____________ 19

At ____________ Street ____________ City ____________ County ____________ State

the property described below, in apparent good order, except as noted (contents and condition of contents of packages unknown) marked, consigned and destined as shown below, which said company (the word company being understood throughout this contract as meaning any person or corporation in possession of the property under the contract) agrees to carry to its usual place of delivery at said destination, if within the scope of its lawful operations, otherwise to deliver to another carrier on the route to said destination. It is mutually agreed, as to each carrier of all or any of said property over all or any portion of said route to destination, and as to each party at any time interested in all or any of said property, that every service to be performed hereunder shall be subject to all the conditions not prohibited by law, whether printed or written, herein contained, including the conditions on back hereof, which are hereby agreed to by the shipper and accepted for himself and his assigns.

The surrender of this Original ORDER Bill of Lading properly indorsed shall be required before the delivery of the property. Inspection of property covered by this bill of lading will not be permitted unless provided by law or unless permission is indorsed on this original Bill of lading or given in writing by the shipper.

Consigned to Order of ____________

Destination ____________ Street, ____________ City, ____________ County, ____________ State

Notify ____________

At ____________ Street, ____________ City, ____________ County, ____________ State

I.C.C. No. ____________ Vehicle No. ____________

Routing ____________

No. Pack-ages	Description of Articles, Special Marks, and Exceptions	*Weight (Subject to Correction)	Class or Rate	Check Column
	SAMPLE			

Subject to Section 7 of Conditions, if this shipment is to be delivered to the consignee without recourse on the consignor, the consignor shall sign the following statement:

The carrier shall not make delivery of this shipment without payment of freight and all other lawful charges.

____
(signature of consignor.)

If charges are to be prepaid write or stamp here, "To be Prepaid."

Received $ ____________
to apply in prepayment of the charges of the property described hereon.

____
Agent or Cashier.

Per ____________
(the signature here acknowledges only the amount prepaid.)

Charges advanced:

$ ____________

*If the shipment moves between two ports by a carrier by water, the law requires that the bill of lading shall state whether it is "carrier's or shipper's weight."

Note--Where the rate is dependent on value, shippers are required to state specifically in writing the agreed or declared value of the property.

The agreed or declared value of the property is hereby specifically stated by the shipper to be not exceeding

____________ per ____________

____________ Shipper ____________ Agent.

Per ____________ Per ____________

Permanent address of Shipper ____________ Street ____________ City, ____________ State

MOORE BUSINESS FORMS, INC. WACO, TEX. M

Note: Historically, this form was printed in yellow to warn holders that it is an order bill of lading. The back of the form permits negotiation by indorsement.

EXHIBIT 11–2 ■ A SAMPLE NONNEGOTIABLE WAREHOUSE RECEIPT

HART

Warehouse Receipt – Not Negotiable

Agreement No. ________ Vault No. ______________________________

Service Order ________ ______________________________

Receipt and Lot Number ________ Date of Issue ______________ 19____

Received for the account of and deliverable to • ______________________________

whose latest known address is ______________________________

SAMPLE

______________________________ the goods enumerated on the inside or attached schedule to be

stored in Company warehouse, located at ______________________________
which goods are accepted only upon the following conditions set forth below:

READ CAREFULLY That the value of all goods stored, including the contents of any container, and all goods hereafter stored for Depositor's account to be not over $ per pound† per article unless a higher value is noted in the schedule, for which an additional monthly storage charge of ________¢ on each $__________ valuation in excess of $ per pound † per article or fraction thereof will be made.

If there are any items enumerated in this receipt valued in excess of the above limitations per pound per article and not so noted in the schedule, return this receipt within 10 days with proper values so indicated in writing in order that the receipt may be re-issued and proper higher storage rates assessed.

OWNERSHIP. The Customer, Shipper, Depositor, or Agent represents and warrants that he is lawfully possessed of goods to be stored and/or has the authority to store or ship said goods. (If the goods are mortgaged, notify the Company the name and address of the mortgagee.)

PAYMENT OF CHARGES. Storage bills are payable monthly in advance for each month's storage or fraction thereof. Labor charges, cartage and other services rendered are payable upon completion of work. All charges shall be paid at the warehouse location shown hereon, and if delinquent, shall incur interest monthly at the rate of per cent ( ) per year.

The Depositor will pay reasonable attorney's fee incurred by The Company in collecting delinquent accounts.

LIABILITY OF COMPANY. The company shall be liable for any loss or injury to the goods caused by its failure to exercise such care as a reasonably careful man would exercise under like circumstances. The company will not be liable for loss or damage to fragile articles not packed, or articles packed or unpacked by other than employees of this company. Depositor specifically agrees that the warehouse will not be liable for contamination of or for insect damage to articles placed in drawer of furniture by the depositor. Periodic spraying of the warehouse premises shall constitute ordinary and proper care, unless the depositor requests in writing and pays for anti-infestation treatment of articles in drawers and compartments of stored furniture.

CHANGE OF ADDRESS. Notice of change of address must be given the Company in writing, and acknowledged in writing by the Company.

TRANSFER OR WITHDRAWAL OF GOODS. The warehouse receipt is not negotiable and shall be produced and all charges must be paid before delivery to the Depositor, or transfer of goods to another person; however, a written direction to the Company to transfer the goods to another person or deliver the goods may be accepted by the Company at its option without requiring tender of the warehouse receipt

ACCESS TO STORAGE PARTIAL WITHDRAWAL. A signed order from the person in whose name the receipt is issued is required to enable others to remove or have access to goods. A charge is made for stacking and unstacking, and for access to stored goods.

BUILDING-FIRE-WATCHMAN. The Company does not represent or warrant that its building cannot be destroyed by fire or that the contents of said buildings including the said property cannot be destroyed by fire. The Company shall not be required to maintain a watchman or sprinkler system and its failure to do so shall not constitute negligence.

CLAIMS OR ERRORS. All claims for non-delivery of any article or articles and for damage, breakage, etc., must be made in writing within ninety (90) days from delivery of goods stored or they are waived. Failure to return the warehouse receipt for correction within ( ) days after receipt thereof by the depositor will be conclusive that it is correct and delivery will be made only in accordance therewith.

FUTURE SERVICE. This Contract shall extend and apply to future services rendered to the Depositor by the Company and to any additional goods deposited with the Company by the Depositor.

WAREHOUSEMAN'S LIEN. The Company reserves the right to sell the goods stored, in accordance with the provisions of the Uniform Commercial Code (Business and Commerce Code if stored in Texas), for all lawful charges in arrears.

TERMINATION OF STORAGE. The Company reserves the right to terminate the storage of the goods at any time by giving to the Depositor thirty (30) days' written notice of its intention so to do, and, unless the Depositor removes such goods within that period, the Company is hereby empowered to have the same removed at the cost and expense of the Depositor, or the Company may sell them at auction in accordance with state law.

DEPOSITOR WILL PAY REASONABLE LEGAL FEES INCURRED BY WAREHOUSE IN COLLECTING DELINQUENT CHARGES.

THIS DOCUMENT CONTAINS THE WHOLE CONTRACT BETWEEN THE PARTIES AND THERE ARE NO OTHER TERMS, WARRANTIES, REPRESENTATIONS, OR AGREEMENTS OF EITHER DEPOSITOR OR COMPANY NOT HEREIN CONTAINED.

Storage per month or fraction thereof	$________
Warehouse labor	$________
Cartage.	$________
Packing at residence . . .	$________
Wrapping and preparing for storage.	$________
Charges advanced	$________
________________	$________
________________	$________

By ______________________________

• Insert "Mr. and/or Mrs." or, if military personnel, appropriate rank or grade.
†Delete the words "per pound" if the declared value is per article.
For goods stored for military personnel under PL 245, the contractor's liability for care of goods is as provided in Basic Agreement with U.S. Goverment

THIS PROPERTY HAS NOT BEEN INSURED BY THIS COMPANY FOR FIRE OR ANY OTHER CASUALTY
SCHEDULE OF GOODS ON FOLLOWING PAGE OR ATTACHED

HART

W-1 (9-81) Approved by SW WT4© Re-order from Hart Graphics, Austin, Texas

SOURCE: Reprinted with permission of Hart Graphics, Inc., of Austin, Texas. © 1985 Hart Graphics, Inc.

passes at the time and place the sales contract is made, if the goods have already been identified. If the goods have not been identified, title does not pass until identification occurs. Consider an example. Rogers sells lumber to Bodan. It is agreed that Bodan will pick up the lumber at the yard. If the lumber has been identified (segregated, marked, or in any other way distinguished from all other lumber), title passes to Bodan when the contract is signed. If the lumber is still in storage bins at the mill, title does not pass to Bodan until the particular pieces of lumber to be sold under this contract are identified [UCC 2–401(3)].

RISK OF LOSS

Under the UCC, risk of loss does not necessarily pass with title. When risk of loss passes from a seller or lessor to a buyer or lessee is generally determined by the contract between the parties. Sometimes, the contract states expressly when the risk of loss passes. At other times, it does not, and a court must interpret the existing terms to determine whether the risk has passed.

DELIVERY WITH MOVEMENT OF THE GOODS—CARRIER CASES When there is no specification in the agreement, the following rules apply to cases involving movement of the goods (carrier cases). In a shipment contract, if the seller or lessor is required or authorized to ship goods by carrier (but not required to deliver them to a particular destination), risk of loss passes to the buyer or lessee when the goods are duly delivered to the carrier [UCC 2–509(1)(a), 2A–219(2)(a)]. In a destination contract, the risk of loss passes to the buyer or lessee when the goods are tendered to the buyer or lessee at the specified destination [UCC 2–509(1)(b), 2A–219(2)(b)].

DELIVERY WITHOUT MOVEMENT OF THE GOODS The UCC also addresses situations in which the seller or lessor is required neither to ship nor to deliver the goods. Frequently, the buyer or lessee is to pick up the goods from the seller or lessor, or the goods are to be held by a bailee. A *bailment* is a temporary delivery of personal property, without passage of title, into the care of another, called a *bailee*. Under the UCC, a bailee is a party who, by a bill of lading, warehouse receipt, or other document of title, acknowledges possession of goods and contracts to deliver them. A warehousing company, for example, or a trucking company that normally issues documents of title for the goods it receives is a bailee.

Goods Held by the Seller. If the goods are held by the seller, a document of title is usually not used. If the seller is a merchant, risk of loss to goods held by the seller passes to the buyer when the buyer *actually takes physical possession of the goods* [UCC 2–509(3)]. If the seller is not a merchant, the risk of loss to goods held by the seller passes to the buyer on *tender of delivery* [UCC 2–509(3)].

In respect to leases, the risk of loss passes to the lessee on the lessee's receipt of the goods if the lessor is a merchant. Otherwise, the risk passes to the lessee on tender of delivery [UCC 2A–219(c)].

Goods Held by a Bailee. When a bailee is holding goods for a person who has contracted to sell them and the goods are to be delivered without being moved, the goods are usually represented by a negotiable or nonnegotiable document of title (a bill of lading or a warehouse receipt—see Exhibits 11–1 and 11–2). Risk of loss passes to the buyer when (1) the buyer receives a negotiable document of title for the goods, or (2) the bailee acknowledges the buyer's right to possess the goods, or (3) the buyer receives a nonnegotiable document of title *and* has had a *reasonable time* to present the document to the bailee and demand the goods. Obviously, if the bailee refuses to honor the document, the risk of loss remains with the seller [UCC 2–503(4)(b), 2–509(2)].

In respect to leases, if goods held by a bailee are to be delivered without being moved, the risk of loss passes to the lessee on acknowledgment by the bailee of the lessee's right to possession of the goods [UCC 2A–219(2)(b)].

CONDITIONAL SALES Buyers and sellers sometimes form sales contracts that are conditioned either on the buyer's approval of the goods or on the buyer's resale of the goods. Under such contracts, the buyer is in possession of the goods. Sometimes, however, problems arise as to whether the buyer or seller should bear the loss if, for example, the goods are damaged or stolen while in the possession of the buyer.

Sale or Return. A **sale or return** (sometimes called a *sale and return*) is a type of contract by which the buyer purchases the goods but has a conditional right to return the goods (undo the sale) within a specified time period. When the buyer receives possession at the time of sale, the title and risk of loss pass to the buyer. Title and risk of loss remain with the buyer until the buyer returns the goods to the seller within the time period specified. If the buyer fails to return the goods within this time period, the sale is finalized. The return of the goods is made at the buyer's risk and expense. Goods held under a sale-or-return contract are subject to the claims of the buyer's creditors while they are in the buyer's possession.

The UCC treats a **consignment** as a sale or return. Under a consignment, the owner of goods (the *consignor*) delivers them to another (the *consignee*) for the consignee to sell or to keep. If the consignee sells the goods, the consignee must pay the consignor for them. If the consignee does not sell or keep the goods, they may simply be returned to the consignor. While the goods are in the possession of the consignee, the consignee holds title to them, and creditors of the consignee will prevail over the consignor in any action to repossess the goods [UCC 2–326(3)].

Sale on Approval. Usually, when a seller offers to sell goods to a buyer and permits the buyer to take the goods on a trial basis, a **sale on approval** is made. The term *sale* here is a misnomer, as only an *offer* to sell has been made, along with a bailment created by the buyer's possession.

Therefore, title and risk of loss (from causes beyond the buyer's control) remain with the seller until the buyer accepts (approves) the offer. Acceptance can be made expressly, by any act inconsistent with the *trial* purpose or the seller's ownership, or by the buyer's election not to return the goods within the trial period. If the buyer does not wish to accept, the buyer may notify the seller of that fact within the trial period, and the return is made at the seller's expense and risk [UCC 2–327(1)]. Goods held on approval are not subject to the claims of the buyer's creditors until acceptance.

RISK OF LOSS WHEN A SALES OR LEASE CONTRACT IS BREACHED There are many ways to breach a sales or lease contract, and the transfer of risk operates differently depending on which party breaches. Generally, the party in breach bears the risk of loss.

When the Seller or Lessor Breaches. If the goods are so nonconforming that the buyer has the right to reject them, the risk of loss does not pass to the buyer until the defects are *cured* (that is, until the goods are repaired, replaced, or discounted in price by the seller) or until the buyer accepts the goods in spite of their defects (thus waiving the right to reject). For example, a buyer orders blue widgets from a seller, F.O.B. seller's plant. The seller ships black widgets instead. The black widgets (nonconforming goods) are damaged in transit. The risk of loss falls on the seller. Had the seller shipped blue widgets (conforming goods) instead, the risk would have fallen on the buyer [UCC 2–510(2)].

If a buyer accepts a shipment of goods and later discovers a defect, acceptance can be revoked. Revocation allows the buyer to pass the risk of loss back to the seller, at least to the extent that the buyer's insurance does not cover the loss [UCC 2–510(2)].

In regard to leases, Article 2A states a similar rule. If the lessor or supplier tenders goods that are so nonconforming that the lessee has the right to reject them, the risk of loss remains with the lessor or the supplier until cure or acceptance [UCC 2A–220(1)(a)]. If the lessee, after acceptance, revokes his or her acceptance of nonconforming goods, the revocation passes the risk of loss back to the seller or supplier, to the extent that the lessee's insurance does not cover the loss [UCC 2A–220(1)(b)].

When the Buyer or Lessee Breaches. The general rule is that when a buyer or lessee breaches a contract, the risk of loss *immediately* shifts to the buyer or lessee. There are three important limitations to this rule:

1. The seller or lessor must already have identified the contract goods.
2. The buyer or lessee bears the risk for only a *commercially reasonable time* after the seller or lessor has learned of the breach.
3. The buyer or lessee is liable only to the extent of any deficiency in the seller's or lessor's insurance coverage [UCC 2–510(3), 2A–220(2)].

INSURABLE INTEREST

Parties to sales and lease contracts often obtain insurance coverage to protect against damage, loss, or destruction of goods. Any party purchasing insurance, however, must have a sufficient interest in the insured item to obtain a valid policy. Insurance laws—not the UCC—determine sufficiency. The UCC is helpful, however, because it contains certain rules regarding insurable interests in goods.

A buyer or lessee has an **insurable interest** in *identified* goods. The moment the contract goods are identified by the seller or lessor, the buyer or lessee has a special property interest that allows the buyer or lessee to obtain necessary insurance coverage for those goods even before the risk of loss has passed [UCC 2–501(1), 2A–218(1)].

A seller has an insurable interest in goods as long as he or she retains title to the goods. Even after title passes to a buyer, however, a seller who has a security interest in the goods (a right to secure payment—see Chapter 30) still has an insurable interest and can insure the goods [UCC 2–501(2)]. Hence, both a buyer and a seller can have an insurable interest in identical goods at the same time. Of course, the buyer or seller must sustain an actual loss to have the right to recover from an insurance company. In regard to leases, the lessor retains an insurable interest in leased goods until an option to buy has been exercised by the lessee and the risk of loss has passed to the lessee [UCC 2A–218(3)].

SECTION 7

PERFORMANCE OF SALES AND LEASE CONTRACTS

To understand the obligations of the parties under a sales or lease contract, it is necessary to know the duties and obligations each party has assumed under the terms of the contract. Keep in mind that "duties and obligations" under the terms of the contract include those specified by the agreement, by custom, and by the UCC.

In the performance of a sales or lease contract, the basic obligation of the seller or lessor is to *transfer and deliver conforming goods.* The basic obligation of the buyer or lessee is to *accept and pay for conforming goods* in accordance with the contract [UCC 2–301, 2A-516(1)]. Overall performance of a sales or lease contract is controlled by the agreement between the parties. When the contract is unclear and disputes arise, the courts look to the UCC.

THE GOOD FAITH REQUIREMENT

The obligations of good faith and commercial reasonableness underlie every sales and lease contract within the UCC. These obligations can form the basis for a breach of contract suit later on. The UCC's good faith provision, which can never be disclaimed, reads as follows: "Every contract or duty within this Act imposes an obligation of good faith in its performance or enforcement" [UCC 1–203]. Good faith means honesty in fact. In the case of a merchant, it means honesty in fact *and* the observance of reasonable commercial standards of fair dealing in the trade [UCC 2–103(1)(b)]. In other words, merchants are held to a higher standard of performance or duty than nonmerchants are.

OBLIGATIONS OF THE SELLER OR LESSOR

The major obligation of the seller or lessor under a sales or lease contract is to tender conforming goods to the buyer or lessee. Tender of delivery requires that the seller or lessor have and hold *conforming* goods at the disposal of the buyer or lessee and give the buyer or lessee whatever notification is reasonably necessary to enable the buyer or lessee to take delivery [UCC 2–503(1), 2A–508(1)]. Conforming goods are goods that conform exactly to the description of the goods in the contract.

Tender must occur at a *reasonable hour* and in a *reasonable manner.* For example, a seller cannot call the buyer at 2:00 A.M. and say, "The goods are ready. I'll give you twenty minutes to get them." Unless the parties have agreed otherwise, the goods must be tendered for delivery at a reasonable hour and kept available for a reasonable period of time to enable the buyer to take possession of them [UCC 2–503(1)(a)].

All goods called for by a contract must be tendered in a single delivery unless the parties agree otherwise [UCC 2–612, 2A–510] or the circumstances are such that either party can rightfully request delivery in lots [UCC 2–307].

If the contract does not designate the place of delivery for the goods, and the buyer is expected to pick them up, the place of delivery is the *seller's place of business* or, if the seller has none, the *seller's residence* [UCC 2–308]. If the contract involves the sale of *identified goods,* and the parties know when they enter into the contract that these goods are located somewhere other than at the seller's place of business (such as at a warehouse), then the *location of the goods* is the place for their delivery [UCC 2–308].

THE PERFECT TENDER RULE As previously noted, the seller or lessor has an obligation to ship or tender *conforming goods,* and this entitles the buyer or lessee to accept and pay for the goods according to the terms of the contract. Under the common law, the seller was obligated to deliver goods in conformity with the terms of the contract in every detail. This was called the perfect tender rule. The UCC preserves the perfect tender doctrine by stating that if goods or tender of delivery fail *in any respect* to conform to the contract, the buyer or lessee has the right to accept the goods, reject the entire shipment, or accept part and reject part [UCC 2–601, 2A–509].

EXCEPTIONS TO THE PERFECT TENDER RULE

Because of the rigidity of the perfect tender rule, several exceptions to the rule have been created, some of which are discussed here.

Agreement of the Parties. Exceptions to the perfect tender rule may be established by agreement. If the parties have agreed, for example, that defective goods or parts will not be rejected if the seller or lessor is able to repair or replace them within a reasonable period of time, the perfect tender rule does not apply.

Cure. The UCC does not specifically define the term **cure,** but it refers to the right of the seller or lessor to repair, adjust, or replace defective or nonconforming goods [UCC 2–508, 2A–513]. When any tender of delivery is rejected because of nonconforming goods and the time for performance has not yet expired, the seller or lessor can notify the buyer or lessee promptly of the intention to cure and can then do so *within the contract time for performance* [UCC 2–508(1), 2A–513(1)]. Once the time for performance under the contract has expired, the seller or lessor can still exercise the right to cure if he or she had *reasonable grounds to believe that the nonconforming tender would be acceptable to the buyer or lessee* [UCC 2–508(2), 2A–513(2)].

The right to cure substantially restricts the right of the buyer or lessee to reject goods. For example, if a lessee refuses a tender of goods as nonconforming but does not disclose the nature of the defect to the lessor, the lessee cannot later assert the defect as a defense if the defect is one that the lessor could have cured. Generally, buyers and lessees must act in good faith and state specific reasons for refusing to accept goods [UCC 2–605, 2A–514].

Substitution of Carriers. When an agreed-on manner of delivery (such as the use of a particular carrier to transport the goods) becomes impracticable or unavailable through no fault of either party, but a commercially reasonable substitute is available, this substitute performance is sufficient tender to the buyer and must be used [UCC 2–614(1)].

Commercial Impracticability. Occurrences unforeseen by either party when a contract was made may make performance commercially impracticable. When this occurs, the rule of perfect tender no longer holds. According to UCC 2–615(a) and 2A–405(a), delay in delivery or nondelivery in whole or in part is not a breach when performance has been made impracticable "by the occurrence of a contingency the nonoccurrence of which was a basic assumption on which the contract was made." The seller or lessor must, however, notify the buyer or lessee as soon as practicable that there will be a delay or nondelivery.

An increase in cost resulting from inflation does not in and of itself excuse performance, as this kind of risk is ordinarily assumed by a seller or lessor conducting business. The unforeseen contingency must be one that would have been impossible to contemplate in a given business situation.

Destruction of Identified Goods. The UCC provides that when an unexpected event, such as a fire, totally destroys *goods identified at the time the contract is formed* through no fault of either party and *before risk passes to the buyer or lessee,* the parties are excused from performance [UCC 2–613, 2A–221]. If the goods are only partially destroyed, however, the buyer or lessee can inspect them and either treat the contract as void or accept the damaged goods with a reduction of the contract price.

Assurance and Cooperation. Two other exceptions to the perfect tender doctrine apply equally to parties to sales and lease contracts: the right of assurance and the right to cooperation.

The right of assurance—the right to obtain objective indications that performance will occur—stems from the concept that the essential purpose of a contract is performance by both parties and thus when one party has reason to believe the other party will not perform, forcing the first party to perform would create an undue hardship. The UCC provides that if one of the parties has "reasonable grounds" to believe that the other party will not perform as contracted, he or she may in *writing* "demand adequate assurance of due performance" from the other party. Until such assurance is received, he or she may "suspend" further performance without liability. What constitutes "reasonable grounds" is determined by commercial standards. If such assurances are not forthcoming within a reasonable time (not to exceed thirty days), the failure to respond may be treated as a *repudiation* of the contract [UCC 2–609, 2A–401].

Sometimes the performance of one party depends on the cooperation of the other. The UCC provides that when such cooperation is not forthcoming, the other party can suspend his or her own performance without liability and hold the uncooperative party in breach or proceed to perform the contract in any reasonable manner [see UCC 2–311(3)(b)].

OBLIGATIONS OF THE BUYER OR LESSEE

Once the seller or lessor has adequately tendered delivery, the buyer or lessee is obligated to accept the goods and pay for them according to the terms of the contract.

PAYMENT In the absence of any specific agreements, the buyer or lessee must make payment at the time and place the buyer or lessee *receives* the goods [UCC 2–310(a), 2A–516(1)]. When a sale is made on credit, the buyer is obliged to pay according to the specified credit terms (for example, 60, 90, or 120 days), *not* when the goods are received. The credit period usually begins on the *date of shipment* [UCC 2–310(d)]. Under a lease contract, a lessee must pay the lease payment specified in the contract [UCC 2A–516(1)].

Payment can be made by any means agreed on between the parties—cash or any other method generally acceptable in the commercial world. If the seller demands cash when the buyer offers a check, credit card, or the like, the seller must permit the buyer reasonable time to obtain legal tender [UCC 2–511].

ACCEPTANCE A buyer or lessee can manifest assent to the delivered goods in the following ways, each of which constitutes acceptance:

1. There is an acceptance if the buyer or lessee, after having had a reasonable opportunity to inspect the goods, signifies agreement to the seller or lessor that the goods are either conforming or are acceptable despite their nonconformity [UCC 2–606(1)(a), 2A–515(1)(a)].
2. Acceptance is presumed if the buyer or lessee has had a reasonable opportunity to inspect the goods and has failed to reject them within a reasonable period of time [UCC 2–602(1), 2–606(1)(b), 2A–515(1)(b)].
3. In sales contracts, the buyer will be deemed to have accepted the goods if he or she performs any act inconsistent with the seller's ownership. For example, any use or resale of the goods generally constitutes an acceptance. Limited use for the sole purpose of testing or inspecting the goods is not an acceptance, however [UCC 2–606(1)(c)].

If some of the goods delivered do not conform to the contract and the seller or lessor has failed to cure, the buyer or lessee can make a *partial* acceptance [UCC 2–601(c), 2A–509(1)]. The same is true if the nonconformity was not reasonably discoverable before acceptance. (In the latter situation, the buyer or lessee may be able to revoke the acceptance.) A buyer or lessee cannot accept less than a single commercial unit, however. A *commercial unit* is defined by the UCC as a unit of goods that, by commercial usage, is viewed as a "single whole" for purposes of sale, division of which would materially impair the character of the unit, its market value, or its use [UCC 2–105(6), 2A–103(c)]. A commercial unit can be a single article (such as a machine), a set of articles (such as a suite of furniture or an assortment of sizes), a quantity (such as a bale, a gross, or a carload), or any other unit treated in the trade as a single whole.

ANTICIPATORY REPUDIATION

What if, before the time for contract performance, one party clearly communicates to the other the intention not to perform? Such an action is a breach of the contract by *anticipatory repudiation.* When anticipatory repudiation occurs, the nonbreaching party has a choice of two responses. He or she can treat the repudiation as a final breach by pursuing a remedy; or he or she can wait, hoping that the repudiating party will decide to honor the obligations required by the contract despite the avowed intention to renege [UCC 2–610, 2A–402]. In either situation, the nonbreaching party may suspend performance.

Should the latter course be pursued, the UCC permits the breaching party (subject to some limitations) to "retract" his or her repudiation. This can be done by any method that clearly indicates an intent to perform. Once retraction is made, the rights of the repudiating party under the contract are reinstated [UCC 2–611, 2A–403].

SECTION 8

REMEDIES FOR BREACH OF SALES AND LEASE CONTRACTS

Sometimes circumstances make it difficult for a person to carry out the performance promised in a contract, in which case the contract may be breached. When breach occurs, the aggrieved party looks for remedies. These remedies range from retaining the goods to requiring the breaching party's performance under the contract. The general purpose of these remedies is to put the aggrieved party "in as good a position as if the other party had fully performed." Remedies under the Uniform Commercial Code (UCC) are *cumulative* in nature. In other words, an innocent party to a breached sales or lease contract is not limited to one, exclusive remedy. (Of course, a party still may not recover twice for the same harm.)

REMEDIES OF THE SELLER OR LESSOR

A buyer or lessee breaches a sales or lease contract by any of the following actions: (1) wrongfully rejecting tender of the goods; (2) wrongfully revoking acceptance of the goods; (3) failing to make payment on or before delivery of the goods; or repudiating the contract. On the buyer's or lessee's breach, the seller or lessor is afforded several distinct remedies under the UCC. These include the right to stop or withhold delivery of the goods and the right to recover damages or to recover the purchase price of the goods.

THE RIGHT TO RECOVER THE PURCHASE PRICE OR LEASE PAYMENTS DUE Under the UCC, an unpaid seller or lessor can bring an action to recover the purchase price or the payments due under the lease contract, plus incidental damages, but only under one of the following circumstances:

1. When the buyer or lessee has accepted the goods and has not revoked acceptance.
2. When conforming goods have been lost or damaged after the risk of loss has passed to the buyer or lessee.
3. When the buyer or lessee has breached after the goods have been identified to the contract and the seller or lessor is unable to resell or otherwise dispose of the goods [UCC 2–709(1), 2A–529(1)].

If a seller or lessor sues under these circumstances, the goods must be held for the buyer or lessee. The seller or lessor can resell or dispose of the goods at any time prior to collection of the judgment from the buyer or lessee, but in that situation the net proceeds from the sale must be credited to the buyer or lessee. This is an example of the duty to mitigate damages.

In the following case, the court had to determine whether a seller was entitled to recover the purchase price of specially manufactured goods after the buyer had breached the sales contract.

CASE 11.2 Royal Jones & Associates, Inc. v. First Thermal Systems, Inc.

District Court of Appeal of Florida, 1990. 566 So.2d 853.

BACKGROUND AND FACTS *Royal Jones & Associates, Inc., ordered three steel rendering tanks from First Thermal Systems, Inc., for use in its business of constructing rendering plants (factories that process livestock carcasses into hides, fertilizer, and so on). The contract provided that First Thermal would manufacture the tanks according to Royal Jones's specifications for a price of $64,350. When the manufacture of the tanks was completed, Royal Jones refused to accept or pay for the tanks. First Thermal brought an action in a Florida state court for the contract price of the tanks. The trial court, finding that Royal Jones had breached the contract and that the specially manufactured goods were not suitable for sale in the ordinary course of First Thermal's business, awarded First Thermal the full contract price as damages. Royal Jones appealed.*

IN THE LANGUAGE OF THE COURT

ZEHMER, Judge.

* * * *

* * * First Thermal proved that any effort at resale would have been unavailing because these were the only rendering tanks First Thermal ever made, the tanks were manufactured according to Royal Jones's specifications, First Thermal had no other customers to which it could resell the tanks, and it was unaware how the tanks could have been marketed for resale. Also, the tanks were built without needed internal components and to a special size in accordance with Royal Jones's specifications and could not be used as rendering tanks without special engineering to which First Thermal had no access. Finally, there was testimony that the tanks had only scrap value to First Thermal of about $700 if they were processed for a scrap dealer.

DECISION AND REMEDY

The Florida appellate court affirmed the trial court's ruling: First Thermal was entitled to the full contract price of the specially manufactured tanks as damages because the evidence showed that efforts to resell the tanks would be useless.

THE RIGHT TO RECOVER DAMAGES If a buyer or lessee repudiates a contract or wrongfully refuses to accept the goods, a seller or lessor can maintain an action to recover the damages sustained. Ordinarily, the amount of damages equals the difference between the contract price or lease payments and the market price or lease payments at the time and place of tender of the goods, plus incidental damages [UCC 2–708(1), 2A–528(1)].

If the difference between the contract price or payments due under the lease contract and the market price or payments due under the lease contract is too small to place the seller or lessor in the position that he or she would have been in if the buyer or lessee had fully performed, the proper measure of damages is the lost profits of the seller or lessor, including a reasonable allowance for overhead and other expenses [UCC 2–708(2), 2A–528(2)].

REMEDIES OF THE BUYER OR LESSEE

A seller or lessor breaches a sales or lease contract by failing to deliver conforming goods or repudiating the contract prior to delivery. On the breach, the buyer or lessee has a choice of several remedies under the UCC. These remedies include the right to reject nonconforming or improperly delivered goods; to *cover* (that is, to buy the goods elsewhere and recover from the seller the extra cost of obtaining the substitute goods); to recover damages; and, in certain circumstances, to obtain specific performance of the contract.

THE RIGHT TO OBTAIN SPECIFIC PERFORMANCE A buyer or lessee can obtain specific performance when the goods are unique or when the remedy at law is inadequate [UCC 2–716(1), 2A–521(1)]. Ordinarily, an award of money damages is sufficient to place a buyer or lessee in the position he or she would have occupied if the seller or lessor had fully performed. When the contract is for the purchase of a particular work of art or a similarly unique item, however, money damages may not be sufficient. Under these circumstances, equity will require that the seller or lessor perform exactly by delivering the particular goods identified to the contract (a remedy of specific performance).

THE RIGHT TO RECOVER DAMAGES If a seller or lessor repudiates the sales contract or fails to deliver the goods, or if the buyer is justified in rejecting goods that the seller or lessor tenders, then the buyer or lessee has several options under the UCC. The buyer or lessee may cancel the contract and recover as much of the price as has been paid to the seller or lessor. Following cancellation, the buyer or lessee may either (1) cover by obtaining goods from another seller or lessor and seeking reimbursement for the extra costs incurred or (2) recover damages for breach of the contract.

If the buyer or lessee elects to sue for damages, the measure of recovery is the difference between the contract price (or lease payments) and the market price of the goods (or lease payments that could be obtained for the goods) at the time the buyer (or lessee) *learned* of the breach. The market price or market lease payments are determined at the place where the seller or lessor was supposed to deliver the goods. The buyer or lessee can also recover incidental and consequential damages less the expenses that were saved as a result of the breach [UCC 2–713, 2A–519].

THE RIGHT TO REJECT THE GOODS If either the goods or the tender of the goods by the seller or lessor fails to conform to the contract *in any respect*, the buyer or lessee can reject the goods. If some of the goods conform to the contract, the buyer or lessee can keep the conforming goods and reject the rest [UCC 2–601, 2A–509]. The buyer or lessee must reject the goods within a reasonable amount of time after delivery or tender of delivery, and the seller or lessor must be notified seasonably—that is, in a timely fashion or at the proper time [UCC 2–602(1), 2A–509(2)].

If a *merchant buyer or lessee* rightfully rejects goods, and the seller or lessor has no agent or business at the place of rejection, the buyer or lessee is required to follow any reasonable instructions received from the seller or lessor with respect to the goods controlled by the buyer or lessee. The buyer or lessee is entitled to reimbursement for the care and cost entailed in following the instructions [UCC 2–603, 2A–511]. The same requirements hold if the buyer or lessee rightfully revokes his or her acceptance of the goods at some later time [UCC 2–608(3), 2A–517(5)].

If no instructions are forthcoming and the goods are perishable or threaten to decline in value quickly, the buyer or lessee can resell the goods in good faith, taking appropriate reimbursement and a selling commission (not to exceed 10 percent of the gross proceeds) from the proceeds [UCC 2–603(1), (2); 2A–511(1)]. If the goods are not perishable, the buyer or lessee may store them for the seller or lessor or reship them to the seller or lessor [UCC 2–604, 2A–512].

Whether a buyer had the right to keep conforming goods and reject the rest was the issue in the following case.

CASE 11.3 McCalif Grower Supplies, Inc. v. Reed

Supreme Court of Montana, 1995.
272 Mont. 254,
900 P.2d 880.

BACKGROUND AND FACTS *McCalif Grower Supplies, Inc., provides for the supply and shipping of plants from growers to wholesale greenhouses. Wilbur Reed operates a small greenhouse in Missoula, Montana. Reed ordered poinsettias from McCalif. When the poinsettias were delivered, Reed discovered that many of them were damaged because they had not been packed properly. Reed refused to pay for any of the plants. McCalif filed an action in a Montana state court against Reed for the money. Reed claimed that McCalif owed him damages for, among other things, the nonconforming goods. The court awarded McCalif an amount to cover the cost of the plants that had not been damaged and awarded Reed nothing. Reed appealed.*

IN THE LANGUAGE OF THE COURT

WEBER, Justice.

* * * *

With regard to Reed's right to reject a portion of the poinsettias, [UCC 2–601] provides: Buyer's rights on improper delivery. * * * [I]f the goods or the tender of delivery fail in any respect to conform to the contract, the buyer may: (a) reject the whole; or (b) accept the whole; or (c) accept any commercial unit or units and reject the rest. The record demonstrates that Reed accepted a portion of the commercial units of poinsettias and rejected the rest.

DECISION AND REMEDY *The Montana Supreme Court concluded that Reed was entitled to damages for the nonconforming goods, as well as incidental and consequential damages, because the goods did not entirely conform to the contract and Reed was entitled to reject the nonconforming portion of the goods. The court remanded the case for a determination of the amount and the entry of a judgment balancing the awards to McCalif and Reed.*

SECTION 9

SALES AND LEASE WARRANTIES

Warranty is an age-old concept. In sales and lease law, a warranty is an assurance by one party of the existence of a fact on which the other party can rely. Article 2 (on sales) and Article 2A (on leases) of the Uniform Commercial Code (UCC) designate several types of warranties that can arise in a sales or lease contract. These warranties include warranties of title, express warranties, and implied warranties.

Because a warranty imposes a duty on the seller or lessor, a breach of warranty is a breach of the seller's or lessor's promise. If the parties have not agreed to limit or modify the remedies available to the buyer or lessee and if the seller or lessor breaches a warranty, the buyer or lessee can sue to recover damages from the seller or lessor. Under some circumstances, a breach can allow the buyer or lessee to rescind (cancel) the agreement.[4]

WARRANTY OF TITLE

Title warranty arises automatically in most sales contracts. UCC 2–312 imposes three types of warranties of title. In most cases, sellers warrant that they have good and valid title to the goods sold and that transfer of the title is rightful [UCC 2–312(1)(a)].

A second warranty of title provided by the UCC protects buyers who are *unaware* of any encumbrances (claims, charges, or liabilities—usually called *liens*[5]) against goods at the time the contract is made [UCC 2–312(1)(b)]. This warranty protects buyers who, for example, unknowingly purchase goods that are subject to a creditor's security interest (see Chapter 16). If a creditor legally repossesses the goods from a buyer *who had no actual knowledge of the security interest,* the buyer can recover from the seller for breach of warranty. (The buyer who has *actual knowledge* of a security interest has no recourse against a seller.) Article 2A affords similar protection for lessees. Section 2A–211(1) provides that during the term of the lease, no claim of any third party will interfere with the lessee's enjoyment of the leasehold interest.

A merchant seller is also deemed to warrant that the goods delivered are free from any copyright, trademark, or patent claims of a third person [UCC 2–312(3), 2A–211(2)].

In an ordinary sales transaction, the title warranty can be disclaimed or modified only by *specific language* in a contract. For example, sellers may assert that they are transferring only such rights, title, and interest as they have in the goods. In a lease transaction, the disclaimer must "be specific, be by a writing, and be conspicuous" [UCC 2A–214(4)]. In certain cases, the circumstances surrounding the sale are sufficient to indicate clearly to a buyer that no assurances as to title are being made. The classic example is a sheriff's sale, when buyers know that the goods have been seized to satisfy debts, and it is apparent that the goods are not the property of the person selling them [UCC 2–312(2)].

EXPRESS WARRANTIES

A seller or lessor can create an **express warranty** by making representations concerning the quality, condition, description, or performance potential of the goods. Under UCC 2–313 and 2A–210, express warranties arise when a seller or lessor indicates any of the following:

1. That the goods conform to any *affirmation or promise* of fact that the seller or lessor makes to the buyer or lessee about the goods. Such affirmations or promises are usually made during the bargaining process. Statements such as "these drill bits will *easily* penetrate stainless steel—and without dulling" are express warranties.
2. That the goods conform to any *description* of them. For example, a label that reads "Crate contains one 150-horsepower diesel engine" or a contract that calls for the delivery of a "wool coat" creates an express warranty that the content of the goods sold conforms to the description.
3. That the goods conform to any *sample or model* of the goods shown to the buyer or lessee.

Express warranties can be found in a seller's or lessor's advertisement, brochure, or promotional materials, in addition to being made orally or in an express warranty provision in a sales or lease contract. To create an express warranty, a seller or lessor does not have to use formal words such as *warrant* or *guarantee.* It is only necessary that a reasonable buyer or lessee would regard the representation as part of the basis of the bargain [UCC 2–313(2), 2A–210(2)]. Therefore, if an express warranty is not

4. Rescission restores the parties to the positions they were in before the contract was made.

5. Pronounced *leens.* Liens are discussed in detail in Chapter 16.

intended, the marketing agent or salesperson should not promise too much.

BASIS OF THE BARGAIN The UCC requires that for an express warranty to be created, the affirmation, promise, description, or sample must become part of the "basis of the bargain" [UCC 2–313(1), 2A–210(1)]. Just what constitutes the basis of the bargain is hard to say. The UCC does not define the concept, and it is a question of fact in each case whether a representation was made at such a time and in such a way that it induced the buyer or lessee to enter into the contract.

In the following case, the issue was whether warranties contained in a booklet in the glove compartment of a new truck were part of the basis of the bargain for the purchase of the truck.

CASE 11.4 Harris v. Ford Motor Co.

United States District Court, Middle District of Alabama, 1994. 845 F.Supp. 1511.

HISTORICAL AND SOCIAL SETTING *The first pickup trucks, in the 1910s and 1920s, were Ford Model Ts with a platform in place of a back seat. They were used almost exclusively by farmers for hauling. Pickups remained solely practical, functional workhorses for farmers, cowboys, and oil-rig workers until the mid-1970s, when they became fashionable for some suburbanites. By the late 1980s, pickups were as likely to be used to commute to white-collar jobs as they were to do chores on a farm or a ranch. Today, 20 percent of all new vehicles bought in the United States are pickups. Some of these are strictly show vehicles, unsuited to any useful task besides transportation. They may be coated with expensive paint, outfitted with fancy wheels, and upholstered in velour.*

BACKGROUND AND FACTS *William Harris purchased a new 1989 Ford F350 pickup truck from Quality Motors, Inc. The truck came with a "New Car Warranty" booklet, which had been placed in the glove compartment of the truck. A few months later, after the right rear fender on the truck had begun to discolor, Harris discovered that the truck's fender had been scratched in transit from the manufacturer (Ford Motor Company) to the dealership (Quality Motors) and that Quality Motors had repaired the scratched fender and repainted the truck before it sold the truck to Harris. Harris sued Quality Motors and Ford in a federal district court for, among other things, breach of express warranty, claiming in part that the truck was represented as being "new" when in fact it was not—it was damaged. In defending against Harris's claim, the defendants pointed to a clause in the "New Car Warranty" booklet. The clause provided as follows: "A defect or damage may occur in an appearance item while a vehicle is being assembled at the factory or shipped to the dealer. Usually such a defect or damage is found and repaired during the inspection processes at the factory and the dealership." Harris, in response, contended that the warranty booklet was not a part of the "basis of the bargain," because the booklet was delivered long after Harris had obligated himself to purchase the vehicle. All of the parties filed motions for summary judgment.*

IN THE LANGUAGE OF THE COURT

De MENT, District Judge.

* * * *

* * * The evidence demonstrates that, at the time William Harris purchased the vehicle, the "New Car Warranty" was in the glove compartment of the truck, and that the plaintiff was aware of its presence. Based upon this testimony, the court finds that the warranty was delivered to the plaintiff at the time of the sale and was part of the "basis of the bargain."

DECISION AND REMEDY *The federal district court granted summary judgment in favor of the defendants. Because at the time of the sale the warranty booklet was in the truck and the plaintiff was aware of its presence there, the warranty was part of the basis of the bargain.*

STATEMENTS OF OPINION AND VALUE If the seller or lessor merely makes a statement that relates to the value or worth of the goods, or makes a statement of opinion or recommendation about the goods, the seller or lessor is not creating an express warranty [UCC 2–313(2), 2A–210(2)].

For example, a seller claims that "this is the best used car to come along in years; it has four new tires and a 150-horsepower engine just rebuilt this year." The seller has made several *affirmations of fact* that can create a warranty: the automobile has an engine; it has a 150-horsepower engine; the engine was rebuilt this year; there are four tires on the automobile; and the tires are new. The seller's *opinion* that the vehicle is "the best used car to come along in years," however, is known as "puffing" and creates no warranty. (*Puffing* is an expression of opinion by a seller or lessor that is not made as a representation of fact.) A statement relating to the value of the goods, such as "it's worth a fortune" or "anywhere else you'd pay $10,000 for it," does not usually create a warranty.

Although the ordinary seller or lessor can give an opinion that is not a warranty, if the seller or lessor is an expert and gives an opinion as an expert to a layperson, then a warranty may be created. For example, Saul is an art dealer and an expert in seventeenth-century paintings. If Saul states to Lauren, a purchaser, that in his opinion a particular painting is a Rembrandt, Saul has warranted the accuracy of his opinion.

It is not always easy to determine what constitutes an express warranty and what constitutes puffing. The reasonableness of the buyer's or lessee's reliance appears to be the controlling criterion in many cases. For example, a salesperson's statements that a ladder will "never break" and will "last a lifetime" are so clearly improbable that no reasonable buyer should rely on them. Additionally, the context within which a statement is made might be relevant in determining the reasonableness of a buyer's or lessee's reliance. For example, a reasonable person is more likely to rely on a written statement made in an advertisement than on a statement made orally by a salesperson.

IMPLIED WARRANTIES

An **implied warranty** is one that *the law derives* by inference from the nature of the transaction or the relative situations or circumstances of the parties. For example, Kaplan buys an ax at Enrique's Hardware Store. No express warranties are made. The first time she chops wood with it, the ax handle breaks, and she is injured. She immediately notifies Enrique. Examination shows that the wood in the handle was rotten but that the rottenness could not have been noticed by either Enrique or Kaplan. Nonetheless, Kaplan notifies Enrique that she will hold him responsible for the medical bills. Enrique is responsible, because a merchant seller of goods warrants that the goods he or she sells are fit for the ordinary purposes for which such goods are used. This ax was obviously not fit for those purposes.

IMPLIED WARRANTY OF MERCHANTABILITY An **implied warranty of merchantability** automatically arises in every sale or lease of goods made *by a merchant* who deals in goods of the kind sold or leased [UCC 2–314, 2A–212]. Thus, a merchant who is in the business of selling ski equipment makes an implied warranty of merchantability every time the merchant sells a pair of skis, but a neighbor selling his or her skis at a garage sale does not.

To be *merchantable*, goods must be "reasonably fit for the ordinary purposes for which such goods are used." They must be of at least average, fair, or medium-grade quality. The quality must be comparable to quality that will pass without objection in the trade or market for goods of the same description. To be merchantable, the goods must also be adequately packaged and labeled as provided by the agreement, and they must conform to the promises or affirmations of fact made on the container or label, if any.

An implied warranty of merchantability also imposes on the merchant liability for the safe performance of the product. It makes no difference whether the merchant knew of or could have discovered a defect that makes the product unsafe—he or she is liable in either situation. Of course, merchants are not absolute insurers against *all* accidents arising in connection with the goods. For example, a bar of soap is not unmerchantable merely because a user could slip and fall by stepping on it.

In the following case, the court considered whether a loose cap on a bottle of bleach was enough to support a claim for a breach of the implied warranty of merchantability.

CASE 11.5 Keaton v. A.B.C. Drug Co.

Supreme Court of Georgia, 1996. 266 Ga. 385, 467 S.E.2d 558.

BACKGROUND AND FACTS *Marilyn Keaton entered an A.B.C. Drug store to buy a half-gallon bottle of liquid bleach. The bottles were stacked at a height above her eye level. She reached up, grasped the handle of one of the bottles, and began pulling it down from the shelf. The cap was loose, however, causing bleach to splash into her face, injuring her eye. Keaton filed a suit in a Georgia state court against A.B.C., alleging, in part, breach of the implied warranty of merchantability. She claimed that the bleach had not been adequately packaged. A.B.C. argued, in part, that Keaton had failed to exercise care for her own safety. The jury returned a verdict for Keaton, and the court entered a judgment in her favor. On A.B.C.'s appeal, the state intermediate appellate court reversed. The case was appealed to the Supreme Court of Georgia.*

IN THE LANGUAGE OF THE COURT

BENHAM, Chief Justice.

* * * *

* * * ABC, as a merchant of bleach, was required to adequately contain and package the bleach that it sold. Because bleach which spills via a loose cap is not adequately contained or packaged, a claim [for breach of the implied warranty of merchantability] is supported. * * *

* * *

Keaton's claim for breach of implied warranty of merchantability is not defeated by an alleged failure to exercise care for her own safety. * * * The bleach in this case was located at a height above Keaton's eye-level, and it is undisputed that the top was not off nor was there anything noticeably wrong with the bottle. Therefore, there was no patent or obvious defect. It was a jury question as to whether Keaton failed to exercise caution for her own safety * * * .

DECISION AND REMEDY *The Georgia Supreme Court reversed the judgment of the court of appeals. The judgment in Keaton's favor was reinstated because bleach that spills because of a loose cap is not properly packaged, and A.B.C. thus breached the implied warranty of merchantability.*

IMPLIED WARRANTY OF FITNESS FOR A PARTICULAR PURPOSE The **implied warranty of fitness for a particular purpose** arises when *any seller or lessor* (merchant or nonmerchant) knows the particular purpose for which a buyer or lessee will use the goods *and* knows that the buyer or lessee is relying on the skill and judgment of the seller or lessor to select suitable goods [UCC 2–315, 2A–213].

A "particular purpose" of the buyer or lessee differs from the "ordinary purpose for which goods are used" (merchantability). Goods can be merchantable but unfit for a particular purpose. For example, suppose that you need a gallon of paint to match the color of your living room walls—a light shade somewhere between coral and peach. You take a sample to your local hardware store and request a gallon of paint of that color. Instead, you are given a gallon of bright blue paint. Here, the salesperson has not breached any warranty of implied merchantability—the bright blue paint is of high quality and suitable for interior walls—but he or she has breached an implied warranty of fitness for a particular purpose.

A seller or lessor does not need to have actual knowledge of the buyer's or lessee's particular purpose. It is sufficient if a seller or lessor "has reason to know" the purpose. The buyer or lessee, however, must have *relied* on the skill or judgment of the seller or lessor in selecting or furnishing suitable goods for an implied warranty to be created.

For example, Bloomberg leases a computer from Future Tech, a technical business equipment lessor. Bloomberg tells the clerk that she wants a computer with enough memory to operate certain brands of software and produce and store complicated engineering graphics and plans. Future Tech leases Bloomberg an Architex One computer. The computer works, but its memory is too limited. Bloomberg wants her money back. Here, Future Tech has breached the implied warranty of fitness for a particular purpose, and Bloomberg normally will be able to recover. The clerk knew specifically that Bloomberg wanted a computer with enough memory to run certain software and store certain information. Furthermore, Bloomberg relied on the clerk to furnish a computer that would fulfill this purpose. Because Future Tech did not do so, the warranty was breached.

IMPLIED WARRANTY ARISING FROM COURSE OF DEALING OR TRADE USAGE Implied warranties can also arise (or be excluded or modified) as a result of course of dealing, course of performance, or usage of trade [UCC 2–314(3), 2A–212(3)]. In the absence of evidence to the contrary, when both parties to a sales or lease contract have knowledge of a well-recognized trade custom, the courts will infer that both parties intended for that custom to apply to their contract. For example, if an industry-wide custom is to lubricate a new car before it is delivered and a dealer fails to do so, the dealer can be held liable to a buyer for damages resulting from the breach of an implied warranty. (This, of course, would also be negligence on the part of the dealer.)

WARRANTY DISCLAIMERS

Because each type of warranty is created in a special way, the manner in which warranties can be disclaimed or qualified by a seller or lessor varies with the type of warranty.

EXPRESS WARRANTIES As already stated, any affirmation of fact or promise, description of the goods, or use of samples or models by a seller or lessor creates an express warranty. Obviously, then, express warranties can be excluded if the seller or lessor carefully refrains from making any promise or affirmation of fact relating to the goods, describing the goods, or using a sample or model.

The UCC does permit express warranties to be negated or limited by specific and unambiguous language, provided that this is done in a manner that protects the buyer or lessee from surprise. Therefore, a written disclaimer in language that is clear and conspicuous, and called to a buyer's or lessee's attention, could negate all oral express warranties not included in the written sales or lease contract [UCC 2–316(1), 2A–214(1)]. This allows the seller or lessor to avoid false allegations that oral warranties were made, and it ensures that only representations made by properly authorized individuals are included in the bargain.

IMPLIED WARRANTIES Generally speaking, unless circumstances indicate otherwise, the implied warranties of merchantability and fitness are disclaimed by the expressions "as is," "with all faults," and other similar expressions that in common understanding for *both* parties call the buyer's or lessee's attention to the fact that there are no implied warranties [UCC 2–316(3)(a), 2A–214(3)(a)].

The UCC also permits a seller or lessor to specifically disclaim an implied warranty either of fitness or of merchantability [UCC 2–316(2), 2A–214(2)]. To disclaim an implied warranty of fitness for a particular purpose, the disclaimer *must* be in writing and be conspicuous. The word *fitness* does not have to be mentioned in the writing; it is sufficient if, for example, the disclaimer states, "THERE ARE NO WARRANTIES THAT EXTEND BEYOND THE DESCRIPTION ON THE FACE HEREOF." A merchantability disclaimer must be more specific; it must mention *merchantability*. It need not be written; but if it is, the writing must be conspicuous [UCC 2–316(2), 2A–214(4)].

TERMS AND CONCEPTS TO REVIEW

consignment 229
cure 231
express warranty 236
firm offer 222
identification 224
implied warranty 238
implied warranty of fitness for a particular purpose 239
implied warranty of merchantability 238
insurable interest 230
lease agreement 219
lessee 219
lessor 219
sale 218
sale on approval 229
sale or return 228

QUESTIONS AND CASE PROBLEMS

11–1. OFFERS BETWEEN MERCHANTS. A. B. Zook, Inc., is a manufacturer of washing machines. Over the telephone, Zook offers to sell Radar Appliances one hundred model Z washers at a price of $150 per unit. Zook agrees to keep this offer open for ninety days. Radar tells Zook that the offer appears to be a good one and that it will let Zook know of its acceptance within the next two to three weeks. One week later, Zook sends and Radar receives notice that Zook has withdrawn its offer. Radar immediately thereafter telephones Zook and accepts the $150-per-unit offer. Zook claims, first, that no sales contract was ever formed between it and Radar and, second, that if there is a contract, the contract is unenforceable. Discuss Zook's contentions.

11–2. ACCOMMODATION SHIPMENTS. Flint, a retail seller of television sets, orders one hundred Color-X sets from manufacturer Martin. The order specifies the price and that the television sets are to be shipped by Humming Bird Express on or before October 30. The order is received by Martin on October 5. On October 8, Martin writes Flint a letter indicating that the order was received and that the sets will be shipped as directed, at the specified price. This letter is received by Flint on October 10. On October 28, Martin, in preparing the shipment, discovers it has only ninety Color-X sets in stock. Martin ships the ninety Color-X sets and ten television sets of a different model, stating clearly on the invoice that the ten are being shipped only as an accommodation. Flint claims Martin is in breach of contract. Martin claims the shipment was not an acceptance, and therefore no contract was formed. Explain who is correct and why.

11–3. RISK OF LOSS. On May 1, Sikora goes into Carson's retail clothing store to purchase a suit. Sikora finds a suit he likes for $190 and buys it. The suit needs alteration. Sikora is to pick up the altered suit at Carson's store on May 10. Consider the following separate sets of circumstances:

(a) One of Carson's major creditors obtains a judgment on the debt Carson owes and has the court issue a writ of execution (a court order to seize a debtor's property to satisfy a debt) to collect on that judgment all clothing in Carson's possession. Discuss Sikora's rights in the suit under these circumstances.

(b) On May 9, through no fault of Carson's, the store burns down, and all contents are a total loss. Between Carson and Sikora, who suffers the loss of the suit destroyed by fire? Explain.

11–4. REMEDIES OF THE BUYER OR LESSEE. McDonald has contracted to purchase five hundred pairs of shoes from Vetter. Vetter manufactures the shoes and tenders delivery to McDonald. McDonald accepts the shipment. Later, on inspection, McDonald discovers that ten pairs of the shoes are poorly made and will have to be sold to customers as seconds. If McDonald decides to keep all five hundred pairs of shoes, what remedies are available to her? Discuss.

11–5. STATUTE OF FRAUDS. GPL Treatment, Ltd., orally agreed to sell a large quantity of cedar shakes to Louisiana-Pacific Corp. (L-P). GPL sent L-P order confirmation forms that stated the prices and quantities of shakes ordered. Each form also contained a "sign and return" clause, asking L-P to sign and return one copy. L-P did not sign or return any of the forms, but it also did not object to any of the terms. When L-P accepted only about 15 percent of the orders, GPL filed a suit in an Oregon state court against the buyer for breach of contract. Do GPL's confirmation forms satisfy the requirement of a writing under the Statute of Frauds? Are they enforceable against L-P? Discuss fully. [*GPL Treatment, Ltd. v. Louisiana-Pacific Corp.*, 323 Or. 116, 914 P.2d 682 (1996)]

11–6. ANTICIPATORY REPUDIATION. Bryant Lewis contracted to sell Ross Cattle Co. four hundred head of cattle at $47.50 per hundredweight. Ross made an $8,000 down payment. Before delivery, Lewis heard a rumor that Ross was in poor financial condition, and Lewis demanded that he receive full payment before delivering the animals. Ross told Lewis the balance would be paid on delivery, based on the weight of the cattle delivered. Lewis refused to deliver the cattle and sold them to a third party. Ross filed suit. Lewis claimed that the refusal of Ross to pay was an anticipatory repudiation of the contract. Discuss whether Lewis was correct and what action Lewis could have taken on the basis of the rumor. [*Ross Cattle Co. v. Lewis*, 415 So.2d 1029 (Miss. 1982)]

11–7. TENDER OF DELIVERY. Rheinberg-Kellerei GMBH, a German wine producer and export seller, sold 1,245 cases of wine to Vineyard Wine Co., a U.S. company. The contract did not specify delivery to any particular destination, and Rheinberg, through its agent, selected the port of Wilmington for the port of entry. Rheinberg delivered the wine to the boat carrier in early December 1978. On or about January 24, 1979, Vineyard learned that the wine had been lost in the North Atlantic sometime between December 12 and December 22, when the boat sank with all hands aboard. Vineyard refused to pay Rheinberg. Rheinberg filed an action for the purchase price, claiming that risk of loss had passed to the buyer, Vineyard, on delivery of the wine to the carrier. Vineyard claimed that because of Rheinberg's failure to give prompt notice of shipment (notice had not been given until after the ship was lost at sea), risk of loss had not passed to the buyer. Discuss fully who is correct. [*Rheinberg-Kellerei GMBH v. Vineyard Wine Co.*, 281 S.E.2d 425 (N.C.App. 1981)]

11–8. COMMERCIAL IMPRACTICABILITY. Bobby Murray Chevrolet, Inc., contracted to supply 1,200 school bus chassis to local school boards. The contract stated that "products of any manufacturer may be offered," but Bobby Murray submitted its orders exclusively to General Motors Corp. (GMC). When a shortage in automatic transmissions occurred, GMC informed the dealer that it could not fill the orders. Bobby Murray told the school boards, which bought the chassis from another dealer. The boards filed a suit in a North Carolina state court against Bobby Murray on the ground of breach of contract. The dealer responded that its obligation to perform was excused under the doctrine of commercial impracticability, in part because of GMC's failure to fill its orders. Was it? Why or why not? [*Alamance County Board of Education v. Bobby Murray Chevrolet, Inc.*, 121 N.C.App. 222, 465 S.E.2d 306 (1996)]

11–9. IMPLIED WARRANTIES. Robert Levondosky was a patron at Harrah's Marina Hotel Casino, an Atlantic City casino owned by Marina Associates. While playing at one of the casino's tables, he ordered a cocktail, which was served free of charge—it was the casino's custom to give complimentary drinks to patrons at the gambling tables. Levondosky alleged that he swallowed a few thin chips of glass from the rim of the glass in which the drink was served and, as a result, suffered internal injuries. Levondosky sued the casino, contending that the casino had breached an implied warranty of merchantability. In evaluating this claim, the court had to determine (1) whether a "sale" had in fact occurred, which is prerequisite to the creation of an implied warranty of merchantability, and (2) whether the casino gave an implied warranty as to the glass as well as to the drink within it. Review UCC 2–314, and discuss how the court should rule on both issues. [*Levondosky v. Marina Associates*, 731 F.Supp. 1210 (D.N.J. 1990)]

11–10. WARRANTIES. Prestige Motorcar Imports, Inc., advertised a used 1984 Aston Martin Lagonda for sale for $57,600. The car came with a written warranty that covered specific items. Gary Davenport had the car inspected, then bought it. Over the next couple of days, he had the car inspected further and learned that it needed $13,000 worth of repairs, none of which was covered by the written warranty. He complained to Irvin David, owner of Prestige, who offered to refund Davenport's money or fix the car. Davenport refused both and filed a suit in a Florida state court against David and Prestige, in part for breach of warranty. On what grounds might the court issue a judgment against Davenport? [*David v. Davenport*, 656 So.2d 952 (Fla.App.3d 1995)]

11–11. A QUESTION OF ETHICS

Arvo Lake, a retired seventy-one-year-old man, bought an air conditioner in May 1986. The unit was installed and operated according to the manufacturer's instructions. Unbeknownst to Lake, the unit contained a hole in the refrigeration system that allowed Freon, the coolant, to escape from the unit. By August, the unit had ceased cooling, and Lake's residence reached a temperature of at least ninety-six degrees Fahrenheit. The heat caused Lake to suffer from hyperthermia, which caused circulatory failure and death. The executor of Lake's estate, David Garavalia, sued the manufacturer of the air conditioner for damages. The circuit court dismissed the suit, and Garavalia appealed. The appellate court found for the plaintiff, alleging that the risk of death from an air conditioner that failed to operate properly was foreseeable, given Lake's age and the climate in southern Illinois in the summer. [*Garavalia v. Heat Controller, Inc.*, 212 Ill.App.3d 380, 570 N.E.2d 1227, 156 Ill.Dec. 505 (1991)]

1. For a manufacturer to be liable for consequential damages caused by a breach of warranty, the consequential damages must be foreseeable to the manufacturer. Do you agree with the court that Lake's death was a foreseeable consequence of the air conditioner's failure to operate properly?
2. In determining whether Lake's death was a foreseeable result of the malfunctioning air conditioner, the court considered such circumstances as the heat of the Illinois summer, Lake's age, and the high crime rate in Lake's neighborhood. Should these factors have any bearing on

whether the manufacturer should be held liable for Lake's death? Why or why not?

3. One of the judges in this case dissented, stating that "[f]oreseeability means that which is objectively reasonable to expect, not merely what might conceivably occur." He went on to state that an air conditioner is "a rather benign machine" and that the manufacturer of such an appliance could not reasonably foresee that an air conditioner's failure to cool would result in death. Do you agree with this analysis? Discuss.

Accessing the Internet

The Legal Environment of Business

For the most updated information on the Uniform Commercial Code, including drafts of revised articles, go to

http://www.law.cornell.edu/ucc/ucc.table.html

Or go to

http://www.kentlaw.edu/

You can obtain information on current commercial law topics from the law firm of Hale and Dorr at

http://www.haledorr.com/

Cornell Law School's Legal Information Institute offers online access to the Uniform Commercial Code as enacted in several of the states at

http://www.law.cornell.edu/statutes.html#state

To review bills of lading, access the following Web site:

http://www.showtrans.com/bl.htm

CHAPTER 12

TORTS AND STRICT LIABILITY

PART OF DOING BUSINESS TODAY—and, indeed, part of everyday life—is the risk of being involved in a lawsuit. A normal and ever-increasing business operating cost is that of liability insurance to protect against lawsuits. The list of circumstances in which businesspersons can be sued is long and varied. An employee injured on the job may attempt to sue the employer because of an unsafe working environment. A consumer who is injured while using a product may attempt to sue the manufacturer because of a defect in the product. At issue in these examples is alleged wrongful conduct by one person that causes injury to another. Such wrongful conduct is covered by the law of **torts** (the word *tort* is French for "wrong").

Tort law covers a wide variety of injuries. Society recognizes an interest in personal physical safety, and tort law provides remedies for acts that cause physical injury or that interfere with physical security and freedom of movement. Society recognizes an interest in protecting personal property, and tort law provides remedies for acts that cause destruction or damage to property. Society also recognizes an interest in protecting certain intangible interests, such as personal privacy, family relations, reputation, and dignity, and tort law provides remedies for invasion of these *protected interests*.

Certain torts normally occur only in the business context. The important area of business torts will be treated in Chapter 13. In this chapter, we discuss torts that can occur in any context, including the business environment. In fact, as you will see in later chapters of this book, many of the lawsuits brought by or against business firms are based on the tort theories discussed in this chapter.

SECTION 1

THE BASIS OF TORT LAW

Two notions serve as the basis of all torts: wrongs and compensation. Tort law recognizes that some acts are wrong because they cause injuries to others. Of course, a tort is not the only type of wrong that exists in the law. Crimes also involve wrongs, as do breaches of contract.

TORTS AND CRIMES COMPARED

As discussed in Chapter 1, a crime is an act so reprehensible that it is considered a wrong against the state or against society as a whole, as well as against the individual victim. Therefore, the *state* prosecutes a person accused of committing a criminal act. In contrast, a tort action is a *civil* action in which one person brings a personal suit against another to obtain compensation (money damages) or other relief for the harm suffered.

Some torts, such as assault and battery (to be discussed shortly), provide a basis for a criminal prosecution as well as a tort action. For example, Jonas is walking down the street, minding his own business, when suddenly a person attacks him. In the ensuing struggle, the attacker stabs Jonas several times, seriously injuring him. A police officer restrains and arrests the wrongdoer. In this situation, the attacker may be subject both to criminal prosecution by the state and to a tort lawsuit brought by Jonas. Exhibit 12–1 illustrates how the same wrongful act can result in both a civil (tort) action and a criminal action against the wrongdoer.

TORTS AND BREACHES OF CONTRACT COMPARED

If a party breaches a contract, the other party may suffer harmful consequences from the breach. Contract actions differ from tort actions, however,

EXHIBIT 12–1 ■ TORT LAWSUIT AND CRIMINAL PROSECUTION FOR THE SAME ACT

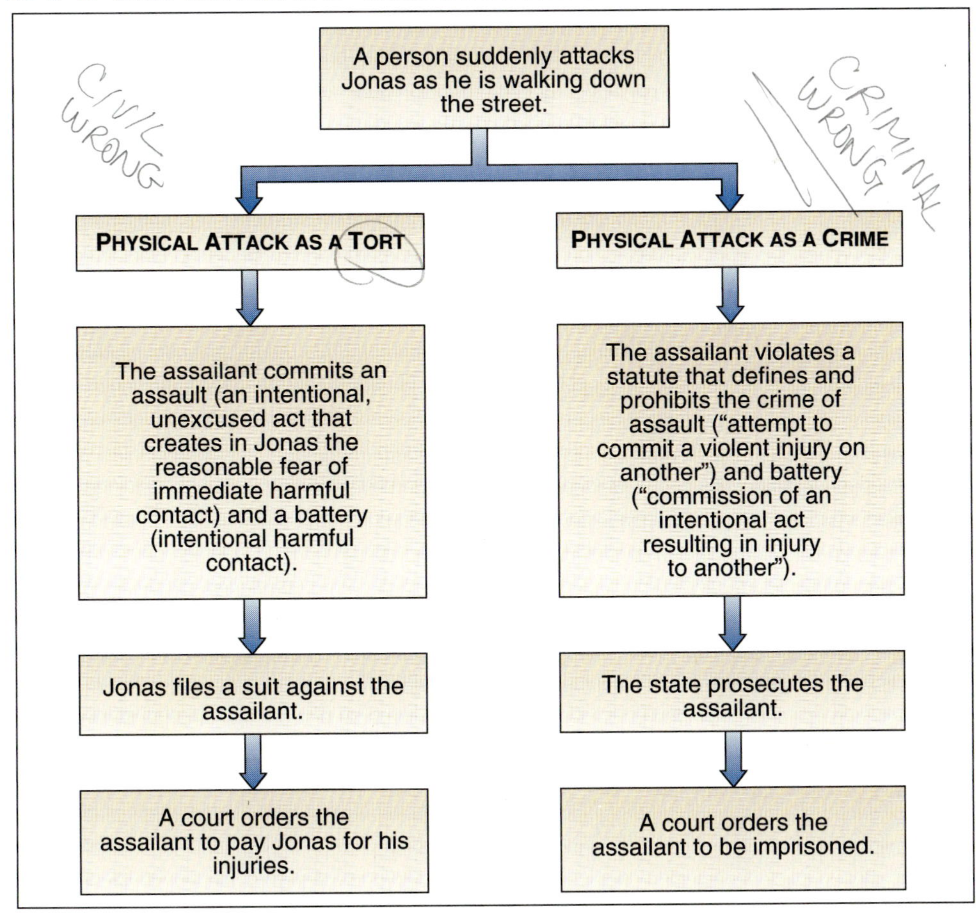

in that a breach of contract violates *an obligation created by the parties themselves.* In contrast, a tort involves a violation of *a duty imposed by law.*

Because of the different purposes and functions of contract and tort law, *punitive damages* (damages designed to punish the wrongdoer and deter others from similar actions—discussed later in this chapter) may be awarded in tort cases but are rarely granted under contract law. Note that a breach of contract may also involve a tort, however. For example, a professional (such as a physician, lawyer, or accountant) who fails to perform his or her duties properly may be sued both for breach of contract and the tort of negligence (negligence is discussed later in this chapter).

SECTION 2 INTENTIONAL TORTS AGAINST PERSONS

An **intentional tort,** as the term implies, requires *intent.* The **tortfeasor** (the one committing the tort) must intend to commit an act, the consequences of which interfere with the personal or business interests of another in a way not permitted by law. An evil or harmful motive is not required—in fact, the actor may even have a beneficial motive for committing what turns out to be a tortious act. In tort law, intent only means that the actor intended the consequences of his or her act or knew with substantial certainty that certain consequences would result from the act. The law generally assumes that individuals intend the *normal* consequences of their actions. Thus, forcefully pushing another—even if done in jest and without any evil motive—is an intentional tort (if injury results), because the object of a strong push can ordinarily be expected to go flying.

Intentional torts against persons include assault and battery, false imprisonment, infliction of emotional distress, defamation, invasion of the right to privacy, and misrepresentation. We discuss these torts in the following subsections.

ASSAULT AND BATTERY

Any intentional, unexcused act that creates in another person a reasonable apprehension or fear of immediate harmful or offensive contact is an **assault.** Note that apprehension is not the same as fear. If a contact is such that a reasonable person would want to avoid it, and if there is a reasonable basis for believing that the contact will occur, then the plaintiff suffers apprehension whether or not he or she is afraid. The interest protected by tort law concerning assault is the freedom from having to expect harmful or offensive contact. The arousal of apprehension is enough to justify compensation.

The *completion* of the act that caused the apprehension, if it results in harm to the plaintiff, is a **battery,** which is defined as an unexcused and harmful or offensive physical contact *intentionally* performed. For example, Ivan threatens Jean with a gun, then shoots her. The pointing of the gun at Jean is an assault; the firing of the gun (if the bullet hits Jean) is a battery. The interest protected by tort law concerning battery is the right to personal security and safety.

A battery can be harmful, or it can be merely offensive (such as an unwelcome kiss or smoke intentionally blown in one's face). The contact can involve any part of the body or anything attached to it—for example, a hat or other item of clothing, a purse, or a chair or an automobile in which one is sitting. Whether the contact is offensive or not is determined by the *reasonable person* standard.[1] The contact can be made by the defendant or by some force the defendant sets in motion—for example, a rock thrown, food poisoned, or a stick swung.

COMPENSATION If the plaintiff shows that there was contact, and the jury agrees that the contact was offensive, the plaintiff has a right to compensation. There is no need to show that the defendant acted out of malice; the person could just have been joking or playing around. The underlying motive does not matter, only the intent to bring about the harmful or offensive contact to the plaintiff. In fact, proving a motive is never necessary. A plaintiff may be compensated for the emotional harm or loss of reputation resulting from a battery, as well as for physical harm.

DEFENSES TO ASSAULT AND BATTERY A number of legally recognized defenses can be raised by a defendant who is sued for assault, battery, or both:

1. *Consent.* When a person consents to the act that damages him or her, there is generally no liability for the damage done.

1. The reasonable person standard is an objective test of how a reasonable person would have acted under the same circumstances. See the subsection entitled "The Duty of Care and Its Breach" later in this chapter.

2. *Self-defense.* An individual who is defending his or her life or physical well-being can claim self-defense. In a situation of either *real* or *apparent* danger, a person may normally use whatever force is *reasonably* necessary to prevent harmful contact.
3. *Defense of others.* An individual can act in a reasonable manner to protect others who are in real or apparent danger.
4. *Defense of property.* Reasonable force may be used in attempting to remove intruders from one's home, although force that is likely to cause death or great bodily injury normally cannot be used just to protect property.

FALSE IMPRISONMENT

False imprisonment is defined as the intentional confinement or restraint of another person's activities without justification. It involves interference with the freedom to move without restraint. The confinement can be accomplished through the use of physical barriers, physical restraint, or threats of physical force. Moral pressure does not constitute false imprisonment. Furthermore, it is essential that the person being restrained not comply with the restraint willingly. In other words, the person being restrained must not agree to the restraint.

Businesspersons are often confronted with suits for false imprisonment after they have attempted to confine a suspected shoplifter for questioning. Under the privilege to detain granted to merchants in some states, a merchant can use the defense of *probable cause* to justify delaying a suspected shoplifter. Probable cause exists when the evidence to support the belief that a person is guilty outweighs the evidence against that belief. The detention, however, must be conducted in a *reasonable* manner and for only a *reasonable* length of time.

INTENTIONAL INFLICTION OF EMOTIONAL DISTRESS

The tort of *intentional infliction of emotional distress* can be defined as an intentional act that amounts to extreme and outrageous conduct resulting in severe emotional distress to another.[2] The tort is also referred to as the *tort of outrage.* For example, a prankster telephones an individual and says that the individual's spouse has just been in a horrible accident. As a result, the individual suffers intense mental pain or anxiety. The caller's behavior is deemed to be extreme and outrageous conduct that exceeds the bounds of decency accepted by society and is therefore **actionable** (capable of serving as the ground for a lawsuit).

As the intentional infliction of emotional distress is a relatively new tort, it poses some problems. One major problem is that emotional distress claims must be subject to some limitation, or they could flood the courts with lawsuits. A society in which individuals are rewarded if they are unable to endure the normal emotional stresses of day-to-day living is obviously undesirable. Therefore, the law usually focuses on the nature of the acts that come under this tort. Indignity or annoyance alone is usually not enough to support a lawsuit based on intentional infliction of emotional distress.

Many times, however, repeated annoyances (such as those experienced by a person who is being stalked), coupled with threats, are enough. In a business context, for example, the repeated use of extreme methods to collect a delinquent account may be actionable. Also, an event causing an unusually severe emotional reaction, such as the extreme distress of a woman incorrectly informed that her husband and two sons have been killed, may be actionable. (Some courts recognize *negligent* infliction of emotional distress.) Because it is difficult to prove the existence of emotional suffering, a court may require that the emotional distress be evidenced by some physical symptom or illness or some emotional disturbance that can be documented by a psychiatric consultant or other medical professional.

DEFAMATION

As discussed in Chapter 5, the freedom of speech guaranteed by the First Amendment is not absolute. In interpreting the First Amendment, the courts must balance the vital guarantee of free speech against other pervasive and strong social interests—including society's interest in preventing and redressing attacks on reputation.

Defamation of character involves wrongfully hurting a person's good reputation by anything published or spoken. The law imposes a general duty on all persons to refrain from making false, defamatory statements of fact about others. Breaching this duty orally involves the tort of **slander**; breaching it in writing

2. *Restatement (Second) of Torts,* Section 46, Comment d. The *Restatement (Second) of Torts* is a compilation of the common law of torts by the American Law Institute.

involves the tort of **libel.** The tort of defamation also arises when a false statement of fact is made about a person's product, business, or title to property. We deal with these torts in the following chapter.

THE PUBLICATION REQUIREMENT The basis of the tort of defamation is the publication of a statement or statements that hold an individual up to contempt, ridicule, or hatred. *Publication* here means that the defamatory statements are communicated to persons other than the defamed party. If Thompson writes Andrews a private letter falsely accusing him of embezzling funds, the action does not constitute libel. If Peters falsely states that Gordon is dishonest and incompetent when no one else is around, the action does not constitute slander. In neither case was the message communicated to a third party.

The courts have generally held that even dictating a letter to a secretary constitutes publication, although the publication may be privileged (a concept that will be explained shortly). Moreover, if a third party overhears defamatory statements by chance, the courts usually hold that this also constitutes publication. Defamatory statements made via the Internet are actionable as well. Note also that any individual who repeats (republishes) defamatory statements is liable even if that person reveals the source of the statements.

The following case raises an interesting issue concerning the publication requirement: Can a plaintiff establish the publication of defamatory statements without the testimony of a third person regarding what he or she heard or understood?

CASE 12.1 Food Lion, Inc. v. Melton

Supreme Court of Virginia, 1995. 250 Va. 144, 458 S.E.2d 580.

BACKGROUND AND FACTS *In April 1991, after shopping at a Food Lion grocery store, sixty-eight-year-old Christine Melton was walking out of the store when a Food Lion security guard stopped her in the parking lot. The guard accused her of leaving with meat belonging to the store in her purse. According to Melton, the guard questioned her repeatedly, loudly, and in an accusatory manner, and "there were people stopping to listen and see what was going on." Finally, Melton allowed the guard to search her purse. No meat was found. Melton filed a suit against Food Lion in a Virginia state court, in part on the ground of defamation. Food Lion in effect denied that the incident had ever happened. Melton was not able to identify any of the people who had "stopped to listen" and could not offer proof as to what they had heard. On the defamation claim, the court entered a judgment in favor of Food Lion, and Melton appealed to the Virginia Supreme Court.*

IN THE LANGUAGE OF THE COURT

KEENAN, Justice.

* * * *

* * * [T]o establish *prima facie* evidence of publication, a plaintiff is not required to present testimony from a third party regarding what that person heard and understood, or to identify the person to whom the defamatory words were published. Instead, a plaintiff may prove publication of defamatory remarks by * * * evidence that the remarks were heard by a third party who understood these remarks as referring to the plaintiff in a defamatory sense.

* * * Melton testified that the security guard stood very close to her and made his accusations in a "very loud tone" of voice * * * . She also testified that, during this time, people were close by, and they stopped "to listen and see what was going on." We hold that, when considered in the light most favorable to Melton, this evidence was sufficient to permit a reasonable inference that the accuser's words were heard and understood by a third party as referring to Melton and as imputing the commission of a crime.

DECISION AND REMEDY *The Virginia Supreme Court held that a plaintiff does not need to present testimony from any third person, or even to identify any such person, to prove publication of defamatory remarks. The court reversed the judgment of the lower court and remanded the case.*

DAMAGES FOR DEFAMATION Traditionally, under the common law, "malice" (wrongful intent stemming from hatred, ill will, a desire for revenge, or other motive) was a required element for damages to be recovered in a defamation action. Over time, the courts began to assume that any statements that were defamatory on their face implied malice. Today, the general rule is that once a defendant's liability for defamation is established, "general damages" are presumed as a matter of law. General damages are designed to compensate the plaintiff for general harms such as disgrace or dishonor in the eyes of the community, humiliation, injured reputation, emotional distress, and so on—harms that are difficult to measure. In other words, to recover damages in a defamation case, the plaintiff need not prove that he or she was actually injured in any way from the libelous statement.

Under tort law, slander is treated differently than libel with respect to damages. In a case alleging slander, the plaintiff must prove "special damages" to establish the defendant's liability. The plaintiff must show that the slanderous statement caused the plaintiff to suffer actual economic or monetary losses. Unless this initial hurdle of proving special damages is overcome, a plaintiff alleging slander normally cannot go forward with the suit and recover any damages. This requirement is imposed in cases involving slander because slanderous statements have a transient quality. In contrast, a libelous (written) statement has the quality of permanence, can be circulated more widely, and usually results from some degree of deliberation on the part of the author.

Exceptions to the burden of proving special damages in cases alleging slander are made for certain types of slanderous statements. If a false statement constitutes "slander *per se*," no proof of special damages is required for it to be actionable. The following four types of utterances are considered to be slander *per se:*

1. A statement that another has a loathsome communicable disease.
2. A statement that another has committed improprieties while engaging in a profession or trade.
3. A statement that another has committed or has been imprisoned for a serious crime.
4. A statement that an unmarried woman is unchaste.

DEFENSES TO DEFAMATION Truth is normally an absolute defense against a defamation charge. In other words, if a defendant in a defamation case can prove that the allegedly defamatory statement of fact was actually true, no tort has been committed. Other defenses to defamation may exist if the speech is privileged or concerns a public figure.

Privileged Speech. In some circumstances, a person will not be liable for defamatory statements because he or she enjoys a **privilege,** or immunity. Privileged communications are of two types: absolute and qualified. Only in limited cases, such as in judicial and legislative proceedings, is *absolute* privilege granted. For example, statements made by attorneys and judges during a trial are absolutely privileged. So are statements made by legislators during congressional floor debate, even if the legislators make such statements maliciously—that is, knowing them to be untrue. An absolute privilege is granted in these situations because judicial and legislative personnel deal with matters that are so much in the public interest that the parties involved should be able to speak out fully and freely and without restriction.

In other situations, a person will not be liable for defamatory statements because he or she has a *qualified*, or conditional, privilege. For example, statements made in recommendation letters or in written evaluations of employees are qualifiedly privileged. Generally, if the communicated statements are made in good faith and the publication is limited to those who have a legitimate interest in the communication, the statements fall within the area of qualified privilege. The concept of conditional privilege rests on the common law assumption that in some situations, the right to know or speak is equal in importance to the right not to be defamed. If a communication is conditionally privileged, to recover damages, the plaintiff must show that the privilege was abused.

Public Figures. In general, false and defamatory statements that are made about **public figures** (public officials who exercise substantial governmental power and any persons in the public limelight) and are published in the press are privileged if they are made without "actual malice." To be made with **actual malice,** a statement must be made *with either knowledge of falsity or a reckless disregard of the truth.*[3]

Statements made about public figures, especially when they are made via a public medium, are usually related to matters of general public interest; they are made about people who substantially affect all of us. Furthermore, public figures generally have some access to a public medium for answering disparaging falsehoods about themselves; private individuals do not. For these reasons, public figures have a greater burden of proof in defamation cases (they must prove actual malice) than do private individuals.

ONLINE DEFAMATION As mentioned, any defamatory statement that is communicated to a third party is considered "published" under defamation law and thus actionable. What about defamatory statements made via the Internet in a "chat" group? Suppose, for example, that two persons are exchanging thoughts online. One of them falsely accuses her boss of sexual misconduct. Does this statement constitute defamation? Yes. This is because what may seem like a private online "conversation" between just two persons is, in fact, a very public exchange, accessible to millions of people. The fact that those people are unseen at the time a defamatory statement is made makes no difference. The defamed person (the boss, in this example) could suffer serious harm from the statement—loss of reputation and perhaps even the loss of a job. The person who made the defamatory statement could be sued in tort for damages.

As in other areas, it is difficult to adapt traditional laws to communications in cyberspace because of the unique qualities of the online medium. In the area of defamation, for example, does a defamatory statement in an online communication constitute libel or slander? Generally, legal authorities tend to assume that such a statement constitutes libel. This is because computerized text and images that are "published" online, like printed written publications, have a quality of permanence—they can be stored electronically, transmitted, copied, and so on. Statements made in online conversations held in "chat boxes" or "virtual rooms," however, might be considered slander, because of the spontaneous and transient nature of the speech and because those engaging in such conversations would likely regard them as being the equivalent of spoken words.

If an online statement is regarded as slander, then, as discussed earlier, special damages must be proved for the statement to be actionable—unless the statement qualifies as slander *per se.* Accusing a seller of motorbikes of being a "sleazy jerk who sells stolen motorbikes" would be slander *per se* because essentially it is a statement that another has committed improprieties while engaging in a profession or trade. Merely accusing a seller of motorbikes of being a "sleazy jerk," however, would probably not even qualify as slander.

INVASION OF THE RIGHT TO PRIVACY

A person has a right to solitude and freedom from prying public eyes—in other words, to privacy. As mentioned in Chapter 5, the courts have held that certain amendments to the U.S. Constitution imply a right to privacy. Some state constitutions explicitly provide for privacy rights. Additionally, a number of federal and state statutes have been enacted to protect individual privacy rights in specific areas. Tort law also protects these rights through the tort of *invasion of privacy.* Four acts qualify as invasion of privacy:

1. *The use of a person's name, picture, or other likeness for commercial purposes without permission.* For example, using without permission someone's picture to advertise a product or someone's name to enhance a company's reputation invades the person's privacy. (This tort, which is usually referred to as the tort of *appropriation,* will be examined in the next chapter.)
2. *Intrusion on an individual's affairs or seclusion.* For example, invading someone's home or illegally searching someone's briefcase is an invasion of privacy. This tort has been held to extend to eavesdropping by wiretap, unauthorized scanning of a bank account, compulsory blood testing, and window peeping.
3. *Publication of information that places a person in a false light.* This could be a story attributing to a person ideas not held or actions not taken by that person. (The publication of such a story could involve the tort of defamation as well.)

3. *New York Times Co. v. Sullivan,* 376 U.S. 254, 84 S.Ct. 710, 11 L.Ed.2d 686 (1964).

4. *Public disclosure of private facts about an individual that an ordinary person would find objectionable.* A newspaper account of a private citizen's sex life or financial affairs could be an actionable invasion of privacy.

FRAUDULENT MISREPRESENTATION

A misrepresentation leads another to believe in a condition that is different from the condition that actually exists. This is often accomplished through a false or an incorrect statement. Misrepresentations may be innocently made by someone who is unaware of the facts. The tort of **fraudulent misrepresentation,** or **fraud,** however, involves intentional deceit for personal gain. The tort includes several elements:

1. A misrepresentation of material facts or conditions with knowledge that they are false or with reckless disregard for the truth.
2. An intent to induce another to rely on the misrepresentation.
3. A justifiable reliance on the misrepresentation by the deceived party.
4. Damages suffered as a result of that reliance.
5. A causal connection between the misrepresentation and the injury suffered.

For fraud to occur, more than mere **puffery,** or *seller's talk,* must be involved. Fraud exists only when a person represents as a fact something he or she knows is untrue. For example, it is fraud to claim that the roof of a building does not leak when one knows it does. Facts are objectively ascertainable, whereas seller's talk is not. "I am the best architect in town" is seller's talk. The speaker is not trying to represent something as fact, because the term *best* is a subjective, not an objective, term.

Normally, the tort of fraudulent misrepresentation only occurs when there is reliance on a *statement of fact.* Sometimes, however, reliance on a *statement of opinion* may involve the tort of fraudulent misrepresentation if the individual making the statement of opinion has a superior knowledge of the subject matter. For example, when a lawyer makes a statement of opinion about the law, a court would construe reliance on such a statement to be equivalent to reliance on a statement of fact.

A growing problem in the online era is fraudulent misrepresentation in Internet transactions, such as those made by purported investment brokers who induce people to invest in enterprises that do not exist. Recovering damages for fraud conducted via the Internet is often impossible because the perpetrator's identity is difficult to discover. Fraudulent and nonfraudulent misrepresentation was already discussed in Chapter 9, in the context of contract law.

damage recovery may be greater

SECTION 3
INTENTIONAL TORTS AGAINST PROPERTY

Intentional torts against property include trespass to land, trespass to personal property, and conversion. These torts are wrongful actions that interfere with individuals' legally recognized rights with regard to their land or personal property. The law distinguishes real property from personal property (see Chapter 48). *Real property* is land and things permanently attached to the land. *Personal property* consists of all other items, which are basically movable. Thus, a house and lot are real property, whereas the furniture inside a house is personal property. Money and securities are also personal property.

TRESPASS TO LAND

The tort of **trespass to land** occurs any time a person, without permission, enters onto, above, or below the surface of land that is owned by another; causes anything to enter onto the land; or remains on the land or permits anything to remain on it. Note that actual harm to the land is not an essential element of this tort, because the tort is designed to protect the right of an owner to exclusive possession. Common types of trespass to land include walking or driving on the land; shooting a gun over the land; throwing rocks or spraying water on a building that belongs to someone else; building a dam across a river, thus causing water to back up on someone else's land; and placing part of one's building on an adjoining landowner's property.

In the past, the right to land gave exclusive possession of a space that extended from "the center of the earth to the heavens," but this rule has been relaxed. Today, reasonable intrusions are permitted. Thus, aircraft can normally fly over privately owned land. Society's interest in air transportation preempts the individual's interest in the airspace.

TRESPASS CRITERIA, RIGHTS, AND DUTIES

Before a person can be a trespasser, the real property

owner (or other person in actual and exclusive possession of the property) must establish that person as a trespasser. For example, "posted" trespass signs expressly establish as a trespasser a person who ignores these signs and enters onto the property. A guest in your home is not a trespasser—unless he or she has been asked to leave but refuses. Any person who enters onto your property to commit an illegal act (such as a thief entering a lumberyard at night to steal lumber) is established impliedly as a trespasser, without posted signs.

At common law, a trespasser is liable for damages caused to the property and generally cannot hold the owner liable for injuries that the trespasser sustains on the premises. This common law rule is being abandoned in many jurisdictions in favor of a "reasonable duty" rule that varies depending on the status of the parties. For example, a landowner may have a duty to post a notice that the property is patrolled by guard dogs. Also, under the "attractive nuisance" doctrine, a landowner may be held liable for injuries sustained by young children on the landowner's property if the children were attracted to the premises by some object, such as a swimming pool or an abandoned building. Finally, an owner can remove a trespasser from the premises—or detain a trespasser on the premises for a reasonable time—through the use of reasonable force without being liable for assault and battery or false imprisonment.

DEFENSES AGAINST TRESPASS TO LAND

Trespass to land involves wrongful interference with another person's real property rights. If it can be shown that the trespass was warranted, however, as when a trespasser enters to assist someone in danger, a defense exists. Another defense is to show that the purported owner did not actually have the right to possess the land in question.

TRESPASS TO PERSONAL PROPERTY

Whenever any individual, without consent, harms the personal property of another or otherwise interferes with the personal property owner's right to exclusive possession and enjoyment of that property, **trespass to personal property**—also called *trespass to personalty*—occurs. Trespass to personal property involves intentional meddling. If Kelly takes Ryan's business law book as a practical joke and hides it so that Ryan is unable to find it for several days prior to a final examination, Kelly has engaged in a trespass to personal property.

If it can be shown that trespass to personal property was warranted, then a complete defense exists. Most states, for example, allow automobile repair shops to hold a customer's car (under what is called an *artisan's lien*, discussed in Chapter 16) when the customer refuses to pay for repairs already completed.

CONVERSION

Conversion is defined as any act that deprives an owner of personal property without that owner's permission and without just cause and that places the property in the service of the trespasser or other person. Conversion is the civil side of crimes related to theft. A store clerk who steals merchandise from the store commits a crime and engages in the tort of conversion at the same time. When conversion occurs, the lesser offense of trespass to personal property usually occurs as well. If the initial taking of the property was a trespass, retention of that property is conversion. If the initial taking of the property was permitted by the owner or for some other reason is not a trespass, failure to return it may still be conversion.

Even if a person mistakenly believed that he or she was entitled to the goods, a tort of conversion may still have occurred. In other words, good intentions are not a defense against conversion; in fact, conversion can be an entirely innocent act. Someone who buys stolen goods, for example, is guilty of conversion even if he or she did not know the goods were stolen.

A successful defense against the charge of conversion is that the purported owner does not in fact own the property or does not have a right to possess it that is superior to the right of the holder. Necessity is another possible defense against conversion. If Abrams takes Mendoza's cat, Abrams is guilty of conversion. If Mendoza sues Abrams, Abrams must return the cat or pay damages. If, however, the cat had rabies and Abrams took the cat to protect the public, Abrams has a valid defense—necessity.

SECTION 4
NEGLIGENCE

In contrast to intentional torts, in torts involving **negligence**, the tortfeasor neither wishes to bring about the consequences of the act nor believes that they will occur. The actor's conduct merely creates a *risk* of such consequences. If no risk is created, there is no negligence. Moreover, the risk must be foresee-

CONCEPT SUMMARY 12.1 Intentional Torts

CATEGORY	NAME OF TORT
Intentional Torts against Persons	1. *Assault and battery*—Any unexcused and intentional act that causes another person to be apprehensive of immediate harm is an assault. An assault resulting in physical contact is battery. 2. *False imprisonment*—An intentional confinement or restraint of another person's movement without justification. 3. *Intentional infliction of emotional distress*—An intentional act that amounts to extreme and outrageous conduct resulting in severe emotional distress to another. 4. *Defamation (libel or slander)*—A false statement of fact, not made under privilege, that is communicated to a third person and that causes damage to a person's reputation. For public figures, the plaintiff must also prove that the statement was made with actual malice. 5. *Invasion of privacy*—Publishing or otherwise making known or using information relating to a person's private life and affairs, with which the public had no legitimate concern, without that person's permission or approval. 6. *Fraudulent misrepresentation (fraud)*—A false representation made by one party, through misstatement of facts or through conduct, with the intention of deceiving another and on which the other reasonably relies to his or her detriment.
Intentional Torts against Property	1. *Trespass to land*—The invasion of another's real property without consent or privilege. Specific rights and duties apply once a person is expressly or impliedly established as a trespasser. 2. *Trespass to personal property*—The intentional interference with an owner's right to use, possess, or enjoy his or her personal property without the owner's consent. 3. *Conversion*—The wrongful taking and use of another person's personal property for the benefit of the tortfeasor or another.

able; that is, it must be such that a reasonable person engaging in the same activity would anticipate the risk and guard against it. In determining what is reasonable conduct, courts consider the nature of the possible harm. A very slight risk of a dangerous explosion might be unreasonable, whereas a distinct possibility of someone's burning his or her fingers on a stove might be reasonable.

To succeed in a negligence action, the plaintiff must prove the following:

1. That the defendant owed a duty of care to the plaintiff.
2. That the defendant breached that duty.
3. That the plaintiff suffered a legally recognizable injury.
4. That the defendant's breach caused the plaintiff's injury.

We discuss here each of these four elements of negligence.

THE DUTY OF CARE AND ITS BREACH

Central to the tort of negligence is the concept of a **duty of care.** This concept arises from the notion that if we are to live in society with other people, some actions can be tolerated and some cannot; some actions are right and some are wrong; and some actions are reasonable and some are not. The basic principle underlying the duty of care is that people are free to act as they please so long as their actions do not infringe on the interests of others.

Tort law defines and measures the duty of care by the **reasonable person standard.** In determining whether a duty of care has been breached, for example, the courts ask how a reasonable person would have acted in the same circumstances. The reasonable person standard is said to be (though in an absolute sense it cannot be) objective. It is not necessarily how a particular person would act. It is society's judgment on how an ordinarily prudent person should act. If the so-called reasonable person existed, he or she would be careful, conscientious, prudent, even tempered, and honest. That individuals are required to exercise a reasonable standard of care in their activities is a pervasive concept in business law, and many of the issues dealt with in subsequent chapters of this text have to do with this duty.

In negligence cases, the degree of care to be exercised varies, depending on the defendant's occupation or profession, his or her relationship with the plaintiff, and other factors. Generally, whether an action constitutes a breach of the duty of care is determined on a case-by-case basis. The outcome depends on how the court judge (or jury, if it is a jury trial) decides a reasonable person in the position of the defendant would act in the particular circumstances of the case. In the following subsections, we examine the degree of care typically expected of landowners and professionals.

DUTY OF LANDOWNERS Landowners are expected to exercise reasonable care to protect from harm individuals coming onto their property. As mentioned earlier in this chapter, in some jurisdictions, landowners are held to have a duty to protect even trespassers against certain risks. Landowners who rent or lease premises to tenants are expected to exercise reasonable care to ensure that the tenants and their guests are not harmed in common areas, such as stairways, entryways, and laundry rooms.

Retailers and other firms that explicitly or implicitly invite persons to come onto their premises are usually charged with a duty to exercise reasonable care to protect these **business invitees.** For example, if you entered a supermarket, slipped on a wet floor, and sustained injuries as a result, the owner of the supermarket would be liable for damages if, when you slipped, there was no sign warning that the floor was wet. A court would hold that the business owner was negligent because the owner failed to exercise a reasonable degree of care in protecting the store's customers against foreseeable risks about which the owner knew or *should have known*. That a patron might slip on the wet floor and be injured as a result was a foreseeable risk, and the owner should have taken care to avoid this risk or warn the customer of it.[4]

Some risks, of course, are so obvious that an owner need not warn of them. For example, a business owner does not need to warn customers to open a door before attempting to walk through it. Other risks, however, even though they may seem obvious to a business owner, may not be so in the eyes of another, such as a child. For example, a hardware store owner may not think it is necessary to warn customers that, if climbed, a stepladder leaning against the back wall of the store could fall down and harm them. It is possible, though, that a child could tip the ladder over while climbing it and be hurt as a result.

In the following case, the court has to decide whether a restaurant owner should be held liable for a customer's injuries on the premises.

4. A business owner can warn of a risk in a number of ways—for example, by placing a sign, traffic cone, sawhorse, board, or the like near a hole in the business's parking lot. See *Hartman v. Walkertown Shopping Center, Inc.*, 113 N.C.App. 632, 439 S.E.2d 787 (1994).

CASE 12.2 Bray v. Kate

Supreme Court of Nebraska, 1990. 235 Neb. 315, 454 N.W.2d 698.

BACKGROUND AND FACTS *Lowell Bray was about to open the door of a restaurant owned by Kate, Inc., when he slipped on some ice and fell, injuring his shoulder. He stated that he could not see the ice but felt it when he slipped. Bray sued Kate, Inc., for damages, alleging that Kate, Inc., by failing to remove the ice from in front of its restaurant door, had breached its duty of care to Bray and was thus negligent. The trial court held for Bray, and Kate, Inc., appealed.*

WHITE, Justice.

* * * *

Summarized, defendant [Kate, Inc.] contends on appeal that the trial court erred * * * because the evidence showed that, as a matter of law, defendant owed no duty to plaintiff. * * *

IN THE LANGUAGE OF THE COURT

In its brief, defendant urges this court to adopt a possessor's duty of care other than the duty which is now required under Nebraska law. We decline to do so. * * *

In view of this court's decisions [in previous cases], the correct statement of Nebraska law is: A possessor of land is subject to liability for injury caused to a business invitee by a condition on the land if (1) the possessor defendant either created the condition, knew of the condition, or by the exercise of reasonable care would have discovered the condition; (2) the defendant should have realized the condition involved an unreasonable risk of harm to a business invitee; (3) the defendant should have expected that a business invitee such as the plaintiff, either (a) would not discover or realize the danger, or (b) would fail to protect himself or herself against the danger; (4) the defendant failed to use reasonable care to protect the plaintiff invitee against the danger; and (5) the condition was a proximate cause of damage to the plaintiff.

* * * *

As to the existence of a duty to the invitee * * * , a clear factual issue was presented and resolved by the jury verdict.

DECISION AND REMEDY

The Supreme Court of Nebraska affirmed the lower court's judgment for Bray. Kate, Inc., owed a duty to its patron, Bray, and because it had breached that duty, it was liable to Bray for damages.

ETHICAL CONSIDERATIONS

It is not uncommon for a court to hold a business owner liable when a customer is harmed by what may seem to be an obvious risk. To a certain extent, such decisions rest on the public policy that business owners are in a better position both to protect against the risks and to bear the costs associated with customers' injuries. Many, however, question whether it is fair to hold businesspersons responsible in these situations.

DUTY OF PROFESSIONALS If an individual has knowledge, skill, or intelligence superior to that of an ordinary person, the individual's conduct must be consistent with that status. Professionals—including doctors, dentists, psychiatrists, architects, engineers, accountants, and lawyers, among others—are required to have a standard minimum level of special knowledge and ability. Therefore, in determining what constitutes reasonable care in the case of professionals, the court takes their training and expertise into account. In other words, an accountant cannot defend against a lawsuit for negligence by stating, "But I was not familiar with that general principle of accounting."

If a professional violates his or her duty of care toward a client, the client may bring a **malpractice** suit against the professional. For example, a patient might sue a physician for *medical malpractice*. A client might sue an attorney for *legal malpractice*.

NO DUTY TO RESCUE Although the law requires individuals to act reasonably and responsibly in their relations with others, if a person fails to come to the aid of a stranger in peril, that person will not be considered negligent under tort law. For example, assume that you are walking down a city street and notice that a pedestrian is about to step directly in front of an oncoming bus. You realize that the person has not seen the bus and is unaware of the danger. Do you have a legal duty to warn that individual? No. Although most people would probably concede that in this situation, the observer has an *ethical* duty to warn the other, tort law does not impose a general duty to rescue others in peril. Duties may be imposed in regard to certain types of peril, however. For example, most states require a motorist involved in an automobile accident to stop and render aid. Failure to do so is both a tort and a crime.

When discussing the distinction between legal and ethical duties in Chapter 2, we pointed out that ethical duties exist beyond the scope of the law. In regard to the duty to rescue, the distinction is clear. Although the law might not require a passerby to save a drowning toddler in a wading pool, society expects that people will aid others who are in danger and cannot help themselves.

THE INJURY REQUIREMENT AND DAMAGES

To recover damages (receive compensation), the plaintiff in a tort lawsuit must prove that he or she suffered a *legally recognizable* injury. That is, the plaintiff must have suffered some loss, harm, wrong, or invasion of a protected interest. This is true in lawsuits for intentional torts as well as lawsuits for negligence. Essentially, the purpose of tort law is to compensate for legally recognized injuries resulting from wrongful acts. If no harm or injury results from a given negligent action, there is nothing to compensate—and no tort exists. For example, if you carelessly bump into a passerby, who stumbles and falls as a result, you may be liable in tort if the passerby is injured in the fall. If the person is unharmed, however, there normally can be no suit for damages, because no injury was suffered. Although the passerby might be angry and suffer emotional distress, few courts recognize negligently inflicted emotional distress as a tort unless it results in some physical disturbance or dysfunction.

As already mentioned, the purpose of tort law is not to punish people for tortious acts but to compensate the injured parties for damages suffered. **Compensatory damages** are intended to compensate, or reimburse, a plaintiff for actual losses—to make the plaintiff whole. Occasionally, however, punitive damages are also awarded in tort lawsuits. **Punitive damages,** or *exemplary damages,* are intended to punish the wrongdoer and deter others from similar wrongdoing. Punitive damages are rarely given in lawsuits for ordinary negligence but may be awarded in suits involving *gross negligence,* which can be defined as an intentional failure to perform a manifest duty in reckless disregard of the consequences of such a failure for the life or property of another.

In recent years, tort litigation has often resulted in high punitive damages awards. In some cases, these awards have been hundreds of times higher than the compensatory damages awarded to the plaintiffs. Some defendants have claimed that such awards violate the Eighth Amendment's prohibition against excessive fines or the defendants' constitutional rights to due process. The constitutionality of a high punitive damages award is at issue in the following case.

CASE 12.3 BMW of North America, Inc. v. Gore

Supreme Court of the United States, 1996. ___ U.S. ___, 116 S.Ct. 1589, 134 L.Ed.2d 809.

BACKGROUND AND FACTS *After Dr. Ira Gore bought a new BMW from an authorized dealer, he discovered that the car had been damaged by acid rain and repainted before its delivery to him. Gore filed a suit in an Alabama state court against BMW of North America, Inc., the car's distributor, and others, based on the failure to disclose the damage and repair. BMW admitted that its policy was not to tell customers of damage to new cars if the cost of repairing the damage was not more than 3 percent of the car's price. After a trial, the jury awarded Gore $4,000 in compensatory damages and $4 million in punitive damages. On appeal, the Alabama Supreme Court reduced the punitive damages award to $2 million. The defendants appealed to the United States Supreme Court, arguing that the award was grossly excessive in violation of the due process clause of the Fourteenth Amendment.*

IN THE LANGUAGE OF THE COURT

Justice *STEVENS* delivered the opinion of the Court.

* * * *

Elementary notions of fairness * * * dictate that a person receive fair notice * * * of the severity of the penalty that a State may impose. Three guideposts, each of which indicates that BMW did not receive adequate notice * * * , lead us to the conclusion that the $2 million award against BMW is grossly excessive: the degree of reprehensibility of the nondisclosure; the disparity between the harm or potential harm suffered by Dr. Gore and his punitive damages award; and the difference between this remedy and the civil penalties authorized or imposed in comparable cases. * * *

* * * *

In this case, none of the aggravating factors associated with particularly reprehensible conduct is present. * * * BMW's conduct evinced no indifference to or reckless disregard for the health and safety of others. * * *

* * * *

The $2 million in punitive damages * * * is 500 times the amount of [Gore's] actual harm * * * . [T]here is no suggestion that [he] * * * was threatened with any additional potential harm * * * .

* * * *

* * * [The] sanction imposed on BMW is substantially greater than the statutory fines * * * for similar malfeasance [misconduct].

DECISION AND REMEDY *The United States Supreme Court held that the award of $2 million in punitive damages was grossly excessive. The Court reversed the state court's ruling and remanded the case.*

CAUSATION

Another element necessary to a tort is *causation.* If a person breaches a duty of care and someone suffers injury, the wrongful activity must have caused the harm for a tort to have been committed.

CAUSATION IN FACT AND PROXIMATE CAUSE

In deciding whether the requirement of causation is met, the court must address two questions:

1. *Is there causation in fact?* Did the injury occur because of the defendant's act, or would it have occurred anyway? If an injury would not have occurred without the defendant's act, then there is causation in fact. **Causation in fact** can usually be determined by use of the *but for* test: "but for" the wrongful act, the injury would not have occurred.
2. *Was the act the proximate cause of the injury?* Theoretically, causation in fact is limitless. One could claim, for example, that "but for" the creation of the world, a particular injury would not have occurred. Thus, as a practical matter, the law has to establish limits, and it does so through the concept of proximate cause. **Proximate cause,** or legal cause, exists when the connection between an act and an injury is strong enough to justify imposing liability. Consider an example. Ackerman carelessly leaves a campfire burning. The fire not only burns down the forest but also sets off an explosion in a nearby chemical plant that spills chemicals into a river, killing all the fish for a hundred miles downstream and ruining the economy of a tourist resort. Should Ackerman be liable to the resort owners? To the tourists whose vacations were ruined? These are questions of proximate cause that a court must decide.

FORSEEABILITY Questions of proximate cause are linked to the concept of foreseeability, because it would be unfair to impose liability on a defendant unless the defendant's actions created a foreseeable risk of injury. Probably the most cited case on the concept of foreseeability as a requirement for proximate cause—and as a measure of the extent of the duty of care generally—is the *Palsgraf* case. The question before the court was as follows: Does the defendant's duty of care extend only to those who may be injured as a result of a foreseeable risk, or does it extend also to persons whose injuries could not reasonably be foreseen?

CASE 12.4 Palsgraf v. Long Island Railroad Co.

Court of Appeals of New York, 1928. 248 N.Y. 339, 162 N.E. 99.

BACKGROUND AND FACTS *The plaintiff, Palsgraf, was waiting for a train on a station platform. A man carrying a package was rushing to catch a train that was moving away from a platform across the tracks from Palsgraf. As the man attempted to jump aboard the moving train, he seemed unsteady and about to fall. A railroad guard on the car reached forward to grab him, and another guard on the platform pushed him from behind to help him board the train. In the process, the man's package, which (unknown to the railroad guards) contained fireworks, fell on the railroad tracks and exploded. There was nothing about the package to indicate its contents. The repercussions of the explosion caused*

scales at the other end of the train platform to fall on Palsgraf, causing injuries for which she sued the railroad company. At the trial, the jury found that the railroad guards had been negligent in their conduct. The railroad company appealed. The appellate court affirmed the trial court's judgment, and the railroad company appealed to New York's highest state court.

IN THE LANGUAGE OF THE COURT

CARDOZO, C. J. [Chief Justice].

* * * *

The conduct of the defendant's guard, if a wrong in its relation to the holder of the package, was not a wrong in its relation to the plaintiff, standing far away. Relatively to her it was not negligence at all. * * *

* * * *

* * * What the plaintiff must show is "a wrong" to herself; i.e., a violation of her own right, and not merely a wrong to someone else[.] * * * The risk reasonably to be perceived defines the duty to be obeyed[.] * * * Here, by concession, there was nothing in the situation to suggest to the most cautious mind that the parcel wrapped in newspaper would spread wreckage through the station. If the guard had thrown it down knowingly and willfully, he would not have threatened the plaintiff's safety, so far as appearances could warn him. His conduct would not have involved, even then, an unreasonable probability of invasion of her bodily security. Liability can be no greater where the act is inadvertent.

* * * One who seeks redress at law does not make out a cause of action by showing without more that there has been damage to his person. If the harm was not willful, he must show that the act as to him had possibilities of danger so many and apparent as to entitle him to be protected against the doing of it though the harm was unintended. * * * The victim does not sue * * * to vindicate an interest invaded in the person of another. * * * He sues for breach of a duty owing to himself.

* * * [To rule otherwise] would entail liability for any and all consequences, however novel or extraordinary.

DECISION AND REMEDY

Palsgraf's complaint was dismissed. The railroad had not been negligent toward her, because injury to her was not foreseeable. Had the owner of the fireworks been harmed, and had he filed suit, there could well have been a different result.

INTERNATIONAL CONSIDERATIONS

Differing Standards of Proximate Cause *The concept of proximate cause is common among countries of the globe, but its application differs from country to country. French law uses the phrase "adequate cause." An event breaks the chain of adequate cause if the event is both unforeseeable and irresistible. England has a "nearest cause" rule that attributes liability based on which event was nearest in time and space. Mexico bases proximate cause on the foreseeability of the harm but does not require that an event be reasonably foreseeable.*

DEFENSES TO NEGLIGENCE

The basic defenses to liability in negligence cases are (1) assumption of risk, (2) superseding intervening cause, and (3) contributory negligence or comparative negligence.

ASSUMPTION OF RISK A plaintiff who voluntarily enters into a risky situation, knowing the risk involved, will not be allowed to recover. This is the defense of **assumption of risk.** For example, a driver entering an automobile race knows there is a risk of being killed or injured in a crash. The driver has assumed the risk of injury. The requirements of this defense are (1) knowledge of the risk and (2) voluntary assumption of the risk.

The risk can be assumed by express agreement, or the assumption of risk can be implied by the plaintiff's knowledge of the risk and subsequent conduct. Of course, the plaintiff does not assume a risk different from or greater than the risk normally carried by the activity. In our example, the race driver assumes the risk of being injured in the race but not the risk that the banking in the curves of the racetrack will give way during the race because of a construction defect.

Risks are not deemed to be assumed in situations involving emergencies. Neither are they assumed when a statute protects a class of people from harm and a member of the class is injured by the harm. For example, courts have generally held that an employee cannot assume the risk of an employer's violation of safety statutes passed for the benefit of employees.

SUPERSEDING INTERVENING CAUSE An unforeseeable intervening event may break the causal connection between a wrongful act and an injury to another. If so, it acts as a *superseding cause*—that is, it relieves a defendant of liability for injuries caused by the intervening event. For example, suppose that Derrick, while riding his bicycle, negligently hits Julie, who is walking on a sidewalk. As a result of the impact, Julie falls and fractures her hip. While she is waiting for help to arrive, a small aircraft crashes nearby and explodes, and some of the fiery debris hits her, causing her to sustain severe burns. Derrick will be liable for damages caused by Julie's fractured hip, but normally he will not be liable for the wounds caused by the plane crash—because the risk of a plane crashing nearby and injuring Julie was not foreseeable.

CONTRIBUTORY AND COMPARATIVE NEGLIGENCE Traditionally, under the common law, if a plaintiff's own negligence contributed to his or her injury, the defendant could raise the defense of **contributory negligence.** Contributory negligence on the part of the plaintiff was a complete defense to liability for negligence (but not for intentional torts or suits based on strict liability, a topic that will be covered later in this chapter). Today, contributory negligence can be used as a defense in only a very few states.

In those jurisdictions that do allow the defense of contributory negligence, the *last clear chance* doctrine can excuse the effect of a plaintiff's negligence. The last clear chance doctrine allows the plaintiff to recover full damages despite his or her failure to exercise care. This rule operates when, through his or her own negligence, the plaintiff is endangered (or his or her property is endangered) by a defendant who has an opportunity to avoid causing damage but fails to take advantage of that opportunity. For example, if Murphy walks across the street against the light, and Lewis, a motorist, sees her in time to avoid hitting her but hits her anyway, Lewis (the defendant) is not permitted to use Murphy's (the plaintiff's) prior negligence as a defense. The defendant negligently missed the opportunity to avoid injuring the plaintiff.

Neither the complete defense of contributory negligence nor the last clear chance doctrine applies in states that have adopted a comparative negligence standard, as the majority of states have done. Under the doctrine of **comparative negligence,** both the plaintiff's negligence and the defendant's negligence are taken into consideration, and damages are awarded accordingly. Some jurisdictions have adopted a "pure" form of comparative negligence that allows the plaintiff to recover damages even if his or her fault is greater than that of the defendant. For example, if the plaintiff was 80 percent at fault and the defendant was 20 percent at fault, the plaintiff may recover 20 percent of his or her damages. Many states' comparative negligence statutes, however, contain a "50 percent" rule, under which the plaintiff recovers nothing if he or she was more than 50 percent at fault.

SPECIAL NEGLIGENCE DOCTRINES AND STATUTES

There are a number of special doctrines and statutes relating to negligence that are important. We examine a few of them here.

RES IPSA LOQUITUR Generally, in lawsuits involving negligence, the plaintiff has the burden of proving that the defendant was negligent. In certain situations, the courts may presume that negligence has occurred, in which case the burden of proof rests on the defendant—that is, the defendant must prove that he or she was *not* negligent. The presumption of the defendant's negligence is known as the doctrine of ***res ipsa loquitur,***[5] which translates as "the facts speak for themselves."

This doctrine is applied only when the event creating the damage or injury is one that ordinarily does not occur in the absence of negligence. For example,

5. Pronounced *rihz ihp*-suh *low*-kwuh-duhr.

EMERGING TRENDS

THE ENHANCED-INJURY THEORY

If a defendant can show contributory negligence on the part of the plaintiff, in a few states this is a complete defense (under common law rules). In most states, however, the doctrine of comparative negligence applies, in which both the plaintiff's and the defendant's negligence are computed and the liability for damages distributed accordingly. What about a situation in which the plaintiff's damages can be clearly broken down into two parts—an initial event and a subsequent, injury-enhancing event?

For example, assume that the plaintiff's damages resulting from an automobile accident can be broken down into (1) those sustained from the initial collision and (2) those sustained from a second "collision," which occurred when the plaintiff smashed her head on the windshield because of a defectively designed seat belt. Even if the plaintiff's own negligence contributed to the

initial collision (for example, suppose that she had been driving at night with her lights off), she was in no way negligent with respect to the second collision, which enhanced the extent and seriousness of her injuries. Thus, under what is becoming known as the *enhanced-injury theory,* the manufacturer of the defectively designed seat belt would be liable for the damages caused by the second event.

THE ENHANCED-INJURY THEORY AS A SWORD

The enhanced-injury theory can be a valuable weapon for plaintiffs in comparative negligence states. In one case, the operator of corn-harvesting equipment negligently placed his hand in the area of the rollers when the machine suddenly stopped operating. It started up again, pulling his hand and arm into the mechanism. He was unable to prevent further injury because there was no device on the machine that allowed for emergency stops.

The court isolated what had happened into two separate events. The first one occurred when the plaintiff negligently placed his hand in the area of the rollers. The enhancing event (the second "collision," as it were) occurred when he received further injuries (more of his body was pulled into the rollers) because the manufacturer had not provided an emergency stop device. Although the plaintiff could not recover for the first event (the initial entanglement), he was able to recover damages from the manufacturer for the injuries he sustained from the injury-

if a person undergoes knee surgery and following the surgery has a severed nerve in the knee area, that person can sue the surgeon under a theory of *res ipsa loquitur.* In this case, the injury would not have occurred but for the surgeon's negligence.[6] For the doctrine of *res ipsa loquitur* to apply, the event must have been within the defendant's power to control, and it must not have been due to any voluntary action or contribution on the part of the plaintiff.

NEGLIGENCE *PER SE* Certain conduct, whether it consists of an action or a failure to act, may be treated as **negligence *per se*** ("in or of itself"). Negligence *per se* may occur if an individual violates a statute or an ordinance providing for a criminal penalty and that violation causes another to be injured. The injured person must prove (1) that the statute clearly sets out what standard of conduct is expected, when and where it is expected, and of whom it is expected; (2) that he or she is in the class intended to be protected by the statute; and (3) that the statute was designed to prevent the type of injury that he or she suffered. The standard of conduct required by the statute is the duty that the defendant owes to the plaintiff, and a violation of the statute is the breach of that duty.

For example, a statute may require a landowner to keep a building in safe condition and may also subject the landowner to a criminal penalty, such as a

6. *Edwards v. Boland,* 41 Mass.App.Ct. 375, 670 N.E.2d 404 (1996).

EMERGING TRENDS

THE ENHANCED-INJURY THEORY (CONTINUED)

enhancing event, which was caused by a design defect.[a]

THE ENHANCED-INJURY THEORY AS A SHIELD

The enhanced-injury theory can also be used by defendants to prevent unfair allocations of damages. Consider a hypothetical example: A woman is riding a motorized scooter without a helmet. She is inadvertently cut off by an automobile driver. As a result, she loses control and is tossed from the scooter, landing headfirst onto the pavement. She sustains serious injuries. The automobile driver also sustains injuries. During trial, it is demonstrated that virtually all of the woman's injuries occurred because she was not wearing a legally required helmet. In certain circumstances, the defendant automobile driver may escape liability for most of the plaintiff's injuries in this particular situation because most of the plaintiff's injuries were the direct and proximate result of the failure to wear a helmet.

In an increasing number of cases, courts are instructing juries to focus on separating the damages caused by an injury-enhancing event from those caused by the initial injury-producing event. At a minimum, the plaintiff's damages may be reduced (relative to the amount sought by the plaintiff) in such cases—and a growing number of jury awards have been so reduced.[b]

IMPLICATIONS FOR THE BUSINESSPERSON

1. Before initiating a lawsuit against another party for negligence, a businessperson should ask his or her attorney about whether the enhanced-injury theory could apply to the facts of the case.
2. A businessperson should also be aware of the possibility of using the enhanced-injury theory as a defense to negligence.

FOR CRITICAL ANALYSIS

1. How can the same legal theory operate in favor of both plaintiffs and defendants?
2. When the enhanced-injury theory applies, how can the party arguing the theory (or the court, for that matter) determine which damages result from the initial event and which were caused by the injury-enhancing event?

a. *Farrell v. John Deere Co.*, 151 Wis.2d 45, 443 N.W.2d 50 (App. 1989).

b. See, for example, *Vonch v. American Standard Insurance Co.*, 151 Wis.2d 138, 442 N.W.2d 598 (App. 1989).

fine, if the building is not kept safe. The statute is meant to protect those who are rightfully in the building. Thus, if the owner, without a sufficient excuse, violates the statute and a tenant is thereby injured, then a majority of courts will hold that the owner's unexcused violation of the statute conclusively establishes negligence—that is, that the owner's violation is negligence *per se*.

"DANGER INVITES RESCUE" DOCTRINE Under the "danger invites rescue" doctrine, if a person commits an act that endangers another, the person committing the act will be liable for any injuries the other party suffers as well as any injuries suffered by a third person in an attempt to rescue the endangered party. For example, if Ludlam commits an act that endangers Schwaller, and Yokem sustains an injury trying to protect Schwaller, then Ludlam will be liable for Yokem's injury, as well as for any injuries Schwaller may sustain. Rescuers can injure themselves, or the persons rescued, or even bystanders, but the original wrongdoers will still be liable.

SPECIAL NEGLIGENCE STATUTES A number of states have enacted statutes prescribing duties and responsibilities in certain circumstances, the violation of which will impose civil liability. For example, most states now have what are called **Good Samaritan statutes.** Under these statutes, persons whom others aid voluntarily cannot turn around and sue the "Good Samaritans" for negligence. These laws were passed largely to protect physicians and

CONCEPT SUMMARY 12.2 Negligence

TERM	DESCRIPTION
Definition of Negligence	The careless performance of a legally required duty or the failure to perform a legally required act.
Elements of Negligence	**1.** The defendant owed a duty of care to the plaintiff. **2.** The defendant breached that duty. **3.** The plaintiff suffered a legally recognizable injury. **4.** The defendant's breach of the duty of care caused the plaintiff's injury.
Defenses to Negligence	**1.** Assumption of risk. **2.** Superseding intervening cause. **3.** Contributory or comparative negligence.
Special Negligence Doctrines and Statutes	**1.** *Res ipsa loquitur*—A doctrine under which a plaintiff need not prove negligence on the part of the defendant because "the facts speak for themselves." **2.** *Negligence per se*—A type of negligence that may occur if a person violates a statute or an ordinance providing for a criminal penalty and the violation causes another to be injured. **3.** *Special negligence statutes*—State statutes that prescribe duties and responsibilities in certain circumstances, the violation of which will impose civil liability. Good Samaritan statutes and dram shop acts are examples of special negligence statutes.

medical personnel who voluntarily render their services in emergency situations to those in need, such as individuals hurt in car accidents.

Many states have also passed **dram shop acts,** under which a tavern owner or bartender may be held liable for injuries caused by a person who became intoxicated while drinking at the bar or who was already intoxicated when served by the bartender. Nearly half the states now have statutes that impose liability on *social hosts* (persons hosting parties) for injuries caused by guests who became intoxicated at the hosts' homes. Under these statutes, it is unnecessary to prove that the tavern owner, bartender, or social host was negligent. Sometimes, the definition of a "social host" is fashioned broadly. For example, in one case, a person who hosted a "bring your own bottle" party was held liable for injuries caused by a drunken guest.[7] In another case, a passenger in a car who gave the driver an alcoholic beverage was held liable for injuries later caused by the driver after he became intoxicated, even though the driver was sober at the time the passenger offered him the drink.[8]

7. *Dower v. Gamba*, 276 N.J.Super. 319, 647 A.2d 1364 (1994).
8. *Wheeler v. Murphy*, 452 S.E.2d 416 (W.Va. 1994).

SECTION 5
STRICT LIABILITY

Another category of torts is called **strict liability,** or *liability without fault.* Intentional torts and torts of negligence involve acts that depart from a reasonable standard of care and cause injuries. Under the doctrine of strict liability, liability for injury is imposed for reasons other than fault.

THE ORIGINS OF STRICT LIABILITY

The modern concept of strict liability traces its origins, in part, to the 1868 English case of *Rylands v. Fletcher.* In the coal-mining area of Lancashire, England, the Rylands, who were mill owners, had constructed a reservoir on their land. Water from the reservoir broke through a filled-in shaft of an abandoned coal mine nearby and flooded the connecting passageways in an active coal mine owned by Fletcher. Fletcher sued the Rylands, and the court held that the defendants (the Rylands) were liable, even though the circumstances did not fit within existing tort liability theories. In justifying its decision, the court compared the situation to the trespass of dangerous animals: "the true rule of law is, that the person who for his own purposes brings on his land and collects and keeps there anything likely to do mischief if it escapes, must keep it at his peril, and, if he does not do so, is *prima facie* [at first sight; on the face of it] answerable for all the damage which is the natural consequence of its escape."[9]

The Rylands appealed to the House of Lords. The House of Lords had to decide whether one is responsible for the consequences of any extraordinary or dangerous process, even if one is as careful as possible—that is, as careful as "the reasonable person." The House of Lords affirmed the ruling of the lower reviewing court but limited the ruling to apply only to the "nonnatural" use of the defendants' land.[10] In this case, the emphasis was placed on the abnormal and inappropriate character of a reservoir in coal-mining country, rather than on the mere tendency of water to "escape."

The doctrine that emerged from *Rylands v. Fletcher* was liberally applied by British courts. Initially, few U.S. courts accepted the doctrine, presumably because the courts were worried about the doctrine's effect on the expansion of American businesses. Today, however, the doctrine of strict liability is the norm rather than the exception.

ABNORMALLY DANGEROUS ACTIVITIES

The influence of *Rylands v. Fletcher* can be seen in the strict liability rule for abnormally dangerous activities, which is one application of the strict liability doctrine. Abnormally dangerous activities have three characteristics:

1. The activity involves potential harm, of a serious nature, to persons or property.
2. The activity involves a high degree of risk that cannot be completely guarded against by the exercise of reasonable care.
3. The activity is not commonly performed in the community or area.

Clearly, the primary basis of liability is the creation of an extraordinary risk. For example, even if blasting with dynamite is performed with all reasonable care, there is still a risk of injury. Balancing that risk against the potential for harm, it is fair to ask the person engaged in the activity to pay for any injury it causes. Although there is no fault, there is still responsibility because of the dangerous nature of the undertaking. In other words, it is reasonable to require the person engaged in the activity to stand prepared to compensate anyone who suffers as a result of the activity.

OTHER APPLICATIONS OF STRICT LIABILITY

Persons who keep wild animals are strictly liable for any harm inflicted by the animals. The basis for applying strict liability is the fact that wild animals, should they escape from confinement, pose a serious risk of harm to persons in the vicinity. An owner of domestic animals (such as dogs, cats, cows, or sheep) may be strictly liable for harm caused by those animals if the owner knew, or should have known, that the animals were dangerous or had a propensity to harm others.

A significant application of strict liability is in the area of *product liability*—liability of manufacturers and sellers for harmful or defective products. This topic will be treated in detail in Chapter 14. Strict liability is also applied in certain types of *bailments* (a bailment exists when goods are transferred temporarily into the care of another).

9. *Fletcher v. Rylands*, L.R. 1 Ex. 265 (1866).
10. *Rylands v. Fletcher*, L.R. 3 H.L. 330 (1868).

TERMS AND CONCEPTS TO REVIEW

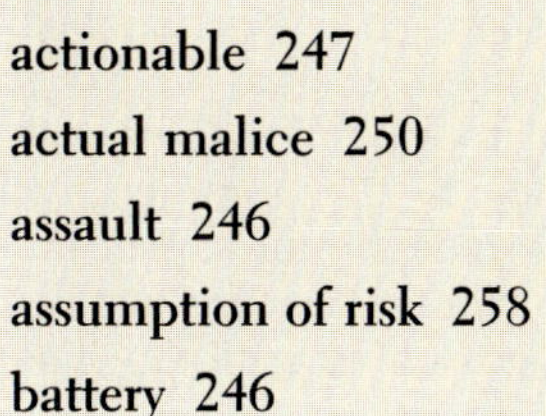

actionable 247
actual malice 250
assault 246
assumption of risk 258
battery 246
business invitee 254
causation in fact 257
comparative negligence 259
compensatory damages 256
contributory negligence 259
conversion 252
defamation 247
dram shop act 262
duty of care 253
fraud 251

TERMS AND CONCEPTS TO REVIEW (CONTINUED)

fraudulent misrepresentation 251
Good Samaritan statute 261
intentional tort 246
libel 248
malpractice 255
negligence 252
negligence *per se* 260
privilege 249
proximate cause 257
public figure 250
puffery 251
punitive damages 256
reasonable person standard 253
res ipsa loquitur 259
slander 247
strict liability 262
tort 244
tortfeasor 246
trespass to land 251
trespass to personal property 252

QUESTIONS AND CASE PROBLEMS

12–1. DEFAMATION. Kendro is an employee of the Dun Construction Corp. While delivering materials to a construction site, he carelessly runs Dun's truck into a passenger vehicle driven by Lowenstein. This is Kendro's second accident in six months. When Dun learns of this latest accident, a heated discussion ensues, and Dun fires Kendro. Dun is so angry at Kendro that he immediately writes a letter to the union of which Kendro is a member and to all other construction outfits in the community, stating that Kendro is the "worst driver in the city" and that "anyone who hires him is asking for legal liability." Kendro files suit against Dun, alleging libel on the basis of the statements made in the letter. Discuss the results.

12–2. DEFENSES TO NEGLIGENCE. Corinna was riding her bike on a city street. While she was riding, she frequently looked behind her to verify that the books that she had fastened to the rear part of her bike were still attached. On one occasion, she was looking behind her and failed to notice a car that was entering an intersection just as she was crossing it. The car hit her, causing her to sustain numerous injuries. Three eyewitnesses stated that the driver of the car had failed to stop at the stop sign before entering the intersection. Corinna sued the driver of the car for negligence. What defenses might the defendant driver raise in this lawsuit? Discuss fully.

12–3. NEGLIGENCE. In which of the following situations will the acting party be liable for the tort of negligence? Explain fully.

(a) Shannon goes to the golf course on Sunday morning, eager to try out a new set of golf clubs she has just purchased. As she tees off on the first hole, the head of her club flies off and injures a nearby golfer.

(b) Shannon goes to the golf course on Sunday morning. While she is teeing off at the eleventh hole, her golf ball veers off toward a roadway next to the golf course and shatters the windshield of a car.

(c) Shannon's doctor gives her some pain medication and tells her not to drive after she takes it, as the medication induces drowsiness. In spite of the doctor's warning, Shannon decides to drive to the store while on the medication. Owing to her lack of alertness, she fails to stop at a traffic light and crashes into another vehicle, causing a passenger in that vehicle to be injured.

12–4. CAUSATION. Ruth carelessly parks her car on a steep hill, leaving the car in neutral and failing to engage the parking brake. The car rolls down the hill, knocking down an electric line. The sparks from the broken line ignite a grass fire. The fire spreads until it reaches a barn one mile away. The barn houses dynamite, and the burning barn explodes, causing part of the roof to fall on and injure a passing motorist, Jim. Can Jim recover damages from Ruth? Why or why not?

12–5. TRESPASS TO LAND. Theo is a former employee of ABC Auto Repair Co. He enters the property of ABC, claiming that the company owes him $1,000 in back wages. An argument ensues, and the ABC general manager, Steward, orders Theo off the property. Theo refuses to leave, and Steward orders two mechanics to throw him off the property, which they do. Theo sues the mechanics, Steward, and ABC for assault and battery. Will Theo succeed in his claim? Explain.

12–6. TORT THEORIES. The Yommers operated a gasoline station. In December 1967, their neighbors, the McKenzies, noticed a smell in their well water, which proved to be caused by gasoline in the water. The McKenzies complained to the Yommers, who arranged to have one of their underground storage tanks replaced. Nevertheless, the McKenzies were unable to use their water for cooking or bathing until they had a filter and water softener installed. At the time of the trial, in December 1968, they were still bringing in drinking water from an outside source. The McKenzies sued the Yommers for damages. The Yommers claimed that the McKenzies had not proved that there was any intentional wrongdoing or negligence on their part and that therefore they should not be held liable. Under what theory might the McKenzies recover damages even in the absence of any negligence on the Yommers' part? Explain. [*Yommer v. McKenzie*, 255 Md. 220, 257 A.2d 138 (1969)]

12–7. STRICT LIABILITY. Danny and Marion Klein were injured when an aerial shell at a public fireworks exhibit went astray and exploded near them. They sued Pyrodyne Corp., the pyrotechnic company that was hired to set up and discharge the fireworks, alleging, among other things, that the company should be strictly liable for damages caused by the fireworks display. Will the court agree with the Kleins? What factors will the court consider in making its decision? Discuss fully. [*Klein v. Pyrodyne Corp.*, 117 Wash.2d 1, 810 P.2d 917 (1991)]

12–8. DUTY OF CARE. As pedestrians exited at the close of an arts and crafts show, Jason Davis, an employee of the show's producer, stood near the exit. Suddenly and without warning, Davis turned around and collided with Yvonne Esposito, an eighty-year-old woman. Esposito was knocked to the ground, fracturing her hip. After hip-replacement surgery, she was left with a permanent physical impairment. Esposito filed a suit in a federal district court against Davis and others, alleging negligence. What are the factors that indicate whether or not Davis owed Esposito a duty of care? What do those factors indicate in these circumstances? [*Esposito v. Davis*, 47 F.3d 164 (5th Cir. 1995)]

12–9. NEGLIGENCE *PER SE*. A North Carolina Department of Transportation regulation prohibits the placement of telephone booths within public rights of way. Despite this regulation, GTE South, Inc., placed a booth in the right of way near the intersection of Hillsborough and Sparger Roads in Durham County. Laura Baldwin was using the booth when an accident at the intersection caused a dump truck to cross the right of way and smash into the booth. To recover for her injuries, Baldwin filed a suit in a North Carolina state court against GTE and others. Was Baldwin within the class of persons protected by the regulation? If so, did GTE's placement of the booth constitute negligence *per se?* [*Baldwin v. GTE South, Inc.*, 335 N.C. 544, 439 S.E.2d 108 (1994)]

12–10. TORT THEORIES. On the morning of October 2, 1989, a fire started by an arsonist broke out in the Red Inn in Provincetown, Massachusetts. The inn had smoke detectors, sprinklers, and an alarm system, all of which alerted the guests, but there were no emergency lights or clear exits. Attempting to escape, Deborah Addis and James Reed, guests at the inn, found the first-floor doors and windows locked. Ultimately, they forced open a second-floor window and jumped out. To recover for their injuries, they filed a suit in a Massachusetts state court against Tamerlane Corporation, which operated the inn under a lease, and others (including Duane Steele, who worked for the owner of the inn). Under what tort theory discussed in this chapter might Addis and Reed recover damages from Tamerlane and the others? What must they prove to recover damages under this theory? Discuss fully. [*Addis v. Steele*, 38 Mass.App.Ct. 433, 648 N.E.2d 773 (1995)]

12–11. A QUESTION OF ETHICS

Ernesto Parra chocked to death on a piece of food while eating at a restaurant. The administrator of Parra's estate sued the restaurant, claiming, among other things, that the restaurant breached its duty to rescue Parra while he was choking. The court stressed that under the common law, there is no general duty to aid a person in peril: "A mere bystander incurs no liability where he fails to take any action, however negligently or even intentionally[,] to rescue another in distress." If Parra had been injured by a dangerous condition in the restaurant, such as a slippery floor, then the restaurant would have had a duty to come to Parra's assistance and ensure that he received any medical treatment necessary. But in the circumstances of the case before the court, the restaurant had not been responsible for placing Parra in danger; the fact that Parra choked was totally personal to Parra. According to the court, "As a general rule, a restaurateur is not an insurer of his customers' safety against all personal injuries. He has no duty as to 'conditions or risks which are ordinary and are, or should be, known or obvious to the patrons.' " [*Parra v. Tarasco, Inc.*, 230 Ill.App.3d 819, 595 N.E.2d 1186, 172 Ill.Dec. 516 (1992)]

1. Do you agree with the court's decision that the restaurant had no duty to rescue Parra? Why or why not?
2. Do you think that the law should impose a duty on all persons to rescue others in distress? What would be some of the implications of such a law for society? Discuss fully.

ACCESSING THE INTERNET

THE LEGAL ENVIRONMENT OF BUSINESS

Within the legal interest group on the commercial service America Online, there is a subcategory on torts and contracts. If you subscribe to America Online, the key word is

LEGAL

Standards established by professional associations play an important role in determining the minimum standard of care expected of the members of those professions—and thus are an important factor in negligence cases. You can locate the professional standards for various professional organizations at the following Internet site:

http:www.lib.uwaterloo.ca/society/standards.html

Cornell Law School also provides business and professional codes for a number of states. To find these, go to

http://www.law.cornell.edu/statutes.html#state

CHAPTER 13

TORTS AND CRIMES RELATED TO BUSINESS

OUR ECONOMIC SYSTEM OF FREE enterprise is predicated on the ability of businesspersons to compete for customers and for sales. Unfettered competitive behavior has been shown to lead to economic efficiency and economic progress. Businesses may, generally speaking, engage in whatever is *reasonably* necessary to obtain a fair share of a market or to recapture a share that has been lost. They are not allowed to use the motive of completely eliminating competition to justify certain business activities, however. Thus, an entire area of what is called business torts has arisen.

Remember that a tort is a breach of a duty owed to an individual or to a group. As mentioned in Chapter 12, many of the torts discussed there also occur in the business context. In Chapter 14, we will look at product liability, which also involves tort actions. Certain other torts that relate to business will be treated in Chapter 15. The torts examined here, in Chapter 13, traditionally have been referred to as **business torts,** which are defined as wrongful interferences with the business rights of others. Included in business torts are such vaguely worded concepts as *unfair competition* and *wrongfully interfering with the business relations of others.*

Following our discussion of these torts, we consider the subject of crime. A crime is a breach of a duty owed to society as a whole. Bribery, money laundering, insider trading, and corporate crime are included, as well as robbery, burglary, forgery, embezzlement, and other property crimes. We conclude the chapter with a section on the application of the Racketeer Influenced and Corrupt Organizations Act (known more popularly as RICO) to fraudulent and other unlawful business activities.

SECTION 1

TORTS RELATED TO BUSINESS

We restrict our discussion in this chapter to the following causes of action:

1. Wrongful interference with another's business rights.
2. Appropriation of another's name or likeness without permission.
3. Disparagement of business property or reputation.
4. Business defamation in cyberspace.

WRONGFUL INTERFERENCE

Torts involving wrongful interference with another's business rights generally fall into two categories—interference with a contractual relationship and interference with a business relationship.

WRONGFUL INTERFERENCE WITH A CONTRACTUAL RELATIONSHIP The body of tort law relating to *wrongful interference with a contractual relationship* has increased greatly in recent years. A landmark case in this area involved an opera singer, Joanna Wagner, who was under contract to sing for a man named Lumley for a specified period of years.[1] A man named Gye, who knew of this contract, nonetheless "enticed" Wagner to refuse to carry out the agreement, and Wagner began to sing for Gye. Gye's action constituted a tort, because it interfered with the contractual relationship between Wagner and Lumley. (Of course, Wagner's refusal to carry out the agreement also entitled Lumley to sue Wagner for breach of contract.)

In principle, any lawful contract can be the basis for an action of this type. The plaintiff must prove that the defendant actually knew of the contract's existence and intentionally *induced* the breach of the contractual relationship, not merely that the defendant reaped the benefits of a broken contract. For example, suppose that Kharkhin has a contract with Sutton that calls for Sutton to do gardening work on Kharkhin's large estate every week for fifty-two weeks at a specified price per week. Minnick, who needs gardening services, contacts Sutton and offers to pay Sutton a wage that is substantially higher than that offered by Kharkhin—although Minnick knows nothing about the Sutton-Kharkhin contract. Sutton breaches his contract with Kharkhin so that he can work for Minnick. Kharkhin cannot sue Minnick, because Minnick knew nothing of the Sutton-Kharkhin contract and was totally unaware that the higher wage he offered induced Sutton to breach that contract.

Three elements are necessary for wrongful interference with a contractual relationship to occur:

1. A valid, enforceable contract must exist between two parties.
2. A third party must *know* that this contract exists.
3. This third party must *intentionally* cause one of the two parties to the contract to break the contract, and the interference must be for the purpose of advancing the economic interest of the third party.

The contract may be between a firm and its employees or a firm and its customers, suppliers, competitors, or other parties. Sometimes a competitor of a firm draws away a key employee. If the original employer can show that the competitor induced the breach of the employment contract—that is, that the employee would not normally have broken the contract—damages can be recovered. In a famous case in the 1980s, Texaco, Inc., was found to have wrongfully interfered with an agreement between the Pennzoil Company and the Getty Oil Company. After Pennzoil had agreed to purchase a portion of Getty Oil, Texaco made an offer to purchase Getty Oil, and Getty Oil accepted Texaco's offer. Pennzoil then successfully sued Texaco for wrongful interference with Pennzoil's contractual relationship with Getty Oil.[2]

WRONGFUL INTERFERENCE WITH A BUSINESS RELATIONSHIP Individuals devise countless schemes to attract business, but they are forbidden by the courts to interfere unreasonably with another's business in their attempts to gain a share of the market. There is a difference between *competition* and *predatory behavior.* The distinction usually depends on whether a business is attempting to attract customers in general or to solicit only those customers who have already shown an interest in the similar product or service of a specific competitor. If a shopping center contains two shoe stores, an employee of Store A cannot be positioned at the entrance of Store B for the purpose of diverting customers to Store A. This type of activity constitutes the tort of wrongful

1. *Lumley v. Gye,* 118 Eng.Rep. 749 (1853).

2. *Texaco, Inc. v. Pennzoil Co.,* 725 S.W.2d 768 (Tex.App.—Houston [1st Dist.] 1987), writ ref'd n.r.e.). See footnote 9 in Chapter 10 for an explanation of "writ ref'd n.r.e." in Texas citations.

interference with a business relationship, often referred to as interference with a prospective (economic) advantage, and it is commonly considered to be an unfair trade practice. If this type of activity were permitted, Store A would reap the benefits of Store B's advertising.

Generally, a plaintiff must prove the following elements to recover damages for the tort of wrongful interference with a business relationship:

1. There was an established business relationship.
2. The tortfeasor, by use of predatory methods, intentionally caused this business relationship to end.
3. The plaintiff suffered damages as a result of the tortfeasor's actions.

DEFENSES TO WRONGFUL INTERFERENCE A person will not be liable for the tort of wrongful interference with a contractual or business relationship if it can be shown that the interference was justified, or permissible. Bona fide competitive behavior is a permissible interference even if it results in the breaking of a contract. If Jerrod's Meats advertises so effectively that it induces Sam's Restaurant to break its contract with Burke's Meat Company, Burke's Meat Company will be unable to recover against Jerrod's Meats on a wrongful interference theory. After all, the public policy that favors free competition in advertising definitely outweighs any possible instability that such competitive activity might cause in contractual relations. Therefore, although luring customers away from a competitor through aggressive marketing and advertising strategies obviously interferes with the competitor's relationship with his or her customers, such activity is permitted by the courts.

In the following case, two drugstore owners sued Wal-Mart Stores, Inc., alleging that Wal-Mart's sales tactics (selling products below cost, holding frequent sales, and so on) amounted to predatory behavior. Wal-Mart contended that its activities were not predatory and in fact promoted competition.

CASE 13.1 Wal-Mart Stores, Inc. v. American Drugs, Inc.

Supreme Court of Arkansas, 1995.
319 Ark. 214,
891 S.W.2d 30.

BACKGROUND AND FACTS *Wal-Mart Stores, Inc., prices some of its products below cost. This is known as a loss-leader strategy. Wal-Mart—or any seller who uses this strategy—hopes that the low prices will attract customers who will then buy other, higher-priced products. Part of Wal-Mart's strategy is to change which products it offers below cost in response to competitors' prices for those same products. American Drugs, Inc., and two other competitors of the Conway Wal-Mart Store in Faulkner County, Arkansas, filed a suit in an Arkansas state court against Wal-Mart, alleging that its loss-leader strategy violated the Arkansas Unfair Practices Act.*[a] *This act prohibits below-cost pricing that is used "for the purpose of injuring competitors and destroying competition." The court ordered Wal-Mart to stop its below-cost sales. Wal-Mart appealed to the Arkansas Supreme Court.*

IN THE LANGUAGE OF THE COURT

BROWN, Justice.

* * * *

* * * A firm that cuts its prices or substantially reduces its profit margin is not necessarily engaging in predatory pricing. * * * Indeed, there is a real danger in mislabeling such practices as predatory, because consumers generally benefit from the low prices resulting from aggressive price competition.

* * * *

* * * [T]he loss-leader strategy employed by Conway Wal-Mart is readily justifiable as a tool to foster competition and to gain a competitive edge as opposed to simply being viewed as a stratagem to eliminate rivals altogether. * * * Certainly legitimate competition in the market place can, and often does, result in economic injury to competitors. A competitor that has been injured by legitimate competitive pricing, though, should not be permitted to use the Arkansas [Unfair

a. Arkansas Code Sections 4-75-201 *et seq.*

Practices] Act as a fountain for recouping its losses. In short, the circumstances of this case are not sufficiently egregious [outstandingly bad] to prove that Conway Wal-Mart crossed the line with regard to predatory prices and purposeful destruction of competition.

DECISION AND REMEDY *The Arkansas Supreme Court held that the use of a loss-leader strategy is not enough to show an intent to destroy competition. The court reversed the order of the lower court and dismissed the suit against Wal-Mart.*

APPROPRIATION

The use of another person's name, likeness, or other identifying characteristic, without permission and for the benefit of the user, constitutes the tort of **appropriation.** Under the law, normally an individual's right to privacy includes the right to the exclusive use of his or her identity. For example, in a case involving a Ford Motor Company television commercial in which a Bette Midler "sound-alike" sang a song that Midler had made famous, the court held that Ford "for their own profit in selling their product did appropriate part of her identity."[3]

A court ruled similarly in a case brought by Vanna White, the hostess of the popular television game show *Wheel of Fortune*, against Samsung Electronics America, Inc. Without White's permission, Samsung included in an advertisement for Samsung videocassette recorders a depiction of a robot dressed in a wig, gown, and jewelry, posed in a setting that resembled the *Wheel of Fortune* set, in a stance for which White is famous. The court held in White's favor, holding that the tort of appropriation does not require the use of a celebrity's name or likeness. The court stated that Samsung's robot ad left "little doubt" as to the identity of the celebrity that the ad was meant to depict.[4]

Often, cases alleging appropriation require the courts to balance a celebrity's right to the exclusive use of his or her identity against the First Amendment right to freedom of speech. For example, in one case, a California newspaper reproduced in poster form pages from various issues that contained photographs and an artist's renditions of Joe Montana, who was at that time a well-known professional quarterback. In Montana's suit against the newspaper for the commercial misappropriation of his name, photograph, and likeness, however, the court held that the defendant newspaper's reproduction and sale of the posters was protected speech under the First Amendment.[5]

Other sports-related commercial misappropriation cases have involved the rights of those who invest time and money in the creation and broadcast of sports events. In the following case, the court considered whether the transmission of real-time information about National Basketball Association games in progress via America Online constituted commercial misappropriation.

3. *Midler v. Ford Motor Co.*, 849 F.2d 460 (9th Cir. 1988).

4. *White v. Samsung Electronics America, Inc.*, 971 F.2d 1395 (1992).

5. *Montana v. San Jose Mercury News, Inc.*, 34 Cal.App.4th, 40 Cal.Rptr.2d 639 (1995).

CASE 13.2 National Basketball Association v. Motorola, Inc.

United States Court of Appeals, Second Circuit, 1997. 105 F.3d 841.

HISTORICAL AND ECONOMIC SETTING *The commercial value and appeal of National Basketball Association (NBA) games can be attributed to years of successful promotion. NBA games reach the peak of their value while they are being played. In the mid-1990s, 80 percent of NBA revenues were derived from the sale of broadcast distribution licenses and admission fees to the arenas. The NBA licenses rights to real-time game data to select local, regional, and national media, including television and radio broadcasters, a satellite service, and a company that provides audio descriptions of games via an 800 number.*

BACKGROUND AND FACTS *Sports Team Analysis and Tracking Systems, Inc. (Stats), provides information about sports to the media—including ESPN and NBC Sports—and to the public. One of Stats's methods is to disseminate real-time information about NBA games in progress via its site on America Online, Inc. (AOL). Users who access the site see point-by-point changes in scores, game time remaining, and such player and team statistics as field goals, free throws, rebounds, three-point shots, total points, and minutes played. The information is updated as frequently as every fifteen seconds. Stats does not have the NBA's permission to transmit this information, however. The NBA and NBA Properties, Inc., filed a suit in a federal district court against Stats and others (including Motorola, Inc., which sells pagers that display similar information), alleging, in part, commercial misappropriation. The defendants argued that because they did not replicate entire broadcasts of NBA games, they were doing nothing wrong. The court ruled in favor of the NBA, and the defendants appealed.*

IN THE LANGUAGE OF THE COURT

WINTER, Circuit Judge:

* * * *

We conclude that Motorola and Stats have not engaged in unlawful misappropriation * * * .

* * * *

With regard to the NBA's primary products—producing basketball games with live attendance and licensing copyrighted broadcasts of those games—there is no evidence that anyone regards [Motorola's pagers] or the AOL site as a substitute for attending NBA games or watching them on television. * * *

* * * *

* * * The use of pagers to transmit real-time information about NBA games requires: (i) the collecting of facts about the games; (ii) the transmission of these facts on a network; (iii) the assembling of them by the particular service; and (iv) the transmission of them to pagers or an on-line computer site. * * * Motorola and Stats expend their own resources to collect purely factual information generated in NBA games * * * . They have their own network and assemble and transmit data themselves.

DECISION AND REMEDY *The court held that Stats's transmission of real-time NBA game information on AOL did not constitute commercial misappropriation.*

DISPARAGEMENT OF PROPERTY

Disparagement of property occurs when economically injurious falsehoods are made not about another's reputation but about another's *product* or *property*. *Disparagement of property* is a general term for torts that can be more specifically referred to as *slander of quality* or *slander of title*.

SLANDER OF QUALITY Publishing false information about another's product, alleging it is not what its seller claims, constitutes the tort of **slander of quality.** This tort has also been given the name **trade libel.** The plaintiff must prove that actual damages proximately resulted from the slander of quality. That is, it must be shown not only that a third person refrained from dealing with the plaintiff because of the improper publication but also that the plaintiff suffered damages because the third person refrained from dealing with him or her. The economic calculation of such damages—they are, after all, conjectural—is often extremely difficult.

It is possible for an improper publication to be both a slander of quality and a defamation. For example, a statement that disparages the quality of a product may also, by implication, disparage the character of a person who would sell such a product. In one case, for instance, claiming that a product that was marketed as a sleeping aid contained "habit-forming drugs" was held to constitute defamation.[6]

6. *Harwood Pharmacal Co. v. National Broadcasting Co.*, 9 N.Y.2d 460, 174 N.E.2d 602, 214 N.Y.S.2d 725 (1961).

SLANDER OF TITLE When a publication falsely denies or casts doubt on another's legal ownership of property, and when this results in financial loss to the property's owner, the tort of **slander of title** may exist. Usually, this is an intentional tort in which someone knowingly publishes an untrue statement about another's ownership of certain property with the intent of discouraging a third person from dealing with the person slandered. For example, it would be difficult for a car dealer to attract customers after competitors published a notice that the dealer's stock consisted of stolen autos.

BUSINESS DEFAMATION IN CYBERSPACE

As discussed in Chapter 12, the tort of defamation occurs when an individual makes a false statement that injures another's reputation. Defamation may take the form of libel (defamatory statements in written or printed form) or slander (defamatory statements made orally). Defamation becomes a business tort when the defamatory matter injures someone in a profession, business, or trade or when it adversely affects a business entity in its credit rating and other dealings.

In today's online world, one of the most significant legal issues regarding defamation in the business context concerns the liability of online service providers (OSPs), such as America Online, CompuServe, and Prodigy. OSPs that author materials and publish them online are, of course, liable for any defamatory statements they include in these publications. Should OSPs also be liable for speech generated by the third party users of their services? The answer to this question depends, in large part, on whether an OSP is classified as a publisher or a distributor of the materials.

Traditionally, the courts have held that libraries, bookstores, newsstands, and other distributors of books and periodicals have no duty to monitor every book or periodical that they distribute. As the United States Supreme Court has held, this would be an unreasonable demand on the seller and a restriction on the public's access to reading matter.[7] Therefore, *distributors* of defamatory materials are not themselves liable for the defamation—unless they happened to know or had reason to know of the defamatory contents. A *publisher,* in contrast, *can* be held liable for defamatory contents in books and periodicals. This is because, under tort law governing defamation, one who repeats or otherwise republishes a defamatory statement is subject to liability as if he or she had originally published it.

THE STATUS OF ONLINE SERVICE PROVIDERS Should OSPs be considered distributors or publishers of information? Two significant cases decided in the 1990s addressed this question. In the first case, *Cubby, Inc. v. CompuServe, Inc.,*[8] the plaintiffs alleged that CompuServe should be held liable for defamatory statements made against them on one of the information sources provided through CompuServe Information Service (CIS). The court held that CompuServe was a distributor of information and thus could not be held liable for the defamatory statements *unless* there was a showing that it knew or had reason to know of the statements.

In the second case, *Stratton Oakmont, Inc. v. Prodigy Services Co.,*[9] the court held that Prodigy was a publisher and thus could be held liable for defamatory statements posted on its "Money Talk" bulletin board by an unidentified Prodigy user. The court reached this conclusion largely because Prodigy, starting in 1990, had held itself out—in its policy statements and in various national newspaper articles—as an online service that exercised editorial control over the content of messages posted on its computer bulletin boards. Prodigy expressly differentiated itself from its competition and expressly likened itself to a newspaper. Prodigy also instructed "board leaders" to monitor bulletin board postings and delete notes from its computer bulletin boards if they were offensive or in "bad taste," in accordance with Prodigy's guidelines.

THE COMMUNICATIONS DECENCY ACT OF 1996 As discussed in Chapter 5, the Communications Decency Act (CDA) was passed in 1996, as part of the Telecommunications Act of that year, to regulate the transmission of obscene and pornographic materials. Although the "indecency" provisions of the act have been declared unconstitutional, other provisions have not. Among the CDA's other provisions are those relating to the liability of online service providers.

Section 230(c) of the CDA reads as follows: "No provider or user of an interactive computer service shall be treated as the publisher or speaker of any information provided by another information

7. *Smith v. California,* 361 U.S. 147, 80 S.Ct. 215, 4 L.Ed.2d 205 (1959).

8. 776 F.Supp. 135 (S.D.N.Y. 1991).

9. Supreme Court of New York, May 24, 1995 (1995 WL 323710). This decision is not published in a reporter. It can be accessed on WESTLAW by use of the citation given here.

content provider." Section 230(c) also states that providers and users of interactive computer services are not subject to civil liability "on account of any action taken voluntarily in good faith to restrict access to or availability of" any materials online that the provider deems "objectionable." In other words, an online service provider may not be held liable as a publisher simply because it attempts, as Prodigy did, to exercise editorial control over the content of transmitted materials. In fact, the specific purpose of this section of the CDA was to overrule the court's decision in the *Stratton Oakmont* case.

Section 230(c) does not distinguish between online service providers that have knowledge of defamatory content being transmitted online and providers that do not. Thus, if the words of this section are taken literally, online service providers now have absolute immunity with respect to defamatory statements by third party users of their services.

SECTION 2

CRIMES RELATED TO BUSINESS

A discussion of criminal law is appropriate to a study of business law because the prevention of crime and the effort of capturing and prosecuting those accused of crimes are time-consuming and costly activities. Consequently, it is important that we understand the nature and extent of such activities and their impact on businesses.

The law imposes various sanctions in attempting to ensure that individuals engaging in business in our society can compete and flourish. These sanctions include those imposed by the civil law, such as damages for various types of tortious conduct (as discussed in the preceding chapter); damages for breach of contract (as discussed in Chapter 10); and the equitable remedies discussed in Chapter 1. Additional sanctions are imposed under criminal law.

Recall from Chapter 1 that *civil law* pertains to the duties that exist between persons or between citizens and their governments. *Criminal law,* in contrast, has to do with crime. A **crime** can be defined as a wrong against society proclaimed in a statute and punishable by a fine and/or imprisonment—or, in some cases, death. Many statutes regulating business provide for criminal as well as civil sanctions. Therefore, criminal law joins civil law as an important element in the legal environment of business. The prerequisites for establishing *fault* or *guilt* in criminal cases differ from those in civil cases, as do the sanctions and penalties.

CLASSIFICATION OF CRIMES

Depending on their degree of seriousness, crimes are classified as felonies or misdemeanors. **Felonies** are serious crimes punishable by death or by imprisonment in a federal or state penitentiary for more than a year. The Model Penal Code[10] provides for four degrees of felony: (1) capital offenses, for which the maximum penalty is death; (2) first degree felonies, punishable by a maximum penalty of life imprisonment; (3) second degree felonies, punishable by a maximum of ten years' imprisonment; and (4) third degree felonies, punishable by up to five years' imprisonment.

Under federal law and in most states, any crime that is not a felony is considered a **misdemeanor.** Misdemeanors are crimes punishable by a fine or by confinement for up to a year. If incarcerated (imprisoned), the guilty party goes to a local jail instead of a penitentiary. Disorderly conduct and trespass are common misdemeanors. Some states have several classes of misdemeanors. For example, in Illinois, misdemeanors are either Class A (confinement for up to a year), Class B (not more than six months), or Class C (not more than thirty days). Whether a crime is a felony or a misdemeanor can also determine whether the case is tried in a magistrate's court (for example, by a justice of the peace) or a general trial court.

In most jurisdictions, **petty offenses** are considered to be a subset of misdemeanors. Petty offenses are minor violations, such as violations of building codes. Even for petty offenses, however, a guilty party can be put in jail for a few days, fined, or both, depending on state law.

THE ESSENTIALS OF CRIMINAL LIABILITY

Two elements must exist simultaneously for a person to be convicted of a crime: (1) the performance of a

10. The American Law Institute issued the Official Draft of the Model Penal Code in 1962. The Model Penal Code is not a uniform code. Uniformity in criminal law among the states is not as important as uniformity in other areas of the law. Crime varies with local circumstances, and it is appropriate that punishments vary accordingly. The Model Penal Code contains four parts: (1) general provisions, (2) definitions of special crimes, (3) provisions concerning treatment and corrections, and (4) provisions on the organization of correction.

prohibited act and (2) a specified state of mind, or intent, on the part of the actor.

THE CRIMINAL ACT Every criminal statute prohibits certain behavior. Most crimes require an act of *commission;* that is, a person must *do* something in order to be accused of a crime. In criminal law, a prohibited act is referred to as the ***actus reus,***[11] or guilty act. In some cases, an act of *omission* can be a crime, but only when a person has a legal duty to perform the omitted act. Failure to file a tax return is an example of an omission that is a crime.

The *guilty act* requirement is based on one of the premises of criminal law—that a person is punished for *harm done* to society. Thinking about killing someone or about stealing a car may be wrong, but the thoughts do no harm until they are translated into action. Of course, a person can be punished for attempting murder or robbery, but only if substantial steps toward the criminal objective have been taken.

STATE OF MIND A wrongful mental state ***(mens rea)***[12] is as necessary as a wrongful act in establishing guilt. The mental state, or requisite *intent,* required to establish guilt of a crime is indicated in the applicable statute or law. Murder, for example, involves the guilty act of killing another human being, and the guilty mental state is the desire, or intent, to take another's life. For theft, the guilty act is the taking of another person's property, and the mental state involves both the awareness that the property belongs to another and the desire to deprive the owner of it.

The elements required to establish a guilty mental state include purpose, knowledge, negligence, and recklessness. A defendant is said to have *purposefully* committed a criminal act when he or she desires to engage in certain criminal conduct or to cause a certain criminal result. For a defendant to have *knowingly* committed an illegal act, he or she must be aware of the illegality, must believe that the illegality exists, or must correctly suspect that the illegality exists but fail to do anything to dispel (or confirm) his or her belief. Criminal *negligence* involves the mental state in which the defendant grossly deviates from the standard of care that a reasonable person would use under the same circumstances. The defendant is accused of taking an unjustified, substantial, and foreseeable risk that resulted in harm.[13]

A defendant who commits an act *recklessly* is more blameworthy than one who is criminally negligent. The Model Penal Code defines criminal recklessness as "consciously disregard[ing] a substantial and unjustifiable risk."[14] Some courts, such as those adhering to the Model Penal Code, will not find criminal recklessness on the part of a defendant who was not subjectively aware of the risk when he or she acted.

CRIMINAL PROCEDURES

Criminal law brings the force of the state, with all its resources, to bear against the individual. Criminal procedures are designed to protect the constitutional rights of individuals and to prevent the arbitrary use of power on the part of the government.

CONSTITUTIONAL SAFEGUARDS The U.S. Constitution provides specific safeguards for those accused of crimes. The United States Supreme Court has ruled that most of these safeguards apply not only in federal but also in state courts by virtue of the due process clause of the Fourteenth Amendment. These safeguards include the following:

1. The Fourth Amendment protection from unreasonable searches and seizures.
2. The Fourth Amendment requirement that no warrant for a search or an arrest be issued without probable cause.
3. The Fifth Amendment requirement that no one be deprived of "life, liberty, or property without due process of law."
4. The Fifth Amendment prohibition against **double jeopardy** (trying someone twice for the same criminal offense).[15]

11. Pronounced *ak*-tuhs *ray*-uhs.
12. Pronounced mehns *ray*-uh.

13. Under Model Penal Code Section 2.02(2)(d), a defendant is negligent if he or she *should be* aware of the risk.
14. Model Penal Code Section 2.02(2)(c). In other words, a defendant is reckless if he or she *is actually* aware of the risk.
15. The prohibition against double jeopardy means that once a criminal defendant is found not guilty of a particular crime, the government may not reindict the person and retry him or her for the same crime. The prohibition against double jeopardy does not preclude a *civil* suit's being brought against the same person by the crime victim to recover damages. For example, a person found not guilty of assault and battery in a criminal case may be sued by the victim in a civil tort case for damages. Additionally, a state's prosecution of a crime will not prevent a separate federal prosecution of the same crime, and vice versa. For example, a defendant found not guilty of violating a state law can be tried in federal court for the same act, if the act is defined as a crime under federal law.

5. The Fifth Amendment requirement that no person be required to be a witness against (incriminate) himself or herself.
6. The Sixth Amendment guarantees of a speedy trial, a trial by jury, a public trial, the right to confront witnesses, and the right to a lawyer at various stages in some proceedings.
7. The Eighth Amendment prohibitions against excessive bail and fines and cruel and unusual punishment.

The Exclusionary Rule. Under what is known as the **exclusionary rule,** all evidence obtained in violation of the constitutional rights spelled out in the Fourth, Fifth, and Sixth Amendments normally is not admissible at trial. All evidence derived from the illegally obtained evidence is known as the "fruit of the poisonous tree," and such evidence normally must also be excluded from the trial proceedings. For example, if a confession is obtained after an illegal arrest, the arrest is "the poisonous tree," and the confession, if "tainted" by the arrest, is the "fruit."

The purpose of the exclusionary rule is to deter police from conducting warrantless searches and from other misconduct. The rule is sometimes criticized because it can lead to injustice. Many a defendant has "gotten off on a technicality" because law enforcement personnel failed to observe procedural requirements based on the above-mentioned constitutional amendments. Even though a defendant may be obviously guilty, if the evidence of that guilt is obtained improperly (without a valid search warrant, for example), it cannot be used against the defendant in court.

The courts, however, can exercise a certain amount of discretion in determining whether evidence has been obtained improperly, thus balancing the scales somewhat. For example, in a 1995 case heard by the U.S. Court of Appeals for the Ninth Circuit, the judges had to decide whether evidence obtained from a wiretap surveillance operation overseas violated the defendant's Fourth Amendment rights. If it did, the evidence would be inadmissible under the exclusionary rule. The defendant was a U.S. citizen, and the operation would have been illegal in the United States, but it was legal in the country where it was conducted. The court held that even though the wiretapping would have been illegal in the United States, the evidence legally obtained overseas was admissible. The court stated that the extent to which an American is protected from surveillance in another country is determined by the law of that country.[16]

The Miranda Rule. In regard to criminal procedure, one of the questions many courts faced in the 1950s and 1960s was not whether suspects had constitutional rights—that was not in doubt—but how and when those rights could be exercised. Could the right to be silent (under the Fifth Amendment's prohibition against self-incrimination) be exercised during pretrial interrogation proceedings, or only during the trial? Were confessions obtained from suspects admissible in court if the suspects had not been advised of their right to remain silent and other constitutional rights? To clarify these issues, the United States Supreme Court issued a landmark decision in 1966 in *Miranda v. Arizona,* presented below.

16. *United States v. Barona,* 56 F.3d 1087 (9th Cir. 1995).

CASE 13.3 Miranda v. Arizona

Supreme Court of the United States, 1966.
384 U.S. 436,
86 S.Ct. 1602,
16 L.Ed.2d 694.

BACKGROUND AND FACTS *On March 13, 1963, Ernesto Miranda was arrested at his home for the kidnapping and rape of an eighteen-year-old woman. Miranda was taken to a Phoenix, Arizona, police station and questioned by two officers. Two hours later, the officers emerged from the interrogation room with a written confession signed by Miranda. A paragraph at the top of the confession stated that the confession had been made voluntarily, without threats or promises of immunity, and "with full knowledge of my legal rights, understanding any statement I make may be used against me." Miranda was at no time advised that he had a right to remain silent and a right to have a lawyer present. The confession was admitted into evidence at the trial, and Miranda was convicted and sentenced to prison for twenty to thirty years. Miranda appealed the decision, claiming that he had not been informed of his constitutional rights. The Supreme Court of Arizona held that Miranda's constitutional rights had not been violated and affirmed his conviction.*

The Miranda *case was subsequently consolidated with three other cases involving similar issues and reviewed by the United States Supreme Court.*

IN THE LANGUAGE OF THE COURT

Mr. Chief Justice WARREN delivered the opinion of the Court.

The cases before us raise questions which go to the roots of our concepts of American criminal jurisprudence; the restraints society must observe consistent with the Federal Constitution in prosecuting individuals for crime. * * *

* * * *

At the outset, if a person in custody is to be subjected to interrogation, he must first be informed in clear and unequivocal terms that he has the right to remain silent. * * *

* * * *

The warning of the right to remain silent must be accompanied by the explanation that anything said can and will be used against the individual in court. This warning is needed in order to make him aware not only of the privilege, but also of the consequences of forgoing it. * * *

The circumstances surrounding in-custody interrogation can operate very quickly to overbear the will of one merely made aware of his privilege by his interrogators. Therefore the right to have counsel present at the interrogation is indispensable to the protection of the Fifth Amendment privilege under the system we delineate today.

* * * *

In order fully to apprise a person interrogated of the extent of his rights under this system then, it is necessary to warn him not only that he has the right to consult with an attorney, but also that if he is indigent [without funds] a lawyer will be appointed to represent him. * * * The warning of a right to counsel would be hollow if not couched in terms that would convey to the indigent—the person most often subjected to interrogation—the knowledge that he too has a right to have counsel present.

DECISION AND REMEDY

The Supreme Court held that Miranda could not be convicted of the crime on the basis of his confession because his confession was inadmissible as evidence. For any statement made by a defendant to be admissible, the defendant must be informed of certain constitutional rights prior to police interrogation. If the accused waives his or her rights to remain silent and to have counsel present, the government must demonstrate that the waiver was made knowingly, voluntarily, and intelligently.

INTERNATIONAL CONSIDERATIONS

The Right to Remain Silent in Great Britain *The right to remain silent has long been a legal hallmark in Great Britain as well as in the United States. In 1994, however, the British Parliament passed an act that provides that a criminal defendant's silence may be interpreted as evidence of the defendant's guilt. British police officers are now required, when making arrests, to inform the suspects, "You do not have to say anything. But if you do not mention now something which you later use in your defense, the court may decide that your failure to mention it now strengthens the case against you. A record will be made of everything you say, and it may be given in evidence if you are brought to trial."*

The Erosion of the* Miranda *Rule. The Supreme Court and lower courts have enforced the *Miranda* rule hundreds of times since the *Miranda* decision. Over time, however, several exceptions to the rule have been created. Congress in 1968 passed the Omnibus Crime Control and Safe Streets Act, which provided—among other things—that in federal cases a voluntary confession could be used in evidence even if the accused was not informed of his or her rights. The United States Supreme Court has carved out other exceptions. In 1984, for example, the Court recognized a "public safety" exception to the

Miranda rule. The need to protect the public warranted the admissibility of statements made by the defendant (in this case, indicating where he placed the gun) as evidence in a trial, even when the defendant had not been informed of his *Miranda* rights.[17] Today, juries can even accept confessions without being convinced of their voluntariness.

CRIMINAL PROCESS As mentioned, a criminal prosecution differs significantly from a civil case in several respects. These differences reflect the desire to safeguard the rights of the individual against the state. Exhibit 13–1 summarizes the major steps in processing a criminal case. We discuss below in more detail three phases of the criminal process—arrest, indictment or information, and trial.

Arrest. Before a warrant for arrest can be issued, there must be probable cause for believing that the individual in question has committed a crime. As discussed in Chapter 5, *probable cause* can be defined as a substantial likelihood that the person has committed or is about to commit a crime. Note that probable cause involves a likelihood, not just a possibility. Arrests may sometimes be made without a warrant if there is no time to get one, but the action of the arresting officer is still judged by the standard of probable cause.

Indictment or Information. Individuals must be formally charged with having committed specific crimes before they can be brought to trial. If issued by a grand jury, such a charge is called an **indictment.**[18] A **grand jury** does not determine the guilt or innocence of an accused party; rather, its function is to determine, after hearing the state's evidence, whether a reasonable basis (probable cause) exists for supposing that a crime has been committed and whether a trial ought to be held.

Usually, grand juries are called in cases involving serious crimes, such as murder. For lesser crimes, an individual may be formally charged with a crime by an **information,** or criminal complaint. An information will be issued by a magistrate (a public official vested with judicial authority) if the magistrate determines that there is sufficient evidence to justify bringing the individual to trial.

Trial. At a criminal trial, the accused person does not have to prove anything; the entire burden of proof is on the prosecutor (the state). As discussed in Chapter 1, the burden of proof in a criminal case is higher than that in a civil case.

In a civil case, a defendant's liability is usually decided based on a *preponderance of the evidence*—meaning that the evidence offered in support of a certain claim must outweigh the evidence offered to negate that claim. In contrast, in a criminal case, the prosecution must show that, based on all the evidence, the defendant's guilt is established *beyond a reasonable doubt.* If there is any reasonable doubt that a criminal defendant did not commit the crime with which he or she has been charged, then the verdict must be "not guilty." Note that giving a verdict of "not guilty" is not the same as stating that the defendant is innocent; it merely means that not enough evidence was properly presented to the court to prove guilt beyond all reasonable doubt. The higher standard of proof in criminal cases reflects a fundamental social value—a belief that it is worse to convict an innocent individual than to let a guilty person go free.

Courts have complex rules about what types of evidence may be presented and how the evidence may be brought out in criminal cases, especially in jury trials. These rules are designed to ensure that evidence in trials is relevant, reliable, and not prejudicial against the defendant.

FEDERAL SENTENCING GUIDELINES Traditionally, persons who had committed the same crime might have received very different sentences, depending on the judge hearing the case, the jurisdiction in which it was heard, and many other factors. In 1984, however, Congress passed the Sentencing Reform Act. This act created the U.S. Sentencing Commission, which was charged with the task of standardizing sentences for federal crimes. The commission's guidelines, which became effective in 1987, established a range of possible penalties for each federal crime. Judges must select a sentence from within this range when sentencing criminal defendants, taking into consideration the defendant's criminal record, the seriousness of the offense, and other factors specified in the guidelines.[19]

17. *New York v. Quarles,* 467 U.S. 649, 104 S.Ct. 2626, 81 L.Ed.2d 550 (1984).

18. Pronounced in-*dyte*-ment.

19. In *Melendez v. United States,* ___ U.S. ___, 116 S.Ct. 2057, 135 L.Ed.2d 427 (1996), the United States Supreme Court held that a federal judge may not depart from the applicable range specified in the guidelines even in response to a federal prosecutor's request. In this case, the prosecutor had recommended a lower sentence than the minimum sentence imposed by the guidelines based on the defendant's substantial assistance in prosecuting the case.

EXHIBIT 13–1 ■ MAJOR STEPS IN PROCESSING A CRIMINAL CASE

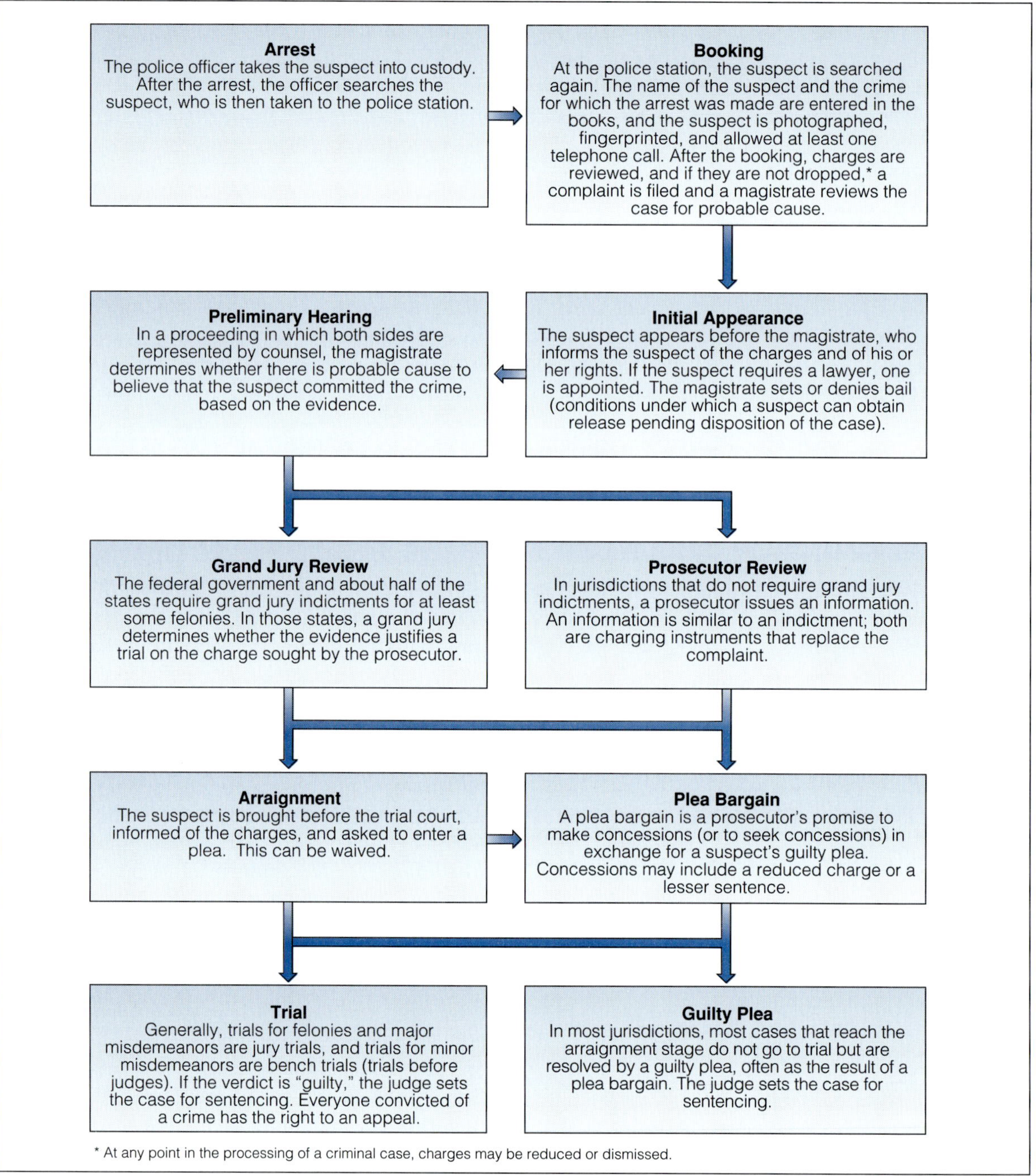

The commission also created specific guidelines for the punishment of crimes committed by corporate employees (white-collar crimes). These guidelines, which went into effect in 1991, established stiffer penalties for mail and wire fraud, commercial bribery and kickbacks, and money laundering (these crimes will be discussed later in this chapter), as well as for criminal violations of employment laws (see Chapters 20 and 21), securities laws (see Chapter 28), and antitrust laws (see Chapters 26 and 27). The guidelines allow judges to take into consideration a number of factors when selecting from the range of possible penalties for a specified crime. These factors include the defendant company's history of past violations, the extent of management's cooperation with federal investigators, and the extent to which the firm has undertaken specific programs and procedures to prevent criminal activities by its employees.

CRIMES AFFECTING BUSINESS

Some types of crimes, such as robbery and burglary, occur in the business world just as they do elsewhere. Other types of crimes, such as bribery and mail fraud, occur most frequently in the business context and, for that reason, often are referred to as white-collar crimes. Although there is no official definition of **white-collar crime,** the term is popularly used to mean an illegal act or series of acts committed by an individual or business entity using some nonviolent means to obtain a personal or business advantage. Usually, this kind of crime is committed in the course of a legitimate occupation.

In this section, we present the basic requirements for a variety of crimes, including several types of white-collar crimes. Other white-collar crimes include actions that violate criminal provisions of laws governing intellectual property (discussed in Chapter 15).

FORGERY The fraudulent making or altering of any writing in a way that changes the legal rights and liabilities of another is **forgery.** If, without authorization, Severson signs Bennett's name to the back of a check made out to Bennett, Severson is committing forgery. Forgery also includes changing trademarks, falsifying public records, counterfeiting, and altering a legal document.

ROBBERY At common law, **robbery** was defined as forcefully and unlawfully taking personal property of any value from another. The use of force or intimidation is usually necessary for an act of theft to be considered a robbery. Thus, picking pockets does not constitute robbery, because the action is unknown to the victim. Typically, states have more severe penalties for *aggravated* robbery—robbery with the use of a deadly weapon.

BURGLARY At common law, **burglary** was defined as breaking and entering the dwelling of another at night with the intent to commit a felony. ("Breaking" required the use of force to get in, or get out, but the slightest force—even pushing open a closed door—was enough.) Originally, the definition was aimed at protecting an individual's home and its occupants. Most state statutes have eliminated some of the requirements found in the common law definition. The time at which the breaking and entering occurs, for example, is usually immaterial. State statutes frequently omit the element of breaking, and some states do not require that the building be a dwelling. Aggravated burglary—which is defined as burglary with the use of a deadly weapon, burglary of a dwelling, or both—incurs a greater penalty.

LARCENY (THEFT) Any person who wrongfully or fraudulently takes and carries away another person's personal property is guilty of **larceny.** Larceny includes the fraudulent intent to deprive an owner permanently of property. Many business-related larcenies entail fraudulent conduct. Whereas robbery involves force or fear, larceny does not. Therefore, picking pockets is larceny, not robbery.

As society becomes more complex, questions often arise as to what property is. In most states, the definition of property that is subject to larceny statutes has expanded. Stealing computer programs may constitute larceny even though the "property" consists of magnetic impulses. Stealing computer time may also constitute larceny. So, too, may the theft of natural gas. Trade secrets may be subject to larceny statutes. Intercepting cellular phone calls to obtain another's phone card number—and then using that number to place long-distance calls, often overseas—is a form of property theft. These types of larceny are covered by "theft of services" statutes in many jurisdictions.

The common law makes a distinction between grand and petit larceny based on the value of the property taken. Many states have abolished this distinction, but in those that have not, grand larceny is a felony and petit larceny, a misdemeanor.

OBTAINING GOODS BY FALSE PRETENSES It is a criminal act to obtain goods by false pretenses—for example, to buy groceries with a check, knowing that one has insufficient funds to cover it. Statutes dealing with such illegal activities vary widely from state to state.

RECEIVING STOLEN PROPERTY It is a crime to receive stolen goods. The recipient of such goods need not know the true identity of the owner or the thief. All that is necessary is that the recipient knows or should know that the goods are stolen, which implies an intent to deprive the owner of those goods.

EMBEZZLEMENT When a person entrusted with another person's property or money fraudulently appropriates that property or money, **embezzlement** occurs. Typically, embezzlement involves an employee who steals money. Banks face this problem, and so do a number of businesses in which corporate officers or accountants "doctor" the books to cover up the fraudulent conversion of money for their own benefit. Embezzlement is not larceny, because the wrongdoer does not physically take the property from the possession of another, and it is not robbery, because no force or fear is used.

It does not matter whether the accused takes the money from the victim or from a third person. If, as the financial officer of a large corporation, Carlson pockets a certain number of checks from third parties that were given to her to deposit into the corporate account, she is embezzling.

Ordinarily, an embezzler who returns what has been taken will not be prosecuted, because the owner usually will not take the time to make a complaint, give depositions, and appear in court. That the accused intended eventually to return the embezzled property, however, does not constitute a sufficient defense to the crime of embezzlement.

ARSON The willful and malicious burning of a building (and in some states, personal property) owned by another is the crime of **arson.** At common law, arson applied only to burning down another person's house. The law was designed to protect human life. Today, arson statutes have been extended to cover the destruction of any building, regardless of ownership, by fire or explosion.

Every state has a special statute that covers a person's burning a building for the purpose of collecting insurance. If Shaw owns an insured apartment building that is falling apart and sets fire to it himself or pays someone else to do so, he is guilty not only of arson but also of defrauding insurers, which is an attempted larceny. Of course, the insurer need not pay the claim when insurance fraud is proved.

MAIL AND WIRE FRAUD One of the most potent weapons against white-collar criminals is the Mail Fraud Act of 1990.[20] Under this act, it is a federal crime to use the mails to defraud the public. Illegal use of the mails must involve (1) mailing or causing someone else to mail a writing—something written, printed, or photocopied—for the purpose of executing a scheme to defraud and (2) contemplating or organizing a scheme to defraud by false pretenses. If, for example, Johnson advertises by mail the sale of a cure for cancer that he knows to be fraudulent because it has no medical validity, he can be prosecuted for fraudulent use of the mails.

Federal law also makes it a crime to use wire, radio, or television transmissions to defraud.[21] Violators may be fined up to $1,000, imprisoned for up to five years, or both. If the violation affects a financial institution, the violator may be fined up to $1 million, imprisoned for up to thirty years, or both.

BRIBERY Basically, three types of bribery are considered crimes: bribery of public officials, commercial bribery, and bribery of foreign officials. The attempt to influence a public official to act in a way that serves a private interest is a crime. As an element of this crime, intent must be present and proved. The bribe can be anything the recipient considers to be valuable. Realize that the *crime of bribery occurs when the bribe is offered.* It does not matter whether the person to whom the bribe is offered accepts the bribe or agrees to perform whatever action is desired by the person offering the bribe. *Accepting a bribe* is a separate crime.

Typically, people make commercial bribes to obtain proprietary information, cover up an inferior product, or secure new business. Industrial espionage sometimes involves commercial bribes. For example, a person in one firm may offer an employee in a competing firm some type of payoff in exchange for trade secrets or pricing schedules. So-called kickbacks, or payoffs for special favors or services, are a form of commercial bribery in some situations.

Bribing foreign officials to obtain favorable business contracts is a crime. This crime was discussed in detail in Chapter 8, along with the Foreign Corrupt Practices Act of 1977, which was passed to curb the use of bribery by American businesspersons in securing foreign contracts.

BANKRUPTCY FRAUD Today, federal bankruptcy law (see Chapter 16) allows individuals and businesses to be relieved of oppressive debt through bankruptcy proceedings. Numerous white-collar crimes may be committed during the many phases of

20. 18 U.S.C. Sections 1341–1342.

21. 18 U.S.C. Section 1343.

a bankruptcy proceeding. A creditor, for example, may file a false claim against the debtor, which is a crime. Also, a debtor may fraudulently transfer assets to favored parties before or after the petition for bankruptcy is filed. For example, a company-owned automobile may be "sold" at a bargain price to a trusted friend or relative. Closely related to the crime of fraudulent transfer of property is the crime of fraudulent concealment of property, such as the hiding of gold coins.

MONEY LAUNDERING The profits from illegal activities amount to billions of dollars a year, particularly the profits from illegal drug transactions and, to a lesser extent, from racketeering, prostitution, and gambling. Under federal law, banks, savings and loan associations, and other financial institutions are required to report currency transactions of over $10,000. Consequently, those who engage in illegal activities face difficulties in placing their cash profits from illegal transactions.

As an alternative to simply placing cash from illegal transactions in bank deposits, wrongdoers and racketeers have invented ways to launder "dirty" money to make it "clean." This **money laundering** is done through legitimate businesses. For example, a successful drug dealer might become a partner with a restaurateur. Little by little, the restaurant shows an increasing profit. As a shareholder or partner in the restaurant, the wrongdoer is able to report the "profits" of the restaurant as legitimate income on which federal and state taxes are paid. The wrongdoer can then spend those monies without worrying about whether his or her lifestyle exceeds the level possible with his or her reported income.

The Federal Bureau of Investigation estimates that organized crime alone has invested tens of billions of dollars in as many as a hundred thousand business establishments in the United States for the purpose of money laundering. Globally, it is estimated that $300 billion in illegal money moves through the world banking system every year.

INSIDER TRADING An individual who obtains "inside information" about the plans of large corporations can often make stock-trading profits by using the information to guide decisions relating to the purchase or sale of corporate securities. *Insider trading* is a violation of securities law and will be considered more fully in Chapter 28. At this point, it may be said that one who possesses inside information and who has a duty not to disclose it to outsiders may not profit from the purchase or sale of securities based on that information until the information is available to the public.

THE THEFT OF TRADE SECRETS As will be discussed in Chapter 15, trade secrets constitute a form of intellectual property that for many businesses can be extremely valuable. The Economic Espionage Act of 1996[22] makes the theft of trade secrets a federal crime. The act also makes it a federal crime to buy or possess trade secrets of another person, knowing that the trade secrets were stolen or otherwise acquired without the owner's authorization.

The act defines a trade secret to incorporate the new methods of creating and storing trade secrets that technology has made possible:

> [T]he term "trade secret" means all forms and types of financial, business, scientific, technical, economic, or engineering information, including patterns, plans, compilations, program devices, formulas, designs, prototypes, methods, techniques, processes, procedures, programs or codes, whether tangible or intangible, and whether or how stored, compiled, or memorialized physically, electronically, graphically, photographically, or in writing if
> (A) the owner thereof has taken reasonable measures to keep such information secret; and
> (B) the information derives independent economic value, actual or potential, from not being generally known to, and not being readily ascertainable through proper means by the public.

Violations of the act can result in steep penalties. The act provides that an individual who violates the act can be imprisoned for up to ten years and fined up to $500,000. If a corporation or other organization violates the act, it can be fined up to $5 million. Additionally, the law provides that any property acquired as a result of the violation and any property used in the commission of the violation is subject to criminal forfeiture—meaning that the government can take the property. A theft of trade secrets conducted via the Internet, for example, could result in the forfeiture of every computer, printer, or other device used to commit or facilitate the violation.

COMPUTER CRIME The American Bar Association defines **computer crime** as any act that is directed against computers and computer parts, that

22. 18 U.S.C. 1831–1839.

uses computers as instruments of crime, or that involves computers and constitutes abuse. A variety of different types of crime can be committed with or against computers.

Types of Computer Crime. Many computer crimes fall into the broad category of financial crimes. Computer networks provide opportunities for employees and others to commit crimes that can involve serious economic losses. For example, employees of accounting and computer departments can transfer monies among accounts with little effort and often with less risk than that involved in transactions evidenced by paperwork. Not only is the potential for crime in the area of financial transactions great, but also most monetary losses from computer crime are suffered in this area.

The theft of computer equipment and the theft of goods with the aid of computers (such as by manipulating inventory records to disguise the theft of goods) are subject to the same criminal and tort laws as thefts of other physical property. In many jurisdictions, the unauthorized use of computer data or services is considered larceny. Other computer crimes include vandalism and destructive programming. A knowledgeable individual, such as an angry employee whose job has just been terminated, can do a considerable amount of damage to computer data and files. Destructive programming in the form of "viruses" presents an ongoing problem for businesspersons and other computer users today.

Another major problem for businesspersons today, as will be discussed in Chapter 15, is software piracy. Under most state laws, software piracy is classified as a crime. At the federal level, the laws protecting intellectual property (such as patent and copyright laws, discussed in Chapter 15) also cover computer programs. In 1990, in an attempt to control further the unauthorized copying of computer programs, the federal government passed a law that prohibits, with some exceptions, the renting, leasing, or lending of computer software without the express permission of the copyright holder.

Prosecuting Computer Crime. At the federal level, the Counterfeit Access Device and Computer Fraud and Abuse Act of 1984, as amended, prohibits unauthorized access to certain types of information, such as restricted government information, information contained in a financial institution's financial records, and information contained in a consumer reporting agency's files on consumers. Penalties for violations include up to five years' imprisonment and a fine of up to $250,000 or twice the amount that was gained by the thief or lost by the victim as a result of the crime. Several states also have laws specifically addressing the problem of computer crime.

One of the problems presented by computer crime is its relative invisibility. Even when it is apparent that a computer crime has occurred, tracing the crime to the individual who committed it can be difficult, because the individual's identity is hidden by the "faceless" nature of computer networks, particularly the Internet. Another problem is that the law is always a step or two behind technological developments, and thus traditional laws may not always apply to activities conducted using computers.

SECTION 3
RICO

Businesses have often been sued for fraudulent or other tortious activities under the Racketeer Influenced and Corrupt Organizations Act.[23] The act, which is commonly known as RICO, was passed by Congress in 1970 as part of the Organized Crime Control Act. The purpose of the act was to curb the apparently increasing entry of organized crime into the legitimate business world.

ACTIVITIES PROHIBITED BY RICO

Under RICO, it is a federal crime (1) to use income obtained from racketeering activity to purchase any interest in an enterprise, (2) to acquire or maintain an interest in an enterprise through racketeering activity, (3) to conduct or participate in the affairs of an enterprise through racketeering activity, or (4) to conspire to do any of the preceding activities.

Racketeering activity is not a new type of substantive crime created by RICO; rather, RICO incorporates by reference twenty-six separate types of federal crimes and nine types of state felonies[24] and states that if a person commits two of these offenses, he or she is guilty of "racketeering activity." The act provides for both criminal liability and civil liability.

23. 18 U.S.C. Sections 1961–1968.

24. See 18 U.S.C. Section 1961(1)(A).

CIVIL LIABILITY UNDER RICO

The penalties for violations of the RICO statute are harsh. In the event of a violation, the statute permits the government to seek civil penalties, including the divestiture of a defendant's interest in a business (called forfeiture) or the dissolution of the business. Perhaps the most controversial aspect of RICO is that in some cases, private individuals are allowed to recover three times their actual losses (treble damages), plus attorneys' fees, for business injuries caused by a violation of the statute.

The broad language of RICO has allowed it to be applied in cases that have little or nothing to do with organized crime, and an aggressive trial attorney may attempt to show that any business fraud constitutes "racketeering activity." In its 1985 decision in *Sedima, S.P.R.L. v. Imrex Co.*,[25] the United States Supreme Court interpreted RICO broadly and set a significant precedent for subsequent applications of the act. Plaintiffs have used the RICO statute in numerous commercial fraud cases because of the inviting prospect of being awarded treble damages if they win. The most frequent targets of civil RICO lawsuits are insurance companies, employment agencies, commercial banks, and stockbrokerage firms.

One of the requirements of RICO is that there be more than one offense—there must be a "pattern of racketeering activity." What constitutes a "pattern" has been the subject of much litigation. According to the interpretation of some courts, a pattern must involve, among other things, continued criminal activity. This is known as the "continuity" requirement. Part of this requirement is that the activity occur over a "substantial" period of time. The court in the following case considered whether the actions of the defendants met this requirement.

25. 473 U.S. 479, 105 S.Ct. 3275, 87 L.Ed.2d 346 (1985).

CASE 13.4 ☒ Tabas v. Tabas

United States Court of Appeals, Third Circuit, 1995.
47 F.3d 1280.

BACKGROUND AND FACTS *Charles and Daniel Tabas formed a partnership to conduct real estate and other business ventures. They agreed that if either partner died, the other would distribute the partnership income equally to himself and to the estate of the deceased partner. When Charles died, Daniel agreed to mail monthly partnership income checks to Charles's widow, Harriette. Daniel mailed monthly checks in the same amount to himself. In addition, Daniel drew a salary and paid a variety of personal expenses from partnership income. When Harriette and the executors of Charles's estate learned of Daniel's activities, they confronted him, and he agreed to dissolve the partnership and sell the assets. Continuing dissatisfaction with Daniel's conduct prompted Harriette and the executors (the plaintiffs) to file a suit in a federal district court against Daniel and others (the defendants), alleging, among other things, that acts of fraud over the previous three and a half years constituted violations of RICO. Daniel filed a motion for summary judgment, which the court granted. The court found no "continuity," reasoning that as soon as the partnership assets were sold, all of the alleged fraud would stop. The plaintiffs appealed.*

IN THE LANGUAGE OF THE COURT

ROTH, Circuit Judge:

* * * *

* * * Each time defendants misrepresented the business nature of an expense, made a questionable charge, or received compensation to which they were not entitled, they lessened the income available to the Estate. Plaintiffs have provided evidence that these activities, which implemented defendants' purported scheme to defraud the Estate, lasted more than three and a half years * * * . We conclude that a scheme lasting over three years extends over a "substantial" period of time and therefore constitutes the type of "long-term criminal conduct"

that RICO was enacted to address. Accordingly, we find, from the strictly durational aspect of the scheme, that plaintiffs in the present case have made a sufficient showing to survive summary judgment on the "continuity" prong of the pattern analysis.

DECISION AND REMEDY *The U.S. Court of Appeals for the Third Circuit reversed the district court's ruling and remanded the case for further proceedings.*

CRIMINAL RICO VIOLATIONS

Many criminal RICO offenses, such as gambling, arson, and extortion, have little, if anything, to do with normal business activities. But securities fraud (involving the sale of stocks and bonds) and mail and wire fraud also may constitute criminal RICO violations, and RICO has become an effective tool in attacking these white-collar crimes in recent years. Under the criminal provisions of RICO, any individual found guilty of a violation is subject to a fine of up to $25,000 per violation, imprisonment for up to twenty years, or both.

TERMS AND CONCEPTS TO REVIEW

actus reus 274
arson 280
appropriation 270
burglary 279
business tort 267
computer crime 281
crime 273
disparagement of property 271
double jeopardy 274
embezzlement 280
exclusionary rule 275
felony 273
forgery 279
grand jury 277
indictment 277
information 277
larceny 279
mens rea 274
misdemeanor 273
money laundering 281
petty offense 273
robbery 279
slander of quality 271
slander of title 272
trade libel 271
white-collar crime 279

QUESTIONS AND CASE PROBLEMS

13–1. WRONGFUL INTERFERENCE. Lothar owns a bakery. He has been trying to obtain a long-term contract with the owner of Martha's Tea Salons for some time. Lothar starts a local advertising campaign on radio and television and in the newspaper. This advertising campaign is so persuasive that Martha decides to break the contract she has had with Harley's Bakery so that she can patronize Lothar's bakery. Is Lothar liable to Harley's Bakery for the tort of wrongful interference with a contractual relationship? Is Martha liable for this tort? For anything?

13–2. BUSINESS TORT THEORIES. Red Stripe Airlines negotiates a lease at an airport for gates on the same concourse as Green Top Airlines. In fact, for passengers to get to Green Top's gates, they must walk past Red Stripe's gates. Red Stripe puts up a large sign that states, "Passengers of other airlines—turn in your tickets or cancel your reservations, and we will give you 25 percent off the price of your trip if you fly on Red Stripe Airlines." In addition, Red Stripe's ticket agents solicit business from travelers on their way to Green Top's gates. At this time, only Red Stripe and Green Top have operative gates on the concourse. Discuss fully any business tort theories under which Green Top can recover against Red Stripe for the latter's actions. (Remember: A ticket is a contract.)

13–3. BUSINESS TORT THEORIES. Luigi owns and operates a famous Italian restaurant in New York City.

Luigi hires chef Toni to prepare the pasta and other dishes on his menu. Toni also contributes a column to *Gourmet Eating* magazine in which he discusses Italian food and restaurants in the area and rates all restaurants with stars. The ratings range from one star (the lowest rating) to five stars (the highest rating). Toni is prohibited from discussing or rating Luigi's restaurant in his column as long as he is employed by Luigi. One day, Luigi and Toni have a dispute over Toni's salary, and Toni, in front of a substantial number of regular customers who are well known in New York society, accuses Luigi of watering his house wine and of not making his own pasta. Luigi has on occasion purchased some pasta from a pasta shop in the neighborhood, but he has never watered his wine. Toni quits on the spot and later, in *Gourmet Eating*, rates Luigi's restaurant with only one star, adding a notation that Luigi's wine and pasta are inferior to the wine and pasta offered by other restaurants. Under what tort theories, if any, can Luigi file suit against Toni? Discuss fully.

13–4. Types of Crimes. The following situations are similar (in all of them, Juanita's television set is stolen), yet three different crimes are described. Identify the three crimes, noting the differences among them.

(a) While passing Juanita's house one night, Sarah sees a portable television set left unattended on Juanita's lawn. Sarah takes the television set, carries it home, and tells everyone she owns it.

(b) While passing Juanita's house one night, Sarah sees Juanita outside with a portable television set. Holding Juanita at gunpoint, Sarah forces her to give up the set. Then Sarah runs away with it.

(c) While passing Juanita's house one night, Sarah sees a portable television set in a window. Sarah breaks the front-door lock, enters, and leaves with the set.

13–5. Wrongful Interference. DBI Services, Inc., provided oil-field trucking services, brine water, and drilling mud to oil producers in the Seminole area of Texas. From 1983 to 1986, the major oil producer in the area, Amerada Hess Corp. (AH), regularly contracted with DBI for its services. AH learned in a 1986 audit of its contractors that DBI had engaged in lavish entertainment of certain AH employees who were responsible for awarding job contracts. Disturbed by this discovery, AH thereafter refused to deal with DBI. AH also refused to accept contract bids from any firms that planned to subcontract work out to DBI, even if the firms had submitted the lowest bids for the contracts. DBI sued AH for tortious interference with its contractual relationships with these other firms. AH claimed that it was not obligated to accept the lowest bids for contracts and that it had a right to determine with whom it would do business. How will the court decide the issue? Discuss. [*DBI Services, Inc. v. Amerada Hess Corp.*, 907 F.2d 506 (5th Cir. 1990)]

13–6. Wrongful Interference. Bombardier Capital, Inc., provides financing to boat and recreational vehicle dealers. Bombardier's credit policy requires dealers to forward immediately to Bombardier the proceeds of boat sales. When Howard Mulcahey, Bombardier's vice president of sales and marketing, learned that a dealer was not complying with this policy, he told Frank Chandler, Bombardier's credit director, of his concern. Before Chandler could obtain the proceeds, Mulcahey falsely told Jacques Gingras, Bombardier's president, that Chandler was, among other things, trying to hide the problem. On the basis of Mulcahey's statements, Gingras fired Chandler and put Mulcahey in charge of the credit department. Under what business tort theory discussed in this chapter might Chandler recover damages from Mulcahey? Explain. [*Chandler v. Bombardier Capital, Inc.*, 44 F.3d 80 (2d Cir. 1994)]

13–7. RICO. During the 1980s, the Mutual Trading Corp. (MTC) bought and sold tires made by the Uniroyal Goodrich Tire Co. In the 1990s, Uniroyal discovered that MTC had perpetrated at least four separate schemes to swindle money from Uniroyal. As part of one scheme, for example, MTC had submitted fraudulent claims for reimbursement for amounts it had refunded to customers in Saudi Arabia. As part of another scheme, MTC had obtained from Uniroyal twice as much for its advertising costs in Nigeria as the parties had previously agreed on. Uniroyal filed a suit against MTC and others in a federal district court, alleging, among other things, that these schemes violated RICO. MTC responded in part that the allegations depicted only a single scheme perpetrated on a single victim and that thus there was no "pattern of racketeering activity." What constitutes a pattern of activity to satisfy RICO? Is RICO satisfied in this case? [*Uniroyal Goodrich Tire Co. v. Mutual Trading Corp.*, 63 F.3d 516 (7th Cir. 1995)]

13–8. Embezzlement. Faulkner, a truck driver, was hauling a load of refrigerators from San Diego to New York for the trucking company that employed him. He departed from his assigned route and stopped in Las Vegas, where he attempted to display and sell some of the refrigerators to a firm. Although the refrigerators never left the truck, to display them he had to break the truck's seals, enter the cargo department, and open two refrigerator cartons. The store owner refused to purchase the appliances, and when Faulkner left the store, he was arrested. He was later convicted under federal law for the embezzlement of an interstate shipment. Faulkner appealed, claiming that the charge of embezzlement should not apply because the property had not been physically removed from the owner's possession. Will the appellate court agree with Faulkner? Explain. [*United States v. Faulkner*, 638 F.2d 129 (9th Cir. 1981)]

13–9. Criminal Liability. In January 1988, David Ludvigson was hired as chief executive officer of Leopard Enterprises, a group of companies that owned funeral homes and cemeteries in Iowa and sold "pre-need" funeral contracts. Under Iowa law, 80 percent of the monies obtained under such a contract must be set aside in trust until the death of the person for whose benefit the funds were paid. Shortly after Ludvigson was hired, the firm began having financial difficulties. Ludvigson used money from the funeral contracts to pay operating expenses until the company went bankrupt and was placed in receivership. Ludvigson was charged and found guilty on five counts of second degree theft stemming from the misappropriation of these funds. He appealed, alleging, among other things, that he was not guilty of any crime, because he had not intended to permanently deprive any of the clients of their trust funds. Furthermore, because none of the victims whose trust funds were used to cover operating expenses was denied services, no injury was done. Will the court agree with Ludvigson? Explain. [*State v. Ludvigson*, 482 N.W.2d 419 (Ia. 1992)]

13–10. A QUESTION OF ETHICS

A troublesome issue concerning the constitutional privilege against self-incrimination has to do with "jail plants"—that is, undercover police officers placed in cells with criminal suspects to gain information from the suspects. For example, in one case, the police placed an undercover agent, Parisi, in a jail cell block with Lloyd Perkins, who had been imprisoned on charges unrelated to the murder that Parisi was investigating. When Parisi asked Perkins if he had ever killed anyone, Perkins made statements implicating himself in the murder. Perkins was then charged with the murder. [*Illinois v. Perkins*, 496 U.S. 292, 110 S.Ct. 2394, 110 L.Ed.2d 243 (1990)]

1. Review the discussion and case presentation of *Miranda v. Arizona* (Case 13.3). Should Perkins's statements be suppressed—that is, not be treated as admissible evidence at trial—because he was not "read his rights" (as required by the *Miranda* decision) prior to making his self-incriminating statements? Does *Miranda* apply in Perkins's situation?
2. Do you think that it is fair for the police to resort to trickery and deception to bring those who have committed crimes to justice? Why or why not? What rights or public policies must be balanced in deciding this issue?

ACCESSING THE INTERNET
THE LEGAL ENVIRONMENT OF BUSINESS

A good starting place to find information on criminal law on the Internet is

http://www.fsu.edu/~crimdo/cj.html

This site, which is updated regularly, offers the most extensive collection of criminal law links on the Internet, including links to local, state, federal, and international resources, as well as to other crime-related Web sites.

Another site with a large number of links to crime-related topics is

http://dpa.state.ky.us:80/

If you are interested in looking at the text of the *U.S. Sentencing Guidelines Manual*, go to

http://www.ussc.gov

The Bureau of Justice Statistics in the U.S. Department of Justice offers an impressive collection of statistics on crime, including data on crimes and victims, drugs and crimes, criminal courts, criminal prosecution, sentencing, and corrections facilities. You can find this collection at

http://www.ojp.usdoj.gov/bjs

For information on criminal justice programs and initiatives, as well as other information on the criminal justice system, go to the U.S. Department of Justice's home page at

http://usdoj.gov

The Justice Information Center is an excellent source for information on criminal and juvenile justice throughout the world. To access this information, go to

http://www.ncjrs.org

The Federal Bureau of Investigation (FBI) offers abundant information and statistics on crime, including information concerning FBI investigations, international crime, wiretapping, electronic surveillance, and economic espionage. You can locate the FBI's home page at

http://www.fbi.gov

One of the goals of the National Institute of Justice, the research arm of the U.S. Department of Justice, is "to prevent and reduce crime and to improve the criminal justice system." To learn about the institute's research and its various projects (in such areas as community policing, violence against women, and drug courts), go to

http://ncjrs.org/nijhome.htm

You can find information on the operations of the American Civil Liberties Union (ACLU) and obtain some information on the protection of constitutional rights within the criminal justice system at

http://www.aclu.org/issues/criminal/hmcj.html

If you would like to learn more about criminal procedures, the following site offers an "Anatomy of a Murder: A Trip through Our Nation's Legal Justice System":

http://tqd.advanced.org/2760

Chapter 14

Product Liability

Product liability refers to the liability incurred by manufacturers and sellers of products when product defects cause injury or property damages to consumers, users, or bystanders (people in the vicinity of the product). Product liability encompasses the tort theories of negligence, misrepresentation, and strict liability—all of which were discussed in Chapter 12. For example, if a product is defective because of the manufacturer's negligence, an injured user of the product can sue the manufacturer for negligence in a product liability suit. If a user is injured by a product as a result of the seller's fraudulent misrepresentation of the nature of that product, the basis of the product liability suit is fraud. In the last several decades, the doctrine of strict liability often has been applied in product liability suits.

In this chapter, we examine each of these bases for product liability. Note that product liability can also be based on warranty theory, a topic we treated in Chapter 11.

SECTION 1
NEGLIGENCE

In Chapter 12, we defined *negligence* as the failure to exercise the degree of care that a reasonable, prudent person would have exercised under the circumstances. If a manufacturer fails to exercise "due care" to make a product safe, a person who is injured by the product may sue the manufacturer for negligence.

Due care must be exercised in designing the product, in selecting the materials, in using the appropriate production process, in assembling and testing the product, and in placing adequate warnings on the label informing the user of dangers of which an ordinary person might not be aware. The duty of care also extends to the inspection and testing of any purchased products that are used in the final product sold by the manufacturer.

PRIVITY OF CONTRACT NOT REQUIRED

A product liability action based on negligence does not require the injured plaintiff and the negligent defendant-manufacturer to be in **privity of contract.** That is, the plaintiff and the defendant need not be directly involved in a contractual relationship. A manufacturer is liable for its failure to exercise due care to *any person* who sustains an injury proximately caused by a negligently made (defective) product. Relative to the long history of the common law, this exception to the privity requirement is a fairly recent development, dating to the early part of the twentieth century.[1]

VIOLATION OF STATUTORY DUTY

Numerous federal and state laws impose duties on manufacturers of cosmetics, drugs, foods, toxic substances, and flammable materials. These duties involve appropriate description of contents, labeling, branding, advertising, and selling. For example, federal statutes include the Flammable Fabrics Act (1953); the Federal Food, Drug and Cosmetic Act (1938); and the Hazardous Substances Labeling Act (1960). In a tort action for damages, a violation of statutory duty is often held to constitute *negligence per se* (negligence in itself, or inherent negligence), as discussed in Chapter 12.

1. A landmark case in this respect is *MacPherson v. Buick Motor Co.*, 217 N.Y. 382, 111 N.E. 1050 (1916).

SECTION 2
MISREPRESENTATION

When a fraudulent misrepresentation has been made to a user or consumer and that misrepresentation ultimately results in an injury, the basis of liability may be the tort of fraud. In this case, the misrepresentation must have been made knowingly or with reckless disregard for the facts. An example is the intentional concealment of a product's defects. In contrast to actions based on negligence and strict liability, in a suit based on fraudulent misrepresentation, the plaintiff does not have to show that the product was defective or that it malfunctioned in any way.[2]

Nonfraudulent misrepresentation, which occurs when a merchant *innocently* misrepresents the character or quality of goods, can also provide a basis of liability. In this situation, it does not have to be proved that the misrepresentation was made knowingly. A famous example involved a drug manufacturer and a victim of addiction to a prescription medicine called Talwin. The manufacturer, Winthrop Laboratories, a division of Sterling Drug, Inc., innocently indicated to the medical profession that the drug was not physically addictive. Using this information, a physician prescribed the drug for his patient, who developed an addiction that turned out to be fatal. Even though the addiction was a highly uncommon reaction resulting from the victim's unusual susceptibility to this product, the drug company was still held liable.[3]

Whether fraudulent or nonfraudulent, the misrepresentation must be of a material fact (a fact concerning the quality, nature, or appropriate use of the product on which a normal buyer may be expected to rely). There must also have been an intent to induce the buyer's reliance. Misrepresentation on a label or advertisement is enough to show an intent to induce the reliance of anyone who may use the product. The buyer also must rely on the misrepresentation. If the buyer is not aware of the misrepresentation or if it does not influence the transaction, there is no liability.

2. See, for example, *Khan v. Shiley, Inc.*, 217 Cal.App.3d 848, 266 Cal.Rptr. 106 (1990).

3. *Crocker v. Winthrop Laboratories, Division of Sterling Drug, Inc.*, 514 S.W.2d 429 (Tex. 1974).

SECTION 3
STRICT LIABILITY

Under the doctrine of *strict liability* (discussed in Chapter 12), people may be held liable for the results of their acts regardless of their intentions or their exercise of reasonable care. For example, a company that uses dynamite in constructing a road is strictly liable for any damages that result, even if it takes reasonable and prudent precautions to prevent such damages. In essence, the blasting company becomes liable for any personal injuries it causes and thus is an absolute insurer—that is, the company is liable for damages regardless of fault.

In several landmark cases involving manufactured goods in the 1960s, courts applied the doctrine of strict liability, and it has since become a common method of holding manufacturers liable. Some states, however, such as Massachusetts, have refused to recognize strict product liability. Additionally, some courts limit the application of the strict liability doctrine to cases in which personal injuries have occurred. Thus, when a defective product causes only *property damage*, depending on the law of the particular jurisdiction, the seller may not be liable under a theory of strict liability. Until recently, recovery for economic loss was not available in an action based on strict liability (and even today it is rarely available).

The *Restatement (Second) of Torts* designates how the doctrine of strict product liability should be applied. It is a precise and widely accepted statement of the liabilities of sellers of goods (including manufacturers, processors, assemblers, packagers, bottlers, wholesalers, distributors, and retailers) and deserves close attention.

THE *RESTATEMENT (SECOND) OF TORTS*

Section 402A of the *Restatement (Second) of Torts* states as follows:

> (1) One who sells any product in a defective condition unreasonably dangerous to the user or consumer or to his property is subject to liability for physical harm thereby caused to the ultimate user or consumer or to his property, if
> (a) the seller is engaged in the business of selling such a product, and
> (b) it is expected to and does reach the user or consumer without substantial change in the condition in which it is sold.
>
> (2) The rule stated in Subsection (1) applies although
> (a) the seller has exercised all possible care in the preparation and sale of his product, and
> (b) the user or consumer has not bought the product from or entered into any contractual relation with the seller.

Strict liability is imposed by law as a matter of public policy. This public policy rests on the threefold assumption that (1) consumers should be protected against unsafe products, (2) manufacturers and distributors should not escape liability for faulty products simply because they are not in privity of contract with the ultimate users of those products, and (3) manufacturers and sellers of products are in a better position to bear the costs associated with injuries caused by their products—costs that they can ultimately pass on to all consumers in the form of higher prices.

REQUIREMENTS OF STRICT PRODUCT LIABILITY—SUMMARIZED

The basis for an action in strict liability as set forth in Section 402A of the *Restatement (Second) of Torts* and as the doctrine is commonly applied can be summarized as a series of six requirements:

1. The product must be in a defective condition when the defendant sells it.
2. The defendant must normally be engaged in the business of selling (or otherwise distributing) that product.
3. The product must be unreasonably dangerous to the user or consumer because of its defective condition (in most states).
4. The plaintiff must incur physical harm to self or property by use or consumption of the product.
5. The defective condition must be the proximate cause of the injury or damage.
6. The goods must not have been substantially changed from the time the product was sold to the time the injury was sustained.

Thus, in any action against a manufacturer or seller, the plaintiff does not have to show why or in what manner the product became defective. To recover damages, however, the plaintiff must show that the product was so defective as to be unreasonably dangerous; that the product caused the plaintiff's injury; and that at the time the injury was sustained, the condition of the product was essentially the same as when it left the hands of the defendant manufacturer or seller.

The plaintiff does not need to be in privity of contract with the manufacturer or seller to sue in strict product liability. Although the drafters of the *Restatement (Second) of Torts*, Section 402A, did not take a position on **bystanders** (those within the vicinity of a product), all courts extend the strict liability of manufacturers and other sellers to such persons. For example, the manufacturer of an automobile was held liable for injuries caused by the explosion of the car's motor while the car was in traffic. A cloud of steam that resulted from the explosion caused multiple collisions, because it kept other drivers from seeing well.[4] In the following classic case, the court indicates some policy reasons for extending the protections of Section 402A to bystanders whose injuries from defective products are reasonably foreseeable.

4. *Giberson v. Ford Motor Co.*, 504 S.W.2d 8 (Mo. 1974).

CASE 14.1 Embs v. Pepsi-Cola Bottling Co. of Lexington, Kentucky, Inc.

Court of Appeals of Kentucky, 1975. 528 S.W.2d 703.

BACKGROUND AND FACTS *Janice Embs was buying some groceries at Stamper's Cash Market. Unnoticed by her, a carton of 7-Up was sitting on the floor at the edge of the produce counter about one foot from where she was standing. Several of the 7-Up bottles exploded. Embs's leg was injured severely enough that Embs had to be taken to the hospital by a managing agent of the store. Embs brought an action in a Kentucky state court against the manufacturer, but the trial court dismissed her claim. Embs appealed.*

IN THE LANGUAGE OF THE COURT

JUKOWSKY, Judge.

* * * *

Our expressed public policy will be furthered if we minimize the risk of personal injury and property damage by charging the costs of injuries against the manufacturer who can procure liability insurance and distribute its expense among the public as a cost of doing business; and since the risk of harm from defective products exists for mere bystanders and passersby as well as for the purchaser or user, there is no substantial reason for protecting one class of persons and not the other. The same policy requires us to maximize protection for the injured third party and promote the public interest in discouraging the marketing of products having defects that are a menace to the public by imposing strict liability upon retailers and wholesalers in the distributive chain responsible for marketing the defective product which injures the bystander. *The imposition of strict liability places no unreasonable burden upon sellers because they can adjust the cost of insurance protection among themselves in the course of their continuing business relationship.* [Emphasis added.]

We must not shirk from extending the rule to the manufacturer for fear that the retailer or middleman will be impaled on the sword of liability without regard to fault. Their liability was already established under Section 402A of the *Restatement of Torts 2d*. As a matter of public policy the retailer or middleman as well as the manufacturer should be liable since the loss for injuries resulting from defective products should be placed on those members of the marketing chain best able to pay the loss, who can then distribute such risk among themselves by means of insurance and indemnity agreements. * * *

The result which we reach does not give the bystander a "free ride." When products and consumers are considered in the aggregate, bystanders, as a class, purchase most of the same products to which they are exposed as bystanders. Thus, as a class, they indirectly subsidize the liability of the manufacturer, middleman and retailer and in this sense do pay for the insurance policy tied to the product.

Public policy is adequately served if parameters are placed upon the extension of the rule so that it is limited to bystanders whose injury from the defect is reasonably foreseeable.

For the sake of clarity we restate the extension of the rule. The protections of Section 402A of the *Restatement of Torts 2d* extend to bystanders whose injury from the defective product is reasonably foreseeable.

DECISION AND REMEDY *The appellate court reversed the trial court's dismissal of Embs's claim. The case was remanded to the lower court for a new trial.*

PRODUCT DEFECT AND STRICT LIABILITY CLAIMS

One requirement for a strict product liability action, in most states, as noted, is that the product be unreasonably dangerous to the user or consumer because of its defective condition. A court may consider a product so defective as to be an **unreasonably dangerous product** if either (1) the product was dangerous beyond the expectation of the ordinary consumer or (2) a less dangerous alternative was economically feasible for the manufacturer, but the manufacturer failed to produce it. Generally, claims that a product is so defective as to be unreasonably dangerous fall into the three categories discussed here.

FLAW IN THE MANUFACTURING PROCESS A plaintiff may allege that a product was unreasonably dangerous because of a flaw in the manufacturing process. As discussed earlier, manufacturers are required to use due care in the manufacture, assembly, and testing of the goods they produce. The failure to exercise proper care in manufacturing a product is an act of negligence. If that negligence causes a product to be defective and unreasonably dangerous, the manufacturer may be strictly liable for harms suffered by users of the product.

DESIGN DEFECT A product, although perfectly manufactured, may nonetheless be unreasonably dangerous because of a defect in design. Generally, a plaintiff claiming a design defect must show that a safer alternative was available and economically feasible for the manufacturer but the manufacturer failed to produce it. When determining whether a less dangerous alternative was economically feasible for the manufacturer, courts will consider a number of factors, including the product's social utility and desirability, the availability of—and economic feasibility of producing—a safer alternative, the obviousness of the danger posed by the product, the probability of injury and its likely seriousness, and the possibility of eliminating the danger without appreciably impairing the product's function.

For example, people often cut themselves on knives, but there is no way to prevent injuries without making the product useless, and the danger is obvious to users. Therefore, a court normally would not find a knife to be unreasonably dangerous and would not hold a supplier of knives liable. In contrast, a court may consider a snowblower without a safety guard over the opening through which the snow is blown to be in a condition that is unreasonably dangerous, even if the snowblower carries warnings to stay clear of the opening. The danger may be within users' expectations, but the court will also consider the likelihood of injury and its probable seriousness, as well as the cost of putting a guard over the opening and the guard's effect on the blower's operation.

Some products are safe when used as their manufacturers and distributors intend but not safe when used in other ways. Suppliers are generally required to expect reasonably foreseeable misuses and to design products that are safe when misused or that include some protective device—for example, a child-proof cap. The following case required the court to determine whether a misuse of a product was reasonably foreseeable.

CASE 14.2 Lutz v. National Crane Corp.

Supreme Court of Montana, 1994. 884 P.2d 455.

BACKGROUND AND FACTS *Gerald Lutz and another employee of Montana Ready-Mix were using a crane to retrieve drilling pipe from beneath power lines when the crane cable touched one of the lines. The cable did not have an insulated link and thus conducted electricity from the line to the pipe, electrocuting Lutz. Lutz's widow, Lori Lutz, filed a suit in a Montana state court against the National Crane Corporation, which manufactured the crane, and others, alleging, among other things, that the crane—without an insulated link—was defectively designed and unreasonably dangerous. National Crane argued, among other things, that the employees had been using the crane to sideload (a prac-*

tice that causes the crane's cable to extend its slack in unpredictable ways) and that sideloading was an unreasonable misuse. The court awarded Lori Lutz $815,400, less 20 percent, which it attributed, in part, to Gerald Lutz's unreasonable misuse. Both parties appealed. Lori Lutz sought the full $815,400. She admitted that sideloading was a misuse but claimed that the misuse was reasonably foreseeable.

IN THE LANGUAGE OF THE COURT

HARRISON, Justice.

* * * *

* * * [C]ranes are often operated in close proximity to live electrical lines and * * * sideloading is not an uncommon, albeit improper, practice of crane operators and groundcrews. * * *

* * * *

National Crane admits that the cranes which it manufactures can be misused through sideloading. National Crane also knows that if sideloading occurs in the vicinity of power lines, the possibility exists that its crane cables might contact power lines. It is undisputed that a crane/power line contact was foreseeable to National Crane. * * *

It being admitted that the alleged misuse of the crane through sideloading was reasonably foreseeable to National Crane, we hold that, as a matter of law, the * * * defense of unreasonable misuse is unavailable to National Crane.

DECISION AND REMEDY

The Supreme Court of Montana remanded the case to the lower court with the instruction to reinstate the full award.

INADEQUATE WARNING A plaintiff in a strict liability action may claim that a product is unreasonably dangerous because it lacks adequate warnings or instructions. Manufacturers and other suppliers of products have a duty to warn product users of product-associated risks and dangers, unless the risks and dangers are commonly known, and the breach of this duty constitutes negligence. (As will be discussed later in this chapter, an assertion that a danger is commonly known can be used as a defense to product liability.) A pharmaceutical company, for example, must warn of the possible side effects of its drugs and of the risks associated with using particular drugs in conjunction with other medications.

Generally, a manufacturer must warn those who purchase its products of the harms that can result from the *misuse* of the products as well. If a particular misuse of a product is foreseeable, a court normally will hold that the manufacturer has a duty to warn of the dangers associated with such misuse.

MARKET-SHARE LIABILITY

Generally, in cases involving product liability, a plaintiff must prove that the defective product that caused his or her injury was the product of a specific defendant. In the last decade or so, in cases in which plaintiffs could not prove which of many distributors of a harmful product supplied the particular product that caused their injuries, courts have dropped this requirement.

This has occurred, for example, in several cases involving DES (diethylstilbestrol), a drug administered in the past to prevent miscarriages. DES's harmful character was not realized until, a generation later, daughters of the women who had taken DES developed health problems, including vaginal carcinoma, that were linked to the drug. Partly because of the passage of time, a plaintiff-daughter often could not prove which pharmaceutical company—out of as many as three hundred—had marketed the DES her mother had ingested. In these cases, some courts applied **market-share liability,** holding that all firms that manufactured and distributed DES during the period in question were liable for the plaintiffs' injuries in proportion to the firms' respective shares of the market.[5]

Market-share liability has also been applied in other situations. In one case, for example, a plaintiff who was a hemophiliac received injections of a blood protein known as antihemophiliac factor

5. See, for example, *Martin v. Abbott Laboratories*, 102 Wash.2d 581, 689 P.2d 368 (1984).

(AHF) concentrate. The plaintiff later tested positive for the AIDS (acquired immune deficiency syndrome) virus. Because it was not known which manufacturer was responsible for the particular AHF received by the plaintiff, the court held that all of the manufacturers of AHF could be held liable under a market-share theory of liability.[6] In another case, the New York Court of Appeals (that state's highest court) held that even if a firm can prove that it did not manufacture the particular product that caused injuries to the plaintiff, the firm can be held liable based on the firm's share of the national market.[7]

OTHER APPLICATIONS OF STRICT LIABILITY

Under the rule of strict liability in tort, the basis of liability has been expanded to include suppliers of component parts. Thus, if General Motors buys brake pads from a subcontractor and puts them in Chevrolets without changing their composition, and if those pads are defective, both the supplier of the brake pads and General Motors will be held strictly liable for the damages caused by the defects.

Liability for personal injuries caused by defective goods also extends to those who lease such goods (lessors). Lessors are liable both under negligence theory and under warranty theory (discussed in Chapter 11). Thus, if Hertz Rent-a-Car leases a car that has been improperly maintained, and a passenger in the car is injured in an accident as a result, the passenger can sue Hertz for negligence or for breach of warranty.

Certain courts have adopted the **crashworthiness doctrine,** which imposes liability for defects in the design or construction of motor vehicles that increase the extent of injuries to passengers if an accident occurs. The doctrine holds even when the defects do not actually cause the accident.[8]

SECTION 4
DEFENSES TO PRODUCT LIABILITY

Defendants in product liability suits can raise a number of defenses. One defense, of course, is to show that there is no basis for the plaintiff's claim. For example, in a product liability case based on negligence, if a defendant can show that the plaintiff has not met the requirements (such as causation) for an action in negligence, the defendant will not be liable. In regard to strict liability, a defendant can claim that the plaintiff failed to meet one of the requirements for an action in strict liability. For example, if the defendant establishes that the goods have been subsequently altered, the defendant will not be held liable.[9] Defendants may also assert the defenses discussed next.

ASSUMPTION OF RISK

Assumption of risk can sometimes be used as a defense in a product liability action. To establish such a defense, the defendant must show that (1) the plaintiff knew and appreciated the risk created by the product defect, and (2) the plaintiff voluntarily assumed the risk, even though it was unreasonable to do so. (See Chapter 12 for a more detailed discussion of assumption of risk.)

PRODUCT MISUSE

Similar to the defense of voluntary assumption of risk is that of **product misuse.** Here, the injured party *does not know that the product is dangerous for a particular use* (contrast this with assumption of risk), but the use is not the one for which the product was designed. The courts have severely limited this defense. Even if the injured party does not know about the inherent danger of using the product in a wrong way, if the misuse is foreseeable, the seller must take measures to guard against it.

COMPARATIVE NEGLIGENCE

As discussed in Chapter 12, under the doctrine of comparative negligence, a defendant in a product liability suit may avoid liability in whole or in part if the plaintiff's own negligence contributed to the injury for which the plaintiff seeks damages. The comparative negligence standard has also been applied in strict liability cases. Whereas previously the plaintiff's conduct was not a defense to strict liability, today some jurisdictions consider the negligent or intentional actions of both the plaintiff and

6. *Smith v. Cutter Biological, Inc.*, 72 Haw. 416, 823 P.2d 717 (1991).

7. *Hymowitz v. Eli Lilly and Co.*, 73 N.Y.2d 487, 539 N.E.2d 1069, 541 N.Y.S.2d 941 (1989).

8. *Turner v. General Motors Corp.*, 514 S.W.2d 497 (Tex. Civ.App. 1974).

9. Under some state laws, the failure to properly maintain a product may constitute a subsequent alteration. See, for example, *LaPlante v. American Honda Motor Co.*, 27 F.3d 731 (1st Cir. 1994).

the defendant in the apportionment of liability and damages.

COMMONLY KNOWN DANGERS

The dangers associated with certain products (such as matches and guns) are so commonly known that manufacturers need not warn users of those dangers. If a defendant succeeds in convincing the court that a plaintiff's injury resulted from a *commonly known danger*, the defendant will not be liable.

A classic case on this issue involved a plaintiff who was injured when an elastic exercise rope that she had purchased slipped off her foot and struck her in the eye, causing a detachment of the retina. The plaintiff claimed that the manufacturer should be liable because it had failed to warn users that the exerciser might slip off a foot in such a manner. The court stated that to hold the manufacturer liable in these circumstances "would go beyond the reasonable dictates of justice in fixing the liabilities of manufacturers." After all, stated the court, "[a]lmost every physical object can be inherently dangerous or potentially dangerous in a sense. . . . A manufacturer cannot manufacture a knife that will not cut or a hammer that will not mash a thumb or a stove that will not burn a finger. The law does not require [manufacturers] to warn of such common dangers."[10]

A related defense is the *knowledgeable user* defense. If a particular danger (such as electrical shock) is or should be commonly known by particular users (such as electricians) of a product (such as electrical equipment), the manufacturer need not warn these users of the danger. The following case illustrates this concept.

10. *Jamieson v. Woodward & Lothrop*, 247 F.2d 23 (D.C. 1957).

CASE 14.3 ■ Travelers Insurance Co. v. Federal Pacific Electric Co.

Supreme Court of New York, Appellate Division, First Department, 1995.
211 A.D.2d 40,
625 N.Y.S.2d 121.

COMPANY PROFILE *Federal Pacific Electric Company makes electrical equipment, including Stab-Lok circuit breakers. Reliance Electric Company bought Federal from UV Industries Liquidating Trust, Inc., in 1979. In 1980, Federal revealed that it had obtained Underwriters Laboratories (UL) certification for its Stab-Lok circuit breakers by cheating on UL tests. Reliance sued UV Industries. A cash settlement ended the lawsuit in 1984. Two years later, Reliance sold Federal to Challenger Electric Equipment Corporation. The Consumer Product Safety Commission, a federal regulatory commission, later concluded that the Stab-Lok circuit breakers "did not present a serious risk of injury."*

BACKGROUND AND FACTS *A water pipe burst, flooding a switchboard at the offices of RCA Global Communications, Inc. This tripped the switchboard circuit breakers. RCA employees assigned to reactivate the switchboard included an electrical technician with twelve years of on-the-job training, a licensed electrician, and an electrical engineer with twenty years of experience who had studied power engineering in college. The employees attempted to switch one of the circuit breakers back on without testing for short circuits, which they later admitted they knew how to do and should have done. The circuit breaker failed to engage but ignited an explosive fire. RCA filed a claim with its insurer, Travelers Insurance Company. Travelers paid the claim and filed a suit in a New York state court against, among others, Federal Pacific Electric Company, the supplier of the circuit breakers. Travelers alleged that Federal had been negligent in failing to give RCA adequate warnings and instructions regarding the circuit breakers. The court apportioned 15 percent of the responsibility for the fire to Federal. Federal appealed.*

IN THE LANGUAGE OF THE COURT

NARDELLI, Justice.

* * * *

* * * [T]here is no necessity to warn a customer already aware—through common knowledge or learning—of a specific hazard and, in the proper case, the

court can decide as a matter of law that there is no duty to warn or that the duty has been discharged. * * *

* * * *

Given the * * * common knowledge of the minimal accepted practices in the field and the level of expertise, training and experience of the RCA electricians which encompassed the specific situation they faced, the * * * court should have found that there was no necessity on the part of Federal to warn RCA, which was already aware of the specific hazard, and the court should have granted Federal's motion entering judgment in its favor * * * .

DECISION AND REMEDY *The Supreme Court of New York, Appellate Division, reversed the judgment of the lower court and dismissed the complaint against Federal.*

FEDERAL PREEMPTION

If a manufacturer, such as an automobile manufacturer, complies with federal safety standards in manufacturing its products, it may be able to avoid liability under state product liability laws. As discussed in Chapter 5, when Congress chooses to act exclusively in an area in which the federal government and the states have concurrent powers, it is said to have *preempted* the area, thus precluding claims brought under a conflicting state or local law on the same subject.

THE *CIPOLLONE* CASE A leading case on this issue, *Cipollone v. Liggett Group, Inc.*,[11] was decided by the United States Supreme Court in 1992. In that case, the Court held that the Federal Cigarette Labeling and Advertising Act of 1965, which requires specific warnings to be included on cigarette packages, preempted state laws requiring cigarette manufacturers to sufficiently warn consumers of the potential dangers associated with cigarette smoking. The Court stated, however, that there was no indication that Congress had intended to preempt state laws that fall *outside* the scope of the federal law, such as laws governing fraudulent misrepresentation.

DETERMINING CONGRESSIONAL INTENT In *Cipollone* and other cases involving preemption issues, the courts must decide whether Congress, when enacting a particular statute, *intended* to preempt the area and thus preclude plaintiffs from bringing claims under state law. In determining congressional intent, courts look at the wording of the statute itself, as well as at the legislative history of the statute (such as congressional committee reports on the topic).

For example, in *Tebbetts v. Ford Motor Co.*,[12] a plaintiff alleged that a 1988 Ford Escort was defectively designed because it did not contain an air bag on the driver's side. The defendant-manufacturer contended that it had complied with federal safety regulations authorized by the National Traffic and Motor Vehicle Safety Act (NTMVSA) of 1966 and that those regulations preempted recovery under state product safety laws. The court interpreted House and Senate reports on the issue, as well as a clause included in the act itself, to mean that not all state law claims were preempted by the federal regulations. (The relevant clause stated that "[c]ompliance with any Federal motor vehicle safety standard issued under this [act] does not exempt any person from any liability under common law.") Thus, the plaintiff in *Tebbetts* was not precluded by the NTMVSA from suing Ford under state product liability laws.

Generally, it is difficult to predict whether a defendant will be subject to liability under state laws notwithstanding the defendant's compliance with federally mandated product safety standards. Courts differ in their interpretations of congressional intent, and the outcomes in cases involving similar facts can thus also differ.

STATUTES OF LIMITATIONS AND REPOSE

As discussed in Chapter 1, *statutes of limitations* restrict the time within which an action may be brought. A typical statute of limitations provides that

11. 505 U.S. 504, 112 S.Ct. 2608, 120 L.Ed.2d 407 (1992).

12. 665 A.2d 345 (N.H. 1995).

an action must be brought within a specified period of time after the cause of action accrues. Generally, a cause of action is held to accrue when some damage occurs. Sometimes the running of the prescribed period is *tolled* (that is, suspended) until the party suffering an injury has discovered it (or should have discovered it).

Many states have passed laws placing outer time limits on some claims so that the defendant will not be left vulnerable to lawsuits indefinitely. These **statutes of repose** may limit the time within which a plaintiff can file a product liability suit. Typically, a statute of repose begins to run at an earlier date and runs for a longer time than a statute of limitations. For example, a statute of repose may require that claims must be brought within twelve years from the date of sale or manufacture of the defective product. It is immaterial that the product is defective or causes an injury if the injury occurs after this statutory period has lapsed. In addition, some of these legislative enactments have limited the application of the doctrine of strict liability to new goods.

TERMS AND CONCEPTS TO REVIEW

- **bystander** 291
- **crashworthiness doctrine** 294
- **market-share liability** 293
- **privity of contract** 289
- **product liability** 288
- **product misuse** 294
- **statute of repose** 297
- **unreasonably dangerous product** 292

QUESTIONS AND CASE PROBLEMS

14–1. THEORIES OF LIABILITY. Chen buys a television set manufactured by Quality TV Appliance, Inc. She is going on vacation, so she takes the set to her mother's house for her mother to use. Because the set is defective, it explodes, causing her mother to be seriously injured. Chen's mother sues Quality to obtain compensation for her injury and for the damage to her house. Under what theory or theories discussed in this chapter might Chen's mother recover damages from Quality?

14–2. NEGLIGENCE. Perfect Drug Co. manufactures and has placed on the market a drug for airsickness. Boro purchases the drug from Alban's Drugstore. Boro is going on a trip and takes two of the tablets as directed. Boro loses consciousness because of the side effects of the drug, and he falls down a flight of stairs at the airport, breaking an arm and a leg. Perfect Drug knew of the possible side effects but did not place any warning on the label. Also, it is learned that Perfect Drug failed to meet minimum federal drug standards in the manufacture of the drug—standards that would have reduced the side effects. Boro wants to file an action based on Perfect's negligence.

(a) Discuss Boro's burden of proof.

(b) Discuss how the situation would be different if a warning had been placed on the package and minimum standards had been met.

14–3. LIABILITY IN TORT. Colt manufactures a new pistol. The firing of the pistol depends on an enclosed high-pressure device. The pistol has been thoroughly tested in two laboratories in the Midwest, and its design and manufacture are in accord with current technology. Wayne purchases one of the new pistols from Hardy's Gun and Rifle Emporium. When he uses the pistol in the high altitude of the Rockies, the difference in pressure causes the pistol to misfire, resulting in serious injury to Wayne. Colt can prove that all due care was used in the manufacturing process, and it refuses to pay for Wayne's injuries. Discuss Colt's liability in tort.

14–4. LIABILITY TO THIRD PARTIES. Baxter manufactures electric hair dryers. Julie purchases a Baxter dryer from her local Ace Drugstore. Cox, a friend and guest in Julie's home, has taken a shower and wants to dry her hair. Julie tells Cox to use the new Baxter hair dryer that she has just purchased. As Cox plugs in the dryer, sparks fly out from the motor, and sparks continue to fly as she operates it. Despite this, Cox begins drying her hair. Suddenly, the entire dryer ignites into flames, severely burning Cox's scalp. Cox sues Baxter on the basis of negligence and strict liability in tort. Baxter admits the dryer was defective but denies liability, particularly because Cox was not the person who purchased the dryer. In other words, Cox had no contractual relationship with Baxter. Discuss the validity of Baxter's defense. Are there any other defenses that Baxter might assert to avoid liability? Discuss.

14–5. STRICT LIABILITY. Gina is standing on a street corner waiting for a ride to work. Gomez has just purchased a new car manufactured by Optimal Motors.

Gomez is driving down the street when suddenly the steering mechanism breaks, causing him to run over Gina. Gina suffers permanent injuries. Gomez's total income per year has never exceeded $15,000. Gina files suit against Optimal under the theory of strict liability in tort. Optimal pleads no liability because (1) due care was used in the manufacture of the car, (2) Optimal is not the manufacturer of the steering mechanism (Smith is), and (3) the *Restatement* governing strict liability applies only to users or consumers, and Gina is neither. Discuss the validity of the defenses claimed by Optimal.

14–6. NEGLIGENCE. A two-year-old child lost his leg when he became entangled in a grain auger on his grandfather's farm. The auger had a safety guard that prevented any item larger than 4⅝ inches from coming into contact with the machine's moving parts. The child's foot was smaller than the openings in the safety guard. Was such an injury reasonably foreseeable? Discuss. [*Richelman v. Kewanee Machinery & Conveyor Co.*, 59 Ill.App.3d 578, 375 N.E.2d 885, 16 Ill.Dec. 778 (1978)]

14–7. THEORIES OF LIABILITY. Frances Ontai entered the Straub Clinic and Hospital to have an X-ray examination of the colon. Ontai was placed in a vertical position on a table manufactured by General Electric. The footrest on the table broke, and Ontai fell to the floor of the examination room, suffering injuries. Ontai filed suit against Straub and General Electric. Ontai's suit against General Electric was based on negligence and strict liability in tort. Discuss briefly each of these theories of liability. Should General Electric be held liable under either theory? Discuss fully. [*Ontai v. Straub Clinic and Hospital, Inc.*, 66 Haw. 237, 659 P.2d 734 (1983)]

14–8. LIABILITY. James Patterson, who worked as a clerk in a convenience store in Dallas, was shot and killed during a robbery of the store in 1980. The revolver used by the robber was a .38 caliber "Saturday Night Special" manufactured by a West German company, Rohm Gesellschaft. Patterson's mother brought a product liability action against Rohm and the Florida distributor of the handgun, claiming that the handgun was "defective and unreasonably dangerous" in design because its potential for injury and death far outweighed any social utility it might have. The defendant moved for summary judgment, contending that it could not be liable for Patterson's death because the handgun was not defective—the gun did not malfunction, nor did it lack any essential safety features. What was the result? Discuss fully. [*Patterson v. Rohm Gesellschaft*, 608 F.Supp. 1206 (N.D.Tex.—Dallas Div. 1985)]

14–9. PRODUCT LIABILITY. John Whitted bought a Chevrolet Nova from General Motors Corp. (GMC). Six years later, Whitted crashed the Nova into two trees. During the impact, the seat belt broke, and Whitted was thrust against the steering wheel, which broke, and the windshield, which shattered. He suffered fractures in his left arm and cuts to his forehead. Whitted sued GMC and the manufacturer, asserting, among other things, that because the seat belt broke, the defendants were strictly liable for his injuries. What does Whitted have to show in order to prove his case? [*Whitted v. General Motors Corp.*, 58 F.3d 1200 (7th Cir. 1995)]

14–10. DUTY TO WARN. Judy Dunne, who weighed between 450 and 500 pounds, received an exercise bike from her children as a birthday present. The bike had been purchased from Wal-Mart Stores, Inc. When Dunne received the bike, she rode it only for a moment. Later, she mounted the bike for a second time and pedaled for three or four rotations. The bike then collapsed, and Dunne fell off, sustaining numerous injuries. The bike was designed for use by people who weigh under 250 pounds (which is 99 percent of the population) and had been tested up to 440 pounds. The manufacturer did not specify any weight limit in marketing the bike, however, and there was no way that Dunne could have known of this weight limit. Under what theory of product liability discussed in this chapter might Dunne recover damages for her injuries? What defense or defenses might Wal-Mart and the bike's manufacturer assert in an attempt to avoid liability? Who will likely win the suit, and why? [*Dunne v. Wal-Mart Stores, Inc.*, 679 So.2d 1034 (La.App.1st 1996)]

14–11. A QUESTION OF ETHICS

William Mackowick, who had worked as an electrician for thirty years, was installing high-voltage capacitors in a switchgear room in a hospital when he noticed that a fellow electrician had removed the cover from an existing capacitor manufactured by Westinghouse Electric Corp. Westinghouse had placed a warning label inside the cover of the metal box containing the capacitor on which users were instructed to ground the electricity before handling. Nothing was said on the label about the propensity of electricity to "arc." (Arcing occurs when electricity grounds itself by "jumping" to a nearby object or instrument.) Mackowick walked over to warn the other electricians of the danger associated with the exposed capacitor, and, while talking, pointed his screwdriver toward the capacitor box. The electricity flowing through the fuses arced to the screwdriver and sent a high-voltage electric current through Mackowick's body. As a result, he sustained severe burns and was unable to return to work for three months. Discuss. [*Mackowick v. Westinghouse Electric Corp.*, 575 A.2d 100 (Pa. 1990)]

1. An appellate court held that even though the manufacturer did not include with its capacitor a warning about arcing, the product was not defective for failure to warn of inherent product dangers. The rationale of the court was that the product would only be used by experienced electricians who would be aware of the dangers of arcing. Was this a reasonable assumption?
2. It is ethical for a company not to include such a warning if it is even remotely possible that an inexperienced user of the product would not understand its inherent dangers?

CHAPTER 15

INTELLECTUAL PROPERTY AND CYBERLAW

MOST PEOPLE THINK OF WEALTH in terms of houses, land, cars, stocks, and bonds. Wealth, however, also includes **intellectual property,** which consists of the products of individuals' minds—products that result from intellectual, creative processes. Although it is an abstract term for an abstract concept, intellectual property is nonetheless wholly familiar to virtually everyone. *Trademarks, service marks, copyrights,* and *patents* are all forms of intellectual property. The book you are reading is copyrighted. Undoubtedly, the personal computer you use at home is trademarked. The study of intellectual property law is valuable because intellectual property has taken on an increasing importance, not only within the United States but globally as well. Today, ownership rights in intangible intellectual property are more important to the prosperity of many U.S. companies than are their tangible assets.

The need to protect creative works was voiced by the framers of the U.S. Constitution over two hundred years ago: Article I, Section 8, of the Constitution authorized Congress "[t]o promote the Progress of Science and useful Arts, by securing for limited Times to Authors and Inventors the exclusive Right to their respective Writings and Discoveries." Laws protecting patents, trademarks, and copyrights are explicitly designed to protect and reward inventive and artistic creativity. Although intellectual property law limits the economic freedom of some individuals, it does so to protect the freedom of others to enjoy the fruits of their labors—in the form of profits.

In the first part of this chapter, we examine trademark, patent, and copyright laws, as well as the legal protection available for intellectual property that consists of *trade secrets*. We then examine an issue of increasing significance to businesspersons: the protection of intellectual property rights in today's online environment.

SECTION 1 TRADEMARKS AND RELATED PROPERTY

A **trademark** is a distinctive mark, motto, device, or implement that a manufacturer stamps, prints, or otherwise affixes to the goods it produces so that they may be identified on the market and their origin vouched for. Statutory protection of trademarks and related property is provided at the federal level by the Lanham Trademark Act of 1946.[1] The Lanham Act was enacted in part to protect manufacturers from losing business to rival companies that used confusingly similar trademarks. The Lanham Act incorporates the common law of trademarks and provides remedies for owners of trademarks who wish to enforce their claims in federal court. Many states also have trademark statutes.

At common law, the person who used a symbol or mark to identify a business or product was protected in the use of that trademark. Clearly, if one used the trademark of another, it would lead consumers to believe that one's goods were made by the other. The law seeks to avoid this kind of confusion. In the following famous case concerning Coca-Cola, the defendants argued that the Coca-Cola trademark was entitled to no protection under the law, because the term did not accurately represent the product.

1. 15 U.S.C. Sections 1051–1127.

CASE 15.1 The Coca-Cola Co. v. The Koke Co. of America

Supreme Court of the United States, 1920.
254 U.S. 143,
41 S.Ct. 113,
65 L.Ed. 189.

COMPANY PROFILE *John Pemberton, an Atlanta pharmacist, invented a caramel-colored, carbonated soft drink in 1886. His bookkeeper, Frank Robinson, named the beverage Coca-Cola after two of the ingredients, coca leaves and kola nuts. Asa Candler bought the Coca-Cola Company in 1891, and within seven years, he made the soft drink available in all of the United States, as well as in parts of Canada and Mexico. Candler continued to sell Coke aggressively and to open up new markets, reaching Europe before 1910. In doing so, however, he attracted numerous competitors, some of whom tried to capitalize directly on the Coke name.*

BACKGROUND AND FACTS *The Coca-Cola Company sought to enjoin (prevent) the Koke Company of America and other beverage companies from, among other things, using the word* Koke *for their products. The Koke Company of America and other beverage companies contended that the Coca-Cola trademark was a fraudulent representation and that Coca-Cola was therefore not entitled to any help from the courts. The Koke Company and the other defendants alleged that the Coca-Cola Company, by its use of the Coca-Cola name, represented that the beverage contained cocaine (from coca leaves), which it no longer did. The trial court granted the injunction against the Koke Company, but the appellate court reversed the lower court's ruling. Coca-Cola then appealed to the United States Supreme Court.*

IN THE LANGUAGE OF THE COURT

Mr. Justice *HOLMES* delivered the opinion of the Court.

* * * *

* * * Before 1900 the beginning of [Coca-Cola's] good will was more or less helped by the presence of cocaine, a drug that, like alcohol or caffeine or opium, may be described as a deadly poison or as a valuable item of the pharmacopeia

according to the rhetorical purposes in view. The amount seems to have been very small,[a] but it may have been enough to begin a bad habit and after the Food and Drug Act of June 30, 1906, if not earlier, long before this suit was brought, it was eliminated from the plaintiff's compound. * * *

* * * Since 1900 the sales have increased at a very great rate corresponding to a like increase in advertising. The name now characterizes a beverage to be had at almost any soda fountain. It means a single thing coming from a single source, and well known to the community. It hardly would be too much to say that the drink characterizes the name as much as the name the drink. In other words Coca-Cola probably means to most persons the plaintiff's familiar product to be had everywhere rather than a compound of particular substances. * * * [B]efore this suit was brought the plaintiff had advertised to the public that it must not expect and would not find cocaine, and had eliminated everything tending to suggest cocaine effects except the name and the picture of [coca] leaves and nuts, which probably conveyed little or nothing to most who saw it. It appears to us that it would be going too far to deny the plaintiff relief against a palpable fraud because possibly here and there an ignorant person might call for the drink with the hope for incipient cocaine intoxication. The plaintiff's position must be judged by the facts as they were when the suit was begun, not by the facts of a different condition and an earlier time.

DECISION AND REMEDY *The district court's injunction was allowed to stand. The competing beverage companies were enjoined from calling their products* Koke.

a. In reality, until 1903 the amount of active cocaine in each bottle of Coke was equivalent to one "line" of cocaine.

TRADEMARK REGISTRATION

Trademarks may be registered with the state or with the federal government. To register for protection under federal trademark law, a person must file an application with the U.S. Patent and Trademark Office in Washington, D.C. Under current law, a mark can be registered (1) if it is currently in commerce or (2) if the applicant intends to put it into commerce within six months.

Under extenuating circumstances, the six-month period can be extended by thirty months, giving the applicant a total of three years from the date of notice of trademark approval to make use of the mark and file the required use statement. Registration is postponed until the mark is actually used. Nonetheless, during this waiting period, any applicant can legally protect his or her trademark against a third party who previously has neither used the mark nor filed an application for it. Registration is renewable between the fifth and sixth years after the initial registration and every ten years thereafter (every twenty years for trademarks registered before 1990).

Registration of a trademark with the U.S. Patent and Trademark Office gives notice on a nationwide basis that the trademark belongs exclusively to the registrant. The registrant is also allowed to use the symbol ® to indicate that the mark has been registered. Whenever that trademark is copied to a substantial degree or used in its entirety by another, intentionally or unintentionally, the trademark has been *infringed* (used without authorization). When a trademark has been infringed, the owner of the mark has a cause of action against the infringer. A person need not have registered a trademark in order to sue for trademark infringement, but registration does furnish proof of the date of inception of the trademark's use.

DISTINCTIVENESS OF MARK

A central objective of the Lanham Act is to reduce the likelihood that registered marks will be so similar to one another that consumers cannot distinguish among them. The Lanham Act states, "No trademark by which the goods of the applicant may be distinguished from the goods of others shall be refused registration."[2]

2. 15 U.S.C. Section 1052.

Only those trademarks that are deemed sufficiently distinctive from all competing trademarks will be protected, however. The trademarks must be sufficiently distinct to enable consumers to identify the manufacturer of the goods easily and to differentiate among competing products.

STRONG MARKS Fanciful, arbitrary, or suggestive trademarks are generally considered to be the most distinctive (strongest) trademarks, because they are normally taken from outside the context of the particular product and thus provide the best means of distinguishing one product from another.

Fanciful trademarks include invented words, such as Xerox for one manufacturer's copiers and Kodak for another company's photographic products. Arbitrary trademarks include actual words used with products that have no literal connection to the words, such as English Leather used as a name for an after-shave lotion (and not for leather processed in England). Suggestive trademarks are those that suggest something about a product without describing the product directly. For example, the trademark Dairy Queen suggests an association between the products and milk, but it does not directly describe ice cream.

SECONDARY MEANING Descriptive terms, geographical terms, and personal names are not inherently distinctive and do not receive protection under the law until they acquire a secondary meaning. A secondary meaning may arise when customers begin to associate a specific term or phrase (such as London Fog) with specific trademarked items (coats with London Fog labels). Whether a secondary meaning becomes attached to a term or name usually depends on how extensively the product is advertised, the market for the product, the number of sales, and other factors. Once a secondary meaning is attached to a term or name, a trademark is considered distinctive and is protected. Even a shade of color can qualify for trademark protection, once customers associate the color with the product.[3]

GENERIC TERMS Generic terms, such as *bicycle* and *computer*, receive no protection, even if they acquire secondary meanings. A particularly thorny problem arises when a trademark acquires generic use. For example, *aspirin* and *thermos* were originally the names of trademarked products, but today the words are used generically. Other examples are *escalator, trampoline, raisin bran, dry ice, lanolin, linoleum, nylon,* and *corn flakes*. Even so, the courts will not allow another firm to use those marks in such a way as to deceive a potential consumer.

THE FEDERAL TRADEMARK DILUTION ACT OF 1995

In 1995, Congress amended the Lanham Act by passing the Federal Trademark Dilution Act.[4] Until the passage of this amendment, federal trademark law only prohibited the unauthorized use of the same mark on competing (or on noncompeting but "related") goods or services when such use would likely confuse consumers as to the origin of those goods and services. Trademark dilution laws, which about half of the states have enacted, protect "distinctive" or "famous" trademarks (such as Jergens, McDonald's, RCA, and Macintosh) from certain unauthorized uses of the marks *regardless* of a showing of competition or a likelihood of confusion. The Federal Trademark Dilution Act extended the protection available to trademark owners by creating a federal cause of action for trademark dilution.

In one of the first cases to be decided under the 1995 act's provisions, a federal court held that a famous mark may be diluted not only by the use of an *identical* mark but also by the use of a *similar* mark. The case was brought by Ringling Bros.–Barnum & Bailey, Combined Shows, Inc., against the state of Utah. Ringling Bros. claimed that Utah's use of the slogan "The Greatest Snow on Earth"—to attract visitors to the state's recreational and scenic resorts—diluted the distinctiveness of the circus's famous trademark, "The Greatest Show on Earth." Utah moved to dismiss the suit, arguing that the 1995 provisions only protect owners of famous trademarks against the unauthorized use of identical marks. The court disagreed and refused to grant Utah's motion to dismiss the case.[5]

TRADE DRESS

The term **trade dress** refers to the image and overall appearance of a product—for example, the distinctive decor, menu, layout, and style of service of a par-

3. *Qualitex Co. v. Jacobson Products Co.*, 514 U.S. 159, 115 S.Ct. 1300, 131 L.Ed.2d 248 (1995).

4. 15 U.S.C. Section 1125.

5. *Ringling Bros.–Barnum & Bailey, Combined Shows, Inc. v. Utah Division of Travel Development*, 935 F.Supp. 736 (E.D.Va. 1996).

ticular restaurant. Basically, trade dress is subject to the same protection as trademarks. In cases involving trade dress infringement, as in trademark infringement cases, a major consideration is whether consumers are likely to be confused by the allegedly infringing use. The issue in the following case was whether a golf course owner was liable for trade dress infringement for replicating on its course, without permission, the most prominent feature of a different, famous golf course.

CASE 15.2 Pebble Beach Co. v. Tour 18 I, Ltd.

United States District Court, Southern District of Texas, 1996. 942 F.Supp. 1513.

BACKGROUND AND FACTS *Sea Pines Company, Inc., operates Harbour Town Golf Links—one of the most famous golf courses in the United States—on Hilton Head Island, South Carolina. Tour 18 I, Limited, operates golf courses in Texas. For its courses, Tour 18 intentionally copied golf holes from famous courses, including Harbour Town's Hole 18, without the permission of the owners. Tour 18 even built replicas of the Harbour Town lighthouse, which is the distinctive feature of the Harbour Town course. Tour 18 markets its courses aggressively, featuring especially the replicas of the lighthouse. Sea Pines and others, including Pebble Beach Company, filed a suit in federal district court against Tour 18. The plaintiffs alleged, among other things, that Tour 18's use of the replica lighthouses constituted trade dress infringement.*

IN THE LANGUAGE OF THE COURT

HITTNER, District Judge.

* * * *

* * * Tour 18 is liable for trade dress infringement if there is a likelihood of confusion generated by Tour 18's replication and use of [Sea Pines's] trade dress. * * * [T]hat there is an identity of customers, identity of advertising, and similarity between the parties' goods and services * * * support a finding of likelihood of confusion. Additionally, * * * the trade dress of the lighthouse is a strong, distinctive identifier * * * for Harbour Town Golf Links. Tour 18's intent in copying the trade dress of the lighthouse and Harbour Town Hole 18 also weighs in favor of a likelihood of confusion.

* * * [M]any golfers [have been] confused into believing Tour 18 received permission or approval from plaintiffs to replicate their golf holes. * * * Therefore, in this Court's view, Tour 18's adoption of Sea Pines' trade dress creates confusion among golfers as to whether Tour 18 sought and received assistance, approval, or permission from Sea Pines to replicate the Harbour Town lighthouse and 18th Hole.

DECISION AND REMEDY *The federal district court held that Tour 18 was liable for trade dress infringement. The court ordered Tour 18 to remove its replicas of the Harbour Town lighthouse from its courses and to disclaim prominently, in all of its marketing, "any association, affiliation, sponsorship, or permission from" Sea Pines.*

SERVICE, CERTIFICATION, AND COLLECTIVE MARKS

A **service mark** is similar to a trademark but is used to distinguish the services of one person or company from those of another. For example, each airline has a particular mark or symbol associated with its name. Titles and character names used in radio and television are frequently registered as service marks.

Other marks protected by law include certification marks and collective marks. A **certification mark** is used by one or more persons other than the owner to certify the region, materials, mode of manufacture, quality, or accuracy of the owner's goods or services. When used by members of a cooperative, association, or other organization, it is referred to as a **collective mark.** Examples of certification marks are the phrases

"Good Housekeeping Seal of Approval" and "UL Tested." Collective marks appear at the ends of the credits of movies to indicate the various associations and organizations that participated in the making of the movies. The union marks found on the tags of certain products are also collective marks.

TRADE NAMES

Trademarks apply to *products*. The term **trade name** is used to indicate part or all of a business's name, whether the business is a sole proprietorship, a partnership, or a corporation. Generally, a trade name is directly related to a business and its goodwill. A trade name may be protected as a trademark if the trade name is the same as the name of the company's trademarked product—for example, Coca-Cola. Unless also used as a trademark or service mark, a trade name cannot be registered with the federal government. Trade names are protected under the common law, however. As with trademarks, words must be unusual or fancifully used if they are to be protected as trade names. The word *Safeway*, for example, was held by the courts to be sufficiently fanciful to obtain protection as a trade name for a food-store chain.[6]

SECTION 2

PATENTS

A **patent** is a grant from the government that gives an inventor the exclusive right to make, use, and sell an invention for a period of twenty years from the date of filing the application for a patent. Patents for a fourteen-year period are given for designs, as opposed to inventions. For either a regular patent or a design patent, the applicant must demonstrate to the satisfaction of the U.S. Patent and Trademark Office that the invention, discovery, process, or design is genuine, novel, useful, and not obvious in light of current technology. A patent holder gives notice to all that an article or design is patented by placing on it the word *Patent* or *Pat.* plus the patent number.

PATENT INFRINGEMENT

If a firm makes, uses, or sells another's patented design, product, or process without the patent owner's permission, the tort of patent infringement occurs. Patent infringement may occur even though not all features or parts of an invention are copied. (With respect to a patented process, however, all steps or their equivalents must be copied in order for infringement to occur.) Often, litigation for patent infringement is so costly that the patent holder will instead offer to sell to the infringer a license to use the patented design, product, or process. Indeed, in many cases, the costs of detection, prosecution, and monitoring are so high that patents are valueless to their owners, because the owners cannot afford to protect them.

Until recently, parties involved in patent litigation also faced another problem: it was often hard to predict the outcome of litigation because jurors found it difficult to understand the issues in dispute. This was particularly true when the claims involved patents on complicated products—such as sophisticated technological or biotechnological products. In a significant case decided in 1996, *Markman v. Westview Instruments, Inc.*,[7] the United States Supreme Court held that it is the responsibility of judges, not juries, to interpret the scope and nature of patent claims. In other words, before a case goes to the jury, the judge must interpret the nature of the claim and give the jury instructions based on that interpretation.

Determining the nature and scope of a patent claim is a key element in most patent cases. Many observers thus predict that the likely result of the Supreme Court's decision will be that the majority of patent cases will be decided on motions for summary judgment. Many also predict that the Court's decision will also lead to greater clarity and uniformity in the case law in this area.

PATENTS FOR SOFTWARE

At one time, it was difficult for developers and manufacturers of software to obtain patent protection because many software products simply automate procedures that can be performed manually. In other words, the computer programs do not meet the "novel" and "not obvious" requirements previously mentioned. Also, the basis for software is often a mathematical equation or formula, which is not patentable. In 1981, however, the United States Supreme Court held that it is possible to obtain a patent for a *process* that incorporates a computer program—providing, of course, that the process itself

6. *Safeway Stores v. Suburban Foods*, 130 F.Supp. 249 (E.D.Va. 1955).

7. ___ U.S. ___, 116 S.Ct. 1384, 134 L.Ed.2d 577 (1996).

is patentable.[8] Subsequently, many patents have been issued for software-related inventions.

Another obstacle to obtaining patent protection for software is the procedure for obtaining patents. The process can be expensive and slow. The time element is a particularly important consideration for someone wishing to obtain a patent on software. In light of the rapid changes and improvements in computer technology, the delay could undercut the product's success in the marketplace.

Despite these difficulties, patent protection is used in the computer industry. If a patent is infringed, the patent holder may sue for an injunction, damages, and the destruction of all infringing copies, as well as attorneys' fees and court costs.

SECTION 3

COPYRIGHTS

A **copyright** is an intangible property right granted by federal statute to the author or originator of a literary or artistic production of a specified type. Currently, copyrights are governed by the Copyright Act of 1976,[9] as amended. Works created after January 1, 1978, are automatically given statutory copyright protection for the life of the author plus fifty years. For copyrights owned by publishing houses, the copyright expires seventy-five years from the date of publication or one hundred years from the date of creation, whichever is first. For works by more than one author, the copyright expires fifty years after the death of the last surviving author.

Copyrights can be registered with the U.S. Copyright Office in Washington, D.C. A copyright owner no longer needs to place the symbol © or the term *Copr.* or *Copyright* on the work, however, to have the work protected against infringement. Chances are that if somebody created it, somebody owns it.

WHAT IS PROTECTED EXPRESSION?

Works that are copyrightable include books, records, films, artworks, architectural plans, menus, music videos, product packaging, and computer software. To obtain protection under the Copyright Act, a work must be original and fall into one of the following categories: (1) literary works; (2) musical works; (3) dramatic works; (4) pantomimes and choreographic works; (5) pictorial, graphic, and sculptural works; (6) films and other audiovisual works; and (7) sound recordings. To be protected, a work must be "fixed in a durable medium" from which it can be perceived, reproduced, or communicated. Protection is automatic. Registration is not required.

Section 102 of the Copyright Act specifically excludes copyright protection for any "idea, procedure, process, system, method of operation, concept, principle, or discovery, regardless of the form in which it is described, explained, illustrated, or embodied." Note that it is not possible to copyright an *idea*. The underlying ideas embodied in a work may be freely used by others. What is copyrightable is the particular way in which an idea is *expressed*. Whenever an idea and an expression are inseparable, the expression cannot be copyrighted. Generally, anything that is not an original expression will not qualify for copyright protection. Facts widely known to the public are not copyrightable. Page numbers are not copyrightable, because they follow a sequence known to everyone. Mathematical calculations are not copyrightable.

Compilations of facts, however, are copyrightable. Section 103 of the Copyright Act defines a compilation as "a work formed by the collection and assembling of preexisting materials or data that are selected, coordinated, or arranged in such a way that the resulting work as a whole constitutes an original work of authorship." The key requirement in the copyrightability of a compilation is originality. Thus, the White Pages of a telephone directory do not qualify for copyright protection when the information that makes up the directory (names, addresses, and telephone numbers) is not selected, coordinated, or arranged in an original way.[10] In one case, even the Yellow Pages of a telephone directory did not qualify for copyright protection.[11]

Copyright law protects song lyrics as literary works. When recording a song, notice of copyright must be included, and royalties must be paid. In addition, the lyrics cannot be published without permission. These principles are not in doubt. What is sometimes in doubt is how they apply to new technology. At issue in the following case was how they applied to a new development in the karaoke industry.

---

8. *Diamond v. Diehr*, 450 U.S. 175, 101 S.Ct. 1048, 67 L.Ed.2d 155 (1981).

9. 17 U.S.C. Sections 101 *et seq.*

10. *Feist Publications, Inc. v. Rural Telephone Service Co.*, 499 U.S. 340, 111 S.Ct. 1282, 113 L.Ed.2d 358 (1991).

11. *Bellsouth Advertising & Publishing Corp. v. Donnelley Information Publishing, Inc.*, 999 F.2d 1436 (11th Cir. 1993).

CASE 15.3 ABKCO Music, Inc. v. Stellar Records, Inc.

United States Court of Appeals, Second Circuit, 1996. 96 F.3d 60.

BACKGROUND AND FACTS *ABKCO Music, Inc., owns the copyrights to seven songs by Mick Jagger and Keith Richards. Performance Tracks, Inc., is in the karaoke industry. Using new technology, Tracks encodes the audio rendition of a song with a simultaneous video display of the lyrics on "compact discs + graphics" (CD+Gs).*[a] *Tracks and Stellar Records, Inc., distributed their versions of ABKCO's Jagger-Richards tunes on CD+Gs, including, without ABKCO's permission, the songs' lyrics. ABKCO filed a suit in a federal district court against the distributors, alleging in part copyright infringement. The court ordered Tracks to stop "publishing" the lyrics. In effect, this prohibited Tracks from distributing its discs. Tracks appealed.*

IN THE LANGUAGE OF THE COURT

OWEN, * * * Judge:

* * * *

A time-honored method of facilitating singing along with music has been to furnish the singer with a printed copy of the lyrics. Copyright holders have always enjoyed exclusive rights over such copies. While projecting lyrics on a screen and producing printed copies of the lyrics, of course, have their differences, there is no reason to treat them differently for purposes of the Copyright Act.

* * * *

Tracks * * * contends that the Copyright Act has not kept pace with new technology, and that Congress * * * would include [CD+Gs] within the definition of "phonorecords" if it were to redefine "phonorecord" today. It would, however, seem to be a sufficient answer to Tracks' contention to observe that Tracks' product is not within the statutory definition of "phonorecord," and what Congress may or may not do in the future to redefine the term is not for us to speculate.

DECISION AND REMEDY *The U.S. Court of Appeals for the Second Circuit affirmed the lower court's order.*

a. The primary difference between CD+Gs and other karaoke discs is that CD+Gs display only the lyrics. Other discs include other images, such as a picture of a beach.

COPYRIGHT INFRINGEMENT

Whenever the form or expression of an idea is copied, an infringement of copyright has occurred. The reproduction does not have to be exactly the same as the original, nor does it have to reproduce the original in its entirety. If a substantial part of the original is reproduced, there is copyright infringement.

Those who infringe copyrights may be liable for damages or criminal penalties. These range from actual damages or statutory damages, imposed at the court's discretion, to criminal proceedings for willful violations. Actual damages are based on the harm caused to the copyright holder by the infringement, while statutory damages, not to exceed $100,000, are provided for under the Copyright Act. Criminal proceedings may result in fines and/or imprisonment.

An exception to liability for copyright infringement is made under the "fair use" doctrine. In certain circumstances, a person or organization can reproduce copyrighted material without paying royalties (fees paid to the copyright holder for the privilege of reproducing the copyrighted material). Section 107 of the Copyright Act provides as follows:

> [T]he fair use of a copyrighted work, including such use by reproduction in copies or phonorecords or by any other means specified by [Section 106 of the Copyright Act], for purposes such as criticism, comment, news reporting, teaching (including multiple copies for classroom use), scholarship, or research, is not an infringement of copyright. In determining

whether the use made of a work in any particular case is a fair use the factors to be considered shall include—

(1) the purpose and character of the use, including whether such use is of a commercial nature or is for nonprofit educational purposes;
(2) the nature of the copyrighted work;
(3) the amount and substantiality of the portion used in relation to the copyrighted work as a whole; and
(4) the effect of the use upon the potential market for or value of the copyrighted work.

Because these guidelines are very broad, the courts determine whether a particular use is fair on a case-by-case basis. Thus, anyone reproducing copyrighted material may still be subject to a violation. In determining whether a use is fair, courts have often considered the fourth factor to be the most important.

A question that sometimes comes up is the extent to which copying material for classroom use is a fair use. That was the question in the following case.

CASE 15.4 Princeton University Press v. Michigan Document Services, Inc.

United States Court of Appeals, Sixth Circuit, 1996. 99 F.3d 1381.

HISTORICAL AND SOCIAL SETTING *To previous generations of students, the coursepack was a rare educational tool. Because of advances in technology, however, coursepacks have become almost as common as textbooks. Coursepacks are produced by commercial copyshops, which typically obtain permission before including copyrighted materials. Profits from coursepack sales can be high, and copyshops often compete intensely for business.*

BACKGROUND AND FACTS *James Smith, the owner of Michigan Document Services, Inc. (MDS), a commercial copyshop, concluded that it was unnecessary to obtain the copyright owners' permission to reproduce copyrighted materials in coursepacks. Smith publicized his conclusion, claiming that professors would not have to worry about any delay in production at his shop. MDS then compiled, bound, and sold coursepacks to students at the University of Michigan without obtaining the permission of copyright owners. Princeton University Press and two other publishers filed a suit in a federal district court against MDS, alleging copyright infringement. MDS claimed that its coursepacks were covered under the fair use doctrine. The court ruled in favor of the copyright owners, and MDS appealed.*

IN THE LANGUAGE OF THE COURT

DAVID A. NELSON, Circuit Judge.

* * * *

* * * To negate fair use, one need only show that if the challenged use should become widespread, it would adversely affect the potential market for the copyrighted work. Under this test, * * * it is reasonably clear that the plaintiff publishers have succeeded in negating fair use.

* * * [M]ost of the copyshops that compete with MDS in the sale of coursepacks pay permission fees for the privilege of duplicating and selling excerpts from copyrighted works. The three plaintiffs together have been collecting permission fees at a rate approaching $500,000 a year. If copyshops across the nation were to start doing what [MDS has] been doing here, this revenue stream would shrivel and the potential value of the copyrighted works of scholarship published by the plaintiffs would be diminished accordingly.

DECISION AND REMEDY *The U.S. Court of Appeals for the Sixth Circuit held in part that MDS's practice of preparing coursepacks without obtaining the copyright owners' permission was not a fair use and ordered MDS to stop.*

COPYRIGHT PROTECTION FOR SOFTWARE

In 1980, Congress passed the Computer Software Copyright Act, which amended the Copyright Act of 1976 to include computer programs in the list of creative works protected by federal copyright law. The 1980 statute, which classifies computer programs as "literary works," defines a computer program as a "set of statements or instructions to be used directly or indirectly in a computer in order to bring about a certain result."

Because of the unique nature of computer programs, the courts have had many problems in applying and interpreting the 1980 act. In a series of cases decided in the 1980s, the courts held that copyright protection extended not only to those parts of a computer program that can be read by humans, such as the "high-level" language of a source code, but also to the binary-language object code of a computer program, which is readable only by the computer.[12] Additionally, such elements as the overall structure, sequence, and organization of a program were deemed copyrightable.[13]

By the early 1990s, the issue had evolved into whether the "look and feel"—the general appearance, command structure, video images, menus, windows, and other screen displays—of computer programs should also be protected by copyright. Although the courts have disagreed on this issue, the tendency has been not to extend copyright protection to look-and-feel aspects of computer programs. For example, in 1992 a federal district court held that the user interface of Apple's Macintosh computer is not protected under a look-and-feel theory and that Apple's use of windows, icons, and menus—and generally the series of images that Apple calls a "desktop metaphor"—is an unprotectible "idea."[14] Similarly, in 1995, the Court of Appeals for the First Circuit held that Lotus Development Corporation's menu command hierarchy for its Lotus 1-2-3 spreadsheet is not protectable under the Copyright Act. The court deemed that the menu command hierarchy is a "method of operation," and Section 102 of the Copyright Act specifically excludes methods of operation from copyright protection.[15] The decision was affirmed by the United States Supreme Court in 1996.[16]

SECTION 4
TRADE SECRETS

Some business processes and information that are not, or cannot be, patented, copyrighted, or trademarked are nevertheless protected against appropriation by competitors as trade secrets. **Trade secrets** consist of customer lists, plans, research and development, pricing information, marketing techniques, production techniques, and generally anything that makes an individual company unique and that would have value to a competitor. Unlike copyright and trademark protection, protection of trade secrets extends both to ideas and to their expression. (For this reason, and because a trade secret involves no registration or filing requirements, trade secret protection may be well suited for software.)

The most widely used definition of a trade secret is found in the *Restatement of Torts*, Section 757(b):

> A trade secret may consist of any formula, pattern, device, or compilation of information which is used in one's business, and which gives him an opportunity to obtain an advantage over competitors who do not know or use it. It may be a formula for a chemical compound, a process of manufacturing, treating or preserving materials, . . . or a list of customers.

Of course, the secret formula, process, or other information must be disclosed to some persons, particularly to key employees. Businesses generally attempt to protect their trade secrets by having all employees who use the process or information agree in their contracts never to divulge it. (Such agreements are called *nondisclosure agreements.*) Thus, if a salesperson tries to solicit the company's customers for noncompany business, or if an employee copies the employer's unique method of manufacture, he or she has appropriated a trade secret and has also broken a contract—two separate wrongs. Theft of confi-

12. See *Stern Electronics, Inc. v. Kaufman*, 669 F.2d 852 (2d Cir. 1982); and *Apple Computer, Inc. v. Franklin Computer Corp.*, 714 F.2d 1240 (3d Cir. 1983).

13. *Whelan Associates, Inc. v. Jaslow Dental Laboratory, Inc.*, 797 F.2d 1222 (3d Cir. 1986).

14. *Apple Computer, Inc. v. Microsoft Corp.*, 799 F.Supp. 1006 (D.N.Cal. 1992). The district court's ruling was not upset on appeal.

15. *Lotus Development Corp. v. Borland International, Inc.*, 49 F.3d 807 (1st Cir. 1995).

16. *Lotus Development Corp. v. Borland International, Inc.*, ___ U.S. ___, 116 S.Ct. 804, 113 L.Ed.2d 610 (1996). This issue may again come before the Supreme Court for a decision, because only eight justices heard the case, and there was a tied vote; the effect of the tie was to affirm the lower court's decision.

dential business data by industrial espionage, as when a business taps into a competitor's computer, is a theft of trade secrets without any contractual violation and is actionable in itself.

Under Section 757 of the *Restatement of Torts*, "One who discloses or uses another's trade secret, without a privilege to do so, is liable to the other if (1) he discovered the secret by improper means, or (2) his disclosure or use constitutes a breach of confidence reposed in him by the other in disclosing the secret to him."

The Economic Espionage Act of 1996 made the theft of trade secrets a federal crime. We examined the provisions and significance of this act in Chapter 13, in the context of crimes related to business.

SECTION 5

CYBERLAW: PROTECTING INTELLECTUAL PROPERTY IN CYBERSPACE

Not surprisingly, because of the unique nature of the Internet, its use creates unique legal questions and issues—particularly with respect to intellectual property rights. What exactly constitutes an infringing use of another's intellectual property rights in the online environment? How can the owners of intellectual property rights know when, and by whom, those rights are being infringed in this context? Should online service providers bear legal responsibility for infringing actions by users of their services? These are just a few of the questions raised by the presence of intellectual property in cyberspace.

The emerging body of law governing cyberspace is often referred to as *cyberlaw.* We have already examined, in previous chapters, cyberlaw as it relates to court jurisdiction, constitutional issues, and the tort of defamation. Here we look at cyberlaw as it applies to the types of intellectual property discussed in this chapter.

TRADEMARK PROTECTION ON THE INTERNET—DOMAIN NAMES

One of the initial trademark issues involving intellectual property in cyberspace has been whether **domain names** (Internet addresses) should be treated as trademarks or simply as a means of access, similar to street addresses in the physical world. Increasingly, the courts are holding that the principles of trademark law should apply to domain names on the Internet. Before looking at trademark infringement and dilution issues, we need to briefly discuss some of the special characteristics of domain names and how they are registered.

DOMAIN NAMES A domain name consists of a series of "domains" separated by periods. A business's domain name typically consists of two domains. The top-level domain indicates the type of organization that is using the name—such as ".com" for a commercial entity (although noncommercial entities also use this name); ".net" for a network; ".edu" for an educational organization; or ".gov" for a government organization. The second-level domain usually consists of the name of the firm that maintains the site. Companies that do business on the Internet often use their names as domain names because this allows customers to access their sites without extensive searching. Consumers who want to locate those companies' World Wide Web sites also benefit from this practice.

DOMAIN NAME REGISTRATION The entity responsible for registering domain names is Network Solutions, Inc. (NSI), which is funded by the U.S. National Science Foundation. NSI acts on behalf of the Internet Network Information Center (InterNIC), which, in turn, handles the daily administration of the domain name system in the United States. The top-level domains handled by the NSI apply worldwide. A new organization has developed an additional set of top-level domain names that may be in effect by the time you read this book.

Initially, domain names were handed out on a first-come, first-served basis, with few questions asked. Since 1995, however, the NSI has required any party seeking to register a domain name to state that the party's use of the name will not infringe on the intellectual property rights of any other party, that the party intends to use the name on "a regular basis on the Internet" (NSI may require a party that does not use the name for more than ninety days to relinquish the name), and that the party's use of the name will not be unlawful. If the party violates these representations made in the application, the NSI may cancel the domain name.

TRADEMARK INFRINGEMENT One of the problems in applying trademark law to Internet domain names is that trademark law allows multiple parties to use the same mark—as long as the mark is used for different goods or services and will not cause customer confusion. On the Internet as it is currently structured, however, only one party can use a particular domain name, regardless of the type of goods or services offered. In other words, although two or more businesses can own the trademark Acme, only one business can operate on the Internet with the domain name "acme.com." Because of this restrictive feature of domain names, there is a question as to whether domain names should function as trademarks.

To date, the courts that have considered this question have held that the unauthorized use of another's mark in a domain name may constitute trademark infringement. In one case, for example, a publishing company, the Comp Examiner Agency (CEA), used "juris.com" as its domain name. Juris, Inc., contended that CEA's use of the domain name infringed on its trademark Juris, which it used in connection with software, because the use would likely cause customer confusion. The court agreed and granted an injunction against CEA's further use of the "juris.com" domain name.[17]

TRADEMARK DILUTION Owners of famous trademarks also have succeeded in preventing others from using their marks as domain names under the Federal Trademark Dilution Act of 1995. For example, in one case, Hasbro, Inc., the maker of the famous children's board game Candy Land, sued a company that used the domain name "candyland.com." Hasbro contended that the company's commercial use of its mark diluted the mark's distinctiveness in violation of the federal dilution law. The court agreed and issued a preliminary injunction requiring the other party to relinquish the domain name.[18]

The 1995 act exempts from its coverage certain conduct, including noncommercial uses of marks. Thus, if a party registers another's famous mark as a domain name for a Web site that is not used for commercial purposes (to advertise or sell products and services), the owner of the famous mark will have no federal cause of action for trademark dilution. One of the significant questions concerning this exemption is whether "cybersquatting" constitutes a commercial use of a domain name. Cybersquatting occurs when a party registers another party's famous mark as a domain name and then holds the other party hostage—that is, the first party offers to forfeit its rights to the domain name to the owner of the famous mark in exchange for a sum of money. In the following case, the court addressed this issue.

17. *Comp Examiner Agency, Inc. v. Juris, Inc.* (C.D.Cal. 1996)[1996 WL 376600]. This decision, which is not reported in West's *Federal Supplement*, can be accessed by use of the WESTLAW (WL) citation.

18. *Hasbro, Inc. v. Internet Entertainment Group, Ltd.* (W.D.Wash. 1996)[1996 WL 84853]. This decision, which is not reported in West's *Federal Supplement*, can be accessed by use of the WESTLAW (WL) citation.

CASE 15.5 Panavision International, L.P. v. Toeppen

United States District Court, Central District of California, 1996. 945 F.Supp. 1296.

BACKGROUND AND FACTS *Panavision International, Limited Partnership, is a supplier of photographic equipment. Panavision owns several famous trademarks, including Panavision, which it advertises to the public and to movie and television studios, networks, and production companies. Panavision's "Filmed with Panavision" credit appears at the end of many movies and television shows. Dennis Toeppen registered "panavision.com" as a domain name, precluding Panavision from using the name to identify its own Web site. Toeppen told Panavision that he would sell the name for $13,000. Panavision filed a suit in a federal district court against Toeppen, charging in part that he was in violation of the Federal Trademark Dilution Act of 1995.*

IN THE LANGUAGE OF THE COURT

PREGERSON, District Judge.

* * * *

Registration of a trademark as a domain name, without more, is not a commercial use of the trademark and therefore is not within the prohibitions of the [Federal

Trademark Dilution] Act. In the case before the Court, however, Toeppen has made a commercial use of the Panavision marks.

Toeppen's "business" is to register trademarks as domain names and then to sell the domain names to the trademarks' owners. * * * His "business" is premised on the desire of the companies to use their trademarks as domain names and the calculation that it will be cheaper to pay him than to sue him. * * *

* * * *

* * * As a result of the current state of Internet technology, Toeppen was able * * * to eliminate the capacity of the Panavision marks to identify and distinguish Panavision's goods and services on the Internet. * * * Toeppen's conduct, which prevented Panavision from using its marks in a new and important business medium, has diluted Panavision's marks within the meaning of the statute.

DECISION AND REMEDY *The court ordered Toeppen to, among other things, transfer the registration of "panavision.com" to Panavision.*

PATENTS FOR CYBERPRODUCTS

Almost every day, we hear of some innovation in communications technology, particularly Internet technology. It therefore is not surprising that new cyberproducts to meet the needs of Internet users and online service providers are being developed and patented at an unprecedented rate. Cyberproducts include data-compression software, encryption programs, software facilitating information linking and retrieval systems, and other forms of network software.

The problem faced by the developers of cyberproducts, who normally invest substantial time and money resources in the research and development of those products, is how to protect their exclusive rights to the use of the products.

A patent owner whose product is featured on the Internet may find it particularly difficult to prevent the unauthorized use of the patented property. For example, a video game maker might agree to provide part of a game on the Internet, through a third party's Web site, to give potential purchasers a sample of the product. How can the game maker prevent the third party from using, or letting others use, the product for other purposes (such as making and selling illegal copies of the game)?

Licensing the use of a product has proved to be one of the best ways to protect intellectual property on the Internet. In the context of a patent, a *license* is permission granted by the patent owner to another (the *licensee*) to make, sell, or use the patented item. Any license that a patent holder grants can be restricted to certain specified purposes and can be limited to the licensee only. Of course, because the Internet does not have any geographical boundaries, a licensing agreement should be made only in consideration of all U.S., foreign, and international laws. These same principles apply to the owners and licensees of other intellectual property, including copyrights and trademarks.

COPYRIGHTS IN CYBERSPACE

Uploading, downloading, browsing—any of these activities conducted in cyberspace can infringe on a copyright owner's rights. The following subsections identify some of the many copyright issues that arise in cyberspace and discuss the liability of online providers for copyright infringement.

ONLINE ISSUES The rights granted to copyright owners in the Copyright Act include the right to make copies of a copyrighted work, the right to publicly distribute those copies, and the right to perform or display copyrighted works. How those rights apply in cyberspace is still being debated.

A copyright owner might argue that the right to make copies of a work is infringed each time the work is stored in a computer's memory. Does software stored in a computer constitute a copy in this sense? A few courts have held that it does.[19] What about the digital storage of photographs, music, and other works? A few courts have held that these are also copies.[20]

Does the online transmission of a copyrighted work without permission violate the right to publicly

19. See, for example, *MAI Systems Corp. v. Peak Computer, Inc.*, 991 F.2d 511 (9th Cir. 1993).

20. See, for example, *Religious Technology Center v. Netcom On-Line Communications Services, Inc.*, 907 F.Supp. 1361 (N.D.Cal. 1995).

EMERGING TRENDS

ONLINE COPYRIGHT INFRINGEMENT

Intellectual property is big business. Indeed, some researchers estimate that the market value of intellectual property—copyrights, trademarks, patents, and the like—exceeds the value of physical property in the world today. Most intellectual property does not sell for the cost of production plus a normal profit. Rather, intellectual property is sold at a price that reflects heavy research costs for ingenious ideas. Any property that involves high development costs and low production costs is vulnerable to "piracy"—the unauthorized copying and use of the property.

In the past, copying intellectual products was time consuming, and the pirated copies were worse than the originals. Think about copying software today, though, via the Internet. The pirated copy of software obtained via the Internet is exactly the same as the original—after all, it is digitized. The only difference may be that the pirated version is not accompanied by a user's manual, the lack of which can diminish the usefulness and application of the software.

FASTER TRANSFER SPEEDS EXPAND THE SCOPE OF POSSIBILITIES FOR PIRACY

When the Internet first became popular, modems were slow, and computer central processing units (CPUs) were slow, too. Thus, the transmission and downloading of files were time consuming. Over time, however, modem and CPU speeds have increased, and as a result, it takes much less time to copy a pirated software program (or a legitimate one, for that matter). As technology improves and digital satellite systems, cable modems, faster CPUs, and the like make transfer rates even faster, the rapid digital transfer of first audio, and then video with audio, will be possible. While this bodes well for the online transmission of, say, new compact discs (CDs), it also opens the door to greater piracy possibilities: higher transfer speeds make it easier to deliver intellectual property to vast numbers of individuals on the World Wide Web.

HOW BIG IS THE PROBLEM?

The Business Software Alliance estimates that half of the global market for software is supplied today by pirated products. The International Federation of the Phonographic Industry believes that 20 percent of recorded music is pirated. Much of the piracy of intellectual property, especially software and music, is deemed "altruistic." People illegally give intellectual property away not to make any money but because they want to be generous. There is also a problem with respect to copyright law, which makes a distinction between reproduction for public use (which requires the copyright holder's permission) and reproduction for private use (which, within limits, does not require the copyright holder's permission). The difficulty here is distinguishing between private and public use.

distribute the work? Some might claim that no right is violated because no physical copy is transferred. Others might argue that there is a violation if the recipient downloads what is transmitted to the hard disk drive of his or her computer.[21]

21. See *Agee v. Paramount Communications, Inc.*, 59 F.3d 317 (2d Cir. 1995), for a further discussion of this issue. The court recommended that the Copyright Act be amended to answer the question.

Some of the most controversial questions concern the right to perform copyrighted works. Does downloading a copy of a musical recording constitute a performance? What about playing it back after downloading? Questions also arise in relation to the right to publicly display a work. Is a work publicly displayed when it is visually browsed online? Most observers would agree that it is. Probably most would also agree that browsing is a "fair use," particularly if it is a noncommercial use and there is no downloading.

EMERGING TRENDS

ONLINE COPYRIGHT INFRINGEMENT (CONTINUED)

Current copyright law also only controls the first sale of a particular work. It applies to your new textbook but not to any subsequent sales of the textbook as a used piece of intellectual property. In the digital world, an initial copy can be perfectly copied again and again.

Finally, current copyright law is based on national boundaries. A right to distribute copies of a CD in one country does not automatically include the right to distribute the CD in another country. The Internet, however, knows no national boundaries.

HOW CAN THE PROBLEM BE SOLVED?

Is there any current solution to the increasing problem of the piracy of intellectual property via the Internet? The simple answer is no. Efforts to find such a solution are underway, nonetheless. A technological effort is being made to develop pirate-proof ways of transmitting materials. For example, IBM has developed so-called secure "packaging" for sending digital information over the Internet. In the digital world, however, every time someone comes up with a new technology, experts (often hackers) soon manage to get around it.

Many argue that the government should crack down more on piracy. It is relatively easy to discover piracy on the Internet by using one of the powerful search engines that exist today. By keying in a couple of sentences from a copyrighted work, for example, and then searching online databases, you can quickly find out what Web sites contain pirated copies of the article. It takes resources to do such research, however, and many nations are unwilling to invest their resources in efforts to reduce online piracy. Furthermore, even if the source is tracked down, it is difficult to determine who is liable. Perhaps the only long-term solution is to make the "real thing"—the original—more valuable than the pirated version. One way to do this is to continually update works that are online—most individuals will not pirate a financial newsletter that is updated every day. Alternatively, some companies will attempt to figure out different ways to make money from their intellectual property. This is certainly true on the Internet, where many services are provided free of charge, and the provider obtains revenues by selling advertising on the particular Web site.

IMPLICATIONS FOR THE BUSINESSPERSON

1. Anybody who owns intellectual property has to be aware that it is increasingly possible that the property may be pirated via the Internet.
2. Nonetheless, businesspersons must weigh potential benefits against potential costs when deciding how many resources should be devoted to combating online piracy of intellectual property.

FOR CRITICAL ANALYSIS

1. Can the distribution through the Internet of intellectual property be regulated by copyright laws? Should it?
2. What argument would you present to convince somebody that stealing information is no different from stealing tangible property?

ONLINE LIABILITY One current controversy is whether online providers—including Internet access services, bulletin board service (BBS) operators, and others—should be liable for the unauthorized copying, distribution, and performance or display of copyrighted work.

The most significant factor seems to be whether a provider is directly involved in the unauthorized use. An important case concerned the unauthorized uploading of literary works through an Internet access service.[22] The court held that the service was not liable for copyright infringement because, like a self-service photocopier, it only provided the system that permitted unauthorized copying.

In a second case, a BBS operator's customers uploaded and downloaded copyrighted photos, to and from the bulletin board, without the copyright

22. *Religious Technology Center v. Netcom On-Line Communications Services, Inc.*, 907 F.Supp. 1361 (N.D.Cal. 1995).

owner's permission. The court held the operator liable for infringement of the owner's rights, in part because some of the photos were altered to include ads for the bulletin board.[23] In a third case, a bulletin board service encouraged its users to upload unauthorized copies of video game software. The court held the service liable because it knew that the copies were unauthorized and were being uploaded into its storage media.[24]

Many online providers believe that the Copyright Act needs to be amended to impose liability only when a provider knows that a use of its service is infringing on a copyright owner's rights and does nothing about it. Copyright owners favor imposing liability in *all* circumstances. The debate continues.

SECTION 6 INTERNATIONAL PROTECTION FOR INTELLECTUAL PROPERTY

For many years, the United States has been a party to various international agreements relating to intellectual property rights. For example, the Paris Convention of 1883, to which about ninety countries are signatory, allows parties in one country to file for patent and trademark protection in any of the other member countries. Other international agreements in this area include the Berne Convention and the TRIPS agreement.

THE BERNE CONVENTION

Under the Berne Convention of 1886, an international copyright agreement, if an American writes a book, his or her copyright in the book must be recognized by every country that has signed the convention. Also, if a citizen of a country that has not signed the convention first publishes a book in a country that has signed, all other countries that have signed the convention must recognize that author's copyright. Copyright notice is not needed to gain protection under the Berne Convention for works published after March 1, 1989.

The Berne Convention and other international agreements have given some protection to intellectual property on a worldwide level. None of them, however, has been as significant and far reaching in scope as the Trade-Related Aspects of Intellectual Property Rights—or, more simply, TRIPS—agreement.

THE TRIPS AGREEMENT

The TRIPS agreement was signed by representatives from over one hundred nations in 1994, following the eighth and final round (called the Uruguay Round) of negotiations among nations that were signatory to the General Agreement on Tariffs and Trade, or GATT.[25] The TRIPS agreement was one of several documents that were annexed to the agreement that created the World Trade Organization, or WTO, which replaced GATT as of 1995. The TRIPS agreement established, for the first time, standards for the international protection of intellectual property rights, including patents, trademarks, and copyrights for movies, computer programs, books, and music.

Prior to the TRIPS agreement, one of the difficulties faced by U.S. sellers of intellectual property in the international market was that another country might either lack laws to protect intellectual property rights or fail to enforce what laws it had. To address this problem, the TRIPS agreement provides that each member country must include in its domestic laws broad intellectual property rights and effective remedies (including civil and criminal penalties) for violations of those rights.

Generally, the TRIPS agreement provides that member nations must not discriminate (in terms of the administration, regulation, or adjudication of intellectual property rights) against foreign owners of such rights. In other words, a member nation cannot give its own nationals (citizens) favorable treatment without offering the same treatment to nationals of all member countries. For example, if a U.S. software manufacturer brings a suit for the infringement of intellectual property rights under Japan's national laws, the U.S. manufacturer is entitled to receive the same treatment as a Japanese domestic manufacturer. Each member nation must also ensure that legal procedures are available for parties who wish to bring actions for infringement of intellectual prop-

23. *Playboy Enterprises, Inc. v. Frena,* 839 F.Supp. 1552 (M.D.Fla. 1993).

24. *Sega Enterprises, Ltd. v. MAPHIA,* 857 F.Supp. 679 (N.D.Cal. 1994).

25. GATT was originally negotiated in 1947 to minimize trade barriers among nations. Between 1947 and 1994, the GATT nations undertook seven more rounds of negotiations relating to tariffs and trade.

erty rights. Additionally, in a related document, the Uruguay Round of GATT established a mechanism for settling disputes among member nations.

Particular provisions of the TRIPS agreement refer to patent, trademark, and copyright protection for intellectual property. The agreement specifically provides copyright protection for computer programs by stating that compilations of data, databases, and other materials are "intellectual creations" and are to be protected as copyrightable works. Other provisions relate to trade secrets and the rental of computer programs and cinematographic works.

CYBERSPACE ISSUES

Because cyberspace has no national boundaries, the Internet is an international communications medium. For this reason, intellectual property in cyberspace may be subject to the laws of many countries, including the United States, and to international law.

Currently, the laws of many countries and international laws are being updated to reflect changes in technology and the spread of the Internet. Copyright holders and other owners of intellectual property generally agree that changes in the law are needed to stop the increasing international piracy of their property (see this chapter's *Emerging Trends*). The World Intellectual Property Organization (WIPO) is attempting to update international law by suggesting proposals for its member countries to ratify, although widespread ratification and implementation could take a decade or more.

Among the WIPO proposals for protecting copyrights in cyberspace are provisions that could extend the rights that exist under current U.S. copyright law to the distribution and performance of their works to copyright holders in other countries. Other proposals concern issues that are discussed elsewhere in this chapter—fair use in cyberspace, temporary digital copying, and the liability of online providers—as well as technological copy protection methods.

TERMS AND CONCEPTS TO REVIEW

certification mark 303	**intellectual property** 299	**trade name** 304
collective mark 303	**patent** 304	**trade secret** 308
copyright 305	**service mark** 303	**trademark** 300
domain name 309	**trade dress** 302	

QUESTIONS AND CASE PROBLEMS

15–1. FAIR USE DOCTRINE. Professor Wise is teaching a summer seminar in business torts at State University. Several times during the course, he makes copies of relevant sections from business law texts and distributes them to his students. Wise does not realize that the daughter of one of the textbook authors is a member of his seminar. She tells her father about Wise's copying activities, which have been done without her father's or his publisher's permission. Her father sues Wise for copyright infringement. Wise claims protection under the fair use doctrine. Who will prevail? Explain.

15–2. TRADEMARKS. Otro, Inc., has been doing business since 1962 in more than fifty locations throughout the United States. Otro manufactures and distributes a wide variety of electronic products, which prominently bear the Otro trademark. Otro advertises its products nationally. Paul is not affiliated with Otro. Without Otro's permission, Paul registers the domain name "Otro.com," intending to profit by reselling or licensing it to Otro. Paul then sets up a Web site at the Otro.com address featuring a picture of himself. When Otro learns that it cannot register its mark as a domain name, Otro asks a court to order Paul to assign his registration of the name to Otro. Will the court give Otro what it wants? Why or why not?

15–3. COPYRIGHT INFRINGEMENT. In which of the following situations would a court likely hold Ursula liable for copyright infringement?

(a) From a scholarly journal at the library, Ursula photocopies ten pages relating to a topic on which she is writing a term paper.

(b) Ursula makes blouses, dresses, and other clothes and sells them in her small shop. She advertises some of the outfits as Guest items, hoping that customers might mistakenly assume that they were made by Guess, the well-known maker of clothing.

(c) Ursula operates a bulletin board on the Internet. She encourages the board's customers to upload scanned copies of magazines and add their own comments. With each magazine displayed on her board, she includes her board's Internet address in place of the title of the publication.

(d) Ursula teaches Latin American history at a small university. She has a VCR and frequently tapes television programs relating to Latin America. She then takes the videos to her classroom so that her students can watch them.

15–4. COPYRIGHT PROTECTION. One day during algebra class, Diedra, an enterprising fourteen-year-old student, began drawing designs on her shoelaces. By the end of the class, Diedra had decorated her shoelaces with the name of the school, Broadson Junior High, written in blue and red (the school colors) and with pictures of bears, the school's mascot. After class, Mrs. Laxton, Diedra's teacher, reprimanded Diedra for not paying attention in class and asked Diedra what she had been doing during the lecture. Diedra showed Mrs. Laxton her shoelaces. When Diedra got home that night, she wrote about the day's events in her diary. She also drew her shoelace design in the diary. Mrs. Laxton had been trying to think of how she could build school spirit. She thought about Diedra's shoelaces and decided to go into business for herself. She called her business Spirited Shoelaces and designed shoelaces for each of the local schools, decorating the shoelaces in each case with the school's name, mascot, and colors. The business became tremendously profitable. Even though Diedra never registered her idea with the patent or copyright office, does she nonetheless have intellectual property rights in the shoelace design? Will her diary account be sufficient proof that she created the idea? Discuss fully.

15–5. FAIR USE DOCTRINE. Original Appalachian Artworks, Inc. (OAA), makes and distributes the very successful product called Cabbage Patch Kids—soft, sculptured dolls that were in great demand in the early 1980s. The dolls are unique in appearance, and the name is registered as a trademark to OAA. The design, too, is protected under a copyright registration. In 1986, Topps Chewing Gum, Inc., had an artist copy many of the features of the dolls for Topps's new product—stickers that depicted obnoxious cartoon characters called Garbage Pail Kids. The stickers, along with another product line that Topps developed, proved very lucrative; in fact, Topps expanded the product line to include T-shirts, balloons, and school notebooks. Topps claimed that its product was actually a satire of (critical comment on) OAA's product and therefore a fair use of a protected work. Did Topps's use of OAA's product constitute a fair use of the product, or did it constitute trademark and copyright infringement? [*Original Appalachian Artworks, Inc. v. Topps Chewing Gum, Inc.*, 642 F.Supp. 1031 (N.D.Ga. 1986)]

15–6. TRADEMARK INFRINGEMENT. In 1987, Quality Inns International, Inc., announced a new chain of economy hotels to be marketed under the name McSleep Inns. McDonald's wrote Quality Inns a letter stating that the use of this name infringed on the McDonald's family of trademarks characterized by the prefix *Mc* attached to a generic term. Quality Inns claimed that *Mc* had come into generic use as a prefix and therefore McDonald's had no trademark rights to the prefix itself. Quality Inns filed an action seeking a declaratory judgment from the court that the mark McSleep Inns did not infringe on McDonald's federally registered trademarks or common law rights to its marks and would not constitute an unfair trade practice. What factors must the court consider in deciding this issue? What will be the probable outcome of the case? Explain. [*Quality Inns International, Inc. v. McDonald's Corp.*, 695 F.Supp. 198 (D.Md. 1988)]

15–7. TRADEMARK INFRINGEMENT. CBS, Inc., owns and operates Television City, a television production facility in Los Angeles that is home to many television series. The name Television City is broadcast each week in connection with each show. CBS sells T-shirts, pins, watches, and so on emblazoned with "CBS Television City." CBS registered the name Television City with the U.S. Patent and Trademark Office as a service mark "for television production services." David and William Liederman wished to open a restaurant in New York City using the name Television City. Besides food, the restaurant would sell television memorabilia such as T-shirts, sweatshirts, and posters. When CBS learned of the Liedermans' plans, it asked a federal district court to order them not to use the name Television City in connection with their restaurant. Does CBS's registration of the Television City mark ensure its exclusive use in all markets and for all products? If not, what factors might the court consider to determine whether the Liedermans can use the name Television City in connection with their restaurant? [*CBS, Inc. v. Liederman*, 866 F.Supp. 763 (S.D.N.Y. 1994)]

15–8. TRADE SECRETS. William Redmond, as the general manager for PepsiCo, Inc., in California, had access to the company's inside information and trade secrets. In 1994, Redmond resigned to become chief operating officer for the Gatorade and Snapple Company, which makes and markets Gatorade and Snapple and is a subsidiary of the Quaker Oats Company. PepsiCo brought an action in a federal district court against Redmond and Quaker Oats, seeking to prevent Redmond from disclosing PepsiCo's secrets. The court ordered Redmond not to assume new duties that were likely to trigger disclosure of those secrets. The central issue on appeal was whether a plaintiff can obtain relief for trade secret misappropriation on showing that an ex-employee's new employment will *inevitably* lead him or her to rely on the plaintiff's trade secrets. How should the court rule on this issue? Discuss fully. [*PepsiCo v. Redmond*, 54 F.3d 1262 (7th Cir. 1995)]

15–9. TRADEMARKS. Sara Lee Corp. manufactures pantyhose under the L'eggs trademark. Originally, L'eggs were sold in egg-shaped packaging, a design that Sara Lee continues to use with its product. Sara Lee's only nationwide competitor in the same pantyhose markets is Kayser-Roth Corp. When Kayser-Roth learned of Sara Lee's plan to introduce L'eggs Everyday, a new line of hosiery, Kayser-Roth responded by simultaneously introducing a new product, Leg Looks. Sara Lee filed a complaint in a federal district court against Kayser-Roth, asserting that the name Leg Looks infringed on the L'eggs mark. Does Kayser-Roth's Leg Looks infringe on Sara Lee's L'eggs? Why or why not? [*Sara Lee Corp. v. Kayser-Roth Corp.*, 81 F.3d 455 (4th Cir. 1996)]

15–10. A QUESTION OF ETHICS

Texaco, Inc., conducts research to develop new products and technology in the petroleum industry. As part of the research, Texaco employees routinely photocopy articles from scientific and medical journals without the permission of the copyright holders. The publishers of the journals brought a copyright infringement action against Texaco in a federal district court. The court ruled that the copying was *not* fair use. The U.S. Court of Appeals for the Second Circuit affirmed this ruling "primarily because the dominant purpose of the use is 'archival'—to assemble a set of papers for future reference, thereby serving the same purpose for which additional subscriptions are normally sold, or . . . for which photocopying licenses may be obtained." [*American Geophysical Union v. Texaco, Inc.*, 37 F.3d 881(2d Cir. 1994)]

1. Do you agree with the court's decision that the copying was not a fair use? Why or why not?
2. Do you think that the law should impose a duty on every person to obtain permission to photocopy or reproduce any article under any circumstance? What would be some of the implications of such a duty for society? Discuss fully.

ACCESSING THE INTERNET
THE LEGAL ENVIRONMENT OF BUSINESS

Information on intellectual property law is available at the following site:

http://www.legal.net/intellct.htm

To perform patent searches and to access information on the patenting process, go to

http://sunsite.unc.edu/patents/intropat.html

You can find answers to frequently asked questions about patents at

http://www.sccsi.com/DaVinci/patentfaq.html

The U.S. Patent and Trademark Office provides online access to a broad range of U.S. and international trademark resources, including forms, links to relevant statutes, recent regulations, trademark registration forms, and links to international patent and trademark offices in such places as Japan, New Zealand, and Sweden. You can even order a trademark registration by e-mail using this site, which is located at

http://www.uspto.gov/

You can also access information on patent law at the following Internet site:

http://www.patents.com

An interesting Web site has recently been developed by three George Washington University lawyers in intellectual property law. The site offers information on trademarks and Internet domain names and examines some of the legal issues involved. The site includes background information on a number of well-known domain-name disputes, as well as links to other resources. You can access this site at

http://www.law.georgetown.edu/lc/

The Legal Information Institute at Cornell University's School of Law has developed a database containing United States Supreme Court decisions concerning intellectual property issues. You can find these decisions at

http://www.law.cornell.edu/syllabi?copyright+patent+trademark

Another online magazine that deals, in part, with intellectual property issues is *Law Technology Product News*. The address for this publication is

http://www.ljextra.com/ltpn/

The Cyberspace Law Institute (CLI) offers articles and information on topics such as copyright infringement, privacy and trade secrets, trademarks, and domain names. Find this site at

http://www.cli.org

The World Intellectual Property Organization (WIPO) Arbitration Center is an extensive site containing the full text of its rules, recommended contract clauses and arbitration agreements, and other information concerning the arbitration of intellectual property disputes. You can find this site at

http://www.uspto.gov/web/

CHAPTER 16

CREDITOR-DEBTOR RELATIONS AND BANKRUPTCY

HISTORICALLY, DEBTORS AND THEIR FAMILIES have been subjected to punishment, including involuntary servitude and imprisonment, for their inability to pay debts. The modern legal system, however, has moved away from a punishment philosophy in dealing with debtors. In fact, many observers say that it has moved too far in the other direction, to the detriment of creditors.

Normally, creditors have no problem collecting the debts owed to them. When disputes arise over the amount owed, however, or when the debtor simply cannot or will not pay, what happens? What remedies are available to creditors when debtors default? And what laws assist and protect debtors? The first part of this chapter provides the answers to these questions. It deals with the various rights and remedies available through statutory laws, common law, and contract law to assist the debtor and creditor in resolving their disputes without the debtor's having to resort to bankruptcy. The second part of this chapter discusses bankruptcy as a last resort in resolving debtor-creditor problems.

SECTION 1

LAWS ASSISTING CREDITORS

Both the common law and statutory laws create various rights and remedies for creditors. We discuss here some of these rights and remedies, including liens, garnishment, creditors' composition agreements, mortgage foreclosure, and a debtor's assignment of assets for the benefit of creditors.

LIENS

A **lien** is a claim or charge on a debtor's property that must be satisfied before the property (or its proceeds) is available to satisfy the claims of other creditors. As mentioned, liens may arise under statutory law or under the common law. Statutory liens include *mechanic's liens.* Liens created at common law include *artisan's liens* and *innkeeper's liens. Judicial liens* include those that represent a creditor's efforts to collect on a debt before or after a judgment is entered by a court.

Generally, a lien creditor has priority over an unperfected security interest but not over a perfected security interest. Thus, a person who becomes a lien creditor before another security interest in the same property is perfected has priority, but one who acquires the lien after perfection does not have priority. Mechanic's and artisan's liens, however, have priority over perfected security interests unless a statute provides otherwise.

MECHANIC'S LIEN When a person contracts for labor, services, or material to be furnished for the purpose of making improvements on real property but does not immediately pay for the improvements, the creditor can place a **mechanic's lien** on the property. This creates a special type of debtor-creditor relationship in which the real estate itself becomes security for the debt.

For example, a painter agrees to paint a house for a homeowner for an agreed-on price to cover labor and materials. If the homeowner cannot pay or pays only a portion of the charges, a mechanic's lien against the property can be created. The painter is the lienholder, and the real property is encumbered with a mechanic's lien for the amount owed. If the homeowner does not pay the lien, the property can be sold to satisfy the debt. Notice of the *foreclosure* (the enforcement of the lien) must be given to the debtor in advance, however.

The procedures by which a mechanic's lien is created are controlled by state law. Generally, the lienholder must file a written notice of lien against the particular property involved. The notice of lien must be filed within a specific time period, measured from the last date on which materials or labor were provided (usually within 60 to 120 days). Failure to pay the debt entitles the lienholder to foreclose on the real estate on which the improvements were made and to sell it to satisfy the amount of the debt. Of course, as mentioned, the lienholder is required by statute to give notice to the owner of the property prior to foreclosure and sale. The sale proceeds are used to pay the debt and the costs of the legal proceedings; the surplus, if any, is paid to the former owner.

ARTISAN'S LIEN An **artisan's lien** is a security device created at common law through which a creditor can recover payment from a debtor for labor and materials furnished in the repair of personal property. For example, Whitney leaves her diamond ring at the jewelry shop to be repaired and to have her initials engraved on the band. In the absence of an agreement, the jeweler can keep the ring until Whitney pays for the services that the jeweler provides. Should Whitney fail to pay, the jeweler has a lien on Whitney's ring for the amount of the bill and can sell the ring in satisfaction of the lien.

In contrast to a mechanic's lien, an artisan's lien is *possessory.* The lienholder ordinarily must have retained possession of the property and have expressly or impliedly agreed to provide the services on a cash, not a credit, basis. The lien remains in existence as long as the lienholder maintains possession, and the lien is terminated once possession is voluntarily surrendered—unless the surrender is only temporary. With a temporary surrender, there must be an agreement that the property will be returned to the lienholder. Even with such an agreement, if a third party obtains rights in that property while it is out of the possession of the lienholder, the lien is lost.

Modern statutes permit the holder of an artisan's lien to foreclose and sell the property subject to the lien to satisfy payment of the debt. As with the mechanic's lien, the lienholder is required to give notice to the owner of the property prior to foreclosure and sale. In some states, holders of artisan's liens must give notice to title lienholders of automobiles prior to foreclosure. The sale proceeds are used to pay the debt and the costs of the legal proceedings, and the surplus, if any, is paid to the former owner. The artisan's lien has priority over a filed statutory lien (such as a title lien on an automobile or a lien filed under Article 9 of the UCC) as well as priority over a bailee's lien (such as a storage lien).

JUDICIAL LIENS A debt must be past due before a creditor can commence legal action against a debtor. Once legal action is brought, the debtor's property may be seized to satisfy the debt. If the property is seized prior to trial proceedings, the seizure is referred to as an *attachment* of the property. The seizure may also occur following a court judgment in the creditor's favor. In that case, the court's order to seize the property is referred to as a *writ of execution*.

Attachment. **Attachment** refers to a court-ordered seizure and taking into custody of property prior to the securing of a judgment for a past-due debt. Attachment rights are created by state statutes. Normally a *prejudgment* remedy, attachment occurs either at the time of or immediately after the commencement of a lawsuit and before the entry of a final judgment. By statute, the restrictions and requirements for a creditor to attach before judgment are specific and limited. The due process clause of the Fourteenth Amendment to the Constitution limits the courts' power to authorize seizure of a debtor's property without notice to the debtor or a hearing on the facts. In recent years, a number of state attachment laws have been held to be unconstitutional.

To use attachment as a remedy, the creditor must have an enforceable right to payment of the debt under law, and the creditor must follow certain procedures. Otherwise, the creditor can be liable for damages for wrongful attachment. He or she must file with the court an *affidavit* (a written or printed statement, made under oath or sworn to) stating that the debtor is in default and stating the statutory grounds under which attachment is sought. A bond must be posted by the creditor to cover at least court costs, the value of the loss of use of the good suffered by the debtor, and the value of the property attached. When the court is satisfied that all the requirements have been met, it issues a **writ of attachment,** which is similar to a writ of execution (to be discussed shortly) in that it directs the sheriff or other officer to seize nonexempt property. If the creditor prevails at trial, the seized property can be sold to satisfy the judgment.

Writ of Execution. If a creditor is successful in a legal action against a debtor, the court awards the creditor a judgment against the debtor (usually for the amount of the debt plus any interest and legal costs incurred in obtaining the judgment). Frequently, the creditor finds it easy to secure a judgment against the debtor but nevertheless fails to collect the awarded amount. If the debtor will not or cannot pay the judgment, the creditor is entitled to go back to the court and obtain a **writ of execution,** which is an order, usually issued by the clerk of the court, directing the sheriff to seize (levy) and sell any of the debtor's nonexempt real or personal property that is within the court's geographical jurisdiction (usually the county in which the courthouse is located). The proceeds of the sale are used to pay off the judgment and the costs of the sale. Any excess is paid to the debtor.

The debtor can pay the judgment and redeem the nonexempt property any time before the sale takes place. Because of exemption laws (which cover the debtor's homestead and designated items of personal property) and bankruptcy laws, however, many judgments are virtually uncollectible.

GARNISHMENT An order for **garnishment** permits a creditor to collect a debt by seizing property of the debtor (such as wages or money in a bank account) that is being held by a third party (such as an employer or a bank). Typically, a garnishment judgment is served on a debtor's employer so that part of the debtor's usual paycheck will be paid to the creditor.

The legal proceeding for a garnishment action is governed by state law. As a result of a garnishment proceeding, as noted, a third party (such as the debtor's employer) is ordered by the court to turn over property owned by the debtor (such as wages) to pay the debt. Garnishment can be a prejudgment remedy, requiring a hearing before a court, or a postjudgment remedy. According to the laws in some states, the judgment creditor needs to obtain only one order of garnishment, which will then continuously apply to the judgment debtor's weekly wages until the entire debt is paid. In other states, the judgment creditor must go back to court for a separate order of garnishment for each pay period.

Both federal laws and state laws limit the amount of money that can be taken from a debtor's weekly take-home pay through garnishment proceedings. Federal law provides a minimal framework to protect debtors from losing all their income in order to pay judgment debts.[1] State laws also provide dollar exemptions, and these amounts are often larger than those provided by federal law.[2] State and federal statutes can be applied together to help create a pool of funds sufficient to enable a debtor to continue to provide for family needs while also reducing the amount of the judgment debt in a reasonable way.

1. For example, the federal Consumer Credit Protection Act of 1968, 15 U.S.C. Sections 1601–1693r, provides that a debtor can retain either 75 percent of the disposable earnings per week or the sum equivalent to thirty hours of work paid at federal minimum wage rates, whichever is greater.

2. A few states (for example, Texas) do not permit garnishment of wages by private parties except under a child-support order.

Under federal law, garnishment of an employee's wages for any one indebtedness cannot be grounds for dismissal of an employee.

One of the questions courts have faced in recent years has to do with whether a debtor's pension fund can be attached by creditors, through garnishment or other proceedings, to satisfy a debt. Under the Employee Retirement Income Security Act (ERISA) of 1974,[3] certain types of pension funds "may not be alienated [transferred]," or attached. The law is less clear, however, on whether pension funds, *after* they have been received by a retiree, can be subject to attachment by creditors. This issue is before the court in the following case.

3. 29 U.S.C. Sections 1001–1461.

CASE 16.1 United States v. Smith

United States Court of Appeals, Fourth Circuit, 1995. 47 F.3d 681.

BACKGROUND AND FACTS *For nine years, Charles Smith asked his friends and acquaintances to invest their money in his business schemes. Smith used most of the money—estimated to be more than $350,000—for personal expenses. Smith was indicted for criminal fraud and pleaded guilty to that crime in a federal district court. The court imposed a prison sentence and ordered Smith to repay his victims as much as possible by turning over, each month, the entire amount of his pension benefits. Smith appealed the order, claiming that it violated the "anti-alienation" provision of ERISA.*

IN THE LANGUAGE OF THE COURT

ERVIN, Chief Judge:

* * * *

This court has long recognized a strong public policy against the alienability of * * * ERISA [pension] benefits. The Supreme Court, as well, has found that it is not "appropriate to approve any * * * exception * * * ."

* * * *

* * * The government * * * cannot require Smith to turn over his pension benefits * * * . Understandably, there may be a natural distaste for the result we reach here. The statute, however, is clear. Congress has made a policy decision to protect the ERISA income of retirees, even if that decision prevents others from securing relief for the wrongs done them.

DECISION AND REMEDY *The U.S. Court of Appeals for the Fourth Circuit vacated the lower court's order and remanded the case. The appellate court ordered the lower court to redetermine the amount that Smith was to pay to his victims, based on "a balance of the victims' interest in compensation and Smith's other financial resources."*

MORTGAGE FORECLOSURE

Mortgage holders have the right to foreclose on mortgaged property in the event of a debtor's default. The usual method of foreclosure is by judicial sale of the property, although the statutory methods of foreclosure vary from state to state. If the proceeds of the foreclosure sale are sufficient to cover both the costs of the foreclosure and the mortgaged debt, any surplus is received by the debtor. If the sale proceeds are insufficient to cover the foreclosure costs and the mortgaged debt, however, the **mortgagee** (the creditor-lender) can seek to recover the difference from the **mortgagor** (the debtor) by obtaining a deficiency judgment representing the difference between the mortgaged debt plus foreclosure costs and the amount actually received from the proceeds of the foreclosure sale. A deficiency judgment is obtained in a separate legal action that is pursued subsequent to the foreclosure action. It entitles the creditor to recover from other property owned by the debtor. Some states do not permit deficiency judgments for some types of real estate interests.

Before the foreclosure sale, a defaulting mortgagor can redeem the property by paying the full amount of the debt, plus any interest and costs that have accrued. This right is known as the **equity of redemption.** In some states, a mortgagor may even redeem the property within a certain period of time—called a **statutory period of redemption**—after the sale. In these states, the deed to the property is not usually delivered to the purchaser until the statutory period has expired.

SECTION 2

SURETYSHIP AND GUARANTY

When a third person promises to pay a debt owed by another in the event the debtor does not pay, either a *suretyship* or a *guaranty* relationship is created. The third person's credit becomes the security for the debt owed.

SURETYSHIP

A contract of strict **suretyship** is a promise made by a third person to be responsible for the debtor's obligation. It is an express contract between the **surety** and the creditor. The surety in the strictest sense is *primarily* liable for the debt of the principal. The creditor can demand payment from the surety from the moment that the debt is due. A suretyship contract is not a form of indemnity; that is, it is not merely a promise to make good any loss that a creditor may incur as a result of the debtor's failure to pay. The creditor need not exhaust all legal remedies against the principal debtor before holding the surety responsible for payment. Moreover, a surety agreement does not have to be in writing to be enforceable, although usually such agreements are in writing.

For example, Jason Oller wants to borrow money from the bank to buy a used car. Because Jason is still in college, the bank will not lend him the money unless his father, Stacey Oller, who has dealt with the bank before, will *cosign* the note (add his signature to the note, thereby becoming jointly liable for payment of the debt). When Mr. Oller cosigns the note, he becomes primarily liable to the bank. On the note's due date, the bank can seek payment from Jason Oller, Stacey Oller, or both jointly.

GUARANTY

A guaranty contract is similar to a suretyship contract in that it includes a promise to answer for the debt or default of another. With a suretyship arrangement, however, the surety is primarily liable for the debtor's obligation. With a guaranty arrangement, the **guarantor**—the third person making the guaranty—is *secondarily* liable. The guarantor can be required to pay the obligation only after the principal debtor defaults, and usually only after the creditor has made an attempt to collect from the debtor.

For example, a corporation, BX Enterprises, needs to borrow money to meet its payroll. The bank is skeptical about the creditworthiness of BX and requires Dawson, its president, who is a wealthy businessperson and owner of 70 percent of BX Enterprises, to sign an agreement making himself personally liable for payment if BX does not pay off the loan. As a guarantor of the loan, Dawson cannot be held liable until BX Enterprises is in default.

The Statute of Frauds requires that a guaranty contract between the guarantor and the creditor must be in writing to be enforceable unless the *main purpose exception* applies. Briefly, this exception provides that if the main purpose of the guaranty agreement is to benefit the guarantor, then the contract need not be in writing to be enforceable.

The guaranty contract terms determine the extent and time of the guarantor's liability. For example, the guaranty can be *continuing*, designed to cover a series of transactions by the debtor. Also, the guaranty can be *unlimited* or *limited* as to time and amount. In addition, the guaranty can be *absolute*, in which case the guarantor becomes liable immediately on the debtor's default, or *conditional*, in which case the guarantor becomes liable only on the happening of a certain event.

DEFENSES OF THE SURETY AND THE GUARANTOR

The defenses of the surety and the guarantor are basically the same. Therefore, the following discussion applies to both, although it refers only to the surety.

Certain actions will release the surety from the obligation. For example, making any material modification in the terms of the original contract between the principal debtor and the creditor, including the awarding of a binding extension of time for making payment, without first obtaining the consent of the surety will discharge a gratuitous surety (one who receives no consideration in return for acting as a surety) completely and a surety who is compensated to the extent that the surety suffers a loss.

Naturally, if the principal obligation is paid by the debtor or by another person on behalf of the debtor, the surety is discharged from the obligation. Similarly, if valid tender of payment is made, and the creditor for some reason rejects it with knowledge of the surety's existence, then the surety is released from any obligation on the debt.

Generally, any defenses available to a principal debtor can be used by the surety to avoid liability on the obligation to the creditor. Defenses available to the principal debtor that the surety *cannot* use include the principal debtor's incapacity or bankruptcy and the statute of limitations. The ability of the surety to assert any defenses the debtor may have against the creditor is the most important concept in suretyship, because most of the defenses available to the surety are also those of the debtor.

Obviously, a surety may also have his or her own defenses—for example, incapacity or bankruptcy. If the creditor fraudulently induced the surety to guarantee the debt, the surety can assert fraud as a defense. In most states, the creditor has a legal duty to inform the surety, prior to the formation of the suretyship contract, of material facts known by the creditor that would substantially increase the surety's risk. Failure to so inform is fraud and makes the suretyship obligation voidable.

In addition, if a creditor surrenders or impairs the debtor's collateral while knowing of the surety and without the surety's consent, the surety is released to the extent of any loss suffered from the creditor's actions. The primary reason for this is to protect the surety who agreed to become obligated only because the debtor's collateral was in the possession of the creditor.

RIGHTS OF THE SURETY AND THE GUARANTOR

The rights of the surety and the guarantor are basically the same. Therefore, again, the following discussion applies to both.

When the surety pays the debt owed to the creditor, the surety is entitled to certain rights. First, the surety has the legal **right of subrogation.** Simply stated, this means that any right the creditor had against the debtor now becomes the right of the surety. Included are creditor rights in bankruptcy, rights to collateral possessed by the creditor, and rights to judgments secured by the creditor. In short, the surety now stands in the shoes of the creditor and may pursue any remedies that were available to the creditor against the debtor.

Second, the surety has a right to be reimbursed by the debtor. This **right of reimbursement** may stem either from the suretyship contract or from equity. Basically, the surety is entitled to receive from the debtor all outlays made on behalf of the suretyship arrangement. Such outlays can include expenses incurred, as well as the actual amount of the debt paid to the creditor.

Third, in the case of **co-sureties** (two or more sureties on the same obligation owed by the debtor), the **right of contribution** allows a surety who pays more than his or her proportionate share on a debtor's default to recover from the co-sureties the amount paid above the surety's obligation. Generally, a co-surety's liability either is determined by agreement or, in the absence of agreement, is set at the maximum liability under the suretyship contract.

For example, assume that two co-sureties are obligated under a suretyship contract to guarantee the debt of a debtor. Together, the sureties' maximum liability is \$25,000. Surety A's maximum liability is \$15,000, and surety B's is \$10,000. The debtor owes \$10,000 and is in default. Surety A pays the creditor the entire \$10,000. In the absence of agreement, surety A can recover \$4,000 from surety B (\$10,000 ÷ \$25,000 × \$10,000 = \$4,000, surety B's obligation).

SECTION 3

PROTECTION FOR DEBTORS

The law protects debtors, as well as creditors. Certain property of the debtor, for example, is exempt from creditors' actions. Consumer protection statutes also protect debtors' rights. Of course, bankruptcy laws, which will be discussed in the next chapter, are designed specifically to assist debtors in need of help.

EXEMPTIONS

In most states, certain types of real and personal property are exempt from levy of execution or attachment. Probably the most familiar of these exemptions is the **homestead exemption.** Each state permits the debtor to retain the family home, either in its entirety or up to a specified dollar amount, free from the claims of unsecured creditors or trustees in bankruptcy. The purpose is to ensure that the debtor will retain some form of shelter.

Suppose that Beere owes Veltman $40,000. The debt is the subject of a lawsuit, and the court awards Veltman a judgment of $40,000 against Beere. Beere's homestead is valued at $50,000, and the homestead exemption is $25,000. There are no outstanding mortgages or other liens on his homestead. To satisfy the judgment debt, Beere's family home is sold at public auction for $45,000. The proceeds of the sale are distributed as follows:

1. Beere is given $25,000 as his homestead exemption.
2. Veltman is paid $20,000 toward the judgment debt, leaving a $20,000 deficiency judgment (that is, "leftover debt") that can be satisfied from any other nonexempt property (personal or real) that Beere may have, if allowed by state law.

In a few states, statutes permit the homestead exemption only if the judgment debtor has a family. The policy behind this type of statute is to protect the family. If a judgment debtor does not have a family, a creditor may be entitled to collect the full amount realized from the sale of the debtor's home.

State exemption statutes usually include both real and personal property. Personal property that is most often exempt from satisfaction of judgment debts includes the following:

1. Household furniture up to a specified dollar amount.
2. Clothing and certain personal possessions, such as family pictures or a Bible.
3. A vehicle (or vehicles) for transportation (at least up to a specified dollar amount).
4. Certain classified animals, usually livestock but including pets.
5. Equipment that the debtor uses in a business or trade, such as tools or professional instruments, up to a specified dollar amount.

SPECIAL PROTECTION FOR CONSUMER-DEBTORS

There are a number of consumer protection statutes and rules that apply to the debtor-creditor relationship. A brief listing and discussion here of some of the most important of these laws will illustrate their breadth and significance.

CONSUMER CREDIT PROTECTION ACT Commonly known as the Truth-in-Lending Act, Title I of the Consumer Credit Protection Act is basically a *disclosure law.* Administered by the Federal Reserve Board, this law requires sellers and lenders to disclose credit terms on loans so that a consumer-debtor can shop around for the best financing arrangements. Essentially, it requires that the creditor clearly indicate to the consumer-debtor what charges are being made for the privilege of paying the debt over a period of time, including the total annual interest percentage rate and finance charges.

UNIFORM CONSUMER CREDIT CODE In an attempt to make consumer credit laws at the state level uniform, the National Conference of Commissioners on Uniform State Laws proposed legislation called the Uniform Consumer Credit Code (UCCC). Its essential points are as follows:

1. To place statutory ceilings on interest rates and other charges.
2. To require disclosure similar to that required by the Truth-in-Lending Act.
3. To limit garnishment actions against take-home wages to a certain amount and to prohibit discharge of an employee solely because of garnishment proceedings.
4. To allow cancellation of a contract solicited by a seller in the consumer-debtor's home within three business days of the solicitation.
5. To prohibit referral sales, which are sales in which a seller offers a rebate or discount to a buyer

for furnishing the names of other prospective purchasers.
6. To provide criminal as well as civil penalties for violations.

Only a handful of states have adopted the UCCC, even though it has undergone numerous drafts. Some other states have passed laws similar to some of the provisions of the UCCC, such as laws concerning home-solicitation sales.

FEDERAL TRADE COMMISSION RULE In many modern consumer transactions buyers make purchases on credit, taking the seller's good and promising to pay the full debt at a later time. The buyer in such transactions often becomes a debtor by executing a *note*—a promise to pay a definite amount within a certain time. Such notes are often transferred to a third party, who purchases the notes from the seller-creditor and is then entitled to payment on the notes when due. If the person holding the note is deemed to be a *holder in due course* (HDC), then he or she is free of all claims to and most defenses against payment on the note—including those of the buyer-debtor who executed the note. The Federal Trade Commission (FTC) promulgated a rule that limits the rights of an HDC when the buyer-debtor executes a note as part of a consumer transaction. The FTC rule provides basically that any defenses the buyer can assert against the seller can also be asserted against an HDC. The seller is also required to disclose this information clearly to the buyer in its sales agreement.

The rule basically eliminates the use of a buyer's waiver-of-defense clause in a consumer transaction. These clauses waive any claim or defense the debtor might have against a third party who, for example, purchases the buyer's note from the seller.

SECTION 4
BANKRUPTCY AND REORGANIZATION

The basic law of bankruptcy in the United States is the federal Bankruptcy Code. The Bankruptcy Code has two goals—to protect a debtor by giving him or her a fresh start, free from creditors' claims, and to ensure equitable treatment to creditors who are competing for a debtor's assets.

The United States Constitution confers on Congress the power to establish uniform laws on bankruptcy.[4] When the Constitution vests power over certain matters in the federal government, as it does with respect to bankruptcy law, the federal law on that subject takes precedence over any state law on the same subject. The Constitution also forbids states from enacting laws that impair contractual obligations, which naturally includes contractual obligations between debtors and creditors. But although the Bankruptcy Code is federal law, the Code incorporates much state law regulating matters important in bankruptcy. State laws on secured transactions, liens, judgments, and exemptions, for example, play a significant role in federal bankruptcy proceedings.

Bankruptcy proceedings are held in specialized federal bankruptcy courts. A bankruptcy court's primary function is to hold *core proceedings*[5] dealing with the procedures required to administer the estate of the debtor in bankruptcy. Bankruptcy courts are under the authority of U.S. district courts, and rulings from bankruptcy courts can be appealed to the district courts. Fundamentally, a bankruptcy court fulfills the role of an administrative court for the district court concerning matters in bankruptcy. Decisions on personal injury, wrongful death, and other civil proceedings affecting the debtor are resolved in other federal or state courts.

The remaining sections in this chapter deal with the most frequently used bankruptcy plans allowed under the various chapters of the Bankruptcy Code: Chapter 7 liquidations, Chapter 11 reorganizations, and Chapter 13 plans. The latter two chapters are sometimes referred to as *rehabilitation chapters.* As you read the following sections on bankruptcy, be sure to keep in mind that references to Chapter 7, Chapter 9, and Chapter 13 are references to chapters contained in the Bankruptcy Code, not references to chapters within this textbook.

Throughout the various chapters of the Bankruptcy Code, a distinction is made between secured and unsecured creditors. A secured creditor is one in whose favor there is a **security interest**—an interest in personal property or fixtures that secures, or serves as collateral for, payment of a debt. Unsecured creditors do not have a security interest in property that serves as collateral to the underlying debt.

Even though a creditor may have a security interest in certain personal property, additional steps must be

4. U.S. Constitution, Article I, Section 8. See Appendix B.
5. Core proceedings are procedural functions, such as allowance of claims, decisions on preferences, automatic stay proceedings, confirmation of bankruptcy plans, discharge of debts, and so on.

taken to ensure that the creditor's security interest in collateral takes *priority* over claims made on the collateral by third parties, such as other secured or general creditors, trustees in bankruptcy, and later purchasers of the collateral. A secured creditor establishes priority over such third party claims by taking steps to *perfect* the security interest. Although there are other means of perfecting a security interest, the most common one is by filing with an appropriate public office a *financing statement*, signed by the debtor, describing the collateral and giving the names and addresses of the debtor and the creditor.[6]

As will be seen, because bankruptcy generally occurs when the debtor's obligations exceed the debtor's assets, the priority of claims to the available assets is frequently crucial to the outcome of a bankruptcy proceeding.

LIQUIDATION PROCEEDINGS

Liquidation under Chapter 7 of the Bankruptcy Code is generally the most familiar type of bankruptcy proceeding and is often referred to as an *ordinary*, or *straight, bankruptcy.* Put simply, a debtor in a liquidation bankruptcy turns all assets over to a **trustee.** The trustee sells the nonexempt assets and distributes the proceeds to creditors. With certain exceptions, the remaining debts are then **discharged** (extinguished), and the debtors are relieved of their obligation to pay the debts.

Any "person"—defined as including individuals, partnerships, and corporations[7]—may be a debtor in a liquidation proceeding. Railroads, insurance companies, banks, savings and loan associations, investment companies licensed by the Small Business Administration, and credit unions cannot be debtors in a liquidation bankruptcy, however. Rather, other chapters of the Bankruptcy Code or federal or state statutes apply to them.

FILING THE PETITION

A straight bankruptcy may be commenced by the filing of either a voluntary or an involuntary **petition in bankruptcy**—the document that is filed with a bankruptcy court to initiate bankruptcy proceedings.

Voluntary Bankruptcy. When a voluntary petition in bankruptcy is brought by the debtor, he or she files official forms designated for that purpose in the bankruptcy court. The Code requires a consumer-debtor who has opted for liquidation bankruptcy proceedings to state in the petition, at the time of filing, that he or she understands the relief available under other chapters of the Code and has chosen to proceed under Chapter 7. If the consumer-debtor is represented by an attorney, the attorney must file an affidavit stating that he or she has informed the debtor of the relief available under each chapter. A debtor does not have to be insolvent[8] to file for bankruptcy relief. Anyone liable to a creditor can declare bankruptcy.

The voluntary petition contains the following schedules:

1. A list of both secured and unsecured creditors, their addresses, and the amount of debt owed to each.
2. A statement of the financial affairs of the debtor.
3. A list of all property owned by the debtor, including property claimed by the debtor to be exempt.
4. A listing of current income and expenses. (This schedule provides creditors and the court with relevant information on the debtor's ability to pay creditors a reasonable amount from future income. This information *could* permit a court, on its own motion, to dismiss a debtor's Chapter 7 petition after a hearing and to encourage the filing of a repayment plan under Chapter 13, when that would substantially improve the chances that creditors would be paid.)

The official forms must be completed accurately, sworn to under oath, and signed by the debtor. To conceal assets or knowingly supply false information on these schedules is a crime under the bankruptcy laws. If the voluntary petition for bankruptcy is found to be proper, the filing of the petition will itself constitute an **order for relief.** (An order for relief is a court's grant of assistance to a complainant. In the context of bankruptcy, relief consists of discharging a complainant's

6. There are basically three methods of perfection. First, the debtor may transfer possession of the collateral to the secured creditor. Second, the security interest may be perfected automatically at the time of a credit sale (that is, at the moment the security interest is created under a written security agreement). Third, and most commonly, a security interest may be perfected by the creditor's filing a financing statement.

7. The definition of *corporation* includes unincorporated companies and associations. It also covers labor unions.

8. The inability to pay debts as they become due is known as *equitable* insolvency. A *balance sheet* insolvency, which exists when a debtor's liabilities exceed assets, is not the test. Thus, it is possible for debtors to voluntarily petition for bankruptcy or to be thrown into involuntary bankruptcy even though their assets far exceed their liabilities. This may occur when a debtor's cash flow problems become severe.

debts.) Once a consumer-debtor's voluntary petition has been filed, the clerk of the court or other appointee must give the trustee and creditors mailed notice of the order for relief not more than twenty days after entry of the order. A husband and wife may file jointly for bankruptcy under a single petition.

As mentioned above, debtors do not have to be insolvent to file for voluntary bankruptcy. Debtors do not have unfettered access to bankruptcy proceedings under Chapter 7, however. Section 707(b) of the Bankruptcy Code allows a bankruptcy court to dismiss a petition for relief under Chapter 7 if the granting of relief would constitute "substantial abuse" of Chapter 7. In the following case, the court had to decide whether granting a Chapter 7 discharge to the debtor would constitute substantial abuse.

CASE 16.2 Matter of Blair

United States Bankruptcy Court, Northern District of Alabama, Eastern Division, 1995. 180 Bankr. 656.

BACKGROUND AND FACTS *James Blair, Jr., owed primarily consumer debts of less than $7,000, and his income exceeded his living expenses by more than $200 a month. When he filed a petition for relief under Chapter 7, the court concluded that if he filed a repayment plan under Chapter 13, his debts would be paid off in forty months. The bankruptcy administrator filed a motion to dismiss Blair's petition.*

IN THE LANGUAGE OF THE COURT

JAMES S. SLEDGE, Bankruptcy Judge.

* * * *

* * * [T]he substantial abuse determination must be made on a case by case basis, in light of the totality of the circumstances. * * * [F]actors [that] should be considered * * * [include:] (1) Whether the bankruptcy petition was filed because of sudden illness, calamity, disability, or unemployment; (2) Whether the debtor incurred cash advances and made consumer purchases far in excess of his ability to pay; (3) Whether the debtor's proposed family budget is excessive or unreasonable; (4) Whether the debtor's schedules and statement of current income and expenses reasonably and accurately reflect the true financial condition; and (5) Whether the petition was filed in good faith.

* * * *

* * * [T]his Court concludes that granting this debtor relief under Chapter 7 would be a substantial abuse of the provisions of the chapter as well as perverting the purpose of the Bankruptcy Code: to give a fresh start to the honest but unfortunate debtor.

DECISION AND REMEDY *The court dismissed Blair's petition. He could pay most, if not all, of his debts under a Chapter 13 repayment plan.*

Involuntary Bankruptcy. An involuntary bankruptcy occurs when the debtor's creditors force the debtor into bankruptcy proceedings. An involuntary case cannot be commenced against a farmer[9] or a charitable institution. For an involuntary action to be filed against other debtors, the following requirements must be met: If the debtor has twelve or more creditors, three or more of these creditors having unsecured claims totaling at least $10,000 must join in the petition. If a debtor has fewer than twelve creditors, one or more creditors having a claim of $10,000 may file.

If the debtor challenges the involuntary petition, a hearing will be held, and the bankruptcy court will enter an order for relief if it finds either of the following:

1. The debtor is generally not paying debts as they become due.
2. A general receiver, assignee, or custodian took possession of, or was appointed to take charge of, substantially all of the debtor's property within 120 days before the filing of the petition.

9. The definition of *farmer* includes persons who receive more than 80 percent of their gross income from farming operations, such as tilling the soil, dairy farming, ranching, or the production or raising of crops, poultry, or livestock. Corporations and partnerships may qualify under certain conditions.

If the court grants an order for relief, the debtor will be required to supply the same information in the bankruptcy schedules as in a voluntary bankruptcy.

An involuntary petition should not be used as an everyday debt-collection device, and the Code provides penalties for the filing of frivolous petitions against debtors. Judgment may be granted against the petitioning creditors for the costs and attorneys' fees incurred by the debtor in defending against an involuntary petition that is dismissed by the court. If the petition is filed in bad faith, damages can be awarded for injury to the debtor's reputation. Punitive damages may also be awarded.

AUTOMATIC STAY The moment a petition, either voluntary or involuntary, is filed, there exists an **automatic stay,** or suspension, of virtually all litigation and other action by creditors against the debtor or the debtor's property. In other words, once a petition has been filed, creditors cannot commence or continue most legal actions, such as foreclosure of liens, execution on judgments, trials, or any action to repossess property in the hands of the debtor. A secured creditor, however, may petition the bankruptcy court for relief from the automatic stay in certain circumstances. Also, the automatic stay does not apply to paternity, alimony, maintenance, and support debts, and to certain other actions, such as criminal proceedings, against the debtor. The Code provides that if a creditor *knowingly* violates the automatic stay (a willful violation), any party injured, including the debtor, is entitled to recover actual damages, costs, and attorneys' fees and may be entitled to recover punitive damages as well.

Underlying the Code's automatic stay provision for a secured creditor is a concept known as *adequate protection.* The **adequate protection doctrine,** among other things, protects secured creditors from losing their security as a result of the automatic stay. The bankruptcy court can provide adequate protection by requiring the debtor or trustee to make periodic cash payments or a one-time cash payment (or to provide additional collateral or replacement liens) to the extent that the stay may actually cause the value of the property to decrease. Or the court may grant other relief that is the "indubitable equivalent" of (that is, equivalent to, without any doubt) the secured party's interest in the property, such as a guaranty by a solvent third party to cover losses suffered by the secured party as a result of the stay.

PROPERTY OF THE ESTATE On the commencement of a liquidation proceeding under Chapter 7, an *estate in property* is created. The estate consists of all the debtor's legal and equitable interests in property presently held, wherever located, together with community property, property transferred in a transaction voidable by the trustee, proceeds and profits from the property of the estate, and certain after-acquired property. Interests in certain property—such as gifts, inheritances, property settlements (divorce), and life insurance death proceeds—to which the debtor becomes entitled *within 180 days after filing* may also become part of the estate. Thus, the filing of a bankruptcy petition generally fixes a dividing line: property acquired prior to the filing of the petition becomes property of the estate, and property acquired after the filing of the petition, except as just noted, remains the debtor's.

The issue in the following case is whether payments made under a covenant not to compete should be included in a debtor's estate. The covenant was entered into *before* the petition was filed, but the payments were due *after* the filing.

CASE 16.3 In re Andrews

United States Court of Appeals, Fourth Circuit, 1996. 80 F.3d 906.

BACKGROUND AND FACTS *Tarmac Acquisition, Inc., bought AMAX Corporation, a ready-mix concrete company. As part of the deal, the AMAX owners, including John Andrews, signed agreements not to compete with Tarmac. Andrews was to receive $1 million, payable in quarterly installments over a five-year period. Three years later, Andrews filed a bankruptcy petition. He asked the federal bankruptcy court not to include, in the property of his estate (which would ultimately be distributed to creditors), any future installments. The court refused, and a federal district court affirmed this decision. Andrews appealed to the U.S. Court of Appeals for the Fourth Circuit.*

IN THE LANGUAGE OF THE COURT

ELLIS, District Judge:

* * * *

* * * Pre-petition assets, like the NCA [noncompetition agreement] payments, are those assets rooted in the debtor's pre-petition activities, including any proceeds that may flow from those assets in the future. These assets belong to the estate and ultimately to the creditors. Post-petition assets are those that result from the debtor's post-petition activities and are his to keep free and clear of the bankruptcy proceeding.

* * * *

Seen in this light, the NCA payments due Andrews fall clearly on the pre-bankruptcy or "past" side of the bright line. These payments are plainly rooted in, and grow out of, Andrews's pre-petition activities. * * * [B]ut for the [AMAX] sale, there would have been no NCA and no quarterly payments to Andrews. * * * Given this close connection between the NCA and the pre-petition sale of the debtor's share in the concrete business, we are persuaded that the payments were well rooted in the pre-bankruptcy past. * * * [T]hey should be included in Andrews's estate.

DECISION AND REMEDY *The U.S. Court of Appeals for the Fourth Circuit affirmed the lower court's decision. Andrews's future installments were to be included in the property of his bankruptcy estate because they were "rooted in the debtor's pre-petition activities."*

CREDITORS' MEETING AND CLAIMS Within a reasonable time after the order for relief has been granted (not less than ten days or more than thirty days), the bankruptcy court must call a meeting of creditors listed in the schedules filed by the debtor. The bankruptcy judge does not attend this meeting.

The debtor is required to attend the meeting (unless excused by the court) and to submit to examination under oath by the creditors and the trustee. Failing to appear when required or making false statements under oath may result in the debtor's being denied a discharge in bankruptcy. At the meeting, the trustee ensures that the debtor is aware of the potential consequences of bankruptcy and of his or her ability to file for bankruptcy under a different chapter.

To be entitled to receive a portion of the debtor's estate, each creditor must normally file a *proof of claim* with the bankruptcy court clerk within ninety days of the creditors' meeting.[10] The proof of claim lists the creditor's name and address, as well as the amount that the creditor asserts is owed to the creditor by the debtor. If a creditor fails to file a proof of claim, the bankruptcy court or trustee may file the proof of claim on the creditor's behalf but is not obligated to do so.

Generally, any legal obligation of the debtor is a claim. In the case of a disputed, or unliquidated, claim, the bankruptcy court will set the value of the claim. Any creditor holding a debtor's obligation can file a claim against the debtor's estate. These claims are automatically allowed unless contested by the trustee, the debtor, or another creditor. A creditor who files a false claim commits a crime.

The Code, however, does not allow claims for breach of employment contracts or real estate leases for terms longer than one year. Such claims are limited to one year's wages or rent, despite the remaining length of either contract in breach.

EXEMPTIONS The trustee takes control over the debtor's property, but an individual debtor is entitled to exempt certain property from the bankruptcy. The Bankruptcy Code exempts the following property (the dollar amounts stated in the Bankruptcy Code will be adjusted automatically on April 1, 1998, and every three years thereafter based on changes in the Consumer Price Index):[11]

1. Up to $15,000 in equity in the debtor's residence and burial plot (the homestead exemption).

10. This ninety-day rule applies in Chapter 13 bankruptcies as well.

11. A debtor cannot avoid a judicial lien for paternity, alimony, maintenance, and support debts, however, even if the lien is imposed on exempt property.

2. Interest in a motor vehicle up to $2,400.
3. Interest, up to $400 for a particular item, in household goods and furnishings, wearing apparel, appliances, books, animals, crops, and musical instruments (the aggregate total of all items is limited, however, to $8,000).
4. Interest in jewelry up to $1,000.
5. Interest in any other property up to $800, plus any unused part of the $15,000 homestead exemption up to $7,500.
6. Interest in any tools of the debtor's trade up to $1,500.
7. Any unmatured life insurance contract owned by the debtor.
8. Certain interests in accrued dividends and interest under life insurance contracts owned by the debtor.
9. Professionally prescribed health aids.
10. The right to receive Social Security and certain welfare benefits, alimony and support, and certain pension benefits.
11. The right to receive certain personal injury and other awards up to $15,000.

Individual states have the power to pass legislation precluding debtors from using the federal exemptions within the state; a majority of the states have done this. In those states, debtors may use only state, not federal, exemptions. In the rest of the states, an individual debtor (or a husband and wife filing jointly) may choose either the exemptions provided under state law or the federal exemptions.[12]

THE TRUSTEE Promptly after the order for relief in the liquidation proceeding has been entered, an interim, or provisional, trustee is appointed by the **U.S. Trustee** (a government official who performs appointing and other administrative tasks that a bankruptcy judge would otherwise have to perform). The interim, or provisional, trustee presides over the debtor's property until the first meeting of creditors. At this first meeting, either a permanent trustee is elected or the interim trustee becomes the permanent trustee.

The basic duty of the trustee is to collect the debtor's available estate and reduce it to money for distribution, preserving the interests of both the debtor and unsecured creditors. This requires that the trustee be accountable for administering the debtor's estate. To enable the trustee to accomplish this duty, the Code gives the trustee certain powers, stated in both general and specific terms. These powers must be exercised within two years of the order for relief.

Trustee's Powers. The general powers of the trustee are described by the statement that the trustee occupies a position *equivalent* in rights to that of certain other parties. For example, the trustee has the same rights as a *lien creditor* who could have obtained a judicial lien on the debtor's property or who could have levied execution on the debtor's property. This means that a trustee has priority over an unperfected secured party to the debtor's property. This right of a trustee, equivalent to that of a lien creditor, is known as the *strong-arm power.* A trustee also has power equivalent to that of a *bona fide purchaser* of real property from the debtor.

Nevertheless, a creditor with a purchase-money security interest may prevail against a trustee, if the creditor files within ten days (twenty days, in many states) of the debtor's receipt of the collateral, even if the bankruptcy petition is filed before the creditor perfects. For example, Baker loaned Newbury $20,000 on January 1, taking a security interest in the machinery Newbury purchased with the $20,000 and delivered on that same date. On January 27, before Baker had perfected her security interest, Newbury filed for bankruptcy. The trustee can invalidate Baker's security interest, because it was unperfected when Newbury filed the bankruptcy petition. Baker can only assert a claim as an unsecured creditor. But if Newbury had filed for bankruptcy on January 7, and Baker had perfected her security interest on January 8, she would have prevailed, because she would have perfected her purchase-money security interest within ten days of Newbury's receipt of the machinery.

The trustee has the power to require persons holding the debtor's property at the time the petition is filed to deliver the property to the trustee. (A trustee does not usually take actual possession of a debtor's property. Instead, a trustee's possession is constructive. For example, to obtain control of a debtor's business inventory, a trustee might change the locks on the doors to the business and hire a security guard.) The trustee also has specific *powers*

12. State exemptions may or may not be limited with regard to value. Under state exemption laws, a debtor may enjoy an unlimited value exemption on a motor vehicle, for example, even though the federal bankruptcy scheme exempts a vehicle only up to a value of $2,400. A state's law may also define the property coming within an exemption differently than the federal law or may exclude, or except, specific things from an exemption, making it unavailable to a debtor who fits within the exception.

of avoidance—that is, the trustee can set aside a sale or other transfer of the debtor's property, taking it back as a part of the debtor's estate. These powers include any voidable rights available to the debtor, preferences, certain statutory liens, and fraudulent transfers by the debtor. Each of these powers is discussed in more detail below.

The debtor shares most of the trustee's avoidance powers. Thus, if the trustee does not take action to enforce one of his or her rights (for example, to recover a preference), the debtor in a liquidation bankruptcy can nevertheless enforce that right.[13]

Voidable Rights. A trustee steps into the shoes of the debtor. Thus, any reason that a debtor can use to obtain the return of his or her property can be used by the trustee as well. These grounds include fraud, duress, incapacity, and mutual mistake.

For example, Ben sells his boat to Tara. Tara gives Ben a check, knowing that there are insufficient funds in her bank account to cover the check. Tara has committed fraud. Ben has the right to avoid that transfer and recover the boat from Tara. Once an order for relief under Chapter 7 of the Code has been entered for Ben, the trustee can exercise the same right to recover the boat from Tara, and the boat becomes a part of the debtor's estate.

Preferences. A debtor is not permitted to transfer property or to make a payment that favors—or gives a **preference** to—one creditor over others. The trustee is allowed to recover payments made both voluntarily and involuntarily to one creditor in preference over another.

To have made a preferential payment that can be recovered, an *insolvent* debtor generally must have transferred property, for a *preexisting* debt, within *ninety days* of the filing of the petition in bankruptcy. The transfer must give the creditor more than the creditor would have received as a result of the bankruptcy proceedings. The trustee does not have to prove insolvency, as the Code provides that the debtor is presumed to be insolvent during this ninety-day period.

Sometimes the creditor receiving the preference is an **insider**—an individual, a partner, a partnership, a corporation, or an officer or a director of a corporation (or a relative of one of these) who has a close relationship with the debtor. If this is the situation, the avoidance power of the trustee is extended to transfers made within *one year* before filing; however, the *presumption* of insolvency is confined to the ninety-day period. Therefore, the trustee must prove that the debtor was insolvent at the time of a transfer that occurred prior to the ninety-day period.

Not all transfers are preferences. To be a preference, the transfer must be made for something other than current consideration. Therefore, it is generally assumed by most courts that payment for services rendered within ten to fifteen days prior to the payment of the current consideration is not a preference. If a creditor receives payment in the ordinary course of business, such as payment of last month's telephone bill, the payment cannot be recovered by the trustee in bankruptcy. To be recoverable, a preference must be a transfer for an antecedent (preexisting) debt, such as a year-old printing bill. In addition, the Code permits a consumer-debtor to transfer any property to a creditor up to a total value of $600, without the transfer's constituting a preference. Also, payment of paternity, alimony, maintenance, and support debts is not a preference.

If a preferred creditor has sold the property to an innocent third party, the trustee cannot recover the property from the innocent party. The creditor, however, generally can be held accountable for the value of the property.

Liens on Debtor's Property. The trustee has the power to avoid certain statutory liens against the debtor's property, such as a landlord's lien for unpaid rent. The trustee can avoid statutory liens that first became effective against the debtor when the bankruptcy petition was filed or when the debtor became insolvent. The trustee can also avoid any lien against a bona fide purchaser that was not perfected or enforceable on the date of the bankruptcy filing.

Fraudulent Transfers. The trustee may avoid fraudulent transfers or obligations if they are made within one year of the filing of the petition or if they are made with actual intent to hinder, delay, or defraud a creditor. Transfers made for less than a reasonably equivalent consideration are also vulnerable if by making them, the debtor became insolvent, was left engaged in business with an unreasonably small

13. Under Chapter 11 (to be discussed later), for which no trustee other than the debtor generally exists, the debtor has the same avoidance powers as a trustee under Chapter 7. Under Chapter 13 (also to be discussed later), a trustee must be appointed.

amount of capital, or intended to incur debts that he or she could not pay. When a fraudulent transfer is made outside the Code's one-year limit, creditors may seek alternative relief under state laws. State laws often allow creditors to recover for transfers made up to three years prior to the filing of a petition.

DISTRIBUTION OF PROPERTY The rights of perfected secured creditors were discussed above. The Code provides that a consumer-debtor, either within thirty days of filing a liquidation petition or before the date of the first meeting of the creditors (whichever is first), must file with the clerk a statement of intention with respect to the secured collateral. The statement must indicate whether the debtor will retain the collateral or surrender it to the secured party.[14] The trustee is obligated to enforce the debtor's statement within forty-five days after it is filed.

If the collateral is surrendered to the perfected secured party, the secured creditor can enforce the security interest either by accepting the property in full satisfaction of the debt or by foreclosing on the collateral and using the proceeds to pay off the debt. Thus, the perfected secured party has priority over unsecured parties as to the proceeds from the disposition of the collateral. Indeed, the Code provides that if the value of the collateral exceeds the perfected secured party's claim and if the security agreement so provides, the secured party also has priority as to the proceeds in an amount that will cover reasonable fees and costs incurred because of the debtor's default. Fees include reasonable attorneys' fees. Any excess over this amount is used by the trustee to satisfy the claims of unsecured creditors. Should the collateral be insufficient to cover the secured debt owed, the secured creditor becomes an unsecured creditor for the difference.

Bankruptcy law establishes an order of priority for classes of debts owed to *unsecured* creditors, and they are paid in the order of their priority. Each class must be fully paid before the next class is entitled to any of the remaining proceeds. If there are insufficient proceeds to pay fully all the creditors in a class, the proceeds are distributed *proportionately* to the creditors in the class, and classes lower in priority receive nothing. The order of priority among classes of unsecured creditors is as follows:

1. Administrative expenses—including court costs, trustee fees, and attorneys' fees.
2. In an involuntary bankruptcy, expenses incurred by the debtor in the ordinary course of business from the date of the filing of the petition up to the appointment of the trustee or the issuance by the court of an order for relief.
3. Unpaid wages, salaries, and commissions earned within ninety days of the filing of the petition, limited to $4,000 per claimant. Any claim in excess of $4,000 or earned before the ninety-day period is treated as a claim of a general creditor (listed as item 9 below).
4. Unsecured claims for contributions to be made to employee benefit plans, limited to services performed during 180 days prior to the filing of the bankruptcy petition and $4,000 per employee.
5. Claims by farmers and fishers, up to $4,000, against debtor operators of grain storage or fish storage or processing facilities.
6. Consumer deposits of up to $1,800 given to the debtor before the petition was filed in connection with the purchase, lease, or rental of property or purchase of services that were not received or provided. Any claim in excess of $1,800 is treated as a claim of a general creditor (listed as item 9 below).
7. Paternity, alimony, maintenance, and support debts.
8. Certain taxes and penalties due to government units, such as income and property taxes.
9. Claims of general creditors.

If any amount remains after the priority classes of creditors have been satisfied, it is turned over to the debtor. Exhibit 16–1 illustrates graphically the collection and distribution of property in most voluntary bankruptcies.

In a bankruptcy case in which the debtor has no assets,[15] creditors are notified of the debtor's petition for bankruptcy but are instructed not to file a claim. In such a case, the unsecured creditors will receive no payment, and most, if not all, of these debts will be discharged.

14. Also, if applicable, the debtor must specify whether the collateral will be claimed as exempt property and whether the debtor intends to redeem the property or reaffirm the debt secured by the collateral (the reaffirmation of debts will be discussed shortly).

15. This type of bankruptcy is called a "no asset" case.

EXHIBIT 16–1 ■ COLLECTION AND DISTRIBUTION OF PROPERTY IN MOST VOLUNTARY BANKRUPTCIES

This exhibit illustrates the property that might be collected in a debtor's voluntary bankruptcy and how it might be distributed to creditors. Involuntary bankruptcies and some voluntary bankruptcies could include additional types of property and other creditors.

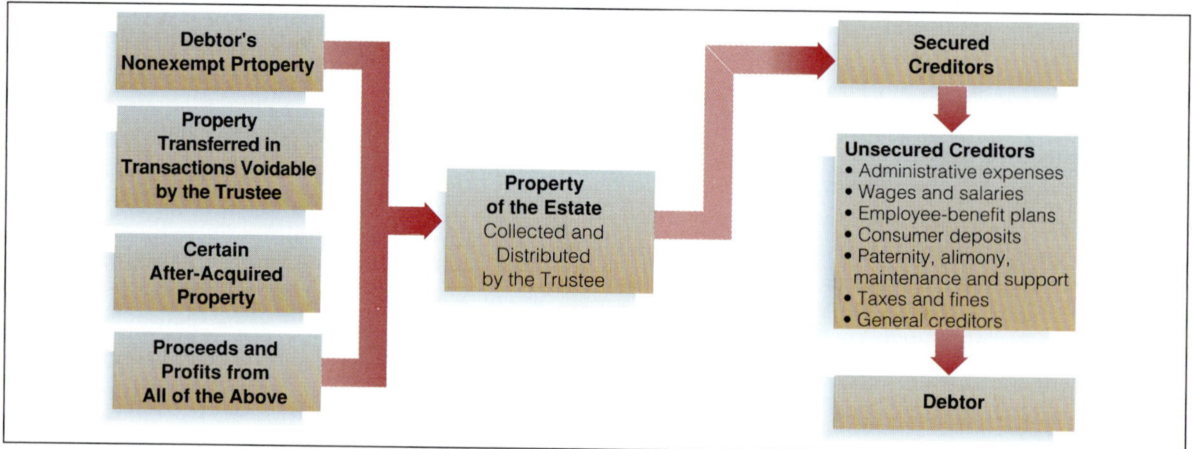

DISCHARGE From the debtor's point of view, the primary purpose of liquidation is to obtain a fresh start through a discharge of debts.[16] Certain debts, however, are not dischargeable in bankruptcy. Also, certain debtors may not qualify to have all debts discharged in bankruptcy. These situations are discussed below.

Exceptions to Discharge. Discharge of a debt may be denied because of the nature of the claim or the conduct of the debtor. Claims that are not dischargeable in a liquidation bankruptcy include the following:

1. Claims for back taxes accruing within three years prior to bankruptcy.
2. Claims for amounts borrowed by the debtor to pay federal taxes.
3. Claims against property or money obtained by the debtor under false pretenses or by false representations.
4. Claims by creditors who were not notified and did not know of the bankruptcy; these claims did not appear on the schedules the debtor was required to file.
5. Claims based on fraud or misuse of funds by the debtor while he or she was acting in a fiduciary capacity or claims involving the debtor's embezzlement or larceny.
6. Alimony, child support, and (with certain exceptions) property settlements.
7. Claims based on willful or malicious conduct by the debtor toward another or the property of another.
8. Certain government fines and penalties.
9. Certain student loans, unless payment of the loans imposes an undue hardship on the debtor and the debtor's dependents.
10. Consumer debts of more than $1,000 for luxury goods or services owed to a single creditor incurred within sixty days of the order for relief. This denial of discharge is a *rebuttable presumption* (that is, the denial may be challenged by the debtor), however, and any debts reasonably incurred to support the debtor or dependents are not classified as luxuries.
11. Cash advances totaling more than $1,000 that are extensions of open-end consumer credit obtained by the debtor within sixty days of the order for relief. A denial of discharge of these debts is also a rebuttable presumption.
12. Judgments or consent decrees against a debtor as a result of the debtor's operation of a motor vehicle while intoxicated.

In the following case, the question of the discharge of a student loan is at issue.

16. Discharges are granted under Chapter 7 only to *individuals*, not to corporations or partnerships. The latter may use Chapter 11, or they may terminate their existence under state law.

CASE 16.4 In re Baker

United States Bankruptcy Court, Eastern District of Tennessee, 1981. 10 Bankr. 870.

HISTORICAL AND SOCIAL SETTING *In 1980, about 53 percent of married women in the United States were working, compared with about 41 percent ten years earlier. More than 60 percent of wives who were separated from their husbands worked outside the home in 1980, compared with about 52 percent in 1970; for divorced women, the figures were about 74 percent and 72 percent, respectively. On average, however, in 1980, women earned only 62 cents for every dollar that men earned. In American families, husbands averaged nearly $21,000 in earnings, and wives, $8,600. At the same time, of mothers who were entitled to child support, less than 75 percent actually received any payments. Of mothers living below the poverty line, more than 60 percent received nothing at all.*

BACKGROUND AND FACTS *Mary Lou Baker attended three different institutions of higher learning, the University of Tennessee at Chattanooga, Cleveland State Community College, and the Baroness Erlanger School of Nursing. At these three schools, she received educational loans totaling $6,635. After graduation, she was employed, but her monthly take-home pay was less than $650. Monthly expenses for herself and her three children were approximately $925. Her husband had left town and provided no child or other financial support. She received no public aid and had no other income. In January 1981, just prior to this action, Mary Lou Baker's church paid her gas bill so that she and her children could have heat in their home. One child had difficulty reading, and another required expensive shoes. Baker had not been well and had been unable to pay her medical bills. She filed for bankruptcy. In her petition, she sought a discharge of her educational loans based on the hardship provision, which is the issue before the court.*

IN THE LANGUAGE OF THE COURT

RALPH H. KELLEY, Bankruptcy Judge.

* * * *

In 1976 the Congress passed the Educational Amendments which restricted a discharge in bankruptcy [of student loans]. The restriction was designed to remedy an abuse by students who, immediately upon graduation, would file bankruptcy to secure a discharge of educational loans. These students often had no other indebtedness and could easily pay their debts from future wages.

* * * *

The court concludes that under the circumstances of this case, requiring the debtor to repay the debts owed to the *three* defendants in the amount of $6,635.00 plus interest would impose upon her and her dependents an undue hardship. In passing the Educational Amendments of 1976 and including these amendments in the Bankruptcy Reform Act of 1978, Congress intended to correct an abuse. It did not intend to deprive those who have truly fallen on hard times of the "fresh start" policy of the new Bankruptcy Code.

DECISION AND REMEDY *The debtor's student loans were discharged. Given the fact that she had "truly fallen on hard times," Baker should be allowed to have her debts discharged in bankruptcy to avoid undue hardship.*

Objections to Discharge. In addition to the exceptions to discharge previously listed, a bankruptcy court may also deny the discharge of the *debtor* (as opposed to the debt). In the latter situation, the assets of the debtor are still distributed to the creditors, but the debtor remains liable for the unpaid portion of all claims. Some grounds for the denial of discharge of the debtor follow.

1. The debtor's concealment or destruction of property with the intent to hinder, delay, or defraud a creditor.
2. The debtor's fraudulent concealment or destruction of financial records.
3. The granting of a discharge to the debtor within six years of the filing of the petition.

Effect of Discharge. The primary effect of a discharge is to void any judgment on a discharged debt and enjoin any action to collect a discharged debt. A discharge does not affect the liability of a co-debtor.

Revocation of Discharge. The Code provides that a debtor may lose his or her bankruptcy discharge by revocation on petition by the trustee or a creditor. The bankruptcy court may, within one year, revoke the discharge decree if it is discovered that the debtor acted fraudulently or dishonestly during the bankruptcy proceedings. The revocation renders the discharge void, allowing creditors not satisfied by the distribution of the debtor's estate to proceed with their claims against the debtor.

REAFFIRMATION OF DEBT A debtor may wish to pay a debt—such as, for example, a debt owed to a family member, family doctor, bank, or some other creditor—notwithstanding the fact that the debt could be discharged in bankruptcy. An agreement to pay a debt dischargeable in bankruptcy is called a **reaffirmation agreement.** To be enforceable, reaffirmation agreements must be made before the debtor is granted a discharge. The agreement must be filed with the court. Approval by the court is required unless the debtor's attorney files an affidavit stating that the reaffirmation agreement is voluntarily made, that the debtor understands the consequences of the agreement and of a default under the agreement, and that the agreement will not result in an undue hardship on the debtor or the debtor's family. If court approval is required, a separate hearing will be held.

The agreement must contain a clear and conspicuous statement advising the debtor that reaffirmation is not required. The debtor can rescind, or cancel, the agreement at any time prior to discharge or within sixty days of the filing of the agreement, whichever is *later.* This rescission period must be stated *clearly* and *conspicuously* in the reaffirmation agreement.

REORGANIZATIONS

The type of bankruptcy proceeding used most commonly by corporate debtors is the Chapter 11 *reorganization.* In a reorganization, the creditors and the debtor formulate a plan under which the debtor pays a portion of his or her debts and is discharged of the remainder. The debtor is allowed to continue in business. Although this type of bankruptcy is commonly a corporate reorganization, any debtors (including individuals but excluding stockbrokers and commodities brokers)[17] who are eligible for Chapter 7 relief are eligible for relief under Chapter 11.[18] In 1994, Congress established a "fast track" Chapter 11 for small business debtors whose liabilities do not exceed $2 million and who do not own or manage real estate. This permits bankruptcy proceedings without the appointment of committees and can save time and costs.

The same principles that govern the filing of a liquidation petition apply to reorganization proceedings. The case may be brought either voluntarily or involuntarily. The same principles govern the entry of the order for relief. The automatic stay and adequate protection provisions are applicable in reorganizations as well.

In some instances, creditors may prefer private, negotiated adjustments of creditor-debtor relations, also known as **workouts,** to bankruptcy proceedings. Often, these out-of-court workouts are much more flexible and thus more conducive to a speedy settlement. Speed is critical, because delay is one of the most costly elements in any bankruptcy proceeding. Another advantage of workouts is that they avoid the various administrative costs of bankruptcy proceedings.

Under Section 305(a) of the Bankruptcy Code, a court, after notice and a hearing, may dismiss or sus-

17. In *Toibb v. Radloff,* 501 U.S. 157, 111 S.Ct. 2197, 115 L.Ed.2d 145 (1991), the Supreme Court ruled that a nonbusiness debtor may petition for relief under Chapter 11.
18. In addition, railroads are eligible for Chapter 11 relief.

pend all proceedings in a case at any time if dismissal or suspension would better serve the interests of the creditors. Section 1112 also allows a court, after notice and a hearing, to dismiss a case under reorganization "for cause." Cause includes the absence of a reasonable likelihood of rehabilitation, the inability to effect a plan, and an unreasonable delay by the debtor that is prejudicial to (may harm the interests of) creditors.[19] In the following case, creditors of the Johns-Manville Corporation sought to dismiss, under Section 1112, a voluntary petition filed by Manville.

19. See 11 U.S.C. Section 1112(b). Debtors are not prohibited from filing successive petitions, however. A debtor whose petition is dismissed, for example, can file a new Chapter 11 petition (which may be granted unless it is filed in bad faith).

CASE 16.5 In re Johns-Manville Corp.

United States Bankruptcy Court, Southern District of New York, 1984. 36 Bankr. 727.

COMPANY PROFILE *In 1858, H. W. Johns founded a roofing materials business in Brooklyn. By 1901, Johns had patented a line of products containing asbestos and merged with the Manville Covering Company, which had begun in 1886 in Milwaukee to produce pipe coverings and insulation materials. The renamed Johns-Manville Company concentrated on making building materials. Johns-Manville moved to Colorado in the early 1970s. In 1974, nearly 500 men who had worked with Johns-Manville products in the construction of ships during World War II filed the first major asbestos lawsuit against the company. By 1982, Johns-Manville had settled more than 4,000 asbestos-related lawsuits but faced a backlog of nearly 17,000.*

BACKGROUND AND FACTS *On August 26, 1982, the Johns-Manville Corporation filed for protection under Chapter 11 of the Bankruptcy Code. This filing came as quite a surprise to some of Manville's creditors, as well as to some of the other corporations that were being sued, along with Manville, for injuries caused by asbestos exposure. Manville asserted that the nearly 17,000 lawsuits pending as of the filing date and the potential lawsuits of people who had been exposed to asbestos but who would not manifest asbestos-related diseases until some time in the future necessitated its filing. The creditors of Manville, including people harmed by asbestos exposure who had won lawsuits or settlements, contended that Johns-Manville had not filed in good faith and that the voluntary reorganization petition should thus be dismissed under Section 1112 of the Bankruptcy Code.*

IN THE LANGUAGE OF THE COURT

BURTON R. LIFLAND, Bankruptcy Judge.

* * * *

In determining whether to dismiss under Code Section 1112(b), a court is not necessarily required to consider whether the debtor has filed in "good faith" because that is not a specified [requirement] under the Code for filing. Rather, according to Code Section 1129(a)(3), good faith emerges as a requirement for the confirmation of a plan. * * * It is thus logical that the good faith of the debtor be deemed a predicate primarily for emergence out of a Chapter 11 case. It is after confirmation of a concrete and immutable reorganization plan that creditors are foreclosed from advancing their distinct and parochial interests in the debtor's estate.

* * * *

In the instant case, not only would liquidation be wasteful and inefficient in destroying the utility of valuable assets of the companies as well as jobs, but, more importantly, liquidation would preclude just compensation of some present asbestos victims and all future asbestos claimants. This unassailable reality represents all the more reason for this Court to adhere to this basic potential liquidation avoidance aim of Chapter 11 and deny the motions to dismiss. Manville must not be required to wait until its economic picture has deteriorated beyond salvation to file for reorganization.

DECISION AND REMEDY *The motions to dismiss the Manville petition were denied. The court concluded that a bankruptcy proceeding was appropriate in this situation.*

DEBTOR IN POSSESSION On entry of the order for relief, the debtor generally continues to operate his or her business as a **debtor in possession (DIP).** The court, however, may appoint a trustee (often referred to as a *receiver*) to operate the debtor's business if gross mismanagement of the business is shown or if appointing a trustee is in the best interests of the estate.

CREDITORS' COMMITTEES As soon as practicable after the entry of the order for relief, a creditors' committee of unsecured creditors is appointed. The committee may consult with the trustee or the DIP concerning the administration of the case or the formulation of the plan. Additional creditors' committees may be appointed to represent special interest creditors. Orders affecting the estate generally will be entered only with either the consent of the committee or after a hearing in which the judge hears the position of the committee.

Businesses with debts of less than $2 million that do not own or manage real estate can avoid creditors' committees. In these cases, orders can be entered without a committee's consent.

THE REORGANIZATION PLAN A reorganization plan to rehabilitate the debtor is a plan to conserve and administer the debtor's assets in the hope of an eventual return to successful operation and solvency. The plan must be fair and equitable and must do the following:

1. Designate classes of claims and interests.
2. Specify the treatment to be afforded the classes. (The plan must provide the same treatment for all claims in a particular class.)
3. Provide an adequate means for execution.

Only the debtor may file a plan within the first 120 days after the date of the order for relief. If the debtor does not meet the 120-day deadline, however, or if the debtor fails to obtain the required creditor consent (discussed below) within 180 days, any party may propose a plan. If a small-business debtor chooses to avoid creditors' committees, the time for the debtor's filing is shortened to 100 days, and any other party's plan must be filed within 160 days.

Once the plan has been developed, it is submitted to each class of creditors for acceptance. Each class must accept the plan unless the class is not adversely affected by the plan. A class has accepted the plan when a majority of the creditors, representing two-thirds of the amount of the total claim, vote to approve it.

Even when all classes of claims accept the plan, the court may refuse to confirm it if it is not "in the best interests of the creditors."[20] A spouse or child of the debtor can block the plan if it does not provide for payment of their claims in cash.

The plan is binding on confirmation. The debtor is given a reorganization discharge from all claims not protected under the plan. This discharge does not apply to any claims that would be denied discharge under liquidation.

CHAPTER 13 PLANS

Chapter 13 of the Bankruptcy Code provides for "Adjustment of Debts of an Individual with Regular Income." Individuals (not partnerships or corporations) with *regular income* who owe fixed unsecured debts of less than $250,000 or fixed secured debts of less than $750,000 may take advantage of bankruptcy repayment plans. This includes salaried employees; individual proprietors; and individuals who live on welfare, Social Security, fixed pensions, or investment income. Many small-business debtors have a choice of filing a plan for reorganization or for repayment. There are several advantages, however, with repayment plans. One advantage is that they are less

20. The plan need not provide for full repayment to unsecured creditors. Instead, creditors receive a percentage of each dollar owed to them by the debtor.

expensive and less complicated than reorganization proceedings or, for that matter, even liquidation proceedings.

FILING THE PETITION A repayment plan case can be initiated only by the filing of a voluntary petition by the debtor. Certain liquidation and reorganization cases may be converted to repayment plan cases with the consent of the debtor.[21] A trustee, who will make payments under the plan, must be appointed. On the filing of a repayment plan petition, the automatic stay previously discussed takes effect. Although the stay applies to all or part of a consumer debt, it does not apply to any business debt incurred by the debtor.

THE REPAYMENT PLAN A plan of rehabilitation by repayment must provide for the following:

1. The turnover to the trustee of such future earnings or income of the debtor as is necessary for execution of the plan.
2. Full payment in deferred cash payments of all claims entitled to priority.[22]
3. The same treatment of all claims within a particular class. (The Code permits the debtor to list co-debtors, such as guarantors or sureties, as a separate class.)

Filing the Plan. Only the debtor may file for a repayment plan. This plan may provide either for payment of all obligations in full or for payment of a lesser amount. The time for payment under the plan may not exceed three years unless the court approves an extension. The term, with extension, may not exceed five years.

The Code requires the debtor to make "timely" payments, and the trustee is required to ensure that the debtor commences these payments. The debtor must commence making payments under the proposed plan within thirty days after the plan has been *filed.* If the plan has not been confirmed, the trustee is instructed to retain the payments until the plan is confirmed and then distribute them accordingly. If the plan is denied, the trustee will return the payments to the debtor less any costs. Failure of the debtor to make timely payments or to commence payments within the thirty-day period will allow the court to convert the case to a liquidation bankruptcy or to dismiss the petition.

Confirmation of the Plan. After the plan is filed, the court holds a confirmation hearing, at which interested parties may object to the plan. The court will confirm a plan with respect to each claim of a secured creditor under any of the following circumstances:

1. If the secured creditors have accepted the plan.
2. If the plan provides that creditors retain their liens and if the value of the property to be distributed to them under the plan is not less than the secured portion of their claims.
3. If the debtor surrenders the property securing the claims to the creditors.

Objection to the Plan. Unsecured creditors do not have a vote to confirm a repayment plan, but they can object to it. The court can approve a plan over the objection of the trustee or any unsecured creditor only in either of the following situations:

1. When the value of the property to be distributed under the plan is at least equal to the amount of the claims.
2. When all the debtor's projected disposable income to be received during the three-year plan period will be applied to making payments. Disposable income is all income received *less* amounts needed to support the debtor and dependents and/or amounts needed to meet ordinary expenses to continue the operation of a business.

Modification of the Plan. Prior to completion of payments, the plan may be modified at the request of either the debtor, the trustee, or an unsecured creditor. If there is an objection to the modification by any interested party, the court must hold a hearing to determine approval or disapproval of the modified plan.

DISCHARGE After completion of all payments, the court grants a discharge of all debts provided for by the repayment plan. Except for allowed claims not provided for by the plan, certain long-term debts provided for by the plan, and claims for alimony and child support, all other debts are dischargeable. A discharge of debts under a Chapter

21. A Chapter 13 case may be converted to a Chapter 7 case either at the request of the debtor or, under certain circumstances, "for cause" by a creditor. A Chapter 13 case may be converted to a Chapter 11 case after a hearing.

22. As with a Chapter 11 reorganization plan, full repayment of all claims is not always required.

13 repayment plan is sometimes referred to as a "super-discharge." One of the reasons for this is that the law allows a Chapter 13 discharge to include fraudulently incurred debt and claims resulting from malicious or willful injury. Therefore, a discharge under Chapter 13 may be much more beneficial to some debtors than a liquidation discharge under Chapter 7.

Even if the debtor does not complete the plan, a hardship discharge may be granted if failure to complete the plan was due to circumstances beyond the debtor's control and if the value of the property distributed under the plan was greater than would have been paid in a liquidation. A discharge can be revoked within one year if it was obtained by fraud.

TERMS AND CONCEPTS TO REVIEW

adequate protection doctrine 329
artisan's lien 320
attachment 321
automatic stay 329
co-surety 324
debtor in possession (DIP) 338
discharge 327
equity of redemption 323
garnishment 321
guarantor 323
homestead exemption 325
insider 332
lien 320
liquidation 327
mechanic's lien 320
mortgagee 323
mortgagor 323
order for relief 327
petition in bankruptcy 327
preference 332
reaffirmation agreement 336
right of contribution 324
right of reimbursement 324
right of subrogation 324
security interest 326
statutory period of redemption 323
surety 323
suretyship 323
trustee 327
U.S. Trustee 331
workout 336
writ of attachment 321
writ of execution 321

QUESTIONS AND CASE PROBLEMS

16–1. LIENS. Sylvia takes her car to Crank's Auto Repair Shop. A sign in the window states that all repairs must be paid for in cash unless credit is approved in advance. Sylvia and Crank agree that Crank will repair Sylvia's car engine and put in a new transmission. No mention is made of credit. Because Crank is not sure how much engine repair will be necessary, he refuses to give Sylvia an estimate. He repairs the engine and puts in a new transmission. When Sylvia comes to pick up her car, she learns that the bill is $995. Sylvia is furious, refuses to pay Crank that amount, and demands possession of her car. Crank demands payment. Discuss the rights of the parties in this matter.

16–2. CREDITORS' REMEDIES. Kanahara is employed by the Cross-Bar Packing Corp. and earns take-home pay of $400 per week. He is $2,000 in debt to the Holiday Department Store for goods purchased on credit over the past eight months. Most of this property is nonexempt and is presently located in Kanahara's apartment. Kanahara is in default on his payments to Holiday. Holiday learns that Kanahara has a girlfriend in another state and that he plans on giving her most of this property for Christmas. Discuss what actions are available and should be taken by Holiday to resolve the debt owed by Kanahara.

16–3. GUARANTY. Natalie is a student at Slippery Stone University. In need of funds to pay for tuition and books, she attempts to secure a short-term loan from West Bank. The bank agrees to make a loan if Natalie will have someone financially responsible guarantee the loan payments. Sheila, a well-known businesswoman and a friend of Natalie's family, calls the bank and agrees to pay the loan if Natalie cannot. Because of Sheila's reputation, the loan is made. Natalie is making the payments, but because of illness she is not able to work for one month. She requests that West Bank extend the loan for three months. West Bank agrees, raising the interest rate for the extended period. Sheila is not notified of the extension (and therefore does not consent to it). One month later Natalie drops out of school. All attempts to collect from Natalie fail. West Bank wants to hold Sheila liable. Discuss West Bank's claim against Sheila.

16–4. PRIORITY OF CREDITORS. Sam is a retail seller of television sets. He sells Gracen a $900 set on a retail installment security agreement in which she pays $100 down and agrees to pay the balance in equal installments. Sam retains a security interest in the set, and he perfects that interest by filing a financing statement locally. Two months later, Gracen is in default on her payments to Sam and is involuntarily petitioned into bankruptcy by her creditors. Sam wants to repossess the television set, as provided for in the security agreement, and he wants to have priority over the trustee in bankruptcy as to any proceeds from the disposal of the set. Discuss fully Sam's right to repossess and whether he has priority over the trustee in bankruptcy as to any proceeds from the disposal of the set.

16–5. DISTRIBUTION OF ASSETS. Montoro petitioned himself into voluntary bankruptcy. There were three major claims against his estate. One was made by Carlton, a friend who held Montoro's negotiable promissory note for $2,500; one was made by Elmer, an employee who was owed three months' back wages of $4,500; and one was made by the United Bank of the Rockies on an unsecured loan of $5,000. In addition, Dietrich, an accountant retained by the trustee, was owed $500, and property taxes of $1,000 were owed to Rock County. Montoro's nonexempt property was liquidated, with proceeds of $5,000. Discuss fully what amount each party will receive, and why.

16–6. ARTISAN'S LIEN. Air Ruidoso, Ltd., operated a commuter airline and air charter service between Ruidoso, New Mexico, and airports in Albuquerque and El Paso. Executive Aviation Center, Inc., provided services for airlines at the Albuquerque International Airport. When Air Ruidoso failed to pay more than $10,000 that it owed for fuel, oil, and oxygen, Executive Aviation took possession of Air Ruidoso's plane. Executive Aviation claimed that it had a lien in the plane and filed a suit in a New Mexico state court to foreclose. Do supplies such as fuel, oil, and oxygen qualify as "materials" for the purpose of creating an artisan's lien? Why or why not? [*Air Ruidoso, Ltd. v. Executive Aviation Center, Inc.*, 122 N.M. 71, 920 P.2d 1025 (1996)]

16–7. PREFERENCES. Fred Currey purchased cattle from Itano Farms, Inc. As payment for the cattle, Currey gave Itano Farms worthless checks in the amount of $50,250. Currey was later convicted of passing bad checks, and the state criminal court ordered him to pay Itano Farms restitution in the amount of $50,250. About four months after this court order, Currey and his wife filed for Chapter 7 bankruptcy protection. During the ninety days prior to the filing of the petition, Currey had made three restitution payments to Itano, totaling $14,821. The Curreys sought to recover these payments as preferences. What should the court decide? Explain. [*In re Currey*, 144 Bankr. 490 (D.Ida. 1992)]

16–8. DISMISSAL OF CHAPTER 7 CASE. Ellis and Bonnie Jarrell filed a Chapter 7 petition. The reason for the filing was not calamity, sudden illness, disability, or unemployment—both Jarrells were employed. Their petition was full of inaccuracies that understated their income and overstated their obligations. For example, they declared as an expense a monthly contribution to an investment plan. The truth was that they had monthly income of $3,197.45 and expenses of $2,159.44. They were attempting to discharge a total of $15,391.64 in unsecured debts. Most of these were credit-card debts, at least half of which had been taken as cash advances. Should the court dismiss the petition? If so, why? Discuss. [*In re Jarrell*, 189 Bankr. 374 (M.D.N.C. 1995)]

16–9. AUTOMATIC STAY. David Sisco had about $600 in an account in Tinker Federal Credit Union. Sisco owed DPW Employees Credit Union a little more than $1,100. To collect on the debt, DPW obtained a garnishment judgment and served it on Tinker. The next day, Sisco filed a bankruptcy petition. Tinker then told DPW that, because of the bankruptcy filing, it could not pay the garnishment. DPW objected, and Tinker asked an Oklahoma state court to resolve the issue. What effect, if any, does Sisco's bankruptcy filing have on DPW's garnishment action? [*DPW Employees Credit Union v. Tinker Federal Credit Union*, 925 P.2d 93 (Okla.App.4th 1996)]

16–10. A QUESTION OF ETHICS

In September 1986, Edward and Debora Davenport pleaded guilty in a Pennsylvania court to welfare fraud and were sentenced to probation for one year. As a condition of their probation, the Davenports were ordered to make monthly restitution payments to the county probation department, which would forward the payments to the Pennsylvania Department of Public Welfare, the victim of the Davenports' fraud. In May 1987, the Davenports filed a petition for Chapter 13 relief and listed the restitution payments among their debts. The bankruptcy court held that the restitution obligation was a dischargeable debt. On appeal, the district court reversed, holding that state-imposed criminal restitution obligations cannot be discharged in Chapter 13 bankruptcy. The Court of Appeals for the Third Circuit reversed the district court's decision, concluding that "the plain language of the chapter" demonstrated that restitution orders are debt within the meaning of the Code and hence dischargeable in proceedings under Chapter 13. Ultimately, the case was reviewed by the United States Supreme Court, which affirmed the Third Circuit's ruling. The Court noted that under the Bankruptcy Code, a debt is defined as a liability on a claim, and a claim is defined as a right to payment. Because the restitution obligations clearly constituted a right to payment, the Court held that the obligations were dischargeable in bankruptcy. [*Pennsylvania Department of Public Welfare v. Davenport*, 495 U.S. 552, 110 S.Ct. 2126, 109 L.Ed.2d 588 (1990)]

1. Critics of this decision contend that the Court adhered to the letter, but not the spirit, of bankruptcy law in arriving at its conclusion. In what way, if any, did the Court not abide by the "spirit" of bankruptcy law?
2. Do you think that individuals' repayment plans, which allow nearly all types of debts to be discharged, tip the scales of justice too far in favor of debtors?

ACCESSING THE INTERNET
THE LEGAL ENVIRONMENT OF BUSINESS

The Legal Information Institute at Cornell University offers a collection of law materials concerning debtor-creditor relationships, including federal statutes and recent Supreme Court decisions on this topic, at

http://www.law.cornell.edu/topics/debtor_creditor.html

The U.S. Bankruptcy Code is online at

http://www.law.cornell.edu:80/uscode/11

Cornell Law School's Legal Information Institute provides a general introduction to bankruptcy law and links to related Internet resources at

http://www.law.cornell.edu/topics/bankruptcy.html

You can find links to an extensive number of bankruptcy resources on the Internet by accessing the Bankruptcy Lawfinder at

http://www.agin.com/lawfind/

The American Bankruptcy Institute (ABI) is also a good resource for bankruptcy information. The ABI site includes a collection of selected bankruptcy court decisions, daily and weekly summaries of important bankruptcy news, legislative updates, and so on. You can access the site at

http://www.abiworld.org

For a discussion of alternatives to bankruptcy, go to

http://apocalypse.berkshire.net/~mkb/

The site includes information on the following alternatives: Debt Workout, Do Nothing, and Pay Creditors.

Dockets, records, and some of the decisions of the bankruptcy courts can be accessed online through the federal courts' electronic bulletin board system, PACER (see the *Accessing the Internet* section at the end of Chapter 3 for information on PACER).

CHAPTER 17

BUSINESS ORGANIZATIONS

EVERY BUSINESS ACTIVITY INVOLVES—implicitly or explicitly—a form of business organization, whether it be a sole proprietorship, a partnership, a corporation, or some hybrid form. Each form provides different degrees of flexibility and different rights and liabilities, and it is important to be aware of these differences when choosing and structuring one's business organization. In this chapter, we examine the basic features of sole proprietorships, partnerships, corporations, limited liability companies, limited liability partnerships, and limited liability limited partnerships. We also touch on joint ventures, syndicates, joint stock companies, business trusts, cooperatives, and private franchises.

Note that there is great variety in the sizes and functions of business organizations even within the same category. For example, businesses conducted as sole proprietorships can range from a small mail order business run out of the owner's home to a multimillion-dollar manufacturing operation occupying acres of an industrial complex. Similarly, partnerships can range from an informal arrangement between two individuals to a formal organization with hundreds of partners. Also, most of the wealthiest U.S. business firms are organized as corporations, but the majority of corporations are small. It has been estimated that over 90 percent of the corporations have ten or fewer shareholders.

The sizes of businesses may differ considerably within a category, but tax liabilities and other obligations faced by the businesses within each category typically are constant. A sole proprietorship doing $22,000 worth of business faces the same federal tax laws as a sole proprietorship doing $10 million worth of business.

SECTION 1
SOLE PROPRIETORSHIPS

The simplest form of business is a **sole proprietorship.** In this form, the owner is the business; thus, anyone who does business without creating a separate business organization has a sole proprietorship. Sole proprietorships constitute over two-thirds of all American businesses. They are also usually small enterprises—less than 1 percent of the sole proprietorships existing in the United States have revenues that exceed $1 million per year. Sole proprietors can own and manage any type of business from an informal, home-office undertaking to a large restaurant or construction firm.

A major advantage of the sole proprietorship is that the proprietor receives all of the profits (because he or she assumes all of the risk). In addition, it is often easier and less costly to start a sole proprietorship than to start any other kind of business, as few legal forms are involved. This type of business organization also entails more flexibility than does a partnership or a corporation. The sole proprietor is free to make any decision he or she wishes to concerning the business—whom to hire, when to take a vacation, what kind of business to pursue, and so on. A sole proprietor pays only personal income taxes on profits, which are reported as personal income on the proprietor's personal income tax form. Sole proprietors are also allowed to establish tax-exempt retirement accounts in the form of Keogh plans.[1]

The major disadvantage of the sole proprietorship is that, as sole owner, the proprietor alone bears the burden of any losses or liabilities incurred by the business enterprise. In other words, the sole proprietor has unlimited liability, or legal responsibility, for all obligations incurred in doing business. This unlimited liability is a major factor to be considered in choosing a business form. Another disadvantage is that the proprietor's opportunity to raise capital is limited to personal funds and the funds of those who are willing to make loans. The sole proprietorship also has the disadvantage of lacking continuity on the death of the proprietor. When the owner dies, so does the business—it is automatically dissolved. If the business is transferred to family members or other heirs, a new proprietorship is created.

SECTION 2
PARTNERSHIPS

A **partnership** arises from an agreement, express or implied, between two or more persons to carry on a business for profit. Partners are co-owners of a business and have joint control over its operation and the right to share in its profits.

One advantage of the partnership is that it can be organized easily and inexpensively. No particular form of partnership agreement is necessary to create a partnership, but for practical reasons, the agreement should be in writing. Basically, the partners may agree to almost any terms when establishing the partnership so long as they are not illegal or contrary to public policy. Another advantage of the partnership is that the firm itself does not pay federal income taxes, although the firm must file an **information return** with the Internal Revenue Service (IRS). A partner's profit from the partnership (whether distributed or not) is taxed as individual income to the individual partner.

The main disadvantage of the partnership is that the partners are subject to personal liability for partnership obligations. In other words, if the partnership cannot pay its debts, the personal assets of the partners are subject to creditors' claims.

A partnership is a legal entity only for limited purposes, such as the partnership name and title of ownership and property.

SECTION 3
LIMITED PARTNERSHIPS

Traditionally, partnerships have been classified as either *general partnerships* or *limited partnerships.* The type of partnership that was discussed in the preceding section is a general partnership. The **limited partnership** is a special and, at one time, quite popular form of partnership consisting of at least one general partner and one or more limited partners. The general partner or partners assume responsibility for the management of the partnership and liability for all partnership debts. The limited partners have no right to participate in the management or operation of the partnership and assume no liability for partnership debts beyond the amount of capital they have contributed.

1. A *Keogh plan* is a retirement program designed for self-employed persons. A certain percentage of income can be contributed to the plan, and interest earnings will not be taxed until funds are withdrawn.

One of the major benefits of becoming a limited partner is this limitation on liability, both with respect to lawsuits brought against the partnership and with respect to the amount of money placed at risk. The maximum money at risk is defined by the limited partnership agreement, which specifically states how much each limited partner must contribute to the partnership.

Unlike a general partnership, a limited partnership is completely a creature of statute. The limited partnership does not come into existence until a *certificate of partnership* is filed with the appropriate state office. If the statutory requirements are not followed almost to the letter, the courts will hold that a general partnership exists instead. Then those who thought their liability was limited by their investment in a limited partnership will be held generally liable to the full extent of their personal net worth.

The exemptions from personal liability of the limited partners rest on their not participating in management. Indeed, the surname of a limited partner cannot be included in the partnership name. A violation of this provision renders the limited partner just as liable as a general partner to any creditor who does not know that he or she is a limited partner. Note that no law expressly bars the participation of limited partners in the management of the partnership. Rather, the threat of personal liability normally deters their participation.

How much actual review and advisement a limited partner can engage in before being exposed to liability is an unsettled question. Despite the restriction on the participation of limited partners in the management of a firm, however, all of the partners continue to have a fiduciary obligation to the other partners. In the following case, two limited partners filed suit against a general partner of the limited partnership. The issue before the court is whether the general partner breached his fiduciary obligation to the other partners.

CASE 17.1 Drucker v. Mige Associates II

Supreme Court,
Appellate Division,
First Department, 1996.
639 N.Y.S.2d 365.

BACKGROUND AND FACTS *Mige Associates II was a limited partnership. Mige owned an apartment building that could have been converted into a cooperative (a housing complex jointly owned by the residents) at a substantial profit. The conversion required, under the voting provisions of the partnership agreement, the consent of Jon Meadow, one of the general partners. Before consenting, Meadow demanded that he receive more money than the other general partners. When his demand was rejected, he blocked the conversion. Ronald Drucker and Ronald Schaffer, two of the limited partners, filed a suit in a New York state court against Meadow. The court ruled in Meadow's favor. Drucker and Schaffer appealed.*

IN THE LANGUAGE OF THE COURT

MEMORANDUM DECISION.

* * * *

* * * Meadow breached his fiduciary responsibility to the general and limited partners of Mige II Associates. Meadow effectively derailed the profitable conversion of the partnership's building into a cooperative apartment through his unwarranted demands * * * . Meadow's conduct was neither economically nor otherwise justified and can only fairly be viewed as an attempt to use the voting provisions of the partnership agreement for personal gain in contravention of the fundamental implied covenant of good faith and fair dealing governing the partners' fiduciary obligations to one another, and as a threat of irreparable harm to his own as well as plaintiffs' partnership interests.

* * * *

* * * Accordingly, while the court-ordered removal of a partner or judicial dissolution of a partnership are rarely invoked remedies, the totality of the circumstances lead us to conclude that the interests of the partnership would be best served by Meadow's removal as a general partner * * * .

DECISION AND REMEDY *The New York state appellate court terminated Meadow's rights as a general partner. Meadow had breached his fiduciary duty to the other partners.*

INTERNATIONAL CONSIDERATIONS **Liability of Limited Partners in Argentina** *Many nations permit businesspersons to establish limited partnerships. In Argentina, the limited partnership is called a* sociedad en comandita *and is closely regulated by the government. Limited partners, known as "sleeping partners," have limited liability so long as they do not participate in management. Argentinian law, however, does permit limited partners to inspect the books, express their views to managers, and offer advice at partnership meetings.*

SECTION 4
CORPORATIONS

A widely used type of business organizational form is the **corporation.** Corporations are owned by *shareholders*—those who have purchased ownership shares in the business. A *board of directors,* elected by the shareholders, manages the business. The board of directors normally employs *officers* to oversee day-to-day operations.

The corporation is a creature of statute. A corporation is an artificial being, existing in law only and neither tangible nor visible. Its existence depends generally on state law, although some corporations, especially public organizations, can be created under federal law. Each state has its own body of corporate law, and these laws are not entirely uniform. The Model Business Corporation Act (MBCA) is a codification of modern corporation law that has been influential in the codification of state corporation statutes. Today, the majority of state statutes are guided by the most recent version of the MBCA, often referred to as the Revised Model Business Corporation Act (RMBCA). You should keep in mind, however, that there is considerable variation among the statutes of the states that have used the MBCA or the RMBCA as a basis for their statutes, and several states do not follow either act. Because of this, individual state corporation laws should be relied on to determine corporate law rather than the MBCA or RMBCA

Under modern law, except as limited by charters, statutes, or constitutions, *a corporation can engage in any act and enter into any contract available to a natural person in order to accomplish the purposes for which it was created.* When a corporation is created, the express and implied powers necessary to achieve its purpose also come into existence.

THE NATURE OF THE CORPORATION

A corporation can consist of one or more *natural* persons (as opposed to the artificial "person" of the corporation) identified under a common name. The corporation substitutes itself for its shareholders in conducting corporate business and in incurring liability, yet its authority to act and the liability for its actions are separate and apart from the individuals who own it. (In certain limited situations, the "corporate veil" can be pierced; that is, liability for the corporation's obligations can be extended to shareholders, a topic that is important to small corporations.)

CORPORATE PERSONNEL Responsibility for the overall management of the corporation is entrusted to a board of directors, which is elected by the shareholders. The board of directors hires corporate officers and other employees to run the daily business operations of the corporation.

When an individual purchases a share of stock in a corporation, that person becomes a shareholder and an owner of the corporation. Unlike the members in a partnership, the body of shareholders can change constantly without affecting the continued existence of the corporation. A shareholder can sue the corporation, and the corporation can sue a shareholder. Additionally, under certain circumstances, a shareholder can sue on behalf of a corporation. The rights and duties of all corporate personnel will be examined in the following chapter.

CORPORATE TAXATION Corporate profits are taxed by state and federal governments. Corporations can do one of two things with corporate profits—retain them or pass them on to shareholders in the form of dividends. The corporation receives no tax deduction for dividends distributed to shareholders. Dividends are again taxable (except when they represent distributions of capital) as ordinary income to the shareholder receiving them. This double-taxation feature of the corporation is one of its major disadvantages.

Profits not distributed are retained by the corporation. These **retained earnings,** if invested properly, will yield higher corporate profits in the future and thus cause the price of the company's stock to rise. Individual shareholders can then reap the benefits of the retained earnings in the capital gains they receive when they sell their shares.

CLASSIFICATION OF CORPORATIONS

The classification of a corporation normally depends on its location, purpose, and ownership characteristics.

DOMESTIC AND FOREIGN CORPORATIONS A corporation is known as a *domestic corporation* in its home state (the state in which it incorporates). A corporation that is formed in one state but doing business in another is referred to in that other state as a *foreign corporation.* A corporation formed in another country (say, Mexico) but doing business in the United States is referred to in the United States as an *alien corporation.*

A corporation does not have an automatic right to do business in a state other than its state of incorporation. A corporation normally is required to obtain a *certificate of authority* in any state in which it plans to do business. Once the certificate has been issued, the powers conferred on the corporation by its home state generally can be exercised in the other state. Should a foreign corporation do business without obtaining a certificate of authority, the state can fine the corporation; deny it the privilege of using state courts; and even hold its officers, directors, or agents personally liable for corporate obligations, including contractual obligations, incurred in that state.[2]

PUBLIC AND PRIVATE CORPORATIONS A corporation formed by the government to meet some political or governmental purpose is a public corporation. Cities and towns that incorporate are common examples. In addition, many federal government organizations, such as the U.S. Postal Service, the Tennessee Valley Authority, and AMTRAK, are public corporations.

Private corporations, in contrast, are created either wholly or in part for private benefit. Most corporations are private. Although they may serve a public purpose, as a public utility does, they are owned by private persons rather than by the government.

NONPROFIT CORPORATIONS Corporations formed for purposes other than making a profit are called *nonprofit* or *not-for-profit* corporations. Nonprofit corporations are usually (although not necessarily) private corporations. Private hospitals, educational institutions, charities, religious organizations, and the like are frequently organized as nonprofit corporations. The nonprofit corporation is a convenient form of organization that allows various groups to own property and to form contracts without the individual members' being personally exposed to liability.

CLOSE CORPORATIONS A **close corporation** is one whose shares are held by members of a family or by relatively few persons. Close corporations are also referred to as *closely held, family,* or *privately held* corporations. Usually, the members of the small group constituting a close corporation are personally known to one another. Because the number of shareholders is so small, there is no trading market for the shares. In practice, a close corporation is often operated like a partnership. A few states recognize this similarity in special statutory provisions that cover close corporations.

Some states have enacted special statutory provisions that apply to close corporations. These provisions expressly permit close corporations to depart significantly from certain formalities required by traditional corporation law.[3] Additionally, Section 7.32 of the RMBCA—a provision added to the RMBCA in 1991 and adopted in several states—gives close corporations a substantial amount of flexibility in determining the rules by which they will operate. Under Section 7.32, if all of the shareholders of a corporation agree in writing, the corporation can operate without directors, bylaws, annual or special shareholders' or directors' meetings, stock certifi-

2. *Robertson v. Levy,* 197 A.2d 443 (D.C.App. 1964).

3. For example, in some states (such as Maryland), the close corporation need not have a board of directors.

cates, or formal records of shareholders' or directors' decisions.[4]

Management of Close Corporations. The close corporation has a single shareholder or a closely knit group of shareholders, who usually hold the positions of directors and officers. Management of a close corporation resembles that of a sole proprietorship or a partnership. As a corporation, however, the firm must meet whatever specific legal requirements are set forth in state statutes.

To prevent a majority shareholder from dominating a close corporation, the corporation may specify that action can be taken by the board only on approval of more than a simple majority of the directors. Typically, this would not be required for ordinary business decisions but only for extraordinary actions, such as changing the amount of dividends or dismissing an employee-shareholder. Additionally, in some cases, courts have held that majority shareholders owe a fiduciary duty to minority shareholders (see Chapter 18 for a further discussion of the duties of majority shareholders).

Transfer of Shares in Close Corporations. Because, by definition, a close corporation has a small number of shareholders, the transfer of one shareholder's shares to someone else can cause serious management problems. The other shareholders may find themselves required to share control with someone they do not know or like.

Consider an example. Three brothers, Terry, Damon, and Henry Johnson, are the only shareholders of Johnson's Car Wash, Inc. Henry wants to sell his shares to an unknown third person, Terry and Damon object to Henry's idea, and a dispute ensues. What could they have done to avoid this situation? The articles of incorporation could have restricted the transferability of shares to outside persons by stipulating that shareholders offer their shares to the corporation or other shareholders before selling them to an outside purchaser. In fact, a few states have statutes under which close corporation shares cannot be transferred unless certain persons—including shareholders, family members, and the corporation—are first given the opportunity to purchase the shares for the same price.

Another way that control of a close corporation can be stabilized is through the use of a shareholder agreement. A shareholder agreement can provide that when one of the original shareholders dies, his or her shares of stock in the corporation will be divided in such a way that the proportionate holdings of the survivors, and thus their proportionate control, will be maintained.

S CORPORATIONS In 1982, Congress enacted the Subchapter S Revision Act "to minimize the effect of federal income taxes on choices of the form of business organizations and to permit the incorporation and operation of certain small businesses without the incidence of income taxation at both the corporate and shareholder level."[5] Also, corporations were divided into two groups: **S corporations,** which have elected Subchapter S treatment, and C *corporations,* or all other corporations, which are subject to Subchapter C of the Internal Revenue Code. Close corporations that meet the qualifying requirements specified in Subchapter S of the Code can operate as S corporations. If a corporation has S corporation status, it can avoid the imposition of income taxes at the corporate level while retaining many of the advantages of a corporation, particularly limited liability.

Qualification Requirements for S Corporations. Among the numerous requirements for S corporation status, the following are the most important:[6]

1. The corporation must be a domestic corporation.
2. The corporation must not be a member of an affiliated group of corporations.
3. The shareholders of the corporation must be individuals, estates, or certain trusts. Corporations, partnerships, and nonqualifying trusts cannot be shareholders.
4. The corporation must have seventy-five or fewer shareholders.
5. The corporation must have only one class of stock, although not all shareholders need have the same voting rights.
6. No shareholder of the corporation may be a nonresident alien.

4. Shareholders cannot agree, however, to eliminate certain rights of shareholders, such as the right to inspect corporate books and records or the right to bring derivative actions (lawsuits on behalf of the corporation—see Chapter 18).

5. Senate Report No. 640, 97th Congress, 1st Session (1981).

6. The Small Business Job Protection Act of 1996 relaxed some of the qualifying requirements for S corporation status. For example, prior to the 1996 act, an S corporation could have only thirty-five or fewer shareholders.

Benefits of S Corporations. At times, it is beneficial for a regular corporation to elect S corporation status. Benefits include the following:

1. When the corporation has losses, the S election allows the shareholders to use the losses to offset other income.
2. As mentioned, a single tax on corporate income is imposed at individual income tax rates at the shareholder level. (The income is taxable to shareholders whether or not it is actually distributed.)
3. When the stockholder's tax bracket is lower than the tax bracket for regular corporations, the S election causes the corporation's entire income to be taxed in the shareholder's bracket (because it is taxed as personal income), whether or not it is distributed. This is particularly attractive when the corporation wants to accumulate earnings for some future business purpose.

As mentioned later in this chapter, limited liability companies and limited liability partnerships offer the advantages of the S corporation (taxation benefits and limited liability) without the disadvantages (shareholder restrictions). Thus, as limited liability companies and partnerships become more widespread, the significance of the S corporation as a business form will likely diminish.

CORPORATE FORMATION

Up to this point, we have discussed some of the general characteristics of corporations. We now examine the process by which corporations come into existence. Generally, this process involves two steps: (1) preliminary organizational and promotional undertakings (particularly, obtaining capital for the future corporation) and (2) the legal process of incorporation.

Before a corporation becomes a reality, people invest in the proposed corporation as subscribers, and contracts are frequently made by promoters on behalf of the future corporation. *Promoters* are those who, for themselves or others, take the preliminary steps in organizing a corporation. One of the tasks of the promoter is to issue a *prospectus*, which is a document required by federal or state securities laws (see Chapter 28) that describes the financial operations of the corporation, thus allowing an investor to make an informed decision. The promoter also secures the corporate charter.

PROMOTER'S LIABILITY A promoter may purchase or lease property with a view toward selling it to the corporation when the corporation is formed. In addition, a promoter may enter into contracts with attorneys, accountants, architects, and other professionals whose services will be needed in planning for the proposed corporation. Finally, a promoter induces people to purchase stock in the corporation.

As a general rule, a promoter is held personally liable on preincorporation contracts. Courts simply hold that promoters are not agents when a corporation has yet to come into existence. If, however, the promoter secures the contracting party's agreement to hold only the corporation (not the promoter) liable on the contract, the promoter will not be liable in the event of any breach of contract.

Once the corporation is formed (the charter issued), the promoter remains personally liable until the corporation assumes the preincorporation contract by *novation*. Novation releases the promoter and makes the corporation liable for performing the contractual obligations. In some cases, the corporation adopts the promoter's contract by undertaking to perform it. Most courts hold that adoption in and of itself does not discharge the promoter from contractual liability. A corporation cannot normally ratify a preincorporation contract, as no principal was in existence at the time the contract was made.

SUBSCRIBERS AND SUBSCRIPTIONS Prior to the actual formation of the corporation, the promoter can contact potential individual investors, and they can agree to purchase capital stock in the future corporation. This agreement is often referred to as a *subscription agreement*, and the potential investor is called a *subscriber*. Depending on state law, subscribers become shareholders as soon as the corporation is formed or as soon as the corporation accepts the agreement. This way, if Corporation X becomes insolvent, the trustee in bankruptcy (see Chapter 16) can collect the consideration for any unpaid stock from a preincorporation subscriber.

Most courts view preincorporation subscriptions as continuing offers to purchase corporate stock. On or after its formation, the corporation can choose to accept the offer to purchase stock. Many courts also treat a subscription as a contract between the subscribers, making it irrevocable except with the consent of all of the subscribers. Under the RMBCA, a subscription is irrevocable for a period of six months unless otherwise provided in the subscription agreement or unless all the subscribers agree to the revocation of the subscription. In other jurisdictions, the preincorporation subscriber can revoke the offer to purchase before acceptance without liability, however.

INCORPORATION PROCEDURES

Exact procedures for incorporation differ among the states, but the basic requirements are similar.

STATE CHARTERING The first step in the incorporation procedure is to select a state in which to incorporate. Because state incorporation laws differ, individuals have found some advantage in looking for the states that offer the most advantageous tax or incorporation provisions. Delaware has historically had the least restrictive laws. Consequently, many corporations, including a number of the largest, have incorporated there. Delaware's statutes permit firms to incorporate in Delaware and carry out business and locate operating headquarters elsewhere. (Most other states now permit this as well.) Closely held corporations, however, particularly those of a professional nature, generally incorporate in the state in which their principal stockholders live and work.

ARTICLES OF INCORPORATION The primary document needed to begin the incorporation process is called the *articles of incorporation* (see Exhibit 17–1). The articles include basic information about the corporation and serve as a primary source of authority for its future organization and business functions. The person or persons who execute the articles are called *incorporators* and will be discussed shortly. Generally, the information indicated below should be included in the articles of incorporation.

Corporate Name. The choice of a corporate name is subject to state approval to ensure against duplication or deception. State statutes usually require that the secretary of state run a check on the proposed name in the state of incorporation. Some states require that the incorporators, at their own expense, run a check on the proposed name for the newly formed corporation. Once cleared, a name can be reserved for a short time, for a fee, pending the completion of the articles of incorporation. All corporate statutes require the corporation name to include the word *Corporation*, *Incorporated*, *Company*, or *Limited* or an abbreviation of one of these terms.

The new corporation's name may not be the same as, or deceptively similar to, the name of an existing corporation doing business within the state. For example, if an existing corporation is named General Dynamics, Inc., the state will not allow another corporation to be called General Dynamic, Inc., because that name is deceptively similar to the first, and it would impliedly transfer a part of the goodwill established by the first corporate user to the second corporation. (See Chapter 15 for a fuller discussion of trade names.)

Nature and Purpose. The intended business activities of the corporation must be specified in the articles, and naturally, they must be lawful. Stating a general corporate purpose is usually sufficient to give rise to all of the powers necessary or convenient to the purpose of the organization. The corporate charter can state, for example, that the corporation is organized "to engage in the production and sale of agricultural products." There is a trend toward allowing corporate charters to state that the corporation is organized for "any legal business." A broadly stated purpose creates greater flexibility and avoids unnecessary future amendments to the corporate charter should the corporation change or modify its line of business.

Duration. A corporation can have perpetual existence under the corporate statutes of most states. A few states, however, prescribe a maximum duration, after which the corporation must formally renew its existence.

Capital Structure. The capital structure of the corporation is generally set forth in the articles. A few state statutes require a very small capital investment for ordinary business corporations but a greater capital investment for those engaged in insurance or banking. The articles must also indicate the number of shares of stock the corporation is authorized to issue and may include other information, such as the valuation of the shares and the types or classes of stock authorized for issuance.

Internal Organization. The articles should describe the internal management structure of the corporation, although this can be included in bylaws adopted after the corporation is formed. The articles of incorporation commence the corporation; the bylaws are formed after commencement by the board of directors. Bylaws are subject to, and cannot conflict with, the incorporation statute or the corporation's charter.

EXHIBIT 17–1 ■ ARTICLES OF INCORPORATION

ARTICLE ONE

The name of the corporation is ______________________________.

ARTICLE TWO

The period of its duration is __________ (may be "perpetual," a number of years, or until a certain date).

ARTICLE THREE

The purpose (or purposes) for which the corporation is organized is (are) ______________________________
______________________________.

ARTICLE FOUR

The aggregate number of shares that the corporation shall have authority to issue is ________ of the par value of ________ dollar(s) each (or "without par value").

ARTICLE FIVE

The corporation will not commence business until it has received for the issuance of its shares consideration of the value of _______ (can be any sum not less than $1,000).

ARTICLE SIX

The address of the corporation's registered office is ______________________________, and the name of its registered agent at such address is ______________________________
______________________________.
(Use the street or building or rural address of the registered office, not a post office box number.)

ARTICLE SEVEN

The number of initial directors is ______________, and the names and addresses of the directors are
____
______________________________.

ARTICLE EIGHT

The name and address of the incorporator is ______________________________
______________________________.

(signed) ______________________________
Incorporator

Sworn to on ______________ by the above-named incorporator.
(date)

____
Notary Public

(Notary Seal)

Under the RMBCA, shareholders may amend or repeal bylaws. The board of directors may also amend or repeal bylaws unless the articles of incorporation or provisions of the incorporation statute reserve that power to shareholders exclusively. Typical bylaw provisions describe voting procedures and requirements for shareholders, the election of the board of directors, the methods of replacing directors, and the manner and time of scheduling shareholders' meetings and board meetings.

Registered Office and Agent. The corporation must indicate the location and address of its registered office within the state. Usually, the registered office is also the principal office of the corporation. The corporation must give the name and address of a specific person who has been designated as an agent and who can receive legal documents on behalf of the corporation. These legal documents include service of process (the delivery of a court order requiring an appearance in court).

Incorporators. Each incorporator must be listed by name and must indicate an address. An incorporator is a person—often, the corporate promoter—who applies to the state on behalf of the corporation to obtain its corporate charter. The incorporator need not be a subscriber and need not have any interest at all in the corporation. Many states do not impose residency or age requirements for incorporators. States vary as to the required number of incorporators; it can be as few as one or as many as three. Incorporators are required to sign the articles of incorporation when they are submitted to the state; often, this is their only duty. In some states, they participate at the first organizational meeting of the corporation.

CERTIFICATE OF INCORPORATION Once the articles of incorporation have been prepared, signed, and authenticated by the incorporators, they are sent to the appropriate state official, usually the secretary of state, along with the appropriate filing fee. In many states, the secretary of state will then issue a *certificate of incorporation* representing the state's authorization for the corporation to conduct business. (This may be called the *corporate charter*.) The certificate and a copy of the articles are returned to the incorporators, who then hold the initial organizational meeting, which completes the details of incorporation.

CORPORATE FINANCING Corporations are financed by the issuance and sale of corporate securities—bonds and stock. A detailed description of the types of securities that can be issued and the difference between stocks and bonds is given in Chapter 28.

IMPROPER INCORPORATION

The procedures for incorporation are very specific. If they are not followed precisely, others may be able to challenge the existence of the corporation.

Errors in the incorporation procedures can become important when, for example, a third person who is attempting to enforce a contract or bring suit for a tort injury fortuitously learns of them. On the basis of improper incorporation, the plaintiff could seek to make the would-be shareholders personally liable. Also, when the corporation seeks to enforce a contract against a defaulting party, if the defaulting party learns of a defect in the incorporation procedure, he or she may be able to avoid liability on that ground.

To prevent injustice, courts will sometimes attribute corporate existence to an improperly formed corporation by holding it to be a *de jure* corporation or a *de facto* corporation, as discussed below. In some cases, corporation by estoppel may also occur.

DE JURE AND *DE FACTO* CORPORATIONS In the event of substantial compliance with all conditions precedent to incorporation, a corporation is said to have *de jure* existence in law. In most states, the certificate of incorporation is viewed as evidence that all mandatory statutory provisions have been met. This means that the corporation is properly formed, and neither the state nor a third party can attack its existence. If, for example, an incorporator's address was incorrectly listed, this would mean that the corporation was improperly formed. The law, however, does not regard such inconsequential procedural defects as detracting from substantial compliance, and courts will uphold the *de jure* status of the corporate entity.

Sometimes there is a defect in complying with statutory mandates—for example, the corporation charter may have expired. Under these circumstances, the corporation may have a *de facto* status, meaning that its existence cannot be challenged by third persons except the state. The following elements are required for *de facto* status:

1. There must be a state statute under which the corporation can be validly incorporated.
2. The parties must have made a good faith attempt to comply with the statute.
3. The enterprise must already have undertaken to do business as a corporation.

CORPORATION BY ESTOPPEL If an association that is neither an actual corporation nor a *de facto* or *de jure* corporation holds itself out as being a corporation, it will be estopped from denying corporate status in a lawsuit by a third party. This usually occurs when a third party contracts with an association that claims to be a corporation but does not hold a certificate of incorporation. When the third party brings suit naming the so-called corporation as the defendant, the association may not escape from liability on the ground that no corporation exists. When justice requires, the courts treat an alleged corporation as if it were an actual corporation for the purpose of determining the rights and liabilities involved in a particular situation. Corporation by estoppel is thus determined by the situation. It does not extend recognition of corporate status beyond the resolution of the problem at hand.

DISREGARDING THE CORPORATE ENTITY

In some unusual situations, a corporate entity is used by its owners to perpetrate a fraud, circumvent the law, or in some other way accomplish an illegitimate objective. In these cases, the court will ignore the corporate structure by "piercing the corporate veil," exposing the shareholders to personal liability.

The following are some of the factors that may cause the courts to pierce the corporate veil:

1. A party is tricked or misled into dealing with the corporation rather than the individual.
2. The corporation is set up never to make a profit or always to be insolvent, or it is too "thinly" capitalized—that is, it has insufficient capital at the time it is formed to meet its prospective debts or potential liabilities.
3. Statutory corporate formalities, such as holding required corporation meetings, are not followed.
4. Personal and corporate interests are mixed together, or commingled, to the extent that the corporation has no separate identity.

To elaborate on the fourth factor in the preceding list, consider a close corporation that is formed according to law by a single person or by a few family members. In such a case, the corporate entity and the sole stockholder (or family-member stockholders) must carefully preserve the separate status of the corporation and its owners. Certain practices invite trouble for the one-person or family-owned corporation: the commingling of corporate and personal funds; the failure to remit taxes, including payroll and sales taxes; and the shareholders' continuous personal use of corporate property (for example, vehicles).

Corporation laws usually do not specifically prohibit a stockholder from lawfully lending money to his or her corporation. When an officer, director, or majority shareholder lends the corporation money and takes back security in the form of corporate assets, however, the courts will scrutinize the transaction closely. Any such transaction must be made in good faith and for fair value.

When the corporate privilege is abused for personal benefit and the corporate business is treated in such a careless manner that the corporation and the shareholder in control are no longer separate entities, the court usually will require the shareholder to assume personal liability to creditors for the corporation's debts. In short, when the facts show that great injustice would result from the use of a corporation to avoid individual responsibility, a court of equity will look behind the corporate structure to the individual stockholder. Whether a trial court properly "pierced the corporate veil" is at issue in the following case.

CASE 17.2 J-Mart Jewelry Outlets, Inc. v. Standard Design

Court of Appeals of Georgia, 1995. 218 Ga.App. 459, 462 S.E.2d 406.

BACKGROUND AND FACTS *Jim Halter, the sole shareholder of J-Mart Jewelry Outlets, Inc., knew that as a result of financial difficulties, J-Mart would soon go out of business. Eight days before the firm stopped doing business, it paid the balance due on Halter's personal credit card. At the same time, Halter paid J-Mart $1 for a Cadillac that the firm had bought new for his personal use and on which it had made three payments. Four of J-Mart's creditors, including Standard Design, filed a suit in a Georgia state court against Halter and others to recover for J-Mart's unpaid debts. The jury "pierced the corporate veil" to hold Halter personally responsible. Halter appealed.*

IN THE LANGUAGE OF THE COURT

BLACKBURN, Judge.

* * * *

The concept of piercing the corporate veil is applied in Georgia to remedy injustices which arise where a party has over extended his privilege in the use of a corporate entity in order to defeat justice, perpetrate fraud or to evade contractual or tort responsibility. * * *

* * * *

Halter knew as early as late April but not later than June 1991 that J-Mart would have to cease operations as a result of its financial difficulties. * * * [T]he $6,902.87 balance on Halter's American Express personal account was paid by J-Mart on December 23, 1991, eight days before it ceased doing business. * * * J-Mart, with knowledge that it would soon cease doing business, purchased a new Cadillac for Halter's use. It thereafter made three payments on the vehicle before transferring it to Halter for $1 and allowing him to assume the remaining payments * * * . In light of the evidence presented, the trial court properly [ruled against Halter].

DECISION AND REMEDY *The Court of Appeals of Georgia affirmed the judgment of the lower court and upheld the awards to the creditors. The trial court properly pierced the corporate veil to hold the shareholder personally liable.*

INTERNATIONAL CONSIDERATIONS **Piercing the Corporate Veil in Europe** *Other nations that recognize limited liability entities also provide for "piercing the corporate veil" to prevent abuse. When there is a single controlling shareholder, some European cases have established a presumption that the shareholder is personally liable. The shareholder bears the burden of proving that the company was truly a separate entity.*

CORPORATE MANAGEMENT—DIRECTORS

Every corporation is governed by a board of directors. Few legal requirements exist concerning directors' qualifications. Only a handful of states impose minimum age and residency requirements. A director is sometimes a shareholder, but this is not a necessary qualification—unless, of course, statutory provisions or corporate articles or bylaws require ownership.

Subject to statutory limitations, the number of directors is set forth in the corporation's articles or bylaws. Historically, the minimum number of directors has been three, but today many states permit fewer. Indeed, the RMBCA permits corporations with fewer than fifty shareholders to eliminate the board of directors.

ELECTION OF DIRECTORS The first board of directors is normally appointed by the incorporators on the creation of the corporation, or directors are named by the corporation itself in the articles. The first board serves until the first annual shareholders' meeting. Subsequent directors are elected by a majority vote of the shareholders.

The term of office for a director is usually one year—from annual meeting to annual meeting. Longer and staggered terms are permissible under most state statutes. A common practice is to elect one-third of the board members each year for a three-year term. In this way, there is greater management continuity.

A director can be removed *for cause* (that is, for failing to perform a required duty), either as specified in the articles or bylaws or by shareholder action. Even the board of directors itself may be given power to remove a director for cause, subject to shareholder review. In most states, unless the shareholders have reserved the right at the time of election, a director cannot be removed without cause.

Vacancies can occur on the board of directors because of death or resignation or when a new position is created through amendment of the articles or bylaws. In these situations, either the shareholders or the board itself can fill the position, depending on state law or on the provisions of the bylaws.

BOARD OF DIRECTORS' MEETINGS The board of directors conducts business by holding formal meetings with recorded minutes. The date on which regular meetings are held is usually established in the articles or bylaws or by board resolution, and no further notice is customarily required. Special meetings can be called, with notice sent to all directors.

Quorum requirements can vary among jurisdictions. (A **quorum** is the minimum number of members of a body of officials or other group that must be present in order for business to be validly transacted.) Many states leave the decision as to quorum requirements to the corporate articles or bylaws. In the absence of specific state statutes, most states provide that a quorum is a majority of the number of directors authorized in the articles or bylaws. Voting is done in person (unlike voting at shareholders' meetings, which can be done by proxy, as discussed later in this chapter).[7] The rule is one vote per director. Ordinary matters generally require a simple majority vote; certain extraordinary issues may require a greater-than-majority vote.

DIRECTORS' MANAGEMENT RESPONSIBILITIES

Directors have responsibility for all policymaking decisions necessary to the management of all corporate affairs. Just as shareholders cannot act individually to bind the corporation, the directors must act as a body in carrying out routine corporate business. One director has one vote, and generally the majority rules. The general areas of responsibility of the board of directors include the following:

1. Authorization for major corporate policy decisions—for example, the initiation of proceedings for the sale or lease of corporate assets outside the regular course of business, the determination of new product lines, and the overseeing of major contract negotiations and major management-labor negotiations.
2. Appointment, supervision, and removal of corporate officers and other managerial employees and determination of their compensation.
3. Financial decisions, such as the declaration and payment of dividends to shareholders and the issuance of authorized shares and bonds.

Most states permit the board of directors to elect an executive committee from among the directors to handle the interim management decisions between board of directors' meetings, as provided in the bylaws. The executive committee is limited to making management decisions about ordinary business matters.

The board of directors can delegate some of its functions to an executive committee or to corporate officers. In doing so, the board is not relieved of its overall responsibility for directing the affairs of the corporation, but corporate officers and managerial personnel are empowered to make decisions relating to ordinary, daily corporate affairs within well-defined guidelines.

CORPORATE OFFICERS AND EXECUTIVES

Officers and other executive employees are hired by the board of directors or, in rare instances, by the shareholders. In addition to carrying out the duties articulated in the bylaws, corporate and managerial officers act as agents of the corporation, and the ordinary rules of agency (discussed in Chapter 19) normally apply to their employment. The qualifications required of officers and executive employees are determined at the discretion of the corporation and are included in the articles or bylaws. In most states, a person can hold more than one office and can be both an officer and a director of the corporation.

The rights of corporate officers and other high-level managers are defined by employment contracts, because these persons are employees of the company. Corporate officers, though, can normally be removed by the board of directors at any time with or without cause and regardless of the terms of the employment contracts—although in so doing, the corporation may be liable for breach of contract.

CORPORATE MANAGEMENT—SHAREHOLDERS

The acquisition of a share of stock makes a person an owner and shareholder in a corporation. Shareholders thus own the corporation. Although they have no legal title to corporate property vested in the corporation, such as buildings and equipment, they do have an *equitable* (ownership) interest in the firm.

As a general rule, shareholders have no responsibility for the daily management of the corporation, although they are ultimately responsible for choosing the board of directors, which does have such control. Ordinarily, corporate officers and other employees owe no direct duty to individual stockholders. Their duty is to the corporation as a whole. A director, however, is in a fiduciary relationship to the corporation and therefore serves the interests of the shareholders as a whole. Generally, there is no legal relationship between shareholders and

7. Except in Louisiana, which allows a director to vote by proxy under certain circumstances. Some states, such as Michigan and Texas, and Section 8.20 of the RMBCA permit telephone conferences for board of directors' meetings.

creditors of the corporation. Shareholders can, in fact, be creditors of the corporation and have the same rights of recovery against the corporation as any other creditor.

In this section, we look at the powers, rights, and liabilities of shareholders, which may be established in the articles of incorporation and under the state's general incorporation law.

SHAREHOLDERS' POWERS Shareholders must approve fundamental changes affecting the corporation before the changes can be effected. Hence, shareholders are empowered to amend the articles of incorporation (charter) and bylaws, approve a merger or the dissolution of the corporation, and approve the sale of all or substantially all of the corporation's assets. Some of these powers are subject to prior board approval.

Election and removal of the board of directors are accomplished by a vote of the shareholders. The first board of directors is either named in the articles of incorporation or chosen by the incorporators to serve until the first shareholders' meeting. From that time on, selection and retention of directors are exclusively shareholder functions.

Directors usually serve their full terms; if they are unsatisfactory, they are simply not reelected. Shareholders have the inherent power, however, to remove a director from office *for cause* (breach of duty or misconduct) by a majority vote.[8] Some state statutes even permit removal of directors *without cause* by the vote of a majority of the holders of outstanding shares entitled to vote.[9] Some corporate charters also expressly provide that shareholders, by majority vote, can remove a director at any time without cause.

SHAREHOLDERS' MEETINGS Shareholders' meetings must occur at least annually, and in addition, special meetings can be called to take care of urgent matters. Shareholders are notified of the date and hour of a shareholders' meeting in a written announcement that is sent a reasonable length of time prior to the date of the meeting.[10] Notices of special meetings must include a statement of the purpose of the meeting; business transacted at a special meeting is limited to that purpose.

SHAREHOLDER VOTING For shareholders to act during a meeting, a quorum must be present. Generally, this condition is met when shareholders holding more than 50 percent of the outstanding shares are present. Corporate business matters are presented in the form of resolutions, which shareholders vote to approve or disapprove. If a state statute sets forth specific voting requirements, the corporation's articles or bylaws must be consistent with these statutory limitations. Some states provide that obtaining the unanimous written consent of shareholders is a permissible alternative to holding a shareholders' meeting.

Once a quorum is present, voting can proceed. A majority vote of the shares represented at the meeting is usually required to pass resolutions. Assume that Novo Pictures, Inc., has 10,000 outstanding shares of voting stock. Its articles of incorporation set the quorum at more than 50 percent of outstanding shares and provide that a majority vote of the shares present is necessary to pass on ordinary matters. Therefore, for this firm, at the shareholders' meeting, a quorum of stockholders representing 5,000 outstanding shares must be present to conduct business, and a vote of at least 2,501 of those shares is needed to pass ordinary resolutions. If 6,000 shares are represented, a vote of 3,001 will be required, and so on.

At times, more than a simple majority vote will be required either by statute or by corporate charter. Extraordinary corporate matters, such as a merger, a consolidation, or the dissolution of the corporation, require approval by a higher percentage of the representatives of all corporate shares entitled to vote, not just a majority of those present at that particular meeting.

Voting Lists. A voting list is prepared by the corporation prior to each shareholders' meeting. Persons

8. A director can often demand court review of removal for cause.
9. Most states allow *cumulative voting* (which will be discussed shortly) for directors. If cumulative voting is authorized, a director may not be removed if the number of votes sufficient to elect him or her under cumulative voting is voted against his or her removal. See, for example, California Corporate Code Section 303A. Also see Section 8.08(c) of the RMBCA.

10. The shareholder can waive the requirement of written notice by signing a waiver form. A shareholder who does not receive written notice but who learns of the meeting and attends without protesting the lack of notice is said to have waived notice by such conduct. State statutes and corporate bylaws typically set forth the time within which notice must be sent, what methods can be used, and what the notice must contain.

whose names appear on the corporation's stockholder records as owners are the ones ordinarily entitled to vote.[11] The voting list contains the name and address of each shareholder as shown on the corporate records on a given cutoff date, or record date. (Under RMBCA 7.07, the record date may be as much as seventy days before the meeting.) The voting list also includes the number of voting shares held by each owner. The list is usually kept at the corporate headquarters and is available for shareholder inspection.

Cumulative Voting. Most states permit or require shareholders to elect directors by *cumulative voting*, a method of voting designed to allow minority shareholders representation on the board of directors.[12] When cumulative voting is allowed or required, the number of members of the board to be elected is multiplied by the total number of voting shares. The result equals the number of votes a shareholder has, and this total can be cast for one or more nominees for director. All nominees stand for election at the same time. When cumulative voting is not required either by statute or under the articles, the entire board can be elected by a majority of shares at a shareholders' meeting.

Suppose, for example, that a corporation has 10,000 shares issued and outstanding. The minority shareholders hold only 3,000 shares, and the majority shareholders hold the other 7,000 shares. Three members of the board are to be elected. The majority shareholders' nominees are Alomon, Beasley, and Caravel. The minority shareholders' nominee is Dovrik. Can Dovrik be elected to the board by the minority shareholders?

If cumulative voting is allowed, the answer is yes. The minority shareholders have 9,000 votes among them (the number of directors to be elected times the number of shares equals 3 times 3,000, which equals 9,000 votes). All of these votes can be cast to elect Dovrik. The majority shareholders have 21,000 votes (3 times 7,000 equals 21,000 votes), but these votes have to be distributed among their three nominees. The principle of cumulative voting is that no matter how the majority shareholders cast their 21,000 votes, they will not be able to elect all three directors if the minority shareholders cast all of their 9,000 votes for Dovrik, as illustrated in Exhibit 17–2.

Other Voting Techniques. A group of shareholders can agree in writing prior to a shareholders' meeting, in a *shareholder voting agreement*, to vote their shares together in a specified manner. Such agreements usually are held to be valid and enforceable.

Because it usually is not practical for owners of only a few shares of stock of publicly traded corporations to attend a shareholders' meeting, such stockholders normally give third parties written authorization to vote their shares at the meeting. This authorization is called a **proxy** (from the Latin *procurare*, "to manage, take care of"). Proxies are often solicited by management, but any person can solicit proxies to concentrate voting power. Proxies have been used by a group of shareholders as a device for taking over a corporation. Proxies are normally revocable (that is, they can be withdrawn), unless they are specifically designated as irrevocable.

Another technique is for shareholders to enter into a *voting trust*, which is an agreement (a trust contract) under which legal title (recorded ownership on the corporate books) is transferred to a trustee who is responsible for voting the shares. The agreement can specify how the trustee is to vote, or it can allow the trustee to use his or her discretion. The trustee takes physical possession of the stock

11. When the legal owner is deceased, bankrupt, incompetent, or in some other way under a legal disability, his or her vote can be cast by a person designated by law to control and manage the owner's property.

12. See, for example, California Corporate Code Section 708. Under RMBCA 7.28, however, no cumulative voting rights exist unless the articles of incorporation so provide.

EXHIBIT 17–2 ■ RESULTS OF CUMULATIVE VOTING

BALLOT	MAJORITY SHAREHOLDER VOTES			MINORITY SHAREHOLDER VOTES	DIRECTORS ELECTED
	Alomon	*Beasley*	*Caravel*	*Dovrik*	
1	10,000	10,000	1,000	9,000	Alomon, Beasley, Dovrik
2	9,001	9,000	2,999	9,000	Alomon, Beasley, Dovrik
3	6,000	7,000	8,000	9,000	Beasley, Caravel, Dovrik

EMERGING TRENDS

LIMITED LIABILITY COMPANIES

For many entrepreneurs and investors, the ideal business form would combine the tax advantages of the partnership form of business with the limited liability feature of the corporate enterprise. Traditionally, two types of business forms partially addressed these needs.

One is the limited partnership. Limited partners enjoy both the tax benefits of the partnership and limited liability. Yet the limited liability of limited partners is conditional: it exists only so long as the limited partner does not participate in management.

The other business form is the S corporation. S corporation status allows small corporations to avoid the double-taxation feature of corporations. Like partnerships, S corporations are "pass-through" entities with regard to taxes. S corporation shareholders pay taxes personally on their respective shares of the profits, and the corporation itself is not taxed. The problem with S corporations is that there are several restrictions regarding who

can be shareholders, what type of stock can be issued, and so on.

The creation of the limited liability company (LLC) has been a boon for businesspersons because this business form provides for *both* limited liability and pass-through taxation. The rapid growth in the use of LLCs is expected to continue, particularly in view of new rules issued by the Internal Revenue Service (IRS) in 1997 regarding the taxation of these entities.

THE ROLE OF THE IRS

The IRS has played a key role in the emergence of the LLC as a significant business form. This is because even though a state law may allow businesspersons to form an LLC, unless the IRS agrees to tax the entity as a partnership, the tax advantages will be lost. Consider that prior to 1988, only two states had authorized LLCs: Wyoming (in 1977) and Florida (in 1982). In 1988, the IRS ruled that Wyoming LLCs would be taxed as partnerships. This ruling encouraged other states to enact LLC statutes, and in less than a decade, all states had done so.

It is predicted that new IRS rules that went into effect on January 1, 1997, will encourage even more widespread use of LLCs in the business world. The new regulations provide that any unincorporated business will automatically be taxed as a partnership unless it indicates otherwise on the tax form. The exceptions involve publicly traded companies, companies formed under a state incorporation statute, and certain foreign-owned companies. If a business chooses to be taxed as a corporation, it can indicate this choice by "checking a box" on the IRS form.

The rules also provide that any business that has only one owner,

certificate and in return gives the shareholder a *voting trust certificate.* The shareholder retains all of the rights of ownership (for example, the right to receive dividend payments) except for the power to vote the shares.

SECTION 5

LIMITED LIABILITY COMPANIES

The **limited liability company (LLC)** is a relatively new form of business enterprise that offers the limited liability of a corporation and the tax advantages of a partnership. Although LLCs have existed for over a century in other areas, including several European and South American nations, it was only in 1977 that they first appeared in the United States. In that year, Wyoming passed legislation authorizing the creation of an LLC. Interest in LLCs mushroomed after a 1988 ruling by the Internal Revenue Service (IRS) that Wyoming LLCs would be taxed as partnerships instead of as corporations. Because of this tax advantage, by 1997 all states had enacted LLC statutes.

Like the limited partnership and the corporation, an LLC must be formed and operated in com-

Emerging Trends

Limited Liability Companies (Continued)

including a single-member LLC, will be taxed as a sole proprietorship unless it chooses to be taxed as a corporation. Although nearly half of the states allow for the creation of one-member LLCs, many businesspersons were reluctant to form them because they were uncertain how the IRS would treat them. The new rules largely remove this uncertainty, and thus, very likely, one-member LLCs will become more common in the future.

The "Four-Factor Test" No Longer Applies

The 1997 IRS rule greatly simplified the creation and operation of LLCs by abolishing certain requirements that previously had to be met in order to qualify for partnership tax treatment. Under those requirements, if an LLC possessed more than two of the following four characteristics, the LLC as an entity would be liable for income taxes, and the benefits of pass-through taxation would be lost:

- Limited liability.
- Continuity of life.
- Free transferability of interest.
- Centralization of management.

By abolishing this four-factor test for partnership tax status, the IRS gave much greater flexibility to businesspersons in terms of how they form and operate their firms.

State Statutes

Most of the states are currently in the process of revising their LLC statutes to conform with the new IRS regulations. They are eliminating certain "hoops" that business organizations had to jump through in order to qualify for LLC status, including the four-factor test just discussed. Some states, though, may continue to use the four-factor test for determining whether a business entity should be treated as a corporation or as a partnership for *state* income tax purposes.

Implications for the Businessperson

1. Certainly, for closely held businesses, the regular corporate form of organization will gradually become less significant. Business attorneys increasingly will suggest the LLC form of organization because LLCs are now much easier to establish and can operate with greater flexibility.
2. Every state still has its own set of rules and regulations for LLCs. Therefore, the formation of this type of business organization must still conform with state law.

For Critical Analysis

1. What is the major benefit of an LLC relative to, say, a sole proprietorship?
2. If you were running a business with distinct divisions, could you imagine wanting to create an LLC for just one of those divisions? Explain why you might.

pliance with state law. To form an LLC, *articles of organization* must be filed with a central state agency, such as the secretary of state's office. The business's name must include the words "Limited Liability Company" or the initials "L.L.C."

A major advantage of the LLC is that it does not pay taxes as an entity; rather, profits are "passed through" the LLC and paid personally by the owners of the company, who are called *members*. Another advantage is that the liability of members is limited to the amount of their investments. In an LLC, members are allowed to participate fully in management activities, and under at least one state's statute, the firm's managers need not even be members of the LLC. Yet another advantage is that corporations and partnerships, as well as foreign investors, can be LLC members. Additionally, in contrast to S corporations, there is no limit on the number of shareholder-members of the LLC. Finally, part of the LLC's attractiveness to businesspersons is the flexibility it offers. The members can themselves decide how to operate the various aspects of the business through a simple operating agreement.

The disadvantages of the LLC are relatively few. Some of the initial disadvantages no longer exist as a result of an IRS regulation that became effective in January 1997. (See this chapter's *Emerging Trends* for details.) A remaining disadvantage of the LLC is that state statutes are not uniform. Until state LLC statutes are revised to correspond to the new IRS rules, as they probably will be in the near future, businesses must comply with existing requirements. Additionally, state laws may continue to vary with respect to *state* taxation.

SECTION 6

LIMITED LIABILITY PARTNERSHIPS

The **limited liability partnership (LLP)** is similar to the LLC. The difference between an LLP and an LLC is that the LLP is designed more for professionals who normally do business as partners in a partnership. The first state to enact an LLP statute was Texas, in 1991. Other states quickly followed suit, and by 1997, virtually all of the states had enacted LLP statutes. Like LLCs, LLPs must be formed and operated in compliance with state statutes. The appropriate form must be filed with a central state agency, usually the secretary of state's office, and the business's name must include either "Limited Liability Partnership" or "L.L.P."

The major advantage of the LLP is that it allows a partnership to continue as a pass-through entity for tax purposes but limits the personal liability of the partners for partnership tort liability. Consider a group of lawyers operating as a partnership. A client sues one of the attorneys for malpractice and wins a large judgment, and the firm's malpractice insurance is insufficient to cover the obligation. Under traditional partnership law, the partners are jointly and severally (individually) liable. This means, in the example here, that when the attorney's personal assets are exhausted, the personal assets of the other, innocent partners can be used to satisfy the judgment.

Although LLP statutes vary from state to state, generally each state statute limits in some way the liability of partners. For example, Delaware law protects each innocent partner from the "debts and obligations of the partnership arising from negligence, wrongful acts, or misconduct." In North Carolina, Texas, and Washington, D.C., the statutes protect innocent partners from obligations arising from "errors, omissions, negligence, incompetence, or malfeasance."

In most states, it is relatively easy to convert a traditional partnership into an LLP because the firm's basic organizational structure remains the same. Additionally, all of the statutory and common law rules governing partnerships still apply (apart from those modified by the LLP statute). Normally, LLP statutes are simply amendments to a state's already existing partnership law.

SECTION 7

LIMITED LIABILITY LIMITED PARTNERSHIPS

A **limited liability limited partnership (LLLP)** is a type of limited partnership. The difference between a limited partnership and an LLLP is that the liability of a general partner in an LLLP is the same as the liability of a limited partner. That is, the liability of all partners is limited to the amount of their investments in the firm.

A few states provide expressly for LLLPs.[13] In states that do not provide for LLLPs but do allow for limited partnerships and limited liability partnerships, a limited partnership should probably still be able to register with the state as an LLLP.

SECTION 8

OTHER ORGANIZATIONAL FORMS

Besides the business forms already discussed, several other forms can be used to organize a business. For the most part, these other business forms are hybrid organizations—that is, they have characteristics similar to those of partnerships or corporations or combine features of both.

JOINT VENTURE

A **joint venture,** which is sometimes referred to as a joint adventure, is a relationship in which two or more persons or business entities combine their efforts or their property for a single transaction or project or a related series of transactions or projects. Unless otherwise agreed, joint venturers share profits and losses equally. For example, when several contractors combine their resources to build and sell houses in a single development, their relationship is a joint venture.

A joint venture resembles a partnership and is taxed like a partnership. The essential difference is that a joint venture typically involves the pursuit of a single

13. See, for example, Colorado Rev. Stat. Ann. Section 7-62-109. Other states that provide expressly for limited liability limited partnerships include Delaware, Florida, Missouri, Pennsylvania, Texas, and Virginia.

project or series of transactions, and a partnership usually concerns an ongoing business. Of course, a partnership may be created to conduct a single transaction. For this reason, most courts apply the same principles to joint ventures as they apply to partnerships.

Joint ventures range in size from very small activities to huge, multimillion-dollar joint actions undertaken by some of the world's largest corporations. Large organizations often investigate new markets or new ideas by forming joint ventures with other enterprises. For instance, General Motors Corporation and Volvo Truck Corporation were involved in a joint venture—Volvo GM—to manufacture heavy-duty trucks and market them in the United States.

SYNDICATE

A group of individuals getting together to finance a particular project, such as the building of a shopping center or the purchase of a professional basketball franchise, is called a **syndicate,** or an *investment group*. The form of such groups varies considerably. A syndicate may exist as a corporation or as a general or limited partnership. In some cases, the members merely own property jointly and have no legally recognized business arrangement.

JOINT STOCK COMPANY

A **joint stock company** is a true hybrid of a partnership and a corporation. It has many characteristics of a corporation in that (1) its ownership is represented by transferable shares of stock, (2) it is usually managed by directors and officers of the company or association, and (3) it can have a perpetual existence. Most of its other features, however, are more characteristic of a partnership, and it is usually treated like a partnership. As with a partnership, it is formed by agreement (not statute), property is usually held in the names of the members, shareholders have personal liability, and generally the company is not treated as a legal entity for purposes of a lawsuit. In a joint stock company, however, shareholders are not considered to be agents of each other, as would be the case if the company were a true partnership (see Chapter 38).

BUSINESS TRUST

A **business trust** is created by a written trust agreement that sets forth the interests of the beneficiaries and the obligations and powers of the trustees. With a business trust, legal ownership and management of the property of the business stay with one or more of the trustees, and the profits are distributed to the beneficiaries.

The business trust was started in Massachusetts in an attempt to obtain the limited liability advantage of corporate status while avoiding certain restrictions on a corporation's ownership and development of real property. The business trust resembles a corporation in many respects. Beneficiaries of the trust, for example, are not personally responsible for the trust's debts or obligations. In fact, in a number of states, business trusts must pay corporate taxes.

COOPERATIVE

A **cooperative** is an association, either incorporated or not, that is organized to provide an economic service, without profit, to its members (or shareholders). An incorporated cooperative is subject to state laws governing nonprofit corporations. It makes distributions of dividends, or profits, to its owners on the basis of their transactions with the cooperative rather than on the basis of the amount of capital they contribute. Cooperatives that are unincorporated are often treated like partnerships. The members have joint liability for the cooperative's acts.

The cooperative form of business is generally adopted by groups of individuals who wish to pool their resources to gain some advantage in the marketplace. Consumer purchasing co-ops are formed to obtain lower prices through quantity discounts. Seller marketing co-ops are formed to control the market and thereby obtain higher sales prices from consumers. Often, because of their special status, cooperatives are exempt from certain federal laws, such as antitrust laws (laws prohibiting anticompetitive practices—see Chapters 26 and 27).

SECTION 9

PRIVATE FRANCHISES

A **franchise** is defined as any arrangement in which the owner of a trademark, a trade name, or a copyright licenses others to use the trademark, trade name, or copyright in the selling of goods or services. A **franchisee** (a purchaser of a franchise) is generally legally independent of the **franchisor** (the seller of the franchise). At the same time, the franchise is economically dependent on the franchisor's integrated business system. In other words, a franchisee can operate as an independent businessperson but still obtain the advantages of a regional or national organization. Well-known franchises include McDonald's, KFC, and Burger King.

TYPES OF FRANCHISES

Because the franchising industry is so extensive and so many different types of businesses sell franchises, it is difficult to summarize the many types of franchises that now exist. Generally, though, franchises fall into one of the following three classifications: distributorships, chain-style business operations, and manufacturing or processing-plant arrangements.

DISTRIBUTORSHIP A *distributorship* arises when a manufacturing concern (franchisor) licenses a dealer (franchisee) to sell its product. Often, a distributorship covers an exclusive territory. An example is an automobile dealership.

CHAIN-STYLE BUSINESS OPERATION A *chain-style business operation* exists when a franchise operates under a franchisor's trade name and is identified as a member of a select group of dealers that engage in the franchisor's business. The franchisee is generally required to follow standardized or prescribed methods of operations. Often, the franchisor requires that the franchisee maintain certain standards of operation. In addition, sometimes the franchisee is obligated to deal exclusively with the franchisor to obtain materials and supplies. Examples of this type of franchise are McDonald's and most other fast-food chains.

MANUFACTURING OR PROCESSING-PLANT ARRANGEMENT A *manufacturing or processing-plant arrangement* exists when the franchisor transmits to the franchisee the essential ingredients or formula to make a particular product. The franchisee then markets it either at wholesale or at retail in accordance with the franchisor's standards. Examples of this type of franchise are Coca-Cola and other soft-drink bottling companies.

LAWS GOVERNING FRANCHISING

Because a franchise relationship is primarily a contractual relationship, it is governed by contract law. If the franchise exists primarily for the sale of products manufactured by the franchisor, the law governing sales contracts as expressed in Article 2 of the Uniform Commercial Code applies (see Chapter 11). Additionally, the federal government and most states have enacted laws governing certain aspects of franchising. Generally, these laws are designed to protect prospective franchisees from dishonest franchisors and to prohibit franchisors from terminating franchises without good cause.

FEDERAL PROTECTION FOR FRANCHISEES Automobile dealership franchisees are protected from automobile manufacturers' bad faith termination of their franchises by the Automobile Dealers' Franchise Act[14]—also known as the Automobile Dealers' Day in Court Act—of 1965. If a manufacturer-franchisor terminates a franchise because of a dealer-franchisee's failure to comply with unreasonable demands (for example, failure to attain an unrealistically high sales quota), the manufacturer may be liable for damages.

Another federal statute is the Petroleum Marketing Practices Act (PMPA)[15] of 1979, which prescribes the grounds and conditions under which a franchisor may terminate or decline to renew a gasoline station franchise. Federal antitrust laws (discussed in Chapters 26 and 27), which prohibit certain types of anticompetitive agreements, may also apply in certain circumstances.

In 1979, the Federal Trade Commission (FTC) issued regulations that require franchisors to disclose material facts necessary to a prospective franchisee's making an informed decision concerning the purchase of a franchise.

STATE PROTECTION FOR FRANCHISEES State legislation tends to be similar to federal statutes and the FTC regulations. For example, to protect franchisees, a state law might require the disclosure of information that is material to making an informed decision regarding the purchase of a franchise. This could include such information as the actual costs of operation, recurring expenses, and profits earned, along with facts substantiating these figures. State deceptive trade practices acts may also prohibit certain types of actions on the part of franchisors.

In response to the need for a uniform franchise law, the National Conference of Commissioners on Uniform State Laws drafted a model law that standardizes the various state franchise regulations. Because the uniform law represents a compromise of so many diverse interests, it has met with little success in being adopted as law by the various states.

THE FRANCHISE CONTRACT

The franchise relationship is defined by a contract between the franchisor and the franchisee. The fran-

14. 15 U.S.C. Sections 1221–1225.
15. 15 U.S.C. Sections 2801-2841.

chise contract specifies the terms and conditions of the franchise and spells out the rights and duties of the franchisor and the franchisee. If either party fails to perform the contractual duties, that party may be subject to a lawsuit for breach of contract. Furthermore, if a franchisee is induced to enter into a franchise contract by the franchisor's fraudulent misrepresentation, the franchisor may be liable for damages.

Because each type of franchise relationship has its own characteristics, it is difficult to describe the broad range of details a franchising contract may include. Typically, though, the major issues addressed in franchising contracts relate to payment, location and business organization, price and quality controls, and termination.

PAYMENT FOR THE FRANCHISE The franchisee ordinarily pays an initial fee or lump-sum price for the franchise license (the privilege of being granted a franchise). This fee is separate from the various products that the franchisee purchases from or through the franchisor. In some industries, the franchisor relies heavily on the initial sale of the franchise for realizing a profit. In other industries, the continued dealing between the parties brings profit to both. In most situations, the franchisor will receive a stated percentage of the annual sales or annual volume of business done by the franchisee. The franchise agreement may also require the franchisee to pay a percentage of advertising costs and certain administrative expenses.

LOCATION AND BUSINESS ORGANIZATION OF THE FRANCHISE Typically, the franchisor will determine the territory to be served. The franchise agreement may specify whether the premises for the business must be leased or purchased outright. In some cases, construction of a building is necessary to meet the terms of the agreement. Often, the franchise contract will indicate whether the franchisee has exclusive rights, or "territorial rights," to a certain geographical area. Exclusive territory is important to a franchisee because nearby competition can reduce profits.

Certainly, the agreement will specify whether the franchisor supplies equipment and furnishings for the premises or whether this is the responsibility of the franchisee. When the franchise is a service operation, such as a motel, the contract often provides that the franchisor will establish certain standards for the facility and will make inspections to ensure that the standards are being maintained in order to protect the franchise's name and reputation.

The business organization of the franchisee is of great concern to the franchisor. Depending on the terms of the franchise agreement, the franchisor may specify particular requirements for the form and financing of the business. The franchise agreement may provide that standards of operation—relating to such aspects of the business as sales quotas, quality, and record keeping—be met by the franchisee. Furthermore, a franchisor may wish to retain stringent control over the training of personnel involved in the operation and over administrative aspects of the business. Although the day-to-day operation of the franchise business is normally left up to the franchisee, the franchise agreement may provide for whatever amount of supervision and control is agreed on by the parties.

Generally, the statutory and case law governing franchising tend to emphasize the importance of good faith and fair dealing in franchise relationships. In the following case, the franchisee did not have any exclusive territorial rights under the franchise contract. When the franchisor built a competing operation nearby, the franchisee sued the franchisor. At issue in the case was whether the franchisor had breached an implied covenant of good faith and fair dealing.

CASE 17.3 Vylene Enterprises, Inc. v. Naugles, Inc.

United States Court of Appeals, Ninth Circuit, 1996. 90 F.3d 1472.

BACKGROUND AND FACTS *Vylene Enterprises, Inc., entered into a ten-year franchise agreement with Naugles, Inc., to operate a restaurant. Under the agreement, Vylene could extend the franchise "on terms and conditions to be negotiated." The agreement did not forbid Naugles from building a restaurant nearby. Shortly after Vylene asked for the extension, Naugles built a new restaurant less than a mile and a half away. The new restaurant offered a different menu with lower prices and discount coupons. Vylene's restaurant lost money. In Vylene's subsequent bankruptcy proceedings, the court held, among other things, that Naugles had breached an implied covenant of good faith and fair dealing. Naugles appealed. The appellate court ruled in favor of Naugles, and Vylene appealed.*

IN THE LANGUAGE OF THE COURT

T. G. NELSON, Circuit Judge:

* * * *

* * * [A] franchisee, although not entitled to an exclusive territory, [is] still entitled to expect that the franchisor [will] not act to destroy the right of the franchisee to enjoy the fruits of the contract.

* * * Vylene did not have any rights to exclusive territory under the terms of the franchise agreement, and we do not impliedly read any such rights into the contract. However, Naugles' construction of a competing restaurant within a mile and a half of Vylene's restaurant was a breach of the covenant of good faith and fair dealing. The bad faith character of the move becomes clear when one considers that building the competing restaurant had the potential to not only hurt Vylene, but also to reduce Naugles' royalties from Vylene's operations.

DECISION AND REMEDY

The U.S. Court of Appeals for the Ninth Circuit vacated the lower court's ruling and remanded the case for consideration of other issues. The franchisor breached an implied covenant of good faith and fair dealing by attempting to compete with the franchisee.

PRICE AND QUALITY CONTROLS OF THE FRANCHISE Franchises provide the franchisor with an outlet for the firm's goods and services. Depending on the nature of the business, the franchisor may require the franchisee to purchase certain supplies from the franchisor at an established price.[16] A franchisor cannot, however, set the prices at which the franchisee will resell the goods, because this is a violation of state or federal antitrust laws, or both. A franchisor can suggest retail prices but cannot mandate them.

As a general rule, the validity of a provision permitting the franchisor to enforce certain quality standards is unquestioned. Because the franchisor has a legitimate interest in maintaining the quality of the product or service to protect its name and reputation, it can exercise greater control in this area than would otherwise be tolerated. Increasingly, however, franchisors are finding that if they exercise too much control over the operations of their franchisees, they may incur liability, as principals, for the torts of their franchisees' employees.

TERMINATION OF THE FRANCHISE The duration of the franchise is a matter to be determined between the parties. Generally, a franchise relationship starts with a short trial period, such as a year, so that the franchisee and the franchisor can determine whether they want to stay in business with one another. Usually, the franchise agreement specifies that termination must be "for cause," such as death or disability of the franchisee, insolvency of the franchisee, breach of the franchise agreement, or failure to meet specified sales quotas. Most franchise contracts provide that notice of termination must be given. If no set time for termination is specified, then a reasonable time, with notice, is implied. A franchisee must be given reasonable time to wind up the business—that is, to do the accounting and return the copyright or trademark or any other property of the franchisor.

Because a franchisor's termination of a franchise often has adverse consequences for the franchisee, much franchise litigation involves claims of wrongful termination. Generally, the termination provisions of contracts are more favorable to the franchisor. This means that the franchisee, who normally invests a substantial amount of time and money in the franchise operation to make it successful, may receive little or nothing for the business on termination. The franchisor owns the trademark and hence the business.

It is in this area that statutory and case law become important. The federal and state laws discussed earlier attempt, among other things, to protect franchisees from the arbitrary or unfair termination of their franchises by the franchisors. Generally, both statutory and case law emphasize the importance of good faith and fair dealing in terminating a franchise relationship.

In determining whether a franchisor has acted in good faith when terminating a franchise agreement,

---

16. Although a franchisor can require franchisees to purchase supplies from it, requiring a franchisee to purchase exclusively from the franchisor may violate federal antitrust laws (see Chapters 26 and 27). For two landmark cases in this area, see *United States v. Arnold, Schwinn & Co.*, 388 U.S. 365, 87 S.Ct. 1956, 18 L.Ed.2d (1967); and *Fortner Enterprises, Inc. v. U.S. Steel Corp.*, 394 U.S. 495, 89 S.Ct. 1252, 22 L.Ed.2d 495 (1969).

the courts generally try to balance the rights of both parties. If a court perceives that a franchisor has arbitrarily or unfairly terminated a franchise, the franchisee will be provided with a remedy for wrongful termination. If a franchisor's decision to terminate a franchise was made in the normal course of the franchisor's business operations, however, and reasonable notice of termination was given to the franchisee, normally a court would not consider the termination wrongful. At issue in the following case is whether Domino's Pizza, Inc., acted wrongfully when it terminated one of its franchises.

CASE 17.4 Bennett Enterprises, Inc. v. Domino's Pizza, Inc.

United States Court of Appeals, District of Columbia Circuit, 1995. 45 F.3d 493.

BACKGROUND AND FACTS *Bennett Enterprises, Inc., entered into a franchise agreement with Domino's Pizza, Inc., to operate a Domino's pizza store. The agreement stated that Domino's had the right to terminate the franchise if Bennett failed to comply with any provision, including a promise to comply with "all applicable laws." For most of its first year in business, Bennett did not make a profit and did not pay any taxes. Domino's told Bennett that if it did not resolve its tax problems, Domino's would terminate the franchise. Bennett did not pay the taxes or work out a payment plan with the government but instead sold the franchise and filed a suit against Domino's in a federal district court. Bennett charged Domino's with, among other things, breach of contract, on the ground that the franchise agreement did not entitle Domino's to declare Bennett in default on the basis of unpaid taxes. The court ruled in Bennett's favor. Domino's appealed.*

IN THE LANGUAGE OF THE COURT

SENTELLE, Circuit Judge:

* * * *

The language of [the franchise agreement] is not ambiguous * * * because it is not reasonably or fairly susceptible to an interpretation that does not encompass compliance with state and federal tax laws. * * * [A]ny reasonable construction of the language "all applicable laws" in a business franchise agreement must include tax statutes at the very minimum. To that extent the contract is unambiguous, and that is the only extent with which we are concerned. * * * Under the franchise agreement Domino's had the right to place Bennett in default for failure to pay taxes.

DECISION AND REMEDY *The U.S. Court of Appeals for the District of Columbia Circuit reversed the lower court's judgment. The franchisee violated the franchise agreement, and thus the franchisor did not act wrongfully in terminating the franchise.*

TERMS AND CONCEPTS TO REVIEW

business trust 361
close corporation 347
cooperative 361
corporation 346
franchise 361
franchisee 361
franchisor 361
joint stock company 361
joint venture 360
limited liability company (LLC) 358
limited liability limited partnership (LLLP) 360
limited liability partnership (LLP) 360
limited partnership 344
partnership 344
proxy 357
quorum 355
retained earnings 347
S corporation 348
sole proprietorship 344
syndicate 361

QUESTIONS AND CASE PROBLEMS

17–1. CHOICE OF BUSINESS FORM. Suppose that Subir, Brad, and Lori are college graduates, and Subir has come up with an idea for a new product that he believes could make the three of them very rich. His idea is to manufacture soft-drink dispensers for home use, and his goal is to market them to consumers throughout the Midwest. Subir's personal experience qualifies him to be both first-line supervisor and general manager of the new firm. Brad is a born salesperson. Lori has little interest in sales or management but would like to invest a large sum of money that she has inherited from her aunt. Discuss fully what factors Subir, Brad, and Lori should consider in deciding which form of business organization to adopt.

17–2. CHOICE OF BUSINESS FORM. In the situation described in Question 17–1, assume that Lori is willing to put her inherited money in the business but does not want any further liability should the business fail. Alternatively, the bank is willing to lend some capital at a 12 percent interest rate, but it will do so only if certain restrictions are placed on management decisions. The bank's plan is not satisfactory to Subir or Brad, and the two decide to bring Lori into the business. Under these circumstances, discuss which types of business organizations are best suited to meet Lori's needs.

17–3. BUSINESS FORMS AND LIABILITY. The limited liability of corporate shareholders is one of the most important reasons that firms choose to organize as corporations rather than as partnerships or sole proprietorships. Limited liability means that if a corporation is not able to meet its obligations with corporate assets, creditors will not be allowed to look to the owners (stockholders) of the corporation to satisfy their claims. Assume that Subir and Brad (in Question 17–1) do not have a wealthy friend like Lori who wishes to go into business with them. They therefore must borrow money to start their business. Subir and Brad decide to incorporate. What do you think a lender will ask them when they seek a loan? What effect does this have on the "advantage" of limited liability under incorporation?

17–4. LIABILITY OF LIMITED PARTNERS. Asner and Burton form a limited partnership with Asner as the general partner and Burton as the limited partner. Burton puts up $15,000, and Asner contributes some office equipment that he owns. A certificate of limited partnership is properly filed, and business is begun. One month later, Asner becomes ill. Instead of hiring someone to manage the business, Burton takes over complete management himself. While Burton is in control, he makes a contract with Thomas involving a large sum of money. Asner returns to work. Because of other commitments, the Thomas contract is breached. Thomas contends that Asner and Burton will be personally liable for damages caused by the breach if the damages cannot be satisfied out of the assets of the limited partnership. Discuss this contention.

17–5. SUBSCRIPTION AGREEMENTS. As a promoter forming a new corporation, Peterson enters into three preincorporation subscription agreements with Mary, Anne, and Harry. The three subscribers each agree to purchase one thousand shares of stock of the future corporation for $2,000. Two months later, just prior to the issuance of the corporate charter, Mary tells Peterson she is withdrawing from the agreement. The charter is issued the next week. Just before the first organizational meeting of the corporation, Harry also withdraws from the agreement. Discuss fully whether Mary, Harry, or both can withdraw from the subscription agreements without liability.

17–6. FRANCHISE TERMINATION. Ormsby Motors, Inc. (OMI), was a General Motors Corp. (GM) dealership. Their agreement provided for termination if OMI submitted "false . . . claims for any payment." Larry Kain was in charge of OMI's warranty claims. After several years of excessive claims, GM complained to OMI. When nothing changed, GM conducted a dealer audit. The audit uncovered, among other things, over eighty claims in one ten-day period for paint repair work that was never done. OMI denied knowledge of Kain's activities. GM terminated its dealership agreement with OMI. OMI asked a federal district court to stop the termination, arguing in part that GM did not have good cause. Did GM have good cause? Explain. [*Ormsby Motors, Inc. v. General Motors Corp.*, 842 F.Supp. 344 (N.D.Ill. 1994)]

17–7. GOOD FAITH IN FRANCHISE RELATIONS. Barn-Chestnut, Inc. (BCI), entered into a franchise agreement with Grocers Development Corp. (GDC) for a Convenient Food Mart "for as long as [BCI] . . . shall have a good and valid lease" to the property. GDC sold its interest in the franchise and the property to CFM Development Corp. When the lease was about to expire, CFM offered to enter into a new lease and franchise agreement with BCI at a significantly higher price. BCI refused. When CFM refused to make another deal, BCI filed a suit against CFM in a West Virginia state court on the ground that CFM had to offer BCI a lease because the franchise was contingent on a lease. The court did not agree. BCI then argued that the implied obligation of good faith required CFM to offer to renew the lease. Essentially, the question on appeal was whether the franchisor had an obligation to renew the franchise even though there was no clause in the contract requiring that the lease/franchise be renewed. Was BCI correct in contending that the franchisor did have such an obligation? Explain. [*Barn-Chestnut, Inc. v. CFM Development Corp.*, 193 W.Va. 565, 457 S.E.2d 502 (1995)]

17–8. LIABILITY FOR PREINCORPORATION CONTRACTS. Skandinavia, Inc., manufactured and sold polypropylene underwear. Following two years of poor sales,

Skandinavia entered into negotiations to sell the business to Odilon Cormier, an experienced textile manufacturer. Skandinavia and Cormier agreed that Cormier would take Skandinavia's underwear inventory and use it in a new corporation, which would be called Polypro, Inc. In return, Skandinavia would receive a commission on future sales from Polypro. Polypro was subsequently established and began selling the underwear. Skandinavia, however, never received any commissions from the sales. It therefore brought suit against Polypro and Cormier to recover its promised commissions. The claim against Polypro was dismissed by the trial court, but the trial court found Cormier to be personally liable for the commissions owed. Cormier appealed to the Supreme Court of New Hampshire. Is Cormier personally liable for the contract he signed in the course of setting up a new corporation? Discuss. [*Skandinavia, Inc. v. Cormier*, 128 N.H. 215, 214 A.2d 1250 (1986)]

17–9. Corporate Status. Pat Daniels, John Daniels, and Bill Mandell (the defendants) planned to purchase a tavern and restaurant business in St. Charles, Illinois, and to organize their business in the form of a corporation under the name of D&M, Inc. The defendants negotiated with Howard Realty Group to lease the premises on which the tavern and restaurant were located. While the sale of the business and the negotiation of the lease were proceeding, neither the seller of the business nor Howard contemplated personal guarantees from the defendants. On January 18, 1987, although D&M had not yet been incorporated, the lease was signed in the name of D&M, Inc., by Pat Daniels and Bill Mandell, in their capacities as president and secretary, respectively, of the future corporation. On February 11, 1987, the defendants filed the articles of incorporation for D&M with the secretary of state's office because the name "D&M, Inc." was already in use by another Illinois corporation. The defendants then decided to file the articles of incorporation under the name of The Lodge at Tin Cup Pass, Inc. (the Lodge). They first checked with the landlord to see if they could use that name, because it was similar to the name of the property, Tin Cup Pass. The Lodge was duly incorporated on March 5, 1987. In late 1988, when the Lodge defaulted on its lease payments, Tin Cup Pass Limited Partnership, to whom Howard had assigned the lease, sued the defendants personally to recover the lease payments due, alleging that the defendants should be held liable as corporate promoters for D&M, Inc., a corporation that was never formed. What will result in court? Discuss fully. [*Tin Cup Pass Limited Partnership v. Daniels*, 195 Ill.App.3d 847, 553 N.E.2d 82, 142 Ill.Dec. 732 (1990)]

17–10. A Question of Ethics

On November 3, 1981, Garry Fox met with a representative of Coopers & Lybrand (Coopers), a national accounting firm, to obtain tax advice from Coopers and other accounting services on behalf of a corporation Fox was in the process of forming. Coopers agreed to perform the services. The new corporation, G. Fox and Partners, Inc., was incorporated on December 4, 1981. Coopers completed its work by mid-December and billed G. Fox and Partners for $10,827 for its accounting services. When neither the new corporation nor Fox paid the bill, Coopers sued Garry Fox personally for the amount. Coopers claimed that Fox had breached express and implied contracts and that, as a corporate promoter, Fox was liable for the unpaid debt. Fox argued that Coopers had agreed to look solely to the corporation for payment. The trial court found that there was no agreement, either express or implied, that would obligate Fox individually to pay Coopers's fee, because Coopers failed to prove the existence of any such agreement. On appeal, however, the trial court's judgment was reversed. Fox was held liable as a corporate promoter for the unpaid debt. [*Coopers & Lybrand v. Fox*, 758 P.2d 683 (Colo. 1988)]

1. In view of the fact that Coopers & Lybrand knew that Fox was acting on behalf of a future corporation, do you think that it is fair that Fox should be held personally liable for the contract?
2. Undertaking preliminary corporate organization and promotion is an essential step in the process of corporate formation. Do you think that the risks imposed on promoters by holding them personally liable for preincorporation contracts counter the public policy of promoting business enterprises?
3. What might result if corporate promoters could never be held personally liable for preincorporation contracts? Would such a law also pose a barrier to commerce by increasing the difficulty in obtaining necessary preincorporation contracts, such as for office space, equipment, credit, and so on?

Accessing the Internet
The Legal Environment of Business

The Web site of the law firm of Reinhart et al. provides extensive information about business organizations. The URL for this site is

http://www.rbvdnr.com/

For information on limited liability companies, go to

http://www.mgovg.com/

You can find the full text of the Internal Revenue Service rule concerning the taxation of limited liability companies and limited liability partnerships by accessing the Treasure Chest of Important Documents at the following site:

http://www.LWeekly.com

To learn how the U.S. Small Business Administration assists in forming, financing, and operating businesses, go to

http://www.sbaonline.sba.gov/

The Center for Corporate Law at the University of Cincinnati College of Law is a good source of information on corporate law. Go to

http://www.law.uc.edu/CCL/

At last count, the corporation statutes of about one-fourth of the states were online. Cornell University's Legal Information Institute has links to these statutes at

http://fatty.law.cornell.edu/topics/state_statutes.html

You can find an online newsletter dealing with corporate officers' and employees' personal liability for business taxes at

http://www.integritax.com

Hoover's Online has an extensive collection of data on U.S. corporations. To access this site, go to

http://www.hoovers.com

Switchboard, a nationwide residential and business directory, can be accessed at

http://www.switchboard.com/

For daily news on the world of business, including corporate activities, you can access Money Online at

http://www.money.com

You can find nearly all of the stories from the printed editions of the *Wall Street Journal* at

http://wsj.com

Fortune magazine also is now on line. Go to

http://fortune.com

To access the current edition of *Business Week*, go to

http://www.businessweek.com/

CNN, the financial network, provides features and news briefs of interest to businesspersons at

http://www.cnnfn.com/

CHAPTER 18

RIGHTS AND DUTIES WITHIN THE CORPORATION

CORPORATE DIRECTORS, OFFICERS, and shareholders all play different roles within the corporate entity. The directors play a key role, because they control the firm. They decide on corporate policy and appoint corporate officers to manage the day-to-day affairs of the firm. Because they bear responsibility for running the corporation, directors and officers are charged with fiduciary duties, including a duty of loyalty to the corporation and its shareholder-owners and a duty to exercise reasonable care in corporate decision making. The shareholders also play a vital role, albeit a less direct one. They indirectly exercise control over the corporation because they elect the board of directors. Additionally, as owners of the corporation, they are entitled to have a say in matters involving major corporate changes.

Sometimes, actions that may benefit the corporation as a whole do not coincide with the separate interests of the individuals making up the corporation. In such situations, it is important to know the rights and duties of all participants in the corporate enterprise. This chapter focuses on these rights and the ways in which conflicts among corporate participants are resolved.

SECTION 1
ROLE OF DIRECTORS AND OFFICERS

Directors, representing the interests of the shareholders, manage the corporation through the officers whom they choose. Directors and officers are deemed *fiduciaries* of the corporation, because their relationship with the corporation and its shareholders is one of trust and confidence. As fiduciaries, directors and officers owe ethical—and legal—duties to the corporation and the shareholders. These fiduciary duties include the duty of care and the duty of loyalty.

DUTY OF CARE

Directors and officers must exercise due care in performing their duties. The standard of *due care* has been variously described in judicial decisions and codified in many corporation codes. Generally, a director or officer is expected to act in good faith, to exercise the care that an ordinarily prudent person would exercise in similar circumstances, and to act in what he or she considers to be the best interests of the corporation. Directors and officers who have not exercised the required duty of care can be held liable for the harms suffered by the corporation as a result of their negligence.

DUTY TO MAKE INFORMED AND REASONABLE DECISIONS Directors and officers are expected to be informed on corporate matters. To be informed, a director or officer must do what is necessary to become informed: attend presentations, ask for information from those who have it, read reports, review other written materials such as contracts—in other words, carefully study a situation and its alternatives. Depending on the nature of the business, directors and officers are often expected to act in accordance with their own knowledge and training. Most states and Section 8.30(b) of the RMBCA, however, allow a director to make decisions in reliance on information furnished by competent officers or employees, professionals such as attorneys and accountants, or even an executive committee of the board without being accused of acting in bad faith or failing to exercise due care if such information turns out to be faulty.

Directors are also expected to make reasonable decisions. For example, a director should not accept a tender offer (an offer to purchase shares in the company that is made by another company directly to the shareholders) with only a moment's consideration based solely on the market price of the corporation's shares.

DUTY TO EXERCISE REASONABLE SUPERVISION Directors are also expected to exercise a reasonable amount of supervision when they delegate work to corporate officers and employees. For example, suppose that a corporate bank director fails to attend any board of directors' meetings for five years, never inspects any of the corporate books or records, and generally fails to supervise the efforts of the bank president and the loan committee. Meanwhile, a corporate officer, the bank president, makes various improper loans and permits large overdrafts. In this situation, the corporate director may be held liable to the corporation for losses resulting from the unsupervised actions of the bank president and the loan committee.

DISSENTING DIRECTORS Directors are expected to attend board of directors' meetings, and their votes should be entered into the minutes of corporate meetings. Unless a dissent is entered, the director is presumed to have assented. Directors who dissent are rarely held individually liable for mismanagement of the corporation. For this reason, a director who is absent from a given meeting sometimes registers with the secretary of the board a dissent to actions taken at the meeting.

DUTY OF LOYALTY

Loyalty can be defined as faithfulness to one's obligations and duties. In the corporate context, the duty of loyalty requires directors and officers to subordinate their personal interests to the welfare of the corporation.

For example, directors may not use corporate funds or confidential corporate information for personal advantage. Similarly, they must refrain from putting their personal interests above those of the corporation. For instance, a director should not oppose a transaction that is in the corporation's best interest simply because its acceptance may cost the director her or his position. Cases dealing with fiduciary duty typically involve one or more of the following:

1. Competing with the corporation.
2. Usurping (taking personal advantage of) a corporate opportunity.
3. Having an interest that conflicts with the interest of the corporation.

4. Engaging in insider trading (using information that is not public to make a profit trading securities, as discussed in Chapter 28).
5. Authorizing a corporate transaction that is detrimental to minority shareholders.
6. Selling control over the corporation.

In the following case, a corporation sued two of its former officers, alleging that they had breached their duty of loyalty by planning and creating a competing enterprise while still employed by the corporation.

CASE 18.1 Veco Corp. v. Babcock

Appellate Court of Illinois, First District, Second Division, 1993. 243 Ill.App.3d 153, 611 N.E.2d 1054, 183 Ill.Dec. 406.

BACKGROUND AND FACTS *Two high-ranking officers of Veco Corporation, an Illinois financial services company, started talking about forming their own financial services company, to be called CorMac, Inc. The officers, Robert Babcock and Margaret Michails, expanded their discussions to include other employees of Veco, including Jeanne Tucker and Patricia Walker. While they were still working for Veco, Babcock prepared the business plan for CorMac, and Michails typed it up. The plan listed the Veco employees who would join CorMac and also detailed the "taking over" of an important Veco client. When Veco's founder and sole shareholder, David Vear, discovered what Babcock had done, he summarily fired him. Immediately thereafter, Michails, Tucker, and Walker resigned and began working with CorMac. In the wake of those resignations, Veco was left with no personnel experienced in handling one of its major accounts (National Exchange Benefit Trust, or N.E.B.T.). As a result, according to Veco, it suffered losses totaling at least $100,000. Veco sued Babcock and Michails, alleging that they had breached their fiduciary duty of loyalty by forming their business plan and recruiting other key Veco employees to join their new competing entity while they were still employed by Veco. The trial court held for Babcock and the others. The court did not see their actions as illegal, even though they may have been unethical. Veco appealed.*

IN THE LANGUAGE OF THE COURT

Justice *HARTMAN* delivered the opinion of the court:

* * * *

* * * Corporate officers are liable for breaching their fiduciary duties where, while still affiliated with the company, they solicit fellow employees to join a rival business or orchestrate a mass exodus of employees to follow shortly the officer's resignation from the company. In the present case, it is undisputed that Babcock recruited Michails, Tucker, and Walker to join him prior to his termination; he also cautioned them not to tell Vear of their plans. At Babcock's direction and while still employed at Veco, Michails retrieved, copied, and typed various documents belonging to Veco for CorMac. While still employed at Veco, Tucker joined Babcock in a meeting where Babcock solicited N.E.B.T. members for CorMac. After Vear fired Babcock, Michails, Tucker, and Walker immediately resigned. This evidence is uncontradicted. Clearly, defendants secretly solicited Veco employees for CorMac and orchestrated a mass exodus of Veco's N.E.B.T. servicing employees to follow Babcock's resignation. Such conduct is a breach of fiduciary duties.

DECISION AND REMEDY *The appellate court, holding that the trial court's ruling was against the "manifest weight of the evidence," reversed the trial court's decision and remanded the case for further proceedings consistent with its opinion. The officers breached their fiduciary duty of loyalty by planning and creating a competing enterprise while employed by the corporation.*

CONFLICTS OF INTEREST

Corporate directors often have many business affiliations, and a director can sit on the board of more than one corporation. Of course, directors are precluded from entering into or supporting businesses that operate in direct competition with corporations on whose boards they serve. Their fiduciary duty requires them to make a full disclosure of any potential conflicts of interest that might arise in any corporate transaction.

Sometimes a corporation enters into a contract or engages in a transaction in which an officer or director has a personal interest. The director or officer must make a *full disclosure* of that interest and must abstain from voting on the proposed transaction. For example, Ballo Corporation needs office space. Stephan Colson, one of its five directors, owns the building adjoining the corporation's headquarters. He negotiates a lease with Ballo for the space, making a full disclosure to Ballo and the other four board directors. The lease arrangement is fair and reasonable, and it is unanimously approved by the other members of the corporation's board of directors. In such a case, the contract is valid. The rule is one of reason; otherwise, directors would be prevented from ever giving financial assistance to the corporations they serve.

State statutes contain different standards, but a contract will generally not be voidable if it was fair and reasonable to the corporation at the time it was made, if there was a full disclosure of the interest of the officers or directors involved in the transaction, and if the contract was approved by a majority of the disinterested directors or shareholders.

Often, contracts are negotiated between corporations having one or more directors who are members of both boards. Such transactions require great care, as they are closely scrutinized by the courts. (As will be discussed in Chapter 27, in certain circumstances—if two large corporations are competing with each other, for example—it may constitute a violation of antitrust laws for a director to sit on the boards of both companies.)

SECTION 2 LIABILITY OF DIRECTORS AND OFFICERS

Directors and officers are exposed to liability on many fronts. Shareholders may perceive that the corporate directors are not acting in the best interests of the corporation and may sue the directors, in what is called a *shareholder's derivative suit,* on behalf of the corporation. (This type of action is discussed later in this chapter, in the context of shareholders' rights.) In addition, corporate directors and officers may be held liable not only for their own torts and crimes but also for torts and crimes committed by corporate employees under their supervision.

In this section, we examine the so-called *business judgment rule,* under which a corporate director or officer may be able to avoid liability to the corporation or to its shareholders for exercising poor business judgment. We also look at the liability of corporate directors and officers for torts and crimes.

THE BUSINESS JUDGMENT RULE

Directors and officers are expected to exercise due care and to use their best judgment in guiding corporate management, but they are not insurers of business success. Honest mistakes of judgment and poor business decisions on their part do not make them liable to the corporation for resulting damages. This is the **business judgment rule.** The rule generally immunizes directors and officers from liability for the consequences of a decision that is within managerial authority, as long as the decision complies with management's fiduciary duties and as long as acting on the decision is within the powers of the corporation. Consequently, if there is a reasonable basis for a business decision, it is unlikely that the court will interfere with that decision, even if the corporation suffers as a result.

To benefit from the rule, directors and officers must act in good faith, in what they consider to be the best interests of the corporation, and with the care that an ordinarily prudent person in a similar position would exercise in similar circumstances. This requires an informed decision, with a rational basis, and with no conflict between the decision maker's personal interest and the interest of the corporation.

LIABILITY FOR TORTS AND CRIMES

The corporation as an entity is liable for the torts and crimes that corporate agents and employees commit when they are acting within the scope of their employment. Liability for the actions of its corporate agents and employees is imputed to the corporation (the principal) under agency law. Furthermore, directors, officers, and corporate employees are personally liable for the torts and crimes that they commit within the scope of their employment. In other words, even though the corporation as an entity may assume liability for, say, a corporate agent's tort, that does not mean that the agent can avoid personal liability for the tort. Additionally, directors and officers can be held criminally liable under certain federal or state statutes, such as environmental or employment laws.

Corporate directors and officers may also be held personally liable for the torts and crimes committed by corporate personnel under their direct supervision. Normally, the court must show that the wrongful actions were committed at the officer's direction or with his or her permission. Increasingly, however, liability is imposed on corporate officers because of their failure to supervise their employees adequately or because of their ability to exercise such pervasive control over corporate affairs that they should be treated as employers.

THE "RESPONSIBLE PERSON" DOCTRINE Under what is known as the "responsible person" doctrine, a court may impose criminal liability on a corporate officer regardless of whether he or she participated in, directed, or even knew about a given criminal violation. In *United States v. Park*,[1] for example, the chief executive officer of a national supermarket chain was held personally liable for sanitation violations in corporate warehouses in which food was exposed to contamination by rodents. The court imposed personal liability on the corporate officer not because he intended the crime[2] or even knew about it. Rather, liability was imposed because the officer was in a "responsible relationship" to the corporation and had the power to prevent the violation.

Since the *Park* decision, courts have applied this "responsible person" doctrine numerous times to hold corporate officers liable for statutory violations committed by others. An example is *O'Callaghan v. United States*.[3] James O'Callaghan was the president and a majority shareholder of Cafe Society, Inc., which owned a restaurant. The day-to-day operations of the restaurant were run by a management company. When the restaurant filed for bankruptcy, O'Callaghan asked the company's bankruptcy lawyer to be sure that the corporation's delinquent withholding taxes were paid. The lawyer informed O'Callaghan that the payments were being made, but in fact, they were not. Even though O'Callaghan was not involved in the daily operations of Cafe Society, he was nonetheless held liable by the court, as a "responsible person," for the unpaid taxes.

PERVASIVENESS OF CONTROL Corporate directors and officers may also be subject to liability as employers if they exercise sufficient control over the workplace. In *United States v. Cusack*,[4] for example, the court held that a corporate officer's control over corporate operations was so pervasive that, in effect, the officer was not only a corporate agent-employee but also an employer. Therefore, as an employer, the officer could be subject to liability for the statutory violations of corporate employees.

Whether an officer will be subject to liability as an employer usually depends on how the relevant statute defines the term *employer*. For example, most federal antidiscrimination statutes (including Title VII of the Civil Rights Act of 1964, the Age Discrimination in Employment Act, and the Americans with Disabilities Act) define an employer as a "person engaged in an industry affecting commerce" who "employs" a certain number of people. In contrast, the Family and Medical Leave Act (FMLA) extends employer status to "any person who acts, directly or indirectly, in the interest of an employer to any of the employees of such employer." Therefore, corporate officers acting in a supervisory capacity may be held liable as employers under the FMLA.[5]

SECTION 3
RIGHTS OF DIRECTORS

A director of a corporation has a number of rights, including the rights of participation, inspection, compensation, and indemnification.

PARTICIPATION AND INSPECTION

A corporate director must have certain rights to function properly in that position. The main right is one

1. 421 U.S. 658, 95 S.Ct. 1903, 44 L.Ed.2d 489 (1975).
2. Two elements must be present for a crime to exist: a criminal act and criminal intent. In *Park*, the court dispensed with the latter requirement.
3. 943 F.Supp. 320 (S.D.N.Y. 1996).
4. 806 F.Supp. 47 (D.N.J. 1992).
5. See, for example, *Freemon v. Foley*, 911 F.Supp. 326 (N.D.Ill. 1995).

of participation—meaning that the director must be notified of board of directors' meetings so as to participate in them. As pointed out earlier in this chapter, regular board meetings are usually established by the bylaws or by board resolution, and no notice of these meetings is required. If special meetings are called, however, notice is required unless waived by the director.

A director must have access to all of the corporate books and records to make decisions and to exercise the necessary supervision over corporate officers and employees. This right of inspection is virtually absolute and cannot be restricted.

COMPENSATION AND INDEMNIFICATION

Nominal sums are often paid as honorariums to directors. In many corporations, directors are also chief corporate officers (president or chief executive officer, for example) and receive compensation in their managerial positions. Most directors also gain through indirect benefits, such as business contacts, prestige, and other rewards. There is a trend toward providing more than nominal compensation for directors, especially in large corporations in which directorships can be enormous burdens in terms of time, work, effort, and risk. Many states permit the corporate articles or bylaws to authorize compensation for directors, and in some cases the board can set its own compensation unless the articles or bylaws provide otherwise.

Corporate directors may become involved in lawsuits by virtue of their positions and their actions as directors. Most states (and RMBCA 8.51) permit a corporation to indemnify (guarantee reimbursement to) a director for legal costs, fees, and judgments involved in defending corporation-related suits. Many states specifically permit a corporation to purchase liability insurance for the directors and officers to cover indemnification. When the statutes are silent on this matter, the power to purchase such insurance is usually considered to be part of the corporation's implied power.

SECTION 4
RIGHTS OF OFFICERS AND MANAGERS

As noted earlier, corporate officers' duties are the same as the duties of directors because their respective corporate positions involve both of them in decision making and place them in similar positions of control. Hence, they are viewed as having the same fiduciary duties of care and loyalty in their conduct of corporate affairs. Also, they are subject to the same obligations concerning corporate opportunities and conflicts of interest as directors are, but they do not have a defense that directors have—the business judgment rule.

The rights of corporate officers and other high-level managers are defined by employment contracts, because they are employees of the company.

SECTION 5
RIGHTS OF SHAREHOLDERS

Shareholders possess numerous rights. A significant right—the right to vote their shares—has already been discussed. In addition to voting rights, a shareholder has the rights, based on ownership of stock, to receive stock certificates (depending on the jurisdiction), to purchase newly issued stock, to receive dividends, to inspect corporate records, to transfer shares (with some exceptions), to receive a proportionate share of corporate assets on corporate dissolution, and to file suit on behalf of the corporation. These rights are discussed in the following subsections.

STOCK CERTIFICATES

A **stock certificate** is a certificate issued by a corporation that evidences ownership of a specified number of shares in the corporation. In jurisdictions that require the issuance of stock certificates, shareholders have the right to demand that the corporation issue certificates and record their names and addresses in the corporate stock record books. In most states (and under RMBCA 6.26), boards of directors may provide that shares of stock be uncertificated (that is, that no actual, physical stock certificates need be issued). In that circumstance, it may be required that the corporation send the holders of uncertificated shares letters or some other form of notice containing the same information required to be included on the face of stock certificates.

Stock is intangible personal property, and the ownership right exists independently of the certificate itself. A stock certificate may be lost or destroyed, but ownership is not destroyed with it. A new certificate can be issued to replace one that has been lost or destroyed.[6] Notice of shareholder meetings, dividends, and operational and financial reports are all distributed according to the recorded ownership listed in the corporation's books, not on the basis of possession of the certificate.

PREEMPTIVE RIGHTS

A **preemptive right** is a common law concept under which a preference is given to a shareholder over all other purchasers to subscribe to or purchase a prorated share of a new issue of stock. This right does not apply to **treasury shares**—shares previously authorized and issued but later reacquired by the corporation. This allows the shareholder to maintain his or her portion of control, voting power, or financial interest in the corporation. Most statutes either (1) grant preemptive rights but allow them to be negated in the corporation's articles or (2) deny preemptive rights except to the extent that they are granted in the articles. The result is that the articles of incorporation determine the existence and scope of preemptive rights. Generally, preemptive rights apply only to additional, newly issued stock sold for cash and must be exercised within a specified time period (such as thirty days).

For example, Tron Corporation authorizes and issues 1,000 shares of stock, and Omar Loren purchases 100 shares, making him the owner of 10 percent of the company's stock. Subsequently, Tron, by vote of its shareholders, authorizes the issuance of another 1,000 shares (amending the articles of incorporation). This increases its capital stock to a total of 2,000 shares. If preemptive rights have been provided, Loren can purchase one additional share of the new stock being issued for each share currently owned—or 100 additional shares. Thus, he can own 200 of the 2,000 shares outstanding, and his relative position as a shareholder will be maintained. If preemptive rights are not reserved, his proportionate control and voting power will be diluted from that of a 10 percent shareholder to that of a 5 percent shareholder because of the issuance of the additional 1,000 shares.

Preemptive rights can be very important for shareholders in close corporations. This is because of the relatively small number of shares and the substantial interest that each shareholder controls in a close corporation. Without preemptive rights, it would be possible for a shareholder to lose his or her proportionate control over the firm.

STOCK WARRANTS

Usually, when preemptive rights exist and a corporation is issuing additional shares, each shareholder is given **stock warrants,** which are transferable options to acquire a given number of shares from the corporation at a stated price. Warrants are often publicly traded on securities exchanges. When the warrant option is for a short period of time, the stock warrants are usually referred to as *rights*.

DIVIDENDS

A **dividend** is a distribution of corporate profits or income *ordered by the directors* and paid to the shareholders in proportion to their respective shares in the corporation. Dividends can be paid in cash, property, stock of the corporation that is paying the dividends, or stock of other corporations.[7]

State laws vary, but every state determines the general circumstances and legal requirements under which dividends are paid. State laws also control the sources of revenue to be used; only certain funds are legally available for paying dividends. Once declared, a cash dividend becomes a corporate debt enforceable at law like any other debt. Depending on state law, dividends may be paid from the following sources:

1. *Retained earnings.* All state statutes allow dividends to be paid from the undistributed net profits earned by the corporation, including capital gains from the sale of fixed assets. The undistributed net profits are called *retained earnings*.
2. *Net profits.* A few state statutes allow dividends to be issued from current net profits without regard to deficits in prior years.
3. *Surplus.* A number of state statutes allow dividends to be paid out of any kind of surplus.

ILLEGAL DIVIDENDS Sometimes dividends are improperly paid from an unauthorized account, or

6. For a lost or destroyed certificate to be reissued, a shareholder normally must furnish an indemnity bond (a guaranty of payment) to protect the corporation against potential loss should the original certificate reappear at some future time in the hands of a bona fide purchaser [UCC 8–302, 8–405(2)].

7. Technically, dividends paid in stock are not dividends. They maintain each shareholder's proportional interest in the corporation. On one occasion, a distillery declared and paid a "dividend" in bonded whiskey.

their payment causes the corporation to become insolvent. Generally, in such cases, shareholders must return illegal dividends only if they knew that the dividends were illegal when they received them. A dividend paid while the corporation is *insolvent* is automatically an illegal dividend, and shareholders may be liable for returning the payment to the corporation or its creditors. In all cases of illegal and improper dividends, the board of directors can be held personally liable for the amount of the payment. When directors can show that a shareholder knew a dividend was illegal when it was received, however, the directors are entitled to reimbursement from the shareholder.

DIRECTORS' FAILURE TO DECLARE A DIVIDEND When directors fail to declare a dividend, shareholders can ask a court of equity for an injunction to compel the directors to meet and to declare a dividend. For the injunction to be granted, it must be shown that the directors have acted so unreasonably in withholding the dividend that their conduct is an abuse of their discretion.

Often, large money reserves are accumulated for a bona fide purpose, such as expansion, research, or some other legitimate corporate use. The mere fact that sufficient corporate earnings or surplus is available to pay a dividend is not enough to compel directors to distribute funds that, in the board's opinion, should not be distributed.[8] The courts are hesitant to interfere with corporate operations and will not compel directors to declare dividends unless abuse of discretion is clearly shown.

8. A striking exception to this rule was made in *Dodge v. Ford Motor Co.*, 204 Mich. 459, 170 N.W. 668 (1919), when Henry Ford, the president and major stockholder of Ford Motor Company, refused to declare a dividend notwithstanding the firm's large capital surplus. The court, holding that Ford had abused his discretion, ordered the company to declare a dividend.

INSPECTION RIGHTS

Shareholders in a corporation enjoy both common law and statutory inspection rights. The shareholder's right of inspection is limited, however, to the inspection and copying of corporate books and records for a *proper purpose*, provided the request is made in advance. Either the shareholder can inspect in person, or an attorney, accountant, or other type of assistant can do so as the shareholder's agent. The RMBCA requires the corporation to maintain an alphabetical voting list of shareholders with addresses and number of shares owned; this list must be kept open at the annual meeting for inspection by any shareholder of record.

The power of inspection is fraught with potential abuses, and the corporation is allowed to protect itself from them. For example, a shareholder can properly be denied access to corporate records to prevent harassment or to protect trade secrets or other confidential corporate information. Some states require that a shareholder must have held his or her shares for a minimum period of time immediately preceding the demand to inspect or must hold a minimum number of outstanding shares. The RMBCA provides that every shareholder is entitled to examine specified corporate records.

A shareholder who is denied the right of inspection can seek a court order to compel the inspection. At issue in the following case is whether a person who does not own shares in a corporation can obtain an order to compel an inspection of the corporate books.

CASE 18.2 ☒ Shaw v. Agri-Mark, Inc.

Supreme Court of Delaware, 1995.
663 A.2d 464.

HISTORICAL AND SOCIAL SETTING *The salaries of officers and directors of corporations have skyrocketed since 1980. In some instances, employees, shareholders, and others who have an interest in a corporation have protested the high pay. In part, they assert that the money could be spent in other ways to benefit their corporation. To protest—or support—the level of executive salaries, however, those who are interested must first discover how much the pay is.*

BACKGROUND AND FACTS *Agri-Mark, Inc., was incorporated in Delaware. Agri-Mark handles dairy products under exclusive contracts with farmers. The farmers are considered "members" of the corporation, but only its directors are shareholders. Karen Shaw and other members filed a suit in a federal district court against Agri-Mark, seeking to inspect its books and records. They sought in part salary information concerning the five highest-paid executives. When the court ruled in their favor, Agri-Mark appealed to the U.S. Court of Appeals for the Second Circuit. The appellate court asked the Supreme Court of Delaware whether the right of inspection of corporate books and records under Delaware law is exclusively reserved to shareholders.*

IN THE LANGUAGE OF THE COURT

WALSH, Justice:

* * * *

* * * While the appellants may assert certain rights arising out of the fiduciary relationship between themselves * * * and those who manage the affairs of the corporation, those rights do not extend to or include the attributes of record stockholders. Our corporate law has traditionally limited the rights of stockholders to stockholders of record. * * *

* * * *

In this case, appellants are not stockholders of Agri-Mark, let alone stockholders of record. * * * As the only stockholders of Agri-Mark, the directors exclusively enjoy the rights incident to their share ownership, including the right of inspection * * * .

DECISION AND REMEDY *The Supreme Court of Delaware held that a person must be a "stockholder of record"—his or her name must be listed in the corporate stock ledger—to be entitled to inspect the books and records of the corporation.*

TRANSFER OF SHARES

Corporate stock represents an ownership right in intangible personal property. The law generally recognizes the right of an owner to transfer property to another person unless there are valid restrictions on its transferability. Although stock certificates are negotiable and freely transferable by indorsement and delivery, transfer of stock in closely held corporations is generally restricted by the bylaws, by a restriction stamped on the stock certificate, or by a shareholder agreemen. The existence of any restrictions on transferability must always be noted on the face of the stock certificate, and these restrictions must be reasonable.

Sometimes, corporations or their shareholders restrict transferability by reserving the option to purchase any shares offered for resale by a shareholder. This **right of first refusal** remains with the corporation or the shareholders for only a specified time or a reasonable time. Variations on the purchase option are possible. For example, a shareholder might be required to offer the shares to other shareholders or to the corporation first.

When shares are transferred, a new entry is made in the corporate stock book to indicate the new owner. Until the corporation is notified and the entry is complete, voting rights, notice of shareholders' meetings, dividend distribution, and so forth are all held by the current record owner.

RIGHTS ON DISSOLUTION

When a corporation is dissolved and its outstanding debts and the claims of its creditors have been satisfied, the remaining assets are distributed on a pro rata basis among the shareholders. If no preferences in distribution of assets on liquidation are given to any class of stock, then all of the stockholders share the remaining assets.

Shareholders also have the right to petition the court to dissolve the corporation. Suppose that a minority shareholder knows that the board of directors is mishandling corporate assets or is permitting a deadlock to threaten or irreparably injure the corporation's finances. The minority shareholder is not powerless to intervene. He or she can petition a court to appoint a receiver and to liquidate the business assets of the corporation.

The RMBCA permits any shareholder to initiate such an action in any of the following circumstances:

1. The directors are deadlocked in the management of corporate affairs, shareholders are unable to break that deadlock, and irreparable injury to the corporation is being suffered or threatened.
2. The acts of the directors or those in control of the corporation are illegal, oppressive, or fraudulent.
3. Corporate assets are being misapplied or wasted.
4. The shareholders are deadlocked in voting power and have failed, for a specified period (usually two annual meetings), to elect successors to directors whose terms have expired or would have expired with the election of successors.

In the following case, one of a corporation's only two shareholders petitioned a court to dissolve the corporation because the shareholders could not agree on how to run the corporation.

CASE 18.3 Black v. Graham

Supreme Court of Georgia, 1996. 464 S.E.2d 814.

HISTORICAL AND ECONOMIC SETTING *Despite the continued expansion of the economy in the early 1990s, there was declining demand in the market for construction materials. At the time, there were nearly 72,000 building materials and garden supplies establishments in the United States. At the same time, there were more than 500,000 construction contractors. Most construction contracting and building supplies firms are small businesses. In the construction industry, a business is classified as small if it has gross annual receipts between $7 million and $15 million.*

BACKGROUND AND FACTS *Black and Graham each owned 50 percent of the stock of a building supplies corporation; they also served as the corporation's directors. When the two shareholder-directors deadlocked over differences of opinion on how to run their business, Graham filed a petition in a Georgia state court to dissolve the corporation. The parties agreed to the appointment of a custodian to run their firm while the court considered Graham's petition. Ultimately, the court ordered each shareholder to offer to buy the other out. This attempt to resolve the matter failed. The court then converted the custodian into a receiver, directed him to wind up the affairs of the business, and told him to liquidate the corporation. Both parties appealed to the Supreme Court of Georgia.*

IN THE LANGUAGE OF THE COURT

HINES, Justice.

* * * *

* * * A deadlock occurs [w]here stock of [a] corporation is owned in equal shares by two contending parties, which condition threatens to result in destruction of business, and it appears that [the] parties cannot agree upon management of [the] business, and under existing circumstances neither one is authorized to impose its views upon the other * * * . The evidence in this case portrays a classic situation of deadlock. Black and Graham as sole and equal shareholders functioned as *de facto* directors who were wholly unable to agree on the management of the business. Neither had the authority to prevail in his view and the hostile and static situation threatened irreparable injury to the corporation. Under these circumstances, the appointment of a receiver and dissolution was warranted.

DECISION AND REMEDY *The Supreme Court of Georgia affirmed the orders of the lower court. The corporation would be dissolved because the shareholders could not agree on how to run the firm.*

SHAREHOLDER'S DERIVATIVE SUITS

When those in control of a corporation—the corporate directors—fail to sue in the corporate name to redress a wrong suffered by the corporation, shareholders are permitted to do so "derivatively" in what is known as a **shareholder's derivative suit.** Some wrong must have been done to the corporation, and before a derivative suit can be brought, the shareholders must first state their complaint to the board of directors. Only if the directors fail to solve the problem or to take appropriate action can the derivative suit go forward.

The right of shareholders to bring a derivative action is especially important when the wrong suffered by the corporation results from the actions of corporate directors. This is because the directors and officers would probably be unwilling to take any action against themselves.

The shareholder's derivative suit is singular in that those suing are not pursuing rights or benefits for themselves personally but are acting as guardians of the corporate entity. Therefore, any damages recovered by the suit normally go into the corporation's treasury, not to the shareholders personally.

SECTION 6 LIABILITY OF SHAREHOLDERS

One of the hallmarks of the corporate organization is that shareholders are not personally liable for the debts of the corporation. If the corporation fails, shareholders can lose their investments, but that is generally the limit of their liability. As discussed in Chapter 17, in certain instances of fraud, undercapitalization, or careless observance of corporate formalities, a court will pierce the corporate veil (disregard the corporate entity) and hold the shareholders individually liable. But these situations are the exception, not the rule.

Although rare, there are certain other instances in which a shareholder can be personally liable. One relates to illegal dividends, which were discussed previously. Two others relate to *stock subscriptions* and *watered stock.*

STOCK-SUBSCRIPTION AGREEMENTS

Sometimes, stock-subscription agreements—written contracts by which one agrees to buy capital stock of a corporation—exist prior to incorporation. Normally, these agreements are treated as continuing offers and are irrevocable (for up to six months under RMBCA 6.20). Once the corporation has been formed, it can sell shares to investors. In either case, once the subscription agreement or stock offer is accepted, a binding contract is formed. Any refusal to pay constitutes a breach resulting in the personal liability of the shareholder.

WATERED STOCK

Shares of stock can be paid for with property or services rendered instead of cash. (Shares cannot be purchased with promissory notes, however.) The general rule is that for **par-value shares** (that is, shares that have a specific face value, or formal cash-in value, written on them, such as one penny or one dollar), the corporation must receive a value at least equal to the par-value amount. For **no-par shares** (that is, shares without a par value), the corporation must receive the value of the shares as determined by the board or the shareholders.

For either par-value or no-par shares, the setting of the value is based on the same factors: tax rates, whether the corporation needs capital surplus, and what the corporation will receive for the shares (money, property, or services). When shares are issued by the corporation for less than these stated values, the shares are referred to as **watered stock.**[9] In most cases, the shareholder who receives watered stock must pay the difference to the corporation (the shareholder is personally liable). In some states, the shareholder who

9. The phrase *watered stock* was originally used to describe cattle that—kept thirsty during a long drive—were allowed to drink large quantities of water just prior to their sale. The increased weight of the "watered stock" allowed the seller to reap a higher profit.

receives watered stock may be liable to creditors of the corporation for unpaid corporate debts.

To illustrate the concept of watered stock: Suppose that during the formation of a corporation, Gomez, as one of the incorporators, transfers his property, Sunset Beach, to the corporation for 10,000 shares of stock at a par value of $100 per share for a total price of $1 million. After the property is transferred and the shares are issued, Sunset Beach is carried on the corporate books at a value of $1 million. On appraisal, it is discovered that the market value of the property at the time of transfer was only $500,000. The shares issued to Gomez are therefore watered stock, and he is liable to the corporation for the difference between the value of the shares and the value of the property.

SECTION 7 DUTIES OF MAJORITY SHAREHOLDERS

In some cases, a majority shareholder is regarded as having a fiduciary duty to the corporation and to the minority shareholders. This occurs when a single shareholder (or a few shareholders acting in concert) owns a sufficient number of shares to exercise *de facto* (actual) control over the corporation. In these situations, majority shareholders owe a fiduciary duty to minority shareholders and creditors when they sell their shares, because such a sale represents, in fact, a transfer of control of the corporation.

TERMS AND CONCEPTS TO REVIEW

business judgment rule 372
dividend 375
no-par share 379
par-value share 379
preemptive right 375
right of first refusal 377
shareholder's derivative suit 379
stock certificate 374
stock warrant 375
treasury share 375
watered stock 379

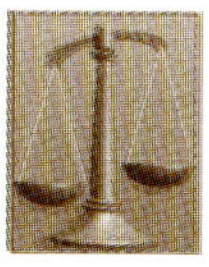

QUESTIONS AND CASE PROBLEMS

18–1. DUTIES OF DIRECTORS. Otts Corp. is negotiating with the Wick Construction Co. for the renovation of the Otts corporate headquarters. Wick, owner of the Wick Construction Co., is also one of the five members of the board of directors of Otts. The contract terms are standard for this type of contract. Wick has previously informed two of the other directors of his interest in the construction company. The contract is approved by Otts's board on a three-to-two vote, with Wick voting with the majority. Discuss whether this contract is binding on the corporation.

18–2. DUTIES OF DIRECTORS. AstroStar, Inc., has a board of directors consisting of three members (Eckhart, Golum, and Macero) and has approximately five hundred shareholders. At a regular meeting of the board, the board selects Galiard as president of the corporation by a two-to-one vote, with Eckhart dissenting. The minutes of the meeting do not register Eckhart's dissenting vote. Later, on an audit, it is discovered that Galiard is a former convict and has openly embezzled $500,000 from AstroStar, Inc. This loss is not covered by insurance. The corporation wants to hold directors Eckhart, Golum, and Macero liable. Eckhart claims no liability. Discuss the personal liability of the directors to the corporation.

18–3. RIGHTS OF SHAREHOLDERS. Superal Corp. authorized 100,000 shares and issued all of them during its first six months in operation. Avril purchased 10,000 of the shares (10 percent). Later, Superal reacquired 10,000 of the shares it originally issued. With shareholder approval, Superal has now amended its articles so as to authorize and issue another 100,000 shares. It has also, by a resolution of the board of directors, made plans to reissue the 10,000 shares of treasury stock (the shares reacquired by the corporation). There is no provision in the corporate articles dealing with shareholders' preemptive rights. Because of her ownership of 10 percent of Superal, Avril claims that she has the preemptive right to purchase 10,000 shares of the new issue and 1,000 shares of the stock being reissued. Discuss her claims.

18–4. RIGHTS OF SHAREHOLDERS. Lucia has acquired one share of common stock of a multimillion-dollar corporation with over 500,000 shareholders. Lucia's ownership is so small that she is questioning what her rights are as a shareholder. For example, she wants to know whether this one share entitles her to

(1) attend and vote at shareholders' meetings, (2) inspect the corporate books, and (3) receive yearly dividends. Discuss Lucia's rights in these three matters.

18–5. LIABILITY OF SHAREHOLDERS. Riddle has made a preincorporation subscription agreement to purchase 500 shares of a newly formed corporation. The shares have a par value of $100 per share. The corporation is formed, and Riddle's subscription is accepted by the corporation. Riddle transfers a piece of land he owns to the corporation, and the corporation issues 250 shares for it. One year later, with the corporation in serious financial difficulty, the board declares and pays a dividend of $5 per share. It is now learned that the land transferred by Riddle had a market value of $18,000 at the time of transfer. Discuss any liability that shareholder Riddle has to the corporation or to creditors of the corporation.

18–6. RIGHTS OF SHAREHOLDERS. Jacob Schachter and Herbert Kulik, the founders of Ketek Electric Corp., each owned 50 percent of the corporation's shares, and they served as the corporation's only officers. Arnold Glenn, as trustee, and Kulik brought a shareholder's derivative suit in a New York state court against Schachter, alleging that Schachter had diverted Ketek assets and opportunities to Hoteltron Systems, Inc., a corporation wholly owned by Schachter. The trial court held for Glenn and Kulik, and it awarded damages to Kulik, not to Ketek. On appeal, the appellate court ruled that the damages should be awarded to the injured corporation, Ketek, rather than to the innocent shareholder, Kulik. Kulik appealed to the state supreme court, arguing that awarding damages to the corporation was inequitable because Schachter, as a shareholder of Ketek, would ultimately share in the proceeds of the award. How should the state supreme court rule, and why? [*Glenn v. Hoteltron Systems, Inc.*, 74 N.Y.2d 386, 547 N.E.2d 71, 547 N.Y.S.2d 816 (1989)]

18–7. RIGHTS OF SHAREHOLDERS. Melissa and Gary Callicoat each owned 50 percent of Callicoat, Inc. They were also Callicoat's only directors. They could not agree on the day-to-day management of the firm. Neither could they agree on whether a debt owed to Arthur Baz was a personal or a corporate debt. Melissa suggested that they dissolve the corporation. Gary refused and shut her out from the operations of the firm. Melissa filed a petition in an Ohio state court against Gary and Callicoat, asking the court to dissolve the corporation. On what basis might the court order the dissolution? [*Callicoat v. Callicoat*, 73 Ohio Misc.2d 38, 657 N.E.2d 874 (1994)]

18–8. BUSINESS JUDGMENT RULE. William Bear was the president of the William R. Bear Agency, Inc. (Bear Agency). Timothy Schirmer was a shareholder. In 1990, the YMCA was an important client of Bear Agency, and Bear spent company funds for family memberships in the YMCA. The same year, Bear put his wife on the payroll because, at the time, she was the only one in the office with computer experience. He decided not to declare a bonus for the employees in 1990, in part to invest the money in computers for the firm. The next April, Bear bought a BMW with company funds to use as a company car. Disapproving these actions, Schirmer filed a suit against Bear, Bear Agency, and others in an Illinois state court, asking the court to dissolve the corporation, among other things. Discuss how a decision not to dissolve Bear Agency might be supported by the business judgment rule. [*Schirmer v. Bear*, 271 Ill.App.3d 778, 648 N.E.2d 1131, 208 Ill.Dec. 209 (1994)]

18–9. DUTY OF LOYALTY. Mackinac Cellular Corp. offered to sell Robert Broz a license to operate a cellular phone system in Michigan. Broz was a director of Cellular Information Systems, Inc. (CIS). CIS, as a result of bankruptcy proceedings, was in the process of selling its cellular holdings. Broz did not formally present the opportunity to the CIS board, but he told some of the firm's officers and directors, who replied that CIS was not interested. At the time, PriCellular, Inc., a firm that was interested in the Michigan license, was attempting to buy CIS. Without telling PriCellular, Broz bought the license himself. After PriCellular took over CIS, the company filed a suit in a Delaware state court against Broz, alleging that he had usurped a corporate opportunity. For what reasons might a court decide that Broz had done nothing wrong? Discuss. [*Broz v. Cellular Information Systems, Inc.*, 673 A.2d 148 (Del. 1996)]

18–10. A QUESTION OF ETHICS

Abe Schultz, Sol Schultz, and Lawrence Newfeld were the managing directors and officers of Chemical Dynamics, Inc., a close corporation. In 1967, the corporation leased a building in which to house its offices and operations. Included in the lease agreement was a provision giving Chemical Dynamics an option to purchase the property for $300,000. In 1970, because the corporation was experiencing financial problems and could not pay its rent, it assigned the lease and the purchase option to Newfeld in return for Newfeld's loan to the corporation of approximately $21,500. In 1973, Newfeld purchased the property. Eventually, when the corporation's financial situation had improved and its debts were paid, Abe Schultz sued Newfeld on behalf of the corporation, claiming that Newfeld had breached his fiduciary duty by usurping a corporate opportunity to purchase the property. Given these facts, consider the following questions. [*Chemical Dynamics, Inc. v. Newfeld*, 728 S.W.2d 590 (Mo.App. 1987)]

1. In Schultz's suit against Newfeld, the trial court held that Newfeld has not usurped a corporate opportunity because the corporation "knowingly, willingly, and voluntarily sold bargained, granted and transferred its entire interest in the lease, including the option to purchase the real estate, to Newfeld as consideration for the lease." The court placed emphasis on the language of the corporation's assignment, which was titled a "Bill of Sale," and stated that the corporation was

"surrendering . . . all benefits of the lease" to Newfeld as consideration for the loan. Schultz countered, however, that the language of the agreement was merely to give Newfeld the greatest degree of protection from creditors—ostensibly, by keeping the lease separate from the corporation's other assets by assigning it wholly to Newfeld. Schultz stated that, notwithstanding the language of the assignment, his understanding was that Newfeld was taking the lease *on behalf of, and in the name of, the corporation.* Is it possible that Newfeld could have led the other directors into this belief and merely demanded the language in the agreement to protect the lease from the corporation's many creditors? If so, was the subsequent purchase a violation of a legal or ethical duty?

2. Neither the trial court nor the appellate court considered it significant that the option to purchase the lease had expired before Newfeld's eventual purchase of the property. Because Newfeld had acquired the option in the original loan-for-lease transaction, the court held that it was his right to make the eventual purchase free from any latent interest that the corporation might have. If the option had expired, though, was it not legally required that the corporation be given first opportunity to buy the real estate? Does it matter legally and ethically that the corporation was not in a position to buy the real estate at the time the owners offered it to Newfeld?

18–11. Case Briefing Assignment

Examine Case A.4 [*Maschmeier v. Southside Press, Ltd.*, 435 N.W.2d 377 (Iowa App. 1989)] in Appendix A. The case has been excerpted there in great detail. Review and then brief the case, making sure that you include answers to the following questions in your brief.

1. What was the primary reason for this lawsuit?
2. What restriction did the corporate bylaws place on the transfer of corporate shares? On transfer, how was the price of shares to be determined?
3. How did the majority shareholders (the parents) effectively "freeze out" or "squeeze out" the minority shareholders (the sons)?
4. Why was it necessary for the court to determine the fair value of shares, as the shareholders had agreed in the bylaws on a method for accomplishing this?
5. Why was it necessary to establish that the majority shareholders had acted oppressively toward the minority shareholders or wasted corporate assets before the court could fashion its particular remedy in this case?

Unit Three—Cumulative Hypothetical Problem

18–12.. *Samuel Polson has an idea for a new software application. Polson hires an assistant and invests a considerable amount of his own time and money developing the application. To develop other software, and to manufacture and market his applications, Polson needs capital.*

1. Polson borrows $5,000 from his friend, Michael Brant. Polson promises to repay Brant the $5,000 in three weeks. Brant, in urgent need of money, borrows $5,000 from his friend Mary Viva and assigns his rights to the $5,000 Polson owes him to Viva in return for the loan. Viva notifies Polson of the assignment. Polson pays Brant the $5,000 on the date stipulated in their contract. Brant refuses to give the money to Viva, and Viva sues Polson. Is Polson obligated to pay Viva $5,000 also? Discuss.
2. Polson learns that a competitor, Trivan, Inc., has already filed for a patent on a nearly identical program and has manufactured and sold the software to some customers. Polson learns from a reliable source that Trivan paid Polson's assistant a substantial sum of money to obtain a copy of the program. What legal recourse does Polson have against Trivan? Discuss fully.
3. While Polson is developing his idea and founding his business, he has no income. He continues to have living expenses, however, as well as payments due on his mortgage, various credit-card debts, and some loans that he took out to pay for his son's college tuition. As his business begins to make money, Polson files for Chapter 7 liquidation to be rid of his personal debts entirely, even though he believes that he could probably pay them off over a four-year period if he scrimped and used every cent available to pay his creditors. Are all of Polson's personal debts dischargeable under Chapter 7, including the debts incurred for his son's education? Given the fact that Polson could foreseeably pay off his debts over a four-year period, will the court allow Polson to obtain relief under Chapter 7? Why or why not?
4. Polson is the sole owner of the business and pays no business income taxes. What is the form of Polson's business organization? What other options, in terms of business organizational forms, does Polson have? What are the advantages and disadvantages of each option? If Polson decides to incorporate the business under the name Polson Software, Inc., what steps will he need to take to do so?

FOCUS ON ETHICS

THE PRIVATE ENVIRONMENT

Many aspects of the private environment lend themselves to ethical analysis. Businesspersons certainly face ethical questions when they deal with the application of black-letter law to contracts. (*Black-letter law* is an informal term for the principles of law that courts generally accept or that are embodied in statutes.) Courts, for example, generally will not inquire into the adequacy of the consideration given in a contract. In other words, a court will not reevaluate a contract to determine whether what each party gave is equivalent to what each party received.

Ethical questions are also at the core of many principles of the law of sales. Many of the UCC provisions such as good faith and commercial reasonableness, though designed to meet the practical needs of business dealings, express ethical standards as well. Product liability also involves ethics. Many of the principles of product liability are based on principles designed to aid individuals injured, without extensive inquiry into issues of fault.

Ethical issues are not only prevalent in dealings between the firm and others outside the firm, they also are fundamental to relations within the firm. Ethical considerations, for example, underlie the fiduciary duties owed by corporate directors and managers to shareholders. The fiduciary duties are central to the relationship between the owners of a corporation and those charged

with managing its affairs. In this *Focus on Ethics,* we examine selected areas in which ethical problems relate to the private environment of business.

ETHICS AND FREEDOM OF CONTRACT

In Chapter 2, we pointed out that in general, the responsible business manager will evaluate a business transaction on the basis of three criteria—legality, profitability, and ethics. But what does acting ethically mean in the area of contracts? If an individual with whom you enter into a contract fails to look after his or her own interests, is that your fault, and should you therefore be doing something about it? If the contract happens to be to your advantage and therefore to the other party's detriment, do you have a responsibility to correct the situation?

For example, assume that a neighbor whom you rarely see places a "for sale" sign on her car, offering to sell it for $3,000. You learn that she is moving to another state and needs the extra cash to help finance the move. You know that she could easily get $6,000 for the car, and you congratulate yourself on your good fortune. Even if you do not need a car, you can purchase it and then sell it at a profit. But you also learn that your neighbor has failed to do the preliminary research—checking Blue Book prices and so on—that most reasonable individuals would undertake when selling a car, and therefore she is unaware that the car is underpriced.

Are you obligated to tell her that she is essentially giving away $3,000 if she sells you the car for only $3,000? Do you have an ethical responsibility toward this woman—whom you will probably never see again—simply because she failed to look after her own interests? This kind of situation, transplanted into the world of commercial transactions, raises an obvious question: At what point should the savvy businessperson cease looking after his or her own economic welfare and become "his brother's keeper," so to speak?

The answer to this question is not simple. On the one hand, a common ethical assumption in our society is that individuals should be held responsible for the consequences of their own actions, including their contractual promises. This principle is expressed in the legal concept of freedom of contract, a topic discussed in Chapter 9. Applying this ethical precept to the above example, you could justify not saying anything about the true value of the car to your neighbor by stating that you were upholding the principle of freedom of contract. On the other hand, a common assumption in our society

Focus on Ethics

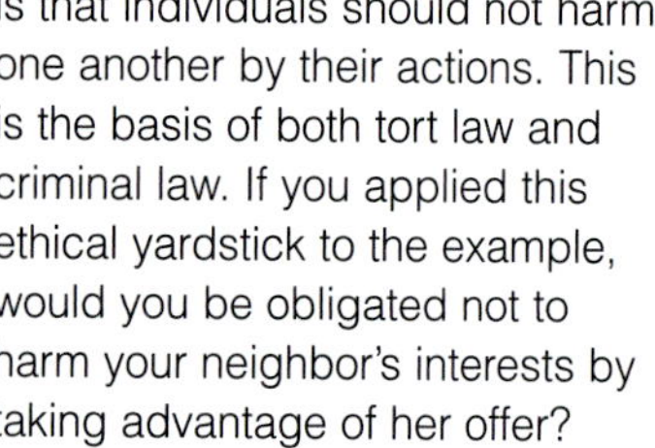

is that individuals should not harm one another by their actions. This is the basis of both tort law and criminal law. If you applied this ethical yardstick to the example, would you be obligated not to harm your neighbor's interests by taking advantage of her offer? How would you balance these two ethical principles?

In the area of contract law, ethical behavior often involves just such a "balancing act." In the example, if you purchased the car and the neighbor later learned its true value and sued you for the difference, very likely no court of law would agree that the contract should be rescinded. In other words, the law would not "answer" your ethical question in this case. The court probably would not come to the aid of the neighbor, because she could easily have prevented the injustice by learning, as a "reasonable person" would have, the market value of the car. There are times, however, when courts will hold that the principle of freedom of contract should give way to the principle that people should not be harmed by the actions of others. We look below at some examples of how parties to contracts may be excused from performance under their contracts if that is the only way injustice can be prevented.

Unconscionability

The doctrine of unconscionability represents a good example of how the law attempts to enforce ethical behavior. Under this doctrine, a contract may be deemed to be so unfair to one party as to be unenforceable—even though that party voluntarily agreed to the contract's terms. Unconscionable action, like unethical action, is incapable of precise definition. Information about the particular facts and specific circumstances surrounding the contract is essential. For example, a contract with a marginally literate consumer might be seen as unfair and unenforceable, whereas the same contract with a major business firm would be upheld by the courts.

Section 2–302 of the Uniform Commercial Code, which incorporates the common law concept of unconscionability, similarly does not define the concept with any precision. Rather, it leaves it to the courts to determine when a contract is so one sided and unfair to one party as to be unconscionable and thus unenforceable.

Usually, courts will do all they can to save contracts rather than render them unenforceable. Thus, only in extreme situations, as when a contract or clause is so one sided as to "shock the conscience" of the court, will a court hold a contract or contractual clause unconscionable.

Ethics and Sales: Good Faith and Commercial Reasonableness

Good faith and commercial reasonableness are two key concepts that permeate the UCC and help to prevent unethical behavior by businesspersons. These two concepts are read into every contract and impose certain duties on all parties. Section 2–311(1) of the UCC indicates that when parties leave the particulars of performance to be specified by one of the parties, "[a]ny such specification must be made in good faith and within limits set by commercial reasonableness."

The requirement of commercial reasonableness means that the term subsequently supplied by one party should not come as a surprise to the other. The party filling in the missing term may not take advantage of the opportunity to add a contractual term that will be beneficial to himself or herself (and detrimental to the other party) and then demand contractual performance of the other party that was totally unanticipated. Under the UCC, the party filling in the missing term may not deviate from what is commercially reasonable in the context of the transaction. Courts frequently look to course of dealing, usage of trade, and the surrounding circumstances in determining what is commercially reasonable in a given situation.

Good Faith

The obligation of good faith is particularly important in so-called output and requirements contracts. UCC 2–306 states that "quantity" in these contracts "means such actual output or requirements as may occur in good faith." For example, if General Motors contracts with Jalin's Fuel Injectors to purchase all of Jalin's output, Jalin's cannot then increase its production from one eight-hour shift per day to three eight-hour shifts per day to make greater

Focus on Ethics

profits under the contract. As another example, assume that Mandrow's Machines has fifty employees assembling IBM clones. Mandrow's has a requirements contract with Advanced Tech Circuit Boards under which Advanced Tech is to supply Mandrow's with all of the circuit boards it needs. If all of a sudden Mandrow's quadruples the size of its business, it cannot insist that Advanced Tech supply it with all of its requirements as specified in the original contract.

In many situations, parties may find it advantageous (profitable) to avoid a legal obligation. Without the counterobligation of good faith, the potential for abuse in the area of sales contracts exists. Suppose, for example, that the market price of the goods subject to a requirements contract rises rapidly and dramatically because of a shortage of materials necessary to their production. The buyer could claim that his or her needs are equivalent to the entire output of the seller. Then, after buying all of the seller's output at the contract price, which is substantially below the market price, the buyer could turn around and sell the goods that he or she does not need at the higher market price. Under the UCC, this type of unethical behavior is prohibited—even though the buyer in this instance has not technically breached the contract.

The Ethical Considerations of Debt

We are certainly many years away from that period in our history when debtors' prisons existed. Today, debtors are in a much more favorable position. If a creditor fails to exercise care in all aspects of the creditor-debtor relationship, the creditor may end up being accused of fraud, negligence, breach of contract, breach of the duty of good faith, or some other claim that may render the debt uncollectible. If worst comes to worst, the debtor can file for protection under bankruptcy law. Indeed, some now say that we have proceeded too far in the direction of protecting debtors and have made it too easy for debtors to avoid paying what they legally owe. Clearly, it is difficult to ensure the rights of both debtors and creditors at the same time, and laws governing debtor-creditor relationships are frequently perceived, by one group or another, as being unfair.

Creditors are given numerous remedies under both the common law and statutory law to protect their legitimate interests. When these rights and remedies are invoked, however, the creditor is often considered by the general public to be employing unfair tactics. For many, the question of fairness revolves around the purpose for which the debt was incurred. If the debt was incurred for a needed item, such as a refrigerator, then common opinion seems to be that the debtor should be dealt with leniently. If, however, the debt was incurred for a trip to the Bahamas, the issue appears to be significantly different.

There is obviously no way in which the law can protect both debtors and creditors at all times under all circumstances. Trade-offs must be made in attempting to balance the rights of both groups, and the trade-offs made often lead to questions of fairness and justice. We look below at several aspects of debtor-creditor relationships that frequently pose ethical questions.

Ethics and Bankruptcy

The first goal of bankruptcy law is to provide relief and protection to debtors who have "gotten in over their heads." Society has generally concluded that everyone should be given the chance to start over again. Thus, bankruptcy law is a balancing act between providing such a chance and ensuring that creditors are given "a fair shake." Understandably, ethical issues arise in the process.

Is Bankruptcy Too Easy?

The total number of bankruptcies has increased dramatically since the Bankruptcy Code was revised in 1978 to make it easier to petition for bankruptcy relief. In 1976, for example, 193,000 debtors petitioned for bankruptcy. By 1997, bankruptcy filings exceeded 1.1 million per year. An estimated 90 to 95 percent of that number are personal bankruptcies. Additionally, the average amount owed by debtors when they file for bankruptcy has risen significantly in the past decade—from about $75,000 in 1988 to more than $130,000 in 1997. Has the law gone too far in providing relief for debtors?

Consider the concept of bankruptcy from the point of view of the creditor. The creditor has

FOCUS ON ETHICS

extended a transfer of purchasing power from himself or herself to the debtor. That transfer of purchasing power represents a transfer of an asset for an asset. The debtor obtains the asset of money, goods, or services, and the creditor obtains the asset called a *secured* or *unsecured* legal obligation to pay. Once the debtor is in bankruptcy, voluntarily or involuntarily, the asset that the creditor owns most often has a diminished value. Indeed, in many circumstances, that asset has no value. Yet the easier it becomes for debtors to hide behind bankruptcy laws, the greater will be the incentive for debtors to use such laws to avoid payment of legally owed sums of money.

Bankruptcy and Economics

Among other things, the increasing number of bankruptcies means that creditors incur higher risks in making loans, because bankruptcy shifts the cost of the debt from the debtor to the creditor. To compensate for these higher risks, creditors will do one or more of the following: increase the interest rates charged to everyone, require more security (collateral), or be more selective in the granting of credit. Thus, the more lenient bankruptcy laws are, the better off will be those debtors who find themselves in bankruptcy; but those debtors who will never be in bankruptcy will be worse off. Ethical concerns here must be matched with the economic concerns of other groups of individuals affected by the law.

Consequences for Debtors

Some contend that debtors take unfair advantage of bankruptcy law and see bankruptcy as an easy solution to their financing problems. While it is true that there is less of a stigma attached to bankruptcy today than there once was, bankruptcy is never easy for debtors. Many debtors feel a sense of shame and failure when they petition for bankruptcy. They also have to face the consequences of bankruptcy—blemished credit ratings for up to ten years, higher interest charges for new debts, such as those incurred through the purchase of cars or homes, and so on. They may even find it difficult to get jobs.

There is no law prohibiting private employers from discriminating against job applicants on the basis of the applicants' prior bankruptcy status. The Bankruptcy Code does provide that the *government* may not "deny employment to, terminate the employment of, or discriminate with respect to employment against" a person who has been a bankruptcy debtor. In the parallel provision concerning private employers, however, the Code omits the phrase "deny employment to." Therefore, although a private employer may not fire an employee who has filed for bankruptcy protection, the employer may refuse to hire a job applicant who has done so. The courts provide little relief for job applicants who encounter such an experience, generally holding that the wording of the Code's provisions in these respects reflects the specific intentions of the legislators who drafted those provisions.[1]

Clearly, balancing the rights of debtors and creditors is not easy. Because of the consequences of bankruptcy, debtors do not always get the "fresh start" promised by bankruptcy law. At the same time, creditors rarely are able to recover all of the money owed them once a debtor petitions for bankruptcy.

Student Loans and Chapter 13

Many students rely on government-guaranteed loans to help them meet college tuition and other expenses. Repaying these loans may be difficult for those individuals who obtain jobs but, for one reason or another, have insufficient income to cover their debts. If they enter bankruptcy proceedings, however, they will find that, unless repaying government-guaranteed loans creates an undue hardship, the loans are not dischargeable. The Bankruptcy Code, by prohibiting the dischargeability of student loans in bankruptcy, expresses the policy that the public should not have to bear the burden of covering, through taxes, these loans.

In effect, this policy has shifted the burden of student-loan default to the other creditors of the individuals in bankruptcy. Under a Chapter 13 repayment plan, for

1. See, for example, *Pastore v. Medford Savings Bank,* 186 Bankr. 553 (D.Mass. 1995).

FOCUS ON ETHICS

example, if 100 percent of a student-loan debt must be paid off, there may not be enough assets left over to pay other creditors. Some courts have recently held that giving student loans priority unfairly discriminates against unsecured creditors. In *Groves v. LaBarge,*[2] for example, the district court affirmed the bankruptcy court's refusal to confirm a repayment plan in which student loans were to be repaid in full yet other, unsecured claims were to receive only 10 to 40 percent of the total amount due. The court held that the plan unfairly discriminated against the class of general creditors and stated that "to allow discrimination solely on the basis of non-dischargeability enables the debtor to exit bankruptcy free of student loan liability at the expense of other unsecured creditors, and [i]n essence . . . [to] shift the student loan non-dischargeability burden from herself on to her general unsecured creditors." Other courts have also rejected the principle that the payment of student loans should take priority over the payment of general creditors.[3]

As we have emphasized, bankruptcy law represents an attempt to balance the interests of debtors and creditors. When one of those creditors is the government (as the guarantor of student loans), the rights of the tax-paying public must also be weighed. Although Congress, through the Bankruptcy Code, has deemed it fair that student loans must be paid off at the expense of other creditors, clearly, some courts, including the court hearing the *Groves* case, do not agree.

2. 160 Bankr. 121 (E.D.Mo. 1993).

3. See, for example, *McCullough v. Brown,* 162 Bankr. 506 (N.D.Ill. 1993).

Business and Fiduciary Duties Revisited

An important duty that arises in the law of agency, and that applies to all partners and corporate directors, officers, and management personnel, is the duty of loyalty. As caretakers of the shareholders' wealth, corporate directors and officers also have a fiduciary duty to exercise care when making decisions affecting the corporate enterprise.

The Duty of Loyalty

Every individual has his or her own personal interests, which may at times conflict with the interests of the partnership or corporation with which he or she is affiliated. In particular, a partner or a corporate director may face a conflict between personal interests and the interests of the business entity. Corporate officers may find themselves in a position to acquire assets that would also benefit the corporation if acquired in the corporation's name.

In one landmark case, *Guth v. Loft, Inc.,*[4] Charles G. Guth, the president and a director of Loft, Inc., a soft-drink bottling company, negotiated with the Coca-Cola Company for a discount on its syrups. When negotiations with Coca-Cola failed to result in a discount for Loft, Guth decided to see what Pepsi Cola could offer. During his investigation of this possibility, Guth set up a new corporation to acquire the secret formula and trademark for the manufacture of Pepsi Cola. He did so without offering the opportunity to Loft. A shareholder brought a suit against Guth, arguing that the shares of the new corporation should belong to Loft, and not to Guth personally. The shareholder prevailed. The court ruled that Guth had *usurped* a corporate opportunity in violation of his duty of loyalty to the corporation.

4. 5 A.2d 503 (Del. 1939).

The Duty of Care

In addition to the duty of loyalty, every corporate director or officer has a duty of care, which involves a duty to be informed and to make informed decisions. Traditionally, though, the duty of care did not include a duty to monitor the behavior of corporate employees to detect and prevent wrongdoing unless the directors had some reason to suspect that wrongful acts were in fact occurring. For example, in a leading case on the issue, the Delaware Supreme Court held in 1963 that corporate directors did not have a duty "to install and operate a corporate system of espionage to ferret out wrongdoing which they have no reason to suspect exists."[5]

Enter the corporate sentencing guidelines in 1991. Under these

5. *Graham v. Allis-Chalmers Manufacturing Co.,* 188 A.2d 125 (Del. 1963).

Focus on Ethics

guidelines, the courts may impose—and have been imposing fairly regularly—substantial penalties on corporations and corporate directors for criminal wrongdoing. The guidelines, though, allow these penalties to be mitigated if a company can show that it has a compliance program in place—an effective program to detect and prevent wrongdoing by corporate personnel. The question here is, do the guidelines imply that directors have a *duty* to have such a program in place?

In 1996, a Delaware chancery (trial) court suggested that corporate directors do have such a duty. The case involved criminal behavior on the part of a company's middle-level and lower-level employees, and the question was whether the directors, who were apparently unaware of the actions, had breached their oversight duties. Under the traditional rule, as mentioned, directors had no duty to detect and "ferret out" wrongdoing. According to the court in this case, though, the corporate sentencing guidelines have changed this standard. The court stated that "a director's obligation includes a duty to attempt in good faith to assure that a corporation information and reporting system, which the board concludes is adequate, exists." The court also noted that in view of the potential impact of the sentencing guidelines on any business organization, "[a]ny rational person attempting in good faith to meet an organizational governance responsibility would be bound to take into account this development and the enhanced penalties and the opportunities for reduced sanctions that it offers." [6]

Clearly, the corporate sentencing guidelines are altering the business and legal environment in which directors operate. In the case just discussed, the directors were able to avoid liability because there *was* a compliance program in place—which the company agreed to modify so that it would be more effective in the future.

Discussion Questions

1. Suppose that you contract to purchase steel at a fixed price per ton. There is a lengthy steelworkers' strike, which causes the price of steel to triple from the price specified in the contract. If you demand that the supplier fulfill the contract, the supplier will go out of business. What are your ethical obligations in this situation? What are your legal rights?

2. How can a court objectively measure good faith and commercial reasonableness?

3. Merchants may "huff and puff" their wares as they traditionally have and still—in most instances—not violate their duty of dealing honestly and in good faith with the buyers of their products. Do you think that the customary practice of puffing is a fundamentally dishonest practice that should be abandoned? Is there anything the law can, or should, do to ensure that buyers and lessees will not be taken in by sellers' and lessors' statements of opinion?

4. Do you think that the law favors debtors at the expense of creditors, or vice versa? Is there any way a better balance between creditors' and debtors' interests could be achieved?

5. Three decades ago, prosecution of corporations and corporate directors for crimes was a rare event, and penalties for corporate crime were relatively light. Today, this is no longer true. According to the U.S. Sentencing Commission, companies are being sentenced under the corporate sentencing guidelines at a rate of more than two a week, and corporate fines reaching hundreds of millions of dollars are not especially uncommon. Does this development mean that corporations are committing more crimes today than in the past? Or is the government just getting tougher on corporate crime? How can a company avoid liability for crimes committed by its employees?

---

6. *In re Caremark International, Inc. Derivative Litigation* (Del.Ch. 1996)[1996 WL 549894]. This decision, which has not been published in a reporter, can be accessed by use of the WESTLAW (WL) citation.

UNIT FOUR

THE EMPLOYMENT ENVIRONMENT

CONTENTS

CHAPTER 19

AGENCY

ONE OF THE MOST COMMON, IMPORTANT, and pervasive legal relationships is that of **agency.** In an agency relationship between two parties, one of the parties, called the *agent,* agrees to represent or act for the other, called the *principal.* The principal has the right to control the agent's conduct in matters entrusted to the agent. By using agents, a principal can conduct multiple business operations simultaneously in various locations. Thus, for example, contracts that bind the principal can be made at different places with different persons at the same time.

A familiar example of an agent is a corporate officer who serves in a representative capacity for the owners of the corporation. In this capacity, the officer has the authority to bind the principal (the corporation) to a contract. Indeed, agency law is essential to the existence and operation of a corporate entity, because only through its agents can a corporation function and enter into contracts. Because agency relationships permeate the business world, an understanding of the law of agency is crucial to understanding business law.

SECTION 1

AGENCY RELATIONSHIPS

Section 1(1) of the *Restatement (Second) of Agency*[1] defines *agency* as "the fiduciary relation which results from the manifestation of consent by one person to another that the other shall act in his behalf and subject to his control, and consent by the other so to act." The term **fiduciary** is at the heart of agency law. The term can be used both as a noun and as an adjective. When used as a noun, it refers to a person having a duty created by his or her undertaking to act primarily for another's benefit in matters connected with the undertaking. When used as an adjective, as in "fiduciary relationship," it means that the relationship involves trust and confidence.

In a principal-agent relationship, the parties have agreed that the agent will act *on behalf and instead of* the principal in negotiating and transacting business with third persons. Agency relationships commonly exist between employers and employees. A salesperson in a department store, for example, is an agent of the store owner (the principal) and acts on the owner's behalf. Any sale of goods made by the salesperson to a customer is binding on the principal. Similarly, representations of fact made by the salesperson with respect to the goods sold are usually binding on the principal. Agency relationships may sometimes also exist between employers and independent contractors who are hired to perform special tasks or services.

EMPLOYER-EMPLOYEE RELATIONSHIPS

Normally, all employees who deal with third parties are deemed to be agents. All employment laws (state and federal) apply only to the employer-employee relationship. Statutes governing Social Security, withholding taxes, workers' compensation, unemployment compensation, workplace safety laws, employment discrimination, and the like (see Chapters 20 and 21) are applicable only when there exists an employer-employee relationship. *These laws do not apply to the independent contractor.*

Because employees may be deemed agents of their employers, agency law and employment law overlap considerably. Agency relationships, though, as will become apparent, can exist outside an employee-employer relationship and thus have a broader reach than employment laws do.

EMPLOYER–INDEPENDENT CONTRACTOR RELATIONSHIPS

Independent contractors are not employees, because by definition, those who hire them have no control over the details of their work performance. Section 2 of the *Restatement (Second) of Agency* defines an **independent contractor** as follows:

> [An independent contractor is] a person who contracts with another to do something for him but who is not controlled by the other nor subject to the other's right to control with respect to his physical conduct in the performance of the undertaking. He may or may not be an agent.

Building contractors and subcontractors are independent contractors, and a property owner does not control the acts of either of these professionals. Truck drivers who own their equipment and hire out on a per-job basis are independent contractors, but truck drivers who drive company trucks on a regular basis are usually employees.

The relationship between a principal and an independent contractor may or may not involve an agency relationship. To illustrate: An owner of real estate who hires a real estate broker to negotiate a sale of his or her property not only has contracted with an independent contractor (the real estate broker) but also has established an agency relationship for the specific purpose of assisting in the sale of the property. Another example is an insurance agent, who is both an independent contractor and an agent of the insurance company for which he or she sells policies.

CRITERIA FOR ESTABLISHING EMPLOYEE STATUS

A question that frequently comes before the courts has to do with whether a worker should be deemed an employee or an independent contractor. How a court decides this issue can have a significant effect on the rights and liabilities of the parties.

For example, employers normally are held liable as principals for the actions of their employee-agents if those actions are carried out within the scope of employment. Additionally, federal and state statutory laws governing employment discrimination, workplace safety, and compensation for on-the-job injuries normally apply only to employees—not independent

1. The *Restatement (Second) of Agency* is an authoritative summary of the law of agency and is often referred to by jurists in their decisions and opinions.

contractors. The tax liability of employers is also affected by the determination of worker status. Whereas employers are responsible for certain taxes, such as Social Security and unemployment taxes, with respect to employees, they are not responsible for these taxes if their workers are classified as independent contractors.

In deciding whether a worker is deemed to be an employee or an independent contractor, courts often consider the following questions:

1. How much control can the employer exercise over the details of the work? (If an employer can exercise considerable control over the details of the work and the day-to-day activities of the worker, this indicates employee status. This is perhaps the most important factor weighed by the courts in determining employee status.)
2. Is the worker engaged in an occupation or business distinct from that of the employer? (If so, this points to independent-contractor status, not employee status.)
3. Is the work usually done under the employer's direction or by a specialist without supervision? (If the work is usually done under the employer's direction, this indicates employee status.)
4. Does the employer supply the tools at the place of work? (If so, this indicates employee status.)
5. For how long is the person employed? (If the person is employed for a long period of time, this indicates employee status.)
6. What is the method of payment—by time period or at the completion of the job? (Payment by time period, such as once every two weeks or once a month, indicates employee status.)
7. What degree of skill is required of the worker? (If a great degree of skill is required, this may indicate that the person is an independent contractor hired for a specialized job and not an employee.)

Often, the criteria for determining employee status are established by a statute or administrative agency regulation. The Internal Revenue Service (IRS), for example, has guidelines for its auditors to follow in determining whether a worker is an independent contractor or an employee. In the past, auditors were to consider twenty factors in making such a decision. New guidelines effective in 1997, however, encourage IRS examiners to look closely at just one of those factors—the degree of control the business exercises over the worker. The IRS tends to scrutinize closely a firm's classification of a worker as an independent contractor rather than an employee, because employers can avoid certain tax liabilities by hiring independent contractors rather than employees.

In the following case, an insurance broker who lost her job wanted to take advantage of the protection against discrimination offered to employees under a state statute. Because that statute governed only employer-employee relationships, the plaintiff tried to convince the court that she was an employee rather than an independent contractor.

CASE 19.1 Scott v. Massachusetts Mutual Life Insurance Co.

Court of Appeals of New York, 1995. 86 N.Y.2d 429, 657 N.E.2d 769, 633 N.Y.S.2d 754.

BACKGROUND AND FACTS *James Blatt hired Marilyn Scott to sell insurance for the Massachusetts Mutual Life Insurance Company. Their contract stated, "Nothing in this contract shall be construed as creating the relationship of employer and employee." The contract was terminable at will by either party. Scott hired and trained other agents according to Massachusetts Mutual's guidelines, but she financed her own office and staff, was paid according to performance, had no taxes withheld from her checks, and could sell products of Massachusetts Mutual's competitors. When Blatt terminated their contract, Scott filed a suit in a New York state court against him and Massachusetts Mutual. Scott claimed that she had been discriminated against on the basis of her gender, age, and marital status in violation of a state law prohibiting employment discrimination. The defendants filed a motion for summary judgment on the ground that the law applied only to employees and Scott was an independent contractor. The court granted the motion, which an appellate court upheld. Scott appealed to New York's highest state court.*

IN THE LANGUAGE OF THE COURT

TITONE, Judge.

* * * *

* * * [P]laintiff was responsible for financing her own operating expenses and support staff, was paid by performance rather than a salary, did not have

Federal, State or local taxes withheld from her pay, could sell competitors' products and had agreed by contract to operate as an independent contractor. Although plaintiff alleges that she was required to recruit and train agents according to defendant Massachusetts Mutual's guidelines, that was true only for agents whose hiring was financed by defendant and not by plaintiff, and, in any event, reflects only minimal control over plaintiff's own work. Additionally, the fact that plaintiff was compelled to attend regular company meetings and was asked to draw up a job description for her position are not inconsistent with her status as an independent contractor. * * * [A]t most, * * * defendants exercised minimal control over plaintiff's own daily work product.

The only conclusion to be drawn from these facts is that plaintiff operated her office with a high degree of independence not found in a traditional employer/employee relationship.

DECISION AND REMEDY *The Court of Appeals of New York dismissed Scott's claim. Because her employer exercised only minimal control over her work, Scott was not considered to be an "employee."*

SECTION 2

FORMATION OF THE AGENCY RELATIONSHIP

Agency relationships are *consensual;* that is to say, they come about by voluntary consent and agreement between the parties. Generally, the agreement need not be in writing, and consideration is not required.

A principal must have contractual capacity. A person who cannot legally enter into contracts directly should not be allowed to do so indirectly through an agent. Because an agent derives the authority to enter into contracts from the principal and because a contract made by an agent is legally viewed as a contract of the principal, it is immaterial whether the agent personally has the legal capacity to make that contract. Thus, a minor can be an agent but in some states cannot be a principal appointing an agent.[2] (When a minor is permitted to be a principal, however, any resulting contracts will be voidable by the minor principal but not by the adult third party.) In sum, any person can be an agent, regardless of whether he or she has the capacity to contract. Even a person who is legally incompetent can be appointed an agent.

An agency relationship can be created for any legal purpose. An agency relationship created for a purpose that is illegal or contrary to public policy is unenforceable. If LaSalle (as principal) contracts with Burke (as agent) to sell illegal narcotics, the agency relationship is unenforceable, because selling illegal narcotics is a felony and is contrary to public policy. It is also illegal for medical doctors and other licensed professionals to employ unlicensed agents to perform professional actions.

Generally, there are four ways in which an agency relationship can arise: by agreement of the parties, by ratification, by estoppel, and by operation of law. We look here at each of these possibilities.

AGENCY BY AGREEMENT

An agency agreement can take the form of an express written contract. An agency relationship can also be implied by conduct. For example, a hotel expressly allows only Hans Cooper to park cars, but Hans has no employment contract there. The hotel's manager tells Hans when to work, as well as where and how to park the cars. The hotel's conduct amounts to a manifestation of its willingness to have Hans park its customers' cars, and Hans can infer from the hotel's conduct that he has authority to act as a parking valet. It can be inferred that Hans is an agent for the hotel, his purpose being to provide valet parking services for hotel guests.

There are two main exceptions to oral agency agreements. In many states, the Statute of Frauds (discussed in Chapter 9) requires that whenever agency authority empowers the agent to enter into a contract that the Statute of Frauds requires to be in writing, the agent's authority from the principal must also be in writing. This is known as the **equal dignity rule.** It

2. Some courts have granted exceptions to allow a minor to appoint an agent for the limited purpose of contracting for the minor's necessities of life. See *Casey v. Kastel,* 237 N.Y. 305, 142 N.E. 671 (1924).

Exhibit 19–1 ■ A Sample General Power of Attorney

POWER OF ATTORNEY

GENERAL

Know All Men by These Presents: That I, ______________________________

____

the undersigned (jointly and severally, if more than one) hereby make, constitute and appoint ______________

____

as a true and lawful Attorney for me and in my name, place and stead and for my use and benefit:

(a) To ask, demand, sue for, recover, collect and receive each and every sum of money, debt, account, legacy, bequest, interest, dividend, annuity and demand (which now is or hereafter shall become due, owing or payable) belonging to or claimed by me, and to use and take any lawful means for the recovery thereof by legal process or otherwise, and to execute and deliver a satisfaction or release therefore, together with the right and power to compromise or compound any claim or demand;

(b) To exercise any or all of the following powers as to real property, any interest therein and/or any building thereon: To contract for, purchase, receive and take possession thereof and or evidence of title thereto; to lease the same for any term or purpose, including leases for business, residence, and oil and/or mineral development; to sell, exchange, grant or convey the same with or without warranty; and to mortgage, transfer in trust, or otherwise encumber or hypothecate the same to secure payment of a negotiable or non-negotiable note or performance of any obligation or agreement;

(c) To exercise any or all of the following powers as to all kinds of personal property and goods, wares and merchandise, choses in action and other property in possession or in action: To contract for, buy, sell, exchange, transfer and in any legal manner deal in and with the same; and to mortgage, transfer in trust, or otherwise encumber or hypothecate the same to secure payment of a negotiable or non-negotiable note or performance of any obligation or agreement;

(d) To borrow money and to execute and deliver negotiable or non-negotiable notes therefore with or without security; and to loan money and receive negotiable or non-negotiable notes therefore with such security as he shall deem proper;

(e) To create, amend, supplement and terminate any trust and to instruct and advise the trustee of any trust wherein I am or may be trustor or beneficiary; to represent and vote stock, exercise stock rights, accept and deal with any dividend, distribution or bonus, join in any corporate financing, reorganization, merger, liquidation, consolidation or other action and the extension, compromise, conversion, adjustment, enforcement or foreclosure, singly or in conjunction with others, of any corporate stock, bond, note, debenture or other security; to compound, compromise, adjust, settle and satisfy any obligation, secured or unsecured, owing by or to me and to give or accept any property and/or money whether or not equal to or less in value than the amount owing in payment, settlement or satisfaction thereof;

(f) To transact business of any kind or class and as my act and deed to sign, execute, acknowledge and deliver any deed, lease, assignment of lease, covenant, indenture, indemnity, agreement, mortgage, deed of trust, assignment of mortgage or of the beneficial interest under deed of trust, extension or renewal of any obligation, subordination or waiver of priority, hypothecation, bottomry, charter-party, bill of lading, bill of sale, bill, bond, note, whether negotiable or non-negotiable, receipt, evidence of debt, full or partial release or satisfaction of mortgage, judgment and other debt, request for partial or full reconveyance of deed of trust and such other instruments in writing of any kind or class as may be necessary or proper in the premises.

Giving and Granting unto my said Attorney full power and authority to do so and perform all and every act and thing whatsoever requisite, necessary or appropriate to be done in and about the premises as fully to all intents and purposes as I might or could do if personally present, hereby ratifying all that my said Attorney shall lawfully do or cause to be done by virtue of these presents. The powers and authority hereby conferred upon my said Attorney shall be applicable to all real and personal property or interests therein now owned or hereafter acquired by me and wherever situated.

My said Attorney is empowered hereby to determine in his sole discretion the time when, purpose for and manner in which any power herein conferred upon him shall be exercised, and the conditions, provisions and covenants of any instrument or document which may be executed by him pursuant hereto; and in the acquisition or disposition of real or personal property, my said Attorney shall have exclusive power to fix the terms thereof for cash, credit and/or property, and if on credit with or without security.

The undersigned, if a married woman, hereby further authorizes and empowers my said Attorney, as my duly authorized agent, to join in my behalf, in the execution of any instrument by which any community real property or any interest therein, now owned or hereafter acquired by my spouse and myself, or either of us, is sold, leased, encumbered, or conveyed.

When the context so requires, the masculine gender includes the feminine and/or neuter, and the singular number includes the plural.

WITNESS my hand this ____________ day of ______________________, 19____

______________________________ ______________________________

______________________________ ______________________________

State of California } SS.
County of ______________________

On ______________________________, before me, the undersigned, a Notary Public in and for said State, personally appeared ______________________________

____

known to me to be the person __________ whose name ______________________ subscribed to the within instrument and acknowledged that ______________________ executed the same.

Witness my hand and official seal. (Seal) ______________________________
Notary Public in and for said State.

applies most frequently to contracts for the sale of an interest in land or contracts that cannot be performed within one year. An exception to the equal dignity rule exists in modern business practice; an executive of a corporation, when acting for the corporation in an ordinary business situation, is not required to obtain written authority from the corporation.

Another agency agreement that must be in writting is a power of attorney. A **power of attorney** grants an agent either full or restricted authority to act in the principal's behalf and often is executed in a notarized writing.[3] The power of attorney can be special—permitting the agent to do specified acts only—or it can be general—permitting the agent to transact all business dealings for the principal. Of course, if the appointment comes within the Statute of Frauds, it must be in writing to be enforceable. See Exhibit 19–1.

AGENCY BY RATIFICATION

On occasion, a person who is in fact not an agent may make a contract on behalf of another (a principal). If the principal approves or affirms that contract by word or by action, an agency relationship is created by *ratification*. Ratification involves a question of intent, and intent can be expressed by either words or conduct.

AGENCY BY ESTOPPEL

When a principal causes a third person to believe that another person is his or her agent, and the third person acts to his or her detriment in reasonable reliance on that belief, the principal is "estopped to deny" the agency relationship. In such a situation, the principal's actions have created the *appearance* of an agency that does not in fact exist. The third person must prove that he or she *reasonably* believed that an agency relationship existed, however. (These concepts also apply when a person who is in fact an agent undertakes an action that is beyond the scope of his or her authority, as will be discussed later in this chapter.)

Suppose that Jerry accompanies Grant, a seed sales representative, to call on a customer, Palko, the proprietor of the Neighborhood Seed Store. Jerry has performed independent sales work but has never signed an employment agreement with Grant. Grant boasts to Palko that he wishes he had three more assistants "just like Jerry." Palko has reason to believe from Grant's statements that Jerry is an agent for Grant, because Grant's representation to Palko created the impression that Jerry was Grant's agent and had authority to solicit orders. Palko then places seed orders with Jerry. If Grant does not correct the impression that Jerry is an agent, Grant will be bound to fill the orders just as if Jerry were really Grant's agent. The acts or declarations of a purported agent in and of themselves do not create an agency by estoppel. Rather, it is the deeds or statements of the *principal* that create an agency by estoppel. If Jerry walked into Palko's store and claimed to be Grant's agent, when in fact he was not, and Grant had no knowledge of Jerry's representations, Grant would not be bound to any deal struck by Jerry and Palko.

The court in the following case considered whether an agency existed by estoppel between the owner of a jewelry cart in a mall and the seller of "The Only Completely Safe, Sterile Ear Piercing Method."

3. An agent who holds the power of attorney is called an *attorney in fact* for the principal. Despite the use of the word "attorney" here, *an agent does not have to be an attorney at law to hold a power of attorney.*

CASE 19.2 Williams v. Inverness Corp.

Supreme Judicial Court of Maine, 1995.
664 A.2d 1244.

COMPANY PROFILE *Inverness Corporation is the world's largest maker of body-piercing equipment. Sam Mann founded Inverness in 1975 with a design for piercing equipment that was more sterile and less threatening than the products then in use. The first year, sales totaled more than $750,000. Today, the company makes disposable ear-piercing kits, skin-care products, hair-removal waxes, electrolysis kits, and jewelry dips. Based in Fair Lawn, New Jersey, Inverness sells its products in fifty-two countries.*

BACKGROUND AND FACTS *Inverness Corporation markets the Inverness Ear Piercing System, which includes a training course, an "eye-catching assortment* *of selling aids" such as counter displays, and release forms that tout the system as "The Only Completely Safe, Sterile Ear Piercing Method." Margaret Barrera, the owner of a jewelry cart in a mall, bought the system, took the course, and set up the displays. Seventeen-year-old Angela Williams paid Barrera to pierce Williams's ear. The ear became infected, which led to complications. Williams's mother filed a suit on Angela's behalf in a Maine state court against Inverness and Barrera, claiming in part that Inverness was liable on a theory of agency by estoppel. The court issued a judgment in Williams's favor. Inverness appealed to Maine's highest state court.*

IN THE LANGUAGE OF THE COURT

DANA, Justice.

* * * *

* * * There are critical pieces of evidence in the record that can fairly be interpreted as leading to an inference that Inverness did hold Barrera out as its agent. Most important, a jury reasonably could infer that Inverness knew, or should have known, that Barrera distributed Inverness's release forms * * * .

* * * A jury reasonably could infer * * * that Inverness knew, or should have known, that Barrera was using the Inverness Ear Piercing System, that she displayed Inverness's "eye-catching assortment of selling aids," and that she used Inverness's training program.

Finally, there was evidence that Angela believed that Barrera was Inverness's agent, that Angela relied on Inverness's manifestations of agency, and that Angela's reliance on Barrera's care and skill was justifiable. * * * The release form and display promote the Inverness Ear Piercing System as "The Only Completely Safe, Sterile Ear Piercing Method."

DECISION AND REMEDY

The Supreme Judicial Court of Maine affirmed the lower court's judgment. Inverness was liable for Williams's injury because Inverness's actions created the appearance of an agency between it and Barrera.

AGENCY BY OPERATION OF LAW

There are other situations also in which the courts will find an agency relationship in the absence of a formal agreement. This may occur in family relationships. For example, suppose one spouse purchases certain basic necessaries and charges them to the other spouse's charge account. The courts will often rule that the latter is liable for payment of the necessaries, either because of a social policy of promoting the general welfare of the spouse or because of a legal duty to supply necessaries to family members.

Agency by operation of law may also occur in emergency situations, when the agent's failure to act outside the scope of his or her authority would cause the principal substantial loss. If the agent is unable to contact the principal, the courts will often grant this emergency power. For example, a railroad engineer may contract on behalf of his or her employer for medical care for an injured motorist hit by the train.

SECTION 3 DUTIES OF AGENTS AND PRINCIPALS

Once the principal-agent relationship has been created, both parties have duties that govern their conduct. As discussed previously, the principal-agent relationship is *fiduciary*—one of trust. In a fiduciary relationship, each party owes the other the duty to act with the utmost good faith. In this section, we examine the various duties of agents and principals.

AGENT'S DUTIES TO THE PRINCIPAL

Generally, the agent owes the principal five duties—performance, notification, loyalty, obedience, and accounting.

PERFORMANCE An implied condition in every agency contract is the agent's agreement to use reasonable diligence and skill in performing the work. When an agent fails to perform his or her duties, liability for breach of contract may result. The degree of skill or care required of an agent is usually that expected of a reasonable person under similar circumstances. Generally, this is interpreted to mean ordinary care. An agent may, however, have represented himself or herself as possessing special skills or, by virtue of his or her profession, be expected to exercise certain skills (such as those that an accountant or attorney possesses). Similarly, a corporate director, as an agent of the corporation, is expected to exercise a reasonable degree of diligence and oversight in the performance of his or her duties. In these situations, the agent is expected to exercise the skill or skills claimed. Failure to do so constitutes a breach of the agent's duty.

Not all agency relationships are based on contract. In some situations, an agent acts gratuitously—that is, without payment. A gratuitous agent cannot be liable for breach of contract, as there is no contract; he or she is subject only to tort liability. Once a gratuitous agent has begun to act in an agency capacity, he or she has the duty to continue to perform in that capacity in an acceptable manner and is subject to the same standards of care and duty to perform as other agents. For example, Bower's friend Alcott is a real estate broker. Alcott offers to sell Bower's farm at no charge. If Alcott never attempts to sell the farm, Bower has no legal cause of action to force Alcott to do so. If Alcott does find a buyer, however, but fails to provide a sales contract within a reasonable period of time, thus causing the buyer to seek other property, then Bower has a cause of action in tort against Alcott for negligence.

NOTIFICATION There is a maxim in agency law that notice to the agent is notice to the principal. An agent is thus required to notify the principal of all matters that come to his or her attention concerning the subject matter of the agency. This is the duty of notification. The law assumes that the principal knows of any information acquired by the agent that is relevant to the agency—regardless of whether the agent actually passes on this information to the principal.

LOYALTY Loyalty is one of the most fundamental duties in a fiduciary relationship. Basically stated, the agent has the duty to act solely for the benefit of his or her principal and not in the interest of the agent or a third party. For example, an agent cannot represent two principals in the same transaction unless both know of the dual capacity and consent to it. The duty of loyalty also means that any information or knowledge acquired through the agency relationship is confidential. It would be a breach of loyalty to disclose such information either during the agency relationship or after its termination. Typical examples of confidential information are trade secrets and customer lists compiled by the principal.

In short, the agent's loyalty must be undivided. The agent's actions must be strictly for the benefit of the principal and must not result in any secret profit for the agent. For example, suppose that Remington contracts with Averly, a real estate agent, to sell Remington's property. Averly knows that he can find a buyer who will pay substantially more for the property than Remington is asking. If Averly secretly purchased Remington's property, however, and then sold it at a profit to another buyer, Averly would breach his duty of loyalty as Remington's agent. Averly has a duty to act in Remington's best interests and can only become the purchaser in this situation with Remington's knowledge and approval.

OBEDIENCE When an agent is acting on behalf of the principal, a duty is imposed on that agent to follow all lawful and clearly stated instructions of the principal. Any deviation from such instructions is a violation of this duty. During emergency situations, however, when the principal cannot be consulted, the agent may deviate from the instructions without violating this duty. Whenever instructions are not clearly stated, the agent can fulfill the duty of obedience by acting in good faith and in a manner reasonable under the circumstances.

ACCOUNTING Unless an agent and a principal agree otherwise, the agent has the duty to keep and make available to the principal an account of all property and money received and paid out on behalf of the principal. The agent has a duty to maintain separate accounts for the principal's funds and the agent's personal funds, and no intermingling of these accounts is allowed. Whenever a licensed professional (such as an attorney) violates this duty to account, he or she may be subject to disciplinary proceedings carried out by the appropriate regulatory institution (such as the state bar association) in addition to being liable to the principal (the professional's client) for failure to account.

PRINCIPAL'S DUTIES TO THE AGENT

The principal also has certain duties to the agent. These duties relate to compensation, reimbursement and indemnification, cooperation, and safe working conditions.

COMPENSATION In general, when a principal requests certain services from an agent, the agent reasonably expects payment. The principal therefore has a duty to pay the agent for services rendered. For example, when an accountant or an attorney is asked to act as an agent, an agreement to compensate the agent for this service is implied. The principal also has a duty to pay that compensation in a timely manner. Except in a gratuitous agency relationship, in which the agent does not act for money, the principal must pay the agreed-on value for the agent's services. If no amount has been expressly agreed on, then the principal owes the agent the customary compensation for such services.

REIMBURSEMENT AND INDEMNIFICATION Whenever an agent disburses sums of money to fulfill the request of the principal or to pay for necessary expenses in the course of a reasonable performance of his or her agency duties, the principal has the duty to reimburse the agent for these payments. Agents cannot recover for expenses incurred by their own misconduct or negligence, however.

Subject to the terms of the agency agreement, the principal has the duty to *indemnify* (compensate) an agent for liabilities incurred because of authorized and lawful acts and transactions. For example, if the agent, on the principal's behalf, forms a contract with a third party, and the principal fails to perform the contract, the third party may sue the agent for damages. In this situation, the principal is obligated to compensate the agent for any costs incurred by the agent as a result of the principal's failure to perform the contract. Additionally, the principal must indemnify (pay) the agent for the value of benefits that the agent confers on the principal. The amount of indemnification is usually specified in the agency contract. If it is not, the courts will look to the nature of the business and the type of loss to determine the amount.

COOPERATION A principal has a duty to cooperate with the agent and to assist the agent in performing his or her duties. The principal must do nothing to prevent such performance. For example, when a principal grants an agent an exclusive territory, creating an *exclusive agency*, the principal cannot compete with the agent or appoint or allow another agent to so compete in violation of the exclusive agency. If the principal did so, he or she would be exposed to liability for the agent's lost sales or profits.

SAFE WORKING CONDITIONS The common law requires the principal to provide safe working premises, equipment, and conditions for all agents and employees. The principal has a duty to inspect working conditions and to warn agents and employees about any unsafe areas. When the agency is one of employment, the employer's liability is frequently covered by state workers' compensation insurance, which is the primary remedy for an employee's injury on the job (see Chapter 20).

SECTION 4 REMEDIES AND RIGHTS OF AGENTS AND PRINCIPALS

It is said that every wrong has its remedy. In business situations, disputes between agents and principals may arise out of either contract or tort laws and carry corresponding remedies. These remedies include monetary damages, termination of the agency relationship, injunction, and required accountings.

AGENT'S RIGHTS AND REMEDIES AGAINST PRINCIPAL

For every duty of the principal, the agent has a corresponding right. Therefore, the agent has the right to be compensated, reimbursed, and indemnified and to work in a safe environment. An agent also has the right to perform agency duties without interference by the principal.

Remedies of the agent for breach of duty by the principal follow normal contract and tort remedies. For example, under appropriate circumstances, an agent can lawfully withhold further performance and demand that the principal give an accounting.

When the principal-agent relationship is not contractual, an agent has no right to specific performance. An agent can recover for past services and future damages but cannot force the principal to allow him or her to continue acting as an agent.

PRINCIPAL'S RIGHTS AND REMEDIES AGAINST AGENT

In general, a principal has contract remedies for an agent's breach of fiduciary duties. The principal also has tort remedies for fraud, misrepresentation, negligence, deceit, libel, slander, and trespass committed by the agent. In addition, any breach of a fiduciary duty by an agent may justify the principal's termination of the agency. The main actions available to the principal are constructive trust, avoidance, and indemnification.

CONSTRUCTIVE TRUST Anything an agent obtains by virtue of the employment or agency relationship belongs to the principal. It is a breach of an agent's fiduciary duty to retain secretly benefits or profits that, by right, belong to the principal. For example, Andrews, a purchasing agent, gets cash rebates from a customer. If Andrews keeps the rebates, he violates his fiduciary duty to his principal, Metcalf. On finding out about the cash rebates, Metcalf can sue Andrews and recover them.

An agent is also prohibited from taking advantage of the agency relationship to obtain goods or property that the principal wants to purchase. For example, Peterson (the principal) wants to purchase property in the suburbs. Cox, Peterson's agent, learns that a valuable tract of land has just become available. Cox cannot buy the land for herself. Peterson gets the right of first refusal. If Cox purchases the land for her own benefit, the courts will impose a constructive trust on the land; that is, the land will be held for, and on behalf of, the principal despite the fact that the agent attempted to buy it in her own name.

AVOIDANCE When an agent breaches the agency agreement or agency duties under a contract, the principal has a right to avoid any contract entered into with the agent. This right of avoidance is at the election of the principal.

In the following case, a real estate agent was supposedly acting on behalf of a landowner for the sale of real estate. The trial court decided that the agent had breached his fiduciary duties, and therefore the principal could avoid the contract.

CASE 19.3 Ramsey v. Gordon

Court of Civil Appeals of Texas—Waco, 1978.
567 S.W.2d 868.

BACKGROUND AND FACTS *Ramsey, the plaintiff, was a licensed real estate broker and was also in the business of buying and holding land for resale. Gordon, the defendant, was the owner of approximately 181 acres of land and engaged Ramsey's services as a broker to find a buyer for the property. Ramsey, when he heard that the land was rapidly appreciating in value, told Gordon that he would buy the land himself. Gordon then agreed to sell Ramsey the tract of land for $800 per acre. A contract of sale to convey the property was drawn up; but before the contract was executed, Gordon conveyed the property to a third party for the same price ($800 per acre). Meanwhile, Ramsey, acting for himself, began negotiating for the resale of the property to another customer for a price of $1,250 per acre. Naturally, when Ramsey learned that Gordon had conveyed the property to another buyer, he blamed Gordon for his lost profits. Ramsey claimed that he had lost over $90,000 in profits on the resale of the property and brought an action against Gordon to recover this amount. Gordon maintained that Ramsey had breached his fiduciary duties as Gordon's agent by not finding a purchaser for the best price available. The trial court held for Gordon, and Ramsey appealed.*

IN THE LANGUAGE OF THE COURT

HALL, Justice.

* * * *

Ramsey does not challenge the finding that the property was increasing in value when the contract was being negotiated and made with Gordon, nor the findings that he knew the value was increasing and failed to disclose that fact to Gordon. Indeed, he may not do so because [the findings] are amply supported by the evidence and its inferences. His response to the conclusion that he breached his duties as Gordon's agent is to argue that he was only a purchaser and to cite Gordon's testimony that Gordon believed $800.00 per acre was a fair price when he made the contract. The over-all import of the record is that when it served Ramsey's purposes he would claim that under the contract he was Gordon's agent, but that in fact he used the contract to speculate with the property to his personal advantage without disclosure to Gordon. As we have said, the [trial] court found that Ramsey was Gordon's agent. Ramsey's testimony supports that finding.

Whenever an agent breaches his duty to his principal by becoming personally interested in an agency agreement, the contract is voidable at the election of the principal without full knowledge of all the facts surrounding the agent's interest. [Emphasis added.] * * * [It is a] settled rule that an agent in dealing with a principal on his own account owes it to the principal not only to make no misstatements concerning the subject matter of the transaction, but also to disclose to him fully and completely all material facts known to the agent which might affect the principal; and that unless this duty on the part of the agent has been met, the principal cannot be held to have ratified the transaction.

DECISION AND REMEDY *The judgment of the trial court was affirmed. Ramsey was denied recovery because an agency relationship had existed between Ramsey and Gordon, and Ramsey had breached his duties under this relationship.*

INDEMNIFICATION In certain situations, when a principal is sued by a third party for an agent's negligent conduct, the principal can sue the agent for an equal amount of damages. This is called *indemnification*. The same holds true if the agent violates the principal's instructions. For example, Lewis (the principal) tells his agent Moore, who is a used-car salesman, to make no warranties for the used cars. Moore is eager to make a sale to Walters, a third party, and makes a warranty for the car's engine. Lewis is not absolved from liability to Walters for engine failure, but if Walters sues Lewis, Lewis normally can then sue Moore for indemnification for violating his instructions.

Sometimes it is difficult to distinguish between instructions of the principal that limit an agent's authority and those that are merely advice. For example, Willis (the principal) owns an office supply company; Jones (the agent) is the manager. Willis tells Jones, "Don't order any more inventory this month." Willis goes on vacation. A large order comes in from a local business, and the present inventory is insufficient to meet it. What is Jones to do? In this situation, Jones probably has the inherent authority to order more inventory despite Willis's command. It is unlikely that Jones would be required to indemnify Willis in the event that the local business subsequently canceled the order.

SECTION 5

SCOPE OF AGENT'S AUTHORITY

Once the principal-agent relationship is created, attention focuses on the rights of third persons who deal with the agent. A principal's liability in a contract with a third party arises from the authority given the agent to enter legally binding contracts on the principal's behalf. An agent's authority can be either *actual* (express or implied) or *apparent*.

ACTUAL AUTHORITY—EXPRESS AND IMPLIED

Express authority is embodied in that which the principal has engaged the agent to do. Express authority can be given orally or in writing. The equal dignity rule in most states requires that if the contract being executed is or must be in writing, then the agent's authority must also be in writing. Failure to comply with the equal dignity rule can make a contract voidable *at the option of the principal*. The law regards the contract at that point as a mere offer. If the principal decides to accept the offer, acceptance must be ratified, or affirmed, in writing. Assume that Pattberg (the principal) orally asks Austin (the agent) to sell a ranch that Pattberg owns. Austin finds a buyer and signs a sales contract (a contract for an interest in realty must be in writing) on behalf of Pattberg to sell the ranch. The buyer cannot enforce the contract unless Pattberg subsequently ratifies Austin's agency status in writing. Once the contract is ratified, either party can enforce rights under the contract.

Implied authority is conferred by custom, can be inferred from the position the agent occupies, or is implied by virtue of being reasonably necessary to carry out express authority. For example, Carlson is employed by Packard Grocery to manage one of its stores. Packard has not specified (expressly stated) Carlson's authority to contract with third persons. In this situation, though, authority to manage a business implies authority to do what is reasonably required (as is customary or can be inferred from a manager's position) to operate the business. This includes making contracts for obtaining employee help, for buying merchandise and equipment, and even for advertising the products sold in the store.

Because implied authority is conferred on the basis of custom, it is important for third persons to be familiar with the custom of the trade. The list of rules that have developed to determine what authority is implied based on custom or on the agent's position is extensive. In general, implied authority is authority customarily associated with the position occupied by the agent or authority that can be inferred from the express authority given to the agent to perform fully his or her duties. For example, an agent who has authority to solicit orders for goods sold by the principal has no authority to collect payments for the goods unless the agent possesses the goods. The test is whether it was reasonable for the agent to believe that he or she had the authority to enter the contract in question.

APPARENT AUTHORITY AND ESTOPPEL

Actual authority (express or implied) arises from what the principal manifests *to the agent.* An agent has **apparent authority** when the principal, by either word or action, causes a *third party* reasonably to believe that the agent has authority to act, even though the agent has no express or implied authority. If the third party changes his or her position in reliance on the principal's representations, the principal may be *estopped* from denying that the agent had authority.

For example, assume that Adam is a traveling sales agent for a pesticide company. Adam neither possesses the goods ordered nor delivers them, and he has no express or implied authority to collect payments from customers. Now assume that a customer, Ling, pays Adam for a solicited order. Adam then takes the payment to the principal's accounting department. An accountant accepts payment and sends Ling a receipt. This procedure is thereafter followed for other orders solicited by Adam and paid for by Ling. Later, Adam solicits an order, and Ling pays Adam as before. This time, however, Adam absconds with the money. Can Ling claim that the payment to Adam was authorized and thus, in effect, a payment to the principal? The answer is yes, because the principal's *repeated* acts of accepting Ling's payments through Adam led Ling reasonably to believe that Adam had authority to receive payments for goods solicited. Although Adam did not have express or implied authority, the principal's conduct gave Adam apparent authority to collect.

There are other ways in which agency by estoppel may arise based on apparent authority. If, for example, the principal has "clothed the agent" with both possession and apparent ownership of the principal's property, the agent has very broad powers and can deal with the property as if he or she were the true owner. For example, to deceive certain creditors, Sikora (the principal) and Hunter (the agent) agree verbally that Hunter will hold certain stock certificates for Sikora. Because the certificates are bearer paper (that is, they do not require indorsement to be transferred), Hunter's possession and apparent ownership of the stock certificates are such strong indications of ownership that a reasonable person would conclude that Hunter was the actual owner. If Hunter negotiates the stock certificates to a third person, Sikora will be estopped from denying Hunter's authority to transfer the stock.

When land is involved, courts have held that possession alone is not a sufficient indication of ownership. If, however, the agent also possesses the deed to the property and sells the property against the principal's wishes to an unsuspecting buyer, the principal normally cannot cancel the sale or assert a claim to title.

The following case illustrates a situation dealing with apparent authority.

CASE 19.4 Cargill, Inc. v. Mountain Cement Co.

Supreme Court of Wyoming, 1995. 891 P.2d 57.

BACKGROUND AND FACTS *Cargill, Inc., hired Charlie Mandry to work as a sales representative. Cargill provided Mandry with an office, a telephone, and an expense account. Through Mandry, Salt Creek Welding ordered steel from Cargill to build a silo for Mountain Cement Company. Mandry arranged to have some of the steel supplied by another company. The other firm's product was defective, which caused the silo to collapse. Mountain Cement filed a suit in a Wyoming state court against Cargill and others. The court ruled in favor of Mountain Cement. On appeal, one of the issues was whether Mandry acted as Cargill's agent in arranging the sale of the defective steel to Salt Creek.*

IN THE LANGUAGE OF THE COURT

TAYLOR, Justice.

* * * *

Apparent authority is created when the principal holds the agent out as possessing the authority to bind the principal or when the principal allows the agent to claim such authority. * * * To recover on this theory [apparent authority] the third party must establish two facts: (1) the principal was responsible for the appearance of authority in the agent to conduct the transaction in question, and (2) the third party reasonably relied on the representations of the agent. * * *

* * * *

* * * Cargill provided Mandry with a telephone, an expense account and office space. These facts indicate that Cargill intended to hold Mandry out as an agent who possessed the authority to bind Cargill. Further, Salt Creek reasonably relied on that apparent authority when it ordered steel from Cargill. Thus, both prongs of the apparent authority test are satisfied.

DECISION AND REMEDY *The Supreme Court of Wyoming affirmed the lower court's decision on this issue and upheld the ruling in favor of Mountain Cement. Cargill held Mandry out as its agent, and Salt Creek reasonably relied on that apparent authority.*

EMERGENCY POWERS

When an unforeseen emergency demands action by the agent to protect or preserve the property and rights of the principal, but the agent is unable to communicate with the principal, the agent has emergency power.

For example, Fulsom is an engineer for Pacific Railroad. While Fulsom is acting within the scope of his employment, he falls under the train many miles from home and is severely injured. Dusky, the conductor, directs Thompson, a doctor, to give medical aid to Fulsom and to charge Pacific for the medical services. Dusky, an agent, has no express or implied authority to bind the principal, Pacific Railroad, for the services of Thompson. Because of the emergency situation, however, the law recognizes Dusky as having authority to act appropriately under the circumstances.

RATIFICATION

In agency relationships, a principal is not liable to a third party if an agent acts outside of his or her authority. **Ratification** occurs when the principal affirms an agent's unauthorized act. Ratification binds the principal to the agent's act and creates a situation in which the act is treated as if it had been authorized by the principal *from the outset.* With respect to a contract, if the principal does not ratify, the contract does not bind the principal, and the third party's agreement with the agent is viewed merely as an unaccepted offer. Because the third party's agreement is treated as an unaccepted offer, the third party can revoke the offer (rescind the agreement) at any time before the principal ratifies, without liability. The agent, however, may well be liable to the third party for misrepresenting his or her authority.

For ratification to be effective, the principal must be aware of all material facts. If a principal ratifies a contract *without knowledge* of all its terms, the principal can thereafter rescind (cancel) the ratification—unless, of course, the third party has proceeded to change position to his or her detriment in reliance on the contract. Suppose that an agent, without authority, contracts with a third person on behalf of a principal for repair work to the principal's office building. The principal learns of the contract from the agent and agrees to "some repair work," thinking that it will involve only patching and painting the exterior of the building. In fact, the contract includes resurfacing the parking lot, which the principal does not want done. On learning of the additional provision, the principal rescinds the contract. If the third party has made no preparations to do the work (such as purchasing materials, hiring additional workers, or renting equipment), then the principal can still rescind. If the third party has made preparations in reliance on the principal's ratification, the principal must reimburse the third party for the cost of the preparations.

Two important points must be stressed. First, it is immaterial whether the principal's lack of knowledge results from the agent's fraud or is simply a mistake on the principal's part. If the third party has not changed position in reliance on the principal's ratification, the principal can repudiate the ratification. The unauthorized contract remains an offer, and there is no contract, because contract law provides that one cannot accept terms about which one does not know. Second, the entire transaction must be ratified; a principal cannot affirm the desirable parts of a contract and reject the undesirable parts.

Death or incapacity of the third party *before* ratification will void an unauthorized contract. Most courts will also recognize an intervening and extraordinary change of circumstances as a basis for setting aside a principal's ratification to permit a third party to revoke. Assume that Abend, without authority, enters into a contract with a third party who wants to purchase Paula's shopping center. The following night, the shopping center is destroyed by fire. Paula's subsequent ratification will not be effective to bind the third party. The courts will reason that it is unjust to hold a third party liable in such a case and will permit the transaction to be avoided despite ratification. As to the principal's capacity, the principal must have the legal capacity to authorize the transaction at the time the agent engages in the act and at the time the principal ratifies that act.

SECTION 6
LIABILITY FOR CONTRACTS

Liability for contracts formed by an agent depends on how the principal is classified and on whether the actions of the agent were authorized or unauthorized.

Principals are classified as disclosed, partially disclosed, or undisclosed.[4] A **disclosed principal** is a principal whose identity is known by the third party at the time the contract is made by the agent. A **partially disclosed principal** is a principal whose identity is not known by the third party, but the third party knows that the agent is or may be acting for a principal at the time that the contract is made. An **undisclosed principal** is a principal whose identity is totally unknown by the third party, and the third party has no knowledge that the agent is acting in an agency capacity at the time the contract is made.

AUTHORIZED ACTS

If an agent acts within the scope of his or her authority, a disclosed or partially disclosed principal is liable to a third party for a contract made by the agent. If the principal is disclosed, an agent has no contractual liability for the nonperformance of the principal or of the third party. If the principal is partially disclosed, in most states the agent is also treated as a party to the contract, and the third party can hold the agent liable for contractual nonperformance.[5]

When neither the fact of agency nor the identity of the principal is disclosed, the undisclosed principal is fully bound to perform just as if the principal had been fully disclosed at the time the contract was made. Exceptions to this rule are made in the following circumstances:

1. The undisclosed principal was expressly excluded as a party in the contract. For example, an agent contracts for a lease of a building with a landlord. The landlord does not know of the agency, and the lease specially lists the agent as tenant, with no right of assignment without the landlord's consent. The undisclosed principal cannot enforce the lease.
2. The contract is a negotiable instrument, such as a check or a promissory note. Here, the UCC provides that only the agent is liable if the instrument neither names the principal nor shows that the agent signed in a representative capacity.

4. *Restatement (Second) of Agency*, Section 4.
5. *Restatement (Second) of Agency*, Section 321.

3. The performance of the agent is personal to the contract, allowing the third party to refuse the principal's performance. Typical examples involve extensions of credit and highly personal services, such as surgery.
4. The third party would not have entered into a contract with the principal had the third party known the principal's identity, the agent or the principal knew this, and the third party rescinds the contract.

When a principal's identity is undisclosed and the agent is forced to pay the third party, the agent is entitled to indemnification by the principal. It was the principal's duty to perform, even though his or her identity was undisclosed,[6] and failure to do so will make the principal ultimately liable. Once the undisclosed principal's identity is revealed, the third party generally can elect to hold either the principal or the agent liable on the contract.

UNAUTHORIZED ACTS

If an agent has no authority but nevertheless contracts with a third party, the principal cannot be held liable to the contract. It does not matter whether the principal was disclosed, partially disclosed, or undisclosed. The agent is liable, however. For example, Scammon signs a contract for the purchase of a truck, purportedly acting as an agent under authority granted by Johnson. In fact, Johnson has not given Scammon any such authority. Johnson refuses to pay for the truck, claiming that Scammon had no authority to purchase it. The seller of the truck is entitled to hold Scammon liable for payment.

If the principal is disclosed or partially disclosed, the agent's liability to the third party is based on the theory of breach of implied warranty of authority, not on breach of the contract itself.[7] The agent's implied warranty of authority can be breached intentionally or by a good faith mistake.[8] The agent is liable, as long as the third party relied on the agency status. Conversely, if the third party knows at the time the contract is made that the agent is mistaken about the extent of his or her authority, or the agent indicates to the third party *uncertainty* about the extent of authority, the agent is not personally liable for breach of warranty.

SECTION 7 LIABILITY FOR AGENT'S TORTS

Obviously, an agent is liable for his or her own torts. A principal may also be liable for an agent's torts if they result from one of the following:

1. The principal's own tortious conduct.
2. The principal's authorization of a tortious act.
3. The agent's unauthorized but tortious misrepresentation.

If the agent is an employee, whose conduct the principal-employer controls, the employer may also be liable for torts committed by the employee in the course of employment under the doctrine of *respondeat superior*, as discussed below.

PRINCIPAL'S TORTIOUS CONDUCT

A principal conducting an activity through an agent may be liable for harm resulting from the principal's own negligence or recklessness, which may include giving improper instructions; authorizing the use of improper materials, tools, or the like; establishing improper rules; or failing to prevent others' tortious conduct while they are on the principal's property or using the principal's equipment, materials, or tools. For instance, if Jack knows that Kathy cannot drive but nevertheless authorizes her to use the company truck to deliver some equipment to a customer, he will be liable for his own negligence to anyone injured by her negligent driving.

PRINCIPAL'S AUTHORIZATION OF AGENT'S TORTIOUS CONDUCT

Similarly, a principal who authorizes an agent to commit a tortious act may be liable to persons or property injured thereby, because the act is considered to be the principal's. For example, Selkow directs Warren—an agent Selkow retained to oversee the harvest of crops he bought—to cut the corn on specific acreage, which neither of them has the right to do. The harvest is therefore a trespass, and Selkow is liable to whoever owns the corn.

In the same light, assume that Victoria instructs Guthrie, her real estate agent, to tell prospective purchasers that there is oil beneath her property, when she

6. If the agent is a gratuitous agent, and the principal accepts the benefits of the agent's contract with a third party, then the principal will be liable to the agent on the theory of quasi contract (see Chapter 9).
7. The agent is not liable on the contract because the agent was never intended personally to be a party to the contract.
8. If the agent intentionally misrepresents his or her authority, then the agent can also be liable in tort for fraud.

knows there is not. Victoria will be liable to anyone who buys the property in reliance on the statements.

MISREPRESENTATION

A principal is exposed to tort liability whenever a third person sustains a loss due to the agent's misrepresentation. The principal's liability depends on whether the agent was actually or apparently authorized to make representations and whether such representations were made within the scope of the agency.

FRAUDULENT MISREPRESENTATION Assume that Bassett is a demonstrator for Moore's products. Moore sends Bassett to a home show to demonstrate products and to answer questions from consumers. Moore has given Bassett authority to make statements about the products. If Bassett makes only true representations, all is fine; but if he makes false claims, Moore will be liable for any injuries or damages sustained by third parties in reliance on Bassett's false representations.

An interesting series of cases has arisen on the theory that when a principal has placed an agent in a position to defraud a third party, the principal is liable for the agent's fraudulent acts. For example, Frendak is a loan officer at First Security Bank. In the ordinary course of the job, Frendak approves and services loans and has access to the credit records of all customers. Frendak falsely represents to a borrower, McMillan, that the bank feels insecure about McMillan's loan and intends to call it in unless McMillan provides additional collateral, such as stocks and bonds. McMillan gives Frendak numerous stock certificates, which Frendak keeps in her own possession and later uses to make personal investments. The bank is liable to McMillan for losses sustained on the stocks even though the bank had no direct role in or knowledge of the fraudulent scheme.

The legal theory used here is that the agent's position conveys to third persons the impression that the agent has the authority to make statements and perform acts consistent with the ordinary duties that are within the scope of the position. When an agent appears to be acting within the scope of the authority that the position of agency confers but is actually taking advantage of a third party, the principal who placed the agent in that position is liable. In the example above, if a bank teller or a security guard had told McMillan that the bank required additional security for the loan, McMillan would not have been justified in relying on either person's authority to make that representation. McMillan, however, could reasonably expect that the loan officer was telling the truth.

INNOCENT MISREPRESENTATION Tort liability based on fraud requires proof that a material misstatement was made knowingly and with the intent to deceive. An agent's innocent mistakes occurring in a contract transaction or involving a warranty contained in the contract can provide grounds for the third party's rescission of the contract and the award of damages. Moreover, justice dictates that when a principal knows that an agent is not accurately advised of facts but does not correct either the agent's or the third party's impressions, the principal is directly responsible to the third party for resulting damages. The point is that the principal is always directly responsible for an agent's misrepresentation made within the scope of authority.

THE DOCTRINE OF *RESPONDEAT SUPERIOR*

Under the doctrine of ***respondeat superior***,[9] the principal-employer is liable for any harm caused to a third party by an agent-employee in the scope of employment. This doctrine imposes **vicarious liability** on the employer—that is, liability without regard to the personal fault of the employer for torts committed by an employee in the course or scope of employment.[10] Third persons injured through the negligence of an employee can sue either the employee who was negligent or the employer, if the employee's negligent conduct occurred while the employee was acting within the scope of employment.

At early common law, a servant (employee) was viewed as the master's (employer's) property. The master was deemed to have absolute control over the servant's acts and was held strictly liable for them no matter how carefully the master supervised the servant. The rationale for the doctrine of *respondeat superior* is based on the principle of social duty that requires every person to manage his or her affairs, whether accomplished by the person or through agents, so as not to injure another. Liability is imposed on employers because they are deemed to be in a better financial position to bear the loss. The

9. Pronounced ree-*spahn*-dee-uht soo-*peer*-ee-your. The doctrine of *respondeat superior* applies not only to employer-employee relationships but also to other principal-agent relationships in which the principal has the right of control over the agent.

10. The theory of *respondeat superior* is similar to the theory of strict liability covered in Chapter 12.

Emerging Trends

The Use of "Intelligent Agents"

Intelligent agents are semiautonomous Internet computer programs that are capable of executing specific tasks. For example, intelligent agents on the World Wide Web can search through many databases and retrieve only relevant information for the user. Some intelligent agents are used to make purchases on the Internet. A user might use BargainFinder (Andersen Consulting, Chicago), for example, to search the many Internet Web sites that offer compact discs (CDs) and seek out the lowest price for a particular album. Once found, the intelligent agent links the user directly to the appropriate Web site. Other shopping agents locate other specific products in online catalogues and actually negotiate product acquisition, as well as delivery.

What Agency Law Applies?

Intelligent agents may be just that, but standard agency principles have only applied to *human* agents, who have express or implied authority to enter into specific contracts. Many questions in agency law revolve around whether the human agent acted within the scope of his or her authority. What does this concept mean when dealing with an electronic intelligent agent?

Consider a not-too-uncommon example. Software that an intelligent agent might find for its user will undoubtedly involve a "click-on" agreement (see the discussion of electronic sales contracts in the *Emerging Trends in Business Law* presented in Chapter 21). Intelligent agents searching the Internet may run into a wide variety of such "click-on" agreements, which, by necessity, contain many different terms and conditions. If the intelligent agent ignores the terms and conditions of a licensing agreement outlined in the "click-on" setting, is the user of the agent nonetheless bound by the agreement? Conversely, many "click-on" agreements exempt third parties from any liability resulting from the underlying product or service. Is the user of the intelligent agent bound by this particular term? With respect to human agents, the courts occasionally have found that an agent could not

superior financial position carries with it the duty to be responsible for damages.

Today the doctrine continues, but employers carry liability insurance and spread the cost of risk over the entire business enterprise. Public policy requires that an injured person be afforded effective relief, and recovery from a business enterprise provides far more effective relief than recovery from an individual employee. Liability rights exist under law because of public-policy protections of third parties. Thus, a master (employer) cannot contract with a servant (employee) to disclaim responsibilities for injuries resulting from the servant's acts, because such disclaimers are against public policy.

LIABILITY FOR EMPLOYEE'S NEGLIGENCE

For the employer to be liable for an employee's negligence, the employee's injury-causing act must have occurred within the course and scope of the employee's employment.

Scope of Employment. The *Restatement (Second) of Agency*, Section 229, indicates the following general factors that courts will consider in determining whether or not a particular act occurred within the course and scope of employment:

1. Whether the employee's act was authorized by the employer.
2. The time, place, and purpose of the act.
3. Whether the act was one commonly performed by employees on behalf of their employers.
4. The extent to which the employer's interest was advanced by the act.

EMERGING TRENDS

THE USE OF "INTELLIGENT AGENTS" (CONTINUED)

agree to such a term without explicit authority.[a]

THE PROPOSED UCC ARTICLE 2B

The National Conference of Commissioners on Uniform State Laws has drafted a proposed Article 2B, entitled "Licenses," for the Uniform Commercial Code (UCC). This proposed UCC article does address the issue of intelligent agents. According to the Reporters' Notes, any company or individual that creates and sets out or adopts the intelligent agent ultimately takes responsibility for its conduct and is bound by its performances and messages.[b] Unfortunately, no distinction is made between the person or business that developed and programmed the intelligent agent and the user. As currently used, most electronic agents are automatically agreeing to whatever terms are included in a click-on contract.

THE MARKET REACTS

One way the market on the Internet has reacted to intelligent agents is by engaging in "agent blocking." Some online stores have blocked the BargainFinder intelligent agent from accessing pricing information. Other online stores are developing click-on agreements that can be understood by a computer and that are therefore more conspicuous for intelligent agents.

IMPLICATIONS FOR THE BUSINESSPERSON

1. Any businessperson contemplating the use of an Internet intelligent agent must proceed with caution. Time may be saved, but users of such agents must consider the possibility that they might be bound to terms of which they are unaware.
2. Because intelligent agents are not yet at a high enough level of sophistication, they probably will continue to have more contracting authority than any businessperson wants them to have. User beware!

FOR CRITICAL ANALYSIS

1. What are the costs and benefits of using an intelligent shopping agent?
2. How might online shopping-site owners develop standardized click-on agreements?

a. *Bernstein v. Seacliff Beach Club, Inc.*, 35 Misc.2d 153, 228 N.Y.S.2d 567 (1962).
b. UCC 2B–111, Note 1 (Tentative Draft, September 4, 1996).

5. The extent to which the private interests of the employee were involved.
6. Whether the employer furnished the means or instrumentality (for example, a truck or a machine) by which an injury was inflicted.
7. Whether the employer had reason to know that the employee would do the act in question and whether the employee had done it before.
8. Whether the act involved the commission of a serious crime.

Consider an example. Mandel (the employee) is a delivery driver for Schwartz (the employer). Schwartz provides Mandel with a vehicle and instructs him to use it for making company deliveries. One day, while he is making deliveries, Mandel negligently runs into Chan, a pedestrian, causing Chan to be seriously injured. Because the negligence occurred as part of Mandel's regular duties of employment (making deliveries), Schwartz is liable to Chan for the injuries caused by Mandel's negligence.

An employee going to and from work or to and from meals is usually considered outside the scope of employment. All travel time of traveling salespersons or others whose jobs require them to travel is normally considered within the scope of employment for the duration of the business trip, including the return trip home, unless they depart significantly from the employer's business.

Departures from the Employer's Business. When an employee goes off on his or her own—that is, departs from the employer's business to take care of personal affairs—is the employer liable? The answer depends on whether the employee's activity is a minor departure from the employer's business or a substantial departure akin to an utter abandonment of the employer's business. For example, a traveling salesperson, while driving the employer's vehicle to call on a customer, decides to stop at the post office—which is one block off his route—to mail a personal letter. As the employee approaches the post office, he negligently runs into a parked vehicle owned by Inga. In this situation, because the employee's detour from the employer's business is not substantial, the employee is still within the scope of employment, and the employer is liable.

The result would be different if the employee had decided to pick up a few friends for cocktails in another city and in the process had negligently run his vehicle into Inga's. In this situation, the departure from the employer's business would be substantial, to the point of abandoning the employer's business, and the employer would not be liable to Inga for damages. The employee would be considered to be on a "frolic" of his own, and only the employee could be held liable to Inga.

Courts often refer to the "detour-frolic" distinction when deciding whether a given action was within the course and scope of employment. The distinction was first drawn in the following classic case on "master-servant" (employer-employee) law.

CASE 19.5 Joel v. Morison

Court of Exchequer, England, 1834. 172 Eng. Rep. 1338.

BACKGROUND AND FACTS *The plaintiff was walking across Bishopsgate-street when he was knocked down by a cart driven negligently by a servant of the defendant. The plaintiff suffered a fractured leg and multiple injuries. The plaintiff took the position that the defendant was liable for his injuries because the defendant's servant was driving the cart that caused the injuries. The defendant argued that his cart was never driven in the neighborhood in which the plaintiff was injured. Moreover, it was suggested that the defendant's servant had gone out of his way for his own purposes and might have taken the cart at a time when it was not wanted for business purposes to pay a visit to some friends.*

IN THE LANGUAGE OF THE COURT

PARKE, Judge.

* * * *

* * * This is an action to recover damages for an injury sustained by the plaintiff, in consequence of the negligence of the defendant's servant. * * * If the servants, being on their master's business, took a detour to call upon a friend, the master will be responsible. If * * * the servants lent the cart to a person who was driving without the defendant's knowledge, he will not be responsible. Or, if * * * the young man who was driving took the cart surreptitiously, and was not at the time employed on his master's business, the defendant will not be liable. The master is only liable where the servant is acting in the course of his employment. If he was going out of his way, against his master's implied commands, when driving on his master's business, he will make his master liable; *but if he was going on a frolic of his own, without being at all on his master's business, the master will not be liable.* As to the damages, the master * * * [although not himself] guilty of any offence, * * * is only responsible in law, therefore the amount should be reasonable. [Emphasis added.]

DECISION AND REMEDY *The verdict was for the plaintiff, and he was awarded damages of £30. In this case, the master was held liable for the acts of his servant.*

INTERNATIONAL CONSIDERATIONS ***Respondeat Superior* in Islamic Countries** *The doctrine of* respondeat superior *is well established in the legal systems of the United States and most*

Western countries. Middle Eastern countries, however, do not employ the principle. Islamic law holds to a strict principle that responsibility for human actions lies with the individual and cannot be vicariously extended to others.

Notice of Dangerous Conditions. The employer is charged with knowledge of any dangerous conditions discovered by an employee and pertinent to the employment situation. To illustrate: A maintenance employee in Martin's apartment building notices a lead pipe protruding from the ground in the building's courtyard. The employee neglects either to fix it or to inform the employer of the danger. John falls on the pipe and is injured. The employer is charged with knowledge of the dangerous condition regardless of whether or not the employee actually informed the employer. That knowledge is imputed to the employer by virtue of the employment relationship.

LIABILITY FOR EMPLOYEE'S INTENTIONAL TORTS Most intentional torts that employees commit have no relation to their employment; thus, their employers will not be held liable. Under the doctrine of *respondeat superior*, however, the employer is liable for intentional torts of the employee that are committed within the course and scope of employment, just as the employer is liable for negligence. For example, an employer is liable when an employee (such as a "bouncer" at a nightclub or a security guard at a department store) commits assault and battery or false imprisonment while acting within the scope of employment.

An employee acting at the employer's direction can be liable as a *tortfeasor* (one who commits a wrong, or tort), along with the employer, for committing the tortious act even if the employee was unaware of the wrongfulness of the act. For example, an employer directs an employee to burn out a field of crops. The employee does so, assuming that the field belongs to the employer, which it does not. Both can be found liable to the owner of the field for damages.

An employer who knows or should know that an employee has a propensity for committing tortious acts is liable for the employee's acts even if they would not ordinarily be considered within the scope of employment. For example, the Blue Moon employs Arnold Munn as a bouncer, knowing that he has a history of arrests for assault and battery. While he is working one night, and within the scope of his employment, he viciously attacks a patron who "looks at him funny." The Blue Moon will bear the responsibility for Munn's acts, because it knew that he had a propensity for committing tortious acts.

An employer is also liable for permitting an employee to engage in reckless acts that can injure others. For example, an employer observes an employee smoking while filling containerized trucks with highly flammable liquids. Failure to stop the employee will cause the employer to be liable for any injuries that result if a truck explodes.

To reduce the likelihood of liability losses, employers set up stringent work rules. For example, employees who drive company vehicles may be prohibited from giving rides to other passengers. Employees who violate these rules by being careless or committing unlawful or tortious acts may be subject to discipline, including discharge. Almost without exception, employers purchase liability insurance to cover the actions of certain employees.

SECTION 8

LIABILITY FOR INDEPENDENT CONTRACTOR'S TORTS

The general rule concerning liability for the acts of independent contractors is that the employer is not liable for physical harm caused to a third person by the negligent act of an independent contractor in the performance of the contract. An employer who has no legal power to control the details of the physical performance of a contract cannot be held liable. Here again, the test is the *right to control.* Because an employer bargains with an independent contractor only for results and retains no control over the manner in which those results are achieved, the employer is generally not expected to bear the responsibility for torts committed by an independent contractor. A collection agency is a typical example of an independent contractor. The creditor is generally not liable for the acts of the collection agency, because collection is a distinct business occupation.

Generally, an exception to this doctrine prevails when unusually hazardous activities are involved. Typical examples of such activities include blasting operations, the transportation of highly volatile chemicals, and the use of poisonous gases. In these cases, an employer cannot be shielded from liability merely by using an independent contractor. Strict liability is imposed on the employer-principal as a matter of law. Also, in some states, strict liability is imposed by statute.

In the following case, one of the issues before the court is whether a secured creditor could be held liable for the damages caused by the independent contractor's tortious actions when repossessing collateral.

CASE 19.6 MBank of El Paso v. Sanchez

Supreme Court of Texas, 1992. 836 S.W.2d 151.

BACKGROUND AND FACTS *MBank of El Paso contracted with El Paso Recovery Service (El Paso) to have El Paso repossess Yvonne Sanchez's 1978 Pontiac Trans-Am, which had been purchased through MBank financing. Two men hired by El Paso went to Sanchez's home with a tow truck and proceeded to hook the tow truck to the car, which was in the driveway. Sanchez demanded that they cease their attempt to take the automobile and that they leave the premises. When they ignored her, she locked herself in the car. They then took the vehicle, with Sanchez locked in it, on a high-speed ride from her home to the repossession lot and parked the car in a fenced and locked yard with a loose guard dog. Sanchez filed suit against MBank for damages, alleging that El Paso and its employees were MBank's agents and that they had willfully breached the peace in violation of the self-help provision of UCC 9–503.*[a] *The trial court held that the bank could not be liable because El Paso was an independent contractor. Sanchez appealed, and the appellate court, holding that MBank had a nondelegable duty to repossess the vehicle without a breach of the peace, reversed the trial court's decision and remanded the case. MBank appealed to the state supreme court.*

IN THE LANGUAGE OF THE COURT

MAUZY, Justice.

* * * *

Section 9–503 * * * gives a secured party two choices: it may repossess the collateral "if this can be done without breach of the peace," or it may take legal action. If the secured party chooses the first of those options, it runs the risk that the repossession may, in fact, breach the peace. When that happens, the secured party may be held liable in tort.

* * * *

As a general rule, when a duty is imposed by law on the basis of concerns for public safety, the party bearing the duty cannot escape it by delegating it to an independent contractor. * * *

We believe that section 9–503 of the UCC imposes a duty on secured creditors pursuing nonjudicial repossession to take precautions for public safety. * * * [A] secured creditor is prohibited from delegating this duty to an independent contractor.

* * * *

A secured creditor certainly has a strong interest in obtaining collateral from a defaulting debtor. That interest, however, must be balanced against society's interest in the public peace. If a creditor chooses to pursue self-help, it must be expected

---

a. This "self-help" provision allows secured creditors to repossess collateral on their own initiative, without resorting to judicial assistance.

to take precautions in doing so. If this burden is too heavy, the creditor may seek relief by turning to the courts. By pursuing a legal remedy, a creditor shifts the responsibility for repossession to officers of the law.

DECISION AND REMEDY *The state supreme court affirmed the lower appellate court's judgment. An employer cannot avoid liability for an independent contractor's breach of the peace when repossessing collateral.*

SECTION 9 LIABILITY FOR AGENT'S CRIMES

Obviously, an agent is liable for his or her own crimes. A principal or employer is not liable for an agent's or employee's crime simply because the agent or employee committed the crime while otherwise acting within the scope of authority or employment, unless the principal or employer participated by conspiracy or other action. In some jurisdictions, under specific statutes, a principal may be liable for an agent's violating, in the course and scope of employment, such regulations as those governing sanitation, prices, weights, and the sale of liquor.

SECTION 10 TERMINATION OF AN AGENCY

Agency law is similar to contract law in that both an agency and a contract may be terminated by an act of the parties or by operation of law. Once the relationship between the principal and the agent has ended, the agent no longer has *actual* authority to bind the principal—that is, he or she lacks the principal's consent to act in the principal's behalf. Generally, if the agency is terminated by an act of the parties, the principal can still be bound by the agent's acts if the agent has acted within the scope of his or her *apparent* authority, however. To terminate the agent's apparent authority, third parties must be notified of the agency termination—as will be discussed later.

TERMINATION BY ACT OF THE PARTIES

An agency relationship may be terminated by act of the parties in a number of ways, including those discussed here.

LAPSE OF TIME An agency agreement may specify the time period during which the agency relationship will exist. If so, the agency ends when that time expires. For example, Akers signs an agreement of agency with Jefferson "beginning January 1, 1998, and ending December 31, 1999." The agency is automatically terminated on December 31, 1999. Of course, the parties can agree to continue the relationship, in which case the same terms will apply.

If no definite time is stated, then the agency continues for a reasonable time and can be terminated at will by either party. What constitutes a reasonable time depends on the circumstances and the nature of the agency relationship. For example, Jefferson asks Akers to sell her car. If after two years Akers has not sold Jefferson's car and there has been no communication between Jefferson and Akers, it is safe to assume that the agency relationship has terminated. Akers no longer has the authority to sell Jefferson's car.

PURPOSE ACHIEVED An agent can be employed to accomplish a particular objective, such as the purchase of stock for a cattle rancher. In that situation, the agency automatically ends after the cattle have been purchased. If more than one agent is employed to accomplish the same purpose, such as the sale of real estate, the first agent to complete the sale automatically terminates the agency relationship for all the others.

OCCURRENCE OF A SPECIFIC EVENT An agency can be created to terminate on the happening of a certain event. For example, Jefferson appoints Akers to handle her business affairs while she is away. When Jefferson returns, the agency automatically terminates.

Sometimes one aspect of the agent's authority terminates on the occurrence of a particular event, but the agency relationship itself does not terminate. For example, Jefferson, a banker, permits Akers, the credit manager, to grant a credit line of $5,000 to certain depositors who maintain a balance of $5,000 in a savings account. If any customer's savings account balance falls below $5,000, Akers can no longer make the credit line available to that customer. Akers, however, continues to have the right to extend credit to the other customers maintaining the minimum balance.

MUTUAL AGREEMENT Recall from basic contract law that parties can rescind (cancel) a contract by mutually agreeing to terminate the contractual relationship. The same holds true in agency law regardless of whether the agency contract is in writing or whether it is for a specific duration. For example, Jefferson no longer wishes Akers to be her agent, and Akers does not want to work for Jefferson any more. Either party can communicate to the other the intent to terminate the relationship. Agreement to terminate effectively relieves each of the rights, duties, and powers inherent in the relationship.

TERMINATION BY ONE PARTY As a *general* rule, either party can terminate the agency relationship. The agent's act is said to be a renunciation of authority. The principal's act is a revocation of authority. Although both parties may have the *power* to terminate—because agency is a consensual relationship, and thus neither party can be compelled to continue in the relationship—they may not possess the *right* to terminate and may therefore be liable for breach of contract. Wrongful termination can subject the canceling party to a suit for damages. For example, Akers has a one-year employment contract with Jefferson to act as Jefferson's agent for $25,000. Jefferson can discharge Akers before the contract period expires (Jefferson has the *power* to breach the contract); however, Jefferson will be liable to Akers for money damages, because Jefferson has no *right* to breach the contract.

Even in an agency at will (that is, an agency that either party may terminate at any time), the principal who wishes to terminate must give the agent a reasonable notice—that is, at least sufficient notice to allow the agent to recoup his or her expenses and, in some cases, to make a normal profit.

A special rule applies in an *agency coupled with an interest.* This type of agency is not an agency in the usual sense, because it is created for the agent's benefit instead of for the principal's benefit. For example, suppose that Julie borrows $5,000 from Rob, giving Rob some of her jewelry and signing a letter authorizing Rob to sell the jewelry as her agent if she fails to repay the loan. Julie, after she has received the $5,000 from Rob, then attempts to revoke Rob's authority to sell the jewelry. Julie will not succeed in this attempt, because a principal cannot revoke an agency created for the agent's benefit.

An agency coupled with an interest should not be confused with a situation in which the agent merely derives proceeds or profits from the sale of the subject matter. For example, an agent who merely receives a commission from the sale of real property does not have a beneficial interest in the property itself. Likewise, an attorney whose fee is a percentage of the recovery (a *contingency fee*—see Chapter 4) merely has an interest in the proceeds. These agency relationships are revocable by the principal, subject to any express contractual arrangements between the principal and the agent.

NOTICE OF TERMINATION When an agency has been terminated by act of the parties, it is the principal's duty to inform any third parties who know of the existence of the agency that it has been terminated (although notice of the termination may be given by others).

An agent's authority continues until the agent receives some notice of termination. As previously mentioned, notice to third parties follows the general rule that an agent's *apparent authority* continues until the third person receives notice (from any source of information) that the authority has been terminated. The principal is expected to notify *directly* any third person who the principal knows has dealt with the agent. For third persons who have heard about the agency but have not dealt with the agent, *constructive notice* is sufficient.[11]

No particular form is required for notice of termination of the principal-agent relationship to be effective. The principal can actually notify the agent, or the agent can learn of the termination through some other means. For example, Manning bids on a shipment of steel, and Stone is hired as an agent to arrange transportation of the shipment. When Stone learns that Manning has lost the bid, Stone's authority to make the transportation arrangement terminates.

If the agent's authority is written, it must be revoked in writing, and the writing must be shown to all people who saw the original writing that estab-

11. With *constructive notice* of a fact, knowledge of the fact is imputed by law to a person if he or she could have discovered the fact by proper diligence. Constructive notice is often accomplished by publication in a newspaper.

lished the agency relationship. Sometimes, a written authorization (such as a power of attorney) contains an expiration date. The passage of the expiration date is sufficient notice of termination.

TERMINATION BY OPERATION OF LAW

Certain events will terminate agency authority automatically, because their occurrence makes it impossible for the agent to perform or improbable that the principal would continue to want performance. These events include death, insanity, loss of the agency's subject matter (impossibility), changed circumstances, bankruptcy, and war. When an agency terminates by operation of law, there is no duty to notify third persons—unless the agent's authority is coupled with an interest.[12]

12. There is an exception to this rule in banking. The UCC provides that the bank, as agent, can continue to exercise specific types of authority even after the customer's death or insanity unless it has knowledge of the death or insanity. When the bank has knowledge of the customer's death, it has authority for ten days after the death to pay checks (but not notes or drafts) drawn by the customer unless it receives a stop-payment order from someone who has an interest in the account, such as an heir.

TERMS AND CONCEPTS TO REVIEW

agency 390	**fiduciary** 391	**power of attorney** 395
apparent authority 401	**implied authority** 401	**ratification** 402
disclosed principal 403	**independent contractor** 391	***respondeat superior*** 405
equal dignity rule 393	**partially disclosed principal** 403	**undisclosed principal** 403
express authority 400		**vicarious liability** 405

QUESTIONS AND CASE PROBLEMS

19–1. AGENT'S DUTIES TO PRINCIPAL. Peter hires Alice as an agent to sell a piece of property he owns. The price is to be at least $30,000. Alice discovers that because a shopping mall is planned for the area in which Peter's property is located, the fair market value of the property will be at least $45,000 and could be higher. Alice forms a real estate partnership with her cousin Carl, and she prepares for Peter's signature a contract for sale of the property to Carl for $32,000. Peter signs the contract. Just before closing and passage of title, Peter learns about the shopping mall and the increased fair market value of his property. Peter refuses to deed the property to Carl. Carl claims that Alice, as agent, solicited a price above that agreed on in the creation of the agency and that the contract is therefore binding and enforceable. Discuss fully whether Peter is bound to this contract.

19–2. AGENCY FORMATION. John Paul Corp. made the following contracts:

(a) A contract with Able Construction to build an addition to the corporate office building.
(b) A contract with a certified public accountant (CPA), a recent college graduate, to head the cost accounting section.
(c) A contract with a salesperson to travel a designated area to solicit orders (contracts) for the corporation.

Able contracts with Apex for materials for the addition; the CPA hires an experienced accountant to advise her on certain accounting procedures; and the salesperson contracts to sell a large order to Green, agreeing to deliver the goods in person within twenty days. Later, Able refuses to pick up the materials, the CPA is in default in paying the hired consultant, and the salesperson does not deliver on time. Apex, the accountant, and Green claim John Paul Corp. is liable under agency law. Discuss fully whether an agency relationship was created by John Paul with Able, the CPA, or the salesperson.

19–3. AGENT'S DUTIES TO PRINCIPAL. Ankir is hired by Peters as a traveling salesperson. Ankir not only solicits orders but also delivers the goods and collects payments from his customers. Ankir places all payments in his private checking account and at the end of each month draws sufficient cash from his bank to cover the payments made. Peters is totally unaware of this procedure. Because of a slowdown in the economy, Peters tells all his salespeople to offer 20 percent discounts on orders. Ankir solicits orders, but he offers only 15 percent discounts, pocketing the extra 5 percent paid by customers. Ankir has not lost any orders by this practice, and he is rated one of Peters's top salespersons. Peters learns of Ankir's actions. Discuss fully Peters's rights in this matter.

19–4. Liability for Agent's Contracts. Alice Adams is a purchasing agent–employee for the A & B Coal Supply partnership. Adams has authority to purchase the coal needed by A & B to satisfy the needs of its customers. While Adams is leaving a coal mine from which she has just purchased a large quantity of coal, her car breaks down. She walks into a small roadside grocery store for help. While there, she runs into Will Wilson. Wilson owns 360 acres back in the mountains with all mineral rights. Wilson, in need of money, offers to sell Adams the property at $1,500 per acre. On inspection of the property, Adams forms the opinion that the subsurface contains valuable coal deposits. Adams contracts to purchase the property for A & B Coal Supply, signing the contract "A & B Coal Supply, Alice Adams, agent." The closing date is August 1. Adams takes the contract to the partnership. The managing partner is furious, as A & B is not in the property business. Later, just before closing, both Wilson and the partnership learn that the value of the land is at least $15,000 per acre. Discuss the rights of A & B and Wilson concerning the land contract.

19–5. Undisclosed Principal. Paula Enterprises hires Able to act as its agent to purchase a one-thousand-acre tract of land from Thompson for $1,000 per acre. Paula Enterprises does not wish Thompson to know that it is the principal or that Able is its agent. Paula wants the land for a new country housing development, and Thompson may not sell the land for that purpose or may demand a premium price. Able makes the contract for the purchase, signing only his name as purchaser and not disclosing to Thompson the agency relationship. The closing and transfer of deed are to take place on September 1.

(a) If Thompson learns of Paula's identity on August 1, can Thompson legally refuse to deed the property on September 1? Explain.

(b) Paula gives Able the money for the closing, but Able absconds with the money, causing a breach of Able's contract at the date of closing. Thompson then learns of Paula's identity and wants to enforce the contract. Discuss fully Thompson's rights under these circumstances.

19–6. Principal's Liability for Agent's Torts. Able is hired as a traveling salesperson for the ABC Tire Corp. Able has a designated geographical area and time schedule within which to solicit orders and service customers. Able is given a company car to use in covering the territory. One day, Able decides to take his personal car to cover part of his territory. It is 11:00 A.M., and Able has just finished calling on all customers in the city of Tarrytown. Able's next appointment is in the city of Austex, twenty miles down the road, at 2:00 P.M. Able starts out for Austex, but halfway there he decides to visit a former college roommate who runs a farm ten miles off the main highway. Able is enjoying his visit with his former roommate when he realizes that it is 1:45 P.M. and that he will be late for the appointment in Austex. Driving at a high speed down the country road to reach the main highway, Able crashes his car into Thomas's tractor, severely injuring Thomas, a farmer. Thomas claims he can hold the ABC Tire Corp. liable for his injuries. Discuss fully ABC's liability in this situation.

19–7. Employee versus Independent Contractor. Stephen Hemmerling was a driver for the Happy Cab Co. Hemmerling paid certain fixed expenses and abided by a variety of rules relating to the use of the cab, the hours that could be worked, the solicitation of fares, and so on. Rates were set by the state. Happy Cab did not withhold taxes from Hemmerling's pay. While driving a cab, Hemmerling was injured in an accident and filed a claim against Happy Cab in a Nebraska state court for workers' compensation benefits. Such benefits are not available to independent contractors. On what basis might the court hold that Hemmerling is an employee? Explain. [*Hemmerling v. Happy Cab Co.*, 247 Neb. 919, 530 N.W.2d 916 (1995)]

19–8. *Respondeat Superior.* Justin Jones suffered from genital herpes and sought treatment from Dr. Steven Baisch of Region West Pediatric Services. A nurse's assistant, Jeni Hallgren, who was a Region West employee, told her friends and some of Jones's friends about Jones's condition. This was a violation of the Region West employee handbook, which required employees to maintain the confidentiality of patients' records. Jones filed a suit in a federal district court against Region West, among others, alleging that Region West should be held liable for its employee's actions on the basis of *respondeat superior.* On what basis might the court hold that Region West was not liable for Hallgren's acts? Discuss fully. [*Jones v. Baisch, M.D.*, 40 F.3d 252 (8th Cir. 1994)]

19–9. Undisclosed Principal. John Dunning was the sole officer of the R. B. Dunning Company and was responsible for the management and operation of the business. When the company rented a warehouse from Samuel and Ruth Saliba, Dunning did not say that he was acting for the firm. The parties did not have a written lease. Business faltered, and the firm stopped paying rent. Eventually, it went bankrupt and vacated the property. The Salibas filed a suit in a Maine state court against Dunning personally, seeking to recover the unpaid rent. Dunning claimed the debt belonged to the company because he had only been acting as its agent. Who is liable for the rent, and why? [*Estate of Saliba v. Dunning*, 682 A.2d 224 (Me. 1996)]

19–10. A Question of Ethics

Kimberly Sierra, suffering from a severe asthma attack, went to Southview Hospital & Family Health Center. She was treated in the emergency room by Dr. Thomas Mucci. At the time, as a result of statements by Southview administrators, brochures, and ads, Sierra believed that the physicians at Southview were "hospital doctors." In fact, Mucci's contract with Southview stated, "The relationship between [Southview and Mucci] shall be that of independent contractor." Within a few hours, Sierra was pronounced dead. Sierra's mother, Edna Clark, sued Southview and others, alleging, in part, negligent medical care. Southview argued that it was not responsible for the acts of its independent contractors. The Supreme Court of Ohio heard the case and held that Southview was liable under the doctrine of agency by estoppel, based primarily on its "hold[ing] itself out to the public as a provider of medical services." [*Clark v. Southview Hospital & Family Health Center*, 68 Ohio St.3d 435, 628 N.E.2d 46 (1994)]

1. Could Southview have avoided liability if Sierra had known that Mucci was an independent contractor? Is it ethical for a hospital to attempt to avoid such responsibility?
2. Some department stores rent space in their stores to vendors of individual lines of products, such as cosmetics. In doing so, does a department store hold itself out to the public as a "provider" of cosmetics, subjecting itself to liability for the negligent acts of the independent contractors on its premises? Should the holding in the *Southview* case be applied in such contexts?

ACCESSING THE INTERNET
THE LEGAL ENVIRONMENT OF BUSINESS

The 'Lectric Law Library's Lawcopedia contains a summary of agency laws at

http://www.lectlaw.com/d-a.htm

Scroll down through the A's and select the link to Agent for useful information on this area of the law.

If you are interested in learning more about "intelligent agents," you can read the article entitled "Can Programs Bind Humans to Contracts?" at

http://www.ljx.com/internet/0113shrink.html

CHAPTER 20

EMPLOYMENT RELATIONSHIPS

At one time in the United States, employment relationships were governed primarily by the common law. Under the common law doctrine of **employment at will,** normally either party could terminate the employment relationship at any time and for any reason, unless an employment contract provided to the contrary. Other common law concepts governing employment relationships were those of contract, agency, and tort law.

The industrial revolution of the late nineteenth century significantly altered employment relationships. The growth of large factories and business enterprises increased the bargaining power of employers and diminished that of employees. Child labor laws were nonexistent. By the end of the century, workers were beginning to organize into unions to protect their rights. By the early twentieth century, and particularly during the Great Depression of the 1930s, both state and federal governments began to protect the rights of workers.

Legislation during the 1930s and subsequent decades established the right of employees to unionize and bargain with management for improved working conditions, salaries, and benefits. A succession of other laws during and since the 1930s provided further protection for employees. Today's employers must comply with myriad laws and regulations to ensure that employee rights are protected. Although common law doctrines still apply to employment relationships, their applicability is greatly restricted—because they only apply to those areas not governed by statutory law or administrative agency regulations.

In this chapter, we look at the most significant laws regulating employment relationships. We examine other important laws regulating the workplace—those prohibiting employment discrimination—in the next chapter, and labor law will be discussed in Chapter 22.

SECTION 1 WAGE-HOUR LAWS

In the 1930s, to protect employees against some of the adverse effects of the employment-at-will doctrine, Congress enacted several laws regulating the wages and working hours of employees. In 1931, Congress passed the Davis-Bacon Act,[1] which requires the payment of "prevailing wages" to employees of contractors and subcontractors working on government construction projects. In 1936, the Walsh-Healey Act[2] was passed. This act requires that a minimum wage, as well as overtime pay of time and a half, be paid to employees of manufacturers or suppliers entering into contracts with agencies of the federal government.

In 1938, with the passage of the Fair Labor Standards Act[3] (FLSA), Congress extended wage-hour requirements to cover all employers engaged in interstate commerce or engaged in the production of goods for interstate commerce. We examine here the FLSA's provisions in regard to child labor, maximum hours, and minimum wages.

CHILD LABOR

The FLSA prohibits oppressive child labor. Children under fourteen years of age are allowed to do certain types of work, such as deliver newspapers, work for their parents, and work in the entertainment and (with some exceptions) agricultural areas. Children who are fourteen or fifteen years of age are allowed to work, but not in hazardous occupations. There are also numerous restrictions on how many hours per day and per week they can work. For example, they cannot work during school hours, for more than three hours on a school day (or eight hours on a nonschool day), for more than eighteen hours during a school week (or forty hours during a nonschool week), or before 7 A.M. or after 7 P.M. (9 P.M. during the summer). Most states require persons under sixteen years of age to obtain work permits.

1. 40 U.S.C. Sections 276a–276a-5.
2. 41 U.S.C. Sections 35–45.
3. 29 U.S.C. Sections 201–260.

Persons between the ages of sixteen and eighteen do not face such restrictions on working times and hours, but they cannot be employed in hazardous jobs or in jobs detrimental to their health and well-being. Persons over the age of eighteen are not affected by any of the above-mentioned restrictions.

HOURS AND WAGES

Under the FLSA, any employee who agrees to work more than forty hours per week must be paid no less than one and a half times his or her regular pay for all hours over forty. Certain employees are exempt from the overtime provisions of the act. Exempt employees fall into four categories: executives, administrative employees, professional employees, and outside salespersons. Generally, to fall into one of these categories, an employee must earn more than a specified amount of income per week and devote a certain percentage of work time to the performance of specific types of duties, as determined by the FLSA. To qualify as an outside salesperson, the employee must regularly engage in sales work away from the office and spend no more than 20 percent of work time per week performing duties other than sales.

The FLSA provides that a **minimum wage** of a specified amount ($5.15 per hour as of September 1, 1997) must be paid to employees in covered industries. Congress periodically revises the amount of the minimum wage. Under the FLSA, the term *wages* includes the reasonable costs of the employer in furnishing employees with board, lodging, and other facilities if they are customarily furnished by that employer.

SECTION 2 WORKER HEALTH AND SAFETY

Under the common law, employees injured on the job had to rely on tort law or contract law theories in suits they brought against their employers. Additionally, workers had some recourse under the common law governing agency relationships (discussed in Chapter 19), which imposes a duty on a principal-employer to provide a safe workplace for his or her agent-employee. Today, numerous state and federal statutes protect employees and their families from the risk of accidental injury, death, or disease resulting from their employment. This section discusses the primary federal statute governing health and safety in the workplace, along with state workers' compensation acts.

THE OCCUPATIONAL SAFETY AND HEALTH ACT

At the federal level, the primary legislation for employee health and safety protection is the Occupational Safety and Health Act of 1970.[4] Congress passed this act in an attempt to ensure safe and healthful working conditions for practically every employee in the country. The act provides for specific standards that employers must meet, plus a general duty to keep workplaces safe.

ENFORCEMENT AGENCIES Three federal agencies develop and enforce the standards set by the Occupational Safety and Health Act. The Occupational Safety and Health Administration (OSHA) is part of the Department of Labor and has the authority to promulgate standards, make inspections, and enforce the act. OSHA has safety standards governing many workplace details, such as the structural stability of ladders and the requirements for railings. OSHA also establishes standards that protect employees against exposure to substances that may be harmful to their health.

The National Institute for Occupational Safety and Health is part of the Department of Health and Human Services. Its main duty is to conduct research on safety and health problems and to recommend standards for OSHA to adopt. Finally, the Occupational Safety and Health Review Commission is an independent agency set up to handle appeals from actions taken by OSHA administrators.

PROCEDURES AND VIOLATIONS OSHA compliance officers may enter and inspect facilities of any establishment covered by the Occupational Safety and Health Act.[5] Employees may also file complaints of violations. Under the act, an employer cannot discharge an employee who files a complaint or who, in good faith, refuses to work in a high-risk area if bodily harm or death might result.

Employers with eleven or more employees are required to keep occupational injury and illness records for each employee. Each record must be made available for inspection when requested by an OSHA inspector. Whenever a work-related injury or disease occurs, employers must make reports directly to OSHA. Whenever an employee is killed in a work-related accident or when five or more employees are hospitalized in one accident, the employer must notify the Department of Labor within forty-eight hours. If the company fails to do so, it will be fined. Following the accident, a complete inspection of the premises is mandatory.

Criminal penalties for willful violation of the Occupational Safety and Health Act are limited. Employers may be prosecuted under state laws, however. In other words, the act does not preempt state and local criminal laws.[6]

STATE WORKERS' COMPENSATION LAWS

State **workers' compensation laws** establish an administrative procedure for compensating workers injured on the job. Instead of suing, an injured worker files a claim with the administrative agency or board that administers the local workers' compensation claims.

Most workers' compensation statutes are similar. No state covers all employees. Typically excluded are domestic workers, agricultural workers, temporary employees, and employees of common carriers (companies that provide transportation services to the public). Generally, the statutes cover minors. Usually, the statutes allow employers to purchase insurance from a private insurer or a state fund to pay workers' compensation benefits in the event of a claim. Most states also allow employers to be *self-insured*—that is, employers who show an ability to pay claims do not need to buy insurance.

In general, the right to recover benefits is predicated wholly on the existence of an employment relationship and the fact that the worker's injury was *accidental* and *occurred on the job* or *in the course of employment*, regardless of fault. Intentionally inflicted self-injury, for example, would not be considered accidental and hence would not be covered. If an injury occurred while an employee was commuting to or

4. 29 U.S.C. Sections 553, 651–678.

5. In the past, warrantless inspections were conducted. In 1978, however, the United States Supreme Court held that warrantless inspections violated the warrant clause of the Fourth Amendment to the Constitution. See *Marshall v. Barlow's, Inc.*, 436 U.S. 307, 98 S.Ct. 1816, 56 L.Ed.2d 305 (1978).

6. *Pedraza v. Shell Oil Co.*, 942 F.2d 48 (1st Cir. 1991); *cert.* denied, *Shell Oil Co. v. Pedraza*, 502 U.S. 1082, 112 S.Ct. 993, 117 L.Ed.2d 154 (1992).

from work, it would not usually be considered to have occurred on the job or in the course of employment and hence would not be covered.

An employee must notify his or her employer of an injury promptly (usually within thirty days of the injury's occurrence). Generally, an employee also must file a workers' compensation claim with the appropriate state agency or board within a certain period (sixty days to two years) from the time the injury is first noticed, rather than from the time of the accident.

An employee's acceptance of workers' compensation benefits bars the employee from suing for injuries caused by the employer's negligence. By barring lawsuits for negligence, workers' compensation laws also bar employers from raising common law defenses to negligence, such as contributory negligence. For example, an employer can no longer raise such defenses as contributory negligence or assumption of risk to avoid liability for negligence. A worker may sue an employer who *intentionally* injures the worker, however.

SECTION 3 INCOME SECURITY

Federal and state governments participate in insurance programs designed to protect employees and their families by covering the financial impact of retirement, disability, death, hospitalization, and unemployment. The key federal law on this subject is the Social Security Act of 1935.[7]

SOCIAL SECURITY AND MEDICARE

The Social Security Act provides for old age (retirement), survivors, and disability insurance. The act is therefore often referred to as OASDI. Both employers and employees must "contribute" under the Federal Insurance Contributions Act (FICA)[8] to help pay for the employees' loss of income on retirement. The basis for the employee's and the employer's contribution is the employee's annual wage base—the maximum amount of the employee's wages that are subject to the tax. The employer withholds the employee's FICA contribution from the employee's wages and then matches this contribution. (In 1997, employers were required to withhold 6.2 percent of each employee's wages, up to a maximum amount of $65,400, and to match this contribution.)

Retired workers are eligible to receive monthly payments from the Social Security Administration, which administers the Social Security Act. Social Security benefits are fixed by statute but increase automatically with increases in the cost of living.

Medicare, a health insurance program, is administered by the Social Security Administration for people sixty-five years of age and older and for some under sixty-five who are disabled. It has two parts, one pertaining to hospital costs and the other to nonhospital medical costs, such as visits to doctors' offices. People who have Medicare hospital insurance can obtain additional federal medical insurance if they pay small monthly premiums, which increase as the cost of medical care increases. As with Social Security contributions, both the employer and the employee contribute to Medicare. Currently, 1.45 percent of the amount of all wages and salaries paid to employees, plus a matching amount paid by the employer, go toward financing Medicare. There is no cap on the amount of wages subject to the Medicare tax.

PRIVATE PENSION PLANS

There has been significant legislation to regulate employee retirement plans set up by employers to supplement Social Security benefits. The major federal act covering these retirement plans is the Employee Retirement Income Security Act (ERISA) of 1974.[9] This statute empowers the Labor Management Services Administration of the Department of Labor to enforce its provisions governing employers who have private pension funds for their employees. ERISA does not require an employer to establish a pension plan. When a plan exists, however, ERISA establishes standards for its management.

A key provision of ERISA concerns **vesting.** Vesting gives an employee a legal right to receive pension benefits at some future date when he or she stops working. Before ERISA was enacted, some employees who had worked for companies for as long as thirty years received no pension benefits when their employment terminated, because those benefits had not vested. ERISA establishes complex vesting rules. Generally, however, all employee contributions to pension plans vest immediately, and

7. 42 U.S.C. Sections 301–1397e.

8. 26 U.S.C. Sections 3101–3125.

9. 29 U.S.C. Sections 1001–1461.

employee rights to employer pension-plan contributions vest after five years of employment.

In an attempt to prevent mismanagement of pension funds, ERISA has established rules on how they must be invested. Pension managers must be cautious in their investments and refrain from investing more than 10 percent of the fund in securities of the employer. ERISA also contains detailed record-keeping and reporting requirements.

UNEMPLOYMENT COMPENSATION

The United States has a system of unemployment insurance in which employers pay into a fund, the proceeds of which are paid out to qualified unemployed workers. The Federal Unemployment Tax Act of 1935[10] created a state system that provides unemployment compensation to eligible individuals. Employers that fall under the provisions of the act are taxed at regular intervals. Taxes are typically paid by the employers to the states, which then deposit them with the federal government. The federal government maintains an Unemployment Insurance Fund, in which each state has an account.

SECTION 4 COBRA

Federal legislation also addresses the issue of health insurance for workers whose jobs have been terminated and who are thus no longer eligible for group health-insurance plans. The Consolidated Omnibus Budget Reconciliation Act (COBRA) of 1985[11] prohibits the elimination of a worker's medical, optical, or dental insurance coverage on the voluntary or involuntary termination of the worker's employment. The act includes most workers who have either lost their jobs or had their hours decreased so that they are no longer eligible for coverage under the employer's health plan. Only workers fired for gross misconduct are excluded from protection.

APPLICATION OF COBRA

The worker has sixty days (beginning with the date that the group coverage would stop) to decide whether to continue with the employer's group insurance plan or not. If the worker chooses to discontinue the coverage, then the employer has no further obligation. If the worker chooses to continue coverage, however, the employer is obligated to keep the policy active for up to eighteen months. If the worker is disabled, the employer must extend coverage up to twenty-nine months. The coverage provided must be the same as that enjoyed by the worker prior to the termination or reduction of work. If family members were originally included, for example, COBRA would prohibit their exclusion. This is not a free ride for the worker, however. To receive continued benefits, he or she may be required to pay all of the premium, as well as a 2 percent administrative charge.

EMPLOYERS' OBLIGATIONS UNDER COBRA

Employers, with some exceptions, must comply with COBRA if they employ twenty or more workers and provide a benefit plan to those workers. An employer must inform an employee of COBRA's provisions when a group health plan is established and if that worker faces termination or a reduction of hours that would affect his or her eligibility for coverage under the plan.

An employer is relieved of the responsibility to provide benefit coverage if it completely eliminates its group benefit plan. An employer is also relieved of responsibility when the worker becomes eligible for Medicare, falls under a spouse's health plan, becomes insured under a different plan (with a new employer, for example), or fails to pay the premium.

An employer that fails to comply with COBRA risks substantial penalties. These penalties include a tax of up to 10 percent of the annual cost of the group plan or $500,000, whichever is less.

SECTION 5 FAMILY AND MEDICAL LEAVE

In 1993, Congress passed the Family and Medical Leave Act (FMLA)[12] to protect employees who need time off work for family or medical reasons. A major-

10. 26 U.S.C. Sections 3301–3310.
11. 29 U.S.C. Sections 1161–1169.
12. 29 U.S.C. Sections 2601, 2611–2619, 2651–2654.

ity of the states also have legislation allowing for a leave from employment for family or medical reasons, and many employers maintain private family-leave plans for their workers.

COVERAGE AND APPLICABILITY OF THE FMLA

The FMLA requires employers who have fifty or more employees to provide employees with up to twelve weeks of family or medical leave during any twelve-month period. During the employee's leave, the employer must continue the worker's health-care coverage and guarantee employment in the same position or a comparable position when the employee returns to work. An important exception to the FMLA, however, allows the employer to avoid reinstatement of a *key employee*—defined as an employee whose pay falls within the top 10 percent of the firm's work force. Additionally, the act does not apply to employees who have worked less than one year or less than twenty-five hours a week during the previous twelve months.

Generally, an employee may take family leave when he or she wishes to care for a newborn baby, a newly adopted child, or a foster child just placed in the employee's care.[13] An employee may take medical leave when the employee or the employee's spouse, child, or parent has a "serious health condition" requiring care. For most absences, the employee must demonstrate that the health condition requires continued treatment by a health-care provider and includes a period of incapacity of more than three days. Under regulations issued by the Department of Labor (DOL) in 1995, employees suffering from certain chronic health conditions may take FMLA leave for their own incapacities that require absences of less than three days. For example, an employee who has asthma or diabetes may have periodic episodes of illness, rather than episodes continuing over an extended period of time. Similarly, pregnancy may involve periodic visits to a health-care provider and episodes of morning sickness. According to the DOL's regulations, employees with such conditions are covered by the FMLA.

13. The foster care must be state sanctioned for such an arrangement to fall within the coverage of the FMLA.

REMEDIES FOR VIOLATIONS OF THE FMLA

Remedies for violations of the FMLA include (1) damages for unpaid wages (or salary), lost benefits, denied compensation, and actual monetary losses (such as the cost of providing for care) up to an amount equivalent to the employee's wages for twelve weeks; (2) job reinstatement; and (3) promotion. The successful plaintiff is entitled to court costs, attorneys' fees, and—in cases involving bad faith on the part of the employer—double damages.

SECTION 6

EMPLOYEE PRIVACY RIGHTS

Recall from Chapter 5 that there is no provision in the U.S. Constitution that guarantees a right to privacy. A personal right to privacy, however, has been inferred from other constitutional guarantees provided by the First, Third, Fourth, Fifth, and Ninth Amendments to the Constitution. Additionally, state laws providing for privacy rights may apply in the employment context. Finally, remember from Chapter 12 that the invasion of another's privacy may constitute a tort.

In the last two decades, concerns about the privacy rights of employees have arisen in response to the sometimes invasive tactics used by employers in their efforts to monitor and screen workers. Lie-detector tests, drug tests, and other practices have increasingly been subject to challenge as violations of employee privacy rights.

LIE-DETECTOR TESTS

At one time, many employers required employees or job applicants to take polygraph examinations (lie-detector tests) in connection with their employment. To protect the privacy interests of employees and job applicants, in 1988 Congress passed the Employee Polygraph Protection Act.[14] The statute prohibits employers from (1) requiring or causing employees or job applicants to take lie-detector tests or suggesting or requesting that they do so; (2) using, accepting, referring to, or asking about the results of lie-detector tests taken by employees or applicants; and (3) taking or threatening negative employment-related action

14. 29 U.S.C. Sections 2001–2009.

against employees or applicants based on results of lie-detector tests or on their refusal to take the tests.

Employers excepted from these prohibitions include federal, state, and local government employers; certain security service firms; and companies manufacturing and distributing controlled substances. Other employers may use polygraph tests when investigating losses attributable to theft, including embezzlement and the theft of trade secrets.

DRUG TESTING

In the interests of public safety and to reduce unnecessary costs, many of today's employers, including the government, require their employees to submit to drug testing. Laws relating to the privacy rights of private-sector employees vary from state to state. Some state constitutions prohibit private employers from testing for drugs, and state statutes may restrict drug testing by private employers in any number of ways. A collective bargaining agreement may also provide protection against drug testing. In some instances, employees have brought actions against their employers for the tort of invasion of privacy.

Constitutional limitations apply to the testing of government employees. The Fourth Amendment provides that individuals have the right to be "secure in their persons" against "unreasonable searches and seizures" conducted by government agents. Drug tests have been held constitutional, however, when there was a reasonable basis for suspecting government employees of using drugs. Additionally, when drug use in a particular government job could threaten public safety, testing has been upheld. For example, a U.S. Department of Transportation rule that requires employees engaged in oil and gas pipeline operations to submit to random drug testing was upheld, even though the rule did not require that before being tested the individual must have been suspected of drug use.[15] The court held that the government's interest in promoting public safety in the pipeline industry outweighed the employees' privacy interests.

AIDS TESTING

An increasing number of employers are testing their workers for acquired immune deficiency syndrome (AIDS). Few public issues involve more controversy than this practice. Some state laws restrict AIDS testing, and federal statutes offer some protection to employees and job applicants who have AIDS or have tested positive for the AIDS virus. The federal Americans with Disabilities Act of 1990[16] (discussed in Chapter 21), for example, prohibits discrimination against individuals with disabilities, and the term *disability* has been broadly defined to include those individuals with diseases such as AIDS. The law also requires employers to reasonably accommodate the needs of persons with disabilities. Generally, although the law may not prohibit AIDS testing, it may prohibit the discharge of employees based on the results of those tests.

ELECTRONIC PERFORMANCE MONITORING

A particularly troublesome privacy issue concerns employers' monitoring of their employees' computer files, voice mail, e-mail, or other electronic communications. Electronic monitoring by employers may violate the Electronic Communications Privacy Act (ECPA) of 1986.[17] This act amended existing federal wiretapping law to cover electronic forms of communications, such as communications via cellular telephones or e-mail. The ECPA prohibits the intentional interception of any wire or electronic communication or the intentional disclosure or use of the information obtained by the interception.

The act excludes from coverage, however, any electronic communications through devices that are "furnished to the subscriber or user by a provider of wire or electronic communication service" and that are being used by the subscriber or user, or by the provider of the service, "in the ordinary course of its business." Generally, this "business-extension exception" to the ECPA permits employers to monitor employee telephone conversations in the ordinary course of their businesses. It does not, however, permit employers to monitor employees' personal communications. Under another exception to the ECPA, an employer may also avoid liability under the act if employees consent to having their electronic communications intercepted by the employer.

Generally, there is little specific government regulation of monitoring activities, and an employer may be able to avoid what laws do exist by simply informing employees that they are subject to monitoring.

15. *Electrical Workers Local 1245 v. Skinner*, 913 F.2d 1454 (9th Cir. 1990).

16. 42 U.S.C. Sections 12102–12118.

17. 18 U.S.C. Sections 2510–2521.

Then, if employees challenge the monitoring practice, the employer can raise the defense of consent by claiming that the employees consented to the monitoring. Employers should be cautious when monitoring employees, however, because if an employee brings an action for invasion of privacy, a court may decide that the employee's reasonable expectation of privacy outweighs the employer's need for surveillance. Similarly, an employer should consider alternatives before searching an employee's desk, filing cabinet, or office. If a search is conducted and the employee sues, a court may balance the purposes of the search against its intrusiveness. The court may also consider the availability of less intrusive alternatives that would have accomplished the same purposes.

In a case involving the alleged invasion of employee privacy rights, an important factor to be considered is whether the employee had a reasonable expectation of privacy with regard to the activity involved. A central issue in the following case is whether an employee had a reasonable expectation of privacy in regard to e-mail communications made via the employer's e-mail system.

CASE 20.1 Smyth v. Pillsbury Co.

United States District Court, Eastern District of Pennsylvania, 1996. 914 F.Supp. 97.

BACKGROUND AND FACTS *Pillsbury Company maintained an e-mail system for communications among its employees. Pillsbury told the employees that their e-mail was confidential and would not be used against them. Michael Smyth, a Pillsbury employee, sent e-mail to his supervisor, referring to sales management and threatening to "kill the backstabbing bastards." The e-mail was intercepted, and Smyth was discharged for transmitting inappropriate and unprofessional comments. Smyth filed a suit in a federal district court against Pillsbury, claiming in part that he had been wrongfully discharged in violation of his right to privacy. Pillsbury filed a motion to dismiss.*

IN THE LANGUAGE OF THE COURT

WEINER, District Judge.

* * * *

* * * [W]e do not find a reasonable expectation of privacy in e-mail communications voluntarily made by an employee to his supervisor over the company e-mail system notwithstanding any assurances that such communications would not be intercepted by management. Once plaintiff communicated the alleged unprofessional comments to a second person (his supervisor) over an e-mail system which was apparently utilized by the entire company, any reasonable expectation of privacy was lost. Significantly, the defendant did not require plaintiff, as in the case of an urinalysis or personal property search[,] to disclose any personal information about himself. Rather, plaintiff voluntarily communicated the alleged unprofessional comments over the company e-mail system. We find no privacy interests in such communications.

* * * Moreover, the company's interest in preventing inappropriate and unprofessional comments or even illegal activity over its e-mail system outweighs any privacy interest the employee may have in those comments.

DECISION AND REMEDY *The court granted the employer's motion to dismiss. The employee did not have a reasonable expectation of privacy in his e-mail in these circumstances.*

SCREENING PROCEDURES

An area of concern to potential employees has to do with preemployment screening procedures. What kinds of questions on an employment application or a preemployment test are permissible? What kinds of questions go too far in terms of invading the potential employee's privacy? Is it an invasion of the potential employee's privacy, for example, to ask questions about his or her sexual orientation or religious convictions?

Although an employer may believe that such information is relevant to the job for which the individual has applied, the applicant may feel differently about the matter. Generally, questions on an employment application must have a reasonable nexus, or connection, with the job for which an applicant is applying.[18]

SECTION 7

EMPLOYMENT-RELATED IMMIGRATION LAWS

The most important immigration laws governing employment relationships are the Immigration Reform and Control Act (IRCA) of 1986[19] and the Immigration Act of 1990.[20] The IRCA, which is administered by the U.S. Immigration and Naturalization Service (INS), prohibits employers from hiring illegal immigrants. Employers must complete a special form—called INS Form I-9—for each employee and indicate on it that the employer has verified that the employee is either a U.S. citizen or is otherwise entitled to work in this country.

The Immigration Act of 1990 limits the number of legal immigrants entering the United States by capping the number of visas (entry permits) that are issued each year. Under the act, employers recruiting workers from other countries must complete a certification process and satisfy the Department of Labor that there is a shortage of qualified U.S. workers capable of performing the work. The employer must also establish that bringing immigrants into this country will not adversely affect the existing labor market in that particular area. In this way, the act attempts to serve two purposes: encouraging skilled workers to enter this country and at the same time restricting competition for American jobs.

SECTION 8

WRONGFUL DISCHARGE

Whenever an employer discharges an employee in violation of an employment contract or a statutory law protecting employees, the employee may bring an action for **wrongful discharge.** If an employer's actions do not violate any express employment contract or statute, then the question is whether the employer has violated a common law doctrine. Because of the harsh effects of the employment-at-will doctrine for employees, courts have carved out various exceptions to the doctrine. These exceptions are based on contract theory, tort theory, and public policy.

EXCEPTIONS BASED ON CONTRACT THEORY

Some courts have held that an *implied* employment contract exists between the employer and the employee. If the employee is fired outside the terms of the implied contract, he or she may succeed in an action for breach of contract even though no written employment contract exists.

For example, an employer's manual or personnel bulletin may state that, as a matter of policy, workers will be dismissed only for good cause. If the employee is aware of this policy and continues to work for the employer, a court may find that there is an implied contract based on the terms stated in the manual or bulletin. Promises that an employer makes to employees regarding discharge policy may also be considered part of an implied contract. If the employer fires a worker in a manner contrary to the manner promised, a court may hold that the employer has violated the implied contract and is liable for damages. Most state courts will consider this claim and judge it by traditional contract standards.

A few states have gone further and held that all employment contracts contain an implied covenant of good faith. This means that both sides promise to abide by the contract in good faith. If an employer fires an employee for an arbitrary or unjustified reason, the employee can claim that the covenant of good faith was breached and the contract violated.

In the following case, one of the issues was whether there existed between an employer and its employees an implied-in-fact contract not to demote the employees without good cause.

18. See, for example, *Soroka v. Dayton Hudson Corp.*, 7 Cal.App.4th 203, 1 Cal.Rptr.2d 77 (1991).

19. 29 U.S.C. Section 1802.

20. This act amended various provisions of the Immigration and Nationality Act of 1952, 8 U.S.C. Sections 1101–1524.

CASE 20.2 Scott v. Pacific Gas and Electric Co.

Supreme Court of California, 1995. 11 Cal.4th 454, 904 P.2d 834, 46 Cal.Rptr.2d 427.

HISTORICAL AND SOCIAL SETTING *Faced with more regulations than they can afford to enforce and supported by the popular belief that fewer regulations help businesses prosper, many states are attempting to deregulate some industries. California is leading the way in the deregulation of the power industry. For this reason, utilities in California are facing increased competition. In response, utility firms are cutting costs to increase efficiency. Some of these cuts involve the elimination of jobs. Others involve the investigation of possible employee misconduct, such as time card fraud and conflict of interest.*

BACKGROUND AND FACTS *Pacific Gas and Electric Company (PG&E) had a system called "Positive Discipline" that, according to its personnel manual, was to apply to all employees. The basic principle was to discipline employees only for good cause. Byron Scott and Al Johnson were engineers working for PG&E as senior managers when they were demoted, allegedly for a conflict of interest from their outside consulting practice. They filed a suit in a California state court against PG&E, claiming that there was no good cause for the demotions. The court issued a judgment in their favor, and PG&E appealed. The state appellate court reversed, and the engineers appealed to the Supreme Court of California.*

IN THE LANGUAGE OF THE COURT

MOSK, Justice.

* * * *

* * * PG&E had adopted a detailed system of "Positive Discipline" that was to apply to all employees * * * . PG&E employees had a reasonable expectation that the company would follow its own human resources policy, which had as its basic premise the disciplining of its employees only for good cause.

* * * Scott and Johnson committed no significant conflict of interest violations * * * . PG&E, pursuant to its personnel policies, was obliged to afford Scott and Johnson the opportunity to cure [any] relatively minor offenses through the positive discipline process, but * * * failed to do so * * * . The [trial court] therefore reasonably concluded that PG&E had breached its implied contractual agreement by wrongfully demoting Scott and Johnson.

DECISION AND REMEDY *The Supreme Court of California reversed the decision of the intermediate appellate court and remanded the case. The employer's personnel policies expressed the terms of an implied-in-fact contract between the firm and its employees. Because the employer breached this contract, the employees were entitled to some relief.*

EXCEPTIONS BASED ON TORT THEORY

In a few cases, the discharge of an employee may give rise to an action for wrongful discharge under tort theories. Abusive discharge procedures may result in intentional infliction of emotional distress or defamation. In one case, a restaurant had suffered some thefts of supplies, and the manager announced that he would start firing waitresses alphabetically until the thief was identified. The first waitress fired said that she suffered great emotional distress as a result. The state's highest court upheld her claim as stating a valid cause of action.[21]

21. *Agis v. Howard Johnson Co.*, 371 Mass. 140, 355 N.E.2d 315 (1976).

Some courts have permitted workers to sue their employers under the tort theory of fraud. Under this theory, an employer may be held liable for making false promises to a prospective employee if the employee detrimentally relies on the employer's representations by taking the job. For example, suppose that an employer induces a prospective employee to leave a lucrative job and move to another state by offering "a long-term job with a thriving business." In fact, the employer is having significant financial problems. Furthermore, the employer is planning a merger that will involve the elimination of the position offered to the prospective employee. If the employee takes the job in reliance on the employer's representations and is fired shortly thereafter, the employee may be able to bring an action against the employer for fraud.[22]

EXCEPTIONS BASED ON PUBLIC POLICY

The most widespread common law exception to the employment-at-will doctrine is an exception made on the basis of public policy. Courts may apply this exception when an employer fires a worker for reasons that violate a fundamental public policy of the jurisdiction.

Generally, the courts require that the public policy involved must be expressed clearly in the statutory law governing the jurisdiction. The public policy against employment discrimination, for example, is expressed clearly in federal and state statutes. Thus, if a worker is fired for discriminatory reasons but has no cause of action under statutory law (for example, if the workplace has too few employees to be covered by the statute), that worker may succeed in a suit against the employer for wrongful discharge in violation of public policy.[23]

Sometimes, an employer will direct an employee to perform an illegal act. If the employee refuses to perform the act, the employer may decide to fire the worker. Similarly, employees who "blow the whistle" on the wrongdoing of their employers often find themselves disciplined or even out of a job. **Whistleblowing** occurs when an employee tells a government official, upper-management authorities, or the press that his or her employer is engaged in some unsafe or illegal activity. Whistleblowers on occasion have been protected from wrongful discharge for reasons of public policy. For example, a bank was held to have wrongfully discharged an employee who pressured the employer to comply with state and federal consumer credit laws.[24]

The following case involves an employee who was discharged for violating a company rule in order to save a woman from a life-threatening situation. The employee sued the company, alleging that his discharge violated public policy.

22. See, for example, *Lazar v. Superior Court of Los Angeles Co.*, 12 Cal.4th 631, 909 P.2d 981, 49 Cal.Rptr.2d 377 (1996).

23. See, for example, *Molesworth v. Brandon*, 341 Md. 621, 672 A.2d 608 (1996).

24. *Harless v. First National Bank in Fairmont*, 162 W.Va. 116, 246 S.E.2d 270 (1978).

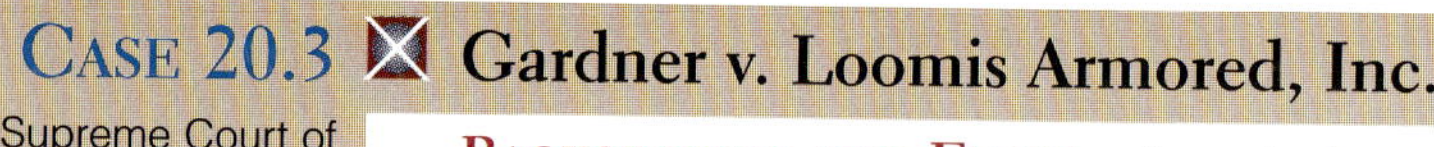

CASE 20.3 Gardner v. Loomis Armored, Inc.

Supreme Court of Washington, 1996. 128 Wash.2d 931, 913 P.2d 377.

BACKGROUND AND FACTS *Loomis Armored, Inc., has a company rule forbidding its armored truck drivers from leaving their trucks unattended. The employee handbook states, "Violations of this rule will be grounds for termination." Kevin Gardner worked for Loomis as a driver. During a scheduled stop at a bank, Gardner left the truck to aid a woman who was being threatened by a man with a knife. Gardner was discharged for violating Loomis's rule. In Gardner's subsequent suit against Loomis, the Supreme Court of Washington was asked whether employment termination in these circumstances violates public policy.*

IN THE LANGUAGE OF THE COURT

DOLLIVER, Justice.

* * * *

The narrow public policy encouraging citizens to rescue persons from life threatening situations clearly evinces [demonstrates] a fundamental societal interest * * * . The value attached to such acts of heroism is plainly demonstrated by the fact that society has waived most criminal and tort penalties stemming from conduct necessarily committed in the course of saving a life. If our society has placed the rescue of a life above constitutional rights and above the criminal code, then such conduct clearly rises above a company's work rule. Loomis' work rule does not provide an overriding justification for firing Gardner when his conduct directly served the public policy encouraging citizens to save persons from serious bodily injury or death.

We find that Gardner's discharge for leaving the truck and saving a woman from an imminent life threatening situation violates the public policy encouraging such heroic conduct. This holding does not create an affirmative legal duty requiring citizens to intervene in dangerous life threatening situations. We simply observe that society values and encourages voluntary rescuers when a life is in danger. Additionally, our adherence to this public policy does nothing to invalidate Loomis' work rule regarding drivers' leaving the trucks. * * * Our holding merely forbids Loomis from firing Gardner when he broke the rule because he saw a woman who faced imminent life threatening harm, and he reasonably believed his intervention was necessary to save her life. Finally, by focusing on the narrow public policy encouraging citizens to save human lives from life threatening situations, we continue to protect employers from frivolous lawsuits.

DECISION AND REMEDY *The Supreme Court of Washington ruled that Gardner's discharge was in violation of the public policy of encouraging citizens to aid others in life-threatening situations.*

SECTION 9 STATUTORY PROTECTION FOR WHISTLEBLOWERS

To encourage workers to report employer wrongdoing, such as fraud, a number of states[25] have enacted so-called whistleblower statutes. These statutes protect whistleblowers from subsequent retaliation on the part of employers. On the federal level, the Whistleblower Protection Act of 1989[26] protects federal employees who blow the whistle on their employers from their employers' retaliatory actions. Whistleblower statutes may also provide an incentive to disclose information by providing the whistleblower with a monetary reward. For example, the federal False Claims Reform Act of 1986[27] requires that a whistleblower who has disclosed information relating to a fraud perpetrated against the U.S. government receive between 15 and 25 percent of the proceeds if the government brings suit against the wrongdoer.

25. At least thirty-seven states now have whistleblower statutes.
26. 5 U.S.C. Section 1201.
27. 31 U.S.C. Sections 3729–3733. This act amended the False Claims Act of 1863.

TERMS AND CONCEPTS TO REVIEW

employment at will 416
minimum wage 417
vesting 419
whistleblowing 426
workers' compensation laws 418
wrongful discharge 424

QUESTIONS AND CASE PROBLEMS

20–1. LABOR LAWS. Calzoni Boating Co. is an interstate business engaged in manufacturing and selling boats. The company has five hundred nonunion employees. Representatives of these employees are requesting a four-day, ten-hours-per-day workweek, and Calzoni is concerned that this would require paying time and a half after eight hours per day. Which federal act is Calzoni thinking of that might require this? Will the act in fact require paying time and a half for all hours worked over eight hours per day if the employees' proposal is accepted? Explain.

20–2. HEALTH AND SAFETY REGULATIONS. Denton and Carlo were employed at an appliance plant. Their job required them to do occasional maintenance work while standing on a wire mesh twenty feet above the plant floor. Other employees had fallen through the mesh, and one of them had been killed by the fall. When Denton and Carlo were asked by their supervisor to do work that would likely require them to walk on the mesh, they refused because of their fear of bodily harm or death. Because of their refusal to do the requested work, the two employees were fired from their jobs. Was their discharge wrongful? If so, under what federal employment law? To what federal agency or department should they turn for assistance?

20–3. UNFAIR LABOR PRACTICES. Suppose that Consolidated Stores is undergoing a unionization campaign. Prior to the union election, management says that the union is unnecessary to protect workers. Management also provides bonuses and wage increases to the workers during this period. The employees reject the union. Union organizers protest that the wage increases during the election campaign unfairly prejudiced the vote. Should these wage increases be regarded as an unfair labor practice? Discuss.

20–4. WORKERS' COMPENSATION. Galvin Strang worked for a tractor company in one of its factories. Near his work station was a conveyor belt that ran through a large industrial oven. Sometimes, the workers would use the oven to heat their meals. Thirty-inch-high flasks containing molds were fixed at regular intervals on the conveyor and were transported into the oven. Strang had to walk between the flasks to get to his work station. One day, the conveyor was not moving, and Strang used the oven to cook a frozen pot pie. As he was removing the pot pie from the oven, the conveyor came on. One of the flasks struck Strang and seriously injured him. Strang sought recovery under the state workers' compensation law. Should he recover? Why or why not?

20–5. HEALTH AND SAFETY REGULATIONS. At an REA Express, Inc., shipping terminal, a conveyor belt was inoperative because an electrical circuit had shorted out. The manager called a licensed electrical contractor. When the contractor arrived, REA's maintenance supervisor was in the circuit breaker room. The floor was wet, and the maintenance supervisor was using sawdust to try to soak up the water. While the licensed electrical contractor was standing on the wet floor and attempting to fix the short circuit, he was electrocuted. Simultaneously, REA's maintenance supervisor, who was standing on a wooden platform, was burned and knocked unconscious. The Occupational Safety and Health Administration (OSHA) sought to fine REA Express $1,000 for failure to furnish a place of employment free from recognized hazards. Will the court uphold OSHA's decision? Discuss fully. [*REA Express, Inc. v. Brennan*, 495 F.2d 822 (2d Cir. 1974)]

20–6. EMPLOYMENT AT WILL. Robert Adams worked as a delivery truck driver for George W. Cochran & Co. Adams persistently refused to drive a truck that lacked a required inspection sticker and was subsequently fired as a result of his refusal. Adams was an at-will employee, and Cochran contended that because there was no written employment contract stating otherwise, Cochran was entitled to discharge Adams at will—that is, for cause or no cause. Adams sought to recover $7,094 in lost wages and $200,000 in damages for the "humiliation, mental anguish and emotional distress" that he had suffered as a result of being fired from his job. Under what legal doctrines discussed in this chapter—or exceptions to those doctrines—might Adams be able to recover damages from Cochran? Discuss fully. [*Adams v. George W. Cochran & Co.*, 597 A.2d 28 (D.C.App. 1991)]

20–7. WORKERS' COMPENSATION. Linda Burnett Kidwell, employed as a state traffic officer by the California Highway Patrol (CHP), suffered an injury at home, off duty, while practicing the standing long jump. The jump is a required component of the CHP's annual physical performance program fitness test. Kidwell filed a claim for workers' compensation benefits. CHP and the California workers' compensation appeals board denied her claim. Kidwell appealed to a state appellate court. What is the requirement for granting a workers' compensation claim? Should Kidwell's claim be granted? [*Kidwell v. Workers' Compensation Appeals Board*, 33 Cal.App.4th 1130, 39 Cal.Rptr.2d 540 (1995)]

20–8. PRIVACY RIGHTS. The city of Los Angeles requires a polygraph examination for police officers who ask to be promoted or transferred into a few specialized divisions where the work is unusually sensitive and requires a high level of integrity. Generally, those who fail the test are not promoted or transferred, but neither are they demoted or otherwise penalized. The Los Angeles Protective League filed a suit against the city in a California state court, asking the court, among other things, to order the city to stop the testing. On what basis might the court grant the league's request? On what basis might it refuse to do so? [*Los Angeles Protective League v. City of Los Angeles*, 35 Cal.App.4th 1535, 42 Cal.Rptr.2d 23 (1995)]

20–9. WHISTLEBLOWING. Gabor Nagy was a car salesperson for Whittlesey Automotive Group. Whittlesey asked Nagy to allow some of his phone conversations with "customers" to be recorded. The "customers" were actually employees of a company Whittlesey had hired to conduct a sales training program. Nagy refused to consent. He was eventually fired for his "negative attitude." Nagy filed a suit in a California state court against Whittlesey. He cited a state statute that makes eavesdropping a crime and alleged in part that he was wrongfully terminated in violation of public policy. Will the court agree? Discuss fully. [*Nagy v. Whittlesey Automotive Group*, 40 Cal.App.4th 1328, 47 Cal.Rptr.2d 395 (1995)]

20–10. PERFORMANCE MONITORING. The Communications Operations Division (COD) of the Milwaukee Police Department (MPD) received incoming emergency calls and coordinated the dispatch of officers. All incoming emergency calls were taped. The taping system was in a glass case in the middle of the COD work area. Also, the employees knew that their supervisors might monitor their calls for evaluation and training purposes. Cynthia Griffin, a COD telecommunicator, filed a suit in a federal district court against the MPD and her supervisors, alleging that they had illegally monitored her personal calls. For what reasons might the court rule in favor of the defendants? [*Griffin v. City of Milwaukee*, 74 F.3d 824 (7th Cir. 1996)]

20–11. A QUESTION OF ETHICS

Paul Luedtke was employed by Nabors Alaska Drilling, Inc., to work on the company's drilling rigs on Alaska's North Slope. Over the course of his employment, Luedtke was promoted to driller, a position in which he was responsible for overseeing the work of an entire drilling crew. Twice during Luedtke's employment he was accused of violating company drug and alcohol policies, and he was once disciplined for taking alcohol to the North Slope in contravention of company regulations. Some time later, Luedtke was ordered to submit to a physical examination, ostensibly to meet the company's physical standards for work on offshore drilling rigs. As part of the examination, Luedtke's urine was tested for drugs. The results indicated marijuana use, and Luedtke was ordered to submit to and pass two subsequent drug tests before continuing employment with the company. Luedtke refused to comply and was fired. Luedtke brought suit against the company on the basis of several legal theories. The Alaska Supreme Court held that the common law of Alaska expressed a public policy of protecting certain "spheres of employee conduct" and " 'private' information" from scrutiny by private employers. The court went on to find, however, that such policy did not protect Luedtke because the drug testing was based on the company's legitimate need to control drug use in a hazardous environment like the one in which Luedtke was employed. [*Luedtke v. Nabors Alaska Drilling, Inc.*, 768 P.2d 1123 (Alaska, 1989)]

1. The court in this case stated that the public policy of the state protected off-the-job activities and that companies could only test employees at times "contemporaneous with the employee's work time" and only if testing was for the limited purpose of "monitoring drug use that may directly affect employee performance." Legal arguments aside, is this a fair restriction on employers? Society seeks to protect against racial and other forms of discrimination in the workplace but generally leaves employers free to choose workers on the basis of whatever other criteria they deem fit. Should private employers be free to discharge or not hire workers on the basis of characteristics they find objectionable—like drug use, for instance—regardless of the relation between those characteristics and work performance?
2. Even if a worker's off-the-job life-style does not "directly affect employee performance," are there other practical considerations that support an employer's wanting to know about certain employee characteristics? Could not certain "private" activities affect a worker's long-term health and life expectancy? This is certainly a practical concern of an employer, if not a moral one. Should any other social goal—the right to privacy, say—take precedence over such practical considerations?
3. Could investigation into the private affairs of an employee be justified as indicating the employee's propensities for other conduct important to the employer? For example, does illegal drug use demonstrate a propensity to break other laws? What about marital infidelity—are unfaithful spouses likely to be employees prone to stealing or embezzling from an employer? In general, how limited should an employee's expectation of privacy be?

20–12. CASE BRIEFING ASSIGNMENT

Examine Case A.5 [*Johnston v. Del Mar Distributing Co.*, 776 S.W.2d 768 (Tex.App.—Corpus Christi 1989)] in Appendix A. The case has been excerpted there in great detail. Review and then brief the case, making sure that you include answers to the following questions in your brief.

1. Why did Del Mar Distributing Co. terminate Nancy Johnston's employment?
2. What defense did Del Mar raise against Johnston's claim of wrongful discharge.
3. On what case precedent did the appellate court base its reasoning?
4. Why did the appellate court conclude that, given the circumstances of this case, it was irrelevant whether the act itself that Johnston was asked to perform was legal or illegal?

ACCESSING THE INTERNET

THE LEGAL ENVIRONMENT OF BUSINESS

BenefitsLink offers extensive information on employee benefits, including the full text of the Employee Retirement Income Security Act (ERISA) and links to other benefits resources on the Internet. You can access BenefitsLink at

http://www.benefitslink.com/index

A site that offers information on health-care benefits for employees can be accessed at

http://www.rbvdnr.com/eb/eb-main.htm

The Web site of the Occupational Safety and Health Administration (OSHA) offers information related to workplace health and safety, including the text of the Occupational Safety and Health Act of 1970, information on how and where to file an OSHA complaint, OSHA standards and regulations, OSHA directives, and more. You can access the site at

http://www.osha-slc.gov

The Bureau of Labor Statistics offers a wide variety of data on employment, including data on employment compensation, working conditions, and productivity. Go to

http://stats.bls.gov/blshome.html

You can find information on whistleblowing at a Web site operated by Philips & Cohen, a law firm that specializes in defending whistleblowers. Go to

http://www.whistleblowers.com/

To read the Fair Labor Standards Act, go to:

http://www.law.cornell.edu/uscode/29/ch8.html

If you want to review proposed OSHA rules, you can access the *Federal Register* at

http://ssdc.ucsd.edu/gpo/

To learn more about Social Security, access the Social Security Administration's home page at

http://www.ssa.gov/

CHAPTER 21

EMPLOYMENT DISCRIMINATION

DURING THE EARLY 1960S, we, as a nation, focused our attention on the civil rights of all Americans, including our rights under the Fourteenth Amendment to the equal protection of the laws. Out of this movement to end racial and other forms of discrimination grew a body of law protecting workers against discrimination in the workplace. This protective legislation further eroded the employment-at-will doctrine, which was discussed in Chapter 20. In the past several decades, judicial decisions, administrative agency actions, and legislation have restricted the ability of employers, as well as unions, to discriminate against workers on the basis of race, color, religion, national origin, gender, age, or disability. A class of persons defined by one or more of these criteria is known as a **protected class.**

Several federal statutes prohibit **employment discrimination** against members of protected classes. The most important statute is Title VII of the Civil Rights Act of 1964.[1] Title VII prohibits employment discrimination on the basis of race, color, religion, national origin, and gender. Discrimination on the basis of age and disability are prohibited by the Age Discrimination in Employment Act of 1967[2] and the Americans with Disabilities Act of 1990,[3] respectively.

This chapter focuses on the kinds of discrimination prohibited by these federal statutes. Note, however, that discrimination against employees on the basis of any of the above-mentioned criteria may also violate state human rights statutes or other state laws prohibiting discrimination.

1. 42 U.S.C. Sections 2000e–2000e-17.
2. 29 U.S.C. Sections 621–634.
3. 42 U.S.C. Sections 12102–12118.

SECTION 1

TITLE VII OF THE CIVIL RIGHTS ACT OF 1964

Title VII of the Civil Rights Act of 1964 and its amendments prohibit job discrimination against employees, applicants, and union members on the basis of race, color, national origin, religion, and gender at any stage of employment. Title VII applies to employers affecting interstate commerce with fifteen or more employees, labor unions with fifteen or more members, labor unions that operate hiring halls (to which members go regularly to be rationed jobs as they become available), employment agencies, and state and local governing units or agencies. A special section of the act prohibits discrimination in most federal government employment.

Title VII applies to any employer that "has fifteen or more employees for each working day in each of twenty or more calendar weeks in the current or preceding calendar year." One of the problems that courts have faced in applying Title VII is how to interpret the phrase "has fifteen or more employees." Does an employer "have" an employee on any working day on which the employer maintains an employment relationship with the employee, or only on working days on which the employee is actually receiving compensation from the employer? In 1997, the United States Supreme Court resolved this issue by holding that the test for when an employer "has" an employee is whether the employer has an employment relationship with the individual on the day in question. This test is generally called the "payroll method," because the employment relationship is most readily demonstrated by the individual's appearance on the employer's payroll as a full-time or part-time worker.[4]

PROCEDURES UNDER TITLE VII

Compliance with Title VII is monitored by the Equal Employment Opportunity Commission (EEOC). A victim of alleged discrimination, before bringing a suit against the employer, must first file a claim with the EEOC. The EEOC may investigate the dispute and attempt to obtain the parties' voluntary consent to an out-of-court settlement. If voluntary agreement cannot be reached, the EEOC may then file a suit against the employer on the employee's behalf. If the EEOC decides not to investigate the claim, the victim may bring his or her own lawsuit against the employer.

Until recently, the EEOC investigated every claim of employment discrimination, regardless of the merits of the claim. In 1996, however, in its National Enforcement Plan, the EEOC stated that it will investigate only "priority cases." The plan contains a list of the types of cases that the EEOC wants to investigate and take to litigation and those that it does not. Generally, priority cases are cases that affect many workers, cases involving retaliatory discharge (firing an employee in retaliation for submitting a claim with the EEOC), and cases involving types of discrimination that are of particular concern to the EEOC.

INTENTIONAL AND UNINTENTIONAL DISCRIMINATION

Title VII prohibits both intentional and unintentional discrimination. Intentional discrimination by an employer against an employee is known as **disparate-treatment discrimination.** Because intent may sometimes be difficult to prove, courts have established certain procedures for resolving disparate-treatment cases. Suppose that a woman applies for employment with a construction firm and is rejected. If she sues on the basis of disparate-treatment discrimination in hiring, she must show that (1) she is a member of a protected class, (2) she applied and was qualified for the job in question, (3) she was rejected by the employer, and (4) the employer continued to seek applicants for the position or filled the position with a person not in a protected class.

If the woman can meet these relatively easy requirements, she makes out a ***prima facie* case** of illegal discrimination. Making out a *prima facie* case of discrimination means that the plaintiff has met her initial burden of proof and will win in the absence of a legally acceptable employer defense (defenses to claims of employment discrimination will be discussed later in this chapter). The burden then shifts to the employer-defendant, who must articulate a legal reason for not hiring the plaintiff. For example, the employer might say that the plaintiff was not hired because she lacked sufficient experience or training. To prevail, the plaintiff must then show that the employer's reason is a *pretext* (not the true reason) and that discriminatory intent actually motivated the employer's decision.

Employers often find it necessary to use interviews and testing procedures to choose from among a large number of applicants for job openings.

4. *Walters v. Metropolitan Educational Enterprises, Inc.*, ___ U.S. ___, 117 S.Ct. 660, 136 L.Ed.2d 644 (1997).

Minimum educational requirements are also common. Employer practices, such as those involving educational requirements, may have an unintended discriminatory impact on a protected class. **Disparate-impact discrimination** occurs when, as a result of educational or other job requirements or hiring procedures, an employer's work force does not reflect the percentage of nonwhites, women, or members of other protected classes that characterizes the pool of qualified individuals in the local labor market. If a person challenging an employment practice having a discriminatory effect can show a connection between the practice and the disparity, he or she makes out a *prima facie* case, and no evidence of discriminatory intent needs to be shown.

DISCRIMINATION BASED ON RACE, COLOR, AND NATIONAL ORIGIN

Title VII prohibits employers from discriminating against employees or job applicants on the basis of race, color, or national origin. This prohibition extends to both intentional (disparate-treatment) and unintentional (disparate-impact) discrimination. If a company's standards or policies for selecting or promoting employees have the effect of discriminating against employees or job applicants on the basis of race, color, or national origin, they are illegal—unless (except for race) they have a substantial, demonstrable relationship to realistic qualifications for the job in question. Discrimination against these protected classes in regard to employment conditions and benefits is also illegal.

Note that victims of racial or ethnic discrimination also may have a cause of action under 42 U.S.C. Section 1981. This section, which was enacted as part of the Civil Rights Act of 1866, prohibits discrimination on the basis of race or ethnicity in the formation or enforcement of contracts. Although Section 1981 remained a dead letter on the books for over a century, since the 1970s many plaintiffs have succeeded in Section 1981 cases against their employers. Unlike Title VII, Section 1981 does not place caps on damages (see the discussion of Title VII remedies later in this chapter). Thus, if an employee can prove that he or she was discriminated against in the formation or enforcement of a contract, the employee may be able to obtain a greater amount in damages under Section 1981 than under Title VII.

A question currently being faced by the courts is whether an employer's English-only policy in the workplace constitutes discrimination on the basis of national origin. In its interpretive guidelines on the issue, the EEOC has stated that any English-only policy that prohibits employees from speaking languages other than English *at all times* (including during breaks, lunch hours, and so on) constitutes impermissible discrimination on the basis of national origin. Furthermore, any English-only policy must be justified by "business necessity" (see the discussion of defenses to discrimination later in this chapter). The courts that have addressed the issue, however, seem to show greater tolerance than the EEOC toward English-only policies. Generally, the courts have held that employees' rights do not include the right to speak their native language in the workplace.[5]

In all disparate-impact cases, there are two basic questions—whether a standard or policy has a discriminatory impact and, if it does, whether the standard or policy nevertheless has a substantial, demonstrable relationship to the job. These questions were at issue in the following case.

5. See the *Focus on Ethics* following Chapter 22 for a further discussion of how the courts have dealt with this issue.

CASE 21.1 Fickling v. New York State Department of Civil Service

United States District Court, Southern District of New York, 1995. 909 F.Supp. 185.

BACKGROUND AND FACTS *Job applicants for the position of Social Welfare Eligibility Examiner for Westchester County, New York, must pass a New York State Department of Civil Service examination. In 1989 and 1990, the exam tested mainly reading comprehension and arithmetic, skills that were of relatively little importance to the job. When it was revealed that fewer than two African Americans and about one Hispanic passed the exam for every three non-Hispanic whites who passed, Juliette Fickling and seven other members of protected classes who had failed the test (the plaintiffs) filed a suit in a federal district court against the state and the county. The plaintiffs alleged violations of, among other things, Title VII.*

IN THE LANGUAGE OF THE COURT

PARKER, District Judge.

* * * *

* * * A selection rate for any race, sex, or ethnic group which is less than four-fifths (4/5) (or eighty percent) of the rate for the group with the highest rate will generally be regarded * * * as evidence of adverse impact * * * ." Here, the disparate racial impact * * * was far below the 80% standard. * * *

* * * *

* * * [T]he examination tested mainly reading comprehension. In addition, 38% of the questions required arithmetic. The ability to do arithmetic, however was found to be unimportant to successful job performance * * * . The examinations did not test written expression or oral expression, except the ability to describe eligibility requirements in a comprehensible manner, despite the fact that these abilities were found to be very important to successful job performance * * * .

DECISION AND REMEDY *The federal district court ruled in favor of the plaintiffs and ordered the parties to submit briefs on the issue of remedies.*

DISCRIMINATION BASED ON RELIGION

Title VII of the Civil Rights Act of 1964 also prohibits government employers, private employers, and unions from discriminating against persons because of their religion. An employer must "reasonably accommodate" the religious practices of its employees, unless to do so would cause undue hardship to the employer's business. For example, if an employee's religion prohibits him or her from working on a certain day of the week or at a certain type of job, the employer must make a reasonable attempt to accommodate these religious requirements. Employers must reasonably accommodate an employee's religious belief even if the belief is not based on the tenets or dogma of a particular church, sect, or denomination. The only requirement is that the belief be sincerely held by the employee.[6]

DISCRIMINATION BASED ON GENDER

Under Title VII, as well as other federal acts, employers are forbidden to discriminate against employees on the basis of gender. Employers are prohibited from classifying jobs as male or female and from advertising in help-wanted columns that are designated male or female unless the employer can prove that the gender of the applicant is essential to the job. Furthermore, employers cannot have separate male and female seniority lists. Generally, to succeed in a suit for gender discrimination, a plaintiff must demonstrate that gender was a determining factor in the employer's decision to hire, fire, or promote him or her. Typically, this involves looking at all of the surrounding circumstances.

The Pregnancy Discrimination Act of 1978,[7] which amended Title VII, expanded the definition of gender discrimination to include discrimination based on pregnancy. Women affected by pregnancy, childbirth, or related medical conditions must be treated—for all employment-related purposes, including the receipt of benefits under employee-benefit programs—the same as other persons not so affected but similar in ability to work. An employer is required to treat an employee temporarily unable to perform her job owing to a pregnancy-related condition in the same manner as the employer would treat other temporarily disabled employees. The employer must change work assignments, grant paid disability leaves, or grant leaves without pay if that is how it would treat other employees with temporary disabilities. Policies concerning an employee's return to work, accrual of seniority, pay increases, and so on must also result in equal treatment.

SEXUAL HARASSMENT

Title VII also protects employees against **sexual harassment** in the workplace. Sexual harassment can take two forms: *quid pro quo* harassment and hostile-environment harassment. *Quid pro quo* is a Latin phrase that is often translated to mean "something in exchange for something else." *Quid pro quo*

6. *Frazee v. Illinois Department of Employment Security*, 489 U.S. 829, 109 S.Ct. 1514, 103 L.Ed.2d 914 (1989).

7. 42 U.S.C. Section 2000e(k).

harassment occurs when job opportunities, promotions, salary increases, and so on are given in return for sexual favors. Hostile-environment harassment occurs when an employee is subjected to sexual conduct or comments that he or she perceives as offensive. The EEOC's guidelines on harassment state that the following types of verbal and physical conduct constitute hostile-environment harassment:

1. Conduct that has the purpose or effect of creating an intimidating, hostile, or offensive working environment.
2. Conduct that has the purpose or effect of unreasonably interfering with an individual's performance in the workplace.
3. Conduct that otherwise adversely affects an individual's employment opportunities.

Prior to the United States Supreme Court's 1993 decision in *Harris v. Forklift Systems, Inc.*,[8] many jurisdictions had held that a worker claiming to be a victim of hostile-environment harassment must establish that he or she suffered serious psychological effects as a result of the offensive conduct. In the *Harris* case, the Supreme Court held that "Title VII bars conduct that would seriously affect a reasonable person's psychological well-being, but the statute is not limited to such conduct. So long as the environment would reasonably be perceived, and is perceived, as hostile or abusive, there is no need for it also to be psychologically injurious."

In *Harris*, the Court also addressed another issue on which the courts had been divided: Should a neutral and objective "reasonable person" standard apply in harassment cases, or should a more subjective "reasonable female" or "reasonable male" standard be used? The Court adopted a broad standard by holding that in cases of alleged sexual harassment, the conduct at issue must be abusive both objectively (as perceived by a reasonable person) and subjectively (as perceived by the victim).

Even if an employee can prove that sexually offensive conduct occurred, at what point does such conduct result in an "intimidating, hostile, or offensive working environment" or otherwise qualify as hostile-environment harassment under the EEOC's guidelines? Courts have had to struggle with such questions and usually render their decisions on a case-by-case basis. In some cases, even one incident of sexually offensive conduct can result in a hostile, offensive working environment.[9]

HARASSMENT BY SUPERVISORS AND CO-WORKERS Generally, employers are held liable for Title VII violations by the firm's managerial or supervisory personnel. Normally, in *quid pro quo* harassment cases, the courts hold employers strictly liable for the harassment. In other words, the employer will be held liable regardless of whether the employer knew about the harassment. In hostile-environment cases, however, the courts tend to hold employers liable only if the employers knew or should have known of the harassment and failed to take prompt remedial action. Employers that *do* take prompt action to remedy the problem, however, often can avoid liability for the harassment. Additionally, employers that provide specific guidelines for their employees on sexual harassment—guidelines indicating how to report incidents of harassment—may not be held liable if employees fail to complain of the harassment through the proper channels.[10]

In some cases, high-level supervisors have been held personally liable for harassment under the theory that they exercised sufficient control to be deemed employers. There is a growing consensus among the courts, however, that supervisors cannot be held liable, as employers, under Title VII.[11]

Often, employees alleging harassment complain that the actions of co-workers, not supervisors, are responsible for creating a hostile working environment. In such cases, the employee still has a cause of action against the employer. Generally, though, the employer will be held liable only if it knew or should have known about the harassment and failed to take immediate remedial action.

The following case raises the issue of whether an employer can be held responsible for doing nothing in a situation involving harassment even though the harassing employee had voluntarily ceased the harassment.

---

8. 510 U.S. 17, 114 S.Ct. 367, 126 L.Ed.2d 295 (1993).

9. See *Radtke v. Everett*, 442 Mich. 368, 501 N.W.2d 155 (1993); and *Nadeau v. Rainbow Rugs, Inc.*, 675 A.2d 973 (Me. 1996).

10. See, for example, *Baskerville v. Culligan International Co.*, 50 F.3d 428 (7th Cir. 1995).

11. See, for example, *Williams v. Banning*, 72 F.3d 552 (7th Cir. 1995); and *Sheridan v. E. I. du Pont de Nemours and Co.*, 74 F.3d 1439 (3d Cir. 1996).

CASE 21.2 Fuller v. City of Oakland, California

United States Court of Appeals, Ninth Circuit, 1995. 47 F.3d 1522.

HISTORICAL AND SOCIAL SETTING *At one time, a fear of false reporting limited the testimony of women in the prosecution of rape cases. In the 1970s, this same fear of false reporting was one of the reasons some observers initially opposed the recognition of sexual harassment as discrimination on the basis of gender. Others believed that harassment reflects a conflict between personalities, or that it is based on sexual attractiveness, not gender. Some felt that even if some conduct is harassment, once it stops, the employer should not be held responsible for it.*

BACKGROUND AND FACTS *Patricia Fuller and Antonio Romero were police officers with the city of Oakland, California, when they had a brief romantic relationship. When Fuller broke it off, Romero—who had been promoted to a supervisory position—began to harass her on and off duty. Fuller complained to their superiors. Romero stopped harassing her, and the superiors took no action, except to officially call Fuller's complaint "unfounded." Fuller resigned and filed a suit against the city in a federal district court under Title VII. The city argued that when the harassment stopped, its own responsibility ceased. The court agreed. Fuller appealed to the U.S. Court of Appeals for the Ninth Circuit.*

IN THE LANGUAGE OF THE COURT

POOLE, Circuit Judge:

* * * *

* * * Once an employer knows or should know of harassment, a remedial obligation kicks in. That obligation will not be discharged until action—prompt, effective action—has been taken. Effectiveness will be measured by the twin purposes of ending the current harassment and deterring future harassment—by the same offender or others. * * *

* * * Title VII does not permit employers to stand idly by once they learn that sexual harassment has occurred. To do so amounts to a ratification of the prior harassment. * * *

DECISION AND REMEDY *The U.S. Court of Appeals for the Ninth Circuit reversed the judgment of the lower court and remanded the case. An employer can be held liable for the actions of an employee who commits sexual harassment, even if the harassment has stopped.*

HARASSMENT BY NONEMPLOYEES Employers may also be liable for harassment by *nonemployees* under certain conditions. For example, if a restaurant owner or manager knows that a certain customer repeatedly harasses a waitress and permits the harassment to continue, the restaurant owner may be liable under Title VII even though the customer is not an employee of the restaurant. The issue turns on the control that the employer exerts over a nonemployee. In the situation just described, a court would likely conclude that the restaurant manager or owner could have taken action to prevent the customer from harassing the waitress.

SAME-GENDER HARASSMENT A number of cases have been brought in which plaintiffs allege same-gender harassment—that is, harassment of males by other males or females by other females. The federal courts are widely split on this issue. In some jurisdictions, courts have held that plaintiffs may bring actions under Title VII for same-gender harassment;[12] in other jurisdictions, courts have held to the contrary.[13]

12. See, for example, *McCoy v. Johnson Controls World Services, Inc.*, 878 F.Supp. 229 (S.D.Ga. 1995).

13. See, for example, *McWilliams v. Fairfax County Board of Supervisors*, 72 F.3d 1191 (4th Cir. 1996).

REMEDIES UNDER TITLE VII

Employer liability under Title VII may be extensive. If the plaintiff successfully proves that unlawful discrimination occurred, he or she may be awarded reinstatement, back pay, retroactive promotions, and damages.[14] Compensatory damages are available only in cases of intentional discrimination. Punitive damages may be recovered against a private employer only if the employer acted with malice or reckless indifference to an individual's rights. The sum of the amount of compensatory and punitive damages is limited by the statute to specific amounts against specific employers—ranging from $50,000 against employers with one hundred or fewer employees to $300,000 against employers with more than five hundred employees.

As noted earlier, 42 U.S.C. Section 1981, which was enacted as part of the Civil Rights Act of 1866, prohibits discrimination on the basis of race or ethnicity in the formation or enforcement of contracts. Because Section 1981 does not place caps on damages, many individuals alleging forms of discrimination prohibited by this section have sought relief under this law.

SECTION 2 EQUAL PAY ACT OF 1963

The Equal Pay Act of 1963 was enacted as an amendment to the Fair Labor Standards Act of 1938. Basically, the act prohibits gender-based discrimination in the wages paid for similar work on jobs. For the equal pay requirements to apply, the male and female employees must work at the same establishment.

It is job content rather than job description that controls in all cases. To determine whether the Equal Pay Act has been violated, a court will thus look to the primary duties of the two jobs. The jobs of a barber and a beautician, for example, are considered essentially equal. So, too, are those of a tailor and a seamstress. Small differences in job content do not justify higher pay for one gender.

A wage differential for equal work is justified if it is shown to be based on (1) seniority, (2) merit, (3) a system that pays according to quality or quantity of production, or (4) any factor other than gender.

14. Damages were not available under Title VII until 1991. The Civil Rights Act of that year amended Title VII to provide for both compensatory and punitive damages, as well as jury trials.

SECTION 3 DISCRIMINATION BASED ON AGE

Age discrimination is potentially the most widespread form of discrimination, because anyone—regardless of race, color, national origin, or gender—could be a victim at some point in life. The Age Discrimination in Employment Act (ADEA) of 1967, as amended, prohibits employment discrimination on the basis of age against individuals forty years of age or older. The act also prohibits mandatory retirement for nonmanagerial workers. For the act to apply, an employer must have twenty or more employees, and the employer's business activities must affect interstate commerce.

The burden-shifting procedure under the ADEA is similar to that under Title VII. If a plaintiff can establish that he or she (1) was a member of the protected age group, (2) was qualified for the position from which he or she was discharged, and (3) was discharged under circumstances that give rise to an inference of discrimination, the plaintiff has established a *prima facie* case of unlawful age discrimination. The burden then shifts to the employer, who must articulate a legitimate reason for the discrimination. If the plaintiff can prove that the employer's reason is only a pretext and that the plaintiff's age was a determining factor in the employer's decision, the employer will be held liable under the ADEA.

Numerous cases of alleged age discrimination have been brought against employers who, to cut costs, replaced older, higher-salaried employees with younger, lower-salaried workers. Whether a firing is discriminatory or simply part of a rational business decision to prune the company's ranks is not always clear. Companies generally defend a decision to discharge a worker by asserting that the worker could no longer perform his or her duties or that the worker's skills were no longer needed. The employee must prove that the discharge was motivated, at least in part, by age bias. Proof that qualified older employees are generally discharged before employees who are younger or that co-workers continually made unflattering age-related comments about the discharged worker may be enough.

In the past, courts sometimes held that to establish a *prima facie* case of age discrimination, the plaintiff had to prove that he or she had been replaced by a person outside the protected class—that is, by a person under the age of forty years. In 1996, however, in *O'Connor v. Consolidated Coin Caterers Corp.*,[15] the United States Supreme Court held that a cause of action for age discrimination under the ADEA does not require the replacement worker to be outside the protected class. Rather, the issue in all ADEA cases turns on whether age discrimination has in fact occurred, regardless of the age of the replacement worker. In the following case, the court had to decide whether there was sufficient evidence to support a jury's finding of discrimination on the basis of age.

15. ___U.S.___, 116 S.Ct. 1307, 134 L.Ed.2d 433 (1996).

CASE 21.3 Rhodes v. Guiberson Oil Tools

United States Court of Appeals, Fifth Circuit, 1996. 75 F.3d 989.

HISTORICAL AND ECONOMIC SETTING *Exploring and drilling for oil is an expensive operation; drills, pipes, pumps, testing and measuring equipment, trucks, tankers, helicopters, and a variety of services are utilized. Suppliers of these products and services depend entirely on the activities of oil companies in the field. If no one is drilling for oil, the suppliers are out of business. In 1986, the oil industry was in the throes of a severe economic downturn.*

BACKGROUND AND FACTS *Calvin Rhodes sold oil-field equipment for Guiberson Oil Tools. When he was discharged in 1986 at age fifty-six, he was told that the discharge was part of a reduction in the work force (RIF) and that he would be considered for reemployment. Within six weeks, Guiberson hired a forty-two-year-old person to do the same job. Rhodes filed a suit in a federal district court against Guiberson under the Age Discrimination in Employment Act. At the trial, Guiberson officials testified that they had not told Rhodes the truth about why they discharged him and that they had intended to replace him. Guiberson offered as a defense Rhodes's "poor work performance" but did not present any company sales records or goals. Rhodes countered with customers' testimony about his expertise and diligence. The jury found that Rhodes had been discharged because of his age. Guiberson appealed to the U.S. Court of Appeals for the Fifth Circuit.*

IN THE LANGUAGE OF THE COURT

W. *EUGENE DAVIS* and *DUHE*, Circuit Judges:

* * * *

Based on [the] evidence, the jury was entitled to find that the reasons given for Rhodes' discharge were pretexts for age discrimination. The jury was entitled to find that Guiberson's stated reason for discharging Rhodes—RIF—was false. Additionally, the reason for discharge that Guiberson Oil proffered in court * * * was countered with evidence from which the jury could have found that Rhodes was an excellent salesman who met Guiberson Oil's legitimate productivity expectations. * * * [A] reasonable jury could have found that Guiberson Oil discriminated against Rhodes on the basis of his age.

DECISION AND REMEDY *The U.S. Court of Appeals for the Fifth Circuit affirmed the jury's finding. The evidence supported the jury's finding in favor of Rhodes.*

SECTION 4

DISCRIMINATION BASED ON DISABILITY

The Americans with Disabilities Act (ADA) of 1990 is designed to eliminate discriminatory employment practices that prevent otherwise qualified workers with disabilities from fully participating in the national labor force. The ADA prohibits discrimination against a "qualified individual with a disability" with regard to job application and hiring procedures, training, compensation, fringe benefits, advancement, and other terms or conditions of employment.

Prior to 1990, the major federal law providing protection to those with disabilities was the Rehabilitation Act of 1973. That act covered only federal government employees and those employed under federally funded programs. The ADA extends federal protection against disability-based discrimination to all employees of firms affecting interstate commerce that have fifteen or more workers. Basically, the ADA requires that employers "reasonably accommodate" the needs of persons with disabilities unless to do so would cause the employer to suffer an "undue hardship."

PROCEDURES AND REMEDIES UNDER THE ADA

To prevail on a claim under the ADA, a plaintiff must show that he or she (1) has a disability, (2) is otherwise qualified for the employment in question, and (3) was excluded from the employment solely because of the disability. As in Title VII cases, a claim alleging violation of the ADA may be commenced only after the plaintiff has pursued the claim through the EEOC. Plaintiffs may sue for many of the same remedies available under Title VII. They may seek reinstatement, back pay, a limited amount of compensatory and punitive damages (for intentional discrimination), and certain other forms of relief. Repeat violators may be ordered to pay fines of up to $100,000.

WHAT IS A DISABILITY?

The ADA is broadly drafted to define persons with disabilities as persons with physical or mental impairments that "substantially limit" their everyday activities. More specifically, the ADA defines *disability* as "(1) a physical or mental impairment that substantially limits one or more of the major life activities of such individuals; (2) a record of such impairment; or (3) being regarded as having such an impairment."

Generally, the determination of whether an individual has a disability as defined by the ADA is made on a case-by-case basis. Unlike plaintiffs in cases brought under Title VII or the ADEA, who clearly are or are not members of the classes protected by those acts, a plaintiff suing under the ADA must *prove* that he or she has a disability and thus falls under the protection of the ADA. Meeting this first requirement for a case of disability-based discrimination may be difficult.

Health conditions that have been considered disabilities under federal law include blindness, alcoholism, heart disease, cancer, muscular dystrophy, cerebral palsy, paraplegia, diabetes, acquired immune deficiency syndrome (AIDS), and morbid obesity (defined as existing when an individual's weight is two times that of the normal person).[16] The ADA excludes from coverage certain conditions, such as kleptomania.

REASONABLE ACCOMMODATION

If a job applicant or an employee with a disability can perform essential job functions with reasonable accommodation, the employer must make the accommodation. Required modifications may include installing ramps for a wheelchair, establishing more flexible working hours, creating or modifying job assignments, and creating or improving training materials and procedures.

Generally, employers should give primary consideration to employees' preferences in deciding what accommodations should be made. If an applicant or employee fails to let the employer know how his or her disability can be accommodated, the employer may avoid liability for failing to hire or retain the individual on the ground that the individual has failed to meet the "otherwise qualified" requirement.[17] Employers should be cautious in making this assumption in cases involving mental illness, though. For example, in one case, an employee was

16. *Cook v. Rhode Island Department of Mental Health*, 10 F.3d 17 (1st Cir. 1993).

17. See, for example, *Beck v. University of Wisconsin Board of Regents*, 75 F.3d 1130 (7th Cir. 1996); and *White v. York International Corp.*, 45 F.3d 357 (10th Cir. 1995).

held to have a cause of action against his employer under the ADA even though the employee never explicitly told the employer how his disability could be accommodated.[18]

JOB APPLICATIONS AND PREEMPLOYMENT PHYSICAL EXAMS Employers must modify their job-application process so that those with disabilities can compete for jobs with those who do not have disabilities. A job announcement that only has a phone number, for example, would discriminate against potential job applicants with hearing impairments. Thus, the job announcement must also provide an address.

Employers are restricted in the kinds of questions they may ask on job-application forms and during preemployment interviews (see this chapter's *Emerging Trends* for examples of prohibited and permissible questions). Furthermore, employers cannot require persons with disabilities to submit to preemployment physicals unless such exams are required of all other applicants. Employers can condition an offer of employment on the employee's successfully passing a medical examination, but disqualifications must result from the discovery of problems that render the applicant unable to perform the job for which he or she is to be hired.

18. *Bultemeyer v. Fort Wayne Community Schools*, 100 F.3d 1281 (7th Cir. 1996).

DANGEROUS WORKERS Employers are not required to hire or retain workers who, because of their disabilities, pose a "direct threat to the health or safety" of their co-workers. In the wake of the AIDS epidemic, many employers are concerned about hiring or continuing to employ a worker who has AIDS under the assumption that the worker might pose a direct threat to the health or safety of others in the workplace. Courts have generally held, however, that AIDS is not so contagious as to disqualify employees in most jobs. Therefore, employers must reasonably accommodate job applicants or employees who have AIDS or who test positive for the human immunodeficiency virus (HIV), the virus that causes AIDS.[19]

The ADA prohibits employers from refusing to hire or retain persons with disabilities who are otherwise qualified for a particular position. The ADA does not require that *unqualified* disabled applicants be hired or retained, however. Employers sometimes argue that persons with AIDS are not "otherwise qualified" for particular positions because they pose a direct threat to the health or safety of others that cannot be eliminated or reduced by reasonable accommodation. This was the employer's argument in the following case.

19. Courts have disagreed on whether HIV-positive persons who do not have any symptoms of AIDS have a disability under the ADA. For two views on this issue, see *Doe v. Kohn Nast & Graf, P.C.*, 866 F.Supp. 190 (E.D.Pa. 1994); and *Ennis v. National Association of Business and Educational Radio, Inc.*, 53 F.3d 55 (4th Cir. 1995).

CASE 21.4 Mauro v. Borgess Medical Center

United States District Court, Western District of Michigan, Southern Division, 1995. 886 F.Supp. 1349.

HISTORICAL AND SOCIAL SETTING *Acquired immune deficiency syndrome (AIDS) was unknown until the first cases were reported in the United States in 1981. AIDS, which is often fatal, is caused by the human immunodeficiency virus (HIV). HIV can be transmitted from one person to another by contact of the infected blood of one person with an open wound of another. A person infected with HIV remains infected for the rest of his or her life. Although an infected person may not show any symptoms for years, he or she can still infect others.*

BACKGROUND AND FACTS *William Mauro was an operating room surgical technician for the Borgess Medical Center. Surgical technicians must occasionally place their hands into a patient's surgical incision. Borgess officials had reason to believe that Mauro was infected with HIV. When Borgess asked Mauro to be tested for HIV, however, Mauro refused. He also refused to accept a job outside the operating room and, as a consequence, was laid off. Mauro filed a* *suit in a federal district court against Borgess, alleging, among other things, discrimination in violation of the Americans with Disabilities Act. Borgess filed a motion for summary judgment. Mauro argued that the probability of transmission of HIV is small and that a reasonable accommodation would be to add a person to the surgical team to work in or near the patient's incision.*

IN THE LANGUAGE OF THE COURT

McKEAGUE, District Judge.

* * * *

* * * Because there is a real possibility of transmission, however small, and because the consequence of transmission is invariably death, the threat to patient safety posed by plaintiff's presence in the operating room performing the functions of a surgical technician is direct and significant. * * * A cognizable risk of permanent duration with lethal consequences suffices to make a surgical technician * * * not "otherwise qualified."

* * * *

* * * [Furthermore] to require Borgess to * * * add another person to the surgical team is not reasonable. The accommodation plaintiff demands would entail a job restructuring in the operating room, a burden the law does not impose on the employer.

DECISION AND REMEDY

The federal district court granted Borgess's motion for summary judgment. Mauro did not show that he was "otherwise qualified" or that his requested accommodation was reasonable.

SUBSTANCE ABUSERS Drug addiction is a disability under the ADA, because drug addiction is a substantially limiting impairment. Those who are currently using illegal drugs are not protected by the act. The ADA only protects persons with *former* drug addictions—those who have completed a supervised drug-rehabilitation program or who are currently in a supervised rehabilitation program. Individuals who have used drugs casually in the past are not protected under the act. They are not considered addicts and therefore do not have a disability (addiction).

People suffering with alcoholism are protected by the ADA. Employers cannot legally discriminate against employees simply because they are living with alcoholism and must treat them in the same way as they treat other employees. For example, an employee with alcoholism who comes to work late because he or she was drinking the night before cannot be disciplined any differently than an employee who comes to work late for another reason. Of course, employers have the right to prohibit the use of alcohol in the workplace and can require that employees not be under the influence of alcohol while working. Employers can also fire or refuse to hire a person with alcoholism if he or she poses a substantial risk of harm either to himself or herself or to others and the risk cannot be reduced by reasonable accommodation.

HEALTH-INSURANCE PLANS Workers with disabilities must be given equal access to any health insurance provided to other employees. Employers can exclude from coverage preexisting health conditions and certain types of diagnostic or surgical procedures, however. An employer can also put a limit, or cap, on health-care payments in its particular group-health policy—as long as such caps are "applied equally to all insured employees" and do not "discriminate on the basis of disability." Whenever a group health-care plan makes a disability-based distinction in its benefits, the plan violates the ADA. The employer must then be able to justify the distinction by proving one of the following:

1. That limiting coverage of certain ailments is required to keep the plan financially sound.
2. That coverage of certain ailments would cause a significant increase in premium payments or their equivalent, making the plan unappealing to a significant number of workers.
3. That the disparate treatment is justified by the risks and costs associated with a particular disability.

EMERGING TRENDS

ACCOMMODATING WORKERS WITH DISABILITIES

When the Americans with Disabilities Act (ADA) was passed in 1990, Congress estimated that disabilities affected about 17 percent of the U.S. population. Prior to 1990, the major federal law providing protection to those with disabilities was the Rehabilitation Act of 1973. That act only covered federal government employees or those employed under federally funded programs. As of 1994, the ADA extended federal protection against disability-based discrimination to all workplaces with fifteen or more workers.

Many employers have been held liable under the ADA simply because they asked the wrong questions when interviewing job applicants with disabilities. Others have been held liable because they concluded, erroneously, that job applicants or employees with disabilities were not otherwise qualified to perform the jobs in question or that it would constitute an undue hardship to accommodate the needs of persons with disabilities.

JOB APPLICATIONS AND INTERVIEWS

The Equal Employment Opportunity Commission (EEOC) has issued guidelines indicating the kinds of questions that employers may—and may not—ask job applicants with disabilities. Often, the line between permissible and impermissible

questions is a fine one, indeed. Consider these examples:

- *Ability to perform the job:* As an employer, you may ask a job applicant, "Can you do the job?" You may also ask whether the applicant can perform specific tasks related to the job. You may *not* ask the candidate, "How would you do the job?"—*unless* the disability is obvious, the applicant brings up the subject during the interview, or you ask the question of all applicants.
- *Absenteeism:* You may ask, "Can you meet our attendance requirements?" or "How many days were you absent last year?" You may *not* ask, "How many days were you sick last year?"
- *Drug use:* Generally, employers may ask about the current or past use of illegal drugs but not about drug addiction. Therefore, as an employer, you may ask, "Have you ever used illegal drugs?" or "Have you used illegal drugs in the last six months?" You may *not* ask, "How often did you use illegal drugs?" or "Have you been treated for drug abuse?"
- *Alcohol use:* Generally, employers may ask about a candidate's drinking habits but not about alcoholism. Therefore, you may ask, "Do you drink alcohol?" or "Have you been arrested for driving while intoxicated?" but you may *not* ask, "How often do you drink?"
- *History of job-related injuries:* Employers may *not* ask a job candidate with a disability any questions about the applicant's previous job-related injuries or about workers' compensation claims submitted in the past.

Once an employer has made a job offer, the employer may ask the applicant questions concerning his or her disability, including questions about previous workers' compensation claims or about the extent of a drinking problem. The employer may also ask for medical documents verifying the nature of the applicant's disability. Generally, though, the employer should ask such questions only if they are asked of all applicants or if they are follow-up questions based on the applicant's disclosure of the disability during the job interview.

REASONABLE ACCOMMODATION VERSUS UNDUE HARDSHIP

The ADA requires employers to accommodate persons with disabilities unless the accommodation would constitute an undue hardship. The difficulty for employers lies in determining the point at which an accommodation ceases being reasonable and becomes an undue hardship. Because this issue is decided by the courts on

EMERGING TRENDS

ACCOMMODATING WORKERS WITH DISABILITIES (CONTINUED)

a case-by-case basis, there is no one standard that will apply to all situations. To avoid liability for violating the ADA, employers generally should be wary of jumping to any conclusions about when an accommodation will constitute an undue hardship.

For example, in one case, a federal employee qualified as being disabled under the ADA because he had severe bouts of depression. His medication caused drowsiness, and he routinely fell asleep on the job. The employer assumed that it would cause undue hardship to accommodate the worker's on-the-job naps. The U.S. Court of Appeals for the Seventh Circuit, however, held that "[t]he government may presumably require its employees to stay awake as a matter of decorum. But that is not necessarily to say that an occasional nap would make any federal employee unfit."[a]

EVALUATING JOB QUALIFICATIONS

A touchstone issue in many disability cases is whether a job applicant or employee with disabilities is "otherwise qualified" to perform the job. In deciding this issue, it is important for employers to focus on the person's *present* ability to perform the job, not his or her *future* ability to do so. One of the first cases brought under the ADA dealt with this issue. The case involved a security company that fired a high-level employee who had brain cancer. The company claimed that the employee was not qualified. Although the employee's condition was deteriorating rapidly and he probably could not have performed the job several months later, he was still performing the job well *at the time he was fired.* For this reason, the court held that the company had violated the ADA and awarded substantial damages to the fired employee.[b]

Naturally, any analysis of whether a person with disabilities can perform essential job functions involves a decision as to what functions are really essential to a particular job. The courts have routinely held that mental stability, the ability to handle stress, and the ability to follow instructions are critical to most jobs. Less clear is whether attendance—appearing at the job site at specified times—is an essential job function. Generally, the courts have held that an individual is not qualified for a job if that person's attendance is irregular and unpredictable. The required levels of attendance and regularity usually depend on the circumstances of each case, however.

IMPLICATIONS FOR THE BUSINESSPERSON

1. Employers should make sure that the ways in which they advertise, word their job applications, and conduct job interviews meet the EEOC's guidelines.
2. In deciding whether they must accommodate the needs of particular job applicants or employees with disabilities, employers should carefully evaluate whether the applicants or employees are otherwise qualified to perform the jobs. Part of this evaluation entails an analysis of which functions are essential to those jobs and which functions are not.

FOR CRITICAL ANALYSIS

1. In what ways do the requirements under the ADA differ from those under other federal laws prohibiting discrimination?
2. In your opinion, does the ADA fairly balance the interests of employers in maintaining a productive and efficient workplace and the rights of otherwise qualified persons with disabilities to be employed?

a. *Overton v. Reilly,* 977 F.2d 1190 (7th Cir. 1992).

b. *EEOC v. AIC Security,* 55 F.3d 1276 (7th Cir. 1995).

UNDUE HARDSHIP

Employers who do not accommodate the needs of persons with disabilities must demonstrate that the accommodations would cause undue hardship. Generally, the law offers no uniform standards for identifying what is an undue hardship other than the imposition of a "significant difficulty or expense" on the employer. Usually, the courts decide whether an accommodation constitutes an undue hardship on a case-by-case basis. In one case, the court decided that paying for a parking space near the office for an employee with a disability was not an undue hardship.[20] In another case, the court held that accommodating the request of an employee with diabetes for indefinite leave until his disease was under control would create an undue hardship for the employer, because the employer would not know when the employee was returning to work. The court stated that reasonable accommodation under the ADA means accommodation so that the employee can perform the job now or "in the immediate future" rather than at some unspecified distant time.[21]

SECTION 5 DEFENSES TO EMPLOYMENT DISCRIMINATION

The first line of defense for an employer charged with employment discrimination is, of course, to assert that the plaintiff has failed to meet his or her initial burden of proof—proving that discrimination in fact occurred. As noted, plaintiffs bringing cases under the ADA may find it difficult to meet this initial burden, because they must prove that their alleged disabilities are disabilities covered by the ADA. Furthermore, plaintiffs in ADA cases must prove that they were otherwise qualified for the job.

Once a plaintiff succeeds in proving that discrimination occurred, then the burden shifts to the employer to justify the discriminatory practice. Often, employers attempt to justify the discrimination by claiming that it was the result of a business necessity, a bona fide occupational qualification, a seniority system, or employee misconduct.

20. See *Lyons v. Legal Aid Society*, 68 F.3d 1512 (2d Cir. 1995).
21. *Myers v. Hase*, 50 F.3d 278 (4th Cir. 1995).

BUSINESS NECESSITY

An employer may defend against a claim of discrimination by asserting that a practice that has a discriminatory effect is a **business necessity.** If requiring a high school diploma, for example, is shown to have a discriminatory effect, an employer might argue that a high school education is required for workers to perform the job at a required level of competence. If the employer can demonstrate to the court's satisfaction that there exists a definite connection between a high school education and job performance, then the employer will succeed in this business necessity defense.

BONA FIDE OCCUPATIONAL QUALIFICATION

Another defense applies when discrimination against a protected class is essential to a job—that is, when a particular trait is a **bona fide occupational qualification (BFOQ).** For example, a women's clothing boutique might legitimately hire only female attendants if part of an attendant's job involves assisting clients in the boutique's dressing rooms. Similarly, the Federal Aviation Administration can legitimately impose age limits for airline pilots. Race, however, can never be a BFOQ. Generally, courts have restricted the BFOQ defense to instances in which the employee's gender or religion is essential to the job.

SENIORITY SYSTEMS

An employer with a history of discrimination may have no members of protected classes in upper-level positions. Even if the employer now seeks to be unbiased, it may face a lawsuit seeking an order that minorities be promoted ahead of schedule to compensate for past discrimination. If no present intent to discriminate is shown, however, and if promotions or other job benefits are distributed according to a fair **seniority system** (in which workers with more years of service are promoted first or laid off last), the employer has a good defense against the suit.

AFTER-ACQUIRED EVIDENCE OF EMPLOYEE MISCONDUCT

In some situations, employers have attempted to avoid liability for employment discrimination on the basis of "after-acquired evidence" of an employee's misconduct. For example, suppose that an employer fires a worker, and the employee sues the employer for employment discrimination. During pretrial investigation, the employer learns that the employee made material misrepresentations on his or her employment application—misrepresentations that, had the employer known about them, would have served as a ground to fire the individual. Can this after-acquired evidence be used as a defense?

According to the United States Supreme Court, after-acquired evidence of wrongdoing should not operate, "in every instance, to bar all relief for an earlier violation" of a federal law prohibiting discrimination.[22] Since this decision, the courts have generally held that after-acquired evidence, at best, can only serve to limit liability. While such evidence cannot be used to shield an employer entirely from liability for employment discrimination, it may be used to limit the amount of damages for which the employer is liable.

SECTION 6 AFFIRMATIVE ACTION

Federal statutes and regulations providing for equal opportunity in the workplace were designed to reduce or eliminate discriminatory practices with respect to hiring, retaining, and promoting employees. **Affirmative action** programs go a step further and attempt to "make up" for past patterns of discrimination by giving members of protected classes preferential treatment in hiring or promotion.

Affirmative action programs have caused much controversy, particularly when they result in what is frequently called "reverse discrimination"—discrimination against "majority" workers, such as white males (or discrimination against other minority groups that are not given preferential treatment under a particular affirmative action program). At issue is whether affirmative action programs, because of their inherently discriminatory nature, violate the equal protection clause of the Fourteenth Amendment to the Constitution.

THE *BAKKE* CASE

An early nonemployment-related case addressing this issue, *Regents of the University of California v. Bakke*,[23] involved an affirmative action program implemented by the University of California at Davis. Allan Bakke, who had been turned down for medical school at the Davis campus, sued the university for reverse discrimination after he discovered that his academic record was better than those of some of the minority applicants who had been admitted to the program.

The United States Supreme Court held that affirmative action programs were subject to intermediate scrutiny. Recall from the discussion of the equal protection clause in Chapter 5 that any law or action evaluated under a standard of intermediate scrutiny, to be constitutionally valid, must be substantially related to important government objectives. Applying this standard, the Court held that the university could give favorable weight to minority applicants as part of a plan to increase minority enrollment so as to achieve a more culturally diverse student body. The Court stated, however, that the use of a quota system, in which a certain number of places are explicitly reserved for minority applicants, violated the equal protection clause of the Fourteenth Amendment.

THE *ADARAND* CASE AND SUBSEQUENT DEVELOPMENTS

Although the *Bakke* case and later court decisions alleviated the harshness of the quota system, today's courts are going even further in questioning the constitutional validity of affirmative action programs. For example, in *Adarand Constructors, Inc. v. Peña*,[24] the plaintiff (Adarand Constructors, Inc.) was not awarded a federal highway construction project even though it had submitted the lowest bid. Instead, the project went to a Hispanic-owned firm in accordance with a federal program designed to give at least 5 percent of highway construction projects to disadvantaged business enterprises. Adarand sued Federico Peña, the secretary of the U.S. Department of Transportation, and others, alleging that the federal program violated the Constitution.

In a landmark decision, the Supreme Court held that any federal, state, or local affirmative action program that uses racial or ethnic classifications as the basis for making decisions is subject to strict scrutiny by the courts. In effect, the Court's opinion in *Adarand* means that an affirmative action program is constitutional only if it attempts to remedy past discrimination and does not make use of quotas or preferences.

22. *McKennon v. Nashville Banner Publishing Co.*, 513 U.S. 352, 115 S.Ct. 879, 130 L.Ed.2d 852 (1995).

23. 438 U.S. 265, 98 S.Ct. 2733, 57 L.Ed.2d 750 (1978).

24. 515 U.S. 200, 115 S.Ct. 2097, 132 L.Ed.2d 158 (1995).

Furthermore, once such a program has succeeded in the goal of remedying past discrimination, it must be changed or dropped.

In 1996, in *Hopwood v. State of Texas,*[25] two white law-school applicants sued the University of Texas School of Law in Austin, alleging that they were denied admission because of the school's affirmative action program. The program allowed admitting officials to take racial and other factors into consideration when determining which students would be admitted. The Court of Appeals for the Fifth Circuit held that the program violated the equal protection clause because it discriminated in favor of minority applicants. In its decision, the court directly challenged the *Bakke* decision by stating that the use of race even as a means of achieving diversity on college campuses "undercuts the Fourteenth Amendment." The United States Supreme Court declined to hear the case, thus letting the lower court's decision stand.

Although the cases just discussed do not directly relate to affirmative action programs in the workplace, clearly they indicate a trend that will affect employers' affirmative action programs as well. Additionally, in 1996, by a voters' initiative known as Proposition 209, California voters amended their state constitution to ban affirmative action policies in state employment, education, and contracting.[26] Similar movements are currently under way in other states. The question in the following case is whether an employer's voluntary affirmative action policy of "racial diversity" violated Title VII of the Civil Rights Act of 1964.

25. 84 F.3d 720 (5th Cir. 1996).

26. The constitutionality of this amendment was upheld in *Coalition for Economic Equity v. Wilson,* 110 F.3d 1431 (9th Cir. 1997).

CASE 21.5 Taxman v. Board of Education of the Township of Piscataway

United States Court of Appeals, Third Circuit, 1996. 91 F.3d 1547.

BACKGROUND AND FACTS *The Board of Education of the Township of Piscataway, New Jersey, decided to reduce the teaching staff at Piscataway High School by one. Between two teachers of equal seniority and qualifications but different races, the board chose to lay off the white teacher, Sharon Taxman. Minority teachers were not underrepresented in the school district work force. The board based its decision on an affirmative action policy that was designed not to remedy discrimination but to promote "racial diversity." Taxman and others filed a suit in a federal district court against the board, challenging the policy as a violation of Title VII. The court granted a summary judgment in favor of the plaintiffs. The case was appealed to the U.S. Court of Appeals for the Third Circuit. (The decision is currently on appeal to the United States Supreme Court.)*

IN THE LANGUAGE OF THE COURT

MANSMANN, Circuit Judge.

* * * *

Title VII was enacted to further two primary goals: to end discrimination on the basis of race, color, religion, sex or national origin, thereby guaranteeing equal opportunity in the workplace, and to remedy the segregation and underrepresentation of minorities that discrimination has caused in our Nation's work force.

* * * *

* * * [T]he Board's sole purpose in applying its affirmative action policy in this case was to obtain an educational benefit which it believed would result from a racially diverse faculty. While the benefits flowing from diversity in the educational context are significant * * * , the Board does not even attempt to show that its affirmative action plan was adopted to remedy past discrimination or as the result of a manifest imbalance in the employment of minorities * * * .

* * * *

* * * [T]he Board's policy, devoid of goals and standards, is governed entirely by the Board's whim, leaving the Board free, if it so chooses, to grant racial

preferences that do not promote even the policy's claimed purpose. Indeed, under the terms of this policy, the Board, in pursuit of a "racially diverse" work force, could use affirmative action to discriminate against those whom Title VII was enacted to protect.

DECISION AND REMEDY *The U.S. Court of Appeals for the Third Circuit affirmed the lower court's judgment in favor of the plaintiffs and awarded Taxman 100 percent of her back pay.*

SECTION 7 STATE ANTIDISCRIMINATION LAWS

Although the focus of this chapter is on federal legislation, most states also have statutes that prohibit employment discrimination. Generally, the kinds of discrimination prohibited under federal legislation are also prohibited by state laws. In addition, state statutes often provide protection for certain individuals, such as homosexuals, who are not protected under Title VII. Furthermore, state laws prohibiting discrimination may provide additional damages, such as damages for emotional distress, that are not provided for under Title VII. Finally, in some cases, a court has allowed a plaintiff to recover damages for wrongful discharge on the ground that the employer's discriminatory practices were contrary to the state's public policy against discrimination.[27]

27. See, for example, *Molesworth v. Brandon,* 341 Md. 621, 672 A.2d 608 (1996).

TERMS AND CONCEPTS TO REVIEW

affirmative action 445

bona fide occupational qualification (BFOQ) 444

business necessity 444

disparate-impact discrimination 433

disparate-treatment discrimination 432

employment discrimination 431

***prima facie* case 432**

protected class 431

seniority system 444

sexual harassment 434

QUESTIONS AND CASE PROBLEMS

21–1. TITLE VII VIOLATIONS. Discuss fully whether any of the following actions would constitute a violation of Title VII of the 1964 Civil Rights Act, as amended.

(a) Tennington, Inc., is a consulting firm and has ten employees. These employees travel on consulting jobs in seven states. Tennington has an employment record of hiring only white males.

(b) Novo Films, Inc., is making a film about Africa and needs to employ approximately one hundred extras for this picture. Novo advertises in all major newspapers in southern California for the hiring of these extras. The ad states that only African Americans need apply.

21–2. DISCRIMINATION BASED ON AGE. Tavo Jones had worked since 1974 for Westshore Resort, where he maintained golf carts. During the first decade, he received positive job evaluations and numerous merit pay raises. He was promoted to the position of supervisor of golf-cart maintenance at three courses. Then a new employee, Ben Olery, was placed in charge of the golf courses. He demoted Jones, who was over the age of forty, to running one of the three cart facilities, and he froze Jones's salary indefinitely. Olery also demoted five other men over the age of forty. Another cart facility was placed under the supervision of Blake Blair. Later, the cart facilities for the three courses were again consolidated, but Blair—not Jones—was put in charge.

At the time, Blair was in his twenties. Jones overheard Blair say that "we are going to have to do away with these . . . old and senile" men. Jones quit and sued Westshore for employment discrimination. Should he prevail? Explain.

21–3. Disparate-Impact Discrimination. Chinawa, a major processor of cheese sold throughout the United States, employs one hundred workers at its principal processing plant. The plant is located in Heartland Corners, which has a population that is 50 percent white and 25 percent African American, with the balance Hispanic American, Asian American, and others. Chinawa requires a high school diploma as a condition of employment for its cleaning crew. Three-fourths of the white population complete high school, compared with only one-fourth of those in the minority groups. Chinawa has an all-white cleaning crew. Has Chinawa violated Title VII of the Civil Rights Act of 1964? Explain.

21–4. Discrimination Based on Disability. Ananda is a hearing-impaired repairperson currently employed with the Southwestern Telephone Company. Her job requires her to drive the company truck to remote rural areas in all kinds of weather, to climb telephone poles, to make general repairs to telephone lines, and so on. She has held this position for five years, a full year longer than any other employee, and she is quite competent. Ananda recently applied for a promotion to the position of repair crew coordinator, a position that would require her to be in constant communication with all repairpersons in the field. Southwestern rejected Ananda's application, stating that the company "needs someone in this critical position who can speak and hear clearly, someone who does not suffer from any hearing disability." Ananda says she could easily perform the essentials of the job if Southwestern would provide her with a sign interpreter. Although Southwestern agrees that Ananda is otherwise qualified for the coordinator position, the company has concluded that the cost of hiring an interpreter would be prohibitive, and therefore it should not be required to accommodate her disability under the Americans with Disabilities Act. Who is correct? Discuss.

21–5. Discrimination Based on National Origin. Phanna Xieng was sent by the Cambodian government to the United States in 1974 for "advanced military training." When the Cambodian government fell in 1975, Xieng remained in the United States and in 1979 was employed by Peoples National Bank of Washington. In performance appraisals from 1980 through 1985, Xieng was rated by his supervisors as "capable of dealing effectively with customers" and qualified for promotion, although in each appraisal it was noted that Xieng might improve his communication skills to maximize his possibilities for future advancement. Xieng sought job promotions on numerous occasions but was never promoted. In 1986, he filed a complaint against the bank, alleging employment discrimination based on national origin. The employer argued that its refusal to promote Xieng because of his accent or communication skills did not amount to discrimination based on national origin. Is it possible to separate discrimination based on an employee's accent and communication skills from discrimination based on national origin? How should the court rule on this issue? [*Xieng v. Peoples National Bank of Washington*, 120 Wash.2d 512, 844 P.2d 389 (1993)]

21–6. Disparate-Impact Discrimination. Local 1066 of the Steamship Clerks Union accepted only new members who were sponsored by existing members. All of the existing members were white. During a six-year period, the local admitted thirty new members, all of whom were relatives of present members and also white. The Equal Employment Opportunity Commission filed a suit in a federal district court against the union, alleging that this practice constituted disparate-impact discrimination under Title VII. The union argued that it was only continuing a family tradition. What does each party have to prove to win its case? Should the union be required to change its practice? [*EEOC v. Steamship Clerks Union, Local 1066*, 48 F.3d 594 (1st Cir. 1995)]

21–7. Discrimination Based on Disability. When the University of Maryland Medical System Corp. learned that one of its surgeons was HIV positive, the university offered him transfers to positions that did not involve surgery. The surgeon refused, and the university terminated him. The surgeon filed a suit in a federal district court against the university, alleging in part a violation of the Americans with Disabilities Act. The surgeon claimed that he was "otherwise qualified" for his former position. What does he have to prove to win his case? Should he be reinstated? [*Doe v. University of Maryland Medical System Corp.*, 50 F.3d 1261 (4th Cir. 1995)]

21–8. Discrimination Based on Race. Theodore Rosenblatt, a white attorney, worked for the law firm of Bivona & Cohen, P.C. When Bivona & Cohen terminated Rosenblatt's employment, he filed a suit in a federal district court against the firm. Rosenblatt claimed that he had been discharged because he was married to an African American and that a discharge for such a reason violated Title VII and other laws. The firm filed a motion for summary judgment, arguing that he was alleging discrimination against his wife, not himself, and thus did not have standing to sue under Title VII for racial discrimination. Should the court grant or deny the motion? Explain. [*Rosenblatt v. Bivona & Cohen, P.C.*, 946 F.Supp. 298 (S.D.N.Y. 1996)]

21–9. A Question of Ethics

Luz Long and three other Hispanic employees (the plaintiffs) worked as bank tellers for the Culmore branch of the First Union Corp. of Virginia. The plaintiffs often conversed with one another in Spanish, their native language. In 1992, the Culmore branch manager adopted an "English-only" policy, which required all employees to speak English during working hours unless they had to speak another language to assist customers. The plaintiffs refused to cooperate with the new policy and were eventually fired. In a suit against the bank, the plaintiffs alleged that the English-only policy discriminated against them on the basis of their national origin. The court granted the bank's motion for summary judgment, concluding that "[t]here is nothing in Title VII which . . . provides that an employee has a right to speak his or her native tongue while on the job." [*Long v. First Union Corp. of Virginia*, 894 F.Supp. 933 (E.D.Va. 1995)]

1. The bank argued that the policy was implemented in response to complaints made by fellow employees that the Spanish-speaking employees were creating a hostile environment by speaking Spanish among themselves in the presence of other employees. From an ethical perspective, is this a sufficient reason to institute an English-only policy?
2. Is it ever ethically justifiable for employers to deny bilingual employees the opportunity to speak their native language while on the job?
3. Might there be situations in which English-only policies are necessary to promote worker health and safety?

CHAPTER 22

LABOR LAW

THROUGH THE FIRST HALF of the nineteenth century, most Americans were self-employed, often in agriculture. For those who were employed by others, the employers generally set the terms of employment. The nature of employment changed with the growth of the industrial revolution, which had begun about 1760. Fewer Americans were self-employed. Terms of employment were sometimes set through bargaining between employees and employers. Most industrial enterprises were in their infancies, however, and to encourage their development, the government gave employers considerable freedom to hire, fire, and determine other employment conditions in response to changing conditions in the marketplace.

With increasing industrialization, the size of workplaces and the number of workplace hazards increased. Workers came to believe that to counter the power and freedom of their employers and to protect themselves, they needed to organize into unions. Employers discouraged—sometimes forcibly—collective activities such as unions. In support of unionization, Congress enacted such legislation as the Railway Labor Act of 1926.[1] These laws were often restricted to particular industries. Beginning in 1932, Congress enacted a number of statutes that increased employees' rights in general. At the heart of these rights is the right to join unions and engage in collective bargaining with management to negotiate working conditions, salaries, and benefits for a group of workers.

1. 45 U.S.C. Sections 151–188.

This chapter describes the development of labor law and legal recognition of the right to form unions. The laws that govern the management-union relationship are set forth in historical perspective. Then we discuss the process of unionizing a company, the collective bargaining required of a unionized employer, the "industrial war" of strikes and lockouts that may result if bargaining fails, and the labor practices that are considered unfair under federal law.

SECTION 1 FEDERAL LABOR LAW

Federal labor laws governing union-employer relations have developed considerably since the first law was enacted in 1932. Initially, the laws were concerned with protecting the rights and interests of workers. Subsequent legislation placed some restraints on unions and granted rights to employers. This section summarizes the four major federal labor law statutes.

NORRIS-LAGUARDIA ACT

Congress protected peaceful strikes, picketing, and boycotts in 1932 in the Norris-LaGuardia Act.[2] The statute restricted federal courts in their power to issue injunctions against unions engaged in peaceful strikes. The act also provided that contracts limiting an employee's right to join a union are unlawful. Such contracts are known as **yellow dog contracts.** (In the early part of the twentieth century, "yellow dog" meant "coward.") In effect, this act declared a national policy permitting employees to organize.

NATIONAL LABOR RELATIONS ACT

The National Labor Relations Act of 1935 (NLRA),[3] also called the Wagner Act, established the right of employees to form unions, the right of those unions to engage in collective bargaining (negotiate contracts for their members), and the right to strike. The act also created the National Labor Relations Board (NLRB) to oversee union elections and to prevent employers from engaging in unfair labor union activities and unfair labor practices.

The purpose of the NLRA was to secure for employees the rights to organize, to bargain collectively through representatives of their own choosing, and to engage in concerted activities for that and other purposes. Section 8(a) of the act specifically defined a number of employer practices as unfair to labor. These unfair labor practices are central to labor law and are discussed throughout the remainder of this chapter.

Another purpose of the act was to promote fair and just settlements of disputes by peaceful processes. The NLRB was granted investigatory powers and was authorized to issue complaints against employers in response to employee charges of unfair labor practices. The NLRB was further empowered to issue cease-and-desist orders—which could be enforced by a federal court of appeals if necessary—when violations were found.

Employers viewed the NLRA as a drastic piece of legislation. Those who opposed the act claimed that the Constitution's commerce clause (Article I, Section 8, Clause 3) did not grant Congress the power to regulate labor relations. They argued that labor was subject to state, not federal, law. Those who were willing to admit that the NLRA did fall under the commerce clause claimed that the NLRA created an undue burden, which rendered it unconstitutional. The constitutionality of the act was tested in 1937 in *NLRB v. Jones & Laughlin Steel Corp.*[4] In its decision, the United States Supreme Court held that the act and its application were constitutionally valid.

To be protected under the NLRA, an individual must be an "employee," as that term is defined in the statute. Courts have long held that job applicants fall within the definition (otherwise, the NLRA's ban on discrimination in regard to hiring would mean nothing). In the following case, the United States Supreme Court considered whether an individual can be a company's "employee" if, at the same time, a union pays the individual to organize the company.

2. 29 U.S.C. Sections 101–115.
3. 29 U.S.C. Sections 151–169.
4. 301 U.S. 1, 57 S.Ct. 615, 81 L.Ed. 893 (1937).

CASE 22.1 NLRB v. Town & Country Electric, Inc.

Supreme Court of the United States, 1995. ___ U.S. ___, 116 S.Ct. 450, 133 L.Ed.2d 371.

BACKGROUND AND FACTS *Town & Country Electric, Inc., advertised for job applicants but refused to interview ten of eleven applicants who were members of a union, the International Brotherhood of Electrical Workers. The applicants were union "salts"—persons paid by the union to apply for a job with a company and then, when hired, to unionize the company (in this case, Town & Country's work force). The applicants filed a complaint with the National Labor Relations Board (NLRB), alleging that the company had committed an unfair labor practice by discriminating against the applicants on the basis of union membership. The issue turned on whether job applicants paid by a union to organize a company could be considered employees under the National Labor Relations Act (NLRA). The NLRB determined that the applicants were employees and ruled in their favor. Town & Country appealed, and the U.S. Court of Appeals for the Eighth Circuit reversed. The applicants appealed to the United States Supreme Court.*

IN THE LANGUAGE OF THE COURT

Justice *BREYER* delivered the opinion of the Court.

* * * *

* * * [T]he Board's decision is consistent with the broad language of the [NLRA] * * * . The ordinary dictionary definition of "employee" includes any "person who works for another in return for financial or other compensation." The phrasing of the [NLRA] seems to reiterate the breadth of the ordinary dictionary definition, for it says "[t]he term 'employee' shall include any employee." * * *

For another thing, the Board's broad, literal interpretation of the word "employee" is consistent with several of the [NLRA's] purposes, such as protecting "the right of employees to organize for mutual aid without employer interference" * * * .

DECISION AND REMEDY *The United States Supreme Court reversed the decision of the appellate court and remanded the case. The Court held that the applicants were employees and thus could not be discriminated against.*

LABOR-MANAGEMENT RELATIONS ACT

The Labor-Management Relations Act of 1947 (LMRA, or the Taft-Hartley Act)[5] was passed to proscribe certain union practices. The Taft-Hartley Act contained provisions protecting employers as well as employees. The act was bitterly opposed by organized labor groups. It provided a detailed list of unfair labor activities that unions as well as management were now forbidden to practice. In addition, the law gave the president the authority to intervene in labor disputes and delay strikes that would "imperil the national health or safety."

An important provision of the LMRA concerned the **closed shop**—a firm that requires union membership of its workers as a condition of obtaining employment. Closed shops were made illegal under the Taft-Hartley Act. The act preserved the legality of the **union shop,** which does not require membership as a prerequisite for employment but can, and usually does, require that workers join the recognized union after a specified amount of time on the job. The act also allowed individual states to pass their own **right-to-work laws**—laws making it illegal for union membership to be required for *continued* employment in any establishment. Thus, union shops are technically illegal in states with right-to-work laws.

LABOR-MANAGEMENT REPORTING AND DISCLOSURE ACT

The Labor-Management Reporting and Disclosure Act of 1959 (the Landrum-Griffin Act)[6] established an employee bill of rights, as well as reporting

5. 29 U.S.C. Sections 141, 504.

6. 29 U.S.C. Sections 153, 1111.

requirements for union activities to prevent corruption. The Landrum-Griffin Act strictly regulated internal union business procedures.

Union elections, for example, are regulated by the Landrum-Griffin Act, which requires that regularly scheduled elections of officers occur and that secret ballots be used. Ex-convicts and Communists are prohibited from holding union office. Moreover, union officials are made accountable for union property and funds. Members have the right to attend and to participate in union meetings, to nominate officers, and to vote in most union proceedings.

COVERAGE AND PROCEDURES

Coverage of the federal labor laws is broad and extends to all employers whose business activity either involves or affects interstate commerce. Some workers are specifically excluded from these laws. Railroads and airlines are not covered by the NLRA but are covered by a separate act, the Railway Labor Act, which closely parallels the NLRA. Other types of workers, such as agricultural workers and domestic servants, are excluded from the NLRA and have no coverage under separate legislation.

When a union or employee believes that the employer has violated federal labor law (or vice versa), the union or employee files a charge with a regional office of the NLRB. The form for an employee to use to file an unfair labor practice charge against an employer is shown in Exhibit 22–1. The charge is investigated, and if it is found worthy, the regional director files a complaint. An administrative law judge (ALJ) initially hears the complaint and rules on it (see Chapter 6). The board reviews the ALJ's findings and decision. If the NLRB finds a violation, it may issue remedial orders (including requiring rehiring of discharged workers). The NLRB decision may be appealed to a U.S. court of appeals.

SECTION 2
THE DECISION TO FORM OR SELECT A UNION

The key starting point for labor relations law is the decision by a company's employees to form a union, which is usually referred to in the law as their bargaining representative. Many workplaces have no union, and workers bargain individually with the employer. If the workers decide that they want the added power of collective union representation, they must follow certain steps to have a union certified. Usually, the employer will fight these efforts to unionize.

PRELIMINARY ORGANIZING

Suppose that a national union, such as the American Federation of Labor and Congress of Industrial Organizations (AFL-CIO), wants to organize workers who produce semiconductor chips. The union would visit a manufacturing plant of a company—SemiCo in this example. If some SemiCo workers are interested in joining the union, they must begin organizing. An essential part of the process is to decide exactly which workers will be covered in the planned union. Will all manufacturing workers be covered or just those engaged in a single step in the manufacturing process?

The first step in forming a union is to get the relevant workers to sign **authorization cards.** These cards usually state that the worker desires to have a certain union, such as the AFL-CIO, represent the work force. If those in favor of the union can obtain authorization cards from a majority of workers, they may present the cards to the employer and ask the employer, SemiCo, to recognize the union formally. SemiCo is not required to do so, however.

More frequently, authorization cards are obtained to justify an election among workers for unionization. If SemiCo refuses to recognize the union based on authorization cards, an election is necessary to determine whether unionization has majority support among the workers. After the unionizers obtain authorization cards from at least 30 percent of the workers to be represented, the unionizers present these cards to the NLRB regional office with a petition for an election.

This 30 percent support is generally considered a sufficient showing of interest to justify an election on union representation. Union backers are not required to employ authorization cards but generally must have some evidence that at least 30 percent of the relevant work force supports a union or an election on unionization.

APPROPRIATE BARGAINING UNIT

The NLRB considers the employees' petition as a basis for calling an election. In addition to a sufficient showing of interest in unionization, the proposed union must represent an **appropriate bargaining unit.**

EXHIBIT 22–1 ■ UNFAIR LABOR PRACTICE COMPLAINT FORM

FORM EXEMPT UNDER 44 U.S.C. 3512

FORM NLRB-501
(8-83)

UNITED STATES OF AMERICA
NATIONAL LABOR RELATIONS BOARD
CHARGE AGAINST EMPLOYER

DO NOT WRITE IN THIS SPACE

Case	Date Filed

INSTRUCTIONS: File an original and 4 copies of this charge with NLRB Regional Director for the region in which the alleged unfair labor practice occurred or is occurring.

1. EMPLOYER AGAINST WHOM CHARGE IS BROUGHT

a. Name of Employer		b. Number of workers employed
c. Address *(street, city, state, ZIP code)*	d. Employer Representative	e. Telephone No.
f. Type of Establishment *(factory, mine, wholesaler, etc.)*	g. Identify principal product or service	

h. The above-named employer has engaged in and is engaging in unfair labor practices within the meaning of section 8(a). subsections (1) and *(list subsections)* ____________________ of the National Labor Relations Act. and these unfair labor practices are unfair practices affecting commerce within the meaning of the Act.

2. Basis of the Charge *(be specific as to facts, names, addresses, plants involved, dates, places, etc.)*

By the above and other acts, the above-named employer has interfered with, restrained, and coerced employees in the exercise of the rights guaranteed in Section 7 of the Act

3. Full name of party filing charge *(if labor organization, give full name, including local name and number)*

4a. Address *(street and number, city, state, and ZIP code)*	4b. Telephone No.

5. Full name of national or international labor organization of which it is an affiliate or constituent unit *(to be filled in when charge is filed by a labor organization)*

6. DECLARATION

I declare that I have read the above charge and that the statements are true to the best of my knowledge and belief.

By ____________________ ________________

(signature of representative or person making charge) *(title if any)*

Address ____________________ ____________ __________

(Telephone No.) *(date)*

WILLFUL FALSE STATEMENTS ON THIS CHARGE CAN BE PUNISHED BY FINE AND IMPRISONMENT (U.S. CODE, TITLE 18, SECTION 1001)

Not every group of workers can form together into a single union. One key requirement of an appropriate bargaining unit is a *mutuality of interest* among all the workers to be represented. Groups of workers with significantly conflicting interests may not be represented in a single union.

JOB SIMILARITY One factor in determining the mutuality of interest is the *similarity of the jobs* of all the workers to be unionized. The NLRB considers factors such as similar levels of skill and qualifications, similar levels of wages and benefits, and similar working conditions. If represented workers have vastly different working conditions, they are unlikely to have the mutuality of interest necessary to bargain as a single unit with their employer.

One issue of job similarity has involved companies that employ both general industrial workers and craft workers (those with specialized skills, such as electricians). On many occasions, the NLRB has found that industrial and craft workers should be represented by different unions, although this is not an absolute rule.

WORK-SITE PROXIMITY A second important factor in determining the appropriate bargaining unit is *geographical*. If workers at only a single manufacturing plant are to be unionized, the geographical factor is not a problem. Even if the workers desire to join a national union, such as the AFL-CIO, they can join together in a single "local" division of that union. Geographical disparity may become a problem if a union is attempting to join workers at many different manufacturing sites together into a single union.

NONMANAGEMENT EMPLOYEES A third factor to be considered is the rule against unionization of *management* employees. The labor laws differentiate between labor and management and preclude members of management from being part of a union. There is no clear-cut definition of management, but supervisors are considered management and may not be included in worker unions. A supervisor is an individual who has the discretionary authority, as a representative of the employer, to make decisions such as hiring, suspending, promoting, firing, or disciplining other workers.[7] Professional employees, including legal and medical personnel, may be considered labor rather than management.

7. *Waldau v. Merit Systems Protection Board,* 19 F.3d 1395 (Fed.Cir. 1994).

MOVING TOWARD CERTIFICATION

A union, then, becomes certified through a procedure that begins with petitioning the NLRB. The proposed union must present authorization cards or other evidence showing an employee interest level of at least 30 percent. The organization must also show that the proposed union represents an appropriate bargaining unit. If the workers are under the NLRA's jurisdiction and if no other union has been certified within the past twelve months for these workers, the NLRB will schedule an election.

SECTION 3 UNION ELECTION

Labor law provides for an election to determine whether employees choose to be represented by a union and, if so, which union. The NLRB supervises this election, ensuring secret voting and voter eligibility. The election is usually held about a month after the NLRB orders the vote (although it may be much longer, if management disputes the composition of an appropriate bargaining unit). If the election is a fair one, and if the proposed union receives majority support, the board certifies the union as the bargaining representative. Otherwise, the board will not certify the union.

Sometimes, a plant with an existing union may attempt to *decertify* the union (de-unionize). Although this action may be encouraged by management, it must be conducted by the employees. This action also requires a petition to the NLRB, with a showing of 30 percent employee support and no certification within the past year. The NLRB may grant this petition and call for a decertification election.

UNION ELECTION CAMPAIGN

Union organizers may campaign among workers to solicit votes for unionization. Considerable litigation has arisen over the rights of workers and outside union supporters to conduct such campaigns.

The employer retains great control over any activities, including unionization campaigns, that take place on company property and company time. Employers may lawfully use this authority to limit the campaign activities of union supporters. For example, management may prohibit all solicitations and distribution of pamphlets on company property as long as it has a legitimate business reason for doing so (such as to ensure safety or to prevent interference with business). The employer may also reasonably limit the places where solicitation occurs (for example, limit it to the lunchroom), limit the times during which solicitation can take place, and prohibit all outsiders from access to the workplace. All these actions are lawful.

Suppose that a union seeks to organize clerks at a department store. Courts have found that an employer can prohibit all solicitation in areas of the store open to the public. Union campaign activities in these circumstances could seriously interfere with the store's business.

There are some legal restrictions on management regulation of union solicitation. The key restriction is the *nondiscrimination* rule. An employer may prohibit all solicitation during work time or in certain places but may not selectively prohibit union solicitation during work time. If the employer permits political candidates to campaign on the employer's premises, for example, it also must permit union solicitation.[8]

Workers have a right to some reasonable opportunity to campaign. For example, the Supreme Court held that employees have a right to distribute a pro-union newsletter in nonworking areas on the employer's property during nonworking time. In this case, management had the burden to show some material harm from this action and could not do so.[9]

MANAGEMENT ELECTION CAMPAIGN

Management may also campaign among its workers against the union (or for decertification of an existing union). Campaign tactics, however, are carefully monitored and regulated by the NLRB. Otherwise, the economic power of management might allow coercion of the workers.

Management still has many advantages in the campaign. For example, management is allowed to call all workers together during work time and make a speech against unionization. Management need not give the union supporters an equal opportunity for rebuttal. The NLRB does restrict what management may say in such a speech, however.

NO THREATS In campaigning against the union, the employer may not make threats of reprisals if employees vote to unionize. A supervisor may not state, "If the union wins, you'll all be fired." This would be a threat. Employers must be very careful on this issue. For example, suppose an employer says, "Our competitor's plant in town unionized, and half the workers lost their jobs." The NLRB might consider this to be a veiled threat and therefore unfair.

An interesting controversy arose over a film that employers showed during union campaigns, *And Women Must Weep*. This film was prepared to help employers fight unionization efforts. The film dramatizes union misconduct during a strike, including vandalism, bomb threats, and attacks on neutral individuals such as a minister and an infant, who is shot and killed. Although this film is arguably inaccurate, courts have found it legal. One court wrote that "the film is a one-sided brief against unionism, devoid of significant rational content perhaps, but nevertheless not reasonably to be construed as threatening retaliation or force."[10]

"LABORATORY CONDITIONS" Obviously, union election campaigns are not like national political campaigns, when a political party can make almost any claim. The NLRB tries to maintain "laboratory conditions" for a fair election that is unaffected by pressure. In establishing such conditions, the board considers the totality of circumstances in the campaign. The NLRB is especially strict about promises (or threats) made by the employer at the last minute, immediately before the election, because the union lacks an opportunity to respond effectively to these last-minute statements.

There is even a specific rule that prohibits an employer from making any election speech on company time, to massed assemblies of workers, within twenty-four hours of the time for voting. Such last-minute speeches are permitted only if employees attend voluntarily and on their own time.[11]

The employer is also prohibited from taking actions that might intimidate its workers. Employers

8. *Nonemployee* union organizers do not have the right to trespass on an employer's property to organize employees, however. See *Lechmere, Inc. v. NLRB*, 502 U.S. 527, 112 S.Ct. 841, 117 L.Ed.2d 79 (1992).

9. *Eastex, Inc. v. NLRB*, 437 U.S. 556, 98 S.Ct. 2505, 57 L.Ed.2d 428 (1978).

10. *Luxuray of New York v. NLRB*, 447 F.2d 112 (2d Cir. 1971).

11. Political party–like electioneering on behalf of a union, on the day of a union election, however, has been held acceptable and does not invalidate the election. See *Overnite Transportation Co. v. NLRB*, 104 F.3d 109 (7th Cir. 1997).

may not undertake certain types of surveillance of workers or even create the impression of observing workers to identify union sympathizers. Management also is limited in its ability to question individual workers about their positions on unionization. These actions are deemed to contain implicit threats.

NLRB OPTIONS If the employer issues threats or engages in other unfair labor practices and then wins the election, the NLRB may invalidate the results. The NLRB may certify the union, even though it lost the election, and direct the employer to recognize the union as the employees' exclusive bargaining representative. Or the NLRB may ask a court to order a new election.

Not every statement that an employer makes against a union during a unionization campaign constitutes an unfair labor practice, however. In the following case, the NLRB argued that certain employer statements contained threats, but the employer contended that the statements were only expressions of opinion about the prospect of unionization.

CASE 22.2 NLRB v. Pentre Electric, Inc.

United States Court of Appeals, Sixth Circuit, 1993. 998 F.2d 363.

BACKGROUND AND FACTS *Pentre Electric, Inc., was an electrical contracting company co-owned by its president, Phil Luff, and its vice president, Pat Meehan. Pentre had nineteen employees. In November 1989, the International Brotherhood of Electrical Workers began a campaign to unionize the employees. At a company meeting in July 1990, Luff told the employees that most of Pentre's customers did not employ union contractors. Luff predicted that Pentre would likely have to build a new customer base in the event of the union's election but that "Pat and I would probably succeed." Later, Meehan met with about ten of the employees individually. Among other things, Meehan said that "if we were a union contractor, we'd have to establish new customers" and "I'm not prepared to do that." The election was held August 20. A majority of the employees voted against union representation. The NLRB and the union charged Pentre with unfair labor practices. After a hearing, an administrative law judge agreed, construing Meehan's statement that he was "not prepared" to face the difficulties of rebuilding a customer base as a threat to close Pentre in retaliation for a pro-union vote. The judge ordered a new election. The NLRB applied to a court for enforcement of the order. Pentre argued that its officers' statements did not constitute an unfair labor practice.*

IN THE LANGUAGE OF THE COURT

BOYCE F. MARTIN, Jr., Circuit Judge.

* * * *

* * * [A]ny statement or prediction by an employer about the effects of unionization * * * must be carefully phrased on the basis of objective fact to convey an employer's belief as to demonstrably probable consequences beyond his control or to convey a management decision already arrived at to close the plant in case of unionization. If there is any implication that an employer may or may not take action solely on his own initiative for reasons unrelated to economic necessities and known only to him, the statement is no longer a reasonable prediction based on available facts but a threat of retaliation based on misrepresentation and coercion. * * *

* * * *

* * * [N]othing in [Luff's] statements intimated that he or Meehan would close the plant as a result of anti-union *animus* [animosity]. Luff's speech conveyed nothing more than his analysis of the likely economic consequences of unionization of Pentre, in light of his knowledge of Pentre's customers and competitors. * * *

* * * Like Luff, Meehan made his predictions about the effect of unionization on Pentre based upon his experience in the electrical contracting industry and his knowledge about the nature of Pentre's customer base. His statement conveyed that the probable consequences of unionization were beyond his control. * * * No employee could reasonably have come away from either speech with the belief that anti-union sentiment on the part of the company could lead to closure if the employees voted in favor of the union.

DECISION AND REMEDY *The court concluded that the statements did not constitute unfair labor practices and denied the NLRB's request for enforcement of the order for a new election.*

SECTION 4 COLLECTIVE BARGAINING

If a fair election is held and the union wins, the NLRB will certify the union as the *exclusive bargaining representative* of the workers polled. Unions may provide a variety of services to their members, but the central legal right of a union is to serve as the sole representative of the group of workers in bargaining with the employer over the workers' rights.

The concept of bargaining is at the heart of the federal labor laws. When a union is officially recognized, it may make a demand to bargain with the employer. The union then sits at the table opposite the representatives of management to negotiate contracts for its workers. The terms of employment that result from the negotiations apply to all workers in the bargaining unit, even those who do not choose to belong to the union. This process is known as **collective bargaining.** Such bargaining is like most other business negotiations, and each side uses its economic power to pressure or persuade the other side to grant concessions.

Bargaining is a somewhat vague term. Bargaining does not mean that either side must give in on demands or even that the sides must always compromise. It does mean that a demand must be taken seriously and considered as part of a package to be negotiated. Importantly, both sides must bargain in "good faith."

SUBJECTS OF BARGAINING

A common issue in collective bargaining concerns the subjects over which the parties can bargain. The law makes certain subjects mandatory for collective bargaining. These topics cannot be "taken off the table" unilaterally but must be discussed and bargained over.

TERMS AND CONDITIONS OF EMPLOYMENT

The NLRA provides that employers may bargain with workers over wages, hours of work, and other terms and conditions of employment. These are broad terms that cover many employment issues. Suppose that a union wants a contract provision granting all workers four weeks of paid vacation. The company need not give in to this demand but must at least consider it and bargain over it.

Many other employment issues are also considered appropriate subjects for collective bargaining. These include safety rules, insurance coverage, pension and other employee benefits plans, procedures for employee discipline, and procedures for employee grievances against the company. The Supreme Court has held that an employer must bargain even over the price of food sold in the company cafeteria.[12]

A few subjects are illegal in collective bargaining. Management need not bargain over a provision that would be illegal if included in a contract. Thus, if a union presents a demand for **featherbedding** (the hiring of unnecessary excess workers) or for an unlawful closed shop, management need not respond to these demands.

CLOSING OR RELOCATING A PLANT Management need not bargain with a union over the decision to close a particular facility. Similarly, management need not bargain over a decision to relocate a plant if the move involves a basic change in the nature of the employer's operation.[13] Management may choose to bargain over such decisions, however, to obtain concessions on other bargaining subjects.

Management must bargain over the economic consequences of such decisions. Thus, issues such as

12. *Ford Motor Co. v. NLRB*, 441 U.S. 488, 99 S.Ct. 1842, 60 L.Ed.2d 420 (1979).

13. *Dubuque Packing Co.*, 303 N.L.R.B. No. 386 (1991).

severance pay (compensation for the termination of employment) in the event of a plant shutdown are appropriate for collective bargaining. Also, if a relocation does *not* involve a basic change in the nature of an operation, management must bargain over the decision unless it can show (1) that the work performed at the new location varies significantly from the work performed at the former plant; (2) that the work performed at the former plant is to be discontinued entirely and not moved to the new location; (3) that the move involves a change in the scope and direction of the enterprise; (4) that labor costs were not a factor in the decision; or (5) that even if labor costs were a factor, the union could not have offered concessions that would have changed the decision to relocate. The following case involves a decision to relocate a significant part of an employer's operations.

CASE 22.3 United Food and Commercial Workers International Union v. NLRB

United States Court of Appeals, District of Columbia Circuit, 1993.
1 F.3d 24.

HISTORICAL AND CULTURAL SETTING *In the late 1970s, the consumption of meat began to drop in the United States. This was due in large part to concerns about the possible harmful effect of meat consumption on human health. By the beginning of the 1980s, Americans were buying less beef and pork and more chicken and fish. Added to the price instability of the livestock that serve as the source for the products, the decline in the consumption of beef and pork caused many companies in the meat-packing industry to look for ways to cut their costs. By the mid-1980s, Americans' consumption of chicken and turkey had surpassed that of beef and pork.*

BACKGROUND AND FACTS *In the late 1970s, Dubuque Packing Company, a processor of beef and pork, began losing money at its plant in Dubuque, Iowa. The company and the United Food and Commercial Workers International Union (UFCW), which represented the employees, negotiated concessions to keep the plant open. In March 1981, the company announced that it planned to close the plant's hog kill and cut operations. Negotiations began again. The UFCW rejected the company's proposal to freeze wages. In June, the company announced that it might relocate—rather than close—the hog department. To assess the situation, the UFCW requested financial information, which the company refused to provide. The company said that the employees could save their jobs by approving the wage freeze proposal, which the union recommended be rejected until the company opened its books. The workers voted against the proposal. Three days later, the company announced that its decision to close the hog department was "irrevocable." On October 1, the company opened a hog operation at a new plant in Rochelle, Illinois, and two days later cut more than five hundred hog jobs at the Dubuque plant. The UFCW complained to the NLRB, claiming that the company had refused to bargain in good faith over the relocation. The NLRB agreed and ordered the company to pay back wages to all employees terminated as a result of the move. The company asked a court to review the case.*

IN THE LANGUAGE OF THE COURT

BUCKLEY, Circuit Judge:

* * * *

Dubuque objects, first, to the [National Labor Relations] Board's finding that its relocation did not constitute a change in the scope and direction of its business.

* * *

The Board's position enjoys ample support in the record. * * * Dubuque used the Rochelle facility to substantially replace the Dubuque facility. As production in Rochelle increased, there was a corresponding reduction at Dubuque until the hog kill and cut processing departments and related operations there were completely phased out. Larry J. Tangeman, general plant superintendent at Dubuque, became superintendent of the Rochelle facility and about 13 members of Dubuque management also were transferred to Rochelle, as was certain production equipment. The purposes of the Rochelle plant, to slaughter hogs, dress carcasses, and to process pork into hams, bacon, and sausage, were the same as at the Dubuque plant. * * *

Dubuque's second contention is that because "the record * * * is very clear that the union would not offer labor concessions," bargaining would have been futile; hence it was not required. * * *

* * * [T]hat principle has no bearing here. * * * [T]he UFCW could, would, and did accept concessions * * * all in a vain attempt to keep the Dubuque facility open. Indeed, the vote that led to Dubuque's "irrevocable" decision to relocate was not a vote to categorically refuse Dubuque's overtures, but a vote to insist on financial disclosure as a prelude to bargaining. The Board's finding that good-faith bargaining between Dubuque and the UFCW might not have been futile was substantially supported by the record.

DECISION AND REMEDY *The court upheld the NLRB's determination that the employer had refused to bargain in good faith over the relocation and enforced the order for the payment of back wages.*

GOOD FAITH BARGAINING

Parties engaged in collective bargaining often claim that the other side is not bargaining in good faith, as required by labor law. Although good faith is a matter of subjective intent, a party's actions are used to evaluate the finding of good or bad faith in bargaining.

Obviously, the employer must be willing to meet with union representatives. Excessive delaying tactics may be proof of bad faith, as is insistence on obviously unreasonable contract terms. Suppose that a company makes a single overall contract offer on a "take-it-or-leave-it" basis and refuses to consider modifications of individual terms. This also is considered bad faith in bargaining.

While bargaining is going on, management may not make unilateral changes in important working conditions, such as wages or hours of employment. These changes must be bargained over. Once bargaining reaches an impasse, management may make such unilateral changes. The law also includes an exception permitting unilateral changes in cases of business necessity.

A series of decisions have found other actions to constitute bad faith in bargaining, including the following:

- Engaging in a campaign among workers to undermine the union.
- Constantly shifting positions on disputed contract terms.
- Sending bargainers who lack authority to commit the company to a contract.

If an employer (or a union) refuses to bargain in good faith without justification, it has committed an unfair labor practice, and the other party may petition the NLRB for an order requiring good faith bargaining. Except in extreme cases, the NLRB does not have authority to require a party to accede to any specific contract terms. The NLRB may require a party to reimburse the other side for its litigation expenses.

A party to collective bargaining may be excused from bargaining when the other party refuses to bargain. The following case illustrates this situation.

CASE 22.4 Stroehmann Bakeries, Inc. v. NLRB

United States Court of Appeals, Second Circuit, 1996. 95 F.3d 218.

BACKGROUND AND FACTS *Stroehmann Bakeries, Inc., operated a distribution center for its baked goods in Syracuse, New York, where employees—known as shippers—loaded the goods onto local delivery trucks. The shippers were represented by a union. When their collective bargaining agreement expired, Stroehmann proposed eliminating their positions. In subsequent negotiations, the company admitted that it could obtain the capital to keep the Syracuse center open and proposed cutting only half of the positions. The union asked Stroehmann for extensive financial information, including lists of customers and sales accounts, accounts payable journals, supplier invoices, production reports, employee compensation, and employee-pension plans. The company refused to comply with the request and, when the union did not return to the negotiations, declared that bargaining was at an impasse. Ten days later, Stroehmann eliminated the shippers' jobs. The National Labor Relations Board ordered the company to reinstate the shippers. Stroehmann asked the U.S. Court of Appeals for the Second Circuit to deny enforcement of the order.*

IN THE LANGUAGE OF THE COURT

WINTER, Circuit Judge:

* * * *

Once Stroehmann conceded that it had access to capital sufficient to continue the Syracuse shipping unit, the Union's need for financial information to bargain intelligently was virtually non-existent. * * * Stroehmann did not enter the negotiations with a closed mind but rather offered proposals in response to the Union's request for ways to save jobs. It was the Union that refused to bargain after it made a request for financial information [that was denied].

The comprehensive and detailed information requested by the Union had virtually no relevance to the issues at stake in bargaining * * * . We conclude, therefore, that Stroehmann was under no obligation to respond to the voluminous requests for information submitted by the Union.

Because Stroehmann's refusal to furnish the information was permissible, it was entitled to declare an impasse when the Union refused to return to the bargaining table. The unilateral decision to close the shipping unit was, therefore, lawful.

DECISION AND REMEDY *The U.S. Court of Appeals for the Second Circuit denied enforcement of the NLRB's order. The company acted within its rights in eliminating the shippers' jobs.*

INTERNATIONAL CONSIDERATIONS

Union Rights in Great Britain *In Great Britain, a union that has been recognized by an employer for collective bargaining purposes has certain rights. These rights include the right to receive information related to collective bargaining issues, the right to time off, the right to appoint a representative to handle safety matters, and the right to be consulted before an employer relocates its place of business.*

SECTION 5

STRIKES

The law does not require parties to reach a contract agreement in collective bargaining. Even when parties have bargained in good faith, they may be unable to reach a final agreement. When extensive collective bargaining has been conducted and the parties still cannot agree, an impasse has been reached.

When bargaining has reached an impasse, the union may call a strike against the employer to pressure it into making concessions. A strike occurs when the unionized workers leave their jobs and refuse to work. The workers also typically picket the plant, standing outside the facility with signs that complain of management's unfairness.

A strike is an extreme action. Striking workers lose their right to be paid. Management loses production and may lose customers, whose orders cannot be filled. Labor law regulates the circumstances and conduct of strikes. Most strikes are "economic strikes," which are initiated because the union wants a better contract. A union may also strike when the employer has engaged in unfair labor practices.

The right to strike is guaranteed by the NLRA, within limits, and strike activities, such as picketing, are protected by the free speech guarantee of the First Amendment to the Constitution. Nonworkers have a right to participate in picketing an employer. The NLRA also gives workers the right to refuse to cross a picket line of fellow workers who are engaged in a lawful strike. Not all strikes are lawful, however.

ILLEGAL STRIKES

An otherwise lawful strike may become illegal because of the conduct of the strikers. Violent strikes (including the threat of violence) are illegal. The use of violence against management employees or substitute workers is illegal. Certain forms of "massed picketing" are also illegal. If the strikers form a barrier and deny management or other nonunion workers access to the plant, the strike is illegal. Similarly, "sit-down" strikes, in which employees simply stay in the plant without working, are illegal.

SECONDARY BOYCOTTS

A strike directed against someone other than the strikers' employer, such as the companies that sell materials to the employer, is a **secondary boycott.** Suppose that the unionized workers of SemiCo (our hypothetical semiconductor company) go out on strike. To increase their economic leverage, the workers picket the leading suppliers and customers of SemiCo in an attempt to hurt the company's business. SemiCo is considered the primary employer, and its suppliers and customers are considered secondary employers. Picketing of the suppliers or customers is a secondary boycott, which was made illegal by the Taft-Hartley Act.

Common Situs Picketing.

A controversy may arise in a strike when both the primary employer and a secondary employer occupy the same job site. In this case, it may be difficult to distinguish between lawful picketing of the primary employer and an unlawful strike against a secondary employer. The law permits a union to picket a site occupied by both primary and secondary employers, an act called **common situs picketing.** If evidence indicates that the strike is directed against the secondary employer, however, it may become illegal. For example, if a union sends a threatening letter to the secondary employer about the strike, that fact may show that the picketing includes an illegal secondary boycott.

Hot-Cargo Agreements.

In what is called a **hot-cargo agreement,** employers voluntarily agree with unions not to handle, use, or deal in non-union-produced goods of other employers. This particular type of secondary boycott was *not* made illegal by the Taft-Hartley Act, because that act only prevented unions from inducing *employees* to strike or otherwise act to force employers not to handle these goods. The Landrum-Griffin Act addressed this problem:

> It shall be [an] unfair labor practice for any labor organization and any employer to enter into any contract or any agreement . . . whereby such employer . . . agrees to refrain from handling, using, selling, transporting or otherwise dealing in any of the products of any other employer, or to cease doing business with any other person.

Hot-cargo agreements are therefore illegal. Parties injured by an illegal hot-cargo agreement or other secondary boycott may sue the union for damages.

A union may legally urge consumer boycotts of the primary employer, even at the site of a secondary employer. Suppose that a union is on strike against SemiCo, which manufactures semiconductors that are bought by Intellect, Inc., a distributor of electronic components. Intellect sells SemiCo's semiconductors to computer manufacturers. The striking workers can urge the manufacturers not to buy SemiCo's products. The workers cannot urge a total boycott of Intellect, as that would constitute a secondary boycott.

WILDCAT STRIKES

A **wildcat strike** occurs when a minority group of workers, perhaps dissatisfied with a union's representation, calls its own strike. The union is the exclusive bargaining representative of a group of workers, and only the union can call a strike. A wildcat strike, unauthorized by the certified union, is illegal.

In one case, several concrete workers left their jobs because it was raining and went on "strike." The court found the strike illegal because it was not preceded by a demand on the employer for action and because the employer had made shelter available for the workers and paid them for waiting time.

STRIKES THAT THREATEN NATIONAL HEALTH OR SAFETY The law also places some restrictions on strikes that threaten national health or safety. The law does not prohibit such strikes, nor does it require the settlement of labor disputes that threaten the national welfare. The Taft-Hartley Act simply provides time to encourage the settlement of these disputes, called the "cooling-off period."

One of the most controversial aspects of the Taft-Hartley Act was the establishment of this **eighty-day cooling-off period**—a provision allowing federal courts to issue injunctions against strikes that would create a national emergency. The president of the United States can obtain a court injunction that will last for eighty days, and presidents have occasionally used this provision. During these eighty days, the president and other government officials can work with the employer and the union to produce a settlement and avoid a strike that may cause a national emergency.

STRIKES THAT CONTRAVENE NO-STRIKE CLAUSES A strike may also be illegal if it contravenes a **no-strike clause.** The previous collective bargaining agreement between a union and an employer may have contained a clause in which the union agreed not to strike (a no-strike clause). The law permits the employer to enforce this no-strike clause and obtain an injunction against the strike in some circumstances.

The Supreme Court held that a no-strike clause could be enforced with an injunction if the contract contained a clause providing for arbitration of unresolved disputes.[14] The Court held that the arbitration clause was an effective substitute for the right to strike. In the absence of an applicable arbitration provision, however, an employer cannot enjoin (forbid) a strike, even if the contract contains a no-strike clause.

REPLACEMENT WORKERS

Suppose that SemiCo's workers go out on strike. SemiCo is not required to shut down its operations but may find substitute workers to replace the strikers, if possible. These substitute workers are often called "scabs" by union supporters. An employer may even give the replacement workers permanent positions with the company.

In the 1930s and 1940s, strikes were powerful in part because employers often had difficulty finding trained replacements to keep their businesses running during strikes. Since the illegal air traffic controller strike in 1981, when President Ronald Reagan successfully hired replacement workers, employers have increasingly used this strategy, with considerable success. Even the National Football League (NFL), when struck by the players in 1987, found replacements to play for the NFL teams. Although some scoffed at the ability of the replacement players, the tactic was largely successful for management, as the strike was called off after only three weeks. An employer can even use an employment agency to recruit replacement workers.[15]

RIGHTS OF STRIKERS AFTER THE STRIKE

An important issue concerns the rights of strikers after the strike ends. In a typical economic strike over working conditions, the strikers have no right to return to their jobs. If satisfactory replacement workers have been found, the strikers may find themselves out of work. The law does prohibit the employer from discriminating against former strikers. Even if the employer fires all the strikers and retains all the replacement workers, former strikers must be rehired to fill any new vacancies. Former strikers who are rehired retain their seniority rights.

Different rules apply when a union strikes because the employer has engaged in unfair labor practices. If an employer is discriminating against a union's workers, they may go out on an unfair labor practice strike. Furthermore, an economic strike may become an unfair labor practice strike if the employer refuses to bargain in good faith. In the case of an unfair labor practice strike, the employer may still hire replacements but must give the strikers back their jobs once the strike is over. An employer may, however, refuse to rehire unfair labor practice strikers if the strike was deemed unlawful or if there is simply no longer any work for them to do.

---

14. *Boys Markets, Inc. v. Retail Clerks Local 770*, 398 U.S. 235, 90 S.Ct. 1583, 26 L.Ed.2d 199 (1970).

15. *Professional Staff Nurses Association v. Dimensions Health Corp.*, 110 Md.App. 270, 677 A.2d 87 (1996).

SECTION 6
LOCKOUTS

Lockouts are the employer's counterpart to the worker's right to strike. A **lockout** occurs when the employer shuts down to prevent employees from working. Lockouts are usually used when the employer believes that a strike is imminent.

Lockouts may be a legal employer response. In the leading Supreme Court case on this issue, a union and an employer had reached a stalemate in collective bargaining. The employer feared that the union would delay a strike until the busy season and thereby cause the employer to suffer more greatly from the strike. The employer called a lockout before the busy season to deny the union this leverage, and the Supreme Court held that this action was legal.[16]

Some lockouts are illegal, however. An employer may not use its lockout weapon as a tool to break the union and pressure employees into decertification. Consequently, an employer must show some economic justification for instituting a lockout.

SECTION 7
UNFAIR LABOR PRACTICES

The preceding sections have discussed unfair labor practices in the significant acts of union elections, collective bargaining, and strikes. Many unfair labor practices may occur within the normal working relationship as well. The most significant of these practices are discussed below. Exhibit 22–2 lists the basic unfair labor practices.

EMPLOYER'S REFUSAL TO RECOGNIZE THE UNION AND TO NEGOTIATE

As noted above, once a union has been certified as the exclusive representative of a bargaining unit, an employer must recognize and bargain in good faith with the union over issues affecting all employees who are within the bargaining unit. Failure to do so is an unfair labor practice. Because the National Labor Relations Act embraces a policy of majority rule, certification of the union as the bargaining unit's representative binds *all* of the employees in that bargaining unit. Thus, the union must fairly represent all the members of the bargaining unit.[17]

PRESUMPTION OF EMPLOYEE SUPPORT Certification does not mean that a union will continue indefinitely as the exclusive representative of the bargaining unit. If the union loses the majority support of those it represents, an employer is not obligated to continue recognition of, or negotiation with, the union. As a practical matter, a newly elected representative needs time to establish itself among the workers and to begin to formulate and implement its programs. Therefore, as a matter of labor policy, a union is immune from attack by employers and from repudiation by the employees for a period of one year after certification. During this period, it is *presumed* that the union enjoys majority support among the

16. *American Ship Building Co. v. NLRB*, 380 U.S. 300, 85 S.Ct. 955, 13 L.Ed.2d 855 (1965).

17. Thus, when an employee has a grievance against the employer, the union cannot arbitrarily ignore it or handle it perfunctorily, although a union does not have to pursue all employee grievances to arbitration. See *Vaca v. Sipes*, 386 U.S. 171, 87 S.Ct. 903, 17 L.Ed.2d 842 (1967).

EXHIBIT 22–2 ■ BASIC UNFAIR LABOR PRACTICES

EMPLOYERS	UNIONS
1. Refuse to recognize a union and to bargain in good faith. 2. Interfere with, restrain, or coerce employees in their efforts to form a union and bargain collectively. 3. Dominate a union. 4. Discriminate against union workers. 5. Agree to participate in a secondary boycott. 6. Punish employees for engaging in concerted activity.	1. Refuse to bargain in good faith. 2. Picket to coerce unionization without the majority support of the employees. 3. Demand the hiring of unnecessary excess workers. 4. Discriminate against nonunion workers. 5. Agree to participate in a secondary boycott. 6. Engage in an illegal strike. 7. Charge excessive membership fees.

employees; the employer cannot refuse to deal with the union as the employees' exclusive representative, even if the employees prefer not to be represented by that union.

Beyond the one-year period, the presumption of majority support continues, but it is *rebuttable*. An employer may rebut (refute) the presumption with objective evidence that a majority of employees do not wish to be represented by the union. If the evidence is sufficient to support a *good faith* belief that the union no longer enjoys majority support among the employees, the employer may refuse to continue to recognize and negotiate with the union.[18]

18. An employer cannot agree to a collective bargaining agreement and later refuse to abide by it, however, on the ground of a good faith belief that the union did not have majority support when the agreement was negotiated. See *Auciello Iron Works, Inc. v. NLRB*, __ U.S. __, 116 S.Ct. 1754, 135 L.Ed.2d 64 (1996).

QUESTIONS OF MAJORITY SUPPORT A delicate question arises during a strike in which an employer hires replacement workers. Specifically, should it be *assumed* that the replacement workers do not support the union? If they do not, and if as a result the union no longer has majority support, the employer need not continue negotiating with the union.

Another question arises when two companies merge or consolidate, when one company buys the assets or stock of another, or when, under any other circumstances, one employer steps into the shoes of another. Is a collective bargaining agreement between a union and a predecessor employer binding on the union and the successor employer? This is the issue in the following case.

CASE 22.5 Canteen Corp. v. NLRB

United States Court of Appeals, Seventh Circuit, 1997. 103 F.3d 1355.

BACKGROUND AND FACTS *The food service employees at the Medical College of Wisconsin were represented by the Hotel Employees and Restaurant Employees Union. When Canteen Corporation took over the food service, it agreed to negotiate a new contract with the union. Meanwhile, without informing the union, Canteen told the employees that their wages would be cut 20 to 25 percent. The employees resigned. Canteen then recruited employees from other sources and refused to negotiate with the union on the ground that it no longer represented the employees. The union filed an unfair labor practice charge with the National Labor Relations Board (NLRB). The NLRB ordered Canteen to reinstate the employees at their previous wage rates until a new contract could be negotiated. Canteen asked the U.S. Court of Appeals for the Seventh Circuit to review the order.*

IN THE LANGUAGE OF THE COURT

RIPPLE, Circuit Judge.

* * * *

* * * A new employer must consult with the union when it is clear that the employer intends to hire the employees of its predecessor as the initial workforce. * * *

* * * *

* * * The totality of Canteen's conduct demonstrated that it was perfectly clear that Canteen planned to retain the predecessor employees. * * *

* * * Canteen's intention to retain the * * * employees was backed by an expectation so strong that it neglected to take serious steps to recruit from other sources until it was informed that they had rejected job offers. * * * Canteen intended from the outset to hire all of the predecessor employees and did not mention in [its] discussions [with the union] the possibility of any other changes in its initial terms and conditions of employment.

DECISION AND REMEDY *The U.S. Court of Appeals for the Seventh Circuit ordered that the NLRB's order be enforced. The employer was required to reinstate the employees at their previous wage rates until a new contract could be negotiated.*

EMPLOYER'S INTERFERENCE IN UNION ACTIVITIES

The NLRA declares it to be an unfair labor practice for an employer to interfere with, restrain, or coerce employees in the exercise of their rights to form a union and bargain collectively. Unlawful employer interference may take a variety of forms.

Courts have found it an unfair labor practice for an employer to make threats that may interfere with an employee's decision to join a union. Even asking employees about their views on the union may be considered coercive. Employees responding to such questioning must be able to remain anonymous and must receive assurances against employer reprisals. Employers also may not prohibit certain forms of union activity in the workplace. If an employee has a grievance with the company, the employer cannot prevent the union's participation in support of the employee, for example.

If an employer has unlawfully interfered with the operation of a union, the NLRB or a reviewing court may issue a cease-and-desist order halting the practice. The company typically is required to post the order on a bulletin board and renounce its past unlawful conduct.

EMPLOYER'S DOMINATION OF UNION

In the early days of unionization, employers fought back by forming employer-sponsored unions to represent employees. These "company unions" were seldom more than the puppets of management. The NLRA outlawed company unions and any other form of employer domination of workers' unions.

A number of acts are considered unfair labor practices under the law against employer domination. For example, an employer can have no say in which employees belong to the union or which employees serve as union officers. Nor may supervisors or other management personnel participate in union meetings.

Company actions that support a union may be considered improper potential domination. For this reason, a company cannot give union workers pay for time spent on union activities, because this is considered undue support for the union. The company may not provide financial aid to a union and may not solicit workers to join a union.

EMPLOYER'S DISCRIMINATION AGAINST UNION EMPLOYEES

The NLRA prohibits employers from discriminating against workers because they are union officers or are otherwise associated with a union. When workers must be laid off, the company cannot consider union participation as a criterion for deciding whom to fire.

The antidiscrimination provisions also apply to hiring decisions. Suppose that certain employees of SemiCo are represented by a union, but the company is attempting to weaken the union's strength. The company cannot require potential new hires to guarantee that they will not join the union.

Discriminatory punishment of union members or officers can be difficult to prove. The company will claim to have good reasons for its action. The NLRB has specified a series of factors to be considered in determining whether an action had an unlawful, discriminatory motivation. These include giving inconsistent reasons for the action, applying rules inconsistently and more strictly against union members, failing to give an expected warning prior to discharge or other discipline, and acting contrary to worker seniority.

In one case, an employer, Wright Line, fired an employee, Bernard Lamoureux, for knowingly altering time reports and payroll records. Lamoureux conceded that he had not worked the precise hours he reported on his time card but claimed that he had worked an equivalent number of hours at other times. Lamoureux had been a leading union advocate. The NLRB found that the company had shown particular dislike for Lamoureux because it considered him to be the "union kingpin" in the company. In addition, the company had never before discharged a worker for this type of violation. The NLRB found that this was sufficient evidence of discrimination to shift the burden of proof to the company to demonstrate that it had not had a discriminatory motive. The company could not meet this burden, and the discharge was held unlawful.[19]

19. *Wright Line, a Division of Wright Line, Inc.*, 251 N.L.R.B. No. 150 (1980).

The decision to close a facility cannot be made with a discriminatory motive. If a company has several facilities and only one is unionized, the company cannot shut down the union plant simply because of the union. The company could shut down the union plant if it were demonstrably less efficient than the other facilities, however.

UNION'S UNFAIR LABOR PRACTICES

Certain union activities are declared to be unfair labor practices by the Taft-Hartley Act. Secondary boycotts, discussed above, are one such union unfair labor practice.

COERCION Another significant union unfair labor practice is coercion or restraint on an employee's decision to participate in or refrain from participating in union activities. Obviously, it is unlawful for a union to threaten an employee or a family with violence for failure to join the union. The law's prohibition includes economic coercion as well. Suppose that a union official declares, "We have a lot of power here; you had better join the union, or you may lose your job." This threat is an unfair labor practice.

The NLRA provides unions with the authority to regulate their own internal affairs, which includes disciplining union members. This discipline cannot be used in an improperly coercive fashion, however. Suppose a disaffected union member feels that the union is no longer providing proper representation for employees and starts a campaign to decertify the union. The union may expel the employee from membership but may not fine or otherwise discipline the worker.

DISCRIMINATION Another significant union unfair labor practice is discrimination. A union may not discriminate against workers because they refuse to join. This provision also prohibits a union from using its influence to cause an employer to discriminate against workers who refuse to join the union. A union cannot force an employer to deny promotions to workers who fail to join the union.

OTHER UNFAIR PRACTICES Other union unfair labor practices include featherbedding, participation in picketing to coerce unionization without majority employee support, and refusal to engage in good faith bargaining with employer representatives.

Unions are allowed to bargain for certain "union security clauses" in contracts. Although closed shops are illegal, a union can bargain for a provision that requires workers to contribute to the union within thirty days after they are hired. This is typically called an agency shop, or union shop, clause.

The union shop clause can compel workers to begin paying dues to the certified union but cannot require the worker to "join" the union. Dues payment can be required to prevent workers from taking the benefits of union bargaining without contributing to the union's efforts. The clause cannot require workers to contribute their efforts to the union, however, or to go out on strike.

Even a requirement of dues payment has its limits. Excessive initiation fees or dues may be illegal. Unions often use their revenues to contribute to causes or to lobby politicians. A nonunion employee subject to a union shop clause who must pay dues cannot be required to contribute to this sort of union expenditure.[20]

SECTION 8

RIGHTS OF NONUNION EMPLOYEES

Most of labor law involves the formation of unions and associated rights. Even nonunion employees have some similar rights, however. Most workers do not belong to unions, so this issue is significant. The NLRA protects concerted employee action, for example, and does not limit its protection to certified unions.

CONCERTED ACTIVITY

Data from the NLRB indicate that growing numbers of nonunion employees are challenging employer barriers to their **concerted action.** Protected concerted action is that taken by employees for their mutual benefit regarding wages, hours, or terms and conditions of employment.

Even an action by a single employee may be protected concerted activity, if that action is taken for the benefit of other employees and if the employee has at least discussed the action with other approving workers. If only a single worker engages in a protest or walkout, the employer will not be liable for an unfair labor practice if it fires the worker unless the employer is aware that this protest or walkout is concerted activity taken with the assent of other

20. *Communication Workers of America v. Beck,* 487 U.S. 735, 108 S.Ct. 2641, 101 L.Ed.2d 634 (1988).

workers. Sometimes the mutual interest of other workers should be obvious to the employer, however.

SAFETY

A common circumstance for nonunion activity is concern over workplace safety. The Labor-Management Relations Act authorizes an employee to walk off the job if he or she has a good faith belief that the working conditions are abnormally dangerous. The employer cannot lawfully discharge the employee under these conditions.

Suppose that Knight Company operates a plant building mobile homes. A large ventilation fan at the plant blows dust and abrasive materials into the faces of workers. The workers have complained, but Knight Company has done nothing. The workers finally refuse to work until the fan is modified, and Knight fires them. The NLRB will find that the walkout is a protected activity and can command Knight to rehire the workers with back pay.

To be protected under federal labor law, a safety walkout must be *concerted* activity. If a single worker walks out over a safety complaint, other workers must be affected by the safety issue for the walkout to be protected under the LMRA.

EMPLOYEE COMMITTEES

Personnel specialists note that worker problems are often attributable to a lack of communication between labor and management. In a nonunion work force, a company may wish to create some institution to communicate with workers and act together with them to improve workplace conditions.

This institution, generally called an **employee committee,** is composed of representatives from both management and labor. The committee meets periodically and has some authority to create rules. The committee gives employees a forum to voice their dissatisfaction with certain conditions and gives management a conduit to inform workers fully of policy decisions.

The creation of an employee committee may be entirely well motivated on the company's part and may serve the interests of workers as well as management. Nevertheless, employee committees are fraught with potential problems under federal labor laws, and management must be aware of these problems.

The central problem with employee committees is that they may become the functional equivalent of unions dominated by management, in violation of the NLRA. Thus, these committees cannot perform union functions. For example, the employee representatives on such a committee should not present a package of proposals on wages and terms of employment, because this is the role of a union negotiating committee.

In the following case, a union complained that an employer had committed an unfair labor practice by maintaining an employee committee.

CASE 22.6 In re Simmons Industries, Inc.

National Labor Relations Board, 1996. 321 N.L.R.B. No. 32.

HISTORICAL AND SOCIAL SETTING *In the 1930s and 1940s, after Congress enacted the first laws protecting unions, union membership as a percentage of the work force grew rapidly, until about a third of all workers belonged to unions. As the size of the work force continued to grow, however, the number of workers belonging to unions did not increase proportionately. By the mid-1990s, union members made up only about 15 percent of the work force. Unions, which have sometimes been frustrated by employees' reluctance to organize, often blame unsuccessful attempts to unionize a particular employer's work force on the employer.*

BACKGROUND AND FACTS *Simmons Industries, Inc., operated chicken processing plants. One of Simmons's customers was Kentucky Fried Chicken (KFC). To satisfy KFC's concerns with quality, Simmons formed at each plant a total quality management (TQM) committee. Simmons appointed managers and employees from a cross-section of the plants to serve on the committees and set the committees' agendas, which included such topics as employee* *bonuses and absences. Later, the United Food and Commercial Workers Union attempted unsuccessfully to organize the employees. The union filed a complaint with the National Labor Relations Board (NLRB), alleging that Simmons had committed unfair labor practices by, among other things, maintaining a TQM committee at its plant in Jay, Oklahoma. The union argued that the committee was a "labor organization" dominated by management in violation of the National Labor Relations Act (NLRA).*

IN THE LANGUAGE OF THE COURT

DECISION AND ORDER

* * * *

* * * [T]he concept of "labor organization" * * * includes very loose, informal, unstructured, and irregular meeting groups. Such a loose organization will meet the [NLRA] definition if: (1) employees participate, (2) the organization exists, at least in part, for the purpose of dealing with employers, and (3) these dealings concern conditions of work or concern other statutory subjects such as grievances, labor disputes, wages, rates of pay, or hours of employment.

* * * *

* * * [E]mployee members [of the TQM committee] were representative of each * * * grouping of employees. * * * [T]he Committee discussed and made proposals solicited by [Simmons] with respect to the formulation and implementation of an incentive bonus pay program, clearly a mandatory bargaining subject. [Simmons] accepted some of the committee's proposal and guided itself by others in formulating the bonus plan. * * * Furthermore, the * * * Committee continued * * * to discuss and make proposals with respect to employee discipline, attendance and punctuality problems and employee courtesy breaks. On recommendations based in large part on employee member complaints, the plant manager issued a set of rules that clearly affected these conditions of employment and mandatory bargaining subjects. Thus the * * * Committee * * * effectively constituted a representational employee committee, in effect a labor organization, which was unlawfully dominated, interfered with in operation and administration, and rendered unlawful assistance to by [Simmons] in violation of [the NLRA].

DECISION AND REMEDY

The NLRB ordered Simmons to, among other things, "[i]mmediately disestablish and cease giving assistance or any other support" to its TQM committee.[a]

a. This decision was an application of the principle declared in the leading case in this area, *Electromation, Inc.*, 309 N.L.R.B. 990 (1992).

TERMS AND CONCEPTS TO REVIEW

appropriate bargaining unit 453
authorization card 453
closed shop 452
collective bargaining 458
common situs picketing 462
concerted action 467
eighty-day cooling-off period 463
employee committee 468
featherbedding 458
hot-cargo agreement 462
lockout 464
no-strike clause 463
right-to-work law 452
secondary boycott 462
severance pay 459
union shop 452
wildcat strike 462
yellow dog contract 451

QUESTIONS AND CASE PROBLEMS

22–1. PRELIMINARY ORGANIZING. A group of employees at the Briarwood Furniture Company's manufacturing plant were interested in joining a union. A representative of the American Federation of Labor and Congress of Industrial Organizations (AFL-CIO) told the group that her union was prepared to represent the workers and suggested that the group begin organizing by obtaining authorization cards from their fellow employees. After obtaining 252 authorization cards from among Briarwood's 500 nonmanagement employees, the organizers requested that the company recognize the AFL-CIO as the official representative of the employees. The company refused. Has the company violated federal labor laws? What should the organizers do?

22–2. APPROPRIATE BARGAINING UNIT. The Briarwood Furniture Company, discussed in the preceding problem, employs 400 unskilled workers and 100 skilled workers in its plant. The unskilled workers operate the industrial machinery used in processing Briarwood's line of standardized plastic office furniture. The skilled workers, who work in an entirely separate part of the plant, are experienced artisans who craft Briarwood's line of expensive wood furniture products. Do you see any problems with a single union's representing all the workers at the Briarwood plant? Explain. Would your answers to Problem 22–1 change if you knew that 51 of the authorization cards had been signed by the skilled workers, with the remainder signed by the unskilled workers?

22–3. UNFAIR LABOR PRACTICES. Suppose that Consolidated Stores is undergoing a unionization campaign. Prior to the election, management says that the union is unnecessary to protect workers. Management also provides bonuses and wage increases to the workers during this period. The employees reject the union. Union organizers protest that the wage increases during the election campaign unfairly prejudiced the vote. Should these wage increases be regarded as an unfair labor practice? Discuss.

22–4. UNFAIR LABOR PRACTICES. SimpCo was engaged in ongoing negotiations over a new labor contract with the union representing the company's employees. As the deadline for expiration of the old labor contract drew near, several employees who were active in union activities were disciplined for being late to work. The union claimed that other employees had not been dealt with as harshly and that the company was discriminating on the basis of union activity. When the negotiations failed to prove fruitful and the old contract expired, the union called a strike. The company claimed the action was an economic strike to press the union's demands for higher wages. The union contended the action was an unfair labor practice strike because of the alleged discrimination. What importance does the distinction have for the striking workers and the company?

22–5. APPROPRIATE BARGAINING UNIT. Westvaco operated plants that manufactured printed folding cartons, and its production and maintenance employees were represented by a union. The company hired four new technicians to work at the facility. The union argued that the technicians should be part of the unionized work force. Westvaco disputed this argument, claiming that the technicians, because of their greater skills, were not properly part of the same bargaining unit as the existing production and maintenance employees—the technicians had previously been put through an extensive and specialized training course that lasted about four months. The National Labor Relations Board agreed with the union and added the new technicians to the bargaining unit. Westvaco appealed to the court. How should the court rule? Explain fully. [*Westvaco, Virginia, Folding Box Division v. NLRB*, 795 F.2d 1171 (4th Cir. 1986)]

22–6. SECONDARY BOYCOTTS. For many years, grapefruit was shipped to Japan from Fort Pierce and Port Canaveral, Florida. In 1990, Coastal Stevedoring Co. in Fort Pierce and Port Canaveral Stevedoring, Ltd., in Port Canaveral—nonunion firms—were engaged in a labor dispute with the International Longshoremen's Association (ILA). The ILA asked the National Council of Dockworkers' Unions of Japan to prevent Japanese shippers from using nonunion stevedores in Florida, and the council warned Japanese firms that their workers would not unload fruit loaded in the United States by nonunion labor. The threat caused all citrus shipments from Florida to Japan to go through Tampa, where they were loaded by stevedores represented by the ILA. Coastal, Canaveral, and others complained to the National Labor Relations Board (NLRB), alleging that the ILA's request of the Japanese unions was an illegal secondary boycott. How should the NLRB rule? [*International Longshoremen's Association, AFL-CIO*, 313 N.L.R.B. No. 53 (1993)]

22–7. UNFAIR LABOR PRACTICES. The Teamsters Union represented twenty-seven employees of Curtin Matheson Scientific, Inc. When a collective bargaining agreement between the union and the company expired, the company made an offer for a new agreement, which the union rejected. The company locked out the twenty-seven employees, and the union began an economic strike. The company hired replacement workers. When the union ended its strike and offered to accept the company's earlier offer, the company refused. The company also refused to bargain further, asserting doubt that the union was supported by a majority of the employees. The union sought help from the National Labor Relations Board (NLRB), which refused to presume that the replacement workers did not support the union. On the company's appeal, a court overturned the NLRB's ruling. The union appealed to the United States Supreme Court. How should the Court rule? [*NLRB v. Curtin Matheson Scientific, Inc.*, 494 U.S. 775, 110 S.Ct. 1542, 108 L.Ed.2d 801 (1990)]

22–8. GOOD FAITH BARGAINING. American Commercial Barge Line Co. was an affiliation made up of a number of barge and towing companies. The Seafarers International Union of North America (SIU) represented workers for Inland Tugs (IT), a separate corporate division of American Commercial Barge Line. When SIU and IT began negotiating a new collective bargaining agreement, SIU demanded that the bargaining unit include all the employees of American Commercial Barge Line. SIU also demanded that any contract include a pledge by other American Commercial Barge Line companies to continue their contributions to SIU funds, which provided for union activities. Unable to agree on these issues, the parties continued to meet for several years. Meanwhile, on the basis of an employee poll, IT changed its system of calculating wages. SIU filed a complaint with the NLRB, claiming that these changes were an unfair labor practice. IT responded that SIU was not bargaining in good faith. How should the NLRB rule? Explain. [*Inland Tugs, A Division of American Commercial Barge Line Co. v. NLRB*, 918 F.2d 1299 (7th Cir. 1990)]

22–9. EMPLOYEE COMMITTEES. Electromation, Inc., a manufacturer of electrical components and related products, cut wages, bonuses, and incentive pay and tightened attendance and leave policies. When the employees complained, Electromation set up "action committees," each consisting of employees and management representatives. No employee was involved in drafting the goals of the committees. The committees were told to suggest solutions, which would be implemented if management "believed they were within budget concerns" and "would be acceptable to the employees." Employee committee members were expected to discuss suggestions with their co-workers. The Teamsters Union, which had been seeking to organize the employees, challenged the establishment of the committees as an unfair labor practice and asked the NLRB to order that they be dissolved. On what basis might the NLRB grant the union's request? [*Electromation, Inc.*, 309 N.L.R.B. 990 (1992)]

22–10. A QUESTION OF ETHICS

Salvatore Monte was president of Kenrich Petrochemicals, Inc. Helen Chizmar had been Kenrich's office manager since 1963. Among the staff that Chizmar supervised were her sister, daughter, and daughter-in-law. In 1987, Chizmar's relatives and four other staff members designated the Oil, Chemical, and Atomic Workers International Union as their bargaining representative. Chizmar was not involved, but when Monte was notified that his office was unionizing, he told Chizmar that someone else could do her job for "$20,000 less" and fired her. He told another employee that one of his reasons for firing Chizmar was that he "was not going to put up with any union bullsh—." During negotiations with the union, Monte said that he planned to "get rid of the whole family." Chizmar's family complained to the National Labor Relations Board (NLRB) that the firing was an unfair labor practice. The NLRB agreed and ordered that Chizmar be reinstated with back pay. Kenrich appealed. In view of these facts, consider the following questions. [*Kenrich Petrochemicals, Inc. v. NLRB*, 907 F.2d 400 (3d Cir. 1990)]

1. The National Labor Relations Act does not protect supervisors who engage in union activities. Should the appellate court affirm the NLRB's order nonetheless?
2. If the appellate court does not affirm the NLRB's order, what message will be sent to the supervisors and employees of Kenrich?
3. Is there anything Kenrich could (legally) do to avoid the unionization of its employees? Would it be ethical to counter the wishes of the employees to unionize?
4. What are the advantages of unionization for employees? Are there any disadvantages?

UNIT FOUR—CUMULATIVE HYPOTHETICAL PROBLEM

22–11. *Falwell Motors, Inc., is a large corporation that manufacturers automobile batteries.*

1. One of Falwell's salespersons, Loren, puts in long hours every week. He spends most of his time away from the office generating sales. Less than 10 percent of his work time is devoted to other duties. Usually, he receives a substantial bonus at the end of each year from his employer, and Loren now relies on this supplement to his annual salary and commission. One year, the employer does not give any of its employees year-end bonuses. Loren calculates the amount of hours he had worked during the year beyond the required forty hours a week. Then he tells Falwell's president that if he is not

paid for these overtime hours, he will sue the company for the overtime pay he has "earned." Falwell's president tells Loren that Falwell is not obligated to pay Loren overtime because Loren is a salesperson. What federal statute governs this dispute? Under this statute, is Falwell required to pay Loren for the "overtime hours"? Why or why not?

2. One day Barry, one of the salespersons, anxious to make a sale, intentionally quotes a price to a customer that is $500 lower than Falwell has authorized for that particular product. The customer purchases the product at the quoted price. When Falwell learns of the deal, it claims that it is not legally bound to the sales contract because it did not authorize Barry to sell the product at that price. Is Falwell bound by the contract? Discuss fully.

3. One day Gina, a Falwell employee, suffered a serious burn when she accidentally spilled some acid on her hand. The accident occurred because another employee, who was suspected of using illegal drugs, carelessly bumped into her. The hand required a series of skin-grafting operations before it healed sufficiently to allow Gina to return to work. Gina wants to obtain compensation for her lost wages and medical expenses. Can she do so? If so, how?

4. After Gina's injury, Falwell decides to conduct random drug tests on all of its employees. Several employees claim that the testing violates their privacy rights. If the dispute is litigated, what factors will the court consider in deciding whether the random drug testing is legally permissible?

5. Aretha, a Falwell employee, is disgusted by the sexually offensive behavior of several male employees. She has complained to her supervisor on several occasions about the offensive behavior, but the supervisor merely laughs at her concerns. Aretha decides to bring a legal action against the company for sexual harassment. Does Aretha's complaint concern *quid pro quo* harassment or hostile-environment harassment? What federal statute protects employees from sexual harassment? What remedies are available under that statute? What procedures must Aretha follow in pursuing her legal action?

ACCESSING THE INTERNET
THE LEGAL ENVIRONMENT OF BUSINESS

The Institute of Labor Relations at Cornell University and *Human Resource Executive* magazine have complied an extensive index of resources on labor law. You can find these resources at

http://www.workindex.com

A similar index of Web links on labor relations is Employee Relations Web Picks at

http://www.webcom.com/~garnet/labor/

The Legal Information Institute at Cornell Law School provides introductions to various labor and employment topics at

http://fatty.law.cornell.edu/topics/topics2.html#employment_law

"A Primer on Labor Relations" is offered by Labor Relations Alternatives of Albany, New York, at

http://www.globalone.net/lra/labor/union1.htm

The site of the American Federation of Labor–Congress of Industrial Organizations (AFL-CIO) provides links to a broad variety of labor-related resources. Go to

http://www.aflcio.org/

The National Labor Relations Board is now online at the following URL:

http://www.doc.gov/nlrb/homepg.html

FOCUS ON ETHICS

THE EMPLOYMENT ENVIRONMENT

The employment environment is one in which individuals come together for the purpose of achieving a common purpose. In this sense, the employment environment is like most others we have examined thus far. Yet in spite of the similarities, the employment environment remains unique.

Part of the uniqueness of the employment environment stems from the close nature of the relationship between employers and employees, a relationship that, as seen in this unit, often involves intricate duties of agency. In earlier times, most individuals were self-employed, usually on the family farm. The farm was the center of the family unit. At any given time, several generations might have their entire social and financial security invested in the family farm.

With the onset of the industrial revolution, this structure gave way to another—one in which individuals worked with and depended on those individuals that did not share the special bonds of family relationship. Yet because employment relationships typically exist for an extended period, there was inevitably a tendency to incorporate aspects of the family into the employment environment. The result has been that there is sometimes a conflict between the impersonal nature of the market—labor is, after all, a factor of production—and the family-like aspect of the close, long-term relation between an employer and employee. Moreover, the aspects that account for the uniqueness of the employment environment generate numerous ethical issues. In this unit's *Focus on Ethics* we examine two such issues. First, we examine the ethical problems surrounding the high degree of loyalty demanded in an agency relationship. Second, we examine the degree to which society should rely on business to utilize affirmative action programs in eliminating the lingering social problem of discrimination against minorities.

THE DUTIES OF AGENTS AND PRINCIPALS

When one person agrees to act on behalf of another, as an agent does in an agency relationship, that person assumes certain ethical responsibilities. An agent acting *on behalf of* a principal implicitly promises to place the principal's interests above his or her own interests. Similarly, a principal in an agency relationship assumes certain ethical duties. If an agent incurs expenses or liability while acting on the principal's behalf, for example, it is only fair that the principal should assume responsibility for those expenses or that liability. In essence, agency law gives legal force to the ethical duties arising in an agency relationship. Although agency law also focuses on the rights of agents and principals, those rights are framed by the concept of duty—that is, an agent's duty becomes a right for the principal and vice versa.

Significantly, most of the duties of the principal and agent described below are negotiable at law. In forming a contract, the principal and the agent can extend or abridge many of the ordinary duties owed in such a relationship. Legal rules generally come into play when the contract is silent or ambiguous on an issue. Allowing the parties to negotiate their relative duties seems ethically fair, as long as the parties are able to understand their rights and make informed decisions.

DISABILITY-BASED DISCRIMINATION

In providing protection for disabled persons in the employment context through the Americans with Disabilities Act (ADA), Congress expressed society's concern that persons with disabilities should be given a fair opportunity to compete in the workplace. This act differs from most other federal antidiscrimination laws in that it requires employers to treat employees with disabilities *unequally* as opposed to equally—under the ADA, a person with a disability is entitled to be reasonably accommodated by the employer.

FOCUS ON ETHICS

The ADA thus forces employers to view their workplaces in a new light. They must view job qualifications with an eye toward determining whether employees with disabilities are qualified to perform certain jobs with reasonable accommodations. They must also analyze job requirements from a different perspective, focusing on which requirements are essential to a job and which are not. Furthermore, employers must be especially careful not to ask job applicants or employees impermissible questions or request certain types of information from them.

The ADA protects not only persons who actually suffer from disabilities but also persons who are *perceived* by employers to have disabilities. For example, in one case, an employee was discharged five weeks after he had a heart attack. Regardless of whether the employee was actually disabled, there was evidence that the company regarded him as disabled, and hence the employee had a cause of action under the ADA.[1]

The ADA clearly offers broad protections to employees. More than anything else, the act requires an attitudinal change. In particular, the act requires employers and employees alike to revise their perceptions of what the term *disability* means in the context of the workplace.

1. *Katz v. City Metal Co.*, 87 F.3d 26 (1st Cir. 1996).

ENGLISH-ONLY POLICIES

As the U.S. population becomes more and more multilingual, so does the work force. In response to this development, many employers have instituted English-only policies in their workplaces. Are such policies fair to non-English-speaking workers? Do they violate Title VII, which prohibits discrimination on the basis of national origin?

Employers seem to be caught between the proverbial "rock and a hard place" with respect to this issue. In one case, for example, an employee sued her employer, claiming that the employer's *failure* to institute an English-only policy violated her rights under Title VII. The federal court declined to dismiss the suit.[2] In several other cases, however, employers who have adopted English-only policies have been sued for Title VII violations even though the reason the policies were implemented was to ease ethnic tensions in the workplace—and thus *deter* discriminatory practices.

Consider the case of *Garcia v. Spun Steak Co.*[3] In that case, the employer faced the following problem: several African American and Chinese American employees complained that the company's Spanish-speaking employees were making racist comments about them. Hoping to resolve the problem, the employer adopted an English-only policy—only to be faced with a lawsuit brought by the Spanish-speaking employees. They claimed that they had been denied their "right" to express their cultural heritage on the job. Additionally, they contended that they had been denied a privilege held by English-speaking employees: the opportunity to speak their native language in the workplace. They also argued that the policy intimidated them and made them feel isolated and inferior.

To date, the courts have shown a fair degree of tolerance of English-only rules. In the *Spun Steak* case, for example, the Court of Appeals for the Ninth Circuit held that Title VII does not protect an employee's right to express his or her cultural heritage on the job. Furthermore, in the court's eyes, the employees had not been denied any privilege enjoyed by the English-speaking employees, because, as bilingual persons, they could elect to speak in English and therefore had the capability to converse in the workplace. Finally, in regard to the claim of "intimidation," which the court regarded as a type of hostile-environment claim, the court stated that it was unwilling to adopt a blanket rule that English-only policies create a hostile work environment.

More recently, a federal district court dismissed a case challenging an English-only rule adopted by a nursery school located in Houston, Texas. The rule prohibited employees (about 50 percent of whom were Spanish speaking) from speaking Spanish anywhere on the school's

2. *McNeil v. Aguilos,* 831 F.Supp. 1079 (S.D.N.Y. 1993).
3. 998 F.2d 1480 (9th Cir. 1993).

Focus on Ethics

premises. The owner of the school had posted signs indicating that failure to comply with the policy would result in immediate termination. Several Hispanic workers sued the school, alleging that the school's policy had a disparate impact on Hispanic employees. The court, however, noting that the rule was adopted for the purpose of encouraging the children to speak English, held that the rule did not violate Title VII.[4]

Generally, the courts seem to be rejecting the EEOC's interpretive guidelines on English-only policies. As mentioned in Chapter 21, the EEOC has taken a stricter approach, stating that blanket English-only policies (policies that prohibit employees from speaking languages other than English *at all times*) constitute discrimination on the basis of national origin in violation of Title VII.

Labor Law and Quality Control

One of the ways in which today's corporations have increased their productivity and product quality—and hence their ability to compete effectively—is by using some type of employee-participation program. Such programs are established into only to promote labor-management cooperation but also to incorporate employee input into the decision-making process in order to improve the quality of the firm's products or services.

While employee-participation programs appear to be an effective approach to the problems of productivity and product quality, they have recently come under attack as violating labor laws. To illustrate: Electromation, Inc., an electrical-components manufacturer, set up a series of committees involving employee and management participation. The committees were initially established to counter employee dissatisfaction with new employment policies that related to absenteeism, nonsmoking rules, and so on.

The workers who participated in these committees involved themselves in developing solutions to these and various other problems, including worker benefits. The Teamster Union, which was attempting to unionize Electromation's work force, successfully argued to the National Labor Relations Board (NLRB) that the committees violated the National Labor Relations Act (NLRA) because, in essence, the committees were labor organizations that were unlawfully "dominated" by the employer.[5]

Because numerous companies throughout the United States use similar action committees, the corporate community felt that it had been dealt a severe blow by the NLRB's decision. Almost any type of employee-participation program, regardless of how beneficial for employer and employee alike, could possibly be characterized as a labor organization as defined under the NLRA. As a result, employers will be wary of employee-participation programs, regardless of how beneficial they are.

The U.S. Constitution is premised on the belief that we benefit as a society by the free exchange of ideas and political beliefs. Should labor laws function to restrict the expression of ideas? Can a balance be struck between the goals of free speech and assembly and the prevention of an employer-dominated workplace in which the employee is underrepresented?

Discussion Questions

1. How much obedience and loyalty does an agent-employee owe an employer? What if the employer engages in an activity—or requests the employee to engage in an activity—that violates the employee's ethical standards but does not necessarily violate any public policy or law? In such a situation, does an employee's duty to abide by his or her own ethical standards override the employee's duty of loyalty to the employer?

2. If an agent injures a third party during the course of employment, under the doctrine of *respondeat superior,* the employer may be held liable for the agent's actions even though the employer did not authorize the action and was not even aware of it. Do you think that it is fair to hold employers liable in

4. *EEOC v. Synell, Inc.*, 91 F.3d 138 (5th Cir. 1996).

5. *Electromation, Inc.*, 309 N.L.R.B. No. 163 (1992).

Focus on Ethics

such situations? Do you think that it would be fairer to hold that the employee alone should bear responsibility for his or her tortious actions to third parties, even when the actions are committed within the scope of employment?

3. Do you think that the Americans with Disabilities Act goes too far in protecting the rights of employees with disabilities (or perceived disabilities)? Does it go far enough?

4. Do you see any need for English-only policies in the workplace? Can such policies ever reduce tensions between different ethnic groups, some of which are caused by the use of different languages?

UNIT FIVE

THE REGULATORY ENVIRONMENT

CONTENTS

Chapter 23
Consumer Protection

All statutes, agency rules, and common law judicial decisions that serve to protect the interest of consumers are classified as **consumer law.** Consumer transactions take a variety of forms but broadly include those that involve an exchange of value for the purpose of acquiring goods, services, land, or credit for personal or family use.

Traditionally, in disputes involving consumers, it was assumed that the freedom to contract carried with it the obligation to live by the deal made. Therefore, the watchword in most such transactions was *caveat emptor*—"let the buyer beware." Over time, this attitude has changed considerably. Today, myriad federal and state laws protect consumers from unfair trade practices, unsafe products, discriminatory or unreasonable credit requirements, and other problems related to consumer transactions. Nearly every agency and department of the federal government has an office of consumer affairs, and most states have one or more such offices to assist consumers. Also, typically the attorney general's office assists consumers at the state level.

Because of the wide variation among state consumer protection laws, our primary focus in this chapter is on federal legislation—specifically, on legislation governing advertising practices, labeling and packaging, sales, health protection, product safety, and credit protection. Realize, though, that state laws often provide more sweeping and significant protections for the consumer than do federal laws. State consumer protection laws are discussed later in this chapter.

SECTION 1

DECEPTIVE ADVERTISING

One of the earliest—and still one of the most important—federal consumer protection laws was the Federal Trade Commission Act of 1914.[1] As mentioned in the preceding chapter, the act created the Federal Trade Commission (FTC) to carry out the broadly stated goal of preventing unfair and deceptive trade practices, including deceptive advertising.[2]

DECEPTIVE ADVERTISING DEFINED

Advertising will be deemed deceptive if a consumer would be misled by the advertising claim. Vague generalities and obvious exaggerations are permissible. These claims are known as *puffing*. When a claim takes on the appearance of literal authenticity, however, it may create problems. Advertising that would *appear* to be based on factual evidence but that in fact is not will be deemed deceptive. A classic example is provided by a 1944 case in which the claim that a skin cream would restore youthful qualities to aged skin was deemed deceptive.[3]

Some advertisements contain "half-truths," meaning that the presented information is true but incomplete, and it leads consumers to a false conclusion. For example, the makers of Campbell's soups advertised that "most" Campbell's soups were low in fat and cholesterol and thus were helpful in fighting heart disease. What the ad did not say was that Campbell's soups are high in sodium, and high-sodium diets may increase the risk of heart disease. The FTC ruled that Campbell's claims were thus deceptive. Advertising that contains an endorsement by a celebrity may be deemed deceptive if the celebrity actually makes no use of the product.

BAIT-AND-SWITCH ADVERTISING

The FTC has promulgated specific rules to govern advertising techniques. One of the most important rules is contained in the FTC's "Guides Against Bait Advertising,"[4] issued in 1968. The rule seeks to prevent **bait-and-switch advertising**—that is, advertising a very low price for a particular item that will likely be unavailable to the consumer, who will then be encouraged to purchase a more expensive item. The low price is the "bait" to lure the consumer into the store. The salesperson is instructed to "switch" the consumer to a different, more expensive item. Under the FTC guidelines, bait-and-switch advertising occurs if the seller refuses to show the advertised item, fails to have in stock a reasonable quantity of the item, fails to promise to deliver the advertised item within a reasonable time, or discourages employees from selling the item.

FTC ACTIONS AGAINST DECEPTIVE ADVERTISING

The FTC receives complaints from many sources, including competitors of alleged violators, consumers, consumer organizations, trade associations, Better Business Bureaus, government organizations, and state and local officials. If enough consumers complain and the complaints are widespread, the FTC will investigate the problem and perhaps take action. If, after its investigations, the FTC believes that a given advertisement is unfair or deceptive, it drafts a formal complaint, which is sent to the alleged offender. The company may agree to settle the complaint without further proceedings.

If the company does not agree to settle the complaint, the FTC can conduct a hearing in which the company can present its defense. As discussed in Chapter 6, a hearing conducted by an administrative agency is held before an administrative law judge instead of a federal district court judge. If the FTC succeeds in proving that an advertisement is unfair or deceptive, it usually issues a **cease-and-desist order** requiring that the challenged advertising be stopped. It might also impose a sanction known as **counteradvertising** by requiring the company to advertise anew—in print, on radio, and on television—to inform the public about the earlier misinformation. The FTC may institute **multiple product orders,** which require a firm to cease and desist from false advertising not only in regard to the product that was the subject of the action but also in regard to all of the firm's other products.

Is it false or misleading to advertise a product as effective when its only effectiveness results from users' belief that it works? The court addresses this issue in the following case.

1. 15 U.S.C. Sections 41–58.
2. 15 U.S.C. Section 45.
3. *Charles of the Ritz Distributing Corp. v. Federal Trade Commission*, 143 F.2d 676 (2d Cir. 1944).
4. 16 C.F.R. Part 238.

CASE 23.1 Federal Trade Commission v. Pantron I Corp.

United States Court of Appeals, Ninth Circuit, 1994. 33 F.3d 1088.

HISTORICAL AND SOCIAL SETTING *Hair has been part of people's self-image since primitive men and women first adorned it with clay, trophies, and badges. Sometimes, an abundance of hair is interpreted as characteristic of virility. At other times, a bald pate is seen as indicating masculinity. Regardless of how it is viewed, male-pattern baldness (the loss of hair from the upper scalp) results from an individual's genetic background and hormone levels. There is no "cure," and even hair transplants may have no lasting effect.*

BACKGROUND AND FACTS *Pantron I Corporation sold the Helsinki Formula as a "cure" for baldness. Pantron claimed that the product reduced hair loss and promoted hair growth. The Federal Trade Commission filed a suit in a federal district court against Pantron and its owner, Hal Lederman, alleging that these claims constituted an unfair or deceptive trade practice. The court concluded in part that the product had a "placebo effect"—that is, that it worked when its users believed it would. The court issued an order that, among other things, allowed Pantron to continue claiming its product "works some of the time for a lot of people." The FTC appealed this order.*

IN THE LANGUAGE OF THE COURT

REINHARDT, Circuit Judge:

* * * *

* * * Where, as here, a product's effectiveness arises solely as a result of the placebo effect, a representation that the product is effective constitutes a false advertisement even though some consumers may experience positive results. In such circumstances, the efficacy claim is misleading because the [product] is not inherently effective, its results being attributable to the psychosomatic effect produced by * * * advertising * * * .

* * * Under the evidence in the record before us, it appears that massaging vegetable oil on one's head would likely produce the same positive results as using the Helsinki Formula. * * * [A] court should not allow a seller to rely on such a placebo effect in supporting a claim of effectiveness * * * . [W]ere we to hold otherwise, advertisers would be encouraged to foist unsubstantiated claims on an unsuspecting public in the hope that consumers would believe the ads and the claims would be self-fulfilling.

DECISION AND REMEDY *The U.S. Court of Appeals for the Ninth Circuit reversed this part of the lower court's order and remanded the case. Pantron could not continue to claim that its product "works some of the time for a lot of people."*

TELEMARKETING AND ELECTRONIC ADVERTISING

The pervasive use of the telephone to market goods and services to homes and businesses led to the passage in 1991 of the Telephone Consumer Protection Act (TCPA).[5] The act prohibits telephone solicitation using an automatic telephone dialing system or a prerecorded voice. Most states also have laws regulating telephone solicitation.[6]

Not surprisingly, the widespread use of facsimile (fax) machines has led to the use of faxes as a tool for direct marketing. Advertising by fax is less expensive

5. 47 U.S.C. Sections 227 *et seq.*

6. For a discussion of the constitutionality of the TCPA, which some plaintiffs have alleged goes too far in restricting free speech, see *Moser v. Federal Communications Commission*, 46 F.3d 970 (9th Cir. 1995); *cert.* denied __ U.S. __, 115 S.Ct. 2615, 132 L.Ed.2d 857 (1995).

than mailing letters, and faxes normally receive greater attention than "junk mail." At the same time, unsolicited fax messages tie up the recipient's fax machine and impose a cost on the recipient, who must pay for fax paper and other supplies. The TCPA also makes it illegal to transmit ads via fax without first obtaining the recipient's permission.

The act is enforced by the Federal Communications Commission and also provides for a private right of action. Consumers can recover any actual monetary loss resulting from a violation of the act or receive $500 in damages for each violation, whichever is greater. If a court finds that a defendant willfully or knowingly violated the act, the court has the discretion to treble the damages awarded.

The Telemarketing and Consumer Fraud and Abuse Prevention Act[7] of 1994 directed the FTC to establish rules governing telemarketing and to bring actions against fraudulent telemarketers. The FTC's Telemarketing Sales Rule[8] of 1995 requires a telemarketer, before making a sales pitch, to inform the recipient that the call is a sales call and to identify the seller's name and the product being sold. The rule makes it illegal for telemarketers to misrepresent information (including facts about their goods or services, earnings potential, profitability, the risk attending an investment, or the nature of a prize). Additionally, telemarketers must inform the people they call of the total cost of the goods being sold, any restrictions on obtaining or using them, and whether a sale will be considered to be final and nonrefundable.

SECTION 2
LABELING AND PACKAGING LAWS

A number of federal and state laws deal specifically with the information given on labels and packages. The restrictions are designed to ensure that labels and packages provide accurate information about products and warn about possible dangers from the products' use or misuse. In general, labels must be accurate. That is, they must use words as those words are understood by the ordinary consumer. For example, a box of cereal cannot be labeled "giant" if that would exaggerate the amount of cereal contained in the box. In some instances, labels must specify the raw materials used in the product, such as the percentage of cotton, nylon, or other fiber used in a garment. In other instances, the product must carry a warning. Cigarette packages and advertising, for example, must include one of several warnings about the health hazards associated with smoking.[9]

Federal laws regulating the labeling and packaging of products include the Wool Products Labeling Act of 1939,[10] the Fur Products Labeling Act of 1951,[11] the Flammable Fabrics Act of 1953,[12] the Fair Packaging and Labeling Act of 1966,[13] the Smokeless Tobacco Health Education Act of 1986,[14] and the Nutrition Labeling and Education Act of 1990.[15] The Smokeless Tobacco Health Education Act, for example, requires that producers, packagers, and importers of smokeless tobacco label their product with one of several warnings about the health hazards associated with the use of smokeless tobacco; the warnings are similar to those contained on other tobacco product packages.

The Fair Packaging and Labeling Act requires that products carry labels that identify the product; the net quantity of the contents, as well as the quantity of servings, if the number of servings is stated; the manufacturer; and the packager or distributor. The act also authorizes requirements concerning words used to describe packages, terms that are associated with savings claims, information disclosures for ingredients in nonfood products, and standards for the partial filling of packages. Food products must bear labels detailing nutritional content, including how much fat a product contains and what kind of fat it is. These restrictions are enforced by the Department of Health and Human Services, as well as the Federal Trade Commission. The Nutrition Labeling and Education Act of 1990 requires standard nutrition facts (including fat content) on food labels; regulates the use of such terms as *fresh* and *low-fat*; and, subject to the federal Food and Drug Administration's approval, authorizes certain health claims.

7. 15 U.S.C. Sections 6101–6108.
8. 16 C.F.R. Sections 310.1–310.8.

9. 15 U.S.C. Sections 1331–1341.
10. 15 U.S.C. Section 68.
11. 15 U.S.C. Section 69.
12. 15 U.S.C. Section 1191.
13. 15 U.S.C. Sections 1451–1461.
14. 15 U.S.C. Sections 4401–4408.
15. 21 U.S.C. Section 343-1.

EMERGING TRENDS

CONSUMER PROTECTION ON THE INTERNET

According to Jodie Bernstein, head of the Federal Trade Commission's Bureau of Consumer Protection, "The Internet will not achieve its commercial potential if [it] becomes the Wild West of fraudulent schemes."[a] Because so much fraud has occurred on the Internet recently, a growing group of concerned individuals and consumer advocacy groups are calling for federal regulations to impose order on the electronic frontier. In opposition are those who fear that any regulation could stunt the growth of the Internet. They argue that the reason the Internet has grown so fast is that it has not been regulated.

a. As quoted in Albert R. Karr, "Critics of Internet Clamor for More Controls," *The Wall Street Journal Europe*, October 2, 1996, p. 4.

ENTER THE FTC

Since the beginning of 1996, the Federal Trade Commission (FTC) has filed dozens of cases, under existing consumer protection statutes, concerning use of the Internet. Many of these cases involve so-called pyramid schemes, in which the early-round participants profit to the detriment of later-round members. In general, then, until now federal government agencies have fought online fraud by looking for violations of existing laws on the Internet. Some states, though, have enacted specific Internet-directed laws. Additionally, the Council of Better Business Bureaus, or BBB, now provides for the online filing of complaints. The BBB also now offers an online seal of approval for online advertising.

The FTC is currently considering whether to regulate the collection of information about visitors to Web sites. The FTC's privacy initiative is available at the FTC's Web site listed in the *Accessing the Internet* feature at the end of this chapter.

DECEPTIVE ADVERTISING IN CYBERSPACE

For years, the FTC has fought deceptive advertising in printed materials and in radio and television broadcasts. In the future, it will spend more of its resources to monitor deceptive advertising on the Internet. In the last few months of 1996, for example, it brought eight enforcement actions against entities that apparently had made false or unsubstantiated claims in their Internet ads. During that year, it brought over two

SECTION 3

SALES

Many of the laws that protect consumers concern the disclosure of certain terms in sales transactions and provide rules governing the various forms of sales, such as door-to-door sales, mail-order sales, referral sales, and the unsolicited receipt of merchandise. Much of the federal regulation of sales is conducted by the FTC under its regulatory authority to curb unfair trade practices. Other federal agencies, however, are involved to various degrees. For example, the Federal Reserve Board of Governors has issued **Regulation Z**,[16] which governs credit provisions associated with sales contracts. Many states have also enacted laws governing consumer sales transactions. Moreover, states have provided a number of consumer protection provisions through the adoption of the Uniform Commercial Code and, in those states that have adopted it, the Uniform Consumer Credit Code.

DOOR-TO-DOOR SALES

Door-to-door sales are singled out for special treatment in the laws of most states, in part because of the nature of the sales transaction. Repeat purchases are

16. 12 C.F.R. Sections 226.1–226.30.

EMERGING TRENDS

CONSUMER PROTECTION ON THE INTERNET (CONTINUED)

dozen cases in all involving online fraud and deceptive advertising.

The FTC has moved particularly quickly on commercial Internet fraud schemes. It has even provided "hot links" on Web sites that it has targeted. A hot link takes the user to the FTC's own Web site, on which the complaint, restraining order, and other documents in the case can be read and downloaded.

OTHER AGENCIES FIGHT ONLINE FRAUD AND FALSE ADVERTISING

The Securities and Exchange Commission (SEC) also has been active in prosecuting online scams. One fraudulent scheme involved twenty thousand investors, who lost in all more than $3 million. Other cases have involved false claims about the earnings potential of home business programs, such as the claim that one could "earn $4,000 or more each month." Others have involved claims for "guaranteed credit repair."

The Department of Transportation (DOT), as well as the Food and Drug Administration (FDA), have also brought actions against purported online violators of advertising and disclosure laws. The DOT fined Virgin Airlines for failing to disclose the true price of a flight that it advertised on the Web. The FDA has not yet brought any actions against apparent online violators of regulations governing drug advertising, however. One issue that the FDA has yet to resolve is the distinction between advertising and labeling.

IMPLICATIONS FOR THE BUSINESSPERSON

1. All business entities must be aware that the laws and government regulations governing standard "paper" commerce and advertising apply equally to the Internet.
2. Businesspersons should realize that even though Internet sites are seemingly infinite in number, the vastness of this number will not prevent federal and state agency "watchdogs" from discovering fraud and false advertising. An increasing percentage of government regulatory dollars are going into policing the Internet.

FOR CRITICAL ANALYSIS

1. How might online industries regulate themselves?
2. How can a set of guidelines for online advertising be developed, given that the technology is changing so rapidly?

not as likely as they are in stores, and thus the seller has less incentive to cultivate the goodwill of the purchaser. Furthermore, the seller is unlikely to present alternative products and their prices. Thus, a number of states have passed "cooling-off" laws that permit the buyers of goods sold door-to-door to cancel their contracts within a specified period of time, usually two to three days after the sale.

An FTC regulation also requires sellers to give consumers three days to cancel any door-to-door sale. Because this rule applies in addition to the relevant state statutes, consumers are given the most favorable benefits of the FTC rule and their own state statutes. In addition, the FTC rule requires that consumers be notified in Spanish of this right if the oral negotiations for the sale were in that language.

TELEPHONE AND MAIL-ORDER SALES

Sales made by either telephone or mail order are the greatest source of complaints to the nation's Better Business Bureaus. Many mail-order firms are far removed from most of their buyers, thus making it more burdensome for buyers to bring complaints against them. To a certain extent, consumers are protected under federal laws prohibiting mail fraud and under state consumer protection laws that parallel and supplement the federal laws.

The FTC Mail or Telephone Order Merchandise Rule of 1993, which amended the FTC Mail-Order Rule of 1975,[17] provides specific protections for consumers who purchase goods via phone lines or through the mails. The 1993 rule extended the 1975 rule to include sales in which orders are transmitted by computer, fax machine, or some similar means involving telephone lines. Among other things, the rule requires mail-order merchants to ship orders within the time promised in their catalogues or advertisements, to notify consumers when orders cannot be shipped on time, and to issue a refund within a specified period of time when a consumer cancels an order.

In addition, the Postal Reorganization Act of 1970[18] provides that *unsolicited* merchandise sent by U.S. mail may be retained, used, discarded, or disposed of in any manner deemed appropriate, without the recipient's incurring any obligation to the sender.

FTC REGULATION OF SPECIFIC INDUSTRIES

Over the last decade, the FTC has begun to target certain sales practices on an industry-wide basis. Two examples involve the used-car business and the funeral-home trade. In 1984, the FTC enacted the Used Motor Vehicle Regulation Rule,[19] which is more commonly known as the used-car rule. This rule requires used-car dealers to affix a buyer's guide label to all cars sold on their lots. The label must disclose the following information: (1) the car's warranty or a statement that the car is being sold "as is," (2) information regarding any service contract or promises being made by the dealer, and (3) a suggestion that the purchaser obtain both an inspection of the car and a written statement of any promises made by the dealer.

In 1984, the FTC also enacted rules requiring that funeral homes provide customers with itemized prices of all charges incurred for a funeral.[20] In addition, the regulations prohibit funeral homes from requiring specific embalming procedures or specific types of caskets for bodies that are to be cremated.

REAL ESTATE SALES

Various federal and state laws apply to consumer transactions involving real estate. These laws are designed to prevent fraud and to provide buyers with certain types of information. In some cases, these protections mirror those provided in non–real estate sales. The disclosure requirements of the Truth-in-Lending Act apply to a number of real estate transactions, as will be discussed shortly.

INTERSTATE LAND SALES FULL DISCLOSURE ACT The Interstate Land Sales Full Disclosure Act[21] was passed by Congress in 1968, and it is administered by the Department of Housing and Urban Development (HUD). The purpose of the act is to ensure disclosure of certain information to consumers so that they can make reasoned decisions about land purchases. The act is similar to the Securities Act of 1933 in both purpose and design. The act requires anyone proposing to sell or lease one hundred or more lots of unimproved land, if the sale or lease is to be part of a common promotional plan, to file an initial statement of record with HUD's Office of Interstate Land Sales Registration.

The act only applies if the promotional plan can be deemed part of interstate commerce. As in cases involving securities, this is generally an easy requirement to meet. For example, even strictly local sales might be considered interstate commerce if transacted in part over the phone; although the calls might be local, the phone lines traverse state boundaries. For the same reason, use of the mail system is likely to ensure that a promotional plan is in the stream of interstate commerce.

Once the initial statement is filed, it must be approved by HUD before the developer can begin to offer the land for sale or lease. The act also provides purchasers with a private right of action for the land promoter's fraud, misrepresentation, or noncompliance with pertinent provisions of the act. Criminal penalties are provided under the act, and HUD is given certain rights with regard to inspections, injunctions, and prosecution of offenses. Three provisions of the act give purchasers rights of rescission (cancellation).

REAL ESTATE SETTLEMENT PROCEDURES ACT For many individuals, purchasing a home involves a bewildering array of procedures and requirements. Settlement (finalizing a real estate transaction) may require title insurance, attorneys' fees, appraisal fees, taxes, insurance, and brokers' fees. To aid home buyers, federal legislation requires specific disclosures regarding settlement procedures. The 1976 revisions

17. 16 C.F.R. Sections 435.1–435.2.
18. 39 U.S.C. Section 3009.
19. 16 C.F.R. Sections 455.1–455.5.
20. 16 C.F.R. Section 453.2.
21. 15 U.S.C. Sections 1701–1720.

of the Real Estate Settlement Procedures Act of 1974[22] make the following stipulations:

1. Within three business days after a person applies for a mortgage loan, the lender must send a booklet prepared by HUD that explains the settlement procedures, describes the costs to the potential buyer, and outlines the applicant's legal rights.
2. Within the three-day period, the lender must give an estimate of most of the settlement costs.
3. The lender must clearly identify individuals or firms that the applicant is required to use for legal or other services, including title search and insurance.
4. If the loan is approved, the lender must provide a truth-in-lending statement that shows the annual percentage rate on the mortgage loan.
5. Lenders, title insurers, and others involved in the transaction cannot pay kickbacks for business referred to them.

SECTION 4 CREDIT PROTECTION

Because of the extensive use of credit by American consumers, credit protection has become an especially important area regulated by consumer protection legislation. One of the most significant statutes regulating the credit and credit-card industry is Title I of the Consumer Credit Protection Act (CCPA),[23] which was passed by Congress in 1968 and is commonly referred to as the Truth-in-Lending Act (TILA).

THE TRUTH-IN-LENDING ACT

The TILA is basically a *disclosure law.* It is administered by the Federal Reserve Board and requires sellers and lenders to disclose credit terms or loan terms so that individuals can shop around for the best financing arrangements. TILA requirements apply only to persons who, in the ordinary course of business, lend money, sell on credit, or arrange for the extension of credit. Thus, sales or loans made between two consumers do not come under the protection of the act. Additionally, only debtors who are *natural* persons (as opposed to the artificial "person" of the corporation) are protected by this law; other legal entities are not.

The disclosure requirements are contained in Regulation Z, which, as mentioned earlier in this chapter, was promulgated by the Federal Reserve Board. If the contracting parties are subject to the TILA, the requirements of Regulation Z apply to any transaction involving an installment sales contract in which payment is to be made in more than four installments. Transactions subject to Regulation Z typically include installment loans, retail and installment sales, car loans, home improvement loans, and certain real estate loans if the amount of financing is less than $25,000.

Under the provisions of the TILA, all of the terms of a credit instrument must be clearly and conspicuously disclosed. The TILA provides for contract rescission (cancellation) if a creditor fails to follow *exactly* the procedures required by the act.[24] TILA requirements are strictly enforced.

In the following case, a consumer sued a lender, alleging TILA violations. The lender claimed that the consumer was not entitled to relief because she had lied on her credit application.

22. 12 U.S.C. Sections 2601–2617.
23. 15 U.S.C. Sections 1601–1693r.

24. Note, however, that amendments to the TILA enacted in 1995 prevent borrowers from rescinding loans for minor clerical errors in closing documents [15 U.S.C. Sections 1605, 1631, 1635, 1640, and 1641].

CASE 23.2 Purtle v. Eldridge Auto Sales, Inc.

United States Court of Appeals, Sixth Circuit, 1996. 91 F.3d 797.

BACKGROUND AND FACTS *Renee Purtle bought a 1986 Chevrolet Blazer from Eldridge Auto Sales, Inc. To finance the purchase through Eldridge, Purtle filled out a credit application on which she misrepresented her employment status. Based on the misrepresentation, Eldridge extended credit. In the credit contract, Eldridge did not disclose the finance charge, the annual percentage rate, or the total sales price or use the term "amount financed," as the TILA and its regulations require. Purtle defaulted on the loan, and Eldridge repossessed the vehicle. Purtle filed a suit in a federal district court against Eldridge, alleging violations of the TILA. The court awarded Purtle $1,000 in damages, plus attorneys'*

fees and costs. Eldridge appealed, arguing in part that Purtle was not entitled to damages because she had committed fraud on her credit application.

IN THE LANGUAGE OF THE COURT

FORESTER, District Judge.

* * * *

* * * [T]he TILA imposes mandatory disclosure requirements on those who extend credit to consumers. * * * In the event that a creditor fails to disclose any of the credit terms required under the TILA and its regulations, a consumer may bring a civil action against the creditor. If a violation is proven, the consumer may recover twice the amount of the finance charge (but not less than $100.00 nor more than $1,000.00). The purpose of the statutory recovery is "to encourage lawsuits by individual consumers as a means of enforcing creditor compliance with the Act." The TILA also permits recovery of reasonable attorney's fees and costs. * * *

* * * *

* * * [O]nce a court finds a violation of the TILA, no matter how technical, the court has no discretion as to the imposition of civil liability. * * * Based on the unambiguous statutory language, it is clear that * * * the district court appropriately awarded Purtle the statutory penalty set out above.

DECISION AND REMEDY

The U.S. Court of Appeals for the Sixth Circuit affirmed the lower court's award. The lender was required to pay damages based on its violation of the TILA, despite the borrower's fraud.

EQUAL CREDIT OPPORTUNITY In 1974, the Equal Credit Opportunity Act (ECOA)[25] was enacted as an amendment to the TILA. The ECOA prohibits the denial of credit solely on the basis of race, religion, national origin, color, sex, marital status, or age. The act also prohibits credit discrimination on the basis of whether an individual receives certain forms of income, such as public-assistance benefits. Under the ECOA, a creditor may not require the signature of an applicant's spouse, other than as a joint applicant, on a credit instrument if the applicant qualifies under the creditor's standards of creditworthiness for the amount and terms of the credit request.

Creditors are permitted to request any information from a credit applicant except that which would be used for the type of discrimination covered in the act or its amendments. In the following case, the issue concerns whether a creditor violated the ECOA by requiring the signature of an applicant's spouse on a loan guaranty.

25. 15 U.S.C. Section 1691–1691f.

CASE 23.3 Federal Deposit Insurance Corp. v. Medmark, Inc.

United States District Court, District of Kansas, 1995. 897 F.Supp. 511.

BACKGROUND AND FACTS *Bruce Shalberg was a director of Medmark, Inc., a small medical equipment supply company. As a condition of a loan to Medmark, the Merchants Bank asked Shalberg—whom the bank found to be independently creditworthy—to sign a guaranty of repayment. Later, for another loan, the bank required Shalberg's wife, Mary—who had nothing to do with Medmark—to sign the guaranty. When the bank failed, the Federal Deposit Insurance Corporation (FDIC) took over its assets. The FDIC filed a suit in a federal district court against Medmark and the Shalbergs to recover the amount of the loans. Mary Shalberg filed a motion for summary judgment, contending that the bank, in requiring her to sign the guaranty, had violated the Equal Credit Opportunity Act (ECOA).*

IN THE LANGUAGE OF THE COURT

VRATIL, District Judge.

* * * *

[A regulation issued under the ECOA] specifically provides that a creditor may not require the signature of an applicant's spouse if the applicant qualifies under the creditor's standards of creditworthiness for the amount and terms of the credit requested. The FDIC argues that the Bank "obviously" did not believe Mr. Shalberg to be independently creditworthy * * * . [But the] record contains no evidence that Mr. Shalberg was not creditworthy, in his own right, in the Bank's eyes. Summary judgment in favor of Mrs. Shalberg is therefore appropriate.

DECISION AND REMEDY *The federal district court issued a summary judgment in favor of Mary Shalberg, relieving her from any obligation on the loans. The creditor violated the ECOA by requiring Shalberg's signature on the loan guaranty.*

CREDIT-CARD RULES The TILA also contains provisions regarding credit cards. One provision limits the liability of a cardholder to $50 per card for unauthorized charges made before the creditor is notified that the card has been lost. Another provision prohibits a credit-card company from billing a consumer for any unauthorized charges if the credit card was improperly issued by the company. For example, if a consumer receives an unsolicited credit card in the mail and the card is later stolen and used by the thief to make purchases, the consumer to whom the card was sent will not be liable for the unauthorized charges.

Further provisions of the act concern billing disputes related to credit-card purchases. If a debtor thinks that an error has occurred in billing or wishes to withhold payment for a faulty product purchased by credit card, the act outlines specific procedures for both the consumer and the credit-card company to follow in settling the dispute.

CONSUMER LEASES The Consumer Leasing Act (CLA) of 1988[26] amended the TILA to provide protection for consumers who lease automobiles and other goods. The CLA applies to those who lease or arrange to lease consumer goods in the ordinary course of their business. The act only applies if the goods are priced at $25,000 or less and if the lease term exceeds four months. The CLA and its implementing regulation, Regulation M,[27] require lessors to disclose in writing all of the material terms of the lease.

THE FAIR CREDIT REPORTING ACT

In 1970, to protect consumers against inaccurate credit reporting, Congress enacted the Fair Credit Reporting Act (FCRA).[28] The act provides that consumer credit reporting agencies may issue credit reports to users only for specified purposes, including the extension of credit, the issuance of insurance policies, compliance with a court order, and compliance with a consumer's request for a copy of his or her own credit report. The act further provides that any time a consumer is denied credit or insurance on the basis of the consumer's credit report, or is charged more than others ordinarily would be for credit or insurance, the consumer must be notified of that fact and of the name and address of the credit reporting agency that issued the credit report.

Under the act, consumers may request the source of any information being given out by a credit agency, as well as the identity of anyone who has received an agency's report. Consumers are also permitted to have access to the information contained about them in a credit reporting agency's files. If a consumer discovers that a credit reporting agency's files contain inaccurate information about the consumer's credit standing, the agency, on the consumer's written request, must investigate the matter and delete any unverifiable or erroneous information within a reasonable period of time.

An agency that fails to comply with the act is liable for actual damages, plus additional damages not to exceed $1,000 and attorneys' fees.[29] Damages are also available against anyone who uses a credit report for an improper purpose, as well as banks, credit-card companies, and other businesses that report information to credit agencies and do not respond adequately to customer complaints.

The following case illustrates the liability exposure of companies that maintain credit reports and ratings.

26. 15 U.S.C. Sections 1667–1667e.
27. 12 C.F.R. Part 213.
28. 15 U.S.C. Sections 1681–1681t.
29. 15 U.S.C. Section 1681n.

CASE 23.4 Guimond v. Trans Union Credit Information Co.

United States Court of Appeals, Ninth Circuit, 1995. 45 F.3d 1329.

HISTORICAL AND ECONOMIC SETTING *A credit report reflects a consumer's bill-paying history. It lists the consumer's creditors and whether he or she has made payments on time. Inaccurate information can keep an individual from obtaining credit, because lenders rely on credit reports when deciding whether to extend credit. The major credit reporting agencies include the Trans Union Credit Information Company.*

BACKGROUND AND FACTS *Renie Guimond learned of inaccuracies that Trans Union Credit Information Company had in its file on her. She notified Trans Union, which told her the file would be corrected; however, it was not corrected for a year. Guimond filed a suit in a federal district court against Trans Union, in part to recover damages under the Fair Credit Reporting Act (FCRA) for the company's failure to correct the information more quickly. Trans Union countered that Guimond had no claim, because she had not been denied credit before the information was corrected. The court ruled in favor of Trans Union, and Guimond appealed.*

IN THE LANGUAGE OF THE COURT

FONG, District Judge:

* * * *

[The FCRA] states: Whenever a consumer reporting agency prepares a consumer report it shall follow reasonable procedures to assure maximum possible accuracy of the information * * * .

* * * *

Liability * * * is predicated on the reasonableness of the credit reporting agency's procedures * * * .

* * * [T]he focus should not have been on Guimond's damage claims. Rather the inquiry should have centered on whether Trans Union's procedures for preparing Guimond's file contained reasonable procedures to prevent inaccuracies. Guimond has made out a *prima facie* case under [the FCRA] by showing that there were inaccuracies in her credit report. The district court was then required to consider whether Trans Union was liable under [the FCRA] before it determined that Guimond had suffered no recoverable damages.

DECISION AND REMEDY *The U.S. Court of Appeals for the Ninth Circuit reversed this part of the lower court's ruling and remanded the case for trial. The agency could be held liable if its procedures to assure the accuracy of its information were not reasonable.*

FAIR DEBT COLLECTION PRACTICES ACT

In 1977, Congress enacted the Fair Debt Collection Practices Act (FDCPA)[30] in an attempt to curb what were perceived to be abuses by collection agencies. The act applies only to specialized debt-collection agencies that regularly attempt to collect debts on behalf of someone else, usually for a percentage of the amount owed. Creditors attempting to collect debts are not covered by the act unless, by misrepresenting themselves, they cause debtors to believe they are collection agencies. The act explicitly prohibits a collection agency from using any of the following tactics:

1. Contacting the debtor at the debtor's place of employment if the debtor's employer objects.
2. Contacting the debtor during inconvenient or unusual times (for example, calling the debtor at three o'clock in the morning) or at any time if the debtor is being represented by an attorney.

30. 15 U.S.C. Section 1692.

3. Contacting third parties other than the debtor's parents, spouse, or financial adviser about payment of a debt unless a court authorizes such action.
4. Using harassment or intimidation (for example, using abusive language or threatening violence) or employing false or misleading information (for example, posing as a police officer).
5. Communicating with the debtor at any time after receiving notice that the debtor is refusing to pay the debt, except to advise the debtor of further action to be taken by the collection agency.

The FDCPA also requires a collection agency to include a **validation notice** whenever it initially contacts a debtor for payment of a debt or within five days of that initial contact. The notice must state that the debtor has thirty days within which to dispute the debt and to request a written verification of the debt from the collection agency. The debtor's request for debt validation must be in writing.

The enforcement of the FDCPA is primarily the responsibility of the Federal Trade Commission. The act provides that a debt collector that fails to comply with the act is liable for actual damages, plus additional damages not to exceed \$1,000[31] and attorneys' fees. In the following case, the United States Supreme Court considered whether lawyers engaged in consumer debt-collection litigation were exempt from the FDCPA.

31. According to the U.S. Court of Appeals for the Sixth Circuit, the \$1,000 limit on damages applies to each lawsuit, not to each violation. See *Wright v. Finance Service of Norwalk, Inc.*, 22 F.3d 647 (6th Cir. 1994).

CASE 23.5 Heintz v. Jenkins

Supreme Court of the United States, 1995. 514 U.S. 291, 115 S.Ct. 1489, 131 L.Ed.2d 395.

BACKGROUND AND FACTS *Darlene Jenkins borrowed money from Gainer Bank to buy a car. The terms of the loan required her to keep the car insured. When she let her insurance expire, the bank bought a policy. Jenkins defaulted on the loan, and the bank asked George Heintz, a lawyer, to recover its money. Heintz began legal proceedings against Jenkins to recover the amount due on the loan, plus the cost of the insurance. Jenkins filed a suit in a federal district court against Heintz under the Fair Debt Collection Practices Act (FDCPA), claiming that Heintz was trying to collect an amount that was not part of the loan agreement. The court dismissed the suit, holding that the FDCPA does not apply to lawyers engaging in litigation. Jenkins appealed, and the U.S. Court of Appeals for the Seventh Circuit reversed. Heintz appealed to the United States Supreme Court.*

IN THE LANGUAGE OF THE COURT

Justice *BREYER* delivered the opinion of the Court.

* * * *

There are two rather strong reasons for believing that the [FDCPA] applies to the litigating activities of lawyers. First, the [FDCPA] defines the "debt collector[s]" to whom it applies as including those who "regularly collec[t] or attemp[t] to collect, directly or indirectly, [consumer] debts owed * * * another." In ordinary English, a lawyer who regularly tries to obtain payment of consumer debts through legal proceedings is a lawyer who regularly "attempts" to "collect" those consumer debts.

Second, in 1977, Congress enacted an earlier version of this statute, which contained an express exemption for lawyers. That exemption said that the term "debt collector" did not include "any attorney-at-law collecting a debt as an attorney on behalf of and in the name of a client." In 1986, however, Congress repealed this exemption * * * .

DECISION AND REMEDY *The United States Supreme Court upheld the decision of the appellate court. The Court held that the FDCPA does apply to lawyers engaged in consumer debt-collection litigation.*

GARNISHMENT OF WAGES

Despite the increasing number of protections afforded debtors, creditors are not without means of securing payment on debts. One of these is the right to garnish a debtor's wages after the debt has gone uncollected for a prolonged period. Recall from Chapter 16 that *garnishment* is the legal procedure by which a creditor may collect on a debt by directly attaching, or seizing, a portion of the debtor's assets (such as wages) that are in the possession of a third party (such as an employer).

State law provides the basis for a process of garnishment, but the law varies among the states as to how easily garnishment can be obtained. Indeed, a few states, such as Texas, prohibit garnishment of wages altogether except for child support. In addition, constitutional due process and federal legislation under the TILA provide further protections against abuse.[32] In general, the debtor is entitled to notice and an opportunity to be heard in a process of garnishment. Moreover, wages cannot be garnished beyond 25 percent of the debtor's after-tax earnings, and the garnishment must leave the debtor with at least a specified minimum income.

SECTION 5
CONSUMER HEALTH AND SAFETY

Laws discussed earlier regarding the labeling and packaging of products go a long way toward promoting consumer health and safety. But there is a significant distinction between regulating the information dispensed about a product and regulating the content of the product. The classic example is tobacco products. Tobacco products have not been altered by regulation or banned outright despite their obvious hazards. What has been regulated are the warnings that producers are required to give consumers about the hazards of tobacco.[33] This section focuses on laws that regulate the actual products made available to consumers.

THE FEDERAL FOOD, DRUG AND COSMETIC ACT

The first federal legislation regulating food and drugs was enacted in 1906 as the Pure Food and Drugs Act. That law, as amended in 1938, exists presently as the Federal Food, Drug and Cosmetic Act (FFDCA).[34] The act protects consumers against adulterated and misbranded foods and drugs. More recent amendments have added substantive and procedural requirements to the act. In its present form, the act establishes food standards, specifies safe levels of potentially hazardous food additives, and sets classifications of food and food advertising.

Most of these statutory requirements are monitored and enforced by the Food and Drug Administration (FDA). Under an extensive set of procedures established by the FDA, drugs must be shown to be effective as well as safe before they may be marketed to the public, and the use of some food additives suspected of being carcinogenic is prohibited. A 1976 amendment to the FFDCA[35] authorizes the FDA to regulate medical devices, such as pacemakers and other health devices and equipment, and to withdraw from the market any such device that is mislabeled.

THE CONSUMER PRODUCT SAFETY ACT

Consumer product safety legislation began in 1953 with enactment of the Flammable Fabrics Act, which prohibits the sale of highly flammable clothing or materials. Over the next two decades, Congress enacted legislation regarding the design or composition of specific classes of products. Then, in 1972, Congress, by enacting the Consumer Product Safety Act,[36] created a comprehensive scheme of regulation over matters of consumer safety. The act also established far-reaching authority over consumer safety under the Consumer Product Safety Commission (CPSC).

The CPSC conducts research on the safety of individual products, and it maintains a clearinghouse of information on the risks associated with various consumer products. The Consumer Product Safety Act authorizes the CPSC to set standards for consumer products and to ban the manufacture and

32. 15 U.S.C. Sections 1671–1677.

33. We are ignoring recent civil litigation concerning the liability of tobacco product manufacturers for injuries that arise from the use of tobacco.

34. 21 U.S.C. Sections 301–393.

35. 21 U.S.C. Sections 352(o), 360(j), 360(k), and 360c–360k.

36. 15 U.S.C. Sections 2051–2083.

sale of any product that it deems to be potentially hazardous to consumers. The CPSC also has authority to remove from the market any products it believes to be imminently hazardous and to require manufacturers to report on any products already sold or intended for sale if the products have proved to be hazardous. The CPSC also has authority to administer other product safety legislation, such as the Child Protection and Toy Safety Act of 1969[37] and the Federal Hazardous Substances Act of 1960.[38]

The CPSC's authority is sufficiently broad to allow it to ban any product that it believes poses an "unreasonable risk" to consumers. Some of the products that the CPSC has banned include various types of fireworks, cribs, and toys, as well as many products containing asbestos or vinyl chloride.

SECTION 6 STATE CONSUMER PROTECTION LAWS

Thus far, our primary focus has been on federal legislation. As mentioned, however, state laws often provide more sweeping and significant protections for the consumer than do federal laws. The warranty and unconscionability provisions of the Uniform Commercial Code (discussed in Chapter 11) offer important protections for consumers against unfair practices on the part of sellers and lessors. The Magnuson-Moss Warranty Act, of 1975,[39] supplements the UCC provisions in cases involving both a consumer transaction of at least $10 and an express written warranty.

Far less widely adopted than the UCC is the Uniform Consumer Credit Code (UCCC). The UCCC has provisions concerning truth in lending, maximum credit ceilings, door-to-door sales, fine-print clauses, and other practices affecting consumer transactions.

Virtually all states have specific consumer protection acts, often titled "deceptive trade practices acts." Although state consumer protection statutes vary widely in their provisions, a common thread runs through most of them. Typically, state consumer protection laws are directed at deceptive trade practices, such as a seller's providing false or misleading information to consumers. As just mentioned, some of the legislation provides broad protection for consumers. A prime example is the Texas Deceptive Trade Practices Act of 1973, which forbids a seller from selling to a buyer anything that the buyer does not need or cannot afford.

37. This act consists of amendments to 15 U.S.C. Sections 1261, 1262, and 1274.

38. 15 U.S.C. Sections 1261–1277.

39. 15 U.S.C. Sections 2301–2312.

TERMS AND CONCEPTS TO REVIEW

QUESTIONS AND CASE PROBLEMS

23–1. UNSOLICITED MERCHANDISE. Andrew, a California resident, received a flyer in the U.S. mail announcing a new line of regional cookbooks distributed by the Every-Kind Cookbook Co. Andrew was not interested and threw the flyer away. Two days later, Andrew received in the mail an introductory cookbook entitled *Lower Mongolian Regional Cookbook*, as announced in the flyer, on a "trial basis" from Every-Kind. Andrew was not interested but did not go to the trouble to return the cookbook. Every-Kind demanded payment of $20.95 for the *Lower Mongolian Regional Cookbook*. Discuss whether Andrew can be required to pay for the cookbook.

23–2. CONSUMER PROTECTION. Fireside Rocking Chair Co. advertised in the newspaper a special sale price of $159 on machine-caned rocking chairs. In the advertisement was a drawing of a natural-wood rocking chair with a caned back and seat. The average person would not be able to tell from the drawing whether the rocking chair was machine caned or hand caned. Hand-caned rocking chairs sold for $259. Lowell and Celia

Gudmundson went to Fireside because they had seen the ad for the machine-caned rocking chair and were very interested in purchasing one. The Gudmundsons arrived on the morning the sale began. Fireside's agent said the only machine-caned rocking chairs he had were painted lime green and were priced at $159. He immediately turned the Gudmundsons' attention to the hand-caned rocking chairs, praising their quality and pointing out that for the extra $100, the hand-caned chairs were surely a good value. The Gudmundsons, preferring the natural-wood machine-caned rocking chair for $159 as pictured in the advertisement, said they would like to order one. The Fireside agent said he could not order a natural-wood, machine-caned rocking chair. Discuss fully whether Fireside has violated any consumer protection laws.

23–3. Door-to-Door Sales. On June 28, a sales representative for Renowned Books called on the Gonchars at their home. After a very persuasive sales pitch on the part of the sales agent, the Gonchars agreed in writing to purchase a twenty-volume set of historical encyclopedias from Renowned Books for a total of $299. An initial down payment of $35 was required, with the remainder of the price to be paid in monthly payments over a one-year period. Two days later the Gonchars, having second thoughts, contacted the book company and stated that they had decided to rescind the contract. Renowned Books said this would be impossible. Has Renowned Books violated any consumer law by not allowing the Gonchars to rescind their contract? Explain.

23–4. Truth in Lending. Michael and Patricia Jensen purchased a new 1989 Ford Tempo from Ray Kim Ford, Inc. The Jensens signed a retail installment contract that provided for an estimated trade-in value of $800 for their old car. When the traded-in car turned out to be worth $1,388.08, Ray Kim prepared a second retail installment contract without the Jensens' knowledge. The second contract, although it credited the increased trade-in value of the car, compensated for this credit by increasing the interest rate, increasing the sales price of the car, and making other adjustments so that the second contract basically called for future cash payments by the Jensens of about the same amount as the first contract. In effect, the second contract gave the Jensens almost no benefit for the increased value of their traded-in car. The Jensens made payments under the contract until they noticed the minor difference in monthly payments, asked for a copy of the contract, and realized that it was not the contract that they had signed. The Jensens sued Ray Kim, alleging that the second contract was a forgery and that Ray Kim had violated the Truth-in-Lending Act (TILA) by not disclosing to them the credit terms of the second contract. Has Ray Kim violated the TILA? If the Jensens choose to adopt the terms of the second contract, despite the forgery, has the act been violated? Discuss fully. [*Jensen v. Ray Kim Ford, Inc.*, 920 F.2d 3 (7th Cir. 1990)]

23–5. Deceptive Advertising. Thompson Medical Co. marketed a new cream called Aspercreme that was supposed to help arthritis victims and others suffering from minor aches. Aspercreme contained no aspirin. Thompson's television advertisements stated that the product provided "the strong relief of aspirin right where you hurt" and showed the announcer holding up aspirin tablets as well as a tube of Aspercreme. The Federal Trade Commission held that the advertisements were misleading, because they led consumers to believe that Aspercreme contained aspirin. Thompson Medical Co. appealed this decision and argued that the advertisements never actually stated that the product contained aspirin. How should the court rule? Discuss. [*Thompson Medical Co. v. Federal Trade Commission*, 791 F.2d 189 (D.C. Cir. 1986)]

23–6. Deceptive Advertising. Dennis and Janice Geiger saw an advertisement in a newspaper for a Kimball Whitney spinet piano on sale for $699 at the McCormick Piano & Organ Co. Because the style of the piano drawn in the advertisement matched their furniture, the Geigers were particularly interested in the Kimball. When they went to McCormick Piano & Organ, however, they learned that the drawing closely resembled another, more expensive Crest piano and that the Kimball spinet looked quite different from the piano sketched in the drawing. The salesperson told the Geigers that she was unable to order a spinet piano of the style they requested. When the Geigers asked for the names of other customers who had purchased the advertised pianos, the salesperson became extremely upset and said she would not, under any circumstances, sell the Geigers a piano. The Geigers then brought suit against the piano store, alleging that the store had engaged in deceptive advertising in violation of Indiana law. Was the McCormick Piano & Organ Co. guilty of deceptive advertising? Explain. [*McCormick Piano & Organ Co. v. Geiger*, 412 N.E.2d 842 (Ind.App. 1980)]

23–7. Fair Debt Collection. Josephine Rutyna was a sixty-year-old widow who, in late 1976 and early 1977, incurred a debt for medical treatment of her high blood pressure and epilepsy. She assumed that the cost of the services was paid by either Medicare or her private insurance company. In July 1978, however, she was contacted by an agent of Collection Accounts Terminal, Inc., who stated that Rutyna still owed a debt of $56 for those services. She denied that she owed the debt, and the following month she received a letter from the collection agency threatening to contact her neighbors and employer concerning the debt if the $56 was not paid immediately. Discuss fully whether the collection agency's letter violates any consumer protection law. [*Rutyna v. Collection Accounts Terminal, Inc.*, 478 F.Supp. 980 (N.D.Ill. 1979)]

23–8. Equal Credit Opportunity. The Riggs National Bank of Washington, D.C., lent more than $11 million to Samuel Linch and Albert Randolph. To obtain the loan, Linch and Randolph provided personal financial statements. Linch's statement included substantial assets that he owned jointly with his wife, Marcia. As a condition of the loan, Riggs required that Marcia, as well as Samuel and Albert, sign a personal guaranty for repayment. When the borrowers defaulted, Riggs filed a suit in a federal district court to recover its money, based on the personal guaranties. The court ruled against the borrowers, who appealed. On what basis might the borrowers argue that Riggs violated the Equal Credit Opportunity Act? [*Riggs National Bank of Washington, D.C. v. Linch*, 36 F.3d 370 (4th Cir. 1994)]

23–9. Debt Collection. Equifax A.R.S., a debt-collection agency, sent Donna Russell a notice about one of her debts. The front of the notice stated that "[i]f you do not dispute this claim (see reverse side) and wish to pay it within the next 10 days we will not post this collection to your file." The reverse side set out Russell's rights under the Fair Debt Collection Practices Act (FDCPA), including that she had thirty days to decide whether to contest the claim. Russell filed a suit in a federal district court against Equifax. The court ruled against Russell, who appealed. On what basis might Russell argue that Equifax violated the FDCPA? Did Equifax violate the FDCPA? [*Russell v. Equifax A.R.S.*, 74 F.3d 30 (2d Cir. 1996)]

23–10. A Question of Ethics

On July 16, 1982, the Semars signed a loan contract with Platte Valley Federal Savings & Loan Association, offering a second mortgage on their home as collateral. Under the Truth-in-Lending Act (TILA), borrowers are allowed three business days to rescind, without penalty, a consumer loan that uses their principal dwelling as security. The TILA requires lenders in such situations to state specifically the last date on which the borrower can rescind the loan agreement, and if they fail to include this date, the borrower may rescind the loan within three years after it was made. Platte Valley's form omitted the exact expiration date of the three-day period, although it stated that the rescission right expired three business days after July 16. The Semars ceased making monthly payments on the loan in September 1983 and sent a Notice of Rescission to Platte Valley on February 15, 1984. The Semars claimed that Platte Valley had violated the TILA by failing to specify in the loan contract the exact date of the expiration of the three-day rescission period. Because of this violation, the Semars maintained they had three years in which to rescind the contract. Although the court found the Semars to be "unsympathetic plaintiffs," it nevertheless held that rescission was appropriate for the technical violation of the TILA. [*Semar v. Platte Valley Federal Savings & Loan Association*, 791 F.2d 699 (9th Cir. 1986)]

1. Do you think that the court, by adhering so strictly to the letter of the law, violated the spirit of the law?
2. When deciding issues involving alleged violations of consumer protection legislation, such as the TILA, should courts balance the equities of the cases? That is, should the ethical (or unethical) behavior of the parties to a particular transaction be taken into consideration?
3. How might you justify, on ethical grounds, the court's decision in this case?

Accessing the Internet

The Legal Environment of Business

To view the FTC's Web site, go to

http://www.ftc.gov/

The Nolo Press has a section called Money and Consumer Matters at

http://www.nolo.com/

The Web site of the Consumer Product Safety Commission (CPSC) provides information on the CPSC as well as online versions of CPSC publications, such as its *Consumer Product Safety Review.* To access the CPSC's site, go to

http://www.cpsc.gov/

For information on the advertising guidelines and enforcement policy of the Federal Trade Commission (FTC), go to the Advertising Law Internet Site at

http://www.webcom.com/~lewrose/home.html

For information on the Food and Drug Administration, access

http://www.fda.gov/

The goal of the Better Business Bureau (BBB) is to provide information to consumers so they can make informed buying decisions. To access the BBB's home page, go to

http://www.bbb.org/

The Better Business Bureau now has a special online site, called BBBOnLine, to help consumers who shop on the Internet locate reliable online businesses. You can access this site at

http://www.bbbonline.org/

If you subscribe to the commercial service CompuServe, you have access to its Consumer Forum. Once on CompuServe, type in

Go legal

Then select

Consumer Forum

From the Library Menu, choose

Browse

CHAPTER 24

ENVIRONMENTAL LAW

WE NOW TURN TO A DISCUSSION of the various ways in which businesses are regulated by the government in the interest of protecting the environment. Concern over the degradation of the environment has increased over time in response to the environmental effects of population growth, urbanization, and industrialization. Environmental protection is not without a price, however. For many businesses, the costs of complying with environmental regulations are high, and for some they are too high. There is constant tension between the desirability of increasing profits and productivity and the need to attain higher quality in the environment.

Environmental law—all law pertaining to environmental protection—is not new. Indeed, the federal government began to regulate some activities, such as those involving the pollution of navigable waterways, in the late 1800s. In the last few decades, however, the body of environmental law has expanded substantially as government has attempted to control industrial waste and to protect certain natural resources and endangered species.

In this chapter, we first discuss the common law actions that can be brought against business firms and individuals for damages caused by polluting activities. The remainder of the chapter examines the various statutes and regulations that have been created to protect the environment.

SECTION 1

COMMON LAW ACTIONS

Common law remedies against environmental pollution originated centuries ago in England. Those responsible for operations that created dirt, smoke, noxious odors, noise, or toxic substances were sometimes held liable under common law theories of nuisance or negligence. Today, injured individuals continue to rely on the common law to obtain damages and injunctions against business polluters. (Statutory remedies are also available, a topic that we treat later.)

NUISANCE

Under the common law doctrine of **nuisance,** persons may be held liable if they use their property in a manner that unreasonably interferes with others' rights to use or enjoy their own property. In these situations, it is common for courts to balance the equities between the harm caused by the pollution and the costs of stopping it.

Courts have often denied injunctive relief on the ground that the hardships to be imposed on the polluter and on the community are greater than the hardships to be suffered by the plaintiff. For example, a factory that causes neighboring landowners to suffer from smoke, dirt, and vibrations may be left in operation if it is the core of a local economy. The injured parties may be awarded only money damages. These damages may include compensation for the decreased value of their property that results from the factory's operation.

A property owner may be given relief from pollution in situations in which he or she can identify a distinct harm separate from that affecting the general public. This harm is referred to as a "private" nuisance. Under the common law, citizens were denied standing (access to the courts—see Chapter 3) unless they suffered a harm distinct from the harm suffered by the public at large. Some states still require this. Therefore, a group of citizens who wished to stop a new development that would cause significant water pollution was denied access to the courts on the ground that the harm to them did not differ from the harm to the general public.[1] A public authority (such as a state's attorney general) can sue to abate a "public" nuisance.

In the following case, landowners sued their neighbor, the operator of a gravel pit, under the common law doctrine of nuisance. The landowners contended that the operator's excavation in the gravel pit resulted in the drying up of a spring running under their property.

1. *Save the Bay Committee, Inc. v. Mayor of City of Savannah*, 227 Ga. 436, 181 S.E.2d 351 (1971).

CASE 24.1 Maddocks v. Giles

Supreme Judicial Court of Maine, 1996. 686 A.2d 1069.

BACKGROUND AND FACTS *Sewall and Janice Maddocks owned property next to a gravel pit owned and operated by Elbridge Giles, doing business as E. A. Giles & Son. Below the surface of the Maddockses' property was a subterranean spring that produced large quantities of high-quality water. Giles's excavation in the gravel pit caused the spring to dry up. The Maddockses filed a suit against Giles in a Maine state court, seeking damages on the ground that the excavation was a nuisance because the excavation caused a disruption of the flow of the spring. The court dismissed the complaint, and the Maddockses appealed to the state's highest court, the Supreme Judicial Court of Maine.*

IN THE LANGUAGE OF THE COURT

GLASSMAN, Justice.

* * * *

Although we recognize the general principle that a property owner may use his land as he pleases for all lawful purposes, there is a long standing limitation of this rule preventing a landowner from drastically altering the flow of a watercourse. * * * A watercourse cannot be stopped up or diverted to the injury of other[s]. There is a public or natural [right] in such a stream, belonging to all persons whose lands are benefitted by it. * * * Application of these principles to the facts of this case leads us to conclude that the trial court erred when it dismissed the Maddockses' complaint.

The complaint alleges that Giles' excavation activities created a nuisance that caused a disruption of the flow of a subterranean spring from aquifers beneath Giles' property into the Maddockses' property. * * * [W]e conclude that the complaint sufficiently alleges a nuisance by the disruption of a watercourse * * * .

DECISION AND REMEDY *The Supreme Judicial Court of Maine vacated (set aside) the lower court's dismissal of the Maddockses' complaint. Disruption of the flow of a subterranean spring may constitute a nuisance. The case could proceed to trial.*

NEGLIGENCE AND STRICT LIABILITY

An injured party may sue a business polluter in tort under the negligence and strict liability theories discussed in Chapter 12. The basis for a negligence action is a business's alleged failure to use reasonable care toward a party whose injury was foreseeable and, of course, caused by the lack of reasonable care. For example, employees might sue an employer whose failure to use proper pollution controls contaminated the air, causing the employees to suffer respiratory illnesses. A developing area of tort law involves **toxic torts**—actions against toxic polluters.

Businesses that engage in ultrahazardous activities—such as the transportation of radioactive materials—are strictly liable for whatever injuries the activities cause. In a strict liability action, the injured party does not need to prove that the business failed to exercise reasonable care.

SECTION 2
FEDERAL REGULATION

Congress has passed a number of statutes to control the impact of human activities on the environment. Exhibit 24–1 lists and summarizes the major federal environmental statutes discussed in this chapter. Some of these statutes were passed in an attempt to improve the quality of air and water. Some of them specifically regulate toxic chemicals—including pesticides, herbicides, and hazardous wastes. Some are concerned with radiation.

ENVIRONMENTAL REGULATORY AGENCIES

Much of the body of federal law governing business activities consists of the regulations issued and enforced by administrative agencies. The most well known of the agencies regulating environmental law is, of course, the Environmental Protection Agency (EPA), which was created in 1970 to coordinate federal environmental responsibilities. Other federal agencies with authority for regulating specific environmental matters include the Department of the Interior, the Department of Defense, the Department of Labor, the Food and Drug Administration, and the Nuclear Regulatory Commission. These regulatory agencies—and all other agencies of the federal government—must take environmental factors into consideration when making significant decisions.

ASSESSMENT OF THE IMPACT OF AGENCY ACTIONS ON THE ENVIRONMENT

The National Environmental Policy Act (NEPA) of 1969[2] requires that for every major federal action that significantly affects the quality of the environment, an **environmental impact statement (EIS)** must be prepared. An action qualifies as "major" if it involves a substantial commitment of resources (monetary or otherwise). An action is "federal" if a federal agency has the power to control it. Construction by a private developer of a ski resort on federal land, for example, may require an EIS.[3] Building or operating a nuclear plant, which requires a federal permit,[4] or constructing a dam as part of a federal project would require an EIS.[5] If an agency decides that an EIS is unnecessary, it must issue a statement supporting this conclusion.

An EIS must analyze (1) the impact on the environment that the action will have, (2) any adverse

2. 42 U.S.C. Sections 4321–4370d.

3. *Robertson v. Methow Valley Citizens' Council*, 490 U.S. 332, 109 S.Ct. 1835, 104 L.Ed.2d 351 (1989).

4. *Calvert Cliffs Coordinating Committee v. Atomic Energy Commission*, 449 F.2d 1109 (D.C. Cir. 1971).

5. *Marsh v. Oregon Natural Resources Council*, 490 U.S. 360, 109 S.Ct. 1851, 104 L.Ed.2d 377 (1989).

EXHIBIT 24–1 ■ FEDERAL ENVIRONMENTAL STATUTES

POPULAR NAME	PURPOSE	STATUTE REFERENCE
Rivers and Harbors Appropriations Act (1899)	To prohibit ships and manufacturers from discharging and depositing refuse in navigable waterways.	33 U.S.C. Sections 401–418.
Federal Insecticide, Fungicide, and Rodenticide Act (FIFRA) (1947)	To control the use of pesticides and herbicides.	7 U.S.C. Sections 136–136y.
Federal Water Pollution Control Act (FWPCA) (1948)	To eliminate the discharge of pollutants from major sources into navigable waters.	33 U.S.C. Sections 1251–1387.
Atomic Energy Act (1954)	To limit environmental harm from the private nuclear industry.	42 U.S.C. Sections 2011 to 2297g-4.
Clean Air Act (1963)	To control air pollution from mobile and stationary sources.	42 U.S.C. Sections 7401–7671q.
National Environmental Policy Act (NEPA) (1969)	To limit environmental harm from federal government activities.	42 U.S.C. Sections 4321–4370d.
Marine Protection, Research, and Sanctuaries Act (Ocean Dumping Act) of 1972	To regulate the transporting and dumping of material into ocean waters.	16 U.S.C. Sections 1401–1445.
Noise Control Act (1972)	To regulate noise pollution from transportation and nontransportation sources.	42 U.S.C. Sections 4901–4918.
Endangered Species Act (1973)	To protect species that are threatened with extinction.	16 U.S.C. Sections 1531–1544.
Safe Drinking Water Act (1974)	To regulate pollutants in public drinking water systems.	42 U.S.C. Sections 300f to 300j-25.
Resource Conservation and Recovery Act (RCRA) (1976)	To establish standards for hazardous waste disposal.	42 U.S.C. Sections 6901–6986.
Toxic Substances Control Act (1976)	To regulate toxic chemicals and chemical compounds.	15 U.S.C. Sections 2601–2692.
Comprehensive Environmental Response, Compensation, and Liability Act (CERCLA) (Superfund) (1980)	To regulate the clean-up of hazardous waste-disposal sites.	42 U.S.C. Sections 9601–9675.
Low Level Radioactive Waste Policy Act (1980)	To assign to the states responsibility for nuclear power plants' low-level radioactive waste.	42 U.S.C. Sections 2021b–2021j.
Nuclear Waste Policy Act (1982)	To provide for the designation of a permanent radioactive waste-disposal site.	42 U.S.C. Sections 10101–10270.
Oil Pollution Act (1990)	To establish liability for the clean-up of navigable waters after oil-spill disasters.	33 U.S.C. Sections 2701–2761.

effects on the environment and alternative actions that might be taken, and (3) irreversible effects the action might generate. EISs have become instruments for private citizens, consumer interest groups, businesses, and others to challenge federal agency actions on the basis that the actions improperly threaten the environment.

Other federal laws also require that environmental values be considered in agency decision making. Among the most important of these laws are those that have been enacted to protect fish and wildlife. Under the Fish and Wildlife Coordination Act of 1958,[6] federal agencies proposing to approve the impounding or diversion of the waters of a stream must consult with the Fish and Wildlife Service with a view to preventing the loss of fish and wildlife resources. Also important is the Endangered Species Act of 1973.[7] Under this act, all federal agencies are required to take steps to ensure that their actions "do not jeopardize the continued existence of endangered species" or the habitat of an endangered species. An action may jeopardize the continued existence of a species if it sets in motion a chain of events that reduces the chances that the species will survive.

SECTION 3
AIR POLLUTION

Federal involvement with air pollution goes back to the 1950s, when Congress authorized funds for air-pollution research. In 1963, the federal government passed the Clean Air Act,[8] which focused on multistate air pollution and provided assistance to states. Various amendments, particularly in 1970, 1977, and 1990, strengthened the government's authority to regulate the quality of air. These laws provide the basis for issuing regulations to control pollution coming primarily from mobile sources (such as automobiles) and stationary sources (such as electric utilities and industrial plants).

MOBILE SOURCES

Regulations governing air pollution from automobiles and other mobile sources specify pollution standards and time schedules for meeting the standards. For example, the 1970 Clean Air Act required a reduction of 90 percent in the amount of carbon monoxide and other pollutants emitted by automobiles by 1975. (This did not happen, however, and the 1977 amendments extended the deadline to 1983. Generally, automobile manufacturers met the 90 percent reduction goal by installing catalytic converters on automobiles.)

Under the 1990 amendments, automobile manufacturers must cut new automobiles' exhaust emission of nitrogen oxide by 60 percent and emission of other pollutants by 35 percent. By 1998, all new automobiles must meet these standards. Another set of emission controls may be ordered after 2000. To ensure compliance, the EPA certifies the prototype of a new automobile whose emission controls are effective up to 50,000 miles. The EPA may also inspect production models. If a vehicle does not meet the standards in actual driving, the EPA can order a recall and the repair or replacement of pollution-control equipment at the manufacturer's expense.

Service stations are also subject to environmental regulations. The 1990 amendments require service stations to sell gasoline with a higher oxygen content in forty-one cities that experience carbon monoxide pollution in the winter. Service stations are required to sell even cleaner-burning gasoline in Los Angeles and another eight of the most polluted urban areas.

The EPA attempts to update pollution-control standards when new scientific information becomes available. In light of purported evidence that very small particles (2.5 microns, or millionths of a meter) of soot affect our health as significantly as larger particles, the EPA issued new particulate standards for motor vehicle exhaust systems and other sources of pollution. The EPA also decreased the acceptable standard for ozone, which is formed when sunlight combines with pollutants from cars and other sources. Ozone is the basic ingredient of smog.[9]

STATIONARY SOURCES

The Clean Air Act authorizes the EPA to establish air-quality standards for stationary sources (such as manufacturing plants) but recognizes that the primary responsibility for preventing and controlling air pollution rests with state and local governments. The EPA sets primary and secondary levels of ambient standards—that is, the maximum levels of certain pollutants—and the states formulate plans to achieve those standards. The plans are to provide for the attainment of primary standards within three years and secondary standards within a reasonable time. For economic, political, and technological reasons, however, the deadlines are often subject to change.

Different standards apply to sources of pollution in clean areas and sources in polluted areas. Different standards also apply to existing sources of

6. 16 U.S.C. Sections 661–666c.
7. 16 U.S.C. Sections 1531–1544.
8. 42 U.S.C. Sections 7401–7671q.
9. As of 1997, President Clinton had approved these regulations.

pollution and major new sources. Major new sources include existing sources modified by a change in a method of operation that increases emissions. Performance standards for major sources require use of the *maximum achievable control technology*, or MACT, to reduce emissions from the combustion of fossil fuels (coal and oil). The EPA issues guidelines as to what equipment meets this standard.

Under the 1990 amendments to the Clean Air Act, 110 of the oldest coal-burning power plants in the United States must cut their emissions by 40 percent by the year 2001 to reduce acid rain. Utilities were granted "credits" to emit certain amounts of sulfur dioxide, and those that emit less than the allowed amounts can sell their credits to other polluters. Controls on other factories and businesses are intended to reduce ground-level ozone pollution in ninety-six cities to healthful levels by 2005 (except Los Angeles, which has until 2010). Industrial emissions of 189 hazardous air pollutants must be reduced by 90 percent by 2000. By 2002, the production of chlorofluorocarbons (such as Freon), carbon tetrachloride, and methyl chloroform—used in air conditioning, refrigeration, and insulation and linked to depletion of the ozone layer—must stop.

HAZARDOUS AIR POLLUTANTS

Hazardous air pollutants are those likely to cause an increase in mortality or in serious irreversible or incapacitating illness. As noted, there are 189 of these pollutants, including asbestos, benzene, beryllium, cadmium, mercury, and vinyl chloride. These pollutants may cause cancer as well as neurological and reproductive damage. They are emitted from stationary sources by a variety of business activities, including smelting, dry cleaning, house painting, and commercial baking. Instead of establishing specific emissions standards for each hazardous air pollutant, the 1990 amendments to the Clean Air Act require industry to use pollution-control equipment that represents the maximum achievable control technology, or MACT, to limit emissions. The EPA issues guidelines as to what equipment meets this standard.

In recent years, the EPA has become increasingly concerned with the hazardous air pollutants emitted by landfills. In the past, when environmental regulators considered the pollution caused by landfilling, they generally focused only on groundwater contamination. By the 1990s, however, it had become apparent that emissions (such as toxic gases) from landfills, including hazardous air pollutants, constituted a significant source of air pollution. In 1996, the EPA issued a new rule to regulate these emissions. The rule requires landfills constructed after May 30, 1991, that emit more than a specified amount of pollutants to install landfill gas collection and control systems. The rule also requires the states to impose the same requirements on landfills constructed before May 30, 1991, if they accepted waste after November 8, 1987.[10]

VIOLATIONS OF THE CLEAN AIR ACT

For violations of emission limits under the Clean Air Act, the EPA can assess civil penalties of up to $25,000 per day. Additional fines of up to $5,000 per day can be assessed for other violations, such as failing to maintain the required records. To penalize those for whom it is more cost effective to violate the act than to comply with it, the EPA is authorized to obtain a penalty equal to the violator's economic benefits from noncompliance. Persons who provide information about violators may be paid up to $10,000. Private citizens can also sue violators.

Those who knowingly violate the act may be subject to criminal penalties, including fines of up to $1 million and imprisonment for up to two years (for false statements or failures to report violations). Corporate officers are among those who may be subject to these penalties.

SECTION 4
WATER POLLUTION

Federal regulations governing the pollution of water can be traced back to the Rivers and Harbors Appropriations Act of 1899.[11] These regulations prohibited ships and manufacturers from discharging or depositing refuse in navigable waterways.

NAVIGABLE WATERS

Once limited to waters actually used for navigation, the term *navigable waters* is today interpreted to include coastal and freshwater wetlands (how the

10. 40 C.F.R. Sections 60.750–759.

11. 33 U.S.C. Sections 401–418.

EPA defines wetlands will be discussed shortly), as well as intrastate lakes and streams used by interstate travelers and industries. In 1948, Congress passed the Federal Water Pollution Control Act (FWPCA),[12] but its regulatory system and enforcement proved inadequate. In 1972, amendments to the FWPCA—known as the Clean Water Act—established the following goals: (1) make waters safe for swimming, (2) protect fish and wildlife, and (3) eliminate the discharge of pollutants into the water. The amendments required that municipal and industrial polluters apply for permits before discharging wastes into navigable waters.

They also set forth specific time schedules, which were extended by amendment in 1977 and by the Water Quality Act of 1987.[13] Under these schedules, the EPA establishes limitations for discharges of types of pollutants based on the technology available for controlling them. Regulations, for the most part, specify that the *best available control technology*, or BACT, be installed. The EPA issues guidelines as to what equipment meets this standard, which essentially requires the most effective pollution-control equipment available. New sources must install BACT equipment before beginning operations. Existing sources are subject to timetables for installation of BACT equipment. These sources must immediately install equipment that utilizes the *best practical control technology*, or BPCT. The EPA also issues guidelines as to what equipment meets this standard.

12. 33 U.S.C. Sections 1251–1387.

13. This act amended 33 U.S.C. Section 1251.

WETLANDS The Clean Water Act prohibits the filling or dredging of **wetlands** unless a permit is obtained from the Army Corps of Engineers. The EPA defines wetlands as "those areas that are inundated or saturated by surface or ground water at a frequency and duration sufficient to support, and that under normal circumstances do support, a prevalence of vegetation typically adapted for life in saturated soil conditions." In recent years, federal regulatory policy in regard to wetlands has elicited substantial controversy because of the broad interpretation of what constitutes a wetland subject to the regulatory authority of the federal government. The following case is illustrative.

CASE 24.2 Hoffman Homes, Inc. v. Administrator, United States Environmental Protection Agency

United States Court of Appeals, Seventh Circuit, 1993.
999 F.2d 256.

COMPANY PROFILE *Sam and Jack Hoffman started F&S Construction in 1947. Over the next few years, the company—renamed the Hoffman Group—built thousands of low-priced houses throughout the United States, becoming the nation's third largest builder by 1955. Norman Hassinger, a residential marketing expert, became president of the Hoffman Group in 1982 and gradually took over the firm. In 1987, the Hoffman Group became the Hassinger Companies. Hassinger created Hoffman Homes, Inc., as a home-building subsidiary.*

BACKGROUND AND FACTS *Hoffman Homes, Inc., in preparation for the construction of a housing subdivision, filled and graded a 0.8-acre, bowl-shaped depression ("Area A"). Before Hoffman filled Area A, rainwater periodically collected there. The EPA issued an order stating that Hoffman had filled wetlands without a permit in violation of the Clean Water Act and ordered Hoffman to, among other things, cease its filling activities and pay a fine of $50,000 for violating the act. Hoffman protested that the EPA had no regulatory authority over Area A because the area in no way affected interstate commerce. The EPA stated that it had authority to regulate discharges of fill materials into intrastate wetlands that have a "minimal, potential effect" on interstate commerce and that Area A had such an effect because migratory birds could potentially use the area. Hoffman appealed the decision to the Seventh Circuit Court of Appeals.*

In the Language of the Court

HARLINGTON WOOD, Senior Circuit Judge.

* * * *

* * * It is true, of course, that migratory birds can alight most anywhere. As [a witness] testified, he has seen mallards in parking lot puddles. The ALJ [administrative law judge of the EPA], however, was in the unique position to view the evidence, to hear the testimony, and to judge the credibility of the witnesses. He concluded that the evidence did not support the conclusion that Area A had characteristics whose use by and value to migratory birds is well established. We agree. The migratory birds are better judges of what is suitable for their welfare than are we [or anyone at the EPA]. Having avoided Area A the migratory birds have thus spoken and submitted their own evidence. We see no need to argue with them. No justification whatsoever is seen from the evidence to interfere with private ownership based on what appears to be no more than a well intentioned effort in these particular factual circumstances to expand government control beyond reasonable or practical limits. After April showers not every temporary wet spot necessarily becomes subject to government control.

Decision and Remedy

The court, holding that Area A was not subject to regulation under the Clean Water Act, vacated the EPA's order requiring Hoffman Homes to pay a $50,000 administrative penalty for the filling of Area A.

VIOLATIONS OF THE CLEAN WATER ACT Under the Clean Water Act, violators are subject to a variety of civil and criminal penalties. Civil penalties for each violation range from a maximum of $10,000 per day, and not more than $25,000 per violation, to as much as $25,000 per day. Criminal penalties range from a fine of $2,500 per day and imprisonment for up to one year to a fine of $1 million and fifteen years' imprisonment. Injunctive relief and damages can also be imposed. The polluting party can be required to clean up the pollution or pay for the cost of doing so. Criminal penalties apply only if a violation was intentional.

DRINKING WATER

Another statute governing water pollution is the Safe Drinking Water Act.[14] Passed in 1974, this act requires the EPA to set maximum levels for pollutants in public water systems. Operators of public water supply systems must come as close as possible to meeting the EPA's standards by using the best available technology that is economically and technologically feasible. The EPA is particularly concerned with contamination from underground sources. Pesticides and wastes leaked from landfills or disposed of in underground injection wells are among the more than two hundred pollutants known to exist in groundwater used for drinking in at least thirty-four states. Many of these substances are associated with cancer and damage to the central nervous system, liver, and kidneys.

The act was amended in 1996 to give the EPA greater flexibility in setting regulatory standards governing drinking water. Prior to the 1996 amendments, the EPA had to set standards for twenty-five different drinking water contaminants every three years, which it had largely failed to do. Under the 1996 amendments, the EPA can move at whatever rate it deems necessary to control contaminants that are of greatest concern to the public health. The 1996 amendments also imposed new requirements on suppliers of drinking water. Each supplier must send to every household it supplies with water an annual statement describing the source of its water, the level of any contaminants contained in the water, and any possible health concerns associated with the contaminants.

OCEAN DUMPING

The Marine Protection, Research, and Sanctuaries Act of 1972[15] (known popularly as the Ocean Dumping Act) regulates the transportation and

14. 42 U.S.C. Sections 300f to 300j-25.

15. 16 U.S.C. Sections 1401–1445.

dumping of material into ocean waters. (The term *material* is synonymous with the term *pollutant* as used in the Federal Water Pollution Control Act.) The Ocean Dumping Act prohibits entirely the ocean-dumping of radiological, chemical, and biological warfare agents and high-level radioactive waste. The act establishes a permit program for transporting and dumping other materials. There are specific exemptions—materials subject to the permit provisions of other pollution legislation, wastes from structures regulated by other laws (for example, offshore oil exploration and drilling platforms), sewage, and other wastes. The Ocean Dumping Act also authorizes the designation of marine sanctuaries for "preserving or restoring such areas for their conservation, recreational, ecological, or esthetic values."

Each violation of any provision or permit may result in a civil penalty of not more than $50,000 or revocation or suspension of the permit. A knowing violation is a criminal offense that may result in a $50,000 fine, imprisonment for not more than a year, or both. An injunction may also be imposed.

OIL POLLUTION

In 1989, the supertanker *Exxon Valdez* caused the worst oil spill in North American history in the waters of Alaska's Prince William Sound. A quarter of a million barrels of crude oil—more than ten million gallons—leaked out of the ship's broken hull. In response to the *Exxon Valdez* oil-spill disaster, Congress passed the Oil Pollution Act of 1990.[16] Any onshore or offshore oil facility, oil shipper, vessel owner, or vessel operator that discharges oil into navigable waters or onto an adjoining shore may be liable for clean-up costs, as well as damages. The act created a $1 billion oil clean-up and economic compensation fund and decreed that by the year 2011, oil tankers using U.S. ports must be double hulled to limit the severity of accidental spills.

Under the act, damage to natural resources, private property, and the local economy, including the increased cost of providing public services, is compensable. The act provides for civil penalties of $1,000 per barrel spilled or $25,000 for each day of the violation. The party held responsible for the clean-up costs can bring a civil suit for contribution from other potentially liable parties.

16. 33 U.S.C. Sections 2701–2761.

SECTION 5
NOISE POLLUTION

Regulations concerning noise pollution include the Noise Control Act of 1972.[17] This act requires the EPA to establish noise emission standards (maximum noise levels below which no harmful effects occur from interference with speech or other activity)—for example, for railroad noise emissions. The standards must be achievable by the best available technology, and they must be economically within reason.

The act prohibits, among other things, distributing products manufactured in violation of the noise emission standards and tampering with noise control devices. Either of these activities can result in an injunction or whatever other remedy "is necessary to protect the public health and welfare." Illegal product distribution can also result in a fine and imprisonment. Violations of provisions of the Noise Control Act can result in penalties of not more than $50,000 per day and imprisonment for not more than two years.

SECTION 6
TOXIC CHEMICALS

Originally, most environmental clean-up efforts were directed toward reducing smog and making water safe for fishing and swimming. Over time, however, control of toxic chemicals has become an important part of environmental law.

PESTICIDES AND HERBICIDES

The first toxic chemical problem to receive widespread public attention was that posed by pesticides and herbicides. Using these chemicals to kill insects and weeds has increased agricultural productivity, but their residue remains in the environment. In some instances, accumulations of this residue have killed animals, and scientists have identified potential long-term effects that are detrimental to people.

FEDERAL INSECTICIDE, FUNGICIDE, AND RODENTICIDE ACT (FIFRA) The federal statute regulating pesticides and herbicides is the Federal

17. 42 U.S.C. Sections 4901–4918.

Insecticide, Fungicide, and Rodenticide Act (FIFRA) of 1947.[18] Under FIFRA, pesticides and herbicides must be (1) registered before they can be sold, (2) certified and used only for approved applications, and (3) used in limited quantities when applied to food crops. If a substance is identified as harmful, the EPA can cancel its registration after a hearing. If the harm is imminent, the EPA can suspend registration pending the hearing. The EPA, or state officers or employees, may also inspect factories in which these chemicals are manufactured.

Under 1996 amendments to the Federal Food, Drug and Cosmetic Act, for a pesticide to remain on the market, there must be a "reasonable certainty of no harm" to people from exposure to the pesticide.[19] This means that there must be no more than a one-in-a-million risk to people of developing cancer from exposure in any way, including eating food that contains residues from the pesticide. Pesticide residues are in nearly all fruits and vegetables and processed foods. Under the 1996 amendments, the EPA must distribute to grocery stores brochures on high-risk pesticides that are in food, and the stores must display these brochures for consumers.

VIOLATIONS OF FIFRA It is a violation of FIFRA to sell a pesticide or herbicide that is unregistered, a pesticide or herbicide with a registration that has been canceled or suspended, or a pesticide or herbicide with a false or misleading label. For example, it is an offense to sell a substance that is adulterated (that has a chemical strength different from the concentration declared on the label). It is also an offense to destroy or deface any labeling required under the act. The act's labeling requirements include directions for the use of the pesticide or herbicide, warnings to protect human health and the environment, a statement of treatment in the case of poisoning, and a list of the ingredients.

A private party can petition the EPA to suspend or cancel the registration of a pesticide or herbicide. If the EPA fails to act, the private party can petition a federal court to review the EPA's failure. Penalties for registrants and producers for violating FIFRA include imprisonment for up to one year and a fine of no more than $50,000. Penalties for commercial dealers include imprisonment for up to one year and a fine of no more than $25,000. Farmers and other private users of pesticides or herbicides who violate the act are subject to a $1,000 fine and imprisonment for up to thirty days.

TOXIC SUBSTANCES

The first comprehensive law covering toxic substances was the Toxic Substances Control Act of 1976.[20] The act was passed to regulate chemicals and chemical compounds that are known to be toxic—such as asbestos and polychlorinated biphenyls, popularly known as PCBs—and to institute investigation of any possible harmful effects from new chemical compounds. The regulations authorize the EPA to require that manufacturers, processors, and other organizations planning to use chemicals first determine their effects on human health and the environment. The EPA can regulate substances that may pose an imminent hazard or an unreasonable risk of injury to health or the environment. The EPA may require special labeling, limit the use of a substance, set production quotas, or prohibit the use of a substance altogether.

HAZARDOUS WASTES

Some industrial, agricultural, and household wastes pose more serious threats than others. If not properly disposed of, these toxic chemicals may present a substantial danger to human health and the environment. If released into the environment, they may contaminate public drinking water resources.

RESOURCE CONSERVATION AND RECOVERY ACT In 1976, Congress passed the Resource Conservation and Recovery Act (RCRA)[21] in reaction to an ever-increasing concern with the effects of hazardous waste materials on the environment. The RCRA required the EPA to establish regulations to monitor and control hazardous waste disposal and to determine which forms of solid waste should be considered hazardous and thus subject to regulation. The act authorized the EPA to promulgate various technical requirements for some types of facilities for storage and treatment of hazardous waste. The act also requires all producers of hazardous waste materials to label and package properly any hazardous waste to be transported.

18. 7 U.S.C. Sections 136–136y.
19. 21 U.S.C. Section 346a.
20. 15 U.S.C. Sections 2601–2692.
21. 42 U.S.C. Sections 6901–6986.

The RCRA was amended in 1984 and 1986 to decrease the use of land containment in the disposal of hazardous waste and to require compliance with the act by some generators of hazardous waste—such as those generating less than 1,000 kilograms (2,200 pounds) a month—that had previously been excluded from regulation under the RCRA.

Under the RCRA, a company may be assessed a civil penalty based on the seriousness of the violation, the probability of harm, and the extent to which the violation deviates from RCRA requirements. The assessment may be up to $25,000 for each violation. Criminal penalties include fines up to $50,000 for each day of violation, imprisonment for up to two years (in most instances), or both. Criminal fines and the time of imprisonment can be doubled for certain repeat offenders.

SUPERFUND In 1980, Congress passed the Comprehensive Environmental Response, Compensation, and Liability Act (CERCLA),[22] commonly known as Superfund. The basic purpose of Superfund is to regulate the clean-up of disposal sites in which hazardous waste is leaking into the environment. A special federal fund was created for that purpose.

Potentially Responsible Parties. Superfund provides that when a release or a threatened release of hazardous chemicals from a site occurs, the EPA can clean up the site and recover the cost of the clean-up from the following persons: (1) the person who generated the wastes disposed of at the site, (2) the person who transported the wastes to the site, (3) the person who owned or operated the site at the time of the disposal, or (4) the current owner or operator. A person falling within one of these categories is referred to as a **potentially responsible party (PRP).**

Liability under Superfund is usually joint and several—that is, a PRP who generated only a fraction of the hazardous waste disposed of at the site may nevertheless be liable for all of the clean-up costs. CERCLA authorizes a party who has incurred clean-up costs to bring a "contribution action" against any other person who is liable or potentially liable for a percentage of the costs.

Courts often focus on the meaning of the words "owner or operator" to determine who is a PRP. In one case, a parent company was held liable as an "operator" for clean-up costs for a chemical spill at a plant owned by its subsidiary. The court pointed out that the parent company controlled the subsidiary's finances, real estate transactions, and contact with the government and that the parent company's personnel held most of the subsidiary's officer and director positions.[23] In other cases, courts have held officers and shareholders liable based on their authority to exercise control over their corporations.[24] In the following case, the court considers whether a corporation can be held liable under CERCLA.

22. 42 U.S.C. Sections 9601–9675.

23. *United States v. Kayser-Roth Corp.*, 910 F.2d 24 (1st Cir. 1990).

24. See, for example, *State of New York v. Shore Realty Corp.*, 759 F.2d 1032 (2d Cir. 1985).

CASE 24.3 B. F. Goodrich Co. v. Betkoski

United States Court of Appeals, Second Circuit, 1996. 99 F.3d 505.

BACKGROUND AND FACTS *Terrance and Harold Murtha owned and operated two landfill sites used for the disposal of hazardous substances. The EPA and the state of Connecticut cleaned up the sites and then filed suits in a federal district court to recover the costs from the Murthas and other potentially responsible parties who generated or transported hazardous substances to the sites. Many of the parties, including the Murthas and B. F. Goodrich Company, agreed to, among other things, pay a share of the costs. These parties joined the EPA and the state of Connecticut in a suit against John Betkoski and eighty-seven other defendants who refused to pay. The defendants filed motions for summary judgment, which the court granted, in part based on its decisions concerning successor liability. The plaintiffs appealed.*

IN THE LANGUAGE OF THE COURT

CARDAMONE, Circuit Judge:

* * * *

[CERCLA's] broad remedial purpose would be sharply curtailed if the Act did not encompass successor liability. * * * [A]bsent successor liability, a predecessor could benefit from the illegal disposal of hazardous substances and later evade responsibility for remediation simply by changing the form in which it does business, thereby subverting the Act's purpose of holding responsible parties liable for cleanup costs. * * *

* * * The traditional common law rule states that a corporation acquiring the assets of another corporation * * * takes on its liabilities if * * * the successor is a "mere continuation" of the predecessor * * * .

The [defendants] contend that when determining whether there is a "mere continuation," we should not use the common law test * * * , which requires the existence of a single corporation after the transfer of assets, with an identity of stock, stockholders, and directors between the successor and predecessor corporations. Rather, they urge that we employ the "continuity of enterprise" approach, * * * [under which liability depends on whether] the successor maintains the same business, with the same employees doing the same jobs, under the same supervisors, working conditions, and production processes, and produces the same products for the same customers.

* * * [T]he substantial continuity test is more consistent with the Act's goals * * * . We therefore adopt the substantial continuity test as the appropriate legal test for successor liability under CERCLA.

DECISION AND REMEDY

The U.S. Court of Appeals for the Second Circuit reversed the trial court's grant of summary judgment to those defendants who were successor corporations. The plaintiffs could proceed with their case.

Liability of Lending Institutions and Fiduciaries. In recent years, courts have wrestled with the question of whether lending institutions can be held liable for toxic waste on property they hold as collateral for their loans. Some courts followed the lead of the Court of Appeals for the Eleventh Circuit, which held in 1990 that a bank can be held liable as a PRP if the bank has the "capacity to influence" a borrower's decisions about toxic waste.[25] Other courts held to the contrary. In one case, the court held that to impose liability on a bank for involving itself in the debtor's affairs would be to "punish the Bank for engaging in its normal course of business."[26] To clarify this issue, Congress amended CERCLA in 1996 to provide that banks and other lenders can be held liable under CERCLA for property they hold as collateral only if they actually participate in the management or operational affairs of the borrower.[27]

Another issue on which the courts disagreed was whether certain fiduciaries, such as trustees and executors of estates, could be held liable as PRPs. In at least one case, a federal court held that a trustee could be personally liable for those costs of cleaning up a hazardous waste site that exceeded the value of the trust's assets.[28] The 1996 amendments also addressed this issue by stating that a fiduciary can only be held personally liable as a PRP in limited circumstances—such as when the hazardous waste pollution is caused by the fiduciary's own negligence.[29]

SECTION 7
RADIATION

Nuclear power plants are built and operated by private industry. The nuclear industry is regulated

25. *United States v. Fleet Factors Corp.*, 901 F.2d 1550 (11th Cir. 1990).

26. *Z & Z Leasing, Inc. v. Graying Reel, Inc.*, 873 F.Supp. 51 (E.D.Mich. 1995).

27. 42 U.S.C. Section 9601.

28. *Phoenix v. Garbage Services Co.*, 816 F.Supp. 564 (D.Ariz. 1993).

29. 42 U.S.C. Section 9607.

almost exclusively by the federal government under the Atomic Energy Act of 1954.[30] The Nuclear Regulatory Commission (NRC) is the federal agency responsible for regulating the private nuclear industry. The NRC reviews the plans for each proposed nuclear plant and issues a construction permit only after preparing an environmental impact statement that considers the impact of an accidental release of radiation. After construction, the NRC licenses the plant's operation.

The Environmental Protection Agency sets standards for radioactivity in the overall environment and for the disposal of some radioactive waste. Low-level radioactive waste generated by private facilities is the responsibility of each state under the Low Level Radioactive Waste Policy Act of 1980.[31] The NRC regulates the use and disposal of other nuclear materials and radioactive waste. Some radioactive waste is buried, burned, or dumped in the ocean. Currently, however, most of it is stored at the plants in which it is produced. Under the Nuclear Waste Policy Act of 1982,[32] the government is looking for a permanent disposal site scheduled to be opened in the year 2000.

A common law theory may serve as the basis for liability for harms caused by radiation. For example, in one case, the court held that the party creating a radiation hazard is strictly liable in tort for its cleanup and any damages.[33] Liability for injury resulting from radiation may also arise under one of the statutes discussed elsewhere in this chapter. For example, the release of radioactive materials into the environment may violate the Clean Water Act, the RCRA, or the CERCLA.[34]

30. 42 U.S.C. Sections 2011 to 2297g-4.

31. 42 U.S.C. Sections 2021b–2021j.

32. 42 U.S.C. Sections 10101–10270.

33. *T&E Industries, Inc. v. Safety Light Corp.*, 123 N.J. 371, 587 A.2d 1249 (1991).

34. See, for example, *Ohio v. Department of Energy*, 904 F.2d 1058 (6th Cir. 1990).

Section 8

STATE AND LOCAL REGULATION

Many states regulate the degree to which the environment may be polluted. Thus, for example, even when state zoning laws permit a business's proposed development, the proposal may have to be altered to change the development's impact on the environment. State laws may restrict a business's discharge of chemicals into the air or water or regulate its disposal of toxic wastes. States may also regulate the disposal or recycling of other wastes, including glass, metal, and plastic containers and paper. Additionally, states may restrict the emissions from motor vehicles.

City, county, and other local governments control some aspects of the environment. For instance, local zoning laws control some land use. These laws may be designed to inhibit or direct the growth of cities and suburbs or to protect the natural environment. Other aspects of the environment may be subject to local regulation for other reasons. Methods of waste and garbage removal and disposal, for example, can have a substantial impact on a community. The appearance of buildings and other structures, including advertising signs and billboards, may affect traffic safety, property values, or local aesthetics. Noise generated by a business or its customers may be annoying, disruptive, or damaging to its neighbors. The location and condition of parks, streets, and other public uses of land subject to local control affect the environment and can also affect business.

TERMS AND CONCEPTS TO REVIEW

environmental impact statement (EIS) 497

environmental law 495

nuisance 496

potentially responsible party (PRP) 505

toxic tort 497

wetland 501

QUESTIONS AND CASE PROBLEMS

24–1. CLEAN AIR ACT. The Environmental Protection Agency (EPA) has set ambient standards for several pollutants, including sulfur dioxide, specifying the maximum concentration allowable in the outdoor air. One way to meet these standards is to reduce emissions. Companies discovered, however, that they could also meet the standards at less cost by building very high smokestacks. When emitted from such high stacks, pollutants were more widely dispersed and remained below the concentration level specified by the ambient standards. Environmental groups claimed that the Clean Air Act was designed to reduce pollution, not to disperse it, and argued that industry should not be allowed to rely on tall stacks. Are the environmental groups correct, or should industry be allowed to use the less expensive dispersal method? Discuss.

24–2. CLEAN AIR ACT. Some scientific knowledge indicates that there is no safe level of exposure to a cancer-causing agent. In theory, even one molecule of such a substance has the potential for causing cancer. Section 112 of the Clean Air Act requires that all cancer-causing substances be regulated to ensure a margin of safety. Some environmental groups have argued that all emissions of such substances must be eliminated in order for such a margin of safety to be reached. A total elimination would likely shut down many major U.S. industries. Should the Environmental Protection Agency totally eliminate all emissions of cancer-causing chemicals? Discuss.

24–3. ENVIRONMENTAL LAWS. Moonbay is a real estate development corporation that primarily develops retirement communities. Farmtex owns a number of feedlots in Sunny Valley. Moonbay purchased twenty thousand acres of farmland in the same area and began building and selling retirement homes on this acreage. In the meantime, Farmtex continued to expand its feedlot business, and eventually only five hundred feet separated the two operations. Because of the odor and flies from the feedlots, Moonbay found it difficult to sell the homes in its development. Moonbay wants to enjoin Farmtex from operating its feedlots in the vicinity of the retirement home development. Discuss under what theory Moonbay would file this action. Discuss fully whether Farmtex has violated any federal environmental laws.

24–4. ENVIRONMENTAL LAWS. Fruitade, Inc., is a processor of a soft drink called Freshen Up. Fruitade uses returnable bottles, as well as a special acid to clean its bottles for further beverage processing. The acid is diluted by water and then allowed to pass into a navigable stream. Fruitade crushes its broken bottles and throws the crushed glass into the stream. Discuss fully any environmental laws that Fruitade has violated.

24–5. PESTICIDE REGULATION. The Environmental Protection Agency (EPA) canceled the registration of the pesticide Diazinon for use on golf courses and sod farms because of concern about the effects of Diazinon on birds. The Federal Insecticide, Fungicide, and Rodenticide Act authorizes cancellation of the registration of products that "generally cause unreasonable adverse effects on the environment." The statute further defines "unreasonable adverse effects on the environment" to mean "any unreasonable risk to man or the environment, taking into account the . . . costs and benefits." Thus, in determining whether a pesticide should continue to be used, one must balance the risks and benefits of the use of the pesticide. Does this mean that the pesticide must be found to kill birds more often than not before its use can be prohibited? [*CIBA-Geigy Corp. v. Environmental Protection Agency*, 874 F.2d 277 (5th Cir. 1989)]

24–6. COMMON LAW NUISANCE. Taylor Bay Protective Association is a nonprofit corporation established for the purpose of restoring and improving the water quality of Taylor Bay. Local water districts began operating a flood control project in the area. As part of the project, a pumping station was developed. Testimony at trial revealed that the pumps were operated contrary to the instructions provided in the operation and maintenance manual. The pumps acted as vacuums, sucking up increased amounts of silt and depositing the silt in Taylor Bay. Thus, the project resulted in sedimentation and turbidity problems in the downstream watercourse of Taylor Bay. The association sued the local water districts, alleging that the pumping operations created a nuisance. Do the pumping operations qualify as a common law nuisance? Who should be responsible for the clean-up costs? Discuss both questions fully. [*Taylor Bay Protective Association v. Environmental Protection Agency*, 884 F.2d 1073 (8th Cir. 1989)]

24–7. WATER POLLUTION. The Environmental Protection Agency (EPA) promulgated water-pollution discharge limits for several mining industries. These standards authorized variances exempting mining operations from coverage by the standards if the operations could show that they used special processes or facilities that made the standards inapplicable. Cost was not a consideration in granting the variances. An industry trade association sued, claiming that the EPA should consider costs in granting variances, and the Fourth Circuit Court of Appeals agreed. Discuss whether the United States Supreme Court should overturn this decision or affirm it and let costs be considered in the granting of variances under the Clean Water Act. [*Environmental Protection Agency v. National Crushed Stone Association*, 449 U.S. 64, 101 S.Ct. 295, 66 L.Ed.2d 268 (1980)]

24–8. SUPERFUND. During the 1970s, a number of chemical companies disposed of their wastes at a facility maintained by South Carolina Recycling and Disposal, Inc. Hazardous chemical wastes were stored rather haphazardly; some leaked into the ground, and fires occurred on several occasions. Eventually, the Environmental Protection Agency (EPA) conducted clean-up operations under Superfund and sued companies that had used the site for the costs of the clean-up. Five of the defendant companies claimed that they should not be liable for the clean-up costs because there was no evidence that their waste materials had contributed in any way to the leakage problem or to any other hazard posed by the site. The EPA asserted that causation was not required for the companies' liability, only evidence that the companies had sent waste to the site. Will the EPA succeed in its claim? Discuss. [*United States v. South Carolina Recycling and Disposal, Inc.*, 653 F.Supp. 984 (D.S.C. 1986)]

24–9. COMMON LAW NUISANCE. In 1987, John and Jean Zarlenga purchased a new home in Bloomingdale, Illinois. Bloomingdale Partners (BP) then built an eight-story apartment complex across the street from the Zarlenga home. Each of the 168 apartments had an air conditioner weighing about nine hundred pounds. Over sixty air conditioners were on the side of the complex that faced the Zarlenga home. The Zarlengas testified that the noise from these air conditioners during the summer was a "loud rumbling sound" that was "continuous and monotonous." The machines disrupted their sleep. Jean Zarlenga suffered from headaches and irritability. In her testimony, she stated, "It's made my life miserable. I cannot use my deck. I cannot have company over . . . I can't open my windows in my bedroom. I toss and turn all night." The Zarlengas sued BP for creating a nuisance, claiming that the apartment complex substantially interfered with the use and enjoyment of their home. The Zarlengas sought damages from BP for the devaluation of their home caused by the noise and for their suffering. How should the court decide this case? Discuss fully. [*In re Bloomingdale Partners*, 160 Bankr. 101 (N.D.Ill. 1993)]

24–10. CLEAN WATER ACT. Attique Ahmad owned the Spin-N-Market, a convenience store and gas station. The gas pumps were fed by underground tanks, one of which had a leak at its top that allowed water to enter. Ahmad emptied the tank by pumping its contents into a storm drain and a sewer system. Through the storm drain, gasoline flowed into a creek, forcing the city to clean the water. Through the sewer system, gasoline flowed into a sewage treatment plant, forcing the city to evacuate the plant and two nearby schools. Ahmad was charged with discharging a pollutant without a permit, which is a criminal violation of the Clean Water Act. The act provides that a person who "knowingly violates" the act commits a felony. Ahmad claimed that he had believed he was discharging only water. Did Ahmad commit a felony? Why or why not? Discuss fully. [*U.S. v. Ahmad*, 101 F.3d 386 (5th Cir. 1996)]

24–11. A QUESTION OF ETHICS

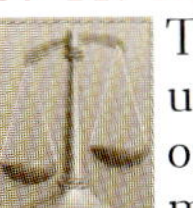

The Endangered Species Act of 1973 makes it unlawful for any person to "take" endangered or threatened species. The act defines *take* to mean to "harass, harm, pursue," "wound," or "kill." The secretary of the interior (Bruce Babbitt) issued a regulation that further defined harm to include "significant habitat modification or degradation where it actually kills or injures wildlife." A group of businesses and individuals involved in the timber industry brought an action against the secretary of the interior and others. The group complained that the application of the "harm" regulation to the red-cockaded woodpecker and the northern spotted owl had injured the group economically, because it prevented logging operations (habitat modification) in Pacific Northwest forests containing these species. The group challenged the regulation's validity, contending that Congress did not intend the word *take* to include habitat modification. The case ultimately reached the United States Supreme Court, which held that the secretary had reasonably construed Congress's intent when he defined harm to include habitat modification. [*Babbitt v. Sweet Home Chapter of Communities for a Great Oregon*, 515 U.S. 687, 115 S.Ct. 2407, 132 L.Ed.2d 597 (1995)]

1. Traditionally, the term *take* has been used to refer to the capture or killing of wildlife, usually for private gain. Is the secretary's regulation prohibiting habitat modification consistent with this definition?
2. One of the issues in this case was whether Congress intended to protect existing generations of species or future generations. How do the terms *take* and *habitat modification* relate to this issue?
3. Three dissenting Supreme Court justices contended that construing the act as prohibiting habitat modification "imposes unfairness to the point of financial ruin—not just upon the rich, but upon the simplest farmer who finds his land conscripted to national zoological use." Should private parties be required to bear the burden of preserving habitats for wildlife?
4. Generally, should the economic welfare of private parties be taken into consideration when environmental statutes and regulations are created and applied?

Accessing the Internet

The Legal Environment of Business

The Virtual Law Library of the Indiana University School of Law provides numerous links to online environmental law resources. Go to

http://www.law.indiana.edu/

Cornell Law School's Legal Information Institute provides access to the *U.S. Code*, which contains the environmental laws discussed in this chapter. Go to

http://www.law.cornell.edu/uscode

Environmental Policy Related Resources offers links to an extensive number of Internet sites dealing with environmental issues. You can access this site at

http://student.ecok.edu/~polsci/resource/environ.html

For information on the standards, guidelines, and regulations of the Environmental Protection Agency, go to

http://www.epa.gov/

Envirofacts is an EPA site that combines data from various EPA programs. Here you can find information on Superfund, the release and transfer of more than 300 toxic chemicals, more than 75,000 water-discharge permits, and much more. To access this site, go to

http://www.epa.gov/enviro/html/ef_home.html

Environmental Information Resources, a site jointly created by the EPA and George Washington University, provides extensive links to environmental resources on the Internet, organized by subject, name, or country. Go to

http://www.gwu.edu/~greenu/index2.html

The site of the Chicago law firm of Ross & Hardies offers a broad overview of existing environmental laws, proposed environmental legislation, and EPA actions, as well as articles on environmental law and an online discussion forum. The URL for this site is

http://www.webcom.com/~staber

Another site with useful information about environmental law is provided by the McCutchen Environmental Group at

http://www.mccutchen.com/env

The environmental law page of *Law Journal Extra!* is a wide-ranging site with a number of useful resources. Access this site at

http://www.ljx.com/practice/environment/index.html

For a catalogue of books about environmental law, go to Cameron May, Environmental Publications, at

http://neon.airtime.co.uk/C-May

For information on the federal Office of Ocean and Coastal Resource Management, go to

http://wave.nos.noaa.gov/ocrm/

For similar information on the U.S. Fish and Wildlife Service, go to

http://www.fws.gov/

You might want to see what is happening at the National Resources Defense Council by accessing

http://www.nrdc.org/nrdc

A useful site with links to environmental law resources worldwide is provided by the International Environmental Liability Management Association at

http://www.magic.ca/ielma/ielma.home.html

CHAPTER 25

LAND-USE CONTROL AND REAL PROPERTY

PROPERTY OWNERSHIP CONFERS certain rights. An owner generally has the right to possess the property; the right either to use the property or to derive profits from another's use of the property; and the right to *alienate*[1] the property—that is, to sell, bequeath (pass on through a will), or give to others the same rights of ownership. Not all forms of ownership provide such a complete bundle of rights, but one or more of these attributes are normally included when we say that property is "owned."

Even for one who possesses the entire bundle of rights we have delineated, however, ownership is not absolute. The law places restrictions on how property may be used. It also imposes duties on the owners regarding how the land is to be maintained. In addition, individual owners may agree with others to restrict or limit the use of their property. Thus, property owners cannot always do with their property whatever they wish. Nuisance and environmental laws, for example, restrict how people carry out certain types of activities on their own land. Briefly stated, the rights of every property owner are subject to certain conditions and limitations.

In this chapter, we first look at the nature of real property and of ownership rights in real property. We then focus on restrictions on ownership in real property. **Real property** (sometimes called *realty* or *real estate*) means the land and everything permanently attached to the land. When structures are *permanently* attached to the land, then everything attached permanently to the structures is also realty. Everything else is **personal property** (or *personalty*). Although real property

1. *Alienate* derives from the Latin word *alienus* (alien), which is from the Latin *alus* (other). In legal terms, *alienate* means to transfer the title to property.

includes more than land, it is generally referred to simply as "land." Hence, the control over ownership and use that we examine in this chapter is commonly referred to as **land-use control.**

SECTION 1
THE NATURE OF REAL PROPERTY

Real property consists of land and the buildings, plants, and trees that it contains. Whereas personal property is movable, real property is immovable. Real property usually means land, but it also includes air and subsurface rights, plant life and vegetation, and *fixtures* (which are explained below).

LAND

Land includes the soil on the surface of the earth and the natural products or artificial structures that are attached to it. It further includes all the waters contained on or under the earth's surface and the air space above it. In other words, absent a contrary statute or case law, a landowner has the right to everything existing permanently below the surface of his or her property to the center of the earth and above it to the heavens (subject to certain qualifications).

AIR SPACE AND SUBSURFACE RIGHTS

The owner of real property has relatively exclusive rights to the air space above the land, as well as to the soil and minerals underneath it. When no limitations on air rights or subsurface rights are indicated on the document transferring title at the time of purchase, a purchaser can generally expect to have an unrestricted right to possession of the property (subject to the limits on ownership rights examined in detail later in this chapter).

Cases involving air rights present questions such as the right of commercial and private planes to fly over property and the right of individuals and governments to seed clouds and produce artificial rain. Flights over private land do not normally violate the property owners' rights unless the flights are low and frequent, causing a direct interference with the enjoyment and use of the land.[2]

Ownership of the surface of land can be separated from ownership of its subsurface. Subsurface rights can be extremely valuable when minerals, oil, or natural gas is located beneath the surface. A subsurface owner's rights would be of little value if he or she could not use the surface to exercise those rights. Hence, a subsurface owner will have a right (called a *profit*—discussed later in this chapter) to use the surface of the land to, for example, find and remove minerals. If the owners of the subsurface rights excavate and their excavation causes the surface to subside, however, they may be liable to the owner of the surface rights.

2. *United States v. Causby*, 328 U.S. 256, 66 S.Ct. 1062, 90 L.Ed. 1206 (1946).

PLANT LIFE AND VEGETATION

Plant life, both natural and cultivated, is also considered to be real property. In many instances, natural vegetation, such as trees, adds greatly to the value of realty. When a parcel of land is sold and the land has growing crops on it, the sale includes the crops, unless otherwise specified in the sales contract. When crops are sold by themselves, however, they are considered to be personal property or goods. Consequently, the sale of crops is a sale of goods, and it is governed by the Uniform Commercial Code (see Chapter 11) rather than by real property law.

FIXTURES

Certain personal property can become so closely associated with the real property to which it is attached that the law views it as real property. Such property is known as a **fixture**—a thing *affixed* to realty. A thing is affixed to realty when it is attached to it by roots; embedded in it; or permanently attached by means of cement, plaster, bolts, nails, or screws. The fixture can be physically attached to real property, can be attached to another fixture, or can even be without any actual physical attachment to the land, as long as the owner *intends* the property to be a fixture.

Fixtures are included in the sale of land if the sales contract does not provide otherwise. The sale of a house includes the land and the house and garage on it, as well as the cabinets, plumbing, and windows. Because these are permanently affixed to the property, they are considered to be a part of it. Unless otherwise agreed, however, the curtains and throw rugs are not included. Items such as drapes and window-unit air conditioners are difficult to classify. Thus, a contract for the sale of a house or commercial realty should indicate which items of this sort are included in the sale. At issue in the following case was whether telephone poles, wires, and other communications equipment qualified as fixtures.

CASE 25.1 New England Telephone and Telegraph Co. v. City of Franklin

Supreme Court of New Hampshire, 1996. 685 A.2d 913.

BACKGROUND AND FACTS *To obtain revenue, cities and towns tax the owners of real property within the municipalities' jurisdiction. The tax is based on an assessment of the value of the property. New England Telephone and Telegraph Company (NETT) and other telephone companies filed a lawsuit in a New Hampshire state court against the City of Franklin and other municipalities challenging the cities' property assessments. NETT and the other plaintiffs objected to the inclusion in their assessments of communications equipment, including telephone poles, wires, and central office equipment. They argued that the equipment was personal property and therefore should not have been taxed. The court granted the telephone companies' motion for summary judgment, and the cities appealed.*

IN THE LANGUAGE OF THE COURT

HORTON, Justice.

* * * *

* * * [W]hether an item of property is properly classified as either personalty or a fixture turns on several factors, including: the item's nature and use; the intent of the party making the annexation; the degree and extent to which the item is specially adapted to the realty; the degree and extent of the item's annexation to the realty; and the relationship between the realty's owner and the person claiming the item. The central factors are the nature of the article and its use, as connected with the use of the underlying land, because these factors provide the basis for ascertaining the intent of the party who affixes or annexes the item in question.

In this case, the items of communications equipment did not constitute fixtures. * * * The poles, wires, and central office equipment, though placed in the ground or bolted to the buildings, were readily removable and transportable without affecting the utility of the underlying land, the buildings, or the equipment itself. * * * In addition, the very nature of telephone poles and wires, as well as their use by the [telephone companies] in connection with integrated telecommunications systems, belies the proposition that the equipment became a permanent and essential part of the underlying realty so as to pass by conveyance [transfer of the title to property] with it.

DECISION AND REMEDY *The Supreme Court of New Hampshire affirmed the trial court's decision. The telephone poles, wires, and central office equipment were not fixtures and thus not subject to taxation by the cities as real property.*

SECTION 2

OWNERSHIP INTERESTS IN REAL PROPERTY

Ownership of property is an abstract concept that cannot exist independently of the legal system. No one actually possesses or *holds* a piece of land, along with the air above, the earth below, and all the water contained on it. One can only possess *rights* in real property. Numerous rights are involved in real property ownership. One who holds the entire bundle of rights owns in *fee simple absolute*. We look first at the fee simple absolute and then at the various types of limited property interests that exist when an owner in fee simple absolute parts with some, but not all, of his or her rights in real property.

FEE SIMPLE

In a **fee simple absolute,** the owner has the greatest aggregation of rights, privileges, and power possible. The owner can give the property away, sell the property for a price, or transfer the property by will to another. The fee simple absolute is limited absolutely to a person and his or her heirs and is assigned forever without limitation or condition. The rights that accompany a fee simple absolute include the right to use the land for whatever purpose the owner sees fit, subject to laws that prevent the owner from unreasonably interfering with another person's land and subject to applicable zoning laws. Furthermore, the owner has the right of *exclusive* possession of the property. A fee simple absolute is potentially infinite in duration and can be disposed of by deed or by will (by selling or by giving away). When there is no will, the fee simple absolute passes to the owner's legal heirs.

Ownership in fee simple may become limited when the property is transferred to another *conditionally*. When this occurs, the fee simple is known as a **fee simple defeasible** (the word *defeasible* means capable of being terminated, or annulled). For example, a **conveyance,** or transfer of real property, "to A and his heirs as long as the land is used for charitable purposes" creates a fee simple defeasible, because ownership of the property is conditioned on the land's being used for charitable purposes. The original owner retains a *partial* ownership interest, because if the specified condition does not occur (if the land ceases to be used for charitable purposes), then the land reverts, or returns, to the original owner. If the original owner is not living at the time, the land passes to his or her heirs. The conveyance of a fee simple defeasible usually includes the words *as long as, until, while,* or *during.*

LIFE ESTATES

A **life estate** is an estate that lasts for the life of some specified individual. A conveyance "to A for his life" creates a life estate.[3] In a life estate, the life tenant (the party who holds the estate) has fewer rights of ownership than the holder of a fee simple defeasible, because the rights necessarily cease to exist on the life tenant's death. The life tenant has the right to use the land, provided no *waste* (injury to the land) is committed. In other words, the life tenant cannot injure the land in a manner that would adversely affect its value to the owner of the future interest in it. The life tenant can use the land to harvest crops or, if mines and oil wells are already on the land, can extract minerals and oil from it, but the life tenant cannot exploit the land by creating new wells or mines.

With few exceptions, the owner of a life estate has an exclusive right to possession during his or her lifetime. In addition, the life tenant has the right to mortgage the life estate and create other interests in the land, but none can extend beyond the life of the tenant.

Along with these rights, the life tenant also has some duties—to keep the property in repair and to pay property taxes. In short, the owner of the life estate has the same rights as a fee simple owner except that he or she must maintain the value of the property during his or her tenancy, less the decrease in value resulting from the normal use of the property allowed by the life tenancy.

At issue in the following case was whether the removal of timber, under a right to do so specifically granted in a deed to a life tenant, constituted waste.

3. A less common type of life estate is created by the conveyance "to A for the life of B." This is known as an estate *pur autre vie*, or an estate for the duration of the life of another.

CASE 25.2 Meadows v. Belknap

Supreme Court of Appeals of West Virginia, 1997. 483 S.E.2d 826.

BACKGROUND AND FACTS *Carma and Derstine Perrine were married in 1942. During their marriage, Mr. Perrine bought, in his name alone, land in West Virginia. In 1989, Mr. Perrine signed a deed that transferred the land to the Perrines' married daughters, Roberta Meadows and Tara Sue Morgan, but reserved, to the Perrines, a life estate and the right to sell the timber on the land. In 1991, Mr. Perrine died. Three years later, Mrs. Perrine sold the timber to Wade Belknap. The daughters filed a suit in a West Virginia state court against Belknap, Mrs. Perrine, and others to stop the timber's removal, which the daughters argued was committing waste. The court ruled that Mrs. Perrine could not remove timber without the daughters' consent. Mrs. Perrine appealed.*

IN THE LANGUAGE OF THE COURT

DAVIS, Justice.

* * * *

* * * [In the deed] Mr. Perrine stated in plain language that he was "retain[ing] the free lifetime usage of all said tracts or parcels of land for and during the lifetime" of himself and Mrs. Perrine. * * * Mr. Perrine specifically set out in the deed that during his lifetime and the lifetime of Mrs. Perrine, each of them retained "the right to use any timber thereon for farm purposes and with the specific right to sell any timber on said tracts[.]" The clarity of the latter passage denudes the argument raised by the daughters. The daughters had no right to interfere with Mrs. Perrine's sale of any or all of the timber on the property. The very words of the deed foreclosed such interference.

DECISION AND REMEDY

The Supreme Court of Appeals reversed the decision of the lower court. The life tenant (Mrs. Perrine) could remove the timber from the land because the deed provided specifically for it.

FUTURE INTERESTS

When an owner in fee simple absolute conveys the estate conditionally to another (such as with a fee simple defeasible) or for a limited period of time (such as with a life estate), the original owner still retains an interest in the land. The owner retains the right to repossess ownership of the land if the conditions of the fee simple defeasible are not met or when the life of the life-estate holder ends. The residuary (or leftover) interest in the property that the owner retains is called a **future interest,** because if it arises, it will only arise in the future.

If the owner retains ownership of the future interest, then the future interest is a **reversionary interest,** because the property will *revert* to the original owner if the condition specified in the fee simple defeasible fails or when the life tenant dies. If, however, the owner of the future interest transfers ownership rights in that future interest to another, the future interest is a **remainder.** For example, a conveyance "to A for life, then to B" creates a life estate for A and a remainder (future interest) for B. An **executory interest** is a type of future interest very similar to a remainder, but an executory interest does not take effect immediately on the expiration of another interest, such as a life estate. For example, a conveyance "to A for life and one year after A's death to B" creates an executory interest for B.

LEASEHOLD ESTATES

A **leasehold estate** is created when a real property owner or lessor (landlord) agrees to convey the right to possess and use the property to a lessee (tenant) for a certain period of time. The tenant has a *qualified* right to exclusive possession (qualified by the right of the landlord to enter on the premises to assure that waste is not being committed). The tenant can use the land—for example, by harvesting crops—but cannot injure it by such activities as cutting down timber for sale or extracting oil. Here we look at the types of leasehold estates, or tenancies, that can be created when real property is leased.

TENANCY FOR YEARS A **tenancy for years** is created by an express contract (which can sometimes be oral) by which property is leased for a specified period of time, such as a month, a year, or a period of years. For example, signing a one-year lease to occupy an apartment creates a tenancy for years. At the end of the period specified in the lease, the lease ends (without notice), and possession of the apartment returns to the lessor. The lease may provide for renewal or extension.

PERIODIC TENANCY A **periodic tenancy** is created by a lease that does not specify how long it is to last but does specify that rent is to be paid at certain intervals. This type of tenancy is automatically renewed for another rental period unless properly terminated. For example, a periodic tenancy is created by a lease that states, "Rent is due on the tenth day of every month." This provision creates a tenancy from month to month. This type of tenancy can also be from week to week or from year to year. A periodic tenancy sometimes arises when a landlord allows a tenant under a tenancy for years to remain in possession after the lease expires and continue paying monthly or weekly rent. At common law, to terminate a periodic tenancy, the landlord or tenant must give one period's notice to the other party. If the tenancy is month to month, for example, one month's notice must be given. State statutes often require a different period for notice of termination in a periodic tenancy, however.

TENANCY AT WILL Suppose a landlord rents an apartment to a tenant "for as long as both agree." In such a case, the tenant receives a **tenancy at will.** At common law, either party can terminate the tenancy without notice (that is, "at will"). This type of tenancy usually arises when a tenant who has been under a tenancy for years retains possession after the termination date of that tenancy with the landlord's consent. Before the tenancy has been converted into a periodic tenancy (by the periodic payment of rent), it is a tenancy at will, terminable by either party without notice. The death of either party or the voluntary commission of waste by the tenant will terminate a tenancy at will.

TENANCY AT SUFFERANCE The mere possession of land without right is called a **tenancy at sufferance.** It is not a true tenancy. A tenancy at sufferance is not an estate, because it is created by a tenant's *wrongfully* retaining possession of property. Whenever a life estate, tenancy for years, periodic tenancy, or tenancy at will ends and the tenant continues to retain possession of the premises without the owner's permission, a tenancy at sufferance is created.

CONCURRENT OWNERSHIP

Persons who share ownership rights simultaneously in particular property are said to be *concurrent owners.* There are two principal types of **concurrent ownership:** *tenancy in common* and *joint tenancy.* Concurrent ownership rights can also be held in a *tenancy by the entirety* or as *community property,* although these latter two types of concurrent ownership are less common.

TENANCY IN COMMON A form of co-ownership in which each of two or more persons owns an undivided portion of the property is a **tenancy in common.** The portions need not be equal. When a tenant in common dies, the property interest passes to the heirs. For example, suppose Henri and Luis own equal interests in a rare coin collection as tenants in common. If Henri dies before Luis, one-half of the coin collection will become the property of Henri's heirs. If instead Henri sells his interest to Stella, Stella and Luis will become co-owners as tenants in common. If Stella dies, her interest in the personal property will pass to her heirs, and they in turn will own the property with Luis as tenants in common.

JOINT TENANCY In a **joint tenancy,** each of two or more persons owns an undivided interest in the whole (personal property), and a deceased joint tenant's interest *passes to the surviving joint tenant or tenants.* Joint tenancy can be terminated at any time before the joint tenant's death by gift or by sale. If no termination occurs, then on the death of a joint tenant, his or her interest transfers to the remaining joint tenants, not to the heirs of the deceased joint tenant. To illustrate: If Henri and Luis from the preceding example are joint tenants and if Henri dies before Luis, the entire collection will become the property of Luis. Henri's heirs will receive absolutely no interest in the collection. If Henri sells his interest to Stella, Stella and Luis will become co-owners. Henri's sale, however, will have terminated the joint tenancy, and Stella and Luis will become owners as tenants in common.

Exhibit 25–1 illustrates the concepts of tenancy in common and joint tenancy.

TENANCY BY THE ENTIRETY A **tenancy by the entirety** is created by a *conveyance* (transfer) of real property to a husband and wife. It is distinguished from a joint tenancy by the inability of either spouse to transfer separately his or her interest during his or her lifetime. In states in which statutes give the wife the right to convey her property, tenancy by the entirety has been effectively abolished. A divorce, either spouse's death, or mutual agreement will terminate a tenancy by the entirety.

COMMUNITY PROPERTY A limited number of states[4] allow property to be owned as **community property.** If property is held as community property, each spouse technically owns an *undivided* one-half interest in it. This type of ownership generally does not apply to property acquired prior to the marriage or to property acquired by gift or inheritance during the marriage.

4. These states include Arizona, California, Idaho, Louisiana, Nevada, New Mexico, Texas, Washington, and Wisconsin, as well as Puerto Rico.

EXHIBIT 25–1 ■ TENANCY IN COMMON AND JOINT TENANCY

If Henri and Luis own equal interests in a coin collection as tenants in common, and Henri dies, one-half of the coin collection will become the property of Henri's heirs. If instead Henri sells his interest to Stella, Stella and Luis will become co-owners as tenants in common. If Henri and Luis own the coin collection as joint tenants, however, and Henri dies, the entire collection will become the property of Luis. If instead Henri sells his interest to Stella, Luis and Stella will become co-owners as tenants in common.

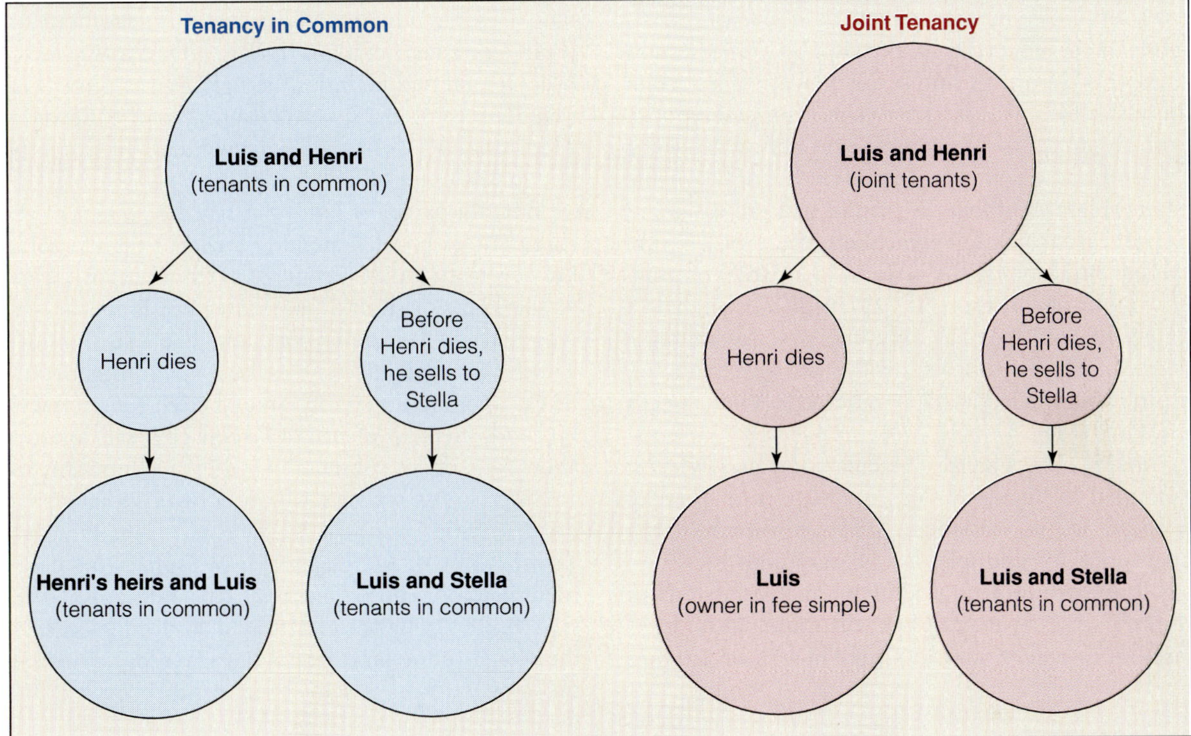

SECTION 3 PRIVATE CONTROL OF LAND USE

One source of land-use control is voluntary agreements between private individuals. A landowner's use of his or her property may be limited by another individual's right to, for example, cross the property. Such interests do not depend on the individual's possession of the property but still limit the use of the property. These interests may be created in a deed. Other promises included in a deed, or in an assignment, lease, mortgage, or other instrument relating to real property, may limit a landowner's use of his or her property in other ways. Here, we examine the ways in which private agreements serve as mechanisms for control of land use.

NONPOSSESSORY INTERESTS

Some interests in land do not include any rights of possession. These interests, known as nonpossessory interests, include *easements*, *profits*, and *licenses*. Because easements and profits are similar, and the same rules apply to both, they will be discussed together.

EASEMENTS AND PROFITS An **easement** is the right of a person to make limited use of another person's real property without taking anything from the property. Suppose Sara, the owner of Whiteacres, has a right to drive her car across Ken's land, Greenacres, which is adjacent to Whiteacres. This right-of-way over Greenacres is an easement. In contrast, a **profit** is the right to go onto land in possession of another and take away some part of the land itself or some product of the land. For example, Chen, the owner of Sea View, gives Loretta the right to go there and remove all the sand and gravel that she needs for her cement business. Loretta has a profit.[5]

Creation of an Easement or Profit. Profits and easements can be created by *deed* or *will* or by *implication*, *necessity*, or *prescription*. Creation by deed or will involves simply the delivery of a deed or a transfer by a will, by the owner of an easement or profit, stating that the grantee (the person receiving the profit or easement) is granted the rights in the easement or profit that the grantor had. An easement or profit is created by *implication* when the circumstances surrounding the division of a parcel of property imply its creation. If Adrian divides in half a parcel of land that has only one well for drinking water and conveys the half without a well to Victor, a profit by implication arises, because Victor needs drinking water.

An easement may also be created by *necessity*. An easement by necessity does not require division of property for its existence. A person who rents an apartment, for example, has an easement by necessity in the private road leading up to it. An easement or profit arises by *prescription* when one person exercises an easement, such as a right-of-way, on another person's land without the landowner's consent, and the use is apparent and continues for a period of time equal to the applicable statute of limitations.

Effect of a Sale of Property. When a parcel of land that is *benefited* by an easement or profit on adjacent land is sold, the property carries the easement or profit along with it. Thus, if Sara sells Whiteacres to MacDonald and includes the right-of-way across her neighbor Ken's land, Greenacres, in the deed to MacDonald, MacDonald will own both the property and the easement that benefits it.

When a parcel of land that has the *burden* of an easement or profit benefiting adjacent land is sold, the new owner must recognize its existence only if he or she knew or should have known of it or if it was recorded in the appropriate office of the county. Thus, if Sara records her easement across Greenacres in the appropriate county office before Ken conveys his land, the new owner of Greenacres will have to allow Sara, or any subsequent owner of Whiteacres, to continue to use the right-of-way across Greenacres.

Termination of an Easement or Profit. An easement or profit can be terminated or extinguished in several ways. The simplest way is to deed it back to the owner of the land that is burdened by it. Also, if the owner of an easement or profit becomes the owner of the property burdened by it, then it is merged into the property. Another way is to abandon the easement with the intent to relinquish the right to use it. In the following case, one of the questions was whether ceasing to use an easement for the purpose for which it was granted constitutes abandonment.

5. Easements and profits may be appurtenant or in gross. An easement or profit appurtenant arises when the owner of one piece of land has a right to go onto (or remove things from) an adjacent piece of land owned by another. An easement or profit in gross simply gives the owner of the easement or profit the right to go onto (or remove something from) land owned by another; there is no requirement that the owner of the easement or profit also own land.

CASE 25.3 Preseault v. United States

United States Court of Appeals, Federal Circuit, 1996. 100 F.3d 1525.

BACKGROUND AND FACTS *In 1899, Rutland-Canadian Railroad Company acquired an easement over land in Burlington, Vermont, on which it laid rails and operated a railroad. Over the years, ownership of the railroad passed through the hands of several different companies. At the same time, the land burdened by the easement also passed to different owners, until J. Paul and Patricia Preseault built a home on it. In 1970, the current owner of the railroad stopped using the line and, in 1975, removed the rails. Eleven years later, the state of Vermont asked the Interstate Commerce Commission (ICC)*[a] *to authorize a lease of the easement to the city of Burlington for use as a hiking and biking trail. The ICC granted the request, and the trail became popular—on warm*

a. The Interstate Commerce Commission was a federal agency with jurisdiction over railroad operations. It was abolished in 1996.

weekends, up to two hundred people per hour passed any given spot. The Preseaults filed a suit in the Court of Federal Claims against the federal government, claiming in part that the easement had been abandoned and thus, by authorizing the trail, the government had taken their property and they should be paid for it. The United States filed a motion for summary judgment, which the court granted. The Preseaults appealed.

IN THE LANGUAGE OF THE COURT

PLAGER, Circuit Judge.

* * * *

* * * [I]n 1986 when the ICC issued its Order authorizing the City to establish a public recreational biking and pedestrian trail on [the Preseaults' land], there was as a matter of state law no railroad easement in existence on [the land], nor had there been for more than ten years. The easement had been abandoned in 1975, and the properties were held by the Preseaults in fee simple, unencumbered by any former property rights of the Railroad. When the City, pursuant to federal authorization, took possession of [the land] and opened [it] to public use, that was a physical taking of the right of exclusive possession that belonged to the Preseaults as an incident of their ownership of the land.

DECISION AND REMEDY

The U.S. Court of Appeals for the Federal Circuit reversed the judgment of the lower court. When the railroad stopped using the line and removed the rails, it abandoned the easement. The court remanded the case for a determination of how much the Preseaults should be paid.

LICENSES A **license** is the revocable right of a person to come onto another person's land. It is a personal privilege that arises from the consent of the owner of the land and that can be revoked by the owner. A ticket to attend a movie at a theater is an example of a license. The ticket is only a revocable license, not a conveyance of an interest in property.

RESTRICTIVE COVENANTS

A private restriction on the use of land is known as a **restrictive covenant.** If the restriction is binding on the party who purchases the property originally as well as on subsequent purchasers—in other words, if its benefit or obligation passes with the land's ownership—it is said to "run with the land."

COVENANTS RUNNING WITH THE LAND A restrictive covenant that runs with the land goes with the land and cannot be separated from it. Consider an example. Owen is the owner of Grasslands, a twenty-acre estate whose northern half contains a small reservoir. Owen wishes to convey the northern half to Arid City, but before he does, he digs an irrigation ditch connecting the reservoir with the lower ten acres, which he uses as farmland. When Owen conveys the northern ten acres to Arid City, he enters into an agreement with the city. The agreement, which is contained in the deed, states, "Arid City, its heirs and assigns, promises not to remove more than five thousand gallons of water per day from the Grasslands reservoir." Owen has created a restrictive covenant running with the land under which Arid City and all future owners of the northern ten acres of Grasslands are limited as to the amount of water they can draw from its reservoir.

Four requirements must be met for a covenant running with the land to be enforceable. If they are not met, the covenant will apply to the two original parties to a contract only and will not run with the land to future owners. The requirements are as follows:

1. The covenant running with the land must be created in a written agreement (covenant). It is usually contained in the document that conveys the land.
2. The parties must intend that the covenant run with the land. In other words, the instrument that contains the covenant must state not only that the promisor is bound by the terms of the covenant but that all the promisor's "successors, heirs, or assigns" will be bound.

3. The covenant must touch and concern the land. That is, the limitations on the activities of the owner of the burdened land must have some connection with the land. For example, a purchaser of land cannot be bound by a covenant requiring him or her to drive only Ford pickups, because such a restriction has no relation to the land purchased.
4. The successors to the original parties to the covenant must have notice of the covenant.

To satisfy the last requirement, the notice may be actual or constructive. For example, in the course of developing a fifty-lot suburban subdivision, Levitt records a declaration of restrictions that effectively limits construction on each lot to one single-family house. In each lot's deed is a reference to the declaration with a provision that the purchaser and his or her successors are bound to those restrictions. Thus, each purchaser assumes ownership with notice of the restrictions. If an owner attempts to build a duplex (or any structure that does not comply with the restrictions) on a lot, the other owners may obtain a court order enjoining the construction.

In fact, Levitt might simply have included the restrictions on the subdivision's map, filed the map in the appropriate public office, and included a reference to the map in each deed. In this way, each owner would have been held to have constructive notice of the restrictions.

ILLEGAL RESTRICTIVE COVENANTS Restrictive covenants have sometimes been used to perpetuate neighborhood segregation, and in these cases they have been invalidated by the courts. In the United States Supreme Court case of *Shelley v. Kraemer,*[6] restrictive covenants proscribing resale to minority groups were declared unconstitutional and could no longer be enforced in courts of law. In addition, the Civil Rights Act of 1968 (also known as the Fair Housing Act) prohibits all discrimination based on race, color, religion, or national origin in the sale and leasing of housing.

SECTION 4

PUBLIC CONTROL OF LAND USE

Land use is subject to regulation by the state within whose political boundaries the land is located. Most states authorize control over land use through various planning boards and zoning authorities at a city or county level. The federal government does not engage in land-use control under normal circumstances, except with respect to federally owned land.[7] The federal government does influence state and local regulation, however, through the allocation of federal funds. Stipulations on land use may be a condition to the states' receiving such funds.

SOURCES OF PUBLIC CONTROL

The states' power to control the use of land through legislation is derived from their *police power* and the doctrine of *eminent domain.* Under their police power, state governments enact legislation that promotes the health, safety, and welfare of their citizens. This legislation includes land-use controls. The power of **eminent domain** is the government's authority to take private property for public use or purpose without the owner's consent. Typically, this is accomplished through a judicial proceeding to obtain title to the land.

POLICE POWER

As an exercise of its police power,[8] a state can regulate the use of land within its jurisdiction. A few states control land use at the state level. Hawaii, for instance, employs a statewide land-use classification scheme. Some states have a land-permit process that operates in conjunction with local control. Florida, for example, uses such a scheme in certain areas of "critical environmental concern" to permit or prohibit development on the basis of available roads, sewers, and so on. Vermont also utilizes a statewide land-permit scheme.

Usually, however, a state authorizes its city or county governments to regulate the use of land within their local jurisdictions. A state confers this power through *enabling legislation.* Enabling legislation normally requires local governments to devise *general plans* before imposing other land-use controls. Enabling acts also typically authorize local bod-

6. 334 U.S. 1, 68 S.Ct. 836, 92 L.Ed. 1161 (1948).

7. Federal (and state) laws concerning environmental matters such as air and water quality, the protection of endangered species, and the preservation of natural wetlands are also a source of land-use control. Some of these laws were discussed in Chapter 24.

8. As pointed out in Chapter 5, the police power of a state encompasses the right to regulate private activities to protect or promote the public order, health, safety, morals, and general welfare.

ies to enact *zoning laws* to regulate the use of land and the types of and specifications for structures. Local planning boards may regulate the development of subdivisions, in which private developers subdivide large tracts of land and construct commercial or residential units for resale to others. Local governments may also enact growth-management ordinances to control development in their jurisdictions.

GOVERNMENT PLANS Most states require that land-use laws follow a local government's general plan. A **general plan** is a comprehensive, long-term scheme dealing with the physical development, and in some cases redevelopment, of a city or community. It addresses such concerns as types of housing, protection of natural resources, provision of public facilities and transportation, and other issues related to land use. A plan indicates the direction of growth in a community and the contributions that private developers must make toward providing such public facilities as roads. If a proposed use is not authorized by the general plan, the plan may be amended to permit the use. (A plan may also be amended to preclude a proposed use.)

Even when a proposed use complies with a general plan, it may not be allowed. Most jurisdictions have requirements in addition to those in the general plan. These requirements are included in specific plans—also called special, area, or community plans. Specific plans typically pertain to only a portion of a jurisdiction's area. For example, a specific plan may concern a downtown area subject to redevelopment efforts, an area with special environmental concerns, or an area with increased public transportation needs arising from population growth.

ZONING LAWS In addition to complying with a general plan and any specific plans, a particular land use must comply with zoning laws. The term **zoning** refers to the dividing of an area into districts to which specific land-use regulations apply. A typical zoning law consists of a zoning map and a zoning ordinance. The zoning map indicates the characteristics of each parcel of land within an area and divides that area into districts. The zoning ordinance specifies the restrictions on land use within those districts.

Zoning ordinances generally include two types of restrictions. One type pertains to the kind of land use—such as commercial versus residential—to which property within a particular district may be put. The second type dictates the engineering features and architectural design of structures built within that district.

Use Restrictions. Districts are typically zoned for residential, commercial, industrial, or agricultural use. Each district may be further subdivided for degree or intensity of use. For example, a residential district may be subdivided to permit a certain number of apartment buildings and a certain number of units in each building. Commercial and industrial districts are often zoned to permit *heavy* or *light* activity. Heavy activity might include the operation of large factories. Light activity might include the operation of professional office buildings or small retail shops. Zoning that specifies the use to which property may be put is referred to as **use zoning.**

Structural Restrictions. Restrictions known as *bulk regulations* cover such details as minimum floor-space requirements and minimum lot-size restrictions. For example, a particular district's minimum floor-space requirements might specify that a one-story building contain a minimum of 1,240 square feet of floor space, and minimum lot-size restrictions might specify that each single-family dwelling be built on a lot that is at least one acre in size. Referred to collectively as **bulk zoning,** these regulations also dictate *setback* (the distance between a building and a street, sidewalk, or other boundary) and the height of buildings, with different requirements for buildings in different areas.

Restrictions related to structure may also be concerned with such matters as architectural control, the overall appearance of a community, and the preservation of historic buildings. An ordinance may require that all proposed construction be approved by a design review board composed of local architects. A community may restrict the size and placement of outdoor advertising, such as billboards and business signs. A property owner may be prohibited from tearing down or remodeling a historic landmark or building. In challenges against these types of restrictions, the courts have generally upheld the regulations.[9]

Variances. A **zoning variance** allows property to be used or structures to be built in some way that varies from the restrictions of a zoning ordinance. A vari-

9. See, for example, *Penn Central Transportation Co. v. New York City*, 438 U.S. 104, 98 S.Ct. 2646, 57 L.Ed.2d 631 (1978).

ance may exempt property from a use restriction to allow, for example, a bakery shop in a residential area. Or a variance may exempt a building from a height restriction so that, for example, a two-story house can be built in a district in which houses are otherwise limited to one floor. Some jurisdictions do not permit variances from use restrictions.

Variances are normally granted by local adjustment boards. In general, a property owner must meet three criteria to obtain a variance:

1. The owner must find it impossible to realize a reasonable return on the land as currently zoned.
2. The adverse effect of the zoning ordinance must be particular to the party seeking the variance and not have a similar effect on other owners in the same zone.
3. Granting the variance must not substantially alter the essential character of the zoned area.

Perhaps the most important of these criteria is whether the variance would substantially alter the character of the area. Courts are more lenient about the other requirements when reviewing decisions of adjustment boards. As the following case illustrates, courts also tend to defer to the discretion of such boards unless there has been a clear abuse of authority.

CASE 25.4 Allegheny West Civic Council, Inc. v. Zoning Board of Adjustment of the City of Pittsburgh

Supreme Court of Pennsylvania, 1997.
689 A.2d 225.

BACKGROUND AND FACTS *Irwin Associates, Inc., contracted to sell, for $431,500, a vacant lot in an area in Pittsburgh, Pennsylvania, zoned for residential use. The deal collapsed when it was learned that the lot was contaminated with petroleum hydrocarbon and benzene in excess of state and federal guidelines. Estimated clean-up costs were $2.5 million to $3 million, with additional annual monitoring costs of $10,000 to $20,000. Irwin asked the Pittsburgh Zoning Board of Adjustment for a variance to use the property as a parking lot. Allegheny West Civic Council wanted residential housing in the area and opposed Irwin's request. The board concluded that Irwin's proposed use would not be detrimental to the neighborhood and granted the variance. Allegheny West appealed to a Pennsylvania state court, which affirmed the board's decision. Ultimately, the case was appealed to the state supreme court.*

IN THE LANGUAGE OF THE COURT

NIGRO, Justice.

* * * *

Irwin Associates' environmental consultant testified that the contamination exceeded state and federal guidelines and that a building on the property may be a health hazard because vapors could accumulate inside. Its real estate financing expert testified that it was unlikely that a financial institution would lend money for a construction project on the property because it would expose itself to potential liability for [clean-up] costs. Irwin Associates' president testified that the relatively small size of the lot precluded other permitted uses not involving improvements. The environmental consultant estimated that the [clean-up] cost would be $2.5 [million] to $3 million and annual monitoring costs would be $10,000 to $20,000. There is thus substantial evidence that Irwin Associates cannot use the property for a permitted purpose or can only conform it for a permitted purpose at a prohibitive cost. Furthermore, * * * there is evidence that the property is now without value as zoned. The local property assessment board assigned the property a fair market value of zero.

The Zoning Board did not abuse its discretion * * * in granting the variance.

DECISION AND REMEDY *The Supreme Court of Pennsylvania affirmed the board's decision to grant the variance. The variant use would not harm the character of the neighborhood, and denying the variance would create unnecessary hardship for the property owner.*

SUBDIVISION REGULATIONS When subdividing a parcel of land into smaller plots, a private developer must comply not only with local zoning ordinances but also with local subdivision regulations. Subdivision regulations are different from zoning ordinances, although they may be administered by the same local agencies that oversee the zoning process. In the design of a subdivision, the local authorities may demand, for example, the allocation of space for a public park or school or may require a developer to construct streets to accommodate a specific level of traffic.

GROWTH-MANAGEMENT ORDINANCES To prevent population growth from racing ahead of the community's ability to provide necessary public services, local authorities may enact a growth-management ordinance to limit, for example, the number of residential building permits. A property owner may thus be precluded from constructing a residential building on his or her property even if the area is zoned for the use and the proposed structure complies with all other requirements. A growth-management ordinance may prohibit the issuance of residential building permits for a specific period of time, until the occurrence of a specific event (such as a decline in the total number of residents in the community), or on the basis of the availability of necessary public services (such as the capacity for drainage in the area or the proximity of hospitals and police stations).

LIMITATIONS ON THE EXERCISE OF POLICE POWER The government's exercise of its police power to regulate the use of land is limited in at least three ways. Two of these limitations arise under the Fourteenth Amendment to the Constitution. The third limitation arises under the Fifth Amendment and requires that, under certain circumstances, the government must compensate an owner who is deprived of the use of his or her property.

Due Process and Equal Protection. A government cannot regulate the use of land in a way that violates either the due process clause or the equal protection clause of the Fourteenth Amendment. A government may be deemed to violate the due process clause if it acts arbitrarily or unreasonably. Thus, there must be a *rational basis* for classifications that are imposed on property. Any classification that is reasonably related to the health or general welfare of the public is deemed to have a rational basis.

Under the equal protection clause, land-use controls cannot be discriminatory. A zoning ordinance is discriminatory if it affects one parcel of land in a way in which it does not affect surrounding parcels and if there is no rational basis for the difference. For example, classifying a single parcel in a way that does not accord with a general plan is discriminatory. Similarly, a zoning ordinance cannot be racially discriminatory. For example, a community may not zone itself to exclude all low-income housing if the intention is to exclude minorities.

The following case involved a challenge to a classification in a zoning ordinance on the ground that there was no rational basis for it.

CASE 25.5 Kirsch v. Prince George's County

Court of Appeals of Maryland, 1993.
331 Md. 89,
626 A.2d 372.

COMPANY PROFILE *The University of Maryland, established in 1807, is an internationally recognized university community that is annually expanding enrollment and its scope of degree offerings. The university's largest campus is within a mile of College Park, Maryland, which is located nine miles from Washington, D.C. The University of Maryland is a public, four-year, coeducational, liberal arts university offering undergraduate and graduate programs. Among its facilities are a center for architectural design and research, a model nuclear reactor, and a wind tunnel. More than two-thirds of the students live off campus.*

BACKGROUND AND FACTS *Donald Kirsch and Martha Kaye Dunn owned residential property in Prince George's County, Maryland. Kirsch and Dunn wished to rent their property to students. Stephanie Stockman and Daniel Cones were students at the University of Maryland who lived off campus in Prince George's County. In 1989, the county council enacted a "mini-dorm"* *zoning ordinance. The ordinance regulated the rental of residential property to persons "who are registered full-time or part-time students at an institution of higher learning." The ordinance imposed restrictions that were intended to address complaints about the noise, litter, and parking of mini-dorm residents from other residents of College Park, near the site of the principal campus of the University of Maryland. The ordinance took effect on July 1, 1990. On July 3, Kirsch, Dunn, Stockman, and Cones filed a lawsuit against the county, seeking a declaration that the ordinance was invalid. The plaintiffs argued in part that the ordinance discriminated against students as a classification in violation of the Fourteenth Amendment. The county filed a motion for summary judgment, and the court granted the motion. The plaintiffs appealed.*

IN THE LANGUAGE OF THE COURT

KARWACKI, Judge.

* * * *

The crucial question for this Court is whether the County by adopting the ordinance's classification advances its objective of clearing residential neighborhoods of noise, litter, and parking congestion within the command of the Equal Protection Clause of the Fourteenth Amendment * * * . We hold that it does not. To differentiate between permissible residential tenant classes by creating more strenuous zoning requirements for some and less for others based solely on the occupation which the tenant pursues away from that residence is that sort of arbitrary classification forbidden under our [Constitution].

* * * *

* * * [T]he Prince George's County "mini-dorm" ordinance does not differentiate based on the nature of the use of the property, such as a fraternity house or a lodging house, but rather on the occupation of the persons who would dwell therein. Therefore, under the ordinance a landlord of a building * * * is permitted to rent the same for occupancy * * * so long as [the tenants] are not pursuing a higher education without incurring the burdens of complying with the arduous requirements of the ordinance. Such occupancy would equally add motor vehicles to a congested parking situation and pose the threat of increased noise and litter. Such a zoning classification of residential property is wholly unrelated to the stated purpose of the ordinance, and its impact upon persons who are registered as full-time or part-time students at an institution of higher learning denies those students equal protection of the laws under the Fourteenth Amendment to the United States Constitution * * * .

DECISION AND REMEDY *The Maryland Court of Appeals reversed the judgment of the lower court and remanded the case for a declaration that the mini-dorm ordinance was invalid.*

Just Compensation. Under the Fifth Amendment, private property may not be taken for a public purpose without the payment of just compensation.[10] If government restrictions on a landowner's property rights are overly burdensome, the regulation may be deemed a **taking.** A taking occurs when a regulation denies an owner the ability to use his or her property for any reasonable income-producing or private purpose for which it is suited. This requires the government to pay the owner.

Suppose Perez purchases a large tract of land with the intent to subdivide and develop it into residential properties. At the time of the purchase, there are no zoning laws restricting use of the land. After Perez has taken significant steps to develop the property, the county attempts to zone the tract "public park-

10. Although the Fifth Amendment pertains to actions taken by the federal government, the Fourteenth Amendment has been interpreted as extending this limitation to state actions.

land only." If this prohibits Perez from developing any of the land, it will be deemed a taking. If the county does not fairly compensate Perez, the regulation will be held unconstitutional and void.

The distinction between an ordinance that merely restricts land use and an outright taking is crucial. A restriction is simply an exercise of the state's police power; even though it limits a property owner's land use, the owner generally need not be compensated for the limitation. An ordinance that completely deprives an owner of use or benefit of property, or an outright governmental taking of property, however, must be compensated.

The United States Supreme Court has held that restrictions do not constitute a taking of an owner's property if they "substantially advance legitimate state interests" and do not "den[y] an owner economically viable use of his land."[11] It is not clear, however, exactly what constitutes a "legitimate state interest" or when particular restrictions "substantially advance" that interest. Furthermore, the term "economically viable use" has not yet been clearly defined. One of the issues in the following case was whether the focus should be on the value of the land or the use to which it could be put.

11. *Agins v. Tiburon*, 447 U.S. 255, 100 S.Ct. 2138, 65 L.Ed. 2d 106 (1980).

CASE 25.6 Del Monte Dunes at Monterey, Ltd. v. City of Monterey

United States Court of Appeals, Ninth Circuit, 1996. 95 F.3d 1422.

BACKGROUND AND FACTS *The owners of ocean-front property in the City of Monterey, California, applied to the city several times for a permit to build a residential development. Del Monte Dunes at Monterey, Limited, bought the property and continued to seek a permit. Each time, the city denied use of more of the property, until no part remained available for any use that would be inconsistent with leaving the property in its natural state. Del Monte sold the property to the state for $800,000 more than it had paid for the property and filed a suit against the city in a federal district court. Del Monte claimed in part that the restrictions on use were an unconstitutional taking. The court awarded Del Monte nearly $1.5 million in damages, and the city appealed, arguing in part that because Del Monte sold the property to the state for more than it had paid, there must have been economically viable uses for the property.*

IN THE LANGUAGE OF THE COURT

WALLACE, Circuit Judge:

* * * *

* * * The fact that [a property owner] received some money from the government in return for his property does not establish as a matter of law that economically viable uses for his property remain or that a taking did not occur.

Focusing the economically viable use inquiry solely on market value or on the fact that a landowner sold his property for more than he paid could inappropriately allow external economic forces, such as inflation, to affect the takings inquiry. * * * [O]ur focus is primarily on use, not value.

* * *

Del Monte contended that the City denied it all economically viable use of the Dunes by requiring it to leave the property in its natural state. * * * . In support of its argument, Del Monte presented evidence establishing that the City progressively denied use of portions of the Dunes until no part remained available for a use inconsistent with leaving the property in its natural state.

* * * *

* * * [T]his evidence, viewed in the light most favorable to Del Monte, supports the jury's finding that the City's actions denied all economically viable use of the Dunes * * * .

DECISION AND REMEDY *The U.S. Court of Appeals for the Ninth Circuit affirmed the jury's award. The restrictions on the property's use amounted to an unconstitutional taking, and Del Monte was entitled to damages.*

INTERNATIONAL CONSIDERATIONS **Takings Law in Germany** *Like the U.S. Constitution, the German constitution places restraints on government's ability to take private property for public use. The German constitution first affirmatively establishes the right of the government to take private property for public use and then requires some payment to the landowner for the property that is taken. The German constitution also states that private property owners have a duty to use their property for the public good.*

EMINENT DOMAIN

As noted above, governments have an inherent power to take property for public use or purpose without the consent of the owner. This is the power of eminent domain, and it is very important in the public control of land use.

Every property owner holds his or her interest in land subject to a superior interest. Just as in medieval England the king was the ultimate landowner, so in the United States the government retains an ultimate ownership right in all land. This right, known as eminent domain, is sometimes referred to as the *condemnation power* of the government to take land for public use. It gives to the government a right to acquire possession of real property in the manner directed by the Constitution and the laws of the state whenever the public interest requires it. Property may not be taken for private benefit, but only for public use.

For example, when a new public highway is to be built, the government must decide where to build it and how much land to condemn. After the government determines that a particular parcel of land is necessary for public use, it brings a judicial proceeding to obtain title to the land.

Under the Fifth Amendment, although the government may take land for public use, it must pay fair and just compensation for it. Thus, in the previous highway example, after the proceeding to obtain title to the land, there is a second proceeding in which the court determines the *fair value* of the land. Fair value is usually approximately equal to market value. The just compensation requirement was at the heart of the following case, in which the court considered a claim for compensation based, in part, on the public's perception of a health risk.

CASE 25.7 Criscuola v. Power Authority of the State of New York

Court of Appeals of New York, 1993. 81 N.Y.2d 649, 621 N.E.2d 1195, 602 N.Y.S.2d 588.

BACKGROUND AND FACTS *Joseph Criscuola owned property in Delaware County in the state of New York. To run a high-voltage power line through the county, the Power Authority of the State of New York (PASNY) acquired an easement across Criscuola's property and the property of his neighbors, through the state's power of eminent domain. In a proceeding to determine how much Criscuola and his neighbors were to be paid, the property owners sought, among other compensation, an amount representing "cancerphobia" and the public's perception that exposure to electromagnetic emissions from power lines poses a health risk. The owners argued that this perception reduced the market value of their property—that the power line meant they would not be able to sell their property except at a low price. The court held that the owners had failed to prove that the public's "cancerphobia" was reasonable and denied the claim. On*

appeal, the owners contended that they did not have to prove that such fears were reasonable to recover compensation in an eminent domain proceeding.

IN THE LANGUAGE OF THE COURT

BELLACOSA, Judge.

* * * *

* * * The issue in a just compensation proceeding is whether or not the market value has been adversely affected. This consequence may be present even if the public's fear is unreasonable. Whether the danger is a scientifically genuine or verifiable fact should be irrelevant to the central issue of its market value impact. * * * Logic and fairness * * * dictate that any loss of market value proven with a reasonable degree of probability should be compensable, regardless of its source. If no one will buy a residential lot because it has a high voltage line across it, the lot is a total loss even though the owner has the legal right to build a house on it. If buyers can be found, but only at half the value it had before the line was installed, the owner has suffered a 50% loss. * * *

* * * *

We, of course, do not hold that claimants are relieved from giving any proof to establish their claims and just compensation damages. * * * This standard protects, as a countermeasure, the legitimate * * * concern against spurious claims and unjust encroachments against the public treasury. Some credible, tangible evidence that a fear is prevalent must be presented to prove the adverse market value impact. * * *

To add the extra component of reasonableness, as PASNY urges, * * * is not supportable or necessary. Thus, while a personal or quirky fear or perception is not proof enough, the public's or the market's relatively more prevalent perception should suffice, scientific certitude or reasonableness notwithstanding.

DECISION AND REMEDY

The New York Court of Appeals reversed the decision of the lower court and remanded the case for a further determination of the amount that the property owners were to be compensated.

TERMS AND CONCEPTS TO REVIEW

QUESTIONS AND CASE PROBLEMS

25–1. OWNERSHIP OF REAL PROPERTY. Glenn is the owner of a lakeside house and lot. He deeds the house and lot to "my wife, Livia, for life, then to my daughter, Sarina." Given these facts, answer the following questions:

(a) Does Glenn have any ownership interest in the lakeside house after making these transfers? Explain.

(b) What is Livia's interest called? Is there any limitation on her rights to use the property as she wishes? Discuss.

(c) What is Sarina's interest called? Explain.

25–2. EASEMENTS AND PROFITS. Murray owns 640 acres of rural land. A new highway is being built nearby by Ajax Corporation, Inc. Ajax purchases from Murray the rights to build and use a road across Murray's land for construction vehicles to pass over and to remove sand and gravel required to build the highway. A deed is prepared and filed in the county by Ajax. Later, a dispute arises between Murray and Ajax, and Murray refuses Ajax the right to use the road or to remove sand and gravel. Ajax claims its property rights cannot be revoked by Murray. Discuss fully what property rights Ajax has in this matter.

25–3. LIMITATIONS ON POLICE POWER. The county intends to rezone an area from industrial use to residential use. Land within the affected area is largely undeveloped, but nonetheless it is expected that the proposed action will reduce the market value of the affected land by as much as 50 percent. Will landowners be successful in suing to have the action declared a taking of their property, entitling them to just compensation?

25–4. SUBDIVISION REGULATIONS. Suppose that as a condition of a developer's receiving approval for constructing a new residential community, the local authorities insist that the developer dedicate, or set aside, land for a new hospital. The hospital would serve not only the proposed residential community but also the rest of the city. If the developer challenges the condition in court, under what standard might the court invalidate the condition?

25–5. GROWTH-MANAGEMENT ORDINANCES. To prevent population growth from racing ahead of the local government's ability to provide adequate police and fire protection, as well as road development for the increase in traffic, the local planning board imposes an ordinance limiting the issuance of residential building permits to one thousand per year for the next three years. A property developer who owns several tracts zoned for residential housing and whose development plans comply with all other existing ordinances challenges the ban in court. Will she succeed? Discuss all the relevant issues. What difference would it make if the developer had already expended considerable resources and taken the last step toward approval of the development project?

25–6. EMINENT DOMAIN AND JUST COMPENSATION. Americana Superfood, Inc., owned a supermarket on East Jefferson Avenue in Detroit. Charles Murphy was a physician and owner of a health-care facility in the same neighborhood. The city of Detroit used the power of eminent domain to acquire land nearby for two urban renewal projects. On the land were more than 1,400 residential properties that were razed as part of the project. This resulted in the relocation of approximately 17,000 residents from the area. When the people moved away, Americana and Murphy lost 75 percent of their business. Americana and Murphy brought an action against Detroit, alleging that the city's acquisition of the surrounding property amounted to a taking of their property interest. They defined their "property interest" as the expectation that the neighborhood would remain a residential area in which their businesses could operate profitably. Is such an expectation a property interest? How should the court rule? [*Charles Murphy, M.D., P.C. v. City of Detroit,* 506 N.W.2d 5 (Mich.App. 1993)]

25–7. EASEMENTS. Merton Peterson owned a golf course, a supper club, and the parking lot between them. Both golfers and club patrons always parked in the lot. Peterson sold the club and the lot to the American Legion, which sold them to VBC, Inc. (owned by Richard Beck and others). When VBC demanded rent from Peterson for use of the lot, Peterson filed a suit in a South Dakota state court to determine title. On what basis might the court hold that Peterson has an easement for the use of the lot? Does Peterson have an easement? [*Peterson v. Beck,* 537 N.W.2d 375 (S.Dak. 1995)]

25–8. TAKING. Richard and Jaquelyn Jackson owned property in a residential subdivision near an airport operated by the Metropolitan Knoxville Airport Authority in Blount County, Tennessee. The Airport Authority considered extending a runway near the subdivision and undertook a study that found that the noise, vibration, and pollution from aircraft using the extension would render the Jacksons' property incompatible with residential use. The airport built the extension, bringing about the predicted results, and the Jacksons filed a suit against the Airport Authority, alleging a taking of their property. The Airport Authority responded that there was no taking because there were no direct flights over the Jacksons' property. In whose favor will the court rule, and why? [*Jackson v. Metropolitan Knoxville Airport Authority,* 922 S.W.2d 860 (Tenn. 1996)]

25–9. LIMITATIONS ON POLICE POWER. John and Florence Dolan owned the A-Boy West Hardware store in downtown Tigard, Oregon. Wanting to expand the store and its parking lot, the Dolans applied to the city for a permit. Under the local zoning regulations, the city could attach conditions to downtown development to provide for projected public needs. The city told the Dolans that they could expand if they would dedicate a portion of their property for the improvement of a storm drainage system and dedicate an additional strip of land as a pedestrian and bicycle path. The dedication would involve about 10 percent of the Dolans' property. The Dolans sought a variance, which the city denied, and the Dolans appealed. The city claimed that there was a sufficient connection between the expansion of the store and the dedication requirements, because the expansion would increase traffic to the area and would also increase storm runoff. The Dolans conceded that there would be increases but contended that the increases would not be enough to justify taking 10 percent of their property. The Dolans claimed that the city's condition was an uncompensated taking of their property in violation of the Fifth Amendment. How should the court rule? Discuss fully. [*Dolan v. City of Tigard*, 512 U.S. 374, 114 S.Ct. 2309, 129 L.Ed.2d 304 (1994)]

25–10. A QUESTION OF ETHICS

Lorenz and his wife purchased a home in Florissant, Missouri. Although the title to the property did not indicate it, the home had been designated as a landmark building. Lorenz later sought a variance that would have allowed him to make certain building changes, such as the installation of vinyl siding on the home. The local council denied the request. Lorenz later learned that the Weslings, an elderly couple whose home was also designated as a landmark building, had been granted a variance similar to the one Lorenz had sought. Lorenz argued that the discrepancy demonstrated that the council's decision had been arbitrary and capricious. The council members contended that they were within their discretion in allowing the Weslings' variance because of the Weslings' advanced age and because the Weslings had apparently been unaware of the ordinance at the time they made their modifications. On review, a court upheld the council's actions as being a proper exercise of discretion. [*Lorenz v. City of Florissant*, 787 S.W.2d 776 (Mo.App. 1990)]

1. Were the Weslings and Lorenz "similarly situated," as Lorenz argued? Lorenz offered evidence that he, too, suffered from physical hardship, but that evidence was contradicted by other evidence. Nonetheless, should the council have limited its inquiry and based its decision solely on property-related issues?
2. Given that the underlying rationale of all zoning and other forms of land-use control is the well-being of the community, do you agree that the council did what was ethically right by allowing special consideration for the Weslings? Alternatively, was Lorenz forced to bear a disproportionate share of the burden by being denied an identical variance? After all, the city could have uniformly enforced the ordinance and simply used tax dollars collected from the community to pay for a change in the structure of the Weslings' home so as to comply with the zoning ordinance. In this way, the landmarks would have been conserved *and* the Weslings would have been protected from hardship.

ACCESSING THE INTERNET
THE LEGAL ENVIRONMENT OF BUSINESS

Cornell Law University's Legal Information Institute has links to state statutes governing property for several of the states. To access these statutes, go to

http://fatty.law.cornell.edu/topics/state_statutes.html

Homes and Communities is a Web site offered by the U.S. Department of Housing and Urban Development. Information of interest to both consumers and businesses is available at this site, which can be accessed at

http://www.hud.gov/

The Internet Law Library of the House of Representatives offers extensive links to sources of law relating to real estate. Go to

http://law.house.gov/home.htm

CHAPTER 26

ANTITRUST AND MONOPOLY

THE ENVIRONMENT OF BUSINESS is generally one of competition among rival firms. In free and open competition, businesses attempt to develop and sell products that are more appealing to customers than are the products of rival firms. Competition among sellers therefore promotes the development of appealing products. When products sold by different firms are similar, firms compete by trying to sell at the lowest price possible while still earning enough after costs to make it worthwhile to remain in that particular endeavor. For example, if Acme, Inc., develops a new digital video disc (DVD) drive that has broad appeal among consumers, it will begin to earn profits greater than those of its rivals—profits commensurate with the appeal of its new product. All else being equal, the greater the appeal of Acme's DVD drive, the greater its profits.

The legal environment of business is premised on encouraging innovative, competitive business behavior. The law attempts to prevent and correct conduct that interferes with free and open competition. The law is concerned with two broad categories of behavior: conduct that leads to or tends to produce *monopoly power* and conduct that is an unreasonable *restraint of trade*. In this chapter, we consider the federal laws that deal with individual firms' behavior leading to or tending to create monopolies. In Chapter 27, we discuss in detail the federal laws that regulate activities that restrain competition.

SECTION 1

MARKET POWER

To encourage innovative behavior, we might feel justified in allowing Acme to have a *monopoly* over the sale of the DVD drive, at least for a while—say seventeen years, which is the duration of a patent. The term **monopoly** is generally used to describe a market in which there is a single seller. In that respect, Acme would be a monopolist, albeit for a limited time, in the DVD drive market. In legal terms, *monopolist* may also describe a firm that, although not the sole seller in the market, can nonetheless substantially ignore rival firms in setting a selling price for its product or can in some way limit rivals from competing in the market (possibly by preventing rivals from entering the market altogether). Acme's monopoly would give it **market power** (the power of a firm to control the market for its product). Acme would have the power during the term of its monopoly to prevent other firms from selling the DVD drive. Acme would be free to charge whatever price it chose to, and it would choose a price that made its profits as large as possible.

COMPETITIVE BEHAVIOR

Another firm might seek to develop a different type of DVD drive, one with appeal equal to or greater than Acme's DVD drive. If it succeeded, it would draw customers away from Acme. It too might seek a legal monopoly over its product. There would then be two monopolies rather than one, but society would have the benefit of two unique and valued products. Moreover, Acme would be concerned that if it charged too high a price for its DVD drive, it would lose customers to its rival. Acme's rival would have the same concern over the price of its product.

Eventually, after the legal monopolies expired, numerous firms would be allowed to market identical products. Each firm would seek to attract customers by charging the lowest price. The only thing that would prevent prices from falling ever lower is that at some point the price of a DVD drive would be so low that new firms would quit trying to enter the market to compete for DVD drive consumers. They would instead devote their efforts and resources to alternative, more profitable ventures. Ultimately, the DVD drive would sell for a competitive price—one that would, of course, cover the costs of production, as well as earn a return equal to that which could be earned by employing the same resources in an alternative industry.

THE GOALS OF ANTITRUST LAW

The scenario described above highlights the benefits to society of having firms develop, produce, and sell goods and services, even though obtaining those benefits may involve conferring a limited monopoly such as that given to Acme. Our scenario should make clear an often overlooked point: market power is not inherently bad. Market power can correlate to high profits, which are the reward for innovation, foresight, and good management. Market power is the prize that motivates firms to benefit society with innovative products and competitive prices.

What is at issue is not market power *per se* but how firms go about acquiring market power and what firms do with that power once they acquire it. **Antitrust law** is the body of statutes and principles that regulate business conduct so as to promote the forms of competition that benefit society while simultaneously seeking to rein in the exercise of market power that often is the fruit of such competition.

SECTION 2

THE COMMON LAW AND THE RESTRAINT OF TRADE

Socially beneficial commercial activity involves cooperation, as well as competition. A business firm, for example, may compete with certain companies in some markets but cooperate with other companies in other markets. A firm that sells finished goods directly to the public may itself act as a consumer by purchasing intermediate products from a second firm. In this sense, the two companies act cooperatively rather than competitively, at least vis-à-vis one another. Similarly, two firms may cooperate to develop or market a new product.

PUBLIC POLICY AND CONTRACTS

Any mutual effort that calls for more than a brief period of sustained cooperation requires commitment from all the parties. The principal means of ensuring such a sustained commitment is through a contract between the parties. Most cooperative efforts among business firms, in fact, are embodied in some form of contract. But a principle of the common law of contracts is that no contract is enforceable if it is against public policy.

ECONOMIC EFFICIENCY Many contracts between business firms promote competition. Because competition, as noted above, is beneficial to society, such contracts are not against public policy. A contract may provide assurances that one firm will be able to obtain necessary inputs from another on a long-term basis. Similarly, a contract may provide assurances to two firms entering into a joint venture that each will continue fulfilling its obligation to the project beyond the initial investment stage. In both these instances, the rights and remedies afforded by contract law promote economic efficiency. Such agreements are not against public policy.

RESTRAINTS OF TRADE Some agreements between business firms, however, may reduce competition. An agreement between two bakers to coordinate their production of bread so as to limit output and charge a uniform, higher price might entirely eliminate competition in the affected market. If the two bakers were the only suppliers in the market, their combining together would in effect create a joint monopoly under which they would share exclusive control over the market. Such an agreement would be condemned under the common law as an *unreasonable restraint of trade.*

Consider, though, a restaurant owner who decides to sell her restaurant to the manager. The manager might demand that, as a condition of the sale, the owner refrain from opening another restaurant across the street. Should such an agreement be condemned as against public policy? At first glance, it is a restraint of trade: it prevents the local community from benefiting from the restauranting skills of the owner. If the agreement were not enforced, however, the manager, who was willing to pay a price commensurate with the current earnings of the restaurant, would not recover the price paid (the investment); customers would probably follow the owner with the established reputation to her new restaurant across the street from the old one.

If the manager knew beforehand that the agreement would not be enforced, it would be the owner who would suffer, because the manager would not be willing to pay a price reflecting the expectation that the earnings of the restaurant would continue at the current level. Society might consider enforcing such agreements in spite of the restraint of trade so that entrepreneurs who contemplate opening new businesses will be ensured of later being able to sell those businesses at full value. If others know that sellers will be held to the promise not to compete, the sellers can sell their businesses for more than they could if such promises were condemned as being against public policy.

INTERFERENCE WITH FREE TRADE

Compare the two agreements just discussed. Both interfere with free trade. The first involves outright collusion between two competitors (the bakers) to completely eliminate competition between themselves. Their agreement calls for artificially driving prices higher by restricting output. The second agreement (the one between the restaurant owner and the manager) also restrains trade, but the restraint is not the primary purpose of the agreement. The restraint is really the only means of ensuring that both parties to the sale of an established restaurant can reap the full benefit of their bargain: the sale of the restaurant for its highest value. The second agreement thus can be viewed as reasonable given that it is the only means of achieving a legitimate end. It also has offsetting benefits in that it encourages entrepreneurship by allowing the owner to sell her business for its highest value.

SECTION 3
THE ORIGINS OF FEDERAL ANTITRUST LEGISLATION

Despite condemning anticompetitive agreements on the basis of public policy, the common law proved to be an ineffective means of protecting free competition. There are temptations for business firms to agree to limit competition or to harm other rivals. Such agreements, to be sure, are unenforceable, because they are held to be against public policy. But the problem under the common law is that such agreements are left unchallenged unless one of the parties to an agreement refuses to abide by its terms. *Unenforceable* means only that a court will not sanction a party that reneges on its promise; it does not mean that a forum will be provided in which anticompetitive agreements can be challenged by others who are not parties to the agreements. These shortcomings became acutely obvious in the United States during the latter half of the 1800s as a concentrated group of powerful individuals began to acquire unrivaled market power by combining competing firms under singular control.

THE TREND TOWARD MONOPOLY

After the Civil War ended, the nation renewed its drive westward. With the movement westward came the expansion of the railroads—which soon developed into monopolies—and the further integration of the economy. The growth of national markets also motivated a number of small companies to combine into large business organizations, many of which gained considerable market power. These large organizations became known as **trusts,** the most famous—or infamous—being John D. Rockefeller's Standard Oil Trust. In general, a trust is an arrangement in which some party, referred to as a trustee, holds legal title to property for the benefit of another. As used by Standard Oil and others around the turn of the century, trusts were a device to amass market power. The participants transferred their stock to a trustee and in return received trust certificates. The trustee then made decisions fixing prices, controlling output, and allocating geographical markets in which specified members could compete free from competition with other members.

In some cases, an entire industry was dominated by a single organization. The public perception was that the trusts used their market power to drive small competitors out of business, leaving the trusts free to raise prices virtually at will.[1]

THE FEDERAL RESPONSE

Congress initially dealt with the railroad monopolies, attempting regulation rather than an outright assault on monopoly power. The result was the Interstate Commerce Act of 1887.[2]

Congress next attempted to deal with trusts in a direct, unified way by passing the Sherman Act in 1890.[3] The Sherman Act is a broadly worded pronouncement that prohibits competitors from making agreements that unreasonably restrain trade and condemns conduct leading to or tending to produce monopoly power. Violations of the Sherman Act are criminal offenses, as well as civil ones.

The Sherman Act, however, failed to end public concerns over monopolies. The United States Supreme Court initially construed the statute too narrowly to give it much effect and subsequently applied it so rigorously as to make the act unworkable. Lackluster enforcement also contributed to the public's dissatisfaction. Concern over the trust problem dominated the 1912 presidential election and eventually, in 1914, led to enactment of the Clayton Act[4] and the Federal Trade Commission Act.[5] This legislation sought to deal with the monopoly problem by proscribing specific acts and providing for more aggressive means of enforcement.

The Clayton Act (as amended by the Robinson-Patman Act in 1936 and the Celler-Kefauver Act of 1950) addresses specific practices that are considered to be anticompetitive. The Federal Trade Commission Act created the Federal Trade Commission and invested it with broad enforcement powers to *prevent,* as well as correct, business behavior broadly defined as *unfair trade practices.*

In the remainder of this chapter, we consider the federal legislation in more detail and examine the means of enforcement. We also examine the narrower area of antitrust law that deals with individual firms' behavior leading to or tending to create monopolies. We reserve for Chapter 27 the broader area of antitrust law that deals with all forms of joint activities that restrain competition.

SECTION 4

OVERVIEW OF THE MAJOR FEDERAL ANTITRUST LAWS

The major pieces of federal antitrust legislation—the Sherman Act, the Clayton Act, and the Federal Trade Commission Act—are briefly outlined below and discussed in more detail later in this chapter and in Chapter 27.

1. There is now a considerable amount of literature that questions whether predatory tactics are economically viable and whether they in fact characterize the activities of Rockefeller and the other "robber barons" of the late nineteenth century.
2. 49 U.S.C. Sections 1–22.
3. 15 U.S.C. Sections 1–7.
4. 15 U.S.C. Sections 12–27.
5. 15 U.S.C. Sections 41–58.

THE SHERMAN ACT

The main provisions of the Sherman Act are contained in Sections 1 and 2 of the act. Both sections describe illegal conduct in very broad terms. Section 1 prohibits a concerted activity on the part of two or more persons to restrain trade:

> Section 1: Every contract, combination in the form of trust or otherwise, or conspiracy, in restraint of trade or commerce among the several States, or with foreign nations, is hereby declared to be illegal [and is a felony punishable by fine or imprisonment].

Section 2 applies to both unilateral and concerted actions:

> Section 2: Every person who shall monopolize, or attempt to monopolize, or combine or conspire with any other person or persons, to monopolize any part of the trade or commerce among the several States, or with foreign nations, shall be deemed guilty of a felony [and is similarly punishable].

Section 1 of the act prohibits concerted activity that unreasonably restrains trade. Section 2 condemns individual anticompetitive behavior that produces, or is intended to produce, monopoly power. Both restraint of trade and monopoly power are fundamental concepts in antitrust law.

A **restraint of trade** is any agreement between firms that has the effect of reducing competition in the marketplace. Some restraints of trade are so blatantly anticompetitive—such as agreements to restrict output or fix prices—that they are condemned without inquiry into any business justification that may be advanced in defense of the agreements. These are known as *per se* violations. Other agreements judge the restraints under a rule of reason (discussed later in this chapter) similar to the common law analysis of the reasonableness of the restraint discussed earlier. Restraints of trade are explored more completely in the next chapter.

Monopoly power is an extreme amount of market power. Recall our initial discussion of Acme's market power in the hypothetical scenario in which Acme was given, for a time, exclusive control over the DVD drive market; specifically, Acme could ignore the effect of raising its product price on the ability of competitors to enter the DVD drive market. Any firm, even if it is not the sole supplier of its product, that is not completely constrained by the potential response of a rival in deciding what price to charge for its product has some degree of market power. Deciding whether such power is great enough to be classified as monopoly power is one of the most difficult tasks encountered in the application of antitrust law.

THE CLAYTON ACT

In contrast to the Sherman Act's broad proscriptions, the Clayton Act's provisions deal with *specific* practices that are not expressly covered by the Sherman Act but that are considered to reduce competition or lead to monopoly power. These practices are divided into four categories—price discrimination, exclusionary practices, corporate mergers, and interlocking directorates. These behaviors violate the Clayton Act only if they substantially tend to lessen competition or create monopoly power. Violations of the Clayton Act are civil, not criminal, violations.

PRICE DISCRIMINATION *Price discrimination* occurs when sellers charge different buyers different prices for identical goods. Section 2 of the Clayton Act prohibits certain classes of price discrimination for reasons other than differences in production or transportation costs. The Clayton Act was amended in 1936 by the Robinson-Patman Act as Congress sought to make it more difficult for businesses to evade the terms of Section 2. To violate Section 2, the seller must be engaged in interstate commerce, and the effect of the price discrimination must be to lessen competition substantially. Under the Robinson-Patman Act, sellers are prohibited from reducing prices to levels substantially below those charged by their competitors unless they can justify the reduction by demonstrating that the lower price was charged "in good faith to meet an equally low price of a competitor."[6]

EXCLUSIONARY PRACTICES Section 3 of the Clayton Act prohibits sellers and lessors from selling or leasing "on the condition, agreement or understanding that the . . . purchaser or lessee thereof shall not use or deal in the goods . . . of a competitor or competitors of the seller." Section 3 in effect prohibits two types of vertical arrangements involving exclusionary tactics: exclusive-dealing contracts and tie-in sales agreements.

6. *United States v. United States Gypsum Co.*, 438 U.S. 422, 98 S.Ct. 2864, 5 L.Ed.2d 854 (1978).

An *exclusive-dealing contract* is one in which a seller forbids the buyer from purchasing products from the seller's competitors. For example, imagine that most soft drinks are produced by one firm, that most soft drinks are marketed by one other firm, and that the producer signs an exclusive-dealing contract with the retail seller. Because the retail seller has committed itself to the established producer, any other soft-drink producer that wants to enter the soft-drink market may find it difficult to do so. Such contracts are prohibited under Section 3 if the effect of the contract will "substantially lessen competition or tend to create a monopoly."

In a *tying arrangement*, or *tie-in sales agreement*, the seller conditions the sale of a product (the tying product) on the buyer's agreeing to purchase another product (the tied product) produced or distributed by the same seller. The legality of such agreements depends on many factors, especially on consideration of the purpose of the arrangement and its likely effect on competition in the relevant markets (consider that there are two markets, because the agreement involves both the tying and the tied product). In the next chapter, we deal in depth with both exclusive-dealing contracts and tying arrangements as part of our analysis of restraints of trade.

CORPORATE MERGERS Under Section 7 of the Clayton Act, a person or business organization is forbidden to hold stock or assets in another business if "the effect . . . may be to substantially lessen competition." This section provides the statutory authorization for the government's challenging corporate mergers that could have an anticompetitive effect. Two crucial considerations are the market shares among firms in the relevant market and barriers to a firm's entry into the market.

INTERLOCKING DIRECTORATES Section 8 of the Clayton Act deals with *interlocking directorates*, which result when individuals serve as directors on the boards of two or more competing companies simultaneously. No person may be a director in two or more corporations at the same time if either of the corporations has capital, surplus, or undivided profits aggregating more than $13,813,000 or competitive sales (gross revenues for all products and services sold by one corporation in competition with the other) of $1,381,300. The threshold amounts are adjusted upward each year by the Federal Trade Commission (FTC). (The amounts given here are those announced by the FTC in 1997.)

THE FEDERAL TRADE COMMISSION ACT

The Federal Trade Commission Act's sole substantive provision is Section 5. It provides, in part, as follows:

> Unfair methods of competition in or affecting commerce, and unfair or deceptive acts or practices in or affecting commerce are hereby declared illegal.

Notice that whereas the Clayton Act prohibits specific forms of anticompetitive behavior, the FTC Act is a "catchall." Section 5 condemns all forms of anticompetitive behavior that are not covered under other federal antitrust laws.

The FTC Act also created the Federal Trade Commission, an administrative agency with functions that include antitrust enforcement, as well as other duties concerning consumer protection.

SECTION 5
ENFORCEMENT OF THE ANTITRUST LAWS

Government agencies enforce the federal antitrust laws. In some circumstances, a private party can sue violators for damages. Before the government can prosecute successfully or a private party can win a lawsuit, however, certain jurisdictional requirements must be met.

JURISDICTIONAL REQUIREMENTS

The Sherman Act applies only to conduct that has a significant impact on commerce. Because Congress can regulate only interstate commerce, in principle only interstate commerce is affected by this act.[7] Courts have generally held that any activity that substantially affects interstate commerce falls under the Sherman Act. Courts have construed the meaning of *interstate commerce* more and more broadly each year, bringing even local activities within the regulatory power of the national government. Whether a seemingly local activity touched sufficiently on interstate commerce to come under the purview of the Sherman Act was at issue in the following case.

7. See the discussion of the commerce clause in Chapter 5.

CASE 26.1 Summit Health, Ltd. v. Pinhas

Supreme Court of the United States, 1991. 500 U.S. 322, 111 S.Ct. 1842, 114 L.Ed.2d 366.

HISTORICAL AND POLITICAL SETTING *The record of the congressional debates on the Sherman Act reveals, in Senator John Sherman's words, an intent to "[go] as far as the Constitution permits Congress to go."*[a] *Congress intended to deal comprehensively and effectively with "the evils resulting from contracts, combinations and conspiracies in restraint of trade, and to that end to exercise all the power it possessed."*[b] *Since the passage of the Sherman Act more than a century ago, the U.S. economy has grown, and the federal power over commerce has experienced similar growth. The United States Supreme Court has long allowed the reach of the Sherman Act to expand with the expanding notions of congressional power.*

BACKGROUND AND FACTS *Dr. Simon Pinhas was an ophthalmologist on the staff of Midway Hospital Medical Center (a subsidiary of Summit Health, Ltd.) in Los Angeles. In February 1986, the administrators of the Medicare program announced that they would no longer reimburse physicians for the services of assistants, and most hospitals in the area abolished their requirements that assistant surgeons be used. Midway refused to do so. For Pinhas, who performed numerous surgeries at Midway, this meant that it would cost him $60,000 a year to pay for assistant surgeons that he did not need. He told Midway that if the requirement was not eliminated, he would leave. In response, the medical staff initiated peer-review proceedings against Pinhas, terminated his staff privileges, and began preparing an adverse report about Pinhas to distribute to all hospitals in the area. Pinhas filed a complaint alleging that the Midway medical staff had entered into a conspiracy to drive him out of business so that other ophthalmologists would obtain a greater share of the market for ophthalmologic services in Los Angeles. The trial court dismissed his complaint on the ground that interstate commerce was not affected by Pinhas's removal from the Midway medical staff, and therefore the Sherman Act did not apply. Pinhas appealed, and ultimately the case was reviewed by the United States Supreme Court.*

IN THE LANGUAGE OF THE COURT

Justice *STEVENS* delivered the opinion of the Court.

* * * *

* * * [T]his case involves the provision of ophthalmological services. It seems clear * * * that these services are regularly performed for out-of-state patients and generate revenues from out-of-state sources; their importance as part of the entire operation of the hospital is evident from the allegations of the complaint. A conspiracy to eliminate the entire ophthalmological department of the hospital, like a conspiracy to destroy the hospital itself, would unquestionably affect interstate commerce. * * * Petitioners [the Midway medical staff] argue that respondent's [Pinhas's] complaint is insufficient because there is no factual nexus between the restraint on this one surgeon's practice and interstate commerce.

There are two flaws in petitioners' argument. First, * * * proper analysis focuses, not upon actual consequences, but rather upon the potential harm that would ensue if the conspiracy were successful. * * * Second, if the conspiracy alleged in the complaint is successful, "as a matter of practical economics" there will be a reduction in the provision of ophthalmological services in the Los Angeles market. * * *

---

a. 20 Congressional Record 1167 (1889).

b. *Atlantic Cleaners & Dyers, Inc. v. United States*, 286 U.S. 427, 52 S.Ct. 607, 76 L.Ed. 1204 (1932).

DECISION AND REMEDY *The United States Supreme Court held that the medical staff's peer-review proceedings affected interstate commerce and thus their actions against Pinhas fell within the jurisdiction of the Sherman Act.*

ETHICAL CONSIDERATIONS *The substantial disagreement on whether essentially local activities—such as the medical staff's actions against Pinhas—should be subject to the "long arm of federal law" is reflected in the Court's five-to-four decision in this case. Justice Scalia, who wrote the dissenting opinion, stated, "As I understand the Court's opinion, the test of Sherman Act jurisdiction is whether the entire line of commerce from which Dr. Pinhas has been excluded affects interstate commerce . . . , which of course it does. This analysis tells us nothing about the substantiality of the impact on interstate commerce generated by the particular conduct at issue here."*

FEDERAL ENFORCEMENT

The federal agencies that enforce the federal antitrust laws are the Department of Justice (DOJ) and the Federal Trade Commission (FTC). The DOJ can prosecute violations of the Sherman Act as either criminal or civil violations. Violations of the Clayton Act are not crimes, and the DOJ can enforce that statute only through civil proceedings. The various remedies that the DOJ has asked the courts to impose include **divestiture** (making a company give up one or more of its operating functions) and **dissolution** (making a company end its operating functions). A group of meat packers, for example, can be forced to divest itself of control or ownership of butcher shops.

The FTC enforces the Clayton Act and has sole authority to enforce the only substantive provision of the Federal Trade Commission Act, Section 5. FTC actions are effected through administrative cease-and-desist proceedings, but the FTC can seek court sanctions for violations of its administrative orders. As part of its enforcement of the Clayton Act, the FTC requires certain persons involved in a merger, consolidation, or other acquisition to notify the agency.[8] The first page of the notification form is shown in Exhibit 26–1 on page 539. Antitrust law as it applies to mergers is discussed in detail in Chapter 27.

PRIVATE ACTIONS

A private party can sue for **treble damages** (three times what he or she has suffered) and attorneys' fees under Section 4 of the Clayton Act if the party is injured as a result of a violation of any of the federal antitrust laws (except Section 5 of the Federal Trade Commission Act). In some instances, private parties may also seek injunctive relief to prevent antitrust violations. The courts have determined that the ability to sue depends on the directness of the injury suffered by the would-be plaintiff. Thus, a person wishing to sue under the Sherman Act must prove (1) that the antitrust violation either directly caused, or was at least a substantial factor in causing, the injury that was suffered and (2) that the unlawful actions of the accused party affected business activities of the plaintiff that were protected by the antitrust laws.

In recent years, more than 90 percent of all antitrust actions have been brought by private plaintiffs. One reason for this is, of course, that successful plaintiffs recover treble damages as a result of the defendants' antitrust law violations. Such recoveries by private plaintiffs for antitrust violations have been rationalized as encouraging "private attorneys general" who will vigorously pursue antitrust violators on their own initiative. This policy consideration has also prompted the courts to ask, in assessing whether a litigant has standing to sue for an alleged antitrust violation, whether the particular plaintiff is properly suited to fulfill the role of a private attorney general.

The court in the following case was asked to decide whether the defendants' alleged antitrust violations were a sufficiently direct cause of injury to the plaintiffs to give the plaintiffs standing (that is, a sufficient stake in the controversy to bring the lawsuit—see Chapter 3).

8. See 15 U.S.C. Section 18a.

CASE 26.2 Amarel v. Connell

United States Court of Appeals, Ninth Circuit, 1997. 102 F.3d 1494.

BACKGROUND AND FACTS *William Amarel and other rice farmers signed contracts to sell their paddy rice (raw rice harvested in the field) to Pacific International Rice Mills, Inc. (PIRMI), for a share of the profits from the sale of the milled rice (rice refined and processed for consumption). PIRMI contracted to sell to the Republic of Korea (South Korea) 200,000 tons of milled Southern rice. Unable to obtain enough Southern rice, PIRMI offered to substitute California rice. Within three days of this offer, Connell Rice & Sugar Company offered South Korea more than seven times as much California rice for a considerably lower per-unit price. In order to match this competitive offer, PIRMI then accepted a reduced price for its rice and lost $12 million on the sale. The farmers filed a lawsuit in a federal district court against Connell's president, Grover Connell, and others. They alleged that the defendants had violated the antitrust laws by, among other things, engaging in predatory pricing in the deal with South Korea. The farmers claimed, as their injury, the reduced return they earned on the rice they sold to PIRMI for export to South Korea. The defendants argued, among other things, that the farmers' alleged injury was indirect and that thus they lacked standing. On most of the allegations, the court ruled against the plaintiffs, who appealed.*

IN THE LANGUAGE OF THE COURT

MICHAEL DALY HAWKINS, Circuit Judge:

* * * *

Defendants * * * assert that plaintiffs' alleged harm is merely "derivative and indirect" because it "derived from the lower prices supposedly obtained for milled rice as a result of defendants' acts." We disagree. * * * Among the particular injuries, plaintiffs allege, are depressed earnings caused by predatorily low prices * * *.

* * * *

* * * Given the close ties between the paddy rice market and the milled rice market, and given that plaintiffs' profits were, in part, a function of profits in the milled rice market, defendants' alleged predatory pricing in the market for milled rice predictably would have impacted the price of paddy rice.

DECISION AND REMEDY *The U.S. Court of Appeals for the Ninth Circuit concluded that the plaintiffs were sufficiently direct victims of the defendants' alleged anticompetitive activities to have standing. The court reversed the judgment in the defendants' favor and remanded the case for a new trial.*

INTERNATIONAL CONSIDERATIONS

Regulation of Purely Foreign Trade *Although U.S. courts have not always been consistent in applying antitrust laws to firms doing business in the United States, they have consistently expressed concern about the anticompetitive practices of firms doing business in other countries. Foreign subsidiaries of U.S. companies often benefit from a lack of enforcement of antitrust laws in other countries. In the mid-1990s, the U.S. Department of Justice expanded its antitrust efforts against foreign firms.*[a] *Sanctions included fines of $10 million and $15 million against two international firms accused of fixing dynamite prices and a total of $170 million in a food-commodities case involving four Asian companies, a U.S. subsidiary of Bayer AG of Germany, and U.S.–based Archer Daniels Midland Company.*

a. See, for example, *United States v. Nippon Paper Industries Co.*, 109 F.3d 1 (1st Cir. 1997), set out as Case 8.2 in Chapter 8.

Exhibit 26–1 ■ FTC Notification Form

16 C.F.R. Part 803 - Appendix

NOTIFICATION AND REPORT FORM FOR CERTAIN MERGERS AND ACQUISITIONS

Approved by OMB
3084-0006
Expires 8-31-97

THE INFORMATION REQUIRED TO BE SUPPLIED ON THESE ANSWER SHEETS IS SPECIFIED IN THE INSTRUCTIONS

FOR OFFICE USE ONLY
TRANSACTION NUMBER

☐ CTO ☐ ETR

➤ Attach the Affidavit required by § 803.5 to this page.

IS THIS ACQUISITION A CASH TENDER OFFER?
☐ YES ☐ NO

DO YOU REQUEST EARLY TERMINATION OF THE WAITING PERIOD? *(Grants of early termination are published in the Federal Register.)*
☐ YES ☐ NO

ITEM 1

(a) NAME AND HEADQUARTERS ADDRESS OF PERSON FILING NOTIFICATION

(b) PERSON FILING NOTIFICATION IS
☐ an acquiring person ☐ an acquired person ☐ both

(c) LIST NAMES OF ULTIMATE PARENT ENTITIES OF ALL ACQUIRING PERSONS

LIST NAMES OF ULTIMATE PARENT ENTITIES OF ALL ACQUIRED PERSONS

(d) THIS ACQUISITION IS *(put an X in all the boxes that apply)*
☐ an acquisition of assets
☐ a merger (see § 801.2)
☐ an acquisition subject to § 802.2(e)
☐ a formation of a joint venture of other corporation (see § 801.40)
☐ a consolidation (see § 801.2)
☐ an acquisition of voting securities
☐ a secondary acquisition
☐ an acquisition subject to § 801.31
☐ an acquisition subject to § 801.30 *(specify type)* ____________
☐ other *(specify)* ____________

(e) INDICATE HIGHEST NOTIFICATION THRESHOLD IN § 801.1(h) FOR WHICH THIS FORM IS BEING FILED *(acquiring person only)*
☐ $15 million ☐ 15% ☐ 25% ☐ 50%

(f) VALUE OF VOTING SECURITIES TO BE HELD AS A RESULT OF THE ACQUISITION

VALUE OF ASSETS

(g) PUT AN "X" IN THE APPROPRIATE BOX TO DESCRIBE PERSON FILING NOTIFICATION
☐ Corporation ☐ Partnership ☐ Other *(specify)* ____________

(h) DATA FURNISHED BY
☐ calendar year ☐ fiscal year (*specify period*) ________ *(month/year)* to ________ *(month/year)*

THIS FORM IS REQUIRED BY LAW and must be filed separately by each person which, by reason of a merger, consolidation or acquisition, is subject to § 7A of the Clayton Act, 15 U.S.C. § 18a, as added by Section 201 of the Hart-Scott-Rodino Antitrust Improvements Act of 1976. Pub. L. No. 94-435, 90 Stat. 1390, and rules promulgated thereunder (hereinafter referred to as "the rules" or by section number). The statute and rules are set forth in the *Federal Register* at 43 FR 33450; the rules may also be found at 18 CFR parts 801-03. Failure to file this **Notification and Report Form,** and to observe the required waiting period before consummating the acquisition, in accordance with the applicable provisions of 15 U.S.C. § 18a and the rules, subjects any "person," as defined in the rules, or any individuals responsible for noncompliance, to liability for a penalty of not more than $10,000 for each day during which such person is in violation of 15 U.S.C. § 18a.

All information and documentary material filed in or with this Form is confidential. It is exempt from disclosure under the Freedom of Information Act, and may be made public only in an administrative or judicial proceeding, or disclosed to Congress or to a duly authorized committee or subcommittee of Congress.

Complete and return *two* notarized copies (with *one* set of documentary attachments) of this **Notification and Report Form** to Premerger Notification Office, Bureau of Competition, Room 303, Federal Trade Commission, Washington, DC 20580, and *three* notarized copies (with *one set* of documentary attachments) to Director of Operations, Antitrust Division, Room 3218, Department of Justice, Washington, D.C. 20530. The central office for information and assistance with respect to matters in connection with this *Notification and Report Form* is Room 303, Federal Trade Commission, Washington, DC 20580, phone (202) 326-3100.

DISCLOSURE NOTICE - Public reporting burden for this report is estimated to vary from 8 to 160 hours per response, with an average of 39 hours per response, including time for reviewing instructions, searching existing data sources, gathering and maintaining the data needed, and completing and reviewing the collection of information. Send comments regarding the burden estimate or any other aspect of this report, including suggestions for reducing this burden to:

Premerger Notification Office,
H-303
Federal Trade Commission
Washington, DC 20580

Office of Information and
Regulatory Affairs,
Office of Management and Budget
Washington, DC 20503

FTC Form C 4 (rev. 09/95)

SECTION 6 EXEMPTIONS

There are many legislative and constitutional limitations on antitrust enforcement. Most are statutory and judicially created exemptions that apply in such areas as labor, insurance, and foreign trade. These exemptions are listed and explained in Exhibit 26–2.

One of the most significant of these exemptions covers joint efforts by businesspersons to obtain legislative, judicial, or executive action. This is often referred to as the ***Noerr-Pennington* doctrine.**[9] For example, video producers might jointly lobby Congress to change the copyright laws without being held liable for attempting to restrain trade. Although selfish rather than purely public-minded conduct is permitted, there is an exception: an action will not be protected if it is clear that the action is "objectively baseless in the sense that no reasonable [person] could reasonably expect success on the merits" and it is an attempt to make anticompetitive use of government processes.[10]

SECTION 7 MONOPOLIES

As noted above, the impetus for the initial federal antitrust legislation was concern over monopolies—specifically, concern that in particular markets a single, dominant firm could acquire and use market power to dictate or influence prices and output. Section 2 of the Sherman Act deals broadly with such cases. Section 2 condemns "every person who shall monopolize or attempt to monopolize." (Note that Section 2 applies to activities in the restraint of trade on the part of a single firm or individual. In contrast, Section 1, as described in the next chapter, applies to certain activities in the restraint of trade on the part of more than one individual or firm.) The essence of a single entity's violation of Section 2 is the entity's willful acquisition or maintenance of monopoly power, or its specifically intended *attempt* to do so, provided the attempt has a reasonable chance of success.

In the remainder of this chapter, we focus on single-firm behavior that is intended either to create or to preserve a monopoly within a particular market. Notice that two distinct types of behavior are subject to sanction under Section 2. First, conduct pursued by a firm that is already a monopolist is condemned as *monopolization* if the conduct interferes with free trade and is intended to preserve the firm's monopoly. Second, conduct intended to capture monopoly power is condemned as an *attempt to monopolize.*

Another Section 2 offense is the act of **predatory pricing.** Predatory pricing involves an attempt by one firm to drive its competitors from the market by selling its product substantially *below* normal costs of production. Once the competitors are eliminated, the firm will attempt to recapture its losses and go on to earn very high profits by driving prices up far above their competitive levels.

MONOPOLIZATION

In *United States v. Grinnell Corp.*,[11] the United States Supreme Court defined the offense of **monopolization** as involving the following two elements: "(1) the possession of monopoly power in the relevant market and (2) the willful acquisition or maintenance of the power as distinguished from growth or development as a consequence of a superior product, business acumen, or historic accident." A violation of Section 2 requires that both these elements be established.

MONOPOLY POWER The Sherman Act does not define *monopoly.* In economic parlance, monopoly refers to control by a single entity of an entire market. It is well established in antitrust law, however, that a firm may be a monopolist even though it is not the sole seller in a market. Nor is monopoly a function of size alone (for example, a "mom and pop" grocery located in an isolated desert town is a geographic monopolist if it is the only grocery serving that particular market). In theory, size in relation to the market is what matters, because monopoly involves power to affect prices and output. The United States Supreme Court has defined monopoly power as "the power to control prices or exclude competition." This definition is of limited help, though, and most scholars generally consider monopoly power to be

9. See *Eastern Railroad Presidents Conference v. Noerr Motor Freight, Inc.*, 365 U.S. 127, 81 S.Ct. 523, 5 L.Ed.2d 464 (1961), and *United Mine Workers of America v. Pennington*, 381 U.S. 657, 89 S.Ct. 1585, 14 L.Ed.2d 626 (1965).

10. *Professional Real Estate Investors Inc. v. Columbia Pictures Industries, Inc.*, 508 U.S. 49, 113 S.Ct. 1920, 123 L.Ed.2d 611 (1993).

11. 384 U.S. 563, 86 S.Ct. 1698, 16 L.Ed.2d 778 (1966).

EXHIBIT 26–2 ■ EXEMPTIONS TO ANTITRUST ENFORCEMENT

EXEMPTION	SOURCE AND SCOPE
Labor	Clayton Act—Permits unions to organize and bargain without violating antitrust laws and specifies that strikes and other labor activities do not normally violate any federal law.
Agricultural Associations	Clayton Act and Capper-Volstead Act of 1992—Allow agricultural cooperatives to set prices.
Fisheries	Fisheries Cooperative Marketing Act of 1976—Allows the fishing industry to set prices.
Insurance Companies	McCarran-Ferguson Act of 1945—Exempts the insurance business in states in which the industry is regulated.
Exporters	Webb-Pomerene Act of 1918—Allows U.S. exporters to engage in cooperative activity to compete with similar foreign associations; Export Trading Company Act of 1982—Permits the Department of Justice to exempt certain exporters.
Professional Baseball	The United States Supreme Court has held that professional baseball is exempt because it is not "interstate commerce."[a]
Oil Marketing	Interstate Oil Compact of 1935—Allows states to set quotas on oil to be marketed in interstate commerce.
Defense Activities	Defense Production Act of 1950—Allows the president to approve, and thereby exempt, certain activities to further the military defense of the United States.
Small Businesses' Cooperative Research	Small Business Administration Act of 1958—Allows small firms to undertake cooperative research.
Joint Ventures' Research or Production	National Cooperative Research Act of 1984 and National Cooperative Production Amendments of 1993—Permit research or production of a product, process, or service by joint ventures consisting of competitors.
State Actions	The United States Supreme Court has held that actions by a state are exempt if the state clearly articulates and actively supervises the policy behind its action.[b]
Regulated Industries	Industries (such as airlines) are exempt when a federal administrative agency (such as the Federal Aviation Administration) has primary regulatory authority.
Businesspersons' Joint Efforts to Seek Government Action	Cooperative efforts by businesspersons to obtain legislative, judicial, or executive action are exempt unless it is clear that an effort is "objectively baseless" and is an attempt to make anticompetitive use of government processes.[c]

a. *Federal Baseball Club of Baltimore, Inc. v. National League of Professional Baseball Clubs,* 259 U.S. 200, 42 S.Ct. 465, 66 L. Ed. 898 (1922). A federal district court has held that this exemption applies only to the game's reserve system. (Under the reserve system, teams hold players' contracts for the players' entire careers. The reserve system is generally being replaced by the free agency system.) See *Piazza v. Major League Baseball,* 831 F.Supp. 420 (E.D.Pa. 1993).
b. See *Packer v. Brown,* 317 U.S. 341, 63 S.Ct. 307, 87 L.Ed. 315 (1943).
c. *Eastern Railroad Presidents Conference v. Noerr Motor Freight, Inc.,* 365 U.S. 127, 81 S.Ct. 523, 5 L.Ed.2d 464 (1961), and *United Mine Workers of America v. Pennington,* 381 U.S. 657, 89 S.Ct. 1585, 14 L.Ed.2d 626 (1965).

simply a *considerable* degree of market power or, otherwise stated, a *significant* degree of freedom from competitive pressure regarding output and pricing decisions. This generally is the way in which the Supreme Court has applied the concept.

As difficult as it is to define market power precisely, it is even more difficult to measure it. As a workable proxy, courts often look to the firm's percentage share of the "relevant market." This is the so-called **market-share test.**[12] The relevant market consists of two elements: (1) a relevant product

12. Other measures have been devised, but the market-share test is the most widely used.

market and (2) a relevant geographical market. A firm generally is considered to have monopoly power if its share of the relevant market is 70 percent or more. This is not an absolute, however. It is only a loose rule of thumb; in some cases, a smaller share may be held to constitute monopoly power.[13] We discuss below examples of the two elements of the market-share test.

PRODUCT MARKET No doubt the relevant product market should include all products that, although produced by different firms, nonetheless have identical attributes. But in determining the relevant market, it must be remembered that products that are not identical may be substituted for one another. Coffee may substitute for tea, cellophane may substitute for waxed paper, and so on. In defining the relevant product market, the key issue is the degree of interchangeability between products. If one product is a sufficient substitute for another, the two are considered to be part of the same product market.

In *United States v. E. I. du Pont de Nemours & Co.*,[14] du Pont was sued for monopolizing the cellophane market. Du Pont controlled about 75 percent of cellophane production but contended that it had no monopoly power, because the relevant market included not only cellophane but also all other flexible packaging materials. The United States Supreme Court found that there was indeed a sufficient degree of interchangeability between cellophane and alternatives such as waxed paper and aluminum foil. The Court noted, for example, that although 35 percent of the snack-food industry used cellophane, an even larger percentage used some other packaging material. Consequently, the Court concluded that du Pont did not control a share of the relevant market sufficient to constitute monopoly power.

Many times, decisions concerning relevant product markets can be interpreted as arbitrary. For example, the FTC blocked a merger between Staples, Inc., and Office Depot, Inc., on the ground that, in the office supply business, they had only one other competitor, OfficeMax, Inc. To eliminate any of the three, the FTC claimed, would violate antitrust laws. Staples contended, however, that, combined with Office Depot, it would control less than 6 percent of a market that included such giant retailers as Wal-Mart Stores, Inc., warehouse clubs, and national catalogue dealers. In other words, the FTC was looking at how office supplies are sold, while Staples was arguing that the agency should look at office supplies as a product. Even after Office Depot agreed to sell sixty-three of its stores to OfficeMax, the FTC still refused to approve the merger and asked a federal district court to block it. The court ruled in favor of the FTC and blocked the merger on antitrust grounds.

The following case demonstrates a court's efforts to determine the relevant product market for replacement parts for machinery manufactured by Caterpillar, Inc.

13. This standard was first articulated by Justice Learned Hand in the famous *Aluminum Co. of America* case discussed later in this chapter. A 90 percent share was held to be clear evidence of monopoly power. Anything less than 64 percent, said Justice Hand, made monopoly power doubtful, and anything less than 30 percent was clearly not monopoly power. This is merely a rule of thumb, however; it is not a binding principle of law.

14. 351 U.S. 377, 76 S.Ct. 994, 100 L.Ed.2d 1264 (1956).

CASE 26.3 Godix Equipment Export Corp. v. Caterpillar, Inc.

United States District Court, Southern District of Florida, Miami Division, 1996. 948 F.Supp. 1570.

COMPANY PROFILE *Caterpillar, Inc., manufactures and sells construction machinery, agricultural machinery, engines, and parts for those machines to customers worldwide. Caterpillar is one of the world's largest companies in this field, with sales exceeding $10 billion annually. As part of its operations, Caterpillar authorizes certain dealers to sell Caterpillar-made replacement parts and provides service and support for those who buy genuine Caterpillar parts through the authorized dealers.*

BACKGROUND AND FACTS *Replacement parts for Caterpillar products are either genuine parts, made by Caterpillar, or "will-fit" parts, made by others to operate in Caterpillar machines. Godix Equipment Export Corporation and Universal Service Company negotiated with some of Caterpillar's authorized dealers to buy genuine Caterpillar parts at a discount and then resold them for* *export. Because Godix and Universal obtained the parts at a discount and did not provide service or other support, they could charge less than the authorized dealers and still profit. To gain control of the sales of its parts, Caterpillar created Caterpillar Export Services (CES). CES compiled a list of "resellers," including Godix and Universal, to whom it refused to sell parts. Godix and Universal filed a lawsuit in a federal district court against Caterpillar, alleging, among other things, that Caterpillar was attempting to monopolize the replacement parts market. Caterpillar filed a motion for judgment as a matter of law.*[a]

IN THE LANGUAGE OF THE COURT

NESBITT, District Judge.

* * * *

In the instant case, Plaintiffs * * * define the relevant product market as comprising replacement parts for Caterpillar equipment. [The plaintiffs' representatives] testified that as buyers in the market place, they choose between genuine and non-genuine Caterpillar replacement parts to resell * * * . [Universal] is currently still in business selling non-genuine "will-fit" parts for Caterpillar machines to customers to whom [it] previously sold the interchangeable genuine Caterpillar parts. * * *

Caterpillar has also presented evidence which would define the relevant product market as the market for replacement Caterpillar parts, either genuine or will-fit. Caterpillar presented [customers] who testified that they choose from either genuine Caterpillar parts or other will-fit parts depending on pricing, quality and service * * * . [S]uppliers of will-fit parts produce interchangeable parts for over ninety percent of the 500,000 genuine Caterpillar replacement parts. That percentage becomes higher when parts that are in low demand are eliminated from the equation. Thus, for purposes of the Motion for Judgment as a Matter of Law, the relevant product market is defined as replacement parts for Caterpillar machines, either genuine or non-genuine will-fit parts.

DECISION AND REMEDY

The court defined the relevant product market as including both genuine and will-fit replacement parts. The court concluded that although Caterpillar could control which dealers sold genuine Caterpillar parts, it could not control who sold will-fit parts. The court granted Caterpillar's motion for judgment as a matter of law on this issue.

a. With this motion, Caterpillar asked the judge to direct a verdict for it on the ground that the plaintiffs had presented no evidence to support their claim. State courts generally use the term *motion for a directed verdict*. See Chapter 3.

GEOGRAPHICAL MARKET The second component of the relevant market is the geographical boundaries of the market. For products that are sold nationwide, the geographical boundaries encompass the entire United States. If transportation costs are significant or if a producer and its competitors sell in only a limited area—one in which customers have no access to other sources of the product—then the geographical market is limited to that area. In this sense, a national firm may compete in several distinct areas, having monopoly power in one but not another. Generally, the geographical market is that section of the country within which a firm can increase its price a bit without attracting new sellers or without losing many customers to alternative suppliers outside that area.

ANTICOMPETITIVE BEHAVIOR Monopoly power is not, in and of itself, illegal. Recall that the monopolization offense has two elements. In addition to monopoly power, there is the requirement of "willful acquisition or maintenance of that power." A dominant market share may be the result of business acumen or the development of a superior product, or it may simply be the result of historical accident. None of these situations should give rise to antitrust concerns. Indeed, it would be counter to society's interest to condemn a firm that had acquired its position on the basis of the first two reasons.

If, however, a firm possesses monopoly power as a result of engaging in some purposeful act to acquire or to maintain that power through anticompetitive means, then the firm is in violation of Section 2. The United States Supreme Court has interpreted this second element as requiring some conduct intended to diminish competition.

Conduct that diminishes competition may not necessarily be anticompetitive. Devising new, low-cost production methods and developing and producing better products all hurt competitors. But they do not injure competition; they are the result of competition. In our initial hypothetical scenario, even if Acme had not received an exclusive monopoly, its DVD drive breakthrough would have given it monopoly power for a period of time until rival firms had had sufficient time to develop and market products that could effectively compete. But ultimately, Acme's innovation would have led to increased competition. Thus, only certain acts are condemned under Section 2, even if the acting firm possesses monopoly power. The hallmark of an action that does violate Section 2 is that, without providing better production or products, the action makes competing in the relevant market more difficult for the acting firm's rivals.

ANTICOMPETITIVE INTENT The qualifier that the sanctioned action have been "willful" is said to require intent, but the intent requirement is difficult to formulate. In most monopolization cases, intent may be inferred from evidence that the firm had monopoly power and engaged in anticompetitive behavior. For example, in *United States v. Aluminum Co. of America*,[15] the seemingly innocent act of expanding the demand for its products ran Alcoa afoul of Section 2. The court found that Alcoa had intentionally and artificially stimulated demand and then increased its own capacity to meet that increased demand.

The Court of Appeals for the Second Circuit[16] relied on the fact that Alcoa clearly possessed a market share sufficient to give it monopoly power (90 percent of what the court determined to be the relevant market) and that the only apparent reason for its expansion was to prevent competitors from entering the aluminum market. This factual conclusion is often criticized, but the principle set out is now well established. Market domination that results from legitimate competitive behavior—such as foresight, innovation, skill, and good management—will not be condemned unless that domination is abused or acquired through behavior that harms, rather than flows from, competition.

A firm's unilateral refusal to deal with another individual or organization is generally permissible.[17] In the following case, however, the refusal to deal was made by a firm possessing monopoly power, and its apparent intent was to injure competition in the relevant market.

15. 148 F.2d 416 (2d Cir. 1945).

16. The Second Circuit acted as the court of final appeal in place of the United States Supreme Court because the latter could not muster a quorum of six qualified justices to hear the case. The case was referred to the court of appeals of the circuit from which it had come under a specially drawn statute (28 U.S.C. Section 2109).

17. Antitrust law does not forbid America Online, Inc., for example, from refusing to deal with advertisers who will not adhere to its rules. See *Cyber Promotions, Inc. v. America Online, Inc.*, 948 F.Supp. 456 (E.D.Pa. 1996).

CASE 26.4 Aspen Skiing Co. v. Aspen Highlands Skiing Corp.

Supreme Court of the United States, 1985.
472 U.S. 585,
105 S.Ct. 2847,
86 L.Ed.2d 467.

BACKGROUND AND FACTS *Aspen, Colorado, is a leading ski resort, and private investors developed four major facilities there for downhill skiing: Ajax, Aspen Highlands, Buttermilk, and Snowmass. The facilities were owned by independent investors, and they jointly offered an "all-Aspen ticket," which could be used for skiing at any of the facilities. Receipts from the tickets were paid to the various facilities according to their use, based on surveys of skiers. By 1977, Aspen Skiing Company (Ski Co.) had acquired ownership of Ajax, Buttermilk, and Snowmass, and Aspen Highlands was owned by the Aspen Highlands Skiing Corporation. At that time, the two companies were engaged in a dispute over the proper distribution of receipts from the all-Aspen ticket. Ski Co. discontinued the*

all-Aspen ticket and replaced it with a three-area ticket that covered only its own facilities. The Aspen Highlands share of the local downhill skiing market declined from over 20 percent in 1976–1977 to 11 percent in 1980–1981. Aspen Highlands filed an antitrust complaint against Ski Co., alleging that Ski Co. had monopolized the market for downhill skiing services at Aspen, in violation of Section 2 of the Sherman Act. Aspen Highlands argued that the discontinuation of the all-Aspen ticket was a purposeful act with intent to monopolize the market. The court issued a judgment in favor of Aspen Highlands, and the Tenth Circuit Court of Appeals affirmed in all respects. Ski Co. appealed to the United States Supreme Court.

IN THE LANGUAGE OF THE COURT

Justice *STEVENS* delivered the opinion of the Court.

* * * *

In this Court, Ski Co. contends that even a firm with monopoly power has no duty to engage in joint marketing with a competitor, that a violation of [Section] 2 cannot be established without evidence of substantial exclusionary conduct, and that none of its activities can be characterized as exclusionary. * * *

* * * *

* * * In the actual case that we must decide, the monopolist did not merely reject a novel offer to participate in a cooperative venture that had been proposed by a competitor. Rather, the monopolist elected to make an important change in a pattern of distribution that had originated in a competitive market and had persisted for several years. The all-Aspen, 6-day ticket with revenues allocated on the basis of usage was first developed when three independent companies operated three different ski mountains in the Aspen area. It continued to provide a desirable option for skiers when the market was enlarged to include four mountains, and when the character of the market was changed by Ski Co.'s acquisition of monopoly power. Moreover, since the record discloses that interchangeable tickets are used in other multimountain areas which apparently are competitive, it seems appropriate to infer that such tickets satisfy consumer demand in free competitive markets.

* * * *

Perhaps most significant, however, is the evidence relating to Ski Co. itself, for Ski Co. did not persuade the jury that its conduct was justified by any normal business purpose. Ski Co. was apparently willing to forgo daily ticket sales both to skiers who sought to exchange the coupons contained in Highlands' Adventure Pack, and to those who would have purchased Ski Co. daily lift tickets from Highlands if Highlands had been permitted to purchase them in bulk. The jury may well have concluded that Ski Co. elected to forgo these short-run benefits because it was more interested in reducing competition in the Aspen market over the long run by harming its smaller competitor.

DECISION AND REMEDY

The United States Supreme Court affirmed the decision of the lower federal courts. The original jury had found that Aspen Highlands had suffered $2.5 million in actual damages, which were trebled under the Sherman Act to an award of $7.5 million. This award was affirmed by the United States Supreme Court.

PREDATORY PRICING

In monopolization cases, predatory pricing—selling below cost—is one form of conduct that continues to receive considerable attention. One reason for this is that a dominant theme in antitrust cases is the promotion of consumer welfare. But consumers benefit from low prices. If a firm sells a valuable product for a price below cost, then it is the firm that loses, not the consumer. Despite the fact that consumers benefit from the low price, predatory pricing is still condemned.

Condemnation of predatory pricing is based on the fear that although it may benefit consumers in the short term, in the longer term, it will harm competition. The harm feared is that a rich rival, by pricing below its competitors' costs, could drive the competitors out of the market by outlasting them during the phase in which prices were below cost. In the subsequent phase, the rich rival would still be in the market but would no longer face any competitors. The firm would then be free to reap large profits by raising the price far above what it had been when the firm faced market competition.

In any event, there are procompetitive reasons not only for low prices but even for prices below cost. Such pricing may be, for example, the only way in which a new firm can gain a "toehold" in a market populated by established firms, especially if the latter have established brand-name recognition in the market. To prevent the entry of new competitors into a market by forbidding them from using low prices, perhaps even prices below cost, would hinder rather than promote competition.

Faced with such uncertainty as to the purpose and effect of firms' pricing decisions, courts have struggled to invent a workable standard for judging predatory pricing. Some courts look at market structure in deciding predatory pricing cases. Under this approach, a court looks at the potential for harm to consumers created by a firm's below-cost pricing. If it appears that a firm pricing below cost will be unable to capture monopoly profits at a later time, the court rejects any attempt to discern intent. The essence of the market approach is that if the firm is unlikely to capture monopoly profits through high prices in the future, intent does not matter.[18] Consumers benefit from the low prices regardless. Moreover, if the firm is pursuing a legitimate objective of trying to gain access to an established market, the efforts should not be hampered by rivals crying foul simply because they lose business to a competitor selling at a lower price.

In an action alleging predatory pricing, a plaintiff must prove that the allegedly predatory prices are below an appropriate measure of its competitor's costs and that the competitor has a reasonable prospect of recouping the difference. This requirement is illustrated in the following case.

18. See, for example, *Brooke Group, Ltd. v. Brown & Williamson Tobacco Corp.*, 509 U.S. 209, 113 S.Ct. 2578, 125 L.Ed.2d 168 (1993), in which the Supreme Court held that a seller's price-cutting policies could not be predatory "[g]iven the market's realities"—the size of the seller's market share, the expanding output by other sellers, and other factors.

CASE 26.5 C.B. Trucking, Inc. v. Waste Management, Inc.

United States District Court, District of Massachusetts, 1996. 944 F.Supp. 66.

BACKGROUND AND FACTS *Every three years, the towns of Franklin and Medway, Massachusetts, publicly solicit bids from private firms to collect residential waste. In 1990, C.B. Trucking, Inc., was the low bidder and was awarded the contracts. On the next round of bidding, Waste Management of Massachusetts, Inc., submitted the low bid. C.B. Trucking filed a lawsuit in a federal district court against Waste Management and others, alleging, among other things, that Waste Management had violated the Sherman Act by attempting to monopolize the residential solid waste business through the practice of predatory pricing. Waste Management filed a motion to dismiss the complaint, in part on the ground that the claims of predatory pricing were "inherently implausible."*

IN THE LANGUAGE OF THE COURT

LASKER, District Judge.

* * * *

In support of its motion, Waste Management has submitted the affidavit of Rory J. Fallon, the officer responsible for preparing, submitting and overseeing the preparation and submission of the municipal bids at issue. Fallon's affidavit * * * explains that Waste Management was able to bid as low as it did because it did not need to make any capital expenditures to perform the * * * contracts.

* * * *

Fallon's affidavit, based as it is on personal knowledge, lowers the boom on C.B. Trucking's case. * * *

Moreover, assuming *arguendo* [for the sake of argument] (in direct contradiction of Fallon's sworn statement) that Waste Management's bid prices were set below its own costs, it is nevertheless economically implausible to conclude that Waste Management had a [reasonable prospect] of recouping its investment in below-cost prices when its contracts * * * were subject to public bidding; limited in duration to three years; and set a fixed price for the services rendered.

DECISION AND REMEDY *The court granted Waste Management's motion and dismissed C.B. Trucking's complaint. Waste Management showed that its prices were not predatory because they were not below its costs. The court reasoned that, even if the prices had been below cost, Waste Management had no reasonable prospect of recouping the difference.*

ATTEMPTS TO MONOPOLIZE

Section 2 also prohibits an **attempt to monopolize** a market. Any action challenged as an attempt to monopolize must have been specifically intended to exclude competitors and garner monopoly power. In addition, the attempt must have had a "dangerous" probability of success; that is, the attempt need not have succeeded but must have posed a *serious* threat of monopolization. A probability cannot be dangerous unless the alleged offender possesses at least some degree of market power. In the following case, the court considered whether, from the facts, a jury could conclude that an attempt to monopolize a certain market had been made and that this attempt had had a dangerous probability of success.

CASE 26.6 Yeager's Fuel, Inc. v. Pennsylvania Power & Light Co.

United States District Court, Eastern District of Pennsylvania, 1997. 953 F.Supp. 617.

HISTORICAL AND TECHNOLOGICAL SETTING *Before electricity became widely available on a commercial scale in the 1880s, other resources served as heating fuels. Today, oil and gas are more cost-efficient heating fuels than electricity. Oil and gas heating systems are generally less expensive to install and operate than electric systems. For example, installation of an electric heat pump costs at least 50 percent more than installation of an oil or gas system, and its operation costs 30 percent to 40 percent more. Electric heating equipment also becomes physically obsolete twice as fast as oil heating equipment.*

BACKGROUND AND FACTS *Pennsylvania Power & Light Company (PP&L) is an electric utility serving central and northeastern Pennsylvania. Between 1983 and 1995, PP&L paid more than $25 million to builders, developers, and others to induce them to use electric home heating in its area. At the time, a PP&L executive remarked, "We're striving for total dominance in the new-home market. We believe you can put electric heat into at least 85 percent of all new homes built in our service area." By 1986, PP&L's share of the new-home heating market was 84 percent. In 1987, PP&L began paying builders, under "all-electric agreements," to construct entire developments of houses heated by electricity only. Yeager's Fuel, Inc., and other fuel oil dealers filed a lawsuit in a federal district court against PP&L, contending, among other things, that the utility was attempting to monopolize the new-home heating market. PP&L filed a motion for summary judgment.*

In the Language of the Court

PADOVA, District Judge.

* * * *

* * * Here, a monopolist with enormous financial resources persuaded builders and developers to exclude competing sources of heat through aggressive marketing strategies * * * .

PP&L essentially used its position to establish itself as a major force in the new construction market by excluding others on some basis other than superior efficiency. Consumers suffered from this conduct because PP&L locked new homeowners into inefficient and expensive sources of heat, restraining their ability to obtain less-costly and more efficient heating systems.

[As to] the question of specific intent, the Court concludes that [the PP&L executive's remark and other] statements could convince a jury that PP&L intended to dominate the new residential heating submarket, that PP&L advanced that intent, and that the all-electric agreements codified PP&L's desire to dominate and assisted in the realization of that objective.

Decision and Remedy

The court ruled that, if the case was allowed to proceed to trial, a jury could conclude that PP&L intended to monopolize the new-home heating market, that it engaged in predatory conduct toward that end, and that this attempt had a dangerous probability of success. The court denied PP&L's motion for summary judgment.

Terms and Concepts to Review

antitrust law 531
attempt to monopolize 547
dissolution 537
divestiture 537
market power 531
market-share test 541
monopolization 540
monopoly 531
monopoly power 534
***Noerr-Pennington* doctrine** 540
predatory pricing 540
restraint of trade 534
treble damages 537
trust 533

Questions and Case Problems

26–1. Exemptions. The Southern Motor Carriers Rate Conference is a private organization that lobbies regulatory commissions in various southern states on behalf of national and regional private commercial carriers. A new carrier claims that the organization is really in the business of setting rates and controlling the issuance of licenses through its influence over the members of the various regulatory boards. How might the organization violate antitrust laws? If the organization does no more than lobby the various agencies, does it run afoul of the antitrust laws in light of the Supreme Court's enunciation of the *Noerr-Pennington* doctrine?

26–2. Predatory Pricing. A car rental firm specializes in renting automobiles to insurance company customers who need temporary replacements while their cars are being repaired. Several other car rental agencies serve the same geographical area. The specialty agency substantially reduces the daily rental fee on its cars. Other firms in the area contend that the reductions amount to predatory pricing. If an antitrust action is brought against the specialty agency, how should the case be decided? Discuss all factors that must be considered.

26–3. Monopolies. Super-Tech Industries presently controls 55 percent of the market in the manufacture and sale of computers. The balance of the market is controlled by five other manufacturers, with Alcan Corp. having 25 percent of the market. Alcan has an innovative research staff, but every time Alcan introduces a faster, more powerful, and more efficient computer in the market, Super-Tech immediately informs its customers of the upcoming development of a competing computer that it will sell at 30 percent below the Alcan price. Alcan claims that these activities on the part of Super-Tech are an antitrust violation. Discuss fully whether this unilateral action by Super-Tech violates antitrust law.

26–4. PUBLIC POLICY AND CONTRACTS. Goodfellows, Inc., is a close corporation with only two shareholders. Goodfellows is engaged in the pizza delivery business. Two other such firms serve the same market, but Goodfellows controls a 75 percent share. The two shareholders agree that one will purchase all of the shares that belong to the other. As a condition of the transaction, the shareholder selling the shares agrees not to open a competing pizza delivery business within a seventy-mile radius or become employed by any rival firm within the same designated area. The covenant is to last five years. Is it an unreasonable restraint of trade? Would a court likely declare unenforceable the promise not to compete?

26–5. ANTICOMPETITIVE BEHAVIOR. Syufy, a movie theater operator, opened a lavish six-screen theater in Las Vegas. All theater owners in Las Vegas obtained films from distributors by submitting bids on first-run movie releases. Successful bidders obtained an exhibition license specifying that the distributor would receive a percentage of the theaters' weekly receipts. Syufy's uniquely opulent theater generated considerable patronage, and soon a price war was under way between Syufy and the other Las Vegas theater owners. Eventually, the competition was reduced to just Syufy and Roberts, a small exhibitor of predominantly second-run films, with the former controlling nearly 100 percent of the Las Vegas theater market. After a major film distributor stopped doing business with Syufy and began to deal exclusively with Roberts, Syufy suffered a reversal of fortunes. Soon thereafter, Roberts became the dominant force in the market. Ultimately, Roberts sold out to a national theater chain. The government sued Syufy, alleging a violation of Section 2 of the Sherman Act. The government argued that Syufy had acquired monopoly power by buying out his competition. Syufy defended by arguing that he could not have violated Section 2 because there were no barriers preventing other firms from entering the Las Vegas theater market. Which side is likely to prevail? [*United States v. Syufy Enterprises*, 903 F.2d 659 (9th Cir. 1990)]

26–6. MONOPOLIES. American Academic Suppliers, Inc., and Beckley-Cardy, Inc., were wholesalers engaged in the sale of school supplies. American's major markets were largely concentrated in the Midwest; Beckley's markets were on a more national scale. American had been started by Beckley's former president on a small initial investment of less than $500,000. American had also hired a number of salespersons away from Beckley. Initially, American had experienced fairly rapid expansion in the markets in which it competed with Beckley. Beckley had responded by giving steep discounts in the prices of some of its products and, according to American, by making disparaging remarks and starting rumors about American's business operations. American sued Beckley, alleging, among other things, that Beckley had violated Section 2 of the Sherman Act by attempting to monopolize the school-supply market. Did Beckley's actions constitute an attempt to monopolize the school-supply market in violation of Section 2 of the Sherman Act? Discuss fully. [*American Academic Suppliers, Inc. v. Beckley-Cardy, Inc.*, 922 F.2d 1317 (7th Cir. 1991)]

26–7. MONOPOLIES. BTR, Inc., owns the patent rights to sorbothane (an elastic polymer with characteristics that make it useful in a variety of products). In 1980, BTR granted Shirley and Larry McQuillan all distribution rights to sorbothane and exclusive rights to buy sorbothane for use in equestrian products. In 1981, BTR split the distribution rights between the McQuillans and Spectrum Sports, Inc. The next year, BTR asked the McQuillans to relinquish more of their distribution rights, but they refused. A few months later, BTR appointed another company as national distributor for sorbothane equestrian products. In August 1983, BTR refused to accept the McQuillans' orders, and Spectrum replaced them as national distributor of some sorbothane products. The McQuillans' business failed. They sued BTR and Spectrum. Did the defendants violate Section 2 of the Sherman Act? [*Spectrum Sports, Inc. v. McQuillan*, 506 U.S. 884, 113 S.Ct. 884, 122 L.Ed.2d 247 (1993)]

26–8. ANTITRUST LAWS. Great Western Directories, Inc. (GW), is an independent publisher of telephone directory Yellow Pages. GW buys information for its listings from Southwestern Bell Telephone Co. (SBT). Southwestern Bell Corp. owns SBT and Southwestern Bell Yellow Pages (SBYP), which publishes a directory in competition with GW. In June 1988, in some markets, SBT raised the price for its listing information, and SBYP lowered the price for advertising in its Yellow Pages. GW feared that these companies would do the same thing in other local markets, and it would then be too expensive to compete in those markets. Because of this fear, GW left one market and declined to compete in another. Consequently, SBYP had a monopoly in those markets. GW and another independent publisher filed a suit in a federal district court against Southwestern Bell Corp. What antitrust law, if any, did Southwestern Bell Corp. violate? Should the independent companies be entitled to damages? [*Great Western Directories, Inc. v. Southwestern Bell Telephone Co.*, 74 F.3d 613 (5th Cir. 1996)]

26–9. A QUESTION OF ETHICS

Mr. Furniture Warehouse, Inc., was a company engaged in the wholesale and retail furniture business. Like many other companies in its line of business, Mr. Furniture frequently obtained its furniture products from manufacturers by making purchases on credit. Credit usually was not provided by the manufacturers themselves but rather by institutions engaged in "commercial factoring." Such institutions typically purchase manufacturers' accounts receivable at a discount and assume direct responsibility for collecting the outstanding debts. Moreover, factored-credit institutions often purchase debt on a nonrecourse basis, meaning that they assume the entire risk of a debtor's failure to repay. The institutions rely on credit ratings and similar criteria in deciding which purchasers should be extended credit. Barclays American/Commercial, Inc., was almost certainly the dominant factored credit institution in the market in which Mr. Furniture operated. Barclays refused to extend credit for Mr. Furniture's inventory purchases from furniture manufacturers. Mr. Furniture's president, Howard Cassett, asserted that the refusal was based on two elements: (1) Barclays's attempt to monopolize the factored-credit market and (2) the personal animosity that Barclays's manager, Jim Stenhouse, harbored toward Cassett. Mr. Furniture sued Barclays, alleging, among other things, violations of the Sherman Act. The trial court ruled that Mr. Furniture lacked standing to bring the antitrust charge; the court held that any alleged monopolization would directly injure other commercial factoring institutions that competed with Barclays, not Mr. Furniture. [*Mr. Furniture Warehouse, Inc. v. Barclays American/Commercial, Inc.*, 919 F.2d 1517 (11th Cir. 1990)]

1. The court's ruling, affirmed on appeal, that Mr. Furniture lacked standing was based on the contention that any antitrust violations committed by Barclays would injure its competitors—other factored-credit institutions—not Mr. Furniture. Should Mr. Furniture have been allowed to complain simply because, as a "consumer" of factored-credit services, it was harmed by the alleged monopoly over credit extension acquired by Barclays? After all, the antitrust laws are supposed to help consumers, not competitors. Does the court's ruling mean that only Barclays's rivals could bring the suit?
2. The court explicitly held that the alleged personal animosity of the Barclays executive toward Mr. Furniture's president was irrelevant. There is something to be said for preventing the antitrust laws, which involve the mechanisms of the judicial process, from being used in a petty way to settle personal feuds. But if monopoly power—assuming Barclays had such power—is used for personal motives, would it be reasonable to allow standing on that basis? Is such abuse any less troubling just because it is done for personal rather than economic reasons?

26–10. Case Briefing Assignment

Examine Case A.6 [*Delaware & Hudson Railway v. Consolidated Rail Corp.*, 902 F.2d 174 (2d Cir. 1990)] in Appendix A. The case has been excerpted there in considerable detail. Review and then brief the case, making sure that you include answers to the following questions in your brief.

1. What was the make-or-buy policy instituted by Conrail, and how did it allegedly disadvantage the Delaware & Hudson Railway?
2. Did the appellate court agree that a policy designed to maximize short-term profits could not, as a matter of law, violate Section 2 of the Sherman Act? On what United States Supreme Court decision was this argument based?
3. Is a monopolist required to aid a competitor?
4. What is the four-factor test for an "essential facility"?

Accessing the Internet

The Legal Environment of Business

The Antitrust Division of the U.S. Department of Justice is online at

http://www.usdoj.gov/

For information on a wide variety of legal issues, including antitrust law, go to the Federal Legal Research Template at

http://www.netrail.net/~sunburst/

CHAPTER 27

ANTITRUST AND RESTRAINTS OF TRADE

THE MAJOR THRUST OF FEDERAL ANTITRUST legislation has been directed at anticompetitive agreements between rival firms. Agreements to fix prices, restrict output, divide markets, exclude other competitors, and otherwise impede the dynamics of a free market have all been condemned as violations of federal antitrust laws. Such joint actions have been prosecuted as impermissible restraints of trade under Section 1 of the Sherman Act and, if the firms possess substantial market power, as conspiracies to monopolize under Section 2 of the same act.

Some agreements may be forced on an unwilling firm by another firm possessing substantial market power. Typical of such agreements are exclusive-dealing contracts and tying arrangements, described in the preceding chapter. Recall that an exclusive-dealing contract conditions one firm's willingness to deal with another on the latter's continued refusal to deal with the former's rivals. Tying arrangements normally require that the purchaser of one product also purchase a second product. Also recall that such agreements violate provisions of the Clayton Act if the contracts or arrangements harm the competitive process or interfere with free trade.

In this chapter, we continue our study of antitrust law by examining in detail the various forms of *concerted behavior* that are condemned as harmful to competition. In particular, we examine how courts attempt to distinguish between those types of trade restrictions that are necessary—perhaps even beneficial—to the competitive process and those that impede competition. We also examine the legal standards for determining whether mergers between firms should be declared illegal on the ground that the result would be to lessen competition.

SECTION 1

RESTRAINTS OF TRADE: OVERVIEW

The underlying assumption of Section 1 of the Sherman Act is that society's welfare is harmed if rival firms are permitted to join in an agreement that consolidates their market power or otherwise restrains competition. Not all agreements between rivals, however, result in enhanced market power or *unreasonably* restrain trade. It is virtually inconceivable that an agreement to fix prices or restrict output could be designed for any purpose other than to diminish interfirm competition. Yet there are numerous instances in which agreements among rivals might actually increase social welfare by making firms more efficient, by making information more readily available, or by creating joint incentives to undertake risky research and development projects.

PER SE VIOLATIONS

Some agreements are considered so blatantly and substantially anticompetitive that they are deemed ***per se*** **violations** of Section 1. For example, if two competitors in a concentrated industry agree to set the prices for their products at the same level, their agreement is considered so anticompetitive that it is deemed a *per se* violation. If an agreement is found to be a *per se* violation, a court is precluded from inquiring whether the agreement should be upheld on the ground that it provides benefits that outweigh its anticompetitive effects. If an agreement is not found to be a *per se* violation of Section 1, then the court proceeds to analyze its legality under what is referred to as a **rule of reason,** according to which the court balances the reasons for the agreement against its potentially anticompetitive effects.

THE RULE OF REASON

In determining whether a specific agreement that is not a *per se* violation should nonetheless be condemned as a Section 1 offense, a court will consider several factors. The court must evaluate the parties' purposes in effecting the agreement, determine whether the parties have power to implement the agreement's purposes, and assess what the effect or potential effect of the agreement is. Some antitrust scholars maintain that case law suggests that courts will also consider a fourth element: whether the parties could have relied on less restrictive means to achieve their goals.

THE SOFT *PER SE* RULE, OR NARROW RULE OF REASON

Sometimes, it is not clear whether a restraint of trade is being judged under the *per se* rule or is being subjected to a rule-of-reason analysis. In some cases, for example, the United States Supreme Court has stated, or at least implied, that it is applying a *per se* rule, and yet a careful reading of its analysis suggests that it is weighing benefits against harms under a rule of reason.[1] Some have termed this a "soft," or "limited," *per se* rule. Others have termed it a "narrow" rule of reason. Perhaps the most that can be said with certainty is that although the distinction between the two rules seems clear in theory, in the actual application of antitrust laws, the distinction has not always been so clear.

SECTION 2

HORIZONTAL RESTRAINTS

The term **horizontal restraint** is encountered frequently in antitrust law. A horizontal restraint is any agreement that in some way restrains competition between rival firms competing in the same market. Whenever firms at the same level of operation and in direct competition with one another (for example, retailers of a similar product located in the same geographical market) agree to operate in a way that restricts their market activities, they are said to have imposed a horizontal restraint on trade. Some horizontal restraints are *per se* violations of Section 1, but others may be permissible; those that are not *per se* violations are tested under the rule of reason.

PRICE FIXING

Consider the scenario presented in Chapter 26 involving the introduction of a new digital video disc (DVD) drive. Suppose our hypothetical firm, Acme, had instead sought large profits by some means other than arduous and financially risky research into

1. See, for example, *Fashion Originator's Guild of America, Inc. v. Federal Trade Commission*, 312 U.S. 457, 61 S.Ct. 703, 85 L.Ed. 949 (1941); *Klor's, Inc. v. Broadway-Hale Stores, Inc.*, 359 U.S. 207, 79 S.Ct. 705, 3 L.Ed.2d 741 (1959); and *Silver v. New York Stock Exchange*, 373 U.S. 341, 83 S.Ct. 1246, 10 L.Ed.2d 389 (1963).

innovative DVD drive technology. Assume that advanced DVD drive technology does not yet exist. Acme's managers decide to make life easy for themselves. They go to other DVD drive producers and say, "Let's not work to one another's disadvantage. There's enough demand for DVD drives for all of us to charge higher prices if we don't undercut one another's prices." Acme's plan calls for each producer to charge a price higher than an established minimum. The minimum price is set as the total cost of the least productive producer plus a 10 percent profit margin. More efficient firms (that is, firms that can produce at lower cost) will, of course, enjoy higher profits.

Although not all such schemes are as simple or as blatant as our hypothetical example suggests, they all involve some means of eliminating competition between rivals to sell at the lowest price while still earning a normal profit (that is, one commensurate with the profit that could be earned in some alternative endeavor using the same resources). By eliminating price competition in which firms seek to sell more by charging less than their rivals, firms restrict output. This is the essence of **price fixing.**

***PER SE* VIOLATION** Perhaps the definitive case regarding price-fixing agreements remains the 1940 case of *United States v. Socony-Vacuum Oil Co.*, also known as the *Madison Oil* case.[2] In this case, a group of independent oil producers in Texas and Louisiana were caught between falling demand due to the Great Depression and increasing supply from newly discovered oil fields in the region. In response, a group of the major refining companies agreed to buy "distress" gasoline (excess supplies) from the independents so as to dispose of it in an "orderly manner." Although there was no explicit agreement as to price, it was clear that the purpose of the agreement was to limit the supply of gasoline on the market, thereby raising prices.

There may have been good reasons for such an agreement. The refiners may simply have wanted to avoid a temporary situation that would have driven the independent suppliers out of business, thus making it difficult to secure crude oil supplies later, after the economic climate had improved. Nonetheless, the threats posed by such agreements to open and free competition were deemed significant. The United States Supreme Court recognized these dangers in the *Socony-Vacuum* case. The Court held that the asserted reasonableness of a price-fixing agreement is never a defense; any agreement that restricts output or artificially fixes price is a *per se* violation of Section 1. The rationale of the *per se* rule was best stated in what is now the most famous portion of the Court's decision: footnote 59 of Justice William O. Douglas's opinion. In it, he compared a freely functioning price system to a body's central nervous system, condemning price-fixing agreements as threats to "the central nervous system of the economy."

2. 310 U.S. 150, 60 S.Ct. 811, 84 L.Ed.2d 1129 (1940).

IDENTIFYING A PRICE-FIXING ARRANGEMENT Price-fixing arrangements are not always easy to identify. An otherwise legitimate arrangement may unintentionally result in price fixing. Price fixing also may be difficult to detect because the parties wish to conceal their scheme. The following case provides an illustration.

CASE 27.1 In re Medical X-ray Film Antitrust Litigation

United States District Court, Eastern District of New York, 1996. 946 F.Supp. 209.

BACKGROUND AND FACTS *Eastman Kodak Company; E. I. du Pont de Nemours & Company; Miles, Inc.; Fuji Medical Systems, U.S.A., Inc.; and other companies sell medical X-ray film. During the late 1980s and early 1990s, Kodak, du Pont, Miles, and Fuji increased the prices of their film every year. The increases, which were generally close in time and amount, were announced late each year. Before the announcements, supervisors with the various companies would tell their employees that their competitors were going to raise prices. Sometimes they distributed copies of competitors' intracompany memos concerning the increases. At meetings of the American Association of Radiological Technicians, some of the competitors' sales representatives exchanged pricing information, including copies of their respective companies' internal memos*

regarding proposed increases. Victoria Orthopedic Associates and other buyers of the film filed a suit in a federal district court against Kodak and the others, alleging price fixing in violation of the Sherman Act. In response to the plaintiffs' evidence of exchange of information among competitors, the defendants argued in part that prices were set before any of the information was exchanged, that none of the individuals involved had any authority to set prices, and that the contacts were random, unplanned encounters. The defendants filed a motion for summary judgment.

IN THE LANGUAGE OF THE COURT

SIFTON, Chief Judge.

* * * *

* * * [P]laintiffs have presented a basis upon which the existence of a price-fixing agreement or conspiracy among defendants can reasonably be inferred. Despite the plausibility of defendants' innocent explanations for the circumstantial evidence plaintiffs have presented * * * , this evidence * * * tends to exclude the possibility that defendants acted independently in setting their prices for medical x-ray film each year. * * * [T]here is sufficient evidence in this case to infer that the market of medical x-ray film dealers and customers, in conjunction with the ease of interfirm communications, served as a kind of clearinghouse from which competitors could gather information regarding current prices and impending price increases in order to coordinate their pricing activities.

DECISION AND REMEDY

The court denied the defendants' motion for summary judgment. There was a reasonable basis from which to infer a price-fixing agreement. The case could proceed to trial.

HORIZONTAL MARKET DIVISIONS

Prices can be controlled indirectly through agreements to restrict output, as well as explicitly through agreements to fix prices. Because the former type of agreement operates to decrease the supplies available to consumers, it has the same effect as a direct agreement to raise prices. Efforts to control prices are often effected by **horizontal market divisions**—that is, agreements to divide the market up among rival firms. The allocation may be geographical (for example, letting one firm serve the Midwest, another the East Coast, and so on), or it may be functional, by class of customer (for example, having one firm deal exclusively with retailers and a second firm deal solely with wholesalers).

In some respects, market divisions may have an even greater impact on competition than do price-fixing agreements. Each firm has a monopoly over its allocated share of the market for that particular brand—it is the sole supplier. The sole supplier is free not only from price competition for that brand but also from competition for that brand regarding quality, customer service, and all other dimensions of competition.

APPLYING THE *PER SE* RULE Consider once again our hypothetical scenario involving Acme and its rival DVD drive producers. Suppose that, flush with the initial success of their price-fixing agreement, the producers agree that each firm that begins selling DVD drives to dealers in remote communities in which DVD drives have not been available will thereafter have an exclusive right to sell at retail or through dealers in that area. Initially, there is intense competition to find such virgin markets. After all the profitable markets have been taken, however, conditions in the exclusive markets may change. Suppliers may begin to limit the warranties they offer. Prices may begin to rise despite the lack of warranties. And service may diminish. Because of such potential effects, agreements like that made by the DVD drive producers are generally treated as *per se* violations of Section 1.

The following case considers whether an allocation of customers is a horizontal restraint that should be treated as a *per se* violation of Section 1 of the Sherman Act. The case also shows the procedural effects of characterizing conduct as a *per se* violation.

CASE 27.2 United States v. Suntar Roofing, Inc.

United States Circuit Court of Appeals, Tenth Circuit, 1990. 897 F.2d 469.

BACKGROUND AND FACTS *Suntar Roofing, Inc., and Ronan's Roofing, Inc., built roofs on new homes in and around Kansas City, Kansas. Some of Suntar's and Ronan's officers and owners agreed to a customer allocation plan that would divide roofing customers in the area between the two corporations. The U.S. government brought criminal charges against some of the officers and owners. During the trial, the judge ruled that all customer allocation schemes are* per se *violations of Section 1 of the Sherman Act. This ruling prevented the defendants from introducing evidence to show the reasonableness of their agreement. The defendants were found guilty of violating federal antitrust laws, and they appealed.*

IN THE LANGUAGE OF THE COURT

BRORBY, Circuit Judge.

* * * *

* * * [S]ince the passage of the Sherman Act, the courts have formulated and applied a *per se* rule of illegality for certain restrictive practices that are deemed to be manifestly anticompetitive. As the Supreme Court explained * * * , "there are certain agreements or practices which because of their pernicious [harmful] effect on competition and lack of any redeeming virtue are conclusively presumed to be unreasonable and therefore illegal without elaborate inquiry as to the precise harm they have caused or the business excuse for their use." Here, appellants [Suntar and Ronan's] argue that the indictment in this case did not justify the trial court's application of *per se* analysis * * * .

* * * [T]he government argued that the conduct charged in the indictment, a "horizontal" customer allocation agreement, represented conduct which is illegal *per se*. Prior to trial, the trial court ruled that the indictment did in fact allege a *per se* violation of the Sherman Act, and that, assuming the government could present evidence establishing the violation charged in the indictment, the defendants would therefore be precluded from introducing evidence of reasonableness or justification at trial. At trial, the court concluded that the government had established the violation charged and therefore precluded defendants' additional evidence. Consistent with the analysis of the Supreme Court and previous holdings of this court and of other circuits, we concur with the determination of the trial court and hold that the activity alleged in the indictment in this case, an agreement to allocate or divide customers between competitors within the same horizontal market, constitutes a *per se* violation of Section 1 of the Sherman Act.

DECISION AND REMEDY *The appellate court sustained the trial judge's ruling that a customer allocation scheme is a* per se *violation of Section 1 of the Sherman Act. Therefore, the trial judge's exclusion of evidence regarding the reasonableness of, or business justification for, the scheme was not an error.*

CRITICISMS OF APPLYING THE *PER SE* RULE

The *per se* rule regarding market divisions has been criticized in certain circumstances, and its future status is uncertain. Some actual cases have involved circumstances very dissimilar to those presented in our hypothetical scenario involving DVD drive production and sales. In one instance, a group of small- and medium-sized grocery stores agreed to market a common brand of grocery products by allocating regional territories to members of the group so that individual members could focus their marketing efforts on a single territory. The group accounted for only about 6 percent of sales in its market and directly competed with such large chain stores as A&P and Safeway, which carried their own brand-name products.[3] A similar venture using territorial restrictions involved a group of small firms attempting to market mattresses under the trademark Sealy.[4]

3. See *United States v. Topco Associates, Inc.*, 405 U.S. 596, 92 S.Ct. 1126, 31 L.Ed.2d 515 (1972).

4. See *United States v. Sealy, Inc.*, 388 U.S. 350, 87 S.Ct. 1847, 18 L.Ed.2d 1238 (1967).

In both these cases, the individual firms did not have sufficient resources to create their own brands individually and joined together so as to compete with larger, established firms selling their own brand-name products. Nonetheless, both cases were treated as *per se* violations of Section 1. It is possible that the United States Supreme Court will ultimately adopt a rule of reason for judging such horizontal restraints. As shown by some cases considered later in this chapter, the Court has been more willing in recent years to consider economic factors rather than relying solely on mechanical characterizations in judging concerted business conduct.

TRADE ASSOCIATIONS

The common interests of firms or individuals within an industry or profession are frequently promoted by trade associations or professional organizations. These organizations may provide for the exchange of information among the members, the enhancement of the public image of the trade or profession, the setting of industry or professional standards, or the pooling of resources to represent the members' interests to various governmental bodies. Some of these activities benefit society, as well as the individual members. Even those activities that benefit the members' general economic well-being may not necessarily be anticompetitive.

For example, lumber producers might be concerned about whether or not they are cutting more trees than expected future demand would warrant given the cutting levels of rival firms. The market for lumber might be widely dispersed over the whole nation, making it especially difficult for small firms to gauge overall demand conditions in the lumber market. Lumber firms might thus decide to form a trade association that could amass data on the output and price levels of its members in various markets.[5] The association would be of economic benefit to lumber firms by reducing the costs of projecting market demand. Such knowledge could also benefit society by making the lumber market function more smoothly, dampening cycles of oversupply and undersupply of lumber output. Even if it did not make the industry function more smoothly, such knowledge would be unlikely to harm competition in the industry unless the industry was *concentrated.*

A **concentrated industry** is one in which either a single firm or a small number of firms controls a large percentage of market sales. In concentrated industries, trade associations can be, and have been, used as a means to facilitate anticompetitive actions, such as fixing prices, allocating markets, or, as discussed in the next section, conducting boycotts—all with the clear objective of lessening competition. For example, consider again the lumber association. Such an association would provide information that members could use to determine whether a secret agreement to fix prices was being adhered to by the conspirators. Thus, such associations offer possibilities of both great benefit and substantial harm.

In most instances, the rule of reason is applied in evaluating such practices and agreements. If a court finds that a particular practice or agreement that restrains trade involves no apparent intent to fix prices or limit output, and that it benefits the public as well as the association, then the court will weigh those benefits against the harms to competition under the rule of reason. As in other cases, however, if the harm to competition is substantial, a trade association's activities will be condemned as a Section 1 violation. As shown in the following case, not even action undertaken by a health-care professional organization allegedly for the sole purpose of protecting the public will escape scrutiny if it is likely to harm market competition.

5. See, for example, *American Column & Lumber Co. v. United States*, 257 U.S. 377, 42 S.Ct. 114, 66 L.Ed.2d 284 (1921).

CASE 27.3 Wilk v. American Medical Association

United States Court of Appeals, Seventh Circuit, 1990. 895 F.2d 352.

BACKGROUND AND FACTS *In 1966, the American Medical Association (AMA) passed a resolution labeling chiropractic an unscientific cult. (Chiropractors attempt to cure or relieve bodily ailments by making skeletal adjustments.) In effect, this label prevented physicians from associating with chiropractors, because Principle 3 of the Principles of Medical Ethics—the AMA's code of ethical conduct—provided that a "physician should practice a method of healing founded on a scientific basis; and he should not voluntarily associate with anyone who violates this principle." Medical doctors used Principle 3 to justify their refusal to have anything to do with chiropractors or to*

allow chiropractors to use hospital diagnostic services or become members of hospital medical staffs. Despite the AMA's efforts, chiropractic became licensed in all fifty states; and in a 1980 revision of the AMA's ethical code, Principle 3 was eliminated. Chester Wilk and four other chiropractors brought an action against the AMA, claiming that the boycott had violated Section 1 of the Sherman Act and seeking injunctive relief from the boycott's "lingering effects" on chiropractors. The trial court, holding that the AMA had violated Section 1 of the Sherman Act by conducting an illegal boycott in restraint of trade, granted an injunction that, among other things, required the AMA to publish widely the trial court's order. The AMA appealed.

IN THE LANGUAGE OF THE COURT

MANION, Circuit Judge.

* * * *

Despite the fact that * * * the conspiracy ended in 1980, * * * the illegal boycott's "lingering effects" still threatened plaintiffs with current injury * * * . [T]he boycott caused injury to chiropractors' reputations which had not been repaired, and current economic injury to chiropractors. Further, the AMA never affirmatively acknowledged that there are no impediments to professional association and cooperation between chiropractors and medical physicians * * * .

* * * *

* * * Essentially, the AMA argues that * * * health care consumers almost invariably lack sufficient information needed to evaluate the quality of medical services. This increases the risk of fraud and deception on consumers by unscrupulous health care providers * * * . The AMA's conduct, the theory goes on, * * * allowed consumers to be assured that physicians would use only scientifically valid treatments. This in effect * * * provided consumers with essential information * * * .

Getting information to the market is a fine goal, but * * * the AMA was not motivated solely by such altruistic concerns. Indeed, * * * the AMA intended to "destroy a competitor," namely, chiropractors. It is not enough to carry the day to argue that competition should be eliminated in the name of public safety.

DECISION AND REMEDY

The appellate court affirmed both the trial court's ruling that the AMA had violated Section 1 of the Sherman Act by conducting an illegal boycott of chiropractors and the trial court's decision to grant an injunction against the AMA.

GROUP BOYCOTTS

A **group boycott,** or concerted refusal to deal, is any agreement by which two or more buyers or sellers refuse to engage in any transactions with a particular person or organization, the object of the boycott. An obvious, and indeed frequent, purpose of a boycott is to eliminate or discipline a competitor of the boycotting group. Boycotts are thus a powerful tool for enforcing anticompetitive arrangements among firms.

ANTICOMPETITIVE INTENT Refer again to the DVD drive producers and their hypothetical attempts to fix prices and allocate market territories. After their initial success in obtaining greater profits for the industry, they face at least two problems. The first is how to discipline errant firms that attempt to increase their profits by selling for less than the agreed price or by encroaching on another firm's exclusive territory. The second is how to prevent new firms attracted by the large profits in the DVD drive industry from entering the market and reducing each member's share of profits.

Observe the actions of the group members further. They have now formed the High-Quality DVD Drive Association. The function of the association, at least as stated in its charter, is to "promote the interests of the consumer above all other considerations by ensuring that DVD drives are always manufactured according to the highest possible standards." To facilitate its goals, the association has decided to confer its "seal of approval" on all DVD drive products deemed of worthy quality. In fact, the association has never denied an *original* producer-member's request for approval except in those instances when the producer happens to have failed to abide by the original price and market-allocation terms the group has set.

Things are not so easy, however, for subsequent arrivals into the DVD drive industry. Alleging that the new firms are able to enter the market and compete only by use of "substandard components," the association refuses to bestow any new seals of approval. Moreover, the association urges retail dealers, some of whom have been invited to become members of the association, not to carry or service any products that do not have the association's seal of approval. In concert, the group refuses to have any dealings with any retailers, wholesalers, or other manufacturers who do not exclusively use products carrying the association's seal of approval. This is a group boycott.

PROCOMPETITIVE INTENT Sometimes, however, group boycotts are intended to promote economic efficiency, moral or social causes, or the general well-being of the group, without intending to injure competition. For example, a professional organization or a trade association might seek to promote its public image by sponsoring a program to prevent its members from engaging in deceptive advertising or employing high-pressure sales tactics. A member's failure to abide by the program guidelines could be punished by expulsion from the organization or association or by denial of the group's endorsement, such as withholding of the association's "seal of approval."

Despite the possibility of a procompetitive intent or some other socially valuable objective, concerted refusals to deal—group boycotts—are generally said to be *per se* violations of Section 1. A more accurate statement is that a court will treat a group boycott as a *per se* violation of Section 1 in cases in which the group possesses market power and the boycott is intended to restrict or exclude a competitor. If, however, these elements are missing, the court may be inclined to weigh the benefits of the group's efforts against the harm inflicted by the boycott. The court in the following case emphasizes these principles.

CASE 27.4 Discon, Inc. v. NYNEX Corp.

United States Court of Appeals, Second Circuit, 1996. 93 F.3d 1055.

BACKGROUND AND FACTS *NYNEX Corporation owns New York Telephone Company (NYTel), which provides telephone service to most of New York. NYTel has a monopoly on phone service in the areas that it serves. NYNEX also owns NYNEX Material Enterprises (known as MECo). MECo's business is, among other things, to obtain for NYTel removal services (salvaging and disposing of obsolete equipment). MECo bought these services from AT&T Technologies, Inc., at inflated prices, which it charged to NYTel. NYTel passed the charges onto its customers. MECo later received secret rebates of the excessive charges from AT&T. (Essentially, MECo and NYNEX used NYTel's monopoly to obtain increased revenues.) When the scheme was uncovered, NYTel agreed to refund over $35 million to its customers. Discon, Inc., which also provides removal services in New York, filed a suit in a federal district court against NYNEX and others, alleging, among other things, that as part of their scheme, the defendants had conspired to eliminate Discon from the market, in favor of AT&T, because Discon had refused to participate in the rebate scheme. Discon contended that this amounted to an illegal group boycott. The defendants filed a motion to dismiss, which the court granted. Discon appealed.*

IN THE LANGUAGE OF THE COURT

JON O. NEWMAN, Chief Judge:

* * * *

In the vast majority of cases, the decision to discriminate in favor of one supplier over another will have a pro-competitive intent and effect. Presumably, the purchaser will have chosen a particular supplier because that firm provides certain efficiencies that allow the purchaser to compete more effectively in the market for sales to the ultimate consumer. In this case, however, no such pro-competitive rationale appears on the face of the complaint. Discon alleges that the intent and effect of choosing AT&T Technologies over Discon was entirely anti-competitive. Although the NYNEX Defendants may be able to present some pro-competitive justification for choosing a more costly supplier in order to overcharge captive rate-paying customers, this justification, if it exists, remains unproven. We conclude that Discon has alleged a cause of action under, at least, the rule of reason, and possibly under the *per se* rule applied to group boycotts, if the restraint of trade has no purpose except stifling competition.

DECISION AND REMEDY *The U.S. Court of Appeals for the Second Circuit reversed the judgment of the lower court. The defendants' treatment of Discon constituted a group boycott. The court remanded the case to determine the defendants' intent. If the intent was to stifle competition, the boycott was a* per se *violation of the Sherman Act.*

JOINT VENTURES

A **joint venture** is any undertaking by two or more firms or individuals that, while maintaining their distinct identities, come together for the limited purpose of achieving a specific goal. Antitrust analysis of joint ventures involves two issues: first, whether the joining together is itself a violation of antitrust laws; and second, whether the purpose or means of the joint venture is impermissible. The first issue is covered by Section 7 of the Clayton Act, as well as Section 1 of the Sherman Act. An important consideration is the joint venture's percentage market share. Here we limit our focus to the legality of the joint venture's purpose and actions.

PERMISSIBLE PURPOSES Unlike price-fixing agreements and market divisions, joint ventures are not necessarily anticompetitive. Indeed, many are likely to provide economic efficiencies. For example, it may be beneficial to society, as well as to the individual firms involved, if firms engaging in substantial research and development (R&D) efforts pool their resources. Pooling R&D resources prevents firms from duplicating one another's efforts. Once the R&D phase has been completed, the firms will compete along other dimensions, such as price, quality, and consumer services. Pooling resources also allows the firms to share the risk that the initial efforts may be fruitless. In some cases, a venture that is desirable from society's point of view involves risks so substantial that no single firm would want to undertake the venture alone. When the risk is spread among many firms, individual risk is reduced, and the venture is more appealing.

NO LESS RESTRICTIVE MEANS Investment bankers often form underwriting syndicates to bring issues of new securities to the market. During the initial offering, it is common for the underwriters to "make a market" by agreeing to buy back enough of the securities to keep the price above a predetermined minimum if demand is less than was anticipated initially. Such an arrangement has all the earmarks of price fixing. In *United States v. Morgan*,[6] however, the court held that the arrangement was not an unreasonable restraint of trade.

Sometimes, the *Morgan* case is cited as an exception to the rule that price fixing is a *per se* violation of Section 1. The decision cannot be taken to mean that price fixing is ever reasonable; distinct features of the case make it clear that the court did not view this as ordinary price fixing, which remains a *per se* violation of Section 1.[7] The court took into consideration several unique aspects of the arrangement: the duration of the syndicate was extremely short; new syndicates involving different investment houses were continually being formed for new offerings; there was a competitive process by which investment houses sought to form and join the new syndicates; and competitive pressures were sufficient to ensure that those seeking to raise investment capital were provided a relatively low-cost, efficient vehicle for doing so. What is perhaps most significant in the *Morgan* case is that the government, in challenging the practice, was unable to point to any less restrictive means of raising capital as efficiently.

6. 118 F.Supp. 621 (S.D.N.Y. 1953).

7. The case is more often cited as a classic example of how to judge joint ventures under the rule of reason.

If a joint venture does not involve price fixing or market divisions, the agreement will be analyzed under the rule of reason. Whether the venture will then be upheld under Section 1 depends on an overall assessment of the purposes of the venture, a strict analysis of the potential benefits relative to the likely harms, and in some cases an assessment of whether there are less restrictive alternatives for achieving the same goals.

SECTION 3
VERTICAL RESTRAINTS

Another distinct set of restraints of trade comprises those imposed by the seller on the buyer (or vice versa), as distinct from those imposed *among* sellers or buyers. The latter restraints involve what is termed a vertical relationship. Horizontal relationships occur at the same level of operations. Vertical relationships, by comparison, encompass the entire chain of production: the purchase of inputs, basic manufacturing, distribution to wholesalers, and eventual sale of a product at the retail level. For some products, these distinct phases are carried on by different firms. In other instances, a single firm may carry out two or more of the functional phases. Firms such as the latter are considered to be **vertically integrated firms.**

There are two kinds of vertical integration—backward and forward. A firm that is integrated backward moves down the chain of production toward a supplier. A firm that is integrated forward moves up the chain of production toward the consumer market. For example, if the Red Ball Shoe Manufacturing Company, a shoe manufacturer, owns its source of leather, it is integrated backward; if Red Ball owns its retail outlets, it is integrated forward (see Exhibit 27–1).

Even though firms operating at different functional levels do not directly compete with one another, each does compete with other firms operating at its own level of operation. Thus, agreements between firms standing in a vertical relationship may affect competition. For example, suppose that a contractual agreement between tire manufacturer Firestone and Billy Ray's Automotive Supplies, an independent retailer, conditions Billy Ray's future supply of Firestone tires on its willingness to resell only at a price set by Firestone. This agreement is a form of **vertical restraint**—an anticompetitive agreement between entities operating at different levels of the market structure. Other types of vertical restraints are often encountered, but not all of them necessarily harm competition. Indeed, many are procompetitive.

Marketing decisions within a vertically integrated firm are not subject to attack under Section 1. The legality of certain other classes of vertical restraints is judged under a rule of reason. Still others are deemed *per se* violations of Section 1.

TERRITORIAL OR CUSTOMER RESTRICTIONS

In arranging for the distribution of its product, a manufacturing firm may seek to insulate its dealers or retailers from direct competition with one another. There may be legitimate, procompetitive reasons for doing so. One such reason is to prevent a dealer from lowering costs and undercutting same-brand rivals by providing the product without promotion or customer service, while relying on a nearby same-brand dealer to provide these services. The cost-cutting same-brand dealer could thus enjoy the benefits of the promotional and customer service costs expended by his or her rivals without incurring the associated costs. This is an example of the "free rider" problem.[8] One way of addressing the problem

8. For a discussion of the free rider problem in the context of sports telecasting, see *Chicago Professional Sports Limited Partnership v. National Basketball Association*, 961 F.2d 667 (7th Cir. 1993).

EXHIBIT 27–1 ■ BACKWARD AND FORWARD INTEGRATION

A firm that is integrated backward moves up the chain of production. A firm that is integrated forward moves down the chain of production.

is to restrict same-brand dealers to selling in specific markets or to certain classes of customers. These restrictions are judged under a rule of reason.

The following case, *Continental T.V., Inc. v. GTE Sylvania, Inc.*, overturned the United States Supreme Court's earlier stance, which had been set out in *United States v. Arnold, Schwinn & Co.*[9] In *Schwinn*, the Court had held territorial or customer restrictions to be *per se* violations. The *Continental* case has been heralded as one of the most important antitrust cases since the 1940s. It represents a definite shift away from rigid characterization to a more flexible approach emphasizing economics and efficiency.

9. 388 U.S. 365, 87 S.Ct. 1856, 18 L.Ed.2d 1249 (1967).

CASE 27.5 Continental T.V., Inc. v. GTE Sylvania, Inc.

Supreme Court of the United States, 1977.
433 U.S. 36,
97 S.Ct. 2549,
53 L.Ed.2d 568.

HISTORICAL AND ECONOMIC SETTING *Since the passage of the antitrust laws around the turn of the century, the courts have been skeptical of any business action that appears to restrain commerce, having long agreed that the "heart of our national economic policy [is] faith in the value of competition."*[a] *In determining what is or is not permitted under the antitrust laws, the courts have sometimes applied a rigid standard to business conduct. The trend, however, has been to establish a flexible standard, rather than a rigid one, particularly in regard to conduct that is considered to have procompetitive benefits. Under a flexible standard, a business practice that is considered a criminal offense in one decade may be judged a corporate virtue in the next. In the mid-1970s, for example, the United States Supreme Court began to qualify or overrule many of its previous decisions that prohibits certain business practices as* per se *violations of the antitrust laws. The Court appeared to be focusing on economic considerations, such as consumer welfare,*[b] *economic efficiency,*[c] *and interbrand versus intrabrand competition.*

BACKGROUND AND FACTS *GTE Sylvania, Inc., a manufacturer of television sets, adopted a franchise plan that limited the number of franchises granted in any given geographical area and that required each franchise to sell only Sylvania products from the location or locations at which it was franchised. A franchise did not constitute an exclusive territory, and Sylvania retained sole discretion to increase the number of retailers in an area, depending on the success or failure of existing retailers in developing their market. Continental T.V., Inc., was a retailer under Sylvania's franchise plan. Shortly after Sylvania proposed a new franchise that would compete with Continental, Sylvania terminated Continental's franchise, and a suit was brought in a federal district court for money owed. Continental claimed that Sylvania's vertically restrictive franchise system violated Section 1 of the Sherman Act. The district court ruled in favor of Continental, and Sylvania appealed. The appellate court reversed the trial court's decision. Continental appealed to the United States Supreme Court.*

a. *Standard Oil Co. v. Federal Trade Commission*, 340 U.S. 231, 71 S.Ct. 240, 95 L.Ed. 239 (1951).
b. *Reiter v. Sonotone Corp.*, 442 U.S. 330, 99 S.Ct. 2326, 60 L.Ed.2d 931 (1979).
c. *Broadcast Music, Inc. v. Columbia Broadcasting System, Inc.*, 441 U.S. 1, 99 S.Ct. 1551, 60 L.Ed.2d 1 (1979).

IN THE LANGUAGE OF THE COURT

Mr. Justice *POWELL* delivered the opinion of the Court.

* * * *

Vertical restrictions reduce intrabrand competition by limiting the number of sellers of a particular product competing for the business of a given group of buyers. * * *

Vertical restrictions promote interbrand competition by allowing the manufacturer to achieve certain efficiencies in the distribution of his products. * * * Established manufacturers can use them to induce retailers to engage in promotional activities or to provide service and repair facilities necessary to the efficient marketing of their products. * * * The availability and quality of such services affect a manufacturer's goodwill and the competitiveness of his product. * * *

* * * *

* * * When anticompetitive effects are shown to result from particular vertical restrictions they can be adequately policed under the rule of reason * * * .

DECISION AND REMEDY

The United States Supreme Court upheld the appellate court's reversal of the district court's decision. Sylvania's vertical system, which was not price restrictive, did not constitute a per se *violation of Section 1 of the Sherman Act.*

RESALE PRICE MAINTENANCE AGREEMENTS

Resale price maintenance agreements, also referred to as *fair trade agreements*, occur when a manufacturer seeks to establish a minimum price that a retailer or wholesaler may charge for the manufacturer's product. Under these agreements, the manufacturer conditions sales to the retailer or wholesaler on the latter's reselling only at a price allowed by the manufacturer.

For many years, such agreements were authorized in some states under so-called *fair trade laws.* Federal law eliminated these provisions in 1975. Subsequently, resale price maintenance agreements were usually condemned as *per se* violations of Section 1 of the Sherman Act. During the Reagan administration (1981–1989), there was considerable criticism on the part of some representatives of government enforcement agencies and in some lower-court decisions of the application of the *per se* rule to resale price maintenance agreements. The courts' more common approach, however, has been to apply the *per se* standard.

Manufacturers can determine the retail prices of their products when they are sold through their own stores or outlets, but they may only *suggest* retail prices for their products when they are sold by independent retailers. At issue in the following case is whether an agreement that set a maximum price for the resale of products supplied by a wholesaler to a dealer constituted price fixing in violation of Section 1 of the Sherman Act.

CASE 27.6 Khan v. State Oil Co.

United States Court of Appeals, Seventh Circuit, 1996. 93 F.3d 1358.

BACKGROUND AND FACTS *Barkat Khan leased a gas station under a contract with State Oil Company, which also agreed to supply gas to Khan for resale. Under the contract, State Oil would set a suggested retail price and sell gas to Khan for 3.25 cents per gallon less than that price. Khan could sell the gas at a higher price, but he would then be required to pay State Oil the difference (which would equal the entire profit Khan realized from raising the price). Khan failed to pay some of the rent due under the lease, and State Oil terminated the contract. Khan filed a suit in a federal district court against State Oil, alleging, among other things, price fixing in violation of the Sherman Act. The court granted summary judgment for State Oil. Khan appealed.*

IN THE LANGUAGE OF THE COURT

POSNER, Chief Judge.

* * * *

State Oil * * * denies that the provision in the contract pertaining to Khan's charging a price above the suggested retail price is a form of price fixing. It points out that Khan was free to charge as high a price as he wishes. This is true in the sense that it would not have been a breach of contract for Khan to raise his price. But the contract made it worthless for him to do so[.] * * * .

* * * *

* * * Price fixing has long been illegal *per se*. In its usual and most pernicious form, the term refers to an agreement or conspiracy between competing firms to fix a minimum price for their product. By a modest extension it refers also to an agreement * * * to fix either a minimum or a maximum price for the resale of their product by their dealers.

DECISION AND REMEDY

The U.S. Court of Appeals for the Seventh Circuit reversed this part of the lower court's decision and remanded the case.

INTERNATIONAL CONSIDERATIONS

Regulation in Other Countries *Other countries have begun to adopt their own versions of U.S. antitrust laws. For example, the Japan Fair Trade Commission has adopted a set of guidelines to reduce anticompetitive practices by Japanese companies. Under the guidelines, manufacturers are prohibited from terminating dealers who sell their products for prices below those suggested by the manufacturers. The European Court of Justice has upheld a fine levied against a Dutch company for threatening to engage in below-cost pricing to force a British competitor out of a particular market.*[a] *And newly independent republics that were once part of the Soviet Union have sought the assistance of U.S. economic and technical experts in revamping their centrally planned economies.*

a. *AKZO Chemie BV v. Commission of the European Community*, E.C.Ct.Jus., No. C-62/86, July 3, 1991. (The European Community is now called the European Union, or EU.)

REFUSALS TO DEAL

Group boycotts, as mentioned, are subject to sharp scrutiny under Section 1. In contrast, basic freedom of contract has been held to support the rule that manufacturers, acting unilaterally rather than in concert, as in a group boycott, are free to deal—or not to deal—with whomever they choose. For example, assume that in our hypothetical example, Acme acts alone to set the price for the resale of its DVD drives by refusing to deal with any wholesaler that resells them at a different price. Acme has not violated the Sherman Act; it has only exercised its right to deal with whomever it chooses.

In some instances, however, a refusal to deal will violate antitrust laws. These instances involve offenses proscribed under Section 2 of the Sherman Act and occur only if (1) the firm refusing to deal has, or is likely to acquire, monopoly power and (2) the refusal is likely to have an anticompetitive effect on a particular market.[10]

PRICE DISCRIMINATION

Whenever a seller charges different buyers different prices for identical goods, the seller is engaging in **price discrimination.** Recall from the preceding chapter that such behavior may violate the Robinson-Patman Act, which was enacted in 1936 and amended Section 2 of the Clayton Act. A violation of Section 2 occurs if a seller discriminates in the prices it charges different customers for com-

10. A good example is provided by the *Aspen Skiing* case discussed in the preceding chapter (Case 26.4) in relation to the Section 2 offense of monopolization.

modities of like quality and grade in interstate commerce and the practice results in injury to competition. The act prohibits indirect discrimination, such as variations in the terms of delivery and differences in sales returns, cash discounts, and the like, as well as direct price discrimination.

CUSTOMER PREFERENCES Although the act appears to embrace the goals of fairness and equality in the marketplace, it has often been criticized as being economically unrealistic. For instance, a difference in packaging, labeling, or product quality normally does not exempt the pricing of the differing products from scrutiny under the act if the difference is deemed to be *negligible.* Thus, orange juice containers that differ by one-eighth inch are considered to be of like grade and quality, because they are *functionally* identical in terms of performance. Despite functional equivalence, however, customer perceptions may favor one type of container over another.

In the same vein, identical products sold under different labels are deemed to be of like quality, though some experts note that many customers exhibit strong preferences for better-known brand names even though the products are physically identical. In *Federal Trade Commission v. Borden Co.,*[11] the United States Supreme Court addressed the issue of a milk producer's charging different prices for milk sold under different labels. Borden sold evaporated milk under the Borden label, a well-known brand, and at the same time, it packed and marketed evaporated milk under private labels owned by its customers. Although the milk was physically indistinguishable, Borden charged a higher price for its brand-labeled milk. In spite of obvious customer preference for the Borden brand of milk, the Court concluded that the act applied to the pricing difference because the milk was of like quality and grade in terms of physical attributes. The Court held that preferences due to brand-name recognition created through national advertising should not be considered in resolving whether goods are of like grade and quality.

TIME AND COST CONSIDERATIONS Despite these examples, some economic aspects are taken into account in judging the legality of pricing practices under the Robinson-Patman Act. For example, as noted in the preceding chapter, Section 2 is not violated even though the goods sold are identical if the seller can justify the price differential on the basis of differences in cost, such as the cost of transporting the goods to buyers in disparate locations. Similarly, consideration is given to the fact that prices are not static but fluctuate as market conditions change. Thus, price discrimination occurs only if sales at different price levels are made reasonably close together in time.

Closeness in time is determined by the economic circumstances of the sales. For example, sales of products that are not frequently sold and that involve considerable production costs may be considered close in time even if they occur years apart. Conversely, sales of low-cost products sold in high volume may be considered close in time when they occur a day or even a few hours apart. Jet aircraft typify high-cost, low-volume products. Closeness in time for sales of aircraft could be two years or more. In contrast, sales of bakery goods occur on an almost continuous basis. Closeness in time for sales of such products could be several hours or, at most, a day.

EXCLUSIONARY PRACTICES

Recall also from the preceding chapter that Section 3 of the Clayton Act prohibits sellers and lessors from selling or leasing goods, machinery, supplies, and the like "on the condition, agreement or understanding that the . . . purchaser or lessee thereof shall not use or deal in the goods . . . of a competitor or competitors of the seller." Two types of vertical arrangements involving exclusionary tactics—exclusive-dealing contracts and tying arrangements—are within the reach of Section 3 of the Clayton Act.

EXCLUSIVE-DEALING CONTRACTS Contracts under which a seller forbids the buyer from purchasing products from the seller's competitors are called **exclusive-dealing contracts.** Such contracts are prohibited under Section 3 if the effect of the contract will "substantially lessen competition or tend to create a monopoly."

The leading decision on exclusive-dealing contracts remains the 1949 case of *Standard Oil Co. of California v. United States,*[12] in which the then-largest gasoline seller in the United States was challenged by the government under Section 3 for making exclusive-dealing contracts with independent stations in seven western states. The United States Supreme Court, in assessing the impact of the exclusive-dealing agreement on competition in the

11. 383 U.S. 637, 86 S.Ct. 1092, 16 L.Ed.2d 153 (1966).

12. 337 U.S. 293, 69 S.Ct. 1051, 93 L.Ed. 1371 (1949).

retail market, noted that the "independents" covered under the arrangement constituted 16 percent of all retail outlets and 7 percent of all retail gas sales in the area. The Court also noted that the market was substantially concentrated because the seven largest suppliers all used exclusive-dealing contracts with their independent retailers and together controlled 65 percent of the market. Looking at market conditions after the arrangements were instituted, the Court noted that market shares were extremely stable and entry into the market was apparently restricted. Thus, the Court found that Section 3 had been violated, because competition was "foreclosed in a substantial share" of the relevant market.

TYING ARRANGEMENTS A seller may condition the sale of a product (the tying product) on the buyer's agreeing to purchase another product (the tied product) produced or distributed by the same seller. As noted in the preceding chapter, the legality of such **tying arrangements** depends on factors such as the purpose of the arrangement and its likely effect on competition in the relevant markets. There are two relevant markets, because the agreement involves two distinct products, the tying and the tied product. In 1936, the United States Supreme Court held that International Business Machines and Remington Rand, by requiring purchase of their own machine cards as a condition of leasing their tabulation machines, had violated Section 3 of the Clayton Act. The two firms were the only ones in the market with completely automated tabulation machines, and the Court concluded that each possessed market power sufficient to "substantially lessen competition" through their respective tying arrangements.[13]

Standards of Application. The Clayton Act provisions in Section 3 have been held to apply only to commodities, not to services. But tying arrangements also can be considered agreements that restrain trade in violation of Section 1 of the Sherman Act. Cases involving tying arrangements for services have been brought under Section 1 of the Sherman Act. Although the Court continues to state that many tying arrangements are illegal *per se*, it nonetheless has shown a willingness to look at factors that are important in a rule-of-reason analysis. This is another example of the so-called soft *per se* rule referred to in regard to group boycotts.

Practical Results. The United States Supreme Court held that U.S. Steel Corporation's practice of tying its attractive credit services for home builders to the builders' purchase of U.S. Steel's prefabricated houses did not violate antitrust laws, because U.S. Steel did not possess market power in either the credit market or the prefabricated housing market.[14] A similar result was reached in *Jefferson Parish Hospital District No. 2 v. Hyde.*[15] Most courts today generally judge the legality of tying arrangements involving services or commodities by looking at both the firm's market power in the tying product market and the amount of commerce affected in the tied product market. The firm must have sufficient market power in the tying product to coerce the purchase of the tied product, and the tying arrangement must affect a substantial amount of commerce in the market for the tied product.

What if a tying arrangement affects only one customer? Can the arrangement nonetheless violate Section 1 of the Sherman Act? The following case addresses this issue.

13. *International Business Machines Corp. v. United States*, 298 U.S. 131, 56 S.Ct. 701, 80 L.Ed.2d 1085 (1936).

14. *U.S. Steel Corp. v. Fortner Enterprises, Inc.*, 429 U.S. 610, 97 S.Ct. 861, 51 L.Ed.2d 80 (1977).

15. 466 U.S. 2, 104 S.Ct. 1551, 80 L.Ed.2d 2 (1984).

CASE 27.7 Datagate, Inc. v. Hewlett-Packard Co.

United States Court of Appeals, Ninth Circuit, 1995.
60 F.3d 1421.

HISTORICAL AND TECHNOLOGICAL SETTING *Military investment in the 1940s fueled the growth of the electronics industry. Computers made at this time weighed several tons and required the space of a warehouse to store operating components. With the advent of smaller components in the 1960s, computers and other technological equipment became more compact. Hewlett-Packard Company (HP) produced the first hand-held scientific calculator in 1972. In the decades since then, the growth of the electronics and computer industries has seemed unstoppable. Today, HP makes a variety of electronic products, including computer hardware and software.*

BACKGROUND AND FACTS *Datagate, Inc., provided repair service for computer hardware made by HP. HP offered the same service. HP also offered support for those who used its software, but the company refused to provide software support to those who did not buy its hardware service. Datagate filed a suit in a federal district court against HP, claiming in part that HP's practice constituted an illegal tying arrangement. The arrangement had been imposed on only one HP customer, Rockwell International, but the Rockwell hardware service contract was worth $100,000 per year. The court held that one customer was not enough and entered a judgment in favor of HP. Datagate appealed.*

IN THE LANGUAGE OF THE COURT

BEEZER, Circuit Judge:

* * * *

[One of the] elements [that] must be satisfied to establish that a tying arrangement is illegal *per se* [is that] the tying arrangement affects a not insubstantial volume of commerce. * * *

* * * *

* * * The * * * requirement can be satisfied by the foreclosure of a single purchaser, so long as the purchaser represents a "not insubstantial" dollar-volume of sales.

* * * *

* * * [T]he Rockwell hardware service contract at issue was worth approximately $100,000 per year. * * *

This amount is sufficient.

DECISION AND REMEDY *The U.S. Court of Appeals for the Ninth Circuit reversed the decision of the lower court and remanded the case for trial. A tying arrangement can be illegal even if it is imposed on only one customer.*

MERGERS

Under Section 7 of the Clayton Act, a person or business organization cannot hold stock or assets in another business "where the effect . . . may be to substantially lessen competition." This section is the statutory authority for preventing mergers that could result in monopoly power or a substantial lessening of competition in the marketplace.

A crucial consideration in most merger cases is **market concentration.** Market concentration roughly translates into the allocation of percentage market shares among the various firms in the relevant product market. For example, if the four largest grocery stores in Chicago accounted for 80 percent of all retail food sales, the market clearly would be concentrated in those four firms. Competition, however, is not necessarily diminished solely as a result of market concentration, and other factors will be considered, including whether the merger will make it more difficult for potential competitors to enter the relevant market.

HORIZONTAL MERGERS

Mergers between firms that compete with each other in the same market are called **horizontal mergers.** If a horizontal merger creates an entity with anything other than a small percentage market share, the merger will be presumed illegal. This is because of the United States Supreme Court's interpretation that Congress, in amending Section 7 of the Clayton Act in 1950, intended to prevent mergers that increase market concentration.[16] Three other factors are also considered: overall concentration of the relevant market, the relevant market's history of tending toward concentration, and whether the apparent design of the merger is to establish market power or restrict competition.

Market Share and Market Concentration. The Court's intense focus on market share in horizontal

16. *Brown Shoe v. United States,* 370 U.S. 294, 82 S.Ct. 1502, 8 L.Ed.2d 510 (1962).

merger decisions has made the definition of relevant markets especially critical in most Section 7 cases. As a result, the Federal Trade Commission (FTC) and the Department of Justice (DOJ) have established guidelines indicating which mergers will be challenged.

Under the guidelines, the first factor to be considered in determining whether a merger will be challenged is the degree of concentration in the relevant market. In determining market concentration, the FTC and the DOJ employ what is known as the **Herfindahl-Hirschman index (HHI).** The HHI is computed by summing the squares of the percentage market shares of the firms in the relevant market. For example, if there are four firms with shares of 30 percent, 30 percent, 20 percent, and 20 percent, respectively, then the HHI equals 2,600 (900 + 900 + 400 + 400 = 2,600). If the pre-merger HHI is less than 1,000, then the market is considered unconcentrated, and the merger will not likely be challenged. If the pre-merger HHI is between 1,000 and 1,800, the industry is judged moderately concentrated, and the merger will be challenged only if it increases the HHI by 100 points or more.[17] If the HHI is greater than 1,800, the market is deemed highly concentrated. In a highly concentrated market, a merger that produces an increase in the HHI between 50 and 100 points raises significant competitive concerns for the FTC and DOJ. Mergers that produce an increase in the HHI of more than 100 points in a highly concentrated market are deemed likely to enhance market power.[18]

Other Factors. The guidelines stress that determining market share and market concentration is only the starting point in analyzing the potential anticompetitive effects of a merger. Before deciding to challenge a merger, the FTC and the DOJ will look at a number of other factors, including the ease of entry into the relevant market, economic efficiency, the financial condition of the merging firms, the nature and price of the product or products involved, and so on. If a firm is a leading one—having at least a 35 percent share and twice that of the next leading firm—any merger with a firm having as little as a 1 percent share will be challenged.

POLITICAL CONSIDERATIONS IN DEFINING THE RELEVANT MARKET Not considered in the above discussion are the sometimes unfathomable definitions of the relevant market determined by the federal government. To take an example, reconsider the proposed Office Depot–Staples merger that the Federal Trade Commission (FTC) refused to approve in 1997. Had the two merged as originally planned, they would have accounted for 6 percent of the market for office supplies. When the FTC initially indicated its disapproval, Office Depot agreed to sell sixty-three of its stores to OfficeMax, thereby bringing the proposed merger to only 4 percent of the office supplies market. The FTC decided that the relevant product market was not office supplies, but rather office supplies sold at large specialty discount stores! It then concluded that the proposed merger would seriously weaken competition in the newly defined market. In other words, the decision was evidently political rather than based on any theory of the economics of antitrust law. After all, office supplies are also sold at Costco, Wal-Mart, Sam's Club, Kmart, and elsewhere. To exclude these obvious competitors from the FTC's analysis was indeed baffling.[19]

VERTICAL MERGERS A **vertical merger** occurs when a company at one stage of production acquires a company at a higher or lower stage of production. Courts in the past have almost exclusively focused on "foreclosure" in assessing vertical mergers. Foreclosure occurs because competitors of the merging firms lose opportunities either to sell or to buy products from the merging firms. For example, in *United States v. E. I. du Pont de Nemours & Co.*,[20] du Pont was challenged for acquiring a considerable amount of General Motors (GM) stock. In holding that the transaction was illegal, the United States Supreme Court noted that stock acquisition would enable du Pont to prevent other sellers of fabrics and finishes from selling to GM, which then accounted for 50 percent of all auto fabric and finish purchases.

---

17. Compute the change in the index by doubling the product of the merging firms' pre-merger market shares. For example, a merger between a firm with a 5 percent share and one with a 6 percent share will increase the HHI by 2 × (5 × 6) = 60. For an analysis of the HHI concentration of companies in the credit-card market, see *SCFC ILC, Inc. v. Visa U.S.A. Inc.*, 819 F.Supp. 956 (D.Utah 1993).

18. See, for example, *United States v. United Tote, Inc.*, 768 F.Supp. 1064 (D.Del. 1991), in which the court ordered the divestiture of a firm whose HHI was 3,940 before a merger and 4,640 after the merger.

19. At the FTC's request, a court blocked the merger on antitrust grounds.

20. 353 U.S. 586, 77 S.Ct. 872, 1 L.Ed.2d 1057 (1957).

More recently, whether a vertical merger has been deemed illegal has depended on several factors, including market concentration, barriers to entry into the market, and the apparent intent of the merging parties. Mergers that do not prevent competitors of either of the merging firms from competing in a segment of the market will not be condemned as "foreclosing" competition and are legal.

CONGLOMERATE MERGERS There are three general types of **conglomerate mergers:** market-extension, product-extension, and diversification

CONCEPT SUMMARY 27.1 Restraints of Trade and Their Lawfulness

PER SE ILLEGAL	SUBJECT TO RULE-OF-REASON ANALYSIS[a]	SUBJECT TO "SOFT" *PER SE* RULE/ NARROW RULE-OF-REASON ANALYSIS
Price Fixing Market Division Resale Price Maintenance Agreement	**Trade Association Activity**—Illegal if undertaken in a concentrated industry to facilitate anticompetitive effect. Not illegal if there is no intent to fix prices or limit output and the activity benefits the public. **Joint Venture**—Illegal if undertaken to facilitate anticompetitive effect. Not illegal if there is no intent to fix prices or limit output, the activity benefits the public, and there are no acceptable alternatives to achieve the same goal. **Territorial or Customer Restriction**—Illegal if undertaken to facilitate anticompetitive effect. **Refusal to Deal**—Illegal if the firm that refuses to deal has monopoly power and the refusal has an anticompetitive effect. **Price Discrimination**—Illegal if undertaken to facilitate anticompetitive effect. **Exclusive-Dealing Contract**—Illegal if the effect is to substantially lessen competition or to create a monopoly.	**Group Boycott**—Illegal if the group possesses market power and the boycott is intended to restrict or exclude a competitor. **Tying Arrangement**—Illegal if undertaken to facilitate anticompetitive effect in the tying product market and the tied product market. **Horizontal Merger**—Illegal if undertaken to facilitate anticompetitive effect or if the percentage of the firm's market share after the merger is large in light of the market's concentration and its history of tending toward concentration. **Vertical Merger**—Illegal if undertaken to facilitate anticompetitive effect or actually has such effect in light of the market's concentration and barriers to entry. **Conglomerate Merger**—Illegal if undertaken to facilitate anticompetitive effect or actually has such effect in light of the market's concentration, barriers to entry, whether the firm's entry would have been possible without the merger, and whether other firms are "waiting in the wings."

a. A rule-of-reason analysis generally requires an evaluation of (1) the intent of the parties in practicing the restraint of trade, (2) whether the parties have the power to accomplish that intent, and (3) the practice's actual and potential effect, which includes any benefit to the public. Sometimes, a court will consider whether the parties could have achieved the same result in a less restrictive way.

mergers. Conglomerate mergers are mergers between firms that do not compete with each other because they are in different markets. A market-extension merger occurs when a firm seeks to sell its product in a new market by merging with a firm already established in that market. A product-extension merger occurs when a firm seeks to add a closely related product to its existing line by merging with a firm already producing that product. For example, a manufacturer might seek to extend its product line of household products to include floor wax by acquiring a leading manufacturer of floor wax. Diversification occurs when a firm merges with another firm that offers a product or service wholly unrelated to the first firm's existing activities. An example of a diversification merger would be Chrysler Corporation's acquisition of Holiday Inns.

TERMS AND CONCEPTS TO REVIEW

concentrated industry 556
conglomerate merger 568
exclusive-dealing contract 564
group boycott 557
Herfindahl-Hirschman index (HHI) 567
horizontal market division 554
horizontal merger 566
horizontal restraint 552
joint venture 559
market concentration 566
***per se* violation 552**
price discrimination 563
price fixing 553
resale price maintenance agreement 562
rule of reason 552
tying arrangement 565
vertical merger 567
vertical restraint 560
vertically integrated firm 560

QUESTIONS AND CASE PROBLEMS

27–1. HORIZONTAL RESTRAINTS. Most of the egg wholesalers supplying eggs to grocery stores in a particular area sell eggs to the retailers under various credit terms. The credit terms vary among the different buyers and sellers, but all of the wholesalers follow a common practice of reducing by 10 percent the price charged to a retailer if the retailer pays the wholesaler within three days of delivery. The various wholesalers agree that henceforth the 10 percent discount will be discontinued. If the agreement is indeed carried out by the wholesalers and the discount policy is discontinued, have the wholesalers violated any antitrust laws? Explain. If suit is brought against the wholesalers, what—if any—justification could they offer for the agreement?

27–2. HORIZONTAL RESTRAINTS. Suppose that the wholesale egg suppliers in the preceding problem agree that the three largest suppliers should sell exclusively to the area's large chain-store groceries, leaving the remaining suppliers to sell solely to local individual "mom and pop" stores. Does the agreement violate any antitrust laws? Is it a defense that the larger suppliers, because of their scale of operations, enjoy a cost advantage that allows them to supply the large chain buyers more efficiently?

27–3. VERTICAL RESTRAINTS. Discuss *fully* whether each of the following situations violates the Sherman Act.

(a) Trujillo Foods, Inc., is the leading seller of frozen Mexican foods in three southwestern states. The various retail outlets that sell Trujillo products are in close competition, and customers are very price conscious. Trujillo has conditioned its sales to retailers with the agreement that the retailers will not sell below a minimum price nor above a maximum price. The retailers are allowed to set any price within these limits.

(b) Franklin, Inc., Green, Inc., and Fill-It, Inc., are competitors in the manufacture and sale of microwave ovens sold primarily east of the Mississippi River. As a patriotic gesture and to assist the unemployed, the three competitors agree to lower their prices on all microwave models by 20 percent for a three-month period that includes the Fourth of July and Labor Day.

(c) Foam Beer, Inc., sells its beer to distributors all over the United States. Foam sends each of its distributors a recommended price list, explaining that past records indicate that selling beer at those prices should ensure the distributor a reasonable rate of return. The price list clearly states that the sale of beer by Foam to the distributor is not conditioned on the distributor's reselling the beer at the recommended price and that the distributor is free to set the price.

27–4. Horizontal Restraints. Mickey's Appliance Store was a new retail seller of appliances in Sunwest City. Mickey's innovative sales techniques and financing caused the appliance department of Luckluster Department Store to lose a great many sales. Luckluster was a large department store and part of a large chain with substantial buying power. Luckluster told a number of appliance manufacturers that if they continued to sell to Mickey's, Luckluster would stop purchasing from them. The manufacturers immediately stopped selling appliances to Mickey's. Mickey's filed suit against Luckluster and the manufacturers, claiming their actions constituted an antitrust violation. Luckluster and the manufacturers could prove that Mickey's was a small retailer with a small portion of the market. Because the relevant market was not substantially affected, they claimed they were not guilty of restraint of trade. Discuss *fully* whether there was an antitrust violation.

27–5. Horizontal Restraints. Thomas Blackburn, Raymond Green, Charles Sweeney, and Daniel Pfeiffer practiced law together as partners, relying on advertising to attract clients. When they had a disagreement over the use of partnership funds, they split into separate partnerships—one formed by Blackburn and Green and the other by Sweeney and Pfeiffer. After the split, they negotiated and signed an agreement that included a term restricting, for an indefinite time, the geographical area within which each could advertise. Less than a year later, the Blackburn firm filed a suit in a federal district court against the Sweeney firm, alleging in part that the restriction on advertising was a *per se* violation of the Sherman Act. On what basis might the court hold that the agreement to restrict advertising was a horizontal agreement to divide markets among competitors? [*Blackburn v. Sweeney*, 53 F.3d 825 (7th Cir. 1995)]

27–6. Robinson-Patman Act. The Stelwagon Manufacturing Co. agreed with Tarmac Roofing Systems, Inc., to promote and develop a market for Tarmac's products in the Philadelphia area. In return, Tarmac promised not to sell its products to other area distributors. In 1991, Stelwagon learned that Tarmac had been selling its products to Stelwagon's competitors—the Standard Roofing Co. and the Celotex Corp.—at substantially lower prices. Stelwagon filed a suit against Tarmac in a federal district court. What is the principal factor in determining whether Tarmac violated the Robinson-Patman Act? Did Tarmac violate the act? [*Stelwagon Manufacturing Co. v. Tarmac Roofing Systems, Inc.*, 63 F.3d 1267 (3d Cir. 1995)]

27–7. Vertical Restraints. Business Electronics Corp. was a dealer for Sharp Electronics Corp. authorized to sell Sharp calculators in and around Houston. Business Electronics consistently sold the calculators for prices below those suggested by Sharp. Another dealer authorized to sell Sharp products in the same area complained to Sharp about the pricing policies of Business Electronics. In response to the complaint, Sharp terminated the Business Electronics dealership. Business Electronics brought suit, contending that the termination was the result of a conspiracy between Sharp and the complaining dealer. Business Electronics argued that the alleged conspiracy was a vertical restraint of trade in violation of Section 1 of the Sherman Act. Could the court apply the rule of reason in this case? Why or why not? What might be the result of applying the rule of reason? [*Business Electronics Corp. v. Sharp Electronics Corp.*, 485 U.S. 717, 108 S.Ct. 1515, 99 L.Ed.2d 808 (1988)]

27–8. Horizontal Restraints. Harcourt Brace Jovanovich Legal and Professional Publications (HBJ), the nation's largest provider of bar review materials and lecture services, began offering a Georgia bar review course in 1976 and was in direct, and often intense, competition with BRG of Georgia, Inc., the other main provider of bar review courses in Georgia, from 1977 to 1979. In early 1980, HBJ and BRG entered into an agreement that gave BRG the exclusive right to market HBJ's materials in Georgia and to use its trade name, "Bar/Bri." The parties agreed that HBJ would not compete with BRG in Georgia and that BRG would not compete with HBJ outside Georgia. Immediately after the 1980 agreement was made, the price of BRG's course was increased from $150 to over $400. Jay Palmer, a former law student, brought an action against the two firms, alleging that the 1980 agreement violated Section 1 of the Sherman Act. What will the court decide? Discuss fully. [*Palmer v. BRG of Georgia, Inc.*, 498 U.S. 46, 111 S.Ct. 401, 112 L.Ed.2d 349 (1990)]

27–9. Vertical Restraints. Eastman Kodak Co. has about a 20 percent share of the highly competitive market for high-volume photocopiers and microfilm equipment and controls nearly the entire market for replacement parts for its equipment (which are not interchangeable with parts for other manufacturers' equipment). Prior to 1985, Kodak sold replacement parts for its equipment without significant restrictions. As a result, a number of independent service organizations (ISOs) purchased Kodak parts to use when repairing and servicing Kodak copiers. In 1985, Kodak changed its policy to prevent the ISOs from competing with Kodak's own service organizations. It ceased selling parts to ISOs and refused to sell replacement parts to its customers unless they agreed *not* to have their equipment serviced by ISOs. In 1987, Image Technical Services, Inc., and seventeen other ISOs sued Kodak, alleging that Kodak's policy was a tying arrangement in violation of Section 1 of the Sherman Act. Kodak claimed that its policy was not an illegal tying arrangement because it had no market power with respect to its equipment. Therefore, it did not have market power with respect to replacement parts—it could not raise the price of replacement parts and service beyond competitive rates, because if it did, it would lose customers, who would purchase other manufacturers' equipment. Assuming that Kodak does not have market power in the market for photocopying and microfilm equipment, does Kodak's restrictive policy constitute an illegal tying arrangement? Does it violate antitrust laws in any way? Discuss fully. [*Eastman Kodak Co. v. Image Technical Services, Inc.*, 504 U.S. 451, 112 S.Ct. 2072, 119 L.Ed.2d 265 (1992)]

27–10. A Question of Ethics

A group of lawyers in the District of Columbia regularly acted as court-appointed attorneys for indigent defendants in District of Columbia criminal cases. At a meeting of the Superior Court Trial Lawyers Association (SCTLA), the attorneys agreed to stop providing such representation until the district increased their compensation. Their subsequent boycott had a severe impact on the district's criminal justice system, and the District of Columbia gave in to the lawyers' demands for higher pay. After the lawyers had returned to work, the Federal Trade Commission filed a complaint against the SCTLA and four of its officers and, after an investigation, ruled that the SCTLA's activities constituted an illegal group boycott in violation of antitrust laws. [*Federal Trade Commission v. Superior Court Trial Lawyers Association*, 493 U.S. 411, 110 S.Ct. 768, 107 L.Ed.2d 851 (1990)]

1. The SCTLA obviously was aware of the negative impact its decision would have on the district's criminal justice system. Given this fact, do you think the lawyers behaved ethically?
2. On appeal, the SCTLA claimed that its boycott had been undertaken to publicize the fact that attorneys were underpaid and that the boycott thus constituted an expression protected by the First Amendment. Do you agree with this argument?
3. Labor unions have the right to strike when negotiations between labor and management fail to result in agreement. Do you think that it is fair for members of the SCTLA to be prohibited from "striking" against their employer, the District of Columbia, simply because the SCTLA is a professional organization and not a labor union?

Accessing the Internet

The Legal Environment of Business

If you use the Yahoo browser, you can get valuable information about antitrust law by accessing

http://www.yahoo.com/Government/Law/

To see the American Bar Association's Web page on antitrust law, go to

http://www.abanet.org/antitrust

Chapter 28

Securities Regulation and Investor Protection

THE STOCK MARKET CRASH of October 29, 1929, and the ensuing economic depression caused the public to focus on the importance of securities markets for the economic well-being of the nation. The feverish trading in securities during the preceding decade became the subject of widespread attention, and numerous reports were circulated concerning the speculative, manipulative, and at times unscrupulous trading that occurred in the stock markets.

The public, outraged by such practices, pressured Congress into action. As a result, in 1931 the Senate passed a resolution calling for an extensive investigation of securities trading. The investigation led, ultimately, to the passage by Congress of the Securities Act of 1933[1] and the Securities Exchange Act of 1934.[2] Both acts were designed to provide investors with more information to help them make buying and selling decisions about *securities*—generally defined as any documents evidencing corporate ownership (stock) or debts (bonds)—and to prohibit deceptive, unfair, and manipulative practices in the purchase and sale of securities. Basically, the 1933 act regulates the initial sales of corporate securities by businesses, and the 1934 act regulates subsequent purchases and sales of securities once they have been issued. This chapter discusses the nature of federal securities regulation and its effect on the business world.

1. 15 U.S.C. Sections 77a–77aa.
2. 15 U.S.C. Sections 78a–78mm.

SECTION 1

CORPORATE FINANCING

Corporations are financed by the issuance and sale of corporate securities—bonds and stock. **Securities** evidence the obligation to pay money or the right to participate in earnings and the distribution of corporate assets. **Stocks,** or *equity securities,* represent the purchase of ownership in the business firm. **Bonds** (debentures), or *debt securities,* represent the borrowing of money by firms (and governments). Of course, not all debt is in the form of debt securities. For example, some debt is in the form of accounts payable and notes payable. Accounts and notes payable are typically short-term debts. Bonds are simply a way for a corporation to split up its long-term debt so that it can market the debt more easily.

BONDS

Bonds are issued by business firms and by governments at all levels as evidence of the funds they are borrowing from investors. Bonds almost always have a designated *maturity date*—the date when the principal, or face amount, of the bond (or loan) is returned to the investor—and are sometimes referred to as *fixed-income securities,* because their owners receive fixed-dollar interest payments during the period of time prior to maturity.

The characteristics of corporate bonds vary widely, in part because corporations differ in their ability to generate the earnings and cash flow necessary to make interest payments and to repay the principal amount of the bonds at maturity. Furthermore, corporate bonds are only a part of the total debt and the overall financial structure of corporate business. The various types of corporate bonds are described in Exhibit 28–1.

STOCKS

Issuing stocks is another way for corporations to obtain financing. The ways in which stocks differ from bonds are summarized in Exhibit 28–2. Basically, stocks represent ownership in a business firm, whereas bonds represent borrowing by the firm.

Exhibit 28–3 offers a summary of the types of stocks issued by corporations. The two major types are *common stock* and *preferred stock.*

COMMON STOCK **Common stock** represents the true ownership of a corporation. It provides a proportionate interest in the corporation with regard to (1) control, (2) earnings, and (3) net assets. A shareholder's interest is generally in proportion to the number of shares owned out of the total number of shares issued.

Any person who purchases shares acquires voting rights—one vote per share held. Voting rights in a corporation apply to the election of the firm's board of directors and to any proposed changes in the ownership structure of the firm.[3] For example, a holder of common stock generally has the right to vote in a decision on a proposed merger, as mergers can change the proportion of ownership.

Holders of common stock are a group of investors who assume a *residual* position in the overall financial structure of a business. In terms of receiving returns on their investments, they are last in line. Their earnings depend on the corporation's paying all the other groups—suppliers, employees, managers, bankers, governments, bondholders, and holders of preferred stock—what is due them first. Once

3. State corporation law specifies the types of actions for which shareholder approval must be obtained.

EXHIBIT 28–1 ■ TYPES OF CORPORATE BONDS

TYPE	DEFINITION
Debenture Bonds	Bonds for which no specific assets of the corporation are pledged as backing. Rather, they are backed by the general credit rating of the corporation, plus any assets that can be seized if the corporation allows the debentures to go into default.
Mortgage Bonds	Bonds that pledge specific property. If the corporation defaults on the bonds, the bondholders can foreclose on the property.
Convertible Bonds	Bonds that can be exchanged for a specified number of shares of common stock under certain conditions.
Callable Bonds	Bonds that may be called in and the principal repaid at specified times or under conditions specified in the bond when it is issued.

Exhibit 28–2 ■ How Do Stocks and Bonds Differ?

Stocks	Bonds
1. Stocks represent ownership.	1. Bonds represent debt.
2. Stocks (common) do not have a fixed dividend rate.	2. Interest on bonds must always be paid, whether or not any profit is earned.
3. Stockholders can elect a board of directors, which controls the corporation.	3. Bondholders usually have no voice in or control over management of the corporation.
4. Stocks do not have a maturity date; the corporation does not usually repay the stockholder.	4. Bonds have a maturity date, when the corporation is to repay the bondholder the face value of the bond.
5. All corporations issue or offer to sell stocks. This is the usual definition of a corporation.	5. Corporations do not necessarily issue bonds.
6. Stockholders have a claim against the property and income of a corporation after all creditors' claims have been met.	6. Bondholders have a claim against the property and income of a corporation that must be met before the claims of stockholders.

those groups are paid, the owners of common stock may be entitled to *all* the remaining earnings. But the board of directors is not normally under any duty to declare the remaining earnings as dividends.

PREFERRED STOCK **Preferred stock** is stock with *preferences.* Usually, this means that holders of preferred stock have priority over holders of common stock as to dividends and to payment on dissolution of the corporation. Preferred stockholders may or may not have the right to vote (the trend is toward giving preferred stockholders the right to vote).

From an investment standpoint, preferred stock is more similar to bonds than to common stock. Preferred shareholders receive periodic dividend payments, usually established as a fixed percentage of the face amount of each preferred share. A share of 6 percent preferred stock with a face amount of $100 per share would pay its owner a $6 dividend each year. Payment of these dividends is not a legal obligation on the part of the firm. Preferred stock is not included among the liabilities of a business, because it is technically equity. Like other equity securities, preferred shares have no fixed maturity date on which they must be retired by the firm. Although occasionally firms retire preferred stock, they are not legally obligated to do so. A sample cumulative convertible preferred-stock certificate is shown in Exhibit 28–4.

Exhibit 28–3 ■ Types of Stocks

Type	Definition
Common Stock	Voting shares that represent ownership interest in a corporation. Common stock has the lowest priority with respect to payment of dividends and distribution of assets on the corporation's dissolution.
Preferred Stock	Shares of stock that have priority over common-stock shares as to payment of dividends and distribution of assets on dissolution. Dividend payments are usually a fixed percentage of the face value of the share. Preferred shares are usually nonvoting shares.
Cumulative Preferred Stock	Preferred shares for which required dividends not paid in a given year must be paid in a subsequent year before any common-stock dividends can be paid.
Participating Preferred Stock	Preferred shares entitling the owner to receive (1) the preferred-stock dividend and (2) additional dividends after the corporation has paid dividends on common stock.
Convertible Preferred Stock	Preferred shares entitling the owner to convert his or her shares into a specified number of common shares either in the issuing corporation or, sometimes, in another corporation.
Redeemable, or Callable, Preferred Stock	Preferred shares issued with the express condition that the issuing corporation has the right to repurchase the shares as specified.

EXHIBIT 28–4 ■ CUMULATIVE CONVERTIBLE PREFERRED-STOCK CERTIFICATE

MORE THAN 100 SHARES

Number 640-0000

$1.75 CUMULATIVE CONVERTIBLE PREFERENCE STOCK

INCORPORATED UNDER THE LAWS OF THE STATE OF DELAWARE

Shares

GENERAL MILLS, INC.

THIS CERTIFICATE IS TRANSFERABLE IN COLUMBUS, GA. OR IN NEW YORK, N.Y.

See reverse for certain definitions

This Certifies that **SPECIMEN** *is the owner of*

FULL-PAID AND NON-ASSESSABLE SHARES, OF THE $1.75 CUMULATIVE CONVERTIBLE PREFERENCE STOCK, WITHOUT PAR VALUE, OF

General Mills, Inc., transferable on the books of the Corporation by the holder hereof in person or by duly authorized attorney upon surrender of this Certificate properly endorsed. This Certificate and the shares represented hereby are issued and shall be held subject to all the provisions of the Certificate of Incorporation and By-Laws of the Corporation and all amendments thereof (copies of which are on file with the Corporation and with the Transfer Agent) to all of which the holder by acceptance hereof assents.

This Certificate is not valid until countersigned by the Transfer Agent or Transfer Clerk and registered by the Registrar.

In Witness Whereof the Corporation has caused this Certificate to be signed by its duly authorized officers and its Corporate Seal to be hereto affixed.

CERTIFICATE OF STOCK

Dated

DELAWARE 1928

REGISTERED:
THE CHASE MANHATTAN BANK
(NATIONAL ASSOCIATION), REGISTRAR

By

AUTHORIZED SIGNATURE

COUNTERSIGNED:
FIRST NATIONAL CITY BANK,
TRANSFER AGENT

By

AUTHORIZED OFFICER.

PRESIDENT

SECRETARY

SECTION 2

THE SECURITIES AND EXCHANGE COMMISSION

The 1934 act created the Securities and Exchange Commission (SEC) as an independent regulatory agency whose function was to administer the 1933 and 1934 acts. The SEC plays a key role in interpreting the provisions of these acts (and their amendments) and in creating regulations governing the purchase and sale of securities.

THE BASIC FUNCTIONS OF THE SEC

The SEC regulates the securities industry by undertaking the following activities:

1. Requiring disclosure of facts concerning offerings of securities listed on national securities exchanges and offerings of certain securities traded over the counter (OTC).
2. Regulating the trade in securities on the national and regional securities exchanges and in the OTC markets.
3. Investigating securities fraud.
4. Regulating the activities of securities brokers, dealers, and investment advisers and requiring their registration.
5. Supervising the activities of mutual funds.
6. Recommending administrative sanctions, injunctive remedies, and criminal prosecution in cases involving violations of securities laws. (The Fraud Section of the Criminal Division of the Department of Justice prosecutes violations of federal securities laws.)

THE EXPANDED POWERS OF THE SEC

From the time of its creation until the present, the SEC's regulatory functions have gradually been increased by legislation granting it authority in different areas. During the 1990s, for example, Congress has passed several acts that have significantly expanded the SEC's powers.

To further curb securities fraud, the Securities Enforcement Remedies and Penny Stock Reform Act of 1990[4] amended existing securities laws to expand greatly the types of securities violation cases that SEC administrative law judges can hear and the SEC's enforcement options. The act also provides that courts can bar persons who have engaged in securities fraud from serving as officers and directors of publicly held corporations.

The Securities Acts Amendments of 1990[5] authorized the SEC to seek sanctions against those who violate foreign securities laws. These amendments increase the ability of the SEC to cooperate in international securities law enforcement. Under the Market Reform Act of 1990, the SEC can suspend trading in securities in the event that the prices rise and fall excessively in a short period of time.[6]

The National Securities Markets Improvement Act of 1996 expanded the power of the SEC to exempt persons, securities, and transactions from the requirements of the securities laws.[7] (This part of the act is also known as the Capital Markets Efficiency Act.) The act also limited the authority of the states to regulate certain securities transactions, as well as certain investment advisory firms.[8]

Currently, both Congress and the SEC are in the process of making fundamental changes in the regulatory framework applying to securities transactions. Over the years, as more and more SEC rules were issued, the body of regulations governing securities transactions became increasingly cumbersome and complex. Congress and the SEC are eliminating some rules, revising others, and generally attempting to streamline the regulatory process to make it more efficient and more relevant to today's securities trading practices.

SECTION 3

THE SECURITIES ACT OF 1933

As mentioned, the Securities Act of 1933 governs initial sales of stock by businesses. The act was designed to prohibit various forms of fraud and to stabilize the securities industry by requiring that all essential information concerning the issuance of securities be made available to the investing public.

Basically, the courts have interpreted the act's definition of what constitutes a security[9] to mean that

4. 15 U.S.C. Section 77g.

5. 15 U.S.C. Section 78a.
6. 15 U.S.C. Section 78i(h).
7. 15 U.S.C. Sections 77z-3, 78mm.
8. 15 U.S.C. Section 80b-3a.
9. See 15 U.S.C. Section 77b(a)(1).

a security exists in any transaction in which a person (1) invests (2) in a common enterprise (3) reasonably expecting profits (4) derived *primarily* or *substantially* from others' managerial or entrepreneurial efforts.[10]

For our purposes, it is probably most convenient to think of securities in their most common form—stocks and bonds issued by corporations. Bear in mind, though, that securities can take many forms and have been held to include whiskey, cosmetics, worms, beavers, boats, vacuum cleaners, muskrats, and cemetery lots, as well as investment contracts in condominiums, franchises, limited partnerships, oil or gas or other mineral rights, and farm animals accompanied by care agreements.

REGISTRATION STATEMENT

Section 5 of the Securities Act of 1933 broadly provides that if a security does not qualify for an exemption, that security must be *registered* before it is offered to the public either through the mails or through any facility of interstate commerce, including securities exchanges. Issuing corporations must file a *registration statement* with the SEC. Investors must be provided with a *prospectus* that describes the security being sold, the issuing corporation, and the risk attaching to the security. In principle, the registration statement and the prospectus supply sufficient information to enable unsophisticated investors to evaluate the financial risk involved.

CONTENTS OF THE REGISTRATION STATEMENT The registration statement must include the following:

1. A description of the significant provisions of the security offered for sale, including the relationship between that security and the other capital securities of the registrant. Also, the corporation must disclose how it intends to use the proceeds of the sale.
2. A description of the registrant's properties and business.
3. A description of the management of the registrant; its security holdings; and its remuneration and other benefits, including pensions and stock options. Any interests of directors or officers in any material transactions with the corporation must be disclosed.
4. A financial statement certified by an independent public accounting firm.
5. A description of pending lawsuits.

OTHER REQUIREMENTS Before filing the registration statement and the prospectus with the SEC, the corporation is allowed to obtain an underwriter who will monitor the distribution of the new issue. There is a twenty-day waiting period (which can be accelerated by the SEC) after registration before the sale can take place. During this period, oral offers between interested investors and the issuing corporation concerning the purchase and sale of the proposed securities may take place, and very limited written advertising is allowed. At this time, the so-called **red herring** prospectus may be distributed. It gets its name from the red legend printed across it stating that the registration has been filed but has not become effective.

After the waiting period, the registered securities can be legally bought and sold. Written advertising is allowed in the form of a so-called **tombstone ad,** so named because historically the format resembled a tombstone. Such ads simply tell the investor where and how to obtain a prospectus. Normally, any other type of advertising is prohibited.

EXEMPT SECURITIES

A number of specific securities are exempt from the registration requirements of the Securities Act of 1933. These securities—which can also generally be resold without being registered—include the following:[11]

1. All bank securities sold prior to July 27, 1933.
2. Commercial paper if the maturity date does not exceed nine months.
3. Securities of charitable organizations.
4. Securities resulting from a corporate reorganization issued for exchange with the issuer's existing security holders and certificates issued by trustees, receivers, or debtors in possession under the bankruptcy laws (bankruptcy is discussed in Chapter 16).
5. Securities issued exclusively for exchange with the issuer's existing security holders, provided no commission is paid (for example, stock dividends and stock splits).
6. Securities issued to finance the acquisition of railroad equipment.

10. *SEC v. W. J. Howey Co.*, 328 U.S. 293, 66 S.Ct. 1100, 90 L.Ed. 1244 (1946).

11. 15 U.S.C. Section 77c.

7. Any insurance, endowment, or annuity contract issued by a state-regulated insurance company.
8. Government-issued securities.
9. Securities issued by banks, savings and loan associations, farmers' cooperatives, and similar institutions subject to supervision by governmental authorities.
10. In consideration of the "small amount involved,"[12] an issuer's offer of up to $5 million in securities in any twelve-month period (including up to $1.5 million in nonissuer resales).

For the last exemption, under Regulation A,[13] the issuer must file with the SEC a notice of the issue and an offering circular, which must also be provided to investors before the sale. This is a much simpler and less expensive process than the procedures associated with full registration. Companies are allowed to "test the waters" for potential interest before preparing the offering circular. To *test the waters* means to determine potential interest without actually selling any securities or requiring any commitment on the part of those who are interested. Small-business issuers (companies with less than $25 million in annual revenues and less than $25 million in outstanding voting stock) can also use an integrated registration and reporting system that uses simpler forms than the full registration system.

Exhibit 28–5 summarizes the securities and transactions (discussed next) that are exempt from the registration requirements under the Securities Act of 1933 and SEC regulations.

12. 15 U.S.C. Section 77c(b).
13. 17 C.F.R. Sections 230.251–230.263.

EXHIBIT 28–5 ■ EXEMPTIONS UNDER THE 1933 ACT FOR SECURITIES OFFERINGS BY BUSINESSES

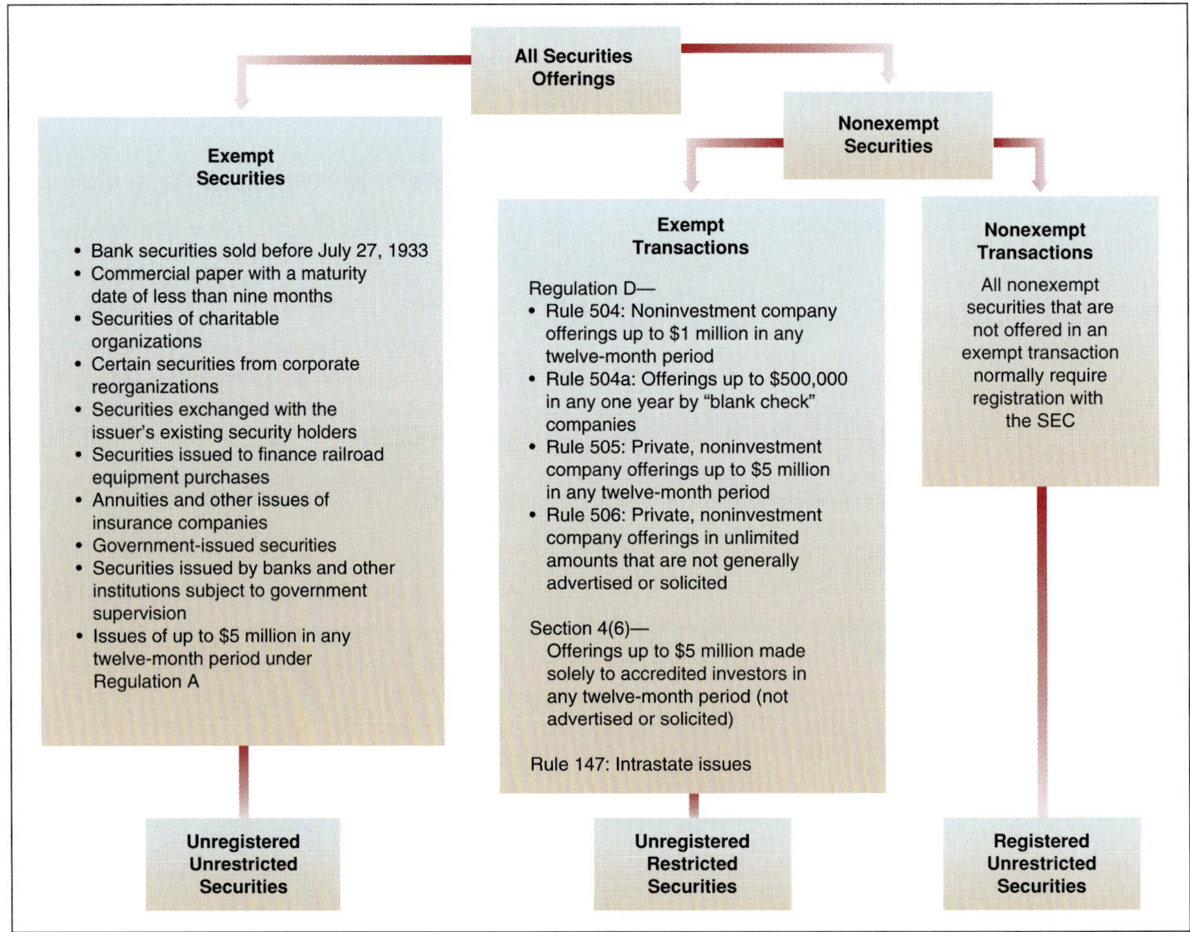

EXEMPT TRANSACTIONS

An issuer of securities that are not exempt under any of the categories listed above can avoid the high cost and complicated procedures associated with registration by taking advantage of certain *exempt transactions*. These exemptions are very broad, and thus many sales occur without registration. Because there is some overlap in the coverage of the exemptions, an offering may qualify for more than one.

SMALL OFFERINGS—REGULATION D

The SEC's Regulation D contains four separate exemptions from registration requirements for limited offers (offers that either involve a small amount of money or are made in a limited manner). Regulation D provides that any of these offerings made during any twelve-month period are exempt from the registration requirements.

Rule 504. Noninvestment company offerings up to $1 million in any twelve-month period are exempt.[14] In contrast to investment companies (discussed later in this chapter), noninvestment companies are firms that are not engaged primarily in the business of investing or trading in securities.

Rule 504a. Offerings up to $500,000 in any one year by so-called blank check companies—companies with no specific business plans except to locate and acquire presently unknown businesses or opportunities—are exempt if no general solicitation or advertising is used; the SEC is notified of the sales; and precaution is taken against nonexempt, unregistered resales.[15] The limits on advertising and unregistered resales do not apply if the offering is made solely in states that provide for registration and disclosure and the securities are sold in compliance with those provisions.[16]

14. 17 C.F.R. Section 230.504. Rule 504 is the exemption used by most small businesses, but that could change under new SEC Rule 1001. This rule permits, under certain circumstances, "testing the waters" for offerings of up to $5 million *per transaction*. These offerings, however, can be made only to "qualified purchasers" (knowledgeable, sophisticated investors).

15. Precautions to be taken against nonexempt, unregistered resales include asking the investor whether he or she is buying the securities for others; before the sale, disclosing to each purchaser in writing that the securities are unregistered and thus cannot be resold, except in an exempt transaction, without first being registered; and indicating on the certificates that the securities are unregistered and restricted.

16. 17 C.F.R. Section 230.504a.

Rule 505. Private, noninvestment company offerings up to $5 million in any twelve-month period are exempt, regardless of the number of **accredited investors** (banks, insurance companies, investment companies, the issuer's executive officers and directors, and persons whose income or net worth exceeds certain limits), so long as there are no more than thirty-five unaccredited investors; no general solicitation or advertising is used; the SEC is notified of the sales; and precaution is taken against nonexempt, unregistered resales. If the sale involves *any* unaccredited investors, *all* investors must be given material information about the offering company, its business, and the securities before the sale. Unlike Rule 506 (discussed next), Rule 505 includes no requirement that the issuer believe each unaccredited investor "has such knowledge and experience in financial and business matters that he is capable of evaluating the merits and the risks of the prospective investment."[17]

Rule 506. Private offerings in unlimited amounts that are not generally solicited or advertised are exempt if the SEC is notified of the sales; precaution is taken against nonexempt, unregistered resales; and the issuer believes that each unaccredited investor has sufficient knowledge or experience in financial matters to be capable of evaluating the investment's merits and risks. There may be no more than thirty-five unaccredited investors, although there may be an unlimited number of accredited investors. If there are *any* unaccredited investors, the issuer must provide to *all* purchasers material information about itself, its business, and the securities before the sale.[18]

This exemption is perhaps most important to those firms that want to raise funds through the sale of securities without registering them. It is often referred to as the *private placement* exemption, because it exempts "transactions not involving any public offering."[19] This provision applies to private offerings to a limited number of persons who are sufficiently sophisticated and in a sufficiently strong bargaining position to be able to assume the risk of the investment (and who thus have no need for federal registration protection), as well as to private offerings to similarly situated institutional investors.

17. 17 C.F.R. Section 230.505.

18. 17 C.F.R. Section 230.506.

19. 15 U.S.C. Section 77d(2).

SMALL OFFERINGS—SECTION 4(6) Under Section 4(6) of the Securities Act of 1933, an offer made *solely* to accredited investors is exempt if its amount is not more than $5 million. Any number of accredited investors may participate, but no unaccredited investors may do so. No general solicitation or advertising may be used; the SEC must be notified of all sales; and precaution must be taken against nonexempt, unregistered resales (because these are restricted securities and may be resold only by registration or in an exempt transaction).[20]

INTRASTATE ISSUES—RULE 147 Also exempt are intrastate transactions involving purely local offerings.[21] This exemption applies to most offerings that are restricted to residents of the state in which the issuing company is organized and doing business. For nine months after the last sale, virtually no resales may be made to nonresidents, and precautions must be taken against this possibility. These offerings remain subject to applicable laws in the state of issue.

RESALES Most securities can be resold without registration (although some resales may be subject to restrictions, which are discussed above in connection with specific exemptions). The Securities Act of 1933 provides exemptions for resales by most persons other than issuers or underwriters. The average investor who sells shares of stock does not have to file a registration statement with the SEC. Resales of restricted securities acquired under Rule 504a, Rule 505, Rule 506, or Section 4(6), however, trigger the registration requirements unless the party selling them complies with Rule 144 or Rule 144A. These rules are sometimes referred to as "safe harbors."

Rule 144. Rule 144 exempts restricted securities from registration on resale if there is adequate current public information about the issuer, the person selling the securities has owned them for at least two years, they are sold in certain limited amounts in unsolicited brokers' transactions, and the SEC is given notice of the resale.[22] "Adequate current public information" consists of the reports that certain companies are required to file under the Securities Exchange Act of 1934. A person who has owned the securities for at least three years is subject to none of these requirements, unless the person is an affiliate. An *affiliate* is one who controls, is controlled by, or is in common control with the issuer. Sales of *nonrestricted* securities by an affiliate are also subject to the requirements for an exemption under Rule 144 (except that the affiliate need not have owned the securities for at least two years).

Rule 144A. Securities that at the time of issue are not of the same class as securities listed on a national securities exchange or quoted in a U.S. automated interdealer quotation system may be resold under Rule 144A.[23] They may be sold only to a qualified institutional buyer (an institution, such as an insurance company, an investment company, or a bank, that owns and invests at least $100 million in securities). The seller must take reasonable steps to ensure that the buyer knows that the seller is relying on the exemption under Rule 144A. A sample restricted stock certificate is shown in Exhibit 28–6.

VIOLATIONS OF THE 1933 ACT

It is a violation of the Securities Act of 1933 to intentionally defraud investors by misrepresenting or omitting facts in a registration statement or prospectus. Liability is also imposed on those who are negligent for not discovering the fraud. Selling securities before the effective date of the registration statement or under an exemption for which the securities do not qualify results in liability.

DEFENSES There are three basic defenses to charges of violations under the 1933 act. A defendant can avoid liability if he or she can prove that, even if a statement was not true or a fact was left out, the statement or omission was not material. A defendant can also avoid liability by proving that the plaintiff knew about the misrepresentation and bought the stock anyway.

Any defendant, except the issuer of the stock, can also assert what is called the *due diligence* defense. To make this defense, a person must prove that he or she reasonably believed, at the time the registration statement became effective, that the statements in it were true and there were no omissions of material facts.

20. 15 U.S.C. Section 77d(6).
21. 15 U.S.C. Section 77c(a)(11); 17 C.F.R. Section 230.147.
22. 17 C.F.R. Section 230.144.
23. 17 C.F.R. Section 230.144A.

EXHIBIT 28–6 ■ A SAMPLE RESTRICTED STOCK CERTIFICATE

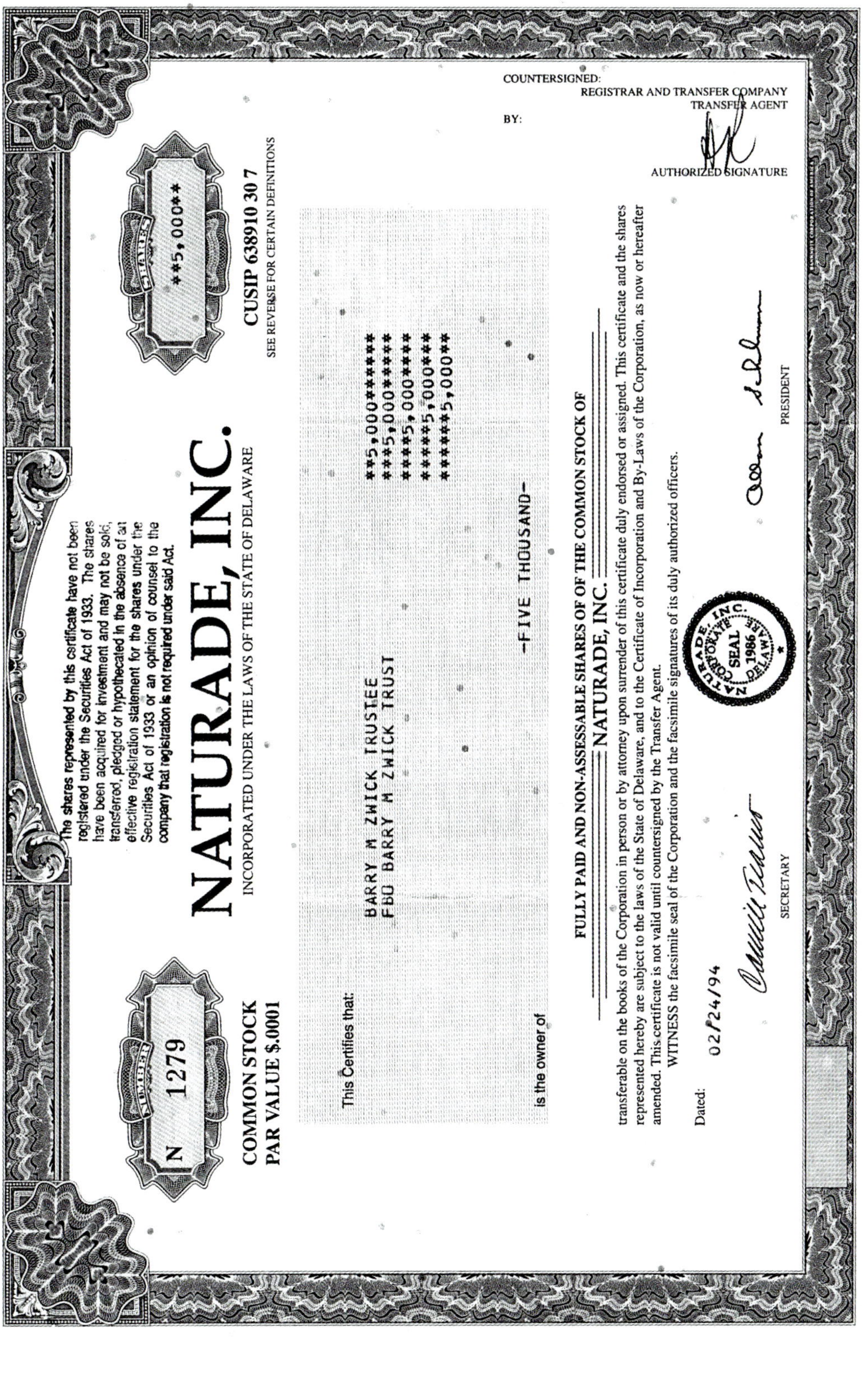

The shares represented by this certificate have not been registered under the Securities Act of 1933. The shares have been acquired for investment and may not be sold, transferred, pledged or hypothecated in the absence of an effective registration statement for the shares under the Securities Act of 1933 or an opinion of counsel to the company that registration is not required under said Act.

NUMBER N 1279

SHARES **5,000**

NATURADE, INC.

INCORPORATED UNDER THE LAWS OF THE STATE OF DELAWARE

COMMON STOCK
PAR VALUE $.0001

CUSIP 638910 30 7
SEE REVERSE FOR CERTAIN DEFINITIONS

This Certifies that:

BARRY M ZWICK TRUSTEE
FBO BARRY M ZWICK TRUST

5,000****
5,000**
****5,000****
*****5,000***
******5,000**

is the owner of

-FIVE THOUSAND-

FULLY PAID AND NON-ASSESSABLE SHARES OF OF THE COMMON STOCK OF
NATURADE, INC.

transferable on the books of the Corporation in person or by attorney upon surrender of this certificate duly endorsed or assigned. This certificate and the shares represented hereby are subject to the laws of the State of Delaware, and to the Certificate of Incorporation and By-Laws of the Corporation, as now or hereafter amended. This certificate is not valid until countersigned by the Transfer Agent.

WITNESS the facsimile seal of the Corporation and the facsimile signatures of its duly authorized officers.

Dated: 02/24/94

NATURADE, INC. CORPORATE SEAL 1986 DELAWARE

SECRETARY

PRESIDENT

COUNTERSIGNED:
REGISTRAR AND TRANSFER COMPANY
TRANSFER AGENT
BY:
AUTHORIZED SIGNATURE

CRIMINAL PENALTIES The U.S. Department of Justice brings criminal actions against those who willfully violate the 1933 act. Violators may be penalized by fines up to $10,000, imprisonment up to five years, or both.

CIVIL SANCTIONS The SEC is authorized to seek, against those who willfully violate the 1933 act, an injunction against further sales of the securities involved. The SEC can also ask the court to grant other relief, such as an order to a violator to refund profits.

Those who purchase the securities and suffer harm as a result of the false or omitted statements, or other violation, may bring a suit in a federal court to recover their losses and other damages. If a registration statement or a prospectus contains material false statements or material omissions, for example, damages may be imposed on those who signed the statement or those who provided information used in preparing the statement (such as accountants and other experts).

SECTION 4 THE SECURITIES EXCHANGE ACT OF 1934

The Securities Exchange Act of 1934 provides for the regulation and registration of securities exchanges, brokers, dealers, and national securities associations, such as the National Association of Securities Dealers (NASD). The SEC regulates the markets in which securities are traded by maintaining a continuous disclosure system for all corporations with securities on the securities exchanges and for those companies that have assets in excess of $10 million and five hundred or more shareholders. These corporations are referred to as Section 12 companies, as they are required to register their securities under Section 12 of the 1934 act.

The act regulates proxy solicitation for voting (see Chapter 17), and it allows the SEC to engage in market surveillance to regulate undesirable market practices such as fraud, market manipulation, misrepresentation, and stabilization. (*Stabilization* is a market-manipulating technique by which securities underwriters bid for securities to stabilize their prices during their issuance.)

SECTION 10(b) AND SEC RULE 10b-5

Section 10(b) is one of the most important sections of the Securities Exchange Act of 1934. This section prohibits the use of any manipulative or deceptive device in violation of SEC rules and regulations. Among the rules that the SEC has prescribed is **SEC Rule 10b-5,** which prohibits the commission of fraud in connection with the purchase or sale of any security. Rule 10b-5 states as follows:

> It shall be unlawful for any person, directly or indirectly, by the use of any means or instrumentality of interstate commerce, or of the mails or of any facility of any national securities exchange,
>
> (a) To employ any device, scheme, or artifice to defraud,
>
> (b) To make any untrue statement of a material fact or to omit to state a material fact necessary in order to make the statements made, in the light of the circumstances under which they were made, not misleading, or
>
> (c) To engage in any act, practice, or course of business which operates or would operate as a fraud or deceit upon any person, in connection with the purchase or sale of any security.[24]

INSIDER TRADING One of the most important purposes of Section 10(b) and SEC Rule 10b-5 relates to so-called **insider trading.** Because of their positions, corporate directors and officers often obtain advance inside information that can affect the future market value of the corporate stock. Obviously, their positions can give them a trading advantage over the general public and shareholders. The 1934 Securities Exchange Act defines inside information and extends liability to officers and directors in their personal transactions for taking advantage of such information when they know that it is unavailable to the person with whom they are dealing.

Section 10(b) of the 1934 act and SEC Rule 10b-5 cover not only corporate officers, directors, and majority shareholders but also any persons having access to or receiving information of a nonpublic nature on which trading is based.

In the following classic case, a shareholder alleged that a corporate officer and a corporate director had breached their fiduciary duties by trading corporate shares on the basis of nonpublic information.

24. 17 C.F.R. Section 240.10b-5.

CASE 28.1 Diamond v. Oreamuno

Court of Appeals of New York, 1969. 24 N.Y.2d 494, 248 N.E.2d 910, 301 N.Y.S.2d 78.

HISTORICAL AND ETHICAL SETTING *Officers and directors owe fiduciary duties to their corporation and its shareholders with respect to corporate business and property. Shares in the corporation are private property, however, and trading in those shares is not usually a corporate transaction. Thus, at common law a century ago, directors and officers were considered to owe no fiduciary duties when they traded in the shares of their corporations. Directors or officers with inside information could trade with impunity without disclosing the information (as long as they avoided outright fraud). Although this rule is sometimes stated to be the majority rule, it has been applied in few cases over the last ninety-five years. Instead, the courts have developed a number of "exceptions." Some state courts apply an agency law theory. According to agency law, an agent may not profit from using the property of his or her principal. It is reasoned by analogy that a director or officer may not profit from using inside information belonging to the corporation.*

BACKGROUND AND FACTS *The defendants in this case were the chairman of the board (Oreamuno) and president (Gonzalez) of Management Assistance, Inc. (MAI), a corporation that bought and leased computers, with maintenance services being provided by IBM. The defendants learned that IBM was going to increase its maintenance prices dramatically, to such an extent that MAI's profits would be cut by 75 percent per month. Just before the IBM maintenance price increase was announced, the defendants sold their MAI stock for $28 per share. After IBM publicly announced its price increase, MAI stock fell to $11 per share. The plaintiff (Diamond) brought a shareholder's derivative lawsuit on behalf of MAI to recover the profits the defendants had made by selling their shares at the higher price. The trial court granted the defendants' motion to dismiss, and the plaintiff appealed.*

IN THE LANGUAGE OF THE COURT

FULD, Chief Judge.

* * * *

Accepting the truth of the complaint's allegations, there is no question but that the defendants were guilty of withholding material information from the purchasers of the shares and, indeed, the defendants acknowledge that the facts asserted constitute a violation of rule 10b-5. * * * Of course, any individual purchaser, who could prove an injury as a result of a rule 10b-5 violation can bring his own action for rescission but we have not been referred to a single case in which such an action has been successfully prosecuted where the public sale of securities is involved. The reason for this is that sales of securities, whether through a stock exchange or over-the-counter, are characteristically anonymous transactions, usually handled through brokers, and the matching of the ultimate buyer with the ultimate seller presents virtually insurmountable obstacles. * * *

* * * There is ample room in a situation such as is here presented for a "private Attorney General" to come forward and enforce proper behavior on the part of corporate officials through the medium of the derivative action brought in the name of the corporation. Only by sanctioning such a cause of action will there be any effective method to prevent the type of abuse of corporate office complained of in this case.

DECISION AND REMEDY *The court of appeals held that when corporate fiduciaries have breached their duty to the corporation by the use of nonpublic information, a shareholder may bring a derivative action for any profit resulting from the breach of duty.*

DISCLOSURE REQUIREMENTS UNDER SEC RULE 10b-5 Any material omission or misrepresentation of material facts in connection with the purchase or sale of a security may violate Section 10(b) and SEC Rule 10b-5. The key to liability (which can be civil or criminal) under this rule is whether the insider's information is *material.* The following are some examples of material facts calling for a disclosure under the rule:

1. Fraudulent trading in the company stock by a broker-dealer.
2. A dividend change (whether up or down).
3. A contract for the sale of corporate assets.
4. A new discovery, a new process, or a new product.
5. A significant change in the financial condition of the firm.
6. Potential litigation against the company.

Ironically, one of the effects of SEC Rule 10b-5 was to deter disclosure. To understand why, consider an example. A company announces that its projected earnings in a certain time period will be X amount. It turns out that the forecast is wrong. The earnings are in fact much lower, and the price of the company's stock is affected—negatively. The shareholders then bring a class-action suit against the company, alleging that the directors violated SEC Rule 10b-5 by disclosing misleading financial information.

In an attempt to rectify this problem and promote disclosure, Congress passed the Private Securities Litigation Reform Act of 1995. Among other things, the act provides a "safe harbor" for publicly held companies that make forward-looking statements, such as financial forecasts. Those who make such statements are protected against federal liability for securities fraud as long as the statements are accompanied by "meaningful cautionary statements identifying important factors that could cause actual results to differ materially from those in the forward-looking statement."[25]

The following is a landmark case interpreting SEC Rule 10b-5. The SEC sued several of Texas Gulf Sulphur Company's directors, officers, and employees under SEC Rule 10b-5 after these persons had purchased large amounts of the corporate stock prior to the announcement of a rich ore discovery by the corporation. At issue was whether the ore discovery was a material fact that had to be disclosed under Rule 10b-5.

25. 15 U.S.C. Sections 77z-2, 78u-5.

CASE 28.2 SEC v. Texas Gulf Sulphur Co.

United States Court of Appeals, Second Circuit, 1968. 401 F.2d 833.

BACKGROUND AND FACTS *Texas Gulf Sulphur Company (TGS) conducted aerial geophysical surveys over more than 15,000 square miles of eastern Canada. The operations indicated concentrations of commercially exploitable minerals. At one site near Timmins, Ontario, TGS drilled a hole that appeared to yield a core with an exceedingly high mineral content. TGS kept secret the results of the core sample. Officers and employees of the company made substantial purchases of TGS's stock or accepted stock options after learning of the ore discovery, even though further drilling was necessary to establish whether there was enough ore to be mined commercially. Several months later, TGS announced that the strike was expected to yield at least 25 million tons of ore, substantially driving up the price of TGS stock. The SEC brought suit against the officers and employees of TGS for violating SEC Rule 10b-5. The officers and employees argued that the information on which they had traded had not been material at the time of their trades because the mine had not then been commercially proved. The trial court held that most of the defendants had not violated SEC Rule 10b-5, and the SEC appealed.*

IN THE LANGUAGE OF THE COURT

WATERMAN, Circuit Judge.

* * * *

* * * [W]hether facts are material within Rule 10b-5 when the facts relate to a particular event and are undisclosed by those persons who are knowledgeable

thereof will depend at any given time upon a balancing of both the indicated probability that the event will occur and the anticipated magnitude of the event in light of the totality of the company activity. Here, * * * knowledge of the possibility, which surely was more than marginal, of the existence of a mine of the vast magnitude indicated by the remarkably rich drill core located rather close to the surface (suggesting mineability by the less expensive openpit method) within the confines of a large anomaly (suggesting an extensive region of mineralization) might well have affected the price of TGS stock and would certainly have been an important fact to a reasonable, if speculative, investor in deciding whether he should buy, sell, or hold.

* * * *

* * * [A] major factor in determining whether the * * * discovery was a material fact is the importance attached to the drilling results by those who knew about it. * * * [T]he timing by those who knew of it of their stock purchases * * *—purchases in some cases by individuals who had never before purchased * * * TGS stock—virtually compels the inference that the insiders were influenced by the drilling results.

DECISION AND REMEDY *The appellate court ruled in favor of the SEC. All of the trading by insiders who knew of the mineral find before its true extent had been publicly announced violated SEC Rule 10b-5.*

APPLICABILITY OF SEC RULE 10b-5 SEC Rule 10b-5 applies in virtually all cases concerning the trading of securities, whether on organized exchanges, in over-the-counter markets, or in private transactions. The rule covers notes, bonds, certificates of interest and participation in any profit-sharing agreement, agreements to form a corporation, and joint-venture agreements; in short, the rule covers just about any form of security. It is immaterial whether a firm has securities registered under the 1933 act for the 1934 act to apply.

SEC Rule 10b-5 is applicable only when the requisites of federal jurisdiction (such as the use of the mails, of stock exchange facilities, or of any instrumentality of interstate commerce) are present. Virtually no commercial transaction, however, can be completed without such contact. In addition, the states have corporate securities laws, many of which include provisions similar to SEC Rule 10b-5.

OUTSIDERS AND SEC RULE 10b-5 The traditional insider-trading case involves true insiders—corporate officers, directors, and majority shareholders who have access to (and trade on) inside information. Increasingly, liability under Section 10(b) of the 1934 act and SEC Rule 10b-5 has been extended to include certain "outsiders"—those who trade on inside information acquired *indirectly*. Two theories have been developed under which outsiders may be held liable for insider trading: the *tipper/tippee theory* and the *misappropriation theory*.

Tipper/Tippee Theory. Anyone who acquires inside information as a result of a corporate insider's breach of his or her fiduciary duty can be liable under SEC Rule 10b-5. This liability extends to **tippees** (those who receive "tips" from insiders) and even remote tippees (tippees of tippees).

The key to liability under this theory is that the inside information be obtained as a result of someone's breach of a fiduciary duty to the corporation whose shares are involved in the trading. Unless there is a breach of a duty not to disclose inside information, the disclosure is made in exchange for personal benefit, and the tippee knows of this breach (or should know of it) and benefits from it, there is no liability under this theory.[26]

Misappropriation Theory. Liability for insider trading may also be established under the misappropriation theory. This theory holds that if an individual wrongfully obtains (misappropriates) inside information and trades on it for his or her personal gain, then the individual should be held liable

26. See, for example, *Chiarella v. United States*, 445 U.S. 222, 100 S.Ct. 1108, 63 L.Ed.2d 348 (1980); and *Dirks v. SEC*, 463 U.S. 646, 103 S.Ct. 3255, 77 L.Ed.2d 911 (1983).

because, in essence, the individual stole information rightfully belonging to another.

The misappropriation theory has been controversial because it significantly extends the reach of SEC Rule 10b-5 to outsiders who would not ordinarily be deemed fiduciaries of the corporations in whose stock they trade. At issue in the following case is whether the misappropriation theory can be applied under Rule 10b-5.

CASE 28.3 United States v. O'Hagan

Supreme Court of the United States, 1997. ___U.S.___, 117 S.Ct. 2199, ___L.Ed.2d___.

BACKGROUND AND FACTS *James O'Hagan was a partner in the law firm of Dorsey & Whitney. Grand Met PLC hired Dorsey & Whitney to assist in a takeover of Pillsbury Company. Before Grand Met made its tender offer, O'Hagan bought shares of Pillsbury stock. When the tender offer was announced, the price of Pillsbury stock increased more than 35 percent. O'Hagan sold his shares for a profit of more than $4 million. The Securities and Exchange Commission (SEC) prosecuted O'Hagan for, among other things, securities fraud in violation of Rule 10b-5 under the misappropriation theory. The SEC contended that O'Hagan breached fiduciary duties he owed to his law firm and Grand Met. When O'Hagan was convicted, he appealed to the U.S. Court of Appeals for the Eighth Circuit, which reversed the convictions. The SEC appealed to the United States Supreme Court.*

IN THE LANGUAGE OF THE COURT

Justice *GINSBURG* delivered the opinion of the Court.

* * * *

* * * [M]isappropriation * * * satisfies [Section] 10(b)'s requirement that chargeable conduct involve a "deceptive device or contrivance" used "in connection with" the purchase or sale of securities. * * * [M]isappropriators * * * deal in deception. A fiduciary who pretends loyalty to the principal while secretly converting the principal's information for personal gain dupes or defrauds the principal.

* * * *

* * * [T]he fiduciary's fraud is consummated * * * when, without disclosure to his principal, he uses the information to purchase or sell securities. * * *

* * * *

* * * An investor's informational disadvantage *vis-à-vis* a misappropriator with material, nonpublic information stems from contrivance, not luck; it is a disadvantage that cannot be overcome with research or skill.

DECISION AND REMEDY *The United States Supreme Court held that liability under Rule 10b-5 can be based on the misappropriation theory, reversed the judgment, and remanded the case.*

INSIDER REPORTING AND TRADING—SECTION 16(b)

Officers, directors, and certain large stockholders[27] of Section 12 corporations are required to file reports with the SEC concerning their ownership and trading of the corporation's securities.[28] To discourage such insiders from using nonpublic information about their company to their personal benefit in the stock market, Section 16(b) of the 1934 act provides for the recapture by the corporation of all profits realized by the insider on any purchase and sale or sale and purchase of the corporation's stock within any six-month period. It is irrelevant whether the insider actually uses inside information; *all such short-swing profits must be returned to the corporation.*

Section 16(b) applies not only to stock but to warrants, options, and securities convertible into stock.

27. Those stockholders owning 10 percent of the class of equity securities registered under Section 12 of the 1934 act.

28. 15 U.S.C. Section 78*l*.

In addition, the courts have fashioned complex rules for determining profits. The SEC exempts a number of transactions under Rule 16b-3.[29] For all of these reasons, corporate insiders are wise to seek competent counsel prior to trading in the corporation's stock. Exhibit 28–7 compares the effects of SEC Rule 10b-5 and Section 16(b).

People resort to various tactics to avoid liability under Section 16(b). These tactics include creative ways of exchanging money for stock, as illustrated by the following case.

29. 17 C.F.R. Section 240.16b-3.

CASE 28.4 Tristar Corp. v. Freitas

United States District Court, Eastern District of New York, 1994. 867 F.Supp. 149.

HISTORICAL AND ETHICAL SETTING *Between 1932 and 1934, the Senate Banking Committee held hearings on the securities markets. It discovered widespread fraud and abuse in securities financing and market practices. This discovery helped to propel the securities acts through Congress. The most important aspect of these acts is their requirement of full disclosure. All important information about a company, its securities, and the transaction must be disclosed. The parties can then make a free choice to deal (or not to deal) based on that information. Because of this unregulated freedom to deal, it is vital that the disclosed information be truthful and complete.*

BACKGROUND AND FACTS *Ross Freitas and Carolyn Kenner were officers and directors of the Tristar Corporation. They were also Tristar shareholders, as they had bought Tristar stock between February 2 and June 15, 1989. Meanwhile, on May 31, they agreed to transfer their Tristar shares to Starion International Ltd. Under a contract titled "Periodic Loan Agreement," Freitas and Kenner gave their shares to Starion's attorney. Starion paid Freitas and Kenner in periodic installments. With each payment, the attorney gave a block of the stock to Starion. When Tristar learned of the deal, the firm filed a suit in a federal district court against Freitas and Kenner, under Section 16(b), to obtain their profits. Tristar filed a motion for summary judgment.*

IN THE LANGUAGE OF THE COURT

DEARIE, District Judge.

* * * *

* * * As a general rule, a sale occurs when the insider has incurred an irrevocable liability to dispose of the stock so that his rights and obligations have become fixed.

The Court has examined the Loan Agreement and finds that on May 31, 1989 defendants did in fact "contract to sell or otherwise dispose of" the Agreement Shares within the meaning of [S]ection 16(b). The Court is persuaded that the Loan Agreement has the ordinary indicia [signs or indications] of an installment sales contract. * * * A common-sense assessment of the mechanics of the Loan Agreement reveals that all of the Agreement Shares were committed on May 31, 1989.

DECISION AND REMEDY *The federal district court ruled in Tristar's favor. The court set for trial the issue of how much money Freitas and Kenner should pay to Tristar.*

EXHIBIT 28–7 ■ COMPARISON OF COVERAGE, APPLICATION, AND LIABILITY UNDER SEC RULE 10b-5 AND SECTION 16(b)

	RULE 10b-5	SECTION 16(b)
Subject matter of transaction	Any security (does not have to be registered).	Any security (does not have to be registered).
Transactions covered	Purchase or sale.	Short-swing purchase and sale or short-swing sale and purchase.
Who is subject to liability?	Virtually anyone with inside information under a duty to disclose—including officers, directors, controlling stockholders, and tippees.	Officers, directors, and certain holders of large amounts of stock.
Is omission or misrepresentation necessary for liability?	Yes.	No.
Any exempt transactions?	No.	Yes, a variety of exemptions.
Is direct dealing with the party necessary?	No.	No.
Who may bring an action?	A person transacting with an insider, the SEC, or a purchaser or seller damaged by a wrongful act.	Corporation and shareholder by derivative action.

PROXY STATEMENTS

Section 14(a) of the Securities Exchange Act of 1934 regulates the solicitation of proxies (see Chapter 17) from shareholders of Section 12 companies. The SEC regulates the content of proxy statements, which are statements sent to shareholders by corporate managers who are requesting authority to vote on behalf of the shareholders in a particular election on specified issues. Whoever solicits a proxy must fully and accurately disclose in the proxy statement all of the facts that are pertinent to the matter on which the shareholders are to vote. SEC Rule 14a-9 is similar to the antifraud provisions of SEC Rule 10b-5. Remedies for violations are extensive, ranging from injunctions to prevent a vote from being taken to monetary damages.

VIOLATIONS OF THE 1934 ACT

Violations of Section 10(b) and Rule 10b-5 of the Securities Exchange Act of 1934 include insider trading. This is a criminal offense, with criminal penalties. Violators of these laws may also be subject to civil liability. For any sanctions to be imposed, however, there must be *scienter*—the violator must have had an intent to defraud or knowledge of his or her misconduct (see Chapter 9). *Scienter* can be proved by showing a defendant made false statements or wrongfully failed to disclose material facts.

Violations of Section 16(b) include the sale by insiders of stock acquired less than six months before the sale. These violations are subject to civil sanctions. Liability under Section 16(b) is strict liability. *Scienter* is not required.

CRIMINAL PENALTIES For violations of Section 10(b) and Rule 10b-5, an individual may be fined up to $1 million, imprisoned up to ten years, or both. A partnership or a corporation may be fined up to $2.5 million.

CIVIL SANCTIONS Both the SEC and private parties can bring actions to seek civil sanctions against violators of the 1934 act.

The Insider Trading Sanctions Act of 1984 permits the SEC to bring suit in a federal district court against anyone violating or aiding in a violation of the 1934 act or SEC rules by purchasing or selling a security while in the possession of material nonpublic information.[30] The violation must occur on or

30. 15 U.S.C. Section 78u(d)(2)(A).

through the facilities of a national securities exchange or from or through a broker or dealer. Transactions pursuant to a public offering by an issuer of securities are excepted. The court may assess as a penalty as much as triple the profits gained or the loss avoided by the guilty party. Profit or loss is defined as "the difference between the purchase or sale price of the security and the value of that security as measured by the trading price of the security at a reasonable period of time after public dissemination of the nonpublic information."[31]

The Insider Trading and Securities Fraud Enforcement Act of 1988 enlarged the class of persons who may be subject to civil liability for insider-trading violations. This act also gave the SEC authority to award **bounty payments** (rewards given by government officials for acts beneficial to the state) to persons providing information leading to the prosecution of insider-trading violations.[32]

Private parties may also sue violators of Section 10(b) and Rule 10b-5. A private party may obtain rescission of a contract to buy securities or damages to the extent of the violator's illegal profits. Those found liable have a right to seek contribution from those who share responsibility for the violations, including accountants, attorneys, and corporations.[33] For violations of Section 16(b), a corporation can bring an action to recover the short-swing profits.

SECTION 5

REGULATION OF INVESTMENT COMPANIES

Investment companies, and mutual funds in particular, grew rapidly after World War II. **Investment companies** act on behalf of many smaller shareholders/owners by buying a large portfolio of securities and managing that portfolio professionally. A **mutual fund** is a specific type of investment company that continually buys or sells to investors shares of ownership in a portfolio. Such companies are regulated by the Investment Company Act of 1940,[34] which provides for SEC regulation of their activities. The 1940 act was expanded by the Investment Company Act Amendments of 1970. Further minor changes were made in the Securities Act Amendments of 1975. The National Securities Markets Improvement Act of 1996 increased the SEC's authority to regulate investment companies by limiting virtually all of the authority of the states to regulate these companies.

The 1940 act requires that every investment company register with the SEC and imposes restrictions on the activities of such companies and persons connected with them. For the purposes of the act, an investment company is defined as any entity that (1) "is . . . engaged primarily . . . in the business of investing, reinvesting, or trading in securities" or (2) is engaged in such business and more than 40 percent of the company's assets consist of investment securities. Excluded from coverage by the act are banks, insurance companies, savings and loan associations, finance companies, oil and gas drilling firms, charitable foundations, tax-exempt pension funds, and other special types of institutions, such as closely held corporations.

All investment companies must register with the SEC by filing a notification of registration. Each year, registered investment companies must file reports with the SEC. To safeguard company assets, all securities must be held in the custody of a bank or stock exchange member, and that bank or stock exchange member must follow strict procedures established by the SEC.

No dividends may be paid from any source other than accumulated, undistributed net income. Furthermore, there are some restrictions on investment activities. For example, investment companies are not allowed to purchase securities on the margin (pay only part of the total price, borrowing the rest), sell short (sell shares not yet owned), or participate in joint trading accounts.

SECTION 6

STATE SECURITIES LAWS

Today, all states have their own corporate securities laws, or "blue sky laws," that regulate the offer and sale of securities within individual state borders. (The phrase *blue sky laws* dates to a 1917 United States Supreme Court decision in which the Court declared that the purpose of such laws was to prevent "speculative schemes which have no more basis than

31. 15 U.S.C. Section 78u(d)(2)(C).
32. 15 U.S.C. Section 78u-1.
33. Note that a private cause of action under Section 10(b) and SEC Rule 10b-5 cannot be brought against accountants, attorneys, and others who "aid and abet" violations of the act. Only the SEC can bring actions against so-called aiders and abettors. See *SEC v. Fehn*, 97 F.3d 1276 (9th Cir. 1996).
34. 15 U.S.C. Sections 80a-1 to 80a-64.

so many feet of 'blue sky.' "[35]) Article 8 of the Uniform Commercial Code, which has been adopted by all of the states, also imposes various requirements relating to the purchase and sale of securities. State securities laws apply only to intrastate transactions. Since the adoption of the 1933 and 1934 federal securities acts, the state and federal governments have regulated securities concurrently. Issuers must comply with both federal and state securities laws, and exemptions from federal law are not exemptions from state laws.

There are differences in philosophy among state statutes, but certain features are common to all state blue sky laws. Typically, state laws have disclosure requirements and antifraud provisions, many of which are patterned after Section 10(b) of the Securities Exchange Act of 1934 and SEC Rule 10b-5. State laws also provide for the registration or qualification of securities offered or issued for sale within the state and impose disclosure requirements. Unless an applicable exemption from registration is found, issuers must register or qualify their stock with the appropriate state official, often called a *corporations commissioner.* Additionally, most state securities laws regulate securities brokers and dealers. The Uniform Securities Act, which has been adopted in part by several states, was drafted to be acceptable to states with differing regulatory philosophies.

The dual federal and state system has not always worked well, particularly during the early 1990s, when there was considerable expansion of the securities markets. The National Securities Markets Improvement Act of 1996 eliminated some of the duplicate regulations. While the states still regulate local and regional matters, the SEC exclusively regulates most of the national securities activities.

SECTION 7

TECHNOLOGY AND SECURITIES LAW

History was made when Spring Street Brewing Company became the first company to conduct an initial public offering over the Internet in 1995. In March 1996, the company again made history when the SEC allowed Spring Street to trade its shares via its Web site without registering as a broker-dealer—provided that the company modified its program. Among other things, the SEC required Spring Street, which had been directly processing the funds received from buyers, to use an independent agent, such as a bank or escrow agent, to receive such funds.

Since that time, a number of other companies have set up Internet sites to facilitate initial offerings and securities trading. Some of these sites are maintained by securities firms that offer the opportunity to invest online. Others are maintained by businesses that also use the Internet to reach millions of potential investors around the world at practically no cost. Many of these businesses offer the delivery of their prospectuses electronically, which further reduces their costs. Some companies also provide information about stock issues on CD-ROM. The SEC now has rules specifying when the electronic delivery of information provides sufficient notice to investors, how an investor can be provided access to information, and what constitutes evidence that electronic delivery has been effected.[36]

An offering can be kept private by placing the issuing company's information at a site protected by a password. Anyone who wants to view the information can be evaluated with respect to investing status before being given the password. The problem with passwords, though, is that they can be given to potentially unevaluated stock purchasers.

Despite the rapid acceptance by the SEC and the investing community of the potential of the Internet, there are many questions to answer. Is it possible to effectively regulate securities information before it is placed online? Does the SEC have the resources to regulate online trading? Are the current securities laws adequate to cope with the new technology? Over the next decade, as these issues are resolved, the Internet may become the most important tool for investors and businesses wishing to attract them.

35. *Hall v. Geiger-Jones Co.*, 242 U.S. 539, 37 S.Ct. 217, 61 L.Ed. 480 (1917).

36. See, for example, "Use of Electronic Media for Delivery Purposes," SEC Release Nos. 33-7233 and 33-7234, October 6, 1996.

TERMS AND CONCEPTS TO REVIEW

accredited investor 579	investment company 589	securities 573
bond 573	mutual fund 589	stock 573
bounty payment 589	preferred stock 574	tippee 585
common stock 573	red herring 577	tombstone ad 577
insider trading 582	SEC Rule 10b-5 582	

QUESTIONS AND CASE PROBLEMS

28–1. REGISTRATION REQUIREMENTS. Estrada Hermanos, Inc., a corporation incorporated and doing business in Florida, decides to sell $1 million worth of its no-par-value common stock to the public. The stock will be sold only within the state of Florida. Jose Estrada, the chairman of the board, says the offering need not be registered with the Securities and Exchange Commission. His brother, Gustavo, disagrees. Who is right? Explain.

28–2. REGISTRATION REQUIREMENTS. Huron Corp. has 300,000 common shares outstanding. The owners of these outstanding shares live in several different states. Huron has decided to split the 300,000 shares two for one. Will Huron Corp. have to file a registration statement and prospectus on the 300,000 new shares to be issued as a result of the split? Explain.

28–3. SEC RULE 10b-5. Danny Cherif was employed by the First National Bank of Chicago in its International Financial Institutions Department from 1979 until 1987, when Cherif's position was eliminated because of an internal reorganization. Cherif, using a forged memo to the bank's security department, caused his magnetic identification (ID) card—which he had received as an employee to allow him to enter the bank building—to remain activated after his employment was terminated. Cherif used his ID card to enter the building at night to obtain confidential financial information from the bank's Specialized Finance Department regarding extraordinary business transactions, such as tender offers. During 1988 and 1989, Cherif made substantial profits through securities trading based on this information. Eventually, Cherif's activities were investigated by the Securities and Exchange Commission (SEC), and Cherif was charged with violating Section 10(b) and SEC Rule 10b-5 by misappropriating and trading on inside information in violation of his fiduciary duties to his former employer. Cherif argued that the SEC had wrongfully applied the misappropriation theory to his activities, because as a former employee, he no longer had a fiduciary duty to the bank. Explain whether Cherif is liable under SEC Rule 10b-5. [*SEC v. Cherif*, 933 F.2d 403 (7th Cir. 1991)]

28–4. SEC RULE 10b-5. Susan Waldbaum was a niece of the president and controlling shareholder of Waldbaum, Inc. Susan's mother (the president's sister) told Susan that the company was going to be sold at a favorable price and that a tender offer was soon to be made. She told Susan not to tell anyone except her husband, Keith Loeb, about the sale. The next day, Susan told her husband of the sale and cautioned him not to tell anyone, because "it could possibly ruin the sale." The day after he learned of the sale, Loeb called Robert Chestman, his broker, and told him that he "had some accurate information" that the company was about to be sold at a price "substantially higher" than the market value of its stock. That day, Chestman purchased shares of the company for himself, as well as for Loeb. Chestman was later convicted by a jury of, among other things, trading on misappropriated inside information in violation of SEC Rule 10b-5. On appeal, the central question in regard to liability under the misappropriation theory was whether Chestman had acquired the inside information about the Waldbaum company as a result of an insider's breach of a fiduciary duty. Essentially, the inquiry focused on whether Loeb owed a fiduciary duty to his wife's family or to his wife to keep the information confidential. How should the court rule? [*United States v. Chestman*, 947 F.2d 551 (2d Cir. 1991)]

28–5. INVESTOR PROTECTION. U.S. News & World Report, Inc., set up a profit-sharing plan in 1962 that allotted to certain employees specially issued stock known as bonus or anniversary stock. The stock was given to the employees for past services and could not be traded or sold to anyone other than the corporate issuer, U.S. News. This special stock was issued only to employees and for no other purpose than as bonuses. Because there was no market for the stock, U.S. News hired an independent appraiser to estimate the fair value of the stock so that the employees could redeem the shares. Charles Foltz and several other employees held stock through this plan and sought to redeem the shares with U.S. News, but Foltz disputed the value set by the appraisers. Foltz sued U.S. News for violation of securities regulations. What defense would allow U.S. News to resist Foltz's claim successfully? [*Foltz v. U.S. News & World Report, Inc.*, 627 F.Supp. 1143 (D.D.C. 1986)]

28–6. SECTION 10(b). In early 1986, FMC Corp. finalized plans to buy some of its own stock as part of a restructuring of its balance statement. Unknown to FMC management, the brokerage firm FMC employed—Goldman, Sachs & Co.—disclosed information on the stock purchase that found its way to Ivan Boesky. FMC was one of the seven major corporations in whose stock Ivan Boesky allegedly traded using inside information. Boesky made purchases of FMC's stock between February 18 and February 21 and between March 12 and April 4. Boesky's purchases amounted to a substantial portion of the total volume of FMC stock traded during these periods. The price of FMC stock increased from $71.25 on February 18, 1986, to $97.00 on April 25, 1986. As a result, FMC paid substantially more for the repurchase of its own stock than anticipated. On the discovery of Boesky's knowledge of FMC's recapitalization plan, FMC sued Boesky for the excess price it had paid—approximately $220 million. Discuss whether FMC should recover under Section 10(b) of the Securities Exchange Act and SEC Rule 10b-5. [*FMC Corp. v. Boesky*, 673 F.Supp. 242 (N.D.Ill. 1987)]

28–7. SHORT-SWING PROFITS. Emerson Electric Co. purchased 13.2 percent of Dodge Manufacturing Co.'s stock in an unsuccessful takeover attempt in June 1967. Later, when Dodge merged with Reliance Electric Co., Emerson decided to sell its shares. To avoid being subject to the restrictions of Section 16 of the Securities Exchange Act of 1934, which pertain to any purchase and sale by any owner of 10 percent or more of a corporation's stock, Emerson decided on a two-step selling plan. First, it sold off sufficient shares to reduce its holdings to 9.96 percent, and then it sold the remaining stock—all within a six-month period. Because under Section 16(b) of the act, the owner must be a 10 percent owner "both at the time of the purchase and sale . . . of the security involved," Emerson thought it had succeeded in avoiding potential liability under Section 16(b). Reliance demanded that Emerson return the profits made on both sales. Emerson sought a declaratory judgment from the court that it was not liable, arguing that because at the time of the second sale it had not owned 10 percent of Dodge stock, Section 16 did not apply. Does Section 16 of the Securities Exchange Act of 1934 apply to Emerson's transactions, and is Emerson liable to Reliance for its profits? [*Reliance Electric Co. v. Emerson Electric Co.*, 404 U.S. 418, 92 S.Ct. 596, 30 L.Ed.2d 575 (1972)]

28–8. SEC RULE 10b-5. Louis Ferraro was the chairman and president of Anacomp, Inc. In June 1988, Ferraro told his good friend Michael Maio that Anacomp was negotiating a tender offer for stock in Xidex Corp. Maio passed on the information to Patricia Ladavac, a friend of both Ferraro and Maio. Maio and Ladavac immediately purchased shares in Xidex stock. On the day that the tender offer was announced—an announcement that caused the price of Xidex shares to increase—Maio and Ladavac sold their Xidex stock and made substantial profits (Maio made $211,000 from the transactions, and Ladavac gained $78,750). The SEC brought an action against the three individuals, alleging that they had violated, among other laws, SEC Rule 10b-5. Maio and Ladavac claimed that they had done nothing illegal. They argued that they had no fiduciary duty either to Anacomp or to Xidex, and therefore they had no duty to disclose or abstain from trading in the stock of those corporations. Had Maio and Ladavac violated SEC Rule 10b-5? Discuss fully. [*SEC v. Maio*, 51 F.3d 623 (7th Cir. 1995)]

28–9. DEFINITION OF A SECURITY. Life Partners, Inc. (LPI), facilitates the sale of life insurance policies that are owned by persons suffering from AIDS (acquired immune deficiency syndrome) to investors at a discount. The investor pays LPI, and LPI pays the policyholder. Typically, the policyholder, in turn, assigns the policy to LPI, which also obtains the right to make LPI's president the beneficiary of the policy. On the policyholder's death, LPI receives the proceeds of the policy and pays the investor. In this way, the terminally ill sellers secure much-needed income in the final years of life, when employment is unlikely and medical bills are often staggering. The SEC sought to enjoin (prevent) LPI from engaging in further transactions on the ground that the investment contracts were securities, which LPI had failed to register with the SEC in violation of securities laws. Do the investment contracts meet the definition of a security discussed in this chapter? Discuss fully. [*SEC v. Life Partners, Inc.*, 898 F.Supp. 14 (D.C. 1995)]

28–10. SECTION 10(b). Joseph Jett worked for Kidder, Peabody & Co., a financial services firm owned by General Electric Co. (GE). Over a three-year period, Jett allegedly engaged in a scheme to generate false profits at Kidder, Peabody to increase his performance-based bonuses. When the scheme was discovered, Daniel Chill and other GE shareholders who had bought stock in the previous year filed a suit in a federal district court against GE. The shareholders alleged that GE had engaged in securities fraud in violation of Section 10(b). They claimed that GE's interest in justifying its investment in Kidder, Peabody gave GE "a motive to willfully blind itself to facts casting doubt on Kidder's purported profitability." On what basis might the court dismiss the shareholders' complaint? Discuss fully. [*Chill v. General Electric Co.*, 101 F.3d 263 (2d Cir. 1996)]

28–11. A QUESTIONS OF ETHICS

Between 1970 and 1981, Sanford Weill had served as the chief executive officer (CEO) of Shearson Loeb Rhodes and several of its predecessor entities (collectively "Shearson"). In 1981, Weill sold his controlling interest in Shearson to the American Express Co. and between 1981 and 1985 served as president of that firm. In 1985, Weill developed an interest in becoming CEO for BankAmerica and secured a commitment from Shearson to invest $1 billion in BankAmerica if he was successful in his negotiations with that firm. In early 1986, Weill met with BankAmerica directors several times, but these contacts were not disclosed publicly until February 20, 1986, when BankAmerica announced that Weill had sought to become its CEO but that BankAmerica was not interested in his offer. The day after the announcement, BankAmerica stock traded at prices higher than they had been during the five weeks preceding the announcement. Weill discussed his efforts to become CEO of BankAmerica with his wife, who discussed the information with her psychiatrist, Dr. Willis, prior to BankAmerica's public announcement of February 20. She also told Dr. Willis about Shearson's decision to invest in BankAmerica if Weill succeeded in becoming its CEO. Willis disclosed to his broker his material, confidential information and purchased BankAmerica common stock. After BankAmerica's public announcement and the subsequent increase in the price of its stock, Willis sold his shares and realized a profit of approximately $27,475.79. The court held that Willis was liable for insider trading under the misappropriation theory. [*United States v. Willis*, 737 F.Supp. 269 (S.D.N.Y. 1990)]

1. The court stated in its opinion in this case that "[i]t is difficult to imagine a relationship that requires a higher degree of trust and confidence than the traditional relationship of physician and patient" and then quoted the concluding words of the Hippocratic oath: "Whatsoever things I see or hear concerning the life of men, in my attendance on the sick or even apart therefrom, which ought not be noised abroad, I will keep silence thereon, counting such things to be as sacred secrets." The court held that Willis had violated his fiduciary duty to Mrs. Weill, his patient, by investing in BankAmerica stock. Do you agree that Willis's private investments, which were based on information learned through his sessions with Mrs. Weill, constituted a violation of his duty to his patient? After all, Willis had not "noised abroad" Mrs. Weill's secrets—that is, he had not told others (except for his stockbroker) about the information. If you had been in Willis's shoes, would you have felt ethically restrained from trading on the information?
2. Can you think of any ways in which Willis's trading could have been harmful to Mrs. Weill's interests? Does your answer to this question have a bearing on how you would answer Question 1 above?
3. Do you think that Willis's liability for his breach of duty should extend only to Mrs. Weill? In other words, do you think that the misappropriation theory of liability imposes too great a burden on outsiders, such as Willis? Why or why not? How might you justify, from an ethical point of view, the application of the misappropriation theory to "outsider trading"?

Unit Five—Cumulative Hypothetical Problem

28–12. *Falwell Motors, Inc., is a large corporation that manufactures automobile batteries.*

1. The Occupational Safety and Health Administration (OSHA) has proposed a new safety rule governing the handling of certain acids in the workplace, including those used by Falwell in its manufacturing operations. Falwell concludes that the rule, which will involve substantial compliance costs, will not significantly increase workplace safety. Falwell sends a letter to OSHA indicating its objections to the proposed rule and enclosing research reports and other data supporting those objections. Does OSHA have any obligation to consider these objections? What procedures must OSHA follow when it makes new rules, such as this one?
2. The Federal Trade Commission (FTC) learns that one of the retail stores that sells Falwell's batteries engages in deceptive advertising practices. What actions can the FTC take against the retailer?
3. For years, Falwell has shipped the toxic waste created by its manufacturing process to a waste-disposal site in the next county. The waste site has become contaminated by leakage from toxic waste containers delivered to the site by other manufacturers. Can Falwell be held liable for clean-up costs, even though its containers were not the ones that leaked? If so, what is the extent of its liability?
4. Falwell faces stiff competition from Alchem, Inc., another battery manufacturer. To acquire control over Alchem, Falwell makes a tender offer to Alchem's shareholders. If Falwell succeeds in its attempt and Alchem is merged into Falwell, will the merger violate any antitrust laws? Suppose the merger falls through. The vice president of Falwell's battery division and the president of Alchem agree to divide up the market between them, so they will not have to compete for customers. Is this agreement legal? Explain.

ACCESSING THE INTERNET

THE LEGAL ENVIRONMENT OF BUSINESS

The Web site for the Securities and Exchange Commission (SEC) is called EDGAR, for Electronic Data Gathering Analysis and Retrieval system. Corporate financial information in the EDGAR database—including initial public offerings, proxy statements, annual corporate reports, registration statements, and other documents filed with the SEC—is available to the public. The site also contains information about the SEC's operations, the statutes it implements, its proposed and final rules, and its enforcement actions. To access EDGAR, go to

http://www.sec.gov/edgarhp.htm

The Center for Corporate Law at the University of Cincinnati College of Law examines all of the acts discussed in this chapter. Go to

http://www.law.uc.edu/CCL/

To find the Securities Act of 1933, go to

http://www.law.uc.edu/CCL/33Act/index.html

To examine the Securities Exchange Act of 1934, go to

http://www.law.uc.edu/CCL/34Act/index.html

For information on investor protection and securities fraud, including answers to frequently asked questions on the topic of securities fraud, go to

http://www.securitieslaw.com

FOCUS ON ETHICS

THE REGULATORY ENVIRONMENT

If this text had been written a hundred years ago, it would have had little to say about federal government regulation. To be sure, by the 1890s, the beginnings of federal antitrust law had been manifested in the form of the Interstate Commerce Act and the Sherman Act, but there was little or no legislation designed to protect consumers or the environment. Today, in contrast, virtually every area of economic activity is regulated by the government.

From a very broad perspective, ethical issues in government regulation arise because regulation, by its very nature, means that some traditional rights and freedoms have to be given up to ensure that other rights and freedoms are protected. Essentially, government regulation brings two ethical principles into conflict. On the one hand, deeply embedded in American culture is the idea that the government should play a limited role in directing our lives. Indeed, this nation was founded so that Americans could be free from the "heavy hand of government" experienced by the colonists under English rule. On the other hand, one of the basic functions of government is to protect the welfare of individuals and the environment in which they live. Ultimately, virtually every law or rule regulating business represents a decision to give up certain rights in order to protect other perceived rights. In this *Focus on Ethics,* we look at some of the ethical aspects of government regulation.

ENVIRONMENTAL LAW

Questions of fairness inevitably arise in regard to environmental law. Has the government gone too far in regulating businesses in the interest of protecting the environment? Has the government gone far enough? At what point do the costs of environmental regulations become too burdensome for society to bear? These are broad questions, but they are ethical in nature, because they ultimately relate to society's notions of what is right, just, or good.

If manufacturers ceased all production and Americans returned to the rural life of earlier times, the environment would certainly benefit. Obviously, Americans do not want to pay that high a cost. Certainly, we want to enjoy the fruits of our advanced economy. But environmental protection means that some sacrifices will have to be made. How much are we willing to sacrifice today to ensure that future generations have a more healthful world in which to live?

Superfund and Toxic Waste

Although everybody is in favor of cleaning up America's toxic waste dumps, nobody has the slightest idea what this task will ultimately cost. Much of the problem in determining the ultimate costs of the Superfund program (CERCLA—see Chapter 24) stems from the difficulty of estimating the costs of cleaning up a site. Until the clean-up is actually undertaken, it is often difficult to assess the extent of contamination. Moreover, there is no agreed-on standard as to how clean these sites need to be before they no longer pose any threat of harm to life. Do you have to remove *all* of the contamination, or would removal of some lesser amount achieve a reasonable degree of environmental quality? On the cost side of the picture, another question exists: If, say, 90 percent of the waste at a given site could be removed for $50,000, but the removal of the other 10 percent would cost $2 million, is it reasonable to remove that remaining 10 percent?

Another aspect of Superfund that raises questions of fairness is the joint and several liability imposed by the act. This means that a party may be liable for the total costs of cleaning up a hazardous waste site, even though that party was responsible for only a small fraction of the toxic waste dumped at the site.

For some time, Congress has been under pressure to overhaul the Superfund legislation for these and other reasons. A bill currently before Congress would, among other things, allow the Environmental Protection Agency to consider what the land is likely to be used for in the future when determining how clean a site has

Focus on Ethics

to be. The bill would also eliminate joint and several liability at most sites and exempt certain small businesses from liability.

Conflicting Regulations

Because various environmental laws and agency rules have been created at different times for different purposes, this body of regulatory law is not always coherent and consistent. The problem of conflicting environmental regulations raises issues of fairness because often, in undertaking a good faith attempt to comply with one regulation, a firm may end up violating another.

Consider, for example, the experience of the Leslie Salt Company, which owned a large tract of land southeast of San Francisco, across the highway from the San Francisco Bay National Wildlife Refuge. Leslie Salt's predecessor had dug various shallow basins to facilitate the manufacture of salt. After Leslie Salt discontinued salt production in 1959, the area remained dry most of the year. During the winter and spring months, however, rainwater occasionally created temporary ponds, which were visited by migratory birds. The usually dry basins created a dust problem, and as a result, Leslie Salt eventually was cited for violating federal air-pollution standards.

To prevent further citations, Leslie Salt began to plow the basins, dig ditches, and discharge fill material into the basins to create conditions more hospitable to plant growth. Ironically, these actions subjected it to penalties under the Clean Water Act. When the Army Corps of Engineers (the Corps) learned of Leslie Salt's filling activities, it issued a cease-and-desist order. The Corps claimed that the filling of the basins violated the Clean Water Act, which prohibits the discharge of any pollutant—including dredged or fill materials—into "navigable waters" without a permit from the Corps. Under a regulation promulgated by the Corps, "navigable waters" include, among other things, "mudflats, sandflats, wetlands, sloughs, prairie potholes, wet meadows, . . . or natural ponds, the use, degradation or destruction of which could affect interstate or foreign commerce."

Leslie Salt, claiming that the ponds had nothing to do with interstate commerce, filed a suit challenging the Corps's jurisdiction over its property. A federal district court concluded that the presence of migratory birds created a sufficient connection to interstate commerce to sustain the Corps's (federal) jurisdiction. On appeal, a federal appellate court affirmed the decision,[1] and the United States Supreme Court refused to grant *certiorari.*

The problem of conflicting regulations is compounded by the sheer volume of environmental regulations governing business activities. As one former federal prosecutor stated, there are so many environmental rules in the book that there "is almost no point in time when a company won't be in violation of some regulation."[2]

Fair Debt Collection

By passing the Fair Debt Collection Practices Act (FDCPA), Congress expressed society's concern with unfair debt-collection practices. The act prohibits those that collect debts for other parties, such as collection agencies, from engaging in certain abusive tactics, as discussed in Chapter 45. Some have argued that the act did not go far enough in the direction of protecting consumer debtors, because the act does not cover creditors that collect their own debts rather than have a third party, such as a collection agency, do so.

Consider, for example, the situation in *Sterling Mirror of Maryland, Inc. v. Gordon.*[3] Sterling Mirror of Maryland, Inc., had installed mirrors in the home of John and Daisy Gordon. Only John signed the contract. Because one of the mirrors was chipped while it was being installed, John Gordon refused to pay the balance due to Sterling Mirror. Sterling Mirror tried to pressure the Gordons into paying for the mirrors by making numerous calls to Daisy at her place of employment. When Sterling Mirror sued the Gordons for the balance due, Daisy counterclaimed for damages under the FDCPA, asserting, among other things, that Sterling

1. *Leslie Salt Co. v. United States,* 55 F.3d 1388 (9th Cir. 1995).

2. David Geneson, as quoted in Max Boot, "A Rotten Fate," *The Wall Street Journal Europe,* December 6, 1995, p. 10.

3. 619 A.2d 64 (D.C.App. 1993).

FOCUS ON ETHICS

Mirror had violated the provisions of that act by contacting her at work. Had Sterling Mirror violated the FDCPA? No, it had not, because Sterling Mirror was not a collection agency, and thus the FDCPA did not apply. Had it been a collection agency, however, it would have violated the FDCPA, because under the act, collection agencies are allowed to contact only the debtor (not the debtor's spouse) at the debtor's place of employment, and then only if the employer does not object.

ANTITRUST LAW AND CONSUMER PROTECTION

From its beginnings in the nineteenth century, antitrust law has sought to maintain a freely competitive business environment so that consumers would not be victimized by monopoly pricing tactics. Consumer welfare has thus from the outset been a touchstone issue in antitrust cases. Sometimes, though, this aspect of antitrust law, which is rooted in ethical notions of fairness, becomes lost in the thicket of antitrust lawsuits among competitors.

The Court of Appeals for the Eighth Circuit emphasized the importance of the consumer perspective in antitrust law in a case involving alleged predatory pricing. The case was brought by Gilbert Bathke and other gasoline retailers (the plaintiffs) located in small Iowa communities against Casey's General Stores, Inc. During the 1980s, Casey's, a multistate retailer of gasoline and other goods, had begun to lose profits to its competitors. In an attempt to increase its sales, Casey's had directed its stores that were losing sales to reduce gas prices. The plaintiffs claimed that Casey's price reductions amounted to predatory pricing in violation of, among other laws, Section 2 of the Sherman Act.

One of the central issues in the case concerned Casey's share of the relevant geographical market. The plaintiffs contended that the relevant geographical market consisted of the small towns in which Casey's operated its stores. After all, contended the plaintiffs, consumers preferred to buy their gasoline in the towns in which they lived, and gasoline retailers' trade came mostly from in-town customers. The court, however, stated that a geographical market is determined not by where consumers actually go for their gasoline but where they *could* go. Evidence of consumers' actual habits is not enough, said the court, to establish the relevant geographical market. To demonstrate the "logic and necessity of applying such a requirement in this case," the court illustrated the difference between a "trade area" and a "relevant market."

"Consider the following illustration," stated the court. "Fifteen miles outside of City A is a small town, Town B, which contains a single shoe store, Smith's Clothing. The only people who ever shop in Smith's Clothing are residents of Town B. When Smith's is accused of monopolization, the plaintiffs argue that Town B defines the relevant geographic market, since all of the store's customers come from there. In that case, Smith's market share is 100%. But further inquiry shows the following. Last year 800 residents of Town B purchased shoes. 400 of them purchased from Smith's Clothing, and the other 400 purchased from the numerous shoe stores in City A. Note that this conclusion is absolutely consistent with the proposition that Smith's 'trade area' is Town B. . . . In sum, 'trade area' considers the extent to which customers will travel in order to do business at Smith's. 'Relevant market' considers the extent to which customers will travel in order to avoid doing business at Smith's."

The court concluded that the plaintiffs' evidence, at best, demonstrated only the "trade area" of Casey's stores. The plaintiffs looked at the issue "only from the perspective of Casey's rivals, not from the perspective of the consumer. This is not the correct approach to use in antitrust cases."[4]

INSIDER TRADING

Only in the last few years have Americans seen rich, successful financiers end up in jail because of some violation of securities laws. One law prohibits the use of inside information to profit in the trading of shares of stock in the corporation from which the information was gleaned. Even a

4. *Bathke v. Casey's General Stores, Inc.*, 64 F.3d 340 (8th Cir. 1995).

FOCUS ON ETHICS

tippee (an outsider) can be liable for insider trading under securities law if the tippee's acquisition of inside information followed from an officer's or director's breach of his or her fiduciary duties. Tippees of tippees (remote tippees) can also be held liable if they knew, or should have known, that they were trading on improperly obtained insider information.

For example, in *SEC v. Musella,*[5] a manager of a law firm passed inside information about corporate mergers and acquisitions planned by the firm's clients to a friend and the friend's stockbroker. The stockbroker passed the information on to a third party. That third party then shared the information with his brother, a police officer. The police officer then recommended to two other police officers that they purchase certain securities. All parties involved, including the latter two police officers, profited substantially from their investments, and other tips and investments followed. Could the two police officers, who never were told (and never inquired about) the source of the information, be held liable for insider trading as remote tippees? Yes, according to the court. Their liability was founded not on the fact that they *knew* that they were trading on improperly acquired inside information but on the fact that they *should have known* that such was the case. The court held that the two police officers "did not ask because they did not want to know." The fact that they had consciously avoided knowledge about the source of the information did not mean that they were not guilty under laws prohibiting insider trading.

Outsiders trading on inside information are normally held liable for violating securities laws only if the trading is related to a breach of some duty. In *Chiarella v. United States,*[6] Chiarella was not held liable for trading on information obtained in the course of his work as a printer because the court held that no fiduciary duty had been breached. Yet, had the jury been instructed to find liability under the misappropriation theory, Chiarella might well have been held liable for violating insider trading laws on the basis that he had violated a duty of loyalty to his employer. In a sense, the development of the misappropriation theory of liability has allowed courts to address more directly the simple ethical question: "Is such behavior right?"

EMINENT DOMAIN: PUBLIC GOOD VERSUS INDIVIDUAL RIGHTS

All law-abiding citizens accept government regulation, though sometimes begrudgingly. Usually we accept regulation because it is to our benefit to do so. For example, we willingly comply with the restriction that cars are to be driven on the right side of the road, and we expect the government to ensure that everyone else does as well. The benefit is that we have at least some assurance that a car will not be careening into us head-on just over the bend or around the next corner.

Other forms of regulation are not as uniformly beneficial, however. Most of us are glad that the government imposes some form of control over the quality of the food we eat. Food processors, though, confront higher costs because of it. Depending on supply and demand conditions in the food market, some or all of the additional costs may be passed on to consumers. In general, we accept these burdens because we believe that the greater good of the public is served by such regulation. But when the burdens of regulation are not distributed evenly over the population, how far does the sentiment for the greater public good carry us? The question is particularly difficult with regard to the "taking" of land through the government's power of eminent domain.

All cultures exhibit an attitude approaching reverence toward "the land." Not surprisingly, ownership of land is one of the most important issues governments face. Where, as in the United States, private ownership and reverence for land go hand in hand, the very idea of "taking" land is controversial. The aversion most feel toward such acts is mitigated by the requirement that the government justly compensate those who must forfeit land for the "public use." But the sentimental attachment often felt toward particular pieces of

5. 678 F.Supp. 1060 (S.D.N.Y. 1988).

6. 445 U.S. 222, 100 S.Ct. 1108, 63 L.Ed.2d 348 (1980).

FOCUS ON ETHICS

land—land on which stands the home to several generations of a family, for example—is seldom compensable. All such takings are made more acceptable by the condition that they be for the public good. But ethically, is it right to have a single individual incur the lion's share of the burden by having to give up his or her parcel of land for the greater good of all? Moreover, who can say without question precisely what the public's interests are and which are so important as to justify the taking of an individual's land?

Some years ago the United States Supreme Court confronted this issue in *Berman v. Parker.*[7] The District of Columbia condemned certain properties for the purpose of urban renewal in the affected area. Controversy arose because the land was subsequently reconveyed to private developers. How could private development of the land be a "public use" as required by the Constitution? The Court held that "use" meant purpose, not who would *physically* use or occupy the land. Moreover, the clearing of slums to make an area more attractive is a legitimate exercise of governmental police powers. Thus it is considered appropriate to take property through eminent domain to carry out those powers and achieve the governmental purpose.

Under the Court's broad interpretation of the doctrine of eminent domain, land may be taken for purely commercial and industrial development and use. In the same vein, the Supreme Court of Michigan upheld the taking of property not in fact "blighted" by urban decay so that the land could be resold to General Motors which planned to erect a manufacturing plant on the land.[8] The purpose that sustained the taking was the creation of new jobs and creation of a tax base for the local government. It is in the nature of government that select individuals must define for the many what the public good is, what purposes should be pursued, and how they should be achieved. But given the wide latitude for discretion in exercising the power of eminent domain, the best safeguard against abuse in taking private property is that governments strive to act ethically even if they do not face strict legal constraints.

7. 348 U.S. 26, 75 S.Ct. 98, 99 L.Ed. 57 (1954).

THE COSTS AND BENEFITS OF GOVERNMENT REGULATION

From an ethical perspective, government regulation has always been problematic because it imposes significant costs on American society. Tax dollars must be spent to pay for the administrative staff required to implement and enforce regulatory laws passed by Congress and rules issued by administrative agencies. In fiscal year 1996 alone, the fifty-six federal regulatory agencies spent over $16 billion to administer their regulations, and they employed nearly 133,000 federal workers to do so. Additionally, businesses subject to these regulations must pay compliance costs, which can be substantial. Some estimate that the total cost to the American public of regulation may be as high as $700 or $800 billion a year, which amounts to 10 percent of the total amount of our gross domestic product.

8. *Poletown Neighborhood Council v. City of Detroit,* 410 Mich. 617, 304 N.W.2d 455 (1981).

Of course, government regulation also provides benefits for society; otherwise, there would be no regulation. The question is, as mentioned previously in the discussion of environmental laws, how much is society willing to pay for those benefits? This question has ethical implications because ultimately, it involves placing a value on certain benefits that cannot really be analyzed quantitatively. For example, how can you put a price on fresh drinking water? On a human life? Is the value of a human life the amount that we are willing to pay to save a human life? If so, then that value is probably not infinite. For example, if consumers were given the choice of reducing the probability of dying in an automobile accident by spending $5,000 more per car, many would choose not to spend the additional money.

It is rarely left up to the public to make these decisions, however. Rather, regulatory agencies, under the authority delegated to them by Congress, are usually the key decision makers in determining such issues as how clean the air should be or how much should be

FOCUS ON ETHICS

spent to save a human life. According to one study, the value of a life, as measured in terms of each cancer case avoided through regulations implementing the Clean Air Act, rose from approximately $15 million in 1987 to $194 million in 1994.

DISCUSSION QUESTIONS

1. Some government regulation, such as antitrust law, may be enforced through lawsuits brought by private parties. Are private suits always ethical and proper, or should we consider the motives of the plaintiff companies? For example, when MCI won a large antitrust award from AT&T, some suggested that federal courts were being used as part of market competition. Might not companies be using antitrust laws to enhance their own market shares and to restrict competition?

2. In the discussion of the Superfund in this *Focus on Ethics,* the following question was raised: "If, say, 90 percent of the waste at a given site could be removed for $50,000, but the removal of the other 10 percent would cost $2 million, is it reasonable to remove that remaining 10 percent?" How would you answer this question?

3. Both environmental and occupational safety laws strive to protect the public health from hazardous substances. Should standards in these two contexts be the same? Or should employees be allowed to voluntarily accept some greater risk in return for a higher wage scale?

4. Assume that removing all asbestos from all public buildings in the nation would save perhaps ten lives per year. If the cost of the asbestos removal were $250 billion, in effect, Americans would be paying $250 million per life saved. Is this too high a price to pay? Should cost ever be a consideration when human lives are at stake?

5. Creditors must comply strictly with the requirements of such consumer protection laws as the Truth-in-Lending Act, the Equal Credit Opportunity Act, and the Fair Debt Collection Practices Act. Even a minor, unintended violation may permit a consumer to sue a creditor for damages. In some cases, consumers have sought damages for violations when the creditor has abided by the "spirit" of the law but not the "letter." Should courts make exceptions when consumers are clearly abusing these protective laws for their own gain? Or should the courts hold creditors liable even when the result is unfair to the creditor?

APPENDIX **A**

BRIEFING CASES—INSTRUCTIONS AND SELECTED CASES

HOW TO BRIEF A CASE

To fully understand the law with respect to business, you need to be able to read and understand court decisions. To make this task easier, you can use a method of case analysis that is called *briefing*. There is a fairly standard procedure that you can follow when you "brief" any court case. You must first read the case opinion carefully. When you feel you understand the case, you can prepare a brief of it.

Although the format of the brief may vary, typically it will present the essentials of the case under headings such as those listed below.

1. **Citation.** Give the full citation for the case, including the name of the case, the date it was decided, and the court that decided it.
2. **Facts.** Briefly indicate (a) the reasons for the lawsuit; (b) the identity and arguments of the plaintiff(s) and defendant(s), respectively; and (c) the lower court's decision—if appropriate.
3. **Issue.** Concisely phrase, in the form of a question, the essential issue before the court. (If more than one issue is involved, you may have two—or even more—questions here.)
4. **Decision.** Indicate here—with a "yes" or "no," if possible—the court's answer to the question (or questions) in the *Issue* section above.
5. **Reason.** Summarize as briefly as possible the reasons given by the court for its decision (or decisions) and the case or statutory law relied on by the court in arriving at its decision.

When you prepare your brief, be sure that you include all of the important facts. The basic format is illustrated below in the briefed version of the sample court case that was presented in Chapter 1 in Exhibit 1–6. We have also annotated the briefed version to indicate the kind of information that is contained in each section.

BRIEFED SAMPLE COURT CASE

ROBINSON v. SHELL OIL CO.
Supreme Court of the United States, 1997.
___ U.S. ___,
117 S.Ct. 843,
136 L.Ed.2d 808.

FACTS Shell Oil Company fired Charles T. Robinson, Sr., in 1991. Shortly thereafter, Robinson filed a charge with the Equal Employment Opportunity Commission (EEOC), alleging that Shell had fired him because of his race. While that charge was pending, Robinson applied for a job with another company. That company contacted

Shell, Robinson's former employer, for an employment reference. Robinson claims that Shell gave him a negative reference in retaliation for his having filed the EEOC charge. Subsequently, Robinson sued Shell, alleging retaliatory discharge in violation of Section 704(a) of Title VII of the Civil Rights Act of 1964. The district court dismissed the case, holding that Section 704(a) does not apply to former employees. Robinson appealed, and the Court of Appeals for the Fourth Circuit affirmed the district court's decision to dismiss the case. Robinson then appealed to the United States Supreme Court.

ISSUE May former employees bring suit under Section 704(a) for retaliation occurring after their employment has been terminated?

DECISION Yes. The Supreme Court reversed the appellate court's decision.

REASON The Supreme Court, finding that the term "employees" in Section 704(a) was ambiguous, looked at the broader context provided by other sections of the statute. The Court pointed out that Section 704(a) "expressly protects employees from retaliation for filing a 'charge' under Title VII." The Court concluded that because a charge for unlawful discharge could only be brought by a former employee, it was "consistent with the broader context of Title VII" and with the purpose of Section 704(a) to hold that former employees are included within the employees protected by Section 704(a).

Review of Sample Court Case

CITATION The name of the case is *Robinson v. Shell Oil Co.* The petitioner (the one bringing the appeal) is Charles T. Robinson, and the respondent (the one against whom the appeal is taken) is Shell Oil Company. The case was decided by the United States Supreme Court in 1997. The first citation is to the *United States Reports.* The volume and page numbers of the reporter are left blank because the opinion has not yet been published in the reporter. The first parallel citation is to the *Supreme Court Reporter* and indicates that the case can be found in Volume 117 of that reporter, on page 843. The second parallel citation is to volume 136, page 808, of the *Lawyers' Edition of the Supreme Court Reports.*

FACTS The *Facts* section identifies the parties to the lawsuit—the petitioner and the respondent—and describes the events leading up to the lawsuit and its appeal. Because this is an appeal to the United States Supreme Court, both the district court and the appellate court decisions are included as part of the history of the case. The petitioners' contention on appeal is included in this section as well.

ISSUE The *Issue* section presents the central issue (or issues) to be decided by the court. In this case, the issue before the Supreme Court was whether the term "employees," as used in Section 704(a) of Title VII of the Civil Rights Act of 1964, should include former employees as well as current employees.

DECISION The *Decision* section, as the term indicates, contains the court's decision on the issue or issues before it. The decision reflects the opinion of the majority of the judges or justices hearing the case. Decisions by appellate courts are frequently phrased in reference to the lower court's decision. That is, the appellate court may "affirm" the lower court's ruling or "reverse" it. In this particular case, the Supreme Court reversed the decision of the lower court (the Court of Appeals for the Fourth Circuit).

REASON The *Reason* section indicates what relevant laws and judicial principles were applied in forming the particular conclusion arrived at in the case at bar ("before the court"). In this case, the relevant law was Section 704(a) of Title VII of the Civil Rights Act of 1964, and the task before the Court was how that section should be interpreted. The Court concluded that it was consistent with the broader context of Title VII to conclude that the term "employees" in Section 704(a) included former employees.

Selected Cases for Briefing

Court opinions can run from a few pages to hundreds of pages in length. For reasons of space, only the essential parts of the opinions are presented in the cases that follow. A series of three asterisks indicates that a portion of the text—other than citations and footnotes—has been omitted. Four asterisks indicate the omission of at least one paragraph.

Case A.1 *Reference: Problem 4–12*

RODRIGUEZ de QUIJAS v. SHEARSON/AMERICAN EXPRESS, INC.
United States Supreme Court, 1989.
490 U.S. 477,
109 S.Ct. 1917,
104 L.Ed.2d 526.

KENNEDY, Justice.

The question here is whether a predispute agreement to arbitrate claims under the Securities Act of 1933 is unenforceable, requiring resolution of the claims only in a judicial forum.

I

Petitioners are individuals who invested about $400,000 in securities. They signed a standard customer agreement with the broker, which included a clause stating that the parties agreed to settle any controversies "relating to [the] accounts" through binding arbitration that complies with ~specified procedures. The agreement to arbitrate these controversies is unqualified, unless it is found to be unenforceable under federal or state law. * * * The investments turned sour, and petitioners eventually sued respondent and its broker-agent in charge of the accounts, alleging that their money was lost in unauthorized and fraudulent transactions. In their complaint they pleaded various violations of federal and state law, including claims under § 12(2) of the Securities Act of 1933, * * * and claims under three sections of the Securities Exchange Act of 1934.

The District Court ordered all the claims to be submitted to arbitration except for those raised under § 12(2) of the Securities Act. It held that the latter claims must proceed in the court action under our clear holding on the point in Wilko v. Swan, 346 U.S. 427, 74 S.Ct. 182, 98 L.Ed. 168 (1953). The District Court reaffirmed its ruling upon reconsideration, and also entered a default judgment against the broker, who is no longer in the case. The Court of Appeals reversed, concluding that the arbitration agreement is enforceable because this Court's subsequent decisions have reduced Wilko to "obsolescence." * * *

II

The Wilko case, decided in 1953, required the Court to determine whether an agreement to arbitrate future controversies constitutes a binding stipulation "to waive compliance with any provision" of the Securities Act, which is nullified by § 14 of the Act. * * * The Court considered the language, purposes, and legislative history of the Securities Act, and concluded that the agreement to arbitrate was void under § 14. But the decision was a difficult one in view of the competing legislative policy embodied in the Arbitration Act, which the Court described as "not easily reconcilable," and which strongly favors the enforcement of agreements to arbitrate as a means of securing "prompt, economical and adequate solution of controversies." * * *

It has been recognized that Wilko was not obviously correct, for "the language prohibiting waiver of 'compliance with any provision of this title' could easily have been read to relate to substantive provisions of the Act without including the remedy provisions." * * * The Court did not read the language this way in Wilko, however, and gave two reasons. First, the Court rejected the argument that "arbitration is merely a form of trial to be used in lieu of a trial at law." * * * The Court found instead that § 14 does not permit waiver of "the right to select the judicial forum" in favor of arbitration, * * * because "arbitration lacks the certainty of a suit at law under the Act to enforce [the buyer's] rights," * * *. Second, the Court concluded that the Securities Act was intended to protect buyers of securities, who often do not deal at arm's length and on equal terms with sellers, by offering them "a wider choice of courts and venue" than is enjoyed by participants in other business transactions, making "the right to select the judicial forum" a particularly valuable feature of the Securities Act. * * *

* * * The shift in the Court's views on arbitration away from those adopted in Wilko is shown by the flat statement in [a prior case]: "By agreeing to arbitrate a statutory claim, a party does not forgo the substantive rights afforded by the statute; it only submits to their resolution in an arbitral, rather than a judicial, forum." * * * To the extent that Wilko rested on suspicion of arbitration as a method of weakening the protections afforded in the substantive law to would-be complainants, it has fallen far out of step with our current strong endorsement of the federal statutes favoring this method of resolving disputes.

Once the outmoded presumption of disfavoring arbitration proceedings is set to one side, it becomes clear that the right to select the judicial forum and the wider choice of courts are not such essential features of the Securities Act that § 14 is properly construed to bar any waiver of these provisions. Nor are they so critical that they cannot be waived under the rationale that the Securities Act was intended to place buyers of securities on an equal footing with sellers. Wilko identified two different kinds of provisions in the Securities Act that would advance this objective. Some are substantive, such as placing on the seller the burden of proving lack of scienter when a buyer alleges fraud. * * * Others are procedural. The specific procedural improvements highlighted in Wilko are the statute's broad venue provisions in the federal courts; the existence of nationwide service of process in the federal courts; the extinction of the amount-in-controversy requirement that had applied to fraud suits when they were brought in federal courts under diversity jurisdiction rather than as a federal cause of action; and the grant of concurrent jurisdiction in the state and federal courts without possibility of removal.

There is no sound basis for construing the prohibition in § 14 on waiving "compliance with any provision" of the Securities Act to apply to these procedural provisions. Although the first three measures do facilitate suits by buyers of securities, the grant of concurrent jurisdiction constitutes explicit authorization for complainants to waive those protections by filing suit in state court without possibility of removal to federal court. These measures, moreover, are present in other federal statutes which have not been interpreted to prohibit enforcement of predispute agreements to arbitrate. * * * [T]he party opposing arbitration carries the burden of showing that Congress intended in a separate statute to preclude a waiver of judicial remedies, or that such a waiver of judicial remedies inherently conflicts with the underlying purposes of that other statute. * * * But as Justice Frankfurter said in dissent in Wilko, so it is true in this case: "There is nothing in the record before us, nor in the facts of which we can take judicial notice, to indicate that the arbitral system . . . would not afford the plaintiff the rights to which he is entitled." * * *

The language quoted above from § 2 of the Arbitration Act also allows the courts to give relief where the party opposing arbitration presents "well-supported claims that the agreement to arbitrate resulted from the sort of fraud or overwhelming economic power that would provide grounds 'for the revocation of any contract.' " * * * This avenue of relief is in harmony with the Securities Act's concern to protect buyers of securities by removing "the disadvantages under which buyers labor" in their dealings with sellers. * * *

III

We now conclude that Wilko was incorrectly decided and is inconsistent with the prevailing uniform construction of other federal statutes governing arbitration agreements in the setting of business transactions. Although we are normally and properly reluctant to overturn our decisions construing statutes, we have done so to achieve a uniform interpretation of similar statutory language * * * and to correct a seriously erroneous interpretation of statutory language that would undermine congressional policy as expressed in other legislation, * * * Both purposes would be served here by overruling the Wilko decision. In this case, for example, petitioners' claims under the 1934 Act were subjected to arbitration, while their claim under the 1933 Act was not permitted to go to arbitration, but was required to proceed in court. That result makes little sense for similar claims, based on similar facts, which are supposed to arise within a single federal regulatory scheme. In addition, the inconsistency * * * undermines the essential rationale for a harmonious construction of the two statutes, which is to discourage litigants from manipulating their allegations merely to cast their claims under one of the securities laws rather than another. For all of these reasons, therefore, we overrule the decision in Wilko.

The judgment of the Court of Appeals is
AFFIRMED.

Case A.2 *Reference: Problem 5–11*

AUSTIN v. BERRYMAN
United States Court of Appeals,
Fourth Circuit, 1989.
878 F.2d 786.

MURNAGHAN, Circuit Judge:

We have before us for *en banc* [by the whole court] reconsideration an appeal taken from an action successfully brought by Barbara Austin in the United States District Court for the Western District of Virginia against the Virginia Employment Commission, challenging a denial of unemployment compensation benefits. * * * In brief, Austin charged, *inter alia* [among other things], that the denial of her claim for unemployment benefits, based on a Virginia statute specifically precluding such benefits for any individual who voluntarily quits work to join his or her spouse in a new location, was an unconstitutional infringement upon the incidents of marriage protected by the fourteenth amendment and an unconstitutional burden on her first amendment right to the free exercise of her religion. Her religion happened to command that she follow her spouse wherever he might go and the sincerity of her religious belief was not questioned. The district court found in Austin's favor and awarded injunctive relief and retroactive benefits.

On appeal, Judge Sprouse, writing for a panel majority, found that the denial of benefits did not implicate Austin's Fourteenth Amendment rights, but that it did unconstitutionally burden Austin's right to the free exercise of her religion. The panel also found, however, that any award of retroactive benefits was barred by the Eleventh Amendment. One panel member concurred with the panel majority as to the Fourteenth and Eleventh Amendment issues, but dissented as to the existence of a free exercise violation. The panel opinion now, of course, has been vacated by a grant of rehearing *en banc*.

After careful consideration of the additional arguments proffered by both sides, the Court, *en banc*, is convinced that the panel majority correctly concluded that denying Austin unemployment benefits did not infringe upon fundamental marital rights protected by the Fourteenth Amendment. To this extent, we adopt the majority panel opinion. We also find, however, that the denial of benefits did not unconstitutionally burden Austin's first amendment right to the free exercise of her religion. We are persuaded that the views expressed on the First Amendment, free exercise of religion claim in the opinion dissenting in part from the panel majority are correct, and we hereby adopt that opinion as that of the *en banc* court. As we find that Austin is not entitled to any relief, we need not address whether the Eleventh Amendment bars an award of retroactive benefits.

The decisive consideration, as we see it, is that the proximate cause of Austin's unemployment is geographic distance, not her religious beliefs. There is no conflict between the circumstances of work and Austin's religious precepts. Austin's religious beliefs do not "require" her "to refrain from the work in question." Austin is unable to work simply because she is now too far removed from her employer to make it practical. In striking contrast, if one, for genuine religious beliefs, moves to a new residence in order to continue to live with a spouse, and that residence is not geographically so removed as to preclude regular attendance at the worksite, no unemployment, and hence no unemployment benefits, will arise. That amounts to proof that extent of geographical non-propinquity, not religious belief, led to Austin's disqualification for unemployment benefits.

Austin voluntarily decided to quit her job and join her spouse in a new geographic location 150 miles away. Virginia has stated that every individual who follows such a course, no matter what the reason, religious or nonreligious, is disqualified for unemployment benefits. To craft judicially a statutory exception only for those individuals who profess Austin's religious convictions, particularly in the absence of a direct conflict between a given employment practice and a religious belief, would, in our view, result in a subsidy to members of a particular religious belief, impermissible under the Establishment Clause.

Accordingly, the judgment of the district court is REVERSED.

Case A.3 *Reference: Problem 10–10*

POTTER v. OSTER

Supreme Court of Iowa, 1988.
426 N.W.2d 148.

NEUMAN, Justice.

This is a suit in equity brought by the plaintiffs to rescind an installment land contract based on the seller's inability to convey title. The question on appeal is whether, in an era of declining land values, returning the parties to the status quo works an inequitable result. We think not. Accordingly, we affirm the district court judgment for rescission and restitution.

The facts are largely undisputed. Because the case was tried in equity, our review is de novo. We give weight to the findings of the trial court, particularly where the credibility of witnesses is concerned, but we are not bound thereby.

The parties, though sharing a common interest in agribusiness, present a study in contrasts. We think the disparity in their background and experience is notable insofar as it bears on the equities of the transaction in issue. Plaintiff Charles Potter is a farm laborer and his wife, Sue, is a homemaker and substitute teacher. They have lived all their lives within a few miles of the real estate in question. Defendant Merrill Oster is an agricultural journalist and recognized specialist in land investment strategies. He owns Oster Communications, a multimillion dollar publishing concern devoted to furnishing farmers the latest in commodity market analysis and advice on an array of farm issues.

In May 1978, Oster contracted with Florence Stark to purchase her 160-acre farm in Howard County, Iowa, for $260,000 on a ten-year contract at seven percent interest. Oster then sold the homestead and nine acres to Charles and Sue Potter for $70,000. Potters paid $18,850 down and executed a ten-year installment contract for the balance at 8.5% interest. Oster then executed a contract with Robert Bishop for the sale of the remaining 151 acres as part of a package deal that included the sale of seventeen farms for a sum exceeding $5.9 million.

These back-to-back contracts collapsed like dominoes in March 1985 when Bishop failed to pay Oster and Oster failed to pay Stark the installments due on their respective contracts. Stark commenced forfeiture proceedings [proceedings to retake the property because Oster failed to perform a legal obligation—payment under the contract—and thus forfeited his right to the land]. Potters had paid every installment when due under their contract with Oster and had included Stark as a joint payee [one of two or more payees—persons to whom checks or notes are payable; see Chapter 25] with Oster on their March 1, 1985, payment. But they were financially unable to exercise their right to advance the sums due on the entire 160 acres in order to preserve their interest in the nine acres and homestead. As a result, their interest in the real estate was forfeited along with Oster's and Bishop's and they were forced to move from their home in August 1985.

Potters then sued Oster to rescind their contract with him, claiming restitution damages for all consideration paid. * * *

Trial testimony * * * revealed that the market value of the property had decreased markedly since its purchase. Expert appraisers valued the homestead and nine acres between $27,500 and $35,000. Oster himself placed a $28,000 value on the property; Potter $39,000. Evidence was also received placing the reasonable rental value of the property at $150 per month, or a total of $10,800 for the six-year Potter occupancy.

The district court concluded the Potters were entitled to rescission of the contract and return of the consideration paid including principal and interest, cost of improvements, closing expenses, and taxes for a total of $65,169.37. From this the court deducted $10,800 for six years' rental, bringing the final judgment to $54,369.37.

On appeal, Oster challenges the judgment. * * * [H]e claims Potters had an adequate remedy at law for damages which should have been measured by the actual economic loss sustained * * *.

* * * *

Rescission is a restitutionary remedy which attempts to restore the parties to their positions at the time the contract was executed. The remedy calls for a return of the land to the seller, with the buyer given judgment for payments made under the contract plus the value of improvements, less reasonable rental value for the period during which the buyer was in possession. The remedy has long been available in Iowa to buyers under land contracts when the seller has no title to convey.

Rescission is considered an extraordinary remedy, however, and is ordinarily not available to a litigant as a matter of right but only when, in the discretion of the court, it is necessary to obtain equity. Our cases have established three requirements that must be met before rescission will be granted. First, the injured party must not be in default. Second, the breach must be substantial and go to the heart of the contract. Third, remedies at law must be inadequate.

The first two tests are easily met in the present case. Potters are entirely without fault in this transaction. They tendered their 1985 installment payment to Oster before the forfeiture, and no additional payments were due until 1986. On the question of materiality, Oster's loss of equitable title [ownership rights protected in equity] to the homestead by forfeiture caused not only substantial, but total breach of his obligation to insure peaceful possession [an implied promise made by a landowner, when selling or renting land, that the buyer or tenant will not be evicted or disturbed by the landowner or a person having a lien or superior title] and convey marketable title under the Oster-Potter contract.

Only the third test—the inadequacy of damages at law—is contested by Oster on appeal. * * *

Restoring the status quo is the goal of the restitutionary remedy of rescission. Here, the district court accomplished the goal by awarding Potters a sum representing all they had paid under the contract rendered worthless by Oster's default. Oster contends that in an era of declining land values, such a remedy goes beyond achieving the status quo and results in a windfall to the Potters. Unwilling to disgorge the benefits he has received under the unfulfilled contract, Oster would have the court shift the "entrepreneural risk" [the risk assumed by one who initiates, and provides or controls the management of, a business enterprise] of market loss to the Potters by limiting their recovery to the difference between the property's market value at breach ($35,000) and the contract balance ($27,900). In other words, Oster claims the court should have awarded * * * damages. * * *

* * * *

* * * [L]egal remedies are considered inadequate when the damages cannot be measured with sufficient certainty. Contrary to Oster's assertion that Potters' compensation should be limited to the difference between the property's fair market value and contract balance at time of breach, * * * damages are correctly calculated as the difference between contract price and market value at the time for performance. Since the time of performance in this case would have been March 1990, the market value of the homestead and acreage cannot be predicted with any certainty, thus rendering such a formulation inadequate.

Most importantly, the fair market value of the homestead at the time of forfeiture is an incorrect measure of the benefit Potters lost. It fails to account for the special value Potters placed on the property's location and residential features that uniquely suited their family. For precisely this reason, remedies at law are presumed inadequate for breach of a real estate contract. Oster has failed to overcome that presumption here. His characterization of the transaction as a mere market loss for Potters, compensable by a sum which would enable them to make a nominal down payment on an equivalent homestead, has no legal or factual support in this record. * * *

* * * *

In summary, we find no error in the trial court's conclusion that Potters were entitled to rescission of the contract and return of all benefits allowed thereunder, less the value of reasonable rental for the period of occupancy * * *.

AFFIRMED.

Case A.4 *Reference: Problem 18–11*

MASCHMEIER v. SOUTHSIDE PRESS, LTD.
Court of Appeals of Iowa, 1989.
435 N.W.2d 377.

HABHAB, Judge.

Defendant Kenneth E. Maschmeier and Charlotte A. Maschmeier created a corporation, Southside Press, Ltd., that did business at 1220 Second Avenue North in Council Bluffs. This building is owned by Kenneth and Charlotte and was leased by them to the corporation.

Kenneth and Charlotte are the majority shareholders, with each having 1300 shares. They are the only officers and directors of the corporation.

They gifted to their two sons [Marty and Larry] each 1200 shares of stock. All the parties were employed by Southside Press until the summer of 1985 when, because of family disagreements, Marty and Larry were terminated as employees. * * *

The parents on August 2, 1985, created a new corporation, Southside Press of the Midlands, Ltd. They are its only officers and directors. As individuals they terminated the lease of their building * * * with Southside and leased the same premises to Midlands. In addition, Kenneth, as president of Southside, entered into a lease with himself as president of Midlands whereby the printing equipment and two of the vehicles were leased to Midlands for $22,372 per year for five years, with an option to buy such assets at the end of the lease term at their fair market value but not to exceed $20,000. In addition, the inventory and two other vehicles owned by Southside were sold by it to Midlands. Notwithstanding the fact that a substantial part of the assets of Southside had been disposed of, the parents still received an annual salary from it of more than $20,000.

After Marty and Larry's employment with Southside had terminated, each obtained employment with other printing companies in the same metropolitan area. The family disagreement continued. All stockholders were employed by companies that were competitive to Southside. Ultimately, the parents, as majority shareholders, offered to buy the sons' shares of stock for $20 per share. Their sons felt that this amount was inadequate. Thus, this lawsuit.

In 1985, Southside Press had gross sales of more than $600,000. The trial court found that in 1985 the corporate assets had a fair market value of $160,745. Shareholders' equity was found to be $236,502.92, and divided by the number of shares equals $47.30 per share. The court found that the majority shareholders had been abusive and oppressive to the minority shareholders by wasting the corporate assets and leaving Southside Press only a shell of a corporation. The court ordered the majority shareholders to pay $47.30 per share to the sons, or $56,760 to each son, plus interest at the maximum legal rate from the date of the filing of the petition.

* * * *

* * * [D]efendants state that the shares were valued at $20 pursuant to the corporate bylaws and should be enforced as an agreement of the shareholders. * * *

* * * *

Whenever a situation exists which is contrary to the principles of equity and which can be redressed within the scope of judicial action, a court of equity will devise a remedy to meet the situation though no similar relief has been granted before. The district court has the power to liquidate a corporation under [Iowa Code] section 496A.94(1). This statute also allows the district court to fashion other equitable relief.

It is contended that, in order for the trial court to have properly invoked the powers under section 496A.94(1), it had to find either the majority shareholders were oppressive in their conduct towards the minority shareholders, or that the majority shareholders misapplied or wasted corporate assets.

* * * The alleged oppressive conduct by those in control of a close corporation must be analyzed in terms of "fiduciary duties" owed by majority shareholders to the minority shareholders and "reasonable expectations" held by minority shareholders in committing capital and labor to the particular enterprise, in light of the predicament in which minority shareholders in a close corporation can be placed by a "freeze-out" situation.

* * * The trial court found * * * here [that] the majority shareholders attempted to "freeze out" or "squeeze out" the minority shareholders by terminating their employment and not permitting them to participate in the business.

* * * *

We concur with the trial court's findings that the majority shareholders acted oppressively toward the minority shareholders and wasted corporate assets. In this respect, we further determine that the trial court properly invoked Iowa Code section 496A.94 when it fashioned the remedy requiring the majority shareholders to purchase the shares of the minority.

But that does not resolve the problem[.] * * * The appellant challenges the method fashioned by the trial court in fixing the value of the stock and payment thereof by asserting it should be governed by the bylaws.

The articles of incorporation of Southside vested in the directors of the corporation the "authority to make provisions in the Bylaws of the corporation restricting the transfer of shares of this corporation." This the board of directors did when they adopted the following bylaw that relates to restrictions on the transferability of stock. * * *

* * * *

Section 3 [of the corporate bylaws] is a restriction on stock transfer. If a shareholder intends to sell his stock, he must first offer it to the corporation at a price "agreed upon by the shareholders at each annual meeting." The shareholders must agree on the value of the stock and if they are unable to do so, each has a right to select an appraiser and the appraisers shall appoint another and in this instance the five appraisers are to act as a Board of Appraisers to value the stock.

* * * Since none of the shareholders requested appraisers, we deem this, as the trial court did, to be a waiver. We concur with this statement from the trial court's ruling: "All parties have left the Court with the burden of evaluating the corporate stock."

* * * *

We agree with the defendants that a contractual formula price is enforceable even if the formula price is less than its fair market value. But here the parties were unable to agree to a price, i.e., at the last meeting of the stockholders. Thus the trial court was called upon to do so.

Courts have generally held that no one factor governs the valuation of shares; but that all factors, such as market value, asset value, future earning prospects, should be considered. In this case, the parties relied rather heavily on what is referred to in the record as book value (shareholders' equity) in arriving at stock value. The trial court likewise used shareholder equity but adjusted that amount by the present day fair market value of corporate assets.

* * * *

We determine that under the circumstances here the valuation per share as fixed by the trial court and the method it employed in arriving at value is fair and reasonable. However, we further conclude that the amount Larry and Marty are to receive must be reduced by the total amount of loans made to them as they appear on the corporate books.

* * * *

We affirm and modify.

Case A.5 *Reference: Problem 20–12*

JOHNSTON v. DEL MAR DISTRIBUTING CO.
Court of Appeals of Texas—Corpus Christi, 1989.
776 S.W.2d 768.

BENAVIDES, Justice.

Nancy Johnston, appellant, brought suit against her employer, Del Mar Distributing Co., Inc., alleging that her employment had been wrongfully terminated. Del Mar filed a motion for summary judgment in the trial court alleging that appellant's pleadings failed to state a cause of action. After a hearing on the motion, the trial court agreed with Del Mar and granted its motion for summary judgment.

* * * *

In her petition, appellant alleged that she was employed by Del Mar during the summer of 1987. As a part of her duties, she was required to prepare shipping documents for goods being sent from Del Mar's warehouse located in Corpus Christi, Texas to other cities in Texas. One day, Del Mar instructed appellant to package a semiautomatic weapon (for delivery to a grocery store in Brownsville, Texas) and to label the contents of the package as "fishing gear." Ultimately, the package was to be given to United Parcel Service for shipping. Appellant was required to sign her name to the shipping documents; therefore, she was concerned that her actions might be in violation of some firearm regulation or a regulation of the United Postal Service. Accordingly, she sought the advice of the United States Treasury Department Bureau of Alcohol, Tobacco & Firearms * * *. A few days after she contacted the Bureau, appellant was fired. Appellant brought suit for wrongful termination alleging that her employment was terminated solely in retaliation for contacting the Bureau.

* * * *

Del Mar asserted in its motion that, notwithstanding the above described facts, appellant's cause of action was barred by the employment-at-will doctrine. Specifically, Del Mar asserted that since appellant's employment was for an indefinite amount of time, she was an employee-at-will and it had the absolute right to terminate her employment for any reason or no reason at all.

It is well-settled that Texas adheres to the traditional employment-at-will doctrine. The Texas Supreme Court [has] held that absent a specific contractual provision to the contrary, either the employer or the employee may terminate their relationship at any time, for any reason.

Today, the absolute employment-at-will doctrine is increasingly seen as a "relic of early industrial times" and a "harsh anachronism." Accordingly, our Legislature has enacted some exceptions to this doctrine * * *.

Recently, the Texas Supreme Court, recognizing the need to amend the employment-at-will doctrine, invoked its judicial authority to create a very narrow common law exception to the doctrine. In [Sabine Pilot Service, Inc. v. Hauck] the Texas Supreme Court was faced with a narrow issue for consideration, i.e., whether an allegation by an employee that he or she was discharged for refusing to perform an illegal act stated a cause of action. The Court held that

> public policy, as expressed in the laws of this state and the United States which carry criminal penalties, requires a very narrow exception to the employment-at-will doctrine * * * [t]hat narrow exception covers only the discharge of an employee for the sole reason that the employee refused to perform an illegal act.

Justice Kilgarlin noted in his concurring opinion to Sabine Pilot that it is against public policy to allow an employer "to require an employee to break a law or face termination. . . ." He elaborated that to hold otherwise "would promote a thorough disrespect for the laws and legal institutions of our society."

* * * *

On appeal, appellant alleges that her petition did state a cause of action pursuant to the public policy exception announced in Sabine Pilot. In her brief, appellant contends that since Texas law currently provides that an employee has a cause of action when she is fired for refusing to perform an illegal act, it necessarily follows that an employee states a cause of action where she alleges that she is fired for simply inquiring into whether or not she is committing illegal acts. To hold otherwise, she argues, would have a chilling [inhibiting, discouraging] effect on the public policy exception announced in Sabine Pilot. We agree.

It is implicit that in order to refuse to do an illegal act, an employee must either know or suspect that the requested act is illegal. In some cases it will be patently obvious that the act is illegal (murder, robbery, theft, etc.); however, in other cases it may not be so apparent. Since ignorance of the law is no defense to a criminal prosecution, it is reasonable to expect that if an employee has a good faith belief that a required act might be illegal, she will try to find out whether the act is in fact illegal prior to deciding what course of action to take. If an employer is allowed to terminate the employee at this point, the public policy exception announced in *Sabine Pilot* would have little or no effect. To hold otherwise would force an employee, who suspects that a requested act might be illegal, to (1) subject herself to possible discharge if she attempts to find out if the act is in fact illegal; or (2) remain ignorant, perform the act and, if it turns out to be illegal, face possible criminal sanctions.

We hold that since the law recognizes that it is against public policy to allow an employer to coerce its employee to commit a criminal act in furtherance of its own interest, then it is necessarily inferred that the same public policy prohibits the discharge of an employee who in good faith attempts to find out if the act is illegal. It is important to note that we are not creating a new exception to the employment-at-will doctrine. Rather, we are merely enforcing the narrow public policy exception which was created in *Sabine Pilot.*

* * * *

Furthermore, it is the opinion of this Court that the question of whether or not the requested act was in fact illegal is irrelevant to the determination of this case. We hold that where a plaintiff's employment is terminated for attempting to find out from a regulatory agency if a requested act is illegal, it is not necessary to prove that the requested act was in fact illegal. A plaintiff must, however, establish that she had a good faith belief that the requested act might be illegal, and that such belief was reasonable. * * *

* * * *

The judgment of the trial court is reversed and remanded for trial.

Case A.6 *Reference: Problem 26–10*

DELAWARE & HUDSON RAILWAY v. CONSOLIDATED RAIL CORP.

United States Court of Appeals, Second Circuit, 1990.
902 F.2d 174.

TIMBERS, Circuit Judge.

* * * *

The dispute leading to this appeal arose when Canadian shippers and railroads sought to lower rates so that rail carriage of newsprint could compete more readily with carriage by truck. Conrail agreed to lower its rates on trips where it was the sole American carrier. It did not decline outright to cooperate in cases where it was the secondary ("short haul") carrier to D & H, but instituted a policy, called "make or buy," that achieved the same effect. Under that policy, Conrail would agree to the reduced rate only if its profit, called "contribution," matched its profit on the route where it was the sole carrier.

Conrail's action placed D & H in a bind between giving up almost all of its profits on a given route and losing entirely the ability to carry freight on the route. It decided not to concur in joint rates where the make or buy policy was in effect. It commenced the instant action in July 1986. In June 1988, D & H sought protection under Chapter 11 of the United States Bankruptcy Code.

After surviving a motion to dismiss and after extensive discovery, D & H's antitrust claims were rejected by the district court on Conrail's motion for summary judgment.

From the summary judgment rejecting these claims, this appeal was taken by D & H which asserts that, since there are genuine issues of material fact with respect to the three claims, summary judgment was improper. We agree.

* * * *

We turn first to the question whether the make or buy policy constituted the offense of monopolization under § 2 of the Sherman Act * * * To establish the defendant's liability, the plaintiff must demonstrate "(1) the possession of monopoly power in the relevant market and (2) the willful acquisition or maintenance of that power as distinguished from growth or development as a consequence of a superior product, business acumen, or historic accident."

Addressing the second element first, we must affirm the district court's ruling unless D & H has demonstrated that there is a genuine issue of material fact as to whether Conrail's make or buy policy constituted willful anticompetitive conduct in the relevant newsprint transportation market. Conrail's most significant contention in this regard is that, since the policy was intended to increase short-term, as well as long-term, profits, Conrail is insulated from liability.

* * * *

A monopolist cannot escape liability for conduct that is otherwise actionable simply because that conduct also provides short-term profits. * * * Our review of the record in the instant case satisfies us that there is evidence which would support a jury finding that Conrail is liable for monopolization. * * * In view of the evidence referred to above, however, we hold that D & H has proffered evidence sufficient to support a verdict in its favor by a reasonable jury on the question whether Conrail's conduct violated § 2. Obviously, therefore, this issue could not properly be decided against D & H on a motion for summary judgment.

* * * *

IV.

We turn next to the question whether the make or buy policy constituted denial of an essential facility and, by implication, a violation of § 2. The alleged essential facility is Conrail's tracks used for short haul routes * * * The district court rejected D & H's claim, relying on the four-factor test set forth [in a previous case]: ((1) control of the essential facility by a monopolist; (2) a competitor's inability practically or reasonably to duplicate the essential facility; (3) the denial of the use of the facility to a competitor; and (4) the feasibility of providing the facility.) * * *

There is no question that Conrail controls the short haul tracks, thus satisfying the first element. With respect to the second element, we agree with the district court's statement that "physical duplication of [Conrail's] lines would be an impractical and unreasonable project to undertake." The fourth element, feasibility, is demonstrated by the fact that D & H was permitted continuous use of the tracks until the make or buy policy foreclosed that use.

The third element—whether Conrail impermissibly denied to D & H the use of the tracks—is the one on which the district court based its decision. The court held correctly that there need not be an outright refusal to deal in order to find that denial of an essential facility occurred. It is sufficient if the terms of the offer to deal are unreasonable. In this context the following passage is particularly appropriate:

"Such plan of reorganization must also provide definitely for the use of the terminal facilities by any other railroad not electing to become a joint owner, upon such just and reasonable terms and regulations as will, in respect of use, character and cost of service, place every such company upon as nearly an equal plane as may be with respect to expenses and charges as that occupied by the proprietary companies."

* * * *

We disagree, however, with the district court's conclusion that the terms of the make or buy policy were reasonable as a matter of law.

We need not determine on this appeal the circumstances under which a legitimate business practice will shield a defendant from liability for conduct that otherwise would constitute denial of an essential facility. * * * In our discussion above on the monopolization claim, we held that there is a genuine issue of material fact with respect to the question whether the make or buy policy was a legitimate practice. That holding is equally applicable here.

V.

D & H also contends that the make or buy policy constituted the § 2 offense of attempted monopolization. To make out a successful claim of attempted monopolization, a plaintiff must demonstrate: (1) anti-competitive conduct; (2) intent to monopolize; and (3) a dangerous probability of obtaining monopoly power. * * * These elements essentially track those required for a successful monopolization claim. We held with respect to the monopolization claim that the development and implementation of the make or buy policy raised triable issues on the questions of conduct and intent. Likewise, evidence of Conrail's monopoly power that is sufficient to withstand a motion for summary judgment also suffices to raise a triable issue as to whether there was a dangerous probability that Conrail would obtain monopoly power.

VI.

To summarize:

We hold that there are genuine issues of material fact with respect to whether the development and implementation by Conrail of its make or buy policy constituted the antitrust offenses of monopolization, denial of essential facilities and attempted monopolization.

Nothing in this opinion is to be construed as an expression of our views on the merits of the issues to be tried. All we hold today is that there are genuine issues of material fact which should not be decided by summary judgment.

REVERSED AND REMANDED.

Appendix B

The Constitution of the United States

Preamble

We the People of the United States, in Order to form a more perfect Union, establish Justice, insure domestic Tranquility, provide for the common defence, promote the general Welfare, and secure the Blessings of Liberty to ourselves and our Posterity, do ordain and establish this Constitution for the United States of America.

Article I

Section 1. All legislative Powers herein granted shall be vested in a Congress of the United States, which shall consist of a Senate and House of Representatives.

Section 2. The House of Representatives shall be composed of Members chosen every second Year by the People of the several States, and the Electors in each State shall have the Qualifications requisite for Electors of the most numerous Branch of the State Legislature.

No Person shall be a Representative who shall not have attained to the Age of twenty five Years, and been seven Years a Citizen of the United States, and who shall not, when elected, be an Inhabitant of that State in which he shall be chosen.

Representatives and direct Taxes shall be apportioned among the several States which may be included within this Union, according to their respective Numbers, which shall be determined by adding to the whole Number of free Persons, including those bound to Service for a Term of Years, and excluding Indians not taxed, three fifths of all other Persons. The actual Enumeration shall be made within three Years after the first Meeting of the Congress of the United States, and within every subsequent Term of ten Years, in such Manner as they shall by Law direct. The Number of Representatives shall not exceed one for every thirty Thousand, but each State shall have at Least one Representative; and until such enumeration shall be made, the State of New Hampshire shall be entitled to chuse three, Massachusetts eight, Rhode Island and Providence Plantations one, Connecticut five, New York six, New Jersey four, Pennsylvania eight, Delaware one, Maryland six, Virginia ten, North Carolina five, South Carolina five, and Georgia three.

When vacancies happen in the Representation from any State, the Executive Authority thereof shall issue Writs of Election to fill such Vacancies.

The House of Representatives shall chuse their Speaker and other Officers; and shall have the sole Power of Impeachment.

Section 3. The Senate of the United States shall be composed of two Senators from each State, chosen by the Legislature thereof, for six Years; and each Senator shall have one Vote.

Immediately after they shall be assembled in Consequence of the first Election, they shall be divided as equally as may be into three Classes. The Seats of the

Senators of the first Class shall be vacated at the Expiration of the second Year, of the second Class at the Expiration of the fourth Year, and of the third Class at the Expiration of the sixth Year, so that one third may be chosen every second Year; and if Vacancies happen by Resignation, or otherwise, during the Recess of the Legislature of any State, the Executive thereof may make temporary Appointments until the next Meeting of the Legislature, which shall then fill such Vacancies.

No Person shall be a Senator who shall not have attained to the Age of thirty Years, and been nine Years a Citizen of the United States, and who shall not, when elected, be an Inhabitant of that State for which he shall be chosen.

The Vice President of the United States shall be President of the Senate, but shall have no Vote, unless they be equally divided.

The Senate shall chuse their other Officers, and also a President pro tempore, in the Absence of the Vice President, or when he shall exercise the Office of President of the United States.

The Senate shall have the sole Power to try all Impeachments. When sitting for that Purpose, they shall be on Oath or Affirmation. When the President of the United States is tried, the Chief Justice shall preside: And no Person shall be convicted without the Concurrence of two thirds of the Members present.

Judgment in Cases of Impeachment shall not extend further than to removal from Office, and disqualification to hold and enjoy any Office of honor, Trust, or Profit under the United States: but the Party convicted shall nevertheless be liable and subject to Indictment, Trial, Judgment, and Punishment, according to Law.

Section 4. The Times, Places and Manner of holding Elections for Senators and Representatives, shall be prescribed in each State by the Legislature thereof; but the Congress may at any time by Law make or alter such Regulations, except as to the Places of chusing Senators.

The Congress shall assemble at least once in every Year, and such Meeting shall be on the first Monday in December, unless they shall by Law appoint a different Day.

Section 5. Each House shall be the Judge of the Elections, Returns, and Qualifications of its own Members, and a Majority of each shall constitute a Quorum to do Business; but a smaller Number may adjourn from day to day, and may be authorized to compel the Attendance of absent Members, in such Manner, and under such Penalties as each House may provide.

Each House may determine the Rules of its Proceedings, punish its Members for disorderly Behavior, and, with the Concurrence of two thirds, expel a Member.

Each House shall keep a Journal of its Proceedings, and from time to time publish the same, excepting such Parts as may in their Judgment require Secrecy; and the Yeas and Nays of the Members of either House on any question shall, at the Desire of one fifth of those Present, be entered on the Journal.

Neither House, during the Session of Congress, shall, without the Consent of the other, adjourn for more than three days, nor to any other Place than that in which the two Houses shall be sitting.

Section 6. The Senators and Representatives shall receive a Compensation for their Services, to be ascertained by Law, and paid out of the Treasury of the United States. They shall in all Cases, except Treason, Felony and Breach of the Peace, be privileged from Arrest during their Attendance at the Session of their respective Houses, and in going to and returning from the same; and for any Speech or Debate in either House, they shall not be questioned in any other Place.

No Senator or Representative shall, during the Time for which he was elected, be appointed to any civil Office under the Authority of the United States, which shall have been created, or the Emoluments whereof shall have been increased during such time; and no Person holding any Office under the United States, shall be a Member of either House during his Continuance in Office.

Section 7. All Bills for raising Revenue shall originate in the House of Representatives; but the Senate may propose or concur with Amendments as on other Bills.

Every Bill which shall have passed the House of Representatives and the Senate, shall, before it become a Law, be presented to the President of the United States; If he approve he shall sign it, but if not he shall return it, with his Objections to the House in which it shall have originated, who shall enter the Objections at large on their Journal, and proceed to reconsider it. If after such Reconsideration two thirds of that House shall agree to pass the Bill, it shall be sent together with the Objections, to the other House, by which it shall likewise be reconsidered, and if approved by two thirds of that House, it shall become a Law. But in all such Cases the Votes of both Houses shall be determined by Yeas and Nays, and the Names of the Persons voting for and against the Bill shall be entered on the Journal of each House respectively. If any Bill shall not be returned by the President within ten Days (Sundays excepted) after it shall have been presented to him, the Same shall be a Law, in like Manner as if he had signed it, unless the Congress by their Adjournment prevent its Return in which Case it shall not be a Law.

Every Order, Resolution, or Vote, to which the Concurrence of the Senate and House of Representatives may be necessary (except on a question of Adjournment) shall be presented to the President of the United States; and before the Same shall take Effect, shall be approved by him, or being disapproved by him, shall be repassed by two thirds of the Senate and House of Representatives, according to the Rules and Limitations prescribed in the Case of a Bill.

Section 8. The Congress shall have Power To lay and collect Taxes, Duties, Imposts and Excises, to pay the Debts and provide for the common Defence and general Welfare of the United States; but all Duties, Imposts and Excises shall be uniform throughout the United States;

To borrow Money on the credit of the United States;

To regulate Commerce with foreign Nations, and among the several States, and with the Indian Tribes;

To establish an uniform Rule of Naturalization, and uniform Laws on the subject of Bankruptcies throughout the United States;

To coin Money, regulate the Value thereof, and of foreign Coin, and fix the Standard of Weights and Measures;

To provide for the Punishment of counterfeiting the Securities and current Coin of the United States;

To establish Post Offices and post Roads;

To promote the Progress of Science and useful Arts, by securing for limited Times to Authors and Inventors the exclusive Right to their respective Writings and Discoveries;

To constitute Tribunals inferior to the supreme Court;

To define and punish Piracies and Felonies committed on the high Seas, and Offenses against the Law of Nations;

To declare War, grant Letters of Marque and Reprisal, and make Rules concerning Captures on Land and Water;

To raise and support Armies, but no Appropriation of Money to that Use shall be for a longer Term than two Years;

To provide and maintain a Navy;

To make Rules for the Government and Regulation of the land and naval Forces;

To provide for calling forth the Militia to execute the Laws of the Union, suppress Insurrections and repel Invasions;

To provide for organizing, arming, and disciplining, the Militia, and for governing such Part of them as may be employed in the Service of the United States, reserving to the States respectively, the Appointment of the Officers, and the Authority of training the Militia according to the discipline prescribed by Congress;

To exercise exclusive Legislation in all Cases whatsoever, over such District (not exceeding ten Miles square) as may, by Cession of particular States, and the Acceptance of Congress, become the Seat of the Government of the United States, and to exercise like Authority over all Places purchased by the Consent of the Legislature of the State in which the Same shall be, for the Erection of Forts, Magazines, Arsenals, dock-Yards, and other needful Buildings;—And

To make all Laws which shall be necessary and proper for carrying into Execution the foregoing Powers, and all other Powers vested by this Constitution in the Government of the United States, or in any Department or Officer thereof.

Section 9. The Migration or Importation of such Persons as any of the States now existing shall think proper to admit, shall not be prohibited by the Congress prior to the Year one thousand eight hundred and eight, but a Tax or duty may be imposed on such Importation, not exceeding ten dollars for each Person.

The privilege of the Writ of Habeas Corpus shall not be suspended, unless when in Cases of Rebellion or Invasion the public Safety may require it.

No Bill of Attainder or ex post facto Law shall be passed.

No Capitation, or other direct, Tax shall be laid, unless in Proportion to the Census or Enumeration herein before directed to be taken.

No Tax or Duty shall be laid on Articles exported from any State.

No Preference shall be given by any Regulation of Commerce or Revenue to the Ports of one State over those of another: nor shall Vessels bound to, or from, one State be obliged to enter, clear, or pay Duties in another.

No Money shall be drawn from the Treasury, but in Consequence of Appropriations made by Law; and a regular Statement and Account of the Receipts and Expenditures of all public Money shall be published from time to time.

No Title of Nobility shall be granted by the United States: And no Person holding any Office of Profit or Trust under them, shall, without the Consent of the Congress, accept of any present, Emolument, Office, or Title, of any kind whatever, from any King, Prince, or foreign State.

Section 10. No State shall enter into any Treaty, Alliance, or Confederation; grant Letters of Marque and Reprisal; coin Money; emit Bills of Credit; make any Thing but gold and silver Coin a Tender in Payment of Debts; pass any Bill of Attainder, ex post facto Law, or Law impairing the Obligation of Contracts, or grant any Title of Nobility.

No State shall, without the Consent of the Congress, lay any Imposts or Duties on Imports or Exports, except what may be absolutely necessary for executing its inspection Laws: and the net Produce of all Duties and Imposts, laid by any State on Imports or Exports, shall be for the Use of the Treasury of the United States; and all such Laws shall be subject to the Revision and Controul of the Congress.

No State shall, without the Consent of Congress, lay any Duty of Tonnage, keep Troops, or Ships of War in time of Peace, enter into any Agreement or Compact with another State, or with a foreign Power, or engage in War, unless actually invaded, or in such imminent Danger as will not admit of delay.

Article II

Section 1. The executive Power shall be vested in a President of the United States of America. He shall hold his Office during the Term of four Years, and, together with the Vice President, chosen for the same Term, be elected, as follows:

Each State shall appoint, in such Manner as the Legislature thereof may direct, a Number of Electors, equal to the whole Number of Senators and Representatives to which the State may be entitled in the Congress; but no Senator or Representative, or Person holding an Office of Trust or Profit under the United States, shall be appointed an Elector.

The Electors shall meet in their respective States, and vote by Ballot for two Persons, of whom one at least shall not be an Inhabitant of the same State with themselves. And they shall make a List of all the Persons voted for, and of the Number of Votes for each; which List they shall sign and certify, and transmit sealed to the Seat of the Government of the United States, directed to the President of the Senate. The President of the Senate shall, in the Presence of the Senate and House of Representatives, open all the Certificates, and the Votes shall then be counted. The Person having the greatest Number of Votes shall be the President, if such Number be a Majority of the whole Number of Electors appointed; and if there be more than one who have such Majority, and have an equal Number of Votes, then the House of Representatives shall immediately chuse by Ballot one of them for President; and if no Person have a Majority, then from the five highest on the List the said House shall in like Manner chuse the President. But in chusing the President, the Votes shall be taken by States, the Representation from each State having one Vote; A quorum for this Purpose shall consist of a Member or Members from two thirds of the States, and a Majority of all the States shall be necessary to a Choice. In every Case, after the Choice of the President, the Person having the greater Number of Votes of the Electors shall be the Vice President. But if there should remain two or more who have equal Votes, the Senate shall chuse from them by Ballot the Vice President.

The Congress may determine the Time of chusing the Electors, and the Day on which they shall give their Votes; which Day shall be the same throughout the United States.

No person except a natural born Citizen, or a Citizen of the United States, at the time of the Adoption of this Constitution, shall be eligible to the Office of President; neither shall any Person be eligible to that Office who shall not have attained to the Age of thirty five Years, and been fourteen Years a Resident within the United States.

In Case of the Removal of the President from Office, or of his Death, Resignation or Inability to discharge the Powers and Duties of the said Office, the same shall devolve on the Vice President, and the Congress may by Law provide for the Case of Removal, Death, Resignation or Inability, both of the President and Vice President, declaring what Officer shall then act as President, and such Officer shall act accordingly, until the Disability be removed, or a President shall be elected.

The President shall, at stated Times, receive for his Services, a Compensation, which shall neither be increased nor diminished during the Period for which he shall have been elected, and he shall not receive within that Period any other Emolument from the United States, or any of them.

Before he enter on the Execution of his Office, he shall take the following Oath or Affirmation: "I do solemnly swear (or affirm) that I will faithfully execute the Office of President of the United States, and will to the best of my Ability, preserve, protect and defend the Constitution of the United States."

Section 2. The President shall be Commander in Chief of the Army and Navy of the United States, and of the Militia of the several States, when called into the actual Service of the United States; he may require the Opinion, in writing, of the principal Officer in each of the executive Departments, upon any Subject relating to the Duties of their respective Offices, and he shall have Power to grant Reprieves and Pardons for Offenses against the United States, except in Cases of Impeachment.

He shall have Power, by and with the Advice and Consent of the Senate to make Treaties, provided two thirds of the Senators present concur; and he shall nominate, and by and with the Advice and Consent of the Senate, shall appoint Ambassadors, other public Ministers and Consuls, Judges of the supreme Court, and all other Officers of the United States, whose Appointments are not herein otherwise provided for, and which shall be established by Law; but the Congress may by Law vest the Appointment of such inferior Officers, as they think proper, in the President alone, in the Courts of Law, or in the Heads of Departments.

The President shall have Power to fill up all Vacancies that may happen during the Recess of the Senate, by granting Commissions which shall expire at the End of their next Session.

Section 3. He shall from time to time give to the Congress Information of the State of the Union, and recommend to their Consideration such Measures as he shall judge necessary and expedient; he may, on extraordinary Occasions, convene both Houses, or either of them, and in Case of Disagreement between them, with Respect to the Time of Adjournment, he may adjourn them to such Time as he shall think proper; he shall receive Ambassadors and other public Ministers; he shall take Care that the Laws be faithfully executed, and shall Commission all the Officers of the United States.

Section 4. The President, Vice President and all civil Officers of the United States, shall be removed from Office on Impeachment for, and Conviction of, Treason, Bribery, or other high Crimes and Misdemeanors.

Article III

Section 1. The judicial Power of the United States, shall be vested in one supreme Court, and in such inferior Courts as the Congress may from time to time ordain and establish. The Judges, both of the supreme and inferior Courts, shall hold their Offices during good Behaviour, and shall, at stated Times, receive for their Services a Compensation, which shall not be diminished during their Continuance in Office.

Section 2. The judicial Power shall extend to all Cases, in Law and Equity, arising under this Constitution, the Laws of the United States, and Treaties made, or which shall be made, under their Authority;—to all Cases affecting Ambassadors, other public Ministers and Consuls;—to all Cases of admiralty and maritime Jurisdiction;—to Controversies to which the United States shall be a Party;—to Controversies between two or more States;—between a State and Citizens of another State;—between Citizens of different States;—between Citizens of the same State claiming Lands under Grants of different States, and between a State, or the Citizens thereof, and foreign States, Citizens or Subjects.

In all Cases affecting Ambassadors, other public Ministers and Consuls, and those in which a State shall be a Party, the supreme Court shall have original Jurisdiction. In all the other Cases before mentioned, the supreme Court shall have appellate Jurisdiction, both as to Law and Fact, with such Exceptions, and under such Regulations as the Congress shall make.

The Trial of all Crimes, except in Cases of Impeachment, shall be by Jury; and such Trial shall be held in the State where the said Crimes shall have been committed; but when not committed within any State, the Trial shall be at such Place or Places as the Congress may by Law have directed.

Section 3. Treason against the United States, shall consist only in levying War against them, or, in adhering to their Enemies, giving them Aid and Comfort. No Person shall be convicted of Treason unless on the Testimony of two Witnesses to the same overt Act, or on Confession in open Court.

The Congress shall have Power to declare the Punishment of Treason, but no Attainder of Treason shall work Corruption of Blood, or Forfeiture except during the Life of the Person attainted.

Article IV

Section 1. Full Faith and Credit shall be given in each State to the public Acts, Records, and judicial Proceedings of every other State. And the Congress may by general Laws prescribe the Manner in which such Acts, Records and Proceedings shall be proved, and the Effect thereof.

Section 2. The Citizens of each State shall be entitled to all Privileges and Immunities of Citizens in the several States.

A Person charged in any State with Treason, Felony, or other Crime, who shall flee from Justice, and be found in another State, shall on Demand of the executive Authority of the State from which he fled, be delivered up, to be removed to the State having Jurisdiction of the Crime.

No Person held to Service or Labour in one State, under the Laws thereof, escaping into another, shall, in Consequence of any Law or Regulation therein, be discharged from such Service or Labour, but shall be delivered up on Claim of the Party to whom such Service or Labour may be due.

Section 3. New States may be admitted by the Congress into this Union; but no new State shall be formed or erected within the Jurisdiction of any other State; nor any State be formed by the Junction of two or more States, or Parts of States, without the Consent of the Legislatures of the States concerned as well as of the Congress.

The Congress shall have Power to dispose of and make all needful Rules and Regulations respecting the Territory or other Property belonging to the United States; and nothing in this Constitution shall be so construed as to Prejudice any Claims of the United States, or of any particular State.

Section 4. The United States shall guarantee to every State in this Union a Republican Form of Government, and shall protect each of them against Invasion; and on Application of the Legislature, or of the Executive (when the Legislature cannot be convened) against domestic Violence.

Article V

The Congress, whenever two thirds of both Houses shall deem it necessary, shall propose Amendments to this Constitution, or, on the Application of the Legislatures of two thirds of the several States, shall call a Convention for proposing Amendments, which, in either Case, shall be valid to all Intents and Purposes, as part of this Constitution, when ratified by the

Legislatures of three fourths of the several States, or by Conventions in three fourths thereof, as the one or the other Mode of Ratification may be proposed by the Congress; Provided that no Amendment which may be made prior to the Year One thousand eight hundred and eight shall in any Manner affect the first and fourth Clauses in the Ninth Section of the first Article; and that no State, without its Consent, shall be deprived of its equal Suffrage in the Senate.

Article VI

All Debts contracted and Engagements entered into, before the Adoption of this Constitution shall be as valid against the United States under this Constitution, as under the Confederation.

This Constitution, and the Laws of the United States which shall be made in Pursuance thereof; and all Treaties made, or which shall be made, under the Authority of the United States, shall be the supreme Law of the Land; and the Judges in every State shall be bound thereby, any Thing in the Constitution or Laws of any State to the Contrary notwithstanding.

The Senators and Representatives before mentioned, and the Members of the several State Legislatures, and all executive and judicial Officers, both of the United States and of the several States, shall be bound by Oath or Affirmation, to support this Constitution; but no religious Test shall ever be required as a Qualification to any Office or public Trust under the United States.

Article VII

The Ratification of the Conventions of nine States shall be sufficient for the Establishment of this Constitution between the States so ratifying the Same.

Amendment I [1791]

Congress shall make no law respecting an establishment of religion, or prohibiting the free exercise thereof; or abridging the freedom of speech, or of the press; or the right of the people peaceably to assembly, and to petition the Government for a redress of grievances.

Amendment II [1791]

A well regulated Militia, being necessary to the security of a free State, the right of the people to keep and bear Arms, shall not be infringed.

Amendment III [1791]

No Soldier shall, in time of peace be quartered in any house, without the consent of the Owner, nor in time of war, but in a manner to be prescribed by law.

Amendment IV [1791]

The right of the people to be secure in their persons, houses, papers, and effects, against unreasonable searches and seizures, shall not be violated, and no Warrants shall issue, but upon probable cause, supported by Oath or affirmation, and particularly describing the place to be searched, and the persons or things to be seized.

Amendment V [1791]

No person shall be held to answer for a capital, or otherwise infamous crime, unless on a presentment or indictment of a Grand Jury, except in cases arising in the land or naval forces, or in the Militia, when in actual service in time of War or public danger; nor shall any person be subject for the same offence to be twice put in jeopardy of life or limb; nor shall be compelled in any criminal case to be a witness against himself, nor be deprived of life, liberty, or property, without due process of law; nor shall private property be taken for public use, without just compensation.

Amendment VI [1791]

In all criminal prosecutions, the accused shall enjoy the right to a speedy and public trial, by an impartial jury of the State and district wherein the crime shall have been committed, which district shall have been previously ascertained by law, and to be informed of the nature and cause of the accusation; to be confronted with the witnesses against him; to have compulsory process for obtaining witnesses in his favor, and to have the Assistance of Counsel for his defence.

Amendment VII [1791]

In Suits at common law, where the value in controversy shall exceed twenty dollars, the right of trial by jury shall be preserved, and no fact tried by jury, shall be otherwise re-examined in any Court of the United States, than according to the rules of the common law.

Amendment VIII [1791]

Excessive bail shall not be required, nor excessive fines imposed, nor cruel and unusual punishments inflicted.

Amendment IX [1791]

The enumeration in the Constitution, of certain rights, shall not be construed to deny or disparage others retained by the people.

Amendment X [1791]

The powers not delegated to the United States by the Constitution, nor prohibited by it to the States, are reserved to the States respectively, or to the people.

Amendment XI [1798]

The Judicial power of the United States shall not be construed to extend to any suit in law or equity, commenced or prosecuted against one of the United States by Citizens of another State, or by Citizens or Subjects of any Foreign State.

AMENDMENT XII [1804]

The Electors shall meet in their respective states, and vote by ballot for President and Vice-President, one of whom, at least, shall not be an inhabitant of the same state with themselves; they shall name in their ballots the person voted for as President, and in distinct ballots the person voted for as Vice-President, and they shall make distinct lists of all persons voted for as President, and of all persons voted for as Vice-President, and of the number of votes for each, which lists they shall sign and certify, and transmit sealed to the seat of the government of the United States, directed to the President of the Senate;—The President of the Senate shall, in the presence of the Senate and House of Representatives, open all the certificates and the votes shall then be counted;—The person having the greatest number of votes for President, shall be the President, if such number be a majority of the whole number of Electors appointed; and if no person have such majority, then from the persons having the highest numbers not exceeding three on the list of those voted for as President, the House of Representatives shall choose immediately, by ballot, the President. But in choosing the President, the votes shall be taken by states, the representation from each state having one vote; a quorum for this purpose shall consist of a member or members from two-thirds of the states, and a majority of all states shall be necessary to a choice. And if the House of Representatives shall not choose a President whenever the right of choice shall devolve upon them, before the fourth day of March next following, then the Vice-President shall act as President, as in the case of the death or other constitutional disability of the President.—The person having the greatest number of votes as Vice-President, shall be the Vice-President, if such number be a majority of the whole number of Electors appointed, and if no person have a majority, then from the two highest numbers on the list, the Senate shall choose the Vice-President; a quorum for the purpose shall consist of two-thirds of the whole number of Senators, and a majority of the whole number shall be necessary to a choice. But no person constitutionally ineligible to the office of President shall be eligible to that of Vice-President of the United States.

AMENDMENT XIII [1865]

Section 1. Neither slavery nor involuntary servitude, except as a punishment for crime whereof the party shall have been duly convicted, shall exist within the United States, or any place subject to their jurisdiction.

Section 2. Congress shall have power to enforce this article by appropriate legislation.

AMENDMENT XIV [1868]

Section 1. All persons born or naturalized in the United States, and subject to the jurisdiction thereof, are citizens of the United States and of the State wherein they reside. No State shall make or enforce any law which shall abridge the privileges or immunities of citizens of the United States; nor shall any State deprive any person of life, liberty, or property, without due process of law; nor deny to any person within its jurisdiction the equal protection of the laws.

Section 2. Representatives shall be apportioned among the several States according to their respective numbers, counting the whole number of persons in each State, excluding Indians not taxed. But when the right to vote at any election for the choice of electors for President and Vice President of the United States, Representatives in Congress, the Executive and Judicial officers of a State, or the members of the Legislature thereof, is denied to any of the male inhabitants of such State, being twenty-one years of age, and citizens of the United States, or in any way abridged, except for participation in rebellion, or other crime, the basis of representation therein shall be reduced in the proportion which the number of such male citizens shall bear to the whole number of male citizens twenty-one years of age in such State.

Section 3. No person shall be a Senator or Representative in Congress, or elector of President and Vice President, or hold any office, civil or military, under the United States, or under any State, who having previously taken an oath, as a member of Congress, or as an officer of the United States, or as a member of any State legislature, or as an executive or judicial officer of any State, to support the Constitution of the United States, shall have engaged in insurrection or rebellion against the same, or given aid or comfort to the enemies thereof. But Congress may by a vote of two-thirds of each House, remove such disability.

Section 4. The validity of the public debt of the United States, authorized by law, including debts incurred for payment of pensions and bounties for services in suppressing insurrection or rebellion, shall not be questioned. But neither the United States nor any State shall assume or pay any debt or obligation incurred in aid of insurrection or rebellion against the United States, or any claim for the loss or emancipation of any slave; but all such debts, obligations and claims shall be held illegal and void.

Section 5. The Congress shall have power to enforce, by appropriate legislation, the provisions of this article.

AMENDMENT XV [1870]

Section 1. The right of citizens of the United States to vote shall not be denied or abridged by the United States or by any State on account of race, color, or previous condition of servitude.

Section 2. The Congress shall have power to enforce this article by appropriate legislation.

Amendment XVI [1913]

The Congress shall have power to lay and collect taxes on incomes, from whatever source derived, without apportionment among the several States, and without regard to any census or enumeration.

Amendment XVII [1913]

Section 1. The Senate of the United States shall be composed of two Senators from each State, elected by the people thereof, for six years; and each Senator shall have one vote. The electors in each State shall have the qualifications requisite for electors of the most numerous branch of the State legislatures.

Section 2. When vacancies happen in the representation of any State in the Senate, the executive authority of such State shall issue writs of election to fill such vacancies: *Provided*, That the legislature of any State may empower the executive thereof to make temporary appointments until the people fill the vacancies by election as the legislature may direct.

Section 3. This amendment shall not be so construed as to affect the election or term of any Senator chosen before it becomes valid as part of the Constitution.

Amendment XVIII [1919]

Section 1. After one year from the ratification of this article the manufacture, sale, or transportation of intoxicating liquors within, the importation thereof into, or the exportation thereof from the United States and all territory subject to the jurisdiction thereof for beverage purposes is hereby prohibited.

Section 2. The Congress and the several States shall have concurrent power to enforce this article by appropriate legislation.

Section 3. This article shall be inoperative unless it shall have been ratified as an amendment to the Constitution by the legislatures of the several States, as provided in the Constitution, within seven years from the date of the submission hereof to the States by the Congress.

Amendment XIX [1920]

Section 1. The right of citizens of the United States to vote shall not be denied or abridged by the United States or by any State on account of sex.

Section 2. Congress shall have power to enforce this article by appropriate legislation.

Amendment XX [1933]

Section 1. The terms of the President and Vice President shall end at noon on the 20th day of January, and the terms of Senators and Representatives at noon on the 3d day of January, of the years in which such terms would have ended if this article had not been ratified; and the terms of their successors shall then begin.

Section 2. The Congress shall assemble at least once in every year, and such meeting shall begin at noon on the 3d day of January, unless they shall by law appoint a different day.

Section 3. If, at the time fixed for the beginning of the term of the President, the President elect shall have died, the Vice President elect shall become President. If the President shall not have been chosen before the time fixed for the beginning of his term, or if the President elect shall have failed to qualify, then the Vice President elect shall act as President until a President shall have qualified; and the Congress may by law provide for the case wherein neither a President elect nor a Vice President elect shall have qualified, declaring who shall then act as President, or the manner in which one who is to act shall be selected, and such person shall act accordingly until a President or Vice President shall have qualified.

Section 4. The Congress may by law provide for the case of the death of any of the persons from whom the House of Representatives may choose a President whenever the right of choice shall have devolved upon them, and for the case of the death of any of the persons from whom the Senate may choose a Vice President whenever the right of choice shall have devolved upon them.

Section 5. Sections 1 and 2 shall take effect on the 15th day of October following the ratification of this article.

Section 6. This article shall be inoperative unless it shall have been ratified as an amendment to the Constitution by the legislatures of three-fourths of the several States within seven years from the date of its submission.

Amendment XXI [1933]

Section 1. The eighteenth article of amendment to the Constitution of the United States is hereby repealed.

Section 2. The transportation or importation into any State, Territory, or possession of the United States for delivery or use therein of intoxicating liquors, in violation of the laws thereof, is hereby prohibited.

Section 3. This article shall be inoperative unless it shall have been ratified as an amendment to the Constitution by conventions in the several States, as provided in the Constitution, within seven years from the date of the submission hereof to the States by the Congress.

Amendment XXII [1951]

Section 1. No person shall be elected to the office of the President more than twice, and no person who has held the office of President, or acted as President, for more than two years of a term to which some other person was elected President shall be elected to the office of President more than once. But this Article shall not apply to any person holding the office of President when this Article was proposed by the Congress, and shall not prevent any person who may be holding the office of President, or acting as President, during the term within which this Article becomes operative from holding the office of President or acting as President during the remainder of such term.

Section 2. This article shall be inoperative unless it shall have been ratified as an amendment to the Constitution by the legislatures of three-fourths of the several States within seven years from the date of its submission to the States by the Congress.

AMENDMENT XXIII [1961]

Section 1. The District constituting the seat of Government of the United States shall appoint in such manner as the Congress may direct:

A number of electors of President and Vice President equal to the whole number of Senators and Representatives in Congress to which the District would be entitled if it were a State, but in no event more than the least populous state; they shall be in addition to those appointed by the states, but they shall be considered, for the purposes of the election of President and Vice President, to be electors appointed by a state; and they shall meet in the District and perform such duties as provided by the twelfth article of amendment.

Section 2. The Congress shall have power to enforce this article by appropriate legislation.

AMENDMENT XXIV [1964]

Section 1. The right of citizens of the United States to vote in any primary or other election for President or Vice President, for electors for President or Vice President, or for Senator or Representative in Congress, shall not be denied or abridged by the United States, or any State by reason of failure to pay any poll tax or other tax.

Section 2. The Congress shall have power to enforce this article by appropriate legislation.

AMENDMENT XXV [1967]

Section 1. In case of the removal of the President from office or of his death or resignation, the Vice President shall become President.

Section 2. Whenever there is a vacancy in the office of the Vice President, the President shall nominate a Vice President who shall take office upon confirmation by a majority vote of both Houses of Congress.

Section 3. Whenever the President transmits to the President pro tempore of the Senate and the Speaker of the House of Representatives his written declaration that he is unable to discharge the powers and duties of his office, and until he transmits to them a written declaration to the contrary, such powers and duties shall be discharged by the Vice President as Acting President.

Section 4. Whenever the Vice President and a majority of either the principal officers of the executive departments or of such other body as Congress may by law provide, transmit to the President pro tempore of the Senate and the Speaker of the House of Representatives their written declaration that the President is unable to discharge the powers and duties of his office, the Vice President shall immediately assume the powers and duties of the office as Acting President.

Thereafter, when the President transmits to the President pro tempore of the Senate and the Speaker of the House of Representatives his written declaration that no inability exists, he shall resume the powers and duties of his office unless the Vice President and a majority of either the principal officers of the executive department or of such other body as Congress may by law provide, transmit within four days to the President pro tempore of the Senate and the Speaker of the House of Representatives their written declaration that the President is unable to discharge the powers and duties of his office. Thereupon Congress shall decide the issue, assembling within forty-eight hours for that purpose if not in session. If the Congress, within twenty-one days after receipt of the latter written declaration, or, if Congress is not in session, within twenty-one days after Congress is required to assemble, determines by two-thirds vote of both Houses that the President is unable to discharge the powers and duties of his office, the Vice President shall continue to discharge the same as Acting President; otherwise, the President shall resume the powers and duties of his office.

AMENDMENT XXVI [1971]

Section 1. The right of citizens of the United States, who are eighteen years of age or older, to vote shall not be denied or abridged by the United States or by any State on account of age.

Section 2. The Congress shall have power to enforce this article by appropriate legislation.

AMENDMENT XXVII [1992]

No law, varying the compensation for the services of the Senators and Representatives, shall take effect, until an election of Representatives shall have intervened.

Appendix C

The Administrative Procedure Act of 1946 [Excerpts]

Section 551. Definitions

For the purpose of this subchapter—

* * * *

(4) "rule" means the whole or a part of an agency statement of general or particular applicability and future effect designed to implement, interpret, or prescribe law or policy or describing the organization, procedure, or practice requirements of an agency and includes the approval or prescription for the future of rates, wages, corporate or financial structures or reorganizations thereof, prices, facilities, appliances, services or allowances therefor or of valuations, costs, or accounting, or practices bearing on any of the foregoing[.]

* * * *

Section 552. Public Information; Agency Rules, Opinions, Orders, Records, and Proceedings

(a) Each agency shall make available to the public information as follows:

(1) Each agency shall separately state and currently publish in the Federal Register for the guidance of the public—

(A) descriptions of its central and field organization and the established places at which, the employees * * * from whom, and the methods whereby, the public may obtain information, make submittals or requests, or obtain decisions;

* * * *

(C) rules of procedure, descriptions of forms available or the places at which forms may be obtained, and instructions as to the scope and contents of all papers, reports, or examinations;

(D) substantive rules of general applicability adopted as authorized by law, and statements of general policy or interpretations of general applicability formulated and adopted by the agency[.]

* * *

* * * *

Section 552b. Open Meetings

* * * *

(j) Each agency subject to the requirements of this section shall annually report to Congress regarding its compliance with such requirements, including a tabulation of the total number of agency meetings open to the public, the total number of meetings closed to the public, the reasons for closing such meetings, and a description of any litigation brought against the agency under this section, including any costs assessed against the agency in such litigation * * *.

* * * *

Section 553. Rule Making

* * * *

(b) General notice of proposed rule making shall be published in the Federal Register, unless persons subject thereto are named and either personally served or otherwise have actual notice thereof in accordance with law. * * *

(c) After notice required by this section, the agency shall give interested persons an opportunity to participate in the rule making through submission of written data, views, or arguments with or without opportunity for oral presentation. * * *

* * * *

Section 554. Adjudications

* * * *

(b) Persons entitled to notice of an agency hearing shall be timely informed of—

(1) the time, place, and nature of the hearing;

(2) the legal authority and jurisdiction under which the hearing is to be held; and

(3) the matters of fact and law asserted.

* * * *

(c) The agency shall give all interested parties opportunity for—

(1) the submission and consideration of facts, arguments, offers of settlement, or proposals of adjustment when time, the nature of the proceeding, and the public interest permit; and

(2) to the extent that the parties are unable so to determine a controversy by consent, hearing and decision on notice * * *.

* * * *

Section 555. Ancillary Matters

* * * *

(c) Process, requirement of a report, inspection, or other investigative act or demand may not be issued, made, or enforced except as authorized by law. A person compelled to submit data or evidence is entitled to retain or, on payment of lawfully prescribed costs, procure a copy or transcript thereof, except that in a nonpublic investigatory proceeding the witness may for good cause be limited to inspection of the official transcript of his testimony.

* * * *

(e) Prompt notice shall be given of the denial in whole or in part of a written application, petition, or other request of an interested person made in connection with any agency proceeding. * * *

Section 556. Hearings; Presiding Employees; Powers and Duties; Burden of Proof; Evidence; Record as Basis of Decision

* * * *

(b) There shall preside at the taking of evidence—

(1) the agency;

(2) one or more members of the body which comprises the agency; or

(3) one or more administrative law judges * * *.

* * * *

(c) Subject to published rules of the agency and within its powers, employees presiding at hearings may—

(1) administer oaths and affirmations;

(2) issue subpoenas authorized by law;

(3) rule on offers of proof and receive relevant evidence;

(4) take depositions or have depositions taken when the ends of justice would be served;

(5) regulate the course of the hearing;

(6) hold conferences for the settlement or simplification of the issues by consent of the parties or by the use of alternative means of dispute resolution as provided in subchapter IV of this chapter;

(7) inform the parties as to the availability of one or more alternative means of dispute resolution, and encourage use of such methods;

* * * *

(9) dispose of procedural requests or similar matters;

(10) make or recommend decisions in accordance with * * * this title; and

(11) take other action authorized by agency rule consistent with this subchapter.

* * * *

Section 702. Right of Review

A person suffering legal wrong because of agency action * * * is entitled to judicial review thereof. An action in a court of the United States seeking relief other than money damages and stating a claim that an agency or an officer or employee thereof acted or failed to act in an official capacity or under color of legal authority shall not be dismissed nor relief therein be denied on the ground that it is against the United States or that the United States is an indispensable party. The United States may be named as a defendant in any such action, and a judgment or decree may be entered against the United States: Provided, [t]hat any mandatory or injunctive decree shall specify the [f]ederal officer or officers (by name or by title), and their successors in office, personally responsible for compliance. * * *

* * * *

Section 704. Actions Reviewable

Agency action made reviewable by statute and final agency action for which there is no other adequate remedy in a court are subject to judicial review. A preliminary, procedural, or intermediate agency action or ruling not directly reviewable is subject to review on the review of the final agency action.

APPENDIX D

UNIFORM COMMERCIAL CODE [EXCERPTS]

Article 2 SALES

Part 1 Short Title, General Construction and Subject Matter

§ 2—101. Short Title.

This Article shall be known and may be cited as Uniform Commercial Code—Sales.

§ 2—102. Scope; Certain Security and Other Transactions Excluded From This Article.

Unless the context otherwise requires, this Article applies to transactions in goods; it does not apply to any transaction which although in the form of an unconditional contract to sell or present sale is intended to operate only as a security transaction nor does this Article impair or repeal any statute regulating sales to consumers, farmers or other specified classes of buyers.

§ 2—103. Definitions and Index of Definitions.

(1) In this Article unless the context otherwise requires

(a) "Buyer" means a person who buys or contracts to buy goods.

(b) "Good faith" in the case of a merchant means honesty in fact and the observance of reasonable commercial standards of fair dealing in the trade.

(c) "Receipt" of goods means taking physical possession of them.

(d) "Seller" means a person who sells or contracts to sell goods.

(2) Other definitions applying to this Article or to specified Parts thereof, and the sections in which they appear are:

"Acceptance". Section 2—606.
"Banker's credit". Section 2—325.
"Between merchants". Section 2—104.
"Cancellation". Section 2—106(4).
"Commercial unit". Section 2—105.
"Confirmed credit". Section 2—325.
"Conforming to contract". Section 2—106.
"Contract for sale". Section 2—106.
"Cover". Section 2—712.
"Entrusting". Section 2—403.
"Financing agency". Section 2—104.
"Future goods". Section 2—105.
"Goods". Section 2—105.
"Identification". Section 2—501.
"Installment contract". Section 2—612.
"Letter of Credit". Section 2—325.
"Lot". Section 2—105.
"Merchant". Section 2—104.

"Overseas". Section 2—323.
"Person in position of seller". Section 2—707.
"Present sale". Section 2—106.
"Sale". Section 2—106.
"Sale on approval". Section 2—326.
"Sale or return". Section 2—326.
"Termination". Section 2—106.

(3) The following definitions in other Articles apply to this Article:

"Check". Section 3—104.
"Consignee". Section 7—102.
"Consignor". Section 7—102.
"Consumer goods". Section 9—109.
"Dishonor". Section 3—507.
"Draft". Section 3—104.

(4) In addition Article 1 contains general definitions and principles of construction and interpretation applicable throughout this Article.

§ 2—104. Definitions: "Merchant"; "Between Merchants"; "Financing Agency".

(1) "Merchant" means a person who deals in goods of the kind or otherwise by his occupation holds himself out as having knowledge or skill peculiar to the practices or goods involved in the transaction or to whom such knowledge or skill may be attributed by his employment of an agent or broker or other intermediary who by his occupation holds himself out as having such knowledge or skill.

(2) "Financing agency" means a bank, finance company or other person who in the ordinary course of business makes advances against goods or documents of title or who by arrangement with either the seller or the buyer intervenes in ordinary course to make or collect payment due or claimed under the contract for sale, as by purchasing or paying the seller's draft or making advances against it or by merely taking it for collection whether or not documents of title accompany the draft. "Financing agency" includes also a bank or other person who similarly intervenes between persons who are in the position of seller and buyer in respect to the goods (Section 2—707).

(3) "Between merchants" means in any transaction with respect to which both parties are chargeable with the knowledge or skill of merchants.

§ 2—105. Definitions: Transferability; "Goods"; "Future" Goods; "Lot"; "Commercial Unit".

(1) "Goods" means all things (including specially manufactured goods) which are movable at the time of identification to the contract for sale other than the money in which the price is to be paid, investment securities (Article 8) and things in action. "Goods" also includes the unborn young of animals and growing crops and other identified things attached to realty as described in the section on goods to be severed from realty (Section 2—107).

(2) Goods must be both existing and identified before any interest in them can pass. Goods which are not both existing and identified are "future" goods. A purported present sale of future goods or of any interest therein operates as a contract to sell.

(3) There may be a sale of a part interest in existing identified goods.

(4) An undivided share in an identified bulk of fungible goods is sufficiently identified to be sold although the quantity of the bulk is not determined. Any agreed proportion of such a bulk or any quantity thereof agreed upon by number, weight or other measure may to the extent of the seller's interest in the bulk be sold to the buyer who then becomes an owner in common.

(5) "Lot" means a parcel or a single article which is the subject matter of a separate sale or delivery, whether or not it is sufficient to perform the contract.

(6) "Commercial unit" means such a unit of goods as by commercial usage is a single whole for purposes of sale and division of which materially impairs its character or value on the market or in use. A commercial unit may be a single article (as a machine) or a set of articles (as a suite of furniture or an assortment of sizes) or a quantity (as a bale, gross, or carload) or any other unit treated in use or in the relevant market as a single whole.

§ 2—106. Definitions: "Contract"; "Agreement"; "Contract for Sale"; "Sale"; "Present Sale"; "Conforming" to Contract; "Termination"; "Cancellation".

(1) In this Article unless the context otherwise requires "contract" and "agreement" are limited to those relating to the present or future sale of goods. "Contract for sale" includes both a present sale of goods and a contract to sell goods at a future time. A "sale" consists in the passing of title from the seller to the buyer for a price (Section 2—401). A "present sale" means a sale which is accomplished by the making of the contract.

(2) Goods or conduct including any part of a performance are "conforming" or conform to the contract when they are in accordance with the obligations under the contract.

(3) "Termination" occurs when either party pursuant to a power created by agreement or law puts an end to the contract otherwise than for its breach. On "termination" all obligations which are still executory on both sides are discharged but any right based on prior breach or performance survives.

(4) "Cancellation" occurs when either party puts an end to the contract for breach by the other and its effect is the same as that of "termination" except that the cancelling party also retains any remedy for breach of the whole contract or any unperformed balance.

§ 2—107. Goods to Be Severed From Realty: Recording.

(1) A contract for the sale of minerals or the like (including oil and gas) or a structure or its materials to be removed from realty is a contract for the sale of goods within this Article if they are to be severed by the seller but until severance a purported present sale thereof which is not effective as a transfer of an interest in land is effective only as a contract to sell.

(2) A contract for the sale apart from the land of growing crops or other things attached to realty and capable of severance without material harm thereto but not described in subsection (1) or of timber to be cut is a contract for the sale of goods within this Article whether the subject matter is to be severed by the buyer or by the seller even though it forms part of the realty at the time of contracting, and the parties can by identification effect a present sale before severance.

(3) The provisions of this section are subject to any third party rights provided by the law relating to realty records, and the contract for sale may be executed and recorded as a document transferring an interest in land and shall then constitute notice to third parties of the buyer's rights under the contract for sale.

Part 2 Form, Formation and Readjustment of Contract

§ 2—201. Formal Requirements; Statute of Frauds.

(1) Except as otherwise provided in this section a contract for the sale of goods for the price of $500 or more is not enforceable by way of action or defense unless there is some writing sufficient to indicate that a contract for sale has been made between the parties and signed by the party against whom enforcement is sought or by his authorized agent or broker. A writing is not insufficient because it omits or incorrectly states a term agreed upon but the contract is not enforceable under this paragraph beyond the quantity of goods shown in such writing.

(2) Between merchants if within a reasonable time a writing in confirmation of the contract and sufficient against the sender is received and the party receiving it has reason to know its contents, its satisfies the requirements of subsection (1) against such party unless written notice of objection to its contents is given within ten days after it is received.

(3) A contract which does not satisfy the requirements of subsection (1) but which is valid in other respects is enforceable

(a) if the goods are to be specially manufactured for the buyer and are not suitable for sale to others in the ordinary course of the seller's business and the seller, before notice of repudiation is received and under circumstances which reasonably indicate that the goods are for the buyer, has made either a substantial beginning of their manufacture or commitments for their procurement; or

(b) if the party against whom enforcement is sought admits in his pleading, testimony or otherwise in court that a contract for sale was made, but the contract is not enforceable under this provision beyond the quantity of goods admitted; or

(c) with respect to goods for which payment has been made and accepted or which have been received and accepted (Sec. 2—606).

§ 2—202. Final Written Expression: Parol or Extrinsic Evidence.

Terms with respect to which the confirmatory memoranda of the parties agree or which are otherwise set forth in a writing intended by the parties as a final expression of their agreement with respect to such terms as are included therein may not be contradicted by evidence of any prior agreement or of a contemporaneous oral agreement but may be explained or supplemented

(a) by course of dealing or usage of trade (Section 1—205) or by course of performance (Section 2—208); and

(b) by evidence of consistent additional terms unless the court finds the writing to have been intended also as a complete and exclusive statement of the terms of the agreement.

§ 2—203. Seals Inoperative.

The affixing of a seal to a writing evidencing a contract for sale or an offer to buy or sell goods does not constitute the writing a sealed instrument and the law with respect to sealed instruments does not apply to such a contract or offer.

§ 2—204. Formation in General.

(1) A contract for sale of goods may be made in any manner sufficent to show agreement, including conduct by both parties which recognizes the existence of such a contract.

(2) An agreement sufficient to constitute a contract for sale may be found even though the moment of its making is undetermined.

(3) Even though one or more terms are left open a contract for sale does not fail for indefiniteness if the parties have intended to make a contract and there is a reasonably certain basis for giving an appropriate remedy.

§ 2—205. Firm Offers.

An offer by a merchant to buy or sell goods in a signed writing which by its terms gives assurance that it will be held open is not revocable, for lack of consideration, during the time stated or if no time is stated for a reasonable time, but in no event may such period of irrevocability exceed three months; but any such term of assurance on a form supplied by the offeree must be separately signed by the offeror.

§ 2—206. Offer and Acceptance in Formation of Contract.

(1) Unless other unambiguously indicated by the language or circumstances

(a) an offer to make a contract shall be construed as inviting acceptance in any manner and by any medium reasonable in the circumstances;

(b) an order or other offer to buy goods for prompt or current shipment shall be construed as inviting acceptance either by a prompt promise to ship or by the prompt or current shipment of conforming or nonconforming goods, but such a shipment of non-conforming goods does not constitute an acceptance if the seller seasonably notifies the buyer that the shipment is offered only as an accommodation to the buyer.

(2) Where the beginning of a requested performance is a reasonable mode of acceptance an offeror who is not notified of acceptance within a reasonable time may treat the offer as having lapsed before acceptance.

§ 2—207. Additional Terms in Acceptance or Confirmation.

(1) A definite and seasonable expression of acceptance or a written confirmation which is sent within a reasonable time operates as an acceptance even though it states terms additional to or different from those offered or agreed upon, unless acceptance is expressly made conditional on assent to the additional or different terms.

(2) The additional terms are to be construed as proposals for addition to the contract. Between merchants such terms become part of the contract unless:

(a) the offer expressly limits acceptance to the terms of the offer;

(b) they materially alter it; or

(c) notification of objection to them has already been given or is given within a reasonable time after notice of them is received.

(3) Conduct by both parties which recognizes the existence of a contract is sufficient to establish a contract for sale although the writings of the parties do not otherwise establish a contract. In such case the terms of the particular contract consist of those terms on which the writings of the parties agree, together with any supplementary terms incorporated under any other provisions of this Act.

§ 2—208. Course of Performance or Practical Construction.

(1) Where the contract for sale involves repeated occasions for performance by either party with knowledge of the nature of the performance and opportunity for objection to it by the other, any course of performance accepted or acquiesced in without objection shall be relevant to determine the meaning of the agreement.

(2) The express terms of the agreement and any such course of performance, as well as any course of dealing and usage of trade, shall be construed whenever reasonable as consistent with each other; but when such construction is unreasonable, express terms shall control course of performance and course of performance shall control both course of dealing and usage of trade (Section 1—205).

(3) Subject to the provisions of the next section on modification and waiver, such course of performance shall be relevant to show a waiver or modification of any term inconsistent with such course of performance.

§ 2—209. Modification, Rescission and Waiver.

(1) An agreement modifying a contract within this Article needs no consideration to be binding.

(2) A signed agreement which excludes modification or rescission except by a signed writing cannot be otherwise modified or rescinded, but except as between merchants such a requirement on a form supplied by the merchant must be separately signed by the other party.

(3) The requirements of the statute of frauds section of this Article (Section 2—201) must be satisfied if the contract as modified is within its provisions.

(4) Although an attempt at modification or rescission does not satisfy the requirements of subsection (2) or (3) it can operate as a waiver.

(5) A party who has made a waiver affecting an executory portion of the contract may retract the waiver by reasonable notification received by the other party that strict performance will be required of any term waived, unless the retraction would be unjust in view of a material change of position in reliance on the waiver.

§ 2—210. Delegation of Performance; Assignment of Rights.

(1) A party may perform his duty through a delegate unless otherwise agreed or unless the other party has a substantial interest in having his original promisor perform or control the acts required by the contract. No delegation of performance relieves the party delegating of any duty to perform or any liability for breach.

(2) Unless otherwise agreed all rights of either seller or buyer can be assigned except where the assignment would materially change the duty of the other party, or increase materially the burden or risk imposed on him by his contract, or impair materially his chance of obtaining return performance. A right to damages for breach of the whole contract or a right arising out of the assignor's due performance of his entire obligation can be assigned despite agreement otherwise.

(3) Unless the circumstances indicate the contrary a prohibition of assignment of "the contract" is to be construed as barring only the delegation to the assignee of the assignor's performance.

(4) An assignment of "the contract" or of "all my rights under the contract" or an assignment in similar general terms is an assignment of rights and unless the language or the circumstances (as in an assignment for security) indicate the contrary, it is a delegation of performance of the duties of the assignor and its acceptance by the assignee constitutes a promise by him to perform those duties. This promise is enforceable by either the assignor or the other party to the original contract.

(5) The other party may treat any assignment which delegates performance as creating reasonable grounds for insecurity and may without prejudice to his rights against the assignor demand assurances from the assignee (Section 2—609).

Part 3 General Obligation and Construction of Contract

§ 2—301. General Obligations of Parties.

The obligation of the seller is to transfer and deliver and that of the buyer is to accept and pay in accordance with the contract.

§ 2—302. Unconscionable Contract or Clause.

(1) If the court as a matter of law finds the contract or any clause of the contract to have been unconscionable at the time it was made the court may refuse to enforce the contract, or it may enforce the remainder of the contract without the unconscionable clause, or it may so limit the application of any unconscionable clause as to avoid any unconscionable result.

(2) When it is claimed or appears to the court that the contract or any clause thereof may be unconscionable the parties shall be afforded a reasonable opportunity to present evidence as to its commercial setting, purpose and effect to aid the court in making the determination.

§ 2—303. Allocations or Division of Risks.

Where this Article allocates a risk or a burden as between the parties "unless otherwise agreed", the agreement may not only shift the allocation but may also divide the risk or burden.

§ 2—304. Price Payable in Money, Goods, Realty, or Otherwise.

(1) The price can be made payable in money or otherwise. If it is payable in whole or in part in goods each party is a seller of the goods which he is to transfer.

(2) Even though all or part of the price is payable in an interest in realty the transfer of the goods and the seller's obligations with reference to them are subject to this Article, but not the transfer of the interest in realty or the transferor's obligations in connection therewith.

§ 2—305. Open Price Term.

(1) The parties if they so intend can conclude a contract for sale even though the price is not settled. In such a case the price is a reasonable price at the time for delivery if

(a) nothing is said as to price; or

(b) the price is left to be agreed by the parties and they fail to agree; or

(c) the price is to be fixed in terms of some agreed market or other standard as set or recorded by a third person or agency and it is not so set or recorded.

(2) A price to be fixed by the seller or by the buyer means a price for him to fix in good faith.

(3) When a price left to be fixed otherwise than by agreement of the parties fails to be fixed through fault of one party the other may at his option treat the contract as cancelled or himself fix a reasonable price.

(4) Where, however, the parties intend not to be bound unless the price be fixed or agreed and it is not fixed or agreed there is no contract. In such a case the buyer must return any goods already received or if unable so to do must pay their reasonable value at the time of delivery and the seller must return any portion of the price paid on account.

§ 2—306. Output, Requirements and Exclusive Dealings.

(1) A term which measures the quantity by the output of the seller or the requirements of the buyer means such actual output or requirements as may occur in good faith, except that no quantity unreasonably disproportionate to any stated estimate or in the absence of a stated estimate to any normal or otherwise comparable prior output or requirements may be tendered or demanded.

(2) A lawful agreement by either the seller or the buyer for exclusive dealing in the kind of goods concerned imposes unless otherwise agreed an obligation by the seller to use best efforts to supply the goods and by the buyer to use best efforts to promote their sale.

§ 2—307. Delivery in Single Lot or Several Lots.

Unless otherwise agreed all goods called for by a contract for sale must be tendered in a single delivery and payment is due only on such tender but where the circumstances give either party the right to make or demand delivery in lots the price if it can be apportioned may be demanded for each lot.

§ 2—308. Absence of Specified Place for Delivery.

Unless otherwise agreed

(a) the place for delivery of goods is the seller's place of business or if he has none his residence; but

(b) in a contract for sale of identified goods which to the knowledge of the parties at the time of contracting are in some other place, that place is the place for their delivery; and

(c) documents of title may be delivered through customary banking channels.

§ 2—309. Absence of Specific Time Provisions; Notice of Termination.

(1) The time for shipment or delivery or any other action under a contract if not provided in this Article or agreed upon shall be a reasonable time.

(2) Where the contract provides for successive performances but is indefinite in duration it is valid for a reasonable time but unless otherwise agreed may be terminated at any time by either party.

(3) Termination of a contract by one party except on the happening of an agreed event requires that reasonable notification be received by the other party and an agreement dispensing with notification is invalid if its operation would be unconscionable.

§ 2—310. Open Time for Payment or Running of Credit; Authority to Ship Under Reservation.

Unless otherwise agreed

(a) payment is due at the time and place at which the buyer is to receive the goods even though the place of shipment is the place of delivery; and

(b) if the seller is authorized to send the goods he may ship them under reservation, and may tender the documents of title, but the buyer may inspect the goods after their arrival before payment is due unless such inspection is inconsistent with the terms of the contract (Section 2—513); and

(c) if delivery is authorized and made by way of documents of title otherwise than by subsection (b) then payment is due at the time and place at which the buyer is to receive the documents regardless of where the goods are to be received; and

(d) where the seller is required or authorized to ship the goods on credit the credit period runs from the time of shipment but post-dating the invoice or delaying its dispatch will correspondingly delay the starting of the credit period.

§ 2—311. Options and Cooperation Respecting Performance.

(1) An agreement for sale which is otherwise sufficiently definite (subsection (3) of Section 2—204) to be a contract is not made invalid by the fact that it leaves particulars of performance to be specified by one of the parties. Any such specification must be made in good faith and within limits set by commercial reasonableness.

(2) Unless otherwise agreed specifications relating to assortment of the goods are at the buyer's option and except as otherwise provided in subsections (1)(c) and (3) of Section 2—319 specifications or arrangements relating to shipment are at the seller's option.

(3) Where such specification would materially affect the other party's performance but is not seasonably made or where one party's cooperation is necessary to the agreed performance of the other but is not seasonably forthcoming, the other party in addition to all other remedies

(a) is excused for any resulting delay in his own performance; and

(b) may also either proceed to perform in any reasonable manner or after the time for a material part of his own performance treat the failure to specify or to cooperate as a breach by failure to deliver or accept the goods.

§ 2—312. Warranty of Title and Against Infringement; Buyer's Obligation Against Infringement.

(1) Subject to subsection (2) there is in a contract for sale a warranty by the seller that

(a) the title conveyed shall be good, and its transfer rightful; and

(b) the goods shall be delivered free from any security interest or other lien or encumbrance of which the buyer at the time of contracting has no knowledge.

(2) A warranty under subsection (1) will be excluded or modified only by specific language or by circumstances which give the buyer reason to know that the person selling does not claim title in himself or that he is purporting to sell only such right or title as he or a third person may have.

(3) Unless otherwise agreed a seller who is a merchant regularly dealing in goods of the kind warrants that the goods shall be delivered free of the rightful claim of any third person by way of infringement or the like but a buyer who furnishes specifications to the seller must hold the seller harmless against any such claim which arises out of compliance with the specifications.

§ 2—313. Express Warranties by Affirmation, Promise, Description, Sample.

(1) Express warranties by the seller are created as follows:

(a) Any affirmation of fact or promise made by the seller to the buyer which relates to the goods and becomes part of the basis of the bargain creates an express warranty that the goods shall conform to the affirmation or promise.

(b) Any description of the goods which is made part of the basis of the bargain creates an express warranty that the goods shall conform to the description.

(c) Any sample or model which is made part of the basis of the bargain creates an express warranty that the whole of the goods shall conform to the sample or model.

(2) It is not necessary to the creation of an express warranty that the seller use formal words such as "warrant" or

"guarantee" or that he have a specific intention to make a warranty, but an affirmation merely of the value of the goods or a statement purporting to be merely the seller's opinion or commendation of the goods does not create a warranty.

§ 2—314. Implied Warranty: Merchantability; Usage of Trade.

(1) Unless excluded or modified (Section 2—316), a warranty that the goods shall be merchantable is implied in a contract for their sale if the seller is a merchant with respect to goods of that kind. Under this section the serving for value of food or drink to be consumed either on the premises or elsewhere is a sale.

(2) Goods to be merchantable must be at least such as

(a) pass without objection in the trade under the contract description; and

(b) in the case of fungible goods, are of fair average quality within the description; and

(c) are fit for the ordinary purposes for which such goods are used; and

(d) run, within the variations permitted by the agreement, of even kind, quality and quantity within each unit and among all units involved; and

(e) are adequately contained, packaged, and labeled as the agreement may require; and

(f) conform to the promises or affirmations of fact made on the container or label if any.

(3) Unless excluded or modified (Section 2—316) other implied warranties may arise from course of dealing or usage of trade.

§ 2—315. Implied Warranty: Fitness for Particular Purpose.

Where the seller at the time of contracting has reason to know any particular purpose for which the goods are required and that the buyer is relying on the seller's skill or judgment to select or furnish suitable goods, there is unless excluded or modified under the next section an implied warranty that the goods shall be fit for such purpose.

§ 2—316. Exclusion or Modification of Warranties.

(1) Words or conduct relevant to the creation of an express warranty and words or conduct tending to negate or limit warranty shall be construed wherever reasonable as consistent with each other; but subject to the provisions of this Article on parol or extrinsic evidence (Section 2—202) negation or limitation is inoperative to the extent that such construction is unreasonable.

(2) Subject to subsection (3), to exclude or modify the implied warranty of merchantability or any part of it the language must mention merchantability and in case of a writing must be conspicuous, and to exclude or modify any implied warranty of fitness the exclusion must be by a writing and conspicuous. Language to exclude all implied warranties of fitness is sufficient if it states, for example, that "There are no warranties which extend beyond the description on the face hereof."

(3) Notwithstanding subsection (2)

(a) unless the circumstances indicate otherwise, all implied warranties are excluded by expressions like "as is", "with all faults" or other language which in common understanding calls the buyer's attention to the exclusion of warranties and makes plain that there is no implied warranty; and

(b) when the buyer before entering into the contract has examined the goods or the sample or model as fully as he desired or has refused to examine the goods there is no implied warranty with regard to defects which an examination ought in the circumstances to have revealed to him; and

(c) an implied warranty can also be excluded or modified by course of dealing or course of performance or usage of trade.

(4) Remedies for breach of warranty can be limited in accordance with the provisions of this Article on liquidation or limitation of damages and on contractual modification of remedy (Sections 2—718 and 2—719).

§ 2—317. Cumulation and Conflict of Warranties Express or Implied.

Warranties whether express or implied shall be construed as consistent with each other and as cumulative, but if such construction is unreasonable the intention of the parties shall determine which warranty is dominant. In ascertaining that intention the following rules apply:

(a) Exact or technical specifications displace an inconsistent sample or model or general language of description.

(b) A sample from an existing bulk displaces inconsistent general language of description.

(c) Express warranties displace inconsistent implied warranties other than an implied warranty of fitness for a particular purpose.

§ 2—318. Third Party Beneficiaries of Warranties Express or Implied.

Note: If this Act is introduced in the Congress of the United States this section should be omitted. (States to select one alternative.)

Alternative A

A seller's warranty whether express or implied extends to any natural person who is in the family or household of his buyer or who is a guest in his home if it is reasonable to expect that such person may use, consume or be affected by the goods and who is injured in person by breach of the warranty. A seller may not exclude or limit the operation of this section.

Alternative B

A seller's warranty whether express or implied extends to any natural person who may reasonably be expected to use, consume or be affected by the goods and who is injured in person by breach of the warranty. A seller may not exclude or limit the operation of this section.

Alternative C

A seller's warranty whether express or implied extends to any person who may reasonably be expected to use, consume or be affected by the goods and who is injured by breach of the warranty. A seller may not exclude or limit the operation of this section with respect to injury to the person of an individual to whom the warranty extends. As amended 1966.

§ 2—319. F.O.B. and F.A.S. Terms.

(1) Unless otherwise agreed the term F.O.B. (which means "free on board") at a named place, even though used only in connection with the stated price, is a delivery term under which

(a) when the term is F.O.B. the place of shipment, the seller must at that place ship the goods in the manner provided in this Article (Section 2—504) and bear the expense and risk of putting them into the possession of the carrier; or

(b) when the term is F.O.B. the place of destination, the seller must at his own expense and risk transport the goods to that place and there tender delivery of them in the manner provided in this Article (Section 2—503);

(c) when under either (a) or (b) the term is also F.O.B. vessel, car or other vehicle, the seller must in addition at his own expense and risk load the goods on board. If the term is F.O.B. vessel the buyer must name the vessel and in an appropriate case the seller must comply with the provisions of this Article on the form of bill of lading (Section 2—323).

(2) Unless otherwise agreed the term F.A.S. vessel (which means "free alongside") at a named port, even though used only in connection with the stated price, is a delivery term under which the seller must

(a) at his own expense and risk deliver the goods alongside the vessel in the manner usual in that port or on a dock designated and provided by the buyer; and

(b) obtain and tender a receipt for the goods in exchange for which the carrier is under a duty to issue a bill of lading.

(3) Unless otherwise agreed in any case falling within subsection (1)(a) or (c) or subsection (2) the buyer must seasonably give any needed instructions for making delivery, including when the term is F.A.S. or F.O.B. the loading berth of the vessel and in an appropriate case its name and sailing date. The seller may treat the failure of needed instructions as a failure of cooperation under this Article (Section 2—311). He may also at his option move the goods in any reasonable manner preparatory to delivery or shipment.

(4) Under the term F.O.B. vessel or F.A.S. unless otherwise agreed the buyer must make payment against tender of the required documents and the seller may not tender nor the buyer demand delivery of the goods in substitution for the documents.

§ 2—320. C.I.F. and C. & F. Terms.

(1) The term C.I.F. means that the price includes in a lump sum the cost of the goods and the insurance and freight to the named destination. The term C. & F. or C.F. means that the price so includes cost and freight to the named destination.

(2) Unless otherwise agreed and even though used only in connection with the stated price and destination, the term C.I.F. destination or its equivalent requires the seller at his own expense and risk to

(a) put the goods into the possession of a carrier at the port for shipment and obtain a negotiable bill or bills of lading covering the entire transportation to the named destination; and

(b) load the goods and obtain a receipt from the carrier (which may be contained in the bill of lading) showing that the freight has been paid or provided for; and

(c) obtain a policy or certificate of insurance, including any war risk insurance, of a kind and on terms then current at the port of shipment in the usual amount, in the currency of the contract, shown to cover the same goods covered by the bill of lading and providing for payment of loss to the order of the buyer or for the account of whom it may concern; but the seller may add to the price the amount of the premium for any such war risk insurance; and

(d) prepare an invoice of the goods and procure any other documents required to effect shipment or to comply with the contract; and

(e) forward and tender with commercial promptness all the documents in due form and with any indorsement necessary to perfect the buyer's rights.

(3) Unless otherwise agreed the term C. & F. or its equivalent has the same effect and imposes upon the seller the same obligations and risks as a C.I.F. term except the obligation as to insurance.

(4) Under the term C.I.F. or C. & F. unless otherwise agreed the buyer must make payment against tender of the required documents and the seller may not tender nor the buyer demand delivery of the goods in substitution for the documents.

§ 2—321. C.I.F. or C. & F.: "Net Landed Weights"; "Payment on Arrival"; Warranty of Condition on Arrival.

Under a contract containing a term C.I.F. or C. & F.

(1) Where the price is based on or is to be adjusted according to "net landed weights", "delivered weights", "out turn" quantity or quality or the like, unless otherwise agreed the seller must reasonably estimate the price. The payment due on tender of the documents called for by the contract is the amount so estimated, but after final adjustment of the price a settlement must be made with commercial promptness.

(2) An agreement described in subsection (1) or any warranty of quality or condition of the goods on arrival places upon the seller the risk of ordinary deterioration, shrinkage and the like in transportation but has no effect on the place or time of identification to the contract for sale or delivery or on the passing of the risk of loss.

(3) Unless otherwise agreed where the contract provides for payment on or after arrival of the goods the seller must before payment allow such preliminary inspection as is feasible; but if the goods are lost delivery of the documents and payment are due when the goods should have arrived.

§ 2—322. Delivery "Ex-Ship".

(1) Unless otherwise agreed a term for delivery of goods "ex-ship" (which means from the carrying vessel) or in equivalent language is not restricted to a particular ship and requires delivery from a ship which has reached a place at the named port of destination where goods of the kind are usually discharged.

(2) Under such a term unless otherwise agreed

(a) the seller must discharge all liens arising out of the carriage and furnish the buyer with a direction which puts the carrier under a duty to deliver the goods; and

(b) the risk of loss does not pass to the buyer until the goods leave the ship's tackle or are otherwise properly unloaded.

§ 2—323. Form of Bill of Lading Required in Overseas Shipment; "Overseas".

(1) Where the contract contemplates overseas shipment and contains a term C.I.F. or C. & F. or F.O.B. vessel, the seller unless otherwise agreed must obtain a negotiable bill of lading stating that the goods have been loaded on board or, in the case of a term C.I.F. or C. & F., received for shipment.

(2) Where in a case within subsection (1) a bill of lading has been issued in a set of parts, unless otherwise agreed if the documents are not to be sent from abroad the buyer may demand tender of the full set; otherwise only one part of the bill of lading need be tendered. Even if the agreement expressly requires a full set

(a) due tender of a single part is acceptable within the provisions of this Article on cure of improper delivery (subsection (1) of Section 2—508); and

(b) even though the full set is demanded, if the documents are sent from abroad the person tendering an incomplete set may nevertheless require payment upon furnishing an indemnity which the buyer in good faith deems adequate.

(3) A shipment by water or by air or a contract contemplating such shipment is "overseas" insofar as by usage of trade or agreement it is subject to the commercial, financing or shipping practices characteristic of international deep water commerce.

§ 2—324. "No Arrival, No Sale" Term.

Under a term "no arrival, no sale" or terms of like meaning, unless otherwise agreed,

(a) the seller must properly ship conforming goods and if they arrive by any means he must tender them on arrival but he assumes no obligation that the goods will arrive unless he has caused the non-arrival; and

(b) where without fault of the seller the goods are in part lost or have so deteriorated as no longer to conform to the contract or arrive after the contract time, the buyer may proceed as if there had been casualty to identified goods (Section 2—613).

§ 2—325. "Letter of Credit" Term; "Confirmed Credit".

(1) Failure of the buyer seasonably to furnish an agreed letter of credit is a breach of the contract for sale.

(2) The delivery to seller of a proper letter of credit suspends the buyer's obligation to pay. If the letter of credit is dishonored, the seller may on seasonable notification to the buyer require payment directly from him.

(3) Unless otherwise agreed the term "letter of credit" or "banker's credit" in a contract for sale means an irrevocable credit issued by a financing agency of good repute and, where the shipment is overseas, of good international repute. The term "confirmed credit" means that the credit must also carry the direct obligation of such an agency which does business in the seller's financial market.

§ 2—326. Sale on Approval and Sale or Return; Consignment Sales and Rights of Creditors.

(1) Unless otherwise agreed, if delivered goods may be returned by the buyer even though they conform to the contract, the transaction is

(a) a "sale on approval" if the goods are delivered primarily for use, and

(b) a "sale or return" if the goods are delivered primarily for resale.

(2) Except as provided in subsection (3), goods held on approval are not subject to the claims of the buyer's creditors until acceptance; goods held on sale or return are subject to such claims while in the buyer's possession.

(3) Where goods are delivered to a person for sale and such person maintains a place of business at which he deals in goods of the kind involved, under a name other than the name of the person making delivery, then with respect to claims of creditors of the person conducting the business the goods are deemed to be on sale or return. The provisions of this subsection are applicable even though an agreement purports to reserve title to the person making delivery until payment or resale or uses such words as "on consignment" or "on memorandum". However, this subsection is not applicable if the person making delivery

(a) complies with an applicable law providing for a consignor's interest or the like to be evidenced by a sign, or

(b) establishes that the person conducting the business is generally known by his creditors to be substantially engaged in selling the goods of others, or

(c) complies with the filing provisions of the Article on Secured Transactions (Article 9).

(4) Any "or return" term of a contract for sale is to be treated as a separate contract for sale within the statute of frauds section of this Article (Section 2—201) and as contradicting the sale aspect of the contract within the provisions of this Article on parol or extrinsic evidence (Section 2—202).

§ 2—327. Special Incidents of Sale on Approval and Sale or Return.

(1) Under a sale on approval unless otherwise agreed

(a) although the goods are identified to the contract the risk of loss and the title do not pass to the buyer until acceptance; and

(b) use of the goods consistent with the purpose of trial is not acceptance but failure seasonably to notify the seller of election to return the goods is acceptance, and if the goods conform to the contract acceptance of any part is acceptance of the whole; and

(c) after due notification of election to return, the return is at the seller's risk and expense but a merchant buyer must follow any reasonable instructions.

(2) Under a sale or return unless otherwise agreed

(a) the option to return extends to the whole or any commercial unit of the goods while in substantially their original condition, but must be exercised seasonably; and

(b) the return is at the buyer's risk and expense.

§ 2—328. Sale by Auction.

(1) In a sale by auction if goods are put up in lots each lot is the subject of a separate sale.

(2) A sale by auction is complete when the auctioneer so announces by the fall of the hammer or in other customary manner. Where a bid is made while the hammer is falling in acceptance of a prior bid the auctioneer may in his discretion reopen the bidding or declare the goods sold under the bid on which the hammer was falling.

(3) Such a sale is with reserve unless the goods are in explicit terms put up without reserve. In an auction with reserve the auctioneer may withdraw the goods at any time until he announces completion of the sale. In an auction without reserve, after the auctioneer calls for bids on an article or lot, that article or lot cannot be withdrawn unless no bid is made within a reasonable time. In either case a bidder may retract his bid until the auctioneer's announcement of completion of the sale, but a bidder's retraction does not revive any previous bid.

(4) If the auctioneer knowingly receives a bid on the seller's behalf or the seller makes or procures such as bid, and notice has not been given that liberty for such bidding is reserved, the buyer may at his option avoid the sale or take the goods at the price of the last good faith bid prior to the completion of the sale. This subsection shall not apply to any bid at a forced sale.

Part 4 Title, Creditors and Good Faith Purchasers

§ 2—401. Passing of Title; Reservation for Security; Limited Application of This Section.

Each provision of this Article with regard to the rights, obligations and remedies of the seller, the buyer, purchasers or other third parties applies irrespective of title to the goods except where the provision refers to such title. Insofar as situations are not covered by the other provisions of this Article and matters concerning title became material the following rules apply:

(1) Title to goods cannot pass under a contract for sale prior to their identification to the contract (Section 2—501), and unless otherwise explicitly agreed the buyer acquires by their identification a special property as limited by this Act. Any retention or reservation by the seller of the title (property) in goods shipped or delivered to the buyer is limited in effect to a reservation of a security interest. Subject to these provisions and to the provisions of the Article on Secured Transactions (Article 9), title to goods passes from the seller to the buyer in any manner and on any conditions explicitly agreed on by the parties.

(2) Unless otherwise explicitly agreed title passes to the buyer at the time and place at which the seller completes his performance with reference to the physical delivery of

the goods, despite any reservation of a security interest and even though a document of title is to be delivered at a different time or place; and in particular and despite any reservation of a security interest by the bill of lading

(a) if the contract requires or authorizes the seller to send the goods to the buyer but does not require him to deliver them at destination, title passes to the buyer at the time and place of shipment; but

(b) if the contract requires delivery at destination, title passes on tender there.

(3) Unless otherwise explicitly agreed where delivery is to be made without moving the goods,

(a) if the seller is to deliver a document of title, title passes at the time when and the place where he delivers such documents; or

(b) if the goods are at the time of contracting already identified and no documents are to be delivered, title passes at the time and place of contracting.

(4) A rejection or other refusal by the buyer to receive or retain the goods, whether or not justified, or a justified revocation of acceptance revests title to the goods in the seller. Such revesting occurs by operation of law and is not a "sale".

§ 2—402. Rights of Seller's Creditors Against Sold Goods.

(1) Except as provided in subsections (2) and (3), rights of unsecured creditors of the seller with respect to goods which have been identified to a contract for sale are subject to the buyer's rights to recover the goods under this Article (Sections 2—502 and 2—716).

(2) A creditor of the seller may treat a sale or an identification of goods to a contract for sale as void if as against him a retention of possession by the seller is fraudulent under any rule of law of the state where the goods are situated, except that retention of possession in good faith and current course of trade by a merchant-seller for a commercially reasonable time after a sale or identification is not fraudulent.

(3) Nothing in this Article shall be deemed to impair the rights of creditors of the seller

(a) under the provisions of the Article on Secured Transactions (Article 9); or

(b) where identification to the contract or delivery is made not in current course of trade but in satisfaction of or as security for a pre-existing claim for money, security or the like and is made under circumstances which under any rule of law of the state where the goods are situated would apart from this Article constitute the transaction a fraudulent transfer or voidable preference.

§ 2—403. Power to Transfer; Good Faith Purchase of Goods; "Entrusting".

(1) A purchaser of goods acquires all title which his transferor had or had power to transfer except that a purchaser of a limited interest acquires rights only to the extent of the interest purchased. A person with voidable title has power to transfer a good title to a good faith purchaser for value. When goods have been delivered under a transaction of purchase the purchaser has such power even though

(a) the transferor was deceived as to the identity of the purchaser, or

(b) the delivery was in exchange for a check which is later dishonored, or

(c) it was agreed that the transaction was to be a "cash sale", or

(d) the delivery was procured through fraud punishable as larcenous under the criminal law.

(2) Any entrusting of possession of goods to a merchant who deals in goods of that kind gives him power to transfer all rights of the entruster to a buyer in ordinary course of business.

(3) "Entrusting" includes any delivery and any acquiescence in retention of possession regardless of any condition expressed between the parties to the delivery or acquiescence and regardless of whether the procurement of the entrusting or the possessor's disposition of the goods have been such as to be larcenous under the criminal law.

(4) The rights of other purchasers of goods and of lien creditors are governed by the Articles on Secured Transactions (Article 9), Bulk Transfers (Article 6) and Documents of Title (Article 7).

Part 5 Performance

§ 2—501. Insurable Interest in Goods; Manner of Identification of Goods.

(1) The buyer obtains a special property and an insurable interest in goods by identification of existing goods as goods to which the contract refers even though the goods so identified are non-conforming and he has an option to return or reject them. Such identification can be made at any time and in any manner explicitly agreed to by the parties. In the absence of explicit agreement identification occurs

(a) when the contract is made if it is for the sale of goods already existing and identified;

(b) if the contract is for the sale of future goods other than those described in paragraph (c), when goods are shipped, marked or otherwise designated by the seller as goods to which the contract refers;

(c) when the crops are planted or otherwise become growing crops or the young are conceived if the contract is for the sale of unborn young to be born within twelve months after contracting or for the sale of crops to be harvested within twelve months or the next normal harvest season after contracting whichever is longer.

(2) The seller retains an insurable interest in goods so long as title to or any security interest in the goods remains in him and where the identification is by the seller alone he may until default or insolvency or notification to the buyer that the identification is final substitute other goods for those identified.

(3) Nothing in this section impairs any insurable interest recognized under any other statute or rule of law.

§ 2—502. Buyer's Right to Goods on Seller's Insolvency.

(1) Subject to subsection (2) and even though the goods have not been shipped a buyer who has paid a part or all of the price of goods in which he has a special property under the provisions of the immediately preceding section may on making and keeping good a tender of any unpaid portion of their price recover them from the seller if the seller becomes insolvent within ten days after receipt of the first installment on their price.

(2) If the identification creating his special property has been made by the buyer he acquires the right to recover the goods only if they conform to the contract for sale.

§ 2—503. Manner of Seller's Tender of Delivery.

(1) Tender of delivery requires that the seller put and hold conforming goods at the buyer's disposition and give the buyer any notification reasonably necessary to enable him to take delivery. The manner, time and place for tender are determined by the agreement and this Article, and in particular

(a) tender must be at a reasonable hour, and if it is of goods they must be kept available for the period reasonably necessary to enable the buyer to take possession; but

(b) unless otherwise agreed the buyer must furnish facilities reasonably suited to the receipt of the goods.

(2) Where the case is within the next section respecting shipment tender requires that the seller comply with its provisions.

(3) Where the seller is required to deliver at a particular destination tender requires that he comply with subsection (1) and also in any appropriate case tender documents as described in subsections (4) and (5) of this section.

(4) Where goods are in the possession of a bailee and are to be delivered without being moved

(a) tender requires that the seller either tender a negotiable document of title covering such goods or procure acknowledgment by the bailee of the buyer's right to possession of the goods; but

(b) tender to the buyer of a non-negotiable document of title or of a written direction to the bailee to deliver is sufficient tender unless the buyer seasonably objects, and receipt by the bailee of notification of the buyer's rights fixes those rights as against the bailee and all third persons; but risk of loss of the goods and of any failure by the bailee to honor the non-negotiable document of title or to obey the direction remains on the seller until the buyer has had a reasonable time to present the document or direction, and a refusal by the bailee to honor the document or to obey the direction defeats the tender.

(5) Where the contract requires the seller to deliver documents

(a) he must tender all such documents in correct form, except as provided in this Article with respect to bills of lading in a set (subsection (2) of Section 2—323); and

(b) tender through customary banking channels is sufficient and dishonor of a draft accompanying the documents constitutes non-acceptance or rejection.

§ 2—504. Shipment by Seller.

Where the seller is required or authorized to send the goods to the buyer and the contract does not require him to deliver them at a particular destination, then unless otherwise agreed he must

(a) put the goods in the possession of such a carrier and make such a contract for their transportation as may be reasonable having regard to the nature of the goods and other circumstances of the case; and

(b) obtain and promptly deliver or tender in due form any document necessary to enable the buyer to obtain possession of the goods or otherwise required by the agreement or by usage of trade; and

(c) promptly notify the buyer of the shipment.

Failure to notify the buyer under paragraph (c) or to make a proper contract under paragraph (a) is a ground for rejection only if material delay or loss ensues.

§ 2—505. Seller's Shipment under Reservation.

(1) Where the seller has identified goods to the contract by or before shipment:

(a) his procurement of a negotiable bill of lading to his own order or otherwise reserves in him a security interest in the goods. His procurement of the bill to the order of a financing agency or of the buyer indicates in addition only the seller's expectation of transferring that interest to the person named.

(b) a non-negotiable bill of lading to himself or his nominee reserves possession of the goods as security but except in a case of conditional delivery (subsection (2) of Section 2—507) a non-negotiable bill of lading naming the buyer as consignee reserves no security interest even though the seller retains possession of the bill of lading.

(2) When shipment by the seller with reservation of a security interest is in violation of the contract for sale it constitutes

an improper contract for transportation within the preceding section but impairs neither the rights given to the buyer by shipment and identification of the goods to the contract nor the seller's powers as a holder of a negotiable document.

§ 2—506. Rights of Financing Agency.

(1) A financing agency by paying or purchasing for value a draft which relates to a shipment of goods acquires to the extent of the payment or purchase and in addition to its own rights under the draft and any document of title securing it any rights of the shipper in the goods including the right to stop delivery and the shipper's right to have the draft honored by the buyer.

(2) The right to reimbursement of a financing agency which has in good faith honored or purchased the draft under commitment to or authority from the buyer is not impaired by subsequent discovery of defects with reference to any relevant document which was apparently regular on its face.

§ 2—507. Effect of Seller's Tender; Delivery on Condition.

(1) Tender of delivery is a condition to the buyer's duty to accept the goods and, unless otherwise agreed, to his duty to pay for them. Tender entitles the seller to acceptance of the goods and to payment according to the contract.

(2) Where payment is due and demanded on the delivery to the buyer of goods or documents of title, his right as against the seller to retain or dispose of them is conditional upon his making the payment due.

§ 2—508. Cure by Seller of Improper Tender or Delivery; Replacement.

(1) Where any tender or delivery by the seller is rejected because non-conforming and the time for performance has not yet expired, the seller may seasonably notify the buyer of his intention to cure and may then within the contract time make a conforming delivery.

(2) Where the buyer rejects a non-conforming tender which the seller had reasonable grounds to believe would be acceptable with or without money allowance the seller may if he seasonably notifies the buyer have a further reasonable time to substitute a conforming tender.

§ 2—509. Risk of Loss in the Absence of Breach.

(1) Where the contract requires or authorizes the seller to ship the goods by carrier

(a) if it does not require him to deliver them at a particular destination, the risk of loss passes to the buyer when the goods are duly delivered to the carrier even though the shipment is under reservation (Section 2—505); but

(b) if it does require him to deliver them at a particular destination and the goods are there duly tendered while in the possession of the carrier, the risk of loss passes to the buyer when the goods are there duly so tendered as to enable the buyer to take delivery.

(2) Where the goods are held by a bailee to be delivered without being moved, the risk of loss passes to the buyer

(a) on his receipt of a negotiable document of title covering the goods; or

(b) on acknowledgment by the bailee of the buyer's right to possession of the goods; or

(c) after his receipt of a non-negotiable document of title or other written direction to deliver, as provided in subsection (4)(b) of Section 2—503.

(3) In any case not within subsection (1) or (2), the risk of loss passes to the buyer on his receipt of the goods if the seller is a merchant; otherwise the risk passes to the buyer on tender of delivery.

(4) The provisions of this section are subject to contrary agreement of the parties and to the provisions of this Article on sale on approval (Section 2—327) and on effect of breach on risk of loss (Section 2—510).

§ 2—510. Effect of Breach on Risk of Loss.

(1) Where a tender or delivery of goods so fails to conform to the contract as to give a right of rejection the risk of their loss remains on the seller until cure or acceptance.

(2) Where the buyer rightfully revokes acceptance he may to the extent of any deficiency in his effective insurance coverage treat the risk of loss as having rested on the seller from the beginning.

(3) Where the buyer as to conforming goods already identified to the contract for sale repudiates or is otherwise in breach before risk of their loss has passed to him, the seller may to the extent of any deficiency in his effective insurance coverage treat the risk of loss as resting on the buyer for a commercially reasonable time.

§ 2—511. Tender of Payment by Buyer; Payment by Check.

(1) Unless otherwise agreed tender of payment is a condition to the seller's duty to tender and complete any delivery.

(2) Tender of payment is sufficient when made by any means or in any manner current in the ordinary course of business unless the seller demands payment in legal tender and gives any extension of time reasonably necessary to procure it.

(3) Subject to the provisions of this Act on the effect of an instrument on an obligation (Section 3—802), payment by check is conditional and is defeated as between the parties by dishonor of the check on due presentment.

§ 2—512. Payment by Buyer Before Inspection.

(1) Where the contract requires payment before inspection non-conformity of the goods does not excuse the buyer from so making payment unless

(a) the non-conformity appears without inspection; or

(b) despite tender of the required documents the circumstances would justify injunction against honor under the provisions of this Act (Section 5—114).

(2) Payment pursuant to subsection (1) does not constitute an acceptance of goods or impair the buyer's right to inspect or any of his remedies.

§ 2—513. Buyer's Right to Inspection of Goods.

(1) Unless otherwise agreed and subject to subsection (3), where goods are tendered or delivered or identified to the contract for sale, the buyer has a right before payment or acceptance to inspect them at any reasonable place and time and in any reasonable manner. When the seller is required or authorized to send the goods to the buyer, the inspection may be after their arrival.

(2) Expenses of inspection must be borne by the buyer but may be recovered from the seller if the goods do not conform and are rejected.

(3) Unless otherwise agreed and subject to the provisions of this Article on C.I.F. contracts (subsection (3) of Section 2—321), the buyer is not entitled to inspect the goods before payment of the price when the contract provides

(a) for delivery "C.O.D." or on other like terms; or

(b) for payment against documents of title, except where such payment is due only after the goods are to become available for inspection.

(4) A place or method of inspection fixed by the parties is presumed to be exclusive but unless otherwise expressly agreed it does not postpone identification or shift the place for delivery or for passing the risk of loss. If compliance becomes impossible, inspection shall be as provided in this section unless the place or method fixed was clearly intended as an indispensable condition failure of which avoids the contract.

§ 2—514. When Documents Deliverable on Acceptance; When on Payment.

Unless otherwise agreed documents against which a draft is drawn are to be delivered to the drawee on acceptance of the draft if it is payable more than three days after presentment; otherwise, only on payment.

§ 2—515. Preserving Evidence of Goods in Dispute.

In furtherance of the adjustment of any claim or dispute

(a) either party on reasonable notification to the other and for the purpose of ascertaining the facts and preserving evidence has the right to inspect, test and sample the goods including such of them as may be in the possession or control of the other; and

(b) the parties may agree to a third party inspection or survey to determine the conformity or condition of the goods and may agree that the findings shall be binding upon them in any subsequent litigation or adjustment.

Part 6 Breach, Repudiation and Excuse

§ 2—601. Buyer's Rights on Improper Delivery.

Subject to the provisions of this Article on breach in installment contracts (Section 2—612) and unless otherwise agreed under the sections on contractual limitations of remedy (Sections 2—718 and 2—719), if the goods or the tender of delivery fail in any respect to conform to the contract, the buyer may

(a) reject the whole; or

(b) accept the whole; or

(c) accept any commercial unit or units and reject the rest.

§ 2—602. Manner and Effect of Rightful Rejection.

(1) Rejection of goods must be within a reasonable time after their delivery or tender. It is ineffective unless the buyer seasonably notifies the seller.

(2) Subject to the provisions of the two following sections on rejected goods (Sections 2—603 and 2—604),

(a) after rejection any exercise of ownership by the buyer with respect to any commercial unit is wrongful as against the seller; and

(b) if the buyer has before rejection taken physical possession of goods in which he does not have a security interest under the provisions of this Article (subsection (3) of Section 2—711), he is under a duty after rejection to hold them with reasonable care at the seller's disposition for a time sufficient to permit the seller to remove them; but

(c) the buyer has no further obligations with regard to goods rightfully rejected.

(3) The seller's rights with respect to goods wrongfully rejected are governed by the provisions of this Article on Seller's remedies in general (Section 2—703).

§ 2—603. Merchant Buyer's Duties as to Rightfully Rejected Goods.

(1) Subject to any security interest in the buyer (subsection (3) of Section 2—711), when the seller has no agent or place of business at the market of rejection a merchant buyer is under a duty after rejection of goods in his possession or control to follow any reasonable instructions received from the seller with respect to the goods and in the absence of such instructions to make reasonable efforts to sell them for the seller's account if they are perishable or threaten to decline in value speedily. Instructions are not reasonable if on demand indemnity for expenses is not forthcoming.

(2) When the buyer sells goods under subsection (1), he is entitled to reimbursement from the seller or out of the proceeds for reasonable expenses of caring for and selling them, and if the expenses include no selling commission then to such commission as is usual in the trade or if there is none to a reasonable sum not exceeding ten per cent on the gross proceeds.

(3) In complying with this section the buyer is held only to good faith and good faith conduct hereunder is neither acceptance nor conversion nor the basis of an action for damages.

§ 2—604. Buyer's Options as to Salvage of Rightfully Rejected Goods.

Subject to the provisions of the immediately preceding section on perishables if the seller gives no instructions within a reasonable time after notification of rejection the buyer may store the rejected goods for the seller's account or reship them to him or resell them for the seller's account with reimbursement as provided in the preceding section. Such action is not acceptance or conversion.

§ 2—605. Waiver of Buyer's Objections by Failure to Particularize.

(1) The buyer's failure to state in connection with rejection a particular defect which is ascertainable by reasonable inspection precludes him from relying on the unstated defect to justify rejection or to establish breach

(a) where the seller could have cured it if stated seasonably; or

(b) between merchants when the seller has after rejection made a request in writing for a full and final written statement of all defects on which the buyer proposes to rely.

(2) Payment against documents made without reservation of rights precludes recovery of the payment for defects apparent on the face of the documents.

§ 2—606. What Constitutes Acceptance of Goods.

(1) Acceptance of goods occurs when the buyer

(a) after a reasonable opportunity to inspect the goods signifies to the seller that the goods are conforming or that he will take or retain them in spite of their non-conformity; or

(b) fails to make an effective rejection (subsection (1) of Section 2—602), but such acceptance does not occur until the buyer has had a reasonable opportunity to inspect them; or

(c) does any act inconsistent with the seller's ownership; but if such act is wrongful as against the seller it is an acceptance only if ratified by him.

(2) Acceptance of a part of any commercial unit is acceptance of that entire unit.

§ 2—607. Effect of Acceptance; Notice of Breach; Burden of Establishing Breach After Acceptance; Notice of Claim or Litigation to Person Answerable Over.

(1) The buyer must pay at the contract rate for any goods accepted.

(2) Acceptance of goods by the buyer precludes rejection of the goods accepted and if made with knowledge of a non-conformity cannot be revoked because of it unless the acceptance was on the reasonable assumption that the non-conformity would be seasonably cured but acceptance does not of itself impair any other remedy provided by this Article for non-conformity.

(3) Where a tender has been accepted

(a) the buyer must within a reasonable time after he discovers or should have discovered any breach notify the seller of breach or be barred from any remedy; and

(b) if the claim is one for infringement or the like (subsection (3) of Section 2—312) and the buyer is sued as a result of such a breach he must so notify the seller within a reasonable time after he receives notice of the litigation or be barred from any remedy over for liability established by the litigation.

(4) The burden is on the buyer to establish any breach with respect to the goods accepted.

(5) Where the buyer is sued for breach of a warranty or other obligation for which his seller is answerable over

(a) he may give his seller written notice of the litigation. If the notice states that the seller may come in and defend and that if the seller does not do so he will be bound in any action against him by his buyer by any determination of fact common to the two litigations, then unless the seller after seasonable receipt of the notice does come in and defend he is so bound.

(b) if the claim is one for infringement or the like (subsection (3) of Section 2—312) the original seller may demand in writing that his buyer turn over to him control of the litigation including settlement or else be barred from any remedy over and if he also agrees to bear all expense and to satisfy any adverse judgment, then unless the buyer after seasonable receipt of the demand does turn over control the buyer is so barred.

(6) The provisions of subsections (3), (4) and (5) apply to any obligation of a buyer to hold the seller harmless against infringement or the like (subsection (3) of Section 2—312).

§ 2—608. Revocation of Acceptance in Whole or in Part.

(1) The buyer may revoke his acceptance of a lot or commercial unit whose non-conformity substantially impairs its value to him if he has accepted it

(a) on the reasonable assumption that its nonconformity would be cured and it has not been seasonably cured; or

(b) without discovery of such non-conformity if his acceptance was reasonably induced either by the difficulty of discovery before acceptance or by the seller's assurances.

(2) Revocation of acceptance must occur within a reasonable time after the buyer discovers or should have discovered the ground for it and before any substantial change in condition of the goods which is not caused by their own defects. It is not effective until the buyer notifies the seller of it.

(3) A buyer who so revokes has the same rights and duties with regard to the goods involved as if he had rejected them.

§ 2—609. Right to Adequate Assurance of Performance.

(1) A contract for sale imposes an obligation on each party that the other's expectation of receiving due performance will not be impaired. When reasonable grounds for insecurity arise with respect to the performance of either party the other may in writing demand adequate assurance of due performance and until he receives such assurance may if commercially reasonable suspend any performance for which he has not already received the agreed return.

(2) Between merchants the reasonableness of grounds for insecurity and the adequacy of any assurance offered shall be determined according to commercial standards.

(3) Acceptance of any improper delivery or payment does not prejudice the party's right to demand adequate assurance of future performance.

(4) After receipt of a justified demand failure to provide within a reasonable time not exceeding thirty days such assurance of due performance as is adequate under the circumstances of the particular case is a repudiation of the contract.

§ 2—610. Anticipatory Repudiation.

When either party repudiates the contract with respect to a performance not yet due the loss of which will substantially impair the value of the contract to the other, the aggrieved party may

(a) for a commercially reasonable time await performance by the repudiating party; or

(b) resort to any remedy for breach (Section 2—703 or Section 2—711), even though he has notified the repudiating party that he would await the latter's performance and has urged retraction; and

(c) in either case suspend his own performance or proceed in accordance with the provisions of this Article on the seller's right to identify goods to the contract notwithstanding breach or to salvage unfinished goods (Section 2—704).

§ 2—611. Retraction of Anticipatory Repudiation.

(1) Until the repudiating party's next performance is due he can retract his repudiation unless the aggrieved party has since the repudiation cancelled or materially changed his position or otherwise indicated that he considers the repudiation final.

(2) Retraction may be by any method which clearly indicates to the aggrieved party that the repudiating party intends to perform, but must include any assurance justifiably demanded under the provisions of this Article (Section 2—609).

(3) Retraction reinstates the repudiating party's rights under the contract with due excuse and allowance to the aggrieved party for any delay occasioned by the repudiation.

§ 2—612. "Installment Contract"; Breach.

(1) An "installment contract" is one which requires or authorizes the delivery of goods in separate lots to be separately accepted, even though the contract contains a clause "each delivery is a separate contract" or its equivalent.

(2) The buyer may reject any installment which is non-conforming if the non-conformity substantially impairs the value of that installment and cannot be cured or if the non-conformity is a defect in the required documents; but if the non-conformity does not fall within subsection (3) and the seller gives adequate assurance of its cure the buyer must accept that installment.

(3) Whenever non-conformity or default with respect to one or more installments substantially impairs the value of the whole contract there is a breach of the whole. But the aggrieved party reinstates the contract if he accepts a non-conforming installment without seasonably notifying of cancellation or if he brings an action with respect only to past installments or demands performance as to future installments.

§ 2—613. Casualty to Identified Goods.

Where the contract requires for its performance goods identified when the contract is made, and the goods suffer casualty without fault of either party before the risk of loss passes to the buyer, or in a proper case under a "no arrival, no sale" term (Section 2—324) then

(a) if the loss is total the contract is avoided; and

(b) if the loss is partial or the goods have so deteriorated as no longer to conform to the contract the buyer may nevertheless demand inspection and at his option either treat the contract as voided or accept the goods with due allowance from the contract price for the deterioration or the deficiency in quantity but without further right against the seller.

§ 2—614. Substituted Performance.

(1) Where without fault of either party the agreed berthing, loading, or unloading facilities fail or an agreed

type of carrier becomes unavailable or the agreed manner of delivery otherwise becomes commercially impracticable but a commercially reasonable substitute is available, such substitute performance must be tendered and accepted.

(2) If the agreed means or manner of payment fails because of domestic or foreign governmental regulation, the seller may withhold or stop delivery unless the buyer provides a means or manner of payment which is commercially a substantial equivalent. If delivery has already been taken, payment by the means or in the manner provided by the regulation discharges the buyer's obligation unless the regulation is discriminatory, oppressive or predatory.

§ 2—615. Excuse by Failure of Presupposed Conditions.

Except so far as a seller may have assumed a greater obligation and subject to the preceding section on substituted performance:

(a) Delay in delivery or non-delivery in whole or in part by a seller who complies with paragraphs (b) and (c) is not a breach of his duty under a contract for sale if performance as agreed has been made impracticable by the occurrence of a contingency the nonoccurrence of which was a basic assumption on which the contract was made or by compliance in good faith with any applicable foreign or domestic governmental regulation or order whether or not it later proves to be invalid.

(b) Where the causes mentioned in paragraph (a) affect only a part of the seller's capacity to perform, he must allocate production and deliveries among his customers but may at his option include regular customers not then under contract as well as his own requirements for further manufacture. He may so allocate in any manner which is fair and reasonable.

(c) The seller must notify the buyer seasonably that there will be delay or non-delivery and, when allocation is required under paragraph (b), of the estimated quota thus made available for the buyer.

§ 2—616. Procedure on Notice Claiming Excuse.

(1) Where the buyer receives notification of a material or indefinite delay or an allocation justified under the preceding section he may by written notification to the seller as to any delivery concerned, and where the prospective deficiency substantially impairs the value of the whole contract under the provisions of this Article relating to breach of installment contracts (Section 2—612), then also as to the whole,

(a) terminate and thereby discharge any unexecuted portion of the contract; or

(b) modify the contract by agreeing to take his available quota in substitution.

(2) If after receipt of such notification from the seller the buyer fails so to modify the contract within a reasonable time not exceeding thirty days the contract lapses with respect to any deliveries affected.

(3) The provisions of this section may not be negated by agreement except in so far as the seller has assumed a greater obligation under the preceding section.

Part 7 Remedies

§ 2—701. Remedies for Breach of Collateral Contracts Not Impaired.

Remedies for breach of any obligation or promise collateral or ancillary to a contract for sale are not impaired by the provisions of this Article.

§ 2—702. Seller's Remedies on Discovery of Buyer's Insolvency.

(1) Where the seller discovers the buyer to be insolvent he may refuse delivery except for cash including payment for all goods theretofore delivered under the contract, and stop delivery under this Article (Section 2—705).

(2) Where the seller discovers that the buyer has received goods on credit while insolvent he may reclaim the goods upon demand made within ten days after the receipt, but if misrepresentation of solvency has been made to the particular seller in writing within three months before delivery the ten day limitation does not apply. Except as provided in this subsection the seller may not base a right to reclaim goods on the buyer's fraudulent or innocent misrepresentation of solvency or of intent to pay.

(3) The seller's right to reclaim under subsection (2) is subject to the rights of a buyer in ordinary course or other good faith purchaser under this Article (Section 2—403). Successful reclamation of goods excludes all other remedies with respect to them.

§ 2—703. Seller's Remedies in General.

Where the buyer wrongfully rejects or revokes acceptance of goods or fails to make a payment due on or before delivery or repudiates with respect to a part or the whole, then with respect to any goods directly affected and, if the breach is of the whole contract (Section 2—612), then also with respect to the whole undelivered balance, the aggrieved seller may

(a) withhold delivery of such goods;

(b) stop delivery by any bailee as hereafter provided (Section 2—705);

(c) proceed under the next section respecting goods still unidentified to the contract;

(d) resell and recover damages as hereafter provided (Section 2—706);

(e) recover damages for non-acceptance (Section 2—708) or in a proper case the price (Section 2—709);

(f) cancel.

§ 2—704. Seller's Right to Identify Goods to the Contract Notwithstanding Breach or to Salvage Unfinished Goods.

(1) An aggrieved seller under the preceding section may

(a) identify to the contract conforming goods not already identified if at the time he learned of the breach they are in his possession or control;

(b) treat as the subject of resale goods which have demonstrably been intended for the particular contract even though those goods are unfinished.

(2) Where the goods are unfinished an aggrieved seller may in the exercise of reasonable commercial judgment for the purposes of avoiding loss and of effective realization either complete the manufacture and wholly identify the goods to the contract or cease manufacture and resell for scrap or salvage value or proceed in any other reasonable manner.

§ 2—705. Seller's Stoppage of Delivery in Transit or Otherwise.

(1) The seller may stop delivery of goods in the possession of a carrier or other bailee when he discovers the buyer to be insolvent (Section 2—702) and may stop delivery of carload, truckload, planeload or larger shipments of express or freight when the buyer repudiates or fails to make a payment due before delivery or if for any other reason the seller has a right to withhold or reclaim the goods.

(2) As against such buyer the seller may stop delivery until

(a) receipt of the goods by the buyer; or

(b) acknowledgment to the buyer by any bailee of the goods except a carrier that the bailee holds the goods for the buyer; or

(c) such acknowledgment to the buyer by a carrier by reshipment or as warehouseman; or

(d) negotiation to the buyer of any negotiable document of title covering the goods.

(3) (a) To stop delivery the seller must so notify as to enable the bailee by reasonable diligence to prevent delivery of the goods.

(b) After such notification the bailee must hold and deliver the goods according to the directions of the seller but the seller is liable to the bailee for any ensuing charges or damages.

(c) If a negotiable document of title has been issued for goods the bailee is not obliged to obey a notification to stop until surrender of the document.

(d) A carrier who has issued a non-negotiable bill of lading is not obliged to obey a notification to stop received from a person other than the consignor.

§ 2—706. Seller's Resale Including Contract for Resale.

(1) Under the conditions stated in Section 2—703 on seller's remedies, the seller may resell the goods concerned or the undelivered balance thereof. Where the resale is made in good faith and in a commercially reasonable manner the seller may recover the difference between the resale price and the contract price together with any incidental damages allowed under the provisions of this Article (Section 2—710), but less expenses saved in consequence of the buyer's breach.

(2) Except as otherwise provided in subsection (3) or unless otherwise agreed resale may be at public or private sale including sale by way of one or more contracts to sell or of identification to an existing contract of the seller. Sale may be as a unit or in parcels and at any time and place and on any terms but every aspect of the sale including the method, manner, time, place and terms must be commercially reasonable. The resale must be reasonably identified as referring to the broken contract, but it is not necessary that the goods be in existence or that any or all of them have been identified to the contract before the breach.

(3) Where the resale is at private sale the seller must give the buyer reasonable notification of his intention to resell.

(4) Where the resale is at public sale

(a) only identified goods can be sold except where there is a recognized market for a public sale of futures in goods of the kind; and

(b) it must be made at a usual place or market for public sale if one is reasonably available and except in the case of goods which are perishable or threaten to decline in value speedily the seller must give the buyer reasonable notice of the time and place of the resale; and

(c) if the goods are not to be within the view of those attending the sale the notification of sale must state the place where the goods are located and provide for their reasonable inspection by prospective bidders; and

(d) the seller may buy.

(5) A purchaser who buys in good faith at a resale takes the goods free of any rights of the original buyer even though the seller fails to comply with one or more of the requirements of this section.

(6) The seller is not accountable to the buyer for any profit made on any resale. A person in the position of a seller (Section 2—707) or a buyer who has rightfully rejected or justifiably revoked acceptance must account for any excess over the amount of his security interest, as hereinafter defined (subsection (3) of Section 2—711).

§ 2—707. "Person in the Position of a Seller".

(1) A "person in the position of a seller" includes as against a principal an agent who has paid or become responsible for the price of goods on behalf of his principal or anyone who otherwise holds a security interest or other right in goods similar to that of a seller.

(2) A person in the position of a seller may as provided in this Article withhold or stop delivery (Section 2—705) and

resell (Section 2—706) and recover incidental damages (Section 2—710).

§ 2—708. Seller's Damages for Non-Acceptance or Repudiation.

(1) Subject to subsection (2) and to the provisions of this Article with respect to proof of market price (Section 2—723), the measure of damages for non-acceptance or repudiation by the buyer is the difference between the market price at the time and place for tender and the unpaid contract price together with any incidental damages provided in this Article (Section 2—710), but less expenses saved in consequence of the buyer's breach.

(2) If the measure of damages provided in subsection (1) is inadequate to put the seller in as good a position as performance would have done then the measure of damages is the profit (including reasonable overhead) which the seller would have made from full performance by the buyer, together with any incidental damages provided in this Article (Section 2—710), due allowance for costs reasonably incurred and due credit for payments or proceeds of resale.

§ 2—709. Action for the Price.

(1) When the buyer fails to pay the price as it becomes due the seller may recover, together with any incidental damages under the next section, the price

(a) of goods accepted or of conforming goods lost or damaged within a commercially reasonable time after risk of their loss has passed to the buyer; and

(b) of goods identified to the contract if the seller is unable after reasonable effort to resell them at a reasonable price or the circumstances reasonably indicate that such effort will be unavailing.

(2) Where the seller sues for the price he must hold for the buyer any goods which have been identified to the contract and are still in his control except that if resale becomes possible he may resell them at any time prior to the collection of the judgment. The net proceeds of any such resale must be credited to the buyer and payment of the judgment entitles him to any goods not resold.

(3) After the buyer has wrongfully rejected or revoked acceptance of the goods or has failed to make a payment due or has repudiated (Section 2—610), a seller who is held not entitled to the price under this section shall nevertheless be awarded damages for non-acceptance under the preceding section.

§ 2—710. Seller's Incidental Damages.

Incidental damages to an aggrieved seller include any commercially reasonable charges, expenses or commissions incurred in stopping delivery, in the transportation, care and custody of goods after the buyer's breach, in connection with return or resale of the goods or otherwise resulting from the breach.

§ 2—711. Buyer's Remedies in General; Buyer's Security Interest in Rejected Goods.

(1) Where the seller fails to make delivery or repudiates or the buyer rightfully rejects or justifiably revokes acceptance then with respect to any goods involved, and with respect to the whole if the breach goes to the whole contract (Section 2—612), the buyer may cancel and whether or not he has done so may in addition to recovering so much of the price as has been paid

(a) "cover" and have damages under the next section as to all the goods affected whether or not they have been identified to the contract; or

(b) recover damages for non-delivery as provided in this Article (Section 2—713).

(2) Where the seller fails to deliver or repudiates the buyer may also

(a) if the goods have been identified recover them as provided in this Article (Section 2—502); or

(b) in a proper case obtain specific performance or replevy the goods as provided in this Article (Section 2—716).

(3) On rightful rejection or justifiable revocation of acceptance a buyer has a security interest in goods in his possession or control for any payments made on their price and any expenses reasonably incurred in their inspection, receipt, transportation, care and custody and may hold such goods and resell them in like manner as an aggrieved seller (Section 2—706).

§ 2—712. "Cover"; Buyer's Procurement of Substitute Goods.

(1) After a breach within the preceding section the buyer may "cover" by making in good faith and without unreasonable delay any reasonable purchase of or contract to purchase goods in substitution for those due from the seller.

(2) The buyer may recover from the seller as damages the difference between the cost of cover and the contract price together with any incidental or consequential damages as hereinafter defined (Section 2—715), but less expenses saved in consequence of the seller's breach.

(3) Failure of the buyer to effect cover within this section does not bar him from any other remedy.

§ 2—713. Buyer's Damages for Non-Delivery or Repudiation.

(1) Subject to the provisions of this Article with respect to proof of market price (Section 2—723), the measure of damages for non-delivery or repudiation by the seller is the difference between the market price at the time when the buyer learned of the breach and the contract price together with any incidental and consequential damages provided in this Article (Section 2—715), but less expenses saved in consequence of the seller's breach.

(2) Market price is to be determined as of the place for

tender or, in cases of rejection after arrival or revocation of acceptance, as of the place of arrival.

§ 2—714. Buyer's Damages for Breach in Regard to Accepted Goods.

(1) Where the buyer has accepted goods and given notification (subsection (3) of Section 2—607) he may recover as damages for any non-conformity of tender the loss resulting in the ordinary course of events from the seller's breach as determined in any manner which is reasonable.

(2) The measure of damages for breach of warranty is the difference at the time and place of acceptance between the value of the goods accepted and the value they would have had if they had been as warranted, unless special circumstances show proximate damages of a different amount.

(3) In a proper case any incidental and consequential damages under the next section may also be recovered.

§ 2—715. Buyer's Incidental and Consequential Damages.

(1) Incidental damages resulting from the seller's breach include expenses reasonably incurred in inspection, receipt, transportation and care and custody of goods rightfully rejected, any commercially reasonable charges, expenses or commissions in connection with effecting cover and any other reasonable expense incident to the delay or other breach.

(2) Consequential damages resulting from the seller's breach include

(a) any loss resulting from general or particular requirements and needs of which the seller at the time of contracting had reason to know and which could not reasonably be prevented by cover or otherwise; and

(b) injury to person or property proximately resulting from any breach of warranty.

§ 2—716. Buyer's Right to Specific Performance or Replevin.

(1) Specific performance may be decreed where the goods are unique or in other proper circumstances.

(2) The decree for specific performance may include such terms and conditions as to payment of the price, damages, or other relief as the court may deem just.

(3) The buyer has a right of replevin for goods identified to the contract if after reasonable effort he is unable to effect cover for such goods or the circumstances reasonably indicate that such effort will be unavailing or if the goods have been shipped under reservation and satisfaction of the security interest in them has been made or tendered.

§ 2—717. Deduction of Damages From the Price.

The buyer on notifying the seller of his intention to do so may deduct all or any part of the damages resulting from any breach of the contract from any part of the price still due under the same contract.

§ 2—718. Liquidation or Limitation of Damages; Deposits.

(1) Damages for breach by either party may be liquidated in the agreement but only at an amount which is reasonable in the light of the anticipated or actual harm caused by the breach, the difficulties of proof of loss, and the inconvenience or nonfeasibility of otherwise obtaining an adequate remedy. A term fixing unreasonably large liquidated damages is void as a penalty.

(2) Where the seller justifiably withholds delivery of goods because of the buyer's breach, the buyer is entitled to restitution of any amount by which the sum of his payments exceeds

(a) the amount to which the seller is entitled by virtue of terms liquidating the seller's damages in accordance with subsection (1), or

(b) in the absence of such terms, twenty per cent of the value of the total performance for which the buyer is obligated under the contract or $500, whichever is smaller.

(3) The buyer's right to restitution under subsection (2) is subject to offset to the extent that the seller establishes

(a) a right to recover damages under the provisions of this Article other than subsection (1), and

(b) the amount or value of any benefits received by the buyer directly or indirectly by reason of the contract.

(4) Where a seller has received payment in goods their reasonable value or the proceeds of their resale shall be treated as payments for the purposes of subsection (2); but if the seller has notice of the buyer's breach before reselling goods received in part performance, his resale is subject to the conditions laid down in this Article on resale by an aggrieved seller (Section 2—706).

§ 2—719. Contractual Modification or Limitation of Remedy.

(1) Subject to the provisions of subsections (2) and (3) of this section and of the preceding section on liquidation and limitation of damages,

(a) the agreement may provide for remedies in addition to or in substitution for those provided in this Article and may limit or alter the measure of damages recoverable under this Article, as by limiting the buyer's remedies to return of the goods and repayment of the price or to repair and replacement of nonconforming goods or parts; and

(b) resort to a remedy as provided is optional unless the remedy is expressly agreed to be exclusive, in which case it is the sole remedy.

(2) Where circumstances cause an exclusive or limited remedy to fail of its essential purpose, remedy may be had as provided in this Act.

(3) Consequential damages may be limited or excluded

unless the limitation or exclusion is unconscionable. Limitation of consequential damages for injury to the person in the case of consumer goods is prima facie unconscionable but limitation of damages where the loss is commercial is not.

§ 2—720. Effect of "Cancellation" or "Rescission" on Claims for Antecedent Breach.

Unless the contrary intention clearly appears, expressions of "cancellation" or "rescission" of the contract or the like shall not be construed as a renunciation or discharge of any claim in damages for an antecedent breach.

§ 2—721. Remedies for Fraud.

Remedies for material misrepresentation or fraud include all remedies available under this Article for non-fraudulent breach. Neither rescission or a claim for rescission of the contract for sale nor rejection or return of the goods shall bar or be deemed inconsistent with a claim for damages or other remedy.

§ 2—722. Who Can Sue Third Parties for Injury to Goods.

Where a third party so deals with goods which have been identified to a contract for sale as to cause actionable injury to a party to that contract

(a) a right of action against the third party is in either party to the contract for sale who has title to or a security interest or a special property or an insurable interest in the goods; and if the goods have been destroyed or converted a right of action is also in the party who either bore the risk of loss under the contract for sale or has since the injury assumed that risk as against the other;

(b) if at the time of the injury the party plaintiff did not bear the risk of loss as against the other party to the contract for sale and there is no arrangement between them for disposition of the recovery, his suit or settlement is, subject to his own interest, as a fiduciary for the other party to the contract;

(c) either party may with the consent of the other sue for the benefit of whom it may concern.

§ 2—723. Proof of Market Price: Time and Place.

(1) If an action based on anticipatory repudiation comes to trial before the time for performance with respect to some or all of the goods, any damages based on market price (Section 2—708 or Section 2—713) shall be determined according to the price of such goods prevailing at the time when the aggrieved party learned of the repudiation.

(2) If evidence of a price prevailing at the times or places described in this Article is not readily available the price prevailing within any reasonable time before or after the time described or at any other place which in commercial judgment or under usage of trade would serve as a reasonable substitute for the one described may be used, making any proper allowance for the cost of transporting the goods to or from such other place.

(3) Evidence of a relevant price prevailing at a time or place other than the one described in this Article offered by one party is not admissible unless and until he has given the other party such notice as the court finds sufficient to prevent unfair surprise.

§ 2—724. Admissibility of Market Quotations.

Whenever the prevailing price or value of any goods regularly bought and sold in any established commodity market is in issue, reports in official publications or trade journals or in newspapers or periodicals of general circulation published as the reports of such market shall be admissible in evidence. The circumstances of the preparation of such a report may be shown to affect its weight but not its admissibility.

§ 2—725. Statute of Limitations in Contracts for Sale.

(1) An action for breach of any contract for sale must be commenced within four years after the cause of action has accrued. By the original agreement the parties may reduce the period of limitation to not less than one year but may not extend it.

(2) A cause of action accrues when the breach occurs, regardless of the aggrieved party's lack of knowledge of the breach. A breach of warranty occurs when tender of delivery is made, except that where a warranty explicitly extends to future performance of the goods and discovery of the breach must await the time of such performance the cause of action accrues when the breach is or should have been discovered.

(3) Where an action commenced within the time limited by subsection (1) is so terminated as to leave available a remedy by another action for the same breach such other action may be commenced after the expiration of the time limited and within six months after the termination of the first action unless the termination resulted from voluntary discontinuance or from dismissal for failure or neglect to prosecute.

(4) This section does not alter the law on tolling of the statute of limitations nor does it apply to causes of action which have accrued before this Act becomes effective.

APPENDIX 

THE NATIONAL LABOR RELATIONS ACT OF 1935 [EXCERPTS]

* * * *

§ 157. **Right of Employees as to Organization, Collective Bargaining, etc.**

Employees shall have the right to self-organization, to form, join, or assist labor organizations, to bargain collectively through representatives of their own choosing, and to engage in other concerted activities for the purpose of collective bargaining or other mutual aid or protection, and shall also have the right to refrain from any or all of such activities except to the extent that such right may be affected by an agreement requiring membership in a labor organization as a condition of employment as authorized in section 158(a)(3) of this title.

§ 158. **Unfair Labor Practices**

(a) Unfair labor practices for an employer

It shall be an unfair labor practice for an employer—

(1) to interfere with, restrain, or coerce employees in the exercise of the rights guaranteed in section 157 of this title;

(2) to dominate or interfere with the formation or administration of any labor organization or contribute financial or other support to it: Provided, [t]hat subject to rules and regulations made and published by the Board pursuant to section 156 of this title, an employer shall not be prohibited from permitting employees to confer with him during working hours without loss of time or pay;

(3) by discrimination in regard to hire or tenure of employment or any term or condition of employment to encourage or discourage membership in any labor organization: Provided, [t]hat nothing in this subchapter, or in any other statute of the United States, shall preclude an employer from making an agreement with a labor organization (not established, maintained, or assisted by any action defined in this subsection as an unfair labor practice) to require as a condition of employment membership therein on or after the thirtieth day following the beginning of such employment or the effective date of such agreement, whichever is the later, (i) if such labor organization is the representative of the employees as provided in section 159(a) of this title, in the appropriate collective-bargaining unit covered by such agreement when made, and (ii) unless following an election held as provided in section 159(e) of this title within one year preceding the effective date of such agreement, the Board shall have certified that at least a majority of the employees eligible to vote in such election have voted to rescind the authority of such labor organization to make such an agreement: Provided further, [t]hat no employer shall justify any discrimination against an employee for nonmembership in a labor organization (A) if he has reasonable grounds for believing that such membership was not available to the employee on the same terms and conditions generally applicable to other members, or (B) if he has reasonable grounds for believing that membership was denied or terminated for reasons

other than the failure of the employee to tender the periodic dues and the initiation fees uniformly required as a condition of acquiring or retaining membership;

(4) to discharge or otherwise discriminate against an employee because he has filed charges or given testimony under this subchapter;

(5) to refuse to bargain collectively with the representatives of his employees, subject to the provisions of section 159(a) of this title.

(b) Unfair labor practices by labor organization

It shall be an unfair labor practice for a labor organization or its agents—

(1) to restrain or coerce (A) employees in the exercise of the rights guaranteed in section 157 of this title: Provided, [t]hat this paragraph shall not impair the right of a labor organization to prescribe its own rules with respect to the acquisition or retention of membership therein; or (B) an employer in the selection of his representatives for the purposes of collective bargaining or the adjustment of grievances;

(2) to cause or attempt to cause an employer to discriminate against an employee in violation of subsection (a)(3) of this section or to discriminate against an employee with respect to whom membership in such organization has been denied or terminated on some ground other than his failure to tender the periodic dues and the initiation fees uniformly required as a condition of acquiring or retaining membership;

(3) to refuse to bargain collectively with an employer, provided it is the representative of his employees subject to the provisions of section 159(a) of this title;

(4) (i) to engage in, or to induce or encourage any individual employed by any person engaged in commerce or in an industry affecting commerce to engage in, a strike or a refusal in the course of his employment to use, manufacture, process, transport, or otherwise handle or work on any goods, articles, materials, or commodities or to perform any services; or (ii) to threaten, coerce, or restrain any person engaged in commerce or in an industry affecting commerce[.] * * *

(5) to require of employees covered by an agreement authorized under subsection (a)(3) of this section the payment, as a condition precedent to becoming a member of such organization, of a fee in an amount which the Board finds excessive or discriminatory under all the circumstances. In making such a finding, the Board shall consider, among other relevant factors, the practices and customs of labor organizations in the particular industry, and the wages currently paid to the employees affected;

(6) to cause or attempt to cause an employer to pay or deliver or agree to pay or deliver any money or other thing of value, in the nature of an exaction, for services which are not performed or not to be performed; and

(7) to picket or cause to be picketed, or threaten to picket or cause to be picketed, any employer where an object thereof is forcing or requiring an employer to recognize or bargain with a labor organization as the representative of his employees, or forcing or requiring the employees of an employer to accept or select such labor organization as their collective bargaining representative[.] * * *

(c) Expression of views without threat of reprisal or force or promise of benefit

The expressing of any views, argument, or opinion, or the dissemination thereof, whether in written, printed, graphic, or visual form, shall not constitute or be evidence of an unfair labor practice under any of the provisions of this subchapter, if such expression contains no threat of reprisal or force or promise of benefit.

(d) Obligation to bargain collectively

For the purposes of this section, to bargain collectively is the performance of the mutual obligation of the employer and the representative of the employees to meet at reasonable times and confer in good faith with respect to wages, hours, and other terms and conditions of employment, or the negotiation of an agreement, or any question arising thereunder, and the execution of a written contract incorporating any agreement reached if requested by either party, but such obligation does not compel either party to agree to a proposal or require the making of a concession: Provided, [t]hat where there is in effect a collective-bargaining contract covering employees in an industry affecting commerce, the duty to bargain collectively shall also mean that no party to such contract shall terminate or modify such contract, unless the party desiring such termination or modification—

(1) serves a written notice upon the other party to the contract of the proposed termination or modification sixty days prior to the expiration date thereof, or in the event such contract contains no expiration date, sixty days prior to the time it is proposed to make such termination or modification;

(2) offers to meet and confer with the other party for the purpose of negotiating a new contract or a contract containing the proposed modifications;

(3) notifies the Federal Mediation and Conciliation Service within thirty days after such notice of the existence of a dispute, and simultaneously therewith notifies any State or Territorial agency established to mediate and conciliate disputes within the State or Territory where the dispute occurred, provided no agreement has been reached by that time; and

(4) continues in full force and effect, without resorting to strike or lock-out, all the terms and conditions of the existing contract for a period of sixty days after such notice is given or until the expiration date of such contract, whichever occurs later[.] * * *

APPENDIX F

THE SHERMAN ACT OF 1890 [EXCERPTS]

Section 1. Every contract, combination in the form of trust or otherwise, or conspiracy, in restraint of trade or commerce among the several States, or with foreign nations, is declared to be illegal. Every person who shall make any contract or engage in any combination or conspiracy hereby declared to be illegal shall be deemed guilty of a felony, and, on conviction thereof, shall be punished by fine not exceeding $10,000,000 if a corporation, or, if any other person, $350,000, or by imprisonment not exceeding three years, or by both said punishments, in the discretion of the court.

Section 2. Every person who shall monopolize, or attempt to monopolize, or combine or conspire with any other person or persons, to monopolize any part of the trade or commerce among the several States, or with foreign nations, shall be deemed guilty of a felony, and, on conviction thereof, shall be punished by fine not exceeding $10,000,000 if a corporation, or, if any other person, $350,000, or by imprisonment not exceeding three years, or by both said punishments, in the discretion of the court.

Section 3. Every contract, combination in form of trust or otherwise, or conspiracy, in restraint of trade or commerce in any Territory of the United States or of the District of Columbia, or in restraint of trade or commerce between any such Territory and another, or between any such Territory or Territories and any State or States or the District of Columbia, or with foreign nations, or between the District of Columbia and any State or States or foreign nations, is declared illegal. Every person who shall make any such contract or engage in any such combination or conspiracy, shall be deemed guilty of a felony, and, on conviction thereof, shall be punished by fine not exceeding $10,000,000 if a corporation, or, if any other person, $350,000, or by imprisonment not exceeding three years, or by both said punishments, in the discretion of the court.

* * * *

Section 7. Every combination, conspiracy, trust, agreement, or contract is declared to be contrary to public policy, illegal, and void when the same is made by or between two or more persons or corporations, either of whom, as agent or principal, is engaged in importing any article from any foreign country into the United States, and when such combination, conspiracy, trust, agreement, or contract is intended to operate in restraint of lawful trade, or free competition in lawful trade or commerce, or to increase the market price in any part of the United States of any article or articles imported or intended to be imported into the United States, or of any manufacture into which such imported article enters or is intended to enter. Every person who shall be engaged in the importation of goods or any commodity from any foreign country in violation of this section, or who shall combine or conspire with another to violate the same, is guilty of a misdemeanor, and on conviction thereof in any court of the United States such person shall be fined in a sum not less than $100 and not exceeding $5,000, and shall be further punished by imprisonment, in the discretion of the court, for a term not less than three months nor exceeding twelve months.

Section 8. The word "person", or "persons", wherever used in sections 1 to 7 of this title shall be deemed to include corporations and associations existing under or authorized by the laws of either the United States, the laws of any of the Territories, the laws of any State, or the laws of any foreign country.

THE CLAYTON ACT OF 1914 [EXCERPTS]

Section 3. That it shall be unlawful for any person engaged in commerce, in the course of such commerce, to lease or make a sale or contract for sale of goods, wares, merchandise, machinery, supplies, or other commodities, whether patented or unpatented, for use, consumption, or resale within the United States or * * * other place under the jurisdiction of the United States, or fix a price charged therefor, or discount from, or rebate upon, such price, on the condition, agreement, or understanding that the lessee or purchaser thereof shall not use or deal in the goods, wares, merchandise, machinery, supplies, or other commodities of a competitor or competitors of the lessor or seller, where the effect of such lease, sale, or contract for sale or such condition, agreement, or understanding may be to substantially lessen competition to tend to create a monopoly in any line of commerce.

Section 4. That any person who shall be injured in his business or property by reason of anything forbidden in the antitrust laws may sue therefor in any district court of the United States in the district in which the defendant resides or is found, or has an agent, without respect to the amount in controversy, and shall recover threefold the damages by him sustained, and the cost of suit, including a reasonable attorney's fee.

Section 4A. Whenever the United States is hereafter injured in its business or property by reason of anything forbidden in the antitrust laws it may sue therefor in the United States district court for the district in which the defendant resides or is found or has an agent, without respect to the amount in controversy, and shall recover actual damages by it sustained and the cost of suit.

Section 4B. Any action to enforce any cause of action under sections 4 or 4A shall be forever barred unless commenced within four years after the cause of action accrued. No cause of action barred under existing law on the effective date of this act shall be revived by this Act.

* * * *

Section 6. That the labor of a human being is not a commodity or article of commerce. Nothing contained in the antitrust laws shall be construed to forbid the existence and operation of labor, agricultural or horticultural organizations, instituted for the purposes of mutual help, and not having capital stock or conducted for profit, or to forbid or restrain individual members of such organizations from lawfully carrying out the legitimate objects thereof; nor shall such organizations or the members thereof, be held or construed to be illegal combinations or conspiracies in restraint of trade, under the antitrust laws.

Section 7. That no person engaged in commerce shall acquire, directly or indirectly, the whole or any part of the stock or other share capital and no corporation subject to the jurisdiction of the Federal Trade Commission shall acquire the whole or any part of the assets of another corporation engaged also in commerce, where in any line of commerce in any section of the country, the effect of such acquisition may be substantially to lessen competition, or to tend to create a monopoly.

No person shall acquire, directly or indirectly, the whole or any part of the stock or other share capital and no corporation subject to the jurisdiction of the Federal Trade Commission shall acquire the whole or any part of the assets of one or more corporations engaged in commerce, where in any line of commerce in any section of the country, the effect of such acquisition, of such stocks or assets, or of the use of such stock by the voting or granting of proxies or otherwise, may be substantially to lessen competition, or to tend to create a monopoly.

This section shall not apply to persons purchasing such stock solely for investment and not using the same by voting or otherwise to bring about, or in attempting to bring about, the substantial lessening of competition * * * .

Section 8. * * * No person at the same time shall be a director in any two or more corporations any one of which has capital, surplus, and undivided profits aggregating more than $1,000,000 engaged in whole or in part in commerce, * * * if such corporations are or shall have been theretofore, by virtue of their business and location of operation, competitors, so that the elimination of competition by agreement between them would constitute a violation of any of the provisions of the antitrust laws. * * *

APPENDIX H

THE FEDERAL TRADE COMMISSION ACT OF 1914 [EXCERPTS]

Section 5. (a)(1) Unfair methods of competition in or affecting commerce, and unfair or deceptive acts or practices in or affecting commerce, are hereby declared unlawful.

(2) The Commission is hereby empowered and directed to prevent persons, partnerships, or corporations from using unfair methods of competition in or affecting commerce and unfair or deceptive acts or practices in or affecting commerce.

(1) Any person, partnership, or corporation who violates an order of the Commission after it has become final, and while such order is in effect, shall forfeit and pay to the United States a civil penalty of not more than $10,000 for each violation, which shall accrue to the United States and may be recovered in a civil action brought by the Attorney General of the United States. Each separate violation of such an order shall be a separate offense, except that in the case of a violation through continuing failure to obey or neglect to obey a final order of the Commission, each day of continuance of such failure or neglect shall be deemed a separate offense. In such actions, the United States district courts are empowered to grant mandatory injunctions and such other and further equitable relief as they deem appropriate in the enforcement of such final orders of the Commission.

APPENDIX I

THE ROBINSON-PATMAN ACT OF 1936 [EXCERPTS]

Section 2. Discrimination in Price, Services, or Facilities—Price; Selection of Customers

(a) It shall be unlawful for any person engaged in commerce, in the course of such commerce, either directly or indirectly, to discriminate in price between different purchasers of commodities of like grade and quality, where either or any of the purchases involved in such discrimination are in commerce, where such commodities are sold for use, consumption, or resale within the United States or any Territory thereof or the District of Columbia or any insular possession or other place under the jurisdiction of the United States, and where the effect of such discrimination may be substantially to lessen competition or tend to create a monopoly in any line of commerce, or to injure, destroy, or prevent competition with any person who either grants or knowingly receives the benefit of such discrimination, or with customers of either of them; *Provided*, That nothing herein contained shall prevent differentials which make only due allowance for differences in the cost of manufacture, sale, or delivery resulting from the differing methods or quantities in which such commodities are to such purchasers sold or delivered: *Provided, however*, That the Federal Trade Commission may, after due investigation and hearing to all interested parties, fix and establish quantity limits, and revise the same as it finds necessary, as to particular commodities or classes of commodities, where it finds that available purchasers in greater quantities are so few as to render differentials on account thereof unjustly discriminatory or promotive of monopoly in any line of commerce; and the foregoing shall then not be construed to permit differentials based on differences in quantities greater than those so fixed and established: *And provided further*, That nothing herein contained shall prevent persons engaged in selling goods, wares, or merchandise in commerce from selecting their own customers in bona fide transactions and not in restraint of trade: *And provided further*, That nothing herein contained shall prevent price changes from time to time where in response to changing conditions affecting the market for or the marketability of the goods concerned, such as but not limited to actual or imminent deterioration of perishable goods, obsolescence of seasonal goods, distress sales under court process, or sales in good faith in discontinuance of business in the goods concerned.

Burden of Rebutting Prima-Facie Case of Discrimination

(b) Upon proof being made, at any hearing on a complaint under this section, that there has been discrimination in price or services or facilities furnished, the burden of rebutting the prima-facie case thus made by showing justification shall be upon the person charged with a violation of this section, and unless justification shall be affirmatively shown, the Commission is authorized to issue an order terminating the discrimination: *Provided, however*, That nothing herein contained shall prevent a seller rebutting the prima-facie case thus made by showing that his [or her] lower price or the furnishing of services or facilities to any purchaser or purchasers was made in good faith to meet an equally low price of a competitor, or the services or facilities furnished by a competitor.

Payment or Acceptance of Commission, Brokerage, or Other Compensation

(c) It shall be unlawful for any person engaged in commerce, in the course of such commerce, to pay or grant, or to receive or accept, anything of value as a commission, brokerage, or other compensation, or any allowance or discount in lieu thereof, except for services rendered in connection with the sale or purchase of goods, wares, or merchandise, either to the other party to such transaction or to an agent, representative, or other intermediary therein where such intermediary is acting in fact for or in behalf, or is subject to the direct or indirect control, of any party to such transaction other than the person by whom such compensation is so granted or paid.

Payment for Services or Facilities for Processing or Sale

(d) It shall be unlawful for any person engaged in commerce to pay or contract for the payment of anything of value to or for the benefit of a customer of such person in the course of such commerce as compensation or in consideration for any services or facilities furnished by or through such customer in connection with the processing, handling, sale or offering for sale of any products or commodities manufactured, sold, or offered for sale by such person, unless such payment or consideration is available on proportionally equal terms to all other customers competing in the distribution of such products or commodities.

Furnishing Services or Facilities for Processing, Handling, etc.

(e) It shall be unlawful for any person to discriminate in favor of one purchaser against another purchaser or purchasers of a commodity bought for resale, with or without processing, by contracting to furnish or furnishing, or by contributing to the furnishing of, any services or facilities connected with the processing, handling, sale, or offering for sale of such commodity so purchased upon terms not accorded to all purchasers on proportionally equal terms.

Knowingly Inducing or Receiving Discriminatory Price

(f) It shall be unlawful for any person engaged in commerce, in the course of such commerce, knowingly to induce or receive a discrimination in price which is prohibited by this section.

Section 3. **Discrimination in Rebates, Discounts, or Advertising Service Charges; Underselling in Particular Localities; Penalties**

It shall be unlawful for any person engaged in commerce, in the course of such commerce, to be a party to, or assist in, any transaction of sale, or contract to sell, which discriminates to his [or her] knowledge against competitors of the purchaser, in that, any discount, rebate, allowance, or advertising service charge is granted to the purchaser over and above any discount, rebate, allowance, or advertising service charge available at the time of such transaction to said competitors in respect of a sale of goods of like grade, quality, and quantity; to sell, or contract to sell, goods in any part of the United States at prices lower than those exacted by said person elsewhere in the United States for the purpose of destroying competition, or eliminating a competitor in such part of the United States; or, to sell, or contract to sell, goods at unreasonably low prices for the purpose of destroying competition or eliminating a competitor.

Any person violating any of the provisions of this section shall, upon conviction thereof, be fined not more than $5,000 or imprisoned not more than one year, or both.

APPENDIX J

SECURITIES ACT OF 1933 [EXCERPTS]

Definitions

Section 2. When used in this title, unless the context requires—

(1) The term "security" means any note, stock, treasury stock, bond, debenture, evidence of indebtedness, certificate of interest or participation in any profit-sharing agreement, collateral-trust certificate, preorganization certificate or subscription, transferable share, investment contract, voting-trust certificate, certificate of deposit for a security, fractional undivided interest in oil, gas, or other mineral rights, any put, call, straddle, option, or privilege on any security, certificate of deposit, or group or index of securities (including any interest therein or based on the value thereof), or any put, call, straddle, option, or privilege entered into on a national securities exchange relating to foreign currency, or, in general, any interest or participation in, temporary or interim certificate for, receipt for, guarantee of, or warrant or right to subscribe to or purchase, any of the foregoing.

Exempted Securities

Section 3. (a) Except as hereinafter expressly provided the provisions of this title shall not apply to any of the following classes of securities:

* * * *

(2) Any security issued or guaranteed by the United States or any territory thereof, or by the District of Columbia, or by any State of the United States, or by any political subdivision of a State or Territory, or by any public instrumentality of one or more States or Territories, or by any person controlled or supervised by and acting as an instrumentality of the Government of the United States pursuant to authority granted by the Congress of the United States; or any certificate of deposit for any of the foregoing; or any security issued or guaranteed by any bank; or any security issued by or representing an interest in or a direct obligation of a Federal Reserve Bank. * * *

(3) Any note, draft, bill of exchange, or banker's acceptance which arises out of a current transaction or the proceeds of which have been or are to be used for current transactions, and which has a maturity at the time of issuance of not exceeding nine months, exclusive of days of grace, or any renewal thereof the maturity of which is likewise limited;

(4) Any security issued by a person organized and operated exclusively for religious, educational, benevolent, fraternal, charitable, or reformatory purposes and not for pecuniary profit, and no part of the net earnings of which inures to the benefit of any person, private stockholder, or individual;

* * * *

(11) Any security which is a part of an issue offered and sold only to persons resident within a single State or Territory, where the issuer of such security is a person resident and doing business within, or, if a corporation,

incorporated by and doing business within, such State or Territory.

(b) The Commission may from time to time by its rules and regulations and subject to such terms and conditions as may be described therein, add any class of securities to the securities exempted as provided in this section, if it finds that the enforcement of this title with respect to such securities is not necessary in the public interest and for the protection of investors by reason of the small amount involved or the limited character of the public offering; but no issue of securities shall be exempted under this subsection where the aggregate amount at which such issue is offered to the public exceeds $5,000,000.

Exempted Transactions

Section 4. The provisions of section 5 shall not apply to—

(1) transactions by any person other than an issuer, underwriter, or dealer.

(2) transactions by an issuer not involving any public offering.

(3) transactions by a dealer (including an underwriter no longer acting as an underwriter in respect of the security involved in such transactions), except—

(A) transactions taking place prior to the expiration of forty days after the first date upon which the security was bona fide offered to the public by the issuer or by or through an underwriter.

(B) transactions in a security as to which a registration statement has been filed taking place prior to the expiration of forty days after the effective date of such registration statement or prior to the expiration of forty days after the first date upon which the security was bona fide offered to the public by the issuer or by or through an underwriter after such effective date, whichever is later (excluding in the computation of such forty days any time during which a stop order issued under section 8 is in effect as to the security), or such shorter period as the Commission may specify by rules and regulations or order, and

(C) transactions as to the securities constituting the whole or a part of an unsold allotment to or subscription by such dealer as a participant in the distribution of such securities by the issuer or by or through an underwriter.

With respect to transactions referred to in clause (B), if securities of the issuer have not previously been sold pursuant to an earlier effective registration statement the applicable period, instead of forty days, shall be ninety days, or such shorter period as the Commission may specify by rules and regulations or order.

(4) brokers' transactions, executed upon customers' orders on any exchange or in the over-the-counter market but not the solicitation of such orders.

* * * *

(6) transactions involving offers or sales by an issuer solely to one or more accredited investors, if the aggregate offering price of an issue of securities offered in reliance on this paragraph does not exceed the amount allowed under Section 3(b) of this title, if there is no advertising or public solicitation in connection with the transaction by the issuer or anyone acting on the issuer's behalf, and if the issuer files such notice with the Commission as the Commission shall prescribe.

Prohibitions Relating to Interstate Commerce and the Mails

Section 5. (a) Unless a registration statement is in effect as to a security, it shall be unlawful for any person, directly or indirectly—

(1) to make use of any means or instruments of transportation or communication in interstate commerce or of the mails to sell such security through the use or medium of any prospectus or otherwise; or

(2) to carry or cause to be carried through the mails or in interstate commerce, by any means or instruments of transportation, any such security for the purpose of sale or for delivery after sale.

(b) It shall be unlawful for any person, directly or indirectly—

(1) to make use of any means or instruments of transportation or communication in interstate commerce or of the mails to carry or transmit any prospectus relating to any security with respect to which a registration statement has been filed under this title, unless such prospectus meets the requirements of section 10, or

(2) to carry or to cause to be carried through the mails or in interstate commerce any such security for the purpose of sale or for delivery after sale, unless accompanied or preceded by a prospectus that meets the requirements of subsection (a) of section 10.

(c) It shall be unlawful for any person, directly, or indirectly, to make use of any means or instruments of transportation or communication in interstate commerce or of the mails to offer to sell or offer to buy through the use or medium of any prospectus or otherwise any security, unless a registration statement has been filed as to such security, or while the registration statement is the subject of a refusal order or stop order or (prior to the effective date of the registration statement) any public proceeding of examination under section 8.

Appendix K

Securities Exchange Act of 1934 [Excerpts]

Definitions and Application of Title

Section 3. (a) When used in this title, unless the context otherwise requires—

* * * *

(4) The term "broker" means any person engaged in the business of effecting transactions in securities for the account of others, but does not include a bank.

(5) The term "dealer" means any person engaged in the business of buying and selling securities for his own account, through a broker or otherwise, but does not include a bank, or any person insofar as he buys or sells securities for his own account, either individually or in some fiduciary capacity, but not as part of a regular business.

* * * *

(7) The term "director" means any director of a corporation or any person performing similar functions with respect to any organization, whether incorporated or unincorporated.

(8) The term "issuer" means any person who issues or proposes to issue any security; except that with respect to certificates of deposit for securities, voting-trust certificates, or collateral-trust certificates, or with respect to certificates of interest or shares in an unincorporated investment trust not having a board of directors or the fixed, restricted management, or unit type, the term "issuer" means the person or persons performing the acts and assuming the duties of depositor or manager pursuant to the provisions of the trust or other agreement or instrument under which such securities are issued; and except that with respect to equipment-trust certificates or like securities, the term "issuer" means the person by whom the equipment or property is, or is to be, used.

(9) The term "person" means a natural person, company, government, or political subdivision, agency, or instrumentality of a government.

Regulation of the Use of Manipulative and Deceptive Devices

Section 10. It shall be unlawful for any person, directly or indirectly, by the use of any means or instrumentality of interstate commerce or of the mails, or of any facility of any national securities exchange—

(a) To effect a short sale, or to use or employ any stop-loss order in connection with the purchase or sale, of any security registered on a national securities exchange, in contravention of such rules and regulations as the Commission may prescribe as necessary or appropriate in the public interest or for the protection of investors.

(b) To use or employ, in connection with the purchase or sale of any security registered on a national securities exchange or any security not so registered, any manipulative or deceptive device or contrivance in contravention of such rules and regulations as the Commission may prescribe as necessary or appropriate in the public interest or for the protection of investors.

APPENDIX L 

TITLE VII OF THE CIVIL RIGHTS ACT OF 1964 [EXCERPTS]

Section 703. **Unlawful Employment Practices.** (a) It shall be an unlawful employment practice for an employer—

(1) to fail or refuse to hire or to discharge any individual, or otherwise to discriminate against any individual with respect to his compensation, terms, conditions, or privileges of employment, because of such individual's race, color, religion, sex, or national origin; or

(2) to limit, segregate, or classify his employees or applicants for employment in any way which would deprive or tend to deprive any individual of employment opportunities or otherwise adversely affect his status as an employee, because of such individual's race, color, religion, sex, or national origin.

(b) It shall be an unlawful employment practice for an employment agency to fail or refuse to refer for employment, or otherwise to discriminate against, any individual because of his race, color, religion, sex, or national origin, or to classify or refer for employment any individual on the basis or his race, color, religion, sex, or national origin.

(c) It shall be an unlawful employment practice for a labor organization—

(1) to exclude or to expel from its membership, or otherwise to discriminate against, any individual because of his race, color, religion, sex, or national origin;

(2) to limit, segregate, or classify its membership or applicants for membership, or to classify or fail or refuse to refer for employment any individual, in any way which would deprive or tend to deprive any individual of employment opportunities, or would limit such employment opportunities or otherwise adversely affect his status as an employee or as an applicant for employment, because of such individual's race, color, religion, sex, or national origin; or

(3) to cause or attempt to cause an employer to discriminate against an individual in violation of this section.

(d) It shall be an unlawful employment practice for any employer, labor organization, or joint labor-management committee controlling apprenticeship or other training or retraining, including on-the-job training programs to discriminate against any individual because of his race, color, religion, sex, or national origin in admission to, or employment in, any program established to provide apprenticeship or other training.

(e) Notwithstanding any other provision of this subchapter—

(1) it shall not be an unlawful employment practice for an employer to hire and employ employees, for an employment agency to classify, or refer for employment any individual, for a labor organization to classify its membership or to classify or refer for employment any individual, or for an employer, labor organization, or joint labor-management committee controlling apprenticeship or other training or retraining programs to admit or employ any individual in any such program, on the basis of his religion, sex, or

national origin in those certain instances where religion, sex, or national origin is a bona fide occupational qualification reasonably necessary to the normal operation of that particular business or enterprise, and

(2) it shall not be an unlawful employment practice for a school, college, university, or other educational institution or institution of learning to hire and employ employees of a particular religion if such school, college, university, or other educational institution or institution of learning is, in whole or in substantial part, owned, supported, controlled, or managed by a particular religion or by a particular religious corporation, association, or society, or if the curriculum of such school, college, university, or other educational institution or institution of learning is directed toward the propagation of a particular religion.

(f) As used in this subchapter, the phrase "unlawful employment practice" shall not be deemed to include any action or measure taken by an employer, labor organization, joint labor-management committee, or employment agency with respect to an individual who is a member of the Communist Party of the United States or of any other organization required to register as a Communist-action or Communist-front organization. * * *

(g) Notwithstanding any other provision of this subchapter, it shall not be an unlawful employment practice for an employer to fail or refuse to hire and employ any individual for any position, for an employer to discharge any individual from any position, or for an employment agency to fail or refuse to refer any individual for employment in any position, or for a labor organization to fail or refuse to refer any individual for employment in any position, if—

(1) the occupancy of such position, or access to the premises in or upon which any part of the duties of such position is performed or is to be performed, is subject to any requirement imposed in the interest of the national security of the United States * * * and

(2) such individual has not fulfilled or has ceased to fulfill that requirement.

(h) Notwithstanding any other provision of this subchapter, it shall not be an unlawful employment practice for an employer to apply different standards of compensation, or different terms, conditions, or privileges of employment pursuant to a bona fide seniority or merit system, or a system which measures earnings by quantity or quality of production or to employees who work in different locations, provided that such differences are not the result of an intention to discriminate because of race, color, religion, sex, or national origin, nor shall it be an unlawful employment practice for an employer to give and act upon the results of any professionally developed ability test provided that such test, its administration or action upon the results is not designed, intended or used to discriminate because of race, color, religion, sex, or national origin. * * *

(j) Nothing contained in this subchapter shall be interpreted to require any employer, employment agency, labor organization, or joint labor-management committee subject to this subchapter to grant preferential treatment to any individual or to any group because of the race, color, religion, sex, or national origin of such individual or group on account of an imbalance which may exist with respect to the total number or percentage of persons of any race, color, religion, sex, or national origin employed by any employer, referred or classified for employment by any employment agency or labor organization, or admitted to, or employed in, any apprenticeship or other training program, in comparison with the total number or percentage of persons of such race, color, religion, sex, or national origin in any community, State, section, or other area, or in the available work force in any community, State, section, or other area.

* * * *

Section 704. **Other Unlawful Employment Practices.**
(a) It shall be an unlawful employment practice for an employer to discriminate against any of his employees or applicants for employment, for an employment agency, or joint labor-management committee controlling apprenticeship or other training or retraining, including on-the-job training programs, to discriminate against any individual, or for a labor organization to discriminate against any member thereof or applicant for membership, because he has opposed any practice made an unlawful employment practice by this subchapter, or because he has made a charge, testified, assisted, or participated in any manner in an investigation, proceeding, or hearing under this subchapter.

(b) It shall be an unlawful employment practice for an employer, labor organization, employment agency, or joint labor-management committee controlling apprenticeship or other training or retraining, including on-the-job training programs, to print or publish or cause to be printed or published any notice or advertisement relating to employment by such an employer or membership or any classification or referral for employment by such a labor organization, or relating to any classification or referral for employment by such an employment agency, or relating to admission to, or employment in, any program established to provide apprenticeship or other training by such a joint-labor-management committee, indicating any preference, limitation, specification, or discrimination, based on race, color, religion, sex, or national origin, except that such a notice or advertisement may indicate a preference, limitation, specification, or discrimination based on religion, sex or national origin when religion, sex, or national origin is a bona fide occupational qualification for employment.

Appendix M

Civil Rights Act of 1991 [Excerpts]

Section 3. Purposes.

The purposes of this Act are—

(1) to provide appropriate remedies for intentional discrimination and unlawful harassment in the workplace;

(2) to codify the concepts of "business necessity" and "job related" enunciated by the Supreme Court in *Griggs v. Duke Power Co.*, 401 U.S. 424 (1971), and in the other Supreme Court decisions prior to *Wards Cove Packing Co. v. Atonio*, 490 U.S. 642 (1989);

(3) to confirm statutory authority and provide statutory guidelines for the adjudication of disparate impact suits under title VII of the Civil Rights Act of 1964 (42 U.S.C. 2000e *et seq.*); and

(4) to respond to recent decisions of the Supreme Court by expanding the scope of relevant civil rights statutes in order to provide adequate protection to victims of discrimination.

Section 101. Prohibition against All Racial Discrimination in the Making and Enforcement of Contracts.

Section 1977 of the Revised Statutes (42 U.S.C. 1981) is amended * * * by adding at the end the following new subsections:

(b) For purposes of this section, the term "make and enforce contracts" includes the making, performance, modification, and termination of contracts, and the enjoyment of all benefits, privileges, terms, and conditions of the contractual relationship.

(c) The rights protected by this section are protected against impairment by nongovernmental discrimination and impairment under color of State law.

Section 102. Damages in Cases of Intentional Discrimination.

The Revised Statutes are amended by inserting after section 1977 (42 U.S.C.1981) the following new section:

Section 1977A. Damages in Cases of Intentional Discrimination in Employment.

(a) Right of Recovery.—

(1) Civil Rights.—In an action brought by a complaining party under section 706 or 717 of the Civil Rights Act of 1964 (42 U.S.C. 2000e-5) against a respondent who engaged in unlawful intentional discrimination (not an employment practice that is unlawful because of its disparate impact) prohibited under section 703, 704, or 717 of the Act (42 U.S.C. 2000e-2 or 2000e-3), and provided that the complaining party cannot recover under section 1977 of the Revised Statutes (42 U.S.C. 1981), the complaining party may recover compensatory and punitive damages as allowed in subsection (b), in addition to any relief authorized by section 706(g) of the Civil Rights Act of 1964, from the respondent.

* * * *

(b) Compensatory and Punitive Damages.—

(1) Determination of Punitive Damages.—A complaining party may recover punitive damages under this section against a respondent (other than a government, government agency or political subdivision) if the complaining party demonstrates that the respondent engaged in a discriminatory practice or discriminatory practices with malice or with reckless indifference to the federally protected rights of an aggrieved individual.

(2) Exclusions from Compensatory Damages.—Compensatory damages awarded under this section shall not include backpay, interest on backpay, or any other type of relief authorized under section 706(g) of the Civil Rights Act of 1964.

(3) Limitations.—The sum of the amount of compensatory damages awarded under this section for future pecuniary losses, emotional pain, suffering, inconvenience, mental anguish, loss of enjoyment of life, and other nonpecuniary losses, and the amount of punitive damages awarded under this section, shall not exceed, for each complaining party—

(A) in the case of a respondent who has more than 14 and fewer than 101 employees in each of 20 or more calendar weeks in the current or preceding calendar year, $50,000;

(B) in the case of a respondent who has more than 100 and fewer than 201 employees in each of 20 or more calendar weeks in the current or preceding calendar year, $100,000; and

(C) in the case of a respondent who has more than 200 and fewer than 501 employees in each of 20 or more calendar weeks in the current or preceding calendar year, $200,000; and

(D) in the case of a respondent who has more than 500 employees in each of 20 or more calendar weeks in the current or preceding calendar year, $300,000.

* * * *

Section 105. Burden of Proof in Disparate Impact Cases.

(a) Section 703 of the Civil Rights Act of 1964 (42 U.S.C. 2000e-2) is amended by adding at the end the following new [subsections to 703(k)(1)]—

(A) An unlawful employment practice based on disparate impact is established under this title only if—

(i) a complaining party demonstrates that a respondent uses a particular employment practice that causes a disparate impact on the basis of race, color, religion, sex, or national origin and the respondent fails to demonstrate that the challenged practice is job related for the position in question and consistent with business necessity; or

(ii) the complaining party makes the demonstration described in subparagraph (C) with respect to an alternative employment practice and the respondent refuses to adopt such alternative employment practice.

* * * *

(C) The demonstration referred to by subparagraph (A)(ii) shall be in accordance with the law as it existed on June 4, 1989, with respect to the concept of "alternative employment practice."

* * * *

Section 107. Clarifying Prohibition against Impermissible Consideration of Race, Color, Religion, Sex, or National Origin in Employment Practices.

(a) In General.—Section 703 of the Civil Rights Act of 1964 (42 U.S.C. 2000e-2) (as amended by sections 105 and 106) is further amended by adding at the end the following new subsection:

(m) Except as otherwise provided in this title, an unlawful employment practice is established when the complaining party demonstrates that race, color, religion, sex, or national origin was a motivating factor for any employment practice, even though other factors also motivated the practice.

* * * *

Section 109. Protection of Extraterritorial Employment.

(a) Definition of Employee.—Section 701(f) of the Civil Rights Act of 1964 (42 U.S.C. 2000e(f)) and section 101(4) of the Americans with Disabilities Act of 1990 (42 U.S.C. 12111(4)) are each amended by adding at the end the following: "With respect to employment in a foreign country, such term includes an individual who is a citizen of the United States."

Appendix N

Americans with Disabilities Act of 1990 [Excerpts]

Title I—EMPLOYMENT

Sec. 101. Definitions.

As used in this title: * * *

(8) **Qualified individual with a disability.**—The term "qualified individual with a disability" means an individual with a disability who, with or without reasonable accommodation, can perform the essential functions of the employment position that such individual holds or desires. For the purposes of this title, consideration shall be given to the employer's judgment as to what functions of a job are essential, and if an employer has prepared a written description before advertising or interviewing applicants for the job, this description shall be considered evidence of the essential functions of the job.

(9) **Reasonable accommodation.**—The term "reasonable accommodation" may include—

(A) making existing facilities used by employees readily accessible to and usable by individuals with disabilities; and

(B) job restructuring, part-time or modified work schedules, reassignment to a vacant position, acquisition or modification of equipment or devices, appropriate adjustment or modifications of examinations, training materials or policies, the provision of qualified readers or interpreters, and other similar accommodations for individuals with disabilities.

(10) **Undue Hardship.**—

(A) **In general.**—The term "undue hardship" means an action requiring significant difficulty or expense, when considered in light of the factors set forth in subparagraph (B).

(B) **Factors to be considered.**—In determining whether an accommodation would impose an undue hardship on a covered entity, factors to be considered include—

(i) the nature and cost of accommodation needed under this Act;

(ii) the overall financial resources of the facility or facilities involved in the provision of the reasonable accommodation; the number of persons employed at such facility; the effect on expenses and resources, or the impact otherwise of such accommodation upon the operation of the facility;

(iii) the overall financial resources of the covered entity; the overall size of the business of a covered entity with respect to the number of its employees; the number, type, and location of its facilities; and

(iv) the type of operation or operations of the covered entity, including the composition, structure, and functions of the workforce of such entity; the geographic separateness, administrative, or fiscal relationship of the facility or facilities in question to the covered entity.

Sec. 102. Discrimination.

(a) **General Rule.**—No covered entity shall discriminate against a qualified individual with a disability because of the disability of such individual in regard to job application procedures, the hiring, advancement, or discharge of employees, employee compensation, job training, and other terms, conditions, and privileges of employment.

(b) **Construction.**—As used in subsection (a), the term "discriminate" includes—

(1) limiting, segregating, or classifying a job applicant or employee in a way that adversely affects the opportunities or status of such applicant or employee because of the disability of such applicant or employee;

(2) participating in a contractual or other arrangement or relationship that has the effect of subjecting a covered entity's qualified applicant or employee with a disability to the discrimination prohibited by this title (such relationship includes a relationship with an employment or referral agency, labor union, an organization providing fringe benefits to an employee of the covered entity, or an organization providing training and apprenticeship programs);

(3) utilizing standards, criteria, or methods of administration—

(A) that have the effect of discrimination on the basis of disability; or

(B) that perpetuate the discrimination of others who are subject to common administrative control;

(4) excluding or otherwise denying equal jobs or benefits to a qualified individual because of the known disability of an individual with whom the qualified individual is known to have a relationship or association;

(5)

(A) not making reasonable accommodations to the known physical or mental limitations of an otherwise qualified individual with a disability who is an applicant or employee, unless such covered entity can demonstrate that the accommodation would impose an undue hardship on the operation of the business of such covered entity; or

(B) denying employment opportunities to a job applicant or employee who is an otherwise qualified individual with a disability, if such denial is based on the need of such covered entity to make reasonable accommodation to the physical or mental impairments of the employee or applicant;

(6) using qualification standards, employment tests or other selection criteria that screen out or tend to screen out an individual with a disability or a class of individuals with disabilities unless the standard, test or other selection criteria, as used by the covered entity, is shown to be job-related for the position in question and is consistent with business necessity; and

(7) failing to select and administer tests concerning employment in the most effective manner to ensure that, when such test is administered to a job applicant or employee who has a disability that impairs sensory, manual, or speaking skills, such test results accurately reflect the skills, aptitude, or whatever other factor of such applicant or employee that such test purports to measure, rather than reflecting the impaired sensory, manual, or speaking skills of such employee or applicant (except where such skills are the factors that the test purports to measure). * * *

Sec. 104. **Illegal Use of Drugs and Alcohol.** * * *

(b) **Rules of Construction.**—Nothing in subsection (a) shall be construed to exclude as a qualified individual with a disability an individual who—

(1) has successfully completed a supervised drug rehabilitation program and is no longer engaging in the illegal use of drugs, or has otherwise been rehabilitated successfully and is no longer engaging in such use;

(2) is participating in a supervised rehabilitation program and is no longer engaging in such use; or

(3) is erroneously regarded as engaging in such use, but is not engaging in such use; except that it shall not be a violation of this Act for a covered entity to adopt or administer reasonable policies or procedures, including but not limited to drug testing, designed to ensure that an individual described in paragraph (1) or (2) is no longer engaging in the illegal use of drugs. * * *

Sec. 107. **Enforcement.**

(a) **Powers, Remedies, and Procedures.**—The powers, remedies, and procedures set forth in sections 705, 706, 707, 709, and 710 of the Civil Rights Act of 1964 (42 U.S.C. 2000e-4, 2000e-5, 2000e-6, 2000e-8, and 2000e-9) shall be the powers, remedies, and procedures this title provides to the Commission, to the Attorney General, or to any person alleging discrimination on the basis of disability in violation of any provision of this Act, or regulations promulgated under section 106, concerning employment.

(b) **Coordination.**—The agencies with enforcement authority for actions which allege employment discrimination under this title and under the Rehabilitation Act of 1973 shall develop procedures to ensure that administrative complaints filed under this title and under the Rehabilitation Act of 1973 are dealt with in a manner that avoids duplication of effort and prevents imposition of inconsistent or conflicting standards for the same requirements under this title and the Rehabilitation Act of 1973. The Commission, the Attorney General, and the Office of Federal Contract Compliance Programs shall establish such coordinating mechanisms (similar to provisions contained in the joint regulations promulgated by the Commission and the Attorney General at part 42 of title 28 and part 1691 of title 29, Code of Federal Regulations, and the Memorandum of Understanding between the Commission and the Office of Federal Contract Compliance Programs dated January 16, 1981 (46 Fed. Reg. 7435, January 23, 1981)) in regulations implementing this title and Rehabilitation Act of 1973 not later than 18 months after the date of enactment of this Act.

Sec. 108. **Effective Date.**

This title shall become effective 24 months after the date of enactment.

APPENDIX O

THE UNIFORM PARTNERSHIP ACT

(Adopted in forty-nine states [all of the states except Louisiana], the District of Columbia, the Virgin Islands, and Guam. The adoptions by Alabama and Nebraska do not follow the official text in every respect, but are substantially similar, with local variations.)

The Act consists of 7 Parts as follows:

I. Preliminary Provisions
II. Nature of Partnership
III. Relations of Partners to Persons Dealing with the Partnership
IV. Relations of Partners to One Another
V. Property Rights of a Partner
VI. Dissolution and Winding Up
VII. Miscellaneous Provisions

An Act to make uniform the Law of Partnerships

Be it enacted, etc.:

Part I Preliminary Provisions

Sec. 1. Name of Act

This act may be cited as Uniform Partnership Act.

Sec. 2. Definition of Terms

In this act, "Court" includes every court and judge having jurisdiction in the case.

"Business" includes every trade, occupation, or profession.

"Person" includes individuals, partnerships, corporations, and other associations.

"Bankrupt" includes bankrupt under the Federal Bankruptcy Act or insolvent under any state insolvent act.

"Conveyance" includes every assignment, lease, mortgage, or encumbrance.

"Real property" includes land and any interest or estate in land.

Sec. 3. Interpretation of Knowledge and Notice

(1) A person has "knowledge" of a fact within the meaning of this act not only when he has actual knowledge thereof, but also when he has knowledge of such other facts as in the circumstances shows bad faith.

(2) A person has "notice" of a fact within the meaning of this act when the person who claims the benefit of the notice:

(a) States the fact to such person, or

(b) Delivers through the mail, or by other means of communication, a written statement of the fact to such person or to a proper person at his place of business or residence.

Sec. 4. Rules of Construction

(1) The rule that statutes in derogation of the common law are to be strictly construed shall have no application to this act.

(2) The law of estoppel shall apply under this act.

(3) The law of agency shall apply under this act.

(4) This act shall be so interpreted and construed as to effect its general purpose to make uniform the law of those states which enact it.

(5) This act shall not be construed so as to impair the obligations of any contract existing when the act goes into effect, nor to affect any action or proceedings begun or right accrued before this act takes effect.

Sec. 5. Rules for Cases Not Provided for in This Act.

In any case not provided for in this act the rules of law and equity, including the law merchant, shall govern.

Part II Nature of Partnership

Sec. 6. Partnership Defined

(1) A partnership is an association of two or more persons to carry on as co-owners a business for profit.

(2) But any association formed under any other statute of this state, or any statute adopted by authority, other than the authority of this state, is not a partnership under this act, unless such association would have been a partnership in this state prior to the adoption of this act; but this act shall apply to limited partnerships except in so far as the statutes relating to such partnerships are inconsistent herewith.

Sec. 7. Rules for Determining the Existence of a Partnership

In determining whether a partnership exists, these rules shall apply:

(1) Except as provided by Section 16 persons who are not partners as to each other are not partners as to third persons.

(2) Joint tenancy, tenancy in common, tenancy by the entireties, joint property, common property, or part ownership does not of itself establish a partnership, whether such co-owners do or do not share any profits made by the use of the property.

(3) The sharing of gross returns does not of itself establish a partnership, whether or not the persons sharing them have a joint or common right or interest in any property from which the returns are derived.

(4) The receipt by a person of a share of the profits of a business is prima facie evidence that he is a partner in the business, but no such inference shall be drawn if such profits were received in payment:

(a) As a debt by installments or otherwise,

(b) As wages of an employee or rent to a landlord,

(c) As an annuity to a widow or representative of a deceased partner,

(d) As interest on a loan, though the amount of payment vary with the profits of the business,

(e) As the consideration for the sale of a good-will of a business or other property by installments or otherwise.

Sec. 8. Partnership Property

(1) All property originally brought into the partnership stock or subsequently acquired by purchase or otherwise, on account of the partnership, is partnership property.

(2) Unless the contrary intention appears, property acquired with partnership funds is partnership property.

(3) Any estate in real property may be acquired in the partnership name. Title so acquired can be conveyed only in the partnership name.

(4) A conveyance to a partnership in the partnership name, though without words of inheritance, passes the entire estate of the grantor unless a contrary intent appears.

Part III Relations of Partners to Persons Dealing with the Partnership

Sec. 9. Partner Agent of Partnership as to Partnership Business

(1) Every partner is an agent of the partnership for the purpose of its business, and the act of every partner, including the execution in the partnership name of any instrument, for apparently carrying on in the usual way the business of the partnership of which he is a member binds the partnership, unless the partner so acting has in fact no authority to act for the partnership in the particular matter, and the person with whom he is dealing has knowledge of the fact that he has no such authority.

(2) An act of a partner which is not apparently for the carrying on of the business of the partnership in the usual way does not bind the partnership unless authorized by the other partners.

(3) Unless authorized by the other partners or unless they have abandoned the business, one or more but less than all the partners have no authority to:

(a) Assign the partnership property in trust for creditors or on the assignee's promise to pay the debts of the partnership,

(b) Dispose of the good-will of the business,

(c) Do any other act which would make it impossible to carry on the ordinary business of a partnership,

(d) Confess a judgment,

(e) Submit a partnership claim or liability to arbitration or reference.

(4) No act of a partner in contravention of a restriction on authority shall bind the partnership to persons having knowledge of the restriction.

Sec. 10. Conveyance of Real Property of the Partnership

(1) Where title to real property is in the partnership name, any partner may convey title to such property by a conveyance executed in the partnership name; but the partnership may recover such property unless the partner's act binds the partnership under the provisions of paragraph (1)

of section 9, or unless such property has been conveyed by the grantee or a person claiming through such grantee to a holder for value without knowledge that the partner, in making the conveyance, has exceeded his authority.

(2) Where title to real property is in the name of the partnership, a conveyance executed by a partner, in his own name, passes the equitable interest of the partnership, provided the act is one within the authority of the partner under the provisions of paragraph (1) of section 9.

(3) Where title to real property is in the name of one or more but not all the partners, and the record does not disclose the right of the partnership, the partners in whose name the title stands may convey title to such property, but the partnership may recover such property if the partners' act does not bind the partnership under the provisions of paragraph (1) of section 9, unless the purchaser or his assignee, is a holder for value, without knowledge.

(4) Where the title to real property is in the name of one or more or all the partners, or in a third person in trust for the partnership, a conveyance executed by a partner in the partnership name, or in his own name, passes the equitable interest of the partnership, provided the act is one within the authority of the partner under the provisions of paragraph (1) of section 9.

(5) Where the title to real property is in the names of all the partners a conveyance executed by all the partners passes all their rights in such property.

Sec. 11. Partnership Bound by Admission of Partner

An admission or representation made by any partner concerning partnership affairs within the scope of his authority as conferred by this act is evidence against the partnership.

Sec. 12. Partnership Charged with Knowledge of or Notice to Partner

Notice to any partner of any matter relating to partnership affairs, and the knowledge of the partner acting in the particular matter, acquired while a partner or then present to his mind, and the knowledge of any other partner who reasonably could and should have communicated it to the acting partner, operate as notice to or knowledge of the partnership, except in the case of a fraud on the partnership committed by or with the consent of that partner.

Sec. 13. Partnership Bound by Partner's Wrongful Act

Where, by any wrongful act or omission of any partner acting in the ordinary course of the business of the partnership or with the authority of his co-partners, loss or injury is caused to any person, not being a partner in the partnership, or any penalty is incurred, the partnership is liable therefor to the same extent as the partner so acting or omitting to act.

Sec. 14. Partnership Bound by Partner's Breach of Trust

The partnership is bound to make good the loss:

(a) Where one partner acting within the scope of his apparent authority receives money or property of a third person and misapplies it; and

(b) Where the partnership in the course of its business receives money or property of a third person and the money or property so received is misapplied by any partner while it is in the custody of the partnership.

Sec. 15. Nature of Partner's Liability

All partners are liable

(a) Jointly and severally for everything chargeable to the partnership under sections 13 and 14.

(b) Jointly for all other debts and obligations of the partnership; but any partner may enter into a separate obligation to perform a partnership contract.

Sec. 16. Partner by Estoppel

(1) When a person, by words spoken or written or by conduct, represents himself, or consents to another representing him to any one, as a partner in an existing partnership or with one or more persons not actual partners, he is liable to any such person to whom such representation has been made, who has, on the faith of such representation, given credit to the actual or apparent partnership, and if he has made such representation or consented to its being made in a public manner he is liable to such person, whether the representation has or has not been made or communicated to such person so giving credit by or with the knowledge of the apparent partner making the representation or consenting to its being made.

(a) When a partnership liability results, he is liable as though he were an actual member of the partnership.

(b) When no partnership liability results, he is liable jointly with the other persons, if any, so consenting to the contract or representation as to incur liability, otherwise separately.

(2) When a person has been thus represented to be a partner in an existing partnership, or with one or more persons not actual partners, he is an agent of the persons consenting to such representation to bind them to the same extent and in the same manner as though he were a partner in fact, with respect to persons who rely upon the representation. Where all the members of the existing partnership consent to the representation, a partnership act or obligation results; but in all other cases it is the joint act or obligation of the person acting and the persons consenting to the representation.

Sec. 17. Liability of Incoming Partner

A person admitted as a partner into an existing partnership is liable for all the obligations of the partnership arising before his admission as though he had been a partner when such obligations were incurred, except that this liability shall be satisfied only out of partnership property.

Part IV Relations of Partners to One Another

Sec. 18. Rules Determining Rights and Duties of Partners

The rights and duties of the partners in relation to the partnership shall be determined, subject to any agreement between them, by the following rules:

(a) Each partner shall be repaid his contributions, whether by way of capital or advances to the partnership property and share equally in the profits and surplus remaining after all liabilities, including those to partners, are satisfied; and must contribute towards the losses, whether of capital or otherwise, sustained by the partnership according to his share in the profits.

(b) The partnership must indemnify every partner in respect of payments made and personal liabilities reasonably incurred by him in the ordinary and proper conduct of its business, or for the preservation of its business or property.

(c) A partner, who in aid of the partnership makes any payment or advance beyond the amount of capital which he agreed to contribute, shall be paid interest from the date of the payment or advance.

(d) A partner shall receive interest on the capital contributed by him only from the date when repayment should be made.

(e) All partners have equal rights in the management and conduct of the partnership business.

(f) No partner is entitled to remuneration for acting in the partnership business, except that a surviving partner is entitled to reasonable compensation for his services in winding up the partnership affairs.

(g) No person can become a member of a partnership without the consent of all the partners.

(h) Any difference arising as to ordinary matters connected with the partnership business may be decided by a majority of the partners; but no act in contravention of any agreement between the partners may be done rightfully without the consent of all the partners.

Sec. 19. Partnership Books

The partnership books shall be kept, subject to any agreement between the partners, at the principal place of business of the partnership, and every partner shall at all times have access to and may inspect and copy any of them.

Sec. 20. Duty of Partners to Render Information

Partners shall render on demand true and full information of all things affecting the partnership to any partner or the legal representative of any deceased partner or partner under legal disability.

Sec. 21. Partner Accountable as a Fiduciary

(1) Every partner must account to the partnership for any benefit, and hold as trustee for it any profits derived by him without the consent of the other partners from any transaction connected with the formation, conduct, or liquidation of the partnership or from any use by him of its property.

(2) This section applies also to the representatives of a deceased partner engaged in the liquidation of the affairs of the partnership as the personal representatives of the last surviving partner.

Sec. 22. Right to an Account

Any partner shall have the right to a formal account as to partnership affairs:

(a) If he is wrongfully excluded from the partnership business or possession of its property by his co-partners,

(b) If the right exists under the terms of any agreement,

(c) As provided by section 21,

(d) Whenever other circumstances render it just and reasonable.

Sec. 23. Continuation of Partnership beyond Fixed Term

(1) When a partnership for a fixed term or particular undertaking is continued after the termination of such term or particular undertaking without any express agreement, the rights and duties of the partners remain the same as they were at such termination, so far as is consistent with a partnership at will.

(2) A continuation of the business by the partners or such of them as habitually acted therein during the term, without any settlement or liquidation of the partnership affairs, is prima facie evidence of a continuation of the partnership.

Part V Property Rights of a Partner

Sec. 24. Extent of Property Rights of a Partner

The property rights of a partner are (1) his rights in specific partnership property, (2) his interest in the partnership, and (3) his right to participate in the management.

Sec. 25. Nature of a Partner's Right in Specific Partnership Property

(1) A partner is co-owner with his partners of specific partnership property holding as a tenant in partnership.

(2) The incidents of this tenancy are such that:

(a) A partner, subject to the provisions of this act and to any agreement between the partners, has an equal right with his partners to possess specific partnership property for partnership purposes; but he has no right to possess such property for any other purpose without the consent of his partners.

(b) A partner's right in specific partnership property is not assignable except in connection with the assignment of rights of all the partners in the same property.

(c) A partner's right in specific partnership property is not subject to attachment or execution, except on a claim against the partnership. When partnership property is attached for a partnership debt the partners, or any of them, or the representatives of a deceased partner, cannot claim any right under the homestead or exemption laws.

(d) On the death of a partner his right in specific partnership property vests in the surviving partner or partners, except where the deceased was the last surviving partner, when his right in such property vests in his legal representative. Such surviving partner or partners, or the legal representative of the last surviving partner, has no right to possess the partnership property for any but a partnership purpose.

(e) A partner's right in specific partnership property is not subject to dower, curtesy, or allowances to widows, heirs, or next of kin.

Sec. 26. Nature of Partner's Interest in the Partnership

A partner's interest in the partnership is his share of the profits and surplus, and the same is personal property.

Sec. 27. Assignment of Partner's Interest

(1) A conveyance by a partner of his interest in the partnership does not of itself dissolve the partnership, nor, as against the other partners in the absence of agreement, entitle the assignee, during the continuance of the partnership, to interfere in the management or administration of the partnership business or affairs, or to require any information or account of partnership transactions, or to inspect the partnership books; but it merely entitles the assignee to receive in accordance with his contract the profits to which the assigning partner would otherwise be entitled.

(2) In case of a dissolution of the partnership, the assignee is entitled to receive his assignor's interest and may require an account from the date only of the last account agreed to by all the partners.

Sec. 28. Partner's Interest Subject to Charging Order

(1) On due application to a competent court by any judgment creditor of a partner, the court which entered the judgment, order, or decree, or any other court, may charge the interest of the debtor partner with payment of the unsatisfied amount of such judgment debt with interest thereon; and may then or later appoint a receiver of his share of the profits, and of any other money due or to fall due to him in respect of the partnership, and make all other orders, directions, accounts and inquiries which the debtor partner might have made, or which the circumstances of the case may require.

(2) The interest charged may be redeemed at any time before foreclosure, or in case of a sale being directed by the court may be purchased without thereby causing a dissolution:

(a) With separate property, by any one or more of the partners, or

(b) With partnership property, by any one or more of the partners with the consent of all the partners whose interests are not so charged or sold.

(3) Nothing in this act shall be held to deprive a partner of his right, if any, under the exemption laws, as regards his interest in the partnership.

Part VI Dissolution and Winding up

Sec. 29. Dissolution Defined

The dissolution of a partnership is the change in the relation of the partners caused by any partner ceasing to be associated in the carrying on as distinguished from the winding up of the business.

Sec. 30. Partnership not Terminated by Dissolution

On dissolution the partnership is not terminated, but continues until the winding up of partnership affairs is completed.

Sec. 31. Causes of Dissolution

Dissolution is caused:

(1) Without violation of the agreement between the partners,

(a) By the termination of the definite term or particular undertaking specified in the agreement,

(b) By the express will of any partner when no definite term or particular undertaking is specified,

(c) By the express will of all the partners who have not assigned their interests or suffered them to be charged for their separate debts, either before or after the termination of any specified term or particular undertaking,

(d) By the expulsion of any partner from the business bona fide in accordance with such a power conferred by the agreement between the partners;

(2) In contravention of the agreement between the partners, where the circumstances do not permit a dissolution under any other provision of this section, by the express will of any partner at any time;

(3) By any event which makes it unlawful for the business of the partnership to be carried on or for the members to carry it on in partnership;

(4) By the death of any partner;

(5) By the bankruptcy of any partner or the partnership;

(6) By decree of court under section 32.

Sec. 32. Dissolution by Decree of Court

(1) On application by or for a partner the court shall decree a dissolution whenever:

(a) A partner has been declared a lunatic in any judicial proceeding or is shown to be of unsound mind,

(b) A partner becomes in any other way incapable of performing his part of the partnership contract,

(c) A partner has been guilty of such conduct as tends to affect prejudicially the carrying on of the business,

(d) A partner willfully or persistently commits a breach of the partnership agreement, or otherwise so conducts himself in matters relating to the partnership business that it is not reasonably practicable to carry on the business in partnership with him,

(e) The business of the partnership can only be carried on at a loss,

(f) Other circumstances render a dissolution equitable.

(2) On the application of the purchaser of a partner's interest under sections 28 or 29 [should read 27 or 28];

(a) After the termination of the specified term or particular undertaking,

(b) At any time if the partnership was a partnership at will when the interest was assigned or when the charging order was issued.

Sec. 33. General Effect of Dissolution on Authority of Partner

Except so far as may be necessary to wind up partnership affairs or to complete transactions begun but not then finished, dissolution terminates all authority of any partner to act for the partnership,

(1) With respect to the partners,

(a) When the dissolution is not by the act, bankruptcy or death of a partner; or

(b) When the dissolution is by such act, bankruptcy or death of a partner, in cases where section 34 so requires.

(2) With respect to persons not partners, as declared in section 35.

Sec. 34. Rights of Partner to Contribution from Copartners after Dissolution

Where the dissolution is caused by the act, death or bankruptcy of a partner, each partner is liable to his copartners for his share of any liability created by any partner acting for the partnership as if the partnership had not been dissolved unless

(a) The dissolution being by act of any partner, the partner acting for the partnership had knowledge of the dissolution, or

(b) The dissolution being by the death or bankruptcy of a partner, the partner acting for the partnership had knowledge or notice of the death or bankruptcy.

Sec. 35. Power of Partner to Bind Partnership to Third Persons after Dissolution

(1) After dissolution a partner can bind the partnership except as provided in Paragraph (3).

(a) By any act appropriate for winding up partnership affairs or completing transactions unfinished at dissolution;

(b) By any transaction which would bind the partnership if dissolution had not taken place, provided the other party to the transaction

(I) Had extended credit to the partnership prior to dissolution and had no knowledge or notice of the dissolution; or

(II) Though he had not so extended credit, had nevertheless known of the partnership prior to dissolution, and, having no knowledge or notice of dissolution, the fact of dissolution had not been advertised in a newspaper of general circulation in the place (or in each place if more than one) at which the partnership business was regularly carried on.

(2) The liability of a partner under paragraph (1b) shall be satisfied out of partnership assets alone when such partner had been prior to dissolution

(a) Unknown as a partner to the person with whom the contract is made; and

(b) So far unknown and inactive in partnership affairs that the business reputation of the partnership could not be said to have been in any degree due to his connection with it.

(3) The partnership is in no case bound by any act of a partner after dissolution

(a) Where the partnership is dissolved because it is unlawful to carry on the business, unless the act is appropriate for winding up partnership affairs; or

(b) Where the partner has become bankrupt; or

(c) Where the partner has no authority to wind up partnership affairs; except by a transaction with one who

(I) Had extended credit to the partnership prior to dissolution and had no knowledge or notice of his want of authority; or

(II) Had not extended credit to the partnership prior to dissolution, and, having no knowledge or notice of his want of authority, the fact of his want of authority has not been advertised in the manner provided for advertising the fact of dissolution in paragraph (1bII).

(4) Nothing in this section shall affect the liability under Section 16 of any person who after dissolution represents himself or consents to another representing him as a partner in a partnership engaged in carrying on business.

Sec. 36. Effect of Dissolution on Partner's Existing Liability

(1) The dissolution of the partnership does not of itself discharge the existing liability of any partner.

(2) A partner is discharged from any existing liability upon dissolution of the partnership by an agreement to that effect between himself, the partnership creditor and the person or partnership continuing the business; and such agreement may be inferred from the course of dealing between the creditor having knowledge of the dissolution and the person or partnership continuing the business.

(3) Where a person agrees to assume the existing obligations of a dissolved partnership, the partners whose obligations have been assumed shall be discharged from any liability to any creditor of the partnership who, knowing of the agreement, consents to a material alteration in the nature or time of payment of such obligations.

(4) The individual property of a deceased partner shall be liable for all obligations of the partnership incurred while he was a partner but subject to the prior payment of his separate debts.

Sec. 37. Right to Wind Up

Unless otherwise agreed the partners who have not wrongfully dissolved the partnership or the legal representative of the last surviving partner, not bankrupt, has the right to wind up the partnership affairs; provided, however, that any partner, his legal representative or his assignee, upon cause shown, may obtain winding up by the court.

Sec. 38. Rights of Partners to Application of Partnership Property

(1) When dissolution is caused in any way, except in contravention of the partnership agreement, each partner, as against his co-partners and all persons claiming through them in respect of their interests in the partnership, unless otherwise agreed, may have the partnership property applied to discharge its liabilities, and the surplus applied to pay in cash the net amount owing to the respective partners. But if dissolution is caused by expulsion of a partner, bona fide under the partnership agreement and if the expelled partner is discharged from all partnership liabilities, either by payment or agreement under section 36(2), he shall receive in cash only the net amount due him from the partnership.

(2) When dissolution is caused in contravention of the partnership agreement the rights of the partners shall be as follows:

(a) Each partner who has not caused dissolution wrongfully shall have,

(I) All the rights specified in paragraph (1) of this section, and

(II) The right, as against each partner who has caused the dissolution wrongfully, to damages for breach of the agreement.

(b) The partners who have not caused the dissolution wrongfully, if they all desire to continue the business in the same name, either by themselves or jointly with others, may do so, during the agreed term for the partnership and for that purpose may possess the partnership property, provided they secure the payment by bond approved by the court, or pay to any partner who has caused the dissolution wrongfully, the value of his interest in the partnership at the dissolution, less any damages recoverable under clause (2a II) of the section, and in like manner indemnify him against all present or future partnership liabilities.

(c) A partner who has caused the dissolution wrongfully shall have:

(I) If the business is not continued under the provisions of paragraph (2b) all the rights of a partner under paragraph (1), subject to clause (2a II), of this section,

(II) If the business is continued under paragraph (2b) of this section the right as against his co-partners and all claiming through them in respect of their interests in the partnership, to have the value of his interest in the partnership, less any damages caused to his co-partners by the dissolution, ascertained and paid to him in cash, or the payment secured by bond approved by the court, and to be released from all existing liabilities of the partnership; but in ascertaining the value of the partner's interest the value of the good-will of the business shall not be considered.

Sec. 39. Rights Where Partnership Is Dissolved for Fraud or Misrepresentation

Where a partnership contract is rescinded on the ground of the fraud or misrepresentation of one of the parties thereto, the party entitled to rescind is, without prejudice to any other right, entitled,

(a) To a lien on, or right of retention of, the surplus of the partnership property after satisfying the partnership liabilities to third persons for any sum of money paid by him for the purchase of an interest in the partnership and for any capital or advances contributed by him; and

(b) To stand, after all liabilities to third persons have been satisfied, in the place of the creditors of the partnership for any payments made by him in respect of the partnership liabilities; and

(c) To be indemnified by the person guilty of the fraud or making the representation against all debts and liabilities of the partnership.

Sec. 40. Rules for Distribution

In settling accounts between the partners after dissolution, the following rules shall be observed, subject to any agreement to the contrary:

(a) The assets of the partnership are:

(I) The partnership property,

(II) The contributions of the partners necessary for the payment of all the liabilities specified in clause (b) of this paragraph.

(b) The liabilities of the partnership shall rank in order of payment, as follows:

(I) Those owing to creditors other than partners,

(II) Those owing to partners other than for capital and profits,

(III) Those owing to partners in respect of capital,

(IV) Those owing to partners in respect of profits.

(c) The assets shall be applied in the order of their declaration in clause (a) of this paragraph to the satisfaction of the liabilities.

(d) The partners shall contribute, as provided by section 18(a) the amount necessary to satisfy the liabilities; but if any, but not all, of the partners are insolvent, or, not being subject to process, refuse to contribute, the other partners shall contribute their share of the liabilities, and, in the relative proportions in which they share the profits, the additional amount necessary to pay the liabilities.

(e) An assignee for the benefit of creditors or any person appointed by the court shall have the right to enforce the contributions specified in clause (d) of this paragraph.

(f) Any partner or his legal representative shall have the right to enforce the contributions specified in clause (d) of this paragraph, to the extent of the amount which he has paid in excess of his share of the liability.

(g) The individual property of a deceased partner shall be liable for the contributions specified in clause (d) of this paragraph.

(h) When partnership property and the individual properties of the partners are in possession of a court for distribution, partnership creditors shall have priority on partnership property and separate creditors on individual property, saving the rights of lien or secured creditors as heretofore.

(i) Where a partner has become bankrupt or his estate is insolvent the claims against his separate property shall rank in the following order:

(I) Those owing to separate creditors,

(II) Those owing to partnership creditors,

(III) Those owing to partners by way of contribution.

Sec. 41. Liability of Persons Continuing the Business in Certain Cases

(1) When any new partner is admitted into an existing partnership, or when any partner retires and assigns (or the representative of the deceased partner assigns) his rights in partnership property to two or more of the partners, or to one or more of the partners and one or more third persons, if the business is continued without liquidation of the partnership affairs, creditors of the first or dissolved partnership are also creditors of the partnership so continuing the business.

(2) When all but one partner retire and assign (or the representative of a deceased partner assigns) their rights in partnership property to the remaining partner, who continues the business without liquidation of partnership affairs, either alone or with others, creditors of the dissolved partnership are also creditors of the person or partnership so continuing the business.

(3) When any partner retires or dies and the business of the dissolved partnership is continued as set forth in paragraphs (1) and (2) of this section, with the consent of the retired partners or the representative of the deceased partner, but without any assignment of his right in partnership property, rights of creditors of the dissolved partnership and of the creditors of the person or partnership continuing the business shall be as if such assignment had been made.

(4) When all the partners or their representatives assign their rights in partnership property to one or more third persons who promise to pay the debts and who continue the business of the dissolved partnership, creditors of the dissolved partnership are also creditors of the person or partnership continuing the business.

(5) When any partner wrongfully causes a dissolution and the remaining partners continue the business under the provisions of section 38(2b), either alone or with others, and without liquidation of the partnership affairs, creditors of the dissolved partnership are also creditors of the person or partnership continuing the business.

(6) When a partner is expelled and the remaining partners continue the business either alone or with others, without liquidation of the partnership affairs, creditors of the dissolved partnership are also creditors of the person or partnership continuing the business.

(7) The liability of a third person becoming a partner in the partnership continuing the business, under this section, to the creditors of the dissolved partnership shall be satisfied out of partnership property only.

(8) When the business of a partnership after dissolution is continued under any conditions set forth in this section the creditors of the dissolved partnership, as against the sepa-

rate creditors of the retiring or deceased partner or the representative of the deceased partner, have a prior right to any claim of the retired partner or the representative of the deceased partner against the person or partnership continuing the business, on account of the retired or deceased partner's interest in the dissolved partnership or on account of any consideration promised for such interest or for his right in partnership property.

(9) Nothing in this section shall be held to modify any right of creditors to set aside any assignment on the ground of fraud.

(10) The use by the person or partnership continuing the business of the partnership name, or the name of a deceased partner as part thereof, shall not of itself make the individual property of the deceased partner liable for any debts contracted by such person or partnership.

Sec. 42. Rights of Retiring or Estate of Deceased Partner When the Business Is Continued

When any partner retires or dies, and the business is continued under any of the conditions set forth in section 41 (1, 2, 3, 5, 6), or section 38(2b) without any settlement of accounts as between him or his estate and the person or partnership continuing the business, unless otherwise agreed, he or his legal representative as against such persons or partnership may have the value of his interest at the date of dissolution ascertained, and shall receive as an ordinary creditor an amount equal to the value of his interest in the dissolved partnership with interest, or, at his option or at the option of his legal representative, in lieu of interest, the profits attributable to the use of his right in the property of the dissolved partnership; provided that the creditors of the dissolved partnership as against the separate creditors, or the representative of the retired or deceased partner, shall have priority on any claim arising under this section, as provided by section 41(8) of this act.

Sec. 43. Accrual of Actions

The right to an account of his interest shall accrue to any partner, or his legal representative, as against the winding up partners or the surviving partners or the person or partnership continuing the business, at the date of dissolution, in the absence of any agreement to the contrary.

Part VII Miscellaneous Provisions

Sec. 44. When Act Takes Effect

This act shall take effect on the ___ day of ___ one thousand nine hundred and ___.

Sec. 45. Legislation Repealed

All acts or parts of acts inconsistent with this act are hereby repealed.

APPENDIX P

THE REVISED UNIFORM PARTNERSHIP ACT [EXCERPTS]

Article 2. GENERAL PROVISIONS

* * * *

§ 201. Partnership as Entity.

A partnership is an entity.

* * * *

§ 203. Partnership Property.

Property transferred to or otherwise acquired by a partnership is property of the partnership and not of the partners individually.

§ 204. When Property is Partnership Property.

(a) Property is partnership property if acquired in the name of:

(1) the partnership; or

(2) one or more partners with an indication in the instrument transferring title to the property of the person's capacity as a partner or of the existence of a partnership but without an indication of the name of the partnership.

(b) Property is acquired in the name of the partnership by a transfer to:

(1) the partnership in its name; or

(2) one or more partners in their capacity as partners in the partnership, if the name of the partnership is indicated in the instrument transferring title to the property.

(c) Property is presumed to be partnership property if purchased with partnership assets, even if not acquired in the name of the partnership or of one or more partners with an indication in the instrument transferring title to the property of the person's capacity as a partner or of the existence of a partnership.

(d) Property acquired in the name of one or more of the partners, without an indication in the instrument transferring title to the property of the person's capacity as a partner or of the existence of a partnership and without use of partnership assets, is presumed to be separate property, even if used for partnership purposes.

Article 3. RELATIONS OF PARTNERS TO PERSONS DEALING WITH PARTNERSHIP

* * * *

§ 302. Transfer of Partnership Property.

(a) Subject to the effect of a statement of partnership authority under Section 303:

(1) Partnership property held in the name of the partnership may be transferred by an instrument of transfer executed by a partner in the partnership name.

(2) Partnership property held in the name of one or more partners with an indication in the instrument transferring the property to them of their capacity as partners or of the existence of a partnership, but without an indication of the name of the partnership, may be transferred by an instrument of transfer executed by the persons in whose name the property is held.

(3) A partnership may recover property transferred under this subsection if it proves that execution of the instrument of transfer did not bind the partnership under Section 301, unless the property was transferred by the initial transferee or a person claiming through the initial transferee to a subsequent transferee who gave value without having notice that the person who executed the instrument of initial transfer lacked authority to bind the partnership.

(b) Partnership property held in the name of one or more persons other than the partnership, without an indication in the instrument transferring the property to them of their capacity as partners or of the existence of a partnership, may be transferred free of claims of the partnership or the partners by the persons in whose name the property is held to a transferee who gives value without having notice that it is partnership property.

(c) If a person holds all of the partners' interests in the partnership, all of the partnership property vests in that person. The person may execute a document in the name of the partnership to evidence vesting of the property in that person and may file or record the document.

* * * *

§ 306. Partner's Liability.

All partners are liable jointly and severally for all obligations of the partnership unless otherwise agreed by the claimant or provided by law.

§ 307. Actions by and Against Partnership and Partners.

(a) A partnership may sue and be sued in the name of the partnership.

(b) An action may be brought against the partnership and any or all of the partners in the same action or in separate actions.

(c) A judgment against a partnership is not by itself a judgment against a partner. A judgment against a partnership may not be satisfied from a partner's assets unless there is also a judgment against the partner.

(d) A judgment creditor of a partner may not levy execution against the assets of the partner to satisfy a judgment based on a claim against the partnership unless:

(1) a judgment based on the same claim has been obtained against the partnership and a writ of execution on the judgment has been returned unsatisfied in whole or in part;

(2) an involuntary case under Title 11 of the United States Code has been commenced against the partnership and has not been dismissed within 60 days after commencement, or the partnership has commenced a voluntary case under Title 11 of the United States Code and the case has not been dismissed;

(3) the partner has agreed that the creditor need not exhaust partnership assets;

(4) a court grants permission to the judgment creditor to levy execution against the assets of a partner based on a finding that partnership assets subject to execution are clearly insufficient to satisfy the judgment, that exhaustion of partnership assets is excessively burdensome, or that the grant of permission is an appropriate exercise of the court's equitable powers; or

(5) liability is imposed on the partner by law or contract independent of the existence of the partnership.

(e) This section applies to any partnership liability or obligation resulting from a representation by a partner or purported partner under Section 308.

* * * *

Article 5.
TRANSFEREES AND CREDITORS OF PARTNER

§ 501. Partner's Interest in Partnership Property not Transferable.

A partner is not a co-owner of partnership property and has no interest in partnership property which can be transferred, either voluntarily or involuntarily.

* * * *

Article 6.
PARTNER'S DISSOCIATION

§ 601. Events Causing Partner's Dissociation.

A partner is dissociated from a partnership upon:

(1) receipt by the partnership of notice of the partner's express will to withdraw as a partner or upon any later date specified in the notice;

(2) an event agreed to in the partnership agreement as causing the partner's dissociation;

(3) the partner's expulsion pursuant to the partnership agreement;

(4) the partner's expulsion by the unanimous vote of the other partners if:

(i) it is unlawful to carry on the partnership business with that partner;

(ii) there has been a transfer of all or substantially all of that partner's transferable interest in the partnership, other than a transfer for security purposes, or a court order charging the partner's interest, which has not been foreclosed;

(iii) within 90 days after the partnership notifies a corporate partner that it will be expelled because it has filed a certificate of dissolution or the equivalent, its charter has been revoked, or its right to conduct business has been suspended by the jurisdiction of its incorporation, there is no revocation of the certificate of dissolution or no reinstatement of its charter or its right to conduct business; or

(iv) a partnership that is a partner has been dissolved and its business is being wound up;

(5) on application by the partnership or another partner, the partner's expulsion by judicial determination because:

(i) the partner engaged in wrongful conduct that adversely and materially affected the partnership business;

(ii) the partner willfully or persistently committed a material breach of the partnership agreement or of a duty owed to the partnership or the other partners under Section 404; or

(iii) the partner engaged in conduct relating to the partnership business which makes it not reasonably practicable to carry on the business in partnership with the partner;

(6) the partner's:

(i) becoming a debtor in bankruptcy;

(ii) executing an assignment for the benefit of creditors;

(iii) seeking, consenting to, or acquiescing in the appointment of a trustee, receiver, or liquidator of that partner or of all or substantially all of that partner's property; or

(iv) failing, within 90 days after the appointment, to have vacated or stayed the appointment of a trustee, receiver, or liquidator of the partner or of all or substantially all of the partner's property obtained without the partner's consent or acquiescence, or failing within 90 days after the expiration of a stay to have the appointment vacated;

(7) in the case of a partner who is an individual:

(i) the partner's death;

(ii) the appointment of a guardian or general conservator for the partner; or

(iii) a judicial determination that the partner has otherwise become incapable of performing the partner's duties under the partnership agreement;

(8) in the case of a partner that is a trust or is acting as a partner by virtue of being a trustee of a trust, distribution of the trust's entire transferable interest in the partnership, but not merely by reason of the substitution of a successor trustee;

(9) in the case of a partner that is an estate or is acting as a partner by virtue of being a personal representative of an estate, distribution of the estate's entire transferable interest in the partnership, but not merely by reason of the substitution of a successor personal representative; or

(10) termination of a partner who is not an individual, partnership, corporation, trust, or estate.

* * * *

Article 7.
PARTNER'S DISSOCIATION WHEN BUSINESS NOT WOUND UP

§ 701. **Purchase of Dissociated Partner's Interest.**

(a) If a partner is dissociated from a partnership without resulting in a dissolution and winding up of the partnership business under Section 801, the partnership shall cause the dissociated partner's interest in the partnership to be purchased for a buyout price determined pursuant to subsection (b).

(b) The buyout price of a dissociated partner's interest is the amount that would have been distributable to the dissociating partner under Section 808(b) if, on the date of dissociation, the assets of the partnership were sold at a price equal to the greater of the liquidation value or the value based on a sale of the entire business as a going concern without the dissociated partner and the partnership were wound up as of that date. In either case, the selling price of the partnership assets must be determined on the basis of the amount that would be paid by a willing buyer to a willing seller, neither being under any compulsion to buy or sell, and with knowledge of all relevant facts. Interest must be paid from the date of dissociation to the date of payment.

(c) Damages for wrongful dissociation under Section 602(b), and all other amounts owing, whether or not presently due, from the dissociated partner to the partnership, must be offset against the buyout price. Interest must be paid from the date the amount owed becomes due to the date of payment.

(d) A partnership shall indemnify a dissociated partner against all partnership liabilities incurred before the dissociation, except liabilities then unknown to the partnership, and against all partnership liabilities incurred after the dissociation, except liabilities incurred by an act of the dissociated partner under Section 702. For purposes of this subsection, a liability not known to a partner other than the dissociated partner is not known to the partnership.

(e) If no agreement for the purchase of a dissociated partner's interest is reached within 120 days after a written demand for payment, the partnership shall pay, or cause to be paid, in cash to the dissociated partner the amount the partnership estimates to be the buyout price and accrued interest, reduced by any offsets and accrued interest under subsection (c).

(f) If a deferred payment is authorized under subsection (h), the partnership may tender a written offer to pay the amount it estimates to be the buyout price and accrued interest, reduced by any offsets under subsection (c), stating the time of payment, the amount and type of security for payment, and the other terms and conditions of the obligation.

(g) The payment or tender required by subsection (e) or (f) must be accompanied by the following:

(1) a statement of partnership assets and liabilities as of the date of dissociation;

(2) the latest available partnership balance sheet and income statement, if any;

(3) an explanation of how the estimated amount of the payment was calculated; and

(4) written notice that the payment is in full satisfaction of the obligation to purchase unless, within 120 days after the written notice, the dissociated partner commences an action to determine the buyout price, any offsets under subsection (c), or other terms of the obligation to purchase.

(h) A partner who wrongfully dissociates before the expiration of a definite term or the completion of a particular undertaking is not entitled to payment of any portion of the buyout price until the expiration of the term or completion of the undertaking, unless the partner establishes to the satisfaction of the court that earlier payment will not cause undue hardship to the business of the partnership. A deferred payment must be adequately secured and bear interest.

(i) A dissociated partner may maintain an action against the partnership, pursuant to Section 406(b)(2)(ii), to determine the buyout price of that partner's interest, any offsets under subsection (c), or other terms of the obligation to purchase. The action must be commenced within 120 days after the partnership has tendered payment or an offer to pay or within one year after written demand for payment if no payment or offer to pay is tendered. The court shall determine the buyout price of the dissociated partner's interest, any offset due under subsection (c), and accrued interest, and enter judgment for any additional payment or refund. If deferred payment is authorized under subsection (h), the court shall also determine the security for payment and other terms of the obligation to purchase. The court may assess reasonable attorney's fees and the fees and expenses of appraisers or other experts for a party to the action, in amounts the court finds equitable, against a party that the court finds acted arbitrarily, vexatiously, or not in good faith. The finding may be based on the partnership's failure to tender payment or an offer to pay or to comply with subsection (g).

APPENDIX 

THE UNIFORM LIMITED LIABILITY COMPANY ACT [EXCERPTS]

[ARTICLE] 2. ORGANIZATION

Section 201. Limited liability company as legal entity.

A limited liability company is a legal entity distinct from its members.

Section 202. Organization.

(a) One or more persons may organize a limited liability company, consisting of one or more members, by delivering articles of organization to the office of the [Secretary of State] for filing.

(b) Unless a delayed effective date is specified, the existence of a limited liability company begins when the articles of organization are filed.

(c) The filing of the articles of organization by the [Secretary of State] is conclusive proof that the organizers satisfied all conditions precedent to the creation of a limited liability company.

Section 203. Articles of organization.

(a) Articles of organization of a limited liability company must set forth:

(1) the name of the company;

(2) the address of the initial designated office;

(3) the name and street address of the initial agent for service of process;

(4) the name and address of each organizer;

(5) whether the company is to be a term company and, if so, the term specified;

(6) whether the company is to be manager-managed, and, if so, the name and address of each initial manager; and

(7) whether one or more of the members of the company are to be liable for its debts and obligations under Section 303(c).

(b) Articles of organization of a limited liability company may set forth:

(1) provisions permitted to be set forth in an operating agreement; or

(2) other matters not inconsistent with law.

(c) Articles of organization of a limited liability company may not vary the nonwaivable provisions of Section 103(b). As to all other matters, if any provision of an operating agreement is inconsistent with the articles of organization:

(1) the operating agreement controls as to managers, members, and members' transferees; and

(2) the articles of organization control as to persons, other than managers, members and their transferees, who reasonably rely on the articles to their detriment.

* * * *

Section 208. Certificate of existence or authorization.

(a) A person may request the [Secretary of State] to furnish a certificate of existence for a limited liability company or a certificate of authorization for a foreign limited liability company.

(b) A certificate of existence for a limited liability company must set forth:

(1) the company's name;

(2) that it is duly organized under the laws of this State, the date of organization, whether its duration is at-will or for a specified term, and, if the latter, the period specified;

(3) if payment is reflected in the records of the [Secretary of State] and if nonpayment affects the existence of the company, that all fees, taxes, and penalties owed to this State have been paid;

(4) whether its most recent annual report required by Section 211 has been filed with the [Secretary of State];

(5) that articles of termination have not been filed; and

(6) other facts of record in the office of the [Secretary of State] which may be requested by the applicant.

(c) A certificate of authorization for a foreign limited liability company must set forth:

(1) the company's name used in this State;

(2) that it is authorized to transact business in this State;

(3) if payment is reflected in the records of the [Secretary of State] and if nonpayment affects the authorization of the company, that all fees, taxes, and penalties owed to this State have been paid;

(4) whether its most recent annual report required by Section 211 has been filed with the [Secretary of State];

(5) that a certificate of cancellation has not been filed; and

(6) other facts of record in the office of the [Secretary of State] which may be requested by the applicant.

(d) Subject to any qualification stated in the certificate, a certificate of existence or authorization issued by the [Secretary of State] may be relied upon as conclusive evidence that the domestic or foreign limited liability company is in existence or is authorized to transact business in this State.

* * * *

[ARTICLE] 3.
RELATIONS OF MEMBERS AND MANAGERS TO PERSONS DEALING WITH LIMITED LIABILITY COMPANY

* * * *

Section 303. Liability of members and managers.

(a) Except as otherwise provided in subsection (c), the debts, obligations, and liabilities of a limited liability company, whether arising in contract, tort, or otherwise, are solely the debts, obligations, and liabilities of the company. A member or manager is not personally liable for a debt, obligation, or liability of the company solely by reason of being or acting as a member or manager.

(b) The failure of a limited liability company to observe the usual company formalities or requirements relating to the exercise of its company powers or management of its business is not a ground for imposing personal liability on the members or managers for liabilities of the company.

(c) All or specified members of a limited liability company are liable in their capacity as members for all or specified debts, obligations, or liabilities of the company if:

(1) a provision to that effect is contained in the articles of organization; and

(2) a member so liable has consented in writing to the adoption of the provision or to be bound by the provision.

* * * *

[ARTICLE] 4.
RELATIONS OF MEMBERS TO EACH OTHER AND TO LIMITED LIABILITY COMPANY

* * * *

Section 404. Management of limited liability company.

(a) In a member-managed company:

(1) each member has equal rights in the management and conduct of the company's business; and

(2) except as otherwise provided in subsection (c) or in Section 801(b)(3)(i), any matter relating to the business of the company may be decided by a majority of the members.

(b) In a manager-managed company:

(1) each manager has equal rights in the management and conduct of the company's business;

(2) except as otherwise provided in subsection (c) or in Section 801(b)(3)(i), any matter relating to the

business of the company may be exclusively decided by the manager or, if there is more than one manager, by a majority of the managers; and

(3) a manager:

(i) must be designated, appointed, elected, removed, or replaced by a vote, approval, or consent of a majority of the members; and

(ii) holds office until a successor has been elected and qualified, unless the manager sooner resigns or is removed.

(c) The only matters of a member or manager-managed company's business requiring the consent of all of the members are:

(1) the amendment of the operating agreement under Section 103;

(2) the authorization or ratification of acts or transactions under Section 103(b)(2)(ii) which would otherwise violate the duty of loyalty;

(3) an amendment to the articles of organization under Section 204;

(4) the compromise of an obligation to make a contribution under Section 402(b);

(5) the compromise, as among members, of an obligation of a member to make a contribution or return money or other property paid or distributed in violation of this [Act];

(6) the making of interim distributions under Section 405(a), including the redemption of an interest;

(7) the admission of a new member;

(8) the use of the company's property to redeem an interest subject to a charging order;

(9) the consent to dissolve the company under Section 801(b)(2);

(10) a waiver of the right to have the company's business wound up and the company terminated under Section 802(b);

(11) the consent of members to merge with another entity under Section 904(c)(1); and

(12) the sale, lease, exchange, or other disposal of all, or substantially all, of the company's property with or without goodwill.

(d) Action requiring the consent of members or managers under this [Act] may be taken without a meeting.

(e) A member or manager may appoint a proxy to vote or otherwise act for the member or manager by signing an appointment instrument, either personally or by the member's or manager's attorney-in-fact.

APPENDIX 

THE GENERAL AGREEMENT ON TARIFFS AND TRADE OF 1994 [EXCERPTS]

Part I

FINAL ACT EMBODYING THE RESULTS OF THE URUGUAY ROUND OF MULTILATERAL TRADE NEGOTIATIONS

1. Having met in order to conclude the Uruguay Round of Multilateral Trade Negotiations, the representatives of the Governments and of the European Communities, members of the Trade Negotiations Committee * * *, *agree* that the Agreement Establishing the Multilateral Trade Organization and the Ministerial Decisions and Declarations * * * embody the results of their negotiations and form an integral part of this Final Act.

* * * *

Part II

AGREEMENT ESTABLISHING THE MULTILATERAL TRADE ORGANIZATION

The *Parties* to this Agreement,

Recognizing that their relations in the field of trade and economic endeavour should be conducted with a view to raising standards of living, ensuring full employment and a large and steadily growing volume of real income and effective demand, and expanding the production and trade in good and services, while allowing for the optimal use of the world's resources in accordance with the objective of sustainable development, seeking both to protect and preserve the environment and enhance the means for doing so in a manner consistent with their respective needs and concerns at different levels of economic development,

Recognizing further that there is need for positive efforts designed to ensure that developing countries * * * secure a share in the growth in international trade commensurate with the needs of their economic development,

Being desirous of contributing to these objectives by entering into reciprocal and mutually advantageous arrangements directed to the substantial reduction of tariffs and other barriers to trade and to the elimination of discriminatory treatment in international trade relations,

Resolved, therefore, to develop an integrated, more viable and durable multilateral trading system encompassing the General Agreement on Tariffs and Trade, the results of the past trade liberalization efforts, and all of the results of the Uruguay Round of multilateral trade negotiations,

Determined to preserve the basic principles and to further the objectives underlying this multilateral trading system,

Agree as follows:

* * * *

The Multilateral Trade Organization [MTO] * * * is hereby established.

* * * *

[The] MTO shall facilitate the implementation, administration, operation, and further the objectives, of this Agreement and of the Multilateral Trade Agreements, and shall also provide the framework for the implementation, administration and operation of the Plurilateral Trade Agreements.

* * * *

[Except] as otherwise provided for under this Agreement or the Multilateral Trade Agreements, the MTO shall be guided by the decisions, procedures and customary practices followed by the contracting parties of the GATT 1947 and the bodies established in the framework of the GATT 1947.

* * * *

AGREEMENT ON AGRICULTURE

* * * *

2. In accordance with the Mid-Term Review Agreement that government measures of assistance, whether direct or indirect, to encourage agricultural and rural development are an integral part of the development programmes of developing countries, investment subsidies which are generally available to agriculture in developing country Members and agricultural input subsidies generally available to low-income or resource poor producers in developing country Members shall be exempt from domestic support reduction commitments that would otherwise be applicable to such measures, as shall domestic support to producers in developing country Members to encourage diversification from growing illicit narcotic crops. * * *

* * * *

AGREEMENT ON TEXTILES AND CLOTHING

* * * *

1. Members agree that circumvention by transshipment, rerouting, false declaration concerning country or place of origin, and falsification of official documents, frustrates the implementation of this Agreement to integrate the textiles and clothing sector into the GATT 1994. Accordingly, Members should establish the necessary legal provisions and/or administrative procedures to address and take action against such circumvention. Members further agree that, consistent with their domestic laws and procedures, they will cooperate fully to address problems arising from circumvention.

* * * *

2. Safeguard action may be taken * * * when, on the basis of a determination by a Member, it is demonstrated that a particular product is being imported into its territory in such increased quantities as to cause serious damage, or actual threat thereof, to the domestic industry producing like and/or directly competitive products. Serious damage or actual threat thereof must demonstrably be caused by such increased quantities in total imports of that product and not by such other factors as technological changes or changes in consumer preference.

* * * *

AGREEMENT ON TECHNICAL BARRIERS TO TRADE

* * * *

2.2 Members shall ensure that technical regulations are not prepared, adopted or applied with a view to or with the effect of creating unnecessary obstacles to international trade. For this purpose, technical regulations shall not be more trade-restrictive than necessary to fulfil a legitimate objective, taking account of the risks non-fulfilment would create. Such legitimate objectives [include] national security requirements; the prevention of deceptive practices; protection of human health or safety, animal or plant life or health, or the environment. In assessing such risks, relevant elements of consideration [include] * * * available scientific and technical information, related processing technology or intended end uses of products.

* * * *

AGREEMENT ON IMPLEMENTATION OF ARTICLE VI OF GATT 1994

* * * *

2.1 For the purpose of this Agreement a product is to be considered as being dumped, i.e., introduced into the commerce of another country at less than its normal value, if the export price of the product exported from one country to another is less than the comparable price, in the ordinary course of trade, for the like product when destined for consumption in the exporting country.

* * * *

3.5 It must be demonstrated that the dumped imports are * * * causing injury within the meaning of this Agreement. The demonstration of a causal relationship between the dumped imports and the injury to the domestic industry shall be based on an examination of all relevant evidence before the authorities. The authorities shall also examine any known factors other than the dumped imports which at the same time are injuring the domestic industry, and the injuries caused by these other factors must not be attributed to the dumped imports. Factors which may be relevant in this respect include * * * the volume and prices of imports not sold at dumping prices, contraction in demand or changes in the patterns of consumption, trade restrictive practices of and competition between the foreign and domestic producers, developments in technology and the export performance and productivity of the domestic industry.

* * * *

9.2 When an anti-dumping duty is imposed in respect of any product, such anti-dumping duty shall be collected in the appropriate amounts in each case, on a non-discriminatory basis on imports of such product from all sources found to be dumped and causing injury, except as to imports from those sources from which price undertakings under the terms of this Agreement have been accepted. The authorities shall name the supplier or suppliers of the product concerned. If, however, several suppliers from the same country are involved, and it is impracticable to name all of these suppliers, the authorities may name the supplying country concerned. If several suppliers from more than one country are involved, the authorities may name either all the suppliers involved, or, if this is impracticable, all the supplying countries involved.

* * * *

AGREEMENT ON PRESHIPMENT INSPECTION

* * * *

12. User Members shall ensure that preshipment inspection entities do not request exporters to provide information regarding:

(a) manufacturing data related to patented, licensed or undisclosed processes, or to processes for which a patent is pending;

(b) unpublished technical data other than necessary to demonstrate compliance with technical regulations or standards;

(c) internal pricing, including manufacturing costs;

(d) profit levels;

(e) the terms of contracts between exporters and their suppliers unless it is not otherwise possible for the entity to conduct the inspection in question. In such cases, the entity shall only request the information necessary for this purpose.

* * * *

AGREEMENT ON SUBSIDIES AND COUNTERVAILING MEASURES

* * * *

3.1 Except as provided in the Agreement on Agriculture, the following subsidies * * * shall be prohibited:

(a) subsidies contingent, in law or in fact, whether solely or as one of several other conditions, upon export performance * * *;

(b) subsidies contingent, whether solely or as one of several other conditions, upon the use of domestic over imported goods.

* * * *

AGREEMENT ON SAFEGUARDS

* * * *

2. A Member may apply a safeguard measure to a product only if that Member has determined * * * that such product is being imported into its territory in such increased quantities, absolute or relative to domestic production, and under such conditions as to cause or threaten to cause serious injury to the domestic industry that produces like or directly competitive products.

* * * *

8. Safeguard measures shall be applied only to the extent as may be necessary to prevent or remedy serious injury and to facilitate adjustment. * * *

* * * *

12. The total period of application of a safeguard measure including the period of application of any provisional measure, the period of initial application and any extension thereof, shall not exceed eight years.

* * * *

19. Safeguard measures shall not be applied against a product originating in a developing country Member as long as its share of imports of the product concerned in the importing Member does not exceed 3 [percent], provided that, developing country Members with less than 3 [percent] import share collectively account for not more than 9 [percent] of total imports of the product concerned.

* * * *

GENERAL AGREEMENT ON TRADE IN SERVICES

* * * *

1. With respect to any measure covered by this Agreement, each Member shall accord immediately and unconditionally to services and service suppliers of any other Member, treatment no less favourable than that it accords to like services and service suppliers of any other country.

* * * *

AGREEMENT ON TRADE-RELATED ASPECTS OF INTELLECTUAL PROPERTY RIGHTS, INCLUDING TRADE IN COUNTERFEIT GOODS

* * * *

1. Members shall ensure that enforcement procedures * * * are available under their national laws so as to permit effective action against any act of infringement of

intellectual property rights covered by this Agreement, including expeditious remedies to prevent infringements and remedies which constitute a deterrent to further infringements. These procedures shall be applied in such a manner as to avoid the creation of barriers to legitimate trade and to provide for safeguards against their abuse.

2. Procedures concerning the enforcement of intellectual property rights shall be fair and equitable. They shall not be unnecessarily complicated or costly, or entail unreasonable time-limits or unwarranted delays.

* * * *

UNDERSTANDING ON RULES AND PROCEDURES GOVERNING THE SETTLEMENT OF DISPUTES

* * * *

2.1 The Dispute Settlement Body (DSB) * * * shall administer these rules and procedures and * * * the consultation and dispute settlement provisions of the covered agreements.

APPENDIX S

THE NORTH AMERICAN FREE TRADE AGREEMENT OF 1993 [EXCERPTS]

Part One: GENERAL PART

Chapter One: Objectives

Article 101: Establishment of the Free Trade Area

The Parties to this Agreement * * * hereby establish a free trade area.

Article 102: Objectives

1. The objectives of this Agreement * * * are to: (a) eliminate barriers to trade in, and facilitate the cross-border movement of, goods and services between the territories of the Parties; (b) promote conditions of fair competition in the free trade area; (c) increase substantially investment opportunities in the territories of the Parties; (d) provide adequate and effective protection and enforcement of intellectual property rights in each Party's territory; (e) create effective procedures for the implementation and application of this Agreement, for its joint administration and for the resolution of disputes; and (f) establish a framework for further trilateral, regional and multilateral cooperation to expand and enhance the benefits of this Agreement.

* * * *

Part Two: TRADE IN GOODS

Chapter Three: National Treatment and Market Access for Goods

* * * *

Article 301: National Treatment

1. Each Party shall accord national treatment to the goods of another Party in accordance with Article III of the General Agreement on Tariffs and Trade (GATT) * * * .

2. [N]ational treatment shall mean, with respect to a state or province, treatment no less favorable than the most favorable treatment accorded by such state or province to any like, directly competitive or substitutable goods, as the case may be, of the Party of which it forms a part.

* * * *

Article 302: Tariff Elimination

1. Except as otherwise provided in this Agreement, no Party may increase any existing customs duty, or adopt any customs duty, on an originating good.

2. [E]ach Party shall progressively eliminate its customs duties on originating goods in accordance with its Schedule * * * .

* * * *

Article 316: Consultations and Committee on Trade in Goods

1. The Parties hereby establish a Committee on Trade in Goods, comprising representatives of each Party.

* * * *

3. The Parties shall convene at least once each year a meeting of their officials responsible for customs, immigration, inspection of food and agricultural products, border inspection facilities, and regulation of transportation for the purpose of addressing issues related to movement of goods through the Parties' ports of entry.

* * * *

Part Three: TECHNICAL BARRIERS TO TRADE

Chapter Nine: Standards-Related Measures

* * * *

Article 904: Basic Rights and Obligations

Right to Take Standards-Related Measures

1. Each Party may * * * adopt, maintain or apply any standards-related measure, including any such measure relating to safety, the protection of human, animal or plant life or health, the environment or consumers, and any measure to ensure its enforcement or implementation. Such measures include those to prohibit the importation of a good of another Party or the provision of a service by a service provider of another Party that fails to comply with the applicable requirements of those measures or to complete the Party's approval procedures.

* * * *

Unnecessary Obstacles

4. No Party may prepare, adopt, maintain or apply any standards-related measure with a view to or with the effect of creating an unnecessary obstacle to trade between the Parties. An unnecessary obstacle to trade shall not be deemed to be created where: (a) the demonstrable purpose of the measure is to achieve a legitimate objective; and (b) the measure does not operate to exclude goods of another Party that meet that legitimate objective.

* * * *

Article 913: Committee on Standards-Related Measures

1. The Parties hereby establish a Committee on Standards-Related Measures, comprising representatives of each Party.

2. The Committee's functions shall include: (a) monitoring the implementation and administration of this Chapter * * * ; (b) facilitating the process by which the Parties make compatible their standards-related measures; (c) providing a forum for the Parties to consult on issues relating to standards-related measures * * * ; (d) enhancing cooperation on the development, application and enforcement of standards-related measures; and (e) considering non-governmental, regional and multilateral developments regarding standards-related measures, including under the GATT.

* * * *

Part Five: INVESTMENT, SERVICES AND RELATED MATTERS

Chapter Eleven: Investment

SECTION A—INVESTMENT

* * * *

Article 1102: National Treatment

* * * *

2. Each Party shall accord to investments of investors of another Party treatment no less favorable than that it accords, in like circumstances, to investments of its own investors with respect to the establishment, acquisition, expansion, management, conduct, operation, and sale or other disposition of investments.

* * * *

4. For greater certainty, no Party may: (a) impose on an investor of another Party a requirement that a minimum level of equity in an enterprise in the territory of the Party be held by its nationals, other than nominal qualifying shares for directors or incorporators of corporations; or (b) require an investor of another Party, by reason of its nationality, to sell or otherwise dispose of an investment in the territory of the Party.

* * * *

Part Six: INTELLECTUAL PROPERTY

Chapter Seventeen: Intellectual Property

Article 1701: Nature and Scope of Obligations

1. Each Party shall provide in its territory to the nationals of another Party adequate and effective protection and enforcement of intellectual property rights, while ensuring that measures to enforce intellectual property rights do not themselves become barriers to legitimate trade.

* * * *

Article 1705: Copyright

* * * *

2. Each Party shall provide to authors and their successors in interest those rights enumerated in the Berne

Convention in respect of works covered by paragraph 1, including the right to authorize or prohibit: (a) the importation into the Party's territory of copies of the work made without the right holder's authorization; (b) the first public distribution of the original and each copy of the work by sale, rental or otherwise; (c) the communication of a work to the public; and (d) the commercial rental of the original or a copy of a computer program. Subparagraph (d) shall not apply where the copy of the computer program is not itself an essential object of the rental. Each Party shall provide that putting the original or a copy of a computer program on the market with the right holder's consent shall not exhaust the rental right.

* * * *

4. Each Party shall provide that, where the term of protection of a work, other than a photographic work or a work of applied art, is to be calculated on a basis other than the life of a natural person, the term shall be not less than 50 years from the end of the calendar year of the first authorized publication of the work or, failing such authorized publication within 50 years from the making of the work, 50 years from the end of the calendar year of making.

5. Each Party shall confine limitations or exceptions to the rights provided for in this Article to certain special cases that do not conflict with a normal exploitation of the work and do not unreasonably prejudice the legitimate interests of the right holder.

* * * *

Article 1706: **Sound Recordings**

1. Each Party shall provide to the producer of a sound recording the right to authorize or prohibit: (a) the direct or indirect reproduction of the sound recording; (b) the importation into the Party's territory of copies of the sound recording made without the producer's authorization; (c) the first public distribution of the original and each copy of the sound recording by sale, rental or otherwise; and (d) the commercial rental of the original or a copy of the sound recording, except where expressly otherwise provided in a contract between the producer of the sound recording and the authors of the works fixed therein. Each Party shall provide that putting the original or a copy of a sound recording on the market with the right holder's consent shall not exhaust the rental right.

* * * *

Article 1708: **Trademarks**

* * * *

4. Each Party shall provide a system for the registration of trademarks, which shall include: (a) examination of applications; (b) notice to be given to an applicant of the reasons for the refusal to register a trademark; (c) a reasonable opportunity for the applicant to respond to the notice; (d) publication of each trademark either before or promptly after it is registered; and (e) a reasonable opportunity for interested persons to petition to cancel the registration of a trademark. A Party may provide for a reasonable opportunity for interested persons to oppose the registration of a trademark.

* * * *

7. Each Party shall provide that the initial registration of a trademark be for a term of at least 10 years and that the registration be indefinitely renewable for terms of not less than 10 years when conditions for renewal have been met.

* * * *

Article 1709: **Patents**

1. Subject to paragraphs 2 and 3, each Party shall make patents available for any inventions, whether products or processes, in all fields of technology, provided that such inventions are new, result from an inventive step and are capable of industrial application. For purposes of this Article, a Party may deem the terms "inventive step" and "capable of industrial application" to be synonymous with the terms "non-obvious" and "useful," respectively.

* * * *

Article 1711: **Trade Secrets**

1. Each Party shall provide the legal means for any person to prevent trade secrets from being disclosed to, acquired by, or used by others without the consent of the person lawfully in control of the information in a manner contrary to honest commercial practices, in so far as: (a) the information is secret in the sense that it is not, as a body or in the precise configuration and assembly of its components, generally known among or readily accessible to persons that normally deal with the kind of information in question; (b) the information has actual or potential commercial value because it is secret; and (c) the person lawfully in control of the information has taken reasonable steps under the circumstances to keep it secret.

* * * *

Article 1714: **Enforcement of Intellectual Property Rights: General Provisions**

* * * *

3. Each Party shall provide that decisions on the merits of a case in judicial and administrative enforcement proceedings shall: (a) preferably be in writing and preferably state the reasons on which the decisions are based; (b) be made available at least to the parties in a proceeding without undue delay; and (c) be based only on evidence in respect of which such parties were offered the opportunity to be heard.

4. Each Party shall ensure that parties in a proceeding have an opportunity to have final administrative decisions

reviewed by a judicial authority of that Party and, subject to jurisdictional provisions in its domestic laws concerning the importance of a case, to have reviewed at least the legal aspects of initial judicial decisions on the merits of a case. Notwithstanding the above, no Party shall be required to provide for judicial review of acquittals in criminal cases.

* * * *

Article 1717: Criminal Procedures and Penalties

1. Each Party shall provide criminal procedures and penalties to be applied at least in cases of willful trademark counterfeiting or copyright piracy on a commercial scale. Each Party shall provide that penalties available include imprisonment or monetary fines, or both, sufficient to provide a deterrent, consistent with the level of penalties applied for crimes of a corresponding gravity.

2. Each Party shall provide that, in appropriate cases, its judicial authorities may order the seizure, forfeiture and destruction of infringing goods and of any materials and implements the predominant use of which has been in the commission of the offense.

Appendix T

The Small Business Regulatory Enforcement Fairness Act of 1996 [Excerpts]

Section 801. Congressional review

(a)(1)(A) Before a rule can take effect, the Federal agency promulgating such rule shall submit to each House of the Congress * * * a report containing—(i) a copy of the rule; (ii) a concise general statement relating to the rule, including whether it is a major rule; and (iii) the proposed effective date of the rule.

* * * *

(C) Upon receipt of a report submitted under subparagraph (A), each House shall provide copies of the report to the chairman and ranking member of each standing committee with jurisdiction under the rules of the House of Representatives or the Senate to report a bill to amend the provision of law under which the rule is issued.

* * * *

(3) A major rule relating to a report submitted under paragraph (1) shall take effect on the latest of—

(A) the later of the date occurring 60 days after the date on which—(i) the Congress receives the report submitted under paragraph (1); or (ii) the rule is published in the *Federal Register*, if so published;

(B) if the Congress passes a joint resolution of disapproval * * * relating to the rule, and the President signs a veto of such resolution, the earlier date—(i) on which either House of Congress votes and fails to override the veto of the President; or (ii) occurring 30 session days after the date on which the Congress received the veto and objections of the President; or

(C) the date the rule would have otherwise taken effect, if not for this section (unless a joint resolution of disapproval * * * is enacted).

* * * *

(b)(1) A rule shall not take effect (or continue), if the Congress enacts a joint resolution of disapproval * * * .

* * * *

Section 657. Oversight of regulatory enforcement

* * * *

(b) (2) The [SBA Enforcement] Ombudsman shall—

(A) work with each agency with regulatory authority over small businesses to ensure that small business concerns that receive or are subject to an audit, on-site inspection, compliance assistance effort, or other enforcement related communication or contact by agency personnel are provided with a means to comment on the enforcement activity conducted by such personnel;

(B) establish means to receive comments from small business concerns regarding actions by agency employees conducting compliance or enforcement activities with respect to the small business concern * * * on a confidential basis * * * ;

(C) based on substantiated comments received from small business concerns and the [Regional Small Business Regulatory Fairness] Boards, annually report to Congress and affected agencies evaluating the enforcement activities of agency personnel including a rating of the responsiveness to small business of the various regional and program offices of each agency; [and]

(D) coordinate and report annually on the activities, findings and recommendations of the [Regional Small Business Regulatory Fairness] Boards to the Administrator [of the Small Business Adminstration] and to the heads of affected agencies[.]

* * * *

(c)(2) Each [Regional Small Business Regulatory Fairness] Board * * * shall—

(A) meet at least annually to advise the Ombudsman on matters of concern to small businesses relating to the enforcement activities of agencies[.]

APPENDIX U

SPANISH EQUIVALENTS FOR IMPORTANT LEGAL TERMS IN ENGLISH

Abandoned property: bienes abandonados
Acceptance: aceptación; consentimiento; acuerdo
Acceptor: aceptante
Accession: toma de posesión; aumento; accesión
Accommodation indorser: avalista de favor
Accommodation party: firmante de favor
Accord: acuerdo; convenio; arregio
Accord and satisfaction: transacción ejecutada
Act of state doctrine: doctrina de acto de gobierno
Administrative law: derecho administrativo
Administrative process: procedimiento o metódo administrativo
Administrator: administrador (-a)
Adverse possession: posesión de hecho susceptible de proscripción adquisitiva
Affirmative action: acción afirmativa
Affirmative defense: defensa afirmativa
After-acquired property: bienes adquiridos con posterioridad a un hecho dado
Agency: mandato; agencia
Agent: mandatorio; agente; representante
Agreement: convenio; acuerdo; contrato
Alien corporation: empresa extranjera
Allonge: hojas adicionales de endosos
Answer: contestación de la demande; alegato
Anticipatory repudiation: anuncio previo de las partes de su imposibilidad de cumplir con el contrato
Appeal: apelación; recurso de apelación
Appellate jurisdiction: jurisdicción de apelaciones
Appraisal right: derecho de valuación
Arbitration: arbitraje
Arson: incendio intencional
Articles of partnership: contrato social
Artisan's lien: derecho de retención que ejerce al artesano
Assault: asalto; ataque; agresión
Assignment of rights: transmisión; transferencia; cesión
Assumption of risk: no resarcimiento por exposición voluntaria al peligro
Attachment: auto judicial que autoriza el embargo; embargo

Bailee: depositario
Bailment: depósito; constitución en depósito
Bailor: depositante
Bankruptcy trustee: síndico de la quiebra
Battery: agresión; física

Bearer: portador; tenedor
Bearer instrument: documento al portador
Bequest or legacy: legado (de bienes muebles)
Bilateral contract: contrato bilateral
Bill of lading: conocimiento de embarque; carta de porte
Bill of Rights: declaración de derechos
Binder: póliza de seguro provisoria; recibo de pago a cuenta del precio
Blank indorsement: endoso en blanco
Blue sky laws: leyes reguladoras del comercio bursátil
Bond: título de crédito; garantía; caución
Bond indenture: contrato de emisión de bonos; contrato del ampréstito
Breach of contract: incumplimiento de contrato
Brief: escrito; resumen; informe
Burglary: violación de domicilio
Business judgment rule: regla de juicio comercial
Business tort: agravio comercial

Case law: ley de casos; derecho casuístico
Cashier's check: cheque de caja
Causation in fact: causalidad en realidad
Cease-and-desist order: orden para cesar y desistir
Certificate of deposit: certificado de depósito
Certified check: cheque certificado
Charitable trust: fideicomiso para fines benéficos
Chattel: bien mueble
Check: cheque
Chose in action: derecho inmaterial; derecho de acción
Civil law: derecho civil
Close corporation: sociedad de un solo accionista o de un grupo restringido de accionistas
Closed shop: taller agremiado (emplea solamente a miembros de un gremio)
Closing argument: argumento al final
Codicil: codicilo
Collateral: guarantía; bien objeto de la guarantía real
Comity: cortesía; cortesía entre naciones
Commercial paper: instrumentos negociables; documentos a valores commerciales
Common law: derecho consuetudinario; derecho común; ley común
Common stock: acción ordinaria
Comparative negligence: negligencia comparada
Compensatory damages: daños y perjuicios reales o compensatorios
Concurrent conditions: condiciones concurrentes
Concurrent jurisdiction: competencia concurrente de varios tribunales para entender en una misma causa
Concurring opinion: opinión concurrente
Condition: condición
Condition precedent: condición suspensiva
Condition subsequent: condición resolutoria
Confiscation: confiscación
Confusion: confusión; fusión
Conglomerate merger: fusión de firmas que operan en distintos mercados
Consent decree: acuerdo entre las partes aprobado por un tribunal
Consequential damages: daños y perjuicios indirectos
Consideration: consideración; motivo; contraprestación
Consolidation: consolidación
Constructive delivery: entrega simbólica
Constructive trust: fideicomiso creado por aplicación de la ley
Consumer protection law: ley para proteger el consumidor
Contract: contrato
Contract under seal: contrato formal o sellado
Contributory negligence: negligencia de la parte actora
Conversion: usurpación; conversión de valores
Copyright: derecho de autor
Corporation: sociedad anómina; corporación; persona juridica
Co-sureties: cogarantes
Counterclaim: reconvención; contrademanda
Counteroffer: contraoferta
Course of dealing: curso de transacciones
Course of performance: curso de cumplimiento
Covenant: pacto; garantía; contrato
Covenant not to sue: pacto or contrato a no demandar
Covenant of quiet enjoyment: garantía del uso y goce pacífico del inmueble
Creditors' composition agreement: concordato preventivo
Crime: crimen; delito; contravención
Criminal law: derecho penal
Cross-examination: contrainterrogatorio
Cure: cura; cuidado; derecho de remediar un vicio contractual
Customs receipts: recibos de derechos aduaneros

Damages: daños; indemnización por daños y perjuicios
Debit card: tarjeta de dé bito
Debtor: deudor
Debt securities: seguridades de deuda
Deceptive advertising: publicidad engañosa
Deed: escritura; título; acta translativa de domino
Defamation: difamación
Delegation of duties: delegación de obligaciones
Demand deposit: depósito a la vista
Depositions: declaración de un testigo fuera del tribunal
Devise: legado; deposición testamentaria (bienes inmuebles)
Directed verdict: veredicto según orden del juez y sin participación activa del jurado
Direct examination: interrogatorio directo; primer interrogatorio
Disaffirmance: repudiación; renuncia; anulación
Discharge: descargo; liberación; cumplimiento
Disclosed principal: mandante revelado
Discovery: descubrimiento; producción de la prueba

Dissenting opinion: opinión disidente
Dissolution: disolución; terminación
Diversity of citizenship: competencia de los tribunales federales para entender en causas cuyas partes intervinientes son cuidadanos de distintos estados
Divestiture: extinción prematture de derechos reales
Dividend: dividendo
Docket: orden del día; lista de causas pendientes
Domestic corporation: sociedad local
Draft: orden de pago; letrade cambio
Drawee: girado; beneficiario
Drawer: librador
Duress: coacción; violencia

Easement: servidumbre
Embezzlement: desfalco; malversación
Eminent domain: poder de expropiación
Employment discrimination: discriminación en el empleo
Entrepreneur: empresario
Environmental law: ley ambiental
Equal dignity rule: regla de dignidad egual
Equity security: tipo de participación en una sociedad
Estate: propiedad; patrimonio; derecho
Estop: impedir; prevenir
Ethical issue: cuestión ética
Exclusive jurisdiction: competencia exclusiva
Exculpatory clause: cláusula eximente
Executed contract: contrato ejecutado
Execution: ejecución; cumplimiento
Executor: albacea
Executory contract: contrato aún no completamente consumado
Executory interest: derecho futuro
Express contract: contrato expreso
Expropriation: expropriación

Federal question: caso federal
Fee simple: pleno dominio; dominio absoluto
Fee simple absolute: dominio absoluto
Fee simple defeasible: dominio sujeta a una condición resolutoria
Felony: crimen; delito grave
Fictitious payee: beneficiario ficticio
Fiduciary: fiduciaro
Firm offer: oferta en firme
Fixture: inmueble por destino, incorporación a anexación
Floating lien: gravamen continuado
Foreign corporation: sociedad extranjera; U.S. sociedad constituída en otro estado
Forgery: falso; falsificación
Formal contract: contrato formal
Franchise: privilegio; franquicia; concesión
Franchisee: persona que recibe una concesión
Franchisor: persona que vende una concesión
Fraud: fraude; dolo; engaño
Future interest: bien futuro

Garnishment: embargo de derechos
General partner: socio comanditario
General warranty deed: escritura translativa de domino con garantía de título
Gift: donación
Gift *causa mortis*: donación por causa de muerte
Gift *inter vivos*: donación entre vivos
Good faith: buena fe
Good faith purchaser: comprador de buena fe

Holder: tenedor por contraprestación
Holder in due course: tenedor legítimo
Holographic will: testamento olográfico
Homestead exemption laws: leyes que exceptúan las casas de familia de ejecución por duedas generales
Horizontal merger: fusión horizontal

Identification: identificación
Implied-in-fact contract: contrato implícito en realidad
Implied warranty: guarantía implícita
Implied warranty of merchantability: garantía implícita de vendibilidad
Impossibility of performance: imposibilidad de cumplir un contrato
Imposter: imposter
Incidental beneficiary: beneficiario incidental; beneficiario secundario
Incidental damages: daños incidentales
Indictment: auto de acusación; acusación
Indorsee: endorsatario
Indorsement: endoso
Indorser: endosante
Informal contract: contrato no formal; contrato verbal
Information: acusación hecha por el ministerio público
Injunction: mandamiento; orden de no innovar
Innkeeper's lien: derecho de retención que ejerce el posadero
Installment contract: contrato de pago en cuotas
Insurable interest: interés asegurable
Intended beneficiary: beneficiario destinado
Intentional tort: agravio; cuasi-delito intenciónal
International law: derecho internaciónal
Interrogatories: preguntas escritas sometidas por una parte a la otra o a un testigo
***Inter vivos* trust:** fideicomiso entre vivos
Intestacy laws: leyes de la condición de morir intestado
Intestate: intestado
Investment company: compañia de inversiones
Issue: emisión

Joint tenancy: derechos conjuntos en un bien inmueble en favor del beneficiario sobreviviente
Judgment *n.o.v.*: juicio no obstante veredicto
Judgment rate of interest: interés de juicio
Judicial process: acto de procedimiento; proceso jurídico
Judicial review: revisión judicial
Jurisdiction: jurisdicción

Larceny: robo; hurto
Law: derecho; ley; jurisprudencia
Lease: contrato de locación; contrato de alquiler
Leasehold estate: bienes forales
Legal rate of interest: interés legal
Legatee: legatario
Letter of credit: carta de crédito
Levy: embargo; comiso
Libel: libelo; difamación escrita
Life estate: usufructo
Limited partner: comanditario
Limited partnership: sociedad en comandita
Liquidation: liquidación; realización
Lost property: objetos perdidos

Majority opinion: opinión de la mayoría
Maker: persona que realiza u ordena; librador
Mechanic's lien: gravamen de constructor
Mediation: mediación; intervención
Merger: fusión
Mirror image rule: fallo de reflejo
Misdemeanor: infracción; contravención
Mislaid property: bienes extraviados
Mitigation of damages: reducción de daños
Mortgage: hypoteca
Motion to dismiss: excepción parentoria
Mutual fund: fondo mutual

Negotiable instrument: instrumento negociable
Negotiation: negociación
Nominal damages: daños y perjuicios nominales
Novation: novación
Nuncupative will: testamento nuncupativo

Objective theory of contracts: teoria objetiva de contratos
Offer: oferta
Offeree: persona que recibe una oferta
Offeror: oferente
Order instrument: instrumento o documento a la orden
Original jurisdiction: jurisdicción de primera instancia
Output contract: contrato de producción

Parol evidence rule: regla relativa a la prueba oral
Partially disclosed principal: mandante revelado en parte
Partnership: sociedad colectiva; asociación; asociación de participación
Past consideration: causa o contraprestación anterior
Patent: patente; privilegio
Pattern or practice: muestra o práctica
Payee: beneficiario de un pago
Penalty: pena; penalidad
Per capita: por cabeza
Perfection: perfeción
Performance: cumplimiento; ejecución
Personal defenses: excepciones personales
Personal property: bienes muebles
Per stirpes: por estirpe
Plea bargaining: regateo por un alegato
Pleadings: alegatos
Pledge: prenda
Police powers: poders de policia y de prevención del crimen
Policy: póliza
Positive law: derecho positivo; ley positiva
Possibility of reverter: posibilidad de reversión
Precedent: precedente
Preemptive right: derecho de prelación
Preferred stock: acciones preferidas
Premium: recompensa; prima
Presentment warranty: garantía de presentación
Price discrimination: discriminación en los precios
Principal: mandante; principal
Privity: nexo jurídico
Privity of contract: relación contractual
Probable cause: causa probable
Probate: verificación; verificación del testamento
Probate court: tribunal de sucesiones y tutelas
Proceeds: resultados; ingresos
Profit: beneficio; utilidad; lucro
Promise: promesa
Promisee: beneficiario de una promesa
Promisor: promtente
Promissory estoppel: impedimento promisorio
Promissory note: pagaré; nota de pago
Promoter: promotor; fundador
Proximate cause: causa inmediata o próxima
Proxy: apoderado; poder
Punitive, or exemplary, damages: daños y perjuicios punitivos o ejemplares

Qualified indorsement: endoso con reservas
Quasi contract: contrato tácito o implícito
Quitclaim deed: acto de transferencia de una propiedad por finiquito, pero sin ninguna garantía sobre la validez del título transferido

Ratification: ratificación
Real property: bienes inmuebles
Reasonable doubt: duda razonable
Rebuttal: refutación
Recognizance: promesa; compromiso; reconocimiento
Recording statutes: leyes estatales sobre registros oficiales
Redress: reporacíon
Reformation: rectificación; reforma; corrección
Rejoinder: dúplica; contrarréplica
Release: liberación; renuncia a un derecho
Remainder: substitución; reversión
Remedy: recurso; remedio; reparación
Replevin: acción reivindicatoria; reivindicación
Reply: réplica
Requirements contract: contrato de suministro
Rescission: rescisión
Res judicata: cosa juzgada; res judicata
Respondeat superior: responsabilidad del mandante o del maestro
Restitution: restitución
Restrictive indorsement: endoso restrictivo
Resulting trust: fideicomiso implícito

Reversion: reversión; sustitución
Revocation: revocación; derogación
Right of contribution: derecho de contribución
Right of reimbursement: derecho de reembolso
Right of subrogation: derecho de subrogación
Right-to-work law: ley de libertad de trabajo
Robbery: robo
Rule 10b-5: Regla 10b-5

Sale: venta; contrato de compreventa
Sale on approval: venta a ensayo; venta sujeta a la aprobación del comprador
Sale or return: venta con derecho de devolución
Sales contract: contrato de compraventa; boleto de compraventa
Satisfaction: satisfacción; pago
***Scienter*:** a sabiendas
S corporation: S corporación
Secured party: acreedor garantizado
Secured transaction: transacción garantizada
Securities: volares; titulos; seguridades
Security agreement: convenio de seguridad
Security interest: interés en un bien dado en garantía que permite a quien lo detenta venderlo en caso de incumplimiento
Service mark: marca de identificación de servicios
Shareholder's derivative suit: acción judicial entablada por un accionista en nombre de la sociedad
Signature: firma; rúbrica
Slander: difamación oral; calumnia
Sovereign immunity: immunidad soberana
Special indorsement: endoso especial; endoso a la orden de una person en particular
Specific performance: ejecución precisa, según los términos del contrato
Spendthrift trust: fideicomiso para pródigos
Stale check: cheque vencido
***Stare decisis*:** acatar las decisiones, observar los precedentes
Statutory law: derecho estatutario; derecho legislado; derecho escrito
Stock: acciones
Stock warrant: certificado para la compra de acciones
Stop-payment order: orden de suspensión del pago de un cheque dada por el librador del mismo
Strict liability: responsabilidad uncondicional
Summary judgment: fallo sumario

Tangible property: bienes corpóreos
Tenancy at will: inguilino por tiempo indeterminado (según la voluntad del propietario)
Tenancy by sufferance: posesión por tolerancia
Tenancy by the entirety: locación conyugal conjunta
Tenancy for years: inguilino por un término fijo
Tenancy in common: specie de copropiedad indivisa
Tender: oferta de pago; oferta de ejecución
Testamentary trust: fideicomiso testamentario
Testator: testador (-a)
Third party beneficiary contract: contrato para el beneficio del tercero-beneficiario
Tort: agravio; cuasi-delito
Totten trust: fideicomiso creado por un depósito bancario
Trade acceptance: letra de cambio aceptada
Trademark: marca registrada
Trade name: nombre comercial; razón social
Traveler's check: cheque del viajero
Trespass to land: ingreso no authorizado a las tierras de otro
Trespass to personal property: violación de los derechos posesorios de un tercero con respecto a bienes muebles
Trust: fideicomiso; trust

***Ultra vires*:** ultra vires; fuera de la facultad (de una sociedad anónima)
Unanimous opinion: opinión unámine
Unconscionable contract or clause: contrato leonino; cláusula leonino
Underwriter: subscriptor; asegurador
Unenforceable contract: contrato que no se puede hacer cumplir
Unilateral contract: contrato unilateral
Union shop: taller agremiado; empresa en la que todos los empleados son miembros del gremio o sindicato
Universal defenses: defensas legitimas o legales
Usage of trade: uso comercial
Usury: usura

Valid contract: contrato válido
Venue: lugar; sede del proceso
Vertical merger: fusión vertical de empresas
Voidable contract: contrato anulable
Void contract: contrato nulo; contrato inválido, sin fuerza legal
***Voir dire*:** examen preliminar de un testigo a jurado por el tribunal para determinar su competencia
Voting trust: fideicomiso para ejercer el derecho de voto

Waiver: renuncia; abandono
Warranty of habitability: garantía de habitabilidad
Watered stock: acciones diluídos; capital inflado
White-collar crime: crimen administrativo
Writ of attachment: mandamiento de ejecución; mandamiento de embargo
Writ of *certiorari*: auto de avocación; auto de certiorari
Writ of execution: auto ejecutivo; mandamiento de ejecutión
Writ of mandamus: auto de mandamus; mandamiento; orden judicial

Glossary

A

Abandoned property Property with which the owner has voluntarily parted, with no intention of recovering it.
Abandonment In landlord-tenant law, a tenant's departure from leased premises completely, with no intention of returning before the end of the lease term.
Abus de droit A doctrine developed in the French courts. The doctrine modified employment at will and protected workers exercising their rights from wrongful discharge and other employer abuses.
Acceleration clause A clause in an installment contract that provides for all future payments to become due immediately on the failure to tender timely payments or on the occurrence of a specified event.
Acceptance In contract law, the offeree's notification to the offeror that the offeree agrees to be bound by the terms of the offeror's proposal. Although historically the terms of acceptance had to be the mirror image of the terms of the offer, the Uniform Commercial Code provides that even modified terms of the offer in a definite expression of acceptance constitute a contract.
Accredited investors In the context of securities offerings, "sophisticated" investors, such as banks, insurance companies, investment companies, the issuer's executive officers and directors, and persons whose income or net worth exceeds certain limits.
Act of state doctrine A doctrine that provides that the judicial branch of one country will not examine the validity of public acts committed by a recognized foreign government within its own territory.
Acquittal A certification or declaration following a trial that the individual accused of a crime is innocent, or free from guilt, and is thus absolved of the charges.
Actionable Capable of serving as the basis of a lawsuit.
Actual authority Authority of an agent that is express or implied.
Actual malice Real and demonstrable evil intent. In a defamation suit, a statement made about a public figure normally must be made with actual malice (with either knowledge of its falsity or a reckless disregard of the truth) for liability to be incurred.
Actus reus (pronounced *ak*-tus *ray*-uhs) A guilty (prohibited) act. The commission of a prohibited act is one of the two essential elements required for criminal liability, the other element being the intent to commit a crime.
Adequate protection doctrine In bankruptcy law, a doctrine that protects secured creditors from losing their security as a result of an automatic stay on legal proceedings by creditors against the debtor once the debtor petitions for bankruptcy relief. In certain circumstances, the bankruptcy court may provide adequate protection by requiring the debtor or trustee to pay the creditor or provide additional guaranties to protect the creditor against the losses suffered by the creditor as a result of the stay.
Adhesion contract A "standard-form" contract, such as that between a large retailer and a consumer, in which the stronger party dictates the terms.
Adjudicate To render a judicial decision. In the administrative process, the proceeding in which an administrative law judge hears and decides on issues that arise when an administrative agency charges a person or a firm with violating a law or regulation enforced by the agency.
Administrative agency A federal or state government agency established to perform a specific function. Administrative agencies are authorized by legislative acts to make and enforce rules to administer and enforce the acts.
Administrative law The body of law created by administrative agencies (in the form of rules, regulations, orders, and decisions) in order to carry out their duties and responsibilities.
Administrative law judge (ALJ) One who presides over an administrative agency hearing and who has the power to administer oaths, take testimony, rule on questions of evidence, and make determinations of fact.
Administrative process The procedure used by administrative agencies in the administration of law.
Administrator One who is appointed by a court to handle the probate (disposition) of a person's estate if that person dies intestate (without a valid will) or if the executor named in the will cannot serve.
Affidavit A written or printed voluntary statement of facts, confirmed by the oath or affirmation of the party making it and made before a person having the authority to administer the oath or affirmation.
Affirm To validate; to give legal force to. *See also* Ratification
Affirmative action Job-hiring policies that give special consideration to members of protected classes in an effort to overcome present effects of past discrimination.
Affirmative defense A response to a plaintiff's claim that does not deny the plaintiff's facts but attacks the plaintiff's legal right to bring an action. An example is the running of the statute of limitations.
After-acquired evidence A type of evidence submitted in support of an affirmative defense in employment discrimination cases. Evidence that, prior to the employer's discriminatory act, the employee engaged in misconduct sufficient to warrant dismissal had the employer known of it earlier.
After-acquired property Property of the debtor that is acquired after the execution of a security agreement.
Agency A relationship between two parties in which one party (the agent) agrees to represent or act for the other (the principal).
Agency by estoppel Arises when a principal negligently allows an agent to exercise powers not granted to the agent, thus justifying others in believing that the agent possesses the requisite agency authority. *See also* Promissory estoppel
Agent A person who agrees to represent or act for another, called the principal.
Aggressor The acquiring corporation in a takeover attempt.
Agreement A meeting of two or more minds in regard to the terms of a contract; usually broken down into two events—an offer by one party to form a contract, and an acceptance of the offer by the person to whom the offer is made.
Alien corporation A designation in the United States for a corporation formed in another country but doing business in the United States.
Alienation In real property law, the voluntary transfer of property from one person to another (as opposed to a transfer by operation of law).
Allegation A statement, claim, or assertion.
Allege To state, recite, assert, or charge.
Alternative dispute resolution (ADR) The resolution of disputes in ways other than those involved in the traditional judicial process. Negotiation, mediation, and arbitration are forms of ADR.
Amend To change and improve through a formal procedure.
American Arbitration Association (AAA) The major organization offering arbitration services in the United States.
Analogy In logical reasoning, an assumption that if two things are similar in some respects, they will be similar in other respects also. Often used in legal reasoning to infer the appropriate application of legal principles in a case being decided by referring to previous cases involving different facts but considered to come within the policy underlying the rule.
Annul To cancel; to make void.
Answer Procedurally, a defendant's response to the plaintiff's complaint.
Anticipatory repudiation An assertion or action by a party indicating that he or she will not perform an obligation that the party is contractually obligated to perform at a future time.
Antitrust law The body of federal and state laws and statutes protecting trade and commerce from unlawful restraints, price discrimination, price fixing, and monopolies. The principal federal antitrust statues are the Sherman Act of 1890, the Clayton Act of 1914, and the Federal Trade Commission Act of 1914.
Apparent authority Authority that is only apparent, not real. In agency law, a person may be deemed to have had the power to act as an agent for another party if the other party's manifestations to a third party led the third party to believe that an agency existed when, in fact, it did not.

Appeal Resort to a superior court, such as an appellate court, to review the decision of an inferior court, such as a trial court or an administrative agency.
Appellant The party who takes an appeal from one court to another.
Appellate court A court having appellate jurisdiction. Each state court system has at least one level of appellate courts. In the federal court system, the appellate courts are the circuit courts of appeals (intermediate appellate courts) and the United States Supreme Court (the highest appellate court in the federal system).
Appellate jurisdiction Courts having appellate jurisdiction act as reviewing courts, or appellate courts, Generally, cases can be brought before appellate courts only on appeal from an order or a judgment of a trial court or other lower court.
Appellee The party against whom an appeal is taken—that is, the party who opposes setting aside or reversing the judgment.
Appraisal right The right of a dissenting shareholder, if he or she objects to an extraordinary transaction of the corporation (such as a merger or consolidation), to have his or her shares appraised and to be paid the fair value of his or her shares by the corporation.
Appropriate bargaining unit A designation based on job duties, skill levels, etc., of the proper entity that should be covered by a collective bargaining agreement.
Appropriation In tort law, the use by one person of another person's name, likeness, or other identifying characteristic without permission and for the benefit of the user.
Arbitrary and capricious test The court reviewing an informal administrative agency action applies this test to determine whether or not that action was in clear error. The court gives wide discretion to the expertise of the agency and decides if the agency had sufficient factual information on which to base its action. If no clear error was made, then the agency's action stands.
Arbitration The settling of a dispute by submitting it to a disinterested third party (other than a court), who renders a decision. The decision may or may not be legally binding.
Arbitration clause A clause in a contract that provides that, in the event of a dispute, the parties will submit the dispute to arbitration rather than litigate the dispute in court.
Arbitrator A disinterested party who, by prior agreement of the parties submitting their dispute to arbitration, has the power to resolve the dispute and (generally) bind the parties.
Arraignment A procedure in which an accused person is brought before the court to plead to the criminal charge in the indictment or information. The charge is read to the person, and he or she is asked to enter a plea—such as "guilty" or "not guilty."
Arson The malicious burning of another's dwelling. Some statutes have expanded this to include any real property regardless of ownership and the destruction of property by other means—for example, by explosion.
Articles of incorporation The document filed with the appropriate governmental agency, usually the secretary of state, when a business is incorporated; state statutes usually prescribe what kind of information must be contained in the articles of incorporation.
Articles of partnership A written agreement that sets forth each partner's rights and obligations with respect to the partnership.
Artisan's lien A possessory lien given to a person who has made improvements and added value to another person's personal property as security for payment for services performed.
Assault Any word or action intended to make another person fearful of immediate physical harm; a reasonably believable threat.
Assignee The person to whom contract rights are assigned.
Assignment The act of transferring to another all or part of one's rights arising under a contract.
Assignor The person who assigns contract rights.
Assumption of risk A defense against negligence that can be used when the plaintiff is aware of a danger and voluntarily assumes the risk of injury from that danger.
Attachment In the context of judicial liens, a court-ordered seizure and taking into custody of property prior to the securing of a judgment for a past-due debt.
Attempt to monopolize Any action by a firm to eliminate competition and gain monopoly power.
Attractive nuisance doctrine A common law doctrine under which a landowner or landlord may be held liable for injuries incurred by children who are lured onto the property by something dangerous and enticing thereon.
Authority In agency law, the agent's permission to act on behalf of the principal. An agent's authority may be actual (express or implied) or apparent. *See also* Actual authority; Apparent authority
Authorization card A card signed by an employee that gives a union permission to act on his or her behalf in negotiations with management once a majority of the employees has signed such cards.
Authorized means In contract law, the means of acceptance authorized by the offeror.
Automatic stay In bankruptcy proceedings, the suspension of virtually all litigation and other action by creditors against the debtor or the debtor's property; the stay is effective the moment the debtor files a petition in bankruptcy.
Award In the context of litigation, the amount of money awarded to a plaintiff in a civil lawsuit as damages. In the context of arbitration, the arbitrator's decision.

B

Bail An amount of money set by the court that must be paid by a criminal defendant to the court before the defendant will be released from custody. Bail is set to assure that an individual accused of a crime will appear for further criminal proceedings. If the accused provides bail, whether in cash or in a surety bond, then he or she is released from jail.
Bailee One to whom goods are entrusted by a bailor. Under the Uniform Commercial Code, a party who, by a bill of lading, warehouse receipt, or other document of title, acknowledges possession of goods and contracts.
Bailee's lien A possessory lien, or claim, that a bailee entitled to compensation can place on the bailed property to ensure that he or she will be paid for the services provided. The lien is effective as long as the bailee retains possession of the bailed goods and has not agreed to extend credit to the bailor. Sometimes referred to as an artisan's lien.
Bailment A situation in which the personal property of one person (a bailor) is entrusted to another (a bailee), who is obligated to return the bailed property to the bailor or dispose of it as directed.
Bailor One who entrusts goods to a bailee.
Bait-and-switch advertising Advertising a product at a very attractive price (the "bait") and then informing the consumer, once he or she is in the store, that the advertised product is either not available or is of poor quality; the customer is then urged to purchase ("switched" to) a more expensive item.
Bankruptcy court A federal court of limited jurisdiction that handles only bankruptcy proceedings. Bankruptcy proceedings are governed by federal bankruptcy law.
Bargain A mutual undertaking, contract, or agreement between two parties; to negotiate over the terms of a purchase or contract.
Basis of the bargain In contract law, the affirmation of fact or promise on which the sale of goods is predicated, creating an express warranty.
Battery The unprivileged, intentional touching of another.
Beachhead acquistion The gradual accumulation of a bloc of a target corporation's shares by an aggressor during an attempt to obtain control of the corporation.
Beyond a reasonable doubt The standard used to determine the guilt or innocence of a person criminally charged. To be guilty of a crime, one must be proved guilty "beyond and to the exclusion of every reasonable doubt." A reasonable doubt is one that would cause a prudent person to hesitate before acting in matters important to him or her.
Bilateral contract A type of contract that arises when a promise is given in exchange for a return promise.
Bill of lading A document that serves both as evidence of the receipt of goods for shipment and as documentary evidence of title to the goods.
Bill of Rights The first ten amendments to the U.S. Constitution.
Binding authority Any source of law that a court must follow when

deciding a case. Binding authorities include constitutions, statutes, and regulations that govern the issue being decided, as well as court decisions that are controlling precedents within the jurisdiction.
Blue laws State or local laws that prohibit the performance of certain types of commercial activities on Sunday.
Blue sky laws State laws that regulate the offer and sale of securities.
Bona fide Good faith. A bona fide obligation is one made in good faith—that is, sincerely and honestly.
Bona fide occupational qualification (BFOQ) Identifiable characteristics reasonably necessary to the normal operation of a particular business. These characteristics can include gender, national origin, and religion, but not race.
Bond A certificate that evidences a corporate (or government) debt. It is a security that involves no ownership interest in the issuing entity.
Bond indenture A contract between the issuer of a bond and the bondholder.
Bounty payment A reward (payment) given to a person or persons who perform a certain service—such as informing legal authorities of illegal actions.
Boycott A concerted refusal to do business with a particular person or entity in order to obtain concessions or to express displeasure with certain acts or practices of that person or business. *See also* Secondary boycott
Breach To violate a law, by an act or an omission, or to break a legal obligation that one owes to another person or to society.
Breach of contract The failure, without legal excuse, of a promisor to perform the obligations of a contract.
Bribery The offering, giving, receiving, or soliciting of anything of value with the aim of influencing an official action or an official's discharge of a legal or public duty or (with respect to commercial bribery) a business decision.
Brief A formal legal document submitted by the attorney for the appellant—or the appellee (in answer to the appellant's brief)—to an appellate court when a case is appealed. The appellant's brief outlines the facts and issues of the case, the judge's rulings or jury's findings that should be reversed or modified, the applicable law, and the arguments on the client's behalf.
Bulk transfer A bulk sale or transfer, not made in the ordinary course of business, of a major part of the materials, supplies, merchandise, or other inventory of an enterprise.
Bulk zoning Zoning regulations that restrict the amount of structural coverage on a particular parcel of land.
Bureaucracy A large organization that is structured hierarchically to carry out specific functions.
Burglary The unlawful entry into a building with the intent to commit a felony. (Some state statutes expand this to include the intent to commit any crime.)
Business ethics Ethics in a business context; a consensus of what constitutes right or wrong behavior in the world of business and the application of moral principles to situations that arise in a business setting.
Business invitees Those people, such as customers or clients, who are invited onto business premises by the owner of those premises for business purposes.
Business judgment rule A rule that immunizes corporate management from liability for actions that result in corporate losses or damages if the actions are undertaken in good faith and are within both the power of the corporation and the authority of management to make.
Business necessity A defense to allegations of employment discrimination in which the employer demonstrates that an employment practice that discriminates against members of a protected class is related to job performance.
Business tort The wrongful interference with the business rights of another.
Buyer in the ordinary course of business A buyer who, in good faith and without knowledge that the sale to him or her is in violation of the ownership rights or security interest of a third party in the goods, purchases goods in the ordinary course of business from a person in the business of selling goods of that kind.
Buy-sell agreement In the context of partnerships, an express agreement made at the time of partnership formation for one or more of the partners to buy out the other or others should the situation warrant—and thus provide for the smooth dissolution of the partnership.
Bylaws A set of governing rules adopted by a corporation or other association.
Bystander A spectator, witness, or person standing nearby when an event occurred and who did not engage in the business or act leading to the event.

C

C.I.F. or C.&F. Cost, insurance, and freight—or just cost and freight. A pricing term in a contract for the sale of goods requiring, among other things, that the seller put the goods in possession of a carrier before risk passes to the buyer.
C.O.D. Cash on delivery. In sales transactions, a term meaning that the buyer will pay for the goods on delivery and before inspecting the goods.
Callable bond A bond that may be called in and the principal repaid at specified times or under conditions specified in the bond when it is issued.
Cancellation The act of nullifying, or making void. *See also* Rescission
Capital Accumulated goods, possessions, and assets used for the production of profits and wealth; the equity of owners in a business.
Carrier An individual or organization engaged in transporting passengers or goods for hire. *See also* Common carrier
Case law The rules of law announced in court decisions. Case law includes the aggregate of reported cases that interpret judicial precedents, statutes, regulations, and constitutional provisions.
Case on point A previous case involving factual circumstances and issues that are similar to the case before the court.
Cash surrender value The amount that the insurer has agreed to pay to the insured if a life insurance policy is canceled before the insured's death.
Categorical imperative A concept developed by the philosopher Immanuel Kant as an ethical guideline for behavior. In deciding whether an action is right or wrong, or desirable or undesirable, a person should evaluate the action in terms of what would happen if everybody else in the same situation, or category, acted the same way.
Causation in fact An act or omission without ("but for") which an event would not have occurred.
Cause of action A situation or state of facts that would entitle a party to sustain a legal action and give the party a right to seek a judicial remedy.
Cease-and-desist order An administrative or judicial order prohibiting a person or business firm from conducting activities that an agency or court has deemed illegal.
Certificate of incorporation The primary document that evidences corporate existence (referred to as articles of incorporation in some states).
Certificate of limited partnership The basic document filed with a designated state official by which a limited partnership is formed.
Certification mark A mark used by one or more persons, other than the owner, to certify the region, materials, mode of manufacture, quality, or accuracy of the owner's goods or services. When used by members of a cooperative, association, or other organization, such a mark is referred to as a collective mark. Examples of certification marks include the "Good Housekeeping Seal of Approval" and "UL Tested."
Certiorari *See* Writ of *certiorari*
Chain-style business franchise A franchise that operates under a franchisor's trade name and that is identified as a member of a select group of dealers that engage in the franchisor's business. The franchisee is generally required to follow standardized or prescribed methods of operation. Examples of this type of franchise are McDonald's and most other fast-food chains.
Chancellor An adviser to the king at the time of the early king's courts of England. Individuals petitioned the king for relief when they could not obtain an adequate remedy in a court of law, and these petitions were decided by the chancellor.
Charging order In partnership law, an order granted by a court to a

judgment creditor that entitles the creditor to attach profits or assets of a partner on dissolution of the partnership.
Charter *See* Corporate charter
Chattel All forms of personal property.
Checks and balances The national government is composed of three separate branches: the executive, the legislative, and the judicial branches. Each branch of the government exercises a check on the actions of the others.
Choice-of-language clause A clause in a contract designating the official language by which the contract will be interpreted in the event of a future disagreement over the contract's terms.
Choice-of-law clause A clause in a contract designating the law (such as the law of a particular state or nation) that will govern the contract.
Citation A reference to a publication in which a legal authority—such as a statute or a court decision—or other source can be found.
Civil law The branch of law dealing with the definition and enforcement of all private or public rights, as opposed to criminal matters.
Civil law system A system of law derived from that of the Roman Empire and based on a code rather than case law; the predominant system of law in the nations of continental Europe and the nations that were once their colonies. In the United States, Louisiana is the only state that has a civil law system.
Claim As a verb, to assert or demand. As a noun, a right to payment.
Close corporation A corporation whose shareholders are limited to a small group of persons, often including only family members. The rights of shareholders of a close corporation usually are restricted regarding the transfer of shares to others.
Closed shop A firm that requires union membership by its workers as a condition of employment. The closed shop was made illegal by the Labor-Management Relations Act of 1947.
Closing The final step in the sale of real estate—also called settlement or closing escrow. The escrow agent coordinates the closing with the recording of deeds, the obtaining of title insurance, and other concurrent closing activities. Several costs must be paid, in cash, at the time of closing, and they can range from several hundred to several thousand dollars, depending on the amount of the mortgage loan and other conditions of sale.
Closing argument An argument made after the plaintiff and defendant have rested their cases. Closing arguments are made prior to the jury charges.
Collateral promise A secondary promise that is ancillary (subsidiary) to a principal transaction or primary contractual relationship, such as a promise made by one person to pay the debts of another if the latter fails to perform. A collateral promise normally must be in writing to be enforceable.
Collective bargaining The process by which labor and management negotiate the terms and conditions of employment, including working hours and workplace conditions.
Collective mark A mark used by members of a cooperative, association, or other organization to certify the region, materials, mode of manufacture, quality, or accuracy of the specific goods or services. Examples of collective marks include the labor union marks found on tags of certain products and the credits of movies, which indicate the various associations and organizations that participated in the making of the movies.
Comity A deference by which one nation gives effect to the laws and judicial decrees of another nation. This recognition is based primarily on respect.
Comment period A period of time following an administrative agency's publication or a notice of a proposed rule during which private parties may comment in writing on the agency proposal in an effort to influence agency policy. The agency takes any comments received into consideration when drafting the final version of the regulation.
Commerce clause The provision in Article I, Section 8, of the U.S. Constitution that gives Congress the power to regulate interstate commerce.
Commercial impracticability A doctrine under which a seller may be excused from performing a contract when (1) a contingency occurs, (2) the contingency's occurrence makes performance impracticable, and (3) the nonoccurrence of the contingency was a basic assumption on which the contract was made. Despite the fact that UCC 2–615 expressly frees only sellers under this doctrine, courts have not distinguished between buyers and sellers in applying it.
Commingle To mix together. To put funds or goods together into one mass so that the funds or goods are so mixed that they no longer have separate identities. In corporate law, if personal and corporate interests are commingled to the extent that the corporation has no separate identity, a court may "pierce the corporate veil" and expose the shareholders to personal liability.
Common carrier A carrier that holds itself out or undertakes to carry persons or goods of all persons indifferently, or of all who choose to employ it.
Common law That body of law developed from custom or judicial decisions in English and U.S. courts, not attributable to a legislature.
Common situs picketing The illegal picketing of an entire construction site by workers who are involved in a labor dispute with a particular subcontractor.
Common stock Shares of ownership in a corporation that give the owner of the stock a proportionate interest in the corporation with regard to control, earnings, and net assets; shares of common stock are lowest in priority with respect to payment of dividends and distribution of the corporation's assets on dissolution.
Community property A form of concurrent ownership of property in which each spouse technically owns an undivided one-half interest in property acquired during the marriage. This form of joint ownership occurs in only nine states and Puerto Rico.
Comparative negligence A theory in tort law under which the liability for injuries resulting from negligent acts is shared by all parties who were negligent (including the injured party), on the basis of each person's proportionate negligence.
Compensatory damages A money award equivalent to the actual value of injuries or damages sustained by the aggrieved party.
Complaint The pleading made by a plaintiff alleging wrongdoing on the part of the defendant; the document that, when filed with a court, initiates a lawsuit.
Complete performance Performance of a contract strictly in accordance with the contract's terms.
Composition agreement *See* Creditors' composition agreement
Computer crime Any wrongful act that is directed against computers and computer parties, or wrongful use or abuse of computers or software.
Concentrated industry An industry in which a large percentage of market sales is controlled by either a single firm or a small number of firms.
Concerted action Action by employees, such as a strike or picketing, with the purpose of furthering their bargaining demands or other mutual interests.
Conciliation A form of alternative dispute resolution in which the parties reach an agreement themselves with the help of a neutral third party, called a conciliator, who facilitates the negotiations.
Concurrent conditions Conditions in a contract that must occur or be performed at the same time; they are mutually dependent. No obligations arise until these conditions are simultaneously performed.
Concurrent jurisdiction Jurisdiction that exists when two different courts have the power to hear a case. For example, some cases can be heard in either a federal or a state court.
Concurrent ownership Joint ownership.
Concurring opinion A written opinion outlining the views of a judge or justice to make or emphasize a point that was not made or emphasized in the majority opinion.
Condition A qualification, provision, or clause in a contractual agreement, the occurrence of which creates, suspends, or terminates the obligations of the contracting parties.
Confession of judgment The act of a debtor in permitting a judgment to be entered against him or her by a creditor, for an agreed sum, without the institution of legal proceedings.
Confiscation A government's taking of privately owned business or per-

sonal property without a proper public purpose or an award of just compensation.
Conforming goods Goods that conform to contract specifications.
Confusion The mixing together of goods belonging to two or more owners so that the separately owned goods cannot be identified.
Conglomerate merger A merger between firms that do not compete with each other because they are in different markets (as opposed to horizontal and vertical mergers).
Consent Voluntary agreement to a proposition or an act of another. A concurrence of wills.
Consequential damages Special damages that compensate for a loss that is not direct or immediate (for example, lost profits). The special damages must have been reasonably foreseeable at the time the breach or injury occurred in order for the plaintiff to collect them.
Consideration Generally, the value given in return for a promise. The consideration, which must be present to make the contract legally binding, must be something of legally sufficient value and bargained for and must result in a detriment to the promisee or a benefit to the promisor.
Consignee One to whom goods are delivered on consignment. *See also* Consignment
Consignment A transaction in which an owner of goods (the consignor) delivers the goods to another (the consignee) for the consignee to sell. The consignee pays the consignor for the goods when they are sold by the consignee.
Consignor One who consigns goods to another. *See also* Consignment
Consolidation A contractual and statutory process in which two or more corporations join to become a completely new corporation. The original corporations cease to exist, and the new corporation acquires all their assets and liabilities.
Constitutional law Law based on the U.S. Constitution and the constitutions of the various states.
Constructive delivery An act equivalent to the actual, physical delivery of property that cannot be physically delivered because of difficulty or impossibility; for example, the transfer of a key to a safe constructively delivers the contents of the safe.
Constructive eviction A form of eviction that occurs when a landlord fails to perform adequately any of the undertakings (such as providing heat in the winter) required by the lease, thereby making the tenant's further use and enjoyment of the property exceedingly difficult or impossible.
Constructive trust An equitable trust that is imposed in the interests of fairness and justice when someone wrongfully holds legal title to property. A court may require the owner to hold the property in trust for the person or persons who rightfully should own the property.
Consumer credit Credit extended primarily for personal or household use.
Consumer-debtor An individual whose debts are primarily consumer debts (debts for purchases made primarily for personal or household use).
Consumer goods Goods that are primarily for personal or household use.
Consumer law The body of statutes, agency rules, and judicial decisions protecting consumers of goods and services from dangerous manufacturing techniques, mislabeling, unfair credit practices, deceptive advertising, and so on. Consumer laws provide remedies and protections that are not ordinarily available to merchants or to businesses.
Contingency fee An attorney's fee that is based on a percentage of the final award received by his or her client as a result of litigation.
Contract An agreement that can be enforced in court; formed by two or more parties, each of whom agrees to perform or to refrain from performing some act now or in the future.
Contract implied in law *See* Quasi contract
Contractual agreement *See* Contract
Contractual capacity The threshold mental capacity required by the law for a party who enters into a contract to be bound by that contract.
Contribution *See* Right of contribution
Contributory negligence A theory in tort law under which a complaining party's own negligence contributed to or caused his or her injuries. Contributory negligence is an absolute bar to recovery in a minority of jurisdictions.
Conversion The wrongful taking, using, or retaining possession of personal property that belongs to another.
Convertible bond A bond that can be exchanged for a specified number of shares of common stock under certain conditions.
Conveyance The transfer of a title to land from one person to another by deed; a document (such as a deed) by which an interest in land is transferred from one person to another.
Conviction The outcome of a criminal trial in which the defendant has been found guilty of the crime with which he or she was charged and on which sentencing, or punishment, is based.
Cooperative An association that is organized to provide an economic service to its members (or shareholders). An incorporated cooperative is a nonprofit corporation. It will make distributions of dividends, or profits, to its owners on the basis of their transactions with the cooperative rather than on the basis of the amount of capital they contributed. Examples of cooperatives are consumer purchasing cooperatives, credit cooperatives, and farmers' cooperatives.
Co-ownership Joint ownership.
Copyright The exclusive right of authors to publish, print, or sell an intellectual production for a statutory period of time. A copyright has the same monopolistic nature as a patent or trademark, but it differs in that it applies exclusively to works of art, literature, and other works of authorship, including computer programs.
Corporate charter The document issued by a state agency or authority (usually the secretary of state) that grants a corporation legal existence and the right to function.
Corporate social responsibility The concept that corporations can and should act ethically and be accountable to society for their actions.
Corporation A legal entity formed in compliance with statutory requirements. The entity is distinct from its shareholders-owners.
Cosign The act of signing a document (such as a note promising to pay another in return for a loan or other benefit) jointly with another person and thereby assuming liability for performing what was promised in the document.
Cost-benefit analysis A decision-making technique that involves weighing the costs of a given action against the benefits of the action.
Co-surety A joint surety. One who assumes liability jointly with another surety for the payment of an obligation.
Counteradvertising New advertising that is undertaken pursuant to a Federal Trade Commission order for the purpose of correcting earlier false claims that were made about a product.
Counterclaim A claim made by a defendant in a civil lawsuit that in effect sues the plaintiff.
Counteroffer An offeree's response to an offer in which the offeree rejects the original offer and at the same time makes a new offer.
Course of dealing Prior conduct between parties to a contract that establishes a common basis for their understanding.
Course of performance The conduct that occurs under the terms of a particular agreement; such conduct indicates what the parties to an agreement intended it to mean.
Court of equity A court that decides controversies and administers justice according to the rules, principles, and precedents of equity.
Court of law A court in which the only remedies that could be granted were things of value, such as money damages. In the early English king's courts, courts of law were distinct from courts of equity.
Covenant not to compete A contractual promise to refrain from competing with another party for a certain period of time (not excessive in duration) and within a reasonable geographic area. Although covenants not to compete restrain trade, they are commonly found in partnership agreements, business sale agreements, and employment contracts. If they are ancillary to such agreements, covenants not to compete will normally be enforced by the courts unless the time period or geographic area is deemed unreasonable.
Covenant not to sue An agreement to substitute a contractual obligation for some other type of legal action based on a valid claim.

Covenant of quiet enjoyment A promise by a grantor (or landlord) that the grantee (or tenant) will not be evicted or disturbed by the grantor or a person having a lien or superior title.
Covenant running with the land An executory promise made between a grantor and a grantee to which they and subsequent owners of the land are bound.
Cover Under the Uniform Commercial Code, a remedy of the buyer or lessee that allows the buyer or lessee, on the seller's or lessor's breach, to purchase the goods from another seller or lessor and substitute them for the goods due under the contract. If the cost of cover exceeds the cost of the contract goods, the breaching seller or lessor will be liable to the buyer or lessee for the difference. In obtaining cover, the buyer or lessee must act in good faith and without unreasonable delay.
Cram-down provision A provision of the Bankruptcy Code that allows a court to confirm a debtor's Chapter 11 reorganization plan even though only one class of creditors has accepted it. To exercise the court's right under this provision, the court must demonstrate that the plan does not discriminate unfairly against any creditors and is fair and equitable.
Crashworthiness doctrine A doctrine that imposes liability for defects in the design or construction of motor vehicles that increase the extent of injuries to passengers if an accident occurs. The doctrine holds even when the defects do not actually cause the accident.
Creditor A person to whom a debt is owed by another person (the debtor).
Creditors' composition agreement An agreement formed between a debtor and his or her creditors in which the creditors agree to accept a lesser sum than that owed by the debtor in full satisfaction of the debt.
Crime A wrong against society proclaimed in a statute and, if committed, punishable by society through fines and/or imprisonment—and, in some cases, death.
Criminal act *See Actus reus*
Criminal intent *See Mens rea*
Criminal law Law that defines and governs actions that constitute crimes. Generally, criminal law has to do with wrongful actions committed against society for which society demands redress.
Cross-examination The questioning of an opposing witness during the trial.
Cumulative voting A method of shareholder voting designed to allow minority shareholders to be represented on the board of directors. With cumulative voting, the number of members of the board to be elected is multiplied by the total number of voting shares held. The result equals the number of votes a shareholder has, and this total can be cast for one or more nominees for director.
Cure Under the Uniform Commercial Code, the right of a party who tenders nonconforming performance to correct his or her performance within the contract period.

D

Damages Money sought as a remedy for a breach of contract or for a tortious act.
Debenture bond A bond for which no specific assets of the corporation are pledged as backing; rather, the bond is backed by the general credit rating of the corporation, plus any assets that can be seized if the corporation allows the debentures to go into default.
Debtor A debtor is any party who owes payment or performance of a secured obligation, whether or not the party actually owns or has rights in the collateral.
Debtor in possession (DIP) In Chapter 11 bankruptcy proceedings, a debtor who is allowed to continue in possession of the estate in property (the business) and to continue business operations.
Declaratory judgment A court's judgment on a justiciable controversy when the plaintiff is in doubt as to his or her legal rights; a binding adjudication of the rights and status of litigants even though no consequential relief is awarded.
Decree The judgment of a court of equity.
Deed A document by which title to property (usually real property) is passed.
Defalcation The misuse of funds.
Defamation Any published or publicly spoken false statement that causes injury to another's good name, reputation, or character.
Default The failure to observe a promise or discharge an obligation. The term is commonly used to mean the failure to pay a debt when it is due.
Default judgment A judgment entered by a court against a defendant who has failed to appear in court to answer or defend against the plaintiff's claim.
Defendant One against whom a lawsuit is brought; the accused person in a criminal proceeding.
Defense That which a defendant offers and alleges in an action or suit as a reason why the plaintiff should not recover or establish what he or she seeks.
Deficiency judgment A judgment against a debtor for the amount of a debt remaining unpaid after collateral has been repossessed and sold.
Delegatee One to whom contract duties are delegated by another, called the delegator.
Delegation The transfer of a contractual duty to a third party. The party delegating the duty (the delegator) to the third party (the delegatee) is still obliged to perform on the contract should the delegatee fail to perform.
Delegation doctrine A doctrine based on Article I, Section 8, of the U.S. Constitution, which has been construed to allow Congress to delegate some of its power to make and implement laws to administrative agencies. The delegation is considered to be proper as long as Congress sets standards outlining the scope of the agency's authority.
Delegator One who delegates his or her duties under a contract to another, called the delegatee.
Delivery In contract law, the one party's act of placing the subject matter of the contract within the other party's possession or control.
Delivery ex ship Delivery from the carrying ship. A contract term indicating that risk of loss will not pass to the buyer until the goods leave the ship or are otherwise properly unloaded.
Delivery order A written order to deliver goods directed to a warehouser, carrier, or other person who, in the ordinary course of business, issues warehouse receipts or bills of lading [UCC 7–102(1)(d)].
Demurrer *See* Motion to dismiss
De novo Anew; afresh; a second time. In a hearing *de novo*, an appellate court hears the case as a court of original jurisidction—that is, as if the case had not previously been tried and a decision rendered.
Deposition The testimony of a party to a lawsuit or a witness taken under oath before a trial.
Destination contract A contract for the sale of goods in which the seller is required or authorized to ship the goods by carrier and deliver them at a particular destination. The seller assumes liability for any losses or damage to the goods until they are tendered at the destination specified in the contract.
Direct examination The examination of a witness by the attorney who calls the witness to the stand to testify on behalf of the attorney's client.
Directed verdict *See* Motion for a directed verdict
Disaffirmance The legal avoidance, or setting aside, of a contractual obligation.
Discharge The termination of an obligation. (1) In contract law, discharge occurs when the parties have fully performed their contractual obligations or when events, conduct of the parties, or operation of the law releases the parties from performance. (2) In bankruptcy proceedings, the extinction of the debtor's dischargeable debts.
Discharge in bankruptcy The release of a debtor from all debts that are provable, except those specifically excepted from discharge by statute.
Disclosed principal A principal whose identity is known to a third party at the time the agent makes a contract with the third party.
Discovery A phase in the litigation process during which the opposing parties may obtain information from each other and from third parties prior to trial.
Disparagement of property An economically injurious falsehood

made about another's product or property. A general term for torts that are more specifically referred to as slander of quality or slander of title.

Disparate-impact discrimination A form of employment discrimination that results from certain employer practices or procedures that, although not discriminatory on their face, have a discriminatory effect.

Disparate-treatment discrimination A form of employment discrimination that results when an employer intentionally discriminates against employees who are members of protected classes.

Dissenting opinion A written opinion by a judge or justice who disagrees with the majority opinion.

Dissolution The formal disbanding of a partnership or a corporation. It can take place by (1) acts of the partners or, in a corporation, of the shareholders and board of directors; (2) the death of a partner; (3) the expiration of a time period stated in a partnership agreement or a certificate of incorporation; or (4) judicial decree.

Distribution agreement A contract between a seller and a distributor of the seller's products setting out the terms and conditions of the distributorship.

Distributorship A business arrangement that is established when a manufacturer licenses a dealer to sell its product. An example of a distributorship is an automobile dealership.

Diversity of citizenship Under Article III, Section 2, of the Constitution, a basis for federal court jurisdiction over a lawsuit between (1) citizens of different states, (2) a foreign country and citizens of a state or of different states, or (3) citizens of a state and citizens or subjects of a foreign country. The amount in controversy must be more than $75,000 before a federal court can take jurisdiction in such cases.

Divestiture The act of selling one or more of a company's parts, such as a subsidiary or plant; often mandated by the courts in merger or monopolization cases.

Dividend A distribution to corporate shareholders of corporate profits or income, disbursed in proportion to the number of shares held.

Docket The list of cases entered on a court's calendar and thus scheduled to be heard by the court.

Document of title Paper exchanged in the regular course of business that evidences the right to possession of goods (for example, a bill of lading or a warehouse receipt).

Domain name The series of letters and symbols used to identify site operators on the Internet; Internet "addresses."

Domestic corporation In a given state, a corporation that does business in, and is organized under the law of, that state.

Domestic relations court A court that deals with domestic (household) relationships, such as adoption, divorce, support payments, child custody, and the like.

Donee beneficiary A third party beneficiary who has rights under a contract as a direct result of the intention of the contract parties to make a gift to the third party.

Double jeopardy A situation occurring when a person is tried twice for the same criminal offense; prohibited by the Fifth Amendment to the Constitution.

Double taxation A feature (and disadvantage) of the corporate form of business. Because a corporation is a separate legal entity, corporate profits are taxed by state and federal governments. Dividends are again taxable as ordinary income to the shareholders receiving them.

Dram shop act A state statute that imposes liability on the owners of bars and taverns, as well as those who serve alcoholic drinks to the public, for injuries resulting from accidents caused by intoxicated persons when the sellers or servers of alcoholic drinks contributed to the intoxication.

Due diligence A required standard of care that certain professionals, such as accountants, must meet to avoid liability for securities violations. Under securities law, an accountant will be deemed to have exercised due diligence if he or she followed generally accepted accounting principles and generally accepted auditing standards and had, "after reasonable investigation, reasonable grounds to believe and did believe, at the time such part of the registration statement became effective, that the statements therein were true and that there was no omission of a material fact required to be stated therein or necessary to make the statements therein not misleading."

Due negotiation The transfer of a document of title in such form that the transferee becomes a holder [UCC 7-501].

Due process clause The provisions of the Fifth and Fourteenth Amendments to the Constitution that guarantee that no person shall be deprived of life, liberty, or property without due process of law. Similar clauses are found in most state constitutions.

Dumping The selling of goods in a foreign country at a price below the price charged for the same goods in the domestic market.

Durable power of attorney A document that authorizes a person to act on behalf of an incompetent persons—write checks, collect insurance proceeds, and otherwise manage the disabled person's affairs, including health care—when he or she becomes incapacitated. Spouses often give each other durable power of attorney and, if they are advanced in age, may give a second such power of attorney to an older child.

Duress Unlawful pressure brought to bear on a person, causing the person to perform an act that he or she would not otherwise perform.

Duty of care The duty of all persons, as established by tort law, to exercise a reasonable amount of care in their dealings with others. Failure to exercise due care, which is normally determined by the "reasonable person standard," constitutes the tort of negligence.

E

Early neutral case evaluation A form of alternative dispute resolution in which a neutral third party evaluates the strengths and weakness of the disputing parties' positions; the evaluator's opinion forms the basis for negotiating a settlement.

Easement A nonpossessory right to use another's property in a manner established by either express or implied agreement.

Eighty-day cooling-off period A provision of the Taft-Hartley Act that allows federal courts to issue injunctions against strikes that might create a national emergency.

Ejectment The eviction of a tenant from leased premises. A remedy at common law to which the landlord can resort when a tenant fails to pay rent for leased premises. To obtain possession of the premises, the landlord must appear in court and show that the defaulting tenant is in wrongful possession.

Electronic fund transfer (EFT) A transfer of funds with the use of an electronic terminal, a telephone, a computer, or magnetic tape.

Embezzlement The fraudulent appropriation of money or other property by a person to whom the money or property has been entrusted.

Eminent domain The power of a government to take land for public use from private citizens for just compensation.

Employee A person who works for an employer for a salary or for wages.

Employee committee Committee created by an employer and composed of representatives of management and nonunion employees to act together to improve workplace conditions.

Employer An individual or business entity that hires employees, pays them salaries or wages, and exercises control over their work.

Employment at will A common law doctrine under which either party may terminate an employment relationship at any time for any reason, unless a contract specifies otherwise.

Employment discrimination Treating employees or job applicants unequally on the basis of race, color, national origin, religion, gender, age, or disability; prohibited by federal statutes.

Enabling legislation A statute enacted by Congress that authorizes the creation of an administrative agency and specifies the name, composition, purpose, and powers of the agency being created.

Entrapment In criminal law, a defense in which the defendant claims that he or she was induced by a public official—usually an undercover agent or police officer—to commit a crime that he or she would otherwise not have committed.

Entrepreneur One who initiates and assumes the financial risks of a new enterprise and who undertakes to provide or control its management.

Environmental impact statement (EIS) A statement required by the National Environmental Policy Act for any major federal action that will significantly affect the quality of the environment. The statement must analyze the action's impact on the environment and explore alternative actions that might be taken.
Environmental law The body of statutory, regulatory, and common law relating to the protection of the environment.
Equal dignity rule In most states, a rule stating that express authority given to an agent must be in writing if the contract to be made on behalf of the principal is required to be in writing.
Equal protection clause The provision in the Fourteenth Amendment to the Constitution that guarantees that no state will "deny to any person within its jurisdiction the equal protection of the laws." This clause mandates that state governments treat similarly situated individuals in a similar manner.
Equitable maxims General propositions or principles of law that have to do with fairness (equity).
Equity of redemption The right of a mortgagor who has breached the mortgage agreement to redeem or purchase the property prior to foreclosure proceedings.
Establishment clause The provision in the First Amendment to the U.S. Constitution that prohibits Congress from creating any law "respecting an establishment of religion."
Estop To bar, impede, or preclude.
Estoppel The principle that a party's own acts prevent him or her from claiming a right to the detriment of another who was entitled to and did rely on those acts. *See also* Agency by estoppel; Promissory estoppel
Ethical reasoning A reasoning process in which an individual links his or her moral convictions or ethical standards to the particular situation at hand.
Ethics Moral principles and values applied to social behavior.
Evidence Proof offered at trial—in the form of testimony, documents, records, exhibits, objects, and so on—for the purpose of convincing the court or jury of the truth of a contention.
Eviction A landlord's act of depriving a tenant of possession of the leased premises.
***Ex parte* contact** Communications with an administrative agency that are not placed in the record.
Ex ship *See* Delivery ex ship
Exclusionary rule In criminal procedure, a rule under which any evidence that is obtained in violation of the accused's constitutional rights guaranteed by the Fourth, Fifth, and Sixth Amendments, as well as any evidence derived from illegally obtained evidence, will not be admissible in court.
Exclusive distributorship A distributorship in which the seller and the distributor of the seller's products agree that the distributor has the exclusive right to distribute the seller's products in a certain geographic area.
Exclusive jurisdiction Jurisdiction that exists when a case can be heard only in a particular court or type of court, such as a federal court or a state court.
Exclusive-dealing contract An agreement under which a seller forbids a buyer to purchase products from the seller's competitors.
Exculpatory clause A clause that releases a contractual party from liability in the event of monetary or physical injury, no matter who is at fault.
Executed contract A contract that has been completely performed by both parties.
Execution An action to carry into effect the directions in a court decree or judgment.
Executive agency An administrative agency within the executive branch of government. At the federal level, executive agencies are those within the cabinet departments.
Executor A person appointed by a testator to see that his or her will is administered appropriately.
Executory contract A contract that has not as yet been fully performed.
Executory interest A future interest, held by a person other than the grantor, that either cuts short or begins some time after the natural termination of the preceding estate.
Export To sell products to buyers located in other countries.
Express authority Authority expressly given by one party to another. In agency law, an agent has express authority to act for a principal if both parties agree, orally or in writing, that an agency relationship exists in which the agent had the power (authority) to act in the place of, and on behalf of, the principal.
Express contract A contract in which the terms of the agreement are fully and explicitly stated in words, oral or written.
Express warranty A seller's or lessor's oral or written promise, ancillary to an underlying sales or lease agreement, as to the quality, description, or performance of the goods being sold or leased.
Expropriation The seizure by a government of privately owned business or personal property for a proper public purpose and with just compensation.

F

F.A.S. Free alongside. A contract term that requires the seller, at his or her own expense and risk, to deliver the goods alongside the ship before risk passes to the buyer.
F.O.B. Free on board. A contract term that indicates that the selling price of the goods includes transportation costs (and that the seller carries the risk of loss) to the specific F.O.B. place named in the contract. The place can be either the place of initial shipment (for example, the seller's city or place of business) or the place of destination (for example, the buyer's city or place of business).
Family limited liability partnership (FLLP) A limited liability partnership (LLP) in which the majority of the partners are persons related to each other, essentially as spouses, parents, grandparents, siblings, cousins, nephews, or nieces. A person acting in a fiduciary capacity for persons so related could also be a partner. All of the partners must be natural persons or persons acting in a fiduciary capacity for the benefit of natural persons.
Featherbedding A requirement that more workers be employed to do a particular job than are actually needed.
Federal form of government A system of government in which the states form a union and the sovereign power is divided between a central government and the member states.
Federal question A question that pertains to the U.S. Constitution, acts of Congress, or treaties. A federal question provides a basis for federal jurisdiction.
Federal Rules of Civil Procedure (FRCP) The rules controlling procedural matters in civil trials brought before the federal district courts.
Federal system A system of government in which power is divided by a written constitution between a central government and regional, or subdivisional, governments. Each level must have some domain in which its policies are dominant and some genuine political or constitutional guarantee of its authority.
Fee simple An absolute form of property ownership entitling the property owner to use, possess, or dispose of the property as he or she chooses during his or her lifetime. On death, the interest in the property descends to the owner's heirs; a fee simple absolute.
Fee simple absolute An ownership interest in land in which the owner has the greatest possible aggregation of rights, privileges, and power. Ownership in fee simple absolute is limited absolutely to a person and his or her heirs.
Fee simple defeasible An estate that can be taken away (by the prior grantor) upon the occurrence or nonoccurrence of a specified event.
Fellow-servant doctrine A doctrine that bars an employee from suing his or her employer for injuries caused by a fellow employee.
Felony A crime—such as arson, murder, rape, or robbery—that carries the most severe sanctions, usually ranging from one year in a state or federal prison to the forfeiture of one's life.
Fiduciary As a noun, a person having a duty created by his or her undertaking to act primarily for another's benefit in matters connected with the undertaking. As an adjective, a relationship founded on trust and confidence.
Fiduciary duty The duty, imposed on a fiduciary by virtue of his or her position, to act primarily for another's benefit.

Final order The final decision of an administrative agency on an issue. If no appeal is taken, or if the case is not reviewed or considered anew by the agency commission, the administrative law judge's initial order becomes the final order of the agency.
Financial institution An organization authorized to do business under state or federal laws relating to financial institutions. For example, under the Electronic Fund Transfer Act, financial institutions include banks, savings and loan associations, credit unions, and other business entities that directly or indirectly hold accounts belonging to consumers.
Financing statement A document prepared by a secured creditor and filed with the appropriate state or local official to give notice to the public that the creditor claims an interest in collateral belonging to the debtor named in the statement. The financing statement must be signed by the debtor, contain the addresses of both the debtor and the creditor, and describe the collateral by type or item.
Firm offer An offer (by a merchant) that is irrevocable without consideration for a period of time (not longer than three months). A firm offer by a merchant must be in writing and must be signed by the offeror.
Fitness for a particular purpose *See* Implied warranty of fitness for a particular purpose
Fixture A thing that was once personal property but that has become attached to real property in such a way that it takes on the characteristics of real property and becomes part of that real property.
Force majeure (pronounced mah-*zhure*) **clause** A provision in a contract stipulating that certain unforeseen events—such as war, political upheavals, acts of God, or other events—will excuse a party from liability for nonperformance of contractual obligations.
Foreclosure A proceeding in which a mortgagee either takes title to or forces the sale of the mortgagor's property in satisfaction of a debt.
Foreign corporation In a given state, a corporation that does business in the state without being incorporated therein.
Foreseeable risk In negligence law, the risk of harm or injury to another that a person of ordinary intelligence and prudence should have reasonably anticipated or foreseen when undertaking an action or refraining from undertaking an action.
Forgery The fraudulent making or altering of any writing in a way that changes the legal rights and liabilities of another.
Forum A jurisdiction, court, or place in which disputes are litigated and legal remedies are sought.
Forum-selection clause A provision in a contract designating the court, jurisdiction, or tribunal that will decide any disputes arising under the contract.
Franchise Any arrangement in which the owner of a trademark, trade name, or copyright licenses another to use that trademark, trade name, or copyright, under specified conditions or limitations, in the selling of goods and services.
Franchisee One receiving a license to use another's (the franchisor's) trademark, trade name, or copyright in the sale of goods and services.
Franchisor One licensing another (the franchisee) to use his or her trademark, trade name, or copyright in the sale of goods or services.
Fraud Any misrepresentation, either by misstatement or omission of a material fact, knowingly made with the intention of deceiving another and on which a reasonable person would and does rely to his or her detriment.
Fraudulent misrepresentation (fraud) Any misrepresentation, either by misstatement or omission of a material fact, knowingly made with the intention of deceiving another and on which a reasonable person would and does rely to his or her detriment.
Free exercise clause The provision in the First Amendment to the U.S. Constitution that prohibits Congress from making any law "prohibiting the free exercise" of religion.
Frustration of purpose A court-created doctrine under which a party to a contract will be relieved of his or her duty to perform when the objective purpose for performance no longer exists (due to reasons beyond that party's control).
Full warranty A warranty as to full performance covering generally both labor and materials.
Fungible goods Goods that are alike by physical nature, by agreement, or by trade usage. Examples of fungible goods are wheat, oil, and wine that are identical in type and quality.
Future interest An interest in real property that is not at present possessory but will or may be possessory in the future. Remainders and reversions are future interests.

G

Garnishment A legal process used by a creditor to collect a debt by seizing property of the debtor (such as wages) that is being held by a third party (such as the debtor's employer).
General jurisdiction Exists when a court's subject-matter jurisdiction is not restricted. A court of general jurisdiction normally can hear any type of case.
General partner In a limited partnership, a partner who assumes responsibility for the management of the partnership and liability for all partnership debts.
General partnership *See* Partnership
General plan A comprehensive document that local jurisdictions are often required by state law to devise and implement as a precursor to specific land-use regulations.
Genuineness of assent Knowing and voluntary assent to the terms of a contract. If a contract is formed as a result of a mistake, misrepresentation, undue influence, or duress, genuineness of assent is lacking, and the contract will be voidable.
Gift Any voluntary transfer of property made without consideration, past or present.
Gift *causa mortis* A gift made in contemplation of death. If the donor does not die of that ailment, the gift is revoked.
Gift *inter vivos* A gift made during one's lifetime and not in contemplation of imminent death, in contrast to a gift *causa mortis.*
Good faith Under the Uniform Commercial Code good faith means honesty in fact; with regard to merchants, good faith means honesty in fact *and* the observance of reasonable commercial standards of fair dealing in the trade.
Good faith purchaser A purchaser who buys without notice of any circumstance that would put a person of ordinary prudence on inquiry as to whether the seller has valid title to the goods being sold.
Good Samaritan statute A state statute that provides that persons who rescue or provide emergency services to others in peril—unless they do so recklessly, thus causing further harm—cannot be sued for negligence.
Grand jury A group of citizens called to decide, after hearing the state's evidence, whether a reasonable basis (probable cause) exists for believing that a crime has been committed and whether a trial ought to be held.
Grant deed A deed that simply recites words of consideration and conveyance. Under statute, a grant deed may impliedly warrant that at least the grantor has not conveyed the property's title to someone else.
Grantee One to whom a grant (of land or property, for example) is made.
Grantor A person who makes a grant, such as a transferor of property or the creator of a trust.
Group boycott The refusal to deal with a particular person or firm by a group of competitors; prohibited by the Sherman Act.
Guarantor A person who agrees to satisfy the debt of another (the debtor) only after the principal debtor defaults; a guarantor's liability is thus secondary.

H

Habitability *See* Implied warranty of habitability
Hearsay An oral or written statement made out of court that is later offered in court by a witness (not the person who made the statement) to prove the truth of the matter asserted in the statement. Hearsay is generally inadmissible as evidence.
Herfindahl-Hirschman index (HHI) An index of market power used to calculate whether a merger of two corporations will result in monopoly power and thus violate antitrust laws.
Homestead exemption A law permitting a debtor to retain the family home, either in its entirety or up to a specified dollar amount, free from

the claims of unsecured creditors or trustees in bankruptcy.
Horizontal market division A market division that occurs when competitors agree to divide up the market for their products or services among themselves, either geographically or by functional class of customers (such as retailers or wholesalers). Such market division constitutes a *per se* violation of the Sherman Act.
Horizontal merger A merger between two firms that are competing in the same market.
Horizontal restraint Any agreement that in some way restrains competition between rival firms competing in the same market.
Hot-cargo agreement An agreement in which employers voluntarily agree with unions not to handle, use, or deal in nonunion-produced goods of other employers; a type of secondary boycott explicitly prohibited by the Labor-Management Reporting and Disclosure Act of 1959.
Hung jury A jury whose members are so irreconcilably divided in their opinions that they cannot come to a verdict by the requisite number of jurors. The judge in this situation may order a new trial.

I

Identification In a sale of goods, the express designation of the goods provided for in the contract.
Illusory promise A promise made without consideration, which renders the promise unenforceable.
Immunity A status of being exempt, or free, from certain duties or requirements. In tort law, freedom from liability for defamatory speech. *See also* Privilege
Implied authority Authority that is created not by an explicit oral or written agreement but by implication. In agency law, implied authority (of the agent) can be conferred by custom, inferred from the position the agent occupies, or implied by virtue of being reasonably necessary to carry out express authority.
Implied warranty A warranty that the law derives by implication or inference from the nature of the transaction or the relative situation or circumstances of the parties.
Implied warranty of fitness for a particular purpose A warranty that goods sold or leased are fit for a particular purpose. The warranty arises when any seller or lessor knows the particular purpose for which a buyer or lessee will use the goods and knows that the buyer or lessee is relying on the skill and judgment of the seller or lessor to select suitable goods.
Implied warranty of habitability An implied promise by a landlord that rented residential premises are fit for human habitation—that is, in a condition that is safe and suitable for people to live in.
Implied warranty of merchantability A warranty that goods being sold or leased are reasonably fit for the general pupose for which they are sold or leased, are properly packaged and labeled, and are of proper quality. The warranty automatically arises in every sale or lease of goods made by a merchant who deals in goods of the kind sold or leased.
Implied-in-fact contract A contract formed in whole or in part from the conduct of the parties (as opposed to an express contract).
Impossibility of performance A doctrine under which a party to a contract is relieved of his or her duty to perform when performance becomes impossible or totally impracticable (through no fault of either party).
In pari delicto At equal fault.
***In personam* jurisdiction** Court jurisdiction over the "person" involved in a legal action; personal jurisdiction.
***In rem* jurisdiction** Court jurisdiction over a defendant's property.
Incidental beneficiary A third party who incidentally benefits from a contract but whose benefit was not the reason the contract was formed; an incidental beneficiary has no rights in a contract and cannot sue to have the contract enforced.
Incidental damages Damages resulting from a breach of contract, including all reasonable expenses incurred because of the breach.
Indemnify To compensate or reimburse another for losses or expenses incurred.
Independent contractor One who works for, and receives payment from, an employer but whose working conditions and methods are not controlled by the employer. An independent contractor is not an employee but may be an agent.
Independent regulatory agency An administrative agency that is not considered part of the government's executive branch and is not subject to the authority of the president. Independent agency officials cannot be removed without cause.
Indictment (pronounced in-*dyte*-ment) A charge by a grand jury that a named person has committed a crime.
Industry-wide liability Product liability that is imposed on an entire industry when it is unclear which of several sellers within the industry manufactured a particular product. *See also* Market-share liability
Information A formal accusation or complaint (without an indictment) issued in certain types of actions (usually criminal actions involving lesser crimes) by a law officer, such as a magistrate.
Information return A tax return submitted by a partnership that only reports the income earned by the business. The partnership as an entity does not pay taxes on the income received by the partnership. A partner's profit from the partnership (whether distributed or not) is taxed as individual income to the individual partner.
Infringement A violation of another's legally recognized right. The term is commonly used with reference to the invasion by one party of another party's rights in a patent, trademark, or copyright.
Initial order In the context of administrative law, an agency's disposition in a matter other than a rulemaking. An administrative law judge's initial order becomes final unless it is appealed.
Injunction A court decree ordering a person to do or refrain from doing a certain act or activity.
Innkeeper An owner of an inn, hotel, motel, or other lodgings.
Innocent misrepresentation A false statement of fact or an act made in good faith that deceives and causes harm or injury to another.
Insider A corporate director or officer, or other employee or agent, with access to confidential information and a duty not to disclose that information in violation of insider-trading laws.
Insider trading The purchase or sale of securities on the basis of "inside information" (information that has not been made available to the public) in violation of a duty owed to the company whose stock is being traded.
Insolvent Under the Uniform Commercial Code, a term describing a person who ceases to pay "his debts in the ordinary course of business or cannot pay his debts as they become due or is insolvent within the meaning of federal bankruptcy law" [UCC 1–201(23)].
Installment contract Under the Uniform Commercial Code, a contract that requires or authorizes delivery in two or more separate lots to be accepted and paid for separately.
Insurable interest An interest either in a person's life or well-being or in property that is sufficiently substantial that insuring against injury to (or the death of) the person or against damage to the property does not amount to a mere wagering (betting) contract.
Intangible property Property that is incapable of being apprehended by the senses (such as by sight or touch); intellectual property is an example of intangible property.
Integrated contract A written contract that constitutes the final expression of the parties' agreement. If a contract is integrated, evidence extraneous to the contract that contradicts or alters the meaning of the contract in any way is inadmissible.
Intellectual property Property resulting from intellectual, creative processes. Patents, trademarks, and copyrights are examples of intellectual property.
Intended beneficiary A third party for whose benefit a contract is formed; an intended beneficiary can sue the promisor if such a contract is breached.
Intentional tort A wrongful act knowingly committed.
***Inter vivos* gift** *See* Gift *inter vivos*
International law The law that governs relations among nations. International customs and treaties are generally considered to be two of the most important sources of international law.
International organization In international law, a term that generally refers to an organization composed mainly of nations and usually established by treaty. The United States is a member of more than one hun-

dred multilateral and bilateral organizations, including at least twenty through the United Nations.

Interpretive rule An administrative agency rule that is simply a statement or opinion issued by the agency explaining how it interprets and intends to apply the statutes it enforces. Such rules are not automatically binding on private individuals or organizations.

Interrogatories A series of written questions for which written answers are prepared and then signed under oath by a party to a lawsuit, usually with the assistance of the party's attorney.

Investment company A company that acts on behalf of many smaller shareholder-owners by buying a large portfolio of securities and professionally managing that portfolio.

Invitee A person who, either expressly or impliedly, is privileged to enter onto another's land. The inviter owes the invitee (for example, a customer in a store) the duty to exercise reasonable care to protect the invitee from harm.

Irrevocable offer An offer that cannot be revoked or recalled by the offeror without liability. A merchant's firm offer is an example of an irrevocable offer.

Issue The first transfer, or delivery, of an instrument to a holder.

J

Joint and several liability In partnership law, a doctrine under which a plaintiff may sue, and collect a judgment from, one or more of the partners separately (severally, or individually) or all of the partners together (jointly). This is true even if one of the partners sued did not participate in, ratify, or know about whatever it was that gave rise to the cause of action.

Joint liability Shared liability. In partnership law, partners incur joint liability for partnership obligations and debts. For example, if a third party sues a partner on a partnership debt, the partner has the right to insist that the other partners be sued with him or her.

Joint stock company A hybrid form of business organization that combines characteristics of a corporation (shareholder-owners, management by directors and officers of the company, and perpetual existence) and a partnership (it is formed by agreement, not statute; property is usually held in the names of the members; and the shareholders have personal liability for business debts). Usually, the joint stock company is regarded as a partnership for tax and other legally related purposes.

Joint tenancy The joint ownership of property by two or more co-owners in which each co-owner owns an undivided portion of the property. On the death of one of the joint tenants, his or her interest automatically passes to the surviving joint tenants.

Joint venture A joint undertaking of a specific commercial enterprise by an association of persons. A joint venture is normally not a legal entity and is treated like a partnership for federal income tax purposes.

Judgment The final order or decision resulting from a legal action.

Judgment *n.o.v.* *See* Motion for judgment *n.o.v.*

Judgment rate of interest A rate of interest fixed by statute that is applied to a monetary judgment from the moment the judgment is awarded by a court until the judgment is paid or terminated.

Judicial lien A lien on property created by a court order.

Judicial process The procedures relating to, or connected with, the administration of justice through the judicial system.

Judicial review The process by which courts decide on the constitutionality of legislative enactments and actions of the executive branch.

Jurisdiction The authority of a court to hear and decide a specific action.

Jurisprudence The science or philosophy of law.

Justiciable (pronounced jus-*tish*-a-bul) **controversy** A controversy that is not hypothetical or academic but real and substantial; a requirement that must be satisfied before a court will hear a case.

K

King's court A medieval English court. The king's courts, or *curiae regis,* were established by the Norman conquerors of England. The body of law that developed in these courts was common to the entire English realm and thus became known as the common law.

L

Laches The equitable doctrine that bars a party's right to legal action if the party has neglected for an unreasonable length of time to act upon his or her rights.

Landlord An owner of land or rental property who leases it to another person, called the tenant.

Landlord's lien A landlord's remedy for a tenant's failure to pay rent. When permitted under a statute or the lease agreement, the landlord may take and keep or sell whatever of the defaulting tenant's property is on the leased premises.

Land-use control The control over the ownership and uses of real property by authorized public agencies.

Larceny The wrongful taking and carrying away of another person's personal property with the intent to permanently deprive the owner of the property. Some states classify larceny as either grand or petit, depending on the property's value.

Last clear chance A doctrine under which a plaintiff may recover from a defendant for injuries or damages suffered, notwithstanding the plaintiff's own negligence, when the defendant had the opportunity—a last clear chance—to avoid harming the plaintiff through the exercise of reasonable care but failed to do so.

Law A body of enforceable rules governing relationships among individuals and between individuals and their society.

Lawsuit The litigation process. *See* Litigation

Lease In real property law, a contract by which the owner of real property (the landlord, or lessor) grants to a person (the tenant, or lessee) an exclusive right to use and possess the property, usually for a specified period of time, in return for rent or some other form of payment.

Lease agreement In regard to the lease of goods, an agreement in which one person (the lessor) agrees to transfer the right to the possession and use of property to another person (the lessee) in exchange for rental payments.

Leasehold estate An estate in realty held by a tenant under a lease. In every leasehold estate, the tenant has a qualified right to possess and/or use the land.

Legal positivists Adherents to the positivist school of legal thought. This school holds that there can be no higher law than a nation's positive law—law created by a particular society at a particular point in time. In contrast to the natural law school, the positivist school maintains that there are no "natural" rights; rights come into existence only when there is a sovereign power (government) to confer and enforce those rights.

Legal rate of interest A rate of interest fixed by statute as either the maximum rate of interest allowed by law or a rate of interest applied when the parties to a contract intend, but do not fix, an interest rate in the contract. In the latter case, the rate is frequently the same as the statutory maximum rate permitted.

Legal realists Adherents to a school of legal thought that was popular in the 1920s and 1930s and that challenged many existing jurisprudential assumptions, particularly the assumption that subjective elements play no part in judicial reasoning. Legal realists generally advocated a less abstract and more realistic approach to the law, an approach that would take into account customary practices and the circumstances in which transactions take place. The school left a lasting imprint on American jurisprudence.

Legal reasoning The process of reasoning by which a judge harmonizes his or her decision with the judicial decisions of previous cases.

Legislative rule An administrative agency rule that carries the same weight as a congressionally enacted statute.

Lessee A person who acquires the right to the possession and use of another's property in exchange for rental payments.

Lessor A person who sells the right to the possession and use of property to another in exchange for rental payments.

Levy The obtaining of money by legal process through the seizure and sale of property, usually done after a writ of execution has been issued.

Liability Any actual or potential legal obligation, duty, debt, or responsibility.
Libel Defamation in writing or other form (such as in a videotape) having the quality of permanence.
License A revocable right or privilege of a person to come on another person's land.
Licensee One who receives a license to use, or enter onto, another's property.
Lien (pronounced leen) An encumbrance on a property to satisfy a debt or protect a claim for payment of a debt.
Lien creditor One whose claim is secured by a lien on particular property, as distinguished from a general creditor, who has no such security.
Life estate An interest in land that exists only for the duration of the life of some person, usually the holder of the estate.
Limited jurisdiction Exists when a court's subject-matter jurisdiction is limited. Bankruptcy courts and probate courts are examples of courts with limited jurisdiction.
Limited liability Exists when the liability of the owners of a business is limited to the amount of their investments in the firm.
Limited liability company (LLC) A hybrid form of business enterprise that offers the limited liability of the corporation but the tax advantages of a partnership.
Limited liability limited partnership (LLLC) A type of limited partnership. The difference between a limited partnership and an LLLP is that the liability of the general partner in an LLLP is the same as the liability of the limited partner. That is, the liability of all partners is limited to the amount of their investments in the firm.
Limited liability partnership (LLP) A form of partnership that allows professionals to enjoy the tax benefits of a partnership while limiting their personal liability for the malpractice of other partners.
Limited partner In a limited partnership, a partner who contributes capital to the partnership but has no right to participate in the management and operation of the business. The limited partner assumes no liability for partnership debts beyond the capital contributed.
Limited partnership A partnership consisting of one or more general partners (who manage the business and are liable to the full extent of their personal assets for debts of the partnership) and one or more limited partners (who contribute only assets and are liable only to the extent of their contributions).
Limited warranty A written warranty that fails to meet one or more of the minimum standards for a full warranty.
Liquidated damages An amount, stipulated in the contract, that the parties to a contract believe to be a reasonable estimation of the damages that will occur in the event of a breach.
Liquidated debt A debt that is due and certain in amount.
Liquidation (1) In regard to bankruptcy, the sale of all of the nonexempt assets of a debtor and the distribution of the proceeds to the debtor's creditors. Chapter 7 of the Bankruptcy Code provides for liquidation bankruptcy proceedings. (2) In regard to corporations, the process by which corporate assets are converted into cash and distributed among creditors and shareholders according to specific rules of preference.
Litigant A party to a lawsuit.
Litigation The process of resolving a dispute through the court system.
Loan workout *See* Workout
Lockout The closing of a plant to employees by an employer to gain leverage in collective bargaining negotiations.
Long arm statute A state statute that permits a state to obtain personal jurisdiction over nonresident defendants. A defendant must have "minimum contacts" with that state for the statute to apply.

M

Magistrate's court A court of limited jurisdiction that is presided over by a public official (magistrate) with certain judicial authority, such as the power to set bail.
Main purpose rule A rule of contract law under which an exception to the Statute of Frauds is made if the main purpose of in accepting secondary liability under a contract is to secure a personal benefit. If this situation exists, the contract need not be in writing to be enforceable.
Majority opinion A court's written opinion, outlining the views of the majority of the judges or justices deciding the case.
Malpractice Professional misconduct or the failure to exercise the requisite degree of skill as a professional. Negligence—the failure to exercise due care—on the part of a professional, such as a physician or an attorney, is commonly referred to as malpractice.
Manufacturing or processing-plant franchise A franchise that is created when the franchisor transmits to the franchisee the essential ingredients or formula to make a particular product. The franchisee then markets the product either at wholesale or at retail in accordance with the franchisor's standards. Examples of this type of franchise are Coca-Cola and other soft-drink bottling companies.
Mark *See* Trademark
Market concentration A situation that exists when a small number of firms share the market for a particular good or service. For example, if the four largest grocery stores in Chicago accounted for 80 percent of all retail food sales, the market clearly would be concentrated in those four firms.
Market power The power of a firm to control the market price of its product. A monopoly has the greatest degree of market power.
Marketable title Title to real estate that is reasonably free from encumbrances, defects in the chain of title, and other events that affect title, such as adverse possession.
Market-share liability A method of sharing liability among several firms that manufactured or marketed a particular product that may have caused plaintiff's injury. This form of liability sharing is used when the true source of the product is unidentifiable. Each firm's liability is proportionate to its respective share of the relevant market for the product. Market-share liability applies only if the injuring product is fungible, the true manufacturer is unidentifiable, and the unknown character of the manufacturer is not the plaintiff's fault.
Market-share test The primary measure of monopoly power. A firm's market share is the percentage of a market that the firm controls.
Marshalling assets The arrangement or ranking of assets in a certain order toward the payment of debts. In equity, when two creditors have recourse to the same property of the debtor, but one has recourse to other property of the debtor, that creditor must resort first to those assets of the debtor that are not available to the other creditor.
Material alteration *See* Alteration
Material fact A fact to which a reasonable person would attach importance in determining his or her course of action. In regard to tender offers, for example, a fact is material if there is a substantial likelihood that a reasonable shareholder would consider it important in deciding how to vote.
Mechanic's lien A statutory lien on the real property of another, created to ensure payment for work performed and materials furnished in the repair or improvement of real property, such as a building.
Mediation A method of settling disputes outside of court by using the services of a neutral third party, called a mediator. The mediator acts as a communicating agent between the parties and suggests ways in which the parties can resolve their dispute.
Mediator A person who attempts to reconcile the differences between two or more parties.
Mens rea (pronounced *mehns ray*-uh) Mental state, or intent. A wrongful mental state is as necessary as a wrongful act to establish criminal liability. What constitutes a mental state varies according to the wrongful action. Thus, for murder, the *mens rea* is the intent to take life; for theft, the *mens rea* must involve both the knowledge that the property belongs to another and the intent to deprive the owner of it.
Merchant A person who is engaged in the purchase and sale of goods. Under the Uniform Commercial Code, a person who deals in goods of the kind involved in the sales contract; for further definitions, see UCC 2–104.
Merchantability *See* Implied warranty of merchantability
Merger A contractual and statutory process in which one corporation (the surviving corporation) acquires all of the assets and liabilities of another corporation (the merged corporation). The shareholders of the

merged corporation receive either payment for their shares or shares in the surviving corporation.

Minimum-contacts requirement The requirement that before a state court can exercise jurisdiction over a foreign corporation, the foreign corporation must have sufficient contacts with the state. A foreign corporation that has its home office in the state or that has manufacturing plants in the state meets this requirement.

Minimum wage The lowest wage, either by government regulation or union contract, that an employer may pay an hourly worker.

Mini-trial A private proceeding in which each party to a dispute argues its position before the other side and vice versa. A neutral third party may be present and act as an adviser if the parties fail to reach an agreement.

Mirror image rule A common law rule that requires, for a valid contractual agreement, that the terms of the offeree's acceptance adhere exactly to the terms of the offeror's offer.

Misdemeanor A lesser crime than a felony, punishable by a fine or imprisonment for up to one year in other than a state or federal penitentiary.

Mislaid property Property with which the owner has voluntarily parted and then cannot find or recover.

Misrepresentation A false statement of fact or an action that deceives and causes harm or injury to another. *See also* Fraudulent misrepresentation (fraud); Innocent misrepresentation

Mitigation of damages A rule requiring a plaintiff to have done whatever was reasonable to minimize the damages caused by the defendant.

Money laundering Falsely reporting income that has been obtained through criminal activity as income obtained through a legitimate business enterprise—in effect, "laundering" the "dirty money."

Monopolization The possession of monopoly power in the relevant market and the willful acquisition or maintenance of the power, as distinguished from growth or development as a consequence of a superior product, business acumen, or historic accident.

Monopoly A term generally used to describe a market in which there is a single seller or a limited number of sellers.

Monopoly power The ability of a monopoly to dictate what takes place in a given market.

Moral minimum The minimum degree of ethical behavior expected of a business firm, which is usually defined as compliance with the law.

Mortgage A written instrument giving a creditor (the mortgagee) an interest in (a lien on) the debtor's (mortgagor's) property as security for a debt.

Mortgage bond A bond that pledges specific property. If the corporation defaults on the bond, the bondholder can take the property.

Mortgagee Under a mortgage agreement, the creditor who takes a security interest in the debtor's property.

Mortgagor Under a mortgage agreement, the debtor who gives the creditor a security interest in the debtor's property in return for a mortgage loan.

Most-favored-nation status A status granted in an international treaty by a provision stating that the citizens of the contracting nations may enjoy the privileges accorded by either party to citizens of the most favored nations. Generally, most-favored-nation clauses are designed to establish equality of international treatment.

Motion A procedural request or application presented by an attorney to the court on behalf of a client.

Motion for a directed verdict In a jury trial, a motion for the judge to take the decision out of the hands of the jury and direct a verdict for the moving party on the ground that the other party has not produced sufficient evidence to support his or her claim; referred to as a motion for judgment as a matter of law in the federal courts.

Motion for a new trial A motion asserting that the trial was so fundamentally flawed (because of error, newly discovered evidence, prejudice, or other reason) that a new trial is necessary to prevent a miscarriage of justice.

Motion for judgment *n.o.v.* A motion requesting the court to grant judgment in favor of the party making the motion on the ground that the jury verdict against him or her was unreasonable and erroneous.

Motion for judgment on the pleadings A motion by either party to a lawsuit at the close of the pleadings requesting the court to decide the issue solely on the pleadings without proceeding to trial. The motion will be granted only if no facts are in dispute.

Motion for summary judgment A motion requesting the court to enter a judgment without proceeding to trial. The motion can be based on evidence outside the pleadings and will be granted only if no facts are in dispute.

Motion to dismiss A pleading in which a defendant asserts that the plaintiff's claim fails to state a cause of action (that is, has no basis in law) or that there are other grounds on which a suit should be dismissed.

Multiple product order An order issued by the Federal Trade Commission to a firm that has engaged in deceptive advertising by which the firm is required to cease and desist from false advertising not only in regard to the product that was the subject of the action but also in regard to all the firm's other products.

Municipal court A city or community court with criminal jurisdiction over traffic violations and, less frequently, with civil jurisdiction over other minor matters.

Mutual assent The element of agreement in the formation of a contract. The manifestation of contract parties' mutual assent to the same bargain is required to establish a contract.

Mutual fund A specific type of investment company that continually buys or sells to investors shares of ownership in a portfolio.

Mutual rescission An agreement between the parties to cancel their contract, releasing the parties from further obligations under the contract. The object of the agreement is to restore the parties to the positions they would have occupied had no contract ever been formed. *See also* Rescission

N

National law Law that pertains to a particular nation (as opposed to international law).

Natural law The belief that government and the legal system should reflect universal moral and ethical principles that are inherent in human nature. The natural law school is the oldest and one of the most significant schools of legal thought.

Negligence The failure to exercise the standard of care that a reasonable person would exercise in similar circumstances.

Negligence *per se* An act (or failure to act) in violation of a statutory requirement.

Negligent misrepresentation Any manifestation through words or conduct that amounts to an untrue statement of fact made in circumstances in which a reasonable and prudent person would not have done (or failed to do) that which led to the misrepresentation. A representation made with an honest belief in its truth may still be negligent due to (1) a lack of reasonable care in ascertaining the facts, (2) the manner of expression, or (3) the absence of the skill or competence required by a particular business or profession.

***Noerr-Pennington* doctrine** A series of cases that permits competitors to lobby for changes in the law to gain greater protection from competition.

Nonconforming goods Goods that do not conform to contract specifications.

No-par shares Corporate shares that have no face value—that is, no specific dollar amount is printed on their face.

No-strike clause Provision in collective bargaining agreement that states the employees will not strike for any reason and labor disputes will be resolved by arbitration.

Notary public A public official authorized to attest to the authenticity of signatures.

Notice-and-comment rulemaking An administrative rulemaking procedure that involves the publication of a notice of a proposed rulemaking in the *Federal Register*, a comment period for interested parties to express their views on the proposed rule, and the publication of the agency's final rule in the *Federal Register*.

Notice of Proposed Rulemaking A notice published (in the *Federal Register*) by an administrative agency describing a proposed rule. The notice must give the time and place for which agency proceedings on the proposed rule will be held, a description of the nature of the proceedings, the legal authority for the proceedings (which is usually the agency's enabling legislation), and the terms of the proposed rule or the subject matter of the proposed rule.

Novation The substitution, by agreement, of a new contract for an old one, with the rights under the old one being terminated. Typically, there is a substitution of a new person who is responsible for the contract and the removal of an original party's rights and duties under the contract.

Nuisance A common law doctrine under which persons may be held liable for using their property in a manner that unreasonably interferes with others' rights to use or enjoy their own property.

O

Objective theory of contracts A theory under which the intent to form a contract will be judged by outward, objective facts (what the party said when entering into the contract, how the party acted or appeared, and the circumstances surrounding the transaction) as interpreted by a reasonable person, rather than by the party's own secret, subjective intentions.

Obligee One to whom an obligation is owed.

Obligor One that owes an obligation to another.

Offer A promise or commitment to perform or refrain from performing some specified act in the future.

Offeree A person to whom an offer is made.

Offeror A person who makes an offer.

Opening statement A statement made to the jury at the beginning of the trial by a party's attorney, prior to the presentation of evidence. The attorney briefly outlines the evidence that will be offered and the legal theory that will be pursued.

Operation of law A term expressing the manner in which certain rights or liabilities may be imposed on a person by the application of established rules of law to the particular transaction, without regard to the actions or cooperation of the party himself or herself.

Opinion A statement by the court expressing the reasons for its decision in a case.

Optimum profits The amount of profits that a business can make and still act ethically, as opposed to maximum profits, defined as the amount of profits a firm can make if it is willing to disregard ethical concerns.

Option contract A contract under which the offeror cannot revoke his or her offer for a stipulated time period, and the offeree can accept or reject the offer during this period without fear that the offer will be made to another person. The offeree must give consideration for the option (the irrevocable offer) to be enforceable.

Order for relief A court's grant of assistance to a complainant. In bankruptcy proceedings, the order relieves the debtor of the immediate obligation to pay the debts listed in the bankruptcy petition.

Ordinance A law passed by a local governing unit, such as a municipality or a county.

Original jurisdiction Courts having original jurisdiction are courts of the first instance, or trial courts—that is, courts in which lawsuits begin, trials take place, and evidence is presented.

Output contract An agreement in which a seller agrees to sell and a buyer agrees to buy all or up to a stated amount of what the seller produces.

P

Partially disclosed principal A principal whose identity is unknown by a third person, but the third person knows that the agent is or may be acting for a principal at the time the agent and the third person form a contract.

Partner A co-owner of a partnership.

Partnership An agreement by two or more persons to carry on, as co-owners, a business for profit.

Partnership by estoppel A judicially created partnership that may, at the court's discretion, be imposed for purposes of fairness. The court can prevent those who present themselves as partners (but who are not) from escaping liability if a third person relies on an alleged partnership in good faith and is harmed as a result.

Par-value shares Corporate shares that have a specific face value, or formal cash-in value, written on them, such as one dollar.

Past consideration An act done before the contract is made, which ordinarily, by itself, cannot be consideration for a later promise to pay for the act.

Patent A government grant that gives an inventor the exclusive right or privilege to make, use, or sell his or her invention for a limited time period. The word *patent* usually refers to some invention and designates either the instrument by which patent rights are evidenced or the patent itself.

Penalty A sum inserted into a contract, not as a measure of compensation for its breach but rather as punishment for a default. The agreement as to the amount will not be enforced, and recovery will be limited to actual damages.

Per se A Latin term meaning "in itself" or "by itself."

***Per se* violation** A type of anticompetitive agreement—such as a horizontal price-fixing agreement—that is considered to be so injurious to the public that there is no need to determine whether it actually injures market competition; rather, it is in itself (*per se*) a violation of the Sherman Act.

Perfect tender rule A common law rule under which a seller was required to deliver to the buyer goods that conformed perfectly to the requirements stipulated in the sales contract. A tender of nonconforming goods would automatically constitute a breach of contract. Under the Uniform Commercial Code, the rule has been greatly modified.

Perfection The legal process by which secured parties protect themselves against the claims of third parties who may wish to have their debts satisfied out of the same collateral; usually accomplished by the filing of a financing statement with the appropriate government official.

Performance In contract law, the fulfillment of one's duties arising under a contract with another; the normal way of discharging one's contractual obligations.

Periodic tenancy A lease interest in land for an indefinite period involving payment of rent at fixed intervals, such as week to week, month to month, or year to year.

Personal jurisdiction *See In personam* jurisdiction

Personal property Property that is movable; any property that is not real property.

Personalty Personal property.

Petition in bankruptcy The document that is filed with a bankruptcy court to initiate bankruptcy proceedings. The official forms required for a petition in bankruptcy must be completed accurately, sworn to under oath, and signed by the debtor.

Petitioner In equity practice, a party that initiates a lawsuit.

Petty offense In criminal law, the least serious kind of criminal offense, such as a traffic or building-code violation.

Pierce the corporate veil To disregard the corporate entity, which limits the liability of shareholders, and hold the shareholders personally liable for a corporate obligation.

Plaintiff One who initiates a lawsuit.

Plea In criminal law, a defendant's allegation, in response to the charges brought against him or her, of guilt or innocence.

Plea bargaining The process by which a criminal defendant and the prosecutor in a criminal case work out a mutually satisfactory disposition of the case, subject to court approval; usually involves the defendant's pleading guilty to a lesser offense in return for a lighter sentence.

Pleadings Statements made by the plaintiff and the defendant in a lawsuit that detail the facts, charges, and defenses involved in the litigation; the complaint and answer are part of the pleadings.

Police powers Powers possessed by states as part of their inherent sovereignty. These powers may be exercised to protect or promote the public order, health, safety, morals, and general welfare.

Policy In insurance law, a contract between the insurer and the insured in which, for a stipulated consideration, the insurer agrees to compensate the insured for loss on a specific subject by a specified peril.

Positive law The body of conventional, or written, law of a particular society at a particular point in time.

Possessory lien A lien that allows one person to retain possession of another's property as security for a debt or obligation owed by the owner of the property to the lienholder. An example of a possessory lien is an artisan's lien.

Potential competition doctrine A doctrine under which a conglomerate merger may be prohibited by law because it would be injurious to potential competition.
Potentially responsible party (PRP) A potentially liable party under the Comprehensive Environmental Response, Compensation and Liability Act (CERCLA). Any person who generated the hazardous waste, transported the hazardous waste, owned or operated a waste site at the time of disposal, or currently owns or operates a site may be responsible for some or all of the clean-up costs involved in removing the hazardous chemicals.
Power of attorney A written document, which is usually notarized, authorizing another to act as one's agent; can be special (permitting the agent to do specified acts only) or general (permitting the agent to transact all business for the principal).
Precedent A court decision that furnishes an example or authority for deciding subsequent cases involving identical or similar facts.
Predatory pricing The pricing of a product below cost with the intent to drive competitors out of the market.
Preemption A doctrine under which certain federal laws preempt, or take precedence over, conflicting state or local laws.
Preemptive rights Rights held by shareholders that entitle them to purchase newly issued shares of a corporation's stock, equal in percentage to shares presently held, before the stock is offered to any outside buyers. Preemptive rights enable shareholders to maintain their proportionate ownership and voice in the corporation.
Preference In bankruptcy proceedings, property transfers or payments made by the debtor that favor (give preference to) one creditor over others. The bankruptcy trustee is allowed to recover payments made both voluntarily and involuntarily to one creditor in preference over another.
Preferred stock Classes of stock that have priority over common stock both as to payment of dividends and distribution of assets on the corporation's dissolution.
Prejudgment interest Interest that accrues on the amount of a court judgment from the time of the filing of a lawsuit to the court's issuance of a judgment.
Preliminary hearing An initial hearing used in many felony cases to establish whether or not it is proper to detain the defendant. A magistrate reviews the evidence and decides if there is probable cause to believe that the defendant committed the crime with which he or she has been charged.
Prenuptial agreement An agreement made before marriage that defines each partner's ownership rights in the other partner's property. Prenuptial agreements must be in writing to be enforceable.
Preponderance of the evidence A standard in civil law cases under which the plaintiff must convince the court that, based on the evidence presented by both parties, it is more likely than not that the plaintiff's allegation is true.
Pretrial conference A conference, scheduled before the trial begins, between the judge and the attorneys litigating the suit. The parties may settle the dispute, clarify the issues, schedule discovery, and so on during the conference.
Pretrial motion A written or oral application to a court for a ruling or order, made before trial.
Price discrimination Setting prices in such a way that two competing buyers pay two different prices for an identical product or service.
Price fixing Fixing—by means of an anticompetitive agreement between competitors—the prices of products or services.
Price-fixing agreement An agreement between competitors in which the competitors agree to fix the prices of products or services at a certain level; prohibited by the Sherman Act.
***Prima facie* case** A case in which the plaintiff has produced sufficient evidence of his or her conclusion that the case can go to to a jury; a case in which the evidence compels the plaintiff's conclusion if the defendant produces no evidence to disprove it.
Principal In agency law, a person who agrees to have another, called the agent, act on his or her behalf.
Principle of rights The principle that human beings have certain fundamental rights (to life, freedom, and the pursuit of happiness, for example). Those who adhere to this "rights theory" believe that a key factor in determining whether a business decision is ethical is how that decision affects the rights of others. These others include the firm's owners, its employees, the consumers of its products or services, its suppliers, the community in which it does business, and society as a whole.
Privatization The replacement of government-provided products and services by private firms.
Privilege In tort law, the ability to act contrary to another person's right without that person's having legal redress for such acts. Privilege may be raised as a defense to defamation.
Privileges and immunities clause Special rights and exceptions provided by law. Article IV, Section 2, of the Constitution requires states not to discriminate against one another's citizens. A resident of one state cannot be treated as an alien when in another state; he or she may not be denied such privileges and immunities as legal protection, access to courts, travel rights, or property rights.
Privity of contract The relationship that exists between the promisor and the promisee of a contract.
Pro rata Proportionately; in proportion.
Probable cause Reasonable grounds to believe the existence of facts warranting certain actions, such as the search or arrest of a person.
Procedural due process The requirement that any government decision to take life, liberty, or property must be made fairly. For example, fair procedures must be used in determining whether a person will be subjected to punishment or have some burden imposed on him or her.
Procedural law Rules that define the manner in which the rights and duties of individuals may be enforced.
Product liability The legal liability of manufacturers, sellers, and lessors of goods to consumers, users, and bystanders for injuries or damages that are caused by the goods.
Product misuse A defense against product liability that may be raised when the plaintiff used a product in a manner not intended by the manufacturer. If the misuse is reasonably foreseeable, the seller will not escape liability unless measures were taken to guard against the harm that could result from the misuse.
Professional corporation A corporation formed by professional persons, such as physicians, lawyers, dentists, and accountants, to gain tax benefits. Subject to certain exceptions (when a court may treat a professional corporation as a partnership for liability purposes), the shareholders of a professional corporation have the limited liability characteristic of the corporate form of business.
Profit In real property law, the right to enter onto and remove things from the property of another (for example, the right to enter onto a person's land and remove sand and gravel therefrom).
Promise A declaration that something either will or will not happen in the future.
Promisee A person to whom a promise is made.
Promisor A person who makes a promise.
Promissory estoppel A doctrine that applies when a promisor makes a clear and definite promise on which the promisee justifiably relies; such a promise is binding if justice will be better served by the enforcement of the promise. *See also* Estoppel
Promoter A person who takes the preliminary steps in organizing a corporation, including (usually) issuing a prospectus, procuring stock subscriptions, making contract purchases, securing a corporate charter, and the like.
Property Legally protected rights and interests in anything with an ascertainable value that is subject to ownership.
Prospectus A document required by federal or state securities laws that describes the financial operations of the corporation, thus allowing investors to make informed decisions.
Protected class A class of persons with identifiable characteristics who historically have been victimized by discriminatory treatment for certain purposes. Depending on the context, these characteristics include age, color, gender, national origin, race, and religion.
Proximate cause Legal cause; exists when the connection between an act and an injury is strong enough to justify imposing liability.
Proxy In corporation law, a written agreement between a stockholder and another under which the stockholder authorizes the other to vote the

stockholder's shares in a certain manner.
Proxy fight A conflict between an individual, group, or firm attempting to take control of a corporation and the corporation's management for the votes of the shareholders.
Public figures Individuals who are thrust into the public limelight. Public figures include government officials and politicians, movie stars, well-known businesspersons, and generally anybody who becomes known to the public because of his or her position or activities.
Public policy A government policy based on widely held societal values and (usually) expressed or implied in laws or regulations.
Public prosecutor An individual, acting as a trial lawyer, who initiates and conducts criminal cases in the government's name and on behalf of the people.
Puffery A salesperson's often exaggerated claims concerning the quality of property offered for sale. Such claims involve opinions rather than facts and are not considered to be legally binding promises or warranties.

Q

Quantum meruit (pronounced *kwahn*-tuhm *mehr*-oo-wuht) Literally, "as much as he deserves"—an expression describing the extent of liability on a contract implied in law (quasi contract). An equitable doctrine based on the concept that one who benefits from another's labor and materials should not be unjustly enriched thereby but should be required to pay a reasonable amount for the benefits received, even absent a contract.
Quasi contract A fictional contract imposed on parties by a court in the interests of fairness and justice; usually, quasi contracts are imposed to avoid the unjust enrichment of one party at the expense of another.
Question of fact In a lawsuit, an issue involving a factual dispute that can only be decided by a judge (or, in a jury trial, a jury).
Question of law In a lawsuit, an issue involving the application or interpretation of a law; therefore, the judge, and not the jury, decides the issue.
Quorum The number of members of a decision-making body that must be present before business may be transacted.
Quota An assigned import limit on goods.

R

Ratification The act of accepting and giving legal force to an obligation that previously was not enforceable.
Reaffirmation agreement An agreement between a debtor and a creditor in which the debtor reaffirms, or promises to pay, a debt dischargeable in bankruptcy. To be enforceable, the agreement must be made prior to the discharge of the debt by the bankruptcy court.
Real property Land and everything attached to it, such as foliage and buildings.
Reasonable care The degree of care that a person of ordinary prudence would exercise in the same or similar circumstances.
Reasonable doubt *See* Beyond a reasonable doubt
Reasonable person standard The standard of behavior expected of a hypothetical "reasonable person." The standard against which negligence is measured and that must be observed to avoid liability for negligence.
Rebuttal The refutation of evidence introduced by an adverse party's attorney.
Receiver In a corporate dissolution, a court-appointed person who winds up corporate affairs and liquidates corporate assets.
Red herring A preliminary prospectus that can be distributed to potential investors after the registration statement (for a securities offering) has been filed with the Securities and Exchange Commission. The name derives from the red legend printed across the prospectus stating that the registration has been filed but has not become effective.
Reformation A court-ordered correction of a written contract so that it reflects the true intentions of the parties.
Regulation Z A set of rules promulgated by the Federal Reserve Board to implement the provisions of the Truth-in-Lending Act.
Reimbursement *See* Right of reimbursement
Rejection In contract law, an offeree's express or implied manifestation not to accept an offer. In the law governing contracts for the sale of goods, a buyer's manifest refusal to accept goods on the ground that they do not conform to contract specifications.
Rejoinder The defendant's answer to the plaintiff's rebuttal.
Release A contract in which one party forfeits the right to pursue a legal claim against the other party.
Relevant evidence Evidence tending to make a fact at issue in the case more or less probable than it would be without the evidence. Only relevant evidence is admissible in court.
Remainder A future interest in property held by a person other than the original owner.
Remanded Sent back. If an appellate court disagrees with a lower court's judgment, the case may be remanded to the lower court for further proceedings in which the lower court's decision should be consistent with the appellate court's opinion on the matter.
Remedy The relief given to an innocent party to enforce a right or compensate for the violation of a right.
Remedy at law A remedy available in a court of law. Money damages are awarded as a remedy at law.
Remedy in equity A remedy allowed by courts in situations where remedies at law are not appropriate. Remedies in equity are based on settled rules of fairness, justice, and honesty, and include injunction, specific performance, rescission and restitution, and reformation.
Remitter A person who sends money, or remits payment.
Reporter A publication in which court cases are published, or reported.
Reply Procedurally, a plaintiff's response to a defendant's answer.
Repudiation The renunciation of a right or duty. The act of a buyer or seller in rejecting a contract either partially or totally. *See also* Anticipatory repudiation
Requirements contract An agreement in which a buyer agrees to purchase and the seller agrees to sell all or up to a stated amount of what the buyer needs or requires.
Res ipsa loquitur (pronounced *rehs ehp*-suh *low*-quuh-duhr) A doctrine under which negligence may be inferred simply because an event occurred, if it is the type of event that would not occur in the absence of negligence. Literally, the term means "the facts speak for themselves."
Resale price maintenance agreement An agreement between a manufacturer and a retailer in which the manufacturer specifies the minimum retail price of its products. Resale price maintenance agreements are illegal *per se* under the Sherman Act.
Rescind (pronounced reh-*sihnd*) To cancel. *See also* Rescission
Rescission (pronounced reh-*sih*-zhen) A remedy whereby a contract is canceled and the parties are returned to the positions they occupied before the contract was made; may be effected through the mutual consent of the parties, by their conduct, or by court decree.
Respondeat superior (pronounced ree-*spahn*-dee-uht soo-*peer*-ee-your) In Latin, "Let the master respond." A doctrine under which a principal or an employer is held liable for the wrongful acts committed by agents or employees while acting within the course and scope of their agency or employment.
Respondent In equity practice, the party who answers a bill or other proceeding.
Restitution An equitable remedy under which a person is restored to his or her original position prior to loss or injury, or placed in the position he or she would have been in had the breach not occurred.
Restraint of trade Any contract or combination that tends to eliminate or reduce competition, effect a monopoly, artificially maintain prices, or otherwise hamper the course of trade and commerce as it would be carried on if left to the control of natural economic forces.
Restrictive covenant A private restriction on the use of land that is binding on the party that purchases the property originally as well as on subsequent purchasers. If its benefit or obligation passes with the land's ownership, it is said to "run with the land."
Retained earnings The portion of a corporation's profits that has not been paid out as dividends to shareholders.
Retaliatory eviction The eviction of a tenant because of the tenant's complaints, participation in a tenant's union, or similar activity with which the landlord does not agree.
Reverse To reject or overrule a court's judgment. An appellate court, for example, might reverse a lower court's judgment on an issue if it feels that the lower court committed an error during the trial or that the jury was improperly instructed.

Reverse discrimination Discrimination against majority groups, such as white males, that results from affirmative action programs, in which preferences are given to minority members and women.

Reversible error An error by a lower court that is sufficiently substantial to justify an appellate court's reversal of the lower court's decision.

Reversionary interest A future interest in property retained by the original owner.

Revocation In contract law, the withdrawal of an offer by an offeror. Unless an offer is irrevocable, it can be revoked at any time prior to acceptance without liability.

Right of contribution The right of a co-surety who pays more than his or her proportionate share on a debtor's default to recover the excess paid from other co-sureties.

Right of entry The right to peaceably take or resume possession of real property.

Right of first refusal The right to purchase personal or real property—such as corporate shares or real estate—before the property is offered for sale to others.

Right of redemption *See* Equity of redemption; Redemption

Right of reimbursement The legal right of a person to be restored, repaid, or indemnified for costs, expenses, or losses incurred or expended on behalf of another.

Right of subrogation The right of a person to stand in the place of (be substituted for) another, giving the substituted party the same legal rights that the original party had.

Right-to-work law A state law providing that employees are not to be required to join a union as a condition of obtaining or retaining employment.

Risk A prediction concerning potential loss based on known and unknown factors.

Risk management Planning that is undertaken to protect one's interest should some event threaten to undermine its security. In the context of insurance, risk management involves transferring certain risks from the insured to the insurance company.

Robbery The act of forcefully and unlawfully taking personal property of any value from another; force or intimidation is usually necessary for an act of theft to be considered a robbery.

Rule of four A rule of the United States Supreme Court under which the Court will not issue a writ of *certiorari* unless at least four justices approve of the decision to issue the writ.

Rule of reason A test by which a court balances the positive effects (such as economic efficiency) of an agreement against its potentially anticompetitive effects. In antitrust litigation, many practices are analyzed under the rule of reason.

Rule 10b-5 *See* SEC Rule 10b-5

Rulemaking The process undertaken by an administrative agency when formally adopting a new regulation or amending an old one. Rulemaking involves notifying the public of a proposed rule or change and receiving and considering the public's comments.

Rules of evidence Rules governing the admissibility of evidence in trial courts.

S

S corporation A close business corporation that has met certain requirements as set out by the Internal Revenue Code and thus qualifies for special income tax treatment. Essentially, an S corporation is taxed the same as a partnership, but its owners enjoy the privilege of limited liability.

Sale The passing of title from the seller to the buyer for a price.

Sale on approval A type of conditional sale in which the buyer may take the goods on a trial basis. The sale becomes absolute only when the buyer approves of (or is satisfied with) the goods being sold.

Sale or return A type of conditional sale in which title and possession pass from the seller to the buyer; however, the buyer retains the option to return the goods during a specified period even though the goods conform to the contract.

Sales contract A contract for the sale of goods under which the ownership of goods is transferred from a seller to a buyer for a price.

Scienter (pronounced *sy-en*-ter) Knowledge by the misrepresenting party that material facts have been falsely represented or omitted with an intent to deceive.

Search warrant An order granted by a public authority, such as a judge, that authorizes law enforcement personnel to search particular premises or property.

Seasonably Within a specified time period, or, if no period is specified, within a reasonable time.

SEC Rule 10b-5 A rule of the Securities and Exchange Commission that makes it unlawful, in connection with the purchase or sale of any security, to make any untrue statement of a material fact or to omit a material fact if such omission causes the statement to be misleading.

Secondary boycott A union's refusal to work for, purchase from, or handle the products of a secondary employer, with whom the union has no dispute, for the purpose of forcing that employer to stop doing business with the primary employer, with whom the union has a labor dispute.

Securities Generally, corporate stocks and bonds. A security may also be a note, debenture, stock warrant, or any document given as evidence of an ownership interest in a corporation or as a promise of repayment by a corporation.

Self-defense The legally recognized privilege to protect one's self or property against injury by another. The privilege of self-defense protects only acts that are reasonably necessary to protect one's self or property.

Seniority system In regard to employment relationships, a system in which those who have worked longest for the company are first in line for promotions, salary increases, and other benefits; they are also the last to be laid off if the work force must be reduced.

Service mark A mark used in the sale or the advertising of services, such as to distinguish the services of one person from the services of others. Titles, character names, and other distinctive features of radio and television programs may be registered as service marks.

Service of process The delivery of the complaint and summons to a defendant.

Settlor One creating a trust.

Severance pay Funds in excess of normal wages or salaries paid to an employee upon termination of his or her employment with a company.

Sexual harassment In the employment context, the granting of job promotions or other benefits in return for sexual favors or language or conduct that is so sexually offensive that it creates a hostile working environment.

Sham transaction A false transaction without substance that is undertaken with the intent to defraud a creditor or the government. An example of a sham transaction is the sale of assets to a friend or relative for the purpose of concealing assets from creditors or a bankruptcy court.

Share A unit of stock. *See also* Stock

Shareholder One who purchases shares of a corporation's stock, thus acquiring an equity interest in the corporation.

Shareholder's derivative suit A suit brought by a shareholder to enforce a corporate cause of action against a third person.

Sharia Civil law principles of some Middle Eastern countries that are based on the Islamic directives that follow the teachings of the prophet Mohammed.

Shipment contract A contract for the sale of goods in which the seller is required or authorized to ship the goods by carrier. The buyer assumes liability for any losses or damage to the goods after they are delivered to the carrier.

Short-form merger A merger between a subsidiary corporation and a parent corporation that owns at least 90 percent of the outstanding shares of each class of stock issued by the subsidiary corporation. Short-form mergers can be accomplished without the approval of the shareholders of either corporation.

Short-swing profits Profits made by officers, directors, and certain large stockholders resulting from the use of nonpublic (inside) information about their companies; prohibited by Section 12 of the 1934 Securities Exchange Act.

Slander Defamation in oral form.

Slander of quality (trade libel) The publication of false information

about another's product, alleging that it is not what its seller claims.
Slander of title The publication of a statement that denies or casts doubt on another's legal ownership of any property, causing financial loss to that property's owner.
Small claims courts Special courts in which parties may litigate small claims (usually, claims involving $2,500 or less). Attorneys are not required in small claims courts, and in many states attorneys are not allowed to represent the parties.
Sole proprietorship The simplest form of business, in which the owner is the business; the owner reports business income on his or her personal income tax return and is legally responsible for all debts and obligations incurred by the business.
Sovereign immunity A doctrine that immunizes foreign nations from the jurisdiction of U.S. courts when certain conditions are satisfied.
Specific performance An equitable remedy requiring exactly the performance that was specified in a contract; usually granted only when money damages would be an inadequate remedy and the subject matter of the contract is unique (for example, real property).
Spot zoning Granting a zoning classification to a parcel of land that is different from the classification given to other land in the immediate area.
Standing to sue The requirement that an individual must have a sufficient stake in a controversy before he or she can bring a lawsuit. The plaintiff must demonstrate that he or she either has been injured or threatened with injury.
Stare decisis (pronounced *ster*-ay dih-*si*-ses) A common law doctrine under which judges are obligated to follow the precedents established in prior decisions.
Statute of Frauds A state statute under which certain types of contracts must be in writing to be enforceable.
Statute of limitations A federal or state statute setting the maximum time period during which a certain action can be brought or certain rights enforced.
Statute of repose Basically, a statute of limitations that is not dependent on the happening of a cause of action. Statutes of repose generally begin to run at an earlier date and run for a longer period of time than statutes of limitations.
Statutory law The body of law enacted by legislative bodies (as opposed to constitutional law, administrative law, or case law).
Statutory lien A lien created by statute.
Statutory period of redemption A time period (usually set by state statute) during which the property subject to a defaulted mortgage, land contract, or other contract can be redeemed by the debtor after foreclosure or judicial sale.
Stock An equity (ownership) interest in a corporation, measured in units of shares.
Stock certificate A certificate issued by a corporation evidencing the ownership of a specified number of shares in the corporation.
Stock option *See* Stock warrant
Stock warrant A certificate that grants the owner the option to buy a given number of shares of stock, usually within a set time period.
Stockholder *See* Shareholder
Strict liability Liability regardless of fault. In tort law, strict liability may be imposed on defendants in cases involving abnormally dangerous activities, dangerous animals, or defective products.
Strike An extreme action undertaken by unionized workers when collective bargaining fails; the workers leave their jobs, refuse to work, and (typically) picket the employer's workplace.
Subject-matter jurisdiction Jurisdiction over the subject matter of a lawsuit.
Submission An agreement by two or more parties to refer any disputes they may have under their contract to a disinterested third party, such as an arbitrator, who has the power to render a binding decision.
Subpoena A document commanding a person to appear at a certain time and place or give testimony concerning a certain matter.
Subrogation *See* Right of subrogation
Subscriber An investor who agrees, in a subscription agreement, to purchase capital stock in a corporation.
Substantial evidence test The test applied by a court reviewing an administrative agency's informal action. The court determines whether the agency acted unreasonably and overturns the agency's findings only if unsupported by a substantial body of evidence.
Substantial performance Performance that does not vary greatly from the performance promised in a contract; the performance must create substantially the same benefits as those promised in the contract.
Substantive due process A requirement that focuses on the content, or substance, of legislation. If a law or other governmental action limits a fundamental right, such as the right to travel or to vote, it will be held to violate substantive due process unless it promotes a compelling or overriding state interest.
Substantive law Law that defines the rights and duties of individuals with respect to each other, as opposed to procedural law, which defines the manner in which these rights and duties may be enforced.
Suit *See* Lawsuit; Litigation
Summary judgment *See* Motion for summary judgment
Summary jury trial (SJT) A method of settling disputes in which a trial is held, but the jury's verdict is not binding. The verdict acts only as a guide to both sides in reaching an agreement during the mandatory negotiations that immediately follow the summary jury trial.
Summons A document informing a defendant that a legal action has been commenced against him or her and that the defendant must appear in court on a certain date to answer the plaintiff's complaint. The document is delivered by a sheriff or any other person so authorized.
Superseding cause An intervening force or event that breaks the connection between a wrongful act and an injury to another; in negligence law, a defense to liability.
Supremacy clause The provision in Article VI of the Constitution that provides that the Constitution, laws, and treaties of the United States are "the supreme Law of the Land." Under this clause, state and local laws that directly conflict with federal law will be rendered invalid.
Surety A person, such as a cosigner on a note, who agrees to be primarily responsible for the debt of another.
Suretyship An express contract in which a third party to a debtor-creditor relationship (the surety) promises to be primarily responsible for the debtor's obligation.
Surviving corporation The remaining, or continuing, corporation following a merger. The surviving corporation is vested with the merged corporation's legal rights and obligations.
Syllogism A form of deductive reasoning consisting of a major premise, a minor premise, and a conclusion.
Symbolic speech Nonverbal conduct that expresses opinions or thoughts about a subject. Symbolic speech is protected under the First Amendment's guarantee of freedom of speech.
Syndicate An investment group of persons or firms brought together for the purpose of financing a project that they would not or could not undertake independently.

T

Takeover The acquisition of control over a corporation through the purchase of a substantial number of the voting shares of the corporation.
Taking The taking of private property by the government for public use. Under the Fifth Amendment to the Constitution, the government may not take private property for public use without "just compensation."
Tangible property Property that has physical existence and can be distinguished by the senses of touch, sight, and so on. A car is tangible property; a patent right is intangible property.
Target corporation The corporation to be acquired in a corporate takeover; a corporation to whose shareholders a tender offer is submitted.
Tariff An tax on imported goods.
Technology licensing Allowing another to use and profit from intellectual property (patents, copyrights, trademarks, innovative products or processes, and so on) for consideration. In the context of international business transactions, technology licensing is sometimes an attractive alternative to the establishment of foreign production facilities.
Tenancy at sufferance A type of tenancy under which one who, after rightfully being in possession of leased premises, continues (wrongfully)

to occupy the property after the lease has been terminated. The tenant has no rights to possess the property and occupies it only because the person entitled to evict the tenant has not done so.
Tenancy at will A type of tenancy under which either party can terminate the tenancy without notice; usually arises when a tenant who has been under a tenancy for years retains possession, with the landlord's consent, after the tenancy for years has terminated.
Tenancy by the entirety The joint ownership of property by a husband and wife. Neither party can transfer his or her interest in the property without the consent of the other.
Tenancy for years A type of tenancy under which property is leased for a specified period of time, such as a month, a year, or a period of years.
Tenancy in common Co-ownership of property in which each party owns an undivided interest that passes to his or her heirs at death.
Tenancy in partnership Co-ownership of partnership property.
Tenant One who has the temporary use and occupation of real property owned by another person, called the landlord; the duration and terms of the tenancy are usually established by a lease.
Tender An unconditional offer to perform an obligation by a person who is ready, willing, and able to do so.
Tender of delivery Under the Uniform Commercial Code, a seller's or lessor's act of placing conforming goods at the disposal of the buyer or lessee and giving the buyer or lessee whatever notification is reasonably necessary to enable the buyer or lessee to take delivery.
Tender offer An offer to purchase made by one company directly to the shareholders of another (target) company; often referred to as a "takeover bid."
Third party beneficiary One for whose benefit a promise is made in a contract but who is not a party to the contract.
Tippee A person who receives inside information.
Tombstone ad An advertisement, historically in a format resembling a tombstone, of a securities offering. The ad informs potential investors of where and how they may obtain a prospectus.
Tort A civil wrong not arising from a breach of contract. A breach of a legal duty that proximately causes harm or injury to another.
Tortfeasor One who commits a tort.
Toxic tort Failure to use or to clean up properly toxic chemicals that cause harm to a person or society.
Trade dress The image and overall appearance of a product—for example, the distinctive decor, menu, layout, and style of service of a particular restaurant. Basically, trade dress is subject to the same protection as trademarks.
Trade fixture The personal property of a commercial tenant that has been installed or affixed to real property for a business purpose. When the lease ends, the tenant can remove the fixture but must repair any damage to the real property caused by the fixture's removal.
Trade libel The publication of false information about another's product, alleging it is not what its seller claims; also referred to as slander of quality.
Trade name A term that is used to indicate part or all of a business's name and that is directly related to the business's reputation and goodwill. Trade names are protected under the common law (and under trademark law, if the name is the same as the firm's trademarked property).
Trade secret Information or a process that gives a business an advantage over competitors who do not know the information or process.
Trademark A distinctive mark, motto, device, or implement that a manufacturer stamps, prints, or otherwise affixes to the goods it produces so that they may be identified on the market and their origins made known. Once a trademark is established (under the common law or through registration), the owner is entitled to its exclusive use.
Treaty An agreement formed between two or more independent nations.
Treble damages Damages consisting of single damages determined by a jury and tripled in amount in certain cases as required by statute.
Trespass to land The entry onto, above, or below the surface of land owned by another without the owner's permission or legal authorization.
Trespass to personal property The unlawful taking or harming of another's personal property; interference with another's right to the exclusive possession of his or her personal property.
Trespasser One who commits the tort of trespass in one of its forms.
Trial court A court in which trials are held and testimony taken.
Trust A voluntary form of business organization in which investors (trust beneficiaries) transfer cash or property to trustees in exchange for trust certificates that represent their investment shares. Management of the business and trust property is handled by the trustees for the use and benefit of the investors. The certificate holders have limited liability (are not responsible for the debts and obligations incurred by the trust) and share in the trust's profits.
Trustee One who holds title to property for the use or benefit of another (the beneficiary).
Tying arrangement An agreement between a buyer and a seller in which the buyer of a specific product or service becomes obligated to purchase additional products or services from the seller.

U

U.S. trustee A government official who performs certain administrative tasks that a bankruptcy judge would otherwise have to perform.
Ultra vires (pronounced *uhl*-trah *vye*-reez) A Latin term meaning "beyond the powers"; in corporate law, acts of a corporation that are beyond its express and implied powers to undertake.
Unanimous opinion A court opinion in which all of the judges or justices of the court agree to the court's decision.
Unconscionable (pronounced un-*kon*-shun-uh-bul) **contract or clause** A contract or clause that is void on the basis of public policy because one party, as a result of his or her disproportionate bargaining power, is forced to accept terms that are unfairly burdensome and that unfairly benefit the dominating party. *See also* Procedural unconscionability; Substantive unconscionability
Undisclosed principal A principal whose identity is unknown by a third person, and the third person has no knowledge that the agent is acting for a principal at the time the agent and the third person form a contract.
Unenforceable contract A valid contract rendered unenforceable by some statute or law.
Uniform law A model law created by the National Conference of Commissioners (NCC) on Uniform State Laws and/or the American Law Institute for the states to consider adopting. If the state adopts the law, it becomes statutory law in that state. Each state has the option of adopting or rejecting all or part of a uniform law.
Unilateral contract A contract that results when an offer can only be accepted by the offeree's performance.
Union shop A place of employment in which all workers, once employed, must become union members within a specified period of time as a condition of their continued employment.
Unitary system A centralized governmental system in which local or subdivisional governments exercise only those powers given to them by the central government.
Unlawful detainer The unjustifiable retention of the possession of real property by one whose right to possession has terminated—as when a tenant holds over after the end of the lease term in spite of the landlord's demand for possession.
Unliquidated debt A debt that is uncertain in amount.
Unreasonably dangerous product In product liability, a product that is defective to the point of threatening a consumer's health and safety. A product will be considered unreasonably dangerous if it is dangerous beyond the expectation of the ordinary consumer or if a less dangerous alternative was economically feasible for the manufacturer, but the manufacturer failed to produce it.
Usage of trade Any practice or method of dealing having such regularity of observance in a place, vocation, or trade as to justify an expectation that it will be observed with respect to the transaction in question.
Use zoning Zoning classifications within a particular municipality that may be distinguished based upon the uses to which the land is to be put.
Usurpation In corporation law, the taking advantage of a corporate opportunity by a corporate officer or director for his or her personal gain

and in violation of his or her fiduciary duties.
Usury Charging an illegal rate of interest.
Utilitarianism An approach to ethical reasoning in which ethically correct behavior is not related to any absolute ethical or moral values but to an evaluation of the consequences of a given action on those who will be affected by it. In utilitarian reasoning, a "good" decision is one that results in the greatest good for the greatest number of people affected by the decision.

V

Valid contract A contract that results when elements necessary for contract formation (agreement, consideration, legal purpose, and contractual capacity) are present.
Validation notice An initial notice to a debtor from a collection agency informing the debtor that he or she has thirty days to challenge the debt and request verification.
Vendee One who purchases property from another, called the vendor.
Vendor One who sells property to another, called the vendee.
Venture capitalist A person or entity that seeks out promising entrepreneurial ventures and funds them in exchange for equity stakes.
Venue (pronounced *ven*-yoo) The geographical district in which an action is tried and from which the jury is selected.
Verdict A formal decision made by a jury.
Vertical merger The acquisition by a company at one stage of production of a company at a higher or lower stage of production (such as a company merging with one of its suppliers or retailers).
Vertical restraint Any restraint on trade created by agreements between firms at different levels in the manufacturing and distribution process.
Vertically integrated firm A firm that carries out two or more functional phases (manufacture, distribution, retailing, and so on) of a product.
Vesting The creation of an absolute or unconditional right or power.
Vicarious liability Legal responsibility placed on one person for the acts of another.
Void contract A contract having no legal force or binding effect.
Voidable contract A contract that may be legally avoided (canceled, or annulled) at the option of one of the parties.
Voidable preference In bankruptcy law, a preference that may be avoided, or set aside, by the trustee.
Voir dire (pronounced *vwahr deehr*) A French phrase meaning, literally, "to see, to speak." In jury trials, the phrase refers to the process in which the attorneys question prospective jurors to determine whether they are biased or have any connection with a party to the action or with a prospective witness.
Voting trust An agreement (trust contract) under which legal title to shares of corporate stock is transferred to a trustee who is authorized by the shareholders to vote the shares on their behalf.

W

Waiver An intentional, knowing relinquishment of a legal right.
Warehouse receipt A document of title issued by a bailee-warehouser to cover the goods stored in the warehouse.
Warehouser One in the business of operating a warehouse.
Warranty A promise that certain facts are truly as they are represented to be.
Warranty disclaimer A seller's or lessor's negation or qualification of a warranty.
Warranty of fitness *See* Implied warranty of fitness for a particular purpose
Warranty of merchantability *See* Implied warranty of merchantability
Warranty of title An implied warranty made by a seller that the seller has good and valid title to the goods sold and that the transfer of the title is rightful.
Waste The abuse or destructive use of real property by one who is in rightful possession of the property but who does not have title to it. Waste does not include ordinary depreciation due to age and normal use.
Watered stock Shares of stock issued by a corporation for which the corporation receives, as payment, less than the stated value of the shares.
Wetlands Areas of land designated by government agencies (such as the Environmental Protection Agency) as protected areas that support wildlife and that therefore cannot be filled in or dredged by private contractors or parties.
Whistleblowing An employee's disclosure to government, the press, or upper-management authorities that the employer is engaged in unsafe or illegal activities.
White-collar crime Nonviolent crime committed by individuals or corporations to obtain a personal or business advantage.
Wildcat strike A strike that is not authorized by the union that ordinarily represents the striking employees.
Willful Intentional.
Winding up The second of two stages involved in the termination of a partnership or corporation. Once the firm is dissolved, it continues to exist legally until the process of winding up all business affairs (collecting and distributing the firm's assets) is complete.
Workers' compensation laws State statutes establishing an administrative procedure for compensating workers' injuries that arise out of—or in the course of—their employment, regardless of fault.
Workout An out-of-court agreement between a debtor and his or her creditors in which the parties work out a payment plan or schedule under which the debtor's debts can be discharged.
Writ of attachment A court's order, prior to a trial to collect a debt, directing the sheriff or other officer to seize nonexempt property of the debtor; if the creditor prevails at trial, the seized property can be sold to satisfy the judgment.
Writ of *certiorari* (pronounced sur-shee-uh-*rah*-ree) A writ from a higher court asking the lower court for the record of a case.
Writ of execution A lcourt's order, after a judgment has been entered against the debtor, directing the sheriff to seize (levy) and sell any of the debtor's nonexempt real or personal property. The proceeds of the sale are used to pay off the judgment, accrued interest, and costs of the sale; any surplus is paid to the debtor.
Wrongful discharge An employer's termination of an employee's employment in violation of an employment contract or laws that protect employees.

Y

Yellow dog contract An agreement under which an employee promises his or her employer, as a condition of employment, not to join a union.

Z

Zoning The division of a city by legislative regulation into districts and the application in each district of regulations having to do with structural and architectural designs of buildings and prescribing the use to which buildings within designated districts may be put.
Zoning variance The granting of permission by a municipality or other public board to a landowner to use his or her property in a way that does not strictly conform with the zoning regulations so as to avoid causing the landowner undue hardship.

TABLE OF CASES

INDEX

E

J

K

L

M

P

S

U

V